Machine Recognition of Patterns

Edited by
Ashok K. Agrawala
Associate Professor of Computer Science
University of Maryland

A volume in the IEEE PRESS Selected Reprint Series

1976

IEEE PRESS

The Institute of Electrical and Electronics Engineers, Inc. New York

PRINTED IN THE UNITED STATES OF AMERICA

IEEE International Standard Book Numbers: Clothbound: 0-87942-091-X
Paperbound: 0-87942-092-8

Library of Congress Catalog Card Number 76-53069

Sole Worldwide Distributor (Exclusive of the IEEE):

JOHN WILEY & SONS, INC.
605 Third Ave.
New York, NY 10016

Wiley Order Numbers: Clothbound: 0-471-03014-7
Paperbound: 0-471-03015-5

Contents

Preface viii

Overview

Patterns in Pattern Recognition: 1968–1974, *L. Kanal* (*IEEE Transactions on Information Theory*, November 1974) 1

Models

An Optimum Character Recognition System Using Decision Functions, *C. K. Chow* (*IRE Transactions on Electronic Computers*, December 1957) 27

Perceptron Simulation Experiments, *F. Rosenblatt* (*Proceedings of the IRE*, March 1960) 35

Speech Recognition: A Model and a Program for Research, *M. Halle and K. Stevens* (*IRE Transactions on Information Theory*, February 1962) 44

Abstraction and Pattern Classification, *R. Bellman, R. Kalaba, and L. Zadeh* (*Journal of Mathematical Analysis and Applications*, 1966) 49

A Note on Learning Signal Detection, *M. Kac* (*IRE Transactions on Information Theory*, February 1962) 56

Computations and Implementations

Interactive Pattern Analysis and Classification Systems: A Survey and Commentary, *L. N. Kanal* (*Proceedings of the IEEE*, October 1972) 59

System Considerations for Automatic Imagery Screening, *T. J. Harley, Jr., L. N. Kanal, and N. C. Randall* (*Pictorial Pattern Recognition*, 1968) 75

A Comparison of Analog and Digital Techniques for Pattern Recognition, *K. Preston, Jr.* (*Proceedings of the IEEE*, October 1972) 92

Feature Extraction and Selection

A Criterion and An Algorithm for Grouping Data, *K. Fukunaga and W. L. G. Koontz* (*IEEE Transactions on Computers*, October 1970) 108

A Comparison of Seven Techniques for Choosing Subsets of Pattern Recognition Properties, *A. N. Mucciardi and E. E. Gose* (*IEEE Transactions on Computers*, September 1971) 115

Feature Extraction on Binary Patterns, *G. Nagy* (*IEEE Transactions on Systems Science and Cybernetics*, October 1969) 124

An Optimal Set of Discriminant Vectors, *D. H. Foley and J. W. Sammon, Jr.* (*IEEE Transactions on Computers*, March 1975) 130

On the Choice of Variables in Classification Problems with Dichotomous Variables, *J. D. Elashoff, R. M. Elashoff, and G. E. Goldman* (*Biometrika*, December 1967) 139

Mean Accuracy

On the Mean Accuracy of Statistical Pattern Recognizers, *G. F. Hughes* (*IEEE Transactions on Information Theory*, January 1968) 142

Comments "On the Mean Accuracy of Statistical Pattern Recognizers" and "Author's Reply," *K. Abend, T. J. Harley, Jr., B. Chandrasekaran, and G. F. Hughes* (*IEEE Transactions on Information Theory*, May 1969) 151

Independence of Measurements and the Mean Recognition Accuracy, *B. Chandrasekaran* (*IEEE Transactions on Information Theory*, July 1971; Correction in January 1972) 155

The Mean Accuracy of Pattern Recognizers with Many Pattern Classes, *R. Y. Kain* (*IEEE Transactions on Information Theory*, May 1969) 160

Mapping
An Optimal Discriminant Plane, *J. W. Sammon, Jr.* (*IEEE Transactions on Computers*, September 1970) . . . 162
A Nonlinear Mapping for Data Structure Analysis, *J. W. Sammon, Jr.* (*IEEE Transactions on Computers*, May 1969) . . . 166
A Projection Pursuit Algorithm for Exploratory Data Analysis, *J. H. Friedman and J. W. Tukey* (*IEEE Transactions on Computers*, September 1974) . . . 175

Dimensionality, Sample Size and Probability of Error
Bibliography on Estimation of Misclassification, *G. T. Toussaint* (*IEEE Transactions on Information Theory*, July 1974) . . . 184
On Dimensionality and Sample Size in Statistical Pattern Classification, *L. Kanal and B. Chandrasekaran* (*Proceedings of the National Electronics Conference*, December 1968) . . . 192
Considerations of Sample and Feature Size, *D. H. Foley* (*IEEE Transactions on Information Theory*, September 1972) . . . 198
Estimation of Error Rates in Discriminant Analysis, *P. A. Lachenbruch and M. R. Mickey* (*Technometrics*, February 1968) . . . 207
On Optimum Recognition Error and Reject Tradeoff, *C. K. Chow* (*IEEE Transactions on Information Theory*, January 1970) . . . 218
Estimation of Classification Error, *K. Fukunaga and D. L. Kessell* (*IEEE Transactions on Computers*, December 1971) . . . 224
Application of Optimum Error-Reject Functions, *K. Fukunaga and D. L. Kessell* (*IEEE Transactions on Information Theory*, November 1972) . . . 231
Nonparametric Bayes Error Estimation Using Unclassified Samples, *K. Fukunaga and D. L. Kessell* (*IEEE Transactions on Information Theory*, July 1973) . . . 235
Independence, Measurement Complexity, and Classification Performance, *B. Chandrasekaran and A. K. Jain* (*IEEE Transactions on Systems, Man, and Cybernetics*, March 1975) . . . 242

Classification
On Pattern Classification Algorithms—Introduction and Survey, *Y. C. Ho and A. K. Agrawala* (*Proceedings of the IEEE*, December 1968) . . . 247
Discriminatory Analysis, Nonparametric Discrimination: Consistency Properties, *E. Fix and J. L. Hodges, Jr.* (*USAF School of Aviation Medicine Project Report*, February 1959) . . . 261
Discriminatory Analysis, Nonparametric Discrimination: Small Sample Performance, *E. Fix and J. L. Hodges, Jr.*, (*USAF School of Aviation Medicine Project Report*, August 1952) . . . 280
The Use of Multiple Measurements in Taxonomic Problems, *R. A. Fisher* (*Annals of Eugenics*, 1936) . . . 323
Nearest Neighbor Pattern Classification, *T. M. Cover and P. E. Hart* (*IEEE Transactions on Information Theory*, January 1967) . . . 333
The Condensed Nearest Neighbor Rule, *P. E. Hart* (*IEEE Transactions on Information Theory*, May 1968) . . . 340
An Algorithm for Finding Nearest Neighbors, *J. H. Friedman, F. Baskett, and L. J. Shustek* (*IEEE Transactions on Computers*, October 1975) . . . 342
A Classifier Design Technique for Discrete Variable Pattern Recognition Problems, *J. C. Stoffel* (*IEEE Transactions on Computers*, April 1974) . . . 348

Applications
The Analysis of Cell Images, *J. M. S. Prewitt and M. L. Mendelsohn* (*Annals of the New York Academy of Sciences*, January 31, 1966) . . . 362
Digital Image-Processing Activities in Remote Sensing for Earth Resources, *G. Nagy* (*Proceedings of the IEEE*, October 1972) . . . 381
Digital Analysis of the Electroencephalogram, the Blood Pressure Wave, and the Electrocardiogram, *J. R. Cox, Jr., F. M. Nolle, and R. M. Arthur* (*Proceedings of the IEEE*, October 1972) . . . 405
Comparative Religion in Character Recognition Machines, *A. W. Holt* (*IEEE Computer Group News*, November 1968) . . . 433

Design of a Linguistic Statistical Decoder for the Recognition of Continuous Speech, *F. Jelinek, L. R. Bahl, and R. L. Mercer (IEEE Transactions on Information Theory,* May 1975) 442
Application of Pattern Recognition to Steady-State Security Evaluation in a Power System, *C. K. Pang, A. J. Koivo, and A. H. El-Abiad (IEEE Transactions on Systems, Man, and Cybernetics,* November 1973) 449

Author Index 459

Subject Index 460

Editor's Biography 463

Preface

Over the years, the field of pattern recognition has attracted workers from a variety of areas such as engineering, system theory, statistics, linguistics, psychology, etc., resulting in a vast literature containing abstract mathematical approaches as well as highly pragmatic techniques. This literature is scattered in a large number of journals in several fields. At least three IEEE journals regularly publish pattern recognition papers. While several textbooks are available for a beginner in the field, a need often arises to go to the source, which, due to the nature of the literature in this field, is not always a straightforward task. This collection of selected readings is not limited to early or "classic" papers. Rather it is designed to be a companion volume to many of the textbooks in pattern recognition and to be a source of useful references for engineers interested in developing the many potential applications of pattern recognition methodology.

The first paper in this volume, "Patterns in Pattern Recognition" by L. N. Kanal, serves not only as an excellent overview of machine pattern recognition, but also as a suitable introduction to this volume. In addition to discussing the status of various aspects of the field as of 1974 and putting different approaches, techniques, and trends in perspective, this paper provides a very useful bibliography.

In the current literature on pattern recognition, one discerns two dominant models: the feature extraction-classification model and the linguistic or syntactic model. As can be seen from the discussion of syntactic methods by Kanal, while ad hoc structural methods have been around from the very beginning of machine pattern recognition, the syntactic formalisms currently receiving much academic attention have not as yet had any significant impact on practical pattern recognition. The current flurry of research activity suggests that in a few years it will probably be desirable to put together a volume of papers devoted to this aspect of pattern recognition methodology. Meanwhile, the discussion by Kanal provides an excellent introduction and references to the literature for those readers who want to explore this aspect further.

In every field of scientific endeavor, some of the landmark work has a tendency of going out of print or becoming very difficult to find. A highlight of this volume is the inclusion of a few papers that fall in this category. The work by Fix and Hodges on discriminatory analysis done in 1951 and 1952 was published as USAF School of Aviation Medicine Technical Reports. This work opened up a whole new area of research in nearest neighbor classification techniques. The original technical reports went out of print some time ago; their inclusion here should prove helpful. The classic paper by R. A. Fisher, although having had a significant impact on the field, is not easily accessible, having been published in the *Annals of Eugenics* in 1936. The inclusion of this paper here may allow the reader to go to the original source.

Pattern recognition is an applied field which tends to discover techniques to solve practical problems. Over the years, however, a lot of theory has been developed with little application of the theory being attempted to the extent that, for a practical problem, the approach to be taken is rarely clear. Within the last few years, there has been a tendency to use interactive systems which allow the user to apply a variety of techniques to the problem at hand. The problems of dimensionality, sample size, and the error rate often tend to limit the design goals. A highlight of this volume is the selections on these topics. Nine papers covering all the major issues involved in these areas are included.

Although pattern recognition techniques can be applied to a variety of problems in a number of fields, only optical character recognition (OCR), blood cell recognition, and isolated speech recognition have reached a stage of commercial use. However, except in the already mature area of OCR, no fully documented case histories are available in the literature. Although the work on OCR is nearly two decades old, the early approaches did not exploit the theoretical advances and relied only on ad hoc techniques. Due to proprietary reasons, most of the more recent commercial applications (e.g., blood cells) described in the literature give general discussions, often leaving out crucial details. The application papers included here are intended to give an indication of potential rather than specific case histories. One hopes that well-developed case histories will appear in the not too distant future.

In closing, I would like to express my gratitude to Professor Laveen Kanal who, in addition to writing the paper which serves as the introduction to this volume, has been a source of many helpful suggestions.

Ashok K. Agrawala
Editor

Patterns in Pattern Recognition: 1968–1974

Invited Paper

LAVEEN KANAL, FELLOW, IEEE

Abstract—**This paper selectively surveys contributions to major topics in pattern recognition since 1968. Representative books and surveys on pattern recognition published during this period are listed. Theoretical models for automatic pattern recognition are contrasted with practical design methodology. Research contributions to statistical and structural pattern recognition are selectively discussed, including contributions to error estimation and the experimental design of pattern classifiers. The survey concludes with a representative set of applications of pattern recognition technology.**

I. Introduction

WHAT IS a pattern that a machine may know it, and a machine that it may know a pattern? That is the fundamental mystery challenging research in automatic pattern recognition. This survey reviews the main paths followed since 1968 and examines some of the research performed in the quest for answers.

This paper complements two 1972 articles. The paper by Kanal and Chandrasekaran (1972) probed theoretical approaches based on alternate models for pattern recognition and assessed contributions to the problem of inferring grammars from samples. To make the present survey somewhat self-contained and accessible to readers not working in pattern recognition, a brief discussion of models is presented in Section III. However, work on interactive pattern analysis and classification systems is mentioned only in passing because the 1972 article in the PROCEEDINGS OF THE IEEE [Kanal (1972)] considered that topic at length.

The topics covered here are grouped under the following section headings:

- II. Journals, Books, and Surveys
- III. Models for Automatic Pattern Recognition
- IV. Design Methodology For Automatic Pattern Recognition Systems
- V. Statistical Feature Extraction, Evaluation, and Selection
- VI. Dimensionality, Sample Size, and Error Estimation
- VII. Statistical Classification
- VIII. Structural Methods
- IX. Applications
- X. Prospects.

Section II gives a representative list of journals, books, and surveys for the period 1968–1974. Section III contrasts two models, the feature extraction statistical-classification model and the linguistic structural model, which have served as the basis for pattern recognition theory; it also briefly introduces a hybrid model. In Section IV, I describe how these theoretical models differ from the practical design methodology which has evolved during the last few years.

Prior to 1968 classification algorithms seemed to be the main output of theoretical research in statistical pattern recognition. Section V reflects the effort devoted since 1968 to theoretical approaches to problems of feature extraction, evaluation, and selection. In Section V, I examine recent approaches to defining pattern representation spaces and to deriving features that enhance class separability; theoretical and experimental investigations of distance measures and error bounds and their use in feature evaluation; and feature subset selection procedures.

Problems in the design and analysis of pattern classification experiments represent another area receiving increased attention since 1968. Section VI summarizes recent investigations and the resulting rules of thumb on the ratio that should be maintained between the number of design samples per class and the number of features. Insights gained from work on how best to use a fixed size sample in designing and testing a classifier are also summarized. In addition, Section VI presents results on the nonparametric estimation of the Bayes error and on the use of unlabeled samples in estimating the error rate.

Section VII is primarily concerned with nonparametric classification. It also briefly describes attempts to compare classification procedures.

Using examples in waveform segmentation and speech recognition in Section VIII, I comment on certain key concepts and differences that distinguish some recent problem-oriented contributions to segmentation, feature extraction, and structural analysis from other general numerical analysis and grammar based approaches. In addition, research on generalizing pattern grammars to overcome the limitations of string grammars is described.

Section IX considers the present status of applications, and Section X comments on how work in pattern recognition is likely to proceed in the near future. References follow Section X.

It is not feasible to cover the waterfront of pattern recognition in a journal article. The aim of the selective discussion of topics and contributions which I present here is to provide a perspective on how pattern recognition theories, techniques, and applications have evolved during the last few years.

Manuscript received July 5, 1974. This work was supported in part by the Air Force Office of Scientific Research under Grant AFOSR 71-1982, in part by the National Science Foundation under Grants GK39905 and GK41602, and in part by L.N.K. Corporation.

The author is with the Department of Computer Science, University of Maryland, College Park, Md. 20742, and with the L.N.K. Corporation, Silver Spring, Md. 20904.

Reprinted from *IEEE Trans. Inform. Theory*, vol. IT-20, pp. 697–722. Nov. 1974.

II. Journals, Books, and Surveys

Since 1968 more than five hundred journal articles on pattern recognition have appeared in the English language engineering literature alone. Within the family of IEEE journals, articles on pattern recognition have been regularly published in the TRANSACTIONS ON COMPUTERS, TRANSACTIONS ON INFORMATION THEORY, TRANSACTIONS ON SYSTEMS, MAN, AND CYBERNETICS, and occasionally in the TRANSACTIONS ON AUTOMATIC CONTROL, TRANSACTIONS ON BIOMEDICAL ENGINEERING, and the PROCEEDINGS OF THE IEEE. Other journals regularly publishing papers in this area include *Pattern Recognition*, *Information Sciences*, and *Information and Control*. Statistical journals that frequently publish papers relevant to pattern classification include the *Journal of the American Statistical Association*, *Biometrics*, *Biometrika*, *Technometrics*, and the *Journal of the Royal Statistical Society*.

For years the closest item to a textbook in pattern recognition was a monograph entitled *Learning Machines* [Nilsson (1965)]. In 1974, one could choose from more than half a dozen textbooks of varying merit on statistical pattern recognition, e.g. [Andrews (1972), Young and Calvert (1974), Chen (1973), Duda and Hart (1973), Fukunaga (1972), Mendel and Fu (1970), Meisel (1972), and Patrick (1972)]; for a book review see [Cover (1973)]. In addition, one could turn to monographs devoted to, or including some discussion of, various aspects of pattern recognition [Anderberg (1973), Bongard (1970), Fu (1968), (1974), Lindsay and Norman (1972), Rosenfeld (1969), Tsypkin (1971), (1973), Uhr (1973), Ullmann (1973), and Watanabe (1969)] and numerous hardcover collections of papers and conference proceedings [e.g., Cacoullous (1973), Cheng *et al.* (1968), Fu (1970), Grasselli (1969), Kanal (1968), Kohlers and Eden (1968), Krishnaiah (1969), Tou (1970), (1971), and Watanabe (1969), (1972)].

The books by Duda and Hart, Meisel, and Ullmann provide broad coverage of the literature up to early 1972. Duda and Hart's bibliographic and historical remarks at the end of each chapter set a high standard of scholarship and give a "who did what, when, and where" picture of the pattern classification and scene analysis literature. Meisel's bibliography is also thorough. Ullmann starts with a description of a 1929 patent for a reading machine and gives the reader a guided tour of 451 references including several patents. Anderberg summarizes literature on clustering techniques, while Fukunaga examines the problems of error estimation in greater depth than the other textbooks. Young and Calvert include a chapter each on two specific applications, viz., electrocardiograms and optical character recognition (OCR).

In addition to these books, many survey articles, reviews, and bibliographies were also published in this period. The PROCEEDINGS OF THE IEEE devoted its October 1972 issue to papers extensively surveying applications of digital pattern recognition [Harmon (1972)]. Earlier survey papers that appeared in the PROCEEDINGS include [Ho and Agrawala (1968), Levine (1969), and Nagy (1968)]. A series of papers [Rosenfeld (1972), (1973), (1974)] covers developments in picture processing by computer during the period 1969 through 1973 and provides an extensive bibliography. For speech recognition, a survey [Hill (1971)], a study committee report [Newell *et al.* (1973)], a recent conference proceeding [Erman (1974)], and a forthcoming book [Reddy (1974)] provide adequate coverage. Additional survey articles on specific topics are cited in subsequent sections of this paper.

III. Models for Automatic Pattern Recognition

An early motivation for work on automatic pattern recognition was to model pattern recognition and intelligence as found in living systems; the Perceptron [Rosenblatt (1960)] and other 1960 vintage "learning" or "self-organizing" networks are examples of models that, at least initially, were biologically motivated. Although the excitement about them had been greatly dampened by 1968, such "bionic" models continued to attract a few circles interested in pattern recognition [Amari (1972)], adaptive control [*Business Week* (1974), Mucciardi (1972)], the implicit storage of a fixed set of patterns [Moore (1971)], modeling the cerebellum [Albus (1971), (1972)], and modeling the input–output relationships of other complex systems [Ivakhnenko (1971), Mucciardi (1974)]. The Proceedings of a 1974 Conference [Conf. on Biologically Motivated Automata (1974)] indicates a revival of interest in biologically motivated automata, neural models, and adaptive networks.

How well the "bionic" networks model the biological systems that served as their motivation is open to question. The point is moot if one accepts the view that recognition is an attainment or a goal rather than a process, method, or technique [Sayre (1965)]. Then machines can "recognize" certain patterns without necessarily having anything in common with the methods used by biological systems to recognize those same patterns [Kanal and Chandrasekaran (1968)]. Most of the theoretical work on machine recognition of patterns has not been biologically motivated but has adopted one or the other of two models, the feature extraction statistical-classification model or the linguistic model.

The period 1960–1968 witnessed extensive activity on decision-theoretic multivariate statistical procedures for the design of classifiers. However, the statistical decision theory approach was justly criticized for focusing entirely on statistical relationships among scalar features and ignoring other structural properties that seemed to characterize patterns. The general feature-extraction classification model, shown in Fig. 1, was also criticized for performing too severe data compression, since it provided only the class designation of a pattern rather than a description that would allow one to generate patterns belonging to a class.

These criticisms led to proposals for a linguistic model for pattern description whereby patterns are viewed as sentences in a language defined by a formal grammar. By 1968 these proposals together with the success of syntax-directed compilers had attracted many to research in pattern grammars. The linguistic or syntactic model for pattern recognition uses a "primitive extractor," which transforms the input data into a string of symbols or some general relational structure. The primitive extractor may itself be a feature extractor classifier. Then a structural pattern

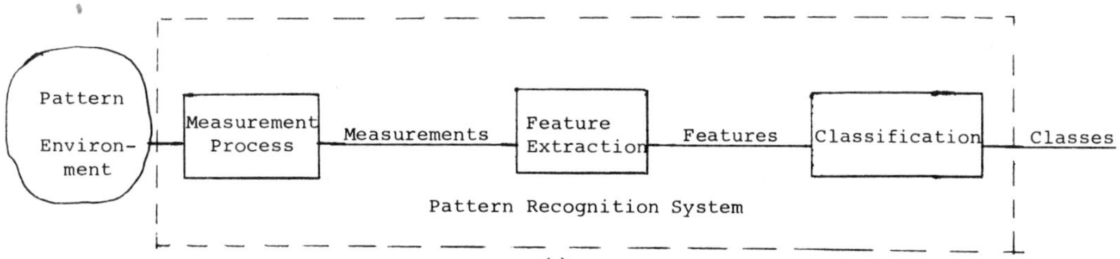

(a)

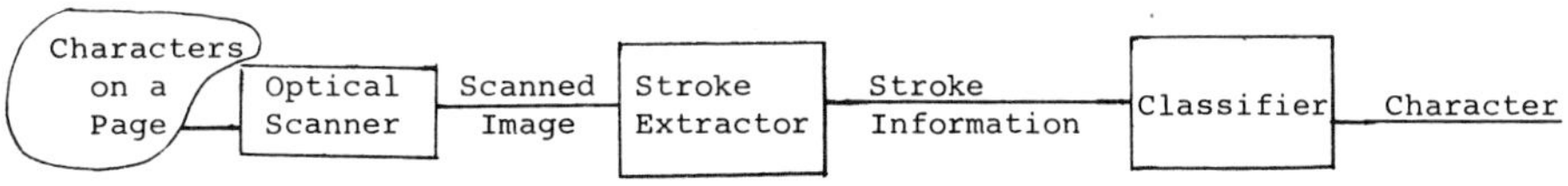

(b)

Fig. 1. (a) Operational system. (b) An example.

analyzer uses a formal grammar to parse the string and thus constructs a description of the pattern.

In the past, much has been made of the apparent difference between the two models. The stress on the distinction between the two models hides many similarities: in practice, in the syntactic model, the extraction of "primitives" can involve statistical classification procedures, and the association of patterns with generative grammars is equivalent to the classification of patterns into categories.

The definition of the formal linguistic model can be enlarged to include other familiar generative mechanisms, such as differential equations, functional equations, and finite-state Markov chains. Stochastic-syntactic models introduce probabilistic aspects into the linguistic model by specifying a discrete probability distribution over productions of a base grammar. For an N class problem, one could develop N stochastic grammars. Each parse provides a structure along with a probability that the structure represents the input pattern; the input is associated with the grammar giving the most probable parse [see, e.g., Fu and Swain (1971), Fu (1972)].

When a formal model is not explicitly present, the terms "ad-hoc" or "heuristic" are used. The phrase "structural pattern recognition" refers to all pattern recognition approaches based on defining primitives and identifying allowable structures in terms of relationships among primitives and substructures that combine primitives. This term represents less a specific set of procedures than an attitude, i.e., that pattern recognition algorithms should be based on the mechanisms that generate and deform patterns.

The structural pattern recognition model is reminiscent of the "analysis by synthesis" model proposed for speech recognition in this TRANSACTIONS [Halle and Stevens (1962)]. In the latter model, a synthetic pattern was generated and matched with the input pattern. The emphasis was on using a generative model that embodied the physical processes thought to govern speech pattern generation in humans, and driving this synthesizer with parameter values obtained from the input pattern. The set of parameter values that provided a match were then used to characterize and recognize the input pattern. The general flavor of the "analysis by synthesis" model and of the structural pattern recognition work now being done is similar, but the emphasis is no longer on identically matching the input pattern nor on matching the physical processes closely. More flexibility is obtained through "black-box" generative models that generate patterns "like" the input pattern without necessarily being closely related to the physical processes about which we may not have much information.

An outline of a formalism that attempts to combine the linguistic and statistical aspects of patterns has been presented in some thought-provoking papers by Grenander (1969), (1970). The major outlines of the proposal are fairly easy to follow but the details of the model are quite ambiguous and much interpretation must be provided by the reader. This model assumes we are given a set of primitive structural objects called signs, which together with known grammars or other known generative mechanisms, produce a set $\mathscr{I}$ of "pure images." Subsets of $\mathscr{I}$ satisfying certain similarity properties (which we do not define here) are called "pure patterns." The pure images are subjected to probabilistic deformations to give a set $\mathscr{I}^D$ of deformed images. Recognition algorithms would then have to define the inverse mappings from the set of deformed images to the pure patterns.

The formalism requires that there exist a method of analysis leading to a unique history of formation for any given image. In practice, in most interesting problems it is only the deformed patterns, further corrupted by noise, that are available, and the deformations and generative mechanism must be discovered from a limited set of samples. Because there will rarely be a unique definition of primitives and generative mechanisms, there will rarely be a unique analysis as required by the model.

In the period being considered, the fuzzy set model proposed by Zadeh (1965) has been applied to classification in a number of theoretical papers. Unlike classical sets, fuzzy sets are defined to have a membership function that can take on any real value between zero and one. This produces a nonexclusive assignment of a pattern to a class. It should be emphasized that this concept is different from a probabilistic assignment of patterns to classes even though a probability also takes on values between zero and one. In the latter case, for a two-class problem, for example, an individual pattern may be probabilistically assigned to one class or the other, but is not thought of as inherently belong-

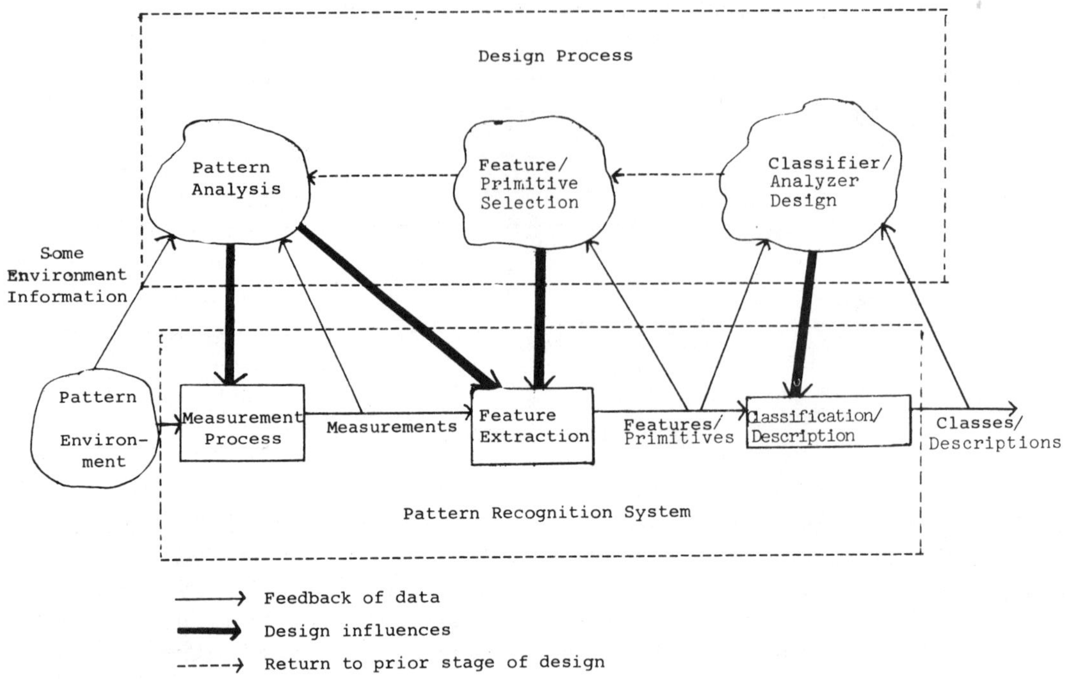

Fig. 2. Development of pattern recognition systems.

ing to both classes simultaneously, as is true in the fuzzy set model. An extensive bibliography on fuzzy sets is given in Kauffman (1973). Zadeh's papers remain the best source for understanding the idea and stimulating thinking about potential applications [Zadeh (1973)].

IV. Design Methodology for Automatic Pattern Recognition Systems

The term "pattern analysis" was not noticeably mentioned prior to 1968 and does not appear in the surveys on pattern recognition published that year in the PROCEEDINGS OF THE IEEE [Nagy (1968) and Ho and Agrawala (1968)]. Its widespread use in the literature seems to have followed the publication of Sammon's reports on the "On-Line Pattern Analysis and Recognition System" (OLPARS) [Sammon (1968)].

As it is understood today, pattern analysis consists of using whatever is known about the problem at hand to guide the gathering of data about the patterns and pattern classes which may exist in the environment being examined, and then subjecting the data to a variety of procedures for inferring deterministic and probabilistic structures that are present in the data. Statisticians call this exploratory data analysis. Histogram plots, scatter plots, cluster analysis routines, linear discriminant analysis, nonlinear mappings, analysis of variance, and regression analysis are examples of procedures used to detect and identify structures and substructures in the data. The purpose is to understand the regularities and peculiarities of a data base to enable better feature definition leading to simpler and better classification or description.

Pattern analysis is now considered an intrinsic and important part of the design process. In contrast, in the literature prior to 1968, automatic pattern recognition system design consisted primarily of designing the classifier. The available features and samples were not explored much but used directly, perhaps in a "learning machine" approach wherein parameters of a fixed structure are sequentially adjusted until correct classification is obtained for all "training" samples or until an error criterion is minimized; or the features were used in a fixed discriminant function the coefficients of which were statistically estimated from the available samples; or assuming parametric forms for the joint densities of feature vectors from each class, sequential and nonsequential statistical estimation procedures were proposed to estimate parameters of the densities for each class and derive classifier designs based on statistical decision theory.

Prior to 1968, it was acknowledged that the boundaries between feature definition, extraction, and classification were not sharp and that feedback between them was needed. However, this was not reflected in the work presented in the literature. At least all the theory-based papers assumed neat partitions between feature extraction and classification. The theoretical research published during the past few years on the syntactic approach to pattern recognition has, for the most part, continued on this path. For example, in the papers on the stochastic syntactic approach to pattern recognition [Fu (1972) and Lee and Fu (1972)], the extractor and analyzer functions are treated independently, which prevents the structural information available to the analyzer from influencing the primitive extraction. Without this feedback the representation provided by the extractor may not be well suited to the patterns being examined. Noting this limitation, models that incorporate feedback between the analyzer/classifier and the extractor have recently been proposed. These are described in Section VIII

A major evolution that has occurred during the last few years is to view the design of a pattern recognition system as a highly iterative process. Fig. 2 illustrates the complex nature of this design process. The theoretical models, in which the flow of data and decisions is in only one direction, from the input pattern environment to the categorizer/structural analyzer, are indicative of the operational pattern recognition system one seeks as an end result.

The advantages of human interaction and intervention in all phases of the iterative design process and the important role of interactive computing and display technology in making this feasible have been elaborated upon in Kanal (1972), which also summarized the data analysis techniques based on clustering, statistical discriminant analysis nonlinear mapping, etc. New graphical representations to enable human understanding of multivariate data continue to be explored, e.g., see Chernoff (1973). While no *radically* new statistical approaches to data analysis have appeared since 1968, effort has been devoted to improving and comparing algorithms and interpreting their relevance to feature extraction, evaluation, and selection. The next section presents some of the results.

V. Feature Extraction, Evaluation, and Selection—"Statistical Methods"

Feature extraction and selection can have a variety of goals. We may be interested in: finding key features that permit the generation or reconstruction of the original patterns, selecting features that parsimoniously characterize patterns, finding features that are effective in discriminating between pattern classes, or some combination of these goals.

In this section, the word "feature" denotes an entity that is derived from some initial measurements; this implies that somehow we know what initial measurements should be made. Reducing the initial measurements can lead to economies in sensor hardware and data processing. A simple approach to discarding measurements might be to examine how closely a linear combination of the selected measurements represents a discarded measurement [Beale, Kendall and Mann (1967), and Allen (1971)]. Clearly, no reduction in measurement effort is achieved if the selection is from features that are combinations of all the initial measurements; this is true of many of the feature extraction selection procedures that have been proposed. However, in the resulting lower-dimensional space, the search for a classifier may be greatly simplified.

Much of the mathematical-statistical work on feature extraction and selection during the past few years has been on:

1) linear and nonlinear transformations to map patterns to lower-dimensional spaces for pattern representation or to enhance class separability;
2) feature evaluation criteria that bound the Bayes error probability and transformations that are optimum with respect to such criteria;
3) search procedures for suboptimal selection of a subset from a given set of measured or derived features.

Pattern Representation Spaces

Many transform techniques, such as Fourier, Walsh–Hadamard, and Haar, have been proposed for deriving feature domains [Andrews (1972)]. The method of principal components, which rank orders the eigenvalues of the pooled covariance matrix of all the classes according to the magnitude of their associated eigenvalues, has a long history in classical multivariate analysis. Some papers in this period have considered nonlinear principal component analysis where, given a class of possible nonlinear coordinates, one finds the coordinate along which the data variance is maximum, and then obtains another coordinate uncorrelated with the first, along which the variance is next largest, etc. [Gnanadesikan and Wilk (1969)].

Among linear transformations, the Karhunen–Loève (K–L) expansion in terms of the eigenvectors of the covariance matrix is in one sense the minimax or "most reliable" feature extractor [Young (1971)]. Watanabe and others have proposed feature domains based on eigenvectors of the pooled autocorrelation matrix and on the eigenvectors of the autocorrelation matrix of a given class [Watanabe (1969)]. A novel K–L type modification of the Fourier transform has been suggested recently for pictures [Fukunaga and Sherman (1973)].

Their "optimality" properties notwithstanding, for a given data set the preceding procedures may or may not provide effective representations. Other candidates to be tried include nonlinear mappings based on multidimensional scaling and intrinsic dimensionality algorithms. Multidimensional scaling and parametric mapping are techniques for finding a configuration of data points in the smallest dimensional space that, according to some defined error criterion, preserves the local structure of the points in the original n-dimensional space. It is possible that the data may tend to lie on a curve in the n-dimensional space; estimation of the parametric form of this curve would indicate the intrinsic dimensionality of the collection of data points.

These nonlinear mappings have been the subject of some investigation during the past few years [Bennett (1969), Calvert and Young (1969), Sammon (1969), Fukunaga and Olsen (1971), Trunk (1972), and Olsen and Fukunaga (1973)]. The basic ideas and references on these mappings were briefly summarized in Kanal (1972). Some recent contributions aimed at simplifying or improving nonlinear mapping algorithms are mentioned next.

Sammon's nonlinear mapping algorithm [Sammon (1969)] involves computing all the $K(K-1)/2$ interpoint distances in the lower-dimensional space. In Chang and Lee (1973) simultaneous adjustment of all the K points to minimize the error function is replaced by a heuristic relaxation procedure in which a pair of points is adjusted at a time.

Iterative algorithms for nonlinear mapping must be repeated for new data points. A noniterative nonlinear mapping is proposed in Koontz and Fukunaga (1972). Noniterative procedures, using K–L expansions for local regions, have also been proposed for estimating the intrinsic dimensionality of the nonlinear surface on which the data may lie [Fukunaga and Olsen (1971) and Olsen and Fukunaga (1973)]. The local dimensionality estimation could be affected by noisy data samples being distributed about their intrinsic dimensional surface, rather than falling exactly on it. In Fukunaga and Hostetler (1973), a method for density gradient estimation is presented, and it is suggested that the samples be moved according to the density gradient so as to condense them onto an intrinsic dimensional skeleton.

Iterative nonlinear mapping algorithms have often been useful for representing pattern data in a lower-dimensional space. Whether or not the noniterative procedures mentioned here truly improve existing implementations of nonlinear mapping and intrinsic dimensionality estimation remains to be seen.

Representations Enhancing Separability

Instead of the information preserving aspects of K–L representations, Fukunaga and Koontz (1970) emphasized the extraction of eigenvectors that enhance class separability. This was done by finding the linear transformation that when applied to the autocorrelation matrix of the mixture of the two classes gives an identity matrix. Then after rank ordering the eigenvalues for class 1, one has $1 \geq \lambda_1^{(1)} \geq \lambda_2^{(1)} \geq \cdots \geq \lambda_n^{(1)} \geq 0$ and for class 2, $\lambda_i^{(2)} = 1 - \lambda_i^{(1)}$. The recommendation that $|\lambda_i - 0.5|$ be the criterion to select the eigenvectors to be used as features has been disputed in Foley (1973) where a three-dimensional two-class counterexample is presented. In this example, there is complete overlap between the two classes along two of the dimensions with very little overlap in the remaining dimension, and it is shown that the Fukunaga–Koontz ranking procedure leads to the two features with zero discriminating power being given the same weight as the one feature that provides high discrimination. As an alternative, a generalization of an optimal discriminant plane [Sammon (1970)] is recommended.

Let

$$R(d) = \frac{\boldsymbol{d}^t(\bar{\boldsymbol{X}}^{(1)} - \bar{\boldsymbol{X}}^{(2)})^2}{\boldsymbol{d}^t A \boldsymbol{d}}$$

where $\boldsymbol{d}$ is the (column) vector (of direction cosines) representing the direction on which the data is to be projected, $(\bar{\boldsymbol{X}}^{(1)} - \bar{\boldsymbol{X}}^{(2)})$ is the difference between sample mean vectors for the two classes, and $A = cW_1 + (1 - c)W_2$, where $0 \leq c \leq 1$ is a weight constant and W_i, $i = 1,2$, is the within-class scatter matrix for class i. Orthogonal discriminant directions are obtained by maximizing this "generalized Fisher ratio" and successively constraining each discriminant direction to be orthogonal to the previous set of discriminant directions. Foley (1973) presents examples in which this "discrim-vector" approach is superior to the Fukunaga–Koontz method.

For the multiclass case most of the work has either cast the M-class problem as $M(M - 1)/2$ two-class problems or employed multidimensional scatter ratios popular in classical statistical multiple discriminant analysis [Duda and Hart (1973)]. While based on linear operator theory, the attempt in Watanabe and Pakvasa (1973) to systemize the generation of orthonormal feature spaces for the multiclass problem, such that separability of the classes is emphasized, is different. Additional investigation is needed before its usefulness can be assessed.

Distance Measures and Error Bounds

If classification rather than description of patterns is the goal, the ultimate test of a set of features is their contribution to the Bayes error probability. The aim of feature selection is to reduce the number of features without adversely affecting error performance. Unfortunately, in most situations, even if the class conditional densities are known, a straightforward analytical relationship between the Bayes error probability and the features used is not available. Hence, various measures of information and distance have been proposed to measure the effectiveness of a given set of features. The major results relating such measures to the Bayes error probability are summarized in Table I.

The primary utility of the distance measures and corresponding bounds in Table I is for theoretical investigations. For example, the Bayesian distance and related bounds led Devijver (1973) to a theoretical justification for the least mean-squared error (LMSE) as a feature selection and ordering criterion [Wee (1968)] and to the relationship of the LMSE criterion to the nearest-neighbor rule. Of course, like the nearest-neighbor (NN) rules, the relationships derived from these bounds represent asymptotic results.

Despite the many papers published in this area, the net result of the extensive investigations on distance measure bounds for P_e seems to be that one should try to estimate the error probability itself in some direct manner.

Subset Selection and Heuristic Search

The feature selection problem can be viewed as a (combinatorial) optimization problem requiring a criterion function and a search procedure. All the literature on feature subset selection can be described in these terms. Some of the procedures were suggested years ago. I will cite here a few recent papers that illustrate the procedures.

In diFigueredo (1974) the probability of misclassification is the criterion functional to be minimized. Within a class of transformations that could include nonlinear transformations, the optimal transformation from the initial space to a feature space of prescribed lower dimension is determined, such that the increased misclassification error in the lower-dimensional space is minimized. The iterative algorithms presented are computationally much more complex than corresponding iterative algorithms for the Bhattacharyya bound [Decell and Quiren (1973)]. The k-NN bound was suggested as an evaluation criterion in Cover (1969) and used in Whitney (1971). Average information content $I(\Omega|X) = H(\Omega) - H(\Omega|X)$ was suggested for feature evaluation at least a decade ago. Experiments with this measure in different contexts continue to be reported [e.g., Simon *et al.* (1972) and Michael and Lin (1973)]. The divergence is another measure with a long history [Kailath

TABLE I
DISTANCE MEASURES AND ERROR BOUNDS

Name	Expression	Relationships
Bayes error probability	$P_e = 1 - \int_{S_x} \max_i [P_i p(X\|w_i)]\, dx$	
		m Class Bounds
1) Equivocation or Shannon entropy	$H(\Omega\|X) = E\left\{-\sum_{i=1}^{m} P_r(w_i\|x) \log P_r(w_i\|x)\right\}$	$\frac{1}{2}[1 - B(\Omega\|X)]$
2) Average conditional quadratic entropy [Vajda (1970)]	$h(\Omega\|X) = E\left\{\sum_{i=1}^{m} P_r(w_i\|x)[1 - P_r(w_i\|x)]\right\}$	$\le [1 - \sqrt{B(\Omega\|X)}] \le \frac{m-1}{m}\left[1 - \sqrt{\frac{mB(\Omega\|X) - 1}{m-1}}\right]$ $\le P_e \le [1 - B(\Omega\|X)]$
3) Bayesian distance [Devijver (1974)]	$B(\Omega\|X) = E\left\{\sum_{i=1}^{m} [P_r(w_i\|x)]^2\right\}$	$= h(\Omega\|X) = R_{NN} = \frac{m-1}{m} - M_0(\Omega\|X)$;
4) Minkowski measures of nonuniformity [Toussaint (1973)]	$M_k(\Omega\|X) = E\left\{\sum_{i=1}^{m} \left\|P_r(w_i\|x) - \frac{1}{m}\right\|^{2(k+1)/2k+1}\right\}$	$P_e \le \cdots \le R_{KNN} \le \cdots \le R_{2NN} \le R_{NN}$ [see Cover and Hart (1967) and Devijver (1974)]
		Two Class Bounds
5) Bhattacharyya bound [see Kailath (1967)]	$b(\Omega\|X) = E\{[P_r(w_1\|x) \cdot P_r(w_2\|x)]^{1/2}\}$	multicategory error: $P_e \le \sum_{i=1}^{m} \sum_{j=i+1}^{m} P_e(w_i,w_j)$;
6) Chernoff bound [see Kailath (1967)]	$C(\Omega\|X; s) = E\{[P_r(w_1\|x)^{1-s} \cdot P_r(w_2\|x)^s]\}$	$\frac{1}{2}\{1 - [J_\alpha(\Omega\|X)]^{1/\alpha}\} \le P_e \le \frac{1}{2}\{1 - J_\alpha(\Omega\|X)\}$, for $\alpha \ge 1$;
7) Kolmogorov variational distance [see Kailath (1967)]	$K(\Omega\|X) = \frac{1}{2}E\{\|P_r(w_1\|x) - P_r(w_2\|x)\|\}$	upper bound equals $[1 - B(\Omega\|X)]$, when $\alpha = 2$; $Q_{n+1} \le Q_n$; $Q_0 = 1 - B(\Omega\|X)$;
8) Generalized Kolmogorov distance [Devijver (1974), Lissack and Fu (1973)]	$J_\alpha(\Omega\|X) = E\{\|P_r(w_1\|x) - P_r(w_2\|x)\|^\alpha\}, \quad 0 < \alpha < \infty$	
9) A family of approximating functions [Ito (1972)]	$Q_n(\Omega\|X) = \frac{1}{2} - \frac{1}{2}[E\{[P_r(w_1\|x) - P_r(w_2\|x)]^{2(n+1)/2n+1}\}]$	
10) The Matusita distance [see Kailath (1967)]	$\gamma = \left[\int_{S_x} \{p(x\|w_1) - p(x\|w_2)\}^2\, dx\right]^{1/2}$	γ gives the same bound as $b(\Omega\|X)$; two-class bound relations: $P_e \le Q_n(\Omega\|X) \le Q_0(\Omega\|X) \le \frac{1}{2}H(\Omega\|X) \le b(\Omega\|X)$ [see Ito (1972) and Hellman and Raviv (1970)]

Notation: $\Omega = (w_i, i = 1,2 \cdots m;\ 2 \le m < \infty)$—a set of pattern classes; P_i is an *a priori* probability of class w_i; X is a n dimensional vector random variable; S_x is a sample space of X; $p(X|w_i)$ is a conditional probability density function; $P_r(w_i|X)$ is a posterior probability of class w_i conditioned on X; $f(X) = \sum_{i=1}^{m} P_i p(x|w_i)$—the mixture distribution; E is an expectation over S_x with respect to $f(X)$; R_{NN} is an m class infinite sample nearest-neighbor risk; R_{KNN} is a k nearest-neighbor risk.

(1967)] on which experiments continue to be reported. Only for a few distributions is it possible to obtain analytical expressions for the distance measures of Table I and use them in feature selection. It is also generally necessary to estimate the distributions.

It is an annoying fact that the set of K individually best discriminating features is not necessarily the best discriminating feature set of size K, even for the case of (conditionally) independent features [Elashoff *et al.* (1967), Toussaint (1971), and Cover (1974)]. Unfortunately, the only way to ensure that the best subset of K features from a set of N is chosen is to explore all $\binom{N}{K}$ possible combinations. Since this is usually infeasible, various suboptimal search procedures are used.

A search procedure which has been used much in the past is the "forward sequential" selection procedure in which the best individual features are chosen on the first round, and then the best pair including the best individual feature are chosen, etc. An example of the use of this selection procedure is the experimental comparison of seven evaluation techniques in Mucciardi and Gose (1971). A much used counterpart to forward selection is the sequential rejection procedure in which one finds the best set of $(n - 1)$ features by discarding the worst one, then the best set of $(n - 2)$ among the preceding $(n - 1)$ selected features is chosen, etc. The dynamic programming formulations for feature selection presented in Fu (1968), Nelson and Levy (1968), and Chang (1973) translate problems of feature selection into the notation of dynamic programming.

Other systematic approaches to feature subset selection, which are likely to receive attention in the near future, are suggested by the possibility of posing many problems in pattern classification as graph searching problems. Branch and bound algorithms [Lawler and Wood (1966)] and heuristic search algorithms [Hart, Nilsson and Raphael (1968) and Nilsson (1972)] can be applied not only to clustering [Koontz *et al.* (1974)] but also to reducing the search involved in feature subset selection. Simple heuristic search procedures have been used with automatic feature generation procedures in Becker (1968) and Simon *et al.* (1972). The usefulness of the result, whether in feature generation or feature reduction, is, of course, dependent on the appropriateness of the evaluation function used in the search procedure.

Further Comments on Statistical Feature Extraction

The preceding approaches to feature extraction and evaluation start with the patterns as points in a multidimensional measurement space that has somehow been defined. The statistical procedures then act as if relationships such as joint probability distributions, interpoint distances, and scatter matrices were the only relationships that mattered in defining patterns and their class memberships. All the optimization, with respect to various criteria, glosses over the fact that the initial representation space (and the "semantic coordinate space") has nothing optimal about it but was arrived at arbitrarily by some accepted convention, or by a combination of intuition, problem knowledge, etc. There is no guarantee that with the representations chosen in a given situation the minimum achievable error will be acceptably low.

The initial representation space and the features selected must be iteratively refined in terms of one another and the classifier as described in Section IV; the proper role of the feature extraction, evaluation, and selection procedures described in this section is that of intermediate tools or subroutines in such a recursive interactive design procedure.

VI. Dimensionality, Sample Size, and Error Estimation

For feature selection and classifier assessment, estimates of the Bayes error probability are of interest, as are estimates of the probability of misclassification of any "suboptimal" classifier that is used. Very often, little is known about the underlying probability distributions, and performance must be estimated using whatever samples are available. In this context various questions arise concerning the relationships between the number of features, the limited size of the sample, the design of the classifier, and the estimation of its performance.

The questions and the answers available to them in 1968 were discussed in Kanal and Chandrasekaran (1968); see also Duda and Hart (1973). Here we summarize some recent results concerning:

1) quantitative estimation of the bias in the error estimate based on the design sample set;
2) whether statistical independence of measurements allows performance to be improved by using additional measurements;
3) how to best use a fixed size sample in designing and testing a classifier;
4) comparison of error estimation procedures based on counting misclassified samples with nonparametric estimation of the Bayes error probability using density estimation techniques;
5) use of unclassified test samples in error estimation.

"Testing on the training set" and "resubstitution" are names for the approach in which the entire set of available samples is first used to design the classifier, and future performance is predicted to be that obtained on the design set. The well-known optimistic bias of this approach was confirmed by various theoretical and experimental demonstrations [Hills (1966) and Lachenbrach and Mickey (1968)]. A classical alternative is the sample-partitioning or "hold-out" method, whereby some samples are used to design the classifier and the remaining to test it. Usually half the samples are held out. An attempt [Highleyman (1962)] at analytically determining the optimal partitioning in order to minimize the variance of the estimated error rate has been shown [Kanal and Chandrasekaran (1968)] to rest on shaky assumptions. Based on experimental comparisons reported in Lachenbruch and Mickey (1968) and elsewhere, the conclusion at the end of 1968 seemed to be that one should use the "leave-one-out" method. In this method, given N samples, a classifier is designed on $N - 1$ samples, tested on the remaining sample, and then the results of all such partitions of size $N - 1$ for the design set and one for the test set are averaged. Except in some special cases, this method takes N times the computation of the hold-out method.

In Glick (1972) it is shown that the resubstitution method is consistent for general nonparametric density estimation schemes, and Wagner (1973) proved that the leave-one-out method is consistent in the nonparametric case under certain mild conditions. As pointed out in Foley (1972), even if a sample partitioning scheme is used during the experimental phase of designing a classifier, the entire set of samples is likely to be used for the final design. Thus one would like to know the conditions under which the estimate using resubstitution is a good predictor of future performance, and the relationship between that and the optimal probability of error achievable by a Bayes classifier.

For two multivariate normal distributions with equal known covariance matrices and estimated mean vectors, Foley (1972) derived the amount of bias of the resubstitution estimate as a function of N/L, the ratio of the number of samples per class to the number of features. The practical qualitative recommendation that emerges from the analysis and simulations is that if N/L is greater than three, then (for the case considered) the expected error rate, using the resubstitution method, is reasonably close to one with an independent test set. An approximate upper bound of $1/8N$ for the variance of the design set error rate suggests that even if just a few features are used, there must be enough samples per class to get a good low-variance estimate of the error rate. Thus, for $N = 50$, regardless of the value of the expectation of the design set error rate, the variance is bounded above by 0.0025. In addition to this, the analysis in Foley (1972) reinforces a well-known result, viz., that by adding more and more features one can keep on decreasing the error rate on the design set and yet have the additional features provide no additional discrimination ability on independent test samples.

As mentioned in Kanal and Chandrasekaran (1968), the less that is known about the underlying probability structure, the larger is the ratio of sample size to dimensionality that is needed. This is borne out by the analyses and results in Mehrotra (1973), which extended the investigation of the N/L ratio in Foley (1972) to the case where the common covariance matrix of two multivariate normal distributions is no longer assumed known but has to be estimated from samples. The nature of the results is similar to those in Foley (1972) but now, even for a N/L ratio as large as five, the expected probability of error on the design set is shown to be considerably optimistically biased. The results of Foley and Mehrotra are based on certain expansions, approximations, and simulations and are meant to provide insight and rules of thumb for practice. They lead to the conclusion that the larger the ratio of training sample size to feature set dimensionality, the better is the error estimate obtained from the training set. Furthermore, a sufficiently large number of samples per class is required in order to have a low-variance error estimate.

What about the number of features? That is, for a given finite design sample size N, is there an optimal measurement complexity? Experimentally it has often been observed, given finite training sets, that as the number of measurements is increased, the performance of the classifier first improves, later reaches a peak, and finally falls off. The analyses in Hughes (1965) and Chandrasekaran and Harley (1969) convincingly demonstrate that, in general, there does exist an optimal measurement complexity at which the mean classification accuracy peaks and that the value of the optimal measurement complexity increases with increasing sample size. Later, the effect of constraining the measurements to be statistically independent was examined in Chandrasekaran (1971) and Chandrasekaran and Jain (1973). In the first paper, Chandrasekaran studied the optimal Bayesian decision function for the case of independent binary variables, with class conditional probabilities $\{p_i, (1 - p_i)\}$ and $\{q_i, (1 - q_i)\}$ under class one and class two, unknown and to be estimated from finite samples from the two classes, using uniform *a priori* distributions for p_i and q_i. His conclusion was that in this case the mean probability of correct classification monotonically increases with N, the number of measurements, giving perfect classification as $N \rightarrow \infty$. The resulting conjecture that independence of measurements guarantees an optimal measurement complexity of infinity was proved invalid in Chandrasekaran and Jain (1973). This second paper presents necessary and sufficient conditions to test whether or not the number of measurements in the statistically independent case should be arbitrarily increased. From this work and from the feature selection example in Elashoff *et al.* (1967), one learns that statistically independent variables can behave more strangely than one might suspect.

The qualitative practical conclusions to be drawn from the aforementioned investigations on dimensionality, sample size, and expected performance seem to be the following. Depending on the probability structure, our degree of knowledge about it, and the estimation procedure used: a) there exists a lower limit on the number N of design samples per class needed to achieve a low enough variance for the error estimate; b) the ratio of N to the dimensionality L must be "large enough" if we are to get a good estimate of the average probability of misclassification; c) for the given sample size there is an optimal value for L, i.e., an optimal measurement complexity consistent with N/L that satisfies b). These conclusions do not, of course, hold for the case of completely known statistics but the latter would be a fortunate situation enabling the use of simple statistical methods. It is apparent that only the surface has been scratched thus far, and the phenomena of dimensionality, sample size, and optimal measurement complexity need to be quantitatively investigated in a variety of contexts not hitherto examined.

Next consider how best to use a given fixed sample of size N in designing and testing a classifier. Toussaint (1974) gives an extensive bibliography on this and related topics in the estimation of misclassification. With the "rotation" or Π method recommended there is a compromise between the hold-out (H) method and the leave-one-out (U) method. It consists of partitioning the total set of N class tagged samples into a test set $\{X\}_i^{Ts} = \{X_1, \cdots, X_k\}$, where $1 \leq k \leq N/2$, N/k an integer, and a training set $\{X\}_i^{Tr} = \{X_{k+1}, \cdots, X_N\}$; and then training the classifier on $\{X\}_i^{Tr}$ and testing it on $\{X\}_i^{Ts}$ to get an error estimate denoted by $\hat{P}_e[\Pi]_i$. The procedure is repeated with additional disjoint test sets $\{X\}_i^{Ts}$, $i = 2, \cdots, N/k$ and corresponding training sets, and the average over the various disjoint test sets results used for the expected error, i.e., $E[\hat{P}_e(\Pi)] = k/N \sum_{i=1}^{N/k} \hat{P}_e[\Pi]_i$. With $k = 1$ this is the leave-one-out method, and with $k = N/2$ this gives a version of the hold-out method well known in statistics as cross validation in both directions [Mosteller and Tukey (1968)]. The rotation method is also related to the "jackknifing" procedures described in Mosteller (1971).

The average resubstitution error rate $E\{\hat{P}_e(R)\}$ provides a lower bound on the true error probability while the other approaches yield upper bounds. In the graphs in Foley (1972) one finds that an average of the design set and test set results gives a good estimate of the true error probability. This leads Toussaint (1974) to recommend the estimate

$$\hat{P}_e^* = \alpha E\{\hat{P}_e(\Pi)\} + (1 - \alpha)\hat{P}_e(R)$$

where $0 \leq \alpha \leq 1$ is a constant depending on the sample size N, the feature size L, and the test set size k. In Toussaint and Sharpe (1973) it is reported that experimental work with $\alpha = 1/2$, $k/N = 1/10$, and $N = 300$, led to $\hat{P}_e^*$ essentially equal to $\hat{P}_e(U)$. To compute the leave-one-out estimate $\hat{P}_e(U)$ would take 300 training sessions, while to compute $\hat{P}_e^*$ takes only 11 training sessions, one for $\hat{P}_e(R)$ and ten for $E\{\hat{P}_e(\Pi)\}$.

Estimation of the Bayes error probability using classified, i.e., class-tagged design samples but unlabeled test samples has been investigated in a number of papers. These investigations use a result of Chow (1970) that, for optimal classification involving a reject option, a surprisingly simple fundamental relation exists between the error and reject rates. In a Bayes strategy, the conditional probability of error is

$$r(X) = 1 - \max_i \frac{P_i p_i(X)}{f(X)}$$

where $f(x)$ is the mixture density $\sum_i P_i p_i(x)$. With rejection allowed, the optimum strategy is to reject whenever $r(X) > t$, where t is the rejection threshold, and decide as before, otherwise. The reject rate $R(t) = \Pr[r(X) > t] = 1 - G(t)$, where $G(t)$ is the cumulative distribution function (cdf) of $r(X)$. The error rate is then given by

$$E(t) = \int_0^t y\, dG(y) = -\int_0^t y\, dR(y).$$

A plot of this relationship gives an error-reject tradeoff curve the slope of which at a given point is the rejection threshold. Chow (1970) noted that this simple integral relation allows the error rate and tradeoff curve to be determined from the empirically observed reject rate function $R(t)$ on unlabeled samples; it can also be used for model validation by comparing the empirical error-reject tradeoff curve with the theoretical one derived from the assumed P_i and $p_i(X)$.

This latter idea was applied in Fukunaga and Kessel (1972), which pointed out that the suggestion was equivalent to a goodness-of-fit test for the distributions $G(t)$ or $R(t)$. One of the methods examined is a test based on the expectation of the conditional probability of error $r(X)$; $E\{r(X)\}$ is just the Bayes error probability P_e, without the reject option. For the M-class case, the estimate

$$E = \frac{1}{N_t} \sum_{i=1}^{N_t} r(X_i)$$

based on N_t independent unlabeled samples from the mixture density $f(X)$, has a variance at least P_e/M less than the variance $P_e(1 - P_e)$ of the estimate based on counting misclassified labeled test samples. This paradoxical behavior, whereby one gets a better estimate by ignoring the class tags on test samples, is attributed to the fact that the error count estimate gives a binary quantization of the error on a test sample, while $r(X_i)$ assigns a real value.

The application in Fukunaga and Kessel (1972) of optimum error-reject rules to two-class multivariate normal problems, for equal and also unequal covariance matrices, provides some interesting comparisons with the work of Foley (1972) and Mehrotra (1973) described earlier, and the remarks made in Kanal and Chandrasekaran (1968) concerning the role of structure.

For the equal covariance case with sample means and sample covariance estimated from a total of $N_1 + N_2 = N_d$ design samples, the analysis in Fukunaga and Kessel (1972) suggests that N_d/L should be ten or greater in order for mean performance to reasonably approximate the optimum. In terms of number of samples per class, this suggestion is consistent with Mehrotra (1973), although the latter's result was obtained by a different approach not involving the reject option.

For the unequal covariance case with unequal as well as equal mean vectors, simulation experiments in Fukunaga and Kessel (1972) showed that the results still depended on the ratio of the number of samples per class to the feature dimensionality but that an even larger number of design samples is needed. Also, with estimated parameters the true error rate is greatly underestimated by the error rate calculated from the empirical reject function. The article concluded that "using the empirical reject rate to predict error rates can produce very inaccurate results if the model used in the classifier design is inaccurate."

As noted earlier, the asymptotic error rate of the nearest-neighbor classification rule provides a bound that is as close or closer to the Bayes error probability than any of the other bounds. Cover (1969) proposed that the number of misclassified samples when using a nearest-neighbor classifier be considered as an estimated bound for the Bayes error probability. As the total number of samples asymptotically increases, for increasing k, the k-NN rules do provide increasingly better asymptotic bounds on the Bayes error probability. Cover's suggestion was followed up in Fralick and Scott (1971) and Fukunaga and Kessel (1973), where nonparametric estimation of the Bayes error probability was investigated via a) error rates resulting when k nearest-neighbor classification was used, and b) error rates of approximate Bayes decision rules based on estimated density functions obtained by using multivariate extensions [Murthy (1965)] of Parzen estimators [Parzen (1962)].

Fukunaga and Kessel (1973) used labeled design samples and unlabeled test samples. For a test sample X_i from the test set of N_t unlabeled samples, consider its k nearest neighbors among the design set N_d. Of these k neighbors, let k_1 be from class w_1 and k_2 from class w_2, and let $r_k(X) = \min\{k_1/k, k_2/k\}$. Then the sample mean $\hat{E}_k = 1/N_t \sum_{i=1}^{N_t} r_k(X_i)$ has an expectation that is a lower bound on the Bayes error. An upper bound is obtained from an unbiased estimate of the conditional k nearest-neighbor error. For N_d very large, the average of the lower bound $r_k(X)$ and the upper bound, over the unlabeled samples, gives a good experimental estimate for the Bayes error. The use of unlabeled test samples results in a lower variance for this estimate than an error estimate based on labeled test samples.

The results in Fukunaga and Kessel (1973) and previous results in Fralick and Scott (1971) suggest that for a small number of design samples the approach using Parzen estimates performs better than the k nearest-neighbor procedures. Further comments are made in Section VII.

When designing a pattern classification device, it is expected that a large labeled design set will have to be gathered. These results suggest a way of estimating the minimum probability of error that is achievable with a given set of features, without having to also label a large set of test samples. The labeling of test samples is not only expensive but can often be an additional source of error, as has been found in some medical applications.

The investigations into dimensionality, sample size, and error estimation described in this section represent perhaps the most useful research in statistical pattern recognition during the period 1968–1974. Although incomplete, they do provide rules of thumb and guidance for designing pattern classification systems and analyzing their experimental performance.

VII. Statistical Classification

The basic assumption underlying statistical classification is that there exists a multivariate probability distribution for each class. Members of a pattern class are then treated as samples from a population, which are distributed in a n-dimensional feature space according to the distribution associated with that population. For two classes an observation x on the vector random variable X representing the features is treated as coming from one of two distributions F_1 or F_2.

This theoretical framework leads to subcategories ranging from complete statistical knowledge of the distributions to no knowledge except that which can be inferred from samples. The subcategories are

a) known distributions;
b) parametric families of distributions for which the functional forms are known, but some finite set of parameters need to be estimated;
c) the nonparametric case in which the distributions are not known.

Under b) and c) there are the possibilities that either some sample patterns of known classification are available, or unlabeled samples are available.

The subcategories a), b), and c) were discussed in Fix and Hodges (1951) and by various other authors in statistics. In Ho and Agrawala (1968) the basic categorization scheme was enlarged to include the additional aspect of unlabeled samples. The paper surveyed work on statistical classification algorithms presented in the engineering literature on pattern recognition through early 1968. Some topics under categories a) and b) that were considered in some detail are sequential and nonsequential statistical decision theoretic algorithms, recursive Bayesian procedures for "learning with a teacher" when labeled samples are available, and the Bayesian formulation of "learning without a teacher" when unlabeled samples are available. Under category c) the paper described: algorithms for learning the coefficients of linear decision functions based on iterative deterministic optimization procedures for solving linear inequalities under some criterion function; extensions of these procedures to deal with nonlinear inequalities or piecewise linear inequalities; algorithms based on stochastic approximation methods to find the coefficients of orthonormal series representations for the difference between the unknown *a posteriori* probability distributions for each class; and some clustering algorithms for unlabeled samples. Also mentioned was the result in Cover and Hart (1967) that for an infinite sample size, using the nearest-neighbor rule for classifying a sample leads to an error rate that is never worse than twice the Bayes error probability.

In the period since 1968, papers on classification under subcategories b) and c) for labeled and unlabeled samples have continued to appear; a survey of statistical classification similar to that in Ho and Agrawala (1968) could now easily be the sole topic of a very long journal article. However, the majority of recently published books in pattern recognition devote almost all their attention to statistical classification, estimation, and clustering procedures, and some of them, Duda and Hart (1973) in particular, provide very good surveys of the literature on these topics through early 1972. Thus I have limited the scope of this section to 1) some recent references and surveys for statistical classification procedures that derive from approaches covered in earlier surveys, and 2) brief descriptions and comments on some recent contributions. Under 2) I focus on topics in nonparametric classification. In recent years, this is the category of classification procedures that has been of greatest interest for work in pattern recognition.

Some Recent References

Prior to 1968 algorithms for the optimal solution of linear inequalities were often proposed in the pattern recognition literature. Papers on this topic continue to appear regularly. A recent example is Warmack and Gonzalez (1973) that claims to have the first direct algorithm, not based on gradient optimization techniques or linear programming, for the optimal solution of consistent and inconsistent strict linear inequalities. An accelerated relaxation-based procedure for finding piecewise linear discriminant functions is described in Chang (1973).

Many papers on decision-directed learning and on various other unsupervised learning schemes such as learning with a "probabilistic teacher" and learning with an "imperfect teacher" have appeared since 1968. In Agrawala (1973) schemes for learning with various types of teachers are reviewed, and simple block diagrams are presented to reveal their interrelationships.

For learning with various types of teachers and for many other problems in statistical pattern classification, e.g., automatic threshold adjustment, taking context into account, intersymbol interference, and distribution-free learning, at least conceptually, compound decision theory provides an integrated theoretical framework. A brief tutorial exposition of compound decision theory procedures appears in Kanal and Chandrasekaran (1969); see also the comments in Cover (1969) and the extended presentation in Abend (1968). In pattern recognition, examples of recent papers based on compound decision theory approaches are Welch and Salter (1971) and Hussain (1974). The optimal processing algorithms based on these approaches are generally unwieldy, and many approximations must be invoked.

Complementing the surveys of clustering presented in the pattern recognition literature is an excellent survey [Har-

TABLE II
NONPARAMETRIC PROBABILITY DENSITY FUNCTION ESTIMATORS [SEE COVER (1972)]

No.	Estimator	Formulation $f(X)$ density function; $X_1 \cdots X_n \cdots$ (independently identically distributed random variable)	Comments
1	Histogram	partition real line into sets $S_1, S_2, \cdots$, let $g_i(x)$ be indicator function for S_i, then $$\hat{f}_n(x) = \sum_i^k g_i(x) \left\{\frac{1}{n} \sum_{j=1}^n g_i(x_j)\right\}$$	variance $\rightarrow 0$ as $\frac{1}{n}$, unbiased 1) selection of S_i's and their number is arbitrary 2) results in piecewise constant $\hat{f}_n(x)$
2	Orthogonal function	$$\hat{f}_n(x) = \sum_{i=1}^k \hat{C}_i^{(n)} \psi_i(x)$$ where $$\hat{C}_i^{(n)} = \frac{1}{n} \sum_{j=1}^n \psi_i(x_j)$$ which minimizes $$J_n = \int (f(x) - \hat{f}_n(x))^2 \, dx$$	1) reduces to histogram approach if $\psi_i = g_i$ 2) possibility of negative values for $\hat{f}_n(x)$ exists 3) scale of ψ_i must be selected before the data is observed [see also Crain (1973)]
3	Rosenblatt estimator	$$\hat{f}_n(x) = \frac{[F_n(x+h) - F_n(x-h)]}{2h}$$ where $$F_n(x) = \frac{1}{n} \sum_{j=1}^n g'(x - x_j)$$ $$g'(x) = \begin{cases} 1, & x \geq 0 \\ 0, & x < 0 \end{cases}$$	$$E\hat{f}_n(x) = f(x) + \frac{h^2}{6} f''(x) + o(h^4)$$ $$E(\hat{f}_n(x) - f(x))^2 = \frac{f(x)}{2hn} + \frac{h^4}{36} \lvert f''(x) \rvert^2 + o\left(\frac{1}{nh} + h^4\right)$$
4	Parzen estimator	$$\hat{f}_n(x) = \frac{1}{h(n)} \sum_{i=1}^n K\left(\frac{x - x_i}{h(n)}\right)$$ K is bounded, absolutely integrable Kernel function $$\lvert xK(x) \rvert \rightarrow 0 \quad \text{as} \quad \lvert x \rvert \rightarrow \infty$$ $$\int K(y) \, dy = 1$$	unbiased, $$\text{var}(\hat{f}_n(x)) \leq \frac{1}{n} E\left(\frac{1}{h(n)} K\left(\frac{x - x_i}{hn}\right)\right)^2$$ rate of convergence $\approx \frac{1}{n}$ (depends on continuity of f)
5	Loftsgaarden and Quesenberry	$$\hat{f}_n(x) = \frac{k_n/n}{2d(n)}$$ where k_n is an integer n, $d(n)$ is the distance to the k_nth closest sample point from x	if $k_n \rightarrow \infty$, $\frac{k_n}{n} \rightarrow 0$ $\Rightarrow$ consistent estimate

tigan (1974)], which provides many interesting recent references not cited in pattern recognition books and articles. The author aptly describes the present status of clustering theory as chaotic and says

> the probabilistic and statistical aspects of clustering are still immature, the principal body of knowledge being clustering algorithms which generate standard clustering structures such as trees or partitions from standard forms of input data such as a distance matrix or data matrix.

Dissatisfaction with heuristic approaches has led to some theoretical analyses of clustering. A recent reference is Wright (1973), who attempts an axiomatic formalization of clustering.

Some recent papers have considered the comparative evaluation of alternative discrimination procedures, a topic that is of direct interest to pattern recognition practice. In Moore (1973), five discriminant functions for binary variables are evaluated. These are the first- and second-order Bahadur approximations, linear and quadratic discriminant functions, and a full multinomial procedure based on estimating the class conditional probability distributions. Among the conclusions drawn is that for binary variables, the quadratic discriminant function rarely performs as well as the linear discriminant function. This confirms the experience reported by many persons working in pattern recognition [Kanal (1972)]. A comparative study of linear and quadratic discriminant functions for independent variables from three nonnormal continuous distributions is reported in Lachenbruck *et al.* (1973). Other comparative studies of some classification procedures are Gessaman and Gessaman (1972) and Odell and Duran (1974).

Many of the comparisons in these studies leave one less than satisfied as to the generality or objectivity of the conclusion. An objective approach suggested by decision theory is to develop admissibility criteria that would eliminate obviously bad algorithms. Admissibility of k-NN algorithms for classification is discussed in Cover and Hart (1967). In a recent study [Fisher and Van Ness (1973)], seven seemingly reasonable admissibility conditions were used in an attempt to compare eight classification procedures including k-NN rules, linear discriminant analysis, quadratic discriminant analysis, and Bayes procedures. Unfortunately, the approach did not provide much comparative information about the alternate algorithms.

Nonparametric Classification Procedures

Nonparametric approaches to classification include:

1) linear, nonlinear, and piecewise linear discriminant functions;
2) stochastic approximation and potential function methods for approximating the decision boundary;
3) clustering procedures;
4) density estimation methods for use in an optimal decision rule;
5) nearest-neighbor classification rules;
6) statistically equivalent blocks;
7) discrete variable methods when there is no inherent metric.

The basic concepts underlying the first five approaches are clearly presented in Duda and Hart (1973) and Fukunaga (1972). These books also briefly deal with discrete variables and present some series approximations for the joint probability function of binary variables. Extensive development and discussion of research contributions to the first five topics, up to 1972, are presented in Patrick (1972), which is the only pattern recognition book with any material on the topic of statistically equivalent blocks. In the following, I briefly describe some recent contributions to topics 4) to 6) that have not been previously surveyed and appear to merit comment.

Five commonly used nonparametric probability density function estimators are examined and compared in Cover (1972), which gives 87 references on nonparametric density estimation. Table II presents a summary of the five estimators. The application of B-splines to multivariate pdf estimation using Parzen estimators is the subject of a recent dissertation [Bennett (1974)]. B-splines are local rather than global approximating functions, so that each point in a set of data points being approximated with the B-spline basis functions has influence on a fixed fraction of the density estimate. For estimating a L dimensional pdf from n random L-vectors of data, Bennett presents an algorithm that uses a L dimensional density kernel estimator with a L-fold tensor product of B-splines as basis functions.

The k nearest-neighbor class of estimators of Loftsgaarden and Quesenberry derive from a method of nonparametric density estimation suggested by Fix and Hodges (1951). In this approach the volume of the region containing the k nearest neighbors of a point is used to estimate the density at that point. Thus the number of observations is fixed and the volume is random. This contrasts with the Parzen estimator approach in which the volume is fixed and the number of data points is random. This symmetry is suggestive and Fralick and Scott (1971) pointed out that the need to choose the kernel K and window (weighting) functions h in the Parzen estimator has its counterpart in the need to choose the number of nearest neighbors and the metric in the k nearest-neighbor approach. Using techniques similar to earlier work on the derivation of the optimum kernel function for Parzen estimators, Fukunaga and Hostetler (1973) obtained a functional form for the optimum k in terms of sample size, dimensionality, and the underlying probability distribution. The optimality is in the sense of minimizing an approximated mean-square error or integrated mean-square error criterion.

A number of papers, many of them published in this TRANSACTIONS, have been concerned with the asymptotic convergence of k-NN rules and certain variations thereof, [Cover (1968), Peterson (1970), Wilson (1972), Wagner (1971), (1973), and Wolverton (1973)]. Of course, the small sample behavior of any nonparametric decision rule is problematical. Cover (1969) has conjectured that

> The failure of the NN rule score to be near its limit is a good indication that every other decision rule based on the n samples will also be doomed to poor behavior. A small sample with respect to the NN rule is probably a smaller sample with respect to more complicated data processing rules.

The experiments of Fralick and Scott (1971) and Fukunaga and Hostetler (1973) would not seem to support that conjecture, as they appear to favor Parzen estimates. However, as Cover has pointed out, Parzen estimates involve a smoothing parameter that the experimenter can adjust after looking at the data. My own experimental comparisons, done in 1964, of nearest-neighbor rules with other competing classification procedures for a specific problem did not favor nearest-neighbor rules. However, these are isolated experiments, and theoretical analysis and systematic experimentation are needed to answer questions about the small sample performance of NN rules and, indeed, all competing classification procedures.

Other than the early work of Fix and Hodges (1952) for univariate and bivariate Gaussian distributions, the only published studies of the small sample performance of the NN rule seem to be Cover and Hart (1967) and the recent paper by Levine, Lustick, and Saltzberg (1973), for the case of samples from two uniform univariate distributions. Not surprisingly, for this case it is shown that the probability of misclassification is close to its asymptotic value even for extremely small samples. An unpublished result by W. Rogers and T. Wagner has been communicated to me by one of the reviewers of an early draft of this paper. For nearest-neighbor classifiers they find that with the leave-one-out method the variance in the risk estimate is less than $5/4n + 3/n^{3/2}$ independent of the underlying distribution. A similar result is claimed for any local classifier. This result is a nonparametric finite sample size result that should allow competing classification procedures to be compared using confidence intervals on the risk estimates.

During the period under consideration, a few papers on nonparametric classification using distribution-free tolerance regions have appeared. Unlike most of the pattern recognition literature, these papers take a non-Bayesian Neyman–Pearson approach to error performance and are thus of some interest.

In 1947, J. W. Tukey used the term "statistically equivalent block" for the multivariate analog of the interval between two adjacent order statistics; to extend the concept of order statistics to the multivariate case, it is necessary to introduce ordering functions. Given n observations from a continuous distribution, the sample space is divided by these observations into $n + 1$ blocks. For any block B_i the proportion of the population covered, referred to as the "coverage," is treated as the value of a random variable U_i. Subject to mild restrictions on the procedure used to divide the sample space, the random variables $U_1 \cdots U_{n+1}$ have a joint distribution that is independent of the distribution giving rise to the sample observations. The distribution is the Dirichlet distribution—a uniform distribution over a set prescribed by simple inequalities. This property of the coverages of the $(n + 1)$ blocks leads to the term statistically equivalent blocks.

Since the sum of any group of the U_i has a beta distribution, the marginal distribution of the proportion of the population that lies in a group of the blocks has the beta distribution. Enough blocks can be chosen to make a probability statement such as "in repeated sampling the probability is p that the region R contains at least α of the population." Thus a distribution-free tolerance region whose coverage has the beta distribution can be constructed in the multivariate case by defining ordering functions to generate statistically equivalent sample blocks.

In Quesenberry and Gessaman (1968), an optimal procedure, in the two-class case, is defined to be one that minimizes the probability of reserve judgment, i.e., rejection, while controlling the conditional error probabilities for each class within prescribed upper bounds. The paper presents a nonparametric classification procedure based on forming regions of reserve judgment from intersections of distribution-free tolerance regions. The choice of the ordering functions determines the usefulness of the procedures; for some families of distributions it is possible to select ordering functions that will make the nonparametric procedure consistent with the optimal procedure for the given family.

In the same context as the preceding paper, Anderson and Benning (1970) present a suboptimum nonparametric classification procedure for the two-class problem. In this paper, the set of ordering functions used to form tolerance regions for the first distribution are based on clusters of the sample drawn from the second distribution, and vice versa. Hyperspherical (Euclidean distance) and hyperelliptical ordering functions are suggested to order observations with respect to cluster means. Note that the general theory of distribution-free tolerance regions does not consider the case where the regions corresponding to a distribution depend on randomness from a source different than the observations on that distribution. Anderson and Benning (1970) prove that the theory does hold for this case.

An earlier paper in this area is Henrichon and Fu (1969). A recent paper is Beakley and Tuteur (1972), which presents three ordering procedures to develop nonparametric tolerance regions and uses them in automatic speaker verification. In Gessaman and Gessaman (1972) reserve judgment procedures based on nonparametric tolerance regions are compared with other standard procedures.

For discrete variables satisfying only a nominal scale (i.e., when there is no inherent metric), a switching theory-based approach is presented in Michalski (1972), (1973) and Stoffel (1972), (1974). In the past, various similarity and clustering metrics have been tried for nominal variables [Anderberg (1973), Goodall (1966), and Hills (1967)]. Sammon (1971) suggested procedures for transforming such discrete variables, termed Discrete Type II variables, into continuous features; the OLPARS Discrete Variable Subsystem commented upon in Kanal (1972) provides a number of such transformations. The contribution of Michalski (1972) and Stoffel (1972) is a feature generation and classification procedure that generates a small set of n-tuples for discrete nominal variables. These n-tuples, called "prime events" in Stoffel (1972), are claimed both to fit a specific class and to discriminate it from other classes.

The independent developments by Michalski and by Stoffel of essentially the same concepts and procedures are based on the idea of the "cover" of two events, and they are related to work on the synthesis of switching functions from incompletely specified input–output relations.

Michalski's work on a "covering theory" approach to switching and classification problems predates Stoffel's 1972 report, but his formulation, development, and exposition are imbedded in complex notation. Here I follow Stoffel's terminology.

An event is an n-tuple $(x_1,x_2,\cdots,x_n)$ in which a subset of the elements have specified values, and the unspecified elements are "don't care" variables. Event e_1 "covers" event e_2, if and only if every element of e_1 which has a specified value equals the value of the corresponding element in e_2. Thus event $e_1 = (2,\cdot,\cdot)$, where $\cdot$ denotes an unspecified element, covers event $e_2 = (2,1,0)$ and event $e_3 = (2,2,\cdot)$, but e_2 does not cover e_1 or e_3, and e_3 does not cover e_1 or e_2. A prime event is an event that covers only those measurement vectors assigned to one class by a Bayes classifier. Also a prime event is not covered by another prime event. An algorithm to generate a sufficient set of prime events that will cover the class is given; the resulting set may not be the smallest possible.

To account for vagaries in the sample, Hamming distance is used as a measure of similarity between events or between a measurement vector and an event. Classification is done by assigning a sample to that class the set of prime events of which covers the sample vector. If the distance from all prime events exceeds a threshold, then the sample is rejected.

The procedure is certainly a systematic approach to the generating of a small set of good templates. However, it generates prime events for each class versus the rest of the classes. It is easy to give examples where by grouping classes together and using a tree classification structure one can do as well with fewer prime events.

The last comment brings up the question as to whether the complexity of patterns and pattern representation schemes can be considered independently of the classification structure adopted.

In an essay on the complexity of patterns and pattern recognition systems [Kanal and Harley (1969)], it is argued that complexity of patterns is in the eye of the beholder and that one can consider evaluating the complexity of different patterns with respect to specific beholders, i.e., specific pattern recognition systems or recognition logics. This is the approach taken by Minsky and Papert (1968), who compute the complexity, or what they call the "order" with respect to single layer threshold logic of a number of interesting geometrical properties. Various aspects of the complexity of patterns and pattern recognition systems are also described heuristically in Kanal and Harley (1969). Cover (1973) represents the beginning of an attempt to obtain a measure of the intrinsic complexity of a pattern so that different beholders, i.e., computational systems, will arrive at the same complexity measure up to an additive constant. Until such time as this effort succeeds, it is likely that problem complexity and system complexity will be matched heuristically in the manner described in Harley *et al.* (1968).

Commentary on Statistical Classification

There has been some tendency to question, in the name of practicality and simplicity, the need for further theoretical studies in the area of statistical classification. No engineer will quarrel with the emphasis on practicality and simplicity but as demonstrated by the attempts to compare classification procedures, not having theoretical guidelines makes it difficult to select between competing techniques without extensive experimentation. A suitable criterion and analysis can be used to analytically decide on the best technique among a set of ad hoc methods. What recent attempts at comparing classification procedures show is that, if anything, more analytical studies are needed so that experimental comparisons can be more meaningfully conducted under theoretical guidelines. The study of classification procedures needs to be extended to cover the combination of hierarchical classification structures and discriminant procedures commonly employed in practice. Finally, the proper role of nonparametric procedures is in the early exploratory stage of a pattern recognition problem. There is no substitute for discovering the underlying structure and taking advantage of it. As an example, the use of a nonparametric tolerance region procedure in speaker verification is warranted in the early phase of an investigation but for such problems considerably more structural knowledge can be used, and approaches such as those considered in the next section seem more appropriate.

VIII. Structural Methods

The linguistic approach views patterns as complexes of primitive structural elements, called words or morphs, and relationships among the words are defined using syntactic or morphological rules. The primitive structural parts are perceptually and conceptually higher level objects than scalar measurements. For instance, the gray levels of individual points of a digitized picture would be too low-level to be meaningful units of that picture, nor would the individual amplitude levels of a digitized waveform be meaningful units for structural analysis.

In practice, the structural approach involves a set of interdependent processes: 1) identification and extraction of morphs—this is the segmentation problem; 2) identification of the relationships to be defined among the morphs; 3) recognition of allowable structures in terms of the morphs and the relationships among them. Two-dimensional line drawings, fingerprints, X-ray images, speech utterances, and other such patterns that exhibit strong deterministic structure and for which *a priori* information in the form of some model can be easily used, are natural candidates for the structural approach.

Ad hoc structural processing has a much longer history in pattern recognition practice than statistical methods, which are based on abstract relationships involving joint probability distributions and distances in multidimensional space among sets of scalar measurements. Commercial print readers involve ad hoc structural processing, and biomedical programs are usually of this kind.

Much of the literature on structural pattern recognition has been devoted to formal methods. Fu and Swain (1971) surveyed the literature prior to 1970 and the November 1971 and January 1972 issues of *Pattern Recognition* together constituted a special issue on syntactic pattern recognition. Much of the published work on structural methods for pattern recognition and scene analysis from 1969 to 1973 is mentioned in Rosenfeld (1972), (1973), (1974). A brief survey also appears in Klinger (1973). A book on *Syntactic Methods in Pattern Recognition* has recently been announced [Fu (1974)].

These general surveys allow us, in this section, to focus on a few key concepts and differences in approach that underlie current work on segmentation and structural analysis.

Segmentation and Structural Analysis

Pattern description has been viewed either as two distinct processes—segmentation followed by structural description, or as an integrated process—segmentation-structural description. The first approach often delegates segmentation to preprocessing and concentrates on formal models for structural description which assume that the patterns are already represented as a segmented structure [Evans (1968), Fu and Swain (1971), and Lee and Fu (1972)].

Piecewise functional approximation is one method for preprocessing waveform data [Pavlidis (1973) and Horowitz (1973)]. The data are fit according to an error criterion with line (or polynomial) segments. The output from the preprocessor is a string of triples $\{(x_i,y_i),A_i,B_i\}$, $i = 1,\cdots,S$, where S is the number of segments, $y = A_ix + B_i$ is the linear approximation to the ith data segment, and (x_i,y_i) is the right endpoint of the line segment. This string is translated into the terminal symbols (tokens) of a grammar under the control of parameters appropriate to the application. The structural analysis is accomplished by a left-to-right

```
<CPW>--><SYSTOLIC><DIASTOLIC>
<SYSTOLIC>-->UPSLOPE <MAXIMA> LARGE-NEG
<MAXIMA>--><M1><M2><M3>/MED-POS <M3>/<M1>MED-NEG
<DIASTOLIC>-->TRAILING-EDGE/<DICROTIC WAVE>TRAILING-EDGE
<DICROTIC WAVE>-->CAP/HOR/PEK/PEK CAP
<M1>-- LSHOLD/<POS-WAVE>
<M2>-- CUP   /<NEG-WAVE>
<M3>-- RSHOLD/CAP
<POS-WAVE>-->CAP/CAP LARGE-NEG
<NEG-WAVE>-->VCUP/VCUP LARGE-POS
```

(a)

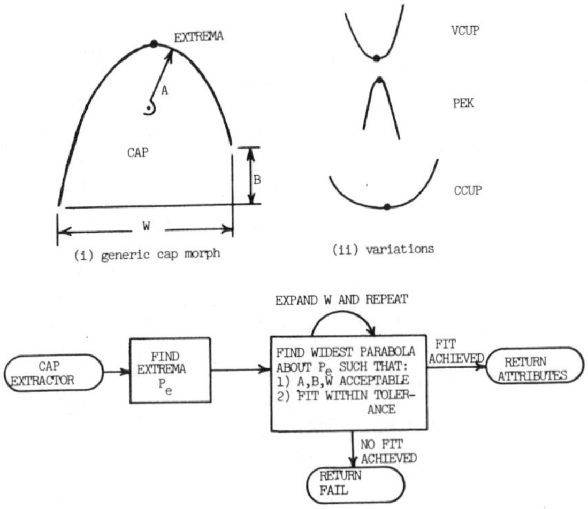

(b)

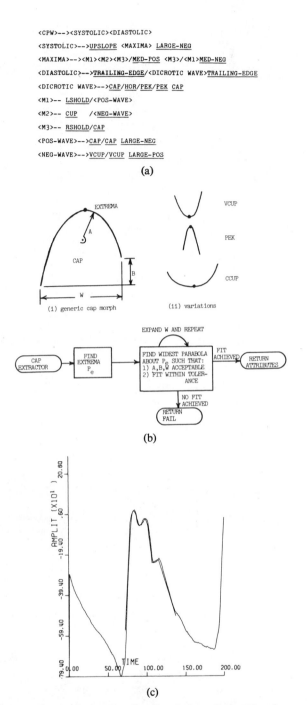

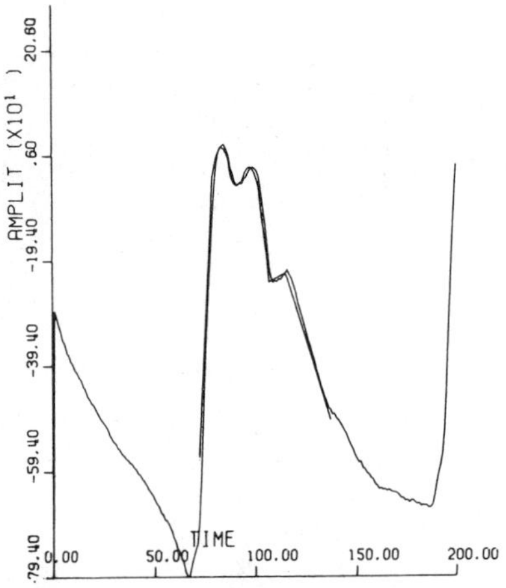

(c)

Fig. 3. (a) Original generative description of carotid pulsewaves through B.N.F. (b) Smooth extrema morphs used in pilot pulsewave analysis and rough extraction procedure. (c) One cycle of raw carotid pulsewave data juxtaposed with fitted representation obtained via parsing.

parser for a grammar that defines more complex relations among the terminal symbols, for example, several appropriate line segments could form a peak.

The advantages of this approach are preprocessing speed, generality, and the mathematical tractibility that approximation theory provides. However, the approach has more the flavor of numerical analysis than pattern analysis. This comment also applies to proposals to use truncated K–L series expansions in pattern analysis [McClure (1974) and Lavin (1972)]. Also such preprocessing usually results in arbitrary segmentations and requires excessive time for scanning and matching of all the data. Furthermore, the segments extracted may not be meaningful in the context of a specific application. In separating the analysis of structure from the extraction of morphs, each process is excluded from information available to the other. That is, the extraction of individual morphs must proceed in ignorance of the *a priori* combinatorial restrictions known by the structural component, and the structural component cannot profit from the intermediate work of extraction.

The alternative approach, integrated segmentation-structural description, is exemplified by the work of Stockman *et al.* (1973), (1974) for carotid artery pulse waveforms and Miller (1973) and Reddy *et al.* (1973) for speech recognition. The salient points of this approach are the following.

a) *Knowledge-based segmentation.* There is *a priori* knowledge of the possible segments in the data. For example, in a carotid pulse wave, it is known that an upslope, a trailing edge, a peak in between, and a dicrotic notch are likely to be found; see Fig. 3. Morphs can be defined that are believed to be of functional importance to the particular problem at hand and can vary in complexity from local extrema to exponential segments.

For scene analysis, Tennenbaum (1973), (1974), discusses the desirability of knowledge-based search for distinguishing features in preference to scanning the entire scene with low-level operators. The term "knowledge-based," currently popular in the artificial intelligence (AI) literature, generally refers to "nonstatistical" *a priori* information, although statistical information and Bayes' theorem are now also acceptable in AI [Yakimovsky and Feldman (1973)].

b) *A priori knowledge is represented by means of decision trees* [Narasimhan and Reddy (1971)], *graph models and decision graphs* [Harlow and Eisenbeis (1973)], *and grammars* [Stockman (1973)].

c) *Several levels of structural information are utilized.* For example, for speech recognition the following types of information have been used.

1) Acoustic-phonetic constraints that limit occurrences of given phonemes in segments of speech in the language under study and specify the phonemic content of vocabulary items.
2) Syntactic constraints in the form of a grammatical model that define what word sequences are allowable utterances of the language.
3) Semantic constraints that allow a hypothesized word sequence to be referred to a particular problem domain so that some measure of its reasonableness can be obtained.

d) *Parsing is bottom-up and top-down and non-left-to-right.* In other words, the more prominent morphs are sought first regardless of their location, and then the grammar is used to predict where other morphs are to be found. In the case of pulse waves, the most prominent morph might be the upslope. Having extracted the upslope, a grammar could be used to predict that the next morph to be scanned is the trailing edge. Having extracted the trailing edge, the next morphs to be scanned might be peaks and a dicrotic notch between the upslope and the trailing edge. In this fashion, the extracted morphs clue the system to the rest of the structures to be searched and also allow future search to be performed over restricted intervals.

In Miller (1973), parse trees are "seeded" by first scanning the entire input utterance for prominent vocabulary items (usually long words). Words in the local context of those found are then sought and partial parse trees (PPT) are assembled anywhere in the input. The PPT represents the grammatical structure of this part of the utterance, while the terminals of the tree are words in the vocabulary believed to exist in the input. PPT's are enlarged by using the grammar to guide the search for hypothesized words in the neighborhood of PPT's and to connect several PPT's into one. Analysis can terminate any time the complete utterance is "covered" by some PPT. The bottom-up non-left-right approach is attractive because of the ability to search first for reliable morphs regardless of location and to guide future analysis accordingly.

There is an analogous technique to this type of parsing, when decision trees rather than grammars are used to represent the possible structures. In the X-ray analysis in Harlow and Eisenbeis (1973), one searches for each lung lobe with respect to those lobes already found before it in the image. If processing leads to an impossible structural outcome, the analysis is backed up and extraction of morphs is taken up again. In Narisimhan and Reddy (1971), isolation of a given morph narrows the structural possibilities, while the present state of structural possibilities dictates the next morph extraction to be attempted.

The parsing approach can also be top-down and left-to-right [Walker (1974), Erman (1974)]. By going top-down only syntactically and semantically acceptable configurations are considered, and very expensive preprocessing can be minimized. By going left-to-right, classical parsing methods can be used and the state of analysis is easily recorded.

One can define a probability (or fit error) that a given morph matches a given segment of raw data. This probability can also be backed up a PPT to yield a figure of merit for a partial parse. The probability of a PPT can be changed by "semantic conditioning" [Erman (1974)]. By maintaining this figure of merit for all partial analyses only the most promising ones need to be extended, or in the case of complete analyses only the most likely cases need to be accepted.

Pattern Grammars

Much of the literature on structural pattern recognition deals with formal string grammars and their multidimensional generalizations. Recall that one of the reasons for introducing linguistic methods was the limited relationships handled in statistical pattern classification. However, phrase-structure string grammars are also severely limited in the relationships they model. Basically, they deal only with concatenation of primitives and immediate constituent structure.

According to a 1971 article [Uhr (1971)], past work on formal linguistic methods for pattern recognition has been either purely theoretical, or merely an incidental portion of some pattern recognition system, or incomplete in the sense of never actually resulting in a running program. As far as applications of purely formal syntactic methods are concerned, the situation remains essentially the same in 1974 as it was in 1971.

An incomplete effort of some interest (because it deals with a real problem) is Moayer and Fu (1973), which describes how a syntactic approach to fingerprint classification might be based on a context-free grammar model. This is one of the few formal grammar-based efforts aimed at obtaining a complete analysis from primitive extraction to classification. It contains: a) a careful study of the data environment yielding the choice of primitive syntactic elements; b) the hierarchical syntactic analysis that permits the one-dimensional concept of concatenation to readily apply to the two-dimensional representations used; and c) the "sequential recognition algorithm" that amalgamates syntactic recognition, primitive feature extraction, and sequential decision-making for computational and logical efficiency. However, no conclusive results have been reported yet on the performance of the technique.

Theoretical research in syntactic pattern recognition has been extensive during the past few years. Various generalizations and new formalisms have been proposed to overcome some of the limitations of string grammars. For example, stochastic finite state and context-free grammars obtained through the specification of a discrete probability distribution over each set of alternative productions have been used as a means of accounting for ambiguities of structure or generation [Fu and Swain (1971)].

We noted earlier the cleavage between the extractor and analyzer that occurs in formal models. In the work based on stochastic formal grammars [Fu and Swain (1971) and Lee and Fu (1972)], while the analyzer is designed to handle ambiguities of structure there seems to be no provision for ambiguities of representations handed over by the extractor. It seems clear that some data objects could be represented by alternative strings of primitives. Also, because the scheme is based on string grammars, it is forced to overemphasize the concatenation relation between primitives.

There have been several proposals for multidimensional generalizations of phrase structure string grammars. For example, in array grammars, instead of replacing one substring by another, rewrite rules are defined to replace a two-dimensional subarray by another subarray. Properties of array grammars and the relationship between array grammars and array automata have been investigated in Milgram and Rosenfeld (1971). In Siromoney *et al.* (1973), rectangular array models are generalized to n dimensions, and three-dimensional array models are used to describe the growth of crystals.

Plex grammars [Feder (1969), (1971)] involve primitive entities called napes. Each nape has a finite number of attaching points, each of which has an associated identifier. Napes are combined by bringing attaching points into coincidence. A picture description language [Shaw (1969, 1970)] can be used to describe pictorial patterns, the primitive elements of which have arbitrary shapes and distinguished heads and tails. The hierarchic structure of a picture is defined by using a "picture description grammar" to combine expressions in the picture description language. In coordinate grammars [Rosenfeld (1973) and Anderson (1968)], morphs have coordinates associated with them, and functions that compute the coordinates of the new morphs from the old morphs are associated with the rewriting rules. Coordinate grammars have been proposed for the description of mathematical notation, shapes, signs, textures, etc. [see, e.g., Chang (1970), (1971), Narasimhan and Reddy (1971), Carlucci (1972), Muchnik (1972), Nake (1971), and Simon and Checroun (1971)]. Graph grammars model various arbitrary relational structures among morphs. These include grammars that generate trees [Brainerd (1969) and Rounds (1969)] and labeled graphs, called webs [Pfaltz and Rosenfeld (1969)]. The notion of graph embedding has been generalized in Ehrig *et al.* (1973).

Bhargava and Fu (1973) present a scheme for representing line drawings in terms of trees. A tree grammar that generates trees is thus a formal description of the corresponding set of patterns. Among the examples given are tree grammars for the chemical structure of a natural rubber molecule and for two electrical circuit diagrams.

There are some problems in using trees and tree grammars in the manner of Bhargava and Fu (1973). First, since trees are acyclic graphs, a single tree cannot completely describe the connectivity of a closed figure. Second, trees introduce ambiguity into a pattern that may not itself be ambiguous. This ambiguity arises because the description of a figure by means of a tree requires a segmentation of the figure described, and an ordering of the segments. A different choice of segments and ordering would result in a different description of the pattern. Graphs and graph grammars are probably more appropriate structures for describing line drawings because cyclic graphs can completely describe the connectivity of closed figures, and a graph description need not order the parts of a figure.

It has often been suggested that transformational rules might be just as useful in pattern analysis as they have been in providing insights into the structure of natural languages. A transformational grammar is defined as $G_\phi = (G,\phi)$, where G is a reasonably simple "base" grammar such as a context-free grammar, and ϕ is a mapping that maps a structure in G, i.e., a tree, into a related tree. Joshi (1973) presents a detailed example of a transformational grammar derivation for a class of polygonal patterns. The example shows how a context-free base grammar and transformational rules for deletion of the interior lines of the generated patterns lead to much simpler derivation than a more direct approach involving a context-sensitive grammar.

Bhargava and Fu (1973) also discuss the application of transformational rules to trees generated by tree grammars. The paper considers transformations: 1) to duplicate patterns, i.e., to represent complex patterns as a periodic repetition of some simple pattern and 2) to relate two occurrences of the same pattern, one of which has undergone a shape-preserving transformation, e.g., rotation, linear translation, or reflection.

In Tauber and Rankin (1972), it is suggested that the syntactic structure of chemical structure diagrams be described by context-free web grammars or array grammars. However, there are some relations between chemical structure diagrams that cannot be described by context-free web grammars, for example, the relation between equivalent structural formulas of the same compound. Transformational rules can be used to transform equivalent diagrams into a canonical form, as well as to combine diagrams and to decompose diagrams into "kernel" diagrams. These are the ideas motivating the work of Underwood and Kanal (1973), which introduces the concept of a transformational web grammar. Because of the potential of graphs for describing patterns of practical interest, graph and transformational graph grammars are likely to receive increasing attention in syntactic pattern recognition.

IX. Applications

It is not difficult to formulate problems from a variety of fields in the terminology of pattern recognition. While that need not imply much about how amenable they are to solution, the terminology and methodology do provide a common framework for investigators in various fields as they become acquainted with work in pattern recognition. Some interesting recent examples are Pang *et al.* (1974), in which each set of measurements describing a state of a power system is treated as a pattern and classifiers, i.e., "security functions" are derived to indicate whether the system is in a secure or alert state; a dissertation in economics that shows how certain models proposed by economists for problems in voting theory and consumer demand can be interpreted and extended via the terminology and methodology of syntactic and decision-theoretic pattern recognition [Piccoli (1974)]; a classification of members of defined categories of stochastic nonlinear systems from input–output data vectors [Saridis and Hofstadter (1973)]; and a use of clustering and discriminant functions to classify characteristics of jobs received by a large digital computer in order to develop dynamic scheduling algorithms [Northouse and Fu (1973)].

Over the years certain investigators in chemistry have been quick to try whatever pattern classification algorithms happened to be popular, from Perceptron algorithms to k nearest-neighbor classifiers, on infrared spectrometric data, NMR spectra, and other chemical data [Kowalski *et al.* (1969, (1972) and Kowalski and Bender (1972), (1973)].

Most of these "applications" of pattern recognition in various fields have been academic demonstrations that suggest the relevance of the methodology. Similarly, many of the "applications" reported in the literature by persons developing pattern recognition techniques are merely incidental to the purpose of demonstrating that a new algorithm "works well," with the demonstration usually being performed on a limited data set. During the past two decades alphanumeric characters have been the favorite data for such "show and tell" experiments with new algorithms.

The focus of most of the published research in pattern recognition has been on techniques. This is very much in evidence in the books that have appeared in the last two years. They are almost entirely technique-oriented, giving a host of techniques with little insight into their comparative utility in different applications. This point is made rather colorfully in a review [Bremermann (1974) of Andrews (1972)]:

> While he should not be blamed for the unsatisfactory state of the art, he can be blamed for not making any attempt to convey to the reader a sense of the effectiveness and ineffectiveness of his methods. There are almost no applications (of 242 pages, only 6 are concerned with actual pattern recognition experiments). Thus a new sacred cow of mathematical machinery is created—its priesthood will probably make a good academic living regardless of whether the cow gives any milk.

Similar comments were also made until recently about information theory but one hears them less often now.

The blame for the state of affairs decried by Bremermann lies in part with the fact that the development of theoretical and heuristic insights, which are relevant to practical applications, requires the type of interaction between theoreticians and experimentalists that is very evident in physics. In pattern recognition, from time to time, such interaction has been fostered in industrial and government research laboratories by organizations interested in applications, such as optical character recognition, target recognition, electrocardiograms, and blood cells. For the most part, however, technique development has occurred without much feedback from experiments, since meaningful experimentation in pattern recognition often requires that significant resources be spent on collection, verification, and handling of large data bases. Some effort at sharing standard data bases is now present [IEEE Computer Society]; this should help. In many application areas, effective use of the data requires close interaction with persons knowledgeable about the processes that generate the data. Also required is a sustained effort devoted to the particular application.

Negative examples abound, wherein inadequate data bases were used and arbitrary operations were performed on data without knowledge of the field, thus leading to unconvincing results. A positive example is the work on the differential diagnosis of white blood cells. Much of the credit for the exploration of this application area goes to the pioneering and sustained work of Prewitt and her colleagues who, with adequate access to data gathering and experimental facilities, established many of the basic ideas for the development of this application [Prewitt and Mendelsohn (1966), Prewitt (1972)]. These ideas and other contributions [e.g., Bacus and Gose (1972), Ingram and Preston (1970), and Young (1969)] have led to the development of commercial products in this area. Whether or not these products of pattern recognition research become either a technical or a market success remains to be seen.

An annual review of progress in cell recognition and related areas occurs at the Engineering Foundation Conference on Automatic Cytology [Engineering Foundation, N.Y.C.]. Other examples of sustained efforts include various projects in electrocardiogram pattern recognition [see Caceres and Driefus (1970) and Zyweitz and Schneider (1973)]. One reason why this applications area is of considerable interest to theoreticians and experimentalists in pattern recognition is the extensive data base gathered by Pipberger [Pipberger *et al.* (1972)]. Although a few programs are supposed to work well, available pattern recognition products in electrocardiography are still undergoing evaluation [Cox *et al.* (1972) and Bailey (1974)]. Other areas of interest in medical pattern recognition include chromosomes [Castleman and Wall (1973)], X-rays [Chien and Fu (1974), Pratt (1973), Harlow and Eisenbeis (1973), and Ballard and Sklansky (1973), (1974)], and the process of diagnosis [Kulikowski (1970), Jacquez (1972), and Patrick *et al.* (1974)]. Only a few recent references have been cited here for these and other applications areas. Through these references, the interested reader can trace the literature in the area. A bibliography of articles on automatic quantitative microscopy is provided in Imanco (1973).

Much data are being gathered by remote sensing using the Earth Resources Technology Satellite (ERTS) and various other elevated platforms for pointing sensors back at the earth. It appears that this particular application grew more out of a need to justify continuation of the space program than out of experimental evidence that the data to be gathered would provide adequate information for discrimination of various phenomena. An excellent survey [Nagy (1972)] and subsequent symposia proceedings [ERTS Summaries, Remote Sensing Symposia] describe the extensive work being done in remote sensing. So far, only a small part of the work in this area is concerned with automatic classification but this is likely to change. Nagy has discussed, rather well, the prospects and pitfalls that await pattern classification studies on data gathered from satellites and aircraft. A study of the application of pattern recognition techniques to weather radar data is reported in Duda and Blackmer (1972) and Blackmer *et al.* (1973).

Table III presents a representative list of pattern recognition problems that have been attempted. It is interesting to note the recent activity in fingerprint and palmprint recognition and also in signature verification, which has been generated by the interest of law enforcement and military base security groups [Eleccion (1973), Nagel and Rosenfeld (1973), Proc. of the Electronic Crime Countermeasures Conf., and Sprouse *et al.* (1974)]. Pattern recognition methodology has also served as the basis for a study of the decision mechanisms used in palmistry [Oda *et al.* (1971)]. A more modern interpretation, viz., the genetic basis of dermatoglyphic patterns, underlies the preliminary pattern classification studies of palm and fingerprint patterns for their potential in diagnosing Down's syndrome, leukemia, and schizophrenia [Stowens and Sammon (1970), and Stowens, Sammon, and Proctor (1970)]; see also Penrose and Loesch (1971).

Applications of pattern recognition in industrial process control are being explored [see, e.g., *Business Week* (1974)].

TABLE III
SOME APPLICATIONS OF PATTERN RECOGNITION

Problem	Input to Pattern Recognition System	Output of Pattern Recognition System
Medical Applications		
Identification and counting of cells	slides of blood samples, microsections of tissue	types of cells
Detection and diagnosis of disease	electrocardiogram waveforms	types of cardiac conditions
	electroencephalogram waveforms	classes of brain conditions
	slides of blood samples	various types and proportions of normal and abnormal cells
Prosthetic control devices	mypotentials	categories of movements of limbs
X-ray diagnosis	X-ray photograph	presence or absence of specific conditions
Military Applications		
Interpretation of aerial reconnaissance imagery	visual, infra-red, radar, multispectral imagery	tanks, personnel carriers, weapons, missile launchers, airfields, campsites
Detection of enemy navy vessels	passive and active sonar waveforms	surface vessels, submarines, whales, fish
Detection of underground nuclear explosions	seismic waveforms	nuclear explosions, conventional explosions, earthquakes
Commercial and Government Applications		
Automatic detection of flaws— impurities in sheet glass, bottles, paper, textiles, printed circuit boards, integrated circuit masks	scanned image (visible on infrared, etc.)	acceptable vs. unacceptable, markings, bubbles, flaws, radiation patterns, etc.
Classification and identification of fingerprints	scanned image	fingerprint descriptions based on Henry system of classification
Traffic pattern study	aerial photographs of highways, intersections, bridges, road sensors	automobiles, trucks, motorcycles, etc., to determine the characteristics of the traffic flow
Natural resource identification	multispectral imagery	terrain forms, agricultural land, bodies of water, forests
Identification of crop diseases	multispectral imagery	normal and diseased crops
Economic prediction	time series of economic indicators	economic conditions
Speech recognition— remote manipulation of processes, parcel post sorting, management information systems, voice input to computers	speech waveform	spoken words, phonemes
Weather forecasting	weather data from various land-based, airborne, ocean, and satellite sensors	categories of weather
Object recognition— parts handling, inspection of parts, assembly	scanned image	object types
Character Recognition		
Bank checks	magnetic response waveform, optical scanned image	numeric characters, special symbols
Automatic processing of documents— utility bills, credit card charges, sale and inventory documents	optical scanned image	alphanumeric characters, special symbols
Journal tape reading	optical scanned image	numeric characters, special symbols
Page readers— automatic type setting, input to computers, reading for the blind	optical scanned image	alphanumeric characters, special symbols
Label readers	optical scanned image	alphanumeric characters, special symbols
Address readers	optical scanned image	letters and numerals combined into zip codes, city and state names, and street addresses
Other readers— licence plate readers, telephone traffic counter readers	optical scanned image	alphanumeric characters, special symbols

In some areas of automatic assembly, flaw detection using simple pattern classification techniques is feasible [Jensen (1973)], but the requirements on precision and low error rate may be quite severe. In other applications, e.g., stock market patterns, the problems are quite difficult but anything better than a 50-percent error rate may justify the effort. Another example is that of postal address readers, a number of which have been operating for several years. Even if they reject a substantial percentage of the letters they process, the sheer volume of mail they correctly sort can still make the installation worthwhile.

Character recognition is the only pattern recognition application area that has led to some commercially viable products. However, as a data entry device for converting written material into computer code, OCR equipment has so far not quite come up to earlier expectations in terms of revenues, customer acceptance, and technical achievement. Now there are new serious competitors to the data entry function performed by OCR; e.g., key-to-tape equipment, typewriter terminals using software editors, or on the near horizon, limited vocabulary isolated-word speech input to computers (also a pattern recognition technology). Also, the past few years have shown that the effectiveness of OCR installations depends upon complex interactions between computer systems, programming, forms design, imprinters, inks, systems and procedures, training, and so forth.

In summary, systems considerations have played a dominant role in the success of an installation, and this is likely to be true of many future pattern recognition products.

A survey of techniques for automatic recognition of print and script appears in Harmon (1972); for an elementary introduction to scanning techniques for OCR see Freedman (1974). Activity in this field continues, as evidenced by patents and papers [see, e.g., Sammon *et al.* (1973), Ullmann (1974)], and by the attendance at annual seminars of the Data Processing Supplies Association [DPSA (1971)] and other meetings. However, it is sobering to note that although many companies entered the OCR market over the last decade, not many have prospered in OCR activity. (Possible reasons why rosy predictions of rich markets did not quite materialize are offered in Kanal (1971).) Fortunately, the OCR experience has not stifled the entry of new companies into other pattern recognition product areas. In addition to blood cell and electrocardiogram recognition devices, isolated-word limited-vocabulary speech recognition devices are now available for trial in various applications. Perhaps these new areas will benefit from the lessons learned in OCR.

X. Prospects

In pattern recognition there have been repeated expressions of concern (similar to those familiar to information theorists) that theoretical research bears little relationship to practical applications. The research described in Sections VI and VIII suggests that this situation is changing. In the coming years, pattern recognition research is likely to intensify efforts to combine heuristic and formal methods and statistical and structural methods. Also likely to increase is the interplay between pattern recognition and various problem-solving techniques in artificial intelligence. The next few years should witness an increasing infiltration of pattern recognition techniques into various disciplines and an increase in serious collaborative investigations involving large data bases, especially in biomedical and remote sensing applications.

The interest in experimenting with real data bases should stimulate further theoretical and experimental studies on the design and analysis of pattern classification experiments. Because of their importance to practice, comparisons of various approaches to multiclass classification will no doubt be further investigated. In syntactic methods, the current interest in scenes, line figures, chemical structure, and electronic circuit diagrams is likely to stimulate further work on graphs and graph grammars.

Challenged by the question, "What is a pattern that a machine may know it?" perhaps someone will come up with a suitable definition of "pattern" in the way that Shannon gave precision to the colloquial word "information." If the resulting theory for such precisely defined patterns were relevant to a larger class of problems than existing theories—that would be a "Kendo" stroke of genius! However, the lack of such a theory does not prevent applied research from producing *now* results that would justify the promise held out by pattern recognition for the last fifteen years. Applications of pattern recognition technology to industrial automation, health care delivery, and other societal problems are being pursued and are likely to play a significant role in the near future.

Acknowledgment

I am grateful to A. K. Agrawala, B. Chandrasekaran, T. Cover, G. D. Forney, J. F. Lemmer, A. Rosenfeld, G. C. Stockman, W. E. Underwood, and two reviewers for their helpful comments on a rough draft of this paper and for their assistance. The construction of the introductory sentence of the paper parallels that used by Warren McCulloch in asking a similar question about numbers and man.

References

[1] K. Abend, "Compound decision procedures for unknown distributions and for dependent states of nature," in *Pattern Recognition*, L. Kanal Ed. Washington, D.C.: Thompson, 1968, pp. 207–249; also available from L.N.K. Corp. Silver Spring, Md.

[2] A. K. Agrawala, "Learning with various types of teachers," Comput. Sci. Center, Univ. Md., College Park, Tech. Rep. TR-276, Dec. 1973; see also *Proc. 1st Int. Joint Conf. Pattern Recognition*, IEEE Publ. no. 73 CHO 821-9c, pp. 453–461.

[3] A. K. Agrawala, "Learning with probabilistic teacher," *IEEE Trans. Inform. Theory*, vol. IT-16, pp. 373–379, July 1970.

[4] R. C. Ahlgren, H. F. Ryan, and C. W. Swonger, "A character recognition application of an iterative procedure for feature selection," *IEEE Trans. Comput.*, vol. C-20, pp. 1067–1075, Sept. 1971.

[5] J. S. Albus, "A theory of cerebellar function," *Math. Biosciences*, vol. 10, pp. 25–61, 1971.

[6] ——, "Theoretical and experimental aspects of a cerebellar model," Ph.d. dissertation, Univ. of Maryland, College Park, 1972.

[7] D. M. Allen, "Mean square error of prediction as a criterion for selecting variables," *Technometrics*, vol. 13, pp. 469–475, Aug. 1972.

[8] S. I. Amari, "Learning patterns and pattern sequences by self-organizing nets of threshold elements," *IEEE Trans. Comput.*, vol. C-21, pp. 1197–1206, Nov. 1972.

[9] M. R. Anderberg, *Cluster Analysis for Applications.* New York: Academic, 1973.

[10] R. H. Anderson, "Syntax-directed recognition of hand printed two dimensional mathematics," Ph.D. dissertation, Harvard Univ., Cambridge, Mass., Jan. 1968; also in *Interactive Systems For Experimental Applied Mathematics.* M. Kefrer and J. Reinfelds, Eds. New York: Academic, 1968, pp. 436–459.

[11] H. Andrews, *Introduction to Mathematical Techniques in Pattern Recognition.* New York: Wiley, 1972.

[12] J. W. Bacus, and E. E. Gose, "Leukocyte pattern recognition," *IEEE Trans. Syst., Man., Cybern.*, vol. SMC-2, Sept. 1972.

[13] J. J. Bailey, M. Horton, and S. Itscoitz, "A method for evaluating computer programs for electrocardiographic applications," Parts 1–3, *Circulation*, vol. XLIX, July 1974.

[14] D. Ballard and J. Sklansky, "Tumor detection in radiographs," *Comput. Biomedical Res.*, vol. 68, pp. 299–321.

[15] ——, "Hierarchic recognition of tumors in chest radiographs," Sch. of Eng., Univ. of Calif., Irvine, Mar. 1974.

[16] G. W. Beakley and F. B. Tuteur, "Distribution-free pattern verification using statistically equivalent blocks," *IEEE Trans. Comput.*, vol. C-21, pp. 1337–1347, Dec. 1972.

[17] E. M. Beale, M. G. Kendall, and D. W. Mann, "The discarding of variables in multivariate analysis," *Biometrica*, vol. 54, pp. 357–366, 1967.

[18] P. W. Becker, "Recognition of patterns using the frequencies of occurrence of binary words," Polyteknisk Forlag, Copenhagen, Denmark, 1968.

[19] J. O. Bennett, "Estimation of multivariate probability density functions using *B*-splines," Ph.D. dissertation, Rice Univ., Houston, Tex., May 1974.

[20] R. S. Bennett, "The intrinsic dimensionality of signal collections," *IEEE Trans. Inform. Theory.*, vol. IT-15, pp. 517–525, Sept. 1969.

[21] R. H. Blackmer, R. O. Duda, and R. Reboh, "Application of pattern recognition techniques to digitized weather radar data," Stanford Res. Inst., Menlo Park, Calif., Contract I-36072, SRI Project 1287, Apr. 1973.

[22] M. Bongard, *Pattern Recognition*, J. K. Hawkins, Ed. Transl. T. Cheron.

[23] W. S. Brainerd, "Tree generating regular systems," *Inform. Contr.*, vol. 14, pp. 217–231, 1969.

[24] H. J. Bremermann, Review of 'An introduction to mathematical techniques in pattern recognition,' by H. C. Andrews, *Amer. Scientist*, vol. 62, pp. 244–245, 1974.

[25] "Controls that learn to make their own decisions," *Business Week*, Apr. 6, 1974.

[26] C. A. Caceres and L. S. Dreifus, Eds., *Clinical Electrocardiography and Computers.* New York: Academic, 1970.
[27] T. Cacoullos, *Discriminant Analysis and Applications.* New, York: Academic, 1973.
[28] T. W. Calvert and T. Y. Young, "Randomly generated nonlinear transformations for pattern recognition," *IEEE Trans. Syst. Sci. Cybern.*, vol. SSC-5, pp. 266–273, Oct. 1969.
[29] L. Carlucci, "A formal system for texture language pattern recognition," vol. 4, no. 1, pp. 53–72, 1972.
[30] K. R. Castleman and R. J. Wall, "Automatic systems for chromosome identification," in Nobel Symp. 23: *Chromosome Identification*, T. Casperson and L. Zech, Eds. Nobel Foundation. New York: Academic, 1973.
[31] B. Chandrasekaran, "Independence of measurements and the mean recognition accuracy," *IEEE Trans. Inform. Theory*, vol. IT-17, pp. 452–456, July 1971. Correction, vol. IT-18, p. 217, Jan. 1972.
[32] B. Chandrasekaran and T. J. Harley, Comments "On the mean accuracy of statistical pattern recognizers," *IEEE Trans. Inform. Theory*, Corresp., vol. IT-15. pp. 421–423, May 1969.
[33] B. Chandrasekaran and A. K. Jain, "Distance functions for independent measurements and finite sample size," in *Proc. 2nd Int. Joint Conf. Pattern Recognition*, 1974; available from IEEE.
[34] ——, "Independence measurement complexity and classification performance," to appear in *IEEE Trans. Syst., Man, Cybern.*, 1974.
[35] B. Chandrasekaran, L. Kanal, and G. Nagy, Rep. on the 1968 IEEE Workshop Pattern Recognition, Delft, The Netherlands, IEEE Special Publ. 68 C 65-C, 1968.
[36] C. L. Chang, "Pattern recognition by piecewise linear discriminant functions," *IEEE Trans. Comput.*, vol. C-22, p. 859, Sept. 1973.
[37] C. L. Chang and R. C. Lee, "A heuristic relaxation method for nonlinear mapping in cluster analysis," *IEEE Trans. Syst., Man, Cybern.*, vol. SMC-3, pp. 197–200, Mar. 1973.
[38] C. Y. Chang, "Dynamic programming as applied to feature subject selection in a pattern recognition system," *IEEE Trans. Syst., Man, Cybern.*, vol. SMC-3, pp. 166–171, Mar. 1973.
[39] S. K. Chang, "A method for the structural analysis of two-dimensional mathematical expressions," *Inform. Sci.*, vol. 2, pp. 253–272, July 1970.
[40] ——, "Picture processing grammar and its applications," *Inform. Sci.*, vol. 3, pp. 121–148, Apr. 1971.
[41] C. H. Chen, *Statistical Pattern Recognition.* New York: Hayden, 1973.
[42] Cheng *et al.*, *Pictorial Pattern Recognition.* Washington, D.C.: Thompson, 1968.
[43] H. Chernoff, "Using faces to represent points in *K*-dimensional space graphically," *J. Amer. Statist. Ass.*, vol. 68, p. 361, June 1973.
[44] Y. T. Chien. "Bibliography on interactive pattern recognition and related topics," School of Eng., Univ. Conn., Storrs, Tech. Rep. CS-74-3, Feb., 1974.
[45] Y. T. Chien, and K. S. Fu, "Recognition of x-ray picture patterns," *IEEE Trans. Syst., Man, Cybern.*, vol. SMC-4, pp. 145–156, Mar. 1974.
[46] C. K. Chow, "On optimum recognition error and reject tradeoff," *IEEE Trans. Inform. Theory*, vol. IT-16, pp. 41–46, Jan. 1970.
[47] T. M. Cover, "Rates of convergence of nearest neighbor decision procedures," in *1968 Hawaii Int. Conf. Systems Theory*, pp. 413–415.
[48] ——, "Learning in pattern recognition," in *Methodologies of Pattern Recognition*, S. Watanabe, Ed. New York: Academic 1969, pp. 111–132.
[49] ——, "A hierarchy of probability density function estimates," in *Frontiers of Pattern Recognition*, S. Watanabe, Ed. New York: Academic, 1972, pp. 83–98.
[50] ——, "Generalization of patterns using Kolmogorov complexity," in *Proc. 1st Joint Int. Conf. Pattern Recognition*, IEEE Publ. no. 73 CHO 821-9C, 1973.
[51] ——, "Recent books on pattern recognition," *IEEE Trans. Inform. Theory*, vol. IT-19, p. 827, Nov. 1973.
[52] ——, "The best two independent measurements are not the two best," *IEEE Trans. Syst., Man, Cybern.* (Corresp.), vol. SMC-4, pp. 116–117, Jan. 1974.
[53] T. M. Cover and P. F. Hart, "Nearest neighbor pattern classification," *IEEE Trans. Inform. Theory*, vol. IT-13, pp. 21–27, Jan. 1967.
[54] J. R. Cox, F. M. Noile, and R. M. Arthur, "Digital analysis of the electroencephalogram, the blood pressure wave, and the electrocardiogram," *Proc. IEEE*, vol. 60, pp. 1137–1164, Oct. 1972.
[55] B. R. Crain, "Density estimation using orthogonal expansions," *J. Amer. Statist. Ass.*, vol. 68, p. 964, Dec. 1973.
[56] R. J. deFigueiredo, "Optimal linear and nonlinear feature extraction based on the minimization of the increased risk of misclassification," in *Proc. 2nd Int. Joint Conf. Pattern Recognition*, 1974.
[57] H. P. Decell, Jr., and J. A. Quierein, "An iterative approach to the feature selection problem," in *Proc. Purdue Univ. Conf. Machine Processing of Remotely Sensed Data*, 1972, pp. 3B1–3B12.
[58] P. A. Devijver, "Relationships between statistical risks and the least-mean-square-error design criterion in pattern recognition," in *Proc. 1st Int. Joint Conf. Pattern Recognition*, IEEE Special Publ. CHO 821-9C, 1973, pp. 139–148.
[59] ——, "On a new class of bounds on Bayes risk in multihypothesis pattern recognition," *IEEE Trans. Comput.*, vol. C-23, pp. 70–80, Jan. 1974.
[60] H. L. Dreyfus, *What Computers Can't Do.* New York: Harper and Row, 1972.
[61] R. O. Duda and R. H. Blackmer, Jr., "Application of pattern recognition techniques to digitized weather radar data," Stanford Res. Inst., Menlo Park, Calif., Contract 1-36072, SRI Project 1287, Mar. 1972.
[62] R. O. Duda and P. E. Hart, *Pattern Classification and Scene Analysis.* New York: Wiley, 1973.
[63] A. R. Dyer, "Discrimination procedures for separate families of hypotheses," *J. Amer. Statist. Ass.*, vol. 68, p. 970, Dec. 1973.
[64] H. Ehrig, M. Pfender, and H. J. Schneider, "Graph grammars: An algebraic approach," in *Proc. 14th Annu. Conf. Switching and Automata Theory*, 1973.
[65] J. D. Elashoff, R. M. Elashoff, and G. E. Goldman, "On the choice of variables in classification problems with dichotomous variables," *Biometrika*, vol. 54, pp. 668–670, 1967.
[66] M. Eleccion, "Automatic fingerprint identification," *IEEE Spectrum*, pp. 36–45, Sept. 1973.
[67] L. Erman, Ed., *1974 IEEE Symp. Speech Recognition*, IEEE Cat. no. 74CHO878-9AE.
[68] T. G. Evans, "A grammar-controlled pattern analyzer," in *1968 Inform. Processing, Proc. IFIP Congr.*, vol. 2, A. J. Moreli, Ed., Amsterdam: North Holland, 1968, pp. 1592–1598.
[69] J. Feder, "Linguistic specification and analysis of classes of line patterns," Dep. Elec. Eng. New York Univ., N.Y.C., Tech. Rep. no. 403-2, Apr. 1969.
[70] ——, "Plex languages," *Inform. Sci.*, vol. 3, pp. 225–241, 1971.
[71] O. Firschein, *et al.*, "Forecasting and assessing the impact of artificial intelligence on society," in *Proc. Int. Joint Conf. Artificial Intelligence*, 1973, pp. 105–120.
[72] L. Fisher and J. W. Van Ness, 1973 "Admissible discriminant analysis," *J. Amer. Statist. Ass.*, vol. 68, pp. 603–607, Sept. 1973.
[73] E. Fix and J. L. Hodges, "Discriminatory analysis small sample performance," USAF Sch. of Aviation Medicine, Randolph Field, Tex., Project 21-49-004, Rep. 11, Contract AF-41-(128)-31, 1952.
[74] D. H. Foley, "Considerations of sample and feature size," *IEEE Trans. Inform. Theory*, vol. IT-18, pp. 618–626, Sept. 1972.
[75] ——, "Orthonormal expansion study for waveform processing system," Rome Air Develop. Center, AF Systems Command, Griffiss AFB, New York, Tech. Rep. RADC-TR-73-168, July 1973.
[76] S. C. Fralick and R. W. Scott, "Nonparametric Bayes-risk estimation," *IEEE Trans. Inform. Theory*, vol. IT-17, pp. 440–444, July 1971.
[77] M. D. Freedman, "Optical character recognition," *IEEE Spectrum*, vol. 11, pp. 44–52, Mar. 1974.
[78] K. S. Fu, *Sequential Methods in Pattern Recognition and Machine Learning.* New York: Academic, 1968.
[79] ——, "On syntactic pattern recognition and stochastic languages," in *Frontiers of Pattern Recognition*, S. Watanabe, Ed. New York: Academic, 1972, pp. 113–137.
[80] ——, *Syntactic Methods in Pattern Recognition.* New York: Academic, 1974.
[81] K. S. Fu and B. K. Bhargava, "Tree systems for syntactic pattern recognition," *IEEE Trans. Comput.*, vol. C-22, pp. 1087–1098, Dec. 1973.
[82] K. S. Fu and P. H. Swain, "On syntactic pattern recognition," in *Software Engineering*, vol. 2, J. T. Tou, Ed. New York: Academic, 1971.
[83] K. S. Fu, Ed. "Pattern recognition and machine learning," in *Proc. Japan–U.S. Seminar Learning Process in Control Systems*, New York: Plenum, 1970.
[84] K. S. Fu, P. J. Min, and T. J. Li, "Feature selection in pattern recognition," *IEEE Trans. Syst. Sci. Cybern.*, vol. SSC-6, p. 33–39, Jan. 1970.
[85] K. Fukunaga, *Introduction To Statistical Pattern Recognition.* New York: Academic, 1972.
[86] K. Fukunaga and L. D. Hostetler, "The estimation of the gradient of a density function and its applications in pattern recognition," presented at Int. Joint Conf. Pattern Recognition, Washington, D.C., Oct. 1973.

[87] ——, "Optimization of k-nearest neighbor density estimates," *IEEE Trans. Inform. Theory*, vol. IT-19, pp. 320–326, May 1973.
[88] K. Fukunaga and D. Kessell, "Application of optimum error-reject functions," *IEEE Trans. Inform. Theory*, (Corresp.), vol. IT-18, pp. 814–817, Nov. 1972.
[89] K. Fukunaga and D. L. Kessell, "Error evaluation and model validation in statistical pattern recognition," Sch. of Elec. Eng., Purdue Univ., Lafayette, Ind., Tech. Rep. TR-EE 72-23, Aug. 1972.
[90] ——, "Nonparametric Bayes error estimation using unclassified samples," *IEEE Trans. Inform. Theory*, vol. IT-19, pp. 434–440, July 1973.
[91] K. Fukunaga and W. Koontz, "Application of the Karhunen–Loève expansion to feature selection and ordering," *IEEE Trans. Comput.*, vol. C-19, pp. 311–318, Apr. 1970.
[92] K. Fukunaga and P. M. Narendra, "A branch and bound algorithm for computing k-nearest neighbors," available from IEEE Comput. Group depository.
[93] K. Fukunaga and D. R. Olsen, "An algorithm for finding intrinsic dimensionality of data," *IEEE Trans. Comput.*, vol. C-20, pp. 176–183, Feb. 1971.
[94] ——, Authors' reply to comments by G. V. Trunk on "An algorithm for finding intrinsic dimensionality of data," *IEEE Trans. Comput.* (Corresp.), vol. C-20, pp. 1615–1616, Dec. 1971.
[95] K. Fukunaga and G. V. Sherman, "Picture representation and classification by pseudo eigenvectors," presented at the IEEE Syst., Man, Cybern. Conf., Boston, Mass., Nov. 1973.
[96] K. Fukushima, "Visual feature extraction by a multilayered network of analog threshold elements," *IEEE Trans. Syst., Sci., Cybern.*, vol. SSC-5, pp. 322–333, Oct. 1969.
[97] ——, "A feature extractor for curvilinear patterns: a design suggested by the mammalian visual system," *Kybernetik*, vol., pp. 153–160, 1970.
[98] M. P. Gessaman and P. H. Gessaman, "Comparison of some multivariate discrimination procedures," *J. Amer. Statist. Ass.*, vol. 67, p. 468, June 1972.
[99] N. Glick, "Sample-based classification procedures derived from density estimators," *J. Amer. Statist. Ass.*, vol. 67, pp. 112–116, Mar. 1972.
[100] R. Gnanadesikan and M. B. Wilk, "Data Analytic Methods in Multivariate Statistical Analysis," in *Multivariate Analysis II*, P. R. Krishnaiah, Ed. New York: Academic, 1969, pp. 593–638.
[101] D. W. Goodall, "On a new similarity index based on probability," *Biometrics*, vol. 22, pp. 668–670, Dec. 1966.
[102] A. Grasselli, Ed. *Automatic Interpretation and Classification of Images*. New York: Academic, 1969.
[103] P. E Green and V. R. Rao, *Applied Multidimensional Scaling–A Comparison of Approaches and Algorithms*. New York: Holt, Rinehart and Winston, 1972.
[104] P. E. Green and F. J. Carmone, *Multidimensional Scaling and Related Techniques in Marketing Analysis*. Boston: Allyn and Bacon, 1970.
[105] U. Grenander, "Foundations of pattern analysis," *Quart. Appl. Math.*, vol. 27, pp. 1–55, Apr. 1969.
[106] U. Grenander, "A unified approach to pattern analysis," in *Advances in Computers*, vol. 10. New York: Academic, 1970.
[107] M. Halle and K. Stevens, "Speech recognition: A model and a program for research," *IRE Trans. Inform. Theory*, vol. IT-8, p. 155, Feb. 1962.
[108] R. M. Haralick, "Glossary and index to remotely sensed image pattern recognition concepts," *Pattern Recognition*, vol. 5, p. 391–403, 1973.
[109] T. J. Harley, L. Kanal, and N. C. Randall, "System considerations for automatic imagery screening," in *Pictorial Pattern Recognition*. Washington D.C.: Thompson, 1968, pp. 15–32.
[110] C. A. Harlow and S. A. Fisenbeis, "The analysis of radiographic images," *IEEE Trans. Comput.*, vol. C-22, pp. 678–689, July 1973.
[111] L. D. Harmon, "*Automatic Reading of Cursive Script Optical Character Recognition*, G. L. Fischer, Jr, *et al.*, Eds. New York: Spartan, 1962, pp. 151–152.
[112] *Special Issue on Digital Pattern Recognition, Proc. IEEE*, vol. 60, Oct. 1972.
[113] P. Hart, N. Nilsson, and B. Raphael, "A formal basis for the heuristic determination of minimal cost paths," *IEEE Trans. Syst. Sci. Cybern.*, vol. SSC-4, pp. 100–107, July 1968.
[114] J. A. Hartigan, "Clustering," *Rev. Biophysics and Bioengineering*, pp. 81–101, 1972.
[115] M. E. Hellman and J. Raviv, "Probability of error, equivocation, and the Chernoff bound," *IEEE Trans. Inform. Theory*, vol. IT-16, pp. 368–372, 1970.
[116] E. G. Henrichon, Jr., and K. S. Fu, "A nonparametric partitioning procedure for pattern classification," *IEEE Trans. Comput.*, vol. C-18, pp. 614–624, July 1969; comments by Beakley and Tuteur, *IEEE Trans. Comput.*, vol. C-19, pp. 362–363, Apr. 1970.
[117] W. H. Highleyman, "The design and analysis of pattern recognition experiments," *Bell Syst. Tech. J.*, vol. 41, pp. 723–744, 1962.
[118] D. R. Hill, "Man-Machine interaction using speech," in *Advances in Computers*, F. L. Alt *et al.*, Eds. New York: Academic, 1971, pp. 165–230.
[119] M. Hills, "Allocation rules and their error rates," *J. Roy. Stat. Soc.*, Ser. B, vol. 28, pp. 1–31, 1968.
[120] ——, "Discrimination and allocation with discrete data," *Appl. Statist.*, vol. 16, 1967.
[121] Y. C. Ho and A. K. Agrawala, "On pattern classification algorithms–Introduction and survey," *Proc. IEEE*, vol. 56, pp. 2101–2114, Dec. 1968.
[122] S. L. Horowitz, "A general peak detection algorithm with applications in the computer analysis of electrocardiograms," Comput. Sci. Lab., Dep. Elec. Eng., Princeton Univ., Princeton, N.J., Tech. Rep. 129, May 1973.
[123] G. F. Hughes, "On the mean accuracy of statistical pattern recognizers," *IEEE Trans. Inform. Theory*, vol. IT-14, pp. 55–63, Jan. 1968.
[124] A. B. Hussain, "Compound sequential probability ratio test for the classification of statistically dependent patterns," *IEEE Trans. Comput.*, vol. C-23, pp. 398–410, Apr. 1974.
[125] A. B. Hussain and R. W. Donaldson, "Suboptimal sequential decision schemes with on-line feature ordering," *IEEE Trans. Comput.*, vol. C-23, pp. 582–590, June 1974.
[126] M. Ichino and K. Hiramatsu, "Suboptimum linear feature selection in multiclass problem," *IEEE Syst., Man, Cybern.*, vol. SMC-4, pp. 28–33, Jan. 1974.
[127] Pattern Recognition Data Bases, available from IEEE Comput. Soc., referenced in Jan. 1974 issue of Computer.
[128] *Special Issue on Feature Extraction and Selection in Pattern Recognition, IEEE Trans. Comput.*, vol. C-20, Sept. 1971.
[129] IMANCO. Bibliography of articles on automatic quantitative microscopy, available from Image Analyzing Computers, Inc., Monsey, New York.
[130] M. Ingram and K. Preston, Jr., "Automatic analysis of blood cells," *Sci. Amer.*, vol. 223, pp. 72–83, Nov. 1970.
[131] T. Ito, "Approximate error bounds in pattern recognition," in *Machine Intelligence*, vol. 7, Edinburgh, Scotland: Edinburgh Univ. Press, Nov. 1972, pp. 369–376.
[132] A. G. Ivakhnenko, "Polynomial theory of complex systems," *IEEE Trans. Syst., Man, Cybern.*, vol. SMC-1, pp. 364–378, Oct. 1971.
[133] J. Jacquez, Ed. *Computer Diagnosis and Diagnostic Methods*. Springfield, Ill.: C. C. Thomas.
[134] N. Jensen, "Practical jobs for optical computers," *Machine Design*, pp. 94–100, Feb. 22, 1973.
[135] A. K. Joshi, "Remarks on some aspects of language structure and their relevance to pattern analysis," *Pattern Recognition*, vol. 5, pp. 365–381, Dec. 1973.
[136] T. Kailath, "The divergence and Bhattacharyya distance measures in signal selection," *IEEE Trans. Commun. Technol.*, vol. COM-15, pp. 52–60, Feb. 1967.
[137] L. Kanal, *Pattern Recognition*. Washington, D.C.: Thompson, also L.N.K., Inc., Silver Spring, Md.
[138] ——, "Generative, descriptive, formal and heuristic modeling in pattern analysis and classification," Rep. Aerosp. Med. Div. AF System Command, Wright-Patterson AFB, Ohio, Contract F33615-69-C-1571; also Univ. Md., College Park, CSC. Tech. Rep. TR-151, Mar. 1971.
[139] ——, "Applications and problems of optical character recognition," in *Proc. Data Processing Supplies Assoc. Annu. Input-Output Systems Meeting*, reprinted as Univ. Md., CSC Tech. Rep. TR-178 AFOSR 71-1982, Mar. 1972.
[140] ——, "Interactive pattern analysis and classification systems: A survey and commentary," *Proc. IEEE*, vol. 60, pp. 1200–1215, Oct. 1972.
[141] ——, Summary of Panel Discussion on Bridging the Gap between Theory and Implementation in Pattern Recognition, Rep. of Special Sessions held at *1st Joint Int. Conf. Pattern Recognition*, NSF, Washington, D.C., Oct. 1973.
[142] L. Kanal and B. Chandrasekaran, "On dimensionality and sample size in statistical pattern classification," in *Proc. Nat. Electronics Conf.*, 1968, pp. 2–7; also appears in *Pattern Recognition*, vol. 3, pp. 225–234, 1971.
[143] ——, "Recognition, machine 'recognition', and statistical approaches," in *Methodologies of Pattern Recognition*. M. S. Watanabe, Ed. New York: Academic, 1969, pp. 317–332.
[144] ——, "On linguistic, statistical and mixed models for pattern recognition," in *Frontiers of Pattern Recognition*. M. S. Watanabe, Ed. New York: Academic, 1972.
[145] L. Kanal and T. J. Harley, "The complexity of patterns and pattern recognition systems," Aerosp. Med. Res. Lab., Wright-Patterson AFB, Ohio, Tech. Rep. AMRI-TR-69-62, Nov. 1969.
[146] A. Kauffman, *Introduction A La Des Sous-Ensembles Flous*, vol. 1, Paris: Masson, 1973.

[147] A. Klinger, "Natural language, linguistic processing, and speech understanding: Recent research and future goals," *Rand Corp.*, R-1377-ARPA, ARPA order no. 189-1, Dec. 1973.
[148] P. A. Kolers and M. Eden, *Recognizing Patterns*. Cambridge, Mass.: M.I.T. Press, 1968.
[149] W. L. Koontz and K. Fukunaga, "A nonlinear feature extraction algorithm using distance transformation," *IEEE Trans. Comput.*, vol. C-21, pp. 56–63, 1972.
[150] W. L. Koontz, P. M. Narendra, and K. Fukunaga, "A branch and bound clustering algorithm," available from IEEE Comput. Group depository.
[151] B. R. Kowalski and C. F. Bender, "The *k*-nearest neighbor classification rule applied to NMR spectra," *Anal. Chem.*, vol. 44, p. 1405, 1972.
[152] B. R. Kowalski and C. F. Bender, "Pattern recognition II: linear and nonlinear methods for displaying chemical data," *J. Amer. Chem. Soc.*, vol. 95, p. 686, 1973.
[153] B. R. Kowalski, P. C. Jurs, and T. L. Isenhour, "Computerized learning machines applied to chemistry problems: Interpretation of infrared spectro metric data," *Anal. Chem.*, vol. 41, p. 1945, 1969.
[154] B. R. Kowalski, T. F. Schatzki, and F. H. Stross, "Classification of archeological artifacts by applying pattern recognition to trace element data," *Anal. Chem.*, vol. 44, p. 2176, 1972.
[155] P. R. Krishnaiah, Ed. *Multivariate Analysis*, vol. II. New York: Academic, 1969.
[156] C. A. Kulikowski, "Pattern recognition approach to medical diagnosis," *IEEE Trans. Syst. Sci. Cybern.*, vol. SSC-6, pp. 173–178, July 1970.
[157] M. C. Kyle and E. D. Freis, "Computer identification of systolic time intervals," *Comput. and Biomed. Res.*, vol. 3, pp. 637–651, 1971.
[158] P. A. Lachenbruch and R. M. Mickey, "Estimation of error rates in discriminant analysis," *Technometrics*, vol. 10, pp. 1–11, 1968.
[159] P. A. Lachenbruch, C. Sneeringer, and L. T. Revo, "Robustness of the linear and quadratic discriminant function to certain types of non-normality," *Commun. in Statist.*, vol. 1, p. 39–56, 1973.
[160] D. G. Lainiotis, "A class of upper bounds on probability of error for multihypotheses pattern recognition," *IEEE Trans. Inform. Theory*. (Corresp.), vol. IT-15, pp. 730–731, Nov. 1969.
[161] D. G. Lainiotis and S. K. Park, "Probability of error bounds," *IEEE Trans. Syst., Man, Cybern.*, vol. SMC-1, pp. 175–178, Apr. 1971.
[162] P. T. Lavin, "Stochastic feature selection," Ph.D. dissertation, Brown Univ., Providence, R.I., 1972; Rep. no. 3 on Pattern Analysis Center for Comp. and Inform. Sci., Div. of Appl. Math., Brown Univ., Providence, R.I.
[163] E. Lawler and D. Wood, "Branch and bound methods: A survey," *Oper. Res.*, vol. 14, pp. 699–719, July–Aug. 1966.
[164] H. C. Lee and K. S. Fu, "A stochastic syntax analysis procedure and its application to pattern classification," *IEEE Trans. Comput.*, vol. C-21, pp. 660–666, July 1972.
[165] A. Levine, L. Lustick, and B. Saltzberg, "The nearest neighbor rule for small samples drawn from uniform distributions," *IEEE Trans. Inform. Theory*, vol. IT-19, p. 697–699, Sept. 1973.
[166] M. D. Levine, "Feature extraction: A survey," *Proc. IEEE*, vol. 57, pp. 1391–1407, Aug. 1969.
[167] P. H. Lindsay and D. Norman, *Human Information Processing–An Introduction To Psychology*. New York: Academic, 1972.
[168] B. S. Lipkin and A. Rosenfeld, Eds. *Picture Processing and Psychopictorics*. New York: Academic, 1970.
[169] T. Lissack and K. S. Fu, "Error estimation and its application to feature extraction in pattern recognition," Purdue Univ. Lafayette, Ind., Rep. TR-EE73-25, Aug. 1973.
[170] H. Marko, "A biological approach to pattern recognition," *IEEE Syst., Man, Cybern.*, vol. SMC-4, pp. 34–39, Jan. 1974.
[171] D. E. McClure, "Problems and methods of nonlinear feature generation in pattern analysis," presented at the 1974 Princeton Conf. on Inform. Sciences and Systems.
[172] K. G. Mehrotra, "Some further considerations on probability of error in discriminant analysis," unpublished Rep. on RADC Contract no. F30602-72-C-0281, 1973.
[173] W. S. Meisel, *Computer-Oriented Approaches to Pattern Recognition*. New York: Academic, 1972.
[174] J. M. Mendel and K. S. Fu, *Adaptive Learning, and Pattern Recognition Systems: Theory and Applications*. New York: Academic, 1970.
[175] M. Michael and W. C. Lin, "Experimental study of information measure and inter-intra class distance ratios on feature selection and orderings," *IEEE Trans. Syst., Man, Cybern.*, vol. SMC-3, pp. 172–181, Mar. 1973.
[176] R. S. Michalski, "A variable-valued logic system as applied to picture description and recognition," in *Graphic Languages*, F. Nake and A. Rosenfeld, Eds. Amsterdam: North Holland, 1972, pp. 20–47.
[177] R. S. Michalski, "Aqval/1–Computer implementation of a variable-valued logic system VL and examples of its application to pattern recognition," in *Proc. 1st Int. Joint Conf. Pattern Recognition*, IEEE Publ. no. 73 CHO 821-90, 1973.
[178] D. Milgram and A. Rosenfeld, "Array automata and array grammars," *Proc. IFIPS Cong.* Amsterdam: North-Holland, Booklet TA-2, 1971, pp. 166–173.
[179] P. L. Miller, "A locally organized parser for spoken output," Lincoln Lab., M.I.T., Cambridge, Tech. Rep. 503, May 2, 1973.
[180] M. Minsky and S. Papert, *Perceptrons: An Introduction to Computational Geometry*. Cambridge, Mass.: M.I.T. Press, 1969.
[181] B. Moayer and K. S. Fu, "A syntactic approach to fingerprint pattern recognition," in *Proc. 1st Int. Joint Conf. Pattern Recognition*, 1973.
[182] W. S. Mohn, Jr, "Two statistical feature evaluation techniques applied to speaker identification," *IEEE Trans. Comput.*, vol. C-20, pp. 979–987, Sept. 1971.
[183] D. H. Moore, II, "Evaluation of five discrimination procedures for binary variables," *J. Amer. Statist. Ass.*, vol. 68, pp. 399–404, June 1973.
[184] F. Mosteller, "The jackknife," *Rev. Int. Stat. Inst.*, vol. 39, no. 3, pp. 363–368, 1971.
[185] F. Mosteller and J. W. Tukey, "Data analysis, including statistics," in *Handbook of Social Psychology*, G. Lindzey and E. Aronsen, Eds. Reading, Mass.: Addison-Wesley, 1968.
[186] A. N. Mucciardi, "Neuromime nets as the basis for the predictive component of robot brains," in *Cybernetics, Artificial Intelligence and Ecology*, E. Robinson and D. Knight, Eds. Washington, D.C.: Spartan, 1972.
[187] A. N. Mucciardi, "New developments in water shed pollution modeling using adaptive trainable networks," presented at 1974 WWEMA Industrial Water and Pollution Conf. and Exposition Sess. Technology Sources and Progress, Detroit, Michigan, Apr. 1–4, 1974.
[188] A. N. Mucciardi and E. E. Gose, "A comparison of seven techniques for choosing subsets of pattern recognition properties," *IEEE Trans. Comput.*, vol. C-20, pp. 1023–1031, Sept. 1971.
[189] I. Muchnik, "Simulation of process of forming the language for description and analysis of the forms of images," *Pattern Recognition*, vol. 4, pp. 101–140, 1972.
[190] V. K. Murthy, "Estimation of probability density," *Ann. Math. Stat.*, vol. 36, pp. 1027–1031, June 1965.
[191] R. N. Nagel and A. Rosenfeld, "Steps toward handwritten signature verification," in *Proc. 1st Int. Joint Conf. Pattern Recognition*, Publ. no. 73 CHO 821-9C, pp. 59–66, 1973.
[192] G. Nagy, "State of the art in pattern recognition," *Proc. IEEE*, vol. 56, pp. 836–862, May 1968.
[193] ——, "Digital image-processing activities in remote sensing for earth resources," *Proc. IEEE*, vol. 60, pp. 1177–1200, Oct. 1972.
[194] F. Nake, "A proposed language for the definition of arbitrary two-dimensional signs," in *Pattern Recognition in Biological and Technical Systems*, Grusser and Klinke, Eds. Berlin: Springer, 1971, pp. 396–402.
[195] R. Narasimhan and V. Reddy, "A syntax-aided recognition scheme for handprinted English letters," *Pattern Recognition*, vol. 3, pp. 345–361, Nov. 1971.
[196] G. D. Nelson and D. M. Levy, "A dynamic programming approach to the selection of pattern features," *IEEE Trans. Syst. Sci. Cybern.*, vol. SSC-4, pp. 145–151, July 1968.
[197] A. Newell, *et al.*, *Speech Understanding Systems*. New York: Elsevier, 1973.
[198] N. J. Nilsson, *Learning Machines*. New York: McGraw-Hill, 1965.
[199] N. J. Nilsson, *Problem-Solving Methods in Artificial Intelligence*. New York: McGraw-Hill, 1971.
[200] ——, "Artificial intelligence," in *Proc. IFIP Cong.*, 1974.
[201] R. A. Northouse and K. S. Fu, "Dynamic scheduling of large digital computer systems using adaptive control and clustering techniques," *IEEE Trans. Syst., Man, Cybern.*, vol. SMC-3, pp. 225–234, May 1973.
[202] M. Oda, B. F. Womack, and K. Tsubouchi, "A pattern recognizing study of palm reading," *IEEE Trans. Syst., Man, Cybern.*, vol. SMC-1, pp. 171–174, Apr. 1971.
[203] P. L. Odell and B. S. Duran, "Comparison of some classification techniques," *IEEE Trans. Comput.*, vol. C-23, pp. 591–596, June 1974.
[204] P. L. Odell, B. S. Duran, and W. A. Coberly, "On the table look-up in discriminate analysis," *J. Statist. Comput. Simul.*, vol. 2, pp. 171–188, 1973.
[205] M. Okamoto, "An asymptotic expansion for the distribution of the linear discriminant function," *Ann. Math. Stat.*, vol. 34, pp. 1286–1301, 1963.
[206] ——, "Correction to an asymptotic expansion for the linear discriminant function," *Ann. Math. Stat.*, vol. 39, pp. 135, 1968.

[207] D. R. Olsen and K. Fukunaga, "Representation of nonlinear data surfaces," *IEEE Trans. Comput.*, vol. C-22, pp. 915–922, Oct. 1973.
[208] P. A. Ota, "Mosaic grammars," Moore Sch. Elec. Eng., Univ. Penn., Philadelphia, Rep. no. 73-13, 1973.
[209] C. K. Pang, A. J. Koivo, and A. H. El-Abiad, "Application of pattern recognition to steady-state security evaluation in a power system," *IEEE Trans. Syst., Man, Cybern.*, vol. SMC-3, pp. 622–631, Nov. 1973.
[210] E. Parzen, "An estimation of a probability density function and mode," *Ann. Math. Stat.*, vol. 33, pp. 1065–1376, 1962.
[211] E. A. Patrick, *Fundamentals of Pattern Recognition.* Englewood Cliffs, N.J.: Prentice-Hall, 1972.
[212] E. A. Patrick and F. P. Fischer, II, "Nonparametric feature selection," *IEEE Trans. Inform. Theory.*, vol IT-15, pp. 577–584, Sept. 1969.
[213] E. A. Patrick, F. P. Stelmack, and L. Y. Shen, "Review of pattern recognition in medical diagnosis and consulting relative to a new system model," *IEEE Syst., Man, Cybern.*, vol. SMC-4, pp. 1–16, Jan. 1974.
[214] T. Pavlidis, "Linguistic analysis of waveforms," in *Software Engineering*, vol. 2, J. T. Tou, Ed. New York: Academic, 1971, pp. 203–225.
[215] T. Pavlidis, "Waveform segmentation through functional approximation," *IEEE Trans. Comput.*, vol. C-22, pp. 689–697, July 1973.
[216] L. S. Penrose and D. Loesch, "Dermatoglyphic patterns and clinical diagnosis by discriminant functions," *Ann. Hum. Genetics*, vol. 35, p. 51, 1971.
[217] L. S. Penrose and D. Loesch, "Diagnosis with dermatoglyphic discriminants," *J. Mental Def. Res.*, vol. 15, p. 185, 1971.
[218] D. W. Peterson, "Some convergence properties of a nearest neighbor decision rule," *IEEE Trans. Inform. Theory*, vol. IT-16, pp. 26–31, Jan. 1970.
[219] J. L. Pfaltz and A. Rosenfeld, "Web grammars," in *Proc. Joint Int. Conf. Artificial Intelligence*, 1969, pp. 609–619.
[220] H. Pipberger, R. Dunn, and J. Cornfield, "First and second generation computer programs for diagnostic ECG and VCG classification," in *Proc. XII Int. Colloquium Vectorcardiography*, Amsterdam: North Holland, 1972.
[221] M. L. Piccoli, "Pattern recognition and social choice theory," Ph.D. dissertation, Purdue Univ., Lafeyette, Ind., May 1974.
[222] J. Prewitt, "Parametric and nonparametric recognition by computer: An application to leukocyte image processing," in *Advances in Computers*, vol. 2. New York: Academic, 1972, pp. 285–414.
[223] J. Prewitt and M. Mendelsohn, "The analysis of cell images," *Ann. N.Y. Acad. Sci.*, vol. 128, pp. 1035–1053, 1966.
[224] C. P. Quesenberry and M. P. Gessaman, "Nonparametric discrimination using tolerance regions," *Ann. Math. Stat.*, vol. 39, no. 2, pp. 664–673, 1968.
[225] D. R. Reddy, *Invited Papers to the IEEE Symposium on Speech Recognition.* New York: Academic, 1974.
[226] D. R. Reddy, *et al.*, "The hearsay speech understanding system," in *Proc. 3rd Int. Joint Conf. Artificial Intelligence*, 1973, pp. 185–193.
[227] E. M. Riseman and A. R. Hanson, "A contextual postprocessing system for error correction using binary *n*-grams," *IEEE Trans. Comput.*, vol. C-23, pp. 480–493, May 1974.
[228] F. Rosenblatt, "Perceptron simulation experiments," *Proc. IRE*, vol. 48, pp. 301–309, Mar. 1960.
[229] A. Rosenfeld, *Picture Processing by Computer.* New York: Academic, 1969.
[230] A. Rosenfeld, "Picture processing: 1972," *Comput. Graphics and Image Processing*, vol. 1, pp. 394–416, 1972.
[231] ——, "Progress in picture processing: 1969–1971," *Computing Surveys*, vol. 5, pp. 81–108, 1973.
[232] ——, "Picture processing: 1973," Comput. Sci. Center, Univ. Md., Tech. Rep. TR-284, Jan. 1974; to appear in *Comput. Graphics and Image Processing.*
[233] P. Ross, "Computers in medical diagnosis," *CRC Critical Reviews in Radiological Science*, vol. 3, p. 197, 1972.
[234] W. C. Rounds, "Context-free grammars on trees," in *Proc. ACM Symp. Theory Computing*, 1969.
[235] J. W. Sammon, *et al.*, "Handprinted character recognition," U.S. Patent 3 755 780, Aug. 1973; also ASTIA document AD 755 936, Jan. 1973.
[236] J. W. Sammon, Jr., "On-line pattern analysis and recognition system (OLPARS)," Rome Air Develop. Center, Tech. Rep. TR-68-263, Aug. 1968.
[237] ——, "A nonlinear mapping for data structure analysis," *IEEE Trans. Comput.*, vol. C-18, pp. 401–409, May 1969.
[238] ——, "An optimal discriminant plane," *IEEE Trans. Comput.* (Short Notes), vol. C-19, pp. 826–829, Sept. 1970.
[239] ——, "Techniques for discrete type-II data processing on-line (AMOLPARS)," Tech. Rep. RADC-TR-71-243, 1971.
[240] G. N. Saridis and R. F. Hofstadter, "A pattern recognition approach to the classification of nonlinear systems from input-output data," presented at the IEEE Conf. Systems, Man, and Cybernetics, 1973.
[241] K. M. Sayre, *Recognition: A Study in the Philosophy of Artificial Intelligence.* Notre Dame, Ind.: Univ. of Notre Dame Press, 1965.
[242] H. J. Scudder, "Probability of error of some adaptive pattern-recognition machines," *IEEE Trans. Inform. Theory*, vol. IT-11, pp. 363–371, July 1965.
[243] A. C. Shaw, "Parsing of graph-representable pictures," *J. Ass. Comput. Mach.*, vol. 17, pp. 453–481, June 1970.
[244] J. C. Simon and A. Checroun, "Pattern linguistic analysis invariant for plane transformations," in *2nd Int. Joint Conf. A.I.*, British Comput. Soc., 1971, pp. 308–317.
[245] J. C. Simon, C. Roche, and G. Sabah, "On automatic generation of pattern recognition operators," in *Proc. 1972 Int. Conf. Cybernetics and Soc.*, pp. 232–238, IEEE Publ. no. 72 CHO647-8SMC.
[246] R. Siromoney, K. Krithivasan, and G. Siromoney, "*n*-dimensional array languages and description of crystal symmetry I and II," *Proc. Indian Acad. Sci.*, vol. 78, pp. 72–78 and 130–139, 1973.
[247] J. Sklansky, Ed. *Pattern Recognition: Introduction and Foundations.* Stroudsburg, Pa.: Dowden, Hutchinson, and Ross, 1973.
[248] L. V. Sprouse, D. L. Zuetle, and C. A. Harlow, "Automatic verification system for human signature images," in *Proc. 1974 Princton Conf. Information Sciences*, Dep. Elec. Eng., Princeton Univ., Princeton, N.J., 1974.
[249] G. Stockman, L. Kanal, and M. Kyle, "The design of a waveform parsing system," in *Proc. 1st Int. Joint Conf. Pattern Recognition*, 1973.
[250] ——, "An experimental waveform parsing system," in *Proc. 2nd Int. Joint Conf. Pattern Recognition*, 1974.
[251] J. C. Stoffel, "On discrete variables in pattern recognition," Ph.D. dissertation, Dep. Elec. Eng., Syracuse Univ., Syracuse, N.Y. Aug. 1972.
[252] ——, "A classifier design technique for discrete variable pattern recognition problems," *IEEE Trans. Comput.*, vol. C-23, pp. 428–441, Apr. 1974.
[253] D. Stowens and J. W. Sammon, Jr., "Dermatoglyphics and leukemia," *Lancet*, pp. 846, Apr. 18, 1970.
[254] D. Stowens, J. W. Sammon, and A. Proctor, "Dermatoglyphics in female schizophrenia," *Psychiatric Quart.*, vol. 44, pp. 516–532, July 1970.
[255] C. W. Swonger, "Property learning in pattern recognition systems using information content measurements," in *Pattern Recognition*, L. Kanal, Ed. Washington, D.C.: Thompson; L.N.K. Silver Spring, Md., 1966, pp. 329–347.
[256] S. J. Tauber and K. Rankin, "Valid structure diagrams and chemical gibberish," *J. Chem. Documentation*, vol. 12, no. 1, pp. 30–34, 1972.
[257] J. M. Tenenbaum, "On locating objects by their distinguishing features in multisensory images," A.I. Center, Stanford Res. Inst., Menlo Park, Calif., Tech. Note 84, SRI Project 1187 and 1530, Sept. 1973.
[258] J. M. Tenenbaum, *et al.*, "An interactive facility for scene analysis research," Artificial Intelligence Center, Stanford Res. Inst., Menlo Park, Calif., Tech. Note 87, SRI Project 1187, Jan. 1974.
[259] J. T. Tou, *Advances in Information Systems Science.* New York: Plenum, 1970.
[260] ——, *Software Engineering*, vol. II, New York: Academic, 1971.
[261] G. T. Toussaint, "Note on optimal selection of independent binary-valued features for pattern recognition," *IEEE Trans. Inform. Theory* (Corresp.), vol. IT-17, p. 618, Sept. 1971.
[262] ——, "Distance measures as measures of certainty and their application to statistical pattern recognition," in *Proc. Annu. Conf. Statistical Science Assoc. Canada*, 1973.
[263] ——, "Bibliography on estimation of misclassification," *IEEE Trans. Inform. Theory*, vol. IT-20, pp. 472–479, July 1974.
[264] G. T. Toussaint and R. W. Donaldson, "Some simple contextual decoding algorithms applied to recognition of handprinted text," in *Proc. Annu. Canadian Comput. Conf.*, 1972.
[265] G. T. Toussaint and P. M. Sharpe, "An efficient method for estimating the probability of misclassification applied to a problem in medical diagnosis," Sch. Comput. Sci., McGill Univ., Montreal, Canada, Nov. 1973.
[266] G. V. Trunk, "Parameter identification using intrinsic dimensionality," *IEEE Trans. Inform. Theory*, vol. IT-18, pp. 126–133, Jan. 1972.
[267] Ya. Z. Tsypkin, *Adaptation and Learning in Control Systems.* New York: Academic, 1971.
[268] ——, *Foundations of the Theory of Learning Systems.* New York: Academic, 1973.
[269] L. Uhr, "Flexible linguistic pattern recognition," in *Pattern*

Recognition, vol. 3, New York: Wiley, Nov. 1971, pp. 363–387.
[270] ——, *Pattern Recognition, Learning, and Thought*. Englewood Cliffs, N.J.: Prentice-Hall, 1973.
[271] J. R. Ullmann, *Pattern Recognition Techniques*. London: Butterworth, 1973.
[272] ——, "The use of continuity in character recognition," *IEEE Trans. Syst., Man, Cybern.*, vol. SMC-4, pp. 294–300, May 1974.
[273] W. E. Underwood and L. Kanal, "Structural descriptions, transformational rules, and pattern analysis," in *Proc. 1st Int. Joint Conf. Pattern Recognition*, Publ. no. 73 CHO 821-9C, 1973, pp. 434–444.
[274] I. Vajda, "Note on discrimination information and variation," *IEEE Trans. Inform. Theory*, vol. IT-16, pp. 771–773, Sept. 1970.
[275] C. J. Verhagen, "Some aspects of pattern recognition in the future," in *Proc. 1st Int. Joint Conf. Pattern Recognition*, IEEE Special Publ. 73 CHO 821-9C, 1973, pp. 541–545.
[276] T. R. Vilmansen, "Feature evaluation with measures of probability dependence," *IEEE Trans. Comput.*, vol. C-22, Apr. 1973.
[277] T. J. Wagner, "Convergence of the edited nearest neighbor," *IEEE Trans. Inform. Theory* (Corresp.), vol. IT-19, pp. 696–697, Sept. 1973.
[278] T. J. Wagner, "Convergence of the nearest neighbor rule," *IEEE Trans. Inform. Theory*, vol. IT-17, pp. 566–571, Sept. 1971.
[279] ——, "Deleted estimates of the Bayes risk," *Ann. Statist.*, vol. 1, pp. 359–362, Mar. 1973.
[280] D. E. Walker, "SRI speech understanding system," Contributed Papers to the *IEEE Symp. on Speech Recognition*, IEEE Catalog no. 74CHO878-9 AE, 1974, pp. 32–37.
[281] R. F. Warmack and R. C. Gonzalez, "An algorithm for the optimal solution of linear equalities and its application to pattern recognition," *IEEE Trans. Comput.*, vol. C-22, pp. 1065–1074, Dec. 1973.
[282] S. Watanabe, *Knowing and Guessing*. New York: Wiley, 1969.
[283] S. Watanabe, Ed., *Methodologies of Pattern Recognition*. New York: Academic, 1969; Review by Richard Duda in *IEEE Trans. Inform. Theory*, vol. IT-17, pp. 633–634, Sept. 1971.
[284] S. Watanabe, Ed., *Frontiers of Pattern Recognition*. New York: Academic, 1972.
[285] S. Watanabe and N. Pakvasa, "Subspace method in pattern recognition," in *Proc. 1st Joint Int. Conf. Pattern Recognition*, IEEE Special Publ. No. 73CHO821-9C, 1974.
[286] W. G. Wee, "Generalized inverse approach to adaptive multiclass pattern classification," *IEEE Trans. Comput.*. vol. C-17, pp. 1157–1164, Dec. 1968.
[287] A. Whitney, "A direct method of nonparametric measurement selection," *IEEE Trans. Comput.* (Short Notes), vol. C-20, pp. 1100–1103, Sept. 1971.
[288] D. L. Wilson, "Asymptotic properties of nearest neighbor rules using edited data," *IEEE Trans. Syst., Man, Cybern.*, vol. SMC-2, pp. 408–421, July 1972.
[289] C. T. Wolverton, "Strong consistency of an estimate of an asymptotic error probability of the nearest neighbor rule," *IEEE Trans. Inform. Theory*, vol. IT-19, p. 119, Jan. 1973.
[290] W. E. Wright, "A formalization of cluster analysis," *Pattern Recognition*, vol. 5, pp. 272–282, Sept. 1973.
[291] Y. Yakimovsky and J. A. Feldman, "A semantics-based decision region analyzer," in Advance Papers of *3rd Int. Joint Conf. Artificial Intelligence*, 1973, pp. 580–588; available from Stanford Res. Inst., Menlo Park, Calif.
[292] I. T. Young, "Automated leucocyte recognition," Ph.D. dissertation, Dep. Elec. Eng., M.I.T., Cambridge, Mass., June 1969.
[293] T. Young, "Reliability of linear feature extractors," *IEEE Trans. Comput.*, vol. C-20, pp. 967–971, Sept. 1971.
[294] T. Y. Young and T. W. Calvert, *Classification, Estimation and Pattern Recognition*. New York: Elsevier, 1974.
[295] L. A. Zadeh, "Fuzzy sets," *Inform. Contr.*, vol. 8, p. 338, 1965.
[296] ——, "Outline of a new approach to the analysis of complex systems and decision processes," *IEEE Trans. Syst., Man, Cybern.*, vol. SMC-3, pp. 28–44, Jan. 1973.
[297] C. Zywietz and B. Schneider, Eds., *Computer Application on ECG and VCG Analysis*. New York: Elsevier, 1973.
[298] Symp. Rec. IEEE Symp. Feature Extraction and Selection in Pattern Recognition, Argonne, Ill. Oct. 5–7, 1970.
[299] Data Processing Supplies Assoc. Ann. Input–Output Systems Meeting, DPSA, Stamford, Conn, 1971.
[300] *Special Issue of Pattern Recognition on Syntactic Pattern Recognition, Pattern Recognition*, vol. 3, 1971.
[301] *1st Int. Electron. Crime Countermeasures Conf.*, IEEE Special Pub. no. 73 CHO 813-6AES, 1973.
[302] *1st Int. Joint Conf. Pattern Recognition*, IEEE Publ. no. 73 CHO 821-9C, 1973.
[303] Symp. significant results obtained from Earth resources technology satellite-1, Goddard Space Flight Center, Greenbelt, Md., S. C. Freden, E. P. Mercanti, and D. E. Whitten, Eds., May 1973.
[304] *Proc. Conf. Biologically Motivated Automata Theory*, IEEE Publ. no. 74CHO889-6C, 1974.

An Optimum Character Recognition System Using Decision Functions*

C. K. CHOW†

Summary—The character recognition problem, usually resulting from characters being corrupted by printing deterioration and/or inherent noise of the devices, is considered from the viewpoint of statistical decision theory. The optimization consists of minimizing the expected risk for a weight function which is preassigned to measure the consequences of system decisions. As an alternative, minimization of the error rate for a given rejection rate is used as the criterion. The optimum recognition is thus obtained.

The optimum system consists of a conditional-probability densities computer; character channels, one for each character; a rejection channel; and a comparison network. Its precise structure and and ultimate performance depend essentially upon the signals and noise structure.

Explicit examples for an additive Gaussian noise and a "cosine" noise are presented. Finally, an error-free recognition system and a possible criterion to measure the character style and deterioration are presented.

* Manuscript received by the PGEC, June 3, 1957.
† Burroughs, Corp., Paoli, Pa.

Introduction

Character recognition has been receiving considerable attention as the result of the phenomenal growth of office automation and the need for translating human language into machine language.[1,2] Broadly speaking, the character printed in conventional form and size on the document (checks, etc.) is first converted to electrical signals, and sufficient information is then extracted from the latter. The purpose of the recognition system is based on the observed data and on *a priori* knowledge of the signal and noise structure

[1] K. R. Eldredge, F. J. Kamphoefner, and P. H. Wendt, "Automatic input for business data processing system," *Proc. Eastern Joint Computer Conf.*, pp. 69–73; December 11, 1956.

[2] E. C. Greanias and Y. M. Hill, "Considerations in the design of character recognition devices," 1957 IRE National Convention Record, pt.4, vol. 5 pp. 119–126.

Reprinted from *IRE Trans. Electron. Comput.*, vol. EC-6, pp. 247–254, Dec. 1957.

to identify which of the possible characters is present, or to reject if the data are ambiguous.

The over-all performance of the recognition system depends not only upon itself, but also upon the number of characters to be recognized, the character style, and noise statistics. In this paper the character style and noise statistics are assumed given and adequate, and the purpose of the paper is to obtain an optimum recognition system. For convenience, the recognition problem is considered one of statistical inference, so that useful results in decision theory can be applied.[3-5] To accomplish this, the notion of risk is employed and proper weights are assigned to various types of error, rejection, and correct recognition to measure the consequences of decisions. This results in an optimum system which minimizes the expected (average) risk function and includes a possible alternate system with a minimum error rate. The results reveal the explicit structure of an optimum system which is determined by the *a priori* noise statistics, the signal structure, and the preassigned weights.

System Approach to the Problem

One practical application of a character recognition system for business documents is to read arabic numerals and selected symbols printed in magnetic ink. A method[1] for achieving this is shown in Fig. 1. The character is first passed through the field of a permanent magnet where it is magnetized in a given direction before being scanned by the read head. From the read head, the printed character is converted into an electrical signal corresponding to the differentiation of the plane area of the character. The function of the recognition system is to examine the amplitude-time signal obtained by the read head and to decide which of the possible characters is being recognized.

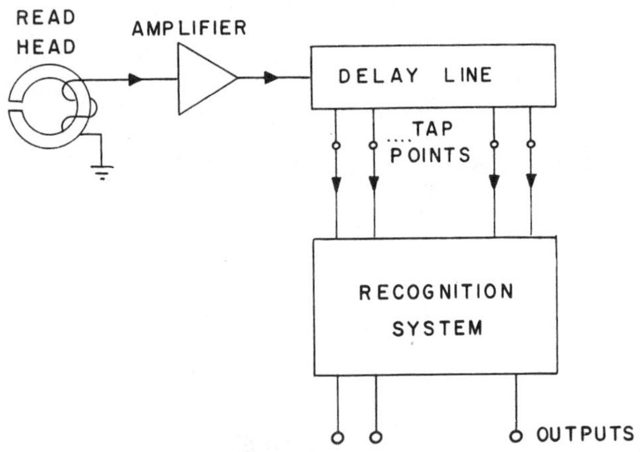

Fig. 1—A recognition system.

It is convenient, at times, to deal with the sampled data rather than the continuous time waveforms. By the sampling theory, if the number of samples is sufficiently large, little information carried by the continuous signal is lost. As shown in Fig. 1, the signal from the read head is first amplified and then fed into a tapped delay line. This serves as a means for sampling and acts as a temporary storage device to convert the series information into parallel information. Although not essential, sampled data are used in the following discussion.

Let the vector $v=(v_1, v_2, \cdots v_s)$ (subscript s being the number of samples) denote voltages on the taps of the delay line at the instant of sampling. (See Appendix I for the meaning of the Symbols.) The vector $a_i=(a_{i1}, a_{i2}, \cdots, a_{is})$ denotes the true sampled signal associated with the ith character where $i=1, 2, \cdots, c$, c being the number of possible characters to be recognized. The vector v constitutes the input to the recognition system. It is assumed that the characters are distinct, *i.e.*, all a_i's are different.

In a simple form, the recognition system may consist of c separate channels, one for each character. Each channel obtains a weighted sum of v_i's, with properly chosen weights, b_{ij}. The output of the ith channel is

$$X_i(v) = \sum_{j=1}^{s} b_{ij}v_j. \tag{1}$$

This operation may be realized by a summing amplifier and possibly with some inverters to provide negative weights, if required. One possible set of weights is:

$$b_{ij} = \frac{a_{ij}}{\left[\sum_{j=1}^{s} a_{ij}^2\right]^{1/2}}. \tag{2}$$

The recognition system is known as a correlation network when the weights are defined by (2).

If the printing is perfect, and the reading devices are noiseless, the observed data v will be identical to one of the a_i's and therefore, it can easily be shown that the right channel of the correlation network has the largest (algebraic) output. Consequently, the recognition system identifies the character with absolute accuracy by the channel having the highest output. However, in practice, there are always, to some degree, deteriorations in printing and inherent noise in the devices. Therefore, the observed data v generally will not be identical to any of the a_i's. In view of this, ambiguities arise which may result in possible misrecognition. To safeguard against the occurrence of error, the recognition system should have provisions for examining the degree of ambiguity and making rejects when required. This function can be achieved in various ways; *e.g.*, whenever the next highest output of the correlation network exceeds some preassigned fraction of the highest output, the system will reject, otherwise the system

[3] A. Wald, "Statistical Decision Functions," John Wiley & Sons, Inc., New York, N. Y., 1950.
[4] D. Van Meter and D. Middleton, "Modern statistical approaches to reception in communication theory," IRE Trans., vol. PGIT-4, pp. 119–145; September, 1954.
[5] D. Middleton and D. Van Meter, "On optimum multiple-alternative detection of signals in noise," IRE Trans., vol. IT-1, pp. 1–9; September, 1955.

identifies the character by the channel having the highest output.

The system described above merely represents one of many possible recognition systems and is not necessarily optimum. A basic problem in the design of recognition systems is to evaluate the system performance in the presence of printing deterioration and inherent noise and to obtain an optimum system. Optimum performance depends primarily upon the character style and permissible deterioration. Greanias and Hill in a recent paper[2] describe the effects of character style and printing deterioration on the character recognition problem from the viewpoint of matching the character with an ideal character and further propose definitions for character quality and style factors. In this paper, the discussion is confined to the problem of obtaining an optimum recognition system for a given set of adequately styled characters and known statistics of character deterioration. The recognition problem is considered to be that of testing multiple hypotheses in the statistical inference. Consequently, the design and evaluation of a recognition system is comparable to a statistical test. Results of decision theory can be applied.[3-5].

In order to judge the relative merit of recognition systems, some criterion of evaluating system performance must be established. The error rate of the system for a given rejection rate is used as the performance criterion for cases where no distinction is made among misrecognitions. Cases may arise where different misrecognitions have different consequences; *e.g.*, the registering of a four as an asterisk may not be as serious an error as registering it as a nine. The criterion of minimum error rate is then no longer appropriate. Instead, the criterion of minimum risk[3] is employed. Proper weights are assigned to measure the consequences of errors, rejections, and correct recognitions. These weights indicate the loss incurred by the system for every possible decision. The loss, which should be regarded as negative utility, may actually represent loss in dollars or unit of utility in measuring the consequence of the system decision. The over-all performance of the system is judged by its expected (or average) risk.

In the following discussion, an optimum system which minimizes the expected risk is derived, and a system having minimum error rate is obtained. Examples are presented for illustration purposes. An error-free system and a possible criterion for judging character style and deterioration are also presented.

The Expected Risk

The vector $a_i=(a_{i1}, a_{i2}, \cdots, a_{is})$ in the s-dimensional space denotes the true sampled signal associated with the ith character ($i=1, 2, \cdots, c$), where c and s are respectively, the number of possible characters to be recognized and the number of samples.* Let $p=(p_1, p_2, \cdots, p_c)$ be the *a priori* distribution of characters (p_i is the *a priori* probability that the ith character occurs). Then, evidently,

$$\sum_{i=1}^{c} p_i = 1, \qquad p_i > 0. \tag{3}$$

The received data are denoted by a s-components vector $v=(v_1, v_2, \cdots, v_s)$. It is the signal corrupted by factors such as the deterioration of printing and inherent noise of the devices. *A priori* noise statistics and the manner in which various signals and noise are combined determine precisely the conditional probability density $F(v|a_i)$ of the observed data v when a_i is the incoming signal.

The space of decisions available to the recognition system consists of $c+1$ possible decisions $d_0, d_1, d_2, \cdots, d_c$. The quantity $d_i(i\neq 0)$ is the decision that the ith character is present while d_0 is the decision for reject. A basic problem in statistical decision theory is the selection of a proper decision rule δ. The rule is expressed as a vector function of the data v, namely, $\delta(v)=(\delta(d_0|v), \delta(d_1|v), \delta(d_2|v) \cdots \delta(d_c|v))$ with $c+1$ components, and satisfies the restriction that:

$$\sum_{i=0}^{c} \delta(d_i | v) = 1 \qquad \text{for all } v, \tag{4}$$

and

$$\delta(d_i | v) \geq 0 \qquad \text{for all } i \text{ and } v. \tag{5}$$

The quantity $\delta(d_i|v)$ is the probability that, for a given observed data v, the decision d_i will be made.

In order to judge the relative merits of the decision rules it is necessary to assign the weight function $W(a_i, d_j)$. This is a function of a_i and d_j, which is the loss incurred by the system if the decision d_j is made when a_i is the true signal. This measure of consequence for various d_j under various a_i is a datum of the problem and is given in advance. Let the weight function be:

$$W(a_i, d_j) = w_{ij} \qquad \begin{array}{l} i = 1, 2 \cdots c \\ j = 0, 1, 2 \cdots c, \end{array} \tag{6}$$

where $w_{ii}(i\neq 0)$ is the weight of correct recognition of the ith character; $w_{ij}(i\neq j\neq 0)$ is the weight of misreading the ith character as the jth one, and $w_{i0}(i\neq 0)$ is the weight of rejecting the ith characters. Therefore, it is required that

$$w_{ij} > w_{i0} > w_{ii} \qquad (i \neq j \neq 0). \tag{7}$$

Usually, w_{ij} is much larger than w_{i0} since the most serious consideration in design of a character recognition system is the occurrence of undetected errors.

In general, w_{ij}'s may all differ, so that various misrecognitions, rejections, and correct recognitions can be properly weighted. The expected risk for any decision rule δ is

$$R(p, \delta) = \sum_{i=1}^{c}\sum_{j=0}^{c} \int_V \delta(d_j | v) p_i w_{ij} F(v | a_i) dv, \tag{8}$$

with integration over the entire observation space V.

* samples are used in the sense of 'sample signal' NOT statistical sense

THE MINIMUM RISK SYSTEM

The problem is then to choose a decision rule to minimize the average risk. By using (4), and since $\int_V F(v|a_i)dv = 1$ for all i, (8) may be written as:

$$R(p, \delta) = R_0(p) + R_1(p, \delta), \tag{9}$$

where

$$R_0 = \sum_{i=1}^{c} p_i w_{i0}, \tag{10}$$

$$R_1 = \int_V \sum_{j=0}^{c} \delta(d_j | v) Z_j(v) dv, \tag{11}$$

and

$$Z_j(v) = \begin{cases} \sum_{i=1}^{c} (w_{ij} - w_{i0}) p_i F(v | a_i); \; j = 1, 2 \cdots c \\ 0 \qquad \text{for } j = 0. \end{cases} \tag{12}$$

The symbol R_0 will express the expected risk when rejection is made for all recognition and R_1 is that part of R which may be adjusted through the choice of δ. Evidently

$$R_1(p, \delta) \geq \int_V \min_j [Z_j(v)] dv, \tag{13}$$

and the equality sign holds if, and only if, the decision rule is chosen as:

$$\delta^*(d_k | v) = 1,$$
$$\delta^*(d_j | v) = 0 \qquad \text{for all } j \neq k \tag{14}$$

whenever

$$\min_j [Z_j(v)] = Z_k(v). \tag{15}$$

This is the optimum decision rule δ^* (the Bayes strategy) which minimizes the expected risk and is nonrandomized since its components are either zero or one. Therefore, R_1 for this decision rule is always nonpositive, and its expected risk (the Bayes risk) is no greater than R_0. The expected risk for the optimum decision rule, δ^*, is

$$R(p, \delta^*) = \sum_{i=1}^{c} p_i w_{i0} + \int_V \min_j [Z_j(v)] dv. \tag{16}$$

Eqs. (14) and (15) reveal that the optimum system for character recognition consists of a computer which evaluates $F(v|a_i)$'s; $(i = 1, 2, \cdots, c)$ for an observed data v; computes the various $Z_j(v)$ $(j = 1, 2, \cdots, c)$; examines and compares these $Z_j(v)$ $(j = 0, 1, 2, \cdots, c)$; selects the smallest (algebraically) one, say $Z_k(v)$; and finally makes the decision d_k [having the same subscript as $Z_k(v)$]. Of course, this method of setting up the computing procedures is not unique; *e.g.*, any ordering-preserving transformation may be used. In any event, the system must be equivalent to the above.

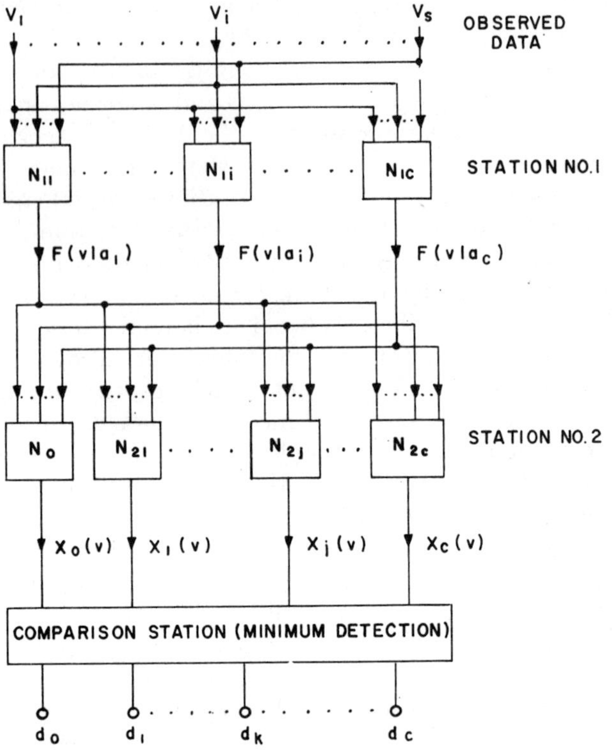

Fig. 2—Functional diagram of an optimum system.

The functional diagram of the optimum system is shown in Fig. 2. Station No. 1 consists of c similar component networks. Each network receives the observed data $v = (v_1, v_2, \cdots, v_s)$ and computes the corresponding conditional probability density $F(v|a_i)$ as its output. This operation depends only upon the *a priori* knowledge of signal and noise structure and on the observed data v; it does not depend upon the weight function $W(a_i, d_j)$ or on *a priori* probability distribution of signals, p.

The outputs of station No. 1 are fed to station No. 2, which consists of c character channels $N_{2j}(j \neq 0)$, and one rejection channel, N_0. They perform the linear operation of weighting each input and then the summing of all weighted inputs. The weights are $p_i w_{ij}$'s and $p_i w_{i0}$'s. The output of the rejection channel is

$$X_0(v) = \sum_{i=1}^{c} w_{i0} p_i F(v | a_i), \tag{17}$$

while the outputs of character channels are

$$X_j(v) = \sum_{i=1}^{c} w_{ij} p_i F(v | a_i) \quad (j = 1, 2 \cdots c). \tag{18}$$

The comparison station receives X's from station No. 2, examines all its inputs, and makes decision by selecting the algebraically smallest of the $c+1$ X's. If the rejection channel has the smallest one, the system rejects. If one of the character channels has the smallest output (say $X_k(v)$, $(k \neq 0)$) then the system recognizes the signal as the kth character.

Since $X_j(v)$ $(j = 0, 1, \cdots, c)$ is equal to $Z_j(v) + X_0(v)$, this system makes decisions in accordance with δ^* as defined by (14) and (15), and thus minimizing the expected risk.

Probabilities of Error and Rejection

The expected risk provides a means for evaluating the performance of a recognition system. At times, it may be desirable to compute the probabilities of error, rejection, and correct recognition as an auxiliary set of merit figures. They are obtained for any decision rule δ as follows:

The probability of correct recognition is:

$$P_c(\delta) = \int_V \sum_{i=1}^{c} \delta(d_i \mid v) p_i F(v \mid a_i) dv; \qquad (19)$$

the probability of rejection, or rejection rate, is:

$$P_r(\delta) = \int_V \delta(d_0 \mid v) \sum_{i=1}^{c} p_i F(v \mid a_i) dv; \qquad (20)$$

and the probability of misrecognition, or error rate, is:

$$P_e(\delta) = 1 - P_c - P_r. \qquad (21)$$

Eqs. (19)–(21) result directly from the fact that $\int_V \delta(d_0|v)F(v|a_i)dv$ and $\int_V \delta(d_i|v)F(v|a_i)dv$ are, respectively, the conditional probabilities of rejection of the ith character and correct recognition of the ith character.

Criterion of Minimum Error Rate

Cases may arise in which the criterion of judging the system performance is the magnitude of its error rate for a given rejection rate. In using this criterion, the optimum recognition system is the one which, for a given rejection rate, α, has a minimum error rate. The optimum decision rule is obtained as: (See Appendix II for proof.)

$$\delta^{**}(d_k \mid v) = 1 \qquad (k \neq 0) \qquad (22)$$

whenever

$$p_k F(v \mid a_k) \geq p_j F(v \mid a_j) \quad \text{for all } j \neq k, \text{ and}$$

$$p_k F(v \mid a_k) \geq \beta \sum_{i=1}^{c} p_i F(v \mid a_i), \qquad (23)$$

and

$$\delta^{**}(d_0 \mid v) = 1, \qquad (24)$$

whenever

$$\beta \sum_{i=1}^{c} p_i F(v \mid a_i) > p_j F(v \mid a_j) \text{ for all } j (j = 1, 2 \cdots c), \qquad (25)$$

where $\beta (0 \leq \beta \leq 1)$ is a nonnegative constant determined by the condition that $P_r(\delta^{**}) = \alpha$; namely,

$$\int_V \delta^{**}(d_0 \mid v) \sum_{i=1}^{c} p_i F(v \mid a_i) dv = \alpha. \qquad (26)$$

The constant β increases with increasing α, and $P_e(\delta^{**})$ and $P_c(\delta^{**})$ are monotonic decreasing functions of α.

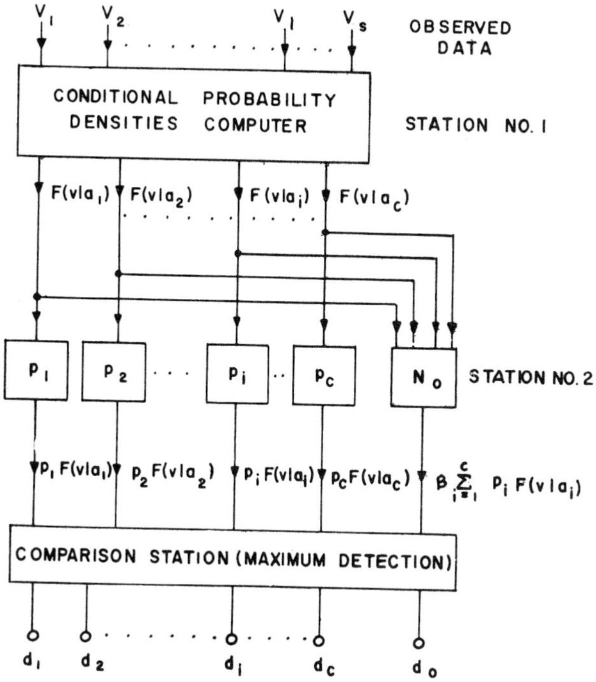

Fig. 3—Functional diagram of the system having the minimum error rate.

The change in the constant β provides a control over the error-reject ratio.

The optimum rule δ^{**} provides the basis for the functional diagram of the system of minimum error rate as shown in Fig. 3. The first station is identical to that of the minimum risk system (see Fig. 2) which computes the conditional probability densities $F(v|a_i)$'s.

The second station for this system is somewhat similar to that shown in the functional diagram for the minimum risk system (see Fig. 2). The c-character channels perform the weighting operation and have $p_i F(v|a_i)$ as outputs. The rejection channel, N_0, performs the operation of weighting and summing and has $\beta \sum_{i=1}^{c} p_i F(v|a_i)$ as its output. All of these $c+1$ outputs are nonnegative. The comparison station then examines these outputs and selects the largest. If the output of the rejection channel is the largest, the system rejects; otherwise the system will identify the character by the channel having the largest output.

It can be shown that the system depicted in Fig. 2 reduces to the system shown in Fig. 3 when β is replaced by $(w_m - w_r)/(w_m - w_c)$, and the following weight function is used.

$$W(a_i, d_j) = \begin{cases} w_c & \text{for } i = j \neq 0 \\ w_r & \text{for } i \neq 0, j = 0. \\ w_m & \text{for } i \neq j \neq 0. \end{cases} \qquad (27)$$

Examples

1) As an illustration, consider a condition where the signals and noise are additive, and the noise has independent normal distribution To be explicit, the probability density function of the noise of the jth component of the ith character is taken as:

$$\frac{1}{\sqrt{2\pi}\sigma_{ij}} \exp\left\{-\frac{(v_j - a_{ij})^2}{2\sigma_{ij}^2}\right\}, \tag{28}$$

where $v_j - a_{ij}$ is the noise and σ_{ij}^2 is the given variance.

The conditional probability density $F(v|a_i)$, under the assumption that noise is statistically independent, is

$$F(v \mid a_i) = \frac{\exp\left\{-\sum_{j=1}^{s} \frac{(v_j - a_{ij})^2}{2\sigma_{ij}^2}\right\}}{(2\pi)^{s/2} \prod_{j=1}^{s} \sigma_{ij}}. \tag{29}$$

Therefore, the last expression dictates the precise structure of station No. 1 for the optimum system. Each component circuit performs the operations of taking differences, squaring, weighting, summing, and taking exponential. This station is common for a minimum risk or minimum error rate system. The structures of the second station and comparison station are indicated in Figs. 2 and 3.

2) In this example, the signal and noise structure are such that the conditional probability density for a given length, $|v|$, of v is directly proportional to the cosine of the angle θ between vectors v and a_i for $|\theta| < \pi/2$ and is zero elsewhere, and that the distributions of $|v|$ for given a_i are identical for all i.[6] [It is denoted as $f(|v|)$.] In other words, $F(v|a_i)$ can be written as

$$F(v \mid a_i) = \rho f(|v|) \frac{a_i \cdot v}{|a_i| \cdot |v|} \quad \text{for } a_i \cdot v > 0$$
$$= 0 \quad \text{elsewhere}, \tag{30}$$

where ρ is a constant independent of i and is determined by the fact that $\int_V F(v|a_i)dv = 1$, and $a_i \cdot v$ denotes the scalar product of vectors a_i and v.

An inspection of the optimum decision rule (δ^* or δ^{**}) reveals that the system remains optimum if the first station is to compute $T[F(v|a_i)]$ instead of $F(v|a_i)$, where T is defined as

$$T(v \mid a_i) = \frac{|v|}{\rho f(|v|)} F(v \mid a_i)$$
$$= \begin{cases} \frac{a_i}{|a_i|} \cdot v = \sum_{j=1}^{s} b_{ij} v_j & \text{for } a_i \cdot v > 0 \\ 0 & \text{for } a_i \cdot v \leq 0, \end{cases} \tag{31}$$

where b_{ij}'s are constants [see (2)]. This operation can be easily realized. Each component of the first station is simply a correlation network followed by a half-wave rectifying circuit. The circuit passes the positive output of the correlation network unaltered and converts its negative output into zero.

The above results also indicate that the recognition system described in the second section of this paper is not optimum for the particular signal and noise structure as given in examples 1 or 2.

[6] This particular signal and noise structure was suggested by the author's colleague, I. M. Sheaffer, Jr., Burroughs Corp., Paoli, Pa.

Error-Free System

For convenience, let V_i denote the set (or region) of all possible observation v when the ith character is present, and let $\tilde{V}_i$ be the largest subset of V_i so that $\tilde{V}_i$'s are nonoverlapping. If noise distributions are so truncated and the signal vectors a_i's are so placed that all $\tilde{V}_i$'s are nonempty, then an error-free system for character recognition does exist. Evidently for any observed data v belonging to $\tilde{V}_k$, only $F(v|a_k)$ is nonzero while all others are zero; the character can then be identified with certainty. On the other hand, if the data v do not belong to any one of the $\tilde{V}_i$'s, then more than one of the $F(v|a_i)$'s will be nonzero. This results in the data being ambiguous for recognition purpose, and an error-free system will reject. Symbolically, the error-free decision rule is:

$$\delta(d_k \mid v) = 1 \quad \text{if } F(v \mid a_k) > 0$$

and

$$F(v \mid a_i) = 0 \quad \text{for all } i \neq k, \tag{32}$$

and

$$\delta(d_0 \mid v) = 1, \quad \text{otherwise},$$

the rejection rate is determined by the probability measures of $\tilde{V}_i$'s, namely $\int_{\tilde{V}_i} F(v|a_i)dv$. The latter is determined by the character style and allowable deterioration. The character style may be considered ideal and the control over the printing perfect, if the resultant $\int_{\tilde{V}_i} F(v|a_i)dv$ is unity for all i, and all characters with allowable deterioration can then be recognized with neither an error nor reject. In this sense, the probability measures of $\tilde{V}_i$'s may be used to evaluate the combined quality of the character style and printing.

Conclusion

The decision theory has been successfully applied to the problem of character recognition. By employing the concept of risk, differences in consequences for various decisions have been taken into consideration. A rejection channel has been introduced to examine the degree of ambiguity of input signal and make rejections when necessary.

As developed, the structure and performance of an optimum system depend upon the signal and noise statistics; therefore, *a priori* knowledge of these statistics is required. Usually, a realistic estimate of noise statistics is not easy to obtain. However, it is sincerely felt that the requirement for high grade performance in character recognition warrants the expenditures in this direction.

Quite often an optimum system may prove to be too expensive for mechanization. Nevertheless, the results presented in this paper are considered useful in that they provide insight into the recognition problem and furnish an ideal system, which actual recognition circuitry may be patterned after.

Although it is recognized as being beyond the scope of this paper, it is worth mentioning that one practical approach to the over-all problem would be to design adequately the character style and to control properly the printing process so that a reliable system would not be too far fetched or difficult to ultimately realize.

Appendix I.

List of Symbols

$a_i = (a_{i1}, a_{i2}, \cdots, a_{is})$, s-dimensional vector associated with the ith character, $(i=1, 2, \cdots, c)$.
a_{ij} = jth sample of the signal of the ith character.
$|a_i| = (\sum_{j=1}^{s} a_{ij}^2)^{1/2}$, the length of vector a_i.
c = number of characters.
d_0 = decision that rejection be made.
d_j = decision that the signal is the jth character $(j=1, 2, \cdots, c)$.
$f(|v|)$ = probability density of the length of v.
$F(v|a_i)$ = conditional probability density for the observed data v when a_i is the incoming signal.
i, j, k = indexes.
N_{1i} = a network of station No. 1, $i=1, 2, \cdots, c$.
N_{2i} = a network of station No. 2, $i=1, 2, \cdots, c$.
N_0 = the network of rejection channel.
P_c = probability of correct recognition.
P_r = probability of rejection (rejection rate).
P_e = probability of misrecognition (error rate).
p_i = *a priori* probability that the ith character occurs, $(i=1, 2, \cdots, c)$.
$p = (p_1, p_2, \cdots, p_c)$.
$R(p, \delta)$ = expected risk of the system; $R = R_0 + R_1$.
$R_0(p)$ = expected risk of the system when rejection is made for all recognition.
$R_1(p, \delta)$ = part of R which is dependent upon δ.
s = number of samples.
T = functional transformation.
V = s-dimension observation space.
V_i = set of all v when the ith character is present.
$\tilde{V}_i$ = largest subset of V_i such that $\tilde{V}_i \cap \tilde{V}_j = 0$ for all $j \neq i$.
$v = (v_1, v_2, \cdots, v_s)$, a vector in V.
$|v| = (\sum_{i=1}^{s} v_i^2)^{1/2}$, the length of vector v.
vi = ith component of the observed data v.
$W(a_i, d_j)$ = weight function.
$w_{ij} = W(a_i, d_j)$.
w_c, w_r, w_m = weights.
$x_i(v)$ = output of the ith channel.
α = permissible rejection rate.
β = constant.
$\delta(v)$ = decision rule, $\delta = [\delta(d_0|v), \delta(d_1|v) \cdots \delta(d_c|v)]$.
$\delta^*(v)$ = optimum decision rule which minimizes the expected risk.
$\delta^{**}(v)$ = optimum decision rule which minimizes the error rate.
θ = angle.
ρ = a normalizing constant.
σ_{ij}^2 = statistical variance of noise.

Appendix II.

To Prove That δ^{**} Has a Minimum Error Rate for a Given Rejection Rate

Without loss of generality, it is assumed that the absolute probability density of the occurrence of v, namely, $\sum_{i=1}^{c} p_i F(v|a_i)$ is nonzero over the entire observation space V. Otherwise, the set over which $\sum_{i=1}^{c} p_i F(v|a_i)$ is zero is first deleted.

Let $m(v)$ be the subscript such that

$$\max [p_i F(v \mid a_i)] = p_m F(v \mid a_m) \tag{33}$$

and let $\delta^1(v)$ be any arbitrary decision rule having the same rejection rate as δ^{**}. It is to be proved that $P_e(\delta^1) \geq P_e(\delta^{**})$.

For every $\delta^1(v)$, a decision rule $\delta^2(v)$ can be constructed as follows:

For every v,

$$\delta^2(d_0 \mid v) = \delta^1(d_0 \mid v)$$

$$\delta^2(d_m \mid v) = 1 - \delta^1(d_0 \mid v) = \sum_{i=1}^{c} \delta^1(d_i \mid v) \tag{34}$$

$$\delta^2(d_i \mid v) = 0 \quad \text{for all } i \neq 0 \neq m.$$

Evidently,

$$P_r(\delta^2) = P_r(\delta^1) = \alpha, \tag{35}$$

and

$$\begin{aligned} P_c(\delta^1) &= \int_V \sum_{i=1}^{c} \delta^1(d_i \mid v) p_i F(v \mid a_i) dv \\ &\leq \int_V \sum_{i=1}^{c} \delta^1(d_i \mid v) p_m F(v \mid a_m) dv \\ &= \int_V \delta^2(d_m \mid v) p_m F(v \mid a_m) dv \\ &= P_c(\delta^2). \end{aligned} \tag{36}$$

It follows from (35) and (36) that

$$P_e(\delta^2) \leq P_e(\delta^1). \tag{37}$$

That is, δ^2 is better than δ^1 (or at least as good) in the sense that for the same rejection rate δ^2 has an error rate smaller than, or equal to, that of δ^1.

The next step is to show that $P_e(\delta^{**}) \leq P_e(\delta^2)$. As shown in (22) ad (23), the decision rule δ^{**} partitions the observation space V into two nonintersecting regions, V_0^{**} and $V - V_0^{**}$, so that for every $v \epsilon V_0^{**}$

$$p_m F(v \mid a_m) < \beta \sum_{i=1}^{c} p_i F(v \mid a_i) \tag{38a}$$

$$\delta^{**}(d_0 | v) = 1, \tag{38b}$$

and for every $v \epsilon V - V_0^{**}$

$$p_m F(v \mid a_m) \geq \beta \sum_{i=1}^{c} p_i F(v \mid a_i) \tag{39a}$$

$$\delta^{**}(d_m \mid v) = 1. \tag{39b}$$

Let V_0^2 be the largest subspace of V such that $\delta^2(d_0 | v)$ is nonzero for all v belonging to V_0^2. V_0^2 is not properly contained in V_0^{**}. This follows readily from the condition that $P_r(\delta^{**}) = P_r(\delta^2)$. The latter may be written as:

$$\int_{V_0^{**}-V_0^{**}\cap V_0^2} \sum_{i=1}^{c} p_i F(v \mid a_i) dv + \int_{V_0^{**}\cap V_0^2} [1 - \delta^2(d_0 \mid v)] \sum_{i=1}^{c} p_i F(v \mid a_i) dv = \int_{V_0^2-V_0^{**}\cap V_0^2} \delta^2(d_0 \mid v) \sum_{i=1}^{c} p_i F(v \mid a_i) dv. \tag{40}$$

Substitution of (38) and (39) in (40) gives:

$$\int_{V_0^{**}-V_0^{**}\cap V_0^2} p_m F(v \mid a_m) dv + \int_{V_0^{**}\cap V_0^2} [1 - \delta^2(d_0 \mid v)] p_m F(v \mid a_m) dv \leq \int_{V_0^2-V_0^{**}\cap V_0^2} \delta^2(d_0 \mid v) p_m F(v \mid a_m) dv. \tag{41}$$

The equality sign prevails if, and only if, $p_m F(v | a_m)$ is equal to $\beta \sum_{i=1}^{c} p_i F(v | a_i)$ throughout the region $V_0^{**} \cup V_0^2$.

The probabilities of correct recognition of δ^{**} and δ^2 may be written respectively as:

$$P_c(\delta^{**}) = \int_{V-V_0^{**}} p_m F(v \mid a_m) dv = \int_{V-(V_0^{**}\cup V_0^2)} p_m F(v \mid a_m) dv + \int_{V_0^2-V_0^{**}\cap V_0^2} p_m F(v \mid a_m) dv, \tag{42a}$$

$$P_c(\delta^2) = \int_V \sum_{i=1}^{c} \delta^2(d_i \mid v) p_i F(v \mid a_i) dv = \int_{V-(V_0^{**}\cup V_0^2)} p_m F(v \mid a_m) dv + \int_{V_0^{**}-V_0^{**}\cap V_0^2} p_m F(v \mid a_m) dv + \int_{V_0^{**}\cap V_0^2} \delta^2(d_m \mid v) p_m F(v \mid a_m) dv + \int_{V_0^2-V_0^{**}\cap V_0^2} \delta^2(d_m \mid v) p_m F(v \mid a_m) dv. \tag{42b}$$

In accordance with (42), (41) is equivalent to $P_e(\delta^{**}) \leq P_e(\delta^2)$. Proof that $P_e(\delta^{**}) \leq \delta P_e(\delta^1)$ is thus completed.

Acknowledgment

This paper is based upon research performed in the Electromechanisms Department of the Burroughs Corporation Research Center at Paoli, Pa. The author wishes to thank his colleagues and Department Manager, G. A. Baird for their encouragement and assistance relative to this paper. The permission of the Burroughs Corporation for release of the material presented here is also acknowledged.

Perceptron Simulation Experiments*

FRANK ROSENBLATT†

Summary—**An experimental simulation program, which has been in progress at the Cornell Aeronautical Laboratory since 1957, is described. This program uses the IBM 704 computer to simulate perceptual learning, recognition, and spontaneous classification of visual stimuli in the perceptron, a theoretical brain model which has been described elsewhere. The paper includes a brief review of the organization of simple perceptrons, and theoretically predicted performance curves are compared with those obtained from the simulation programs, in several types of experiments, designed to study "forced" and "spontaneous" learning of pattern discriminations.**

Introduction

A NUMBER of papers and reports have been published describing the theory of a new brain model called the perceptron. The perceptron is a minimally constrained "nerve net" consisting of logically simplified neural elements, which has been shown to be capable of learning to discriminate and to recognize perceptual patterns [5]–[8]. This paper is concerned with a report of digital simulation experiments which have been carried out on the perceptron, using the IBM 704 computer at the Cornell Aeronautical Laboratory. These experiments are intended to demonstrate the performance of particular systems in typical environmental situations, free from any approximations which have been used in the previously published mathematical analyses. In the simulation programs, the action of every cell and every connection in the network is represented in detail, and visual stimuli are represented by dot patterns corresponding to illuminated points in a retinal mosaic.

Several related experiments have been conducted previously, using a digital computer for the simulation of a nerve net in learning experiments [1], [2], [4]. Rochester and associates, at IBM, have reported on several attempts to simulate the formation of "cell assemblies," in a model based on the work of Hebb [3] Hebb proposes that a set of neurons which is repeatedly activated by a particular sensory stimulus becomes organized into a functional unit, which can be triggered as a whole by sensory patterns sufficiently similar to the original one. Hebb's book, however, does not attempt to specify in a rigorous manner the exact organization or parameters under which the predicted effects would be obtained, so that the IBM group found it necessary to improvise several models and variations of their own, having various degrees of biological plausibility, in an attempt to construct a definite system. The results of these experiments seem ambiguous, not only because of the uncertain relationship of the final model to the nerve net originally suggested, but also because the phenomenon which was sought after has never been defined in a fashion precise enough so that one might say whether or not it has actually occurred. These experiments illustrate the importance of selecting a suitable measure of performance in work of this type; it is essential that a clearly defined test should be specified for the "learning" which has presumably taken place, or else it is impossible to say either how well a particular system has performed or to compare its performance with any other system, or class of systems, in a systematic fashion.

From this standpoint, the experiments reported by Farley and Clark [1], [2] seem to have been better conceived. In this model, a network of eight randomly connected neurons was simulated. Inputs consisted of stimuli applied to one of two disjunct pairs of "input cells," and outputs were measured as the activity of two pairs of "output cells." In later experiments, the size of the network was increased to sixteen cells. It was demonstrated that this system can learn to favor the output from one set of output cells following the presentation of one of the two stimuli, and the alternative output set following presentation of the other stimulus. The problem of generalization was considered only in terms of relatively slight displacements or alterations of the stimulus patterns, and it was suggested that, under these conditions, the response would be most likely to occur which was previously associated to the stimulus having the greatest overlap with the altered stimulus. The problem of generalization to similar but completely disjunct stimuli was not specifically considered. Nonetheless, the process of generalization advocated as a result of these experiments has much in common with our early work on the perceptron. A more thorough consideration of this problem will be published elsewhere [8].

The design of a simulation program for studies of pattern recognition and perceptual generalization in nerve nets should fulfill at least three basic conditions, each of which has been ignored too frequently in previous work along these lines.

1) Simulation should not, in general, be attempted without a theoretical analysis of the nerve net in question, sufficient to indicate suitable parameters and rules of organization, and to indicate questions of theoretical interest. The examination of arbitrary networks in the hope that they will yield something interesting, or the simulation of networks which have been specially designed to compute a particular function by a definite algorithmic procedure seem to be about equally lacking in value.

* Original manuscript received by the IRE, July 16, 1959; revised manuscript received, December 14, 1959. This paper was presented at the 1959 IRE National Convention. The work was supported by the Information Systems Branch, Office of Naval Research, under Contract no. Nonr-2831(00), since July, 1957.

† Cornell Aeronautical Lab., Inc., Buffalo, N. Y.

Reprinted from *Proc. IRE*, vol. 48, pp. 301–309, Mar. 1960.

2) Suitable measures of performance must be defined. This means that some task must be set for the system, the outcome of which can be clearly recognized, and, preferably, counted or quantified in some manner. Signal strengths, waiting times for achievement of a criterion, or percentage of correct decisions are examples of suitable measures.

3) Experiments should be designed with suitable controls against trivial or ambiguous results. If we are interested in teaching a device to generalize a response to visual forms, for example, it is essential that a discrimination test should be made involving at least two different responses, to make sure that the system has not simply generalized the desired response universally to all stimuli, regardless of their similarity to one another. Moreover, it is often important to make sure that the cue for the response is the actual *form* of the stimulus, rather than its location on the retina, or some other unintentional source of information. This last condition is often quite tricky to satisfy, and in most of our current work we make use of Born-von Kármán boundary conditions (in which patterns shifted off of one edge of a retinal field re-enter on the opposite side, as in a toroidally connected space) in order to guarantee the logical equivalence of all points in the retinal space. Given such a retinal field, it is sufficient to place each stimulus pattern with equal probability or frequency at all possible locations in the retinal space, in order to guarantee that the illumination of a particular retinal point does not convey any information about which stimulus is present. It should be noted that this condition is not always observed in the experiments reported in this paper, stimuli often being confined to some subfield of the retina in order to increase the rate of learning. In at least one case (the experiment with the "continuous transducer perceptron" shown in Fig. 8) a discrimination has thus been obtained which would not hold up if the field were uniformly covered with the stimulus patterns.

Organization of a Perceptron

Any perceptron, or nerve net, consists of a network of "cells," or signal generating units, and connections between them. The perceptron is defined by two sets of rules: 1) a set of rules specifying the topological constraints upon the network organization, such as the number of connections to a given unit, or the direction in which connections are made, and 2) a set of rules specifying the dynamic properties of the system, such as thresholds, signal strengths, and memory functions. A "fully random network" would be one in which only the number of cells and the number of connections is specified, each connection being equally likely to originate or terminate on any cell of the system. The topological rules for the organization of a perceptron take the form of constraints applied to such a random network, and it is assumed that all connection properties other than those specified remain "random," in the sense just indicated.

A simplified version of the known features of a mammalian visual system is shown in Fig. 1, for a comparison with the organization of a perceptron, which will be described presently. At the extreme left we see a mosaic of light-sensitive points, or retina, from which signals are transmitted to the visual projection area, in the cerebral cortex. Several intermediate relay stations exist in a typical biological system, which are not shown here. These connections preserve topological characteristics of the stimulus in a reasonably intact form. Beyond the projection area, however, connections appear to be largely random. Impulses are delivered through a large number of paths to the association areas of the cortex, where local feedback loops are activated, so that activity may persist for some time past the termination of the original visual stimulus. From the association area, signals are transmitted to the motor cortex, which again has a clear topological organization corresponding to the location of muscle groups to be controlled.

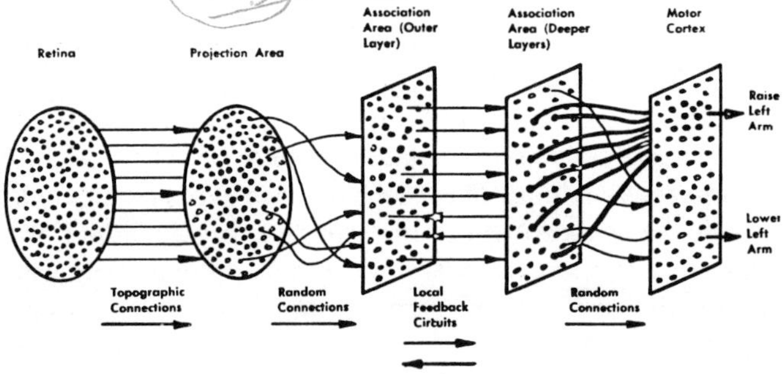

Fig. 1—Organization of a biological brain. (Heavy black areas indicate active cells, responding to the letter X.)

This general plan of organization has been considerably simplified in the perceptron. First of all, we will eliminate the projection area, and assume that the retinal points are directly coupled to association cells, or "A units." The number of input connections to each A unit is specified, but the locations of the origin points for the connections are selected at random from the set of sensory points. Each A unit receives some number, x, of excitatory connections, and some number, y, of inhibitory connections. The connection system from the sensory to association system is a many-to-many system. An excitatory connection from an illuminated sensory point is assumed to transmit a unit positive signal, while an inhibitory connection carries a unit negative signal. Each A unit has a fixed threshold, θ, and is triggered to deliver an output pulse if the algebraic sum (α) of the signals received from the $x+y$ input connections is equal to or greater than θ. A further simplification is introduced at the output side of the association system. Instead of delivering its output signals at random to a large number of "motor area" cells, the cells of the association system are connected to one or more binary response units, which are turned to their "1" state if they receive a positive signal from the association system, or to their "0" state if they receive a negative signal. The magnitude of the output signal generated by an active A unit is called the "value" of that unit, and is represented by the symbol v. The values of the units are stochastic variables, which change as a function of the history of the system. The organization of a simple perceptron with a single binary response is shown in Fig. 2. The total signal delivered by the set of A units is equal to $\Sigma \alpha_i^* v_i$ where α_i^* is equal to 1 if unit a_i is active, and 0 if a_i is inactive, and v_i is the current value of unit a_i. Note that there are two feedback lines from the response unit (or R unit) to the set of A units. These feedbacks control the "reinforcement," or changes in value, of the A units. In general, if the response $R=1$ occurs, active A units will gain in value, while if the response $R=0$ occurs, active units will lose in value. The value of the A unit thus acts as the memory variable for the system. It has been shown to be desirable to further modify the values of the A units by the rule that if some subset of units gains or loses in value, then the remainder of the units must change in the opposite direction just sufficiently to balance out the net change to zero. Thus, one unit can only gain parasitically, at the expense of the other units, and the total value of all of the A units is kept equal to zero at all times. A perceptron with this property is called a "gamma system." The theory of such systems has been considered in detail elsewhere [5], [6].

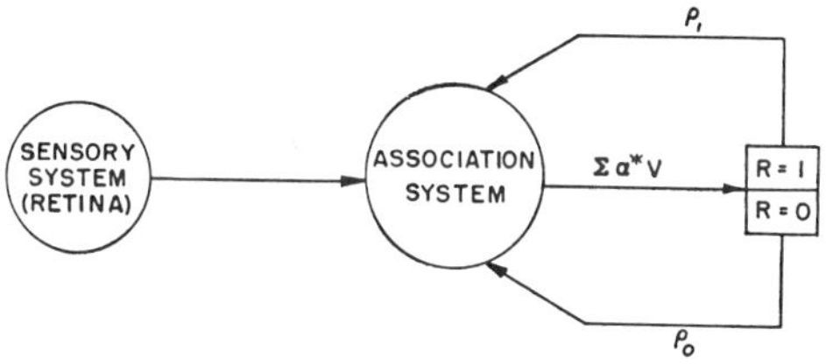

Fig. 2—Organization of a simple perceptron.

Description of Simulation Programs

Fig. 3 shows the organization of a typical simulation program, for the study of perceptron performance in an environment of visual forms. Actually, four basically different programs have so far been written with a number of variations of each, but the two programs which were used for most of the experiments reported here are both organized in the manner illustrated. The third program involves more direct methods of computation rather than true simulation, while the fourth program (designed to study "cross-coupled systems," in which A units may be connected to one another as well as to S points and R units) has proven too slow to be used successfully.[1]

The simulation programs have four main tasks, each of which is actually performed by a separate, self-sufficient program, which is stored on tape, and called into the computer by a supervisory routine. The supervisory routine reads instruction cards provided by the experimenter, which provide information on parameters, and control the sequence of subprograms performed in the course of the experiment. When each subprogram has been completed, control is passed back to the supervisory routine, which reads the next card for further instructions. In a typical experiment, the sequence is as follows:

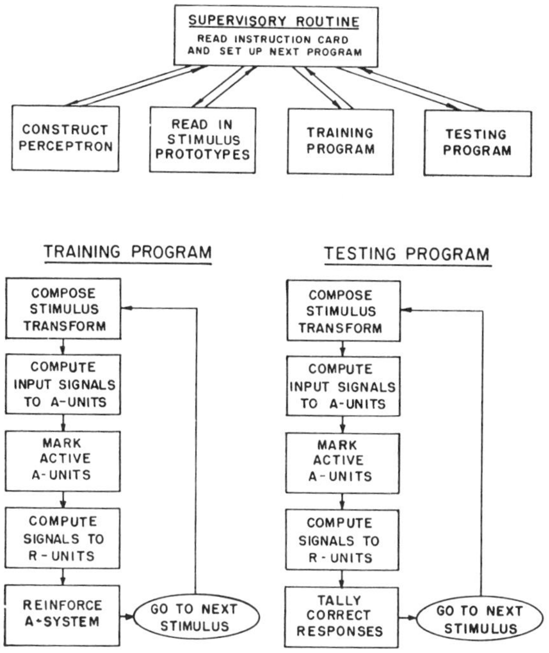

Fig. 3—Flow diagram for simulation program.

1) The perceptron construction routine is called into the core memory, and reads in a set of parameters describing the perceptron to be constructed. These parameters include the number of A units, the number of excitatory and inhibitory connections to each unit, the thresholds of the units, the number of R units, the number of R units connected to each A unit, the decay rate for A unit values (which decay with time in some models) and a random number to be used for priming the pseudo-random-number generator used to control the choice of connections. The program then selects for each A unit a set of $x+y$ sensory points to be assigned as origins for the input connections. This is done by generating a random number number modulo N_s (the number of sensory points) for each connection. This number is used to locate one of the N_s storage locations in which

[1] The cross-coupled system was successfully simulated, and predicted effects obtained in December, 1959, using an improved program. Results will be reported in later publications.

the state of each sensory point is indicated when a "visual" pattern is presented.[2] The perceptron construction routine prepares a table listing all of these connections. In the first simulation program this table was stored on tape; but in the second program, by cutting down the admissible number of A units and connections, it was possible to store the entire table in the core memory, saving a factor of about five in running time of the program. The R units to which each A unit is connected are similarly assigned at random in each of the first two programs, which permit multiple output connections from each A unit. Since, in practice, all experiments have been concerned only with simple binary discrimination problems, more recent programs have been designed with only one R unit, to which all A units are connected. In the second program, it is also possible to assign an initial random distribution of values to the A units, although in most experiments it is assumed that the values start out uniformly from zero.

2) The second stage in the experiment calls for reading a set of "prototype stimulus patterns" into the memory of the computer. These patterns consist of actual dot images of the stimuli to be used, punched as patterns of holes in IBM cards. Thus, if it is planned to teach the perceptron the first four letters of the alphabet, we would read in the images of the letters A, B, C, and D, which are stored for future reference by later routines. These prototypes are never altered, but are used by the stimulus transformation routines which are included in the remaining two programs, to construct variously displaced, rotated, or contracted patterns which are the stimuli actually "shown" to the perceptron.

3) Having constructed the connection tables and read in the prototype stimuli, the computer is ready to begin the actual learning experiment. This consists of an alternation between the two remaining programs, one of which attempts to "teach" the perceptron to recognize the stimulus patterns, while the other evaluates the performance of the perceptron at intervals specified by the control cards. For example, in a typical experiment, the discrimination of the letters "E" and "X," the procedure is as follows. First, a control card calls for the training program to show ten different transformations of the letter "E" (the first stimulus). Each of these is generated by applying a vertical and lateral shift of random magnitudes between zero units of retinal distance and a maximum shift specified by the control card, a rotation between zero degrees and a specified maximum, and a size somewhere between a specified lower and upper bound. Random numbers generated by the routine determine the exact transformation to be applied to each stimulus, and a new image is composed. The control card then specifies that the response "1" is to be reinforced as the appropriate response for the letter "E." The program accordingly calculates the signals received by each A unit from the transformed stimulus, determines which A units are active, and reinforces the units according to the rules for reinforcement of the $R=1$ condition, for the gamma system, *i.e.*, each active A unit gains an increment in value, while the inactive units lose a compensating amount. In the second of the simulation programs, it is also possible for the stimulus to persist for a designated number of cycles, undergoing a random walk during this time, consisting of unit displacements, rotations, or size changes from the position in which it first appeared. This procedure is characteristic of the "forced learning mode" of experiment, which is the only mode possible for the first simulation program. In this mode, the desired response is turned on, or forced, by the training program at the same time that a stimulus is presented. The second program is also designed to permit a "spontaneous learning mode," in which stimuli occur in a random sequence, and the response spontaneously occurring upon presentation of the stimulus is reinforced, regardless of whether or not it is the response ultimately desired. Most of the experiments to be described in this paper were performed in the forced learning mode. After having presented the ten transformations of the letter "E" which were called for, and reinforced the response $R=1$ for each transformation, control is returned to the supervisory routine, which reads the next control card. In this typical experiment, we next call for ten transformations of the letter "X," to be associated to the response $R=0$. This procedure is carried out in the same manner as before.

We now switch to the testing program, which composes a series of stimulus transformations in the same manner as the training program, and goes through an identical set of calculations to determine the active A units in each case. Instead of reinforcing the association units, however, this program merely records the response, and checks it against the desired response for correctness. If the response is correct, it increments a tally of correct responses. Typically, we may look at twenty transformations of the "E" and twenty transformations of the "X," determining in each case the percentage of correct responses ($R=1$ or $R=0$, respectively). During this procedure, a running description of the responses of the system, numbers of active units, and other analytic data, are printed out by the computer. We may now present another ten E's and another ten X's, reinforcing the system as before, then test the performance once more, to find out whether this addi-

[2] In each of the first two simulation programs, multiple connections from the same A unit to the same S point are prohibited. In the second program, an inverse constraint was originally employed, fixing the number of connections originating from each sensory point, and assigning termini at random in the association system. This was later modified by the addition of a scheme to obtain, as nearly as possible, uniform numbers of inputs to each A unit as well as fixed numbers of outputs from the sensory units. These variations have not seriously affected the performance of the program, but it appears that somewhat better performance is obtained with the numbers of inputs to the A units is kept uniform.

tional training has improved the performance, and thus continue alternating between training and testing programs indefinitely. It is also possible to reverse the assigned responses in the middle of the experiment, thus reversing previous learning. In order to obtain unambiguous comparisons of performance in different parts of the training series, the testing series are generally "primed" with the same random number to guarantee that the same stimulus transformations will be used on each repetition of the program. The training programs, on the other hand, continue to select stimuli at random, independently of what has gone before. A comparison of the organization of the training and testing programs is presented in the flow diagrams in Fig. 3.

The two main simulation programs total about 5000 words each. The first program was designed to handle up to 1000 A units, and a 72 by 72 sensory mosaic. It was found that this large sensory system presented stimuli with a fineness of grain considerably better than the limits of discrimination of a thousand-unit perceptron, and at the same time, required an excessive amount of time for stimulus transformations, since each illuminated point in the stimulus must be transformed individually into its image point. The second program reduced the retina to a 20 by 20 mosaic, and limited the number of A units to 500. For the first system, the computing time averaged about 15 seconds per stimulus cycle, while in the second system the time was cut to about 3 seconds per cycle. Subsequent improvements in programming techniques indicate that it should be possible to reduce the computing time still further—say to about one second per cycle—for perceptrons of the size allowed by the second program. At the same time, however, analytic developments have suggested a way of actually calculating the exact performance of a given perceptron of the type discussed above, provided all possible stimuli are known, and a matrix of g coefficients, describing the interactions of each pair of stimuli, is computed for the particular network in question. This technique is discussed in the appendix to [7], and is the method employed in the third of our simulation programs for the analysis of spontaneous learning in infinite perceptrons. In that program, the response of the system is obtained analytically, rather than simulated, but the sequence of stimuli is governed by a series of random numbers generated by the program. We will consider some of the results of this program later in this paper.

Theoretical Predictions and Problems

Before considering the results of the simulation experiments, let us review the main predictions coming from the theory of the perceptron (see [5]–[7]). The simulation experiments were designed in part to verify these predictions, and in part to study problems which were suggested by the theoretical investigations.

Fig. 4 shows a set of theoretical performance curves for perceptrons of three different sizes, in the problem of discriminating a square from a circle. The broken curves (for P_r) show the probability of giving the correct response to a stimulus which is identical in position, size, etc., to one which was shown previously, during the training period. The horizontal axis indicates the number of stimuli of each class (squares and circles) which were presented during the training period. The solid curves indicate the probability of correct response to *any* square or circle, regardless of whether it was used as a training stimulus or not. Note that both sets of curves approach the same asymptotes as the number of training stimuli becomes large. The first task of the simulation program was to check the general character of these learning curves for typical stimulus material, such as letters of the alphabet or geometric patterns. In particular, it was essential to determine whether the rates of learning agreed with the predicted rates, at least to a reasonable approximation.

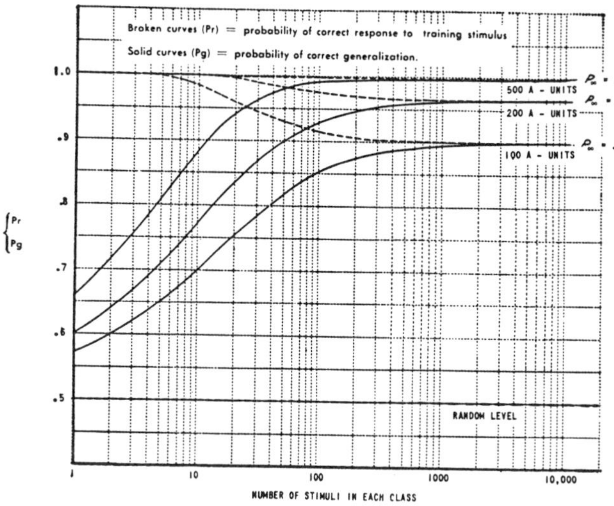

Fig. 4—Learning curves for three typical perceptrons.

A second problem concerned the effect of particular types of transformations, such as shifting of stimuli, rotations, or size changes, upon the learning curves. The original theory did not distinguish among these types of transformations, and it was important to find out whether the system would work equally well for all of them. While sufficient demonstrations have now been made of performance under shifting and rotation conditions, the problem of size changes remains a serious one, with a number of special cases. One such special case involves the assignment of different responses to two stimuli, one of which could be considered a "part" of the other, such as a small circle which could be completely imbedded in a larger one, or the letter "F," which can be considered as an "E" with the lower bar missing. It was predicted that such discriminations would be possible only with a mixture of excitatory and inhibitory input connections, excitatory connections alone being insufficient.[3]

Related to the problem of size variation in the stimuli is the problem of frequency variation, *i.e.*, some kinds of stimuli being more frequent than others. The response assigned to the more frequent stimulus type will generally tend to dominate the response assigned to the less frequent type, unless the system is designed in such a way as to minimize interaction between different classes of stimuli. The extent of this frequency bias was one of the problems originally set for the simulation programs, but a systematic investigation has not yet been completed.

A different problem area concerns the performance of linear systems. At one stage of the perceptron program, we were particularly interested in systems in which no threshold at all was employed in the A units, the output simply being equal to αv (the algebraic product of the input signal and the stored value) rather than $\alpha^* v$, as in the model described above. The values were to be augmented by a quantity equal to α if $R=1$, and diminished by α if $R=0$. It can easily be shown that in such a system, if a stimulus pattern can occur with equal probability anywhere in the retinal space (and eliminating special boundary conditions, as in the toroidally connected model), the expected value of every A unit after a long series of stimulus exposures will be exactly zero. Such a system clearly would not learn at all, if stimuli were distributed uniformly in space. If the stimuli were *not* uniformly distributed, however, the values would tend to correlate with any bias existing in the input signals, and it was predicted that such a system should learn to discriminate. The second simulation program was originally set up to study linear systems of this type, both in forced learning and spontaneous learning experiments. The theory of such systems in spontaneous learning is considered elsewhere [7]. While linear systems have now been abandoned, a typical experiment will be considered presently, as it illustrates several points of interest.

The problem of spontaneous learning—the ability of a perceptron to form meaningful classifications of stimulus patterns without any assignment of "correct" responses by a human experimenter—has prompted an extensive series of experiments. The effect was originally demonstrated with the second simulation program, where two disjunct classes of stimuli were properly separated, in a number of experiments. More interesting results were obtained with the third program, which eventually pointed the way to the development of the "cross-coupled association system," which promises to yield substantially improved performance in a large variety of problems [8]. In studying these spontaneous learning effects, the first question was whether they could actually be obtained at all, and the second was how much experience would be required, a question for which no satisfactory theoretical answer had been found at the time the simulation experiments were undertaken. In this area, there has been particularly close feedback between simulation work and development of the theory, the simulation program frequently demonstrating the existence of special cases, involving particular parameters or particular stimulus forms, which had not been anticipated. More recent theoretical models owe a great deal to this period of empirical exploration.

[3] F. Rosenblatt, "The Perceptron: A Theory of Statistical Separability in Cognitive Systems," Cornell Aero. Lab., Buffalo, N. Y., Rept. no. VG-1196-G-1; January, 1958. See p. 53.

Results of Simulation Experiments

The first experiments which we shall consider are concerned with the discrimination of the letters "E" and "X" in a forced learning situation, and are illustrated in Fig. 5. The stimuli were constrained to a central portion of the field (as shown by the insert) partly to facilitate learning, and partly to prevent truncation at the boundaries, since the toroidal stimulus space was not used in this program. Fig. 5(a) shows the probability of correct generalization (P_g) as measured on a sample of 20 X's and 20 E's. The stimulus sequence consisted of ten X's followed by ten E's, followed by a test of performance; then ten more X's, ten more E's, and a second test, for a total of 100 training stimuli. The data points shown in the figure are means obtained from ten 100 A unit perceptrons, each of them having a different connection network, but exposed to the same sequence of stimuli. The curves in Fig. 5(b) show the performance of a larger (1000 A unit) perceptron, on a more difficult variation of the same problem. In the solid curve, we see the performance of the system for stimuli rotated by some integral number of degrees selected at random between 0 and 30 degrees. This rotation is combined with vertical and horizontal translations selected within the same limits as in the preceding case. For rotations up to 30 degrees, note that the system attains perfect performance after only ten stimuli of each type. The broken curve shows the performance of the same system for rotations up to 359 degrees, combined with translations as above. In this case, there is a definite decline in the perceptron's performance, although it has attained a P_g of better than 0.90 after 30 stimuli of each type.

The next experiment (Fig. 6) was designed to check the hypothesis that performance on outline figures should be better than on solid figures, since unlike figures represented by their contours would have a minimum intersection on the retina, while solid areas might still have a large intersection even though their shape was different. The figures used were squares (illustrated in the inset) and diamonds, which covered the same areas as the squares, rotated 45 degrees. As shown by the two curves, the outline figures did indeed yield a better performance than the solid figures, giving a per-

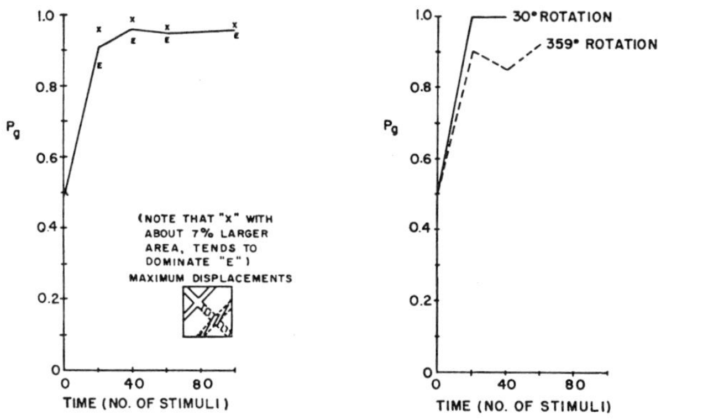

(a) (b)

Fig. 5—(a) Experiment 10. "E" vs "X." No rotation. Centers placed in 13 by 13 field, in 72 by 72 retina. $N_A=100$, $\theta=2$, $x=5$, and $y=5$. (b) Experiments 20, 21. "E" vs "X" with shifting plus rotation. $N_A=1000$, $\theta=4$, $x=10$, and $y=0$.

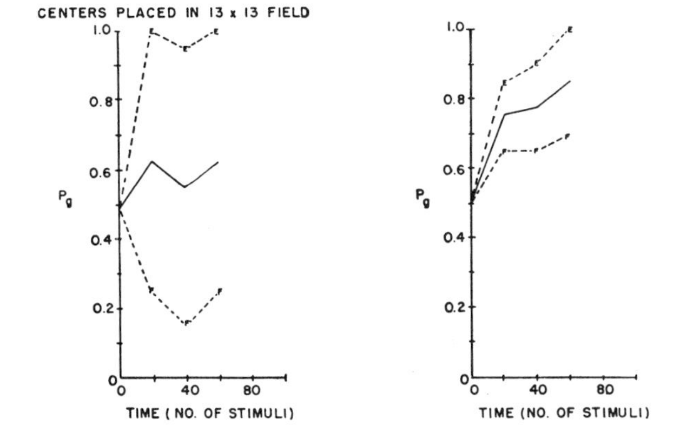

(a) (b)

Fig. 7—(a) Experiment 18. "E" vs "F." $N_A=100$, $x=10$, $\theta=4$, and $y=0$. Centers placed in 13 by 13 field. (b) Experiment 22. "E" vs "F." $N_A=1000$, $x=5$, $\theta=3$, and $y=5$.

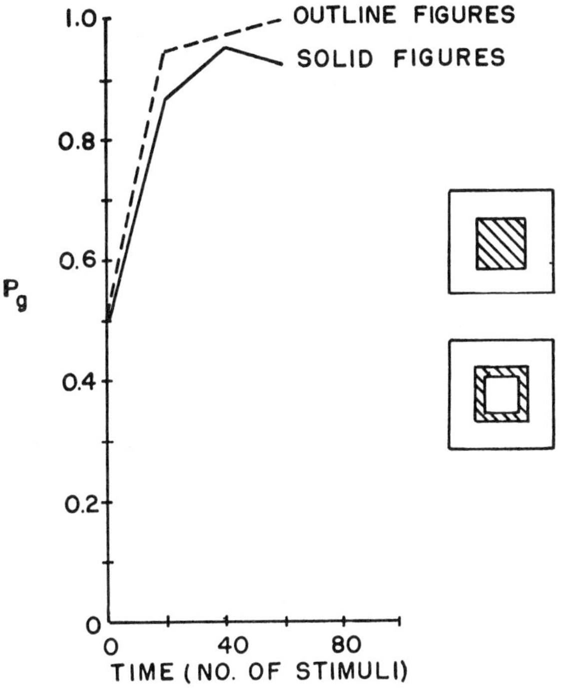

Fig. 6—Experiments 16, 17. Square-diamond discrimination. $N_A=1000$, $x=10$, $y=0$, and $\theta=4$. Centers placed in 13 by 13 field.

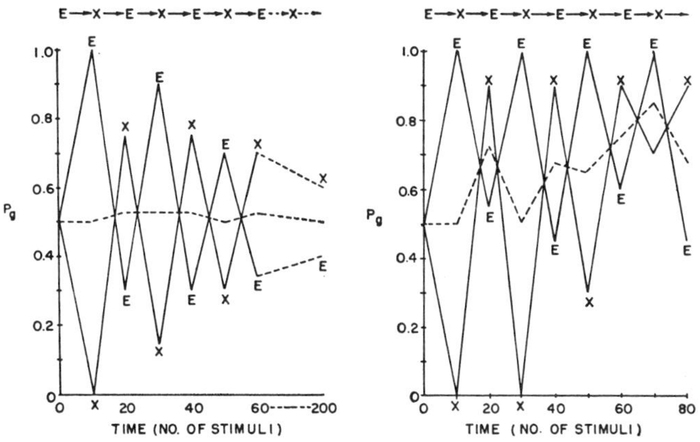

(a) (b)

Fig. 8—Linear system experiments ("E" vs "X"). (a) Experiment 4-14, 15. $N_A=500$, $x=4$, $y=4$. Centers placed in 13 by 13 field. (b) Experiment 4-16. $N_A=500$, $x=4$, and $y=4$. Centers placed in 5 by 5 field.

fect response record after 60 training stimuli (30 of each class). In this experiment, of course, rotation was eliminated to avoid confusion of squares and diamonds, and the figures were merely displaced in the same manner as the E's and X's in the preceding experiment.

Fig. 7 shows two experiments concerned with part-whole discrimination, which was discussed in the preceding section. In Experiment 18, illustrated in Fig. 7(a) a system with only excitatory connections to the A units was simulated. The stimulus is shifted at random in the central portion of the field, as before. In this case, the letter "E" was correctly learned, but the system was unable to learn to give the opposite response to the letter "F." In Experiment 22, shown in Fig. 7(b), we see that a system, in which half of the connections to the A units are inhibitory, is able to learn the correct response to both classes of stimuli, although the F response is considerably less consistent then the E response. Experiments 18 and 22 are, unfortunately, not fully comparable, as the perceptron in the second case was a thousand-unit system, while in Experiment 18 only a hundred A units were used. The character of the curves in these experiments, however, is definitely not a function of the size of the systems, but rather of the stimulus relationships, as shown by supporting evidence from many other cases. These results are in closer agreement with the theoretical predictions referred to earlier.

The next experiment (Fig. 8) was performed with the second simulation program, and represents the learning which is possible with a purely linear model, if the stimuli are constrained to one region of the retinal field. In this experiment, instead of testing the perceptron after every twenty stimuli, as in previous experiments, it was tested after every ten stimuli, which yields the characteristic pattern of converging oscillations shown in the figure. The first ten stimuli were all E's, and after these ten exposures, we find that the system has learned the "E" perfectly, but always gives the wrong response to stimuli of the opposite class (the letter "X"). The perceptron was then shown ten X's, to which the opposite response was forced, and we find at time 20 that it has now learned to give the desired response to the X, but has almost completely forgotten the proper response to the letter E. The amplitudes of such oscillations are apt to be increased by a large decay rate for the values of the A units (which makes more recent reinforcement more effective than earlier experience), but in the experiment illustrated here the decay rate was zero. Note that in Experiment 4-16 [illustrated Fig. 8(b)] the mean learning curve, shown by the broken line, climbs towards a high probability level as experience with both stimuli increases. At the same time, the swings in performance become considerably less pronounced, as each series of ten stimuli represents a progressively diminishing portion of the total experience of the system. The important conclusion from this experiment is that discrimination learning *is* possible for a linear system, provided the stimuli are sufficiently constrained in location. The retinal field in this case was 20 by 20 units, and the centers of the stimuli were constrained to a 5 by 5 region in the center of the retina. In Experiment 4-14 [shown in Fig. 8(a)], where the stimuli were distributed more freely over the retina (with the centers in a 13 by 13 field), no learning was demonstrated even after 200 stimuli. As a methodological experiment, these results indicate the importance of making sure that the stimulus distribution employed does not include "location cues" which are sufficient to indicate which stimulus is present, if we wish to test the ability of the perceptron to discriminate pattern characteristics exclusive of location. This can be fully guaranteed, in general, only by a uniform stimulus distribution over the entire field, with the elimination of special boundary effects by assuming a closed space, or an infinite space, as with the Born-von Kármán boundary conditions referred to in the Introduction.

Experiment 4-36, shown in Fig. 9, was again carried out with the second simulation program, this time with a more conventional perceptron. The threshold of zero, employed here, is sufficient to make the system fundamentally nonlinear, by eliminating the output of A units in the presence of negative input signals. The experiment was designed to show the performance of the system in the presence of a high degree of randomness, or noise, in the initial values of the A units. The stimuli for this experiment were vertical and horizontal bars, 4 units in width and 20 units long. A 5 per cent decay rate was introduced for the values of the A units. Note that in spite of the high decay rate and high initial noise level, the system achieved perfect performance on both classes of stimuli after a total of only 50 stimuli. This should be compared with the performance of very large (or infinite) perceptrons, in a spontaneous learning experiment with the same types of stimuli, which is illustrated in Fig. 10.

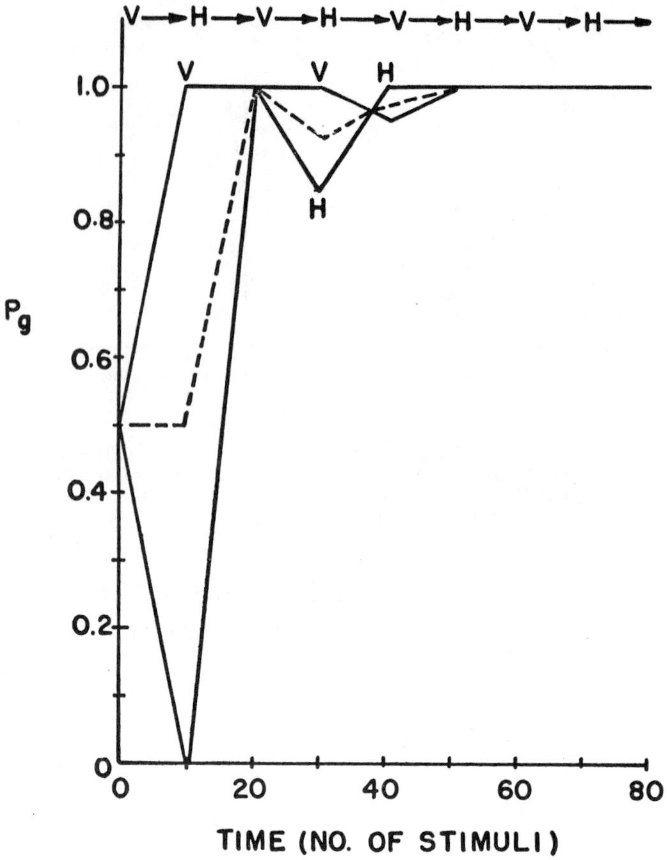

Fig. 9—Experiment 4-36. Forced learning experiment with vertical and horizontal bars. 500 A units. $\delta=0.05$, $\theta=0$, $x=4$, $y=4$, and V_0=between +500 and −500. Centers in 5 by 5 field, in 20 by 20 retina.

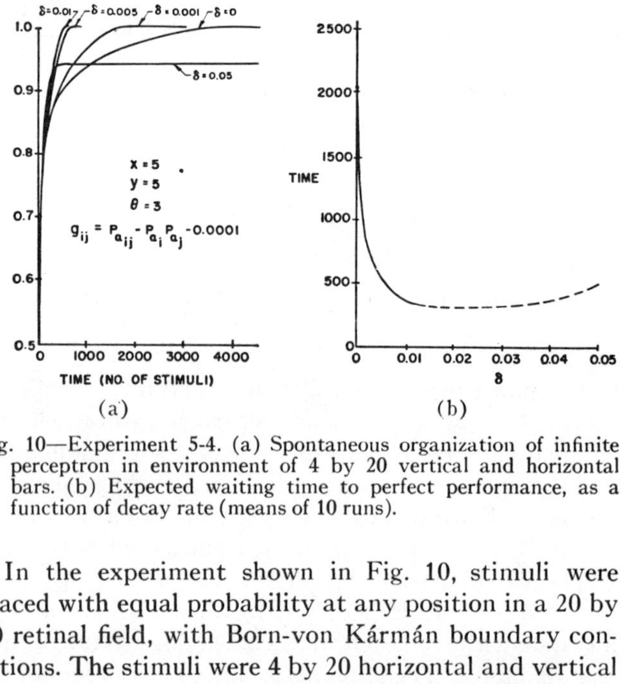

(a) (b)

Fig. 10—Experiment 5-4. (a) Spontaneous organization of infinite perceptron in environment of 4 by 20 vertical and horizontal bars. (b) Expected waiting time to perfect performance, as a function of decay rate (means of 10 runs).

In the experiment shown in Fig. 10, stimuli were placed with equal probability at any position in a 20 by 20 retinal field, with Born-von Kármán boundary conditions. The stimuli were 4 by 20 horizontal and vertical bars, as in the previous case. The perceptron used in this experiment is one in which the A units are reinforced for the response R = 1, but are left unaltered if the response R = 0 occurs. Unlike all of the previously illustrated experiments, this is a spontaneous learning experiment, in which no attempt is made to control the response during the learning procedure, reinforcement being applied for whichever response is elicited by a given stimulus. The perceptron here was assumed to have an infinite number of A units, and the calculations were done with the third program, which was specifically designed to handle these conditions. The family of curves in Fig. 10(a) shows the performance as a function of the decay rate, δ. We find that for a zero decay rate, the system eventually learns to dichotomize the bars correctly 100 per cent of the time, *i.e.*, it learns to assign one response to all horizontal bars, and the opposite response to all vertical bars. However, this takes upwards of 3000 stimuli in most cases.[4] As the decay rate increases, performance improves progressively, until a decay rate is reached (0.05 in this case) for which the system is unstable, and never attains perfect performance. The effect of the decay short of the instability level appears to be to keep previous reinforcements from accumulating to such a degree that they are difficult or impossible to undo, as the system settles into a more satisfactory terminal state; in other words, the decay keeps the system flexible, by making it possible to reverse the effects of previous learning more readily. At the instability level, previous reinforcements are reversed so readily that they are unable to maintain their effect at all, and associations are likely to be lost and reformed continually. The curve in Fig. 10(b) which shows expected waiting time to perfect performance, for the same series of runs, indicates the same phenomenon. We find that there is a clear optimum in performance as a function of the decay rate, for δ = approximately 0.01. Beyond this point, instability begins to occur, as indicated by the broken curve in the figure.

This experiment is the best demonstration to date of the "self-organizing" capability of a perceptron. Nonetheless, it can be demonstrated that minor changes in the stimulus environment will make it impossible for the same perceptron to achieve a satisfactory dichotomy. For example, if the 4 by 20 horizontal bars are replaced by double bars, composed of two 2 by 20 vertical bars separated by a space of 3 units, the perceptron will never spontaneously learn to distinguish the double bars from the single bars. Other classes of stimuli can be set up which are equally difficult, or impossible, for the system to learn spontaneously, although in each of these cases the problem would present no difficulty in a forced learning situation. Moreover, the curves in Fig. 10 are convex, indicating increasing difficulty in correctly associating the last few stimuli after most of the class has been learned. In a human subject faced with this task we would expect concave curves instead. These considerations indicate that the spontaneous learning capability of this perceptron, while interesting, is not sufficient to provide a basis for a biological theory of perceptual organization. This problem is considered in further detail elsewhere [8].

[4] Individual runs differ from one another due to differences in stimulus sequence, even though the perceptrons are infinite; the curves shown are means of ten different runs.

Conclusions

The simulation experiments described above have gone a long way toward demonstrating the feasibility of a perceptron as a pattern-recognizing device. Both forced learning and spontaneous learning performances have been investigated, and some insight has been gained into conditions under which different systems break down, or deviate from typical biological learning phenomena. Although digital simulation is apt to be time-consuming and expensive, particularly for large networks, improved programming methods have cut down the running time considerably, so that for early investigations of all systems proposed up to this time, digital simulation is still competitive with the construction of actual hardware models. As the number of connections in the network increases, however, the burden on a conventional digital computer soon becomes excessive, and it is anticipated that some of the models now under consideration [8] may require actual construction before their capabilities can be fully explored.

Digital programs undertaken to date have been concerned exclusively with the logical properties of the network, rather than with any particular hardware embodiment; that is, there has been no attempt to introduce simulation of electronic noise, component variation, or other factors which might affect the performance of an actual system. The results of these programs, therefore, should be interpreted as indicating performances which might be expected from an "ideal," or perfectly functioning system, and not necessarily as representative of any particular engineering design. A Mark I perceptron, recently completed at the Cornell Aeronautical Laboratory, is expected to provide data on the performance of an actual physical system, which should be useful for comparative study.

A new program is currently being employed to simulate the "cross-coupled perceptron" described elsewhere [8]. The results of this study will be reported separately when they are available.

Bibliography

[1] W. A. Clark and B. G. Farley, "Generalization of Pattern Recognition in a Self-Organizing System," *Proc. W. J. C. C.*, pp. 86–91; 1955.

[2] B. G. Farley and W. A. Clark, "Simulation of self-organizing systems by digital computer," IRE Trans. on Information Theory, vol. IT-4, pp. 76–84; September, 1954.

[3] D. O. Hebb, "The Organization of Behavior," John Wiley and Sons, Inc., New York, N. Y.; 1959.

[4] N. Rochester, J. H. Holland, L. H. Haibt, and W. L. Duda, "Tests on a cell assembly theory of the action of the brain, using a large digital computer," IRE Trans. on Information Theory, vol. IT-6, pp. 80–93; September, 1956.

[5] F. Rosenblatt, "The Perceptron: A Theory of Statistical Separability in Cognitive Systems," Cornell Aero. Lab., Buffalo, N. Y., Rept. no. VG-1196-G-1; January, 1958.

[6] F. Rosenblatt, "The perceptron, a probabilistic model for information storage and organization in the brain," *Psych. Rev.*, vol. 65, pp. 386–408; 1958.

[7] F. Rosenblatt, "Two Theorems of Statistical Separability in the Perceptron," *Proc. of Symposium on the Mechanization of Thought Processes;* 1958. H. M. Stationery Office, London, Eng. Also printed without appendix by Cornell Aero. Lab., Buffalo, N. Y., Rept. no. VG-1196-G-2; September, 1958.

[8] F. Rosenblatt, "Perceptual Generalization Over Transformation Groups," *Proc. of Interdisciplinary Conf. on Self-Organizing Systems;* 1959. Awaiting publication by Pergamon Press, New York, N. Y.

Speech Recognition: A Model and a Program for Research*

M. HALLE† AND K. STEVENS‡, MEMBER, IRE

Summary—**A speech recognition model is proposed in which the transformation from an input speech signal into a sequence of phonemes is carried out largely through an active or feedback process. In this process, patterns are generated internally in the analyzer according to an adaptable sequence of instructions until a best match with the input signal is obtained. Details of the process are given, and the areas where further research is needed are indicated.**

THE FUNDAMENTAL problem in pattern recognition is the search for a *recognition function* that will appropriately pair *signals* and *messages*. The input to the recognizer generally consists of measured physical quantities characterizing each signal to be recognized, while at the output of the recognizer each input signal is assigned to one of a number of categories which constitute the messages. Thus, for instance, in machine translation, the signals are sentences in one language and the messages are sentences in another language. In the automatic recognition of handwriting, the signal is a two-dimensional curve and the message a sequence of letters in a standard alphabet. Similarly, research on automatic speech recognition aims at discovering a recognition function that relates acoustic signals produced by the human vocal tract in speaking to messages consisting of strings of symbols, the phonemes. Such a recognition function is the inverse of a function that describes the production of speech, *i.e.*, the transformation of a discrete phoneme sequence into an acoustic signal.

This paper proposes a recognition model in which mapping from signal to message space is accomplished largely through an active or feedback process. Patterns are generated internally in the analyzer according to a flexible or adaptable sequence of instructions until a best match with the input signal is obtained. Since the analysis is achieved through active internal synthesis of of comparison signals, the procedure has been called "analysis by synthesis."[1]

* Received by the PGIT, September 25, 1961; revised manuscript received, October 12, 1961. This work was supported in part by the U. S. Army Signal Corps, the Air Force Office of Scientific Research, and the Office of Naval Research; in part by the National Science Foundation; and in part by the Air Force (Electronic Systems Division) under Contract AF 19(604)-6102.

† Research Laboratory of Electronics and Department of Modern Languages, Massachusetts Institute of Technology, Cambridge, Mass.

‡ Research Laboratory of Electronics and Department of Electrical Engineering, Massachusetts Institute of Technology, Cambridge, Mass.

The Process of Speech Production

In line with the traditional account of speech production, we shall assume that the speaker has stored in his memory a table of all the phonemes and their actualizations. This table lists the different vocal-tract configurations or gestures that are associated with each phoneme and the conditions under which each is to be used. In producing an utterance the speaker looks up, as it were, in the table the individual phonemes and then instructs his vocal tract to assume in succession the configurations or gestures corresponding to the phonemes.

The shape of man's vocal tract is not controlled as a single unit; rather, separate control is exercised over various gross structures in the tract, *e.g.*, the lip opening, position of velum, tongue position, and vocal-cord vibration. The changing configurations of the vocal tract must, therefore, be specified in terms of parameters describing the behavior of these quasi-independent structures.[2] These parameters will be called *phonetic parameters.*[3]

Since the vocal tract does not utilize the same amount of time for actualizing each phoneme (*e.g.*, the vowel in *bit* is considerably shorter than that in *beat*), it must be assumed that stored in the speaker's memory there is also a schedule that determines the time at which the

[1] The relevance of such analysis procedures to more general perceptual processes has been suggested by several writers. See, for example:
D. M. MacKay, "Mindlike behavior in artefacts," *Brit. J. for Philosophy of Science*, vol. 2, pp. 105–121; 1951.
G. A. Miller, E. Galanter, and K. H. Pribram, "Plans and the Structure of Behavior," Henry Holt and Co., New York, N. Y.; 1960.
M. Halle and K. N. Stevens, "Analysis by synthesis," *Proc. of Seminar on Speech Compression and Processing*, W. Wathen-Dunn and L. E. Woods, Eds., vol. 2, Paper D7: December, 1959.

[2] This view was well understood by the founder of modern phonetics, A. M. Bell, who described utterances by means of symbols ("Visible Speech and The Science of Universal Alphabetics," Simpkin, Marshall and Co., London, Eng.; 1867) from which the behavior of the quasi-independent structures could be read off directly. The subsequent replacement, for reasons of typographical economy, of Bell's special symbols by the Romic of the Internatl. Phonetic Assoc. has served to obscure the above facts and to suggest that phonemes are implemented by controlling the vocal tract as a single unit.

[3] We cannot discuss in detail at this point the nature of the phonetic parameters, and we do not take sides here in the present discussion between proponents of the Jakobsonian distinctive features (R. Jakobson and M. Halle, "Fundamentals of Language," Mouton and Co., The Hague, The Netherlands; 1956) and those of more traditional views ("The Principles of the International Phonetic Association," University College, London, England; 1949). We insist however, that the control of the vocal-tract behavior must be described by specifying a set of quasi-independent phoentic parameters.

Reprinted from *IRE Trans. Inform. Theory*, vol. IT-8, pp. 155–159, Feb. 1962.

vocal tract moves from one configuration to the next, *i.e.*, the time at which one or more phonetic parameters change in value. The timing will evidently differ depending on the speed of utterance—it will be slower for slower speech and faster for faster speech.

Because of the inertia of the structures that form the vocal tract and the limitations in the speed of neural and muscular control, a given phonetic parameter cannot change instantaneously from one value to another; the transitions from one target configuration to the next must be gradual, or smooth. Furthermore, when utterances are produced at any but the slowest rates, a given articulatory configuration may not be reached before motion toward the next must be initiated. Thus the configuration at any given time may be the result of instructions from more than one phoneme. In other words, at this stage in the speech production process, discrete quantities found in the input have been replaced by continuous parameters. A given sequence of phonemes, moreover, may produce a variety of vocal-tract behaviors depending upon such factors as the past linguistic experience of the talker, his emotional state, and the rate of talking.

The continuous phonetic parameters that result from a given phoneme sequence give rise in turn to changes in the geometry and acoustic excitation of the cavities forming the vocal tract. The tract can be visualized as a time-varying linear acoustic system, excited by one or more sound sources, which radiates sound from the mouth opening (and/or from the nose). The acoustic performance of this linear system at a given time and for a given source of excitation can be characterized by the poles and zeros of the transfer function from the source to the output, together with a constant factor.[4] For voiced sounds the vocal tract is excited at the glottis by a quasi-periodic source with high acoustic impedance. Its fundamental frequency varies with time, but the waveform or spectrum of each glottal pulse does not change markedly from one speech sound to another. In addition, the vocal tract may be excited in the vicinity of a constriction or obstruction by a broad-band noise source or by sound.

In the process of generating an acoustic output in response to a sequence of phonemes, a talker strives to produce the appropriate vocal-tract configurations together with the proper type of source, but he does not exert precise control over such factors as the detailed characteristics of the source or the damping of the vocal tract. Consequently, for a given vocal-tract configuration the shape of the source spectrum, the fundamental frequency of the glottal source, and the bandwidths of the poles and zeros can be expected to exhibit some variation for a given talker. Even greater variation is to be expected among different talkers, since the dimensions of the speech-production apparatus are different for different individuals. This variance is superimposed on the already-mentioned variance in articulatory gestures.

[4] G. Fant, "Acoustic Theory of Speech Production," Mouton and Co., The Hague, Neth.; 1960.

Reduction of the Continuous Signal to a Message Consisting of Discrete Symbols; the Segmentation Problem

The analysis procedure that has enjoyed the widest acceptance postulates that the listener first segments the utterance and then identifies the individual segments with particular phonemes. No analysis scheme based on this principle has ever been successfully implemented. This failure is understandable in the light of the preceding account of speech production, where it was observed that segments of an utterance do not in general stand in a one-to-one relation with the phonemes. The problem, therefore, is to devise a procedure which will transform the continuously-changing speech signal into a discrete output without depending crucially on segmentation.

A simple procedure of this type restricts the input to stretches of sound separated from adjacent stretches by silence. The input signals could, for example, correspond to isolated words, or they could be longer utterances. Perhaps the crudest device capable of transforming such an input into phoneme sequences would be a "dictionary" in which the inputs are entered as intensity-frequency-time patterns[5] and each entry is provided with its phonemic representation. The segment under analysis is compared with each entry in the dictionary, the one most closely resembling the input determined, and its phonemic transcription printed out.[6]

The size of the dictionary in such an analyzer increases very rapidly with the number of admissible outputs, since a given phoneme sequence can give rise to a large number of distinct acoustic outputs. In a device whose capabilities would even remotely approach those of a normal human listener, the size of the dictionary would, therefore, be so large as to rule out this approach.[7]

The need for a large dictionary can be overcome if the principles of construction of the dictionary entries are

[5] The initial step in processing a speech signal for automatic analysis usually consists of deriving from the time-varying pressure changes a sequence of short-time amplitude spectra. This transformation, which is commonly performed by sampling the rectified and smoothed outputs of a set of band-pass filters or by computing the Fourier transform of segments of the signal, is known to preserve intact the essential information in the signal, provided that suitable filter bandwidths and averaging times have been chosen.

[6] A model of this type was considered by F. S. Cooper, *et al.*, "Some experiments on the perception of synthetic speech sounds," *J. Acoust. Soc. Am.*, vol. 24, p. 605; November, 1952.

"The problem of speech perception is then to describe the decoding process either in terms of the decoding mechanism or—as we are trying to do—by compiling the code book, one in which there is one column for acoustic entries and another column for message units, whether these be phonemes, syllables, words, or whatever."

[7] This approach need not be ruled out, however, in specialized applications in which a greatly restricted vocabulary of short utterances, such as digits, is to be recognized. See, for example:

H. Dudley and S. Balashek, "Automatic recognition of phonetic patterns in speech," *J. Acoust. Soc. Am.*, vol. 30, pp. 721–732; August, 1958.

P. Denes and M. V. Mathews, "Spoken digit recognition using time-frequency pattern matching," *J. Acoust. Soc. Am.*, vol. 32, pp. 1450–1455; November, 1960.

G. S. Sebestyen, "Recognition of membership in classes," IRE Trans. on Information Theory, vol. IT-6, pp. 44–50; January, 1961.

known. It is then possible to store in the "permanent memory" of the analyzer only the rules for speech production discussed in the previous section. In this model the dictionary is replaced by *generative rules* which can synthesize signals in response to instructions consisting of sequences of phonemes. Analysis is now accomplished by supplying the generative rules with all possible phoneme sequences, systematically running through all one-phoneme sequences, two-phoneme sequences, etc. The internally generated signal which provides the best match with the input signal then identifies the required phoneme sequence. While this model does not place excessive demands on the size of the memory, a very long time is required to achieve positive identification.

The necessity of synthesizing a large number of comparison signals can be eliminated by a *preliminary analysis* which excludes from consideration all but a very small subset of the items which can be produced by the generative rules. The preliminary analysis would no doubt include various transformations which have been found useful in speech analysis, such as segmentation within the utterance according to the type of vocal-tract excitation and tentative identification of segments by special attributes of the signal. Once a list of possible phoneme sequences is established from the preliminary analysis, then the internal signal synthesizer proceeds to generate signals corresponding to each of these sequences.

The analysis procedure can be refined still further by including a *control* component to dictate the order in which comparison signals are to be generated. This control is guided not only by the results of the preliminary analysis but also by quantitative measures of the goodness of fit achieved for comparison signals that have already been synthesized, statistical information concerning the admissible phoneme sequences, and other data that may have been obtained from preceding analyses. This information is utilized by the control component to formulate strategies that would achieve convergence to the required result with as small a number of trials as possible.

It seems to us that an automatic speech recognition scheme capable of processing any but the most trivial classes of utterances must incorporate all of the features discussed above—the input signal must be matched against a comparison signal; a set of generative rules must be stored within the machine; preliminary analysis must be performed; and a strategy must be included to control the order in which internal comparison signals are to be generated. The arrangement of these operations in the proposed recognition model is epitomized in Fig. 1.

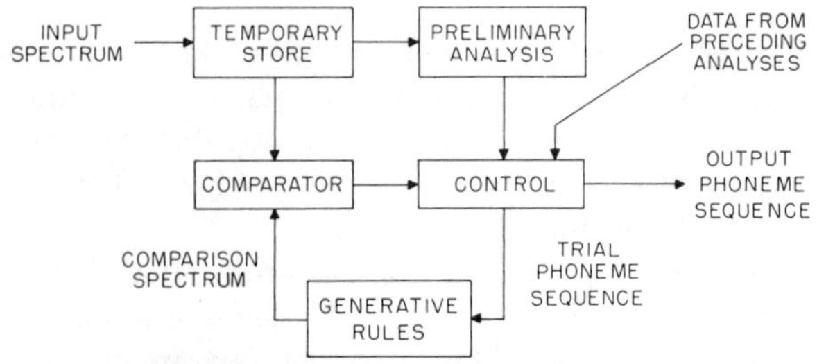

Fig. 1—Block diagram of analysis-by-synthesis procedure for extracting a phoneme sequence from a time-varying input spectrum. The input spectrum, which may be placed in temporary storage pending completion of the analysis, is compared in the comparator with signals synthesized by the generative rules. Instructions as to the phoneme sequences to be tried are communicated to the generative rules by the control component, which bases its decisions on the results of a preliminary analysis of the input signal and on the output of the comparator for previous trials, as well as on other information as noted in the text. When a best match is obtained in the comparator, the control component reads out the phoneme sequence which, through the generative rules, produced that match. This figure also serves to show the arrangement of components in the proposed model for the reduction of speech spectra to continuous phonetic parameters.

Processing of the Speech Signal Prior to Phoneme Identification

In the analysis-by-synthesis procedure just described, it is implied that the comparison between the input and the internally generated signal is made at the level of the time-varying acoustic spectrum. It is clear, however, that the input signal of Fig. 1 could equally well be the result of some transformation of the acoustic spectrum carried out at a previous stage of analysis. Indeed, in any practical speech recognizer, it is essential to subject the spectral pattern to a certain amount of preliminary processing before entering the phonemic analysis stage. The necessity for initial transformations or simplifications stems from the fact that many acoustic signals may correspond to a given sequence of phonemes. To account for all the sources of variance or redundancy in one stage of analysis is much too difficult an undertaking. Through a stepwise reduction procedure, on the other hand, variance due to irrelevant factors can be eliminated a small amount at a time.

The proposed procedure for speech processing contains two major steps. In the first stage the spectral representation is reduced to a set of parameters which describe the pertinent motions and excitations of the vocal tract, *i.e.*, the phonetic parameters. In the second stage, transformation to a sequence of phonemes is achieved. These steps provide a natural division of the analysis procedure into one part concerned primarily with the physical and physiological processes of speech, and the other concerned with those aspects of speech primarily dependent on linguistic and social factors. In the first stage, variance in the signal due to differences in the speech mechanism of different talkers (or of a given talker in different situations) would be largely eliminated. The second stage would account for influences such as rate of talking, linguistic background or dialect of the talker, and contextual variants of phonemes.

Many of the problems involved in the first analysis stage are not unlike those encountered in reducing an utterance to a phoneme sequence. It is not feasible to store all possible spectra together with the corresponding articulatory descriptions. Since, however, rules for generating the spectrum from the articulatory description are known, it is possible to use an analysis-by-synthesis procedure[8] of the type shown in Fig. 1.

The output of this stage is a set of phonetic parameters (rather than the phoneme sequence shown in Fig. 1). The heart of this first-stage analyzer is a signal synthesizer that has the ability to compute comparison spectra when given the phonetic parameters, *i.e.*, an internal synthesizer in which are stored the generative rules for the construction of speech spectra from phonetic parameters. A strategy is required to reduce the time needed to match the input spectrum and the comparison spectrum. The strategy may again depend on the results of a preliminary approximate analysis of the input signal, and on the error that has been computed at the comparator on previous trials. It may also depend on the results that have been obtained for the analysis of signals in the vicinity of the one under direct study. Some of the instructions that are communicated by the control component to the generative rules remain relatively fixed for the matching of spectra generated by a given talker in a given situation. When signals generated by a different talker are presented, the strategy must be able to modify this group of instructions automatically after sufficient data on that talker's speech have been accumulated. The analysis-by-synthesis procedure has the property, therefore, that its strategy is potentially able to adapt to the characteristics of different talkers.

Summary of Model for Speech Recognition

The complete model for speech recognition discussed here takes the form shown in Fig. 2. The input signal is first processed by a peripheral unit such as a spectrum analyzer. It then undergoes reduction in two analysis-by-synthesis loops, and the phoneme sequence appears at the right. In order to simplify the diagram, the group of components performing the functions of storage, preliminary analysis, comparison, and control have been combined in a single block labeled *strategy*.

The procedure depicted here is suitable only for the recognition of sequences of uncorrelated symbols, such as those that control the generation of nonsense syllables. If the speech material to be recognized consists of words, phrases, or continuous text, then the output of the present analysis scheme would have to be processed further to take account of the constraints imposed by the morphological and syntactic structure of the language.

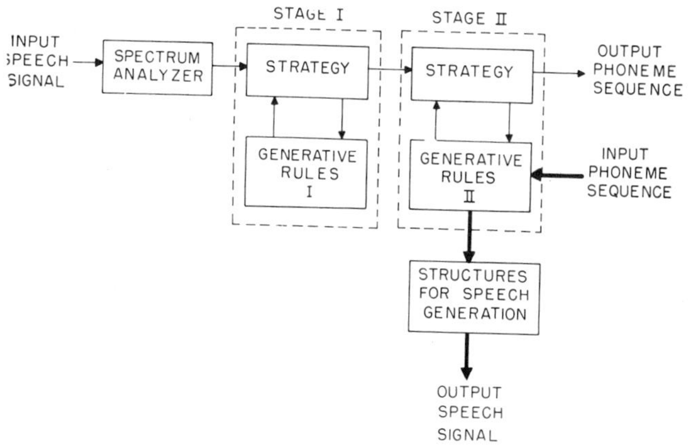

Fig. 2—Block diagram of two-stage scheme for speech processing. Following processing by a spectrum analyzer, the input speech signal is reduced in Stage I to a set of quasi-continuous phonetic parameters, which are processed in Stage II to yield an output phoneme sequence. An analysis-by-synthesis procedure is used for processing the signal at each stage. The heavy lines indicate the operations that are involved in generating a speech signal from a phoneme sequence.

The final analysis stage of Fig. 2 includes, of course, the generative rules for transforming phoneme sequences into phonetic parameters. These are precisely the rules that must be invoked in the production of speech. During speech production the output from these stored rules can be connected directly to the speech mechanism, while the input to the rules is the phoneme sequence to be generated. Addition of peripheral speech-generating structures to Fig. 2 then creates a model that is capable of both speech recognition and speech production. The same calculations are made in the second set of generative rules (and in the generative rules at possible higher levels of analysis) whether speech is being received or generated. It is worthwhile observing that during the recognition process phonetic parameters are merely calculated by the "generative rules II" and direct activation of the speech structures is nowhere required.[9]

For the recognition of continuous speech it may not always be necessary to have recourse to analysis-by-synthesis procedures. A rough preliminary analysis at each of the stages in Fig. 2 may often be all that is required—ambiguities as a result of imprecise analysis at these early stages can be resolved in later stages on the basis of knowledge of the constraints at the morphological, syntactic, and semantic levels.[10]

[8] Partial implementation (or models for implementation) of the analysis-by-synthesis procedure applied at this level, together with discussions of the advantages of the method, have been presented in:
K. N. Stevens, "Toward a model for speech recognition," *J. Acoust. Soc. Am.*, vol. 32, pp. 47–51; January, 1960.
L. A. Chistovich, "Classification of rapidly repeated speech sounds," *Sov. Phys. Acoustics*, vol. 6, pp. 393–398; January–March, 1961 (*Akust. Zhur.*, vol. 6, pp. 392–398; July, 1960).
S. Inomata, "Computational method for speech recognition," *Bull. Electro-Tech. Lab.* (Tokyo), vol. 24, pp. 597–611; June, 1960.
M. V. Mathews, J. E. Miller, and E. E. David, Jr., "Pitch synchronous analysis of voiced sounds," *J. Acoust. Soc. Am.*, vol. 33, pp. 179–186; February, 1961.
C. G. Bell, H. Fujisaki, J. M. Heinz, K. N. Stevens, and A. S. House, "Reduction of speech spectra by analysis-by-synthesis techniques," *J. Acoust. Soc. Am.*, vol. 33; December, 1961.

[9] This point was discussed by A. M. Liberman ("Results of research on speech perception," *J. Acoust. Soc. Am.*, vol. 29, pp. 117–123; January, 1957) who suggested that speech is perceived with reference to articulation, but that "the reference to articulatory movements and their sensory consequences must somehow occur in the brain without getting out into the periphery."

[10] Knowledge of constraints imposed on phoneme sequences by the structure of the language has been incorporated in the design of an automatic speech recognizer described by Fry and Denes (D. B. Fry, "Theoretical aspects of mechanical speech recognition," and P. Denes, "The design and operation of the mechanical speech recognizer at University College, London," *J. Brit. IRE*, vol. 19, pp. 211–234; April, 1959.

Implementation of the Model: Problems for Research

While certain components in both major stages of analysis can be designed from present knowledge, further research is necessary before the remaining components can be realized and before the system can be designed to function as a whole.

In the first stage of analysis, one of the major problems is to devise a procedure for specifying in quantitative terms the "phonetic parameters." These must describe the behavior of structures that control the vocal-tract configuration as well as activities of the lungs and vocal cords. A great deal is known about some parameters, *e.g.*, parameters that relate to voicing, nasalization, interruptedness, and labialization. For others, such as tenseness or the so-called point of articulation, our knowledge is still far from adequate.

A second task is to establish the generative rules describing the conversion of phonetic parameters to time-varying speech spectra. These rules involve a series of relations, namely, those between 1) the phonetic parameters and the vocal-tract geometry and excitation characteristics, 2) the transformation from vocal-tract geometry to the transfer function in terms of poles and zeros, and 3) the conversion from the pole-zero configurations and pertinent excitation characteristics to the speech spectra. The last two of these, which involve application of the theory of linear distributed systems, have been studied in some detail,[6,11,12] whereas the first is less well understood.

The generative rules of the second stage are made up of several distinct parts. First, they embody the relation between what linguists have called a "narrow phonetic transcription of an utterance" and its "phonemic or morphophonemic transcription." The nature of this relation has received a fair amount of attention in the last 30 years and a great deal of valuable information has been gathered. Of especial importance for the present problems are recent phonological studies in which this relation has been characterized by means of a set of ordered rules.[13] Secondly, the generative rules II must describe the utilization of those phonetic parameters that are not governed by the language in question, but are left to the discretion of the speaker. Thus, for instance, it is well known that in English speech, voiceless stops in word final position may or may not be aspirated. The precise way in which individual speakers utilize this freedom is, however, all but unknown. Thirdly, the generative rules II must specify the transformation from discrete to continuous signals that results from the inertia of the neural and muscular structures involved in speech production. There are wide variations in the delay with which different muscular movements can be executed, but the details of the movements are not understood. The study of these problems, which essentially are those of producing continuous speech from phonetic transcriptions, has just begun in earnest. We owe important information to the work of Haskins Laboratory on simplified rules for speech synthesis.[14] This work must now be extended to take physiological factors into consideration more directly, through the use of cineradiography,[15] electromyography, and other techniques. Contributions can also be expected from studies with dynamic analogs of the vocal tract.[16]

Finally, for both stages of analysis, the design of the strategy component is almost completely unknown territory. To get a clearer picture of the nature of the strategy component, it is useful to regard the generative rules as a set of axioms, and the outputs of the generative rules as the theorems that are consequences of these axioms. Viewed in this light the discovery of the phonemic representation of an utterance is equivalent to the discovery of the succession of axioms that was used in proving a particular theorem. The task of developing suitable strategies is related, therefore, to a general problem in mathematics—that of discovering the shortest proof of a theorem when a set of axioms is given. It should be clear, however, that the powerful tools of mathematics will be at our disposal only when we succeed in describing precisely and exhaustively the generative rules of speech. Until such time we can hope only for partially successful analyzers with strategies that can never be shown to be optimal.

[11] T. Chiba and M. Kajiyama, "The Vowel, Its Nature and Structure," Tokyo-Kaiseikan, Tokyo, Jap.; 1941.

[12] H. K. Dunn, "The calculation of vowel resonances, and an electrical vocal tract," *J. Acoust Soc. Am.*, vol. 22, pp. 740–753; November, 1950.

[13] M. Halle, "The Sound Pattern of Russian," Mouton and Co., The Hague, The Netherlands; 1959. N. Chomsky and M. Halle, "The Sound Pattern of English," to be published.

[14] A. M. Liberman, F. Ingemann, L. Lisker, P. Delattre, and F. S. Cooper, "Minimum rules for synthesizing speech," *J. Acoust. Soc. Am.*, vol. 31, pp. 1490–1499; November, 1959.

[15] H. M. Truby, "Acoustico-cineradiographic analysis considerations," *Acta Radiologica*, (Stockholm), Suppl. 182; 1959.

[16] G. Rosen, "Dynamic Analog Speech Synthesizer," Res. Lab. of Electronics, Mass. Inst. Tech., Cambridge, Tech. Rept. No. 353; February 10, 1960.

Abstraction and Pattern Classification

R. Bellman, R. Kalaba, and L. Zadeh

The RAND Corporation, Santa Monica, California

1. Introduction

This note deals in a preliminary way with several concepts and ideas which have a bearing on the problem of pattern classification—a problem which plays an important role in communication and control theories.

There are two basic operations: abstraction and generalization, which appear under various guises is most of the schemes employed for classifying patterns into a finite number of categories. Although abstraction and generalization can be defined in terms of operations on sets of patterns, a more natural as well as more general framework for dealing with these concepts can be constructed around the notion of a "fuzzy" set—a notion which extends the concept of membership in a set to situations in which there are many, possibly a continuum of, grades of membership.

To be more specific, a *fuzzy set* A in a space $\Omega = \{x\}$ is represented by a characteristic function f which is defined on Ω and takes values in the interval [0, 1], with the value of f at x, $f(x)$, representing the "grade of membership" of x in A. Thus, if A is a set in the usual sense, $f(x)$ is 1 or 0 according as x belongs or does not belong to A. When A is a fuzzy set, then the nearer the value of $f(x)$ to 0, the more tenuous is the membership of x in A, with the "degree of belonging" increasing with increase in $f(x)$. In some cases it may be convenient to concretize the belonging of a point to a fuzzy set A by selecting two levels ϵ_1 and ϵ_2 (ϵ_1, $\epsilon_2 \in [0, 1]$) and agreeing that (a) a point x "*belongs*" to A if $f(x) \geqslant 1 - \epsilon_1$; (b) *does not belong* to A if $f(x) \leqslant \epsilon_2$; and (c) x is *indeterminate relative to* A if $\epsilon_2 < f(x) < 1 - \epsilon_1$. In effect, this amounts to using a three-valued characteristic function, with $f(x) = 1$ if $x \in A$; $f(x) = 1/2$, say, if x is indeterminate relative to A; and $f(x) = 0$ if $x \notin A$.

Let A and B be two fuzzy sets in the sense defined above, with f_A and f_B denoting their respective characteristic functions. The *union* of A and B will be denoted in the usual way as

$$C = A \cup B, \tag{1}$$

Reprinted with permission from *J. Math. Anal. Appl.*, vol. 13, pp. 1-7, 1966.

with the characteristic function of C defined by

$$f_C(x) = \text{Max}(f_A(x), f_B(x)). \tag{2}$$

For brevity, the relation expressed by (2) will be written as

$$f_C = f_A \vee f_B \,. \tag{3}$$

Note that when A and B are sets, (2) reduces to the definition of "or."

In a similar fashion, the *intersection* of two fuzzy sets A and B will be denoted by

$$C = A \cap B \tag{4}$$

with the characteristic function of C defined by

$$f_C(x) = \text{Min}(f_A(x), f_B(x)), \tag{5}$$

which for brevity will be written as

$$f_C = f_A \wedge f_B \,. \tag{6}$$

In the case of the intersection, when A and B are sets (5) reduces to the definition of "and." When the characteristic functions are three-valued, (2) and (5) lead to the three-valued logic of Kleene [1].

2. Abstraction and Generalization

Let $x^1, \ldots, x^n$ be given members of a set A in Ω. In informal terms, by abstraction on $x^1, \ldots, x^n$ is meant the identification of those properties of $x^1, \ldots, x^n$ which they have in common and which, in aggregate, define the set A.

The notion of a fuzzy set provides a natural as well as convenient way of giving a more concrete meaning to the notion of *abstraction*. Specifically, let f^i denote the value of the characteristic function, f, of a fuzzy set A at a point x^i in Ω. A collection of pairs $\{(x^1,f^1), \ldots, (x^n,f^n)\}$ or, for short $\{(x^i,f^i)\}^n$, will be called a collection of *samples* or *observations* from A. By an abstraction on the collection $\{(x^i,f^i)\}^n$, we mean the estimation of the characteristic function of A from the samples $(x^1,f^1), \ldots, (x^n,f^n)$. Once an estimate of f has been constructed, we perform a *generalization* on the collection $\{(x^i,f^i)\}^n$ when we use the estimate in question to compute the values of f at points other than $x^1, \ldots, x^n$.

An estimate of f employing the given samples $(x^1,f^1), \ldots, (x^n,f^n)$ will be denoted by $\hat{f}$ or, more explicitly, by $\hat{f}(x; \{x^i,f^i)\}^n)$,and will be referred to as an abstracting function. Clearly, the problem of determining an abstracting function is essentially one of reconstructing a function from the knowledge of its values over a finite set of points. To make this problem meaningful, one must have some a priori information about the class of functions to which f belongs, such that this information in combination with the samples from A would be sufficient to enable one to construct a "good" estimate of f. As in interpolation theory, this approach involves choosing—usually on purely heuristic grounds—a class of estimates of f: $\tilde{F} = \{\tilde{f}(x; \lambda) \mid \lambda \in R^l\}$ and finding that member of this family which fits, or fits "best" (in some specified sense of "best"), the given samples $(x^1, f^1), ..., (x^n, f^n)$. A special case of this procedure which applies to ordinary rather than fuzzy sets is the widely used technique for distinguishing between two sets of patterns via a separating hyperplane. Stated in terms of a single set of patterns, the problem in question is essentially that of finding, if it exists, a hyperplane L passing through the origin of $R^l(\Omega = R^l$, by assumption) such that the given points $x^1, ..., x^n$ belonging to a set A are all on the same side of the hyperplane. (Note that, since A is a set, $f^1 = f^2 = \cdots = f^n = 1$.) In effect, in this case $\tilde{f}(x; \lambda)$ is of the form

$$\begin{aligned} \tilde{f}(x; \lambda) &= 1 \qquad \text{for} \quad \langle x, \lambda \rangle \geqslant 0, \\ \tilde{f}(x; \lambda) &= 0 \qquad \text{for} \quad \langle x, \lambda \rangle < 0, \end{aligned} \tag{7}$$

where $\langle x, \lambda \rangle$ denotes the scalar product of x and λ, and the problem is to find a λ in R^l such that

$$\langle x^i, \lambda \rangle \geqslant 0 \qquad \text{for} \quad i = 1, ..., n. \tag{8}$$

Any $\tilde{f}(x; \lambda)$ whose λ satisfies (8) will qualify as an abstracting function, and the corresponding generalization on $(x^1, 1), ..., (x^n, 1)$ will take the form of the statement "Any x satisfying $\langle x, \lambda \rangle \geqslant 0$ belongs to the same set as the samples $x^1, ..., x^n$." If one is not content with just satisfying (8) but wishes, in addition, to maximize the distance between L and the set of points $x^1, ..., x^n$ (in the sense of maximizing $\text{Min}\langle x^i, \lambda \rangle$), $\| \lambda \| = 1$), then the determination of the corresponding abstracting function requires the solution of a quadratic program, as was shown by Rosen [2] in connection with a related problem in pattern recognition.

In most practical situations, the a priori information about the characteristic function of a fuzzy set is not sufficient to construct an estimate of $f(x)$ which is "optimal" in a meaningful sense. Thus, in most instances one is forced to resort to a heuristic rule for estimating $f(x)$, with the only means of judging the "goodness" of the estimate yielded by such a rule lying in experimentation. In the sequel, we shall describe one such rule for pattern classification and show that a special case of it is equivalent to the "minimum-distance" principle which is frequently employed in signal discrimination and pattern recognition.

3. Pattern Classification

For purposes of our discussion, a *pattern* is merely another name for a point in Ω, and a *category of patterns* is a (possibly fuzzy) set in Ω. When we speak of *pattern classification*, we have in mind a class of problems which can be subsumed under the following formulation and its variants.

Let A and B denote two[1] disjoint sets in Ω representing two categories of patterns. Suppose that we are given n points (patterns) $\alpha^1, \ldots, \alpha^n$ which are known to belong to A, and m points $\beta^1, \ldots, \beta^m$ which are known to belong to B. The problem is to construct estimates of the characteristic functions of A and B based on the knowledge of the samples $\alpha^1, \ldots, \alpha^n$ from A and $\beta^1, \ldots, \beta^m$ from B.

Clearly, one can attempt to estimate f_A without making any use of the β^j, $j = 1, \ldots, m$. However, in general, such an estimate would not be as good as one employing both α's and β's. This is a consequence of an implied or explicit dependence between A and B (e.g., the disjointness of A and B), through which the knowledge of β's contributes some information about f_A. The same applies to the estimation of f_B.

The heuristic rule suggested in the sequel is merely a way of constructing estimates of f_A and f_B, given $\alpha^1, \ldots, \alpha^n$, and $\beta^1, \ldots, \beta^m$, in terms of estimates of f_A and f_B, given a single pair of samples α^i and β^j. Specifically, suppose that with every $\alpha \in A$ and every $\beta \in B$ are associated two sets $\tilde{A}(\alpha; \beta)$ and $\tilde{B}(\beta; \alpha)$ representing the estimates of A and B, given α and β. (In effect, $\tilde{A}(\alpha; \beta)$ defines the set of points in Ω over which the estimate $\tilde{f}_A(\alpha; \beta)$ of f_A is unity, and likewise for $\tilde{f}_B(\beta; \alpha)$ and $\tilde{B}(\beta; \alpha)$. Points in Ω which are neither in $\tilde{A}(\alpha; \beta)$ nor in $\tilde{B}(\beta; \alpha)$ have indeterminate status relative to these sets.)

In terms of the sets in question, the estimates of A and B (or, equivalently, f_A and f_B), given $\alpha^1, \ldots, \alpha^n$ and $\beta^1, \ldots, \beta^m$, are constructed as follows

$$\hat{A} = \bigcap_{j=1}^{m} \bigcup_{i=1}^{n} \tilde{A}(\alpha^i; \beta^j), \tag{9}$$

$$\hat{B} = \bigcap_{i=1}^{n} \bigcup_{j=1}^{m} \tilde{B}(\beta^j; \alpha^i). \tag{10}$$

Thus, under the rule expressed by (9) and (10), we generalize on $\alpha^1, \ldots, \alpha^n$

[1] The restriction to two sets serves merely to simplify the analysis and does not entail any essential loss in generality.

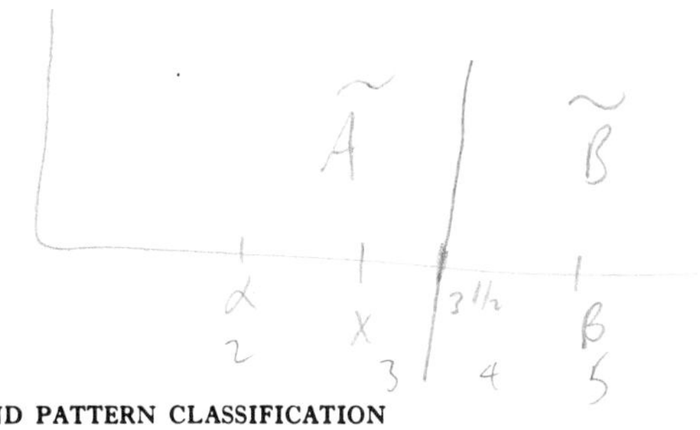

and $\beta^1, \ldots, \beta^m$ by identifying A with $\tilde{A}$ and B with $\tilde{B}$. Note that this rule is consistent in the sense that if α is known to belong to A then $\alpha \in \tilde{A}$, and likewise for a point belonging to B. However, the consistency of this rule does not extend to fuzzy sets. Thus, if (9) and (10) were applied to the estimation of f_A and f_B when A and B are fuzzy sets, it would not necessarily be true that $f_A(\alpha) = \tilde{f}_A(\alpha)$ for all given α in A.

In essence, the rule expressed by (9) and (10) implies that a point x is classified as a member of A if and only if for all β^j there exists an α^i such that x lies in $\tilde{A}(\alpha^i, \beta^j)$. For this reason, the rule in question will be referred to as the "rule of complete dominance."

To illustrate the rule of complete dominance and indicate its connection with the "minimum-distance" principle which is frequently employed in signal discrimination, consider the simple case where Ω is R^l and $\tilde{A}(\alpha; \beta)$ and $\tilde{B}(\beta; \alpha)$ are defined as follows:

$$\tilde{A}(\alpha; \beta) = \left\{ x \,\middle|\, \left\langle x - \frac{(\alpha + \beta)}{2}, \alpha - \beta \right\rangle \geqslant 0 \right\}, \tag{11}$$

$$\tilde{B}(\beta; \alpha) = \left\{ x \,\middle|\, \left\langle x - \frac{(\alpha + \beta)}{2}, \alpha - \beta \right\rangle < 0 \right\}. \tag{12}$$

In effect, $\tilde{A}(\alpha; \beta)$ is the set of all points which are nearer to α than to β or are equidistant from α and β, while $\tilde{B}(\beta; \alpha)$ is the complement of this set with respect to R^l.

Now consider the following "minimum-distance" decision rule. Let A^* and B^* denote the sets of samples $\alpha^1, \ldots, \alpha^n$ and $\beta^1, \ldots, \beta^m$, respectively. Define the distance of a point x in Ω from A^* to be $\text{Min}_i \| x - \alpha^i \|$, where $\| \;\|$ denotes the Euclidean norm and $i = 1, \ldots, n$; do likewise for B^*. Then, given a point x in Ω, decide that $x \in A$ if and only if the distance of x from A^* is less than or equal to the distance of x from B^*.

It is easy to show that this decision rule is a special case of (9) and (10). Specifically, with $\tilde{A}(\alpha; \beta)$ and $\tilde{B}(\beta; \alpha)$ defined by (11) and (12), respectively, the decision rule in question can be expressed as follows:

$$x \in \tilde{A} \Leftrightarrow \forall \beta^j \,\exists\, \alpha^i \{\| x - \alpha^i \| \leqslant \| x - \beta^j \|\}, \qquad \begin{array}{l} i = 1, \ldots, n, \\ j = 1, \ldots, m. \end{array} \tag{13}$$

Now

$$\tilde{A}(\alpha^i; \beta^j) = \{x \mid \| x - \alpha^i \| \leqslant \| x - \beta^j \|\} \tag{14}$$

and consequently (13) defines the set

$$\tilde{A} = \{x \mid \forall \beta^j \,\exists\, \alpha^i (x \in \tilde{A}(\alpha^i; \beta^j))\}. \tag{15}$$

Clearly, (15) is equivalent to

$$\bar{A} = \bigcap_{j=1}^{m} \bigcup_{i=1}^{n} \bar{A}(\alpha^i; \beta^j), \tag{16}$$

and similarly for B. Q.E.D.

In the foregoing discussion of the minimum-distance decision rule, we identified Ω with R^l and used the Euclidean metric in R^l to measure the distance between two patterns in Ω. However, in many cases of practical interest, Ω is a set of line patterns in R^2 such as letters, numerals, etc., to which the Euclidean metric is not applicable. In this case, the distance between two line patterns in R^2, say L_0 and L_1, can be defined by

$$d(L_0, L_1) = \underset{y_0 \in L_0}{\text{Max}} \ \underset{y_1 \in L_1}{\text{Min}} \| y_0 - y_1 \|, \tag{17}$$

where $\| \ \|$ is the Euclidean norm in R^2, and y_0 and y_1 are points in R^2 belonging to L_0 and L_1, respectively.

Now suppose that we agree to regard two patterns L_0 and L_1 as equivalent if one can be obtained from the other through translation, rotation, contraction (or dilation) or any combination of these operations. Thus, let T_δ denote the translation $y \to y + \delta$, where $y, \delta \in R^2$; let T_θ denote the rotation through an angle θ around the origin of R^2; and let T_ρ denote the contraction (or dilation) $x \to \rho x$ where $\rho \in R^1$. Then, we define the *reduced* distance of L_1 from L_0 by the relation

$$d^*(L_1; L_0) = \underset{T_\delta}{\text{Min}} \ \underset{T_\theta}{\text{Min}} \ \underset{T_\rho}{\text{Min}} \ d(L_0, T_\delta T_\theta T_\rho L_1), \tag{18}$$

where $T_\delta T_\theta T_\rho L_1$ denotes the image of L_1 under the operation $T_\delta T_\theta T_\rho$, and $d(L_0, T_\delta T_\theta T_\rho L_1)$ is the distance between L_0 and $T_\delta T_\theta T_\rho L_1$ in the sense of (17). Clearly, it is the reduced distance in the sense of (18) rather than the distance in the sense of (17) that should be used in applying the minimum-distance decision rule to the case where Ω is a set of line patterns in R^2.

To conclude our discussion of pattern classification, we shall indicate how the formulation given in the beginning of this section can be extended to fuzzy sets. Thus, let A and B denote two such sets in Ω, with f_A and f_B denoting their respective characteristic functions. Suppose that we are given n sample triplets $(x^1, f_A{}^1, f_B{}^1), \ldots, (x^n, f_A{}^n, f_B{}^n)$, with $(x^i, f_A{}^i, f_B{}^i)$ representing a sample consisting of x^i and the values of f_A and f_B at x^i. The problem of pattern classification in this context is essentially that of estimating the characteristic functions f_A and f_B from the given collection of samples. Clearly, this formulation of the problem includes as a special case the pattern-classification problem stated earlier for the case where A and B are sets in Ω

References

1. S. C. Kleene, "Introduction to Metamathematics," p. 334. D. Van Nostrand Co., Inc., New York, 1952.
2. J. B. Rosen, "Pattern Recognition by Convex Programming," Tech. Rept. No. 30 (Stanford University, June 1963).

A Note on Learning Signal Detection*

M. KAC†

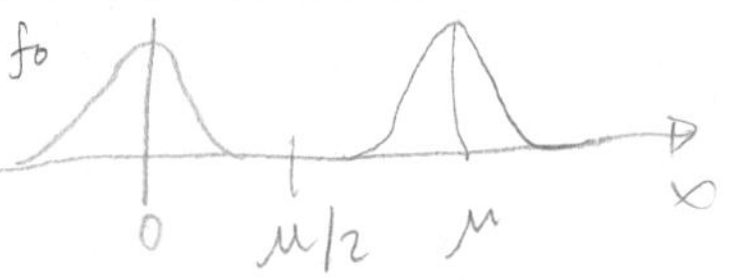

Summary—**This paper considers a threshold detector operating on noisy binary pulses. It is shown that an adaptive error-correction procedure can bring the threshold to the point of equal false alarm and missed detection probabilities.**

1) THE SUBJECT of devices capable of some degree of learning has received considerable attention in recent years. In particular, it has been demonstrated that circuits can be designed which can be "taught" to classify objects by a suitably designed error correcting training procedure.[1]

This paper discusses the applicability of error correcting procedures to the problem of signal detection. The author has chosen the simplest version of the problem to make a rigorous analysis possible and to gain clarity. The reader will notice that the procedure described below is closely related to stochastic approximation methods first introduced by Robbins and Monroe.

2) Let us first review briefly the detection problem from the point of view of the theory of the "ideal observer" (or equivalently, the Neyman-Pearson theory).[2] An observer looking at the radar screen is told that with an a priori probability of, say, 50 per cent a signal may be sent and if it is sent it will appear at a specified point (the so called off-on experiment). The observer is then asked to tell each time whether the signal is present or not.

Let $f_0(x)$ be the probability density of the deflection at the specified point on the screen if the signal is absent (*i.e.*, we have noise alone) and $f_1(x)$ if the signal is present. The optimal detectability criterion is the one which minimizes the probability of making an error.

Any detectability criterion is of the following general type. Let Ω be a set of real numbers (deflections); if the observation falls within Ω we say that the signal is present and if it falls outside Ω (*i.e.*, within the complementary set $\bar{\Omega}$) we say that the signal is absent.

For a given choice of Ω the probability of making an error is

$$\frac{1}{2}\int_{\Omega} f_0(x)\,dx + \frac{1}{2}\int_{\bar{\Omega}} f_1(x)\,dx = \frac{1}{2} + \frac{1}{2}\int_{\Omega}[f_0(x) - f_1(x)]\,dx$$

and, clearly, this is minimum if Ω is the set on which

$$f_0(x) \leq f_1(x). \tag{1}$$

We assume (as is often the case in practice) that $f_0(x) = f_1(x)$ has a unique root θ and that (1) is equivalent to

$$x \geq \hat{\theta}. \tag{2}$$

For example, in case of unrectified signals

$$f_0(x) = \frac{1}{\sigma\sqrt{2\pi}}e^{-x^2/2\sigma^2}, \quad f_1(x) = \frac{1}{\sigma\sqrt{2\pi}}e^{-(x-\mu)^2/2\sigma^2}, \tag{3}$$

we have

$$\hat{\theta} = \frac{\mu}{2}. \tag{4}$$

3) In experiments performed during the war at the Radiation Laboratory[2] the observers were presented with $m(30)$ observations at each time and the optimal detectability criterion in this case is easily seen to be

$$f_0(x_1)\cdots f_0(x_n) \leq f_1(x_1)\cdots f_1(x_n). \tag{5}$$

In the case (3) this criterion is equivalent to

$$\frac{x_1 + x_2 + \cdots + x_m}{m} \geq \frac{\mu}{2}. \tag{6}$$

In a more realistic case

$$f_0(x) = \frac{x}{\sigma^2}e^{-x^2/2\sigma^2}, \quad f_1(x) = \frac{x}{\sigma^2}e^{-\mu^2/2\sigma^2}e^{-x^2/2\sigma^2}I_0\left(\frac{x}{\sigma^2}\right) \tag{7}$$

the detectability criterion is no longer of the simple threshold type (6). However for large m, it is easily seen, a threshold type criterion gives essentially the same (minimal) probability of error. It has been found that human observers, after a period of training performed almost as well as the "ideal observer" and that they were unable to explain clearly the psychological basis for their decisions, which led to a nearly perfect statistical performance.

I shall now show that, under certain conditions, a self-adaptive device can be conceived which too will approach the performance of the "ideal observer".

4) I shall restrict myself to the case $m = 1$. The device operates as follows. It starts with an arbitrarily chosen threshold θ_0 and if the first deflection x_1 is greater than θ_0 it claims that signal is present. If $x_1 < \theta_0$ the device claims that signal is absent. If the answer is correct the threshold is kept for the next observation. If the answer is wrong, the threshold is increased or decreased according to the type of error committed.

The rule for changing the threshold (which falls under the general classification of erro-correcting procedures) can be written as follows:

$$\theta_{n+1} = \theta_n + \Delta(\phi(x_{n+1} - \theta_n) - \epsilon_{n+1}), \tag{8}$$

* Received by the PGIT, August 11, 1961.

† The Rockefeller Institute, New York, N. Y. Also Consultant, Aeronutronic, Division of Ford Motor Co., Newport Beach, Calif.

[1] For an excellent review of certain phases of this work, see H. D. Block, "The perception: A model for brain functioning," to appear in *Rev. Mod. Phys.*

[2] J. L. Lawson and G. E. Uhlenbeck, "Threshold Signals," Rad. Lab. Ser., McGraw-Hill Book Co., New York, N. Y., vol. 24; 1950.

Reprinted from *IRE Trans. Inform. Theory*, vol. IT-8, pp. 126–128, Feb. 1962.

where

$$\phi(x) = \begin{matrix} 1 \\ 0 \end{matrix}\begin{cases} \text{if} \quad x > 0 \\ \text{if} \quad x < 0 \end{cases} \tag{9}$$

and

$$\epsilon_n = \begin{cases} 1 & \text{if signal is present} \\ 0 & \text{if signal is absent.} \end{cases} \tag{10}$$

To simplify the analysis we assume that Δ is small and that the length of the training sequence n is such that

$$n\Delta = t. \tag{11}$$

In the limit $\Delta \rightarrow 0$ we have then a continuous (in time) adjustment process.

5) Let U_n, V_n, ϵ_n be independent random variables such that U_n has probability density $f_1(x)$, V_n has probability density $f_0(x)$ and ϵ_n assumes values 0 and 1 with equal probabilities (*i.e.*, 50 per cent). Let

$$X_n = \epsilon_n U_n + (1 - \epsilon_n) V_n \tag{12}$$

and

$$\theta_{n+1} = \theta_n + \Delta(\phi(X_{n+1} - \theta_n) - \epsilon_{n+1}). \tag{13}$$

Let us now calculate $E\{G(\theta_{n+1})\}$, where the function $G(\theta)$ will be chosen a little later.

We have

$$G[\theta_n + \Delta(\phi(X_{n+1} - \theta_n) - \epsilon_{n+1})] \sim G(\theta_n) + G'(\theta_n)\,\Delta(\phi(X_{n+1} - \theta_n) - \epsilon_{n+1}) \tag{14}$$

and consequently

$$E\{G(\theta_{n+1})\} \sim E\{G(\theta_n)\} + \Delta E\left\{G'(\theta_n)\left[\frac{1}{2}\int_{\theta_n}^{\infty} f_0(x)\,dx - \frac{1}{2}\int_{-\infty}^{\theta_n} f_1(x)\,dx\right]\right\}.$$

Let us now choose $G(\theta)$ in such a way that

$$\lambda G(\theta) = -\tfrac{1}{2}G'(\theta) \cdot\left[\int_{\theta}^{\infty} f_0(x)\,dx - \int_{-\infty}^{\theta} f_1(x)\,dx\right], \qquad \lambda > 0 \tag{15}$$

It is easily seen that log $G(\theta)$ appears as shown in Fig. 1, and consequently $G(\theta)$ appears as in Fig. 2, Here $\tilde{\theta}$ is the (unique) root of

$$\int_{\theta}^{\infty} f_0(x)\,dx = \int_{-\infty}^{\theta} f_1(x)\,dx. \tag{16}$$

With this choice of G we have

$$E\{G(\theta_{n+1})\} \sim (1 - \lambda\,\Delta)E\{G(\theta_n)\}$$

or

$$E\{G(\theta_n)\} \sim G(\theta_0)(1 - \lambda\,\Delta)^n. \tag{17}$$

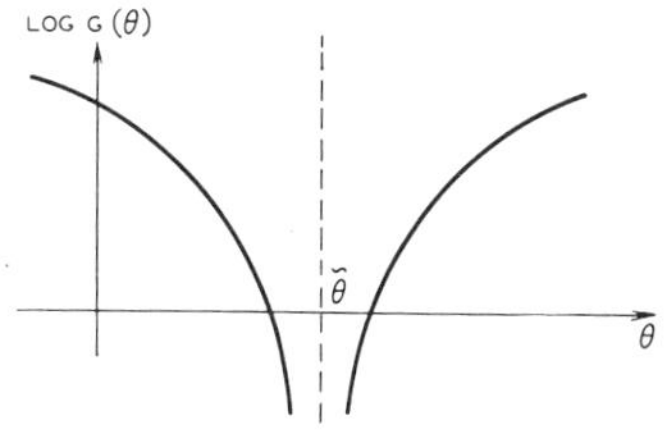

Fig. 1—Log $G(\Theta)$ as a function of Θ.

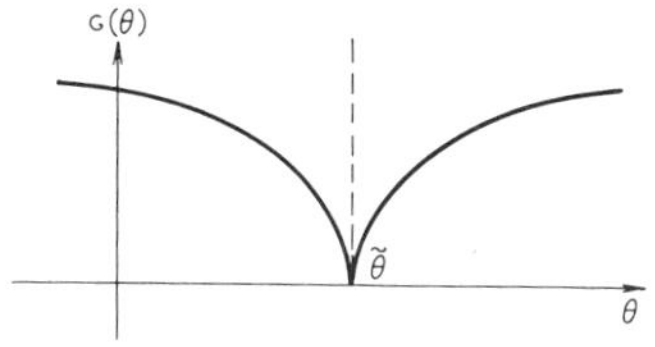

Fig. 2—$G(\Theta)$ as a function of Θ.

In other words, as $\Delta \rightarrow 0$ and $n\,\Delta = t$, we have

$$\lim_{n\rightarrow\infty} E\{G(\theta_n)\} = e^{-\lambda t}G(\theta_0). \tag{18}$$

If $\theta_0 < \tilde{\theta}$ we see that for $\theta < \tilde{\theta}$

$$\frac{G(\theta)}{G(\theta_0)} = \exp\left\{-2\lambda \int_{\theta_0}^{\theta} \frac{d\xi}{g(\xi)}\right\}, \tag{19}$$

where

$$g(\xi) = \int_{\xi}^{\infty} f_0(x)\,dx - \int_{-\infty}^{\xi} f_1(x)\,dx.$$

It now follows easily from (18) and (19) (by an adaptation of Tchebysheff's inequality) that

$$\theta_n \rightarrow \theta_t \tag{20}$$

in probability,[3] where θ_t is the unique root (to the left of θ) of the equation

$$t = 2\int_{\theta_0}^{\theta_t} \frac{d\xi}{g(\xi)}. \tag{21}$$

It is furthermore seen that as $t \rightarrow \infty$

$$\theta_t \rightarrow \tilde{\theta}. \tag{22}$$

It should be noted that, in general, the threshold $\tilde{\theta}$ *will not* be the same as $\hat{\theta}$. The most important case in which both coincide, is the case of normal distributions with different means but the same variance. The case of large m reported by Lawson and Uhlenbeck[2] is essentially equivalent to the case $m = 1$ and normal distributions with different means. Thus a suitably modified device will in the experimental situations[2], perform ultimately as the "ideal observer." It would be of interest to find out whether a human observer faced with a situation in which $\tilde{\theta} \neq \hat{\theta}$ will perform according to $\tilde{\theta}$ or $\hat{\theta}$.

[3] It is most likely that θ_t converges with probability one but in problems of this sort it does not seem to be of crucial importance.

Appendix

In this Appendix I should like to add a few remarks concerning the analysis of Section 5). If θ_0 is an integral multiple of Δ we are dealing with a random walk which is a Markoff chain with infinitely many states.

The rule (13) for changing the threshold gives easily the transition probabilities. In fact, we have (the notation being self-explanatory)

$$P(m\,\Delta \mid (m+1)\,\Delta) = \frac{1}{2}\int_{m\Delta}^{\infty} f_0(x)\,dx \tag{23}$$

$$P(m\,\Delta \mid (m-1)\,\Delta) = \frac{1}{2}\int_{-\infty}^{m\Delta} f_1(x)\,dx \tag{24}$$

$$P(m\,\Delta \mid m\,\Delta) = 1 - \frac{1}{2}\left\{\int_{m\Delta}^{\infty} f_0(x)\,dx + \int_{-\infty}^{m\Delta} f_1(x)\,dx\right\}. \tag{25}$$

Let $W_n(l\Delta)$ be the probability that $\theta_n = l\Delta$. We have

$$\begin{aligned} W_{n+1}(l\,\Delta) = {} & W_n((l-1)\,\Delta)P((l-1)\,\Delta \mid l\,\Delta) \\ & + W_n(l\,\Delta)P(l\,\Delta \mid l\,\Delta) \\ & W_n((l+1)\,\Delta)P((l+1)\,\Delta \mid l\,\Delta) \end{aligned} \tag{26}$$

and the initial condition

$$W_0(l\,\Delta) = \delta(l - l_0), \tag{27}$$

where $\theta_0 = l_0\Delta$ and $\delta(m) = 1$ for $m = 0$ and 0 otherwise.

The difference equation (26) and the initial condition (27) go over in the limit

$$\Delta \to 0 \qquad n\,\Delta = t$$

into

$$\frac{\partial W}{\partial t} = -\frac{1}{2}\frac{\partial}{\partial x}\left[W(x)\int_x^{\infty} f_0(\xi)\,d\xi\right] + \frac{1}{2}\frac{\partial}{\partial x}\left[W(x)\int_{-\infty}^{x} f_1(\xi)\,d\xi\right] \tag{26'}$$

and

$$W(x, 0) = \delta(x - \theta_0), \tag{27'}$$

where δ is now the Dirac δ-function.

We could now appeal to the general theory of partial differential equations of first order and obtain the result of Section 5).

The easiest way to see this is to multiply both sides of (26′) by $G(x)$ and integrate on x. One obtains then, by integration by parts,

$$\frac{g}{dt}\int_{-\infty}^{\infty} G(x)W(x, t)\,dx = \frac{1}{2}\int_{-\infty}^{\infty} G'(x) \cdot\left[\int_x^{\infty} f_0(\xi)\,d\xi - \int_{-\infty}^{x} f_1(\xi)\,d\xi\right]W(x, t)\,dx, \tag{28}$$

and if G is chosen so as to satisfy (15) one gets

$$\frac{d}{dt}\int_{-\infty}^{\infty} G(x)W(x, t)\,dx = -\lambda\int_{-\infty}^{\infty} G(x)W(x, t)\,dx$$

or

$$\int_{-\infty}^{\infty} G(x)W(x, t)\,dx = e^{-\lambda t}G(\theta_0).$$

This, of course, is equivalent to (18) and one gets (for $\theta_0 < \tilde{\theta}$, $x < \tilde{\theta}$)

$$W(x, t) = \delta\left(t - 2\int_{\theta_0}^{x}\frac{d\xi}{g(\xi)}\right)\frac{2}{g(x)}, \tag{29}$$

which can formally be verified to be the solution of (26′) satisfying (27′).

We can now apply the analog of this method to the original system of (26). We introduce an auxiliary function $G(l\Delta)$ and get

$$\begin{aligned} \sum_{l=-\infty}^{\infty} G(l\,\Delta)W_{n+1}(l\,\Delta) = {} & \sum_{l=-\infty}^{\infty} G(l\,\Delta)W_n(l\,\Delta) \\ & + \frac{1}{2}\sum_{l=-\infty}^{\infty} W_n(l\,\Delta)\left\{[G((l+1)\,\Delta) - G(l\,\Delta)]\int_{l\Delta}^{\infty} f_0(x)\,dx \right. \\ & \left. - [G(l\,\Delta) - G((l-1)\,\Delta)]\int_{-\infty}^{l\Delta} f_1(x)\,dx\right\}. \end{aligned}$$

If G is chosen in such a way that

$$\begin{aligned} & (G((l+1)\,\Delta) - G(l\,\Delta))\int_{l\Delta}^{\infty} f_0(x)\,dx \\ & \qquad - (G(l\,\Delta) - G(l-1)\,\Delta))\int_{-\infty}^{l\Delta} f_1(x)\,dx \\ & \qquad = -2\lambda\,\Delta G(l\,\Delta), \end{aligned} \tag{30}$$

we get

$$\sum_{l=-\infty}^{\infty} G(l\,\Delta)W_n(l\,\Delta) = (1 - 2\lambda\,\Delta)^n G(l\,\Delta). \tag{31}$$

Formula (31) should be sufficient to discuss the distribution of θ_n as $n \to \infty$. Unfortunately, the analysis becomes rather involved due mainly to the fact $G(l\Delta)$ changes sign in the neighborhood of $\tilde{\theta}$ (only in the limit $\Delta \to 0$ is $G(l\Delta)$ non-negative). We hope to return to a detailed investigation of the discrete case some time in the future.

Acknowledgment

The author would like to acknowledge the helpful discussions with J. Daly, and Drs. G. R. Cooper, R. D. Joseph, and P. M. Kelly.

Interactive Pattern Analysis and Classification Systems: A Survey and Commentary

LAVEEN N. KANAL, FELLOW, IEEE

Abstract—Starting with the era of learning machines, reasons are presented for the current emergence of graphics-oriented interactive pattern analysis and classification systems (IPACS) as a general approach to practical pattern-recognition problems. A number of representative systems and their application to a wide variety of patterns are surveyed. Various aspects of alternative hardware and software implementations are commented upon and computational algorithms and mappings relevant to interactive analysis and classification of patterns are discussed.

I. Introduction

IN THE Talk of the Town section of the *New Yorker* for December 6, 1958, "our man about town" reported on a conversation with Frank Rosenblatt, the inventor of Perceptrons [151]. The report was titled "Rival," and it reflected the anthropomorphism that was then fashionable in pattern recognition and computers.

Rosenblatt's brilliant conjectures and the colorful names for his "self-organizing" machines attracted wide attention. He had high hopes for his "artificial intelligences." They were to be replacements for human perceivers, recognizers, and problem solvers. Over the next few years there followed a flock of other "adaptive" and "learning" machines such as ADALINE and MADALINE [201], APE (see [91]), MINOS [17], CONFLEX [187], and SOCRATES [188].

Manuscript received February 12, 1972; revised July 14, 1972. This work was supported in part by the Directorate of Mathematical and Information Sciences, Air Force Office of Scientific Research, Air Force Systems Command, USAF, under Grant AFOSR 71-1982 to the University of Maryland.

The author is with the Computer Science Center, University of Maryland, College Park, Md. 20742.

As was to become evident, the true contribution of the brilliant conjectures, catchy names and audacious claims for these machines, was not in providing a general approach to pattern recognition. Rather it was in creating an air of excitement about automatic pattern-recognition and learning machines.

Today there is greater appreciation of the complexities of what is called pattern recognition. But the excitement continues, as does the urge to look for relatively general theoretical and experimental approaches and models which are applicable to a wide class of problems. Aspects of the structural-geometric or linguistic-statistical models for pattern recognition that have recently aroused interest are presented elsewhere [94]. Here we survey graphics-oriented interactive pattern analysis and classification systems, for which we use the abbreviation IPACS. IPACS represent responses to demands for generality in the experimental domain.

Computer-driven interactive graphic displays together with input devices such as the light pen, the Rand tablet, the Sylvania tablet, the mouse, and joy sticks, have improved man–computer communication in recent years. In addition to displaying relationships in two or three dimensions (using perspective) for human inspection, the graphics terminal provides a high data-rate communication link to the computer, enabling dynamic control and manipulation of programs by means of line drawings, as well as character codes or function buttons.

Section II discusses the impact of interactive display technology on approaches to pattern-recognition problems. Section III lists some existing IPACS and gives an idea of the

Reprinted from *Proc. IEEE*, vol. 60, pp. 1200–1215, Oct. 1972.

diversity of applications on which these systems have been tried. The development of an interactive pattern analysis and classification system involves both systems aspects and computational algorithms for pattern analysis and pattern classification. Section IV outlines the overall system features that should be considered when designing IPACS, describes how various specific features have been implemented in existing systems and comments on the desirability and effectiveness of some alternate implementations. Section V describes and comments on the algorithms and mappings being experimented with in some existing systems.

This is a survey of the state of the art of a field in the process of development. Developments in IPACS cited here are those we feel the reader should be aware of, whether or not their descriptions have been published in easily available journals.

II. Reasons for IPACS

For engineers trying to develop practical systems for alphanumeric character recognition, postal address reading, speech recognition, and imagery screening in photointerpretation [26], [72], [97], "self-learning" approaches were at first highly seductive [151], [57], [84], [18]. Looking at classified learning samples, the machines would produce an output which a teacher would tell them was correct or incorrect. And through simple routines they would organize themselves so as to improve their performance. What could be simpler?

Unfortunately, performance on independent test data fell far short of expectation, and after a short detour most optical character recognition (OCR) designers reverted to explicit feature-selection and classification-logic design based on "structural" analysis through intuition and interaction with the misclassifications produced on character reader "test beds" and prototype hardware. Finding the simple Perceptron structures and learning routines wanting, they often proceeded to ignore all subsequent developments in the understanding of statistical classification and feature optimization. The result was that many of the present commercial OCR systems grew like Topsy, and even when adequate performance was achieved the design was often not cost-effective.

When deterministic structural descriptions are the basis of the decision logic, a large amount of information has been transmitted to the recognizer. To statistically "learn" the same type and amount of information would take an inordinately large number of samples. But the within-group variability of patterns in most nontrivial real problems is such that, following a purely structural approach without severe constraints on the input, the performance of practical pattern-recognition systems is unacceptable or marginal. Statistical methods begin where deterministic structural methods leave off—there is a residual core of uncertainty which can be expressed only in terms of probabilistic structures. In most real-life pattern-recognition problems we are faced with the necessity of inferring both deterministic and probabilistic structures governing the patterns and pattern classes in order to achieve good classification performance.

Under the title "Discriminant Analysis," the statistical analysis of data structure had, since the early part of the century, been the subject of a large number of papers; most of these results were summarized by Rao [143]. Rao also related classification into groups to statistical decision theory [191]. He treated classification as a partitioning of a probabilistic feature space into mutually exclusive regions, considered the case of more than two groups, and introduced the concept of a reject region. A 1954 paper [178] on speech recognition, which refers to Rao's book, is perhaps the first pattern-recognition application of this material in the IEEE (IRE) literature. Since 1954, a large number of papers has been published on the subject in the engineering literature, under the title "Pattern Recognition" [120], [82], [113].

All this literature has had but limited impact on the design of optical character readers and other practical pattern-recognition systems. A majority of the papers in the engineering literature on pattern recognition have been solely concerned with the decision theoretic aspects. For many designers of practical systems these papers have been difficult to appreciate, unlike the Perceptron-type learning algorithms which were easy to follow and intuitively appealing even when their underlying mathematics was not understood. In addition, much of the published research represents theoretical studies of specific models under specific assumptions or laboratory-oriented investigations of specific techniques on small nonstandard data sets. Little attention has been given to the constraints on dimensionality and sample size which must be observed in order to have valid estimates of performance [92]. Thus a large percentage of the results suffer from "the love-at-first-sight effect in research" [138].

In problem-oriented pattern-recognition investigations, the starting point is usually some samples of patterns. The question then asked is whether or not the recognition of patterns such as these can be automated, and if it can how complex a machine will be needed [95].

To go from these initial vague questions to an actual pattern-recognition system involves a series of refinements and formalizations concerning the deterministic, probabilistic, or mixed structure that we can infer about the patterns; what level of performance we should strive for; what competing design approaches we think are worth considering; and what manner of implementation is relevant.

The first step in this process is pattern analysis. In order to understand the variability in relatively unconstrained data and to come up with solutions, we need to study the detailed peculiarities of a very large data base. We are no longer content to do what was often done a decade ago, i.e., jump to a hardware implementation of a particular learning machine, an optical spatial filtering system, etc. It is true that one can go a long way, using a problem-oriented approach and a theoretical analysis of requirements, toward rejecting candidate solutions, as was shown [73] for the problem of detecting and locating objects of military interest in aerial reconnaissance photography. That analysis showed what invention was needed before optical spatial filtering techniques would be practical for automatic target detection. It made apparent the electronic methodology and classification design approach that would serve the problem needs. Nevertheless, that type of analysis is limited to certain overall aspects of a problem.

The desirability of an automated interactive approach to pattern analysis and classification logic design can be summarized as follows.

1) It is now recognized that the key to pattern-recognition problems does not lie wholly in learning machines, statistical approaches, spatial filtering, heuristic programming, formal linguistic approaches, or in any other particular solution which has been vigorously advocated by one or another group during the last one and a half decades as *the solution to the*

pattern-recognition problem. No single model exists for all pattern-recognition problems and no single technique is applicable to all problems. Rather what we have in pattern recognition is a bag of tools and a bag of problems.

2) Feature definition and extraction, and pattern classification, are best examined via trial and evaluation. The boundaries between feature selection and classification are not sharp. We need feedback between feature selection, logic design, classification, and testing. And we need many iterations of the feedback process. This is naturally an interactive operation. We cannot preprogram a batch mode operation to go through all the possibilities—it would be too time consuming and costly. So we turn to an on-line and interactive mode of operation.

3) Most data analysis techniques try to answer questions about the structure of the data in a high-dimensional space. Interactive pattern analysis is a way of allowing examination of structure. (Humans are superior in recognizing structure of certain types, especially clusters, where automatic clustering routines are often thrown off by outliers between clusters.) However, to make this examination of structure feasible we must arrange for suitable graphics for displaying relationships among data elements.

4) In many pattern-recognition problems, the human is the standard; we should put him in charge of the design and evaluation process but help him with automation in an interactive mode. For good interaction, the lag between the initiation of some control function and the completion of the requested action should be short enough that it will not interrupt his train of thought.

We would like to have a quick flexible way of analyzing sample patterns, trying out various tools from a versatile tool kit to determine which algorithm or approach should be selected for a given application. This exploratory pattern analysis and evaluation of competing tools is greatly enhanced by automation of known procedures [185] so that they can be applied in a routine fashion. It is further enhanced by an interactive environment. Standardizing the testing of our hypotheses concerning data requires that we incorporate a variety of statistical and nonstatistical procedures; we must understand their theoretical properties, and gain experience regarding their practical limitations and capabilities.

III. Some Representative IPAC "Systems"

Although we call them "systems" only a few IPACS deserve this apellation. For the most part they appear to have been developed piecemeal from software tailored to fairly specific applications without provision for the capabilities which should be incorporated (see Section IV). It should be emphasized that the capability of primary interest is the feedback provided from machine to man or vice versa during the process of designing procedures for feature extraction, pattern analysis, and pattern classification. Thus applications programs such as described in [66] and [67] for recognition of characters handprinted on-line are not discussed.

The IPACS considered here are properly viewed as a subset of a larger group which includes interactive systems for mathematics [98], [171], computer-aided design [37], [106], [153], question answering [118], [169], and computer animation [99], [5], [6], [186]. While each of the above areas has individual requirements, past developments in these fields have strongly influenced the development of existing IPACS, and will continue to exert such an influence.

For the IPACS discussed in this section, a dominating descriptor is the type of input accepted: vectors, images, or waveforms. Interactive image and waveform preprocessors usually produce the data required for the pattern analysis and classification systems which accept vector input. In addition, we have included a discussion of a few interactive systems which are being developed for special applications.

STATPAC [64] is credited with being the forerunner of the group of systems aimed at multivariate statistical analysis and classification of vector data; using clustering, discriminant analysis, and related statistical routines in an interactive-graphics environment. This group is now represented by PROMENADE and OLPARS.

PROMENADE, Stanford Research Institute's (SRI) system for multivariate data analysis, has one clustering option and one clustering based classification routine [69]. With its interactive graphics capability, the limited options have provided insight in the following diverse problem areas: 1) analysis of spectrometer data to perform automatic recognition of chemical compounds; 2) classification of corporations, to predict which companies are likely to become clients for SRI's long-range planning services; 3) utility of cluster analysis relative to regression analysis for producing housing-construction price indexes for apartment projects; and 4) analysis of cloud patterns in weather satellite photographs to obtain brief descriptors of meaningful information in the photographs and to identify and track cloud masses in successive pictures in order to determine wind motions.

OLPARS [155], [157], [29] [159] located at the U. S. Air Force's Rome Air Development Center, is perhaps the foremost system currently in operation. Developed as a sequel to PROMENADE, OLPARS is used for interactive analysis of cluster- and string-type structures in high-dimensional vector data and the design of classification logics using techniques derived from discriminant analysis. OLPARS has made it feasible to experiment with data from a variety of application areas [155]–[157] including radar signature identification, cartographic classification of aerial photographs, analysis of data on personal loans, classification of candidates applying for admission to an Air Force Program, construction of a Document Classification Space for document retrieval, speech recognition for isolated spoken words, handprinted character recognition, and analysis of dermatoglyphic (palm-print) patterns to determine whether there is sufficient information in the palm to discriminate among a variety of diseases [175], [174].

The *IBM Interactive System* for complex data analysis provides some of the features found in OLPARS; it has been used in the study of biomedical data from critically ill patients [60]–[62], [168], and in the further analysis [63], of certain previously studied data on bees [49]. Some of the UCLA biomedical statistical packages are now also said to be available for interactive-graphics mode of operation [38]–[40].

Some IPACS for vector data are being augmented by interactively controlled feature definition and extraction "front ends" to produce vector data. Examples of image-processing-feature-extraction subsystems are the IBM image-processing subsystem for interactive scanning and display [79], and the image feature extraction system (IFES) for OLPARS [128] The IBM system has been used in the development of an interactive man–machine system for reading unformatted typeset text, with all necessary operations being performed on-line at a single sitting [4]. A number of other applications in image processing of line drawings, maps, chromosomes are mentioned in [79].

IFES is described as an extensive software system for online search, feature definition, extraction, and processing of images. Coupling an optical scanning device to OLPARS, it is designed to allow one to interactively perform various global and local picture-processing operations of the type described in [152].

SARF, a signature analysis research facility [172], [123], was designed to display time function and feature space plots to a user and enable him to do interactive feature selection, analysis, and classification. A diffraction pattern sampling system which can be interactively controlled through SARF for image feature extraction from aerial photographs was described recently in the *Proceedings of the IEEE* [108]. Sampling the diffraction pattern results in a sampling signature, which is different for each sampling geometry.

Various applications of SARF are described in [108], [173], and [125], [126]. Because of its emphasis on display, manipulation, and processing of time functions, it is grouped here with other systems and subsystems which have their primary emphasis on interactive waveform analysis.

INTERSPACE [131], [132] like SARF, is designed to accept image data from certain optical scanning devices, but the reports [134] have emphasized its waveform processing capabilities. It incorporates various classical expansions and related user defined operations for waveforms. Past applications include underwater signal processing; the system is presently being directed toward biomedical-image and signal-data processing.

The *Experimental Dynamic Processor, DX-1* [192], [195] was started around the late 1950's to study on-line interactive sensor data processing. This was one of the pioneering efforts in the study of interactive statistical signal analysis using a graphics display and the use of color displays in this context [194], [196]. In addition to radar and biological signal processing and on-line filter design [193], [149], the major use of this system has been in studies of various statistical bandwidth compression schemes.

The *Waveform Processing Subsystem* (WPS) for OLPARS [161] currently under development, is the waveform counterpart of IFES. It is to be an extensive software system for extraction of signal features and manipulation and transformation of waveforms using interactive graphics. The WPS is designed to allow global expansions of waveforms in terms of classical basis functions such as Fourier, Legendre, Laguerre, Hermite, Walsh; user specification and design of digital filters; algebraic and calculus operations on waveforms, such as segmentation differentiation, integration, scaling, zero crossings. A subsystem of WPS allows on-line definition on linguistic features whereby a signal is decomposed into a string of symbols or numbers, and features are defined over this domain [136].

There are a number of man–machine interaction systems for pattern analysis which have a somewhat different flavor. Systems designed specifically for interactive speech analysis,

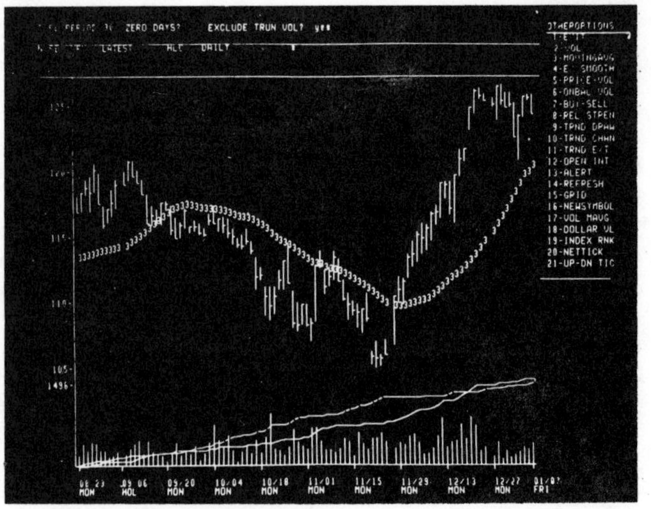

Fig. 1. Merlin display of daily high-close–low-close chart of Xerox stock, with daily volume, buy–sell volume, and a 30-day moving average of closing prices. Options are on right side of display.

synthesis, and recognition are being developed at the University of California at Santa Barbara [33], [76], [77], Carnegie-Mellon University (CMU) [147], and the University of Washington [176]. An informative discussion of the earlier work at Stanford [146], [148], [190] on which the CMU system is based, is included in a recent survey of man–machine interaction using speech [81].

The Bell Laboratories study of a real-time man–machine interactive system for human face identification [59] is concerned with optimizing search and decision strategies: a human describes a face to a computer using features provided by the computer, his own set of features, or some combination thereof; the machine searches a file population to find a stored member which best fits the target. The IBM system for automating the conversion of unformatted typeset text to computer code [4] is concerned with optimum strategies for human intervention in a production-oriented system.

The *Merlin System* [115], [116] demonstrates the power of an interactive system to facilitate analysis of a large data base. A staggering volume of past and current (15-min delayed) data on all stocks listed in the New York and American Stock Exchanges and on an extensive group of commodities is available on-line to the system user in the graphic form appropriate for trying out the various methods of analysis. The system grew out of Project Merlin which Stanford Research Institute (SRI) undertook in the early 1960's under contract from Merrill Lynch, Pierce, Fenner and Smith, for on-line manipulation and display of graphical data. Fig. 1 shows a photo from the storage tube display. The standard methods of "technical analysis" [43], shown on the right side of the display, are available as options. Additional time series methods such as those described in a recently developed interactive time series analysis package [170], and additional methods of data analysis could be incorporated into the menu of available options.

At this stage in the development of IPACS, one of the dangers is that working with inadequate embryonic systems may turn users away from an interactive approach to some problems. The interactive systems discussed in this section use diverse hardware and software to achieve some degree of man–machine symbiosis. Systems under development should provide a higher degree of interactive capability. However, no single system surveyed incorporates all the features desired for effective interactive preprocessing and pattern analysis and classification. In the following section, we review the basic conceptual bases for the implementations and bring out some of the differences of opinion regarding system configurations and options.

IV. Design Considerations and their Realization

The general capabilities that a user would like to have available [70], [172], [155] in an IPACS are not unlike those desired for interactive systems for mathematics [48] or for computer-aided graphics design [87], [140]. The desired capabilities are as follows.

Communication and control of the system through simple procedures, such as: selection of options displayed at each stage of the design process in the form of a menu on the side of the graphic display; selection using a function keyboard; and selection of options through a simple language using an alphanumeric keyboard.

Quick response in an on-line mode, allowing rapid formulation, insertion, and testing of alternate hypotheses.

Easy on-line generation and modification of algorithms and programs; selection, labeling, merging, and splitting of data sets; performing all types of set operations on data sets and subsets; retrieval of selected data for visual inspection and trial design of algorithms.

Ability to go forward and back to any option available in the system; to temporarily store and compare results of applying various optional procedures on a data set; to obtain intermediate and end results while sequencing through options.

Additional requirements for IPACS relate to providing an ability to define and examine "structure" in large sets of high-dimensional multivariate data and to try out statistical and nonstatistical algorithms on mass data, or on user defined subsets of the data.

The large amounts of data which have to be stored in a structured manner and the many programs for implementing user options cannot all be stored in the main core memory of the computer. This together with the interactive interrupts and the limitations on how much data can be displayed at any time on the CRT lead to the requirement of allocating programs and data dynamically to main and auxiliary storage. This situation arises in most interactive graphics applications [189], [203]. The approaches followed by developers of IPACS cover the standard range of solutions for multiprogramming and time-sharing systems [36]. These include static storage allocation by dividing a program into units which "overlay," i.e., replace one another in main storage; automating dynamic storage allocation [14] to provide a "virtual memory" which makes the auxiliary storage look like an extension of the main memory; and programmer-controlled dynamic storage allocation using software and hardware, such as Algol on the stack-oriented Burroughs B5500 [116] to define routines for allocation and deallocation of memory blocks.

The editing, filing, data transformation, display, and other options provided in an IPACS are a function of the type of data to be handled and the relationships and logical associations between data items. To select data on which to execute user options, and have the data resulting from one routine be in a form suitable for the next option, the data must be represented in an organized manner which models structural relationships between data items. Such representations which provide a coupling between problem data and computer analysis are usually referred to as "data structures." Stacks, linked lists, arrays, trees, and rings [100] are examples of structures used for the representation and manipulation of relationships among data items.

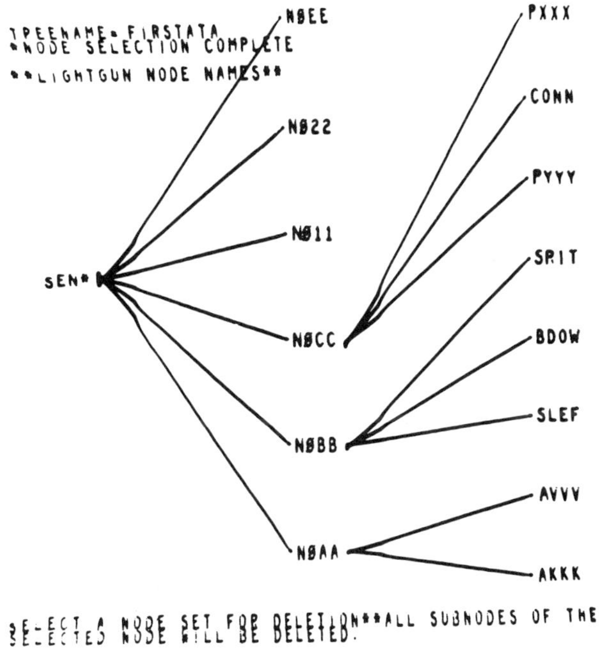

Fig. 2. An OLPARS tree data-structure display.

The OLPARS vector filing system represents *data structure* in the form of a tree or a set of trees. Each node of a tree corresponds to a list of vectors, the list being the union of the lists associated with the nodes of the subtrees of this node. Pointing at a particular node of a data tree displayed on the CRT causes that set of vectors to be selected as the current data set for input to an option at level 1 and subsequent levels of the control tree. The result of applying various transformations and logical operations to user selected nodes of an existing data tree is a new data tree. Fig. 2 shows an OLPARS data tree display.

SARF, which is primarily concerned with waveform inputs, builds a hierarchical ring structure, shown in Fig. 3, to represent the data. This has been the most popular data structure for computer graphics [203], as it permits extensive cross referencing of data with ease.

The *command structure* of an IPACS may also take the form of a tree [14], [70], [157]. The commands available to the user are often presented in the form of lighted words or symbols along the boarders of the display. These light buttons get brighter, when pointed at by a cursor or a light pen, or referenced by the keyboard. The command is then implemented and the next list of options shows up on the display. A user can follow a branch from a node at a given level down to a terminal node, and return to any higher level node on the same path.

SARF and WPS are examples of systems providing user extendibility by adding to preprogrammed subroutines which can be selected by depressing function keys, pointing a light pen, or entering a parameter. In SARF the operators used during the OPERATE function in the EXAMINE data option, and

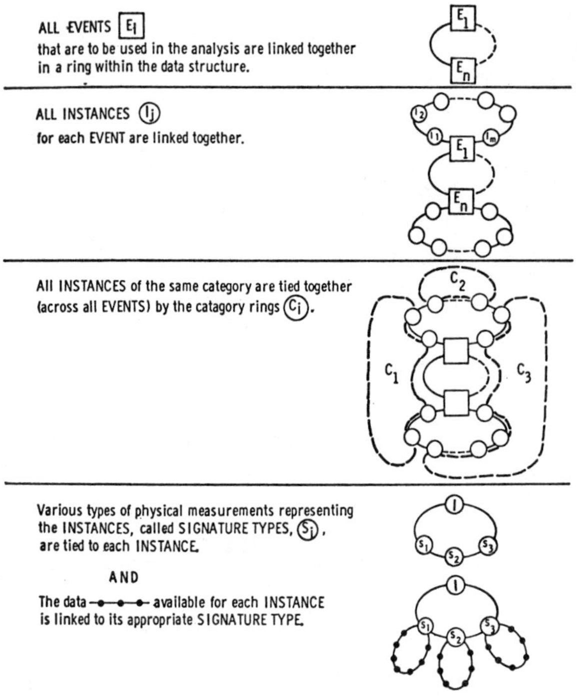
ALL EVENTS Ei
that are to be used in the analysis are linked together in a ring within the data structure.
ALL INSTANCES Ij
for each EVENT are linked together.
All INSTANCES of the same category are tied together (across all EVENTS) by the catagory rings Ci.
Various types of physical measurements representing the INSTANCES, called SIGNATURE TYPES, Si, are tied to each INSTANCE.
AND
The data available for each INSTANCE is linked to its appropriate SIGNATURE TYPE.

Fig. 3. Ring data structure of SARF.

in the definition phase of FEATURE space plot are user supplied routines. In WPS the capability of on-line compilation of algorithms programmed in an interactive session is expected to be implemented using a simple linguistic-feature oriented language called OLWPL (on-line waveform processing language). Each preprogrammed option for segmentation, feature extraction, or transformation has a corresponding predicate in the language. Such extendability approaches the desired goal of allowing any algorithm constructed on-line to be saved in an applications program library.

The need for high-precision graphic display and for dynamic rotation of three-dimensional plots of data has been stressed in some IPACS [70] but disputed by others [197]. The Plot 3-D option included in PROMENADE and OLPARS provides a two-dimensional projection of a three-dimensional space. The center of the CRT represents the center of mass of the three-dimensional data, and a viewer can zoom a window along a radial path toward this center. Combining radial and rotational movement, a viewer gets the illusion of flying about in the three-dimensional data space.

While three-dimentional rotation and tumbling may provide some insight in simulation and modeling studies of well-defined entitities such as space vehicles and chemical structures and is a most impressive demonstration, experience thus far indicates that in IPAC, spinning around, or even just shifting around in three-dimentional data space is confusing and provides no useful insights. While the display should be flicker-free and comfortable to look at, most applications do not require highly precise measurements from the displayed quantities. However, the observation of clustering and related phenomena could be helped by using gray scale and color [70], [197].

Most IPACS use various attention focusing and display manipulation procedures [88] which are becoming standard in computer graphics. These include such options as change of scale, zoom, blink data set, eliminate a data set, eliminate a data point, draw a piecewise-linear boundary, rotate or otherwise transform data, label items on the display. These options are implemented through a graphics executive program which drives the display, processes the interrupts, contains basic graphics routines to generate points, lines, arcs, circles, and alphanumerics, and accesses various items from a library of graphics display routines.

Although the user is primarily interested in the computational algorithms for feature selection, pattern analysis, and pattern classification that are available on a system, the system architecture is what ultimately determines the nature and extent of interactive capability. Most developers of existing IPACS, having come from a pattern-recognition background, have tended to accept various computer-system implementations found useful in other contexts. Usually, the starting point for their systems has been some existing computer hardware rather than a suitably chosen configuration.

Existing and proposed processor configurations for IPACS cover the range from large time-sharing systems and satellite systems, in which a minicomputer or "intelligent" terminal serves as a remote satellite to a central time-shared computer, all the way to dedicated multiprocessors such as used in the experimental dynamic processor, DX-1. In the context of general interactive graphics, various configurations have been discussed in [28], [87], [31].

The emergence of computer networks such as the ARPANET of the Advanced Research Projects Agency and the Education Network of the National Science Foundation raises interesting possibilities for processor configurations. IPACS on such networks would permit many users to share data and programs. However, arguments have been advanced [197] against implementing IPACS in a general-purpose time-sharing environment. These arguments are based on the difficulty of writing efficient general-purpose utility systems which can serve a number of independent users with diverse applications.

Since some minicomputers provide as much computing capability as a large second-generation computer at a reasonable cost, they deserve serious consideration for IPACS. A dedicated minicomputer or one shared by a small number of compatible users, driving a not very high precision display (perhaps just a storage CRT, and a Rand tablet) appears worth investigating.

The extensive computations required in exploring solutions to some practical pattern analysis problems have discouraged the use of interactive processing. While analog techniques for preprocessing have been incorporated in some systems (e.g., [68]) no serious attempts are reported in the literature on the possibility of using analog and hybrid techniques to avoid some of the time-consuming digital computations.

V. Computational Algorithms

The usefulness of an IPACS in exploring solutions to a variety of problems depends on the extent and versatility of the algorithms available on the system. Various *ad hoc* and theoretically derived algorithms for clustering, mapping, classification feature evaluation, etc., are being tried out in different IPACS. Fig. 4 illustrates the organization and computational capabilities of OLPARS. In this section we consider some details of the algorithms available on representative systems. Some applications are also described briefly.

Clustering algorithms attempt to detect and locate the presence of groups of vectors, in a high-dimensional multi-

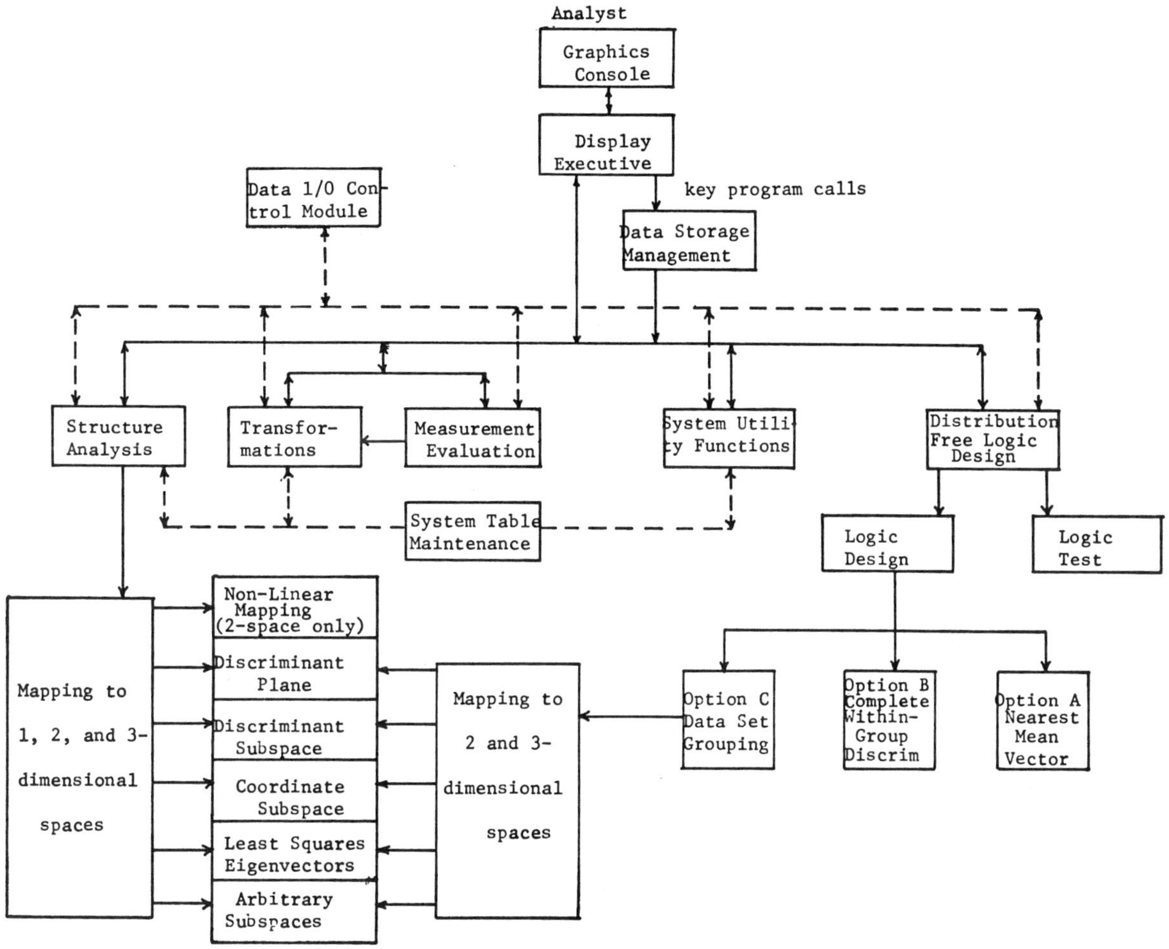

Fig. 4. Organization of OLPARS.

variate space, which share some property of similarity. A large number of similarity measures and other clustering criteria based on general relations among samples have been proposed. Some of these measures and the resulting clustering algorithms are surveyed in [9], [120], [51], and [41].

In these algorithms, based on some clustering criterion, a classification rule is iteratively applied. Rules for creating and destroying classes as the iteration progresses are sometimes incorporated. The ISODATA program [11] for clustering uses the mean distance of each sample from the closest cluster center, and employs merging or splitting rules on each iteration. This program is available in both PROMENADE and OLPARS. An improved version of ISODATA which attempts to incorporate useful features of a number of the cluster-seeking techniques is described in [10].

Clustering criteria based on scatter matrices [202] and invariance under linear transformations of the coordinate system have been examined in [49] and are used in the IBM interactive system [63].

OLPARS also provides a similarity matrix method for data grouping [157] which is related to a number of contributions [15], [75], [120]. The similarity matrix is an approach to representing first-order associations between pairs of data vectors. The ijth element of this matrix is some numerical measure of the "similarity" between the ith and jth vectors. In OLPARS a generalized similarity matrix is defined as a polynomial in terms of powers of the original matrix. The elements of the generalized matrix are replaced by 1 or 0 depending on whether or not they exceed a threshold chosen by the user. The resulting matrix of 0's and 1's becomes the starting point for a procedure to define cluster centers and clustering configurations.

Designers of the INTERSPACE system [131] propose that clustering be performed by a search over partitions of the observation space, in order to maximize the expected value of the natural logarithm of the estimated mixture density. The complexity of this theoretically interesting approach may not be justifiable; reports on its experimental performance compared to other methods mentioned above would be of interest.

In an IPACS, clustering routines can be used for data compression, feature reduction, mode identification, and identification of outliers. Often the large amount of data gathered can only be handled by representing all vectors in a cluster by an appropriately weighted vector. On occasion, feature reduction may be achieved by using these weighted cluster vectors to define a new lower dimensional subspace. Mode identification for density estimation and construction of classification boundaries, and identification of outliers for further examination or rejection are typical uses. OLPARS uses ISODATA to do data compression prior to certain mapping algorithms be-

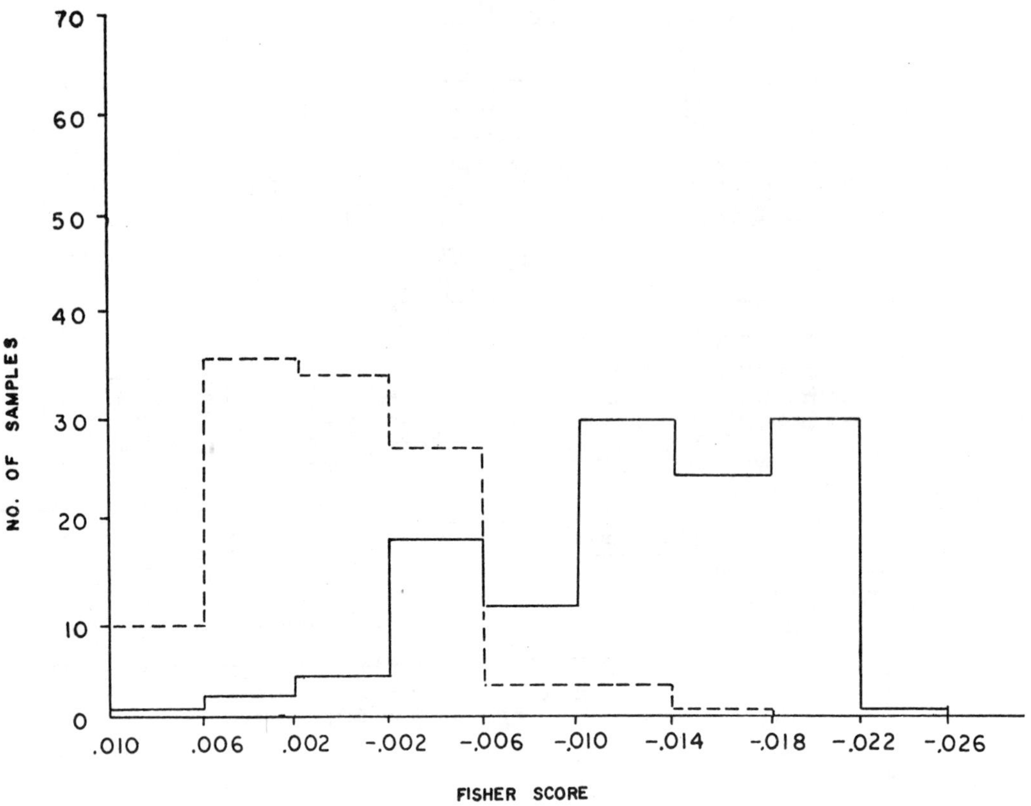

Fig. 5. Histogram of palm-print data along Fisher discriminant for right-handed females, showing separation between normals and downs. Samples used: 295 normals, 263 downs.

cause these algorithms cannot handle more than 250 vectors. Clustering has also been used to avoid the problems involved in preparing an adequate training set [4].

Programs such as ISODATA require the setting of a number of control parameters in an *ad hoc* manner; the merging and splitting rules are heuristic. The evaluation of the resulting cluster configuration also presents a major problem. Both problems are ameliorated in an on-line interactive graphics environment. The display of a graph which shows the user the progress of an iterative clustering procedure is an advantage of the on-line interactive approach. For example, OLPARS allows the user to construct and display scoring and evaluations. The plot of an appropriately defined error function against the number of clusters gives visual identification of the clustering algorithms: the error graph helps bring out the cluster structure of the data. Through trial and error several cluster configurations may be generated until the user is satisfied.

The main advantages of interactive graphics for analysis of clusters in data comes about because of the superiority of humans over mechanistic approaches in recognizing cluster structures and simple linear or curvilinear relationships in one-, two-, and three-space—it is easy to have automatic clustering routines thrown off by isolated "wild shots," strays or outliers bridging clusters, etc.

To make use of this superior ability of humans, the high-dimensional data must be displayed in one, two, or at most three dimensions in such a way that "structure is preserved" or class separability enhanced. Then the user can discover clusters, and identify and classify patterns interactively. Linear and nonlinear mappings which attempt to preserve various aspects of structure in the data while mapping it down to one-, two-, and three-space have been incorporated in various IPACS.

The main categories of *linear and nonlinear mappings for IPACS* which may be discerned from the literature, are the following.

1) Linear mappings to one, two, and three spaces defined by the principal components of the lumped data covariance matrix or correlation matrix.

2) Linear mappings to one and two spaces which emphasize some measure of class separability.

3) Nonlinear mappings, based on multidimensional scaling and intrinsic dimensionality algorithms, which map multivariate data from an n-dimensional space into two dimensions in such a way that some measure of resulting distortion, of intersample distances in the two-space, is minimized.

4) Nonlinear mappings which map data into two-space while enhancing class separability.

5) Mappings of high-dimensional functions into one- and two-space based on the idea of space-filling curves.

6) Miscellaneous.

The method of *principal components*, introduced by Pearson [137] and developed by Hotelling [86], now has an extensive literature devoted to it [2], [202], [144], [145], [127] and is widely used. It shows up indirectly under the terms factor analysis and Karhunen–Loeve expansions [198] and intrinsic analysis [204] for feature selection and ordering. In OLPARS,

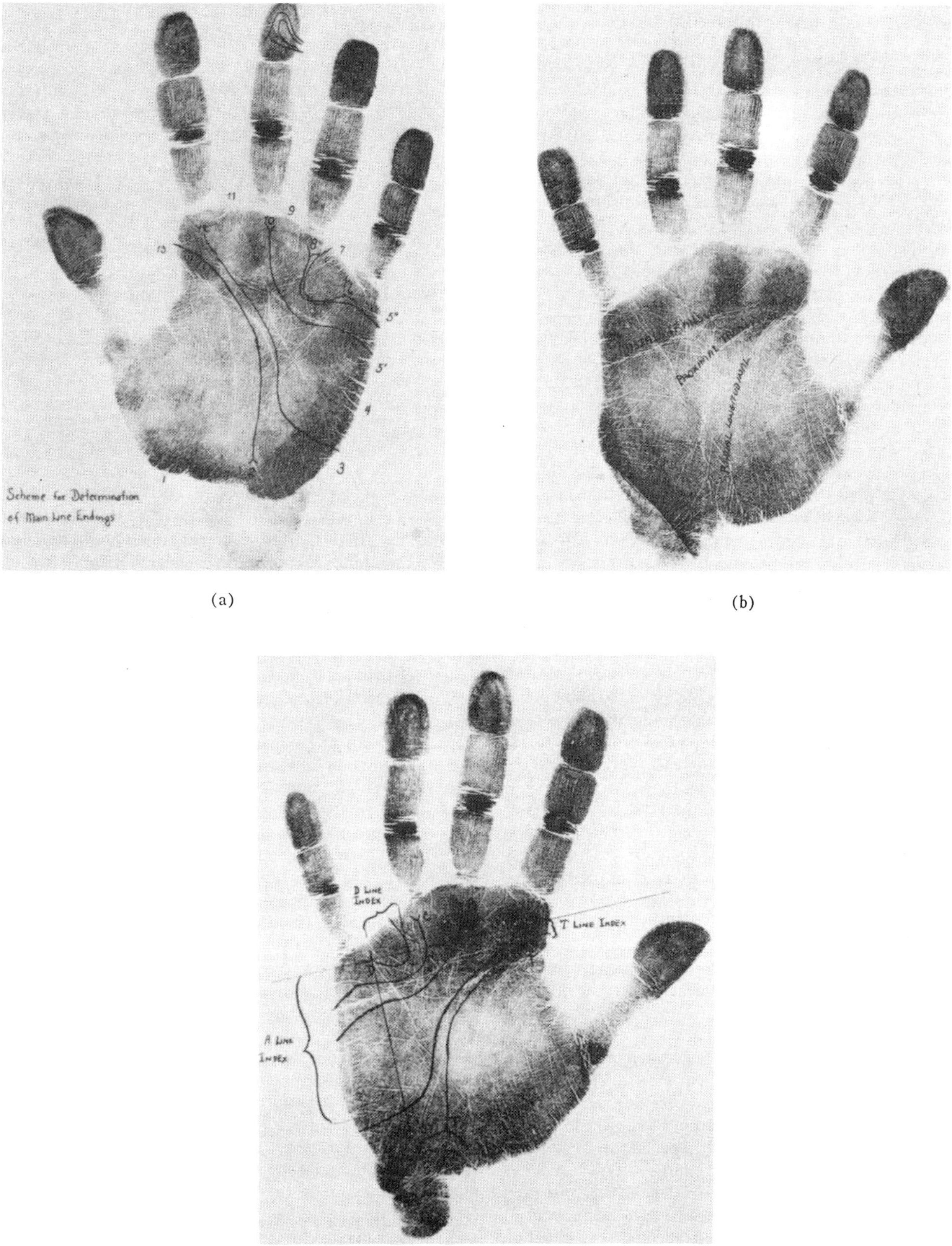

(a) (b)

(c)

Fig. 6. Typical features used in study of relationship of dermatoglyphics to human disease.

it is called the Minimum Residual Distance Method [157]; another example of its use is in the IBM Interactive System [63].

After solving for the eigenvectors of the lumped covariance matrix of the data being considered, the user could select any one, two, or three eigenvectors to define the linear projection subspace. The plane defined by eigenvectors corresponding to the two largest eigenvalues is the two-space which fits the data in the least squares sense. Scatter plots of data on this plane, in the course of interactive analysis, are shown in [29] and [63].

The most widely used *linear mapping which emphasizes class separability* is termed multiple discriminant analysis. It is the subject of an extensive literature [202] and many computer programs [30], [38] exist for it. The discriminant vectors defining the resulting space are obtained by solving a generalized eigenvector equation $(B-\lambda W)d=0$, where B is the between-class covariance matrix and W is the pooled-within-class covariance matrix. This expression results when the ratio of the between-class scatter d^TBd to the sum of the within class scatter d^TWd is maximized with respect to d. The mapping gives a space of dimension one less than the number of classes, or of dimension equal to feature space dimensionality, whichever is smaller. The first is the usual situation encountered in pattern recognition. A plot of 60 talker utterances in the space defined by the two eigenvectors corresponding to the two largest eigenvalues of a $W^{-1}B$ matrix calculated from a 16-dimensional summary associated with each utterance [58] shows that sometimes this method brings out cluster structure rather nicely.

For the two-class case the above gives the well-known Fisher Discriminant Function [47] which is easily understood as the line of projection obtained when the two centers of gravity (means) of the projected samples are separated as far as possible while keeping the total spread (variance) of the combined sample constant. Fig. 5 shows the histogram of samples of palm-print data projected on the Fisher discriminant, indicating the possibility of discriminating between normal subjects and those with Down's syndrome using dermatoglyphic features [174]. The possibility that dermatoglyphics—the ridged skin patterns found on the fingers and toes, the palms of the hand, and the soles of the feet in man—can be used in the diagnosis of mongolism, leukemia, schizophrenia, congenital rubella, and other human diseases, is now the subject of a number of serious investigations [114]. The relationship of certain specific patterns to various chromosome disorders was demonstrated sometime back [34] and the genetic basis of dermatoglyphic patterns is now taken seriously [85].

Studies of palm- and fingerprint patterns using OLPARS have been based on twenty-three features derived from the analysis described in the classic book on the subject [35]. Fig. 6 shows some of the features used. The features represent three groups of measurements: 1) pattern types such as whorls, loops, and arches on fingers and palms; 2) direction and termination of certain skin ridges on the palm; and 3) relative distances between certain reference points located on the palms. Preliminary results of the OLPARS' studies indicating the discriminatory potential of dermatoflyphic patterns have been reported for leukemia [174] and schizophrenia [175].

Additional investigations were carried out to investigate possible links between apparently disparate disorders and test

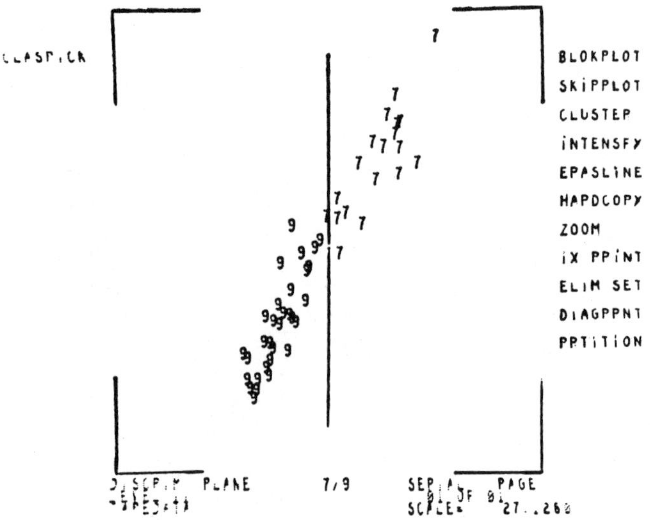

Fig. 7. Optimal discriminant plane mapping. Horizontal axis gives Fisher score. Vertical axis has score along orthogonal direction which satisfies same criterion as Fisher LDF.

the validity of some conjectures on the familial transmission of Down's syndrome. The optimal discriminant plane proved to be a very useful plot in these investigations. The optimal discriminant plane has the Fisher discriminant as one coordinate axis and the second is obtained under the constraint that it be orthogonal to the first while maximizing the same criterion used to derive the first direction. For example, Fig. 7 shows an optimal discriminant plane plot found useful in hand-print character-recognition application.

For the palm-print data, and various other applications of OLPARS, it was necessary to use nominal data, i.e., measurements which satisfied only a nominal scale. Since the OLPARS algorithms applied only to ordinal and cardinal data, termed "Discrete Type I" and "Continuous" measurements, respectively, a *discrete variable subsystem* (DVS) for OLPARS has been developed recently to handle nominal variables, which are called "Discrete Type II" measurements in the OLPARS final report. The DVS subsystem provides a number of suboptimal but feasible derivations of continuous measurements from Discrete Type II measurements. (These discrete to continuous measurement transformations may be viewed as computations estimating certain marginals in the parametric representation of the class conditional joint distributions of the discrete variables.) Mixed discrete and continuous measurements are handled by transforming the discrete measurements and adjoining the resulting variables to the set of continuous variables.

A normalizing transformation can be used [52] to extract the important features for separating two classes by finding the linear transformation which, applied to the autocorrelation matrix of the mixture of two classes, gives an identity matrix. The result is that the eigenvector with the largest eigenvalue for class 1 has the smallest eigenvalue for class 2 and so on. This has been applied to data grouping [53] and seems a good way to define a two-space with the eigenvectors having the largest eigenvalue in each class, respectively, serving as the coordinates.

Various solutions have been proposed to handle singularity of the pooled within-class covariance matrix W which enters into the eigenvector equation for finding the discriminant vectors. The pseudo-inverse matrix method has been a standard one in statistics and has been applied to pattern-recognition problems [199]. It restricts attention to the subspace in which the design samples lie. A modified discriminant analysis method [119] has been used in a speaker identification application. In this approach one first transforms the between class covariance matrix B to eliminate singularities, and in the transformed space sets up the eigenvector equation $B'^{-1}W'$, where the prime indicates a matrix in the transformed space, so that vectors corresponding to small eigenvalues are the desirable directions.

A pseudo-estimate different from the pseudo-inverse solution has been suggested in an imagery screening application [96], [71]. Bayesian arguments for such a pseudoestimate exist [3]. Experimental results obtained with this approach in certain problems were excellent but this has not always been the case [117]. Some IPACS at present offer the pseudo-inverse approach.

There exists substantial literature on the methods of *multidimensional scaling* and *parametric mapping* [165], [166], [101], [102], [167], [104], [25]. These methods have served as the basis for nonlinear mappings from multidimensional space to two- and three-space, for interactive graphic display of data [155], [156], [22]–[24].

Multidimensional scaling and parametric mapping are techniques for finding a configuration of data points, in the smallest dimensional space, that, according to some defined criterion, preserves the local structure of the points in the original n-dimensional space. Shepard's and Kruskal's methods need no more than a measure of similarity between the data points, whereas Shepard and Carroll's and Sammon's approaches require that there be a metric defined on the observation space.

Let d_{ij} be the distance from point i to point j in the original space and D_{ij} the distance between the ith and jth points in the lower dimensional space, and let W_{ij} be weights. The "stress" criterion of [101] is $\sum_{i,j} W_{ij}(d_{ij}-D_{ij})^2$ and the "continuity" criterion used in [167] is $\sum_{i,j} W_{ij}[(d_{ij}/D_{ij})]^2$. The procedure for finding the configuration in the lower dimensional space is to compute the d_{ij} in the original space, and starting with an arbitrary configuration of an equal number of data points in the new space, iteratively move them (using for example a steepest descent method) so as to minimize the criterion.

The mapping algorithms in [22], [23] used the continuity criterion of Shepard and Carroll. The apparent difference between the error criterion of the nonlinear mapping algorithm in OLPARS [156] and a stress criterion used in a particular version of a program for multidimensional scaling [25] has recently been explained [103]. In OLPARS the nonlinear mapping algorithm is specifically designed as an interactive program for mapping to two- and three-space.

It is possible that the data may tend to lie on a curve in the n-dimensional space; estimation of the parametric form of this curve would indicate the intrinsic dimensionality of the collection of data points. The methods for discovering intrinsic dimensionality [13], [181], [182], [184], [54], are closely related to the methods of multidimensional scaling. Bennett's method requires that the observation space be a metric space, and Trunk's method requires that it be a metric space with an inner product. The Fukunaga and Olsen algorithm differs in that it provides a method of specifying variable local regions and relies heavily on interactive operation [183], [55].

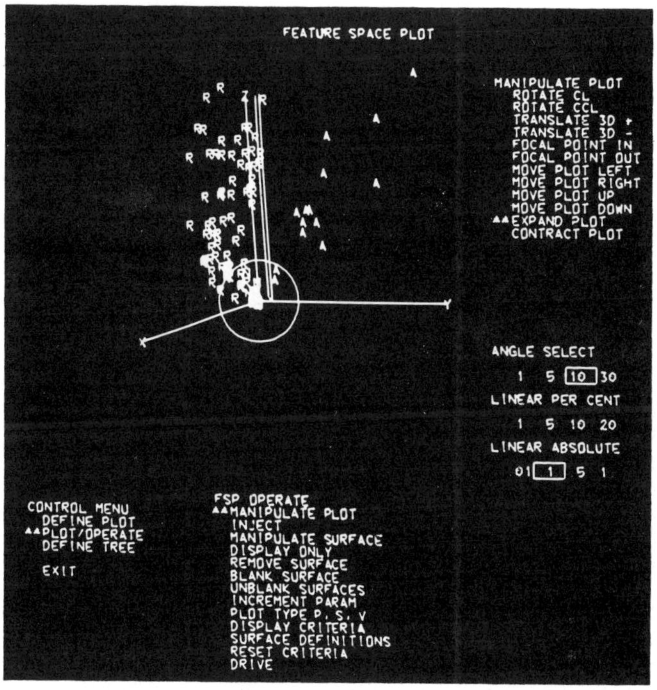

Fig. 8. SARF feature space plot. The circle shown is an inserted boundary.

Nonlinear or *generalized principal component analysis* is considered in [58]. Given a class of possible nonlinear coordinates, this approach, just like linear principal components, finds the coordinate along which the data variance is maximum, then obtains another, uncorrelated with the first, along which the variance is the next largest, and so on. An example of a quadratic principal component analysis is given in [58]. An example of a nonlinear mapping which emphasizes class separability for a two-class case, is the two-dimensional d display [56].

Space-filling curves are continuous mappings from the unit interval onto the n-dimensional unit hypercube. From the time (1891) that examples were provided by Hilbert [80] until recently, they have been of purely mathematical interest. The first application of space-filling curves [1] has been followed by applications in mathematical programming [19], bandwidth reduction [8], and computer-graphic display [133]. An algorithm generalizing Hilbert's curve to n dimensions was provided in [20]; alternative algorithms which are byte oriented are now available [21]. The computer-graphic application maps domains of multidimensional space onto subintervals of the unit interval in order to display an approximated probability density function for each of several classes so that their degree of separability may be visually determined [135].

A variety of *miscellaneous plots*—histograms, scatter plots, contour plots, two- and three-dimensional maps, pair-wise linkage, and association plots, etc.—have been developed to enable on-line graphical display of multidimensional data for interactive analysis. Options available in OLPARS, PROMENADE, and SARF are described in [155], [29], [70], [123], [124], respectively. Some other references related to this section are [62], [44], [109], [179], [32].

Fig. 8 shows a SARF feature space plot (FSP) of events from three categories. The FSP routine displays points in two- or three-dimensional feature spaces, where feature refers to both original and derived features. In this system, as in a number of others, the points to be displayed can be selected by category, subcategory, computational criteria, and/or by position relative to surfaces which are injected from the display into the feature space. In the UCSB speech system [77] scatter plots for two features at a time are used to develop a classification tree. Many of the systems provide the capability of rapidly stepping through a series of such plots.

In addition to the transformations of the original features described above, routines for *rank ordering feature subsets* or individual features have been considered for use in IPACS, and deserve some comment here. Various approaches to *selecting a subset* of a larger *set of features* have been proposed but there are both computational [120] and conceptual problems. For example, it has been demonstrated [180], [42] that the individually best feature out of a set of three binary features need not be a member of the set of two best features.

Raiffa [142] treated the problem of selecting features as a problem in the comparison of experiments [16] and suggested sequential and nonsequential procedures for selecting a subset of properties from a larger set. Bahadur [7] considered the problem of finding a good numerical index which would measure the effectiveness of a given set of properties in classification. Various measures of information, distance, and separation have been posed to serve this need but they may or may not bear any relation to classification error [89], [27], [78], [107]. Bahadur used the symmetric divergence, also called the Kullback–Leibler information number [105], to define an effective distance between two groups, and derived an approximate formula which indicated the contribution of any particular feature, to the distance.

Basically, the above approaches underlie many of the contributions on selecting a subset of features, which have appeared in the literature [74], [50], [122], [200], [110], [112].

The computational problems in using many of these techniques may be appreciated by the report [155] that for OLPARS on the CDC 1604, the estimated computation time for a simple method which uses the symmetric divergence to rank the measurements is about 18 times that estimated for a "discrimination" method which uses the following criterion: discrimination value of feature x_p for differentiating between class i and j, denoted by $M_{ij}(x_p)$, is the squared difference between the mean of x_p in each class, divided by the sum of the weighted variances of each class, with the variances being multiplied respectively, by one less than the number of samples for that class. For discriminating class i from all other classes, the measure used is

$$M_i(x_p) = \sum_{j \neq i} M_{ij}(x_p)$$

and an overall measure for x_p is

$$M(x_p) = \sum_i \sum_{j \neq i} M_{ij}(x_p).$$

It is interesting to note that $M_{ij}(x_p)$, which has been widely used on heuristic grounds, is also, essentially, the measure of separability for univariate distributions, which, following a conjecture [12], has been shown [27] to bear a simple relationship to the probability of error.

The overall measure $M(x_n)$ is of course suboptimal for the multivariate case but it is computationally easy, and is an interactive system where unimodality of classes can be estimated quickly, the method can be practically useful.

Another suboptimal measure of the discrimination ability of a feature, termed the probability of confusion measure, is used [157] where the unimodal class assumption cannot be justified. This method requires estimation of the marginal class distributions from sample data and is therefore computationally not as desirable as the previous method.

A reference of related interest is the article [119] which examines the virtues and faults of analysis of variance as a method for rank-ordering individual features [141]. There are many articles containing examples of stepwise discriminant analysis in which one variable at a time is entered into the set of discriminating variables [117]. Standard programming packages are available for this method [38].

Techniques for *pattern classification* abound. There is a voluminous literature on the subject, part of which has been surveyed in [82], [154], [41], [51]. Much of the rest through 1968 may be found cited in the bibliography [113].

Any worry about having to incorporate a vast number of the techniques covered by this staggering volume of literature into an IPACS should be dispelled by the experience reported thus far. It is well known that the vital difference to performance is made by the appropriateness of the features selected and by the analysis of the details of the within-class and between-class structure present in the data.

Some studies, e.g., [163], for the case of dichotomous variables have found that the Fisher linear discriminant function (LDF) compared rather favorably with certain competing "optimal" techniques. Experience also indicates [96], [93] that "appropriate" use of the Fisher LDF gives performance at least as good or better than most competing techniques, and is far superior to learning algorithms of the Perceptron and stochastic approximation type. If within class clusters and modes are identified, and some estimate of the class overlap can be obtained, then pair-wise-linear discriminants put together into a piecewise-linear decision logic, could be most effective. As we noted the Fisher discriminant and the optimal discriminant plane have proven useful prior to IPACS. With the on-line clustering and mapping capability of an IPACS, the approach has proven even more effective [157].

Following an initial analysis of sample data to determine the potential difficulty of the problem by estimating the modes in each class and the relative overlap of classes, the classes that are easily discriminated are taken care of. Then the more difficult cases are examined in greater detail. The on-line capability facilitates the strategy of designing and trying out simple logics first and determining their inadequacies before going on to more sophisticated methods.

An algorithm [46], [150] which performs an adaptive search for cluster centers while satisfying the constraint of known categories has been used in PROMENADE [70] to allocate a new datum point to the class of the nearest cluster center. It is reported [157] that in each of the many real data applications undertaken with OLPARS the piecewise-linear logic using the Fisher discriminant per each pair of clusters, has outperformed the nearest mean vector solution.

The detection of clusters using a projection option such as nonlinear mapping or eigenvector plot, and the insertion of a decision boundary, e.g., via the feature space plot display in SARF [123], [124], and the principal components or optimal discriminant plane in OLPARS [156], makes it easy to follow the strategy for designing a classification logic recommended earlier. More complicated decision procedures using K-nearest neighbor rules, recursive Bayesian estimation, and stochastic approximation are being proposed for INTERSPACE [131].

The preceding discussion pertains to the techniques which are currently being tried out. The usefulness of some of the simpler methods is well accepted. However, no consensus has been reached on the efficacy of the more sophisticated techniques. One of the major benefits of work on IPACS is likely to be a clearer identification of techniques which are not worth pursuing. This should have a significant impact not only on practical problem solving but also on future directions of theoretical research.

VI. Concluding Remarks

As a result of the developments in computer graphics (e.g., Hobbs [83], Prince [139], [140], Van Dam [189], Secrest and Nievergelt [164], Faiman and Nievergelt [45], Pankhurst [129], Parslow and Green [130]) and man–computer symbiosis (Licklider [111]), the partnership of man and the computer in the solution of problems is now available to investigators in a variety of fields; many of these fields are related to pattern recognition. Indeed, since recognizing patterns is, in one form or another, intrinsic to intelligent activity and since the search for regularities is the principal concern of scientific inquiry, it follows that the field of pattern recognition impinges upon all scientific inquiry and intelligent behavior. This has led, for example, to the comment "Is there—can there be—a field of inquiry devoted to what is called 'pattern recognition'? Almost certainly not . . ." (Neisser [121]).

Such comments have not prevented an influx of theoretical and experimental researchers into what is called pattern recognition—not only to probe further into the meaning of words such as "learning," "identification," "classification," and "recognition" (Sayre [162]) and to see what aspects of these functions could be automated (Kanal [90], Kanal and Chandrasekaran [93])—but also to develop tools for pattern analysis, classification, induction, and problem solving that are applicable to a variety of situations and fields. The interactive systems surveyed in this paper represent some attempts in this direction.

Taking advantage of the experience gained thus far, the next generation of IPACS could be very powerful, experimental facilities for solving practical pattern-recognition problems arising in a wide variety of fields. However, the significant resources needed to implement a truly effective interactive pattern analysis and classification system should not be underestimated. Such IPACS will flourish only in those environments in which the number and variety of problems provides economic viability. Otherwise, an IPACS is likely to go the way of SARF which, having been directed towards a certain area of defense research, fell victim to a lack of funding in that area.

Placing an IPACS in an open environment attracting a wide variety of users with different backgrounds should help the continual evolution of the system. This assumes that the people associated with the effort are capable in both computer systems and pattern recognition.

Because of the impact we feel IPACS will have on problem solving in pattern recognition, it is highly desirable to make this capability inexpensively and widely available. At present, both these attributes are missing. Work remains to be done on processor configurations and system organization to overcome these limitations while still satisfying the large data-handling and computational demands imposed by practical pattern-recognition problems. Also needed is the addition to IPACS of the next natural step, i.e., the development of a capability to do on-line modeling, for rarely is analysis and classification the end of our interest in a body of data.

Even as we sing the praises of experimental interactive pattern analysis classification and modeling, we must keep in mind that these are not a guarantee against poor use of resources nor a substitute for theory and thought. Difficult problems of pattern recognition will continue to require careful planning, time, and effort. However, in this effort we now seek some helping hands—the Rival of 1958 has been replaced by a Partner, the graphics-oriented IPACS.

Acknowledgment

Many people responded quickly to the author's request for papers, reports, and memoranda describing work related to IPACS by themselves and their colleagues. These letters and internal reports were useful in providing a perspective of current work in IPACS. The author thanks those concerned and regrets that limitations of space made it impossible to do full justice to each contribution. For example, descriptions of hardware and peripherals used to implement each IPACS have been omitted.

The author thanks G. G. Lendaris, J. W. Machanik, W. C. Neinow, and J. W. Sammon, Jr., for providing the photographs and illustrations which appear in the paper. The author is also grateful to A. K. Agrawala and A. E. Pottala for their critical reading of earlier drafts and their suggestions which led to many improvements in the paper.

References

[1] K. Abend, T. J. Harley, and L. N. Kanal, "Classification of binary random patterns," *IEEE Trans. Inform. Theory*, vol. IT-11, pp. 538–544, Oct. 1965.

[2] T. W. Anderson, *Introduction to Multivariate Analysis.* New York: Wiley, 1958.

[3] A. Ando and G. M. Kaufmann, "Bayesian analysis of the independent multinormal process—Neither mean nor precision known," *J. Amer. Statist. Ass.*, vol. 60, pp. 347–358, Mar. 1965.

[4] R. N. Ascher, G. M. Koppelman, M. J. Miller, G. Nagy, and G. L. Shelton, Jr., "An interactive system for reading unformatted printed text," *IEEE Trans. Comput.*, vol. C-20, pp. 1527–1543, Dec. 1971.

[5] R. Baecker, "Interactive computer-mediated animation," Project MAC, Tech. Rep. TR-61, June 1969.

[6] ——, "From the animated student to the animated computer to the animated film to the animated student . . . ," in *Proc. Purdue 1971 Symp. Applications of Computers to Electrical Engineering Education.*

[7] R. R. Bahadur, "On classification based on responses to n dichotomous items," in *USAF SAM Series in Statistics* (Randolph AFB, Tex.), 1959; also in *Studies in Item Analysis and Predication*, H. Solomon, Ed. Stanford, Calif.: Stanford Univ. Press, 1961, pp. 169–176.

[8] T. Bially, "Space-filling curves: Their generation and their application to bandwidth reduction," *IEEE Trans. Inform. Theory*, vol. IT-15, pp. 658–664, Nov. 1969.

[9] H. G. Ball, "Data analysis in the social sciences," in *1965 Fall Joint Computer Conf., AFIPS Conf. Proc.* Washington, D. C.: Thompson, 1965, pp. 533–560.

[10] ——, "A comparison of some cluster-seeking techniques," Rome Air Develop. Cen., Tech. Rep. TR-66-514, Nov. 1966.

[11] G. H. Ball and D. J. Hall, "A clustering technique summarizing multivariate data," *Behavior Sci.*, vol. 12, pp. 153–155, Mar. 1967.

[12] P. W. Becker, "Recognition of patterns using the frequencies of occurrence of binary words," *Polyteknisk Forlag* (Copenhagen, Denmark), 1968.

[13] R. S. Bennett, "The intrinsic dimensionality of signal collections," *IEEE Trans. Inform. Theory*, vol. IT-15, pp. 517–525, Sept. 1969.

[14] M. L. Berman, J. W. Machanik, and S. Shellans, "Project Merlin, a graphics operating system," in *Advanced Computer Graphics Economics, Techniques and Applications*, R. D. Parslow and R. E. Green, Eds. New York: Plenum, 1971, pp. 735–773.

[15] R. E. Bonner, "On some clustering techniques," *IBM J. Res. Develop.*, vol. 8, pp. 22–32, Jan. 1964.
[16] D. Blackwell and M. A. Girshick, *Theory of Games and Statistic Decisions.* New York: Wiley, 1956.
[17] A. Brain, G. Forsen, D. Hall, and C. Rosen, "A large self-contained learning machine," in *Proc. 1963 IEEE Western Electronics Conv.* (San Francisco, Calif.), 1963.
[18] J. S. Bryan, "Experiments in adaptive pattern recognition," *IRE Trans. Mil. Electron.*, vol. MIL-7, pp. 174–179, Apr.–July 1963.
[19] A. R. Butz, "Space filling curves and mathematical programming," *Inform. Cont.*, vol. 12, pp. 314–329, Apr. 1968.
[20] ——, "Convergence with Hilbert's space filling curve," *J. Comput. Syst. Sci.*, vol. 3, pp. 128–146, May 1969.
[21] ——, "Alternative algorithm for Hilbert's space-filling curve," *IEEE Trans. Comput.* (Short Notes), vol. C-20, pp. 424–426, Apr. 1971.
[22] T. W. Calvert, "Projections of multidimensional data for use in man-computer graphics," in *1968 Fall Joint Computer Conf., AFIPS Conf. Proc.*, vol. 33, pt. 1. Washington, D. C.: Spartan, 1968, pp. 227–231.
[23] ——, "Nonorthogonal projections for feature extraction in pattern recognition," *IEEE Trans. Comput.* (Short Notes), vol. C-19, pp. 447–452, May 1970.
[24] T. W. Calvert and T. Y. Young, "Randomly generated nonlinear transformations for pattern recognition," *IEEE Trans. Syst. Sci. Cybern.*, vol. SSC-5, pp. 266–273, Oct. 1969.
[25] J. D. Carroll, J. B. Kruskal, and M. Wish, "Multidimensional scaling and closely related topics—Selected, annotated references to papers, programs, and work in progress," Bell Lab. Memo., 1970.
[26] J. B. Chatten and C. F. Teacher, "Character recognition techniques for address reading," in *Optical Character Recognition*, Fischer *et al.*, Eds. New York: Spartan, 1962, pp. 51–59.
[27] H. Chernoff, "A bound on the classification error for discriminating between populations with specified means and variances," Dep. of Statistics, Stanford Univ., Stanford, Calif., Tech. Rep. 66, Jan. 1970.
[28] C. Christensen and E. N. Pinson, "Multi-function graphics for a large computer system," in *1967 Fall Joint Computer Conf., AFIPS Conf. Proc.*, vol. 31. Montvale, N. J.: AFIPS Press, 1967, pp. 697–711.
[29] D. B. Connell, D. W. Clark, B. K. Opitz *et al.*, "Programming package for on-line pattern recognition," Rome Air Develop. Cen., Final Tech. Rep. TR-70-139, Aug. 1970.
[30] W. W. Cooley and P. R. Lohnes, *Multivariate Procedures for the Behavioral Sciences.* New York: Wiley, 1962.
[31] I. W. Cotton and F. S. Greatorex, Jr., "Data structures and techniques for remote computer graphics," in *1968 Fall Joint Computer Conf., AFIPS Conf. Proc.*, vol. 33, pt. 1. Washington, D. C.: Spartan, 1968, pp. 533–544.
[32] G. M. Coulam, W. H. Dunnette, and E. H. Wood, "A computer-controlled scintiscanning system and associated computer graphic techniques for a study of regional distribution of blood flow," *Comput. Biomed. Res.*, vol. 3, pp. 249–273, June 1970.
[33] G. J. Culler, "An attack on the problems of speech analysis and synthesis with the power of an on-line system," in *Proc. Int. Joint Conf. Artificial Intelligence* (Washington, D. C., May 1967), pp. 41–48.
[34] H. Cummins, "Dermatoglyphic stigmata in mongoloid imbeciles," *Am. Neurolog. Ass. Trans.*, Rec. 7, vol. 73, p. 407, 1939.
[35] H. Cummins and C. Midlo, *Finger Prints, Palms and Soles.* New York: Dover, 1943, chs. 4 and 5.
[36] P. J. Denning, "Virtual memory," *Comput. Surveys*, vol. 2, pp. 153–189, Sept. 1970.
[37] M. L. Dertouzos, G. P. Jessel, and J. R. Stinger, "CIRCAL-2: General-purpose on-line circuit design," *Proc. IEEE*, vol. 60, pp. 39–48, Jan. 1972.
[38] W. J. Dixon, "Statistical packages in biomedical computation," in *Computers in Biomedical Research*, R. W. Stacy and B. D. Waxman, Eds. New York: Academic Press, 1965, ch. 3, pp. 47–64.
[39] ——, "Use of displays with packaged statistical programs," in *1967 Fall Joint Computer Conf., AFIPS Conf. Proc.*, vol. 31. Washington, D. C.: Spartan, 1967, pp. 481–484.
[40] ——, "The future of statistics in biomedical sciences," in *The Future of Statistics*, D. G. Watts, Ed. New York: Academic Press, 1968, pp. 47–60.
[41] R. O. Duda and P. E. Hart, *Pattern Classification and Scene Analysis.* New York: Wiley, 1972.
[42] J. D. Elashoff, R. M. Elashoff, and G. E. Goldman, "On the choice of variables in classification problems with dichotomous variables," *Biometrika*, vol. 54, pp. 668–670, 1967.
[43] *Encyclopedia of Stock Market Techniques.* New York: Simon and Schuster.
[44] J. W. Eusebio and G. H. Ball, "Isodata-lines—A program for describing multivariate data by piecewise-linear curves," in *Hawaii Syst. Sci. Conf.*, pp. 135–138, 1968.
[45] M. Faiman and J. Nievergelt, Eds., *Pertinent Concepts in Computer Graphics.* Urbana, Ill.: Univ. of Illinois Press, 1969.
[46] O. Firschein and M. Fischler, "Automatic subclass determination for pattern-recognition applications," *IEEE Trans. Electron. Comput.* (Corresp.), vol. EC-12, pp. 137–141, Apr. 1963.
[47] R. A. Fisher, "The use of multiple measurements in taxonomic problems," *Ann. Eugen.*, vol. 7, pp. 179–188, 1936.
[48] B. D. Fried, "On the user's point of view," in *Interactive Systems for Experimental Applied Mathematics*, M. Klerer and J. Reinfelds, Eds. New York: Academic Press, pp. 11–12, 1968.
[49] H. P. Friedman and J. Rubin, "On some invariant criteria for grouping data," *J. Amer. Statist. Ass.*, vol. 62, pp. 1159–1178, Dec. 1967.
[50] K. S. Fu, Y. T. Chien, and G. P. Cardillo, "A dynamic programming approach to sequential pattern recognition," *IEEE Trans. Electron. Comput.*, vol. EC-16, pp. 790–803, Dec. 1967.
[51] K. Fukunaga, *Introduction to Statistical Pattern Recognition.* New York: Academic Press, 1972.
[52] K. Fukunaga and W. L. G. Koontz, "Application of the Karhunen–Loève expansion to feature selection and ordering," *IEEE Trans. Comput.*, vol. C-19, pp. 311–318, Apr. 1970.
[53] ——, "A criterion and an algorithm for grouping data," *IEEE Trans. Comput.*, vol. C-19, pp. 917–923, Oct. 1970.
[54] K. Fukunaga and D. R. Olsen, "An algorithm for finding intrinsic dimensionality of data," *IEEE Trans. Comput.*, vol. C-20, pp. 176–183, Feb. 1971.
[55] ——, "Authors' reply to comments by G. V. Trunk on 'An algorithm for finding intrinsic dimensionality of data'," *IEEE Trans. Comput.* (Corresp.), vol. C-20, pp. 1615–1616, Dec. 1971.
[56] ——, "A two-dimensional display for the classification of multivariate data," *IEEE Trans. Comput.* (Short Notes), vol. C-20, pp. 917–923, Aug. 1971.
[57] A. Gamba, G. Palmieri, and R. Sanna, "Preliminary experimental results with PAPA, 2," *Suppl. Nuovo Cimento*, vol. 23, ser. X, pp. 280–284, 1960.
[58] R. Gnanadesikan and M. B. Wilk, "Data analytic methods in multivariate statistical analysis," in *Multivariate Analysis II*, P. R. Krishnaiah, Ed. New York: Academic Press, 1969, pp. 593–638.
[59] A. J. Goldstein, L. D. Harmon, and A. B. Lesk, "Man machine interaction in human face identification," *Bell Syst. Tech. J.*, vol. 51, pp. 399–427, 1972.
[60] R. M. Goldwyn, L. Loh, and J. H. Siegel, "The analysis of physiologic abnormalities in the critically ill using a time-sharing system for the conversational manipulation of a large data bank," in *Proc. Annu. Princeton Conf. Information Sciences and Systems*, p. 317, 1969.
[61] R. M. Goldwyn, M. Miller, H. P. Friedman, and J. H. Siegel, "The use of time-sharing and interactive graphics for the assessment of circulation in the critically ill," *IEEE Comput. Commun. Conf. Rec.* (IEEE Cat. 69C67-NVSEC), p. 121, 1969.
[62] R. M. Goldwyn, H. P. Friedman, and J. H. Siegel, "Iteration and interaction in computer data bank analysis: A case study in the physiologic classification and assessment of the critically ill," T. J. Watson Res. Cen., Yorktown Heights, N. Y., IBM Res. RC 3157, Dec. 1970.
[63] R. M. Goldwyn, H. P. Friedman, M. Miller, and J. H. Siegel, "An interactive system for complex data analysis—Command description," T. J. Watson Res. Cen., Yorktown Heights, N. Y., IBM Res. RC 3256, 1971.
[64] J. B. Goodenough, "A light-pen-controlled program for on-line data analysis," *Commun. Ass. Comput. Mach.*, vol. 8, no. 2, pp. 130–134, 1965.
[65] J. C. Gray, "Compound data structure for computer aided design: A survey," in *1967 Proc. Ass. Comput. Mach. Nat. Meeting.* Montvale, N. J.: AFIPS Press, 1967, pp. 355–365.
[66] G. F. Groner, "Realtime recognition of handprinted text," Rand Corp., Santa Monica, Calif., Memo. RM-5016-ARPA, ASTIA Doc. AD-341252, Oct. 1966.
[67] G. F. Groner, J. F. Heafner, and T. W. Robinson, "On-line computer classification of handprinted Chinese characters as a translation aid," *IEEE Trans. Electron. Comput.* (Short Notes), vol. EC-16, pp. 856–860, Dec. 1967.
[68] J. E. Guignon and R. M. Kline, "Development of an on-line image processing system," Comput. Syst. Lab., Washington Univ., St. Louis, Mo., Tech. Rep. TR 5, ASTIA Doc. AD-668966, Feb. 1968.
[69] D. J. Hall, G. H. Ball, and D. E. Wolf, "Applications of PROMENADE data-analysis system," *IEEE Comput. Commun. Conf. Rec.* (IEEE Cat. 69-C67-MUSEC), pp. 101–108, 1969.
[70] D. J. Hall, G. H. Ball, D. E. Wolf, and J. W. Eusebio, "PROMENADE—An improved interactive-graphics man-machine system for pattern recognition," Rome Air Develop. Cen., Tech. Rep. TR-68-572, June 1969.
[71] T. J. Harley, "Pseudoestimates versus pseudo-inverses for singular sample covariance matrices," sec. 2, ASTIA Doc. AD-427172, Sept. 1963.
[72] T. J. Harley, J. Bryan, L. Kanal, and D. Taylor, "Semi-automatic imagery screening—Research study and experimental investigation," Philco Reports, Contract DA-36-039-SC-90742, ASTIA Docs. AD-293616 and AD-4193616, 1962–1963.
[73] T. J. Harley, L. N. Kanal, and N. C. Randall, "System considerations for automatic imagery screening," in *Pictorial Pattern Recog-*

nition, G. C. Cheng *et al.*, Eds. Washington, D. C.: Thompson, 1968, pp. 15–32.

[74] P. E. Hart, "A brief survey of preprocessing for pattern recognition," Defense Documentation Cen., Washington, D. C., ASTIA Doc. AD-647275, 1967.

[75] J. A. Hartigan, "Representation of similarity matrices by trees," *J. Amer. Statist. Ass.*, vol. 62, pp. 1140–1158, Dec. 1967.

[76] D. O. Harris, J. A. Howard, and R. C. Wood, "Research in on-line computation," Univ. of California, Santa Barbara, Calif., Rep. AFCRL-70-0535, June 1970.

[77] ——, "Research in on-line computation," University of California, Santa Barbara, Calif., Final Rep. on AFCRL Contract, Aug. 31, 1971.

[78] T. L. Henderson and D. G. Lainiotis, "Comments on linear feature extraction," *IEEE Trans. Inform. Theory* (Corresp.), vol. IT-15, pp. 728–730, Nov. 1969.

[79] N. M. Herbst and P. M. Will, "An experimental laboratory for pattern recognition and signal processing," *Commun. Ass. Comput. Mach.*, vol. 15, pp. 231–244, Apr. 1972.

[80] D. Hilbert, "Ueber die stetige Abbildung einer Linie auf ein Flachenstuck," *Math. Ann.*, vol. 38, pp. 459–460, Mar. 1891.

[81] D. R. Hill, "Man–machine interaction using speech," in *Advances in Computers*, F. L. Alt *et al.*, Eds. New York: Academic Press, 1971. pp. 165–230.

[82] Y. C. Ho and A. K. Agrawala, "On pattern classification algorithms —Introduction and survey," *Proc. IEEE*, vol. 56, pp. 2101–2114, Dec. 1968.

[83] L. C. Hobbs, "Display applications and technology," *Proc. IEEE*, vol. 54, pp. 1870–1884, Dec. 1966.

[84] A. Hoffman, "The 'whirling dervish,' a simulation study in learning and recognition systems," in *1962 IRE Int. Conv. Rec.*, pt. 4, pp. 153–160, 1962.

[85] S. B. Holt, *The Genetics of Dermal Ridges*. Springfield, Ill.: Charles C Thomas, 1968.

[86] H. Hotelling, "Analysis of a complex of statistical variables into principal components," *J. Educ. Psychol.*, vol. 24, pp. 417–441, 498–520, 1933.

[87] C. I. Johnson, "Interactive graphics in data processing: Principles of interactive systems," *IBM Syst. J.*, vol. 7, nos. 3 and 4, pp. 147–173, 1968.

[88] J. D. Joyce and M. J. Cianciolo, "Reactive displays: Improving man-machine graphical communication," in *1967 Fall Joint Computer Conf., AFIPS Conf. Proc.*, vol. 31. Montvale, N. J.: AFIPS Press, 1967, pp. 713–721.

[89] T. Kailath, "The divergence and Bhattacharya distance measures in signal selection," *IEEE Trans. Commun. Technol.*, vol. COM-15, pp. 52–60, Feb. 1967.

[90] L. N. Kanal, *Pattern Recognition*. Washington, D. C.: Thompson, 1968: Silver Spring, Md.: L.N.K. Inc.

[91] ——, "Review of 'Target detection, prenormalization and learning machines', by M. R. Uffelman," in *Comput. Rev.*, no. 18004, p. 562, Dec. 1969.

[92] L. Kanal and B. Chandrasekaran, "On dimensionality and sample size in statistical pattern classification," in *Proc. Nat. Electronics Conf.*, 1968, pp. 2–7: also in *Pattern Recognition*, vol. 3, 1971, pp. 225–234.

[93] ——, "Recognition, machine 'récognition,' and statistical approaches," in *Methodologies of Pattern Recognition*, M. S. Watanabe, Ed. New York: Academic Press, 1969, pp. 317–332.

[94] ——, "On linguistic, statistical and mixed models for pattern recognition," Univ. of Maryland Comput. Sci. Cen., College Park, Md., Tech. Rep. TR-152, Mar. 1971. To appear in *Frontiers of Pattern Recognition*, M. S. Watanabe, Ed. New York: Academic Press, 1972.

[95] L. Kanal and T. J. Harley, Jr., "The complexity of patterns and pattern recognition systems," Aerosp. Med. Res. Lab., Wright-Patterson AFB, Ohio, Tech. Rep. AMRL-TR-69-62, Nov. 1969.

[96] L. N. Kanal and N. C. Randall, "Recognition system design by statistical analysis," in *Proc. 19th Nat. Ass. Comput. Mach. Conf.* New York: Ass. Comput. Mach., 1964, pp. D2.5-1–D2.5-10.

[97] L. Kanal, F. Slaymaker, D. Smith, and W. Walker, "Basic principles of some pattern recognition systems," in *Proc. Nat. Electronics Conf.* (Chicago, Ill.), 1962, pp. 279–295.

[98] M. Klerer and J. Reinfelds, Eds., *Interactice Systems for Experimental Applied Mathematics*. New York: Academic Press, 1968.

[99] K. C. Knowlton, "Computer-animated movies," in *Emerging Concepts in Computer Graphics*, Secrest and Nievergelt, Eds. New York: Benjamin Publishing Co., 1968, pp. 343–370.

[100] D. E. Knuth, *The Art of Computer Programming*. New York: Addison-Wesley, 1968, vol. I, ch. 2.

[101] J. B. Kruskal, "Multidimensional scaling by optimizing goodness of fit to a nonmetric hypothesis," *Psychometrika*, vol. 29, pp. 1–27, Mar. 1964.

[102] ——, "Nonmetric multidimensional scaling," *Psychometrika*, vol. 29, pp. 115–129, June 1964.

[103] ——, "Comments on 'A nonlinear mapping for data structure analysis'," *IEEE Trans. Comput.* (Corresp.), vol. C-20, p. 1614, Dec. 1971.

[104] J. B. Kruskal and J. D. Carroll, "Geometric models and badness-of-fit functions," in *Multivariate Analysis*, vol. 2. New York: Academic Press, 1969, pp. 639–671.

[105] S. Kullback, *Information Theory and Statistics*. New York: Wiley, 1959.

[106] F. F. Kuo and N. G. Magnuson, Eds., *Computer Oriented Circuit Design*. New York: Prentice-Hall, 1969.

[107] D. G. Lainiotis, "A class of upper bounds on probability of error for multihypotheses pattern recognition," in *IEEE Trans. Inform. Theory* (Corresp.), vol. IT-15, pp. 730–731, Nov. 1969.

[108] G. G. Lendaris and G. L. Stanley, "Diffraction-pattern sampling for automatic pattern recognition," *Proc. IEEE*, vol. 58, pp. 198–216, Feb. 1970.

[109] R. G. Leonard and D. L. Tebbe, "Graphical displays for the interactive analysis of relations between dichotomous variables," in *Proc. SMC Conf.* (San Francisco, Calif.), 1968, pp. 191–200.

[110] P. M. Lewis, II, "The characteristic selection problem in recognition systems," *IRE Trans. Inform. Theory*, vol. IT-8, pp. 171–178, Feb. 1962.

[111] J. C. R. Licklider, "Man–computer symbiosis," *IRE Trans. Hum. Factors Electron.*, vol. HFE-1, pp. 4–11, Mar. 1960.

[112] C. N. Liu, "A programmed algorithm for designing multifont character recognition logics," *IEEE Trans. Electron. Comput.*, vol. EC-13, pp. 586–593, Oct. 1964.

[113] C. J. W. Mason, "Pattern recognition bibliography," *IEEE SMC Group Newsletter*, 1970.

[114] "Dermatoglyphysics," in *Medical World News*, pp. 24–29, July 31, 1970.

[115] Merlin System, "Large data base tapped interactively by storage terminals," *Comput. Decisions*, June 1970.

[116] Merlin System, *User's Guide*. New York: Merlin Systems Corp., 1970.

[117] R. G. Miller "Statistical prediction by discriminant analysis," *Meteorol. Monogr.*, vol. 4, no. 25. Boston, Mass.: Amer. Meteorol. Soc., Oct. 1962.

[118] J. Minker and J. D. Sable, "Relational data system study," Rome Air Develop. Cen., Tech. Rep. TR-70-180, Sept. 1970.

[119] W. S. Mohn, Jr., "Two statistical feature evaluation techniques applied to speaker identification," *IEEE Trans. Comput.*, vol. C-20, pp. 979–987, Sept. 1971.

[120] G. Nagy, "State of the art in pattern recognition," *Proc. IEEE*, vol. 56, pp. 836–862, May 1968.

[121] U. Neisser, Review of "Recognizing patterns: Studies in living and automatic systems," *Amer. Sci.*, vol. 56, no. 4, pp. 464A–465A, 1968.

[122] G. D. Nelson and D. M. Levy, "A dynamic programming approach to the selection of pattern features," *IEEE Trans. Syst. Sci. Cybern.*, vol. SSC-4, pp. 145–151, July 1968.

[123] W. C. Nienow, "Signature analysis research facility (SARF) users' manual," Delco Electron. Rep. OM71-03, June 1971.

[124] ——, "Analysis of engine emission data using SARF," Delco Electron. Publ., Tech. Rep. TR71-45, Sept. 1971.

[125] W. C. Nienow and B. P. Miller, "Analysis of submarine echoes in an ice environment using signature analysis research facility (SARF)," in *Proc. 14th Tech. Conf. on Naval Minefield* (United States Naval Ordnance Lab., White Oak, Md., Jan. 1971).

[126] ——, "Analysis of submarine echoes in an ice environment using SARF II," Delco Electron. Publ., Tech. Rep. TR71–53, Santa Barbara, Calif., Nov. 1971.

[127] M. Okamota, "Optimality of principal components," in *Multivariate Analysis II*, P. R. Krish'naiah, Ed. New York: Academic Press, 1969, pp. 673–685.

[128] B. K. Opitz *et al.*, "Feature definition and extraction," Rome Air Develop. Cen., Tech. Rep. TR-70-179, Sept. 1970.

[129] R. J. Pankhurst, "Computer graphics," in *Advances in Information System Science*, vol. III, J. T. Tou, Ed. New York: Plenum, 1970.

[130] R. D. Parslow and R. E. Green, *Advanced Computer Graphics, Economics, Techniques and Applications*. New York: Plenum, 1971.

[131] E. A. Patrick, "INTERSPACE: Interactive system for pattern analysis, classification and enhancement," in *IEEE Comp. and Commun. Conf. Rec.* (IEEE Cat. 69C67-MVSEC), pp. 113–120, Sept. 1969.

[132] ——, "Interactive pattern analysis and classification utilizing prior knowledge," *Pattern Recogn.*, vol. 3, pp. 53–71, 1971.

[133] E. A. Patrick, D. R. Anderson, and F. K. Bechtel, "Mapping multidimensional space to one dimension for computer output display," *IEEE Trans. Comput.*, vol. C-17, pp. 949–953, Oct. 1968.

[134] E. A. Patrick, F. P. Fischer, and L. Y. L. Shen, "Computer analysis and classification of waveforms and pictures, part I—Waveforms," Rome Air Develop. Cen., Tech. Rep. TR-EE69-23, July 1969.

[135] E. A. Patrick and F. P. Fischer, II, "Cluster mapping with experimental computer graphics," *IEEE Trans. Comput.*, vol. C-18, pp. 987–991, Nov. 1969.

[136] T. Pavlidis, "Linguistic analysis of waveforms," in *Software Engineering*, vol. 2, J. T. Tou, Ed. New York: Academic Press,

1971, pp. 203–225.
[137] K. Pearson, "On line and planes of closest fit to systems of points in space," *Phil. Mag.*, vol. 6, no. 2, pp. 559–572, 1901.
[138] H. Pipberger, M. A. Schneiderman, and J. D. Klingeman, "The love-at-first-sight effect in research," *Circulation*, vol. 38, pp. 822–825, Nov. 1968.
[139] M. D. Prince, "Man-computer graphics for computer-aided design," *Proc. IEEE*, vol. 54, pp. 1698–1708, Dec. 1966.
[140] ——, *Interactive Graphics for Computer-Aided Design.* Reading, Mass.: Addison-Wesley, 1971.
[141] S. Pruzansky and M. V. Mathews, "Talker recognition procedure based on analysis of variance," *J. Acoust. Soc. Amer.*, vol. 36, pp. 2041–2047, Nov. 1964.
[142] H. Raiffa, "Statistical decision theory approach to item selection for dichotomous test and criterion variables," in *Studies in Item Analysis and Prediction*, H. Solomon, Ed. Stanford, Calif.: Stanford Univ. Press, 1957, pp. 187–220.
[143] C. R. Rao, *Advanced Statistical Methods in Biometric Research.* New York: Wiley, 1952.
[144] ——, "The use and interpretation of principal component analysis in applied research," *Sankhya*, vol. A26, pp. 329–358, 1964.
[145] ——, *Linear Statistical Inference and Its Applications.* New York: Wiley, 1965.
[146] D. R. Reddy, "Computer recognition of connected speech," *J. Acoust. Soc. Amer.*, vol. 42, pp. 329–347, 1967.
[147] D. R. Reddy, L. D. Erman, and R. B. Neely, "The CMU speech recognition project," in *Proc. IEEE 1970 Syst. Sci. Cybern. Conf.* (Pittsburgh, Pa.), pp. 234–238, Oct. 1970.
[148] D. R. Reddy and P. J. Vicens, "A procedure for the segmentation of connected speech," *J. Audio Eng. Soc.*, vol. 16, pp. 404–611, 1968.
[149] R. Roper, "An interactive operating system for multivariate data compression and classification," Systems Res. Lab., Dayton, Ohio, Final Rep. AFCRL-71-0462, Contract F19628-70-C-0108, 1971.
[150] C. A. Rosen and D. J. Hall, "A pattern recognition experiment with near-optimum results," *IEEE Trans. Electron. Comput.* (Corresp.), vol. EC-15, pp. 666–667, Aug. 1966.
[151] F. Rosenblatt, (1960), "Perceptron simulation experiments," *Proc. IRE*, vol. 48, pp. 301–309, Mar. 1960.
[152] A. Rosenfeld, *Picture Processing by Computer.* New York: Academic Press, 1969.
[153] D. T. Ross, "AED approach to generalized computer-aided design," in *Proc. Ass. Comput. Mach. Nat. Meet.*, pp. 367–385, 1967.
[154] D. Rutovitz, "Pattern recognition," *J. Roy. Stat. Soc.*, Ser. B, pt. 4, pp. 504–530, 1966.
[155] J. W. Sammon, Jr., "On-line pattern analysis and recognition system (OLPARS)," Rome Air Develop. Cen., Tech. Rep. TR-68-263, Aug. 1968.
[156] ——, "A nonlinear mapping for data structure analysis," *IEEE Trans. Comput.*, vol. C-18, pp. 401–409, May 1969.
[157] ——, "Interactive pattern analysis and classification," *IEEE Trans. Comput.*, vol. C-19, pp. 594–616, July 1970.
[158] ——, "An optimal discriminant plane," *IEEE Trans. Comput.* (Short Notes), vol. C-19, pp. 826–829, Sept. 1970.
[159] J. W. Sammon, Jr., D. B. Connell, and B. K. Opitz, "Programs for on-line pattern analysis," Rome Air Develop. Cen., Tech. Rep. TR-177 (2 vols.), Sept. 1971
[160] J. W. Sammon, Jr., A. H. Proctor, and D. E. Roberts, "An interactive graphic subsystem for pattern analysis," *Pattern Recogn.*, vol. 3, pp. 37–52, 1971.
[161] J. W. Sammon, Jr., and J. H. Sanders, "The waveform processing subsystem (WPS)," P.A.R. Inc., Rep. 72-26, Feb. 1972.
[162] K. M. Sayre, *Recognition-A study in the Philosophy of Artificial Intelligence.* Notre Dame, Ind.: Notre Dame Press, 1965.
[163] E. L. Schaefer, "On discrimination using qualitative variables," Ph.D. dissertation in statistics, Univ. of Michigan (University Microfilms, Inc.), Ann Arbor, Mich., 1966.
[164] D. Secrest and J. Nievergelt, Eds., *Emerging Concepts in Computer Graphics.* New York: Benjamin, 1968.
[165] R. N. Shepard, "The analysis of proximities: Multidimensional scaling with an unknown distance function I," *Psychometrika*, vol. 27, pp. 125–140, June 1962.
[166] ——, "The analysis of proximities: Multidimensional scaling with an unknown distance function II," *Psychometrika*, vol. 27, pp. 219–245, Sept. 1962.
[167] R. N. Shepard and J. D. Carroll, "Parametric representation of nonlinear data structures," in *Multivariate Analysis*, P. R. Krishnarah, Ed. New York: Academic Press, 1966, pp. 561–592.
[168] J. H. Siegel, L. Loh, M. Miller, and R. M. Goldwyn, "An interactive computer system to aid the physician in care oriented clinical research to benefit the critically ill," T. J. Watson Res. Cen., Yorktown Heights, N. Y., Rep. RC 2918, 1970.
[169] R. F. Simmons, "Natural language question-answering systems," *Comm. Assoc. Comput. Mach.*, vol. 13, pp. 15–30, 1969.
[170] R. R. Singers, "TSAP—A time series analysis package for terminal use," M.Sc., thesis, Computer Sci. Cen., Univ. of Maryland, College Park, Md., 1972.
[171] L. B. Smith, "A survey of interactive graphical systems for mathematics," *Comput. Surv.*, vol. 2, pp. 261–301, 1970.
[172] G. L. Stanley, W. C. Nienow, and G. G. Lendaris, "SARF, an interactive signature analysis research facility," in *Purdue Centennial Symp. on Informat. Processing*, vol. 2, pp. 436–448, Apr. 1969.
[173] G. L. Stanley and W. C. Nienow, "Initial investigation of application of SARF to engine diagnostic data," AC Electronics, D. R. L. Publ. S69-13, May 1969.
[174] D. Stowens and J. W. Sammon, Jr., "Dermatoglyphics and leukemia," *Lancet*, pp. 846, Apr. 18, 1970.
[175] D. Stowens, J. W. Sammon, Jr., and A. Proctor, "Dermatoglyphics in female schizophrenia," *Psychiatric Quart.*, vol. 44, pp. 516–532, July 1970.
[176] E. Strassbourger, "The role of the cepstrum in speech recognition," in *Proc. 1972 Int. Conf. on Speech Communication and Processing* (Boston, Mass.), Apr. 1972.
[177] D. Streeter and J. Raviv, "Research on advanced computer methods for biological data processing," Report IBM Corp., Tech. Rep. AMRL TR-66-24, 1966, ASTIA Doc. AD 637 452, 1966.
[178] H. L. Stubbs, "Discriminatory analysis applied to speech sound recognition," in *IRE 1954 Nat. Conv. Rec.*, pt. 4, pp. 41–44, 1954.
[179] H. Thompson, Jr., and M. Woodbury, "Clinical data representation in multidimensional space," *Comput. Biomed. Res.*, vol. 3, pp. 58–73, 1970.
[180] G. T. Toussaint, "Note on optimal selection of independent binary-valued features for pattern recognition," *IEEE Trans. Inform. Theory* (Corresp.), vol. IT-17, p. 618. Sept. 1971.
[181] G. V. Trunk, "Representation and analysis of signals: Statistical estimation of intrinsic dimensionality and parameter identification," *Gen. Syst.*, vol. 13, pp. 49–76, 1968.
[182] ——, "Statistical estimation of the intrinsic dimensionality of data collections," *Inform. Contr.*, vol. 12, pp. 508–525, May–June 1968.
[183] ——, "Comment on 'An algorithm for finding intrinsic dimensionality of data'," *IEEE Trans. Comput.* (Corresp.), vol. C-20, p. 1615, Dec. 1971.
[184] ——, "Parameter identification using intrinsic dimensionality," *IEEE Trans. Inform. Theory*, vol. IT-18, pp. 126–133, Jan. 1972.
[185] J. W. Tukey, "The future of data analysis," *Ann. Math. Stat.*, vol. 33, pp. 1–67, Mar. 1962.
[186] UAIDE (1968–1971), *Proceedings of the 1968, 1969, 1970 and 1971 Users of Automatic Information Display Equipment Conference.* San Diego, Calif.: Stromberg Datagraphic, 1968–1971.
[187] M. R. Uffelman, "CONFLEX 1," in *IRE Int. Conv. Rec.*, vol. 10, pt. 4, 1962.
[188] ——, "Target detection, prenormalization, and learning machines," in *Pictorial Pattern Recognition*, G. C. Cheng *et al.*, Eds. Washington, D. C.: Thompson, 1968, pp. 503–521.
[189] A Van Dam, "Data and storage structure for interactive graphics," in *Proc. Symp. on Data Structure in Programming Languages*, J. T. Tou and P. Wegner, Eds., vol. 6, pp. 237–267, Feb. 1971.
[190] P. Vicens, "Aspects of speech recognition by computer," Stanford Univ., Stanford, Calif., Computer Sci. Dep. Rep. CS127. Apr. 1969.
[191] A. Wald, "Contributions to the theory of statistical estimation and testing hypotheses," *Ann. Math. Stat.*, vol. 10, pp. 299–326, 1939.
[192] C. M. Walter, "The experimental dynamic processor DX-1," in *IRE Int. Conv. Rec.*, vol. 10, pt. 9, pp. 151–156, 1962.
[193] ——, "Signal representation and measurement data manipulation in *N*-space using an on-line PDP system," *Proc. Dig. Equip. Computer Users Soc.* (Maynard, Mass.), 1963.
[194] ——, "Color—A new dimension in man-machine graphics," in *Proc. IFIP Cong. 1965*, vol. 2, pp. 579–581, 1965.
[195] ——, "On-line computer-based aids for the investigation of sensor data compression, transmission and delay problems," in *1966 Proc. Nat. Telemetry Conf.*, May 1966.
[196] ——, "Status report on some applications of processor controlled color displays in signal analysis—1957 to 1967," in *DECUS—Digital Equipment Computer Users Soc. Proc. Spring Symp.*, pp. 21–30, 1967.
[197] ——, "Some comments on interactive systems applied to the reduction and interpretation of sensor data," in *IEEE Computers and Communications Conf. Rec.* (IEEE Special Publ. 69 C67-MVSEC), pp. 109–112, 1969.
[198] S. Watanabe, *Knowing and Guessing.* New York: Wiley, 1969.
[199] W. G. Wee, "Generalized inverse approach to adaptive multiclass pattern classification," *IEEE Trans. Comput.*, vol. C-17, pp. 1157–1164, Dec. 1968
[200] ——, "On feature selection in a class of distribution-free pattern classifiers," *IEEE Trans. Inform. Theory*, vol. IT-16, pp. 47–55. Jan. 1970.
[201] B. Widrow, "Generalization and information storage in networks of Adaline 'neurons'," in *Self-Organizing Systems.* Washington, D. C.: Spartan, 1962.
[202] S. S. Wilks, *Mathematical Statistics.* New York: Wiley, 1962.
[203] R. Williams, "A survey of data structures for computer graphics systems," *Comput. Surv.*, vol. 3, pp. 2–21, Mar. 1971.
[204] T. Young and W. Huggins, "Representation of electrocardiograms by orthogonalized exponentiaos," ASTIA Doc. AD 256 364, 1961.

SYSTEM CONSIDERATIONS FOR AUTOMATIC IMAGERY SCREENING

T. J. HARLEY, JR., L. N. KANAL AND N. C. RANDALL

System Sciences Laboratory
Philco-Ford Corporation
Blue Bell, Pennsylvania

1. INTRODUCTION

There is a large and steadily growing body of literature on the theory and techniques of pattern classification; however, very few papers have dealt with the problems of developing effective systems for real world pattern recognition tasks.

For several years, we have been actively investigating the theoretical aspects of pattern classification and appreciate the need for continued research on theory, techniques and devices in this area. But we have also been deeply involved in programs aimed at the development of useful recognition systems. This paper describes some of the things we have learned.

Our approach is problem oriented; that is, we consider a specific recognition problem that requires a solution and then determine what techniques are suitable for solving it. This is in contrast to a technique-oriented approach in which a specific technique is developed and then attempts are made to find existing problems to which it might be applicable.

The specific problem we consider here is the screening of tactical aerial reconnaissance imagery, primarily photographs. Screening has been defined as: "Gross selection, early in the total interpretation process, to identify those areas in the total supply of imagery which

Reprinted from *Pictorial Pattern Recognition*, pp. 15–31, 1968. Published by Thompson Book Company, Washington D.C., 1968.

meet the minimum qualifications for further interpretation by a human". This type of operation is required in order to reduce the large amounts of imagery that are obtained from aerial reconnaissance. When the amount of information has been sufficiently reduced, a human can then perform the photointerpretation task. It should be noted that no attempt is being made here to design a machine which will actually do photointerpretation. The screening task appears to be a natural one for computer-type machines, since they can provide high speed operation and do not get fatigued or bored as humans do. Furthermore, the operation required is one that can presently be done by humans.

There are a number of aspects to the imagery screening problem. However, the most important and most difficult to solve is that of detecting discrete tactical targets such as armored vehicles, aircraft, fortifications, and artillery. The detection of such small tactical targets can provide the basic language for the performance of more complex tasks. For example, suppose the present locations of all enemy armored vehicles can be made quickly available to a computer. This data can be combined with less volatile information on such items as terrain type, location of strategic targets (e.g., bridges, airfields, villages), and the deployment of friendly forces to establish the location and perhaps the mission of an armored brigade, particularly if repeat cover photography is available over a suitable time scale in order to establish the direction of movement of the armor. Indeed, there are a great number of ways in which the data generated by a target detection device could be used, but consideration of these is not central to the purpose of this paper. Our intent here is to consider the specific problem of quickly and reliably detecting discrete tactical targets in a large amount of imagery.

We attempt to demonstrate in this paper that the constraints of the imagery screening problem lead to the selection of a type of machine implementation, the form of the decision logic, methods for the logic design, and even techniques for evaluating candidate systems.

2. ESTABLISHMENT OF SYSTEM PARAMETERS

In order to clearly illustrate the point of this paper, it is necessary to assume specific values for a set of system parameters. The values selected should be regarded as typical and could vary by a factor of at least two or three in either direction. However, the force of the arguments is not greatly dependent on the exact numbers used.

The first parameter value to be established is that of the resolution, referenced to the object or ground plane, required to detect targets. The question becomes: What resolution is required to reliably detect tactical targets from the air? This parameter is perhaps the most critical of all those to be assigned since its influence on the overall system parameters is very great, perhaps varying as the third or fourth power. One approach to arriving at accurate figures for this parameter is to determine what resolution is required by humans for good performance. On the basis of practical experience, a value of one foot ground resolution seems reasonable; in some imagery, no more resolution is available.

Next, the coverage of a typical frame of photography is established as one thousand feet by one thousand feet, giving rise to a million resolution elements per frame. This is typical of imagery provided by the Army for imagery screening investigations in the early-to-mid-1960's.*

The target size is taken to be 12 ft. by 25 ft., representing typical dimensions of tactical targets, and allowing a small border for improved detection reliability. This means that there are 300 resolution elements in an area occupied by a target.

There is, of course, no *a priori* knowledge about the orientation of the target on the photograph, and there are very few targets with significant rotational symmetry (oil tanks seem to be a favorite object for experiments in target recognition because of their symmetry). Most target detection systems which have been proposed utilize an orientation search in order to ensure detection of the target regardless of which direction it is pointing. It is assumed here that the detection logic will have approximately a plus or minus three degree tolerance. This figure is consistent with the results of experiments performed at Philco-Ford, and also with the fact that a 2 1/2 degree rotation displaces the end element of the 12×25 element array by one element. This means that, at each position on the frame, 60 different orientations must be tested in order to detect the target reliably.

Some people familiar with optical correlators have questioned the

*** It was pointed out by a member of the audience at the Symposium that resolutions approaching 10,000 elements across a frame are now available from military reconnaissance. The ground resolution involved, and the area coverage of a single frame, depend, of course, on the scale factor used. At one foot ground resolution, one would have about 100 million elements to consider per frame. Such figures only serve to strengthen the force of the arguments presented in this paper.**

necessity for a rotation search. It has been suggested that it is only necessary to rotate the target mask (or spatial filter, or hologram, etc.) while integrating the correlation function over all rotations. Then by scanning the integrated correlation function, one may determine the presence or absence of the target in question. However, this reasoning is fallacious, since if the integration is linear, this is exactly equivalent to using, without rotation, a single mask generated by rotating the sample target about its center. A mask of this sort is certainly going to give inferior performance.

Another possibility is to generate scans, such as a spiral, which give signals that are invariant with orientation. However, it will be found that these scans are translation sensitive, and would require more scanning time. Other processing techniques that are rotationally invariant, such as Blum's "grass-fire" [1], cannot be used because they require that the object to be recognized be isolated from its background.

Finally, it is assumed that one hundred distinct target classes must be searched for at any one time. In light of the number and variety of weapons, vehicles, shelters, and other paraphernalia of war used by modern armies, this is a conservative figure.

Notice that this discussion has omitted consideration of scale and aspect angle searches. Scale search should not be required in an automated system because the aircraft altitude and camera focal length are known, thereby enabling calculation of the proper scale to within a few percent. There can be a significant aspect angle problem, especially when low altitude, short focal length imagery is considered. Targets located outside the field center will be seen at a slightly oblique angle, and, of course, targets can be located on irregular or sloped terrain which can alter the aspect angle even at the camera nadir. While it would be theoretically possible and probably desirable to account for the first of these two effects on a point by point basis over the frame, such compensation seems to be a practical impossibility in terms of the presently available implementations.

3. SYSTEM PERFORMANCE SPECIFICATIONS

From the parameter values established in the preceding section, and summarized in Table 1, it is possible to establish the required pattern recognition system performance in terms of probability of false alarm, and probability of false dismissal. From the previous numbers, it can be established that in each frame there are six billion opportunities for a false alarm! This is obtained by multiplying together the number of resolution elements (a decision must be made at each element), 10^6, the number of rotations in the orientation search, 60, and the number of target classes, 100. It is the sheer magnitude of this number that severely constrains the design and evaluation of a screening machine.

It is reasonable to require that a high-performance imagery screening machine produce, on the average, no more than one false alarm in each 100 frames. Performance of this magnitude is highly desir-

Table 1. System Parameters

$$
\left.
\begin{array}{l}
\text{Resolution—1 ft.} \\
\text{Frame Size—1000' x 1000'} \\
\text{Target Size—12' x 25'}
\end{array}
\right\} \quad \text{On ground}
$$

Orientation Tolerance—$\pm 3°$
Target Classes—100
False Alarms—1 in 100 frames
Detection Probability—0.95

able since each frame in which a target is detected is a frame that must be presented to the human photointerpreter, and the whole object of screening is to reduce the number of frames which must be further scrutinized by the photointerpreter. Unfortunately, human psychology seems to dictate that the photointerpreter will not limit his scrutiny to the single area on the frame that the machine designates as the probable target area, and so the false alarm performance must therefore be stipulated in terms of frame rates, and one in a hundred is probably acceptable. From this, one can calculate the equivalent false alarm probability for each separate decision at each point on the film is 1.6×10^{-12}. This is indeed an extremely small false alarm probability.

The magnitude of this false alarm probability should be compared with that reported in many papers on pattern recognition, where an accuracy of 80 or 90 percent is considered very good. However, the basic importance of the severe detection probability constraints is that every effort must be made to achieve superior detection results. It is essential therefore not to compromise on any of the system parameters which influence the detection performance, such as resolution, orientation tolerance, etc. Since these very parameters are the ones that gave rise to the need for such reliability, we can see that we are "locked in" to a rather sophisticated and complex system. Certainly, one cannot escape this dilemma by such shortcut routes as lowering the resolution of the output plane scanner, or detecting all orientations in one fell swoop.

It is somewhat more difficult to establish requirements for false dismissals. Fortunately, within limits, the performance specified does not substantially affect the computations that are relevant to the point of this paper. A probability of detection of 0.95 is assumed in this paper. This specification refers to unobscured, uncamouflaged targets, and must be relaxed in the face of countermeasures. Such performance probably exceeds that achieved by human photointerpreters in a screening operation, but unfortunately the information available on this subject is not definitive.

4. SPEED COMPARISONS OF CANDIDATE SYSTEMS

In addition to requiring extremely reliable detection performance, the large number of resolution elements in a frame dictates that the speed of the machine be considered very carefully. In order to assign some numbers to this problem, let us assume that it takes one microsecond to scan an element of the picture and operate on it. Suppose first that we have a system which operates completely serially and that the 12×25 element target area is scanned at every position in the frame Since the scan must also be repeated 60 times for the orientation search and 100 times for different targets, the total time for this process is 1.8×10^6 seconds, which is approximately 21 days. This time is typical of that required to screen imagery using a general purpose digital computer. Therefore, it can be seen that implementation of an imagery screening system with a sequential device such as a general purpose digital computer is not going to yield adequate results.

In the previous example each element of the picture was scanned 300 times at each rotation and for each target class. This is certainly not efficient, and no one has seriously advocated the use of a completely serial system for tactical target detection. There are many, on the other hand, who advocate optical systems for this application. In these systems, an entire frame is processed in parallel by optically correlating it with a reference pattern. Both noncoherent optical correlators and coherent optical spatial filtering systems perform in this way, although the specific mechanisms involved and the techniques for designing the reference pattern are quite different.

In either case, the amplitude of the illumination at each point in the output plane is proportional to the degree of correlation between the reference pattern and the local target area centered at the corresponding point on the frame. Since the entire 12 $\times$ 25 area is processed into a single correlation value by a parallel operation, the time required to process one frame of imagery would be reduced by a factor of 300 compared to the purely sequential system. In this case, each resolution element of the picture is scanned only once for each reference pattern. However, because only one reference pattern may be processed at a time, each orientation and each target class must be done sequentially.* The total time to process a frame in such a system, using a microsecond per element scan rate, is one hour and forty minutes.

There may be some question as to why any scanning is required in the optical system, since the correlation function for an entire frame is available simultaneously at the output plane. It is important to remember that a decision process is required, which means that the correlation function must be thresholded. Ideally, this could be done in parallel, point by point over the entire output field by making use of a mosaic of photo-sensitive solid state flip-flops, or by use of an electronic image tube. However, such a device must be extremely stable, must have an easily controllable threshold setting, must be uniform in effect over the entire field, compensating in the process for optical vignetting and for variations in average overall illumination, and, most important, must have an input resolution equal to one foot per element referenced to the ground. At the present time, we are not aware that any such device is available, although various investigators are attempting to perfect one.

It thus appears necessary at present to scan the output image, and to threshold electronically. If the output plane transfer function is linear, the resolution of the spot scanning the correlation peaks must be just as good as the scanner used on the input image. This is because the system is completely linear, and interchanging the order of operations does not affect the output at all. Since the spot which is used to scan the output image can be considered as a filter, it can

---

* In a coherent optical system, referenced patterns may be multiplexed by use of different optical "carrier" frequencies. This produces several output images, one for each reference pattern, displaced so that they do not overlap. Note however that the total number of resolution elements in the output plane is limited, and these must now be shared by the various images. This means that only a fraction of a frame can be processed at one time, and the throughput rate is not really increased.

be moved forward in the system without changing the net effect. Thus, we could filter the input image just as readily and obtain the same result. Those who do not object to using a low resolution scanner at the output must certainly object to lowering the resolution of the input image beyond the point of human recognition. In effect, both of these processes have the same result. In practice, the transfer function of camera tubes is not linear, but quadratic; that is, the output signal is proportional to the intensity rather than the amplitude of the illumination. This has the effect of enhancing the correlation peaks, but not nearly as much as is desired. Therefore, while the linear filter analysis suggested here is not entirely valid, the required scanner resolution is not significantly reduced. The time required to optically process a frame in all orientations, and with 100 target classes, while much more reasonable than can be obtained with a strictly sequential system, is still too great, because as described above, the full parallel processing of the optical techniques cannot be realized in practice.

We have been advocates of an electronic implementation in which the input frame is scanned sequentially, and the various target classes in various orientations can all be detected in parallel. In order to understand the system, one must understand the processing of the scanned image. Figure 1 shows this in conceptual form. The sequential scan of the elements of the image is represented by the numbered elements on the tape being stripped off the input frame. The tape is spiralled around a drum and as the scan advances one element, the tape slides one element around the drum. The illustration shows a three-element square window corresponding to a target area. Within the window are elements 3, 4, 5, 13, 14, 15, 23, 24, and 25, which on the original frame formed a similar three-element

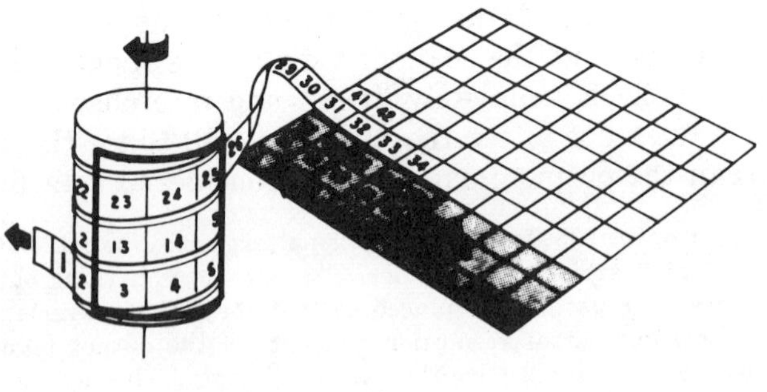

Figure 1. Conceptual Form for Processing of the Scanned Image

square area, as shown outlined in the illustration. As the scan advances one element the strip advances one element, and elements 4, 5, 6, 14, 15, 16, 24, 25, and 26 are in the window, while equivalently, on the frame, the window has moved over one element. Thus, as the element-by-element scan proceeds over the frame, the window also scans over the frame.

In the real world, the frame is much larger—1000 by 1000 elements—and the window also is much larger—perhaps 12 by 25 elements, so that it can contain an entire target. The drum of the illustration is replaced by a dynamic storage medium such as a delay line or a shift register. The elements of the store corresponding to the window area are tapped, and provide the inputs to the recognition logic. The elements on the drum, but outside the window, are not tapped, serving only as a circulating buffer store. Many commercial print readers work on this kind of a scan and store. Because the system is electronic, as many separate detection logics as are desired can be connected in parallel to the taps within the window, with limits set by economic considerations only. In the limit, each element of the frame is scanned only once. Also, because the input transparency can be scanned with a flying-spot scanner rather than a camera tube, much faster scan rates can be used.

For purposes of discussion, let us assume a speed of 0.1 microsecond per element. If all targets and orientations are detected in parallel, the system can process a frame in one hundred milliseconds. However, to do this, a shift register and/or delay line storage of 12000 elements is required. By overlapping scans by fifty percent, so that each element is scanned twice, this requirement can be reduced to 550 elements. The lower limit, in a system with maximum overlap, is 300 elements.

A brief calculation shows that the optimum point of time versus storage tradeoff is obtained at 50 percent scan efficiency. The size of the storage required is $H \cdot W$, where H is the scan height and W is the width of the target in the direction orthogonal to the scan. The relative slowness, or time for different degrees of overlap, is given by $H/(H+1-N)$, where N is the dimension of the target along a scan line. The storage size-time product can be used as a measure of cost. The time-storage product per unit width W is given by $H^2/(H+1-N)$, and this achieves a minimum for $H = 2(N-1)$; i.e., for the case of fifty percent scan efficiency. Table 2 shows the appropriate numbers for the cases where each element is scanned only once (i.e., the completely parallel system); where each element is scanned twice; and the completely serial case in which each element is scanned N times. The minimum is achieved in each case by proper orientation of the target area with respect to the scan.

It is not necessary to implement all targets in all orientations simultaneously. An electronic system which scans at fifty percent efficiency, at 0.1 microsecond per element, and which detects all 100 targets at a single orientation in parallel but requires a complete orientation search with sixty increments, would operate at a rate of

Table 2. Time–Storage Tradeoff

Scan Height	12	22	1,000
Minimum Storage in Elements	300	550	12,000
Relative Processing Time	12	2	1
Time-Storage Product	3,600	1,100	12,000

six seconds per frame. Such a system is entirely feasible. Is such a frame rate necessary, or alternatively, is it adequate?

5. SYSTEM SPEED REQUIREMENTS

In order to determine what the operational speed requirements are, let us consider how fast a reconnaissance aircraft can generate photographic data. Let us assume that the aircraft speed is 600 knots or 1000 feet per second and that the aircraft flies at an altitude of 2000 feet. If a camera using five inch by five inch film is used with a focal length of 10 inches, each frame will show a 1000 $\times$ 1000 foot area. This picture will have a scale of 1:2400 which is typical of tactical imagery. At the speed the aircraft is flying, it will have to take a picture every second in order not to leave gaps in the record. In practice, pictures must be taken more often in order to achieve some degree of overlap for various purposes such as stereo viewing. Let us therefore assume that a picture is taken every 0.6 seconds. With a six second ground processing time by the imagery screening machine, we find that ten hours of processing will be required for each hour of flight. When one considers that more than one reconnaissance aircraft will be flying each day and feeding its photography into the same machine, it is clear that the imagery screening machine will become fully loaded in a very short time even with a six second processing time. Therefore, longer times to process a frame of data should not be considered. In fact, every effort should be made to reduce the processing time still further.

6. DESIGN OF THE DECISION LOGIC

In the context of the system parameters presented, let us now consider some of the approaches we might take to the design of the decision logic. We might consider, for example, the use of optical matched filtering in which we use one example of the target class to generate a matched filter and subsequently use this filter to detect the presence or absence of the target. While requiring only one sample per target class might be considered a virtue, the fact remains that optical matched filtering gives us a linear decision function based upon one sample per target class, and this is just not adequate for the task at hand. When we consider the possibility of using iterative techniques based upon a number of samples for the design of our decision logic, that is, when we consider the use of so called "learning machines," we note that if we are provided with a fixed design sample and all members of the sample are available to us at one time, then any iterative use of these samples can at best only lead us to a terminal state which could have been obtained by an appropriate technique which made use of all the samples at one time. Many of the learning-adaptive algorithms which have been proposed, in the limit of infinite iterations, give essentially a linear discriminant function equivalent to Fisher's discriminant function, which we could have computed from the very beginning in one operation. In fact, there are no advantages to be gained through the use of iterative techniques except in a truly sequential or nonstationary situation where the samples are coming one by one or the statistics of the process are changing. Furthermore, the learning techniques require that all the design samples be used on each iteration, which requires the repeated storage and recovery of each pattern in the design set. While there will usually not be many samples available of the various enemy targets to be detected, there will generally be at least a few, and there will be a large number of "non-target" samples. Therefore, we think that there is little point to using iterative design techniques when in fact one could generate the decision logic quickly and effectively through a combination of statistical classification procedures and heuristics.

Probably the most important criterion for the selection of a design approach, as well as for the selection of an implementation approach, is that it allow for the generation of a hierarchy of logics of increasing power and complexity, so that if an initial, simple logic is not powerful enough for the job, then a more powerful logic can be generated straightforwardly. Polynomial discriminant functions provide such a capability. With good estimates of coefficients, a quadratic discriminant function will do better than a linear one, and in general, a higher order discriminant function will do better yet. The problem is, of course, that the sample size is limited, and therefore the estimates of the coefficients are not very good. If the input consists of 300 variables, then a linear discriminant function requires estimation of 300 coefficients. A general quadratic discriminant function will have close to 45,000 coefficients, although this might be reduced by making use of assumptions about the stochastic nature of imagery.[2] The higher the order of the discriminant function, the more coefficients to be estimated, and generally, the more samples required to achieve the same precision in the estimation of the individual coefficients.[3] With the small sample sizes available, a quadratic discriminant function may perform more poorly than a linear discriminant function because the estimates of the extra coefficients are inherently noisy. Thus, because of the large dimensionality of the problem and the small design samples available, the higher order discriminant function approach must be discarded, in favor of a more heuristic method such as the one we first described a number of years ago.[4,5] The large number of input variables is partitioned into subsets, a classification function is designed for each subset, and then a second layer classification function is designed with the first layer decisions as inputs. Similar techniques have been used in commercial print readers in which simple logics are designed to recognize individual strokes, and a final decision is made using the stroke decisions as inputs.

In the target detection problem, it is not possible to identify, *a priori*, all the significant features, analogous to the character strokes, required to characterize all the target classes. However, because of the spatial structure of the objects to be recognized, it is realistic to assume that the significant features will be local, that is, they will be contained within small well-defined subareas of the target area. The target area is divided up into a number of small local area feature blocks, overlapping each other by about fifty percent. A separate decision logic is statistically designed for each feature block.

Since the feature decisions are independent, based on different areas of the target, it is possible to use the same sample targets to design each feature, and because there are only a small number of elements in each block, fewer target samples are needed to obtain good estimates of coefficients. An additional independent sample set is then used to determine the coefficients of the second decision layer.

The individual feature logics, and the second layer decision, can utilize linear, quadratic or higher order decision functions if desired. For example, suppose that the 12 by 25 element target area were partitioned into 27 overlapping feature blocks, each 5 by 6 elements. The problem of designing 27 linear discriminant feature logics, with 30 variables each, and one 27 input linear discriminant second layer logic is roughly equivalent to that of designing a single linear discriminant function for a 57-element target area. For this problem of tactical target detection, the feature block approach provides the opportunity to use heuristic thinking and yet also includes the possibility of making use of statistical design techniques. In this way, it mitigates both the problem of sample size and the inherent complexity of nonlinear logics which plague the use of statistical techniques.

7. SYSTEM EVALUATION

Despite any claims that may be made in favor of a particular implementation or design technique, one must recognize that claims are no substitute for proof. Certainly, some hardware considerations can be determined straightforwardly from the manufacturers who supply the basic components: scanning tubes, delay lines, logical circuitry, light sources, etc. The one thing that cannot be determined straightforwardly is — can the system recognize targets? An automatic target detection imagery screening machine is going to be very expensive — probably comparable in cost to a large, fast digital computer. Is it possible to determine whether a proposed system is capable of meeting the performance specifications before a full-scale system is designed and built?

Since the object is to solve a real problem, and not just to develop general techniques, it is necessary to evaluate the system performance experimentally on real-world imagery. It is enlightening to consider what such an evaluation requires. First, the experiments must confirm that the system will detect 95 percent of the unobscured targets present in the imagery. Second, on the average, there must not be more than one false alarm every hundred frames.

Of course, performance must be evaluated using test samples which are independent of those used in the design process. That performance on design samples considerably underestimates the probability of error is illustrated by the results in Figure 2 for the cumulative distributions of scores obtained for a feature block discriminant function for design and independent test samples.

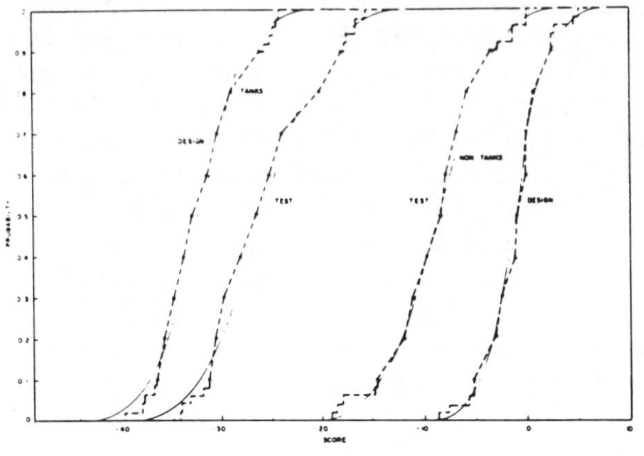

Figure 2. Discriminant Function Scores for Design and Test Samples

It is a well-established principle that a system required to meet some performance specification should be designed to yield much better performance if it is to have much chance of meeting the requirement. Assume for the moment that the target detection logic to be evaluated is in fact infallible; that is, it never misses a target or triggers a false alarm. In practice, of course, such performance is impossible. If the system recognizes 59 consecutive targets of a particular class with no failures, then the recognition specification for that class has been confirmed with a confidence coefficient of 0.95.* On the other hand, about 300 frames of nontarget imagery must be processed by the logics for every target class in all orientations without any false alarms in order to achieve the same confidence that the false alarm specification has been met. This means that a test system built or programmed on a computer to recognize a single target class would have to sequentially scan 30,000 frames of imagery in every orientation without an error in order to confirm the performance. This assumes, of course, that the performance data for a single target class can be extrapolated to one hundred classes. If the system occasionally makes errors, the required sample sizes become much greater. While only 59 target samples are needed with perfect performance, 93 would be needed if the system made only one mistake. While only 300 nontarget frames are needed with perfect per-

* This means that a machine that just fails to meet the specification can be expected to pass the test no more than 5 percent of the time.

formance, 475 would be needed if the system made a single false alarm. If the system is capable of performing at exactly the design specification, the expected number of samples required to verify that it does meet the specifications is infinite. As noted previously, to pass a practical evaluation test, the system must be superior to the specification.

How can such a large number of samples be processed? Computer simulation is not adequate, because based on the figures developed above for a sequential machine, the complete evaluation would require many years of running time. The answer is that an experimental system must be built that approaches real time data rates and exceeds the performance specifications.

The operational frame rate for an electronic target detection system was computed to be ten frames per minute. A frame rate about one-tenth of this should be suitable for system evaluation. Consider for example a prototype capable of recognizing 100 targets in parallel in a single orientation, and capable of a sequential orientation search. Since scanning speeds of ten elements per microsecond and comparable logic circuitry are near the limit of the art, and are therefore quite expensive to achieve, the prototype could reasonably be built to scan at one element per microsecond. Such a prototype would completely process one frame per minute. In about one day, involving only five hours of actual running time, the prototype could test 300 frames for false alarms. If performance were not perfect, it could easily process 3000, or even 10,000 frames within a reasonable period of time in order to achieve the sample size needed to obtain the desired level of confidence. If 10,000 frames could be processed, then the actual machine false alarm rate would have to be one in 120 frames to have a reasonable chance (50 percent) of demonstrating that the performance was one in 100 frames or better.

This is not to say that computer simulations, and evaluations on relatively slow and inexpensive experimental systems, are not called for. Using such techniques, it is possible to rule out many approaches because they fail to perform adequately on even a few samples. Also, it is unwise to undertake to construct an expensive prototype without first performing preliminary experiments to establish the creditability of the approach. But it is clear that it is not possible to confirm the operational capabilities of even a perfect system without building and thoroughly testing a full scale prototype that has all the power, and much of the speed, of the final system.

8. CONCLUSIONS

The problem-oriented approach to the design of an imagery screening target detection system has been used to demonstrate that the system requirements severely constrain the courses of action open to the investigator. In this example, one is led to the following conclusions, which are summarized in Figure 3:

IMPLEMENTATION	DECISION LOGIC	LOGIC DESIGN	SYSTEM EVALUATION
ELECTRONIC	MULTILAYER	STATISTICAL	NEAR-REAL-TIME PROTOTYPE
OPTICAL	ϕ-MACH.	HEURISTIC	
		LEARNING	COMPUTER SIMULATION
		MATCHED FILTER	

Figure 3. Summary of Conclusions

Because of the required frame rates, the system must be implemented electronically.

Because the number of samples of enemy targets available is quite small, the decision logic must be designed by a combination of statistical and heuristic methods.

A two-layer local area feature logic can resolve the sample size problem while still providing logical power.

For evaluation, a prototype system must be built which has all the logical power, and most of the speed capability, of an operational system.

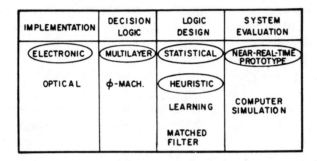

Our purpose in presenting this paper is twofold. First, it has been our experience that too few investigators concerned with target detection appreciate the constraints that the system requirements create. Research on techniques, methods, and devices is necessary and vital, but ultimate success in the application of pattern recognition technology to real world situations requires a problem-oriented approach. Second, too often even the best investigators can become entranced with a particular technique, method, or device and claim that it will solve all the world's problems. We hope that we have conveyed the idea that real world problems are not so easily solved, and that experimental results showing 90, 95, or even 99.9 percent correct recognition, more often than not, demonstrate that a technique is not applicable to the problem being investigated.

ACKNOWLEDGMENT

The preparation of this paper was supported by Contract AF 33(615)–2966 with the 6570th Aerospace Medical Research Laboratories, Aerospace Medical Division, Air Force Systems Command, United States Air Force.

REFERENCES

1. Blum, H., "An Associative Machine for Dealing with the Visual Field and Some of its Biological Implications," in *Biological Prototypes and Synthetic Systems*, Vol. 1, pp. 244–260, Plenum Press, 1962.
2. Abend, K., Harley, T. J. and Kanal, L. N.: Classification of Binary Random Patterns, *IEEE Trans. on Information Theory*, Vol. IT–11, No. 4, pp. 538–544, October 1965.
3. Specht, D. F., "Generation of Polynomial Discriminant Functions for Pattern Recognition," Stanford Electronics Laboratories, Report SU–SEL–66–029, May 1966.
4. Kanal, L. N., and Randall, N. C., "Target Detection in Aerial Photography," Presented at IEEE WESCON, August 26, 1964.
5. Kanal, L. N. and Randall, N. C., "Recognition System Design by Statistical Analysis," *Proceedings of the 19th National Conference of the Association for Computing Machinery*, New York, 1964, pp. D2.5–1 to D2.5–10, Pub. Association for Computing Machinery.

A Comparison of Analog and Digital Techniques for Pattern Recognition

KENDALL PRESTON, JR., SENIOR MEMBER, IEEE

Abstract—Since the computer technology utilized often places limitations on the performance of a particular pattern-recognition task, it is important to compare the state-of-the-art and future trends in both the digital and the analog-computer fields. Electronic, acoustical, and optical analog computers for use in pattern recognition are discussed and their performance compared with that of both general-purpose and special-purpose digital computers.

It is shown that the analog computer offers workers using low-precision high-speed one-dimensional or two-dimensional linear discriminant analysis a significant advantage in hardware performance (equivalent bits per second per dollar) over the digital computer in certain limited but important areas. These areas include fingerprint identification, word recognition, chromosome spread detection, earth-resources and land-use analysis, and broad-band radar signal processing.

A trend analysis is presented which indicates that the advantages of analog computation will probably be overcome in the next few decades by the rapid performance advances being made in digital-computer hardware.

I. Introduction

THE MAIN PURPOSE of this issue of the PROCEEDINGS is to treat *digital* pattern recognition. However, pattern recognition may also be carried out by *analog* means. It is worth comparing the implementation of these two approaches.

This paper rounds out the issue by treating in some detail the use of analog computation—in particular, *optical* analog computation—in pattern recognition. In order to assist the reader in evaluating this alternate approach to pattern recognition, the cost, speed, and accuracy of digital and analog techniques are compared. The comparison not only relates to the current state of the art but also attempts to predict future trends.

The digital approach to problems in pattern recognition has many advantages. Digital computers provide the user with the capability of performing calculations to essentially any degree of precision with almost infinite flexibility as regards the type and scope of the problem addressed. Due to the universality of most major programming languages and the general availability of digital computing facilities, the user also benefits from both ease of programming and the transferability of software. Last but not least, the digital computer ordinarily offers the user absolute repeatability on each execution of a given program. These are the advantages which have led to an almost overwhelming preference for the use of digital computers in carrying out calculations relating to pattern recognition.

In certain limited cases, however, when the pattern-recognition tasks follow the traditional lines of correlation detection of either features or gestalts by matched filtering (linear discrimination), it may be advantageous to use the analog computer. The same is true when performing detection by means of quadratic discrimination. Here analog-computer hardware has a significant speed advantage over most digital hardware. In some cases a considerable cost advantage may also be realized. This is particularly true in the processing of two-dimensional data where optical analog computation may be used to advantage.

This paper argues that, although at present the analog computer offers significant advantages in certain fields, this advantage will eventually be overcome by the digital computer. This may not occur for perhaps three decades. Therefore, it is important for workers in pattern recognition who wish to optimize their their experimental approach to be appraised of both the state of the art and future expectations in the analog pattern-recognition field.

Since the technology utilized often places limitations on performance of a particular recognition task, this paper reviews three major categories of analog technology used in pattern recognition. In addition to analog computers using optical excitation, the electronic analog computer and analog computers using acoustical excitation are discussed. Section II introduces the reader to these three techniques. Section III is concerned with operating systems, illustrating the use of analog computers in pattern recognition and delineating some of their basic characteristics. Section IV, the final section, presents a numerical evaluation of the cost and performance of various analog computers in comparison with electronic digital computers. Future trends are predicted based upon an analysis of the performance advances which have taken place in both the digital and analog fields during the past decade.

II. Basic Technology

This section reviews three means (electronic, acoustical, and optical) which may be used to carry out high-speed analog computations typical of those required in both linear and quadratic discriminant analysis. Since most of the material presented has been extensively described in existing literature, the presentation takes the form of a digest rather than being rigorously analytical or tutorial.

A. Electronic Analog Computers

The development of the operational amplifier by Philbrick [1] and others [2] in the late 1930's opened the era of the electronic analog computer. General-purpose versions of these computers, developed extensively in the 1950's and in the early to mid-1960's [3], [4], are now gradually being displaced by the general-purpose digital computer. Dedicated analog computers and hybrid computers, i.e., those using analog circuitry to obtain high speed, but using digital circuitry for control and programming, are still under active development [5], [6].

The basic components of the electronic analog computer are shown in Fig. 1. Most of these components make use of the

Manuscript received May 12, 1972; revised July 13, 1972.
The author is with the Perkin-Elmer Corporation, Norwalk, Conn. 06856.

Reprinted from *Proc. IEEE*, vol. 60, pp. 1216–1231, Oct. 1972.

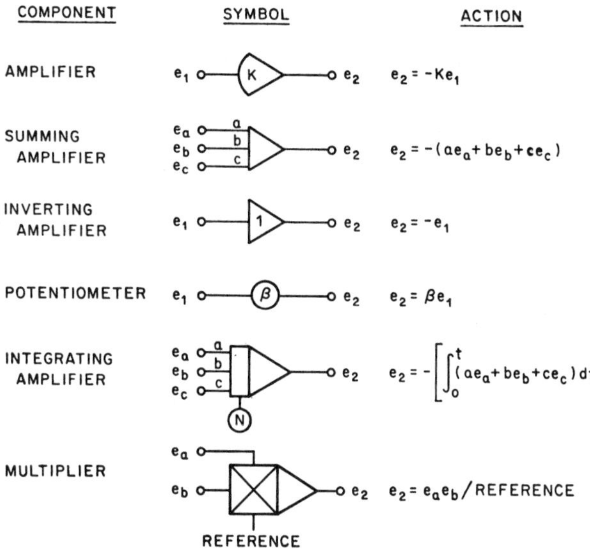

Fig. 1. Symbolic representation of components for use in electronic analog computers.

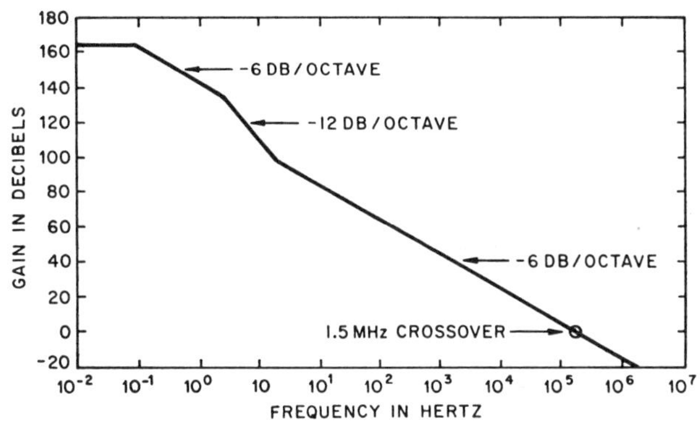

Fig. 2. Gain versus frequency characteristic of a typical operational amplifier.

operational amplifier. By tailoring the inputs to the amplifiers used and by adjusting their feedback networks, it is possible to perform the functions of summation, inversion, multiplication, and integration. Detailed descriptions of these functions are provided in the references.

Fig. 2 shows the frequency response of a typical operational amplifier. Here the dc open-loop gain is 164 dB with a frequency cutoff in the 1- to 10-MHz region. In order to obtain stability and uniformity of response as a function of frequency, a feedback network is usually inserted so that gain is uniform over a frequency band which extends to the 0.1–1.0-MHz range. If the operational amplifier is used as an adder or multiplier within this region, its performance is independent of frequency and, owing to the high loop gain and the large amount of feedback, its stability and accuracy are great. Accuracy, in fact, may be held to within one part in 10 000. Thus the operational amplifier is equivalent to a 14-bit digital adder or multiplier with an operation time of 1–10 μs.

Miniaturization has produced considerable size reduction in analog-computer hardware. In the late 1950's and early 1960's, when the operational amplifier was usually a vacuum-tube device, a single amplifier would occupy 3–4-in on a standard 19-in electronic rack. With the advent of integrated circuitry, many operational amplifiers are now contained in single dual-in-line packages. From 50 to 100 operational amplifiers may be mounted on a single circuit board, thus providing the processing capability of as many digital multipliers working in parallel. In fact, it is this extremely economical parallel-processing capability that still makes analog hardware an attractive means of instrumenting large-scale dedicated pattern-recognition computers (see Section III-A).

In large-scale analog computers, performance is limited by the precision available, which ranges from 4 to 5 decimal digits (0.01 to 0.001 percent), and accuracy, which ranges from about 1 percent on 10-V machines to perhaps 0.1 percent on 100-V machines. Naturally, on both manually programmed and digitally programmed machines, the programs which may be run are strictly limited by the number of components and the available interconnections. It is this restriction that makes the general-purpose analog computer far less attractive than the general-purpose digital computer. However, in machines dedicated to a particular task, the high throughout per dollar (measured in equivalent bits per second per dollar) still makes the dedicated analog computer extremely attractive (see Section IV).

B. Analog Computation Using Acoustical Excitation

In the mid-1960's workers in both the United States [7] and Great Britain [8] devised acoustical-wedge delay lines which could be used in the analog computation of correlation functions. Such devices are useful in pattern-recognition studies using linear discrimination for the detection of signals in noise. Two forms of these delay lines are currently in use for one-dimensional signal detection. These two forms are shown in Fig. 3. In the original form, the signal to be introduced is applied to an electrode along one face of a wedge of homogeneous isotropic material suitable for acoustical propagation within the signal bandwidth utilized. This electrode is designed so as to generate a collimated beam of acoustical radiation over this bandwidth. The device is designed so that the start of the signal to be detected reaches point B at the same time that the latter portion of the signal reaches point A. The face of the device between points A and B contains an output transducer whose electrode structure matches the structure of the signal to be detected. Owing to the simultaneous arrival along AB of acoustical radiation generated by all portions of the signal, a correlation function is generated at the output electrode given ideally by

$$e_2(t) = \sum_{n=1}^{n=N} c_n e_1(t - \tau_n) \tag{1}$$

where $e_1(t)$ is the input signal, τ_n is the transit time to the nth segment of the output electrode, and c_n is the response of the nth segment to continuous-wave excitation anywhere over the signal bandwidth W. If $(\tau_{n+1} - \tau_n) \leq W^{-1}$ for all n, then all resolvable components of $e_1(t)$ are weighted multiplicatively by the corresponding c_n and summed over the interval $T = (\tau_n - \tau_1)$.

If the components of $e_1(t)$ are considered to form a feature vector, then (1) represents the application of a linear discriminant function whose value $e_2(t)$ may be compared to an appropriate threshold. Thus the acoustical-wedge delay line is equivalent to a collection of multipliers and adders operating in parallel whose number equals the time–bandwidth product (TW) of the delay line. Each multiplier and adder

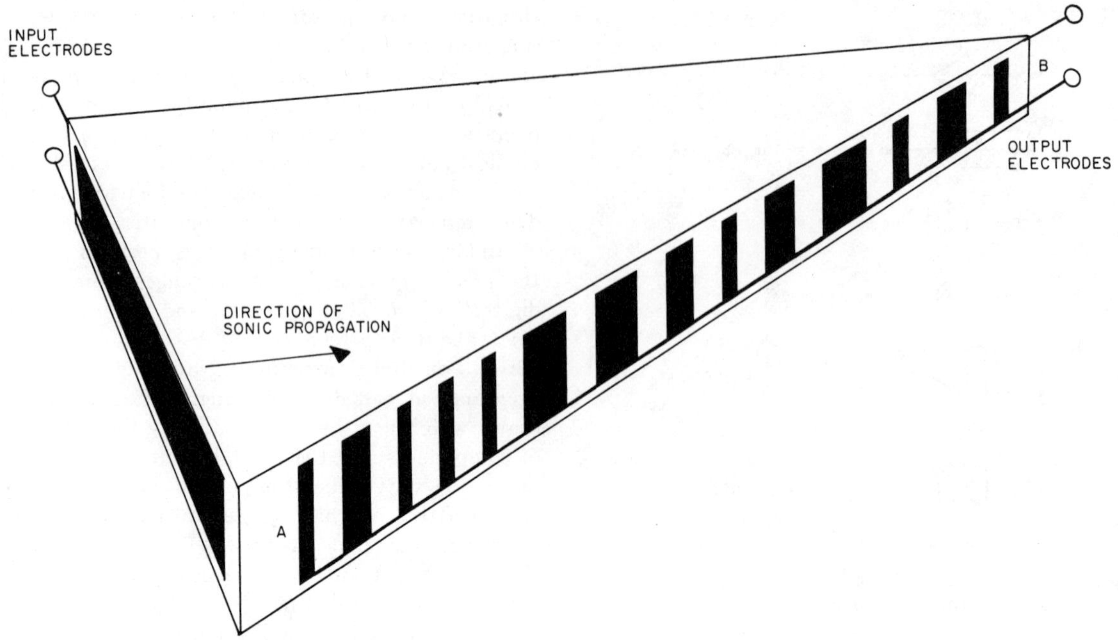

Fig. 3. Acoustic-wedge delay line for use in linear discriminant analysis showing structured output transducer for performing a correlation detection of a known signal waveform.

completes its calculation in an overall computation interval of W^{-1}.

When considering the wedge delay line as a filter matched to the signal $e_1(t)$, the c_n may be found from the frequency-domain equation

$$E_1^*(\omega) = \sum_{n=1}^{n=N} c_n \exp(-j\omega\tau_n) \tag{2}$$

where $E_1(\omega)$ is the Fourier transform of $e_1(t)$ and the asterisk indicates the complex conjugate. However, since $e_1(t)$ is real, a time-domain synthesis of the c_n is usually simpler when it is recognized that the inverse Fourier transform of $E_1^*(\omega)$ is $e_1(-t)$, i.e., the time inverse of $e_1(t)$. Thus the c_n are determined simply from samples of $e_1(-t)$ taken at the Nyquist rate so that the impulse response of the wedge delay line becomes $e_1(-t)$ as required by (2).

Because of the high acoustical velocity in most materials used in wedge delay lines, the time extent of signals which may be handled is usually limited to less than 100 μs. Furthermore, although one can conceive of multiple channels incorporated in a single acoustical structure, fabrication problems make it difficult if not impossible to handle two-dimensional signals in this fashion. Also, although output electrode segments are easily applied by standard photolithographic techniques, they produce a device having, so to speak, a fixed program. These factors limit the use of such devices in pattern-recognition studies. Usually acoustical-wedge delay lines are formed as end items in signal processing systems where the detection tasks to be performed are well defined *a priori*. A typical application is the processing of pulse-Doppler radar signals.

The second structure for use in acoustical matched filtering by correlation detection is shown in Fig. 4. Here the entire interaction is accomplished using surface waves. In this structure the incoming signal is launched as a Rayleigh wave using the input transducer I. As this wave propagates along the surface of the acoustical medium, it interacts with an

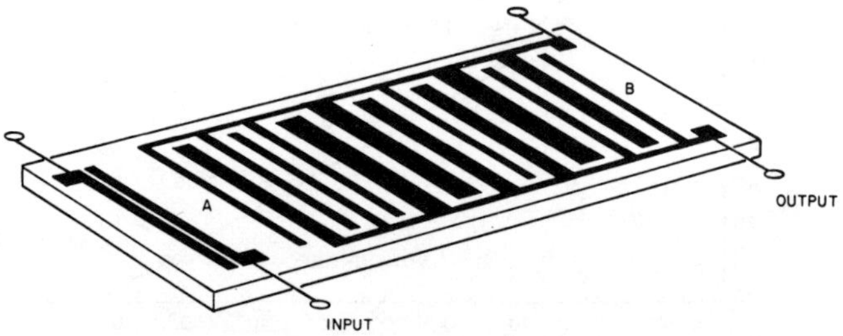

Fig. 4. Drawing of input and output transducer structures for an acoustic surface-wave delay line for use in correlation detection by linear discriminant analysis.

electrode structure AB in much the same fashion as with the wedge delay line. Once again this structure is designed to have a spatial form relating to the inverse time waveform of the signal to be detected. When the configuration and position of the traveling acoustical wave matches that of the electrode structure, a correlation peak occurs in the output signal. Thus just as with the acoustical-wedge structure, it is possible to carry out correlation detection by linear discrimination.

The surface-wave devices have the advantage of smaller size due to the fact that acoustical velocity is lower for surface waves by at least a factor of two. Also, there is the advantage that all photolithography is done on a single surface of the device. This permits one to consider realistically two-dimensional signal processing using many parallel channels.

Transducer width w may be calculated from

$$w = v_s \sqrt{\frac{T}{f_0}} \tag{3}$$

where v_s is the velocity of acoustical propagation and f_0 is the midband frequency. Equation (3) is based on the assumption that all segments of the output transducer must be in the near field of the input transducer. (The length of the output transducer is, of course, simply v_sT.) The literature [9], [10] reports typical transducer widths of 5–50 mm with bandwidths of the order of 5×10^7Hz and $TW\approx10^3$.

One channel of an acoustical-wedge delay line is equivalent to a single digital multiplier–adder combination performing 5×10^{10} computations per second. This type of analog computer is thus two orders of magnitude faster than typical electronic analog computers having 100 operational amplifiers. Also, such devices are far more compact (assuming each output-transducer segment is equivalent to a single operational amplifier). Finally, it should be noted that it may be possible to overcome the fixed-program limitation of the acoustical analog computer by using a second acoustical wave in place of the segment structure of the output transducer, thus forming an "acoustically programmable" system. Experimental versions of such systems are reported in the recent literature [11], [12].

C. Analog Computation Using Optical Excitation

Pattern recognition by matched filtering is feasible, using optical analog computation, because of the Fourier-transform relationship which exists between the electromagnetic radiation fields in the input and output planes of an an appropriately designed lens system [13]. In the ideal case this relationship is given by

$$F(\cos\alpha, \cos\beta) = C\int\int_{-\infty}^{+\infty} f(x, y) \cdot\exp\left[-j\frac{2\pi}{\lambda_L}(x\cos\alpha + y\cos\beta)\right]dxdy \quad (4)$$

where C is a normalizing constant, $f(x, y)$ is the complex amplitude of the radiation field in the input plane, λ_L is the optical wavelength, and $\cos\alpha$ and $\cos\beta$ are the direction cosines of propagation with respect to the x and y axes, respectively. The details of the derivation of this important equation are provided in the Appendix.

The coordinates of the Fourier transform given in (4) may readily be expressed in terms of the spatial coordinates of the output plane using the following geometrical relationships:

$$x_2 = F\cos\alpha/\cos\gamma \quad y_2 = F\cos\beta/\cos\gamma \quad (5)$$

where F is the output focal length of the lens system and $\cos\gamma$ is the direction cosine with respect to the optical axis. Since the direction angle γ is ordinarily small in most optical analog-computer systems, its direction cosine may be set equal to unity. Equation (4) then becomes

$$F(\omega_x, \omega_y) = \int\int_{-\infty}^{+\infty} f(x, y)[\exp -j(\omega_x x + \omega_y y)]dxdy \quad (6)$$

where ω_x and ω_y are the radian spatial frequencies and have units of radians per unit length. These quantities may be expressed either in terms of the direction cosines of optical propagation in the input space or in terms of the output-plane coordinates as follows:

$$\omega_x = 2\pi\cos\alpha/\lambda_L = 2\pi x_2/\lambda_L F$$
$$\omega_y' = 2\pi\cos\beta/\lambda_L = 2\pi y_2/\lambda_L F. \quad (7)$$

Also note that the so-called "spatial frequencies" f_x and f_y are related to ω_x and ω_y as follows:

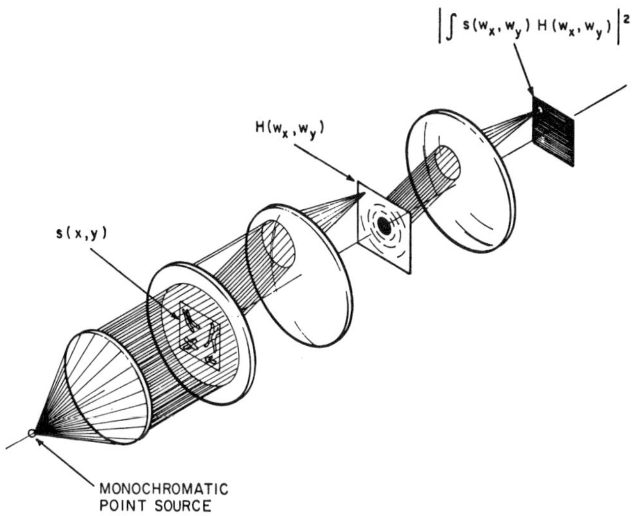

Fig. 5. Typical coherent optical computer configuration for use in two-dimensional matched filtering of the input signal $s(x, y)$ by means of a spatial-frequency-plane filter $H(\omega_x, \omega_y)$.

$$f_x = \omega_x/2\pi \quad f_y = \omega_y/2\pi \quad (8)$$

and have the units of cycles per unit length. If the spatial frequencies present in $f(x, y)$ cover a spatial bandwidth W, and the pupil in the input plane covers a spatial aperture A, then the optical computer is said to exhibit an area space bandwidth equal to $(AW)^2$. The quantity AW is directly related to the time–bandwidth product TW in electronic analog systems [14].

By concatenating lens systems as shown in Fig. 5 successive Fourier transforms may be taken. Therefore, it is possible to design optical analog computers to perform two-dimensional frequency-plane matched filtering as well as two-dimensional spatial-plane correlation.

In certain applications the large-area space bandwidth of the optical computer and the fact that optical systems operate in parallel give optical analog computation a significant advantage over all other techniques. The computation rate R_c at which an optical analog computer performs may be calculated from the expression

$$R_c = \frac{\epsilon\eta P}{h\nu(S/N)^2} \quad (9)$$

where ϵ is the transfer efficiency, η is the quantum efficiency of the output detector, P is the optical input power, h is Planck's constant, ν is the optical frequency, and (S/N) is the desired rms output signal-to-noise ratio at the minimum signal level. For typical values such as $\epsilon=0.5$, $\eta=0.1$, $P=1.0$ W, $\nu=10^{15}$ Hz, and $S/N=10$, R_c is of the order of 10^{14} multiplications per second. This is at least six orders of magnitude faster than electronic analog computers and four orders of magnitude faster than acoustical analog computers.

The main drawbacks to using optical analog computers are 1) the difficulty of I/O conversion and 2) the inaccuracy of the computations performed. New devices for solving I/O problems include such input devices as electrooptic delay lines, membrane light modulators, and photochromic films, as well as such output devices as arrays of light detectors and television pickup tubes. These are discussed extensively by Preston [15].

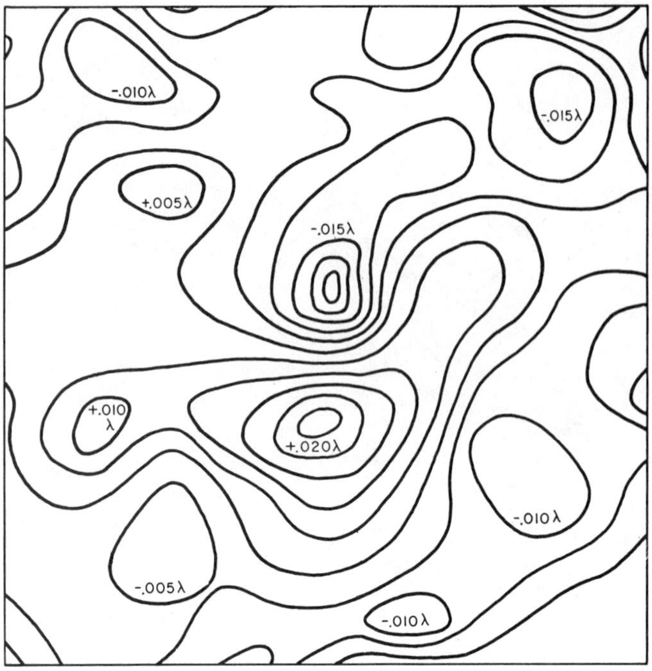

Fig. 6. Graph of the $\phi(x, y, \omega_x, \omega_y)$ function for a highly corrected coherent optical-computer lens system. Courtesy of the Perkin-Elmer Corp. (Excerpted from *Coherent Optical Computers* by permission of publisher, copyright 1972, McGraw-Hill, Inc.)

Aberrations in the optical system cause (6) to become

$$F(\omega_x, \omega_y) = \iint_{-\infty}^{+\infty} f(x, y) \exp\{-j[\omega_x x + \omega_x y + \phi(\omega_x, \omega_y, x, y)]\} dxdy \quad (10)$$

where $\phi(\omega_x, \omega_y, x, y)$ is the function which relates the distortion of the output optical wavefronts to their points of origin in the input plane and to their direction of propagation. It is this aberration function which limits the performance of even the most highly corrected and carefully designed optical computer. The structure of the aberration function for an actual optical-computer lens system for a point on axis ($x=0$, $y=0$) is shown in Fig. 6, in which the peak-to-peak aberration is 0.3 rad with an rms value of 0.06 rad. These values are typical of optical-computer lens systems of the highest quality. This aberration causes a 0.5-percent accuracy in the value of the functions computed [16]. An ordinary lens, such as those used in high-quality cameras, will often exhibit an rms value of the aberration function of 0.5 rad representing an accuracy of only 25 percent.

The optical computer which uses photomultipliers as output transducers has a precision which is limited by the level of scattered light in the output plane. With extreme care in the fabrication of the optical system, a precision of 6 to 7 decimal digits may be reached. Thus the optical analog computer is useful where low to moderate accuracy is acceptable but extremely high speed and precision are required.

III. Analog Pattern-Recognition Systems

Analog computers for use in pattern recognition have been implemented in a variety of operating systems. This section describes certain systems selected by the author for purposes of illustration: one is an electronic analog system; the others, optical analog systems. Systems using acoustical radiation in delay-line matched filters for signal detection are omitted. At present such systems are used primarily for pulse compression in radar and in secure communications and are relatively unsophisticated as regards the pattern-recognition aspects of their performance.

A. Electronic Analog Systems for Pattern Recognition

The system selected here is the Spectral Analyzer and Recognition Computer (SPARC) installation at the Willow Run Laboratories of the University of Michigan. SPARC is a special-purpose analog-computer system of major importance which is used in pattern-recognition studies related to multispectral earth-resources analysis. The sensor, which provides data for SPARC, is a 12-channel spectral scanner which receives energy radiated from the surface of the earth. It uses an aircraft platform carrying a rotating-mirror scanner feeding a 12-channel spectrophotometer. The result is a 12-channel analog recording of a multiplicity of images generated in the spectral bands given in Table I.

TABLE I

Channel Number	Wavelength Interval (nm)
1	400- 440
2	440- 460
3	460- 480
4	480- 520
5	520- 550
6	550- 580
7	580- 620
8	620- 660
9	660- 680
10	680- 720
11	720- 800
12	800- 999

SPARC is used to provide real-time classification of each point in the terrain scanned. Quadratic discrimination is employed with the spectral signature of each point being taken as the input function. Four classes of terrain may be discriminated when using the 12-channel signature. More classes may be included (proportionally) if the number of channels is reduced. Only a single class is addressed during one pass by the computer. The recognition criterion used is the likelihood ratio. The action of the computer is based on the traditional multivariate statistical calculation which uses predetermined covariance matrices for each of the terrain classes treated. Consider a four-class separation constructed using data from the full complement of 12 channels. The likelihood ratio for class A is given by

$$L_A = \frac{p_A f_A}{p_B f_B + p_C f_C + p_D f_D} \quad (11)$$

where p_A is the *a priori* probability that the spectral signature being examined belongs to class A, and f_A is the multivariate normal probability density function for class A evaluated using the instantaneous values of the signals received from all 12 channels. The quantity in the denominator is the probability that the signature belongs to any of the other classes being considered. The expression for the multivariate normal probability function for the Kth class is given by

$$f_K = (2\pi)^{-6} |C^K|^{1/2} \cdot \exp\left[-1/2 \sum_{i=1}^{i=12} \sum_{j=1}^{j=12} (s_i - \bar{s}_i) c_{ij}^K (s_j - \bar{s}_j)\right] \quad (12)$$

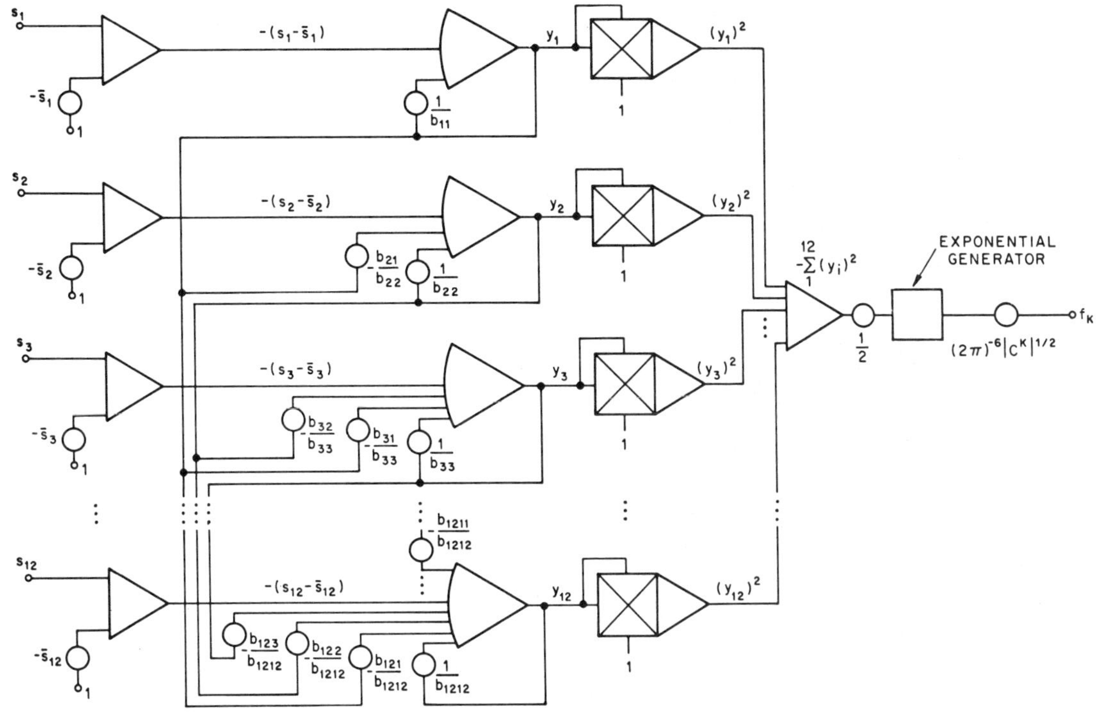

Fig. 7. Schematic diagram of one of the four f computers used in the SPARC system whose purpose is to generate the multivariate normal probability function for the Kth pattern class in real-time from a 12-channel multispectral signature.

where $c_{ij}{}^K$ is the ijth element of the 12×12 inverse covariance matrix for class K, $|C^K|$ is the determinant of the inverse covariance matrix, and $\bar{s}_i$ and $\bar{s}_j$ are the average values of signals from channels i and j, all based on *a priori* data gathered on a "training set" of spectral signatures.

In matrix form (12) becomes

$$f_K = (2\pi)^{-6}|C^K|^{1/2}\exp(-1/2 S^T C^K S). \tag{13}$$

The quantity S is the 12-element signature vector and T indicates transpose. Equation (12) may be simplified as follows by taking into account the fact that the covariance matrix is real and symmetric:

$$f_K = (2\pi)^{-6}|C^K|^{1/2}\exp(-1/2\, Y^T Y) \tag{14}$$

where $Y = SP$ and P is the triangular matrix obtained from $PP^T = C^K$. The elements of Y may be found from the recursion formula

$$y_i = b_{ii}\left[(s_i - \bar{s}_i) + \frac{b_{i1}}{b_{ii}} y_1 + \frac{b_{i2}}{b_{ii}} y_2 + \cdots \frac{b_{i,i-1}}{b_{ii}} y_{i-1}\right] \tag{15}$$

where the b_{ij} are directly related to the elements of P.

This simplification in the matrix multiplication required for the computation of the quantities needed for the calculation of the likelihood ratio results in a considerable simplification of the electronic analog-computer circuitry in SPARC. It leads to the block diagram in Fig. 7, which shows one of the four "f computers" in SPARC. Each f computer contains 12-input operational amplifiers. These amplifiers are used to produce signals equal to the differences between the 12 instantaneous multispectral signal values and the means of these signals as determined from *a priori* data. The next bank of amplifiers and their associated potentiometers is used to compute the product terms needed in the simplified matrix multiplication given in (14). As can be seen, the number of potentiometers and associated inputs increases linearly from spectral channel to spectral channel until, in the final channel, there are 12 potentiometer-controlled inputs including that controlled by the feedback potentiometer. This leads to a total of 90 potentiometers per f computer, 12 of which are set up from data on the means, and 78 from the matrix-multiplier coefficients.

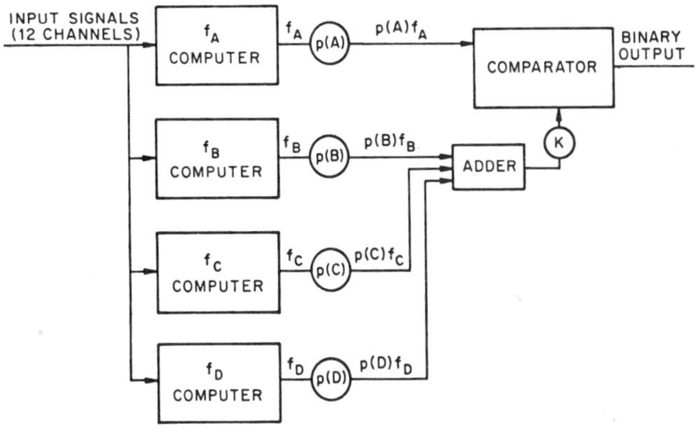

Fig. 8. Block diagram of the Spectral Analyzer and Recognition Computer (SPARC) in use at the Willow Run Laboratories of the University of Michigan for pattern-recognition studies based on multispectral analysis.

Following this bank of amplifiers are 12 function generators for squaring the signals which feed a 12-input summing amplifier. This amplifier is followed by a multiplier for the purpose of exponentiation. A final potentiometer is used for the purpose of applying the normalizing constants required in (14).

The SPARC system is capable of processing input signals having a 50-kHz bandwidth. This is accomplished by using four f computers operating in parallel as shown in Fig. 8. The likelihood ratio for the class being addressed is compared with

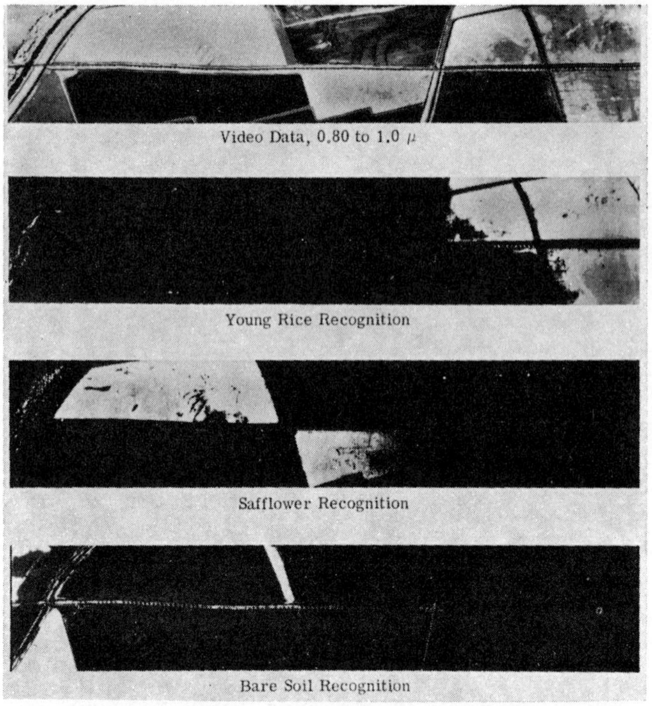

Fig. 9. Photographs of (top to bottom) the SPARC video channel data in the 0.8- to 1.0-μ channel, as well as binary recognition functions generated for areas of rice, safflower, and bare soil as derived from 12-channel multispectral video data of the same scene. Courtesy of the Willow Run Laboratories, University of Michigan.

an adjustable threshold yielding a binary (yes/no) output. The output feeds an image recorder which produces a binary overlay for the terrain images being processed. An example is given in Fig. 9, where the image formed in a single spectral channel is shown in conjunction with three binary overlays corresponding to the following three classes: rice fields, safflower fields, bare soil. In this example the training sets were subsets of picture points for regions of each of the terrain types recognized.

The SPARC electronic analog-computer system described conducts the equivalent of four 12×12 matrix multiplications each 10 μs. This yields a data-processing rate equal to 6×10^7 multiplications per second. A digital system with a single arithmetic unit would require a 10-bit multiplier with a 17-ns computation time to compete with the SPARC system. (Alternatively, of course, a timed-shared bank of digital multipliers could be used which operated at a correspondingly lower rate.)

Note also that the SPARC system is programmable in that the coefficients of all four $\boldsymbol{Y}$ vectors are alterable from their corresponding potentiometers. One of the disadvantages of SPARC is that manual programming is required, but it is understood that the University of Michigan is considering further modifications of the SPARC system which will add electronic control of all potentiometer settings. In such a configuration a digital computer would be used to calculate covariance matrices from spectral samples derived from a training set. This computer would then command the SPARC to assume the proper configuration to process further spectral images at high speed in real time.

B. Optical Analog Systems for Pattern Recognition

This subsection gives examples of the use of optical analog computers for pattern recognition in biology, remote sensing, word recognition, and personnel verification. Other applications, such as character recognition, are also mentioned briefly. Each application is evaluated in terms of data-processing rates achieved and is compared with digital capabilities.

1) Systems Using Wiener-Spectrum Analysis: The simplest operation which can be performed by an optical analog computer is the computation of the Fourier transform of an input pattern as expressed by (6). When the transform is sensed by an energy detector, the result is a measure of the Wiener spectrum of the input pattern, namely,

$$W(\omega_x, \omega_y) = \boldsymbol{F}(\omega_x, \omega)\boldsymbol{F}^*(\omega_x, \omega_y). \quad (16)$$

Only a single lens plus an output detector array is required to construct and record $W(\omega_x, \omega_y)$. As illustrated by the following examples, this rather elementary hardware is all that is required in implementing certain simple but significant pattern-recognition tasks.

a) Chromosome-spread location: One of the most successful applications of optical Wiener-spectrum analysis for pattern recognition is in the high-speed location of chromosome spreads on microscope slides. As indicated by the optically generated Wiener spectra shown in Fig. 10, the chromosome spread has a Wiener spectrum which is unique in comparison with the two other classes of objects ordinarily encountered on the microscope slide. These other objects the are nonmitotic cell and particulate matter, such as ordinary dust and dirt.

Fig. 11 is a graph of the spatial-frequency content of the Wiener spectra corresponding to chromosome spreads (mitotic cells), nonmitotic cells, and "noise." This graph was generated from data taken from a sample consisting of 64 such objects [17]. The Wiener spectra of chromosome spreads contain a relatively high energy content in the 300–400-cycles/mm band with respect to their energy content in the 65–90-cycles/mm band. The Wiener spectra of nonmitotic cells exhibit relatively low energy content over both these spatial-frequency bands, whereas particulate matter, such as dust, has a high energy content in both bands.

To investigate high-speed chromosome location using Wiener-spectrum analysis, the Perkin-Elmer Corporation built an automatic microscope slide scanner (see Fig. 12) incorporating a laser-energized optical computer. This system illuminates a moving microscope slide over an aperture of 50 μm corresponding to the typical diameter of a chromosome spread. Light diffracted by any object within this aperture enters two optical-computer channels. The Wiener spectra generated are annularly integrated and recorded over the two spatial-frequency bands given.

The optical computer is followed by an electronic analog computer which compares the energy detected in the high-spatial-frequency band with a threshold T_1 in order to indicate the presence of a chromosome spread (or dirt). Simultaneously, the electronic computer calculates the ratio of the energy levels detected in both bands and compares this ratio with a threshold T_2. In order to detect the presence of a chromosome spread, the detection criteria are

$$W_H > T_1 \quad W_H/W_L > T_2 \quad (17)$$

where W_L and W_H correspond to the energy content in the high- and low-frequency bands.

One great advantage of utilizing the Wiener spectrum in automatic microscopy is that errors in the focal position of

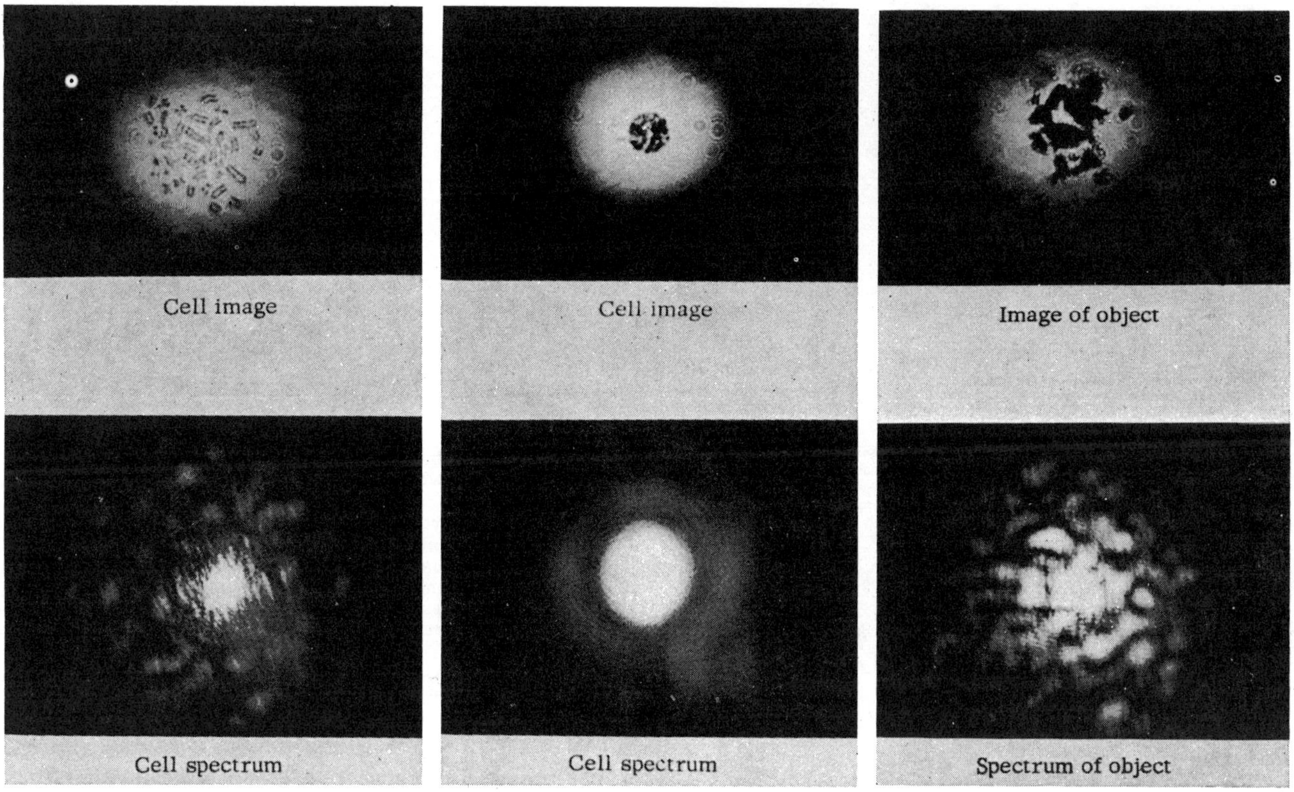

Fig. 10. Wiener spectra generated by means of an optical analog computer analysis of 50-μ diameter regions on a microscope slide containing (left) a chromosome cluster (mitotic cell); (center) a nonmitotic cell; and (right) debris (dust or dirt).

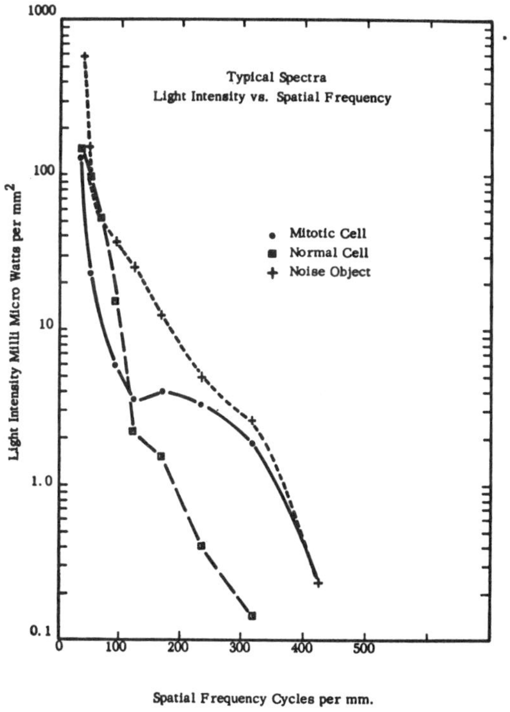

Fig. 11. Graph showing the annularly integrated Wiener spectra of the three types of objects shown in Fig. 10 averaged over a sample of 64 such objects.

Fig. 12. A breadboard optical analog computer constructed for the purpose of high-speed detection of chromosome clusters on microscope slides using two bands in the Wiener spectrum as a signature. From left to right: 1, output aperture of the laser illuminator; 2, illuminating optics; 3, microscope stage; 4, linear traverse mechanism; 5, microscope viewing optics; 6, annular filter for low spatial-frequency band; 7, annular filter for high spatial-frequency band; 8, integrating optics; and 9, photodetectors.

the moving microscope slide have an extremely weak effect on measurement accuracy. For example, only a 10-percent departure from the correct value of the Wiener spectrum occurs if the microscopy slide is displaced along the optical axis by as large an amount as 1 cm. In ordinary microscopy, focal position must be held to between 10^{-3} and 10^{-4} cm to permit a visual image of a chromosome spread to be formed with sufficient clarity so that it can be recognized.

The optical computer shown in Fig. 12 has a slide transport velocity of about 2.5 cm/s. Thus 30 000 50-μm-diam fields are examined per minute and an entire slide (10^6 fields) can be searched in 30 min. The dwell time per field is 2 ms. The calculation of the Wiener spectrum for this system corresponds to taking a 20$\times$20-point Fourier transform (0–400-

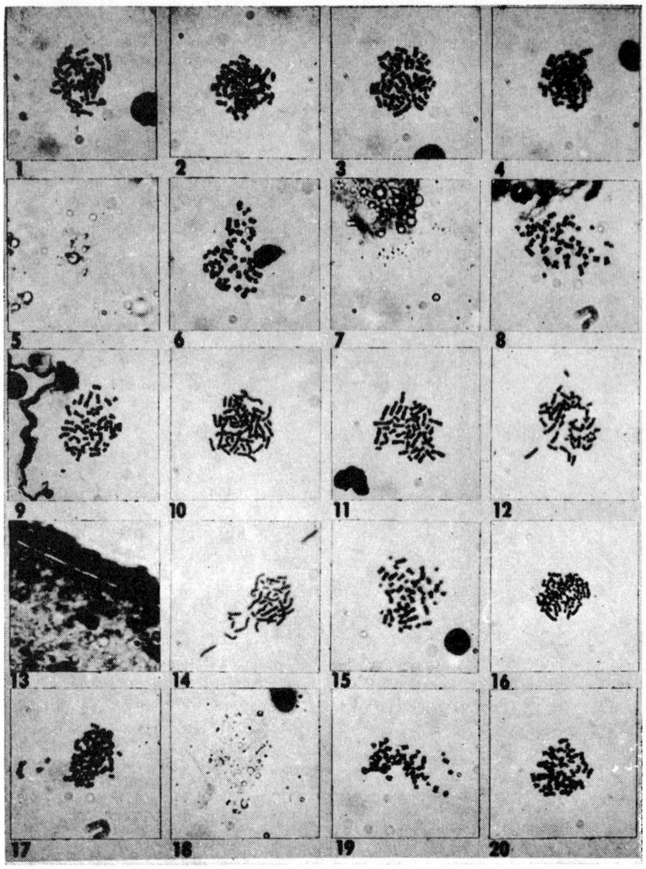

Fig. 13. Microphotographs of the first twenty objects detected by the optical analog computer shown in Fig. 12 when a previously unprocessed slide was loaded on the stage. Of the false positives, three are bubbles in the preparation (5, 7, 18) and one is a fiber (13).

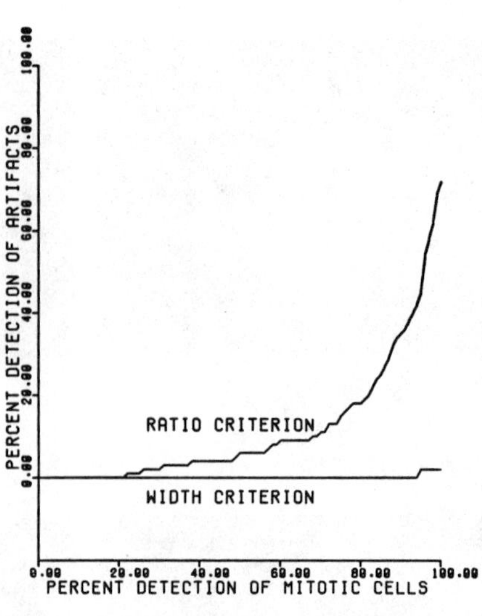

Fig. 14. False-positive rate as a function of false-negative rate for the laser illuminated optical analog-computer portion of the University of Pittsburgh automatic microscope system showing results using a high spatial-frequency versus low spatial-frequency comparison (ratio criterion) in comparison with performance obtained when the time duration of the high spatial-frequency content of the Wiener spectrum is substituted for the value of the low spatial-frequency content (width criterion). Courtesy of the Graduate School of Public Health of the University of Pittsburgh (with permission from "Computers in Biology and Medicine").

cycles/mm bandwidth at a spatial-frequency resolution of 1 cycle/50 μm). Thus this optical computer operates at a rate equivalent to about 10^8 multiplications per second.

The optical-computer system described was used to gather statistical performance data on some six million fields of view taken from portions of about 50 microscope slides which were used in a study for the Graduate School of Public Health of the University of Pittsburgh. It was found that there were several thousand nonmitotic cells per square centimeter on these slides and about 10 chromosome spreads per square centimeter. To maintain a reasonable false-positive rate, the thresholds T_1 and T_2 were adjusted so that about 30 percent of all chromosome spreads were located. It was determined that as many as 80 percent of the false positives occurred due to poor sample-preparation techniques. With improved sample-preparation techniques, a drop in the false-positive rate to 20 percent was demonstrated. This situation is illustrated in Fig. 13, which shows the objects located on the first 20 detections on a previously unscreened microscope slide taken from the test set. Sixteen of the objects are chromosome spreads; three are bubbles in the preparation; one is a piece of fiber.

This approach to high-speed chromosome-spread location has now been implemented as a second-generation automatic microscope for use by the University of Pittsburgh [18]. The technique has been further refined there by including a measurement of the time during which the T_1 threshold is exceeded as the microscope slide is scanned by the optical computer. Use of this signal-width measurement has significantly improved performance (see Fig. 14) so that it now appears that all chromosome spreads may be located with few, if any, false positives. Pittsburgh has also succeeded in upping slide velocity by almost a factor of ten so that the computation rate of the optical analog computer is now of the order of 10^9 multiplications per second.

The complete system under development at the University of Pittsburgh includes not only an optical analog computer for high-speed chromosome-spread location but also a digital cytogenetic-analysis system. Once a chromosome spread is located, its image is converted into binary form by a cathode-ray-tube flying-spot scanner. Pattern-recognition software for on-line digital analysis of the image is then used to determine significant cytogenetic data. The entire system is intended for use in rapid cytogenetic analysis of large populations of individuals. Thus this system represents a melding of analog and digital pattern-recognition technology in its overall implementation.

b) Remote-sensing applications: In addition to using optical analog computation to derive the Wiener spectrum for use in chromosome-spread location, this same technology has been employed in terrain analysis and land-use determinations in the remote-sensing field. In the late 1960's the AC Electronics Defense Research Laboratories of General Motors built an elaborate system for use in applying optical analog-computer techniques in this field [19]. The input to the system was a photographic transparency of the terrain to be analyzed. The optical system took the Fourier transform which was projected into an output plane and scanned by means of a mechanical scanner and photomultiplier so as to record the Wiener spectrum. This information was then delivered to a digital computer which used the structure of the Wiener spectrum to determine the type of land use. Typical categories reported are "buildings, roads, road intersections, and orchards" in one experiment and "residential, agricultural, and natural areas" in another.

This appears to be an excellent application of optical analog-computer techniques due to the fact that the input

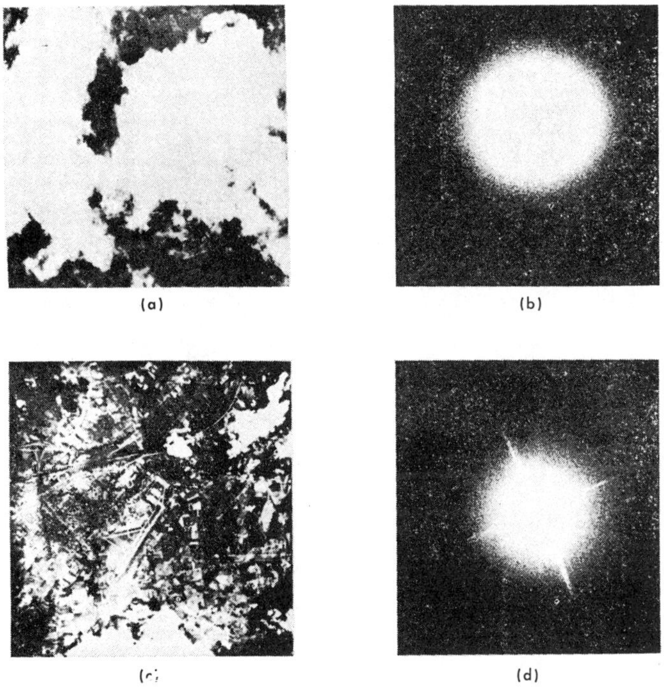

Fig. 15. Photograph comparing the Wiener spectra of an aerial photograph exhibiting cloud cover with one which does not exhibit cloud cover. Courtesy of Recognition Systems, Inc.

data in photographic remote sensing are normally obtained in the form of transparencies which are ideal for direct use as input material. Using the high data-processing rate inherent in optical analog computation, the user may compute Wiener spectra at a much higher rate than can the electronic digital computer. This is particularly useful in all types of reconnaissance (both airborne and satellite-borne) where large quantities of high-resolution imagery are generated.

Similar techniques have been applied by a variety of workers to other tasks in remote sensing. Recognition Systems, Inc., has applied Wiener-spectrum analysis in some recent experiments to distinguish aerial photographs exhibiting cloud cover from those which do not [20]. Fig. 15 provides an example of both types of photographs and the corresponding Wiener spectra. In an experiment involving 2048 such photographs, the Wiener spectrum of each was computed optically. Eight annularly integrated and 32 radially integrated measurements of each spectrum were recorded. A linear discriminant analysis was performed which excluded the total power in the spectrum as a feature and used only the relative spatial-frequency distribution as a signature. The false-positive rate was 10 percent, with a false-negative rate of 4 percent. Recognition Systems estimates that each photograph contains about 10^6 resolvable picture points so that the optical analog computer performed what is equivalent to 10^{12} complex multiplications in producing the Wiener spectrum of each photograph in this experiment.

One final example of the use of Wiener spectra for pattern recognition is illustrated in Fig. 16. This figure is an aerial photograph of a region in the Caribbean which shows a variety of ocean-wave patterns in the vicinity of two islands. The eight inserts in this figure are optically generated Wiener spectra of the ocean-wave structure at their respective locations. The zero spatial-frequency point is at the center of each insert. Measurements taken from these Wiener spectra may be used to distinguish 1) the frequency content of the

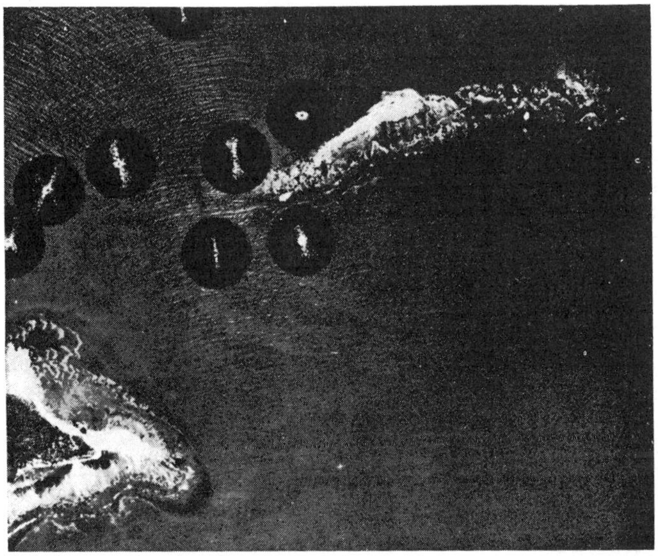

Fig. 16. Wiener spectra (inserts) of various portions of an aerial photograph of an area in the Caribbean Ocean. Both the direction, amplitude, and spatial-frequency contents of the wave structure are displayed. Courtesy of the Optics and Radar Laboratory of the University of Michigan.

wave structure and 2) the relative wave-structure intensity as a function of direction in each region analyzed. As can be seen, one spectrum indicates quiet ocean in the lee of an island; another, wave structure composed of two intersecting patterns traveling in different directions; a third, a highly directional pattern, etc. The work shown here, which was conducted at the Radar and Optics Laboratory of the University of Michigan [21], provides another illustration of the ease with which the optical analog computer may be used to generate Wiener spectra from transparencies produced by aerial photography.

2) Systems Using Optical Analog Matched Filtering: In addition to computation of the Fourier transform, the optical analog computer may be used for both frequency-domain and spatial-domain detection in pattern-recognition systems. An optical computer for frequency-domain matched filtering was shown in Fig. 5. Here a transparency or other equivalent spatial-light modulator is placed in the frequency plane so structured that it is the complex conjugate of the transform of the pattern to be identified. The product formed in the frequency plane is then transformed so that the electric field in the output plane is given by

$$\begin{aligned} E_3(x_3, y_3) &= C \iint S(\omega_x, \omega_y) S^*(\omega_x, \omega_y) \\ &\quad \cdot \exp\left[-j(x_3\omega_x + y_3\omega_y)\right] d\omega_x d\omega_y \\ &= C \iint s(x, y) s^*(x_3 + y, y_3 + y)\, dx\, dy \qquad (18) \end{aligned}$$

where $S(\omega_x, \omega_y)$ is the Fourier transform of the input pattern, $S^*(\omega_x, \omega_y)$ is the complex-conjugate frequency-plane matched filter, and $E_3(x_3, y_3)$ is the output electric-field distribution. Note from the second line of (18) that this type of pattern recognition corresponds to the classical technique of correlation detection.

In a practical sense, the complex quantity $S^*(\omega_x, \omega_y)$ may not be realized as a photographic transparency in that there is no way of producing the controllable phase modulation required or of recording the negative values required. The matched filter must, therefore, be made by some other means. This is usually accomplished by holographic techniques where an intensity-only recording medium is placed in the frequency plane and is illuminated both by the Fourier transform of the pattern to be recognized and by the transform of what is called the "reference function." The reference function usually consists of a point source or, in some cases, a source consisting of several points having a spatially coded structure. In the frequency plane, the optical intensity $I_2(\omega_x, \omega_y)$ to which the recording medium responds is given by

$$\begin{aligned} I_2(\omega_x, \omega_y) &= E_2(\omega_x, \omega_y)E_2^*(\omega_x, \omega_y) \\ &= |\boldsymbol{S}(\omega_x, \omega_y) + \boldsymbol{R}(\omega_x, \omega_y)|^2 \\ &= |\boldsymbol{S}(\omega_x, \omega_y)|^2 + |\boldsymbol{R}(\omega_x, \omega_y)|^2 \\ &\quad + \boldsymbol{S}(\omega_x, \omega_y)\boldsymbol{R}^*(\omega_x, \omega_y) \\ &\quad + \boldsymbol{S}^*(\omega_x, \omega_y)\boldsymbol{R}(\omega_x, \omega_y) \end{aligned} \tag{19}$$

where $\boldsymbol{R}(\omega_x, \omega_y)$ is the Fourier transform of the reference function. The recording medium is exposed to $I_2(\omega_x, \omega_y)$, developed, and placed in the Fourier plane for use as the matched filter. When $s(x, y)$ appears as the input, the output-correlation function results from the $\boldsymbol{S}^*(\omega_x, \omega_y)\boldsymbol{R}(\omega_x, \omega_y)$ term and occurs at an off-axis position in the output plane. In all other respects performance is equivalent to that obtained from the idealized situation given by (18).

Another approach to correlation detection which may be useful when the input recording is moved continuously through the input plane is to employ an optical analog computer using spatial-plane correlation detection. Here an additional lens beyond the x_3, y_3 plane produces a correlation function given by

$$E_4(t, y_4) = \int s(x - v_T t) s_{y_3}(x) dx \tag{20}$$

where v_T is the transport velocity of the input-signal recording and $s_{y_3}(x)$ is a comparison-function transparency located in the x_3, y_3 plane. Since motion is usually in one direction only, the signal detected by such a computer must also be one-dimensional. The signal can, however, be compared with a two-dimensional comparison function consisting of a library of one-dimensional functions.

Ordinarily the most useful optical analog-computer configuration for matched filtering is the one employing frequency-plane rather than spatial-plane detection. This is due to the fact that no mechanical motion is required, the number of optical elements are minimized, and two-dimensional signals may be processed. Furthermore, a frequency-plane matched filter may be created and so arranged as to act as a filter which is matched to a multiplicity of patterns. This is done by using a reference function which takes up different positions and/or structures for each input pattern to be detected. Such a matched filter is simultaneously matched to many signals and can handle a two-dimensional input pattern which is screened for a variety of pattern matches in a single look. A few specific applications are now described which illustrate the use of the optical analog computer operating as a matched filter.

a) Character recognition: One application which has received extensive treatment is optical character recognition. Some of the earlier work reported by IBM demonstrated both the Fourier transforms and correlation functions of fixed fonts [22]. More recent work along these lines, using a matched filter formed from a set of reference functions structured as digital codes, has been reported by Nakajima *et al.* [23]. This employs the approach initially proposed by Gabor [24]. The main deficiency in the use of the optical computer for character recognition is that input material is usually not in the form of a transparency but rather in the form of material printed on a page. This implies that a photographic intermediary must be made. This step makes the entire process unattractive except, perhaps, in reading previously microfilmed pages.

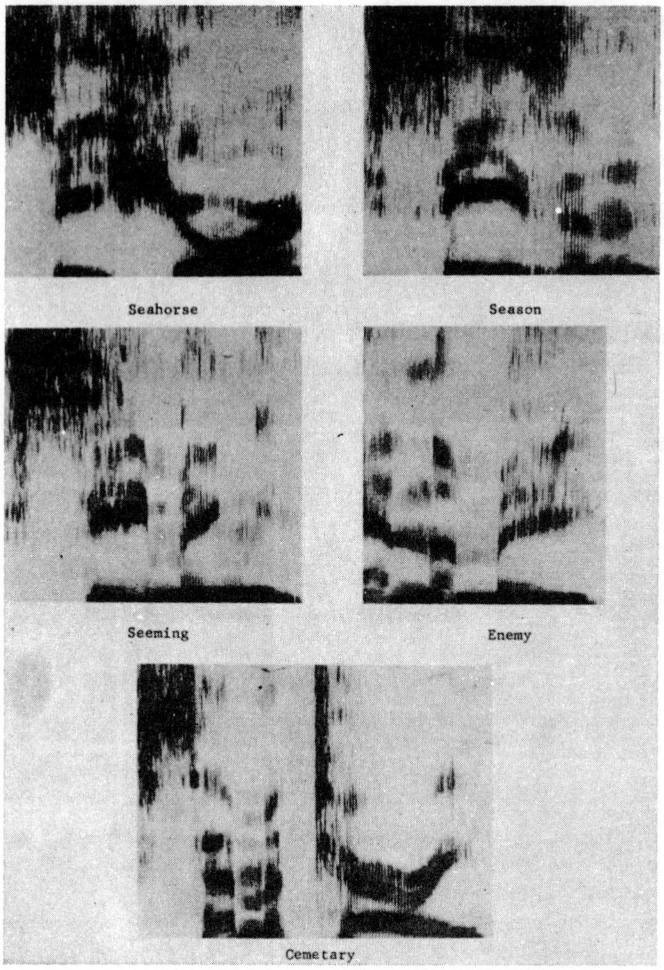

Fig. 17. Speech spectrograms of six words enunciated by the same speaker which contain similar phonemes. Courtesy of Voice Prints, Inc. (Excerpted from *Coherent Optical Computers* by permission of publisher, copyright 1972, McGraw-Hill, Inc.)

To solve the input problem, recent work has been applied to a variety of optical-to-optical converters which may be utilized as input transducers for use in character recognition [25], [26]. These converters are sensitive to the radiation field produced by a noncoherent image of the printed page and are capable of modulating coherent light simultaneously so as to provide a real-time input to an optical computer. None of these devices have been taken past the feasibility stage so that work in this entire area is still confined to the research laboratory. However, if these converters are carried to the point of success in terms of both economy and reliability, then the high data-rate capability of the optical computer may find application in the character-recognition field.

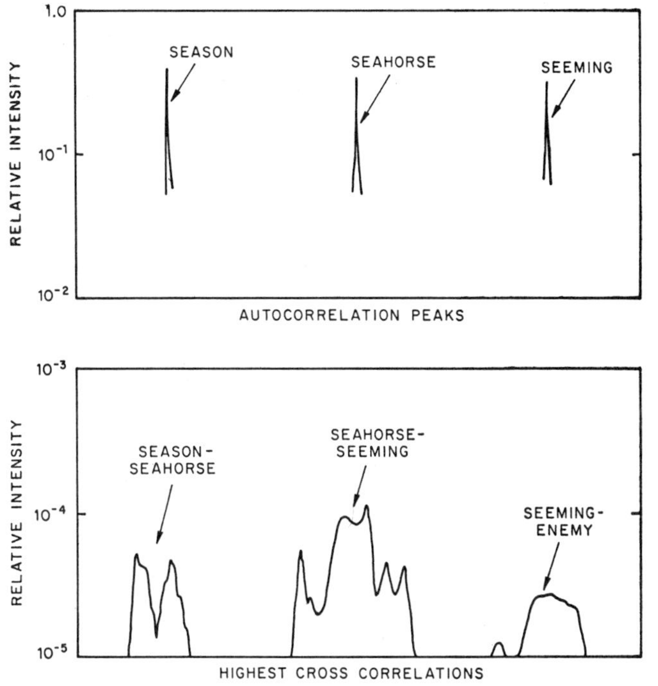

Fig. 18. Autocorrelation and cross-correlation functions for the speech spectrograms shown in Fig. 17 computed by means of an optical analog computer. Courtesy of the Perkin-Elmer Corp. (Excerpted from *Coherent Optical Computers* by permission of publisher, copyright 1972, McGraw-Hill, Inc.)

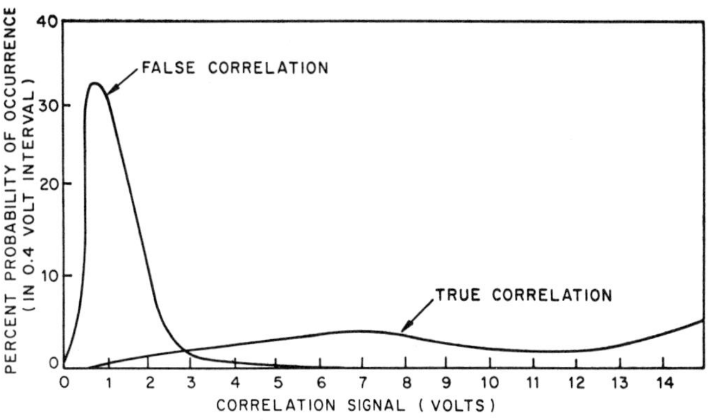

Fig. 19. Cross-correlation functions generated by the optical analog computer incorporated in the KMS Automatic Personnel Verifier for a population of 13 persons. The false correlation curve is based on data taken from 535 trials. The true correlation curve is based on data taken from 429 trials. Courtesy KMS Industries, Inc.

b) Word recognition: Word recognition using optical analog matched filtering of speech spectrograms of words spoken by a known speaker has been pursued by Perkin-Elmer [27]. So far the work reported is exploratory and the samples studied are small. An example is furnished in Fig. 17, which shows the speech spectrograms recorded from the voice of a known speaker enunciating words deliberately chosen to have a marked degree of similarity. Frequency-plane matched filters were constructed holographically for each of the spectrograms. Both the autocorrelation and cross-correlation functions were computed using an optical analog computer. The results of this experiment are given in Fig. 18, which shows, for this small sample, a discrimination margin of 30–40 dB. Clearly, this encouraging result must be backed up with further experimentation before the value of this method of word recognition of a given speaker's vocabulary may be properly evaluated. However, the work is of interest since, with the multiple-pattern matched filter described in Section III-B2), the large area-space–bandwidth product of the optical computer would permit simultaneous interrogation of a vocabulary of 1000 words.

c) Fingerprint recognition: Extensive work has been carried out in the fingerprint-recognition field. A recent investigation of the use of optical analog computers for fingerprint identification by matched filtering has been reported by KMS Industries [28]. Fig. 19 provides probability–density curves for optically generated cross-correlation functions for fingerprints generated from a sample set of 13 persons. These results are taken from an actual operating system where the input pattern is generated by a human forefinger pressed against a window. The front surface of the window forms the input plane to an optical analog computer. The frequency-plane matched filter is introduced into the system in the form of an ID card. Results indicate that, with the threshold adjusted so that the probability of false positives is 0.001, the false-negative probability is about 0.2. Clearly, other threshold values would lead to different results and the actual selection of the threshold value depends on the penalties assigned to the production of false positives and false negatives, respectively. In personnel verification it is usually more desirable to adjust for a very low false-positive rate at the expense of a relatively high false-negative rate.

IV. Summary and Conclusions

From the preceding it is evident that the use of analog techniques in pattern recognition may be advantageous in linear and quadratic discrimination and in recognition based on spectrum analysis. Due to accuracy limitations and the difficulty of obtaining the special-purpose hardware required, this advantage is due primarily to the speed of analog hardware. We should now ask whether the rapid advances in the electronic digital-computer art may soon challenge the speed advantage held by the analog computer.

A. Analog Versus Digital

Cost, as well as speed, is critical. In an attempt to compare analog-computer performance with that of the digital computer, the graph shown in Fig. 20 has been prepared. This graph shows best estimates of the cost performance (in bits per second per dollar) of two of the special-purpose analog-computer systems described. These entries consist of two-pointed arrows, the lower point of which is the best estimate of the price performance of the analog computer in the original system; the upper point, the price performance of the same system in limited-quantity production. Fig. 20 also charts the price trend in general-purpose digital-computer power as a function of time over the past decade [29] and extrapolates this line into the future. Furthermore, the present range of fast Fourier transform (FFT) computers is shown in order to indicate the performance of special-purpose digital computers in comparison with the general-purpose computer systems.

The economic justification for the SPARC electronic analog computer is clear considering the decade in which it was conceived. If electronic-analog-computer device costs can be reduced at the same rate as those of electronic digital computers, then systems such as SPARC will continue to be

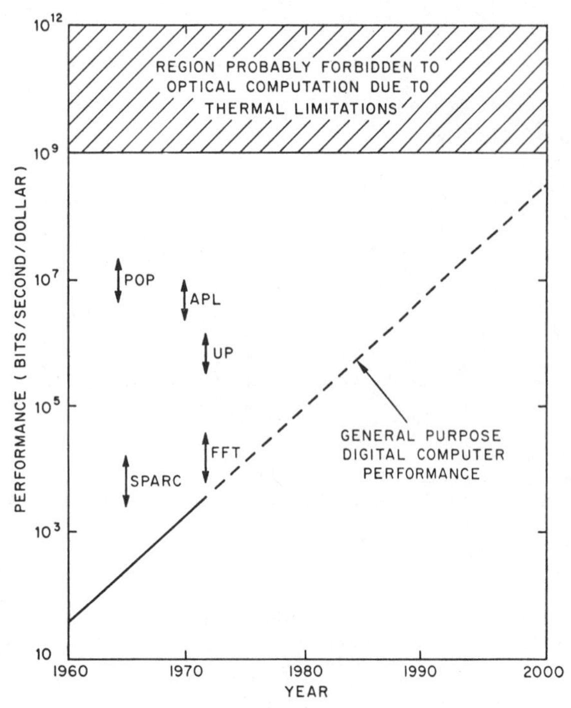

Fig. 20. Performance data (in bits per second per dollar) for a variety of special-purpose analog- and special-purpose digital-computer systems overlaid by the predicted upperbound for optical analog-computer power and an extrapolation of general-purpose digital-computer power for purposes of comparison. A general trend favoring digital electronic systems is evident, but it appears that special-purpose optical analog systems will have an advantage in certain limited areas of application for the next 10 to 30 years.

competitive. Otherwise, it is evident that they will be replaced by digital systems in the 1970's.

The University of Pittsburgh optical analog computer for chromosome-spread detection is seen to be competitive with its digital electronic equivalent. Since the basic components of this system are extremely simple (see Fig. 12), the falloff in laser prices and in the prices of photodetectors (as solid-state detectors replace photomultipliers) should keep such a system competitive for the next decade. The reader interested in commercial biomedical systems using Wiener-spectrum analysis should review the characteristics of the optical cytoanalyzing computers reported by Kamentsky [30].

To add further information to Fig. 20, the price performance of two special-purpose military optical analog computers is also indicated. The Precision Optical Processor (POP) built for the University of Michigan by Perkin-Elmer is a specialized multichannel cross correlator for use in synthetic-aperture radar-signal analysis. This system has the highest equivalent bit rate (10^{12} bit/s) of any optical computer in existence. Its original price is estimated at about 250 000 dollars. Note that this price is for the complete system including laser illuminator, input and output signal film transports, output plane scanner and x–y plotter, the optical system (including auxiliary optics for modifying the processing mode), mounting equipment (a 25-ft-long granite slab), and room air conditioning for both cleanliness and temperature stability.

Another military computer is that fabricated for the Johns Hopkins Applied Physics Laboratory (APL) by Perkin-Elmer [31]. This computer is also used in radar signal processing and is capable of computing a 100-point Fourier transform in 1 μs at a precision equivalent to 10-bit and a 5-bit accuracy. This is equivalent to a processing rate of about 10^{11} bit/s. Its initial price was considerably less than the POP yielding about the same overall performance.

Interestingly, none of the optical analog computers mentioned have achieved the 10^{14}-multiplications-per-second rate predicted by an evaluation of (9) for 1-W laser illumination. This is primarily because of input/output limitations (see Section III-B2)a)).

To complete Fig. 20, the ultimate physical limitations of optical analog computation were taken into account in order to derive a performance bound which would be difficult to penetrate. It was assumed that typical optical analog computer systems will not significantly decrease in price over the next few decades. This will be due to the fact that this type of computer is expected to represent a low-quantity high-price business, to require a significant amount of manual labor in the fabrication and testing of optical systems, and to depend upon precision mechanical-assembly techniques which are not likely to be automated in the same fashion that electronic assembly is now automated. The maximum performance rate, as indicated in Fig. 20, is based on the assumptions that the price for ultimate systems will stay in the 10^5–10^6-dollar range and that thermal considerations, i.e., problems associated with the life of the I/O devices themselves at high illumination levels, will keep laser illumination levels below 10–100 W. This leads to a tentative upper bound in the 10^9–10^{12}-bit/s/dollar range. Therefore, if science and engineering can capitalize upon this type of very specialized computing power for pattern recognition, the special-purpose optical analog computer will probably be competitive with special-purpose digital computers for at least another decade and with general-purpose digital computers perhaps until the end of the 20th century.

Appendix

The basis of optical analog computation is related to the interaction of coherent light with certain pattern input devices called "spatial light modulators." A spatial light modulator is a device which may be used to introduce a two-dimensional function across the input plane of an optical analog computer. Typical spatial light modulators consist of thin films of certain materials which may be used to locally modulate the light passing through them (or reflecting off them) either separately in amplitude, phase, or polarization or in combination. Electrooptic films, silver-halide emulsions, thermoplastic films, liquid-crystal films, deformable-membrane mirrors, etc., are typical spatial light modulators.

The action of any one of these devices may be represented by a complex phase modulating function whose action is characterized by a Jones matrix

$$L = \begin{bmatrix} f_{11}(x_1, y_1) & f_{12}(x_1, y_1) \\ f_{21}(x_1, y_1) & f_{22}(x_1, y_1) \end{bmatrix} \tag{A1}$$

where the x_1, y_1 plane is the input plane. The elements of $\boldsymbol{L}$ relate the xy components of the incident electric-field vector to the electric-field vector generated by the interaction between the incident light and the spatial light modulator. In most cases isotropy prevails so that the off-diagonal terms of the Jones matrix are zero and the diagonal terms are identical. Let each diagonal term be represented in this case by the complex function $f(x_1, y_1)$.

In order to demonstrate the results of the interaction of incident light with the spatial light modulator, expand

$f(x_1, y_1)$ in a Fourier series as follows:

$$f(x_1, y_1) = a_0 + \sum_{k=1}^{k=\infty} \sum_{l=1}^{l=\infty} \left[b_{kl} \cos\left(\frac{2\pi k x_1}{A} + \frac{2\pi l y_1}{A}\right) + c_{kl} \sin\left(\frac{2\pi k x_1}{A} + \frac{2\pi l y_1}{A}\right)\right] \quad \text{(A2)}$$

where the indices k and l are positive integers, A is the linear extent of the spatial light modulator, and the Fourier coefficients a_0, b_{kl}, and c_{kl} are given by

$$a_0 = \frac{1}{A^2} \iint_{-A/2}^{+A/2} f(x_1, y_1) dx_1 dy_1$$

$$b_{kl} = \frac{4}{A^2} \iint_{-A/2}^{+A/2} f(x_1, y_1) \cos\left(\frac{2\pi k x_1}{A} + \frac{2\pi l y_1}{A}\right) dx_1 dy_1$$

$$c_{kl} = \frac{4}{A^2} \iint_{-A/2}^{+A/2} f(x_1, y_1) \cdot \sin\left(\frac{2\pi k x_1}{A} + \frac{2\pi l y_1}{A}\right) dx_1 dy_1. \quad \text{(A3)}$$

Equation (A2) may be rewritten as follows using the imaginary exponential notation:

$$f(x_1, y_1) = a_0 + \frac{1}{2} \sum_{k=1}^{k=\infty} \sum_{l=1}^{l=\infty} \{(b_{kl} - jc_{kl}) \cdot \exp[j(2\pi k x_1/A + 2\pi l y_1/A)] + (b_{kl} + jc_{kl}) \cdot \exp[-j(2\pi k x_1/A + 2\pi l y_1/A)]\}. \quad \text{(A4)}$$

If the electric vector describing the incident light is polarized along the x axis and has a maximum value of E_m and frequency ω_L, then the electric vector generated by the interaction with the spatial light modulator is

$$E(x_1 y_1) = a_0 E_m \exp(-j\omega_L t) + \frac{E_m}{2} \exp(-j\omega_L t) \cdot \sum_{k=1}^{k=\infty} \sum_{l=1}^{l=\infty} \{(b_{kl} - c_{kl}) \cdot \exp[j(2\pi k x_1/A + 2y_1/A)] + (b_{kl} + jc_{kl}) \cdot \exp[-j(2\pi k x_1/A + 2\pi l y_1/A)]\}. \quad \text{(A5)}$$

By expressing the complex Fourier coefficients as follows

$$b_{kl} - jc_{kl} = \frac{4}{A^2} \iint_{-A/2}^{+A/2} f(x_1, y_1) \cdot \exp[-j(2\pi k x_1/A + 2\pi l y_1/A)] dx_1 dy_1$$

$$b_{kl} + jc_{kl} = \frac{4}{A^2} \iint_{-A/2}^{+A/2} f(x_1, y_1) \cdot \exp[j(2\pi k x_1/A + 2\pi l y_1/A)] dx_1 dy_1 \quad \text{(A6)}$$

and recognizing that the above equations are complex conjugates, we may combine (A6) in a single equation given by

$$d_{kl} = \frac{4}{A^2} \iint_{-A/2}^{+A/2} f(x_1, y_1) \cdot \exp[-j(2\pi k x_1/A + 2\pi l y_1/A)] dx_1 dy_1 \quad \text{(A7)}$$

where d_{kl} are the complex Fourier coefficients with the indices

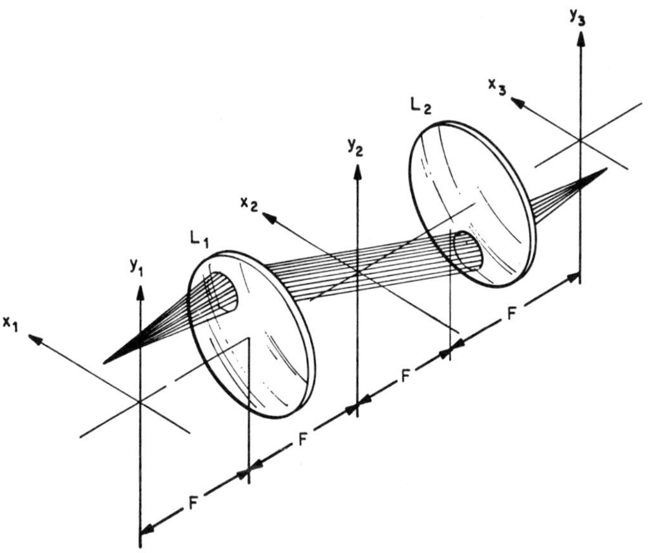

Fig. 21. Schematic of an optical analog computer taking two successive two-dimensional Fourier transforms thus mapping a delta function at x_1, y_1, in the input plane into a delta function at $-x_3$, $-y_3$ in the output plane.

k and l now taking on both positive and negative values. Finally, (A5) becomes

$$E(x_1, y_1) = a_0 E_m \exp(-j\omega_L t) + \frac{E_m}{2} \exp(-j\omega_L t) \cdot \sum_{k=-\infty}^{k=+\infty} \sum_{l=-\infty}^{l=+\infty} d_{kl} \exp[j(2\pi x_1 k/A + 2\pi y_1 l/A)]. \quad \text{(A8)}$$

In order to appreciate the significance of (A8) refer to Fig. 21. This figure shows a typical optical-computer configuration with a spatial light modulator in the input plane plus two lenses which are followed by the output plane. There is also an intermediate plane or "Fourier plane" between the two lenses. Utilize the convention that electromagnetic energy propagates in the direction of the z axis. (This axis is normally called the "optical axis.") In order to clarify the significance of the exponential notation, note that the instantaneous phase of an electromagnetic wave propagating in the z direction may be written $\exp[j(2\pi\omega_L z/c)]$ implying that phase *increases* with z. The quantity c is the velocity of electromagnetic propagation. The complete expression for the exponential is $\exp\{j[2\pi\omega_L(z-ct)/c]\}$. The negative sign is necessitated by the fact that, since it has been assumed that phase increases with z, phase must therefore *decrease* with time as the wave propagates in the positive z direction. (It is, of course, possible to define a phase angle which *decreases* with z which in turn would imply *increasing* phase with time. This, however, is not the usual convention.)

The expression

$$a_0 E_m \exp(-j\omega_L t) \quad \text{(A9)}$$

in (A8) represents the electric field in the input plane ($z=0$) corresponding to the plane wave propagating along the z axis. The expression

$$\frac{E_m}{2} \exp(-j\omega_L t) d_{kl} \exp[j(2\pi x_1 k/A + 2\pi y_1 l/A)] \quad \text{(A10)}$$

represents the electric field in the input plane of one of an infinity of plane waves having the same temporal frequency ω_L and complex amplitudes given by $E_m d_{kl}/2$. Note that each wave is phase shifted by $2\pi k$ radians across the extent A of the input plane in the x direction and by $2\pi l$ radians in the y direction. Since a positive phase shift implies a retrogression in time, those portions of the klth wave having positive values of both kl and xy lag behind the wave at the origin. Thus the wave in question is retarded in the first quadrant of the xy plane. Since a phase shift of $2\pi k$ radians is equivalent to a retardation of k wavelengths, the normal to this plane wave has direction cosines which are given by

$$\cos\alpha = \frac{k\lambda_L}{A} \qquad \cos\beta = \frac{l\lambda_L}{A} \tag{A11}$$

where α and β are the direction angles with respect to the x and y axes, respectively, and λ_L is the wavelength of light. Similarly, a wave with negative values of kl is advanced in the first quadrant, etc.

The above considerations lead to a demonstration of the fact that the primary effect of the spatial light modulator resident in the input plane and whose action is described by $f(x, y)$ is to divide the incident optical radiation into an infinity of new waves whose complex amplitudes are directly related to the complex Fourier coefficients of $f(x, y)$. The directions of propagation of these waves are determined by the corresponding direction cosines. This physical fact is an explanation of the phenomenon called "diffraction." It is this phenomenon which permits the optical analog computer to be used in Fourier analysis. This also permits optical computers to be applied to pattern recognition using correlation detection and matched filtering.

To complete the discussion, let the quantity A become infinite so that k/A and l/A become infinitesimals. A two-dimensional Fourier transform of the function $f(x, y)$ is then obtained which is given by

$$F(\cos\alpha, \cos\beta) = \frac{1}{2}\iint_{-\infty}^{+\infty} f(x, y) \exp\left[-j(2\pi\cos\alpha x/\lambda_L + 2\pi\cos\beta y/\lambda_L)\right] dx\,dy. \tag{A12}$$

The quantities $(2\pi\cos\alpha)/\lambda_L$ and $(2\pi\cos\beta)/\lambda_L$ are called the "radian spatial frequencies" and are symbolized by ω_x and ω_y. This permits the above equation to be written in the form

$$F(\omega_x, \omega_y) = \frac{1}{2\pi}\iint_{-\infty}^{+\infty} f(x, y) \exp\left[-j(\omega_x x + \omega_y y)\right] dx\,dy. \tag{A13}$$

The measure of ω_x and ω_y are radians per unit length. The corresponding "spatial frequencies" whose measure is cycles per unit length are $f_x = \omega_x/2\pi$ and $f_y = \omega_y/2\pi$.

It should be noted that the optical analog computer takes successive two-dimensional Fourier transforms rather than carrying out a Fourier transform followed by its inverse. Thus a delta function in x_1y_1 plane shown in Fig. 21 is mapped into a delta function at $-x_3$, $-y_3$ in the output plane.

The purpose of the lenses in the optical computer is to permit the separation of the Fourier components of $f(x, y)$ at a convenient physical distance from the spatial light modulator. With an input aperture A and no lenses, the Fourier components become separable at the Rayleigh distance given by

$$R_\lambda = A^2/2\lambda_L \tag{A14}$$

which, for typical values of A and λ_L, may range from 10^2 to 10^3 m. When a lens is interposed with the spatial light modulator in its front focal plane, the Fourier components are separably displayed in its back focal plane (A2). Thus except for small values of A and/or large values of λ_L, lenses are a necessity. They are also a necessity when successive Fourier transforms are to be taken for use in correlation detection and matched filtering.

Acknowledgment

The author wishes to thank the members of many organizations who furnished information for inclusion in this paper, as well as the Guest Editor and the referees of this Special Issue, whose suggestions resulted in many worthwhile changes and additions. In particular, G. A. Philbrick Researches, Inc., Electronic Associates, Inc., and the Willow Run Laboratories of the University of Michigan furnished much of the information on electronic analog computers. The Navy Underwater Systems Center (San Diego, Calif.) and Bell Telephone Laboratories (Murray Hill, N. J.) provided data on the use of acoustical delay-line correlators. The Applied Physics Laboratory (Johns Hopkins University), the Institute of Science and Technology (University of Michigan), KMS Industries, Recognition Systems, Inc., the Graduate School of Public Health at the University of Pittsburgh, and many colleagues at Perkin-Elmer supplied much of the information on-optical-analog-computer systems for use in pattern recognition in their fields of specialization. Finally, the assistance of the Technical Documentation Group of Perkin-Elmer is acknowledged for preparation of the photographs and line drawings.

References

[1] G. A. Philbrick, "Designing industrial controllers by analog," *Electronics*, vol. 108, June 1948.
[2] J. R. Ragazzini, R. H. Randall, and F. A. Russell, "Analysis of problems in dynamics by electronic circuits," *Proc. IRE*, vol. 35, pp. 444–452, May 1947.
[3] L. Levine, *Methods for Solving Engineering Problems Using Analog Computers*. New York: McGraw-Hill, 1964.
[4] G. A. Korn and T. M. Korn, *Electronic Analog and Hybrid Computers*. New York: McGraw-Hill, 1964.
[5] G. A. Bekey and W. J. Karplus, *Hybrid Computation*. New York: Wiley, 1968.
[6] A. Hausner, *Analog and Analog Hybrid Computer Programming*. Englewood Cliffs, N. J.: Prentice-Hall, 1971.
[7] R. S. Duncan and M. R. Parker, "The perpendicular diffraction delay line: A new kind of ultrasonic dispersive device," *Proc. IEEE* (Lett.), vol. 53, pp. 413–414, Apr. 1965.
[8] W. S. Mortley, British Patent 988 102, Apr. 7, 1965.
[9] R. H. Tancrell and M. G. Holland, "Acoustic surface wave filters," *Proc. IEEE*, vol. 59, pp. 393–409, Mar. 1971.
[10] E. K. Sittig and G. A. Coquin, "Dispersive-diffraction delay lines with intermediate gratings," *IEEE Trans. Sonics Ultrason.*, vol. SU-17, pp. 23–29, Jan. 1970.
[11] C. F. Quate and R. B. Thomson, "Convolution and correlation in real-time with non-linear acoustics," *Appl. Phys. Lett.*, vol. 16, p. 494, 1970.
[12] W. L. Bongianni, "Pulse compression using nonlinear interaction in a surface acoustic wave convolver," *Proc. IEEE* (Lett.), vol. 59, pp. 713–714, Apr. 1971.
[13] K. Preston, *Coherent Optical Computers*. New York: McGraw-Hill, 1972, p. 77.
[14] *Ibid.*, p. 11.
[15] *Ibid.*, ch. 5.
[16] *Ibid.*, p. 197.
[17] P. E. Norgren, "High speed automatic laser beam detection of chromosome spreads," *Ann. N. Y. Acad. Sci.*, vol. 157, p. 514, 1969.
[18] J. Herron, R. Ranshaw, J. Castle, and N. Wald, "Automatic microscopy for mitotic cell location," in *Computers in Biology and Medicine*, 1972 (in press).
[19] G. G. Lendaris and G. L. Stanley, "Diffraction-pattern sampling for automatic pattern recognition," *Proc. IEEE*, vol. 58, pp. 198–216, Feb. 1970.
[20] H. L. Kasdan, "A distribution-free pattern classification procedure with performance monitoring capability," in *Proc. IFIP Colloq. on Optimization*, Oct. 1971.
[21] R. H. Mitchel and F. B. Rotz, "Applications of coherent optics to

geological imagry," U. S. Air Force Cambridge Res. Lab. Rep. AFCRL-69-0135, Aug. 1969.
[22] L. P. Horwitz and G. L. Shelton, Jr., "Pattern recognition using autocorrelation," *Proc. IRE*, vol. 49, pp. 175–185, Jan. 1961.
[23] M. Nakajima *et al.*, "Automatic character reading using a holographic data processing technique," *Appl. Opt.*, vol. 11, p. 362, 1972.
[24] D. Gabor, "Character recognition by holography," *Nature*, vol. 208, p. 422, 1965.
[25] F. Reizman, "Optical spatial phase modulator array," in *Proc. Electro-Opt. Syst. Design Conf.* (New York), Sept. 1969.
[26] A. D. Jacobson, "The liquid crystal light valve—An optical-to-optical interface device," presented at Conf. on Parallel Image Proc. for Earth Obs. Sys., Goddard Space Flight Cen., Greenbelt, Md., Mar. 1972.
[27] K. Preston, Jr., "Method and apparatus for optical speech correlation," U. S. Patent 3 636 261, Jan. 1972.
[28] C. E. Thomas, "Automatic optical fingerprint identification," in *Proc. Carnahan Conf. on Electron. Crime Countermeasures* (Lexington, Ky.), 1972.
[29] D. L. House and R. A. Hensel, "Semi-conductor memories and mini-computers," *Comput.*, vol. 4, p. 24, 1971.
[30] L. A. Kamentsky, "A flow-through system," in *Proc. 4th Tutorial on Clin. Cytol.* (Univ. of Chicago), Aug. 1971.
[31] K. Preston, Jr., "A coherent optical computer system using the membrane light modulator," *IEEE Trans. Aerosp. Electron. Syst.*, vol. AES-6, pp. 458–467, July 1970.

Bibliography

The following list of supplementary references, which are not specifically cited in the text, is provided for the reader who wishes further background information on electronic, acoustical, and optical analog computers. Regarding electronic analog computers, where the literature is voluminous and the texts, already referenced, adequately describe the state of the art, the supplementary references are of early work taken from *A Palimpsest on the Electronic Analog Art*, prepared by G. A. Philbrick Researchers, Inc., in 1965 (H. M. Paynter, Ed.) and available from Teledyne/Philbrick Research, Allied Drive at Route 128, Boston, Mass. 02026.

Electronic Analog Computers

D. J. Mynall, "Electrical analog computing," *Electron. Eng.* (England), vol. 19, p. 178, June–Sept. 1947.
A. B. MacNee, "An electronic differential analyzer," *Proc. IRE*, vol. 37, pp. 1315–1324, Nov. 1949.
J. M. L. Janssen and L. Ensing, "The electro-analogue, an apparatus for studying regulating systems," *Philips Tech. Rev.*, vol. 12, p. 257, Mar. 1951.
R. C. McMaster, R. L. Merrill, and B. H. List, "Analogous systems in engineering design," *Product Eng.*, vol. 24, p. 184, Jan. 1953.
J. B. Reswick, "Scale factors for analog computers," *Product Eng.*, vol. 25, p. 197, Mar. 1954.

Acoustical Analog Computers

Lord Rayleigh, "On waves propagated along the plane surface of an elastic solid," *Proc. London Math. Soc.*, vol. 17, p. 4, 1885.
J. H. Rowen, "Tapped ultrasonic delay line and uses therefor," U. S. Patent 3 289 144, Nov. 29, 1966; filed Dec. 24, 1963.
J. E. May, "Guided wave ultrasonic delay lines," in *Physical Acoustics*, vol. 1A. New York: Academic Press, 1964, p. 417.
R. S. Duncan and M. R. Parker, "The perpendicular diffraction delay line: A new kind of ultrasonic dispersive device," *Proc. IEEE* (Corresp.), vol. 53, pp. 413–414, Apr. 1965.
G. A. Coquin, and R. Tsu, "Theory and performance of perpendicular diffraction delay lines," *Proc. IEEE*, vol. 53, pp. 581–591, June 1965.
E. K. Sittig, "Dispersive ultrasonic delay lines using multielement arrays," in *Proc. 5th Int. Cong. Acoustics* (Liege, Belgium, Sept. 1965), Paper D22.
D. E. Miller and M. R. Parker, "Dispersion by plane wave excitation of piezoelectric transducer arrays," *Proc. IEEE* (Lett.), vol. 54, pp. 891–892, June 1966.
I. A. Viktorov, *Rayleigh and Lamb Waves*. New York: Plenum, 1967.
E. K. Sittig and G. A. Coquin, "Filters and dispersive delay lines using repetitively mismatched ultrasonic transmission lines," *IEEE Trans. Sonics Ultrason.*, vol. SU-15, pp. 111–119, Apr. 1968.
W. R. Smith *et al.*, "Design of surface wave delay lines with interdigital transducers," *IEEE Trans. Microwave Theory Tech.*, vol. MTT-17, pp. 865–873, Nov. 1969.
P. Hartemann and E. Dieulesaint, "Acoustic surface wave filters," *Electron. Lett.*, vol. 5, p. 657, Dec. 1969.
R. M. White, "Surface elastic waves," *Proc. IEEE*, vol. 58, pp. 1238–1276, Aug. 1970.
W. L. Bond, T. Reeder, and H. J. Shaw, "Wraparound surface wave delay lines," *Electron. Lett.*, vol. 5, p. 657, Feb. 11, 1971.
M. Luukkala and G. S. Kino, "Convolution and time inversion using parametric interactions of acoustic surface waves," *Appl. Phys. Lett.*, vol. 18, p. 393, May 1, 1971.

Optical Analog Computers

P. Elias, "Optics and communication theory," *J. Opt. Soc. Amer.*, vol. 43, p. 229, 1953.
T. P. Cheatham, Jr., and A. Kohlenberg, "Optical filters: Their equivalence to and differences from electrical networks," in *IRE Conv. Rec.*, pt. 4, pp. 6–12, 1954.
E. L. O'Neill, "Spatial filtering in optics," *IRE Trans. Inform. Theory*, vol. IT-2, pp. 56–76, June 1956.
B. J. Howell, "Optical analog computers," *J. Opt. Soc. Amer.*, vol. 49, p. 1012, 1959.
L. J. Cutrona, E. N. Leith, C. J. Palermo, and L. J. Porcello, "Optical data processing and filtering systems," *IRE Trans. Inform. Theory*, vol. IT-6, pp. 386–400, June 1960.
E. N. Leith and J. Upatnieks, "Reconstructed wavefronts and communications theory," *J. Opt. Soc. Amer.*, vol. 52, p. 1123, 1962.
L. B. Lambert, "Wide-band, instantaneous spectrum analyzers employing delay-line light modulators," in *IRE Conv. Rec.*, pt. 6, pp. 69–78, 1962.
D. McLachlan, Jr., "The role of optics in applying correlation functions to pattern recognition," *J. Opt. Soc. Amer.*, vol. 52, p. 454, 1962.
R. E. Williams, "The panchromatic principle in optical filtering," *IEEE Trans. Inform. Theory*, vol. IT-10, pp. 227–234, July 1964.
A. Vander Lugt, "Signal detection by complex spatial filtering," *IEEE Trans. Inform. Theory*, vol. IT-10, pp. 139–145, Apr. 1964.
K. Preston, Jr., "Use of the Fourier transformable properties of lenses for signal spectrum analysis," in *Optical and Electro-Optical Information Processing*. Cambridge, Mass.: M.I.T. Press, 1965, ch. 4.
R. E. Williams, "Partially coherent processing by optical means," *IEEE Trans. Inform. Theory*, vol. IT-11, pp. 499–507, Oct. 1965.
N. F. Izzo, "Optical correlation technique using a variable reference function," *Proc. IEEE* (Corresp.), vol. 53, pp. 1740–1741, Nov. 1965.
E. N. Leith *et al.*, "Coherent optical systems for data processing, spatial filtering, and wavefront reconstruction," in *Optical and Electro-Optical Information Processing*. Cambridge, Mass.: M.I.T. Press, 1965, ch. 8.
A. Kozma and D. L. Kelly, "Spatial filtering for detection of signals submerged in noise," *Appl. Opt.*, vol. 4, p. 387, 1965.
K. Preston, Jr., "Computing at the speed of light," *Electronics*, vol. 72, Sept. 6, 1965.
C. E. Thomas, "Optical spectrum analysis of large space bandwidth signals," *Appl. Opt.*, vol. 5, p. 1782, 1966.
A. Vander Lugt, "Practical considerations for the use of spatial carrier frequency filters," *Appl. Opt.*, vol. 5, p. 1760, 1966.
M. King *et al.*, "Real-time electro-optical signal processors with coherent detection," *Appl. Opt.*, vol. 6, p. 1367, 1967.
A. Offner, "Design and specification criteria for optical data processors," *Appl. Opt.*, vol. 7, p. 2285, 1968.
H. R. Carleton *et al.*, "A simplified coherent optical correlator," *Appl. Opt.*, vol. 7, p. 105, 1968.
H. R. Carleton, W. T. Maloney, and G. Mertz, "Collinear heterodyning in optical processors," *Proc. IEEE*, vol. 57, pp. 769–775, May 1969.
W. D. Squire, H. J. Whitehouse, and J. M. Alsup, "Linear signal processing and ultrasonic transversal filters," *IEEE Trans. Microwave Theory Tech.*, vol. MTT-17, pp. 1020–1040, Nov. 1969.
W. L. Anderson and R. L. Everett, "Electroencephalographic and electrocardiographic data reduction by coherent optical techniques," in *SWIEECO Conf. Rec.*, 1970.
B. J. Pernick and A. Reich, "A holographic system for large time-bandwidth product multichannel spectral analysis," *Appl. Opt.*, vol. 9, p. 229, 1970.
R. G. Eguchi and F. P. Carlson, "Linear vector operations in coherent optical data processing," *Appl. Opt.*, vol. 9, p. 687, 1970.
R. A. Heinz *et al.*, "Matrix multiplication by optical methods," *Appl. Opt.*, vol. 9, p. 2161, 1970.
H. W. Rose *et al.*, "Coherent optical target recognition through a phase distorting medium," *Appl. Opt.*, vol. 10, p. 515, 1971.
W. L. Anderson and R. E. Beissner, "Counting and classifying small objects by far-field light scattering," *Appl. Opt.*, vol. 10, p. 1503, 1971.
J. P. Kirk and A. L. Jones, "Phase-only complex-valued spatial filter," *J. Opt. Soc. Amer.*, vol. 61, p. 1023, 1971.
D. P. Jablonowski *et al.*, "Matrix multiplication by optical methods," *Appl. Opt.*, vol. 11, p. 174, 1972.
H. N. Roberts, "Strain-biased PLZT input devices for optical data processing," *Appl. Opt.*, vol. 11, p. 397, 1972.

A Criterion and an Algorithm for Grouping Data

KEINOSUKE FUKUNAGA, MEMBER, IEEE, AND WARREN L. G. KOONTZ, MEMBER, IEEE

Abstract—Many algorithms for grouping data without supervision depend on some criterion. We state two basic requirements such criteria should meet and we discuss several criteria in terms of these requirements. An attempt to satisfy both requirements simultaneously with a simple criterion leads us to introduce a linear transformation of the data. Although our principal result is for a two category problem, we present discussion and an example for the many category problem as well.

Index Terms—Clustering, data analysis, pattern recognition, unsupervised learning.

I. Introduction

OUR principal results are relevant to the problem of grouping multivariate data without supervision. This problem arises in the design of pattern recognition systems when no preclassified samples are available Even when classified samples are available, it is sometimes necessary to subdivide the known categories without supervision. The importance of data grouping, or clustering, and many approaches to solving this problem are discussed in Ball's survey paper [1].

Data grouping is not a rigorously or uniformly defined concept. Some speak of it as the division of a set of data into subsets whose members are similar in some sense. Others seek subsets exhibiting a cohesiveness which is not entirely related to point-to-point similarity. In the most general case, the proper number of subsets is unknown. However, in this paper we consider the simpler problem where the number of subsets is fixed. Many procedures for solving the general problem combine an algorithm for grouping data into a fixed number of subsets with some procedures for merging or splitting subsets.

It is worth noting at this point that two basic techniques for grouping data appear in the literature. The hierarchical approach is to divide the data into subsets, divide each subset into subsets, and so on, until the desired number of subsets is created. The direct approach, on the other hand, is to subdivide the data into the desired number of subsets in one step. The direct approach seems to yield more reasonable classification but requires more computation. Casey and Nagy [2] advocate a compromise where the data are directly grouped into a small number of subsets and these subsets are subdivided further hierarchically. Hierarchical classification may require only the ability to divide data into two subsets.

Data grouping is often accomplished with the aid of a criterion. This criterion assigns a number to each possible partition of the data. The partition which yields an extreme value of the criterion is chosen as the desired partition. As we see it, the criterion must meet two basic requirements.

1) Performance: The resulting partition must fall along natural boundaries of the data when such boundaries are well defined.
2) Efficiency: There must exist an efficient algorithm for finding the optimum partition.

Another requirement worth noting is uniqueness. We would like to have only one partition which extremizes our criterion. Although uniqueness is an important factor, we will limit our discussion here to performance and efficiency.

In what follows, we will first discuss some criteria which have appeared in the literature. We will then define a linear transformation which can be applied to the original data. Under this transformation, all of the criteria can be expressed in terms of the eigenvalues of a certain matrix. They may, therefore, be compared with one another. Further, it will be shown that for the case of grouping data into only two subsets, all of the criteria are equivalent in terms of the performance requirement. Thus, the choice of criterion for this problem depends entirely on the efficiency of the extremizing algorithm.

We will propose a procedure for grouping data. We will examine our procedure both analytically and numerically. For the case where the data come from two Gaussian distributions, we will derive some useful convergence properties.

II. Criteria and Algorithms for Grouping Data

A. Statistical Scatter

All of the criteria which we will discuss may be defined in terms of the statistical scatter matrices introduced by Wilks [3]. First, we will define these matrices and organize our notation.

Let $\{X_1, X_2, \cdots, X_N\}$, a set of L-dimensional column vectors, be the data set. We wish to divide this set into M groups, $G_1, G_2, \cdots, G_M$, with populations $N_1, N_2, \cdots, N_M$, respectively. The scatter matrices are then defined as follows.

Manuscript received February 4, 1970. This work was supported in part by the Joint Services Program under ARPA Contract N 00014-67-A0226-004.

The authors are with the Department of Electrical Engineering, Purdue University, Lafayette, Ind. 47907.

Reprinted from *IEEE Trans. Comput.*, vol. C-19, pp. 917–923, Oct. 1970.

Total scatter:

$$T \triangleq \sum_{k=1}^{N} X_k X_k^T. \tag{1}$$

Intragroup scatter:

$$W_j \triangleq \sum_{X_k \in G_j} (X_k - C_j)(X_k - C_j)^T \tag{2}$$

where

$$C_j = \frac{1}{N_j} \sum_{X_k \in G_j} X_k. \tag{3}$$

Total intragroup scatter:

$$W \triangleq \sum_{j=1}^{M} W_j. \tag{4}$$

Intergroup scatter:

$$B \triangleq \sum_{j=1}^{M} N_j C_j C_j^T. \tag{5}$$

The superscript T denotes transposition. It is easily shown that

$$T = W + B \tag{6}$$

regardless of the partition. Another important property of the scatter matrices is the fact that the eigenvalues of $W^{-1}B$, $\lambda_1, \cdots, \lambda_L$ are invariant under nonsingular linear transformations of the X_k's.

B. Criteria for Grouping

Several criteria may be defined in terms of the scatter matrices defined above. The intragroup scatter is a measure of the degree of association of the members of the group. The criteria we will discuss are all based on some measure of the "magnitude" of W.

The first, which we denote J_0, is simply

$$J_0 = \operatorname{tr} W = \sum_{j=1}^{M} \sum_{X_k \in G_j} \|X_k - C_j\|^2 \tag{7}$$

where tr W is the trace of the matrix W. J_0 may be interpreted as the mean-squared distance to the group center. The optimum partition is taken as the one which minimizes J_0. This criterion has been used by several authors, including Casey and Nagy [2] and MacQueen [4].

J_0 is not invariant under nonsingular linear transformations of the X_k's. This means that by changing the coordinate system of the original data, one may alter the optimum partition. Friedman and Rubin [5], disturbed by this ambiguity, introduced a family of invariant criteria. A criterion of the form

$$J = f(\lambda_1, \cdots, \lambda_L) \tag{8}$$

is invariant under nonsingular linear transformations. Two such criteria are

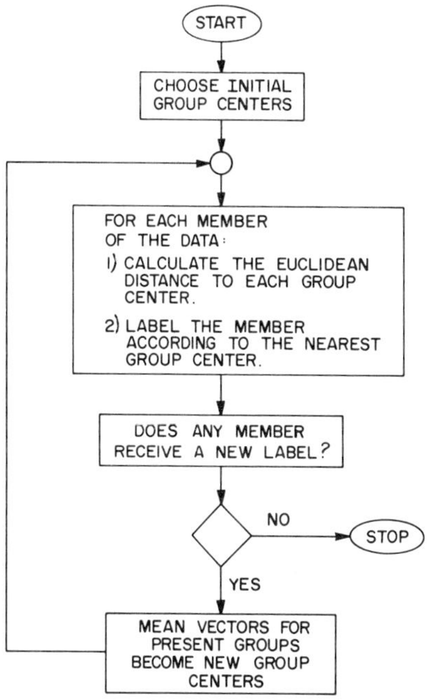

Fig. 1. Basic grouping algorithm.

$$J_1 = \det T / \det W, \tag{9}$$

$$= \prod_{i=1}^{L} (1 + \lambda_i) \tag{10}$$

and

$$J_2 = \operatorname{tr} W^{-1} B, \tag{11}$$

$$= \sum_{i=1}^{L} \lambda_i. \tag{12}$$

Here, the optimum partition is the one which maximizes the criterion.

Several numerical examples were used to show that J_1 and J_2 are superior to J_0 in the sense of the performance requirement. In each example, data of known classification were clustered according to J_0, J_1, and J_2. Fewer misclassified samples resulted when J_1 or J_2 were used. However, any relationship between this performance and the invariance property was not rigorously shown.

A basic assumption in clustering is that the group structure is somehow reflected by the data. If we feel that this structure is reflected in an invariant manner, then we should use an invariant criterion to detect it. This was essentially what Friedman and Rubin assumed, and the notion was supported by their experiments.

Let us simply accept J_1 and J_2 as superior performers, compared to J_0, and turn our attention to the efficiency requirement.

C. Algorithms

The basic algorithm shown in Fig. 1 has been widely used and studied. The well-known ISODATA program [6] is based on this procedure. The asymptotic properties of this algorithm have been studied by MacQueen and others

[4], [7], [8]. It yields a grouping of the data which minimizes, at least locally, J_0.

No such simple algorithm has been proposed to maximize J_1 or J_2. Rather, a process of calculating the change of the criterion due to reassignment of a single data point is used. Since such a process can only guarantee a "single change" maximum, some heuristic modifications are added. The performance of the resulting algorithms is not well understood. Further, time consuming computation of W^{-1} and det W are required at each step.

Thus, J_0 seems superior in terms of the efficiency requirement. In the next section we will show that if the coordinate system is suitably chosen, J_0 becomes a function of $\lambda_1, \cdots, \lambda_L$. For the two group problem, we will show that J_0, J_1, and J_2 become equivalent. This result represents a partial success in our effort to find a criterion which satisfies both of our requirements.

III. The Normalizing Transformation

Let us introduce a nonsingular linear transformation and see how it affects J_0 (recall that it cannot affect J_1 or J_2). From our definitions, it follows that if $N \geq L$, the total scatter T is a positive-definite matrix. Then there exists a nonsingular matrix, A, such that

$$ATA^T = I \tag{13}$$

regardless of the partition.

Fukunaga and Koontz [9] have studied some properties of this same transformation in feature selection and ordering. Under the transformation A we have the following changes:

$$X_k \rightarrow AX_k \triangleq Y_k, \quad k = 1, \cdots, N \tag{14}$$

$$C_j \rightarrow AC_j \triangleq D_j, \quad j = 1, \cdots, M \tag{15}$$

$$W \rightarrow AWA^T \triangleq P \tag{16}$$

$$B \rightarrow ABA^T \triangleq Q \tag{17}$$

$$J_0 \rightarrow \operatorname{tr} P \triangleq J_0'. \tag{18}$$

Equation (6) becomes

$$I = P + Q. \tag{19}$$

Because of their invariance property, $\lambda_1, \cdots, \lambda_L$ can be taken as the eigenvalues of $P^{-1}Q$. The eigenvalues of P, $\mu_1, \cdots, \mu_L$, can be expressed in terms of those of $P^{-1}Q$ as follows:

$$\mu_i = \frac{1}{1 + \lambda_i}, \quad i = 1, \cdots, L. \tag{20}$$

Therefore, J_0' is a function of $\lambda_1, \cdots, \lambda_L$.

$$J_0' = \sum_{i=1}^{L} \frac{1}{1 + \lambda_i}. \tag{21}$$

In our "normalized" coordinate system, we see that the trace of the intragroup scatter matrix belongs to the family of criteria defined by (8). For the two group problem we have a more significant result.

We can choose the origin of our coordinate system so that

$$N_1D_1 + N_2D_2 = 0. \tag{22}$$

The intergroup scatter is now given by

$$Q = N_1D_1D_1^T + N_2D_2D_2^T. \tag{23}$$

The eigenvalues of Q are $1-\mu_1, 1-\mu_2, \cdots, 1-\mu_L$. But since the rank of Q can be no greater than 1 because of (22), we have

$$1 - \mu_i = 0, \quad i = 2, \cdots, L \tag{24}$$

and therefore,

$$\lambda_i = 0, \quad i = 2, \cdots, L. \tag{25}$$

Now our criteria become

$$J_0' = \frac{1}{1 + \lambda_1} + L - 1, \quad \text{(minimize)} \tag{26}$$

$$J_1 = 1 + \lambda_1, \quad \text{(maximize)} \tag{27}$$

$$J_2 = \lambda_1, \quad \text{(maximize).} \tag{28}$$

But, clearly, all three criteria are optimized by the same partition. In fact, any criterion of the form of (8) which is monotonic in λ_1, when $\lambda_2 = \cdots = \lambda_L = 0$ is extremized by this partition. Thus, the algorithm of Fig. 1, which satisfies the efficiency requirement, will yield a partition which extremizes all of the criteria in this family. The performance will equal that of the best criterion in the family.

This equivalence does not hold for the general multigroup problem. However, J_1, J_2, and J_0' of (10), (12), and (21) are similar even for the multigroup problem, when the λ's are small in comparison with 1. Also, we have previously noted the importance of the two group problem in hierarchical partitioning. In addition, we note that the problem of how to scale coordinate axes has been mentioned in the literature. Our normalization is a possible solution to this problem.

IV. Grouping Gaussian Data

The results obtained so far lead us to propose the following procedure for grouping data.

1) Apply the normalizing transformation.
2) Group the data using the algorithm of Fig. 1.

The performance of this procedure can be determined analytically when the data come from two Gaussian distributions. We will establish conditions under which the separating hyperplane converges to a hyperplane perpendicular to the difference-in-mean vector of the original distribution. For the equal covariance case this is shown to be Bayes' optimum hyperplane.

A. Bayes' Classifier for the Equal Covariance Case

Let us assume that the data come from two Gaussian distributions with mean vectors D_1 and D_2, covariance matrices K_1 and K_2, and a priori probabilities p_1 and $p_2(=1-p_1)$. Further, let us assume $K_1=K_2=K$, and that the data are normalized, i.e.,

$$K + p_1 D_1 D_1^T + p_2 D_2 D_2^T = I \tag{29}$$

and

$$p_1 D_1 + p_2 D_2 = 0. \tag{30}$$

Using (29) and (30), we can write the difference-in-mean vector and covariance matrix as

$$D_1 - D_2 = \frac{1}{p_2} D_1 \tag{31}$$

and

$$K = I - \frac{p_1}{p_2} D_1 D_1^T, \tag{32}$$

respectively.

Fig. 2 shows the effect of the normalization on the distribution of the data. In Fig. 2(a) we see an unnormalized distribution. This distribution is one of the troublemakers mentioned by Nagy [10]. Fig. 2(b) shows the normalized distribution.

Bayes' optimum decision surface is a hyperplane of the form

$$(D_1 - D_2)^T K^{-1} X + \text{constant} = 0. \tag{33}$$

Using (31) and (32), we may write this as

$$\frac{1}{p_2} D_1^T \left(I - \frac{p_1}{p_2} D_1 D_1^T \right)^{-1} X + \text{constant} = 0. \tag{34}$$

The inversion in (34) may be easily carried out. The resulting hyperplane is

$$\left[1 + \frac{(p_1/p_2)\|D_1\|^2}{1 - (p_1/p_2)\|D_1\|^2} \right] D_1^T X + \text{constant} = 0. \tag{35}$$

Thus, it can be concluded from (35) that the optimum hyperplane for the equal covariance case is always the direction of D_1, after the transformation of (29) and (30). We will show that the algorithm of Fig. 1 sets a hyperplane perpendicular to the difference-in-mean vector. This property, which the original coordinate system does not have, is a significant advantage of the normalized coordinate system.

B. Convergence for the Equal Covariance Case

For the equal covariance case, we can show that our algorithm converges to a separating hyperplane in the direction of D_1 from a wide range of the initial partitions. After a given iteration, the data are separated by a hyperplane whose direction is, say, V. Suppose the hyperplane is a distance l_1 from D_1 and a distance l_2 from D_2 as shown in Fig. 3. Let U_1 and U_2 be the centers of probability mass to either side of the hyperplane. Then, following the procedure of Fig. 1, the direction of the succeeding hyperplane will be $U_1 - U_2$.

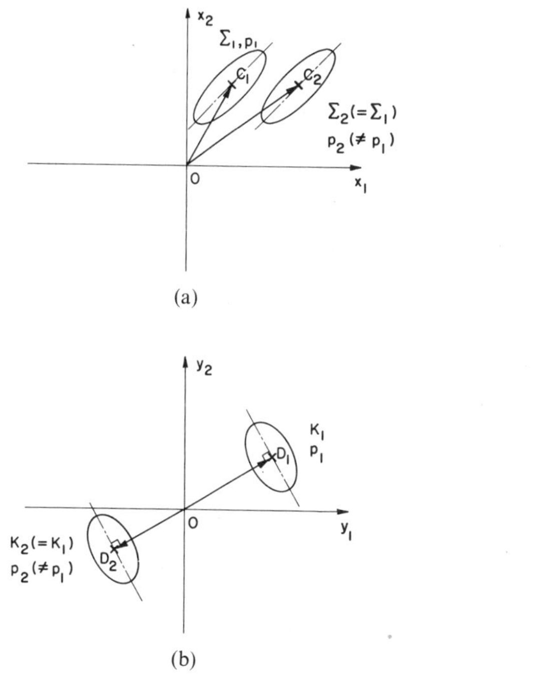

Fig. 2. Normalization of two Gaussian densities with equal covariance matrices. (a) Original densities. (b) Normalized densities.

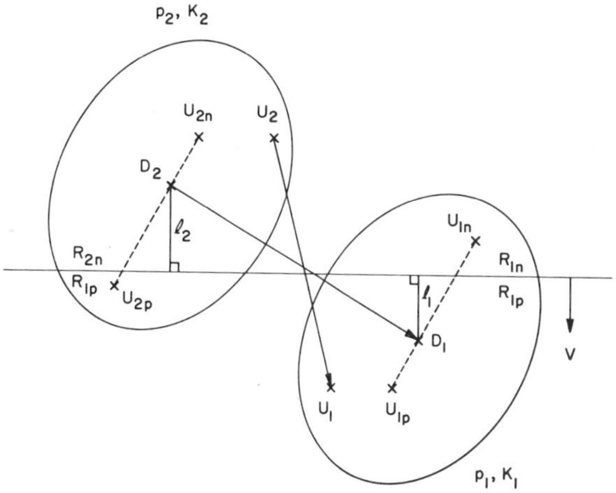
Fig. 3. Separation of two probability distributions.

The hyperplane separates each distribution into two parts, the positive and negative side of the hyperplane. Thus, we have four masses of the data R_{ij} $(i=1,2; j=p,n)$, as shown in Fig. 3. The centers U_{ij} and the populations q_{ij} of these four masses can be obtained as follows:

$$U_{ip} = D_i + \frac{a_i}{s_i b_i} K_i V \tag{36}$$

$$U_{in} = D_i - \frac{a_i}{s_i(1 - b_i)} K_i V \tag{37}$$

$$q_{ip} = p_i b_i \tag{38}$$

$$q_{in} = p_i(1 - b_i) \tag{39}$$

where

$$a_i = \frac{1}{\sqrt{2\pi}} \int_{l_i/s_i}^{\infty} u e^{-u^2/2}\, du = \frac{1}{\sqrt{2\pi}} e^{-l_i^2/2s_i^2} \tag{40}$$

$$b_i = \frac{1}{\sqrt{2\pi}} \int_{\pm l_i/s_i}^{+\infty} e^{-u^2/2}\, du = \operatorname{erf}(\pm l_i/s_i). \tag{41}$$

(If D_i is located in R_{ip}, the positive sign is used. If D_i is located in R_{in}, the negative sign is used.)

$$s_i^2 = V^T K_i V. \tag{42}$$

U_1 is the mass center of R_{1p} and R_{2p}, and U_2 is the one of R_{1n} and R_{2n}. Therefore, U_1 and U_2 are obtained as follows:

$$U_1 = \frac{q_{1p}U_{1p} + q_{2p}U_{2p}}{q_{1p} + q_{2p}} \tag{43}$$

$$U_2 = \frac{q_{1n}U_{1n} + q_{2n}U_{2n}}{q_{1n} + q_{2n}}. \tag{44}$$

Substituting (36) through (41) into (43) and (44),

$$U_1 - U_2 = \frac{p_1p_2(b_1 - b_2)(D_1 - D_2) + \left(\frac{p_1a_1}{s_1}K_1 + \frac{p_2a_2}{s_2}K_2\right)V}{(p_1b_1 + p_2b_2)[1 - (p_1b_1 + p_2b_2)]}. \tag{45}$$

For the equal covariance case,

$$K_1 = K_2 = K \quad \text{and} \quad s_1 = s_2 = s. \tag{46}$$

Furthermore, under our normalization conditions (29) and (30), K and D_2 can be expressed as functions of D_1 so that (45) becomes

$$U_1 - U_2 = c_1D_1 + c_2V \tag{47}$$

where

$$c_1 = \frac{p_1(b_1 - b_2) - \frac{p_1}{sp_2}(p_1a_1 + p_2a_2)D_1^TV}{(p_1b_1 + p_2b_2)[1 - (p_1b_1 + p_2b_2)]} \tag{48}$$

$$c_2 = \frac{\frac{1}{s}(p_1a_1 + p_2a_2)}{(p_1b_1 + p_2b_2)[1 - (p_1b_1 + p_2b_2)]}. \tag{49}$$

The normal of the new hyperplane has a component in the direction of V and another in the direction of D_1. If the coefficient of D_1 has the same sign as D_1^TV, then the successive hyperplanes become more nearly parallel to D_1. To prove this result we must show that the numerator of c_1 of (48) has the same sign as D_1^TV, because c_2 and the denominator of c_1 are always positive. We need only examine in detail the case where $D_1^TV > 0$. The discussion for $D_1^TV < 0$ can be done similarly as for $D_1^TV > 0$. For $D_1^TV > 0$, we see from Fig. 3 that

$$\begin{aligned} l_1 + l_2 &= (D_1 - D_2)^TV \\ &= \frac{1}{p_2} D_1^TV \end{aligned} \tag{50}$$

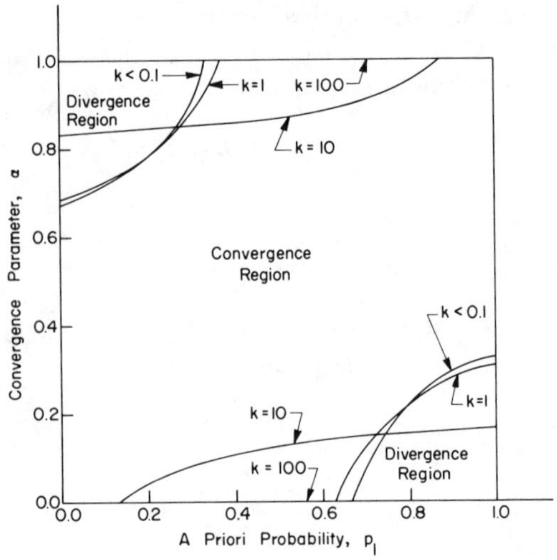

Fig. 4. Regions of convergence.

and our condition for convergence becomes

$$b_1 - b_2 - \frac{l_1 + l_2}{s}(p_1a_1 + p_2a_2) > 0. \tag{51}$$

It is easily seen that the inequality of (51) is not satisfied for certain combinations of parameters. However, the region of parameters where (51) is satisfied can be calculated numerically. The result is shown in Fig. 4. Equations (40), (41), and (46) with (51) show that we have three parameters in (51), l_1/s, l_2/s, and $p_1 (p_2 = 1 - p_1)$, or

$$k = (l_1 + l_2)/s, \quad \alpha = l_1/(l_1 + l_2) \quad \text{and} \quad p_1. \tag{52}$$

In Fig. 4, the convergence regions of α and p_1 are plotted for various k. The figure shows that convergence is quite likely in practice except for either extreme p_1's or α's.

C. *Convergence for the Unequal Covariance Case*

When $K_1 \neq K_2$, it is very difficult to find the convergence region as we did previously. However, the convergence can be proved when the hyperplane passes a certain point. Therefore, it can be said that some convergence region around the point should exist.

For $K_1 \neq K_2$, the normalization leads us to

$$p_1K_1 + p_2K_2 + p_1D_1D_1^T + p_2D_2D_2^T = I \tag{53}$$

instead of (29). Equation (30) is also satisfied.

Let us suppose that the hyperplane passes the point where

$$\frac{a_1}{s_1} = \frac{a_2}{s_1} = \gamma; \tag{54}$$

then, substituting (53) and (31) into (45), we have

$$U_1 - U_2 = \frac{\left[p_1(b_1 - b_2) - \gamma \frac{p_1}{p_2} D^TV\right]D_1 + \gamma V}{(p_1b_1 + p_2b_2)[1 - (p_1b_1 + p_2b_2)]}. \tag{55}$$

Using the same reasoning as before, we obtain the following convergence condition:

$$b_1 - b_2 - \gamma \frac{D_1^T V}{p_2} > 0 \cdot \tag{56}$$

This condition can be expressed, via (50) and (54), as

$$b_1 - \frac{a_1}{s_1} l_1 - b_2 - \frac{a_2}{s_2} l_2 > 0 \tag{57}$$

or

$$\frac{1}{\sqrt{2\pi}}\left[\left[\int_{-l_1/s_1}^{\infty} e^{-u^2/2}\, du - \frac{l_1}{s_1} e^{-l_1^2/2s_1^2}\right.\right.$$
$$\left. - \int_{l_2/s_2}^{\infty} e^{-u^2/2}\, du - \frac{l_2}{s_2} e^{-l_2^2/2s_2^2}\right]$$
$$= \frac{1}{\sqrt{2\pi}}\left[\int_0^{l_1/s_1} (e^{-u^2/2} - e^{-l_1^2/2s_1^2})\, du\right.$$
$$\left. + \int_0^{l_2/s_2} (e^{-u^2/2} - e^{-l_2^2/2s_2^2})\, du\right] > 0. \tag{58}$$

This inequality holds for all l_1/s_1 and l_2/s_2.

Thus, when the hyperplane passes the point where (54) is satisfied, the new difference-in-mean vector, $U_1 - U_2$, approaches $D_1 - D_2$ closer than V. Although we offer no theoretical justification, there should be a region of convergence around the point.

V. Numerical Examples

In addition to our analytical study, we have performed numerical experiments with our procedure. Data were obtained by generating Gaussian random vectors according to a prescribed mean vector and covariance matrix. The means and covariances were taken from Marill and Green's 8-dimensional character data [11]. Various properties of this data are discussed in [12] and [13].

A. Two Groups

For our first experiment, we generate 100 samples each corresponding to A's and B's. We first grouped the data in the original coordinate system according to the basic algorithm. Then we normalized the data and grouped them once again. Table I shows the confusion arrays that result in each case. Fewer misclassified samples result when the data are normalized.

B. Three Groups

In this experiment we have 100 samples each of A's, B's, and C's. The same procedure was applied. The resulting confusion arrays shown in Table II indicate that superior classification may still result.

Fig. 5 is a plot of two coordinates of the data in the original and in the normalized coordinate system.

VI. Summary

We feel that the most systematic approach to data grouping is by means of a criterion. Thus, our study has been aimed at

1) defining the properties of a data grouping criterion, and
2) finding a criterion which has these properties.

TABLE I
Confusion Arrays for A Versus B

Original Coordinates

	Assigned Group 1	Assigned Group 2
Actual Class A	86	14
Actual Class B	30	70

Normalized Coordinates

	Assigned Group 1	Assigned Group 2
Actual Class A	100	0
Actual Class B	19	81

TABLE II
Confusion Arrays for A Versus B Versus C

Original Coordinates

	Assigned Group 1	Assigned Group 2	Assigned Group 3
Actual Class A	84	16	0
Actual Class B	26	73	1
Actual Class C	14	11	75

Normalized Coordinates

	Assigned Group 1	Assigned Group 2	Assigned Group 3
Actual Class A	100	0	0
Actual Class B	27	73	0
Actual Class C	18	0	82

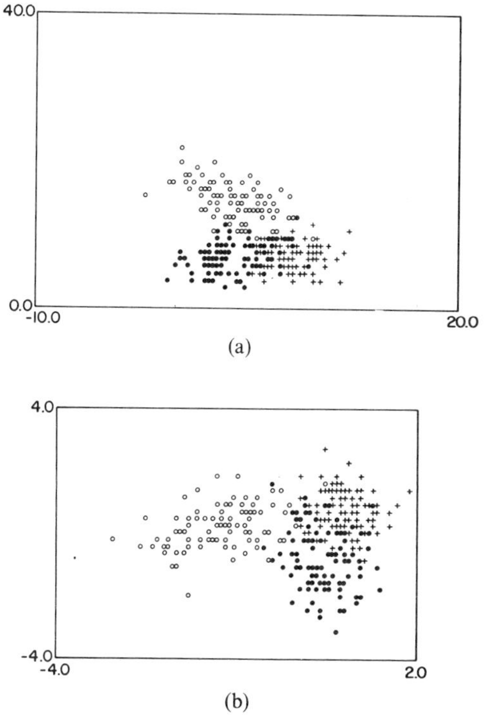

Fig. 5. Scatter plot of the experimental data. (a) Original distribution. (b) Normalized distribution.

We stated two important properties: performance and efficiency. Initially, we compared three criteria, J_0, J_1, and J_2, in terms of these properities. A tradeoff between performance and efficiency was illustrated.

A new criterion J_0' was constructed by applying a linear transformation which unitized the total scatter matrix. J_0' has the same form and efficiency as J_0 and has the invariance property of J_1 and J_2.

For the two group problem, J_0' yields the same optimum partition as J_1 and J_2 with greater efficiency. We therefore feel that J_0' is indeed a promising criterion for dichotomizing data.

For the multigroup problem, we were unable to demonstrate the performance of J_0' analytically. However, its efficiency is still superior to that of J_1 and J_2. J_0' measures the cohesiveness of the subsets according to the mean-squared distance to the group center in the normalized space. The effect of the normalization is to equalize variations in the components of the data vectors. In the original space, J_0 may depend mostly on distance along one or two components. Important structural information in the other components may be ignored. Fig. 2(a) shows such a case. Let us just say that unless we have a priori knowledge that the group structure of our data is reflected by a particular choice of coordinates, we should use an invariant criterion. Then J_0' is a logical choice because

1) it is efficient,
2) it is invariant, and
3) it has a straightforward interpretation.

Finally, we suggest that further study of this problem be carried on. The basic question is: What do we want from a data grouping algorithm? This question may have many answers and, therefore, many valid criteria may exist. Thus, the production of a single criterion does not constitute a solution to the problem.

Acknowledgment

The authors wish to thank T. P. Truitt and J. E. Juliussen for their assistance with the numerical examples.

References

[1] G. H. Ball, "Data analysis in the social sciences: what about the details?" *1965 Fall Joint Computer Conf., AFIPS Proc.*, vol. 27, pt. 1. Washington, D. C.: Spartan, 1965, pp. 533–559.

[2] R. G. Casey and G. Nagy, "An autonomous reading machine," *IEEE Trans. Computers*, vol. C-17, pp. 492–503, May 1968.

[3] S. S. Wilks, "Multidimensional statistical scatter," in *Contributions to Probability and Statistics*, I. Olkin, Ed. Stanford, Calif.: Stanford Publishing, 1960.

[4] J. MacQueen, "Some methods for classification and analysis of multivariate observations," *Proc. 5th Berkeley Symp. on Probability and Statistics*, pp. 281–297, 1967.

[5] H. P. Friedman and J. Rubin, "On some invariant criteria for grouping data," *Amer. Stat. Assoc. J.*, vol. 62, pp. 1159–1178, December 1967.

[6] G. H. Ball and D. J. Hall, "ISODATA, a novel method of data analysis and pattern classification," Stanford Research Inst., Menlo Park, Calif., Tech. Rept., April 1965.

[7] E. M. Braverman, "The method of potential functions in the problem of training machines to recognize patterns without a teacher," *Automat. Remote Contr.*, (USSR), vol. 27, pp. 1748–1771, October 1966.

[8] A. A. Dorofeyuk, "Teaching algorithm for a pattern recognition machine without a teacher, based on the method of potential functions," *Automat. Remote Contr.*, (USSR), vol. 27, pp. 1728–1737, October 1966.

[9] K. Fukunaga and W. L. G. Koontz, "Application of the Karhunen–Loève expansion to feature selection and ordering," *IEEE Trans. Computers*, vol. C-19, pp. 311–318, April 1970.

[10] G. Nagy, "State of the art in pattern recognition," *Proc. IEEE*, vol. 56, pp. 836–862, May 1968.

[11] T. Marill and D. M. Green, "On the effectiveness of receptors in recognition systems," *IEEE Trans. Information Theory*, vol. IT-9, pp. 11–17, January 1963.

[12] K. Fukunaga and T. F. Krile, "Calculation of Bayes recognition error for two multivariate Gaussian distributions," *IEEE Trans. Computers*, vol. C-18, pp. 220–229, March 1969.

[13] K. Fukunaga and D. R. Olsen, "Piecewise linear discriminant functions and classification errors for multiclass problems," *IEEE Trans. Information Theory*, vol. IT-16, pp. 99–100, January 1970.

[14] S. Watanabe, *Knowing and Guessing*. New York: Wiley, 1969, ch. 8.

A Comparison of Seven Techniques for Choosing Subsets of Pattern Recognition Properties

ANTHONY N. MUCCIARDI, MEMBER, IEEE, AND
EARL E. GOSE, SENIOR MEMBER, IEEE

Abstract—The only guaranteed technique for choosing the best subset of N properties from a set of M is to try all $\binom{M}{N}$ possible combinations. This is computationally impractical for sets of even moderate size, so heuristic techniques are required. This paper presents seven techniques for choosing good subsets of properties and compares their performance on a nine-class vectorcardiogram classification problem.

The first technique ranks properties according to their expected probability of error when used separately. The rationale is that a property that has a low error rate when used alone should be a valuable member of a subset of properties.

The second technique is based on the idea that a property that is very similar to another in use adds very little additional discriminatory information. According to this technique, the first of the N properties is chosen arbitrarily or by another technique. The second property selected is the property least correlated with the first. Subsequent properties are those that have the minimum average absolute correlation coefficients with those already chosen.

The third technique is to arbitrarily choose the first property and to determine which two classes are most often confused in a multiclass problem. The property which (when used alone) is the best discriminator between these two classes is the next addition to the set. This procedure is iterated.

The fourth technique is to perform a principal components analysis and to form new properties corresponding to the eigenvectors.

The fifth technique is similar to the fourth, but the original properties that make small contributions to the eigenvectors are omitted from each eigenvector.

The sixth technique chooses those original properties that make the largest average contributions to the eigenvectors.

The seventh technique is a combination of the first two. Properties are ranked according to a weighted sum of their probabilities of error when used alone and their average coefficients of correlation with the other properties. It is shown that this new technique selects properties as well as any of the others, and that it is less expensive to implement than the nearest contender, the eigenvector technique.

All the techniques resulted in lower error rates than did a random selection of properties.

Index Terms—Classification techniques, dimensionality reduction, electrocardiogram classification, feature extraction, Karhunen–Loève expansion, multivariate data analysis, pattern recognition, principal components, property selection, statistical decision making.

Manuscript received November 11, 1970; revised April 1, 1971. This research was supported in part by the U. S. Air Force Office of Scientific Research Directorate of Information Sciences under Grant AF-AFOSR-68-1341, and by the National Institutes of Health. Computational facilities were supplied by the Computer Center, University of Illinois at Chicago Circle, Chicago, Ill., which is partially supported by Grant GP-7275 from the National Science Foundation. A preliminary version of this paper was presented at the IEEE Symposium on Feature Extraction and Selection in Pattern Recognition, Argonne, Ill., October 5–7, 1970.

A. N. Mucciardi is with Adaptronics, Inc., Westgate Research Park, McLean, Va. 22101.

E. E. Gose is with the Department of Information Engineering, University of Illinois at Chicago Circle, Chicago, Ill., and the Department of Physiology, University of Illinois at the Medical Center, Chicago, Ill. 60680.

Introduction

In pattern classification problems, the properties of an object to be classified are measured and combined in a decision rule to render a classification. The selection of properties that contain the most discriminatory information is important because the cost of decision making is directly related to the number of properties used in the decision rule. The problem of selecting a highly discriminatory subset of properties has been approached in a number of ways. Proposed property selection techniques may be divided into three categories: 1) statistical, 2) information theoretic, or 3) sequential.

In the *statistical* category, stepwise multiple linear regression was one of the first techniques examined [23]. A candidate property is admitted to the property set if the incremental increase in the Mahalanobis D^2 measure [21] satisfies a statistical test of significance. The Mahalanobis D^2 measure is the squared distance between the means of two classes normalized by the combined covariance matrices [1]: $D^2=(\bar{\mu}_1-\bar{\mu}_2)'\cdot(\Lambda_1+\Lambda_2)^{-1}\cdot(\bar{\mu}_1-\bar{\mu}_2)$, where $\bar{\mu}$ and Λ denote the mean and covariance, respectively. The D^2 statistical criterion has been used by others [2], [11], [27], [35] to judge the usefulness of individual properties and sets of properties. A second statistical technique examines the correlations between pairs of properties [35]. A third technique, eigenvector analysis (known also as the Karhunen–Loève expansion and principal components analysis), attempts to reduce the dimensionality of the property space by creating new properties that are linear combinations of the original properties [4], [5], [11], [12], [39], [40]. This procedure finds the subspace in which the original sample vectors may be approximated with the least mean-square error for a given dimensionality.

All the proposed statistical property selection techniques possess disadvantages that limit their utility in pattern classification problems. Stepwise multiple regression and the D^2 criterion schemes require the joint probability density functions to be unimodal. The second statistical technique assumes that the two classes are normally distributed with equal covariance matrices. The eigensystem procedure suffers from two disadvantages: the reduction in the number of properties to be used in the decision rule is sometimes offset by the increase in computation necessary to map vectors into the selected subspace; and the dimensionality

Reprinted from *IEEE Trans. Comput.*, vol. C-20, pp. 1023–1031, Sept. 1971.

reduction may be at the expense of separability information between the classes.

The second category of property selection techniques, the *information theoretic* approach, includes those schemes that judge the utility of a property set based on one of two commonly used figures of merit: entropy or divergence. Entropy [19], [20], [36] is a measure of the spread of the samples of each class in the property space. The entropy of a class of samples distributed according to the probability distribution $p(X)$, where X is a property vector, is computed by integrating the quantity $p(X) \log p(X)$ over all X (and negating the result). The entropy is zero if all members of a class have the same vector representation. Divergence [19], [22], [36], [37] is a measure of the distance or differences between pairs of class probability densities in the property space. It is computed by integrating the quantity $[p(X|i)-p(X|j)] \log p(X|i)/p(X|j)$ over all X, where $p(X|i)$ is the conditional probability of observing property vector X on class i. One of the disadvantages of both figures of merit is the amount of computation required to evaluate them: $\binom{M}{N}$ N-fold integrals are required to find the best subset of N out of M properties. Another disadvantage of the two information theoretic methods is that neither is a direct measure of the overall probability of error. It should be noted, however, that for special cases in which the probability distributions are multivariate normal with common covariance matrix, there is a monotonic relation between divergence measure and error probability [22]. A similar property holds for the entropy measure if feature properties are assumed to be statistically independent [20].

The procedures of *sequential analysis* and dynamic programming have also been applied to the property selection problem. Sequential analysis [9], [11], [12], [38] is designed to make decisions using the smallest possible number of properties. Dynamic programming [9], [10], [28] has been used to select the optimal subset of properties as a function of the measurement cost. If the class probability density functions are known, and for given class *a priori* probabilities, both of these procedures will select the subset of properties that minimizes the average decision-making risk [12].

The principal objectives of this research were to search for computationally feasible property selection techniques that require no assumptions about the statistical structure of the data and to compare their utilities to the methods described above. The main product of this research is a property selection technique that considers both the expected probability of error and average correlation coefficient. The technique requires no assumptions about the statistical structure of the classes and is computationally simple.

Electrocardiograms (EKGs) were chosen as a data source with which the developed techniques could be tested. This choice was made for the following reasons: 1) EKG classification is a complex problem involving multigroup classification; 2) a set of properties has been established by clinical and research studies and can form the basis of the original property set; and 3) relating the various properties measured from the electrocardiogram to the diagnostic groups, and evaluating the importance of these various measured properties in making a given diagnosis can contribute to the understanding of the electrocardiogram itself and to its clinical use.

Description and Computation of the Properties

Description of the Electrocardiographic Data

The EKG data used in this study were obtained from Dr. H. V. Pipberger of the Veterans Administration Research Center for Cardiovascular Data Processing, Washington, D. C. The methods of data collection, editing, and confirmation of clinical diagnoses are well documented by Pipberger [17], [29], [33]. In brief, a three-lead corrected Frank lead system was used to record the body surface potentials. The portion of the record with the least noise from muscle tremors and baseline shifts was digitized at a rate of 250 samples/s. The tape obtained from Pipberger contained 1140 records from 9 diagnostic classes. Four-hundred and eighty two records were randomly selected for this study and these were divided into a training and testing set containing 242 and 240 records, respectively. One beat from each record was selected, from which all the property values were measured. The class distribution in each set is presented in Table I.

Three orthogonal leads are used, so vector information can be measured from the waveform as well as single-lead (scalar) information. One-hundred and fifty seven properties were computed from each waveform; some were the measured variables themselves and others were functions of the measured variables. The types of properties used are summarized below. A detailed listing of the 157 properties is given in [25].

The first step in computing the property values is to locate the beginning and end of the QRS complex and the end of the T wave. These points are found by constructing the spatial velocity waveform from the x, y, and z waveforms and then searching the sv waveform for those points that fall below a certain threshold. This technique works very well for the QRS and T waves [30], [31], [34]. A battery of programs similar to those listed in the "Users Guide" provided by Pipberger's group [34] was then used to measure property values 1–147.

The properties are computed by performing the following operations on the EKG waveform: time integrals are computed for the QRS complex and T waves; spatial maxima in both the QRS and T waves are located; instantaneous vectors are computed for the x, y, and z leads; and a single-lead analysis of the QRS waves and $ST-T$ segments is performed. The QRS complex and $ST-T$ segments were both divided into 0.01-s intervals so that instantaneous vectors could be determined at the initial and terminal portions of each complex.

The digital representation of the EKG waveform consists of a number of points. The points from the QRS complex form a vector loop that passes through the origin of the three-dimensional space. Property 148 is the area of the

TABLE I
DISTRIBUTION OF THE TRAINING AND TESTING SET IN EACH OF THE NINE EKG CLASSES

Class	Class Name	Number of Training Samples	Fraction of Data Set	Number of Testing Samples
1	Normal (NOR)	35	0.1446	35
2	Left Ventricular Hypertrophy (LVH)	35	0.1446	35
3	Right Ventricular Hypertrophy (RVH)	27	0.1116	27
4	Biventricular Hypertrophy (BVH)	19	0.0785	19
5	Left Ventricular Conduction Defect (LVCD)	23	0.0950	23
6	Right Ventricular Conduction Defect (RVCD)	23	0.0950	22
7	Apical Infarction (API)	19	0.0785	18
8	Anterior Infarction (ANI)	25	0.1033	25
9	Posterior Infarction (POI)	36	0.1488	36
		242		240

QRS vector loop, defined as the sum of the areas of triangles formed from each adjacent pair of points in the loop and the origin. A least-squares plane was fit to the vector loop points and the rms error between the actual points and those predicted by the plane was used as a measure of the planarity of the QRS vector loop, which is property 149. Property 150 is the difference between the largest and smallest voltages recorded in the QRS loop. Properties 151–157 are angles between certain average vectors [25].

After the 157 property values were obtained for each of the 482 records, the mean and standard deviation of each property was computed based on all 482 records. Each property was then standardized to zero mean and unit variance.

Eigensystem Analysis of the Correlations Among the 157 Properties

The correlation among the 157 properties was determined from a 157×157 correlation matrix. Thirty-five samples from each of the 9 classes were randomly chosen and the correlation matrix was computed from these 315 samples. A convenient method of summarizing the information contained in such a large correlation matrix is to perform an eigensystem analysis. The eigenvector associated with the largest eigenvalue is the axis in the 157-dimensional property space along which the variance (of the 315 points) is a maximum. The eigenvector associated with the second largest eigenvalue is the second axis, orthogonal to the first, which accounts for as much of the remaining variance as possible, and so on. Each new orthogonal axis accounts for a smaller proportion of the original variance. The total variance to be accounted for is

$$\sum_{j=1}^{157} e_j = 157$$

and the amount of variance each axis accounts for can be computed as shown in (1).

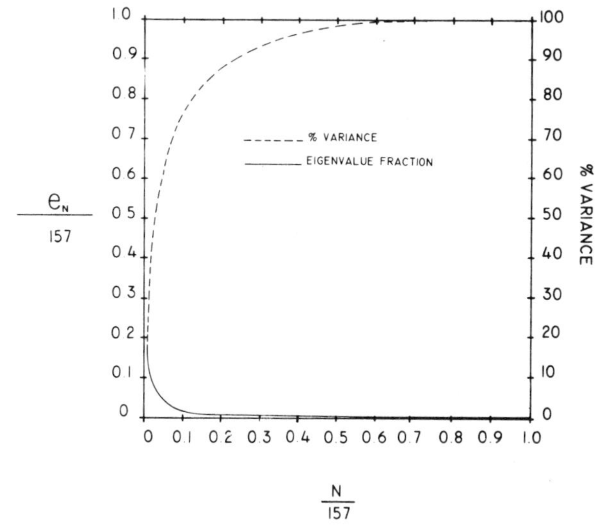

Fig. 1. Eigensystem analysis of the 157-dimensional EKG property space.

$$\text{Fraction of variance accounted for by the } i\text{th axis} = e_i/157 \qquad (1)$$

and the amount of variance accounted for by n of the 157 eigenvectors (ordered with respect to decreasing eigenvalue) is

$$\text{Fraction of variance accounted for by } n \text{ eigenvectors} = \sum_{i=1}^{n} e_i/157 \qquad (2)$$

where e_i is the ith eigenvalue.

A plot of the percentage of the original variance accounted for versus the number of eigenvectors is a convenient method of displaying the amount of correlation among the 157 properties. These data are presented in Fig. 1. The first 35 eigenvalues account for 90 percent of the variance. The possible reduction in dimension from 157 to 35 while maintaining most of the spatial information among the points shows that a great deal of redundancy exists among the 157 properties. This is not unexpected because many of the properties are instantaneous vectors measured at very close intervals on the waveform.

PROPERTY SELECTION TECHNIQUES

Probability of Error

An intuitively appealing approach for finding a good property set is to begin with a large number of candidate properties, individually rank each one by its performance, and eliminate those with low rankings. The expected probability of error (POE) can isolate the best single discriminators. The POE is the fraction of patterns (from K classes) that are misclassified using a single property. This technique has been used by others for property selection [32], [36]. Implicit in this approach is the assumption that a set of properties composed of those properties that *individually* obtain a high ranking with respect to the POE ranking criterion is a good choice. The POE technique has the disadvantage that correlations among the properties are not considered, and hence property sets chosen according to POE may contain redundant members.

Average Correlation Coefficient

The second property selection technique takes correlations into account by ranking the properties according to their average correlation coefficients (ACC). In this case the first property is arbitrarily chosen as that which gives the smallest POE. The second property chosen is that which has the smallest correlation with the first property. The third property is chosen such that its average correlation with the first two is smaller than that of all the remaining candidate properties, and so on. The choice of the ith property on the list depends on its average correlation with the $i-1$ properties already chosen.

Sequential

The third technique requires training and testing for each new property added. The first property is chosen as that which gives the smallest POE. The error rates among the K classes are computed (by a clustering decision rule to be described) and the two classes that are most often confused with each other are noted. The second property selected is that property which is the best discriminator between these two classes when used alone. The error among the K classes is now recomputed using these two properties and the third property is admitted on the basis of its ability to discriminate among the two classes presently most confused. This procedure is iterated.

Eigenvector Analysis

Eigenvector analysis is a technique used by some investigators for property selection [4], [5], [11], [12], [39], [40]. (This procedure is known also as the Karhunen–Loève expansion and principal components analysis.) The idea is to reduce the dimensionality of the property space by creating new properties that are linear combinations of the original properties. The nth eigenvector property is

$$E_n = \sum_{i=1}^{N} u_{ni} x_i \tag{3}$$

where u_{ni} is the ith component of the nth eigenvector. This procedure finds the subspace of the property space in which the original sample vectors may be approximated with the least mean-square error. The subspace is in fact the space spanned by the eigenvectors computed from the sample covariance matrix. (The property values are standardized to unit variance in this study, so the correlation and covariance matrices are identical.) The eigenvector properties can be ordered with respect to the magnitude of their associated eigenvalues as explained above. Eigenvector properties are selected from this ordered list.

Incomplete Eigenvectors

Since each eigenvector property is a linear weighted combination of the 157 standardized EKG properties, the magnitude of the weight on an EKG property is an indication of its importance to a particular eigenvector property. For this property selection technique, some of the N original properties are eliminated from each eigenvector. The *same* properties are eliminated from each eigenvector property. The average absolute weight size was the elimination criterion used; the lowest weighted properties were eliminated first. The average absolute weight size for property i is

$$\bar{u}_i = \frac{1}{NE} \sum_{n=1}^{NE} |u_{ni}| \tag{4}$$

where $i=1,\cdots,N$ and $n=1,\cdots,NE=$number of eigenvectors. If N' of the original properties are retained ($N'<N$), and the remaining properties and their associated weights are relabeled 1 to N', (3) becomes

$$E'_n = \sum_{j=1}^{N'} u_{nj} x_j. \tag{5}$$

Property Weighting by Eigenvector Component

A sixth ordering technique consists of computing the average absolute weight of the ith EKG property over the first 35 eigenvectors. (The first 35 eigenvectors were used because of computational considerations. They account for 90 percent of the variance as shown in Fig. 1.) The EKG properties are then ordered with respect to decreasing average absolute weight size.

Weighted Sum

If POE and ACC have merit as property selection criteria, then it seems reasonable to combine them. The seventh property selection technique combines the two factors in a weighted sum. Property i is ranked according to the value of W:

$$W = w_1\,(\text{POE}) + w_2(\text{ACC}) \tag{6}$$

where w_1, w_2 are two weights with the constraint that $w_1+w_2=1$. The POE values are first scaled to the range (0, 1) as follows:

$$\text{Normalized POE}_i = \frac{\text{POE}_i - \text{POE}_{\min}}{\text{POE}_{\max} - \text{POE}_{\min}}. \tag{7}$$

The first property chosen is the property with smallest POE. The property that produces the smallest value in (6) is chosen second. Before choosing the ith property, the absolute ACC values of the remaining candidate properties at the ith step are rescaled to (0, 1) so that w_1 and w_2 continue to represent the true measure of importance of the terms in (6). The POE and ACC techniques are special cases of this one, in which the weights assume their extreme values ($w_1=1$, $w_2=0$, and $w_1=0$, $w_2=1$, respectively).

EXPERIMENTAL EVALUATION OF THE PROPERTY SELECTION TECHNIQUES

Lower Bound on Testing Set Error Rate

Observer Variation: Error rates of a classificatory system trained to discriminate medical data are determined by comparing the computer's classifications to the physician's classifications. It is therefore important to establish the error rate of the physicians' diagnoses. Most physician errors can be attributed to poorly collected data containing noisy measurements and to variations in methods of measuring waveform properties and in diagnostic criteria [3].

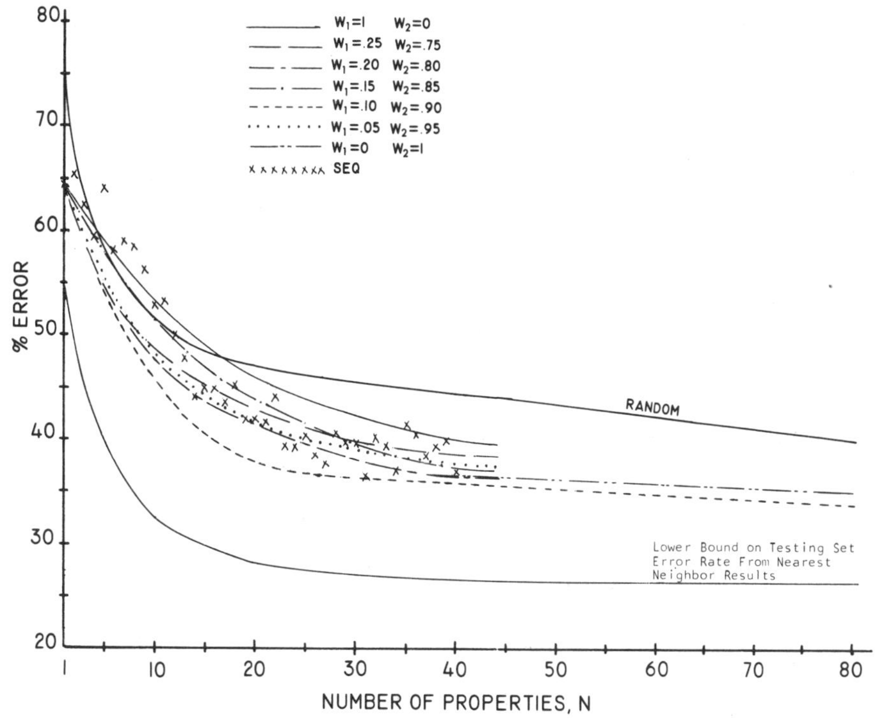

Fig. 2. Testing set error rates of properties ordered by the weighted sum and sequential techniques. The w_1, w_2 data have been smoothed. The error rates of properties randomly ordered are shown for comparative purposes. Nine-class EKG data are used.

For example, it has been reported that two groups of electrocardiographers reading the same set of 561 EKGs disagreed in over 40 percent of the normal–abnormal classifications [13]. In our study, when the data from each of the eight abnormal EKG classes were combined into a single class and the data were processed as a two-class normal–abnormal discrimination problem, a testing set error rate of 7.6 percent was obtained for $N=30$ properties [25]. An attempt was made to increase the reliability of the data used in this study by updating clinical diagnoses upon the availability of pathological reports. Other techniques that were used are described in detail in [32].

Irreducible Error: Another source of error, which relates directly to the properties and diagnostic classes under consideration, has been termed the irreducible error [8] and can be visualized as follows. A set of N properties forms the coordinate axes of an N-dimensional property space and the probability distribution of each class is a surface in this space. Decisions are made by assigning samples to the class with the largest probability at the point in space where the sample lies. If the properties are not perfect discriminators, the surfaces will overlap and some regions of the space will be covered by several classes. If an unknown is observed in one of these regions, any decision rule must at times be in error. This is the irreducible error. If a different set of properties is used, the distributions will change and a new irreducible error results.

If the actual probability distributions for each diagnostic class are known, the irreducible error is equal to

$$\text{Irreducible Error} = \sum_{k=1}^{K} \iint_{\bar{R}_k} \cdots \int P(k)P(X|k)\,dX \qquad (8)$$

where R_k is the region of the N-dimensional property space where samples are classified as members of class k and $\bar{R}_k$ is its complement. When the true distributions are unknown, the irreducible error might be approximated by determining the smallest error produced by a number of different decision procedures, each using the same set of properties. Another way is to compute the error rate of the nearest neighbor decision rule since this error is bounded above by a function of the irreducible error [6], [7]. It has been shown [6] that the nearest neighbor probability of error in the K-category classification problem is

$$\text{IE} \leq \text{NNE} \leq \text{IE}\left[2 - (K/K-1)\text{IE}\right] \qquad (9)$$

where IE and NNE denote the irreducible and nearest neighbor error rate, respectively, and K is the number of classes. Therefore, the nearest neighbor error rate is at most twice the irreducible error regardless of the number of classes and, thus, any other decision rule based on a large data set can decrease the probability of error by at most one half.

A lower bound on the irreducible error rate was estimated from (9) with $K=9$. The nearest neighbor rule error rates are reported in [25] for the properties ranked according to the weighted sum criterion with weights $w_1=0.1$, $w_2=0.9$. The smoothed data are plotted in Figs. 2, 3 and 5. It can be seen in Fig. 2, for example, that this curve reaches the asymptotic value of 26 percent at $N=70$. In this study, the majority of errors occurred when distinguishing between two class pairs: biventricular hypertrophy (BVH) from left ventricular hypertrophy (LVH), and right ventricular conduction defect (RVCD) from right ventricular hypertrophy

(RVH) [25]. These classes are very difficult to discriminate on the basis of electrocardiographic data alone, even for electrocardiographers.

Experimental Results

A histogram for each of the nine classes was constructed for each property based on the training data for each class. A smooth curve, which was a weighted sum of two Gaussian distributions, was fitted to each of the histograms using a steepest ascents routine. These curves are the estimated probability density functions (pdf's) for the nine classes with respect to a given property. The class *a priori* probabilities were taken to be their fractional representations in the training set. For a particular property, each training sample was assigned to one class by computing the probability of membership in each of the nine classes and choosing the class with largest value. (The probability of membership in class k for a training sample having property value x is proportional to the pdf of class k at point x times the *a priori* probability of class k.) The fraction of training samples incorrectly classified is the expected POE for that property.

A number of different weight values were used to evaluate the property listings produced by the weighted combination technique: $w_1 = 1, 0.75, 0.50, 0.25, 0.20, 0.15, 0.10, 0.05$, and 0 (where $w_2 = 1 - w_1$). A ranked list is generated for each set of weight values as explained in the previous section. The error rates on the nine-class *testing* set produced by selecting the top N properties from each of these lists were determined by a clustering decision rule that is described in detail elsewhere [25], [26]. This decision rule consisted of locating the dense clusters of data in the N-dimensional property space for each class and fitting a Gaussian distribution to each cluster of the class. The pdf of class k was a weighted sum of these Gaussian distributions. The weight of each distribution was equal to the fraction of vectors that fell within the cluster. Thus, the pdf of class k evaluated at point X was

$$P(X|k) = \sum_{r=1}^{C_k} (f_{kr}) \frac{1}{\left((2\pi)^{N/2} \left| \prod_{i=1}^{N} \sigma_{ri}^2 \right|^{\frac{1}{2}}\right)} \cdot \exp\left(-\frac{1}{2} \sum_{i=1}^{N} \left(\frac{x_{ri} - \bar{x}_{ri}}{\sigma_{ri}} \right)^2 \right) \quad (10)$$

where C_k is the number of clusters found for class k; f_{kr} is the fraction of class k points in the rth cluster of class k; and $\bar{x}_{ri}$ and σ_{ri} are the center coordinate and standard derivation, respectively, of the rth cluster along dimension i. The probability of membership was computed, knowing the pdf, as described above.

The *testing set* error rates of the weighted sum property selection technique are plotted in Fig. 2. Each of the w_1, w_2 curves has been smoothed. The results of the sequential technique are shown unsmoothed and are indicative of the noise in the w_1, w_2 curves before smoothing. The lowest error rates on the testing data were found using the list of properties obtained with weights of $w_1 = 0.1$ and $w_2 = 0.9$ and the error using the ACC property set ($w_1 = 0$) is smaller than the error using the POE property set ($w_1 = 1$). The high weight on the correlation factor in the best weighted sum may be due to the high redundancy of the property set. The error rates of properties randomly ordered from the list of 157 are also shown in Fig. 2. The utility of the property selection techniques is evident.

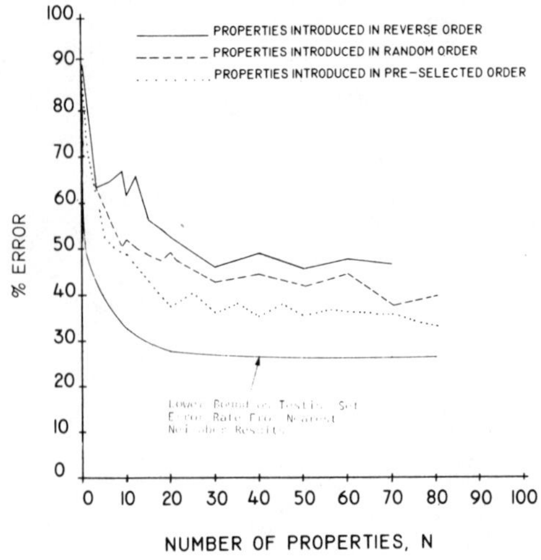

Fig. 3. Testing set error rates of property sets selected in forward, reverse, and random order from the $w_1 = 0.1$, $w_2 = 0.9$ lists. Nine-class EKG data are used.

The sensitivity of the ordering of the weighted sum property list was checked by selecting the properties produced by the $w_1 = 0.1$, $w_2 = 0.9$ ranking in reverse and in random order. If the ordering has utility, the error rates of properties selected in forward order should be lower than those of properties selected in random order and these error rates, in turn, should be lower than those selected in reverse order. This hypothesis is confirmed as shown in Fig. 3.

The results of choosing the first 40 properties according to the sequential technique are examined in detail in Table II. The clustering decision rule was used to determine the error rate among the nine classes at each step in the sequential selection procedure. The first property selected was property 9 because it had the lowest POE. The error rate using property 9 alone is 64.6 percent and classes 5 and 2 are most confused with a total of 16 errors. The best single discriminator among the remaining 156 properties for *these two classes* was property 13. The error was recomputed using properties 9 and 13 and the number of errors between classes 5 and 2 dropped from 16 to 11 while the overall error increased slightly to 65.4 percent. Classes 5 and 2 remained the two most confused classes and property 137 was found to be the best available discriminator. The number of errors between these two classes dropped further to 6 and the overall error decreased to 62.5 percent, and so on. The data in Table II show that after the first 40 property selections, the errors due to the properties selected generally consisted of confusing certain classes with class 2 (22 out of 39 times). The error rates of the property set generated by the sequential technique on this data are not small enough to justify the large amount of computation required for this technique.

The results for both the complete and the incomplete

TABLE II

RESULTS OF THE SEQUENTIAL PROPERTY SELECTION EXPERIMENT

Number of properties chosen, N	Two most confused classes with the $N-1$ properties	Number of errors among these 2 classes	Property chosen	Number of errors among these two classes after property N chosen	Overall percent error using the current N properties
1	—	—	9	—	64.6
2	5&2	16	13	11	65.4
3	5&2	11	137	6	62.5
4	3&1	12	140	11	59.6
5	7&2	14	148	9	64.2
6	5&2	13	131	13	58.3
7	5&2	13	64	11	59.2
8	8&2	14	31	14	58.8
9	8&2	14	20	11	56.3
10	8&2	11	134	8	52.9
11	5&2	11	60	5	53.3
12	6&3	8	76	10	50.0
13	6&3	10	125	7	47.9
14	6&3	7	79	9	44.2
15	6&3	9	37	6	45.0
16	4&2	7	142	7	45.0
17	7&8	9	36	8	43.8
18	6&3	10	73	7	45.4
19	7&8	9	68	4	42.1
20	4&2	6	153	6	42.1
21	6&3	7	58	6	41.7
22	6&3	6	126	10	44.2
23	6&3	10	88	8	39.6
24	6&3	8	52	7	39.6
25	4&2	7	40	7	40.4
26	4&2	7	123	7	38.8
27	4&2	7	146	7	37.9
28	4&2	7	110	8	40.4
29	3&4	8	32	4	39.2
30	4&2	8	47	8	39.2
31	4&2	8	111	6	36.7
32	4&2	6	149	8	40.4
33	4&2	8	136	8	39.6
34	4&2	8	6	7	37.1
35	6&3	8	8	7	41.7
36	4&2	7	120	8	40.8
37	6&3	9	55	9	38.8
38	6&3	9	151	8	39.6
39	6&3	8	121	7	40.0
40	4&2	8	24	7	37.1

eigenvector techniques are shown in Fig. 4. The *same* EKG properties were eliminated from each eigenvector property, with the lowest weighted properties eliminated first, to form the incomplete eigenvector properties. For example, the final experiment used the nine highest average weighted EKG properties in each incomplete eigenvector property. It can be seen that the testing error rate does not increase until half of the EKG properties are eliminated from each eigenvector property. So if eigenvector properties are used in this problem, only 78 of the 157 EKG properties will have to be measured.

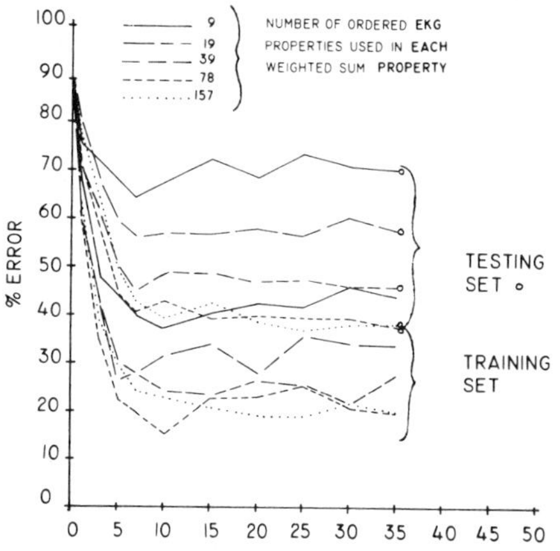

Fig. 4. Error rate as a function of the number of EKG properties used in each eigenvector property. Nine-class EKG data are used.

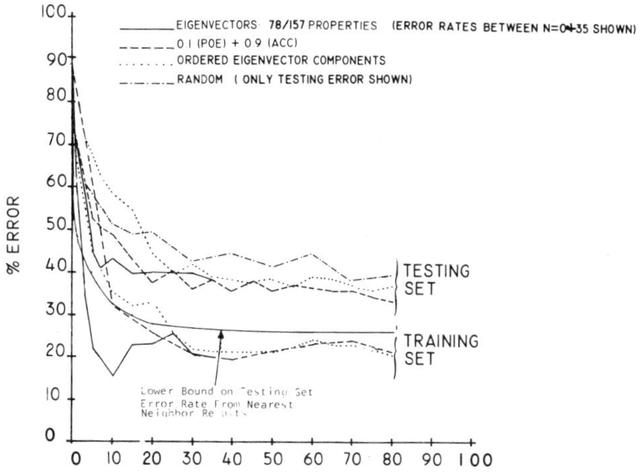

Fig. 5. Comparison of the error rates of properties selected according to the weighted sum, eigenvector, eigenvector component, and random ordering techniques. Nine-class EKG data are used.

The error rates of all the property selection techniques are compared in Fig. 5. Since the weighted sum technique with weights of 0.1 (POE)+0.9 (ACC) produced a better property ranking than either POE or ACC alone, this curve represents the best results of these three techniques. With respect to the testing set, it can be seen that the incomplete eigenvector properties (each a weighted sum of 78 EKG properties) produced the lowest error rates from $N=1$ to $N=20$, with the 0.1 (POE)+0.9 (ACC) ranking next best. The 0.1 (POE)+0.9 (ACC) ranked properties gave the lowest errors beyond $N=20$. While the weighted sum and eigenvector analysis techniques give the best property orderings, the weighted sum technique is to be preferred for $N<78$ since only N original EKG properties need to be measured rather than 78 original EKG properties for each of the (incomplete) eigenvector properties.

Comparison of the Property Lists

A measure of the similarity between two rank-ordered property lists is obtained by correlating the position of given properties within each list. The correlation coefficient between lists i and j, each of which contains 157 entries, is

TABLE III

CORRELATION COEFFICIENTS BETWEEN THE PROPERTY LISTS ORDERED BY FIVE OF THE SEVEN TECHNIQUES. VALUES DERIVED FROM (11).

	POE	ACC	0.1 (POE) +0.9 (ACC)	Sequential	Eigenvector Component	$\lvert C_{j_{avg}}\rvert = \frac{1}{4}\sum_{\substack{i=1 \\ i\neq j}}^{5} \lvert C_{ij}\rvert$
POE	1	−0.091	−0.031	0.323	0.071	0.129
ACC	−0.091	1	0.945	0.260	0.697	0.498
0.1 (POE)+0.9 (ACC)	−0.031	0.945	1	0.203	0.708	0.472
Sequential	0.323	0.260	0.203	1	0.272	0.265
Eigenvector Component	0.071	0.697	0.708	0.272	1	0.439

$$C_{ij} = \frac{\sum_{n=1}^{157} (R_{in} - 78.5)(R_{jn} - 78.5)}{\left[\sum_{n=1}^{157} (R_{in} - 78.5)^2\right]^{\frac{1}{2}} \left[\sum_{n=1}^{157} (R_{jn} - 78.5)^2\right]^{\frac{1}{2}}} \qquad (11)$$

where R_{in} is the position of property n on list i and 78.5 is the mean position on each list. The matrix of correlation coefficients is given in Table III for the five selection techniques that rank-order the original EKG properties. The data show that the property rankings produced by ACC alone and a weighted combination of 0.1 (POE)+0.9 (ACC) are are the two most similar ($C=0.945$) and that the POE criterion, which is the poorest of the seven techniques, gives the most dissimilar list to all others, on the average ($C_{avg}=0.129$).

SUMMARY AND CONCLUSIONS

Seven techniques have been evaluated for choosing pattern recognition properties and their performances were compared on a nine-class electrocardiographic problem. One-hundred and fifty seven properties computed from the vector EKG waveform were used. Seven techniques for ordering the properties were studied. Their respective ranking criteria are: 1) expected probability of error (POE) of individual properties; 2) average correlation coefficient (ACC) of a set of properties; 3) a sequential ordering technique based on minimizing the error between the two most confused classes; 4) eigenvectors, each of which is a linear combination of the 157 properties, ranked according to the magnitude of their associated eigenvalues; 5) eigenvectors from which some of the original properties have been eliminated; 6) largest average contribution to the eigenvectors; and 7) a weighted sum of POE and ACC.

An ordered list of properties is generated when the properties are ranked according to each criterion. Varying numbers of properties chosen from each of the ordered lists were used in a clustering decision rule and the error rates produced by each set of properties were the performance measures used to judge the quality of the selection techniques. The error rates produced by properties chosen according to each of the seven selection techniques were compared with the error rates obtained when the properties are ordered randomly.

The main results of the study are as follows.

1) The error rates of properties selected by each of the seven techniques were lower than the error rates of properties randomly selected.

2) Low mutual correlation among this set of 157 properties is a much stronger criterion for property selection than the single property probability of error.

3) The lowest error rates obtained by the weighted sum technique were found using the list of properties obtained from weights of 0.1 (POE)+0.9 (ACC).

4) The sequential technique requires an excessive amount of computing time.

5) Seventy-nine of the 157 EKG properties could be eliminated from each eigenvector without affecting the error rate of the eigenvector properties.

6) The error rates of the property set ordered by the weighted sum technique are smaller than the property set ordered by the eigenvector technique when the number of properties is greater than 20.

7) For this problem, the weighted sum technique is to be preferred since, for a subset of N properties, only N of the original EKG properties need to be measured rather than 78 of the original EKG properties for each of the N incomplete eigenvector properties.

The results show that the properties selected according to each of the seven techniques contain more discriminatory information about the classes than properties randomly chosen and thus all of the techniques are applicable to pattern classification problems. The choice of a particular selection method will depend on the ease of implementation, economic considerations, and the application.

REFERENCES

[1] T. W. Anderson, *An Introduction to Multivariate Statistical Analysis*. New York: Wiley, 1958.

[2] R. Bakis, N. M. Herbst, and G. Nagy, "An experimental study of machine recognition of hand-printed numerals," *IEEE Trans. Syst. Sci. Cybern.*, vol. SSC-4, July 1968, pp. 119–132.

[3] C. A. Caceres, "A basis for observer variation in electrocardiographic interpretation," *Prog. in Cardiovas. Diseases*, vol. 5, Mar. 1963, pp. 521–532.

[4] Y. T. Chien and K.-S. Fu, "Selection and ordering of feature observations in pattern recognition systems," *Inform. Contr.*, vol. 12, May–June 1968, pp. 394–414.

[5] ——, "On the generalized Karhunen–Loève expansion," *IEEE Trans.*

Inform. Theory, vol. IT-13, July 1967, pp. 518–520.
[6] T. M. Cover and P. E. Hart, "Nearest neighbor pattern classification," *IEEE Trans. Inform. Theory*, vol. IT-13, Jan. 1967, pp. 21–27.
[7] T. M. Cover, "Estimation by the nearest neighbor rule," *IEEE Trans. Inform. Theory*, vol. IT-14, Jan. 1968, pp. 50–55.
[8] J. Edie, W. Floyd, and G. Sebestyen, "Pattern recognition research," Litton Systems, Inc., Waltham, Mass., Sci. Rep. 1, Contract AF 19(628)-1604, June 1963.
[9] K.-S. Fu and Y. T. Chien, "Sequential recognition using a nonparametric ranking procedure," *IEEE Trans. Inform. Theory*, vol. IT-13, July 1967, pp. 484–492.
[10] K.-S. Fu, Y. T. Chien, and G. P. Cardillo, "A dynamic programming approach to sequential pattern recognition," *IEEE Trans. Electron. Comput.*, vol. EC-16,, Dec. 1967, pp. 790–803.
[11] K.-S. Fu and P. J. Min, "On feature selection in multiclass pattern recognition," Purdue Univ. School of Elec. Eng., Lafayette, Ind., Tech. Rep. TR-EE68-17, July 1968.
[12] K.-S. Fu, *Sequential Methods in Pattern Recognition and Machine Learning*. New York: Academic, 1968.
[13] P. A. Gorman, J. B. Calatayud, S. Abraham, and C. A. Caceres, "Observer variation in interpretation of the electrocardiogram," *Med. Ann. District of Columbia*, vol. 33, Mar. 1964, pp. 97–99.
[14] E. E. Gose, "The optimum replacement schedule for an evolving population of pattern recognition properties," in *Proc. 2nd Hawaii Int. Conf. Syst. Sci.*, Weston Periodicals, 1969, pp. 357–360.
[15] ——, "Introduction to biological and mechanical pattern recognition," in *Methodologies of Pattern Recognition*, S. Watanabe, Ed. New York: Academic, 1969, pp. 203–252.
[16] E. E. Gose and A. N. Mucciardi, "Six techniques for choosing pattern recognition properties," presented at the IEEE Comput. Group Symp. Feature Extraction and Selection in Pattern Recognition, Argonne Nat. Lab., Argonne, Ill., Oct. 5–7, 1970.
[17] J. Klingeman and H. V. Pipberger, "Computer classification of electrocardiograms," *Comput. Biomed.Res.*, vol. 1, Mar. 1967, pp. 1–17.
[18] A. H. Klopf and E. E. Gose, "An evolutionary pattern recognition network," *IEEE Trans. Syst. Sci. Cybern.*, vol. SSC-5, July 1969, pp. 247–250.
[19] S. Kullback, *Information Theory and Statistics*. New York: Wiley, 1959.
[20] P. M. Lewis, "The characteristic selection problem in recognition systems," *IRE Trans. Inform. Theory*, vol. 8, Feb. 1962, pp. 171–178.
[21] P. C. Mahalanobis, "On the generalized distance in statistics," *Proc. Nat. Inst. Sci. India*, vol. 122, 1936, pp. 49–55.
[22] T. Marill and D. M. Green, "On the effectiveness of receptors in recognition systems," *IEEE Trans. Inform. Theory*, vol. IT-9, Jan. 1963, pp. 11–17.
[23] R. G. Miller, "Statistical prediction by discriminant analysis," *Meteorol. Monographs*, no. 25, Amer. Meter. Soc., Boston, Mass., Oct. 1962.
[24] A. N. Mucciardi and E. E. Gose, "Evolutionary pattern recognition in incomplete nonlinear multithreshold networks," *IEEE Trans. Electron. Comput.*, vol. EC-15, Apr. 1966, pp. 257–261.
[25] A. N. Mucciardi, "Property selection techniques and decision making efficiency with applications to electrocardiogram classification," Ph.D. dissertation, Univ. Illinois at the Med. Center, Chicago, Ill., 1970.
[26] A. N. Mucciardi and E. E. Gose, "An algorithm for automatic clustering in N-dimensional spaces using hyperellipsoidal cells," *1970 Proc. IEEE Syst. Sci. Cybern. Conf.*, pp. 201–209.
[27] G. Nagy, "State of the art in pattern recognition," *Proc. IEEE*, vol. 56, May 1968, pp. 836–862.
[28] G. D. Nelson and D. M. Levy, "A dynamic programming approach to selection of pattern features," *IEEE Trans. Syst. Sci. Cybern.*, vol. SSC-4, July 1968, pp. 145–150.
[29] H. V. Pipberger, R. J. Arms, and F. W. Stallman, "Automatic screening of normal and abnormal electrocardiograms by means of a digital electronic computer," *Proc. Soc. Exper. Bio. Med.*, vol. 106, 1961, pp. 130–132.
[30] H. V. Pipberger, "Use of computers in interpretation of electrocardiograms," *Circ. Res.*, vol. 11, Sept. 1962, pp. 555–562.
[31] H. V. Pipberger, F. W. Stallman, and A. S. Berson, "Automatic analysis of the P-QRS-T complex of the electrocardiogram by digital computer," *Ann. Intern. Med.*, vol. 57, Nov. 1962, pp. 776–787.
[32] H. V. Pipberger and F. W. Stallman, "Computation of differential diagnosis in electrocardiography," *Ann. N. Y. Acad. Sci.*, vol. 115, art. 2, July 1964, pp. 1115–1128.
[33] H. V. Pipberger, "Computer analysis of the orthogonal electrocardiogram," Vet. Admin. Res. Cent. for Cardiovasc. Data Processing, Washington, D. C., Tech. Rep., 1966.
[34] ——, "Users guide to electrocardiographic data analysis computer programs," Vet. Admin. Res. Cen. for Cardiovasc. Data Processing, Washington, D. C., Tech. Rep., 1966.
[35] P. S. R. Rao, "On selecting variables for pattern classification," Tech. Rep. available from IEEE Comput. Group Repository, 345 East 47 St., New York, N. Y., Dec. 1967.
[36] G. S. Sebestyen and J. Edie, "Pattern recognition research," Litton Systems, Waltham, Mass., Final Rep., Contract AF 19(628)-1604, AD 620 236, July 1965.
[37] J. T. Tou and R. P. Heydorn, "Some approaches to optimum feature extraction," in *Computer and Information Sciences—II*. New York: Academic, 1967, pp. 57–89.
[38] A. Wald, *Sequential Analysis*. New York: Wiley, 1947.
[39] S. Watanabe, "Karhunen–Loève expansion and factor analysis: Theoretical remarks and applications," *Proc. 4th Prague Conf.*, 1965.
[40] S. Watanabe, P. F. Lambert, C. A. Kulikowski, J. L. Buxton, and R. Walker, "Evaluation and selection of variables in pattern recognition, in *Computer and Information Sciences—II*. New York: Academic, 1967, pp. 91–122.

Feature Extraction on Binary Patterns

GEORGE NAGY, MEMBER, IEEE

Abstract—The objects and methods of automatic feature extraction on binary patterns are briefly reviewed. An intuitive interpretation for geometric features is suggested whereby such a feature is conceived of as a cluster of component vectors in pattern space. A modified version of the Isodata or K-means clustering algorithm is applied to a set of patterns originally proposed by Block, Nilsson, and Duda, and to another artificial alphabet. Results are given in terms of a figure-of-merit which measures the deviation between the original patterns and the patterns reconstructed from the automatically derived feature set.

INTRODUCTION

THE CUSTOMARY object of feature extraction in pattern recognition is to secure a more consistent and lower dimensional representation of the differences between the pattern classes than is provided by the primary patterns. This allows the use of relatively simple decision schemes to assign unknown patterns, as characterized by the presence or absence of features, to predetermined classes.

The work reported here is confined to binary patterns and to features of the same species. Each feature is a binary vector of the same dimensionality as the patterns.

This restriction appears to eliminate many of the common pictorial, i.e., those usually defined in two spatial dimensions, measurements, such as height and width, central moments, medial axes or skeletons, lakes and bays, forks and intersections, curve following and line encoding, morpho- and quasi-topological invariants, extrema, local gradients, and the like. On the other hand, it will be seen that the vectorial features are consonant with n-tuples and, in noisy patterns, with threshold logic. The relationship between threshold logic units and the properties sought by more complex measurements has been extensively investigated by Minsky and Papert.

Manuscript received October 20, 1968. This paper was presented at the IEEE Systems Science and Cybernetics Conference, San Francisco, Calif., October 14–16, 1968.

The author is with T. J. Watson Research Center, IBM Corp., Yorktown Heights, N. Y.

Reprinted from *IEEE Trans. Syst. Sci., Cybern.*, vol. SSC-5, pp. 273–278, Oct. 1969.

Our aim is further restricted to finding a minimal set of features capable of reconstructing the input patterns to some desired degree of accuracy. The discriminating power of the features is not taken into account at all. Of course, if a feature set can be used for reconstruction of the patterns, then it is also sufficient to differentiate these patterns from one another, though it may not do this efficiently.

It should be noted that there are always at least two admissible sets of features available: the set of all the individual components, i.e., the unit vectors of the pattern space, and the set of all patterns. The object is to find a sufficient set smaller in number than the smaller of these sets. In some applications there may also be a premium on obtaining features each of which contains as few points as possible.

The problem may also be very simply stated as the decomposition of a binary $M \times N$ pattern matrix P into the Boolean product of an $M \times K$ feature matrix F and a $K \times N$ assignment matrix A in such a way that K is a minimum [7], [8]. The trivial admissible solutions then correspond to the choice of the identity matrix for either F or A.

Alternative Formulations

The problem of designing a highly nonlinear classification system in two stages has been approached in many ways. In terms of adaptive systems, Rosenblatt and Widrow schools, it is equivalent to training a two-layer machine. The two layers are not independent; the modifications in each layer must depend, through some backpropagating error correction or adaptation scheme, on the overall performance of the categorizer. Various probabilistic methods have been suggested to promote the exploration of the vast number of possible weight assignments, but success still seems around the corner.

Viewing the problem as one of dimensionality reduction, one could apply the statistical and algebraic techniques of factor and discriminant analysis, principal components, or Karhunen–Loeve expansions. Unfortunately, all of these depend on the generally nonbinary eigenvectors of the appropriate covariance matrices, and there seems to be no practical method of confining the resulting features to a binary space. There are, to be sure, orthonormal expansions defined on binary spaces, the Rademacher–Walsh functions, for example, which could be used as basis vectors, but here also the coefficients turn out to be real valued variables. In this direction, Chow's investigations of tree-dependence probably represent the best hope.

From the viewpoint of switching theory and Boolean algebra, the task is to reduce the number of conjunctive terms in a series of disjunctions. No systematic methods exist, to our knowledge, to accomplish this for expressions containing of the order of several hundred variables. This also applies to the related fixed word length coding problem.

It is sometimes sufficient merely to select a small subset of features from a pool of intuitively designed or computer generated candidates. Here the information theoretic and statistical distance criteria of Lewis, Allais, Kamentsky, Liu, and others, are available. The serious drawback of this procedure is that no matter how many features are tried, in any situation of practical interest they represent only an infinitesimal fraction of all possible combinations.

Block, Nilsson, and Duda (BND)

The point of departure for the experimental work reported here is a relatively simple set of patterns constructed by Block, Nilsson, and Duda, to evaluate their own feature extraction algorithms, as reported at the 1963 COINS symposium [1]. This excellent pilot study, described in the learning machine idiom, is based on the formation of successive intersections of the Boolean patterns, regarded as subsets of a retinal set, to obtain the core features of the pattern set.

Block *et al.* postulate the existence of a minimal set of features such that 1) each pattern can be synthesized from the features (as a union), and 2) the intersection of all the patterns containing a given feature is that feature. While the first condition is clearly essential, the second condition merely restricts the number of possible solutions to a given problem. In practice it is relatively easy to satisfy both conditions 1) and 2), the main difficulty being the requirement that the features constitute a minimal set.

The sequential algorithm proposed in [1] is shown to obtain features satisfying all the requirements provided that a certain threshold condition, guaranteeing that the size of the smallest feature is much greater than that of the intersection between any two features, is met. None of the examples successfully processed by Block, Nilsson, and Duda satisfy this condition. In fact, it is quite difficult to construct examples to meet the condition without resorting to nonoverlapping features.

The number of computations required by the sequential algorithm, for a known threshold, is proportional to $N \times M \times K^2$, where N is the number of patterns, M is the number of components in each pattern, and K is the number of features. BND also describe, without proof of convergence, a faster parallel algorithm. The features are found here in between $N \times M \times K$ and $N \times M \times K^2$ steps, but each step requires verifying whether the pattern set can be reconstructed with the already derived features.

The pattern set used by BND is shown, together with the unique optimal feature set, in Fig. 1(a) and (b). Notice that if the retina squares are renumbered as in Fig. 1(c), then the features can no longer be easily obtained by inspection.

Feature Determination as a Clustering Problem

In the scheme of [1], each associator or A unit becomes selectively attuned to a set of similar patterns, i.e., those sharing a common feature. Thus this method is in a sense equivalent to clustering the pattern vectors in the space defined by the components.

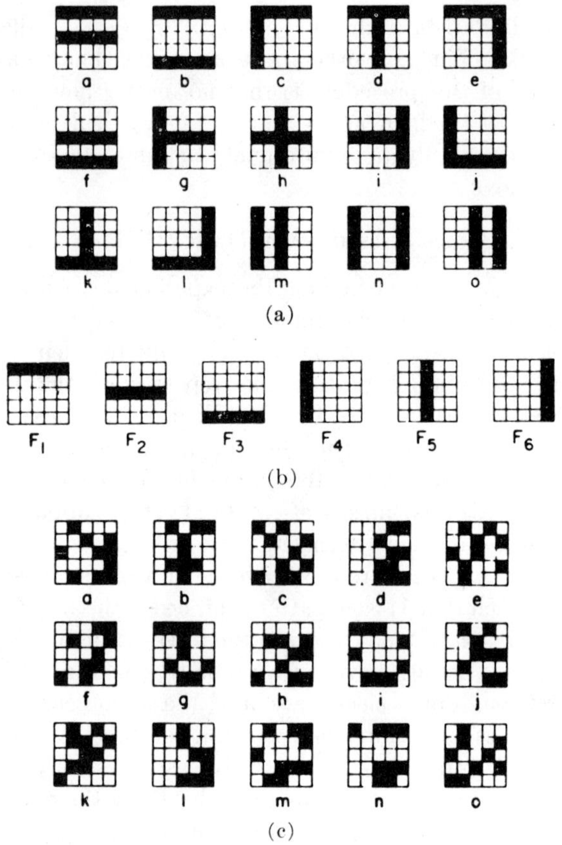

Fig. 1. (a) Pattern set proposed by Block *et al.* to test feature extraction scheme. (b) Smallest set of binary features sufficient to reconstruct the patterns of (a). (c) Scrambled version of pattern set produced by arbitrary renumbering of the retina squares.

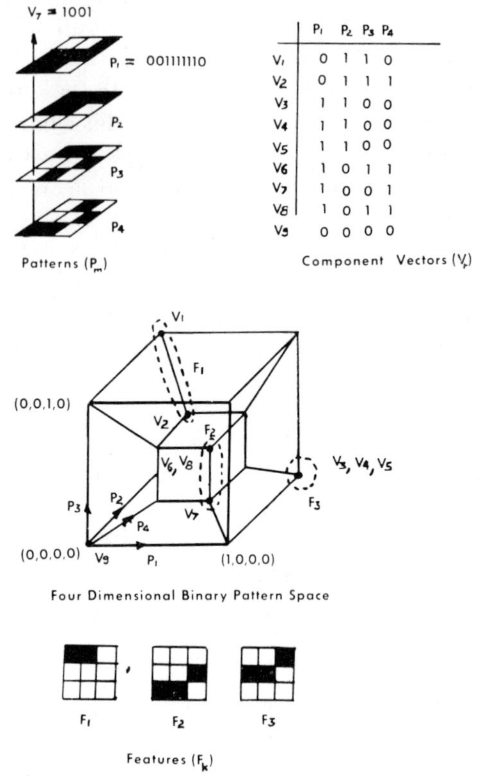

Fig. 2. Four-pattern example of disposition of the nine component vectors V_i in the four-dimensional pattern space, and the features obtained by clustering these vectors by inspection.

The novelty of the approach proposed in this paper resides in the determination of features by the disposition of the component vectors in pattern space rather than vice versa. Tight groups or clusters in this space contain elements which tend to be present or absent in the same patterns. Since this is precisely the intuitive meaning of "feature," success in our endeavour presumably depends only on the availability of adequate clustering techniques.

The idea is illustrated in Fig. 2 by means of a simple example consisting of four patterns on a 3×3 retina. The binary pattern space is schematically represented by a four-dimensional cube. Unfortunately an ordinary three cube could not be used because it is impossible to construct a non-trivial example with only three patterns, and thus, at most, two useful features.

By definition the ith element of the jth component vector is 1 if and only if the jth element is 1 in the ith pattern. Thus if the patterns are considered as the columns of a binary matrix, then the component vectors are the rows of this matrix, as shown at the top of Fig. 2.

The three clusters of component vectors obtained by inspection are circled in dotted lines. The collection of retina points or components in each cluster form the features shown at the bottom of Fig. 2. The reconstruction of the original patterns from these features, although imperfect, is as good as can be possibly achieved with only three features.

The principal clustering method used in the experiments described further on is the popular K-means or Isodata technique [2], [3] modified to allow overlapping clusters. Both randomly assigned and computed starting points were tried in clustering, with the latter proving vastly superior.

The computed starting vectors were derived from a similarity matrix obtained from the pair-wise distances among the component vectors as suggested by Abraham [4]. This procedure corresponds to the determination of the disconnected subgraphs of the undirected graph associated with the similarity matrix. The necessary ultimate connectivity matrix was obtained with Baker's algorithm [5] for Boolean matrix multiplication, although it has been kindly pointed out since, by Prof. P. Robert of the University of Montreal, that a procedure based on Warshall's algorithm would yield the same result more rapidly [6].

Another option allows the experimenter to introduce his own best guesses as starting features to see if the program can improve upon them.

A trivial sufficiency condition for the success of the algorithm is the existence of nonintersecting features corresponding to clusters concentrated at single points. As in Block, Nilsson, and Duda's method, small intersections between the features represent the most favorable conditions. The speed of operation of the least-squares clustering algorithm is proportional to $N \times M \times K$.

A Figure of Merit

Each feature set is automatically evaluated by the program by comparing the pattern set, as reconstructed from the features, to the original set. The figure of merit is the total number of bits, or Hamming distance, in which the synthetic pattern set differs from the original. In the example given earlier, for example, the figure of merit for the three features is two.

The synthetic pattern is the union of all the features assigned to a given pattern. Features are assigned in turn to every pattern, on the basis of closeness in the Hamming distance sense, until the appropriate term in the figure of merit begins to increase. At that point the synthetic pattern is deemed complete.

To render the system less sensitive to false starts and to avoid very similar features in the final set, two routines based on the pattern synthesis portion of the figure of merit computation were added to the program.

1) Whenever two features are similar, i.e., within a given Hamming distance of one another, one of them is replaced by the unreconstructed portion of the least successfully reconstructed pattern.

2) The least used feature, if used in fewer than a specified number of synthetic patterns, is replaced in the same way. In either case, the new set of features are used to form initial cluster centers for a renewed series of iterations.

Neither of these heuristic attempts proved signally successful; to cope with difficult practical problems, more profound changes will have to be introduced.

Results

The algorithm described in the preceding sections was programmed for an IBM 7094 computer, as shown in Fig. 3. The program requires about 1000 FORTRAN statements, with two short machine language subroutines for computing distances between binary vectors. The running time for each experiment is of the order of a few minutes.

For the BND patterns the optimal set of features, as shown in Fig. 1(b), were derived both with random and with computed initial cluster centers. In the latter case, the main clustering algorithm converges in three cycles at an overlap threshold of five. The program tries a full range of overlap thresholds, selecting the final feature set on the basis of the lowest figure of merit. For these patterns a figure of merit of 0 is reached at several values of the threshold.

For a more severe test of the method, the 36-character alphabet shown in Fig. 4(a) was constructed. This set was designed without any regard for reconstructibility in terms of features.

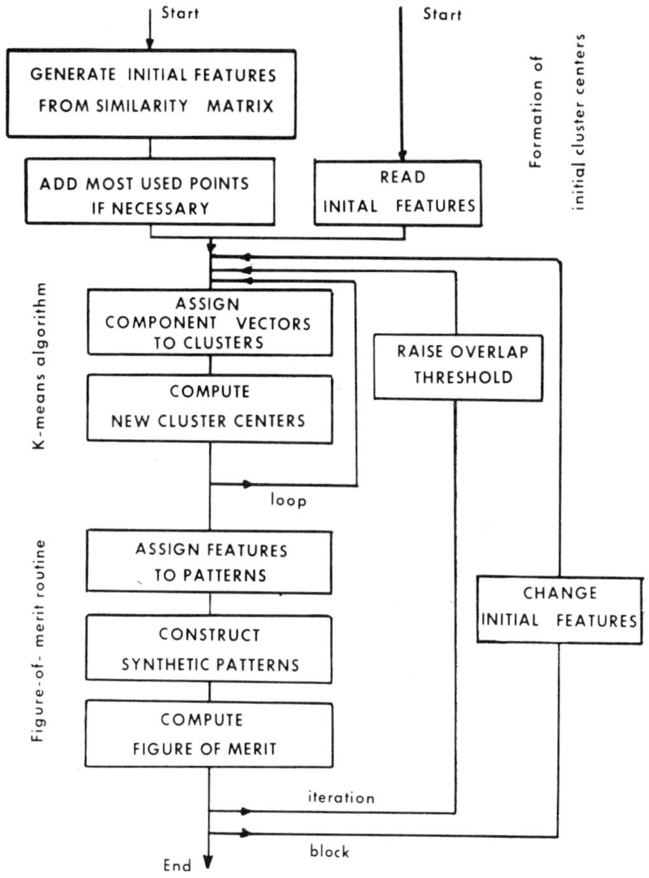

Fig. 3. Major portions of the feature extraction and evaluation program. Tests for leaving the nested loops have been omitted.

TABLE I

Number of Features

	10	15	18	20
Random initial features	140	63	—	—
Best guess features	112	45	—	—
Similarity matrix features	85	42	33	18

Table I shows the figures of merit F obtained with different methods of generating initial features and for varying numbers of features in the final set. By way of comparison, two sets of 10 features proposed by different persons came in at F of 140 and 147, respectively, although eventually the best features of these and the machine generated set were combined to produce an F of 82 with 10 features. Whether this figure is the lowest possible remains unknown.

The best sets of 10 and 15 features generated by the computer are shown in Fig. 4 along with the corresponding synthetic patterns. Of course, with 15 features the synthetic patterns resemble the originals more closely.

It is noteworthy that with the 36-character alphabet the sets of features consistently correspond to nonoverlapping clusters containing all the component vectors. The BND features have a 20-percent overlap.

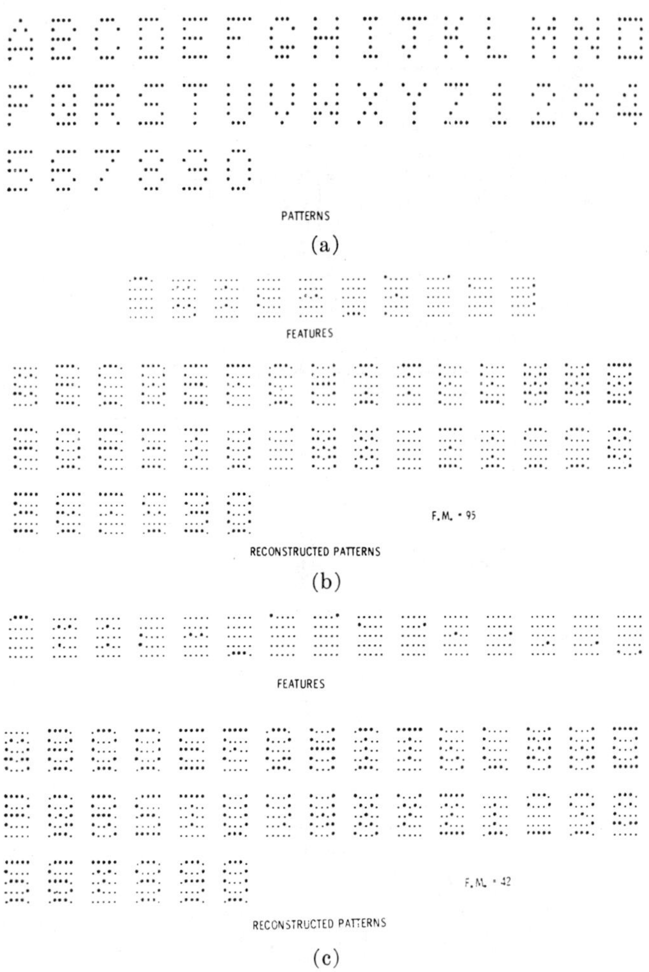

Fig. 4. (a) 36-character alphabet with significant overlap between patterns. (b) 10 automatically derived features and corresponding synthetic patterns. (c) 15 automatically derived features and corresponding synthetic patterns.

Ternary Features

While binary features are in principle adequate for full reconstruction of any binary pattern set, it is clear that for the classification of noisy patterns there is much to be gained by using multilevel features.

Consideration of black, white, or neutral features introduces very little complication in the feature generating portion of the program. The complement of each component vector, which has a 1 in every position corresponding to a pattern which is 0 or white, at that point, is included among the vectors to be clustered. Since the clustering algorithms do not distinguish between the black and the white component vectors, a given feature may include both black and white elements with all others neutral. Contradictions do not arise because a component vector and its complement are always sufficiently far from one another to be included in the same cluster.

The evaluation of a ternary feature set is, however, difficult. The union operation cannot be used for pattern reconstruction, and the figure of merit cannot be based on the Hamming distance. The arbitrary nature of the decisions necessary to circumvent these difficulties renders experimentation with ternary features quite unsatisfying. Much effort was spent on trying to find satisfactory ways of generalizing the reconstruction method and the figure of merit. It soon became clear, for example, that for patterns of interest it is unfructuous to try to treat the black and white points completely symmetrically.

Because in the figure of merit computation weights must be assigned to neutral elements in the synthetic pattern which correspond to black or white elements in the original patterns, the ternary feature sets could not be directly compared to the binary sets derived earlier. Without the weights an all neutral synthetic pattern could be misconstrued for perfect reconstruction.

In spite of our inability to formulate this portion of the problem clearly, it seems worthwhile to continue to try to close the gap between the rudimentary data reduction techniques available for binary channels and their more sophisticated continuous counterparts.

Conclusion

A new way of regarding features in binary patterns has been introduced. An algorithm based on this point of view was programmed for a digital computer, and the feature sets obtained by the algorithm were evaluated by means of a precise error criterion.

The new method seems faster than previous, algorithms. The transposition of the clustering idea from the pattern vectors to the component vectors results in a pleasing duality which is more fully developed in [7].

Although pictorial examples were used to test the method, it is clearly quite general and would encounter no more difficulty with the patterns of Fig. 1(c) than with those of Fig. 1(b). This lack of specialization can be a liability as well as an asset.

A more serious disadvantage is the absence of satisfactory sufficiency and necessity conditions for the correct convergence of the algorithm. This shows up strikingly in the four-pattern example, where there seems no way of extending the set of three plausible features to the four perfect features corresponding to the patterns themselves.

Recent work by Abdali shows that replacing the thresholded Hamming distance by a logical inclusion test leads to firmer theoretical foundations [7]. Since the inclusion method does guarantee complete reconstruction, albeit sometimes with an excessive number of features, perhaps it could advantageously replace the similarity matrix method as a preliminary step. This study also contains a first attempt to apply a mechanistic feature determination rule to automatically scanned handprinted characters.

The calculations in [1, Appendix I] show the amount of data reduction which could be realized by a workable binary feature extraction scheme. Aside from the somewhat questionable applications in pattern recognition, the development of improved feature synthesizing methods could lead to impressive economies in narrow-band image transmission and data compression, particularly where the data exhibits consistency or repetitiousness but the volume transacted exceeds the capability of more conventional coding techniques.

ACKNOWLEDGMENT

The idea of sideways clustering of pattern vectors was first proposed by Dr. Richard Casey of IBM's Watson Research Center. Mr. Louis Loh, also of IBM, suggested numerous improvements in the course of seeing the program through nine successive versions.

REFERENCES

[1] H. D. Block, N. J. Nilsson, and R. O. Duda, "Determination and detection of features in patterns," in *Computers and Information Sciences,* J. T. Tou and R. H. Wilcox, Eds. Washington, D.C.: Spartan, 1964, pp. 75–110.

[2] J. MacQueen, "Some methods for classification and analysis of multivariate observations," *Proc. of the 5th Berkeley Symp. on Statistics and Probability.* Berkeley, Calif.: University of California Press, 1967, pp. 281–297.

[3] G. H. Ball and D. J. Hall, "ISODATA, an iterative method of multivariate analysis and pattern classification," presented at the 1966 Internatl. Communications Conf., Philadelphia, Pa. (also Stanford Res. Inst. Rept., April 1965).

[4] C. Abraham, "Evaluation of clusters on the basis of random graph theory," IBM Corp., Yorktown Heights, N.Y., Res. Memo., 1962.

[5] J. J. Baker, "A note on multiplying Boolean matrices," *Commun. Assoc. for Computing Machinery,* vol. 5, no. 2, 1962.

[6] P. Robert and J. Ferland, "Généralisation de l'algorithme de Warshall," *Rev. Franç. Inform. Rech. Opér.,* vol. 2, no. 7, pp. 71–85, 1968.

[7] S. K. Abdali, "An algorithm for feature extraction and applications to hand-printed characters," Computer Sciences Dept., University of Montreal, P. Q., Canada, Rept., 1968.

[8] N. J. Nilsson, "Some experiments in reconstituting images from features," Stanford Res. Inst., Interim Rept. 1, Proj. 4621, October 1963.

An Optimal Set of Discriminant Vectors

DONALD H. FOLEY, MEMBER, IEEE, AND JOHN W. SAMMON, JR., MEMBER, IEEE

See page 110

***Abstract*—A new method for the extraction of features in a two-class pattern recognition problem is derived. The main advantage is that the method for selecting features is based entirely upon discrimination or separability as opposed to the more common approach of fitting. The classical example of fitting is the use of the eigenvectors of the lumped covariance matrix corresponding to the largest eigenvalues. In an analogous manner, the new technique selects discriminant vectors (or features) corresponding to the largest "discrim-values." The new method is compared to some of the more popular alternative techniques via both data-dependent and mathematical examples. In addition, a recursive method for obtaining the discriminant vectors is given.**

***Index Terms*—Dimensionality reduction, discriminants, eigenvectors, feature extraction, feature ranking, feature selection, Karhunen–Loeve expansions, multivariate data-analysis, pattern classification, pattern recognition.**

I. INTRODUCTION

IN MANY PATTERN recognition applications it is convenient to divide the problem into two parts, feature extraction or selection and pattern classification. Although numerous papers exist in the literature on designing classification logic given a set of features, it is only recently that significant attention has been given to the area of feature extraction. An indication of this emphasis on feature extraction is the special issue of the IEEE TRANSACTIONS ON COMPUTERS devoted entirely to this subject area [1].

Usually, an initial set of raw measurements is taken from examples of each class of interest. For example, the raw measurements might consist of digitized waveforms or images. The number of raw measurements is frequently quite large. Simply stated, the goal of feature extraction is to find a transformation which maps the raw measurements into a smaller set of features which hopefully contain all the relevant or discriminatory information needed to solve the overall pattern recognition problem.

Most of the feature extraction literature has centered around finding linear transformations. The most popular transform is the Karhunen–Loeve or eigenvector orthonormal expansion [2], [3]. Since each eigenvector can be ranked by its corresponding eigenvalue, a subset of the "best" eigenvectors can be chosen as the most "relevant" features. Unfortunately, the subset chosen provides the best fitting subspace. Recognizing that representational accuracy is not the ultimate objective of pattern recognition, Fukunaga and Koontz [4] suggest a modification of the eigenvector technique. A preliminary transformation for a two-class problem is found such that the eigenvectors which best fit class 1 are the poorest for representing class 2.

This paper suggests and derives an algorithm for extracting a set of features for a two-class problem in which the criteria for selecting each feature is based directly on its discriminatory potential. These features are based on an optimal set of discriminant vectors which are an extension of the discriminant plane derived by Sammon [5]. For the remainder of the paper, the term "discriminant vectors" will be used for the new technique.

The following sections of the paper give a quick review and counterexample for both the eigenvector and the Fukunaga–Koontz transforms, a derivation of the discriminant vectors, and a comparison of these different techniques.

Besides the obvious use of discriminant vectors for feature extraction, the discriminant vectors can be used in interactive pattern recognition systems such as the on-line pattern analysis and recognition system (OLPARS) [6]. One objective of OLPARS is to find projections of high dimensional data into one-, two-, or three-spaces so an on-line analyst can both observe the inherent structure of the data and design piecewise linear classification logic. The discriminant vectors provide promising candidates for the directions on which the data could be projected.

II. REVIEW OF KARHUNEN–LOEVE TRANSFORM

Most of the attention in the literature concerning feature selection has centered around the discrete Karhunen–Loeve or eigenvector expansion [2], [3]. In this procedure, the original L-dimensional data vectors are transformed by multiplying by the eigenvectors $\boldsymbol{e}_j$ of the estimated lumped covariance matrix $\sum$. The eigenvectors satisfy the equation

$$\sum \boldsymbol{e}_j = \lambda_j \boldsymbol{e}_j$$

where λ_j is the eigenvalue corresponding to the jth eigenvector. For real data, $\sum$ is a real symmetric matrix and all the eigenvectors are orthogonal, i.e., $\boldsymbol{e}_i{}^t \boldsymbol{e}_j = 0$ for $i \neq j$, and the eigenvalues are all greater than or equal to zero. Hence the eigenvalues can be ordered such that $\lambda_1 \geq$

Manuscript received September 30, 1973; revised August 20, 1974.
The authors are with the Pattern Analysis and Recognition Corporation, Rome, N. Y. 13440.

Reprinted from *IEEE Trans. Comput.*, vol. C-24, pp. 281–289, Mar. 1975.

$\lambda_2 \geq \cdots \geq \lambda_L > 0$. If the eigenvectors are normalized such that $\| e_j \| = e_j^t e_j = 1$, then

$$\Phi = \begin{bmatrix} e_1^t \\ \cdot \\ \cdot \\ \cdot \\ e_L^t \end{bmatrix}$$

is an orthonormal transformation such that $y = \Phi x$ and each $y_j = e_j^t x$ is the jth feature in the new space for the input vector x. The mean square error obtained by projecting all the data into a subspace spanned by only a subset A of $K (K < L)$ eigenvectors is given by

$$\overline{\epsilon^2} = \sum_{j \notin A} \lambda_j$$

where A is the set containing the chosen K eigenvectors.

For any K, this error can be minimized by choosing the eigenvectors corresponding to the K largest eigenvalues. In fact, it is known (e.g., see Fukunaga [7]) that the mean square error in representing a set of random L-dimensional vectors with only K elements of *any* orthonormal transformation (i.e., any K-dimensional subspace) is minimized by selecting the first K elements of the discrete Karhunen–Loeve expansion. Although this transformation is optimal with respect to fitting the data, it is not necessarily optimal with respect to discriminating the data.

Fig. 1 shows a two-class two-dimensional pattern recognition problem. The eigenvector transform would rank direction e_1 as the best fitting direction or feature. However, it would obviously result in a poor recognition rate.

III. FUKUNAGA–KOONTZ TRANSFORM

To avoid the conflict of goals just mentioned, Fukunaga and Koontz [4] suggest in an earlier paper a preliminary transformation for a two-class problem such that the eigenvectors which best fit class 1 are the poorest for representing class 2. In order to briefly describe this method, let R_1 and R_2 be the weighted correlation matrices of class 1 and 2, respectively, i.e.,

$$R_i = P_i(\Sigma_i + \mu_i \mu_i^t), \qquad i = 1,2$$

where P_i, Σ_i, and μ_i are the *a priori* probability, the covariance, and the mean of class i. Let T be a preliminary transform such that

$$T(R_1 + R_2)T^t = I.$$

Fukunaga shows that the eigenvectors of TR_1T^t are the same as the eigenvectors of TR_2T^t and all the eigenvalues are bounded by 0 and 1. Let the eigenvalues for class 1 be ordered such that

$$1 \geq \lambda_1^{(1)} \geq \lambda_2^{(1)} \geq \cdots \geq \lambda_L^{(1)} \geq 0.$$

Fukunaga proves next that $\lambda_i^{(2)} = 1 - \lambda_i^{(1)}$. Consequently, the best fitting eigenvectors for class 1 (e.g., $\lambda_i^{(1)} \cong 1$) are the poorest for class 2 (e.g., $\lambda_i^{(2)} = 1 - \lambda_i^{(1)} \cong 0$). Fukunaga recommends ordering the eigenvectors to be used as features by picking the largest of $| \lambda_j^{(1)} - 0.5 |$.

This implies that an eigenvalue of 0.5 is an extremely poor feature. This may not always be true. The following is a counterexample. Let

$$\mu_1^t = [0 \quad 5 \quad 0]; \quad \mu_2^t = [0 \quad -5 \quad 0]; \quad P_1 = P_2 = 1/2$$

$$\Sigma_1 = \begin{bmatrix} 8 & 0 & 0 \\ 0 & 1 & 0 \\ 0 & 0 & 8 \end{bmatrix}; \qquad \Sigma_2 = \begin{bmatrix} 2 & 0 & 0 \\ 0 & 1 & 0 \\ 0 & 0 & 2 \end{bmatrix}.$$

Note that dimensions one and three have zero means for both classes, while there is considerable separation along dimension two. For example, if the marginal distribution along dimension two was normal, a Bayes error rate of 0.0003 percent would result. Along either dimensions one or three a Bayes error rate of 35 percent would result if the marginal distributions were normal. Also note that a double threshold is required. If a researcher used features which had zero means and different variances for the classes, the classification logic should not be as simple as any of the commonly used linear discriminant functions.

Proceeding with the Fukunaga–Koontz transform,

$$R_1 = 1/2 \begin{bmatrix} 8 & 0 & 0 \\ 0 & 26 & 0 \\ 0 & 0 & 8 \end{bmatrix}; \qquad R_2 = 1/2 \begin{bmatrix} 2 & 0 & 0 \\ 0 & 26 & 0 \\ 0 & 0 & 2 \end{bmatrix}.$$

The matrix[1] T and the matrix TR_1T^t are given by

$$T = \begin{bmatrix} 1/(5)^{1/2} & 0 & 0 \\ 0 & 1/(26)^{1/2} & 0 \\ 0 & 0 & 1/(5)^{1/2} \end{bmatrix}$$

$$TR_1T^t = \begin{bmatrix} 0.8 & 0 & 0 \\ 0 & 0.5 & 0 \\ 0 & 0 & 0.8 \end{bmatrix}$$

Using the Fukunaga–Koontz ranking (i.e., $| \lambda_j^{(1)} - 0.5 |$), dimensions one and three are tied with the highest rating (0.3), while dimension two received the lowest rating possible, i.e., 0.0.

In effect, two features with poor discriminatory information have been chosen over the one feature with almost perfect discriminatory capabilities. In addition, features which prevent the use of a simple linear discriminant have been chosen.

[1] T consists of each eigenvector of R divided by the square root of its corresponding eigenvalue.

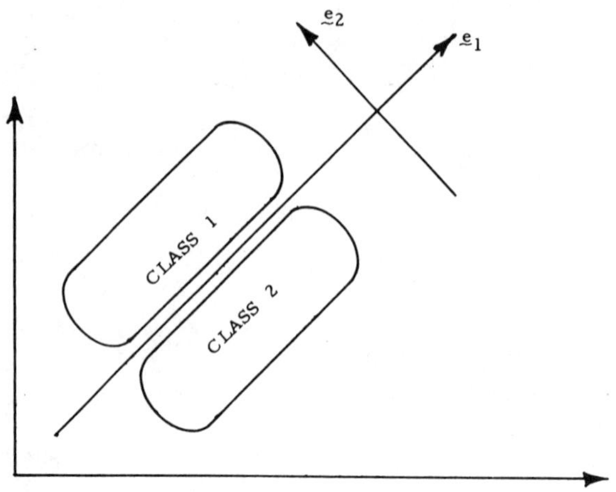

Fig. 1. Illustration of fitting deficiency. Underlined symbols indicate boldfaced symbols in text.

IV. DISCRIMINANT VECTORS

Before proceeding with a derivation of the discriminant vectors, it is worthwhile to place the roles of discrimination and fitting in perspective. Usually if the original set of features is carefully chosen, it is possible to design logic based on the statistics of a design set which achieves a very high recognition rate. In order to cut the error rate even further, the authors have found it practical to use fitting routines in order to create reject strategies. The fitting routines are applied after a class has been tentatively identified by the discrimination logic. Our experience has been to base the routines on the relationships and ranges of certain features. These fitting routines are usually designed from physical knowledge of what must be present if a particular class occurs. If the fitting criteria are not met, a reject decision is output. Other fitting routines based on criteria derived from eigenvector algorithms are also possible.

The objective of the discriminant vectors is to aid in solving the discrimination portion of the task.

In order to find the best vectors for discriminating between two classes, it is necessary to select some optimality criterion. As our measure of discrimination achieved by a vector $\mathbf{d}$, let us choose either 1) the Fisher ratio, that is, the ratio of the projected class differences to the sum of the within-class scatter along $\mathbf{d}$, i.e.,

$$R_1(\mathbf{d}) = \frac{(\mathbf{d}^t\mathbf{\Delta})^2}{\mathbf{d}^t W \mathbf{d}}$$

where

$\mathbf{d}$ = L-dimensional column vector on which the data are projected;
$\mathbf{d}^t$ = transpose of $\mathbf{d}$;
$\mathbf{x}_{ij}{}^t = (x_{ij1}\cdots x_{ijL})$; jth sample vector for class i;
N_i = number of samples in class i;
$\hat{\boldsymbol{\mu}}_i$ = estimated mean of class i, $\hat{\boldsymbol{\mu}}_i = (1/N_i)\sum_{j=1}^{N_i}\mathbf{x}_{ij}$;
$\mathbf{\Delta}$ = difference in the estimated means, $\mathbf{\Delta} = \hat{\boldsymbol{\mu}}_1 - \hat{\boldsymbol{\mu}}_2$;
W_i = within-class scatter for class i, $W_i = \sum_{j=1}^{N_i}(\mathbf{x}_{ij} - \hat{\boldsymbol{\mu}}_i)(\mathbf{x}_{ij} - \hat{\boldsymbol{\mu}}_i)^t$;
W = sum of the within-class scatter, $W = W_1 + W_2$,

or 2) the modified Fisher ratio, that is, the ratio of the projected class differences to the sum of the within-class covariance along $\mathbf{d}$, i.e.,

$$R_2(\mathbf{d}) = (\mathbf{d}^t\mathbf{\Delta})^2/\mathbf{d}^t[\hat{\Sigma}_1 + \hat{\Sigma}_2]\mathbf{d}$$

where

$$\hat{\Sigma}_i = \frac{1}{N_i - 1}\sum_{j=1}^{N_i}(\mathbf{x}_{ij} - \hat{\boldsymbol{\mu}}_i)(\mathbf{x}_{ij} - \hat{\boldsymbol{\mu}}_i)^t = (N_i - 1)^{-1}W_i$$

is the estimated covariance of class i.

This criterion devotes equal attention to minimizing the covariance of each class, while the former devotes more attention to the class with more samples. Since both criteria have the same general form, Anderson and Bahadur [8] have suggested using

$$R(\mathbf{d}) = \frac{(\mathbf{d}^t\mathbf{\Delta})^2}{\mathbf{d}^t A \mathbf{d}}$$

where $A = cW_1 + (1 - c)W_2$ and $0 \leq c \leq 1$. $R(\mathbf{d})$ will be called the generalized Fisher criterion and will be used in the derivation of the discriminant vector. For $c = 0.5$, maximizing $R(\mathbf{d})$ with respect to $\mathbf{d}$ is equivalent to maximizing $R_1(\mathbf{d})$ with respect to $\mathbf{d}$, while for $c = (N_2 - 1)/(N_1 + N_2 - 2)$, maximizing $R(\mathbf{d})$ with respect to $\mathbf{d}$ is equivalent to maximizing $R_2(\mathbf{d})$ with respect to $\mathbf{d}$.

Caution should be exercised in using any pattern recognition technique, such as the Fisher criterion, which inherently makes use of the class means. This is due to the modality problem, and it might be necessary to partition each class into its modes before performing the discriminant vector analysis. If more than two classes are involved, a pairwise voting logic can always be used [5].

With this background, a derivation of the discriminant vectors can begin. Note that the generalized ratio R is independent of the magnitude of the vector $\mathbf{d}$ (since

$R(\boldsymbol{d}) = R(\alpha \boldsymbol{d})$). Consequently, only the direction of $\boldsymbol{d}$ is important and $\boldsymbol{d}$ will be normalized such that $\boldsymbol{d}^t\boldsymbol{d} = 1$. Sammon [5] gives an easily accessible derivation of the first two directions which maximize the Fisher criterion R. The first direction $\boldsymbol{d}_1$ is

$$\boldsymbol{d}_1 = \alpha_1 A^{-1} \boldsymbol{\Delta}$$

where α_1 is chosen such that $\boldsymbol{d}_1{}^t\boldsymbol{d}_1 = 1$ and

$$\alpha_1^2 = (\boldsymbol{\Delta}^t [A^{-1}]^2 \boldsymbol{\Delta})^{-1}.$$

The second best direction for maximizing R subject to the constraint that $\boldsymbol{d}_1$ and $\boldsymbol{d}_2$ are orthogonal (i.e., $\boldsymbol{d}_2{}^t\boldsymbol{d}_1 = 0$ is

$$\boldsymbol{d}_2 = \alpha_2 \{A^{-1} - b_1 [A^{-1}]^2\} \boldsymbol{\Delta}$$

where the constant b_1 is

$$b_1 = \frac{\boldsymbol{\Delta}^t (A^{-1})^2 \boldsymbol{\Delta}}{\boldsymbol{\Delta}^t (A^{-1})^3 \boldsymbol{\Delta}}.$$

See p 163 Eqn. (10)

Now consider the nth discriminant direction $\boldsymbol{d}_n$. Using the method of Lagrange multipliers, we wish to maximize $R(\boldsymbol{d}_n)$ subject to the constraints that $\boldsymbol{d}_i{}^t\boldsymbol{d}_n = 0$ for $i = 1,2,\cdots,n-1$. Let C be

$$C = \frac{(\boldsymbol{d}_n{}^t \boldsymbol{\Delta})^2}{\boldsymbol{d}_n{}^t A \boldsymbol{d}_n} - \lambda_1 \boldsymbol{d}_n{}^t \boldsymbol{d}_1 - \cdots - \lambda_{n-1} \boldsymbol{d}_n{}^t \boldsymbol{d}_{n-1}.$$

Setting the partial of C with respect to $\boldsymbol{d}_n$ equal to zero,

$$\frac{\partial C}{\partial \boldsymbol{d}_n} = 0 \Rightarrow 2K_n \boldsymbol{\Delta} - K_n^2 2A\boldsymbol{d}_n - \lambda_1 \boldsymbol{d}_1 - \cdots - \lambda_{n-1} \boldsymbol{d}_{n-1} = \boldsymbol{0}$$

where

$$K_n = \frac{\boldsymbol{\Delta}^t \boldsymbol{d}_n}{\boldsymbol{d}_n{}^t A \boldsymbol{d}_n} = \frac{\boldsymbol{d}_n{}^t \boldsymbol{\Delta}}{\boldsymbol{d}_n{}^t A \boldsymbol{d}_n}.$$

Therefore,

$$\boldsymbol{d}_n = \frac{1}{K_n} A^{-1} \left[\boldsymbol{\Delta} - \frac{\lambda_1}{2K_n} \boldsymbol{d}_1 - \cdots - \frac{\lambda_{n-1}}{2K_n} \boldsymbol{d}_{n-1} \right]. \quad (1)$$

Applying the constraints, and letting $\beta_i = \lambda_i / 2K_n$ and $s_{ij} = \boldsymbol{d}_i A^{-1} \boldsymbol{d}_j$, we obtain

$$\left.\begin{array}{l} \boldsymbol{d}_1{}^t\boldsymbol{d}_n = 0 \\ \cdot \\ \cdot \\ \cdot \\ \boldsymbol{d}_{n-1}{}^t\boldsymbol{d}_n = 0 \end{array}\right\} \Rightarrow \begin{array}{l} s_{11}\beta_1 + s_{12}\beta_2 + \cdots + s_{1(n-1)}\beta_{n-1} = 1/\alpha_1 \\ \cdot \\ \cdot \\ \cdot \\ s_{i1}\beta_1 + \cdots + s_{i(n-1)}\beta_{n-1} = 0 \\ \cdot \\ \cdot \\ \cdot \\ s_{(n-1)1}\beta_1 + \cdots + s_{(n-1)(n-1)}\beta_{(n-1)} = 0. \end{array} \quad (2)$$

Matrix notation can be used to simplify (1) and (2). For (1), let

$$\boldsymbol{d}_n = \alpha_n A^{-1} \{ \boldsymbol{\Delta} - [\boldsymbol{d}_1 \cdots \boldsymbol{d}_{n-1}] \boldsymbol{\beta} \} \quad (3)$$

where $\boldsymbol{\beta}^t = [\beta_1 \cdots \beta_{n-1}]$ and the constant $(1/K_n)$ has been replaced by the normalizing constant α_n, i.e., α_n is chosen such that $\boldsymbol{d}_n{}^t\boldsymbol{d}_n = 1$. For (2), let

$$S_{n-1}\boldsymbol{\beta} = \begin{bmatrix} 1/\alpha_1 \\ 0 \\ \cdot \\ \cdot \\ \cdot \\ 0 \end{bmatrix} \updownarrow n-1 \quad \text{or} \quad \boldsymbol{\beta} = S_{n-1}^{-1} \begin{bmatrix} 1/\alpha_1 \\ 0 \\ \cdot \\ \cdot \\ \cdot \\ 0 \end{bmatrix} \quad (4)$$

where

$$S_{n-1} = \overbrace{\begin{bmatrix} s_{11} & \cdots & s_{1(n-1)} \\ \cdot & & \cdot \\ \cdot & & \cdot \\ \cdot & & \cdot \\ s_{j1} & \cdots & s_{j(n-1)} \\ \cdot & & \cdot \\ \cdot & & \cdot \\ \cdot & & \cdot \\ s_{(n-1)1} & \cdots & s_{(n-1)(n-1)} \end{bmatrix}}^{n-1} \updownarrow n-1.$$

Combining (3) and (4), a recursive definition for the nth discriminant vector can be obtained:

$$\boldsymbol{d}_n = \alpha_n A^{-1} \left\{ \boldsymbol{\Delta} - [\boldsymbol{d}_1 \cdots \boldsymbol{d}_{n-1}] S_{n-1}^{-1} \begin{bmatrix} 1/\alpha_1 \\ 0 \\ \cdot \\ \cdot \\ \cdot \\ 0 \end{bmatrix} \right\}. \quad (5)$$

The computations involve the inversion of A and S_n. A recursive definition for finding the inverse of S_{n-1} is given in the following equations. A useful identity (e.g., see Rao [9]) for finding the inverse of a symmetric $n \times n$ matrix in terms of an $(n-1) \times (n-1)$ submatrix is given as follows.

Let us partition S_n in the following manner:

$$S_n = \left[\begin{array}{c|c} \begin{matrix} \\ S_{n-1} \\ \\ \end{matrix} & \begin{matrix} s_{1n} \\ \cdot \\ \cdot \\ \cdot \\ s_{(n-1)(n)} \end{matrix} \\ \hline s_{(n)1} \cdots s_{(n)(n-1)} & s_{nn} \end{array}\right] = \left[\begin{array}{c|c} S_{n-1} & \boldsymbol{y}_n \\ \hline \boldsymbol{y}_n{}^t & s_{nn} \end{array}\right]$$

where $\boldsymbol{y}_n{}^t = [s_{(n)1} \cdots s_{(n)(n-1)}]$ and $n \geq 1$. Then

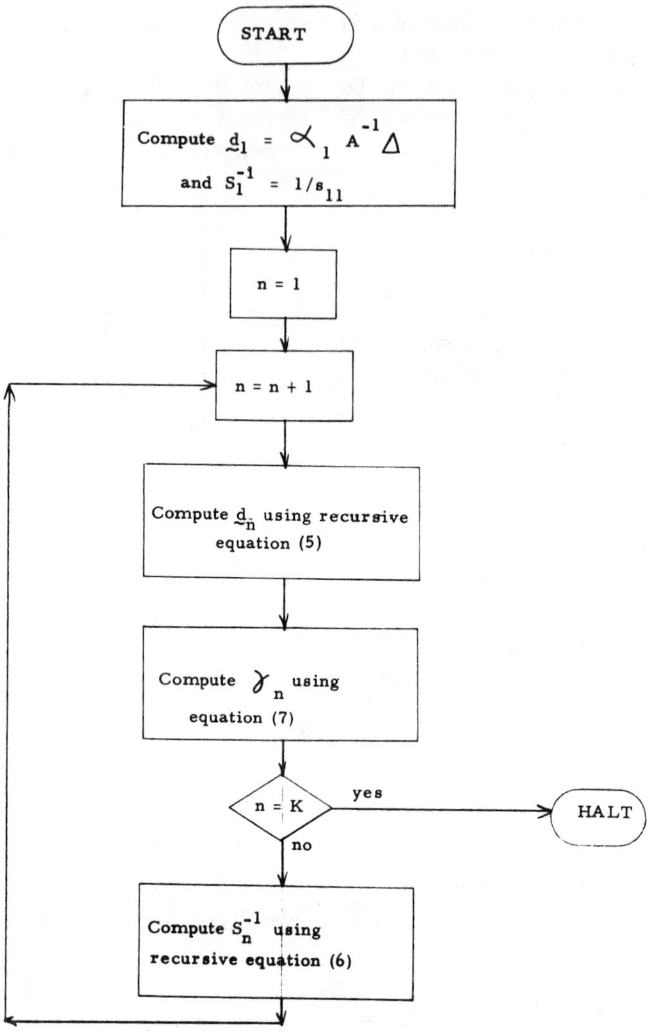

Fig. 2. Recursive procedure for computing K best discriminant vectors and discrim-values. Underlined symbols indicate bold-faced symbols in text.

$$S_n^{-1} = \frac{1}{c_n}\left[\begin{array}{c|c} c_n S_{n-1}^{-1} + S_{n-1}^{-1}\boldsymbol{y}_n\boldsymbol{y}_n{}^t S_{n-1}^{-1} & -S_{n-1}^{-1}\boldsymbol{y}_n \\ \hline -\boldsymbol{y}_n{}^t S_{n-1}^{-1} & 1 \end{array}\right] \tag{6}$$

where the scalar $c_n = s_{nn} - \boldsymbol{y}_n{}^t S_{n-1}^{-1}\boldsymbol{y}_n$.

Note that for each discriminant vector $\boldsymbol{d}_n$ there corresponds a "discrim-value" γ_n, given by

$$\gamma_n = \frac{(\boldsymbol{d}_n{}^t\boldsymbol{\Delta})^2}{\boldsymbol{d}_n{}^t A \boldsymbol{d}_n}. \tag{7}$$

Each γ_n represents the value of the discriminatory criterion $R(\boldsymbol{d}_n)$ for the corresponding discriminant vector $\boldsymbol{d}_n$. Noting that the discriminant vectors can be ordered according to their respective discrim-values such that

$$\gamma_1 \geq \gamma_2 \geq \gamma_3 \geq \cdots \geq \gamma_L \geq 0$$

the analogy between the eigenvectors and the discriminant vectors is complete. The former describes the best fitting subspace while the latter describes the best discriminating subspace.[2] Since the principal purpose of pattern recognition is discrimination, the discriminant vector subspace offers considerable potential as a feature extraction transformation.

Fig. 2 shows the recursive algorithm for computing the first K discriminant vectors and discrim-values.

V. COMPARISON OF FEATURE SELECTION TECHNIQUES

Comparing data-dependent transformations is a difficult task. One method is to assume a distribution for the data. For multivariate class-conditional normal distributions with a common covariance matrix, it is well known that projecting the data on the first discriminant vector yields the optimal Bayes results. Certainly for this case, the discriminant vector technique offers the best results.

[2] Of course, "best-discriminating subspace" is only optimal with respect to the criteria chosen.

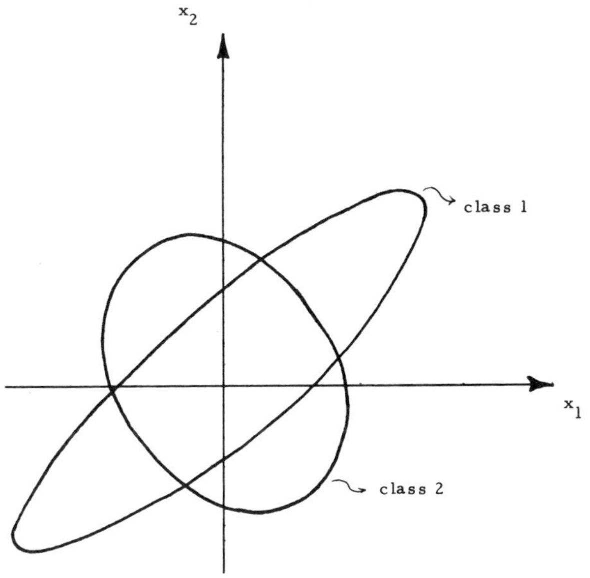

Fig. 3. Illustration of class covariance differences.

A second method of comparison is via a mathematical example. For the example given in Section III, the Fukunaga–Koontz transform fails to rank the features according to their discriminatory usefulness. However, the first discriminant vector $\boldsymbol{d} = k[\Sigma_1 + \Sigma_2]^{-1}\boldsymbol{\Delta}$ lies along the second dimension, which is the most significant feature.

The common factor in the two previous methods of comparison is that the majority of the discriminatory information is contained in differences in the mean vectors as opposed to differences in class covariance. For these cases the discriminant vector technique appears superior.

For those cases in which there is no difference in mean vectors and some difference in class covariance, the Fukunaga–Koontz transform is more effective since the direction chosen by the discriminant vector technique would be based only on sample-size "noise." Fig. 3 shows a typical illustration of this case.

Unfortunately, when these cases occur, the probability of error is usually significant. It has been the authors' experience in practical problems to avoid these cases by designing features whose discriminatory information is reflected in mean vector differences.

However, caution should be exercised in using any pattern recognition technique such as the Fisher criterion which inherently employs mean vector differences. This is caused by the modality problem discussed by Sammon [6] and illustrated here in Fig. 4. In this case the means of classes 1 and 2 are identical, yet significant discriminatory information exists along feature x.

To avoid missing this information, the authors have found it necessary to perform a modal analysis and partition each class into its respective modes before performing any logic design.

Another method of comparison is via a data-dependent example. One difficult data base readily available to the

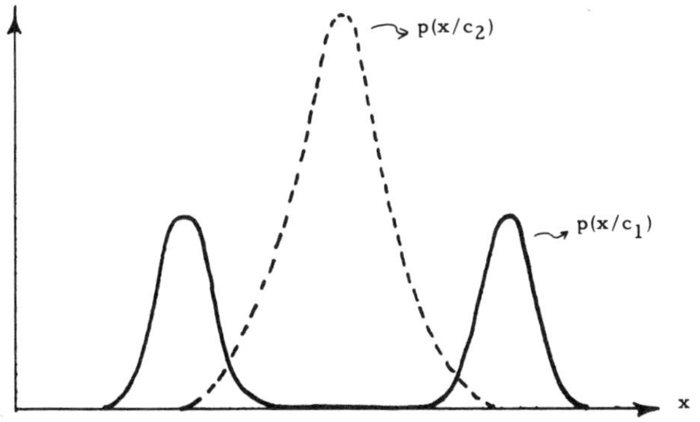

Fig. 4. Illustration of modality problem.

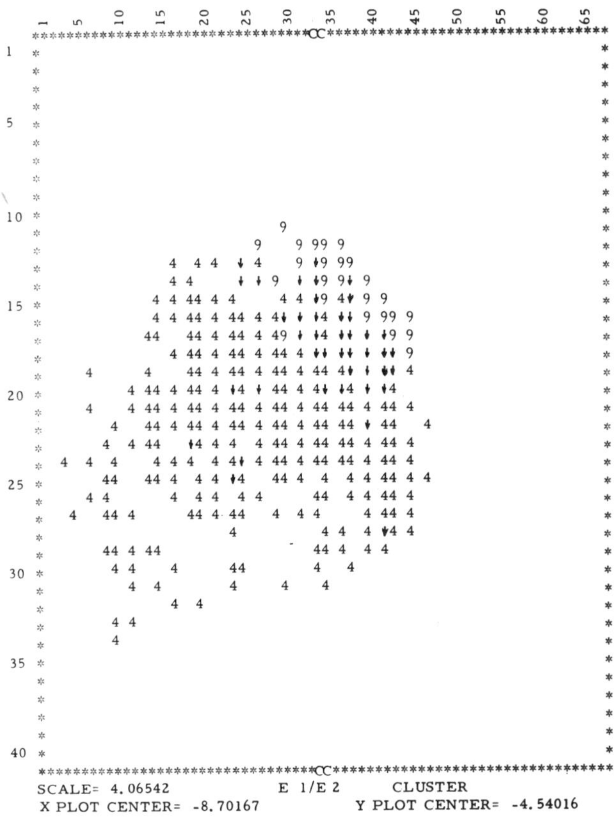

Fig. 5. Eigenvector plot.

authors and also discussed in the open literature (see Sammon [6]) consisted of hand-printed characters for the class of fours and nines. The data base contained 175 fours and 908 nines. Each vector consisted of 40 features. Fig. 5 shows a cluster plot of the data projected on the plane defined by the eigenvectors of the lumped covariance matrix corresponding to the two maximum eigenvalues. A cluster plot is obtained by placing a mesh over the area in the plane spanned by the data. In this figure, each cell in the mesh contains a 4 if only sample vectors from the class of fours are present in the cell, a 9 if only nines are present, and an arrow ($\downarrow$) if samples from both classes

TABLE I
MULTIPLE OVERPRINTS FOR EIGENVECTOR PLOT

Column	Row	Class	# of Samples of Class in Cell	Class	# of Samples of Class in Cell
24	13	4	1	9	1
33	13	4	1	9	1
24	14	4	1	9	1
26	14	4	1	9	1
31	14	4	3	9	1
33	14	4	2	9	3
37	14	4	1	9	1
33	15	4	5	9	3
37	15	4	1	9	2
29	16	4	5	9	1
31	16	4	6	9	2
33	16	4	12	9	1
36	16	4	3	9	2
37	16	4	4	9	4
31	17	4	3	9	1
33	17	4	12	9	1
36	17	4	5	9	3
37	17	4	2	9	2
39	17	4	4	9	14
41	17	4	2	9	9
33	18	4	4	9	1
34	18	4	7	9	1
36	18	4	5	9	1
37	18	4	5	9	3
39	18	4	4	9	7
41	18	4	4	9	14
42	18	4	1	9	5
37	19	4	5	9	6
39	19	4	11	9	6
41	19	4	7	9	4
42	19	4	2	9	1
23	20	4	5	9	1
26	20	4	3	9	1
34	20	4	3	9	1
36	20	4	5	9	1
39	20	4	15	9	1
41	20	4	9	9	1
39	22	4	12	9	1
18	23	4	3	9	1
24	24	4	1	9	1
23	25	4	1	9	1
41	28	4	1	9	1

Note: Only cells containing both classes are shown.

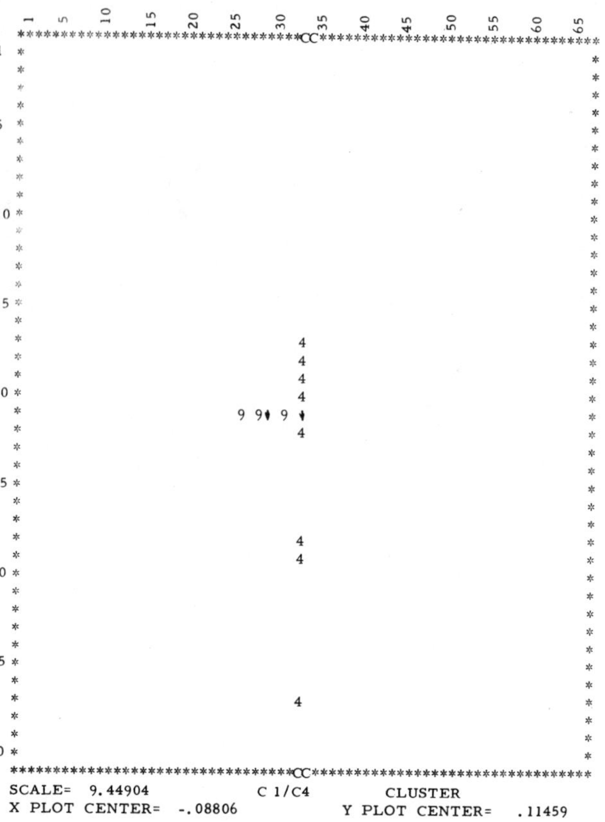

MULTIPLE POINT DISTRIBUTIONS

Fig. 6. Fukunaga–Koontz transform.

TABLE II
MULTIPLE OVERPRINTS FOR FUKUNAGA-KOONTZ TRANSFORM

Column	Row	Class	# of Samples of Class in Cell	Class	# of Samples of Class in Cell
29	21	4	1	9	28
33	21	4	765	9	120

are present. Table I shows a list of cells containing both classes. One logic design procedure which results in a complicated boundary would assign a sample which fell in a cell to the class with the largest number of samples in that cell. Even with this technique, 77 errors would result. (Although this strategy could be used, the authors feel that is an example of overdesigning on the training set.)

Fig. 6 shows a plot of the Fukunaga–Koontz transform using the eigenvectors corresponding to the largest and smallest eigenvalues (essentially 1 and 0). Table II lists the multiple points in each cell. Since this plot may be misleading, it should be noted that the range for the class of nines in the vertical direction is from -0.000007061 to $+0.000004905$. Taking into account the accuracy of the computer, this range is essentially zero. Within this range are 290 fours and, of course, all 175 nines. Using the cell type logic previously mentioned, 121 errors would result.

Fig. 7 shows the data projected on the plane defined by the first and second discriminant vectors, while Table III lists the multiple points in each cell. The vertical boundary shown in the figure would result in only 17 errors. Quite a striking improvement over the two previous methods!

The questions of the type of logic which can be designed and the information contained in higher order discriminant vectors naturally arise. As previously mentioned in

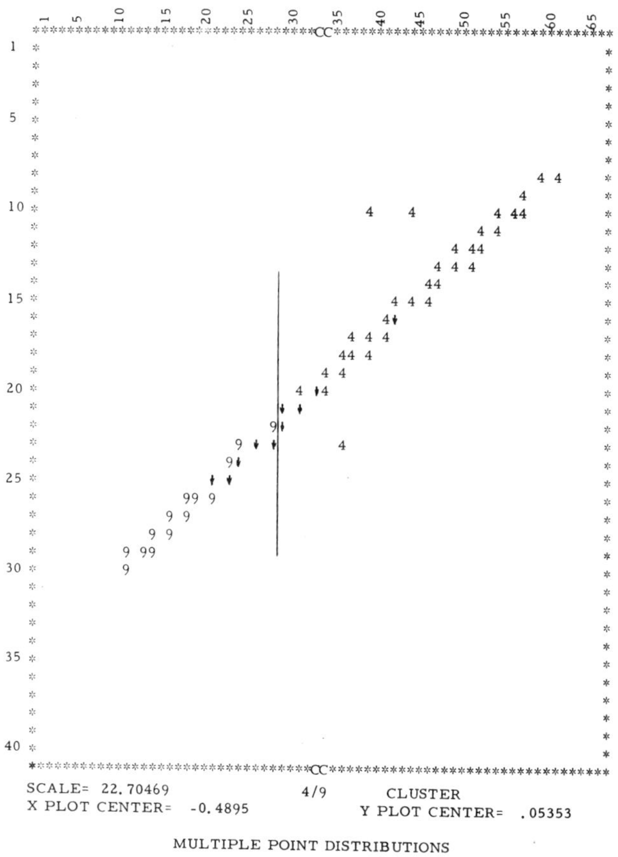

Fig. 7. Projection on first and second discriminant vectors.

TABLE III
MULTIPLE OVERPRINTS FOR FIRST AND SECOND DISCRIMINANT VECTORS

Column	Row	Class	# of Samples of Class in Cell	Class	# of Samples of Class in Cell
42	16	4	89	9	1
33	20	4	19	9	3
29	21	4	2	9	1
31	21	4	16	9	3
29	22	4	7	9	3
26	23	4	2	9	6
28	23	4	1	9	2
24	24	4	1	9	15
21	25	4	1	9	31
23	25	4	1	9	7

the paper, the higher order discriminant vectors can be used to define potentially useful projection planes in such man–machine interactive pattern recognition systems as OLPARS [6]. Fig. 8 contains a projection of this previous data base on the plane defined by the fifth and sixth discriminant vectors. Table IV contains the multiple overprints.

Since the objective of the discriminant vector transformation is to significantly reduce the dimensionality while retaining the discriminatory information, it should be possible to employ sophisticated pattern recognition techniques in the new space that were either computationally impractical or statistically insignificant[3] in the original high dimensional space.

A final justification for selecting the discriminant vectors is the intuitive notion that features based on discrimination should be better than features based on fitting or representing the data.

ACKNOWLEDGMENT

The authors wish to thank A. H. Proctor, Captain

[3] For a discussion of sample size as a function of dimensionality, see Foley [10].

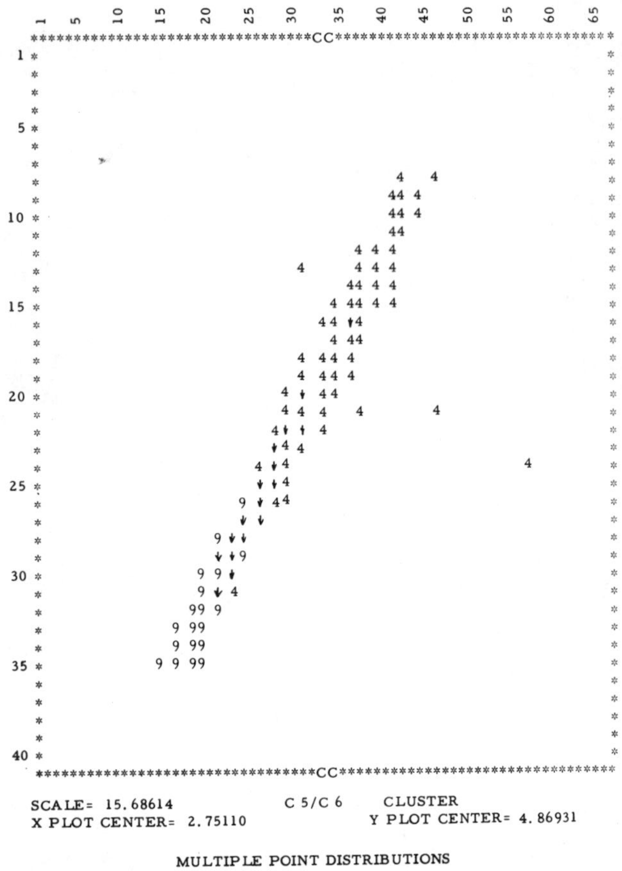

Fig. 8. Projection on fifth and sixth discriminant vectors.

R. D. Bouvier, and G. T. Stevens for their suggestions and programming assistance.

REFERENCES

[1] *IEEE Trans. Comput.* (*Special Issue on Feature Extraction and Selection in Pattern Recognition*), vol. C-20, pp. 967–1117, Sept. 1971.

[2] S. Watanabe, "Karhunen–Loeve expansion and factor analysis," in *Trans. 4th Prague Conf. Information Theory*, 1965.

[3] Y. T. Chien and K. S. Fu, "On the generalized Karhunen–Loève expansion," *IEEE Trans. Inform. Theory* (Corresp.), vol. IT-13, pp. 518–520, July 1967.

[4] K. Fukunaga and W. L. G. Koontz, "Application of the Karhunen-Loève expansion to feature selection and ordering," *IEEE Trans. Comput.*, vol. C-19, pp. 311–318, Apr. 1970.

[5] J. W. Sammon, Jr., "An optimal discriminant plane," *IEEE Trans. Comput.* (Short Notes), vol. C-19, pp. 826–829, Sept. 1970.

[6] ——, "Interactive pattern analysis and classification," *IEEE Trans. Comput.*, vol. C-19, pp. 594–616, July 1970.

[7] K. Fukunaga, *Introduction to Statistical Pattern Recognition.* New York: Academic Press, 1972, ch. 8.

[8] T. W. Anderson and X. X. Bahadur, "Classification into two multivariate normal distributions with different covariance matrices," *Ann. Math. Stat.*, vol. 33, pp. 420–431, 1962.

[9] C. R. Rao, *Linear Statistical Inference and Its Applications.* New York: Wiley, 1965, p. 29.

[10] D. H. Foley, "Considerations of sample and feature size," *IEEE Trans. Inform. Theory*, vol. IT-18, pp. 618–626, Sept. 1972.

TABLE IV

MULTIPLE OVERPRINTS FOR FIFTH AND SIXTH DISCRIMINANT VECTORS

Column	Row	Class	# of Samples of Class in Cell	Class	# of Samples of Class in Cell
36	16	4	31	9	1
31	20	4	18	9	1
29	22	4	22	9	1
31	22	4	47	9	1
28	23	4	2	9	1
28	24	4	18	9	4
26	25	4	8	9	3
28	25	4	15	9	1
26	26	4	14	9	1
24	27	4	2	9	9
26	27	4	2	9	1
23	28	4	1	9	1
24	28	4	5	9	8
21	29	4	1	9	11
23	29	4	1	9	17
23	30	4	1	9	6
21	31	4	1	9	13

On the choice of variables in classification problems with dichotomous variables

By JANET D. ELASHOFF, R. M. ELASHOFF AND G. E. GOLDMAN

Stanford University, University of California,
San Francisco Medical Center, and University of California, Berkeley

SUMMARY

We study how to choose two out of p dichotomous variables in classification problems. Our results show that positive correlation may increase discrimination while negative correlation may decrease discrimination. These results were not predicted from the analysis of the same problems with normally distributed variables.

1. INTRODUCTION

Cochran (1962) investigated the relation between the discriminating power of the linear discriminant function and the discriminating powers of the individual variates used in the function. He assumed the following model. Individuals are assigned to one of two populations on the basis of variables x_j ($j = 1, 2, \ldots, p$). The x_j follow a multivariate normal distribution with the same covariance matrix in each population. Each x_j has variance one in each population and mean zero in population one and mean $\delta_j \geqslant 0$ in population two. The probability that an individual drawn at random from the two combined populations belongs to population one is one-half. Errors in classification have the same cost and the cost of observing variables may be neglected. The 'goodness' of any set of variables is assessed by the probability of a misclassification; and the classification rule is the Bayes rule.

Then, Cochran states the following important results. First, if the x_j are independent, the best set of k variables consists of the k best single variables. Secondly, for a set of two variables, any negative correlation reduces the probability of misclassification, while positive correlation, unless it is sufficiently high, increases the probability of misclassification.

Reprinted with permission from *Biometrika*, vol. 54, pp. 668–670, Dec. 1967.

Cochran's nice results are not generally applicable if the x_j are dichotomous variables. The next sections document this statement for the choice of two out of p variables.

2. Independent variables

If the variables x_j are independent, then the k best variables chosen separately are not generally the best k variables chosen k at a time. Let the variables x_j $(j = 1, 2, 3)$, have probabilities

$$p_j = \text{pr}(x_j = 1|\text{population } 1) \quad \text{and} \quad q_j = \text{pr}(x_j = 1|\text{population } 2)$$

given by $p_1 = 0{\cdot}02$, $q_1 = 0{\cdot}95$; $p_2 = 0{\cdot}04$, $q_2 = 0{\cdot}90$; $p_3 = 0{\cdot}01$, $q_3 = 0{\cdot}80$. Then the variables in order of increasing probability of a misclassification are x_1, x_2, x_3. However, the best two variables chosen jointly are x_1 and x_3, not x_1 and x_2.

Why does this phenomenon occur? By a relabelling of one's and zero's and populations we always have

$$p_j < q_j \quad (j = 1, 2); \tag{1}$$

by a relabelling of the variables we always have

$$q_1 - p_1 > q_2 - p_2. \tag{2}$$

In addition, we assume that

$$\text{the outcome of the Bayes rule depends upon both } x_1 \text{ and } x_2. \tag{3}$$

We 'reform' the parameters as follows: $l_j = (q_j - p_j)$, $h_j = \tfrac{1}{2}(1 - p_j - q_j)$ $(j = 1, 2)$. Then the probability of misclassification is

$$\frac{1}{2}\left\{\frac{1-l_1}{2} + \frac{1-l_2}{2} - l_2|h_1| - l_1|h_2|\right\}. \tag{4}$$

When variables are chosen separately, only the parameters l_1 and l_2 enter into the choice of the variables. However, the probability of misclassification is a decreasing function of each of the four parameters $l_1, l_2, |h_1|$ and $|h_2|$.

3. Dependent variables

If the variables x_j are dependent, then small positive covariances between two variables may be helpful and negative covariances may not be helpful. Let us introduce two covariance parameters ρ_1 and ρ_2 defined by

$$\text{pr}(x_1 = 1 \quad \text{and} \quad x_2 = 1|\text{population } 1) = p_1 p_2 + \rho_1,$$

$$\text{pr}(x_1 = 1 \quad \text{and} \quad x_2 = 1|\text{population } 2) = q_1 q_2 + \rho_2;$$

thus $\rho_1 = E\{(x_1 - p_1)(x_2 - p_2)\}$. We assume that

$$p_1(1 - p_2) - \rho_1 < q_1(1 - q_2) - \rho_2 \tag{5}$$

and

$$p_1 p_2 + \rho_1 < q_1 q_2 + \rho_2. \tag{6}$$

The probability of misclassification is given by expression (4) plus

$$\tfrac{1}{2}(\rho_2 - \rho_1), \tag{7}$$

when (3), (5) and (6) hold and $\rho_1, \rho_2 \geqslant 0$; thus, positive covariances decrease the probability of misclassification for fixed p_j and q_j if and only if $\rho_1 > \rho_2$.

If the inequailty in (5) is reversed, the probability of misclassification becomes expression (4) plus

$$\tfrac{1}{2}(\rho_1 - \rho_2), \tag{8}$$

when (4) and (6) hold. For this situation, positive covariances decrease the probability of misclassification for fixed p_j and q_j if and only if $\rho_2 > \rho_1$.

For negative covariances the probability of misclassification is given by (7), where now $\rho_1, \rho_2 \leqslant 0$. Thus, negative covariances decrease the probability of misclassification for fixed p_j and q_j if and only if $|\rho_1| < |\rho_2|$. These conclusions are reversed when inequality (5) is reversed.

If $\rho_1 = \rho_2 = \rho$, the Bayes rule assuming $\rho = 0$ is the same as the Bayes rule for arbitrary ρ. Thus, the choice of the best two out of p correlated variables is the same as the choice of the best two of p independent variables if $E\{(x_j - p_j)(x_m - p_m)\} = E\{(x_j - q_j)(x_m - q_m)\}$ for all m and j, $m \neq j$.

4. Conclusions

The relatively clear cut results on the choice of variables which hold for the normal theory model do not apply when variables are dichotomous. To choose the best subset of two variables when it is not feasible to compute the $\frac{1}{2}p(p-1)$ possible Bayes rules, a stepwise selection rule (see e.g. Raiffa, 1961) is always at least as good as choosing the two best single variables. Since computation of the stepwise regression rule is facilitated if $E\{(x_1-p_1)(x_j-p_j)\} = E\{(x_1-q_1)(x_j-q_j)\}$ $(j = 2, 3, \ldots, p)$, one might wish to test the null hypotheses that these inequalities hold.

References

Cochran, W. G. (1962). On the performance of the linear discriminant function. *Bull. Int. Statist. Inst.* **39**, 435–47.

Raiffa, H. (1961). Statistical decision theory approach to item selection for dichotomous test and criterion variables. Chapter in *Studies in Item Analysis and Prediction*. Edited by H. Solomon, Stanford.

[*Received December* 1966. *Revised February* 1967]

On the Mean Accuracy of Statistical Pattern Recognizers

GORDON F. HUGHES, MEMBER, IEEE

Abstract—The overall mean recognition probability (mean accuracy) of a pattern classifier is calculated and numerically plotted as a function of the pattern measurement complexity n and design data set size m. Utilized is the well-known probabilistic model of a two-class, discrete-measurement pattern environment (no Gaussian or statistical independence assumptions are made). The minimum-error recognition rule (Bayes) is used, with the unknown pattern environment probabilities estimated from the data relative frequencies. In calculating the mean accuracy over all such environments, only three parameters remain in the final equation: n, m, and the prior probability p_c of either of the pattern classes.

With a fixed design pattern sample, recognition accuracy can first increase as the number of measurements made on a pattern increases, but decay with measurement complexity higher than some optimum value. Graphs of the mean accuracy exhibit both an optimal and a maximum acceptable value of n for fixed m and p_c. A four-place tabulation of the optimum n and maximum mean accuracy values is given for equally likely classes and m ranging from 2 to 1000.

The penalty exacted for the generality of the analysis is the use of the mean accuracy itself as a recognizer optimality criterion. Namely, one necessarily always has some particular recognition problem at hand whose Bayes accuracy will be higher or lower than the mean over all recognition problems having fixed n, m, and p_c.

Manuscript received November 3, 1966; revised July 19, 1967. This work was supported in part by RADC under Contract AF 30(602)-3976.

The author is with Autonetics, a division of North American Rockwell, Inc., Anaheim, Calif. 92803

I. Introduction

SOME consequences of the statistical model of pattern recognition will be presented.[1]–[5] It will be shown that certain useful numerical conclusions can be drawn from rather few assumptions. Basically, the only

Reprinted from *IEEE Trans. Inform. Theory*, vol. IT-14, pp. 55–63, Jan. 1968.

assumption made is that some unknown discrete probability structure underlies the pattern environment. This structure defines the particular recognition problem under consideration. A pattern is obtained by making a sample measurement on the environment. Each possible pattern is to be classified into one of a set of classes by a *recognition rule* having maximal probability of correct classification (Fig. 1).

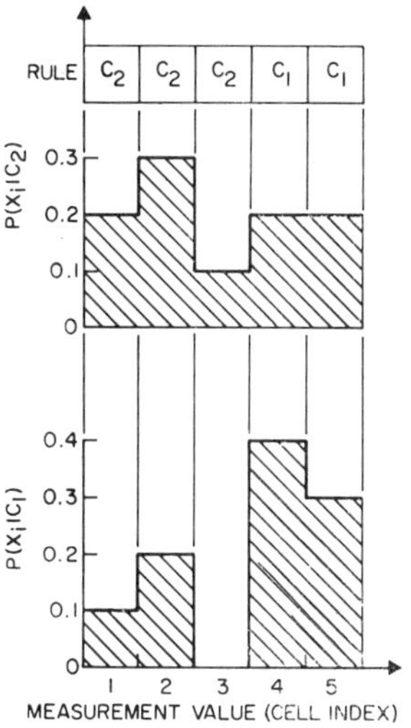

Fig. 1. Known probability example.

It is hoped that this model is sufficiently simple and standard[7],[17] to be readily accepted. The intent of the present analysis is to obtain results which follow from the statistical model itself; e.g., *without* constraining the unknown probabilities to be Gaussian or otherwise parametric. For the same reason, no assumption of statistical independence between pattern measurements will be made. However, only the case of two pattern classes will be treated.

An optimality criterion will be proposed for recognition rules designed from data sets of m sample patterns. The measurement complexity n (total number of discrete values) will also be used as a parameter. It will be shown that it is also desirable to exhibit explicitly the prior probability p_{c1} of class c_1 as the third criterion parameter (where $p_{c2} = 1 - p_{c1}$).

The criterion proposed is the mean correct recognition probability $\bar{P}_{cr}(n, m, p_{c1})$ over all pattern environments. It is obtained by first fixing n, m, and p_{c1} and calculating the accuracy $P_{cr}(n, m, p_{c1})$ of the minimal error-rate Bayes recognition rule for any given environment probability structure.[15] This accuracy is then averaged over all such probability structures, giving the mean accuracy $\bar{P}_{cr}(n, m, p_{c1})$. The resultant equation will be numerically evaluated for practical ranges of n, m, and p_{c1}. Some interesting optimality relationships will thereby be exhibited.

A forewarning should be made of a potential misinterpretation of this criterion. In the literature, the term "mean Bayes accuracy" often refers to averaging only over the possible measurement values of a fixed recognition problem, namely, one having some known environment probability structure.[16] Here, the mean refers to averaging over all recognition problems having fixed measurement complexity n and prior class probability p_{c1}. For example, this includes all subsets of parametric and/or statistically dependent probability structures, as well as all other discrete, normalizable structures. Consequently, the criterion evaluates the *overall* performance of a Bayes recognition rule. Middleton[2] (Section 23.4) presents a useful background discussion on criteria selection.

II. Statistical Model

A statement of the statistical pattern recognition model to be used will first be made. It is fairly standard and contains as few assumptions and constraints as possible. By the term "model" is meant that all the required assumptions are stated, and the applicability of the subsequent analysis to particular recognition problems can be judged on the model itself.

It is assumed that there exist two statistical environments called (caused by) pattern classes c_1 and c_2. Each environment is characterized by a constant but unknown probability distribution over the n discrete values of the pattern measurement variable x. Namely, $P(x_i \mid c_1)$ is the probability of measurement value x_i occurring in environment c_1 for $i = 1, 2, \cdots, n$. These scalars are termed the cell probabilities. Similarily, the unknown distribution $P(x_i \mid c_2)$ characterizes x under the second environment c_2. Vector measurements will be discussed later.

By *unknown*, it is meant that no prior information whatever is given on the $2n$ scalars $P(x_i \mid c_j)$. Any pair of distributions is equally likely a priori. Sample pattern data from the environments is to be measured to estimate the actual $P(x_i \mid c_j)$ existing in any specific recognition problem (the sample relative frequencies will be used).

Thus, the only constraints are that all probabilities be non-negative and that

$$\sum_{i=1}^{n} P(x_i \mid c_1) = \sum_{i=1}^{n} P(x_i \mid c_2) = 1. \tag{1}$$

Whenever a measurement x is made, there is a known prior class probability p_{c1} that class c_1 is in effect and $P(x_i \mid c_1)$ applies. With the complementary probability $p_{c2} = 1 - p_{c1}$, class c_2 and $P(x_i \mid c_2)$ are in effect. However, the particular class in effect for any pattern is not known: only the value x_i produced by the pattern measurement is available.

The pattern recognition problem is to design a recognition rule to predict (recognize) the pattern class most likely in effect for each of the n possible measurement values x_i. Its theoretic solution is known to be a maximal class recognition accuracy Bayes rule.[17] Specifically, this rule is to predict c_1 when x_i occurs if $P(c_1 \mid x_i) > P(c_2 \mid x_i)$;

otherwise predict c_2.[1] This superficially simple rule states to choose the more probable class, given the measurement value x_i which has occurred. The resultant correct recognition probability (accuracy) is then

$$P_{cr}(n, p_{c1}) = \sum_{i=1}^{n} [\max_{j=1,2} P(c_j \mid x_i)]P(x_i) \tag{2}$$

$$= \sum_i \max_j P(c_j, x_i) \tag{3}$$

$$= \sum_i \max_j [P(x_i \mid c_j)p_{cj}]. \tag{4}$$

Note that no assumption of measurement statistical independence is made (Appendix I). Also, a vector of r discrete measurements, each having n_k values, $k = 1, 2, \cdots, r$, is clearly equivalent to a single measurement with

$$n = n_1 n_2 \cdots n_r. \tag{5}$$

Appendix I details this equivalence.

Use of discrete measurement values in the model is dictated by practical considerations. Namely, measurements can be made only to a finite precision and consequently only a finite number n of different values can result. Thus n can be termed the *measurement complexity*. Many recognition problems are explicitly digital, such as the visual patterns usually arising in character recognition.[1]

III. Infinite Data Sets

Although the unknown probabilities $P(x_i \mid c_j)$ must actually be statistically estimated from finite pattern sets, the limiting case of known probabilities ($m = \infty$) will be first developed. For example, the two histograms of Fig. 1 give $P(x_i \mid c_1)$ and $P(x_i \mid c_2)$ for a problem having $n = 5$. Given that the classes are equally likely ($p_{c1} = p_{c2} = \frac{1}{2}$), the optimal recognition rule for the five values is as shown, and the recognition accuracy from (3) and (4) is

$$P_{cr}(5, \tfrac{1}{2})$$

$$= P(c_2, x_1) + P(c_2, x_2) + P(c_2, x_3) + P(c_1, x_4) + P(c_1, x_5)$$

$$= 0.65. \tag{6}$$

It is obvious, but still important to note, that this Bayes accuracy of 65 percent is the best possible for the probability structure of Fig. 1. No amount of "improved recognizer design" can increase this figure. Clearly all accuracies will lie between max $(p_{c1}, 1 - p_{c1})$ and unity, since the former can be obtained with no measurements whatever (the rule would be always to predict the same class, that having higher prior probability). In fact, it will be shown in (16) that the highest average accuracy ($n = \infty$) is only 75 percent for $p_{c1} = \frac{1}{2}$.

Next, it may be observed that the distributions of Fig. 1 possess no particular continuity, symmetry, or modality over the x_i range. No reasonable parametric forms could be assumed for $P(x_i \mid c_1)$ and $P(x_i \mid c_2)$, such as a pair of Gaussian density functions

$$P(x_i \mid c_j) = N(\mu_j, \sigma_j)$$

$$\doteq (1/\sqrt{2\pi\sigma_j^2}) \exp [-(x_i - \mu_j)^2/2\sigma_j^2].$$

This *nonparametric* aspect of the pattern environment appears to be common to many recognition problems. It is further discussed in Section VII, using some sample histograms from photographic recognition data.

Alternative parametric assumptions have been tried by several workers. These include heuristic fitting of an overlapping sequence of multivariate Gaussian densities to the data.[9] Local smoothness assumptions have been made on the densities, according to a metric which leads to a nearest neighbor recognition rule.[1],[8] However, the continuity constraints which would be imposed on the model by these assumptions are of an entirely different nature than the simple normalizing constraints of (1). Also, the validity of such assumptions is often difficult to verify (see Kendall and Stuart,[10] Section 30.63).

In keeping with the desire for minimal constraints on the model, no such continuity or parametric requirements will be imposed at all. Instead, sample pattern data will be used to estimate individually the discrete cell probabilities by computing relative frequencies.

IV. Evaluation Criterion

A natural criterion to evaluate recognition rule performance is the expected or mean Bayes recognition accuracy over all possible environment probabilities $P(x_i \mid c_j)$. Namely, no prior information on each scalar $P(x_i \mid c_j)$ is to be assumed before the sample pattern data are measured. Any set of $2n$ positive real probability values is equally likely as long as (1) is satisfied.[2]

Clearly, if any such set were made more likely than another, then the criterion would emphasize the accuracy on that particular recognition problem. Instead, the criterion is to weigh equally all recognition problems having given values of p_{c1} and n.

It should be remarked that p_{c1} is explicitly exhibited as a parameter because recognition rule performance should be judged against the minimum accuracy of max $(p_{c1}, 1 - p_{c1})$ using *no* measurements. If p_{c1} lies near zero or unity, then any recognizer should have nearly 100 percent accuracy.

Thus the Bayes accuracy of (4) is a statistic, in that it is a function of the random variables

[1] There exist theoretic cases where ties $P(c_1 \mid x_i) = P(c_2 \mid x_i)$ must be more carefully treated, or where randomized decision rules arise.[5] Also, only the direct criterion of maximal recognition accuracy will be used here. No significant change in the analysis results if the misrecognition probabilities are weighted in order to speak of maximizing utility or minimizing risk costs.

[2] This is equivalent to assuming Bayes' postulate (Kendall and Stuart,[10] sec. 8.4). Its use here is fundamentally based on the discrete nature of the distributions.

$$u_i \doteq P(x_i \mid c_1)$$
$$v_i \doteq P(x_i \mid c_2) \qquad i = 1, 2, \cdots, n. \tag{7}$$

To compute its mean or expected value, first note that the u_i and v_i are uniformly distributed due to the "equally likely" assumption of the model:

$$dP(u_1, u_2, \cdots, u_n, v_1, v_2, \cdots, v_n) = N\, du_1\, du_2 \cdots du_{n-1}\, dv_1\, dv_2 \cdots dv_{n-1}. \tag{8}$$

Only $2(n-1)$ differentials appear on the right of (8) because the two normalizing equations (1) fix u_n and v_n in terms of the others. Now, the *boundaries* of the $(n-1)$-order distribution of the u_i alone are given by the intersection of the hypercube $0 \le u_i \le 1$, $i = 1, 2, \cdots, n-1$, and the symmetric hyperplane

$$\sum_{i=1}^{n-1} u_i = 1, \tag{9}$$

which is also caused by (1). An identical boundary structure holds for the v_i, so that the normalizing constant N in (8) is obtained from

$$1 = N\left[\int_0^1 du_1 \int_0^{1-u_1} du_2 \int_0^{1-u_1-u_2} du_3 \cdots \cdot \int_0^{1-u_1-u_2-\cdots-u_{n-2}} du_{n-1}\right] \cdot \left[\int_0^1 dv_1 \int_0^{1-v_1} dv_2 \int_0^{1-v_1-v_2} dv_3 \cdots \cdot \int_0^{1-v_1-v_2-\cdots-v_{n-2}} dv_{n-1}\right]. \tag{10}$$

These two iterated integrals may be easily evaluated, giving

$$N = [(n-1)!]^2. \tag{11}$$

Equation (4) is the recognition accuracy given the u_i, v_i and is multiplied by (8) to obtain a joint probability. This is integrated over the u_i, v_i range to get the mean accuracy. By symmetry, each of the n terms of (4) will have an identical expected value, so that n times the expected value of the first may be taken:

$$\bar{P}_{cr}(n, p_{c1}) = n[(n-1)!]^2 \int_0^1 \int_0^1 \max(p_{c1}u_1, p_{c2}v_1)\, du_1\, dv_1 \cdot \left[\int_0^{1-u_1} du_2 \int_0^{1-u_1-u_2} du_3 \cdots \int_0^{1-u_1-u_2-\cdots-u_{n-2}} du_{n-1}\right] \cdot \left[\int_0^{1-v_1} dv_2 \int_0^{1-v_1-v_2} dv_3 \cdots \int_0^{1-v_1-v_2-\cdots-v_{n-2}} dv_{n-1}\right] \tag{12}$$

$$= n(n-1)^2 \int_0^1 \int_0^1 (1-u_1)^{n-2}(1-v_1)^{n-2} \cdot \max(p_{c1}u_1, p_{c2}v_1)\, dv_1\, du_1. \tag{13}$$

By requiring that $p_{c1} \le p_{c2}$ (without loss of generality), the v_1 integral in (13) may be broken into two ordinary integrals. The first is over the range $0 \le v_1 \le p_{c1}u_1/p_{c2}$, and the second requires an integration by parts. The u_1 integral may be then evaluated as a beta function plus a second, somewhat cumbersome integral whose integrand may be expanded by the binomial theorem and integrated term by term, giving

$$\bar{P}_{cr}(n, p_{c1}) = p_{c1} + p_{c2}(n-1)\left(\frac{p_{c1}}{p_{c2}}\right)^n \cdot \sum_{j=0}^{n} \frac{n!}{j!\,(n-j)!\,(2n-j-1)[p_{c1}/(1-2p_{c1})]^j}, \qquad (p_{c1} < p_{c2}). \tag{14}$$

For the common case $p_{c1} = p_{c2} = \frac{1}{2}$, (14) reduces to

$$\bar{P}_{cr}(n, \tfrac{1}{2}) = \frac{3n-2}{4n-2}. \tag{15}$$

Equation (14) is plotted in Fig. 2 for p_{c1} ranging from 0.1 to 0.9 and n from 1 to 1000. Smooth curves have been drawn for clarity, despite the actual discrete measurement nature.

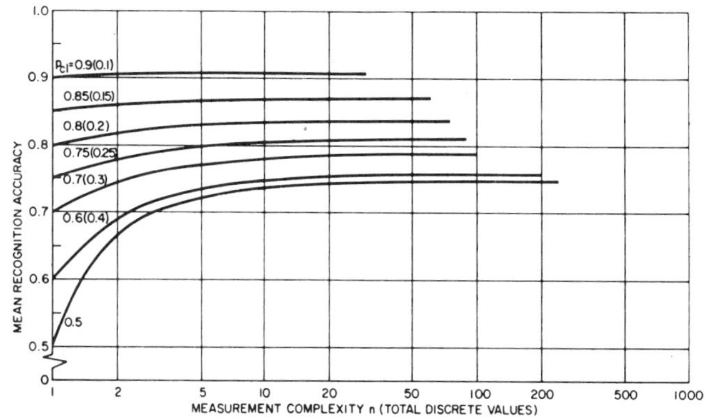

Fig. 2. Infinite data set accuracy.

Note that each recognition accuracy curve begins at $\max(p_{c1}, 1-p_{c1})$ for $n = 1$ (a single measurement value which must always occur and therefore imparts no information). It monotonically increases with the measurement complexity.

Each curve is also near its asymptotic *maximum recognition accuracy* for all $n \gg 2$. This value is *significantly less than* 100 *percent* unless p_{c1} is near zero or unity. In general, the knee of each curve would occur near $n = n_c$, the number of pattern classes defined.

The asymptotic maximum accuracy is obtained by letting $n \to \infty$ in (13):

$$\bar{P}_{cr}(n = \infty, p_{c1}) = p_{c1} + p_{c2}^2 = p_{c2} + p_{c1}^2 = 1 - p_{c1}p_{c2}. \tag{16}$$

V. Finite Data Sets

Equation (14) gives the mean Bayes accuracy in the limiting case where the probability structure is exactly measurable, by means of an infinite set of sample patterns

($m = \infty$). At first glance, it might seem that since only finite data sets exist, the true mean accuracy $\bar{P}_{cr}(n, m, p_{c1})$ could only be approximated. This is because only finite-sample estimates of the true probabilities in (4) can be made. Thus, the statistical model would have to be evaluated by Monte Carlo trials. Experimental sets of testing patterns would be required in order to measure the overall mean accuracy.

It is interesting that this is *not* so. An exact expression for the true mean accuracy can be derived, extending (14) to finite m. Of course this analytic preciseness is obtained at the cost of using a *mean* accuracy criterion. One necessarily always has some *particular* recognition problem at hand with unknown but specific values of $P(x_i \mid c_j)$. It may therefore have an accuracy either higher or lower than the overall mean.

The most direct procedure for employing the m sample patterns to estimate the cell probabilities is to use the *relative frequencies*.[18] If m_1 of the samples are taken under class environment c_1, and measurement value x_1 occurs s times, then the estimate is $P(x_1 \mid c_1) \simeq s/m_1$. Similarly, if r of the $m_2 = m - m_1$ samples taken under c_2 also fall in cell x_1, then $P(x_1 \mid c_2) \simeq r/m_2$.

Such direct use of the relative frequencies is quite natural, as compared to alternate methods using the sample moments.[19] It also offers certain well-known optimality characteristics. For example, the relative frequencies are unbiased and consistent, and also are the maximum-likelihood estimates of the cell probabilities (Appendix I).

To avoid sampling bias, it is necessary that $m_1 = p_{c1}m$ and $m_2 = p_{c2}m$ (truncated to integer values). Consider the first term $i = 1$ in (4). In place of

$$\max\,[P(x_1 \mid c_1)p_{c1},\ P(x_1 \mid c_2)p_{c2}],$$

one has

$$\max\left[\frac{s}{m_1}p_{c1},\ \frac{r}{m_2}p_{c2}\right] = \frac{\max(s, r)}{m}. \tag{17}$$

Thus, the *relative frequency recognition rule* for classifying x_1 is to choose c_1 if $s > r$ and c_2 if $s < r$. If $s = r$, choose the class with higher prior probability. Retaining the previous arbitrary assumption $p_{c1} \le p_{c2}$, choose c_2 for such ties.

In general, the rule for classifying x_i is

$$\text{predict}\begin{cases} c_1 & \text{if } s_i > r_i \\ c_2 & \text{if } s_i \le r_i \qquad (p_{c1} \le p_{c2}). \end{cases} \tag{18}$$

Now, the relative frequencies tend to the true probabilities as $m \to \infty$. Also, the Bayes rule accuracy is the maximum attainable for any rule. Consequently, one expects that the accuracy curves for (18) will lie below those of Fig. 2 and rise into coincidence as $m \to \infty$.

Appendix II gives the derivation of the recognition accuracy for finite m; the result is

$$\bar{P}_{cr}(n, m, p_{c1}) = \sum_{r=0}^{m_2}\sum_{s=0}^{m_1}\left[\frac{(m_2 - r + 1)(m_2 - r + 2)\cdots(m_2 - r + n - 2)}{(m_2 + 1)(m_2 + 2)\cdots(m_2 + n - 1)}\right] \cdot\left[\frac{(m_1 - s + 1)(m_1 - s + 2)\cdots(m_1 - s + n - 2)}{(m_1 + 1)(m_1 + 2)\cdots(m_1 + n - 1)}\right]g(r, s)$$

where

$$g(r, s) = n(n-1)^2\cdot\begin{cases} p_{c1}\dfrac{s+1}{m_1+n} & \text{for } s > r \\[2ex] p_{c2}\dfrac{r+1}{m_2+n} & \text{for } s \le r. \end{cases} \tag{19}$$

Equation (19) is best numerically evaluated by digital computer (compare Appendix II), and is plotted in Fig. 3 for the common case of $p_{c1} = p_{c2} = \frac{1}{2}$, n ranging from 1 to 1000, and m ranging from 2 to 1000. The limiting $m = \infty$ curve from Fig. 2 has been appended. Smooth curves have again been drawn for clarity.

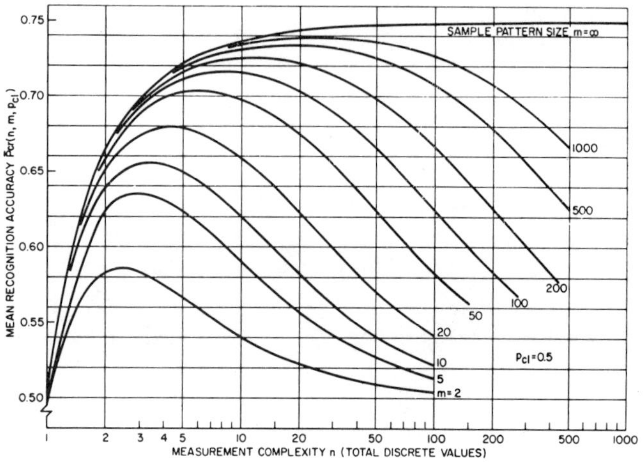

Fig. 3. Finite data set accuracy ($p_{c1} = \frac{1}{2}$).

The most interesting aspect of Fig. 3 is the existence of an *optimal measurement complexity* n_{opt} which maximizes the mean accuracy for any given $m < \infty$. Examples are $n_{\text{opt}} = 17$ for $m = 500$ and $n_{\text{opt}} = 23$ for $m = 1000$ (an interpretation of the relative magnitude of n_{opt} will be made in Section VIII). This behavior is quite reasonable. With m fixed, the accuracy first begins to rise with n as in Fig. 2. It ultimately must fall back as $n/m \to \infty$ because the precision of the probability estimates monotonically degrades. It is shown in Appendix I that this precision degrades as $\sigma(s/m_1)/p(x|c_1)\alpha\sqrt{n/m}$. However, the effect is easy to see when $n \gg m$ because most of the $2n$ cells will contain no samples at all. This then gives zero relative frequencies for these cells, irrespective of the actual cell probabilities. Rule (18) then consists mostly of $r_i = s_i = 0$ ties, which are all resolved by choosing c_2.

Consequently, as n varies from one to infinity, one expects the accuracy to rise to a maximum, fall back, and asymptotically approach max (p_{c1}, p_{c2}). Table I presents the optimal values for equally probable classes.

TABLE I

OPTIMAL MEASUREMENT COMPLEXITY

m	n_{opt}	$\bar{P}_{cr}(m, n_{opt}, \frac{1}{2})$
2	2	0.5833
5	3	0.6350
10	3	0.6548
20	4	0.6791
50	6	0.7031
100	8	0.7161
200	11	0.7257
500	17	0.7345
1000	23	0.7390
∞	∞	0.7500

VI. Unequal Class Probabilities

Equation (19) may also be used to illuminate what appears to be a critical aspect of Bayes recognizers designed from finite sample sets. Namely, if one pattern class is appreciably more likely to occur than another, then there exists a maximum acceptable measurement complexity n_{max}. Its value increases with m. Specifically, for $n > n_{max}(m)$, the recognizer is inferior to simple random guessing (i.e., always predicting the more likely class c_2 irrespective of the measurement value occurring). Note that the actual value of p_{c2} need not be known here, only that it exceeds p_{c1}.

Thus, the general statement is that $\bar{P}_{cr}(n, m, p_{c1}) <$ max (p_{c1}, p_{c2}) for all n exceeding some n_{max}, if p_{c1} sufficiently differs from p_{c2}.

Rather than present an algebraic proof of this statement, it seems more useful to exhibit the effect directly using (19). Fig. 4 presents the accuracy curves for the case of $p_{c1} = 0.2$. The maximum values $n_{max}(m)$ occur where the curves fall below the level $\bar{P}_{cr} = 0.8$. Note that $n_{max}(m) \sim m/2$. Graphically, the curves are similar to Fig. 3 except that the asymptote 0.80 is approached from below. This random-guessing asymptote at $n = \infty$ is due to the ties in (18).[3] An interpretation of the relative magnitude of n_{max} will be made in Section VIII.

It is not difficult to state the reason for this behavior: *If insufficient sample data are available to estimate the pattern probabilities accurately, then a Bayes recognizer is not necessarily optimal.* Stated this simply, of course, the statement is obvious. None the less, the problem is often ignored. In addition, the statement remains qualitatively valid if the probabilities are assumed to be parametric (e.g., Gaussian). The problem is most severe when one pattern class dominates (p_{c2} near unity), and vanishes when both classes are equally likely.

[3] The minimum of each curve thus gives the worst case of a recognizer which is too complex for its design pattern set. In practice, a recognizer inferior to simple random guessing should be rejected. The asymptote line $P_{cr} = 0.80$ would thus apply for all $n > n_{max}$.

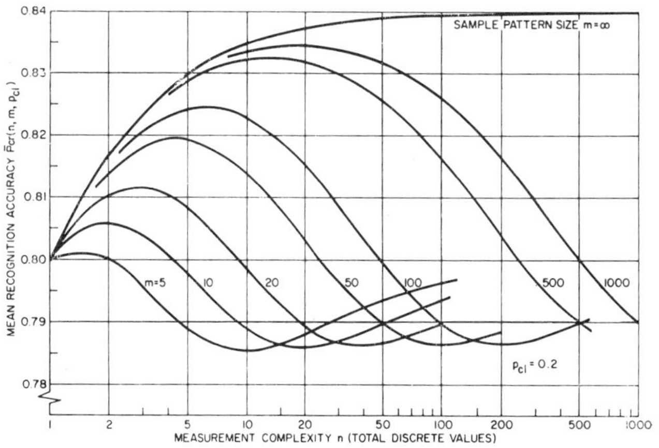

Fig. 4. Finite data set accuracy ($p_{c1} = \frac{1}{5}$).

VII. Experimental

Fig. 5 presents relative frequency (histogram) data gathered from an aerial photograph processor. It was designed to distinguish industrial areas (c_1) from residential urban areas (c_2). The pattern measurement made is the edge density. An edge is defined to exist at any point on the photograph where the two-dimensional intensity-gradient magnitude $|\nabla I|$ exceeds a threshold value. Note that an edge so defined is not necessarily part of a continuous boundary.

Essentially this measurement is able to distinguish between the two classes because homes tend to be small and closely packed, compared to industrial areas. The latter typically contain fewer and larger structures, as well as low-detail areas such as storage yards or parking lots. Consequently, the residential histogram of Fig. 5(a) is concentrated towards the higher edge density values. It is fairly disjoint from the industrial histogram.

Take these histograms as estimates of the cell probabilities and assume $p_{c1} = p_{c2} = \frac{1}{2}$. The Bayes accuracy estimate from (4) is $P_{cr} \cong 0.787$, calculated as in (6). A total of $m = 315$ sample patterns was used in the histograms, and there are $n = 32$ measurement values. From Fig. 3, the mean accuracy is then $\bar{P}_{cr}(32, 315, 0.5) = 0.723$, somewhat below the particular value of 0.787 obtained. Although the choice of 32 measurement values is higher than the optimal value of 13 (Table I), the mean accuracy is not appreciably less than its maximum of 0.729.

As a final experimental topic, one can show that this photographic recognition problem is indeed discontinuous and non-Gaussian. More broadly, it cannot be fitted by reasonable parametric probability functions. This conclusion rests on the large histogram discontinuities shown in Fig. 5; for example, the 210 percent increase from cell 31 to cell 32 under c_2. Or note the 77 percent decrease from cell 14 to cell 15 under c_1.

However, it must be shown that these discontinuities reflect the actual underlying probabilities. They could conceivably be caused merely by random variations due to the finite sample size of 315.

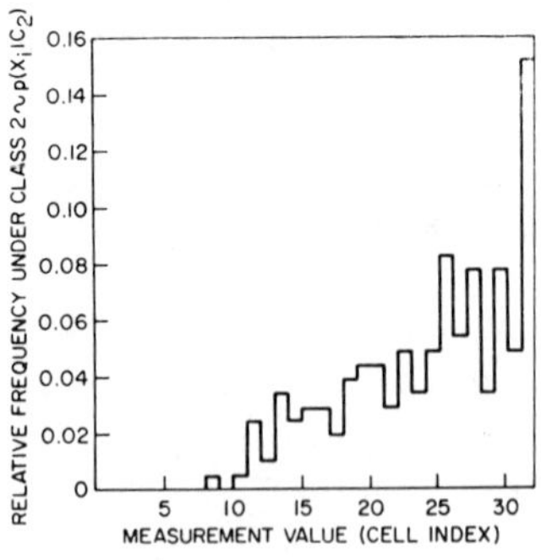

(a)

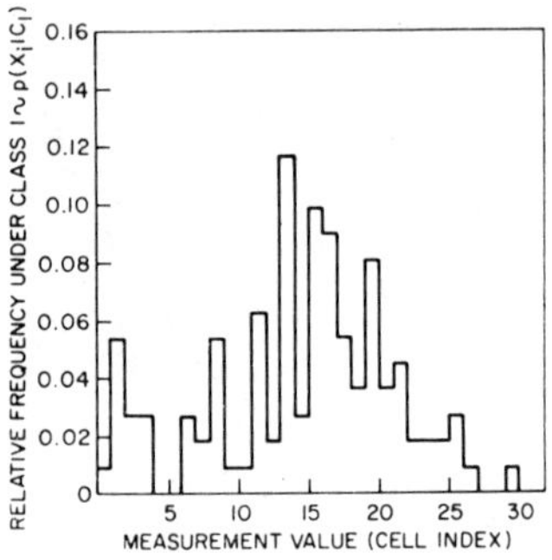

(b)

Fig. 5. Aerial photograph processor histograms.

A rough argument usffices to dispose of this possibility It is well known that the relative frequency r_i/m_1 for each cell of c_1 (say) is a binomially distributed random variable (Appendix I). Its expected value is equal to the true cell probability u_i, and its sampling variance is

$$\begin{aligned} \sigma_i^2 &= u_i(1 - u_i)/m_1 \\ &= r_i(m_1 - r_i)/m_1^3 + O(m_1^{-5/2}). \end{aligned} \tag{20}$$

It is unlikely[4] that the histogram values r_i/m_1 will deviate from the true cell probabilities by more than σ_i. In Fig. 5(a), $m_1 \cong 315/2$ and cell 32 is thus unlikely to have true probability less than $0.152 - \sigma_{32} \cong 0.123$. Cell 31 is unlikely to be more probable than $0.049 + \sigma_{31} \cong 0.066$. Therefore, it is highly likely that a significant discontinuity exists between p_{31} and p_{32} themselves. Roughly, "highly likely" means having probability about $1 - (0.159)^2 = 0.975$.

A more precise binomial argument gives $\Pr[p_{32} < 0.123] = 0.118$ and $\Pr[p_{31} > 0.066] = 0.271$. The discontinuity likelihood is thus nearly $1 - (0.118)(0.271) = 0.968$, rather than 0.975.

VIII. Conclusions

Certain results have been drawn from the statistical model of pattern recognition by using mean value arguments. Most interesting is the existence and size of an optimal measurement complexity, n_{opt}, as well as a maximum acceptable complexity.

If all pattern probabilities were known in advance, the recognition accuracy would be expected to be nearly maximal if $n \gg n_c = 2$ (n_c being the number of pattern classes). More than (say) 20 possible measurement values gives little additional aid in making a simple decision between two dichotomous classes.

The recognition accuracy curves confirm this intuitive feeling. In Fig. 2, the infinite data set curves have substantially reached their asymptotes at $n = 20$. In Fig. 3, n_{opt} ranges from 2 to 23 for $2 \le m \le 1000$ sample patterns.

On the other hand, one can easily envision, with Marill and Green,[7] a vector pattern having 10 component measurements of 10 possible values each. From (5), this gives $n = 10^{10}$, or some twenty billion cell probabilities to estimate, merely to classify patterns into two classes. How is one to reconcile this with (say) the optimal value of $n = 23$ if only 1000 sample patterns are available?

The answer appears to be that only 23 values are statistically significant. A (singular) mapping should be sought to transform the 10^{10} values into 23 before using the sample patterns to compute the recognition rule. In other words, the problem arises because the original measurement structure is incorrectly defined.

Sometimes this mapping can be found by reconsidering the physical origin of the recognition problem at hand. However, statistical assistance in *measurement selection* is often required. Shannons' information measure[2],[12] or Kullbacks' divergence measure[13] might be evaluated for each of the ten pattern vector measurements, and the lowest scoring five discarded.[13],[14] This would leave $n = 10^5$. More directly, score on the estimated accuracy is derived by inserting (17) into (4).

Next, individual *measurement reduction* may be performed on the five remaining measurements. Suppose the ten values of each are reduced to two by forming individual recognition rules. Since the five rules will usually disagree, a final *measurement combination* of the 2^5 values must be made. This value of 32 is not far above the optimum of 23, so that a combining recognition rule can be computed by (18) for a final class prediction.

It should be emphasized that these examples of mapping by measurement selection, reduction, and combination are not proposed as developed techniques. Rather, they are illustrative of a framework for further investigation. Also of interest would be an extension of the present analysis to $n_c > 2$ classes. This is of no conceptual difficulty, yet a general equation giving $\bar{P}_{cr}(n, m, n_c, p_{c1})$ for all n_c has not been found.

Appendix I

Vector Measurements, Statistical Independence, and Sampling Formulas

A discrete vector-pattern measurement $y = (y^r, y^{r-1}, \cdots, y^2, y^1)$ may be nonsingularly mapped to its equivalent

[4] Using the Gaussian approximation to the binomial distribution,[6],[11] the probability of a sampling deviation more than σ_i in *one* direction is about 0.159. It is 0.023 for more than a $2\sigma_i$ deviation.

scalar measurement x by the x_i cell index equation

$$i = j_1 + n_1(j_2 - 1) + n_1n_2(j_3 - 1) + n_1n_2n_3(j_4 - 1) + \cdots + n_1n_2 \cdots n_{r-1}(j_r - 1). \quad (21)$$

Here, j_k is the cell index of component y^k, $1 \leq j_k \leq n_k$, for $k = 1, 2, \cdots, r$. This mapping is quite useful for computer measurement handling, and is inverted by subtracting unity from i and then successively dividing by $n_1, n_2, \cdots, n_r$; extracting the remainders as $j_1 - 1, j_2 - 1, \cdots, j_r - 1$. Indeed, (21) expresses the representation of $i - 1$ in a compound-radix number system having digit radii $n_1, n_2, \cdots, n_r$. Equation (5) follows directly.

To illustrate the probability constraints caused by assuming statistical independence[6] among the measurements y^k, let $r = n_1 = n_2 = 2$. Assume that the component measurements y^2, y^1 are statistically independent under *each* class environment; viz., $P(y^2, y^1 \mid c_i) = P(y^2 \mid c_i) P(y^1 \mid c_i)$ for $i = 1, 2$ and the two values each of y^2 and y^1. Using mapping (21), this leads to the two probability constraints

$$P(x_1 \mid c_i)P(x_4 \mid c_i) = P(x_2 \mid c_i)P(x_3 \mid c_i), \quad (i = 1, 2). \quad (22)$$

This type of constraint would have to be imposed in addition to (1).

Next, the sampling distributions used in the text and Appendix II will be briefly developed. (This is largely a collection of scattered standard results.) Take environment c_1 of the model and let $u_i = P(x_i \mid c_1), i = 1, 2, \cdots, n$. Of m independently sampled patterns, the probability of obtaining a combination with r_i samples in cell i ($i = 1, 2, \cdots, n$) is clearly multinomial[10],[11]:

$$P(r_1, r_2, \cdots, r_n \mid m, u_1, u_2, \cdots, u_n) = \frac{m!}{r_1!\, r_2! \cdots r_n!} u_1^{r_1} u_2^{r_2} \cdots u_n^{r_n} \quad (23)$$

where

$$\sum_{i=1}^{n} r_i = m. \quad (24)$$

For an individual relative frequency r_i/m, the distribution is binomial, since there is probability u_i of falling in cell i and $1 - u_i$ of falling elsewhere:

$$P(r_i \mid m, u_i) = \frac{m!}{r_i!\,(m - r_i)!} u_i^{r_i}(1 - u_i)^{m-r_i}. \quad (25)$$

The relative frequency can thereby be easily shown[11] to have expected value

$$\mu(r_i/m) = u_i \quad (26)$$

and variance

$$\sigma^2(r_i/m) = u_i(1 - u_i)/m. \quad (27)$$

Since the expected value is equal to u_i, the relative frequency is an *unbiased* estimator of u_i. Since the variance vanishes at $m = \infty$, it is also *consistent*. The maximum-likelihood estimator $\hat{u}_i$ of u_i is obtained from the likelihood equation[11]:

$$\frac{\partial[\log P(r_i \mid m, \hat{u}_i)]}{\partial \hat{u}_i} = 0. \quad (28)$$

Using (25), this shows that the *relative frequency is the maximum-likelihood estimator* $\hat{u}_i = r_i/m$.

For a measure of the precision of the relative frequency estimator, one may take σ/μ from (26) and (27):

$$\frac{\sigma(r_i/m)}{\mu(r_i/m)} \sim \sqrt{n/m}. \quad (29)$$

Here, $u_i \sim 1/n$ has been used to get an order of magnitude.

Appendix II

Derivation of Accuracy with Finite Data Set

The derivation of (19) begins analogously to that of (14), except (17) is used instead of the max function in (4). As before, the contribution of measurement value x_1 is equal to any other by symmetry, giving

$$\bar{P}_{cr}(n, m, p_{c1}) = nE\{u_1p_{c1}P[s_1 > r_1 \mid u_1, v_1] + v_1p_{c2}P[s_1 \leq r_1 \mid u_1, v_1]\}, \quad (p_{c1} \leq p_{c2}) \quad (30)$$

where $u_1 = P(x_1 \mid c_1)$, $v_1 = P(x_1 \mid c_2)$. Now s_1 and r_1 arise independently from m_1 samples of environment c_1 and m_2 of c_2 (m_1 is the integral part of $p_{c1}m$ and $m_2 = m - m_1$). Consequently, the joint probability of s_1 and r_1 is the product of two binomial distributions of the form (25):

$$P[s_1, r_1 \mid u_1, v_1] = \frac{m_1!\, m_2!}{s_1!\,(m_1 - s_1)!\, r_1!\,(m_2 - r_1)!} \cdot u_1^{s_1}(1 - u_1)^{m_1-s_1}v_1^{r_1}(1 - v_1)^{m_2-r_1}. \quad (31)$$

The cumulative probability of $s_1 > r_1$ is obtained by simply summing (31) over all r_1, s_1 values obeying the inequality. Interchanging this linear operation with the expectation operator in (30) (representing a $2(n - 1)$-fold integration over the u_i, v_i ranges as in (10), the expected value of a single term of the $s_1 > r_1$ variety may be seen to be

$$n(n - 1)^2p_{c1}(s_1 + 1) \cdot \left[\frac{(m_2 - r_1 + 1)(m_2 - r_1 + 2) \cdots (m_2 - r_1 + n - 2)}{(m_2 + 1)(m_2 + 2) \cdots (m_2 + n - 1)}\right] \cdot \left[\frac{(m_1 - s_1 + 1)(m_1 - s_1 + 2) \cdots (m_1 - s_1 + n - 2)}{(m_1 + 1)(m_1 + 2) \cdots (m_1 + n)}\right]. \quad (32)$$

A term of the $s_1 \leq r_1$ variety is obtained from this by interchanging c_2 and c_1, s_1 and r_1, m_1 and m_2, and the final form of (19) then directly follows.

Numerical evaluation of (19) requires either a three-parameter tabulation or a digital computer. For $n =$

$m = 1000$ in Fig. 3, there are about 10^9 multiplications in the four continued products which range up to magnitude $1500!/500! \cong 10^{2980}$. Consequently, a numerical tabulation is the more reasonable approach (four-place tables for $p_{c1} = \frac{1}{5}$ and $\frac{1}{2}$ are available from the author).

References

[1] C. K. Chow, "An optimum character recognition system using decision functions," *IRE Trans. Electronic Computers*, vol. EC-6, pp. 247–254, December 1957.

[2] D. Middleton, *Statistical Communication Theory*. New York: McGraw-Hill, 1960.

[3] R. G. Miller, "Statistical prediction by discriminant analysis," *Meteorological Monographs*, vol. 4, no. 25, October 1962.

[4] M. Minsky, "A selected descriptor-indexed bibliography to the literature on artificial intelligence," *IRE Trans. Human Factors in Electronics*, vol. HFE-2, pp. 39–56, March 1961.

[5] A. Wald, *Statistical Decision Functions*. New York: Wiley, 1950.

[6] W. B. Davenport and W. L. Root, *The Theory of Random Signals and Noise*. New York: McGraw-Hill, 1958.

[7] T. Marill and D. M. Green, "Statistical recognition functions and the design of pattern recognizers," *IRE Trans. Electronic Computers*, vol. EC-9, pp. 472–477, December 1960.

[8] T. M. Cover and P. E. Hart, "Nearest neighbor pattern classification," *IEEE Trans. Information Theory*, vol. IT-13, pp. 21–27, January 1967.

[9] G. S. Sebestyen, *Decision-Making Processes in Pattern Recognition*. New York: Macmillan, 1962.

[10] M. G. Kendall and A. Stuart, *The Advanced Theory of Statistics*, 2 vols. New York: Hafner, 1958.

[11] H. Cramér, *Mathematical Methods of Statistics*. Princeton, N. J.: Princeton University Press, 1946.

[12] P. M. Lewis, "The characteristic selection problem in recognition systems," *IRE Trans. Information Theory*, vol. IT-8, pp. 171–178, February 1962.

[13] T. Marill and D. M. Green, "On the effectiveness of receptors in recognition systems," *IEEE Trans. Information Theory*, vol. IT-9, pp. 11–17, January 1963.

[14] J. A. Lebo and G. F. Hughes, "Pattern recognition preprocessing by similarity functionals," *1966 Proc. Nat'l Electronics Conf.*, vol. 22.

[15] Davenport and Root,[6] sec. 14–2.

[16] Middleton,[2] sec. 19.1–1.

[17] Davenport and Root,[6] ch. 14.

[18] Davenport and Root,[8] sec. 5–5.

[19] Cramér,[11] sec. 17.6.

Comments "On the Mean Accuracy of Statistical Pattern Recognizers"

K. Abend and T. J. Harley, Jr.

In the above, Hughes [1] presents curves[1] of mean recognition accuracy in which performance[2] using measurements can fall below performance based on prior probabilities alone. He explains this situation with the statement: "If insufficient sample data are available to estimate the pattern probabilities accurately, then a Bayes recognizer is not necessarily optimal." This seemed paradoxical, since the term "Bayes" means minimum average risk (i.e., optimal performance). The problem is that Hughes has *not* used the Bayes procedure for *unknown* cell probabilities. Instead, he employs the Bayes rule that would be appropriate if the cell probabilities were known; but since they are in fact unknown, he substitutes the sample cell frequencies. This procedure is only an ad hoc approximation to a Bayes procedure. A truly Bayes procedure for distributions with unknown parameter values—in this case the cell probabilities of the multinominal distribution—would use the design samples in an optimum manner, and would *maximize* the mean recognition accuracy. In general, such procedures do *not* employ estimates of the parameter values in the same way that the true values would be used if they were known. In the problem treated by Hughes the use of an estimate turns out to be appropriate provided that the expected value of the parameter given the design samples is used rather than an unbiased estimator.

Let y_{cj} represent the set of design samples from class c_j, $j = 1, 2$. The Bayes procedure [2] (which maximizes the probability of

Manuscript received May 1, 1968; revised July 1, 1968. This work was partially supported by U. S. Air Force Contract F33615-67-C-1836 for the Aerospace Medical Research Laboratories, Wright-Patterson Air Force Base, Ohio.

[1] Hughes' Fig. 4.

[2] The terms "performance" and "mean recognition accuracy" are used interchangeably to mean average probability of correct recognition (see [1] for details).

Reprinted from *IEEE Trans. Inform. Theory*, vol. IT-15, pp. 420–423, May 1969.

correct recognition given the design samples) chooses the class that maximizes

$$p(x_i, c_j \mid y_{cj}) = p(x_i \mid y_{cj}, c_j)p_{cj}, \tag{1}$$

where, for example,

$$p(x_i \mid y_{c1}, c_1) = \int u_i f(u_i \mid y_{c1})\, du_i \triangleq \hat{u}_i \tag{2}$$

with $u_i \triangleq p(x_i \mid c_1)$. Thus, it turns out that the Bayes procedure *is* obtainable by using an estimate $\hat{u}_i$ of the ith cell probability. The Bayes procedure differs from the procedure in [1] only in that it specifies the use of the conditional expectation of u_i, given the design samples as the estimate of u_i. We now proceed to solve for $\hat{u}_i$ explicitly.

Let r_i denote[3] the number of samples (out of a total of m from class c_1) for which the measurement value x_i occurs. The probability of $\mathbf{r} = (r_1, \cdots, r_{n-1})$ is multinomial:[4]

$$\begin{aligned} p(\mathbf{r} \mid m, \mathbf{u}) &= p(r_1, \cdots, r_{n-1} \mid m, u_1, \cdots, u_{n-1}) \\ &= \frac{m!}{r_1! r_2! \cdots r_n!} u_1^{r_1} u_2^{r_2} \cdots u_{n-1}^{r_{n-1}} \\ &\qquad \cdot (1 - u_1 - \cdots - u_{n-1})^{r_n}, \end{aligned} \tag{3}$$

where r_n is shorthand for $m - r_1 - \cdots - r_{n-1}$, and u_n is given by

$$\sum_{i=1}^{n} u_i = 1. \tag{4}$$

Assuming a uniform[5] distribution for u_i the prior density of $\mathbf{u} = (u_1, \cdots, u_{n-1})$ is

$$f(u_1, \cdots, u_{n-1}) = \begin{cases} (n-1)! & \mathbf{u} \in S \\ 0 & \mathbf{u} \notin S, \end{cases} \tag{5}$$

where S is the $n - 1$ dimensional simplex

$$\begin{aligned} S = \{(u_1, \cdots, u_{n-1})&: u_i \geq 0, \\ i = 1, \cdots, n-1&; u_1 + \cdots + u_{n-1} \leq 1\} \end{aligned} \tag{6}$$

and u_n is given by (4). The posterior density of $\mathbf{u}$, given the design samples, is

$$\begin{aligned} f(u_1, \cdots, u_{n-1} \mid y_{c1}) &= f(\mathbf{u} \mid m, \mathbf{r}) \\ &= \frac{p(\mathbf{r} \mid m, \mathbf{u}) f(\mathbf{u})}{\int_S p(\mathbf{r} \mid m, \mathbf{u}) f(\mathbf{u})\, du} \\ &= \begin{cases} \dfrac{(n+m-1)!}{r_1! r_2! \cdots r_n!} u_1^{r_1} u_2^{r_2} \cdots u_{n-1}^{r_{n-1}} (1 - u_1 - \cdots - u_{n-1})^{r_n} \\ \qquad\qquad\qquad\qquad \mathbf{u} \in S \\ 0 \qquad\qquad\qquad\qquad \mathbf{u} \notin S \end{cases} \end{aligned} \tag{7}$$

This is the Dirichlet density [3] with parameters $\gamma_i \triangleq 1 + r_i$ (for $n = 2$ it becomes the beta density). Thus, the Bayes rule maximizes (1) with $p(x_i \mid y_{c1}, c_1) = \hat{u}_i$ given by

$$\hat{u}_i = \int_S u_i f(u_1, \cdots, u_{n-1} \mid y_{c1}) \cdot du_1 \cdots du_{n-1} = \frac{1 + r_i}{n + m}. \tag{8}$$

[3] We follow the notation in Appendix I of [1].
[4] [1, (23)].
[5] [1, (8)–(11)].

The Bayes rule is the same as Hughes and Lebo's "maximum mean accuracy" rule [4]. It differs from Hughes' approximate-Bayes rule only in that $(1 + r_i)/(n + m)$ is used instead of r_i/m as the estimator of $p(x_i \mid c_1)$. For equal class probabilities the rules are the same; [1, (19)] gives the maximum recognition accuracy when $p_{c1} = 1/2$.

We hope that this correspondence does nothing to detract from Hughes' excellent paper, which treats a long standing problem in a novel and illuminating manner. The "peaking" of performance at a level of measurement complexity determined by the size of the design set is a fact that has long been observed experimentally. Though we feel that the actual *value* of n at which the peak occurs is much higher in practical pattern recognition problems than that found on the basis of Hughes' model, we concur with the qualitative aspects of his results.

KENNETH ABEND
THOMAS J. HARLEY, JR.
Philco-Ford Corp.
Blue Bell, Pa. 19422

REFERENCES

[1] G. F. Hughes, *IEEE Trans. Information Theory*, vol. IT-14, pp. 55–63, January 1968.
[2] K. Abend, T. J. Harley, Jr., and L. N. Kanal, "Adaptive modelling of likelihood classification—II," Philco-Ford Corp., Blue Bell, Pa., final rept. on Contract AF30 (602)-3623 for Rome Air Development Center, March 1968, section 2, p. 14.
[3] S. S. Wilks, *Mathematical Statistics*. New York: Wiley, 1962.
[4] G. F. Hughes and J. A. Lebo, "Data reduction using information theoretic techniques," RADC Report TR-67-67, final rept. on Contract AF30 (602)-3976, March 1967, pp. 45–46.

B. Chandrasekaran and T. J. Harley, Jr.[6]

In [1] some results concerning the mean accuracy of statistical pattern recognizers were recently presented. The performance curves for the unequal prior class probability case were such that recognition accuracy using measurements can sometimes be lower than max (p_{c1}, p_{c2}), where p_{ci} is the a priori probability of the occurrence of class i. Abend and Harley have traced the source of this paradoxical result to the decision rule in [1] and derived the correct Bayes decision rule that should be used. In this correspondence, we derive the correct expression for the mean recognition accuracy and examine its behavior with respect to measurement complexity. We also show that the correct decision rule does in fact result in performance curves in which the mean probability of correct recognition is never less than max (p_{c1}, p_{c2}). We discuss some relatively strange phenomena that occur when the p_{ci} are unequal.

We follow the notation and approach of Appendix II of [1]. Considering just the measurement value x_1, we assign it to Class 1 or 2 according to the following rule (given by Abend and Harley)

$$\text{predict} \begin{cases} c_1 & \text{if } p_{c1} \dfrac{r_1 + 1}{m_1 + n} > p_{c2} \dfrac{s_1 + 1}{m_2 + n} \\ c_2 & \text{otherwise,} \quad (p_{c1} \leq p_{c2}). \end{cases} \tag{1}$$

The probability of correct recognition is

$$\begin{aligned} P_{cr}(n, m_1, m_2, p_{c1}) &= nE\left\{u_1 P\left[p_{c1} \frac{r_1 + 1}{m_1 + n} > p_{c2} \frac{s_1 + 1}{m_2 + n} \;\middle|\; u_1, v_1\right]\right. \\ &\quad \left. + v_1 P\left[p_{c1} \frac{r_1 + 1}{m_1 + n} \leq p_{c2} \frac{s_1 + 1}{m_2 + n} \;\middle|\; u_1, v_1\right]\right\}. \end{aligned} \tag{2}$$

Equations (31) and (32) of [1] remain unchanged and the expression for the mean recognition accuracy can be seen to be identical to (19) of [1] if we substitute the following expression for $g(r, s)$:

[6] Manuscript received July 2, 1968; revised September 11, 1968. This work was supported by U. S. Air Force Contract F33615-67-C-1836 for the Aerospace Medical Research Laboratories, Wright-Patterson Air Force Base, Ohio.

TABLE I

m_1	m	Applicable Figure
$> \frac{1-2p}{p}$	$< A$	Fig. 1
	$\geq A$	Fig. 2
$< \frac{1-2p}{p}$	$> A$	Fig. 3
	$\leq A$	Fig. 4
$= \frac{1-2p}{p}$	$\leq 2m_1$	Fig. 4
	$> 2m_1$	Fig. 2

$$g(r, s) = n(n-1)^2 \max\left(p_{c1}\frac{s+1}{m_1+n}, p_{c2}\frac{r+1}{m_2+n}\right), \tag{3}$$

that is,

$$\begin{aligned}\bar{P}_{cr}(n, m_1, m_2, p_{c1}) &= \sum_{r=0}^{m_2}\sum_{s=0}^{m_1}\left[\frac{(m_2-r+1)\cdots(m_2-r+n-2)}{(m_2+1)\cdots(m_2+n-1)}\right] \\ &\quad \left[\frac{(m_1-s+1)\cdots(m_2-s+n-2)}{(m_1+1)\cdots(m_1+n-1)}\right]g(r, s) \\ &\triangleq \sum_{r=0}^{m_2}\sum_{s=0}^{m_1} h(m_1, m_2, r, s)g(r, s).\end{aligned} \tag{4}$$

To see that $\bar{P}_{cr}(n) \geq \max(p_{c1}, p_{c2})$, we first note that $\max(a, b)$ is never less than either a or b. Setting $g_1(r, s) = n(n-1)^2 p_{c1}(s+1)/(m_1+n)$ and $g_2(r, s) = n(n-1)^2 p_{c2}(r+1)/(m_2+n)$, it is easy to check that

$$\sum_{r=0}^{m_2}\sum_{s=0}^{m_1} h(m_1, m_2, s, r)g_i(r, s) = p_{ci}, \qquad i = 1, 2$$

and

$$g(r, s) \geq g_i(r, s), \qquad i = 1, 2.$$

Hence

$$\bar{P}_{cr}(n, m_1, m_2, p_{c1}) \geq \max(p_{c1}, p_{c2}). \tag{5}$$

Thus, the correct decision rule does indeed eliminate the paradoxical behavior mentioned earlier. In passing, we mention that (4) gives the mean probability of correct recognition not only for the following particular division of samples into classes, $m_1 = [p_{c1}m]$, $m_2 = m - m_1$ considered in [1], but also for any m_1 and m_2 such that $m_1 + m_2 = m$, the total number of samples.

Some idea of the qualitative behavior of the performance curves can be obtained from the following considerations. We assume, without loss of generality, that $p_{c1} < p_{c2}$. For given m_1, m_2, and p_{c1}, setting $p_{c1} = p$ and $p_{c2} = (1-p)$, $\bar{P}_{cr}(n) = (1-p)$ if

$$\max_s\left(p\frac{s+1}{m_1+n}\right) \leq \min_r\left[(1-p)\frac{r+1}{m_2+n}\right]$$

or

$$p\frac{(m_1+1)}{m_1+n} \leq \frac{(1-p)}{m_2+n}. \tag{6}$$

$\bar{P}_{cr}(n) > (1-p)$ if the inequality (6) is not satisfied. The range of values of n for which (6) is satisfied is given by

$$n < N_1 = \frac{m_1(1+pm_1) - pm(1+m_1)}{(2p+pm_1-1)} \qquad \text{if} \quad m_1 > \frac{1-2p}{p}, \tag{7a}$$

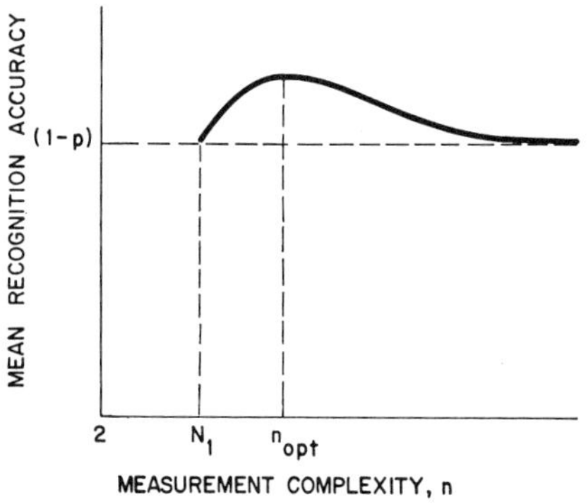

Fig. 1. Mean recognition accuracy: Initial clamping.

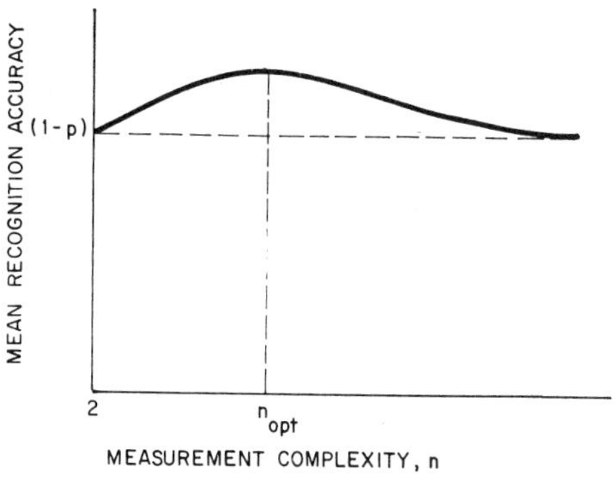

Fig. 2. Mean recognition accuracy: No clamping.

$$n > N_2 = \frac{pm(1+m_1) - m_1(1+pm_1)}{(1-2p-pm_1)} \qquad \text{if} \quad m_1 < \frac{1-2p}{p}. \tag{7b}$$

We consider only values of measurement complexity $n \geq 2$, since there must be a minimum of two measurement values in order to distinguish two classes. The behavior is summarized in Table I and Figs. 1–4. The expressions can be checked by algebraic manipulations of (7), except for the case corresponding to $m_1 = (1-2p)/p$, which can be obtained from (6). For simplicity, the symbol A has been used in Table I to denote the expression

$$\frac{m_1(1+pm_1) + 2 - 4p - 2pm_1}{p(1+m_1)}.$$

Figs. 1 and 3 exhibit what may be called "clamping" phenomena; there are ranges of values of n for which $\bar{P}_{cr}$ is clamped at $\max(p, 1-p)$, and for n outside this range $\bar{P}_{cr} > \max(p, 1-p)$. Fig. 2 is the performance curve we would normally expect and it is attained not only if a sufficient total number of samples is available, but also if there is a sufficient number from Class 1. Further, as long as $m_1 < (1-2p)/p$ for any finite number of total samples, there is a finite value of n after which clamping occurs. If, moreover, the total number of samples is insufficient, performance may never be better than when based on a priori speculation alone, whatever be the measurement complexity. Thus, it appears there are 'thresholds' of the number of samples, for the samples to be effective at all. Below this threshold, the samples have no power to reduce the risk.

Table I summarizes the behavior for any m_1 and m_2. If, however, we use the particular division of the total number of samples into classes given by $m_1 = [pm]$ and $m_2 = m - m_1$, Table I is still valid,

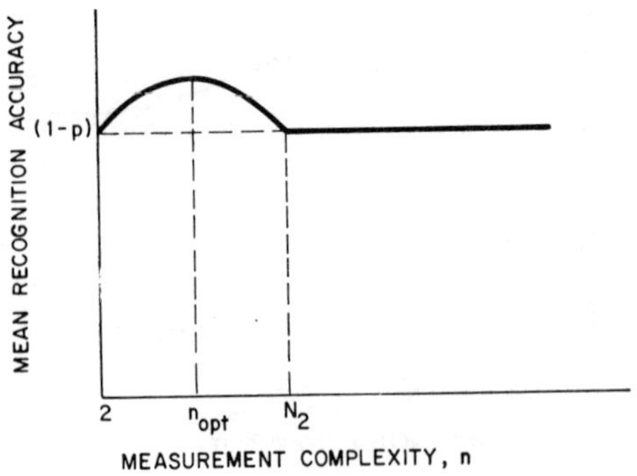

Fig. 3. Mean recognition accuracy: Final clamping.

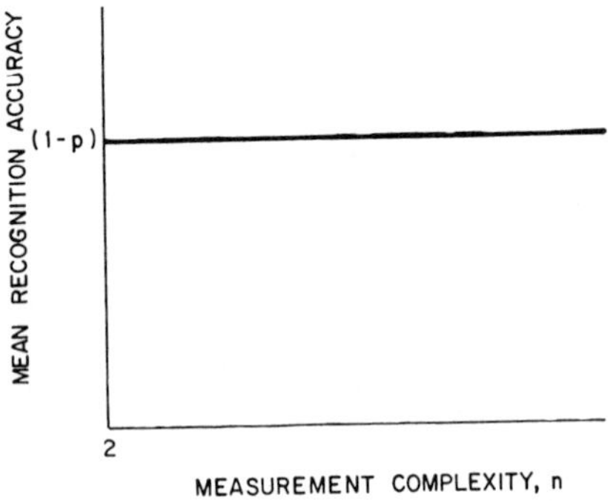

Fig. 4. Mean recognition accuracy: No improvement due to samples.

TABLE II

m	Applicable Figure
$m \geq \dfrac{1-2p}{p^2}$	Fig. 2
$\dfrac{1-2p}{p^2} > m > B$	Fig. 3
$\dfrac{1-2p}{p^2} > m < B$	Fig. 4

but some inequalities become impossible. Table II presents results corresponding to this case. For analytical simplicity, we assume that $[pm] = pm$ and ignore the minor errors associated with this assumption. Also note that the symbol B stands for the expression

$$(-p + \sqrt{5p^2 - 6p + 2})/p(1 - p).$$

Behavior corresponding to Fig. 1 does not occur in this case. Further, if the total number of samples exceeds a certain threshold, $\bar{P}_{cr} \geq \max(p, 1-p)$ for all finite values of measurement complexity. When it is below this threshold for smaller values of n, there is improvement due to samples, while for higher values, there is no improvement at all due to samples.

It is interesting to note that it is sometimes possible to get better performance by a different division of samples than the one corresponding to Table II. For instance, when $m = 7$ and $p = 0.2$, if we use $m_1 = [pm] = 1$ and $m_2 = 6$, we will get behavior corresponding to Fig. 3. On the other hand, if we use $m_1 = 4$ and $m_2 = 3$, the behavior corresponds to Fig. 2, in which case there is no clamping for any value of n.

In spite of these multiple alternatives of behavior, there does exist an optimal measurement complexity n_{opt} demonstrated in Hughes. However, the several qualitative performances that are possible for the unequal prior class probability case make it difficult to make simple general statements about the relationship between measurement complexity and the number of samples.

B. Chandrasekaran
Thomas J. Harley, Jr.
Philco-Ford Corp.
Blue Bell, Pa. 19422

Author's Reply[7]

The above letters make several interesting points about decision procedures for discrete measurement nonparametric pattern recognition in a statistical environment. The areas under discussion appear to be the mean-accuracy criterion [1], and the Maximum Mean-Accuracy recognition rule (MMA rule) [5] as compared to the relative frequency recognition rule [1]. Abend and Harley show that the MMA rule is a Bayes procedure that maximizes the mean accuracy given the data. Chandrasekaran and Harley prove that the expected accuracy of the MMA rule is never lower than the priors, and they discuss an interesting accuracy clamping phenomenon that can arise when the pattern classes do not occur equally in nature. Hughes and Lebo [5] state that it is natural to propose the MMA rule but that an experimental test of it could not be made in their study.

It is important to remark that the line of argument by both Chandrasekaran and Harley and [5] rests on a foundation different from that used to derive the mean-accuracy criterion in [1]. There, the criterion was to evaluate the "*overall* performance of a Bayes recognition rule" by averaging overall recognition problems (equally weighted by Bayes postulate [6]) having fixed measurement complexity n and prior class probability p_{c1}. The mean-accuracy criterion was intended as a theoretic construct that calculates the recognition accuracy one may expect *without using any physical or statistical information specific to the recognition problem at hand* save the pattern measurement complexity n, prior class probabilities p_{cj}, and design data sample size m.

If one accepts the Bayes postulate on which it is based, it allows a numerical estimate of the design patterns to take, without requiring information on the pattern probabilities. However, relative frequencies were used in the criterion to estimate the truly Bayes decision rule (which decides class c_j when x_i occurs if $P[c_j | x_i]$ is maximal over j and achieves maximum accuracy in application). They were chosen simply because they are classical estimators for the underlying probabilities $P[x_i \mid c_j]$.

The above letters suggest that the choice of relative frequency estimators is inconsistent with the choice of optimality criterion; namely, the mean accuracy P_{cr} is maximized by the MMA rule, not the relative frequency rule. This can be seen directly from eq. (19) in [1]. Consequently, I agree with Abend, Harley, and Chandrasekaran that the MMA rule is the correct Bayes decision procedure that should have been used in [1].

Knowledge of probability structure, continuity, or independence can significantly influence the optimal sample size [7]. Performance curves and tables pertinent to the MMA rule have been generated in some independent work [8] in which the partition of the fixed design sample size m between the two classes is also optimized to maximize the mean accuracy.

Gordon F. Hughes
Autonetics Div.
North American Rockwell Corp.
Anaheim, Calif. 92803

References

[5] G. F. Hughes and J. A. Lebo, "Data reduction using information theoretic techniques," RADC Rept. TR-67-67, final rept. on Contract AF30(602)-3976, pp. 45–46, March 1967.
[6] T. Bayes, "Essay towards solving a problem in the doctrine of chances," *Phil. Trans. Roy. Soc.* 1763, vol. 53, pp. 370–418, (reprinted in Biometrica, vol. 45, pp. 293–315, December 1958).
[7] L. Kanal and B. Chandrasekaran, "On dimensionality and sample size in statistical pattern classification," *Proc. 1968 Nat'l Electronics Conf.*, pp. 2–7.
[8] G. F. Hughes, "Number of pattern classifier design samples per class," *IEEE Trans. Information Theory* (to be published).

[7] Manuscript received December 10, 1968.

Independence of Measurements and the Mean Recognition Accuracy

BALAKRISHNAN CHANDRASEKARAN, MEMBER, IEEE

Abstract—A situation of great practical importance in pattern recognition is the case where the designer has only a finite number of sample patterns from each class and the class-conditional density functions are not completely known. Recent results indicate that in this case the dimensionality of the pattern vector, i.e., the number of measurements, should not be arbitrarily increased, since above a certain value (corresponding to the optimal measurement complexity), the performance starts to deteriorate instead of improving steadily. However, whether this phenomenon occurs in the case of independent measurements has been an open question until now. In this paper the following result of practical importance is derived. When the measurements are independent, and a Bayesian approach is taken, one can add extra measurements without fear of this peaking of performance; i.e., the optimal measurement complexity is infinite. In fact, under certain conditions, having just one sample from class 1, and none at all from class 2, can result in a recognition accuracy arbitrarily close to unity for a large enough number of measurements. The implication of these results to practice is discussed, along with the general question of dimensionality and sample size.

Manuscript received March 15, 1970; revised August 19, 1970. This work was supported by Aerospace Medical Research Laboratories, Wright-Patterson AFB, Ohio, Contract F33615-69-C-1571 to Philco-Ford Corporation via a subcontract to LNK Corporation, Blue Bell, Pa., and by NSF Grant GN 534.1 to Ohio State University.

The author is with the Department of Computer and Information Science, Ohio State University, Columbus, Ohio 43210.

I. Introduction and Statement of the Problem

THE RELATIONSHIP between the number of measurements[1] and the performance accuracy of statistical recognition systems, when only a finite number of sample patterns from which to estimate the recognition function is available, has received deserved and increasing attention recently [1]–[4]. A comprehensive discussion of known results is provided in [4]. Most of this work has been the theoretical outgrowth of the observation of the following phenomenon in many practical pattern recognition systems. When the number of measurements is increased, after a certain point performance begins to fall off rather than improve steadily. However, the theoretical models in the above references did not provide for the assumption of independence of measurements. As a result, it was an open question until now whether this phenomenon occurred in the case of independent measurements.

Allais [1] was one of the earliest to consider the problem

[1] In the literature, the terms variables, measurements, and features are used interchangeably. The term dimensionality is used for the cardinality of the set of measurements.

Reprinted from *IEEE Trans. Inform. Theory*, vol. IT-17, pp. 452–456, July 1971. Correction in vol. IT-18, p. 217, Jan. 1972.

mathematically. He showed that this phenomenon was indeed to be expected if the measurements were jointly normally distributed with a nondiagonal covariance matrix and if maximum-likelihood estimates of unknown parameters are used in the decision function, which would be optimal if the parameters were in fact known. These results were not totally satisfying, however, since objections that a nonoptimal decision function was used could be raised. Hughes [2] has considered the problem in greater scope and in a Bayesian context. The model applicable to [2] and [3] can be summarized as follows. Assume that the measurement space has been quantized such that any pattern can be represented by one of n possible measurement states. Notice that n, which is called the measurement complexity, can be increased by increasing not only the number of measurements but also the levels of quantization. However, only the problem associated with increasing the number of measurements is discussed here. A two-class pattern recognition problem can then be defined by the set of numbers $P(x_i \mid c_j)$, $j = 1,2$; $i = 1,\cdots,n$; x_i, the ith measurement state; and c_j, the jth class. For a complete specification, the prior probabilities of the two classes are also needed. However, it is assumed in the sequel that the classes are equiprobable. If one makes suitable *a priori* assumptions over P in particular, a uniform distribution such that all measurement states are *a priori* equally probable, and, further, one has m_j samples from class c_j, then one can derive a mean recognition accuracy, $\bar{P}_{cr}(n,m_1,m_2)$. This is obtained by averaging the accuracy P_{cr} over all problems generatable by the assumed *a priori* assumptions.

Hughes showed that for finite values of m_1 and m_2, there is a finite value for the optimal measurement complexity $n_0(m_1,m_2)$. This is the value at which $\bar{P}_{cr}$ reaches its maximum value. For large values of n, $\bar{P}_{cr}$ approaches $\frac{1}{2}$, no better than a random decision.

Kanal and Chandrasekaran [4] discuss this question of dimensionality and sample size, and indicate that Hughes's results are to be used with care because of the structural assumptions made by the model, even though they explained a long-standing problem in an illuminating manner. The existence of a spectrum of possibilities is demonstrated [4], with Hughes's result occupying the pessimistic end of it. Hughes's model is in a sense quite unstructured. Not only are the possible continuity properties between quantization levels unreflected in the space of measurement states, but because of the way the *a priori* assumptions are made, the problem space contains problems of all degrees of correlation between different measurements.

In this connection, comparison of performance limits for the infinite sample case (i.e., known parameters) for different models is also illuminating. Compare $\bar{P}_{cr} = 0.75$ for the model in [2] with $P_{cr} = 1$ for the case of independent measurements obeying certain conditions [5] or, again, $P_{cr} = 1$ for the case of normal measurements, which need not necessarily be independent, but must obey certain mild correlation conditions [6]. The independence, or more precisely, the degree of correlation, between successive measurements substantially affects the existence and value of n_0 as well as the value of P_{cr}.

The above remarks dealing with the independence of variables suggest the following question of practical importance. In the case of a finite number of samples, if the measurements are independent, can the number of measurements be increased arbitrarily without eventual deterioration of performance? Intuitively it is not clear whether, for a given sample size, this increased structure merely increases n_0 to a higher finite value, or whether this peaking with respect to n vanishes, effectively making n_0 infinite.

This paper investigates this question for independent, binary variables in a Bayesian context. In the interests of analytical simplicity, variables of binary, rather than arbitrary quantization are assumed. Surprisingly, somewhat of a new start has to be made for our investigation; it seems impossible to adapt known results, particularly Hughes's, to this case. However, the analysis has been made very similar as far as possible, so that comparisons can be easily made. Further, consider only a two-class problem, with equal prior probabilities for the classes. It would be a relatively simple matter to extend the analysis to many classes and unequal priors, but it is avoided in order not to detract from the qualitative aspects of the results.

The model to be considered in this paper is the following. The pattern is a binary vector $(x_1,\cdots,x_N)$, where $x_i = 1$ or 0. The dimensionality of the measurement vector is N. The measurement complexity, defined as the total number of measurement states is, in this case, $n = 2^N$. Class c_1 is specified by the set of numbers $\{p_1,\cdots,p_N\}$ where $p_i = Pr(x_i = 1 \mid c_1)$ and class c_2 by $\{q_1,\cdots,q_N\}$, $q_i = Pr(x_i = 1 \mid c_2)$. The variables x_i are independent. A problem is specified by the $2N$ numbers, p_i and q_i, which are assumed unknown. There are available m_1 samples from class c_1 and m_2 samples from class c_2, to estimate the unknown parameters and obtain the optimal decision function. The approach is Bayesian, with uniform prior probability on p_i and q_i, over the interval [0,1], and a zero-one cost function, so that it is sufficient to minimize the mean probability of error. Especially note that the variables are not identically distributed, though the *a prior* probabilities on the p_i and q_i are. The performance measure considered is $\bar{P}_{cr}(N,m_1,m_2)$, the mean probability of correct recognition, for a given N, m_1, and m_2. First consider the case corresponding to known p_i and q_i, i.e., the case where m_1 and m_2 are infinite.

II. Infinite Sample Size

If $f_i(x)$, $i = 1,2$, represent class-conditional density functions, then one can define a distance d_N between f_1 and f_2 by

$$d_N = \sum |f_1(x) - f_2(x)| \, dx. \tag{1}$$

In (1), the subscript N emphasizes the dependence of d on the dimensionality of x. Chu and Chueh [5] show that

$P_{cr}(N)$ can be related to d_N by[2]

$$P_{cr}(N) = \tfrac{1}{2} + \tfrac{1}{4} d_N \quad (2)$$

and hence

$$\bar{P}_{cr}(N) = \tfrac{1}{2} + \tfrac{1}{4} \bar{d}_N. \quad (3)$$

In our case,

$$f_1(x) = \prod_{i=1}^{N} p_i^{x_i}(1 - p_i)^{(1-x_i)}$$

and similarly for f_2, with q_i in place of p_i. Further,

$$\bar{d}_N = \int_{\{p\},\{q\}} \sum_{x_i=0,1} |f_1(x) - f_2(x)| \, dp_1 \cdots dp_N \, dq_1, \cdots, dq_N. \quad (4)$$

Due to the symmetries that exist, it is sufficient to consider $x = (1,\cdots,1)$ and rewrite (4) as

$$\bar{d}_N = 2^N \int | p_1 \cdots p_N - q_1 \cdots q_N | \, dp_1 \cdots dp_N \, dq_1 \cdots dq_N. \quad (5)$$

In the Appendix, the following explicit derivation from (5) has been outlined:

$$\tfrac{1}{2}\bar{d}_N = \sum_{\zeta=0}^{N-1} (2/3)^N (1/3)^\zeta ((N + \zeta - 1)!/(\zeta!(N - 1)!)) - \sum_{\zeta=0}^{N-1} (2/3)^\zeta (1/3)^N ((N + \zeta - 1)!/(\zeta!(N - 1)!)). \quad (6)$$

This quantity increases monotonically with N. In particular,

$$\lim_{N\to\infty} \bar{d}_N = 2. \quad (7)$$

To show this, note that each of the summations can be viewed as arising from negative binomial distributions. From [7], for large N, (6) can be simplified as

$$\bar{d}_N = [\Phi(a_1) + \Phi(a_2)] \quad (8)$$

where Φ is the normal probability integral

$$\Phi(a) = (1/\sqrt{2\pi}) \int_{-\infty}^{a} \exp(-\tfrac{1}{2}x^2) \, dx \quad (9)$$

and a_1 and a_2 for large enough N can be shown to be arbitrarily close to $\sqrt{N/3}$ and $\sqrt{N/6}$, respectively. From this (7) can be obtained directly, leading to the result

$$\lim_{N\to\infty} \bar{P}_{cr}(N) = 1. \quad (10)$$

Paraphrasing (10), for this model, when the p_i and q_i are known, one can achieve arbitrarily close-to-perfect recognition, as the number of independent measurements is increased. Several cautionary remarks are in order. This result, remarkable as it appears, must be viewed in the context of the *a priori* assumptions on the parameters. They essentially lead to the fact that

$$E[|p_i - q_i|] > 0, \qquad \forall i, \quad (11)$$

such that whenever a new variable is added, on the average it has a nonzero distance between classes.

Chu and Chueh [5] derive a result similar to (10), when the measurements are independent, but without any Bayesian assumptions; however, the constraint is that

$$\lim_{N\to\infty} \sum_{i=0}^{N} (|p_i - q_i|) = \infty, \quad (12)$$

which is very similar to (11). See remarks in [4] in connection with the meaning of this type of result to practice. Here (10) is used mainly as a benchmark against which to compare results due to finite sample size. Fig. 1 gives a comparison of our model with the model in [2] for the infinite sample size case. One can see how the structural assumption of independence affects the performance.

III. Finite Sample Size

Here, deriving $\bar{P}_{cr}(N,m_1,m_2)$ is discussed. It can be shown that the Bayes rule for this case can be written as

$$\text{classify as } c_1, \quad \text{if } \prod_{i=1}^{N} \hat{p}_i^{x_i}(1 - \hat{p}_1)^{(1-x_i)} > \prod_{i=1}^{N} \hat{q}_i^{x_i}(1 - \hat{q}_i)^{(1-x_i)}$$
$$\text{classify as } c_2, \quad \text{otherwise.} \quad (13)$$

In (13), the Bayes estimates are

$$\hat{p}_i = (s_i + 1)/(m_1 + 2)$$
$$\hat{q}_i = (r_i + 1)/(m_2 + 2) \quad (14)$$

where s_i and r_i are, respectively, the numbers of times the x_i from classes c_1 and c_2 take on the value unity. Equation (14) can be derived along lines similar to those of Abend and Harley [3].

The derivation for $\bar{P}_{cr}$ is presented; the initial equations are similar to the ones in [2]. If $\{p\} = \{p_1,\cdots,p_N\}$ and $\{q\} = \{q_1,\cdots,q_N\}$ are the true parameters

$$\Pr(s_1,\cdots,s_N, r_1,\cdots,r_N \mid \{p\},\{q\}) = \prod_{i=1}^{N} [(m_1!)^N/(s_i!(m_1 - s_i)!)] p_i^{s_i}(1 - p_i)^{m_1 - s_i} \times [(m_2!)^N/(r_i!(m_2 - r_i)!)] q_i^{r_i}(1 - q_i)^{m_2 - r_i} \quad (15)$$

$$\Pr(s_1 \cdots s_N > r_1 \cdots r_N \mid \{p\},\{q\}) = \sum_{\substack{r_1,\cdots,r_N \\ s_2,\cdots,s_N}} \; \sum_{s_1 > (r_1 \cdots r_N/s_2 \cdots s_N)} \Pr(s_1,\cdots,s_N, r_1,\cdots,r_N). \quad (16)$$

Again, due to the symmetry of the problem it is sufficient to consider $x = (1,\cdots,1)$. Then the probability that it is correctly classified is

$$P_{cr}(x) = \tfrac{1}{2}\{E[p_1 \cdots p_N \Pr(s_1 \cdots s_N > r_1 \cdots r_N) \mid \{p\},\{q\}] + E[q_1 \cdots q_N \Pr(s_1 \cdots s_N \le r_1 \cdots r_N) \mid \{p\},\{q\}]. \quad (17)$$

[2] In this section $P_{cr}(N)$ is shorthand for $P_{cr}(N,\infty,\infty)$. Further, throughout the paper, P_{cr} refers to the recognition accuracy for a specific problem and $\bar{P}_{cr}$ refers to the mean accuracy.

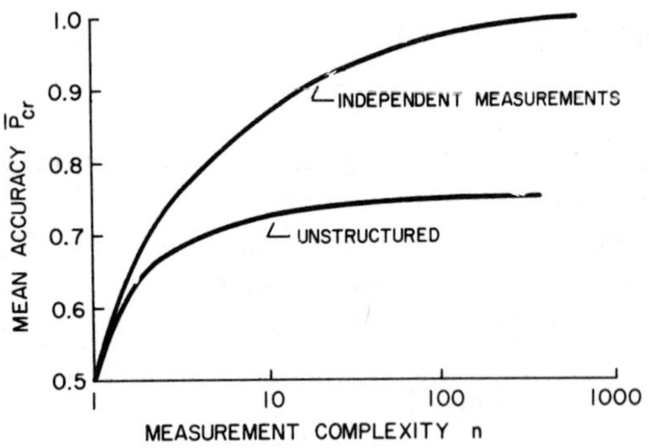

Fig. 1. Effect of independence of measurements; infinite sample size.

Combining (16) and (17),

$$\bar{P}_{cr}(N,m_1,m_2) = (2^{N-1}/(m_1+1)^N(m_2+1)^N) \cdot \sum_{s_1,\cdots,s_N=0}^{m_1} \sum_{r_1,\cdots,r_N=0}^{m_2} g(\bar{r},\bar{s}) \quad (18)$$

where

$$g(\bar{r},\bar{s}) = \max\left\{\prod_{i=1}^{N} [(s_i+1)/(m_1+2)], \prod_{i=1}^{N} [(r_i+1)/(m_2+2)]\right\}. \quad (19)$$

While (18) functionally expresses the variation of $\bar{P}_{cr}$ with N in precise terms, it is, however, rather difficult to interpret directly. It is a subtle function, and it has resisted considerable attempts by the author to reduce its computation to manageable proportions. Even a computer evaluation of $\bar{P}_{cr}$ for, say, $N = 10$, $m_1 = 20$, and $m_2 = 20$ (very reasonable figures), virtually leads to days of computation. However, much of our objective can be achieved, as will be seen, by examining (18) for some interesting values of its arguments.

IV. Effect of Increasing Dimensionality

In order to make the analysis more tractable, examine $\bar{P}_{cr}(N,1,0)$. These extreme values of the arguments have the additional advantage of yielding the following dramatic result.

Proposition:

$$\lim_{N\to\infty} \bar{P}_{cr}(N,1,0) = 1.$$

Proof: From (17) and (18)

$$\bar{P}_{cr}(N,1,0) = \tfrac{1}{2} \sum_{s_1,\cdots,s_N=0}^{1} \max\left\{\prod_{i=1}^{N} ((s_i+1)/3), (1/2^N)\right\}. \quad (20)$$

Choice of j of the s_i to be zero and the remaining $(N-j)$ of the s_i to be unity can be done in $\binom{N}{j}$ ways; hence (20) becomes

$$\bar{P}_{cr}(N,1,0) = \tfrac{1}{2} \sum_{j=0}^{N} \binom{N}{j} \max\{(2^j/3^N),(1/2^N)\}. \quad (21)$$

Note that

$$(2^j/3^N) \gtrless (1/2^N) \text{ according as } j \gtrless N(\log_2 3 - 1) \triangleq aN. \quad (22)$$

For large values of N, (21) can then be approximated by two normal distributions [7], so that

$$\bar{P}_{cr}(N,1,0) \approx \Phi[2\sqrt{N}(a-\tfrac{1}{2})] - \Phi[-\sqrt{N}] + \Phi[\sqrt{\tfrac{1}{2}N}] - \Phi[-((2/3)-a)3(\sqrt{N/2})] \quad (23)$$

where Φ is as defined in (9). Taking the limit of (23) the result follows directly.

Remarks

1) The above proof establishes the monotonicity of $\bar{P}_{cr}(N,1,0)$ after large enough N. A direct evaluation shows that it is true for smaller values of N also.

2) Note that there is just one sample from class c_1, and none at all from class c_2. Still, one can get arbitrarily close to 100 percent recognition accuracy. This is rather remarkable. However, see Section V for the proper perspective on this.

3) As noted earlier, these values for m_1 and m_2 were used both for simplicity as well as for enhancing the point of the result. Through more elaborate processing of (18), the same limit can be shown to hold for $\bar{P}_{cr}(N,1,1)$ and so on. For higher values of m_1 one obtains multinomials in (21) and multidimensional normal distributions in (23). Compare these results with those in [6] and in Section II.

V. Discussion and Conclusions

First, there are a few disclaimers that should serve to place the results in proper perspective. Usually, because of the band-limited nature of all real-world patterns, arbitrarily large numbers of independent measurements are not available. Further, perfect discrimination for infinite N is admittedly a consequence of the *a priori* assumptions on the $\{p\}$ and $\{q\}$. Presumably, one can have *a priori* assumptions such that $\bar{P}_{cr}(N)$ will approach a value less than unity as N tends to infinity. The *a priori* assumptions have the advantage of being similar to those in [2]. The results should be accepted more for their qualitative implications, rather than for their quantitative finality and applicability to design, particularly for large values of N. This is also the case, as was pointed out in [4], for all such results. Hughes's results as well as Gaffey's [6], Chu's and Chueh's [5] are also more valid for understanding certain phenomena, rather than as specific design equations.

What are these qualitative implications? The most important of these is that, in general, one can add any number of independent measurements, however few samples one has. Hughes showed that, in general, this can not be done for measurements of arbitrary correlation. The pessimism of the results for unstructured measurement space is eliminated in our model in two ways: by an effective n_0 of infinity and by a far larger value of $\bar{P}_{cr}$. This was seen already in the infinite sample situation where in place of $\bar{P}_{cr} = 0.75$, $\bar{P}_{cr} = 1$ was obtained. Again in the finite

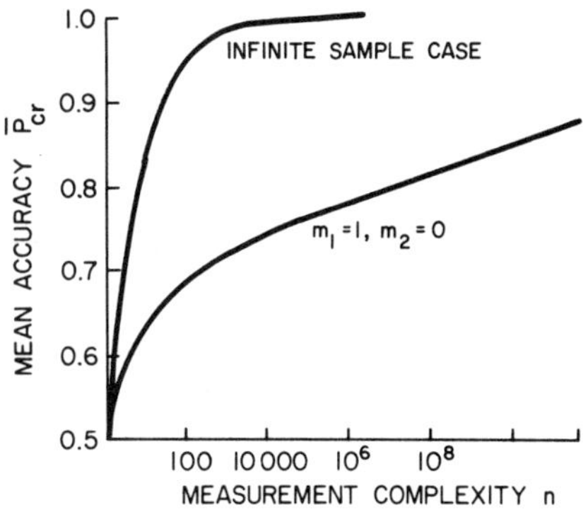

Fig. 2. Comparison of performance rate for infinite and small sample cases; $n = 2^N$.

sample case $\bar{P}_{cr}(\infty,1,0) = 1$, in contrast to hardly any improvement over $\frac{1}{2}$, even for n_0, for the unstructured model. Fig. 2 provides a comparison of these various cases. This figure makes clear the comparative rates at which $\bar{P}_{cr}$ approaches unity for the infinite sample case as against when $m_1 = 1$ and $m_2 = 0$.

Not all the questions relating to independent measurements have been answered, however. Our model is inadequate to handle some of them. A few unanswered questions follow.

1) Do the results remain qualitatively the same, for arbitrary quantization of individual measurements? This situation can be handled by modifying our model suitably. It becomes more elaborate and cumbersome, but it should yield essentially the same qualitative results.

2) Irrespective of the correlation or independence of the variables one has, can the addition of a variable, known to be independent of all the previous ones, be guaranteed not to lead to reduced $\bar{P}_{cr}$, for the same sample size? The modifications in the model necessary to answer this become quite large, and it has not been attempted. Again, the thrust of our results indicates that this question can be answered in the affirmative.

Appendix

In (5), set $p_1 \cdots p_N = z_1$ and $q_1 \cdots q_N = z_2$. It can be shown, after repeated convolutions, that z_1 and z_2, which are identically distributed, have the density function

$$f(z_i) = (1/(N-1)!)(\log(1/z_i))^{N-1}, \qquad 0 \le z \le 1, \quad i = 1,2. \tag{24}$$

One can then write

$$E[|z_1 - z_2|] = \int_{z_2}\int_{z_1=z_2}^{1} (z_1 - z_2) f(z) - \int_{z_2}\int_{0}^{z_1=z_2} (z_1 - z_2) f(z_1) f(z_2)\, dz_1\, dz_2. \tag{25}$$

Substituting (24) in (25) and performing the integration, one obtains from (5)

$$\bar{d}_N = (2^N/3^{2N-1}) \sum_{\nu=0}^{N-1} [2.3^\nu - (3/2)^\nu] \times [\Gamma(2N - \nu - 1)/(\Gamma(N)\Gamma(N-\nu))]. \tag{26}$$

Changing variables in (26) by setting $\nu = N - \zeta$, (6) can be obtained after a few algebraic manipulations.

Acknowledgment

The author is grateful to T. J. Harley, Jr., and K. Abend for discussions relating to this topic.

References

[1] D. C. Allais, "The selection of measurements for prediction," Stanford Electron. Labs., Tech. Rep. 6103–9, Nov. 1964; also available as AD 456770.

[2] G. F. Hughes, "On the mean accuracy of statistical pattern recognizers," *IEEE Trans. Inform. Theory*, vol. IT-14, Jan. 1968, pp. 55–63.

[3] K. Abend, T. J. Harley, Jr., B. Chandrasekaran, and G. F. Hughes, "Comments on 'On the mean accuracy of statistical pattern recognizers'," *IEEE Trans. Inform. Theory* (Corresp.), vol. IT-15, May 1969, pp. 420–423.

[4] L. Kanal and B. Chandrasekaran, "On dimensionality and sample size in statistical pattern classification," in *Proc. 1968 Nat. Electronics Conf.*, pp. 2–7; also, *Pattern Recognition*, to be published.

[5] J. T. Chu and J. C. Chueh, "Error probabilities in decision functions for character recognition," *Ass. Comput. Mach. J.*, vol. 14, Apr. 1967, pp. 273–280.

[6] W. R. Gaffey, "Discriminatory analysis: Perfect discrimination as the number of variables increases," USAF Sch. Aviat. Med., Randolf Field, Tex., Rep. 5, Project 21-49-004, Feb. 1951.

[7] Z. Govindarajulu, "Normal approximations to the classical discrete distributions," in *Classical and Contagious Discrete Distributions*, G. P. Patel, Ed. Calcutta: Statist. Publ. Soc., 1965, pp. 79–108; also, New York: Pergamon.

Correction to "Independence of Measurements and the Mean Recognition Accuracy"

B. CHANDRASEKARAN

In the above paper,[1] on page 157, (16) should read as follows.

$$\Pr\left(\prod_{i=1}^{N} ((s_i+1)/(m_1+2)) > \prod_{i=1}^{N} ((r_i+1)/(m_2+2)) \mid \{p\},\{q\}\right) = \sum_{\text{over } S>R} \Pr(s_1,\cdots,s_N,r_1,\cdots,r_N \mid \{p\},\{q\}), \tag{16}$$

where

$$S = \prod_{i=1}^{N} ((s_i+1)/(m_1+2))$$

$$R = \prod_{i=1}^{N} ((r_i+1)/(m_2+2)).$$

Equation (17) should then become

$$P_{cr}(x) = \tfrac{1}{2}\{E[p_1 \cdots p_N \Pr(S > R) \mid \{p\},\{q\}] + E[q_1 \cdots q_N \Pr(S \le R) \mid \{p\},\{q\}]\}. \tag{17}$$

Equations (18) and (19), as well as the results of the paper, remain unchanged.

Manuscript received July 13, 1971.
The author is with the Department of Computer and Information Science, Ohio State University, Columbus, Ohio 43210.
[1] B. Chandrasekaran, *IEEE Trans. Inform. Theory*, vol. IT-17, July 1971, pp. 452–456.

The Mean Accuracy of Pattern Recognizers with Many Pattern Classes

***Abstract*—Hughes [1] presented some curves relating the mean performance of a pattern classifier averaged over all pattern recognition problems of given complexity, when there are two classes of patterns to be distinguished. In this correspondence the mean recognition probability is computed for the case of q pattern classes when the a priori probabilities of the classes are equal. When the a priori probabilities are unequal, the mean performance will improve over the performance with equal a priori probabilities, so these curves provide a lower bound to the performance of recognizers with more than two pattern classes. Some comments on the appropriateness of these statistics to common recognition problems are made.**

We follow the model of Hughes [1], and let the result of the measurement be expressed as a single discrete quantity having one of the n values, $x_1, x_2, \cdots, x_n$. Then this recognizer solves a recognition problem of *complexity* n. Furthermore, let c_i represent the ith class of patterns. The recognizer can be optimized (maximizing the a posteriori probabilities), if the a priori probabilities of the classes and the conditional probabilities $P(x_j \mid c_i)$ are known, where $P(x_j \mid c_i)$ is the probability that the measurement value x_j is measured from a pattern of class c_i. A recognition problem is specified if these conditional probabilities and the a priori pattern class probabilities are known. We will average over all problems with the same a priori pattern class probabilities. Furthermore, we assume that these problems are all equally likely.

Let p_l be the a priori probability of class l. Then the probability of correct recognition is

$$P_{cr} = \sum_{i=1}^{n} \max_k \left[P(x_i \mid c_k) p_k\right]. \tag{1}$$

The objective is to find the average value of P_{cr} when averaged over all possible unknown patterns, with all possible problems of complexity n.

Let

$$u_{ij} \equiv P(x_i \mid c_j). \tag{2}$$

The mean recognition accuracy is found from [1, (13)]

$$\bar{P} = n(n-1)^q \int_0^1 \int_0^1 \cdots \int_0^1 \prod_{k=1}^{q} (1 - u_{1k})^{n-2} \cdot \max\left[p_1 u_{11}, \cdots, p_q u_{1q}\right] du_{11}\, du_{12} \cdots du_{1q}. \tag{3}$$

When the a priori probabilities p_j are unequal, this integral can only be evaluated as a $(q-1)$-fold summation. Therefore, we will consider the equal a priori case only; where

$$p_j = \frac{1}{q} \qquad (j = 1, \cdots, q). \tag{4}$$

In this case, (3) simplifies to

$$\bar{P}(q, n) = \frac{n(n-1)^q}{q} \int_0^1 \int_0^1 \cdots \int_0^1 \prod_{k=1}^{q} (1 - u_{1k})^{n-2} \cdot \max\left[u_{11}, \cdots, u_{1q}\right] du_{11}\, du_{12} \cdots du_{1q}. \tag{5}$$

We evaluate (5) by finding two recursion relations that must be satisfied, and then by showing the functional forms that satisfy the recursion relations.

Manuscript received October 9, 1968; revised November 5, 1968. This work was performed in connection with Project THEMIS, ONR Contract N00014-68-A-0141-0002.

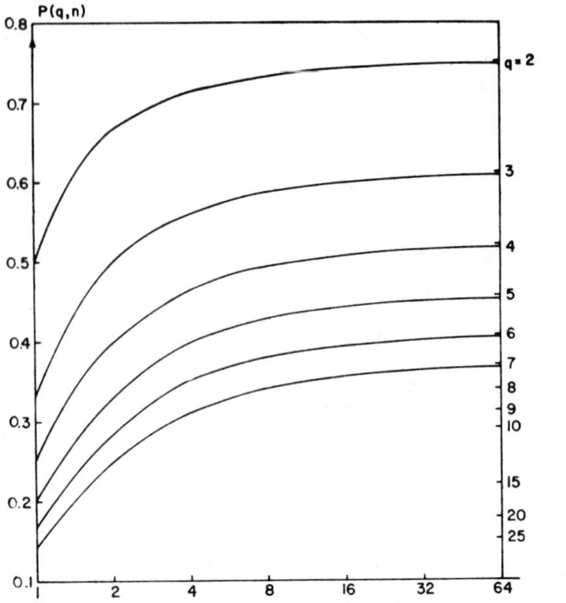

Fig. 1. Average probability of correct recognition among q equiprobable pattern classes, as a function of the complexity of the problem, n. The horizontal dashes indicate the asymptotic values of $\bar{P}$ as $n \to \infty$, for various values of q.

The recursion for $\bar{P}(q, n)$ is obtained by integrating with respect to u_{1q} to obtain

$$\bar{P}(q, n) = \frac{(q-1)}{q} \bar{P}(q-1, n) + \frac{1}{q} R(q, n, n), \tag{6}$$

where

$$R(i, j, n) = (n-1)^i \cdot \int_0^1 \int_0^1 \cdots \int_0^1 \{(1 - \max[u_{11}, \cdots, u_{1i}]\}^j \cdot \prod_{k=1}^{i} \left[(1 - u_{1k})^{n-2}\, du_{1k}\right]. \tag{7}$$

Next we find a recursion relation for the R function, by performing an integration with respect to u_{1i}, to obtain

$$R(i, j, n) = R(i-1, j, n) - \frac{j}{n+j-1} R(i-1, n+j-1, n). \tag{8}$$

The starting values for the recursions are found by direct integration to be

$$\bar{P}(2, n) = \frac{3n-2}{4n-2}, \tag{9}$$

$$R(1, j, n) = \frac{n-1}{n+j-1}. \tag{10}$$

The general forms of P and R are given by

$$\bar{P}(q, n) = \frac{1}{q}\left[1 + \sum_{t=1}^{q-1} \frac{t!(n-1)^t}{\prod_{s=1}^{t} (sn + n - s)}\right] \tag{11}$$

$$R(i, j, n) = \frac{i!(n-1)^i}{\prod_{k=1}^{i} (nk + j - k)}. \tag{12}$$

Reprinted from *IEEE Trans. Inform. Theory*, vol. IT-15, pp. 424–425, May 1969.

Graphs of $\bar{P}(q, n)$ are shown in Fig. 1 for selected values of q. The best average performance is obtained by making n large, in which case $\bar{P}$ is given by

$$\bar{P} = \frac{1}{q}\left[1 + \frac{1}{2} + \frac{1}{3} + \cdots + \frac{1}{q}\right]. \qquad (13)$$

This asymptotic value is indicated by horizontal dashes in Fig. 1 for some values of q. When the complexity is equal to the number of classes, the average performance is approximately 90 percent of the best average performance given by (13).

We have computed the average recognition probability of optimum recognizers for pattern classification problems of given complexity, th q pattern classes, and have shown how the performance deteriorates with increasing q. It is important to observe that there are a large number of pattern classification problems included in the average that are so difficult that humans would not consider the classes so defined to be different. In simple terms, the pattern recognition problems that people care about necessarily lie far above these low means, and the average statistics, though interesting, are not helpful in practical problems.

Acknowledgment

The author has been helped by discussions with Prof. J. H. Park, Jr.

R. Y. Kain
Dept. of Elec. Engrg.
University of Minnesota
Minneapolis, Minn. 55455

References

[1] G. F. Hughes, "On the mean accuracy of statistical pattern recognizers," *IEEE Trans. Information Theory*, vol. IT-14, pp. 55–63, January 1968.

An Optimal Discriminant Plane

JOHN W. SAMMON, JR., MEMBER, IEEE

Abstract—In solving pattern classification problems, many researchers have successfully used the Fisher linear discriminant as the optimal linear method for discriminating between vector samples from two classes. With the introduction of on-line, interactive, graphic systems, it has become conveniently possible to extend the discrimination logic to piecewise linear methods. This paper describes such a method which is being used in the on-line pattern analysis and recognition system (OLPARS).

Index Terms—Dimensionality reductions, discriminants, graphic systems, multivariate data analysis, on-line systems, pattern recognition.

In solving pattern classification problems, many researchers have used the Fisher linear discriminant [1] as the optimal linear method for discriminating between vector samples from two classes. When applying linear discriminant analysis to the two-class problem ($K=2$), we seek to compute a direction $\boldsymbol{d}$ in the L-space defined by a set of L measurements so that orthogonally projected samples from the two classes onto $\boldsymbol{d}$ are maximally discriminated. The orthogonal projection of a vector $\boldsymbol{X}$ onto the direction $\boldsymbol{d}$ is given by (1).

$$z = \langle \boldsymbol{d}, \boldsymbol{X} \rangle = \boldsymbol{d}^T \boldsymbol{X} = \sum_{j=1}^{L} d_j x_j \tag{1}$$

where

$$\sum_{j=1}^{L} d_j^2 = 1$$

$$\boldsymbol{d} = \begin{bmatrix} d_1 \\ d_2 \\ \vdots \\ d_L \end{bmatrix} \updownarrow L \qquad \boldsymbol{X} = \begin{bmatrix} x_1 \\ x_2 \\ \vdots \\ x_L \end{bmatrix} \updownarrow L.$$

The discrimination criterion suggested by Fisher [4] is related to the ratio of the projected class differences relative to the sum of the projected within-class variability. Specifically, the Fisher discriminant is obtained by solving for the unit vector $\boldsymbol{d}$ which maximizes the ratio in (2).

$$R = \frac{\boldsymbol{d}^T B \boldsymbol{d}}{\boldsymbol{d}^T W \boldsymbol{d}}. \tag{2}$$

B is the between-class scatter matrix which is defined in (3) and W is the sum of the within-class scatter matrices defined in (4).

$$\begin{aligned} B &= \sum_{p=1}^{2} N_p [\boldsymbol{\mu}_p - \boldsymbol{\mu}][\boldsymbol{\mu}_p - \boldsymbol{\mu}]^T \\ &= \frac{N_1 N_2}{N} [\boldsymbol{\mu}_1 - \boldsymbol{\mu}_2][\boldsymbol{\mu}_1 - \boldsymbol{\mu}_2]^T \end{aligned} \tag{3}$$

Manuscript received November 17, 1969; revised January 27, 1970.

The author is with Computer Symbolic, Inc., a Division of NCS Computing Corporation, Rome, N. Y., and Syracuse University, Syracuse, N. Y.

where

$\boldsymbol{\mu}_p =$ the mean vector of class p

$\boldsymbol{\mu} = \sum_{p=1}^{2} \frac{N_p}{N} \boldsymbol{\mu}_p =$ the lumped data mean vector

$N_i =$ the number of samples from class i

$N =$ the total number of samples $= N_1 + N_2$.

$$\begin{aligned} W &= S_1 + S_2 \\ S_i &= D_i D_i^T \end{aligned} \tag{4}$$

$$D_i = \overbrace{\left[(\boldsymbol{X}_1^{(i)} - \boldsymbol{\mu}_i)(\boldsymbol{X}_2^{(i)} - \boldsymbol{\mu}_i) \cdots (\boldsymbol{X}_{N_i}^{(i)} - \boldsymbol{\mu}_i) \right]}^{N_i} \updownarrow L$$

$$\boldsymbol{X}_n^{(i)} = \begin{bmatrix} x_{1n}^{(i)} \\ x_{2n}^{(i)} \\ \vdots \\ x_{Ln}^{(i)} \end{bmatrix} = \text{the } n\text{th vector from class } i.$$

In order to solve for the Fisher direction, we take the vector derivative of the ratio R (2) with respect to $\boldsymbol{d}$ and set the resultant equation to zero. This procedure generates the generalized eigenvector equation given in (5).

$$[B - \lambda W]\boldsymbol{d} = 0. \tag{5}$$

The solution is obtained by solving for the eigenvectors of (5). The rank of the between-class scatter matrix for the two-class discrimination problem is one and therefore *only one nonzero* eigenvalue solution to (5) exists. The eigenvector solution corresponding to the nonzero eigenvalue is the Fisher direction and is given in (6).

$$\begin{aligned} \boldsymbol{d} &= \alpha W^{-1}[\boldsymbol{\mu}_1 - \boldsymbol{\mu}_2] = W^{-1}\boldsymbol{\Delta} \\ \boldsymbol{\Delta} &= \boldsymbol{\mu}_1 - \boldsymbol{\mu}_2 \end{aligned} \tag{6}$$

where α is a normalizing constant such that $|\boldsymbol{d}| = 1$. The eigenvalue solution corresponds to the maximum discrimination

$$\lambda = \frac{\boldsymbol{d}^T B \boldsymbol{d}}{\boldsymbol{d}^T W \boldsymbol{d}} = \frac{N_1 N_2}{N} (\boldsymbol{\mu}_1 - \boldsymbol{\mu}_2)^T W^{-1} (\boldsymbol{\mu}_1 - \boldsymbol{\mu}_2). \tag{7}$$

Thus, the optimal Fisher direction is proportional to the inverse of the sum of the within-class scatter matrix times the difference in the mean vectors. It should be noted that W is nonsingular only if the lumped data does not lie in some linear subspace of the L-dimensional measurement space. If this condition approximately exists, the numerical stability of most inversion algorithms becomes tenuous. In these cases, our program will automatically project the data orthogonally onto a linearly independent subspace where W will be nonsingular. The discriminant solution is then computed in the subspace. In order to complete the two-class pattern classification problem a threshold (or thresh-

Reprinted from *IEEE Trans. Comput.*, vol. C-19, pp. 826–829, Sept. 1970.

olds if a reject region is used) must be specified such that the following decision is made: decide class 1 iff $\boldsymbol{d}^T\boldsymbol{X} \geq \theta$, otherwise decide class 2. The threshold θ can be computed using a minimum risk criterion or any other criterion which seems satisfactory to the researcher. In any event, the computation of the direction $\boldsymbol{d}$ and a threshold θ define a hyperplane which divides the L-space into two decision regions.

The distribution-free logic design module of the on-line pattern analysis and recognition system (OLPARS) [2], [3] makes extensive use of the Fisher linear discriminant in solving pattern classification problems. OLPARS is a large interactive graphics-oriented system which is used for both analyzing high-dimensional vector data and for designing decision logic to discriminate between K classes. When solving a pattern classification problem the OLPARS user is given several options for designing and testing decision logic. One such option, in essence, constructs the logic shown in Fig. 1 where $K(K-1)/2$ pairwise Fisher discriminants and their respective thresholds are computed. The output from the d_{ij} box is either zero or one depending on the following criterion:

$$d_{ij}(X) = \begin{cases} 1 & \langle \boldsymbol{d}_{ij}, \boldsymbol{X}\rangle - \theta_{ij} \geq 0 \\ 0 & \text{otherwise.} \end{cases} \tag{8}$$

The signed direction ($\pm$) of $\boldsymbol{d}_{ij}$ and the threshold θ_{ij} are selected so that an output of "one" is interpreted as a vote for class i and a "zero" as a vote for class j. The I box is an inverter which produces a "one" out given a "zero" in, or a "zero" out given a "one" in. The votes for each class are collected and a final decision made in accord with the class having the most votes. Ties are resolved by changing the vote of that discriminant d_{ij} which is involved in the tie whose projected scalar is closest to its respective threshold θ_{ij}. Suppose, for example, that classes i and j are tied (i.e., have the same number of votes) with the maximum number of votes. The system would then examine the set

$$S = \{|\langle \boldsymbol{d}_{pj}, \boldsymbol{X}\rangle - \theta_{pj}|_{p<j}, |\langle \boldsymbol{d}_{jp}, \boldsymbol{X}\rangle - \theta_{jp}|_{p>j}, |\langle \boldsymbol{d}_{pi}, \boldsymbol{X}\rangle - \theta_{pi}|_{p<i}, |\langle \boldsymbol{d}_{ip}, \boldsymbol{X}\rangle - \theta_{ip}|_{p>i}\} \text{ all } p.$$

This set will reference the indices of all the discriminants contributing to the present tie. Next, the system would alter the vote of that discriminant function corresponding to $\min_p S$. Provisions are made to continue this procedure should a new tie situation arise. In addition, the tie breaking algorithm functions so as to guarantee a unique decision; that is, the system forces convergence of this procedure.

In those cases where the Fisher linear discriminant does not yield satisfactory discrimination, it has been found useful to replace the linear logic with piecewise linear logic. In the OLPARS system, this is accomplished by orthogonally projecting the data onto an *optimal discrimination plane* and then designing a decision boundary using piecewise linear line segments. This procedure is easily accomplished by interactive graphic systems such as OLPARS. The user simply designates the pair of classes to be used and

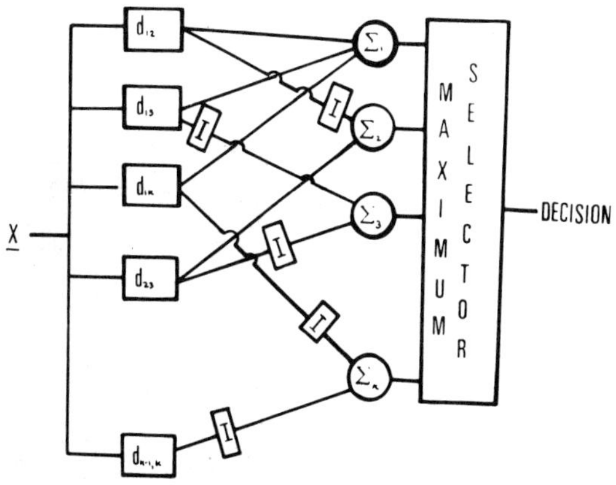

Fig. 1. Discrimination logic.

then requires the system to compute the orthogonal projection of the data onto the optimal discriminant plane. The resultant scatter diagram is then displayed on the CRT. Since OLPARS is an interactive system, the user can designate the discrimination boundary by drawing piecewise linear connected line segments which partition the data in the discriminant plane. The end points of the line segments are designed by using a movable cursor which is appropriately positioned on the CRT display. The OLPARS system, having stored the vector designation of the optimal plane (i.e., two orthogonal unit vectors plus an origin), computes the corresponding piecewise linear hyperplane boundaries. In OLPARS, the user is restricted to using up to five linear segments which must describe a convex boundary with respect to one of the two classes. Once this boundary is specified, the user may replace the corresponding linear discriminant of Fig. 1 with the new piecewise linear boundary.

The discrimination plane used in OLPARS is defined by two orthogonal unit vectors through the data origin. It is considered optimal in the sense that the two unit vectors are determined by maximizing the discrimination ratio R (2) under different constraints. The x axis of the optimal plane is the Fisher discriminant vector $\boldsymbol{d}_1 = \alpha W^{-1}(\boldsymbol{\mu}_1 - \boldsymbol{\mu}_2)$. The second direction is found by maximizing the discrimination ratio R under the constraint that this second direction $\boldsymbol{d}_2$ be orthogonal to the Fisher direction $\boldsymbol{d}_1$. The derivation goes as follows; we wish to maximize

$$\frac{\boldsymbol{d}_2^T B \boldsymbol{d}_2}{\boldsymbol{d}_2^T W \boldsymbol{d}_2} - \lambda[\boldsymbol{d}_2^T \boldsymbol{d}_1] \tag{9}$$

where λ is the Lagrange multiplier. Taking the vector derivative with respect to $\boldsymbol{d}_2$ and solving the resultant equation yields

$$\boldsymbol{d}_2 = \gamma\left[W^{-1} - \frac{\boldsymbol{\Delta}^T[W^{-1}]^2\boldsymbol{\Delta}}{\boldsymbol{\Delta}^T[W^{-1}]^3\boldsymbol{\Delta}}[W^{-1}]^2\right]\boldsymbol{\Delta} \tag{10}$$

where γ is a normalizing constant.

One of the present applications of the OLPARS system is the design of a decision logic for classification of unconstrained handprinted numeric characters. The handprinted character is first located, normalized, edited, and finally

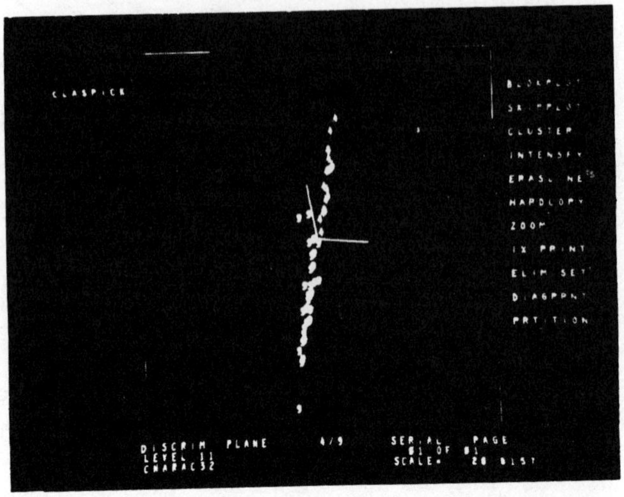

Fig. 2. CRT display of discriminant plane—classes 4 and 9.

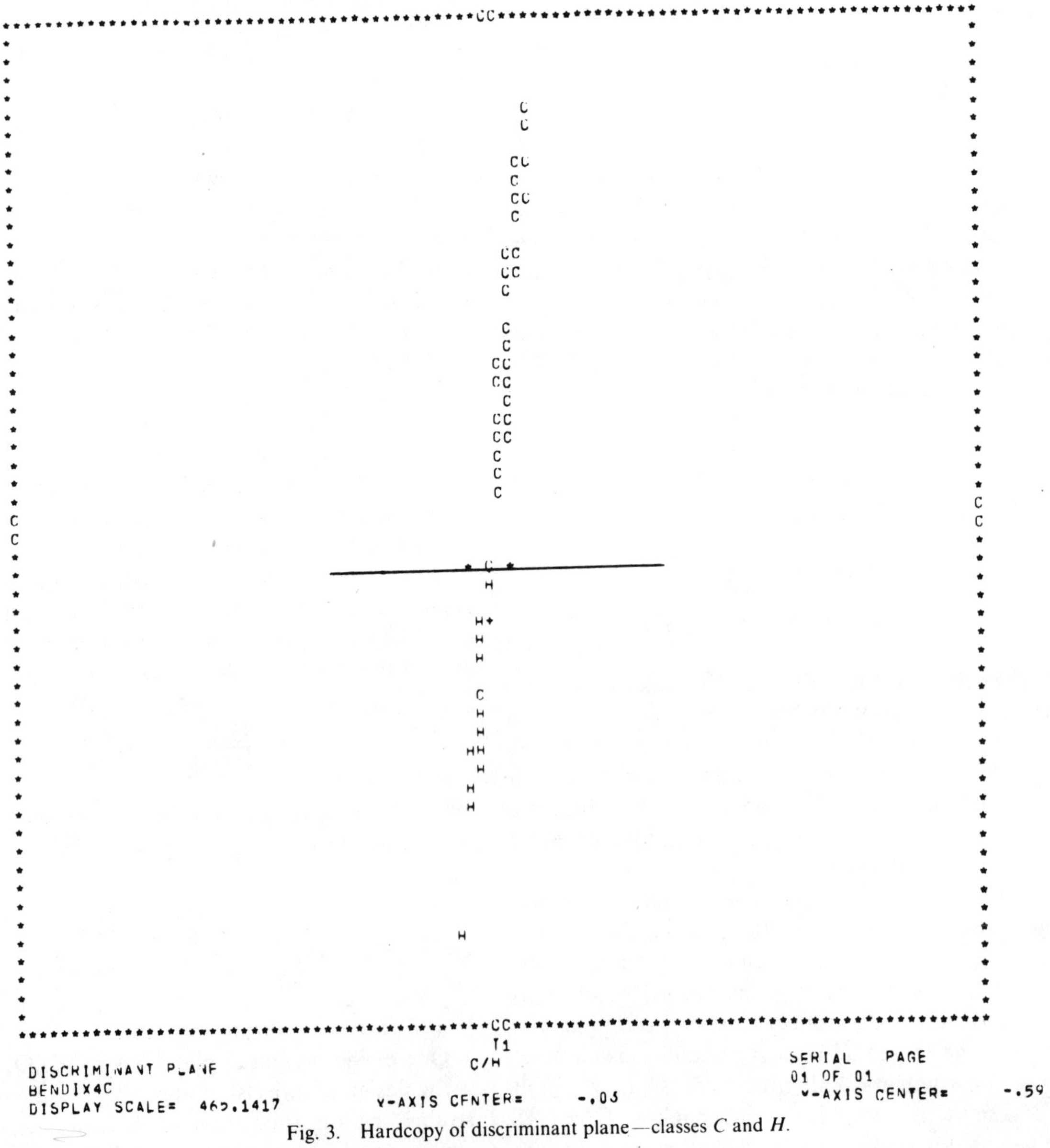

Fig. 3. Hardcopy of discriminant plane—classes C and H.

transformed into a vector composed of 20 measurements.[1] The pairwise Fisher logic shown in Fig. 1 was then computed for all ten numeric classes ($K=10$). In several instances, it was found that the pairwise linear logic used to discriminate a pair of classes produced several errors. In these cases the on-line user requested the system to project the classes in question onto their discriminant plane. Fig. 2 shows the CRT display of the classes four and nine orthogonally projected onto the 4/9 discriminant plane. The Fisher direction corresponds to the x axis and the Fisher linear discrimination boundary is a straight line parallel to the y axis located precisely in the center of the display. The individual variance (or scatter) of the two classes along the x axis is quite small relative to the difference between the class means, thereby accounting for the computation of the x axis as the Fisher direction. An improved discrimination boundary was constructed by drawing the two lines shown in Fig. 2. Upon completing this task, the on-line user selected the partition option by light gunning the PARTITION message displayed along the right side of the display. This action caused the system to replace the previously stored 4/9 Fisher discriminant with the new piecewise linear boundary.

The discriminant plane has proven of enormous value in solving the handprinted character recognition problem. The above example of fours versus nines is not considered particularly unusual since a similar deficiency of the single Fisher discriminant has occurred in approximately 4 percent of all handprinted character pairwise discriminations.

The single Fisher discriminant has occasionally been found lacking for data sets other than the handprint one. OLPARS has been used to design discrimination logic for classifying planimetric features in aerial photography. For this problem, we wished to design logic to automatically recognize four types of planimetric features; namely, hydrographic features H, cultivated features C, vegetated features V, and urban features U. Samples of these classes were obtained by scanning small areas of aerial photographs containing a specified planimetric type [5]. Eventually, 24 measurements related to the spacial frequencies contained in the scanned area were used to represent a sample. The four-class, 24-dimensional data was input to OLPARS and the Fisher pairwise logic computed. The classes of C and H were projected onto the C/H discriminant plane to determine whether the logic could be improved. A hard copy of the resulting display is shown in Fig. 3. As before, the Fisher linear discriminant boundary corresponds to a line parallel to the y axis located precisely in the middle of the display. A + sign in this display corresponds to an overprint of a C and an H. One error was eliminated by replacing the Fisher boundary with the linear boundary connecting the two printed ★'s. (The stars are printed to mark the end points of the lines constructed on the CRT.)

In summary, we have found that the additional degree of freedom provided by the discriminant plane offers a significant advantage over the single Fisher discriminant in those cases where the pair of classes have long elliptically shaped convex hulls relatively placed as shown in Figs. 2 and 3.

[1] A more detailed discussion of the handprinted character recognition problem is contained in [3].

References

[1] R. A. Fisher, "The use of multiple measurements in taxonomic problems," *Ann. Eugen.*, vol. 7, pp. 179–188, September 1936.

[2] J. W. Sammon, Jr., "On-line pattern analysis and recognition system," Rome Air Development Center, Rome, N. Y., Tech. Rept. RADC-TDR-68-263, August 1968.

[3] ——, "Interactive pattern analysis and classification," *IEEE Trans. Computers*, vol. C-19, pp. 594–616, July 1970.

[4] S. S. Wilks, *Mathematical Statistics.* New York: Wiley, 1962, pp. 573–581.

[5] A. E. Whiteside and E. D. Hietanen, "Automatic planimetry extraction," Rome Air Development Center, Rome, N. Y., Tech. Rept. RADC-TR-67-412, October 1967.

A Nonlinear Mapping for Data Structure Analysis

JOHN W. SAMMON, JR.

Abstract—An algorithm for the analysis of multivariate data is presented along with some experimental results. The algorithm is based upon a point mapping of N L-dimensional vectors from the L-space to a lower-dimensional space such that the inherent data "structure" is approximately preserved.

Index Terms—Clustering, dimensionality reduction, mappings, multidimensional scaling, multivariate data analysis, nonparametric, pattern recognition, statistics.

INTRODUCTION

THE purpose of this paper is to describe the nonlinear mapping algorithm (NLM) which has been found to be highly effective in the analysis of multivariate data. The analysis problem is to detect and identify "structure" which may be present in a list of N L-dimensional vectors. Here the word structure refers to geometric relationships among subsets of the data vectors in the L-space. Some examples of structure are hyperspherical and hyperellipsoidal clusters, and linear and certain nonlinear relationships among the vectors of some subset.

The algorithm is based upon a point mapping of the N L-dimensional vectors from the L-space to a lower-dimensional space such that the inherent structure of the data is approximately preserved under the mapping. The approximate structure preservation is maintained by fitting N points in the lower-dimensional space such that their interpoint distances approximate the corresponding interpoint distances in the L-space. We shall be primarily interested in mappings to 2- and 3-dimensional spaces since the resultant data configuration can easily be evaluated by human observations in 3 or less dimensions.

THE NONLINEAR MAPPING

Suppose that we have N vectors in an L-space designated X_i, $i=1, \cdots, N$ and corresponding to these we define N vectors in a d-space ($d=2$ or 3) designated Y_i, $i=1, \cdots, N$. Let the distance[1] between the vectors X_i and X_j in the L-space be defined by $d_{ij}^* \equiv \text{dist}[X_i, X_j]$ and the distance between the corresponding vectors Y_i and Y_j in the d-space be defined by $d_{ij} \equiv \text{dist}[Y_i, Y_j]$. Let us now randomly[2] choose an initial d-space configuration for the Y vectors and denote the configuration as follows:

$$Y_1 = \begin{bmatrix} y_{11} \\ \cdot \\ \cdot \\ \cdot \\ y_{1d} \end{bmatrix} \quad Y_2 = \begin{bmatrix} y_{21} \\ \cdot \\ \cdot \\ \cdot \\ y_{2d} \end{bmatrix} \cdots Y_N = \begin{bmatrix} y_{N1} \\ \cdot \\ \cdot \\ \cdot \\ y_{Nd} \end{bmatrix}$$

Next we compute all the d-space interpoint distances d_{ij}, which are then used to define an error E, which represents how well the present configuration of N points in the d-space fits the N points in the L-space, i.e.,

$$E = \frac{1}{\sum\limits_{i<j} [d_{ij}^*]} \sum_{i<j}^{N} \frac{[d_{ij}^* - d_{ij}]^2}{d_{ij}^*}. \tag{1}$$

Note that the error is a function of the $d \times N$ variables y_{pq}, $p=1, \cdots, N$ and $q=1, \cdots, d$. The next step in the NLM algorithm is to adjust the y_{pq} variables or equivalently change the d-space configuration so as to decrease the error. We use a steepest descent procedure to search for a minimum of the error (see Appendix I for further details).

SOME COMPUTER RESULTS

We have exercised the nonlinear mapping algorithm on several data sets in order to test and evaluate the utility of the program in detecting and identifying structure in data. Some of the results obtained for several different artificially generated data sets[3] are reported for the case where $d=2$. We have also run the algorithm on many real data sets and have achieved highly satisfactory results; however, for demonstration purposes it is useful to work with artificially generated data in order that we can compare our results with the known data structure. The test data sets were as follows.

1) *Straight Line Data:* These data consisted of nine points distributed along a line in a 9-dimensional space. The data points were spaced evenly along the line with an interpoint Euclidean distance of $\sqrt{9}$ units. The initial 2-space configuration was chosen randomly.

Manuscript received August 26, 1968; revised February 2, 1969.
The author was with Rome Air Development Center, Griffiss AFB, Rome, N. Y. He is now with Computer Symbolic, Inc., Rome, N. Y.

[1] Any distance measure could be used; however, if we have no a priori knowledge concerning the data, we would have no reason to prefer any metric over the Euclidean metric. Thus, this algorithm uses the Euclidean distance measure.

[2] For the purpose of this discussion it is convenient to think of the starting configuration as being selected randomly; however, in practice the initial configuration for the vectors is found by projecting the L-dimensional data orthogonally onto a d-space spanned by the d original coordinates with the largest variances.

[3] One exception is data set 3 which is a classical data set. This data set was not artificially generated.

Reprinted from *IEEE Trans. Comput.*, vol. C-18, pp. 401–409, May 1969.

2) *Circular Data:* The data consisted of nine points, eight of which were spaced evenly (45° apart) along a circle of radius 2.5 units in a 2-dimensional space. The ninth point was placed at the center of the circle. The initial 2-space configuration was chosen randomly.

3) *Iris Data:* This data set is fairly well-known since it was used by Fisher [4] in several statistical experiments. The data were originally obtained by making four measurements on Iris flowers. These measurements were then used to classify three different species of Iris flowers. Fifty sample vectors were obtained from each of the three species. Thus, the data set consists of 150 points distributed in a 4-dimensional space.

4) *Gaussian Data Distributed at the Vertices of a Simplex:* These data consist of 75 points distributed in a 4-dimensional space. There are five spherical Gaussian distributions which have their respective mean vectors located at the vertices of a 4-dimensional simplex.[4] The intervertex distance is $\sqrt{5/4}$ units and each covariance matrix is diagonal with a standard deviation along every coordinate of 0.2 unit. Fifteen points were generated from each of the five Gaussian distributions, making a total of 75 points.

5) *Helix Data:* This data set consisted of 30 points distributed along a 3-dimensional helix. The parametric equations for this helix are

$$X = \cos Z$$
$$Y = \sin Z$$
$$Z = \frac{\sqrt{2}}{2} t.$$

The points are distributed at one-unit intervals along the curve (i.e., $t=0, 1, 2, \cdots, 29$).

6) *Nonlinear Data:* This data set consisted of 29 points distributed evenly along a 5-dimensional curve. The parametric equations for this curve are

$$X = \cos Z$$
$$Y = \sin Z$$
$$U = 0.5 \cos 2Z$$
$$V = 0.5 \sin 2Z$$
$$Z = \frac{\sqrt{2}}{2} t.$$

The points were distributed at one-unit intervals along the curve (i.e., $t=0, 1, \cdots, 28$).

Figs. 1 through 9 display the results obtained using the nonlinear mapping algorithm. Convergence was essentially obtained for each case in twenty or less iterations using the gradient searching technique described in Appendix I. As was expected, the data structure inherent in both data sets 1 and 2 was faithfully reproduced under the mapping (see Figs. 1 and 2). This was expected since the data sets are 1- and 2-dimensional, respectively, and therefore a mapping to a 2-space can be accomplished with zero error. In both cases the final error was 10^{-16}.

Observing the result of the Iris data mapping (Fig. 3), we can essentially detect the three species of Iris. The final error was 2×10^{-3} which is considered quite small.

The results obtained on the simplex data (data set 4) were quite interesting. The result of the mapping clearly showed the presence of five clusters (see Fig. 4). However, when we compare this result with the projection of the same data onto the 2-space defined by the two largest eigenvectors of the estimated data covariance matrix, we can only detect four clusters. Two of the clusters overlap completely in the 2-space which fits the data in the least squares sense (see Fig. 5). The resulting NLM error was 0.05. The same experiment has been conducted using Gaussian data distributed at the vertices of higher-dimensional simplexes. Figs. 6 and 7 show the NLM and principal eigenvector plots, respectively, for a 19-dimensional Gaussian simplex distribution. These experiments indicate that for some data sets, the NLM is superior to eigenvector projections for data structure analysis.

The results shown in Figs. 8 and 9 clearly indicate the "string structure" in data sets 5 and 6, respectively. The mapping error for the helix data was 6×10^{-4}. The error for data set 6 was 1.6×10^{-3}.

The utility of any data analysis technique is somehow more convincing when applied to "real" data as opposed to artificially generated data, presuming, of course, that the analysis results are correct. For this reason, the application of the NLM algorithm to an experiment in document retrieval by content is reported here.

The experiment, conducted jointly by Rome Air Development Center (RADC) and the University of Colorado, involved the construction of a document classification space (referred to as the *C*-space) where every document in the library was represented as a 17-dimensional vector. The construction technique devised by Ossorio [8], [9] describes a mapping of 1125 preselected words and phrases into the *C*-space. Documents, or equivalently retrieval requests, were located in the space by computing the vector average of the corresponding key words or phrases which were contained in the document or the request. Retrieval was accomplished by rank-ordering the relevance of the library documents to a given request. The relevance measure was computed using the Euclidean metric between the document vectors and the request vector, the concept being that document vectors which are close in the *C*-space are related by content and therefore should be retrieved together.

[4] The vertices of a simplex are all equidistant from one another as well as from the origin.

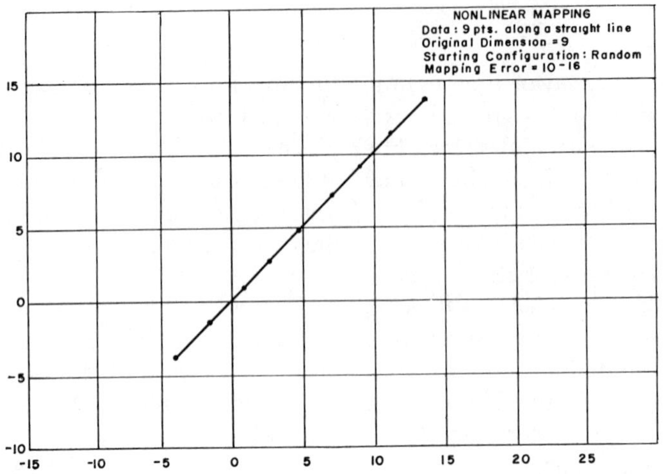

Fig. 1.

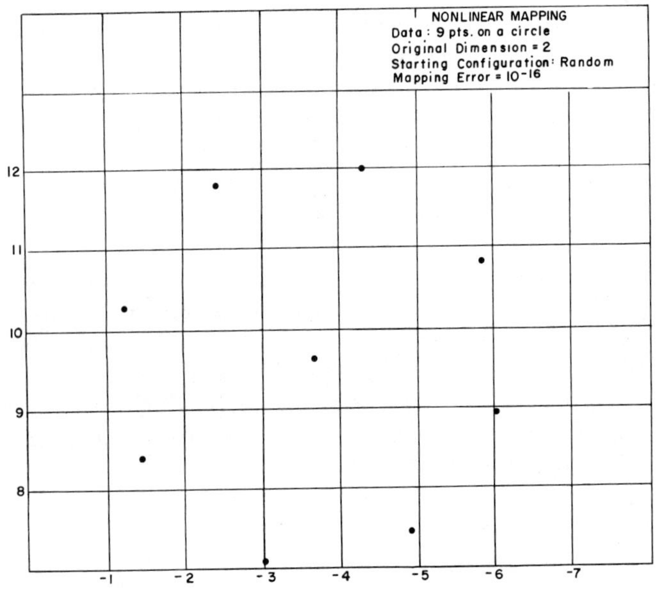

Fig. 2.

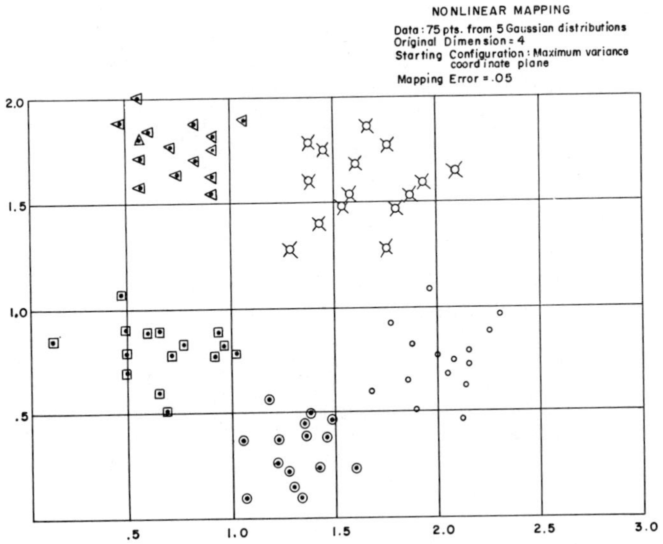

Fig. 4.

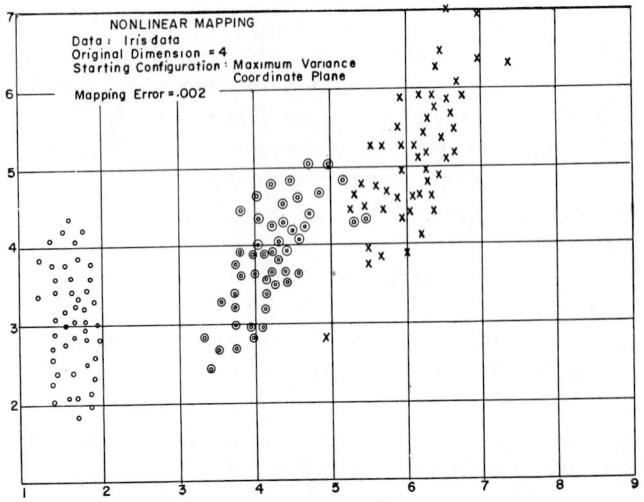

Fig. 3.

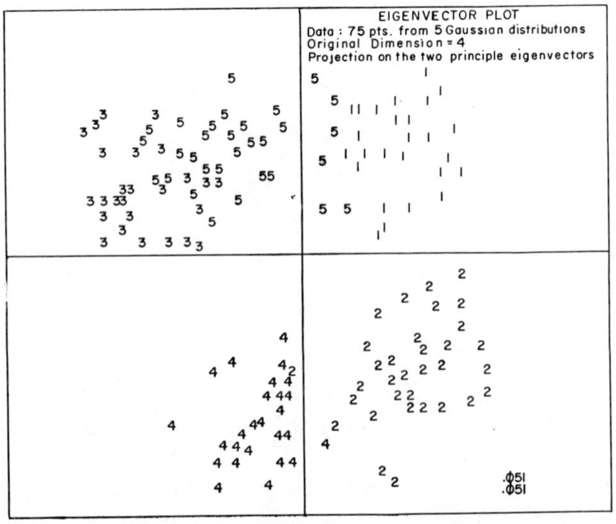

Fig. 5.

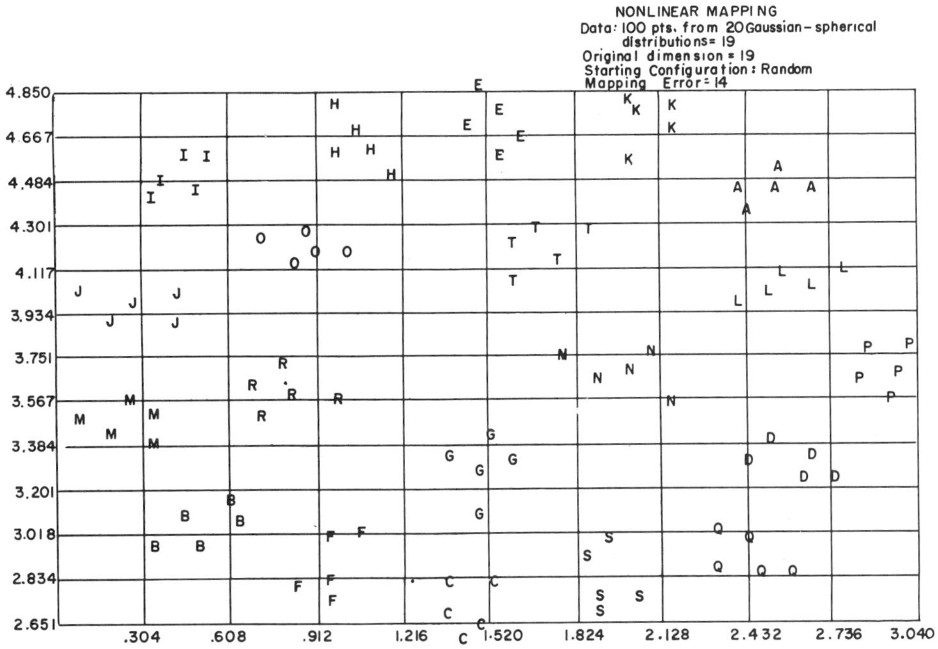

Fig. 6.

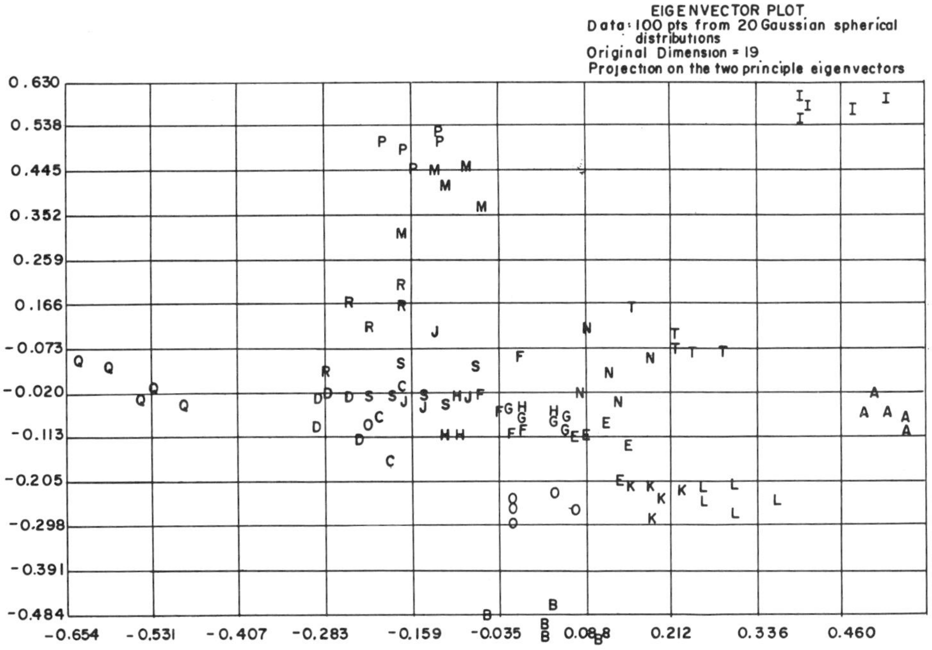

Fig. 7.

Briefly, the C-space construction proceeded as follows. First the subject content covered by the 188 documents in the experimental library was subjectively partitioned into 23 technical fields (see Appendix II for a listing of these fields). Several experts representing each field rated the relevance of each of the 1125 words or phrases to his field, using a scale from 0 to 8. The rating by the experts within each field were then averaged to obtain a word-by-field relevance matrix designated X; the ijth element of X represents the relevance of word or phrase i to field j. (It is convenient to think of the 1125 words or phrases as being represented by vectors in a 23-dimensional space spanned by the 23 coordinate fields.) Next, a 23×23 field correlation matrix C was computed, where the ijth element represented the correlation between the ith and jth fields. C was then factored using the minimum residual method and rotated to a Varimax criterion. Seventeen orthogonal factors were then selected to define the 17-dimensional C-space.

All 1125 words and phrase vectors were mapped into the 17-dimensional C-space using a simple nonlinear formula which tended to emphasize large coordinate

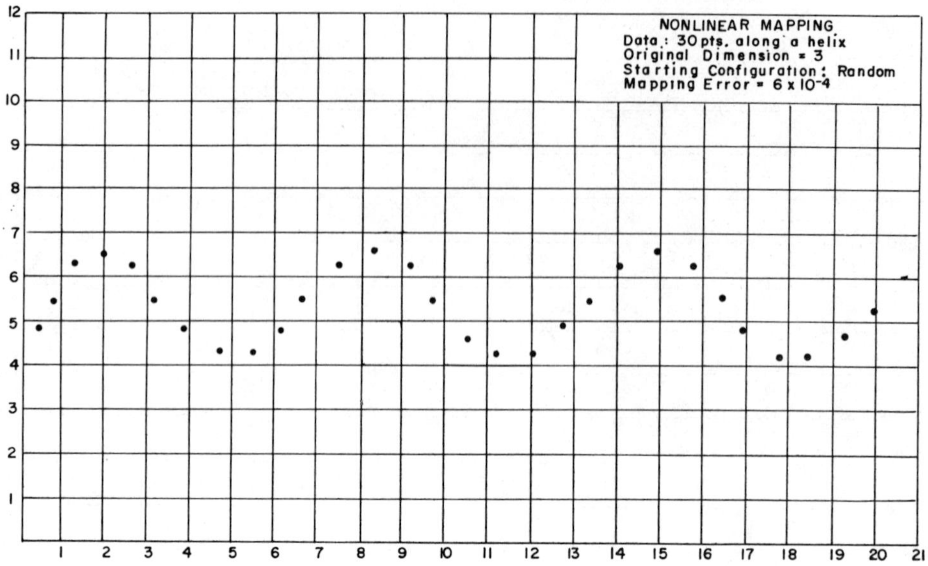

Fig. 8.

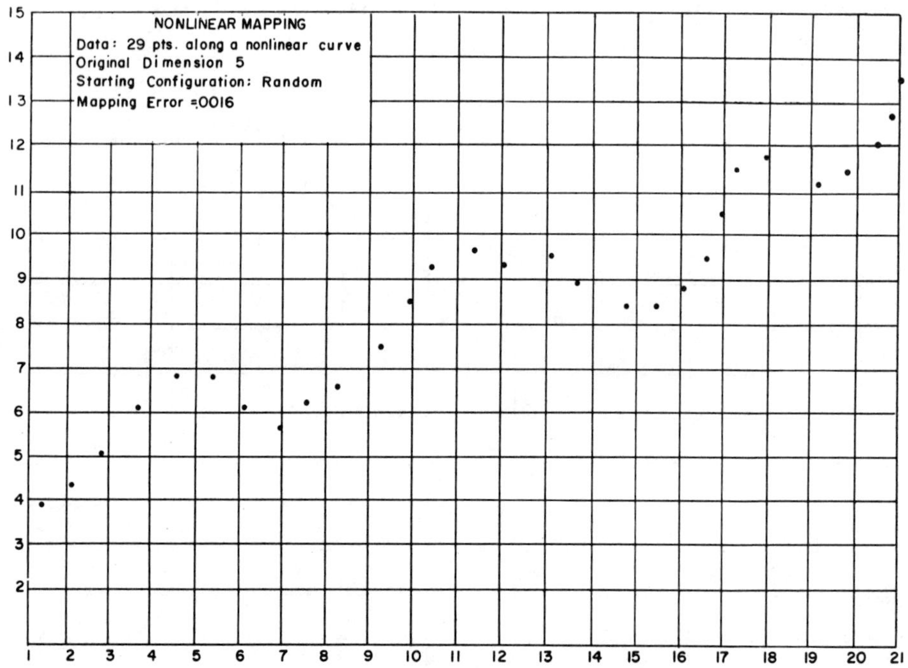

Fig. 9.

projections and minimize small coordinate projections. Finally, the 188 documents were located in the C-space by algebraically averaging the word or phrase vectors corresponding to the word or phrases which appeared in the documents.[5]

In order to evaluate the C-space as a potential method for document indexing, several individuals were asked to generate English queries (see Appendix III for the pertinent queries used here) which were then keypunched, automatically scanned for key word or phrase content, and finally mapped into the C-space. Each requester was then asked to identify those documents of the entire 188 which he felt were most relevant to his query. The C-space was then evaluated by examining the rank ordering of the retrieved documents to compare them to the list of relevant documents specified by the requester. The results of this evaluation can be found in Ossorio [8].

The nonlinear mapping algorithm was used to evaluate the "structure" of the documents in the C-space. Specifically, we were interested in how the documents considered relevant to a particular request were clustered, and further, how these clusters were interrelated to each other and to the entire library. To accomplish

[5] The entire document was never searched for key words or phrases. Rather, for one half of the documents only the abstracts were used, and for the remainder several paragraphs from each document were used.

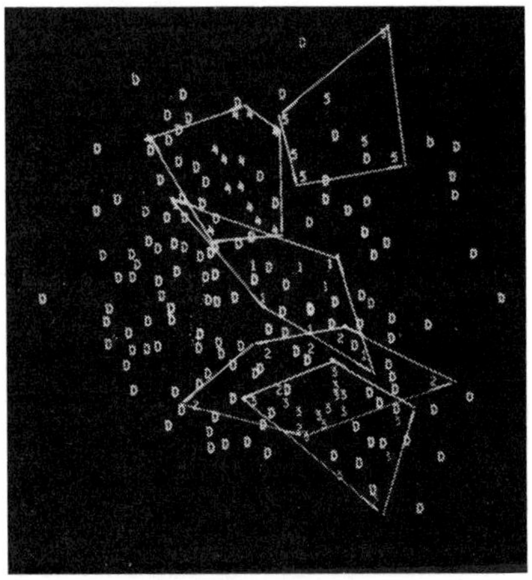

Fig. 10. Nonlinear mapping-photograph of CRT display. Data: 1 = eight Request 1 vectors; 2 = seven Request 2 vectors; 3 = sixteen Request 3 vectors; 4 = thirteen Request 4 vectors; 5 = seven Request 5 vectors. Starting configuration: maximum variance coordinate plane. Mapping error = 0.062.

this analysis, all 188 17-dimensional vectors were used as the input data to the NLM. The numerals 1 through 5 were used in the resulting 2-dimensional mapping to designate the documents labeled relevant to queries 1 through 5. In addition, the symbol D was used to designate the remaining library documents. It is important to note that the NLM algorithm did not utilize the numeric query designations in computing the mapping. Only at the time of plotting the final 2-space configuration of the 188 points were the numeric and symbolic designators used to distinguish the data. The error in achieving the NLM shown in Fig. 10 was 0.062, which was considered to be acceptable for adequate 2-space representation.

The following facts were obtained upon investigation of the NLM result.

1) The documents considered relevant to a given request were clustered, lending evidence to support the hypothesis that related documents have C-space vectors which are close.

2) There does not appear to be any natural C-space structure relating subsets of documents. Instead, the documents tend to be uniformly distributed throughout the space.

3) Clusters 2 and 3 tend to overlap, yet they are well-separated from clusters 4 and 5. This can easily be accounted for since requests 2 and 3 are both concerned with the common subject of statistical data analysis, whereas 4 and 5 involve completely different subjects. In general, the intercluster relationships seem consistent with their respective subject relationships.

In summary, we have found the NLM algorithm to be of considerable value in aiding us in our understanding of the C-space as well as other document spaces. Presently we are planning to incorporate a similar mapping technique in an on-line document retrieval system in order to improve the retrieval via geometric means. The experimental system will operate as follows. The on-line user would examine the 30 highest-ranked documents by retrieving and reading their abstracts. He would then indicate those he considered relevant. Next, a scatter diagram similar to Fig. 10 would be presented upon the CRT display where each of the 30 documents would be indicated by an I or an R, depending upon its relevance. In addition, the original query vector will be displayed as a Q. After examining the relative positions of the documents in the mapping, the user would select (using a light pen) one or more relevant documents to be used to generate a new query vector(s). The concept is that the query vector can be moved to highly relevant regions of the document space by interacting at a display console with a geometric representation of the space.

Relationship of NLM to Other Structure Analysis Algorithms

A mapping algorithm which bears a relationship to the NLM algorithm is one developed by Shepard [11] and later improved by Kruskal [5], [6]. Briefly, the Shepard–Kruskal algorithm seeks to find a configuration of points in a t-space such that the resultant interpoint distances preserve a monotonic relationship to a given set of interelement similarities (or dissimilarities). Specifically, they wish to analyze a set of interelement similarities (or dissimilarities) given by S_{ij}, $i = 1, \cdots, N$, $j = 1, \cdots, N$. Suppose these similarities are ordered in increasing magnitude, such that

$$S_{p_1 q_1} \leq S_{p_2 q_2} \leq \cdots \leq S_{p_n q_n}.$$

The Kruskal-Shepard algorithm seeks to find a set of N t-dimensional vectors y_i, $i = 1, \cdots, N$, such that the order of the interpoint distances $d_{ij} = \text{dist}[y_i, y_j]$ deviates as little as possible from the monotonic ordering of the corresponding similarities. Although the mathematical formulations are similar, the underlying mapping criterions are quite different.

Ball [1] has compiled an excellent survey of clustering and clumping algorithms which are useful in solving the "structure analysis" problem. However, it has been our experience in using clustering techniques that these algorithms suffer to some extent from the following four deficiencies.

1) When using a particular algorithm, the resulting cluster configuration is highly dependent upon a set of control parameters which must be fixed by the user. Some examples of such parameters are:

a) the similarity measure;
b) various similarity thresholds;
c) number of iterations required;
d) thresholds which control the increase or reduction of the number of clusters;
e) the minimum number of vectors required to define a cluster.

When choosing the control parameters for complex data, the user must either have a good deal of a priori information regarding the "structure" of his data, or he must apply the algorithm many times for different values of the control parameters. This second alternative is, at best, tedious.

2) Most of the existing clustering algorithms are particularly sensitive to hyperspherical structure and are inefficient in detecting more complex relationships in the data.

3) Perhaps the most serious deficiency involving present-day clustering algorithms is that there do not exist really good ways for evaluating a resultant cluster configuration.

4) When two clusters are close, the vectors between tend to form a bridge and cause spurious mergers [7].

We feel that the nonlinear mapping is a highly promising structure analysis algorithm since it suffers little from the listed clustering deficiencies. Consider the following facts concerning the algorithm.

1) The routine does not depend upon any control parameters that would require a priori knowledge about the data. Specifically, the user must set the number of iterations and the convergence constant (MF in Appendix I).

2) It is highly efficient in identifying hyperspherical, hyperellipsoidal, and other complex data structures.

3) The resulting mapping (scatter diagram) is easily evaluated by the researcher, thereby taking advantage of the human ability to detect and identify data structure.

4) The problem concerning extraneous data and spurious mergers is not present since humans easily eliminate troublesome data points by making global evaluations (machines have difficulty performing this function).

5) The algorithm is simple and efficient.

Limitations and Extensions

There are, of course, limitations to every algorithm and the nonlinear mapping is no exception. There exist two limitations which we are presently investigating. The first has to do with the reliability of the scatter diagram in displaying extremely complex high-dimensional structure. It is conceivable that the minimum mapping error is too large ($E \gg 0.1$) and the 2-dimensional scatter plot fails to portray the true structure. However, we feel that for data structures composed of superpositions of hyperspherical and hyperellipsoidal clusters, the nonlinear mapping algorithm will, in general, display adequate representations of the true data "structure."

The second limitation of the nonlinear mapping algorithm is related to the number of vectors that it can handle. Since we must compute and store the interdistance matrix, which consists of $N(N-1)/2$ elements, we are limited at present to $N \leq 250$ vectors.[6] In those cases where $N > 250$, we suggest using a data compression technique to reduce the data set to less than 250 vectors. Specifically, we propose to use the Isodata [2] clustering algorithm to perform data compression. This is actually a natural function of clustering since we replace several vectors with a typical representative vector (i.e., the cluster center). Our previous objections to present-day clustering algorithms do not apply here since we are only concerned with fitting the data with 250 cluster centers. We are specifically not using the clustering algorithm to detect structure.

We have used the NLM to analyze multivariate data from two or more classes for the purpose of determining how well the classes can be discriminated from one another. In these cases, it is recommended that the dimensionality be reduced to the smallest number of variables which still preserve discrimination.[7] In many problems certain measurements provide little discriminatory information; yet if these measurements are included, the NLM will attempt to "fit" interpoint distances along these "noisy" directions as well as along discriminating directions. In truly high-dimensional problems, the resulting mapping may show considerable overlap between classes and still a high degree of discrimination may be possible. This phenomena occurred when analyzing a 4-class, 24-dimensional data set. The resulting NLM (the final error was 0.5, which was considered high) showed considerable overlap among the data from three of the classes; yet, using a piecewise linear discrimination technique (based upon the use of a Fisher's linear discriminant between all pairs of classes), 94 percent correct classification was achieved. In this case, the NLM *did not* give an incorrect result since the

[6] The nonlinear map is programmed in FORTRAN IV and runs on a GE-635 computer equipped with 128 K of core. The computation time can be estimated by

$$T \simeq (1.1 \times 10^{-5}) \frac{I \cdot N(N-1)}{2}$$

minutes, where

I = number of iterations
N = number of vectors.

[7] A number of techniques may be used for this purpose. We often use the following:

a) Discriminant measure

$$M(X) \equiv \sum_{i<j} \frac{(\mu_{xi} - \mu_{xj})^2}{\sigma_{xi}^2 + \sigma_{xj}^2}.$$

b) Interpoint measure

$$M(X) \equiv \frac{1}{\sigma_x^2} \sum_{i<j} \frac{1}{N_i N_j} \sum_{p=1}^{N_i} \sum_{q=1}^{N_j} (X_p^{(i)} - X_q^{(j)})^2$$

where

μ_{x_i} = mean of class i along X
$\sigma_{x_i}^2$ = variance of class i along X
σ_x^2 = variance of all data along X
$X_p^{(i)}$ = the pth sample from the ith class along X
N_i = number of samples from the ith class.

c) Multilinear discriminant defined in Wilks [14].

classes greatly overlapped in approximately 20 dimensions and mildly overlapped in the remaining space. The NLM weighted all coordinates equally in an attempt to fit the interpoint distances, and therefore the resulting mapping indicated the predominant overlap which actually existed.

The NLM algorithm described here is one of many algorithms which are being programmed and incorporated into a large on-line graphics-oriented computer system, entitled the On-Line Pattern Analysis and Recognition System (OLPARS) [10].[8] Once the NLM algorithm is incorporated into the OLPARS system, the on-line user will be able to designate a data set, and from the graphics console execute the NLM. The user shall specify a mapping to a 2-space or a 3-space. For $d=2$, the resultant scatter diagram will be displayed upon the CRT; for $d=3$, a perspective scatter plot will be displayed. If the 3-space option is selected, the user will be able to dynamically analyze the resultant perspective scatter diagram by selecting various rotations of the three space. When the user selects $d=2$, he will be given the capability to designate subsets of data (via piecewise linear boundaries drawn on the CRT) representing a collection of points in the scatter diagram which exhibit structure, and thereby partition the initial data list into structured subsets.

Appendix I

Let $E(m)$ be defined as the mapping error after the mth iteration, i.e.,

$$E(m) \equiv \frac{1}{c} \sum_{i<j}^{N} [d_{ij}^* - d_{ij}(m)]^2 / d_{ij}^*$$

where

$$c = \sum_{i<j}^{N} [d_{ij}^*]$$

and

$$d_{ij}(m) = \sqrt{\sum_{k=1}^{d} [y_{ik}(m) - y_{jk}(m)]^2} \, .$$

The new d-space configuration at time $m+1$ is given by

$$y_{pq}(m+1) = y_{pq}(m) - (MF) \cdot \Delta_{pq}(m)$$

where

$$\Delta_{pq}(m) = \frac{\partial E(m)}{\partial y_{pq}(m)} \Bigg/ \left| \frac{\partial^2 E(m)}{\partial y_{pq}(m)^2} \right|$$

and MF is the "magic factor" which was determined empirically to be $MF \approx 0.3$ or 0.4. The partial derivatives are given by

$$\frac{\partial E}{\partial y_{pq}} = \frac{-2}{c} \sum_{\substack{j=1 \\ j \neq p}}^{N} \left[\frac{d_{pj}^* - d_{pj}}{d_{pj} d_{pj}^*} \right] (y_{pq} - y_{jq})$$

and

$$\frac{\partial^2 E}{\partial y_{pq}^2} = \frac{-2}{c} \sum_{\substack{j=1 \\ j \neq p}}^{N} \frac{1}{d_{pj}^* d_{pj}} \cdot \left[(d_{pj}^* - d_{pj}) - \frac{(y_{pq} - y_{jq})^2}{d_{pj}} \left(1 + \frac{d_{pj}^* - d_{pj}}{d_{pj}} \right) \right].$$

In our program we take precautions to prevent any two points in the d-space from becoming identical. This prevents the partials from "blowing up."

[8] For other examples of interactive pattern analysis systems, see Ball and Hall [3], Stanley *et al.* [12], and Walters [13].

Appendix II

Classification Space Fields

1) Adaptive Systems
2) Analog Computers
3) Applied Mathematics
4) Automata Theory
5) Computer Components and Circuits
6) Computer Memories
7) Computer Softwave
8) Display Consoles
9) Human Factors
10) Information Retrieval
11) Information Theory
12) Input–Output Equipment
13) Language Translation
14) Linear Algebra
15) Multivariate Statistical Analysis
16) Nonnumeric Data Processing
17) Numerical Analysis
18) Pattern Recognition
19) Probability and Statistics
20) Programming Languages
21) Stochastic Processes
22) System Design and Evaluation
23) Time-Sharing Systems.

Appendix III

Requests

Request 1: What is known about the statistical distributions of words or concepts in English text? What impact does this knowledge or lack of knowledge have on the effectiveness of standard statistical methods to information retrieval problems? Are nonparametric methods more applicable?

Request 2: I am interested in techniques for data analysis. In particular, I wish information on "cluster-seeking" techniques as opposed to those of factorial analysis and discriminant analysis. "Cluster-seeking" techniques may be classified as follows: probabilistic techniques, signal detection, clustering techniques, clumping techniques, eigenvalue-type techniques, and minimal mode-seeking techniques.

Request 3: I would like any information concerning Bayesian statistics. In particular, I would like to know if one can define or devise multiple-decision procedures from the Bayes approach. Also, how sensitive are Bayes procedures to the prior distribution? Finally, I would like a comparison of the Bayes approach to other classical decision theoretic approaches.

Request 4: What is the structure and characteristics of paging techniques?

Request 5: Are there survey documents (information) available which discuss or detail the relative practicality of memories; for example, capacity versus utilization, density, weight, environmental features, failure rates, economics, etc.?

Acknowledgment

The author expresses his appreciation to D. Elefante for his efforts in developing an efficient FORTRAN IV program for the Nonlinear Mapping Algorithm.

References

[1] G. H. Ball, "A comparison of some cluster-seeking techniques," Rome Air Development Center, Rome, N. Y., Tech. Rept. RADC-TR-66-514, November 1966.
[2] G. H. Ball and D. Hall, "Isodata," portion of Stanford Research Institute (SRI) Final Report to RADC Contract AF30(602)-4196, September, 1967.
[3] ——, "Promenade—an improved interactive graphics man/machine system for pattern recognition," Stanford Research Institute, Menlo Park, Calif., Project 6737, October, 1968.
[4] R. A. Fisher, "The use of multiple measurements in taxonomic problems," *Ann. Eugenics*, vol. 7, pp. 178–188, 1936.
[5] J. B. Kruskal, "Multidimensional scaling by optimizing goodness of fit to a nonmetric hypothesis," *Psychometrika*, pp. 1–27, March 1964.
[6] ——, "Nonmetric multidimensional scaling: a numerical method," *Psychometrika*, vol. 29, pp. 115–129, June 1964.
[7] G. Nagy, "State of the art in pattern recognition," *Proc. IEEE*, vol. 56, pp. 836–861, May 1968.
[8] P. G. Ossorio, "Classification space analysis," RADC-TDR-64-287, October 1964.
[9] ——, "Attribute space development and evaluation," RADC-TDR-67-640, January 1968.
[10] J. W. Sammon, "On-line pattern analysis and recognition system (OLPARS)," RADC-TR-68-263, August 1968.
[11] R. N. Shepard, "The analysis of proximities: multidimensional scaling with an unknown distance function," *Psychometrika*, vol. 27, pp. 125–139, 219–246, 1962.
[12] G. L. Stanley, G. G. Lendaris, and W. C. Nienow, "Pattern recognition program," AC Electronics Defense Research Labs., Santa Barbara, Calif., TR-567-16, November 1967.
[13] C. M. Walters, "On line computer based aids for the investigation of sensor data compression, transmission and delay problems," *1966 Proc. Natl. Telemetry Conf.*, Boston, Mass.
[14] S. S. Wilks, *Mathematical Statistics.* New York: J. Wiley, 1962.

A Projection Pursuit Algorithm for Exploratory Data Analysis

JEROME H. FRIEDMAN AND JOHN W. TUKEY

Abstract—**An algorithm for the analysis of multivariate data is presented and is discussed in terms of specific examples. The algorithm seeks to find one- and two-dimensional linear projections of multivariate data that are relatively highly revealing.**

Index Terms—**Clustering, dimensionality reduction, mappings, multidimensional scaling, multivariate data analysis, nonparametric pattern recognition, statistics.**

INTRODUCTION

MAPPING of multivariate data onto low-dimensional manifolds for visual inspection is a commonly used technique in data analysis. The discovery of mappings that reveal the salient features of the multidimensional point swarm is often far from trivial. Even when every adequate description of the data requires more variables than can be conveniently perceived (at one time) by humans, it is quite often still useful to map the data into a lower, humanly perceivable dimensionality where the human gift for pattern recognition can be applied.

While the particular dimension-reducing mapping used may sometimes be influenced by the nature of the problem at hand, it usually seems to be dictated by the intuition of the researcher. Potentially useful techniques can be divided into three classes.

1) Linear dimension reducers, which can usually be usefully thought of as projections.

2) Nonlinear dimension reducers that are defined over the whole high-dimensional space. (No examples seem as yet to have been seriously proposed for use in any generality.)

3) Nonlinear mappings that are only defined for the given points—most of these begin with the mutual interpoint distances as the basic ingredient. (Minimal spanning trees [2] and iterative algorithms for nonlinear mappings [3], [4] are examples. The literature of clustering techniques is extensive.[1])

While the nonlinear algorithms have the ability to provide a more faithful representation of the multidimensional point swarm than the linear methods, they can suffer from some serious shortcomings; namely, the resulting mapping is often difficult to interpret; it cannot be summarized by a few parameters; it only exists for the data set used in the analysis, so that additional data cannot be identically mapped; and, for moderate to large data bases, its use is extremely costly in computational resources (both CPU cycles and memory).

Our attention here is devoted to linear methods, more specifically to those expressable as projections (although the technique seems extendable to more general linear methods). Classical linear methods include principal components and linear factor analysis. Linear methods have the advantages of straightforward interpretability and computational economy. Linear mappings provide parameters which are independently useful in the understanding of the data, as well as being defined throughout the space, thus allowing the same mapping to be performed on additional data that were not part of the original analysis. The disadvantage of many classical linear methods is that the only property of the point swarm that is used to determine the mapping is a global one, usually the swarm's variance along various directions in the multidimensional space. Techniques that, like projection pursuit, combine global and local properties of multivariate point swarms to obtain useful linear mappings have been proposed by Kruskal [5], [6]. Since projection pursuit uses trimmed global measures, it has the additional advantage of robustness against outliers.

PROJECTION PURSUIT

This paper describes a linear mapping algorithm that uses interpoint distances as well as the variance of the point swarm to pursue optimum projections. This projection pursuit algorithm associates with each direction in the multidimensional space a continuous index that measures its "usefulness" as a projection axis, and then varies the projection direction so as to maximize this index. This projection index is sufficiently continuous to allow the use of sophisticated hill-climbing algorithms for the maximization, thus increasing computational efficiency. (In particular, both Rosenbrock [7] and Powell principal axis [8] methods have proved very successful.) For complex data structures, several solutions may exist, and for each of these, the projections can be visually inspected by the researcher for interpretation and judgment as to their usefulness. This multiplicity is often important.

Computationally, the projection pursuit (PP) algorithm is considerably more economical than the nonlinear

Manuscript received November 28, 1973; revised March 11, 1974. The work of J. H. Friedman was supported by the U. S. Atomic Energy Commission under Contract AT(043)515. The work of J. W. Tukey was prepared in part in connection with research at Princeton University, Princeton, N. J., supported by the U. S. Atomic Energy Commission.

J. H. Friedman is with the Stanford Linear Accelerator Center, Stanford, Calif. 94305.

J. W. Tukey is with the Department of Statistics, Princeton University, Princeton, N. J. 08540 and Bell Laboratories, Murray Hill, N. J. 07974.

[1] See [1] and [2] and their references for a reasonably extensive bibliography on clustering techniques.

Reprinted from *IEEE Trans. Comput.*, vol. C-23, pp. 881–890, Sept. 1974.

mapping algorithms. Its memory requirements are simply proportional to the number of data points N, while the number of CPU cycles required grows as $N \log N$ for increasing N. This allows the PP algorithm to be applied to much larger data bases than is possible with nonlinear mapping algorithms, where both the memory and CPU requirements tend to grow as N^2. Since the mappings are linear, they have the advantages of straightforward interpretability and convenient summarization. Also, once the parameters that define a solution projection are obtained, additional data that did not participate in the search can be mapped onto it. For example, one may apply projection pursuit to a data subsample of size N_s. This requires computation proportional to $N_s \log N_s$. Once a subsample solution projection is found, the entire data set can be projected onto it (for inspection by the researcher) with CPU requirements simply proportional to N.

When combined with isolation [9], projection pursuit has been found to be an effective tool for cluster detection and separation. As projections are found that separate the data into two or more apparent clusters, the data points in each cluster can be isolated. The PP algorithm can then be applied to each cluster separately, finding new projections that may reveal further clustering within each isolated data set. These subclusters can each be isolated and the process repeated.

Because of its computational economy, projection pursuit can be repeated many times on the entire data base, or its isolated subsets, making it a feasible tool for exploratory data analysis. The algorithm has so far been implemented for projection onto one and two dimensions; however, there is no fundamental limitation on the dimensionality of the projection space.

THE PROJECTION INDEX

The choice of the intent of the projection index, and to a somewhat lesser degree the choice of its details, are crucial for the success of the algorithm. Our choice of intent was motivated by studying the interaction between human operators and the computer on the PRIM-9 interactive data display system [10]. This system provides the operator with the ability to rotate the data to any desired orientation while continuously viewing a two-dimensional projection of the multidimensional data. These rotations are performed in real time and in a continuous manner under operator control. This gives the operator the ability to perform manual projection pursuit. That is, by controlling the rotations and viewing the changing projections, the operator can try to discover those data orientations (or equivalently, projection directions) that reveal to him interesting structure. It was found that the strategy most frequently employed by researchers operating the system was to seek out projections that tended to produce many very small interpoint distances while, at the same time, maintaining the overall spread of the data. Such strategies will, for instance, tend to concentrate the points into clusters while, at the same time, separating the clusters.

The P-indexes we use to express quantitatively such properties of a projection axis $\hat{k}$ can be written as a product of two functions

$$I(\hat{k}) = s(\hat{k})d(\hat{k}) \tag{1}$$

where $s(\hat{k})$ measures the spread of the data, and $d(\hat{k})$ describes the "local density" of the points after projection onto $\hat{k}$. For $s(\hat{k})$, we take the trimmed standard deviation of the data from the mean as projected onto $\hat{k}$:

$$s(\hat{k}) = \left[\sum_{i=pN}^{(1-p)N} (X_i \cdot \hat{k} - \bar{X}_k)^2/(1-2p)N\right]^{1/2} \tag{2}$$

where

$$\bar{X}_k = \sum_{i=pN}^{(1-p)N} X_i \cdot \hat{k}/(1-2p)N.$$

Here N is the total number of data points, and $\boldsymbol{X}_i (i = 1,N)$ are the multivariate vectors representing each of the data points, ordered according to their projections $\boldsymbol{X}_i \cdot \hat{k}$. A small fraction p of the points that lie at each of the extremes of the projection are omitted from both sums. Thus, extreme values of $\boldsymbol{X}_i \cdot \hat{k}$ do not contribute to $s(\hat{k})$, which is thus robust against extreme outliers.

For $d(\hat{k})$, we use an average nearness function of the form

$$d(\hat{k}) = \sum_{i=1}^{N} \sum_{j=1}^{N} f(r_{ij}) 1(R - r_{ij}) \tag{3}$$

where

$$r_{ij} = | \boldsymbol{X}_i \cdot \hat{k} - \boldsymbol{X}_j \cdot \hat{k} |$$

and $1(\eta)$ is unity for positive-valued arguments and zero for negative values. (Thus, the double sum is confined to pairs with $0 \le r_{ij} < R$.) The function $f(r)$ should be monotonically decreasing for increasing r in the range $r \le R$, reducing to zero at $r = R$. This continuity assures maximum smoothness of the objective function $I(\hat{k})$.

For moderate to large sample size N, the cutoff radius R is usually chosen so that the average number of points contained within the window, defined by the step function $1(R - r_{ij})$, is not only a small fraction of N, but increases much more slowly than N, say as $\log N$. After sorting the projected point values $\boldsymbol{X}_i \cdot \hat{k}$, the number of operations required to evaluate $d(\hat{k})$ [as well as $s(\hat{k})$] is thus about a fixed multiple of $N \log N$ (probably no more than this for large N). Since sorting requires a number of operations proportional to $N \log N$, the same is true of the entire evaluation of $d(\hat{k})$ and $s(\hat{k})$ combined.

Projections onto two dimensions are characterized by two directions $\hat{k}$ and $\hat{l}$ (conveniently taken to be orthogonal with respect to the initially given coordinates and their scales). For this case, (2) generalizes to

$$s(\hat{k},\hat{l}) = s(\hat{k})s(\hat{l}) \tag{2a}$$

and r_{ij} becomes

$$r_{ij} = [(X_i\cdot\hat{k} - X_j\cdot\hat{k})^2 + (X_i\cdot\hat{l} - X_j\cdot\hat{l})^2]^{1/2} \qquad (3a)$$

in (3).

Repeated application of the algorithm has shown that it is insensitive to the explicit functional form of $f(r)$ and shows major dependence only on its characteristic width

$$\bar{r} = \int_0^R rf(r)\,dr \Big/ \int_0^R f(r)\,dr \qquad \text{(one dimension)} \qquad (4)$$

$$\bar{r} = \int_0^R rf(r)r\,dr \Big/ \int_0^R f(r)r\,dr \qquad \text{(two dimensions)}. \qquad (4a)$$

It is this characteristic width that seems to define "local" in the search for maximum local density. Its value establishes the distance in the projected subspace over which the local density is averaged, and thus establishes the scale of density variation to which the algorithm is sensitive. Experimentation has also shown that when a preferred direction is available, the algorithm is remarkably stable against small to moderate changes in $\bar{r}$, but it does respond to large changes in its value (say a few factors of two).

The projection index $I(\hat{k})$ (or $I(\hat{k},\hat{l})$ for two-dimensional projections) measures the degree to which the data points in the projection are both concentrated locally ($d(\hat{k})$ large) while, at the same time, expanded globally ($s(\hat{k})$ large). Experience has shown that projections that have this property to a large degree tend to be those that are most interesting to researchers. Thus, it seems natural to pursue those projections that maximize this index.

ONE-DIMENSIONAL PROJECTION PURSUIT

The projection index for projection on to an one-dimensional line imbedded in an n-dimensional space is a function of $n - 1$ independent variables that define the direction of the line, conveniently, its direction cosines. These cosines are the n components of a vector parallel to the line subject to the constraint that the squares of these components sum to unity. Thus, we seek the maxima of the P-index $I(\hat{k})$ on the $(n - 1)$-dimensional surface of a sphere of unit radius $S^n(1)$ in an n-dimensional Euclidean space.

One technique for accomplishing this is to apply a solid angle transform (SAT) [11] which reversibly maps such a sphere to an $(n - 1)$-dimensional infinite Euclidean space $E^{n-1}(-\infty,\infty)$ (see the Appendix). This reduces the problem from finding the maxima of $I(\hat{k})$ on the unit sphere in n dimensions to finding the equivalent maxima of $I[\text{SAT}(\hat{k})]$ in $E^{n-1}(-\infty,\infty)$. This replacement of the constrained optimization problem with a totally unconstrained one greatly increases the stability of the algorithm and simplifies its implementation. The variables of the search are the $n - 1$ SAT parameters, and for any such set of parameters, there exists a unique point on the n-dimensional sphere defined by the n components of $\hat{k}$.

The computational resources required by projection pursuit are greatly affected by the algorithm used in the search for the maxima of the projection index. Since the number of CPU cycles required to evaluate the P-index for N data points grows as $N \log N$, it is important for moderate to large data sets to employ a search algorithm that requires as few evaluations of the object function as possible. It is usually the case that the more sophisticated the search algorithm, the smoother the object function is required to be for stability. The P-index $I(\hat{k})$, as defined above, is remarkably smooth, and both Rosenbrock [12] and Powell principal axis [13] search algorithms have been successfully applied without encountering any instability problems. For these algorithms, the number of objective function evaluations per varied parameter required to find a solution projection has been found to vary considerably from instance to instance and to be strongly influenced by the convergence criteria established by the user. Applying a rather demanding convergence criteria, approximately 15–25 evaluations per varied parameter were required to achieve a solution. (Stopping when the P-index changes by only a few percent seems reasonable. A convergence criteria of one percent was used in all of our applications.)

In order to be useful as a tool for exploratory data analysis on data sets with complex structure, it is important that the algorithm find several solutions that represent potentially informative projections for inspection by the researcher. This can be accomplished by applying the algorithm many times with different starting directions for the search. Useful starting directions include the larger principal axes of the data set, the original coordinate axes, and even directions chosen at random. From each starting direction $\hat{k}_s$, the algorithm finds the solution projection axis $\hat{k}_s{}^*$ corresponding to the first maximum of the P-index uphill from the starting point. From these searches, several quite distinct solutions often result. Each of these projections can then be examined to determine their usefulness in data interpretation.

In order to encourage the algorithm to find additional distinct solutions, it is useful to be able to reduce the dimensionality of the sphere to be searched. This can be done by choosing an arbitrary set of directions $\{\hat{o}_i\}_{i=1}{}^m$, $m < n$, which need not be mutually orthogonal, and applying the constraints

$$\hat{k}^*\cdot\hat{o} = o_i \qquad i = 1,m \qquad (4)$$

on the solution direction $\hat{k}^*$. Possible choices for constraint directions might be solution directions found on previous searches, or directions that are known in advance to contain considerable, but well understood, structures. Also, when the choice of scales for the several coordinates is guided by considerations outside the data, one might wish to remove directions with small variance about the mean, since these directions often provide little information about the structure of the data. The introduction of each such constraint direction reduces by one the number of search variables, and thus increases the computational efficiency of the algorithm.

The algorithm can allow for the introduction of an arbitrary number $m < n$ of nonparallel constraint directions. This is accomplished by using Householder reductions [14] to form an orthogonal basis for the $(n - m)$-dimensional orthogonal subspace of the m-dimensional subspace spanned by the m constraint vectors $\{\hat{o}_i\}_{i=1}^m$. The $n - m - 1$ search variables are then the solid angle transform parameters of the unit sphere in this $(n - m)$-dimensional space. The transformation from the original n-dimensional data space proceeds in two steps. First, a linear dimension reducing transformation to the $(n - m)$-dimensional complement subspace, and then the nonlinear SAT that maps the sphere $S^{n-m}(1)$ to $E^{n-m-1}(-\infty,\infty)$.

TWO-DIMENSIONAL PROJECTION PURSUIT

The projection index $I(\hat{k},\hat{l})$ for a two-dimensional plane imbedded in an n-dimensional space is defined by (2a), (3), and (3a). This index is a function of the parameters that define such a plane. Proceeding in analogy with one-dimensional projection pursuit, one could seek the maximum of $I(\hat{k},\hat{l})$ with respect to these parameters. The data projected onto the plane represented by the solution vectors $\hat{k}^*$ and $\hat{l}^*$ can then be inspected by the researcher.

Another useful strategy is to hold one of the directions (for example, $\hat{k}$) constant along some interesting direction, and then seek the maximum of $I(\hat{k},\hat{l})$ with respect to $\hat{l}$ in $\tilde{E}^{n-1}(\hat{k})$, the $(n - 1)$-dimensional subspace orthogonal to $\hat{k}$. This reduces the number of search parameters to $n - 2$. The choice of the constant direction $\hat{k}$ could be motivated by the problem at hand (like one of the original or principal axes), or it could be a solution direction found in an one-dimensional projection pursuit.

A third, intermediate strategy would be to first fix $\hat{k}$ and seek the maximum of $I(\hat{k},\hat{l})$ in $\tilde{E}^{n-1}(\hat{k})$, as described above. Then, holding $\hat{l}$ fixed at the solution value $\hat{l}^*$, vary $\hat{k}$ in $\tilde{E}^{n-1}(l^*)$, seeking a further maximum of $I(\hat{k},\hat{l}^*)$. This process of alternately fixing one direction and varying the other in the orthogonal subspace of the first can be repeated until the solution becomes stable. The final directions $\hat{k}^*$ and $\hat{l}^*$ are then regarded as defining the solution plane. This third strategy, while not as completely general as the first, is computationally much more efficient. This is due to the economies that can be achieved in computing $I(\hat{k},l)$, knowing that one of the directions is constant and that $\hat{k}\cdot\hat{l} = 0$. (Using similar criteria for choosing the cutoff radius as that used for one-dimensional projection pursuit, and sorting the projected values along the constant direction, allows $I(\hat{k},l)$ to be evaluated with a number of operations proportional to $N \log N$.)

As for the one-dimensional case, the two-dimensional P-index $I(\hat{k},\hat{l})$ is sufficiently smooth to allow the use of sophisticated optimization algorithms. Also, constraint directions can be introduced in the same manner as described above for one-dimensional projection pursuit.

TABLE I
SPHERICALLY RANDOM DATA

14 Dimensions — 975 Data Points

Search No.	P-Index Starting	P-Index Solution	Search No.	P-Index Starting	P-Index Solution
1	151.8	156.3	15	150.6	155.8
2	150.7	156.7	16	150.6	156.9
3	149.4	156.0	17	151.0	157.0
4	152.4	159.7	18	152.2	155.6
5	152.3	159.2	19	152.1	160.2
6	151.0	154.4	20	152.9	159.0
7	152.6	155.6	21	150.0	160.8
8	149.6	155.4	22	150.0	157.9
9	150.0	156.1	23	150.7	155.4
10	151.8	153.0	24	151.5	158.4
11	154.0	154.6	25	151.0	155.3
12	151.4	156.7	26	152.8	159.6
13	149.7	154.1	27	151.8	157.0
14	152.1	154.2	28	152.1	157.9

SOME EXPERIMENTAL RESULTS

To illustrate the application of the algorithm, we describe its effect upon several data sets. The first two are artificially generated so that the results can be compared with the known data structure. The third is the well-known Iris data used by Fisher [15], and the fourth is a data set taken from a particle physics experiment. For these examples, $f(r) = R - r$, for one-dimensional projection pursuit (3), while for two-dimensional projection pursuit 3(a), $f(r) = R^2 - r^2$. In both cases R was set to ten percent of the square root of the data variance along the largest principal axis, and the trimming (2) was $P = 0.01$.

A. Uniformally Distributed Random Data

To test the effect of projection pursuit on artificial data having no preferred projection axes, we generated 975 data points randomly from a uniform distribution inside a 14-dimensional sphere, and repeatedly applied one- and two-dimensional projection pursuit to the sample with different starting directions. Table I shows the results of 28 such trials with one-dimensional projection pursuit where the starting directions were the 14 original axes and the 14 principal axes of the data set. The results of the two-dimensional projection pursuit trials were very similar.

The results shown in Table I strongly reflect the uniform nature of the 14-dimensional data set. The standard deviation of the index values for the starting directions is less than one percent, while the increase achieved at the solutions averages four percent. Also, only two searches (runs 13 and 14) appeared to converge to the same solution. The angle between the two directions corresponding to the largest P-indices found (runs 19 and 21) was 67 degrees. The small increase in the P-index from the starting to the solution directions indicates that the algorithm considers these solution directions at most only slightly better projection axes than the starting directions. Visual inspection of the data projections verifies this assessment.

B. *Gaussian Data Distributed at the Vertices of a Simplex*

The previous example shows that projection pursuit finds no seriously preferred projection axes when applied to spherically uniform random data. Another interesting experiment is to test its effect on an artificial data set with considerable multidimensional structure. Following Sammon [4], we applied one-dimensional projection pursuit to a data set consisting of 15 spherical Gaussian clusters of 65 points, each centered at the vertices of a 14-dimensional simplex. The variance of each cluster is one, while the distance between centers is ten. Thus, the clusters are well separated in the 14-dimensional space. Fig. 1(a) shows these data projected onto the direction of their largest principal axis. (For this sample, the largest standard deviation was about 1.15 times the smallest.) As can be seen, this projection shows no hint of the multidimensional structure of the data. Inspection of the one- and two-dimensional projections onto the other principal axes shows the same result.

Using the largest principal axis [Fig. 1(a)] as the starting direction, the one-dimensional PP algorithm yielded the solution shown in Fig. 1(b). The threefold increase in the P-index at the solution indicates that the algorithm considers it a much better projection axis than the starting direction. This is verified by visual inspection of the data as projected onto the solution axis, where the data set is seen to break up into two well-separated clusters of 65 and 910 points.

In order to investigate possible additional structure, we isolated each of the clusters and applied projection pursuit to each one individually. The results are shown in Fig. 1(c) and (d). The solution projection for the 65-point isolate showed no evidence for additional clustering, while the 910-point sample clearly separated into two subclusters of 130 and 780 points. We further isolated these two subclusters and applied projection pursuit to each one individually. The results are illustrated in Fig. 1(e) and (f). The solution for the 130-point subcluster shows it divided into two clusters of 65 points each, while the 780-point cluster separates into a 65-point cluster and 715-point cluster. Continuing with these repeated applications of isolation and projection pursuit, one finds, after using a sequence of linear projections, that the data set is composed of 15 clusters of 65 points each.

Two-dimensional projection pursuit could equally well be applied at each stage in the above analysis. This has the advantage that the solution at a given stage sometimes separates the data set into three apparent clusters. The disadvantage is the increased computational requirements of the two-dimensional projection pursuit algorithm.

C. *Iris Data*

This is a classical data set first used by Fisher [15] and

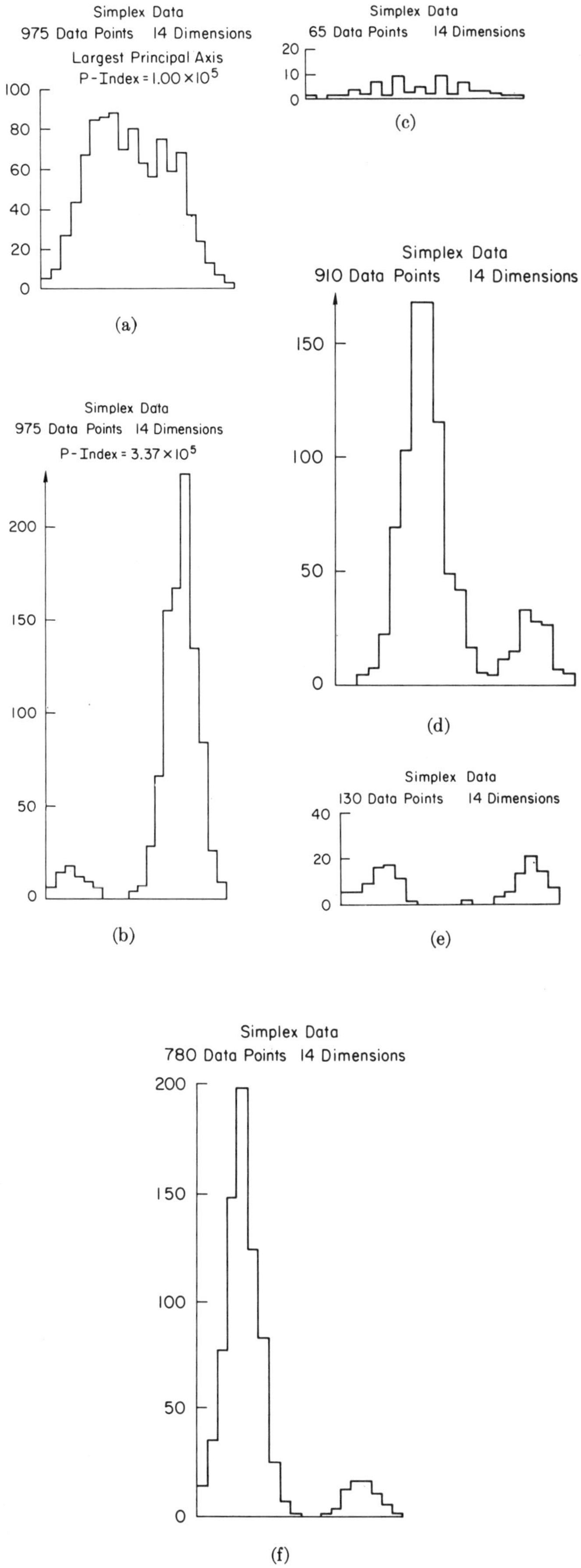

Fig. 1.

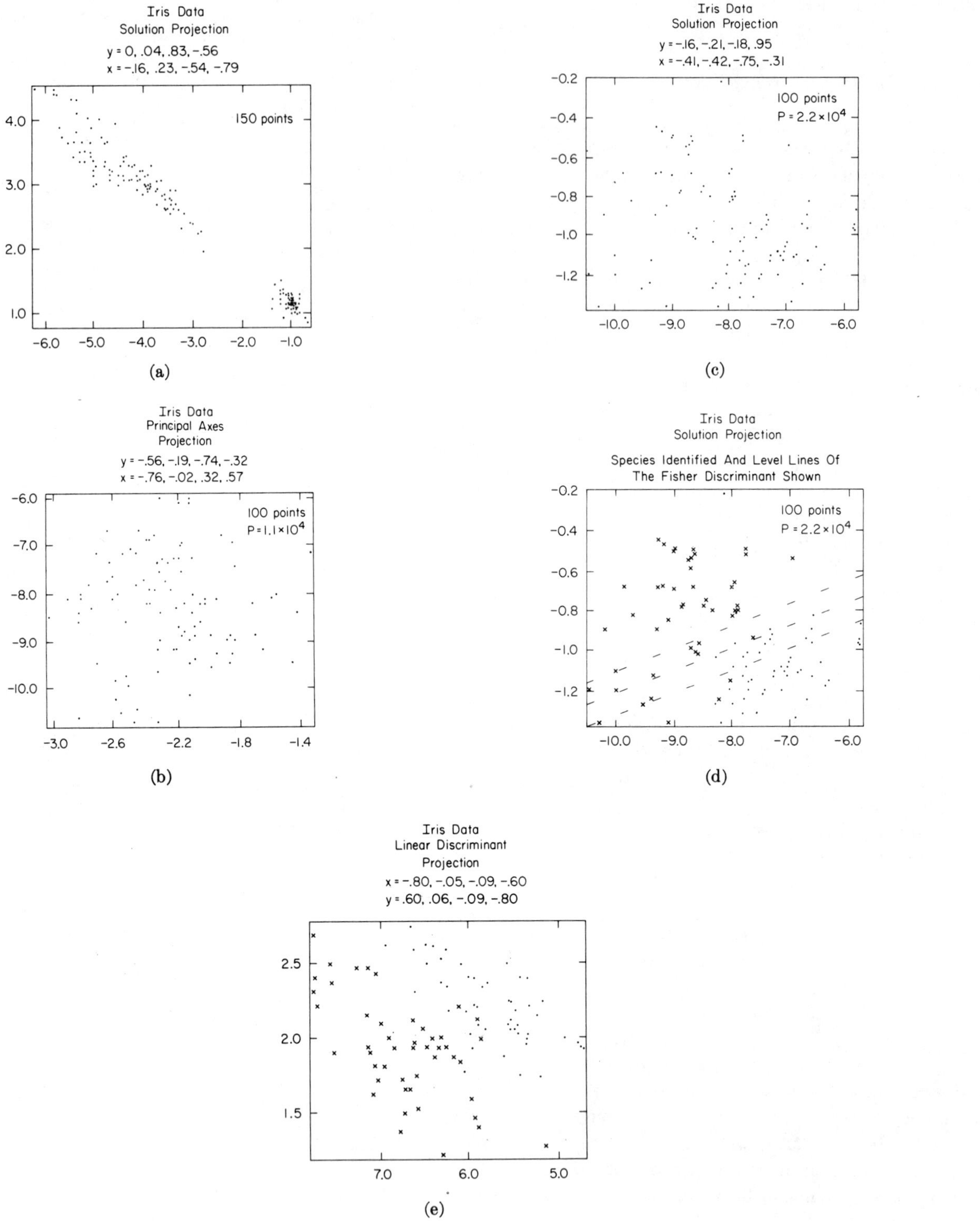

(e)

Fig. 2.

subsequently by many other researchers for testing statistical procedures. The data consist of measurements made on 50 observations from each of three species (one quite different from the other two) of iris flowers. Four measurements were made on each flower, and there were 150 flowers in the entire data set. Taking the largest principal axes as starting directions, we applied projection pursuit to the entire four-dimensional data set. The result for two-dimensional projection pursuit is shown in Fig. 2(a). As can be seen, the data as projected on the solution plane show clear separation into two well-defined clusters of 50 (one species) and 100 (two unresolved species) points. The one-dimensional algorithm also clearly separates the data into these two clusters. However, this two-cluster separation is easy to achieve and is readily apparent from simple inspection of the original data.

Applying the procedure discussed above, we isolate the 100-point cluster (largest standard deviation was about six times the smallest) and reapply projection pursuit, starting with the largest principal axes of the isolate. Fig. 2(b) shows the data projected onto the plane defined by the two largest principal axes. Here the data seem to show no apparent clustering.

One-dimensional projection pursuit, starting with the largest principal axis, was unable to separate this isolate into discernible clusters. Fig. 2(c) shows the results of two-dimensional projection pursuit starting with the plane of Fig. 2(b). This solution plane seems to divide the projected data into two discernible clusters. One in the lower right-hand quadrant with higher than average density seems slightly separated from another, which is somewhat sparser and occupies most of the rest of the projection. In order to see to what extent this apparent clustering corresponds to the different iris species known to be contained in this isolate, Fig. 2(d) tags these species. As can be seen, the two clusters very closely correspond to the two iris species. Also shown in Fig. 2(d) are some level lines of (the projection onto the same plane of) Fisher's linear discriminant function [15] $\hat{f}$ for this isolate, calculated by using the known identities of the two species. In this example, the angle between the direction upon which this linear discriminant function is a projection and this plane is a little more than 45°.

The projection pursuit solution can be compared to a two-dimensional projection of this isolate that is chosen to provide maximum separation of the two species, given the *a priori* information as to which species each data point represents. Fig. 2(e) shows the isolate projected onto such a plane whose horizontal coordinate is the value of Fisher's linear discriminant for the isolate in the full four-dimensional space $\hat{f}$, while the vertical axis is the value of a similar Fisher linear discriminant in $\tilde{E}^3(\hat{f})$, the three-dimensional space orthogonal to $\hat{f}$ [16]. (If the "within variance" were spherical in the initially given coordinate system, this vertical coordinate would not be well defined, since the centers of the two species groups would coincide in $\tilde{E}^3(\hat{f})$. While we may feel that the vertical coordinate adds little to the horizontal one, linear discrimination seems to offer no better choice of a second coordinate, especially since we would like this view also to be a projection of the original data—a projection in terms of the original coordinates and scales—as all two-dimensional projection pursuit views are required to be.) A comparison of Fig. 2(d) and (e) shows that the unsupervised projection pursuit solution achieves separation of the two species equivalent to this discriminant plane. Since these two species are known to touch in the full four-dimensional space [2], [4], it is probably not possible to find a projection that completely separates them.

D. Particle Physics Data

For the final example, we apply projection pursuit to a data set taken from a high-energy particle physics-scattering experiment [17]. In this experiment, a beam of positively charged pi-mesons, with an energy of 16 billion eV, was used to bombard a stationary target of protons contained in hydrogen nuclei. Five hundred examples were recorded of those nuclear reactions in which the final products were a proton, two positively charged pi-mesons, and a negatively charged pi-meson. Such a nuclear reaction with four reaction products can be completely described by seven independent measurables.[2] These data can thus be regarded as 500 points in a seven-dimensional space.

The data projected onto its largest principal axis are shown in Fig. 3(a), while the projection onto the plane defined by the largest two principal axes is shown in Fig. 3(c). (The largest standard deviation was about eight times the smallest.) One-dimensional projection pursuit was applied, starting with the largest principal axis. Fig. 3(b) shows the data projected onto the solution direction. The result of a two-dimensional projection pursuit starting with the plane of Fig. 3(c) is shown in Fig. 3(d).

Although the principal axis projections indicate possible structure within the data set, the projection pursuit solutions are clearly more revealing. This is indicated by the substantial increase in the P-index, and is verified by visual inspection. In particular, the two-dimensional solution projection shows that there are at least three clusters, possibly connected, one of which reasonably separates from the other two. Proceeding as above, one could isolate this cluster from the others and apply projection pursuit to the two samples separately, continuing the analysis.

DISCUSSION

The experimental results of the previous section indicate that the PP algorithm behaves reasonably. That is, it tends to find structure when it exists in the multidimensional data, and it does not find structure when it is known not to exist. When combined with isolation, projection pursuit seems to be an effective tool for the detection of certain types of clustering.

Because projection pursuit is a linear mapping algorithm, it suffers from some of the well-known limitations of linear mapping. The algorithm will have difficulty in detecting clustering about highly curved surfaces in the full dimensionality. In particular, it cannot detect nested spherical clustering. It can, however, detect nested cylin-

[2] For this reaction, $\pi_b{}^+ p_t \rightarrow p \pi_1{}^+ \pi_2{}^+ \pi^-$, the following measurables were used: $X_1 = \mu^2(\pi^-, \pi_1{}^+, \pi_2{}^+)$, $X_2 = \mu^2(\pi^-, \pi_1{}^+)$, $X_3 = \mu^2(p, \pi^-)$, $X_4 = \mu^2(\pi^-, \pi_2{}^+)$, $X_5 = \mu^2(p, \pi_1{}^+)$, $X_6 = \mu^2(p, \pi_1{}^+, -p_t)$, and $X_7 = \mu^2(p, \pi_2{}^+, -p_t)$. Here, $\mu^2(A, B, \pm C) = (E_A + E_B \pm E_C)^2 - (\boldsymbol{P}_A + \boldsymbol{P}_B \pm \boldsymbol{P}_C)^2$ and $\mu^2(A, \pm B) = (E_A \pm E_B)^2 - (\boldsymbol{P}_A \pm \boldsymbol{P}_B)^2$, where E and $\boldsymbol{P}$ represent the particle's energy and momentum, respectively, as measured in billions of electron volts. The notation $(\boldsymbol{p})^2$ represents the inner product $\boldsymbol{P}/\boldsymbol{P}$. The ordinal assignment of the two π^+'s was done randomly.

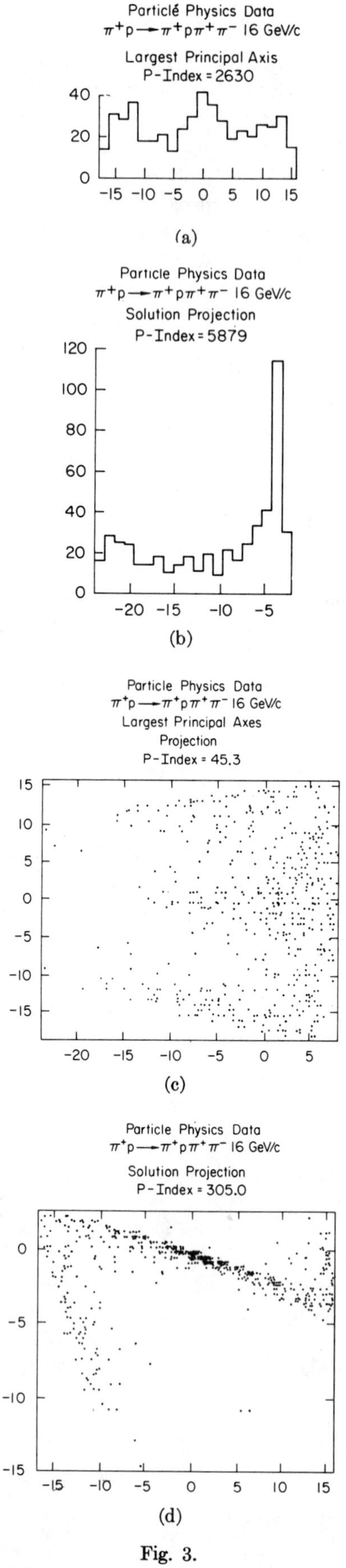

Fig. 3.

drical clustering where the cylinders have parallel generators.

Projection pursuit leaves to the researcher's discretion the choice of measurement variables and metric. The algorithm is, of course, sensitive to change of relative scale of the input measurement variables, as well as to highly nonlinear transformations of them. If there is no *a priori* motivation for a choice of scale for the measurement variables, then they can be independently scaled (standardized) so as to all have the same variance. In the spirit of exploratory data analysis, the researcher might employ projection pursuit to several carefully selected nonlinear transformations of his measurement variables. For example, transformations to various spherical polar coordinate representations [11] would enable projection pursuit to detect nested spherical clustering.

Frequently with multidimensional data, only a few of the measurement variables contribute to the structure or clustering. The clusters may overlap in many of the dimensions and separate in only a few. As pointed out by both Sammon [4] and Kruskal [6], those variables that are irrelevant to the structure or clustering can dilute the effect of those that display it, especially for those mapping algorithms that depend solely on the multidimensional interpoint distances. It is easy to see that the projection pursuit algorithm does not suffer seriously from this effect. Projection pursuit will automatically tend to avoid projections involving those measurement variables that do not contribute to data structure, since the inclusion of these variables will tend to reduce $d(\hat{k})$ while not modifying $s(\hat{k})$ greatly.

In order to apply the PP algorithm, the researcher is not required to possess a great deal of *a priori* knowledge concerning the structure of his data, either for setting up the control parameters for the algorithm or for interpreting its results. The only control parameter requiring care is the characteristic radius $\bar{r}$ defined in (4). Its value establishes the minimum scale of density variation detectable by the algorithm. A choice for its value can be influenced by the global scale of the data, as well as any information that may be known about the nature of the variations in the multivariate density of the points. The sample size is also an important consideration since the radius should be large enough to include, on the average, enough points (in each projection) to obtain a reasonable estimate of the local density. These considerations usually result in a compromise, making $\bar{r}$ as small as possible, consistent with the sample size requirement. Because of the computational efficiency of the algorithm, however, it is possible to apply it several times with different values for $\bar{r}$. Interpretation of the results of projection pursuit is especially straightforward, owing to the linear nature of the mapping.

The researcher also has the choice of the dimensionality of the projection subspace. That is, whether to employ one-, two-, or higher dimensional projection pursuit. The two-dimensional projection pursuit algorithm is slower and slightly less stable than the one-dimensional algorithm; however, the resulting two-dimensional map contains much more information about the data. Experience has shown that a useful strategy is to first find several one-dimensional PP solutions, then use each of these directions as one of the starting axes for two-dimensional projection pursuits.

APPENDIX

This section presents the solid angle transform (SAT) that reversibly maps the surface of a unit sphere in an n-dimensional space $S^n(1)$ to an $(n-1)$-dimensional infinite Euclidean space $E^{n-1}(-\infty,\infty)$. This transformation is derived in [11] and only the results are presented here.

Let $(X_1,X_2,\cdots,X_n)$ be the coordinates of a point lying on the surface of an n-dimensional unit sphere and $(\eta_1,\eta_2,\cdots,\eta_{n-1})$ be the corresponding point in an $(n-1)$-dimensional unit hypercube $E^{n-1}(0,1)$. Then for n even, the transformation is

$$X_{2i} = \left[\prod_{j=1}^{i-1} \eta_{2j}{}^{1/(n-2j)}\right] \cos\left[\sin^{-1}\eta_{2i}{}^{1/(n-2i)}\right] \sin(2\pi\eta_{2i-1}),$$

$$1 \le i \le n/2 - 1$$

$$X_n = \left[\prod_{j=1}^{n/2-1} \eta_{2j}{}^{1/(n-2j)}\right] \sin(2\pi\eta_{n-1})$$

$$X_{2i-1} = X_{2i}\cot(2\pi\eta_{2i-1}), \qquad 1 \le i \le n/2.$$

for n odd, we take

$$X_n = \left[\prod_{j=1}^{(n-3)/2} \eta_{2j}{}^{1/(n-2j)}\right] (2\eta_{n-2} - 1)$$

$$X_{n-1} = \left[\prod_{j=1}^{(n-3)/2} \eta_{2j}{}^{1/(n-2j)}\right] (\eta_{n-2} - \eta_{n-2}{}^2)^{1/2} \sin(2\pi\eta_{n-1})$$

$$X_{2i} = \left[\prod_{j=1}^{i-1} \eta_{2j}{}^{1/(n-2j)}\right] \cos\left[\sin^{-1}\eta_{2i}{}^{1/(n-2i)}\right] \sin(2\pi\eta_{2i-1}),$$

$$1 \le i \le (n-3)/2$$

$$X_{2i-1} = X_{2i}\cot(2\pi\eta_{2i-1}), \qquad 1 \le i \le (n-1)/2.$$

The Jacobian of this transformation,

$$J_n(1) = \frac{2\pi^{n/2}}{\Gamma(n/2)},$$

is a constant, namely, the well-known expression for the surface area of an n-dimensional sphere of unit radius. Adjusted by a factor of the $(n-1)$st root of J_n, the transformation is volume preserving, one to one, and onto. The inverse transformation can easily be obtained by solving the above equations for the η's in terms of the X coordinates. The unit hypercube $E^{n-1}(0,1)$ can be expanded to the infinite Euclidean space $E^{n-1}(-\infty,\infty)$ by using standard techniques [18], specifically, multiple reflection.

ACKNOWLEDGMENT

Helpful discussions with W. H. Rogers and G. H. Golub are gratefully acknowledged.

REFERENCES

[1] L. N. Bolshev, *Bull. Int. Statist. Inst.*, vol. 43, pp. 411–425, 1969.
[2] C. T. Zahn, "Graph-theoretical methods for detecting and describing gestalt clusters," *IEEE Trans. Comput.*, vol. C-20, pp. 68–86, Jan. 1971.
[3] R. N. Shepard and J. D. Carroll, "Parametric representation of nonlinear data structures," in *Multivariate Analysis*, P. Krishnaiah, Ed. New York: Academic, 1966.
[4] J. W. Sammon, Jr., "A nonlinear mapping for data structure analysis," *IEEE Trans. Comput.*, vol. C-18, pp. 401–409, May 1969.
[5] J. B. Kruskal, "Toward a practical method which helps uncover the structure of a set of multivariate observations by finding the linear transformation which optimizes a new 'index of condensation,'" in *Statistical Computation*, R. C. Milton and J. A. Nelder, Ed. New York: Academic, 1969.
[6] ——, "Linear transformation of multivariate data to reveal clustering," in *Multidimensional Scaling: Theory and Application in the Behavorial Sciences*, vol. 1, *Theory*. New York and London: Seminar Press, 1972.
[7] H. H. Rosenbrock, "An automatic method for finding the greatest or least value of a function," *Comput. J.*, vol. 3, pp. 175–184, 1960.
[8] M. J. D. Powell, "An efficient method for finding the minimum of a function of several variables without calculating derivates," *Comput. J.*, vol. 7, pp. 155–162, 1964.
[9] R. L. Mattson and J. E. Dammann, "A technique for determining and coding subclasses in pattern recognition problems," *IBM J.*, vol. 9, pp. 294–302, July 1965.
[10] "PRIM-9," film produced by Stanford Linear Accelerator Cen., Stanford, Calif., Bin 88 Productions, Apr. 1973.
[11] J. H. Friedman and S. Steppel, "Non-linear constraint elimination in high dimensionality through reversible transformations," Stanford Linear Accelerator Cen., Stanford, Calif., Rep. SLAC PUB-1292, Aug. 1973.
[12] S. Derenzo, "MINF-68—A general minimizing routine," Lawrence Berkeley Lab., Berkeley, Calif., Group A Tech. Rep. P-190, 1969.
[13] R. P. Brent, *Algorithms for Minimization Without Derivatives.* Englewood Cliffs, N. J.: Prentice-Hall, 1973.
[14] G. H. Golub, "Numerical methods for solving linear least squares problems," *Numer. Math.*, vol. 7, pp. 206–216, 1965.
[15] R. A. Fisher, "Multiple measurements in taxonomic problems," in *Contributions to Mathematical Statistics.* New York: Wiley.
[16] J. W. Sammon, Jr., "An optimal discriminant plane," *IEEE Trans. Comput.*, vol. C-19, pp. 826–829, Sept. 1970.
[17] J. Ballam, G. B. Chadwick, Z. C. G. Guiragossian, W. B. Johnson, D. W. G. S. Leith, and K. Moriyasu, "Van Hove analysis of the reactions $\pi^-p \rightarrow \pi^-\pi^-\pi^+p$ and $\pi^+p \rightarrow \pi^+\pi^+\pi^-p$ at 16 GeV/C," *Phys. Rev.*, vol. 4, pp. 1946–1947, Oct. 1971.
[18] M. J. Box, *Comput. J.*, vol. 9, pp. 67–77, 1966.

Bibliography on Estimation of Misclassification

GODFRIED T. TOUSSAINT

Abstract—**Articles, books, and technical reports on the theoretical and experimental estimation of probability of misclassification are listed for the case of correctly labeled or preclassified training data. By way of introduction, the problem of estimating the probability of misclassification is discussed in order to characterize the contributions of the literature.**

Introduction

ONE OF THE most important problems in pattern recognition is estimating the probability of misclassification. Before embarking on a description of the literature in this field it is proper to make a distinction between some of the various measures of probabilities of misclassification (error) usually considered.

1) The *optimal or Bayes probability of error*, denoted by P_e^B, is given by $P_e^B = 1 - \int \max_i \{P(X/C_i)P(C_i)\}\, dX$, where $P(X/C_i)$ and $P(C_i)$ are the class-conditional probability density function and the *a priori* probability of the ith class, respectively. This error probability results when one has complete knowledge of the probability density functions with which to construct the optimal decision rule and uses the Bayes decision rule. Knowledge of the underlying distributions could have resulted from observing an infinite number of independent labeled pattern samples. Thus the Bayes error rate can be thought of as the infinite-sample error.

2) The error probability that results when one has complete knowledge of the probability density functions and uses a decision rule other than the Bayes' rule is denoted by P_e^c.

It is clear that $P_e^c \geq P_e^B$, with equality holding when the given classifier is (Bayes) optimal. The term P_e will be used when no distinction is made between P_e^c and P_e^B, and it will be referred to as the "actual" error probability.

In practice one usually obtains a data set which is not only finite, but in fact quite small. Frequently no knowledge is available concerning the underlying distributions. In such situations one would, ideally, like to know what the resulting probability of error is going to be on future pattern samples when the classifier is trained, i.e., its parameters estimated, on the given data set.

3) Denote by $\hat{P}_e$ the probability of error on future performance when the classifier is trained on the given data set.

4) Denote by $E\{\hat{P}_e\}$ the expected error probability on future performance over the distribution of training sets. $\hat{P}_e$ is an estimate of $E\{\hat{P}_e\}$ and both approach the "actual" error probability P_e as the number of pattern samples approaches infinity. $\hat{P}_e$ and $E\{\hat{P}_e\}$ are also known in the literature as error rates of the sample-based classifier design or decision rule. It is obvious that $\hat{P}_e^B \geq P_e^B$, although it is not necessarily true that $\hat{P}_e^c \geq P_e^c$ unless the underlying distributions are such that the given classifier is Bayes optimal.

5) Denote the "apparent" error probability by $P_e(\text{app})$. For example, $P_e^B(\text{app})$ is obtained by estimating the probability distributions or their parameters and subsequently substituting these estimated values into the expression for error probability. The apparent Bayes error probability is given by

$$P_e^B(\text{app}) = 1 - \int \max_i \{\hat{P}(X/C_i)\hat{P}(C_i)\}\, dX$$

where $\hat{P}(X/C_i)$ and $\hat{P}(C_i)$ are estimates of $P(X/C_i)$ and $P(C_i)$, respectively.

Alternately, one can consider the "apparent" error probability to be that obtained when the sample-based classifier design or decision rule is tested on an infinite number of pattern samples coming from distributions, the parameters of which take on the estimated rather than the true values. $P_e^B(\text{app})$ may be greater or less than P_e^B, but has a tendency to be optimistically biased.

6) For 1), 3), 4), and 5) and any classifier considered in 2), denote by $P_{e_{ij}}$ the *transition probability of error* that a pattern belonging to class i is classified into class j, for $i, j = 1,2,\cdots,M$, $i \neq j$, where there are M classes.

7) For 1), 3), 4), and 5) and any classifier considered in 2), denote by $P_{e|C_i}$ the *class-conditional probability of error*, i.e., the probability that any one pattern belonging to class i is misclassified. It follows that

$$P_{e|C_i} = \sum_{\substack{j=1 \\ j\neq i}}^{M} P_{e_{ij}}.$$

8) For 1), 3), 4), and 5) and any classifier considered in 2), denote by $P_{e|X}$ the *conditional probability of error* given a particular unclassified pattern. It follows that

$$P_e = \int P(X)P_{e|X}\, dX$$

where $P(X)$ is the unconditional, or mixture, distribution.

In most pattern recognition problems one is interested in $\hat{P}_e$. However, $\hat{P}_e$ cannot be obtained exactly because, by definition, all the available pattern samples are used for training the classifier and hence none are left for testing it. Several methods are available for estimating $\hat{P}_e$. Some of these methods are described in the following. Emphasis is placed on nonparametric techniques, since usually nothing is known about the distributions.

There are two basic approaches to the problem of estimation of misclassification: the nonparametric approach, which is almost always used in problems such as character recognition; and the parametric approach, in which it is

Manuscript received March 10, 1973; revised January 22, 1974.
The author is with the School of Computer Science, McGill University, Montreal, P.Q., Canada.

Reprinted from *IEEE Trans. Inform. Theory*, vol. IT-20, pp. 472–479, July 1974.

assumed that the unknown distributions belong to a parametric family. The nonparametric methods will be considered first.

Let $\{X,\theta\} = \{X_1, \theta_1; X_2, \theta_2; \cdots; X_N, \theta_N\}$ be the set of N pattern samples available, where X_i and θ_i denote, respectively, the measurement information and the label or classification information of the ith pattern sample. It is assumed that each θ_i associated with X_i is the correct label, i.e., the pattern samples have been correctly preclassified.

Method 1

The first method considered here is the resubstitution, or R method, which consists of the following steps.

1) The classifier is trained on $\{X,\theta\}$.

2) The classifier is tested on $\{X,\theta\}$.

Let the resulting proportion of errors encountered during testing be denoted by $\hat{P}_e[R]$. When pattern recognition as a field of study was still in its infancy, $\hat{P}_e[R]$ was a popular method of estimating $\hat{P}_e$. As a matter of fact, this method of estimating $\hat{P}_e$ was suggested by some statisticians in discriminant analysis long ago [161].

Researchers in the field of pattern recognition soon became interested in the "generalizing" capability of a "learning" machine (adaptive classifier), which gave rise to methods 2)–4). It should be noted that although the three methods are discussed separately for the purpose of clarity and historical perspective, they are all special cases of the method referred to by some statisticians as cross-validation.

Method 2

The second method under investigation is the holdout, or H method, which can be described as follows.

1) Partition $\{X,\theta\}$ into two mutually exclusive sets $\{X,\theta\}_\alpha$ and $\{X,\theta\}_\beta$ such that

$$\{X,\theta\}_\alpha = \{X_1, \theta_1; X_2, \theta_2; \cdots; X_{N(\alpha)}, \theta_{N(\alpha)}\}$$

$$\{X,\theta\}_\beta = \{X_{N(\alpha)+1}, \theta_{N(\alpha)+1}; \cdots; X_N, \theta_N\}$$

and $N(\beta) = N - N(\alpha)$.

2) Train the classifier on $\{X,\theta\}_\alpha$.

3) Test the classifier on $\{X,\theta\}_\beta$.

Let the proportion of errors observed during testing be denoted by $\hat{P}_e[H]$. Traditionally 50 percent of the available samples have been used for training, and 50 percent for testing. The H method was analyzed by Highleyman [89], who indicated a method for obtaining confidence intervals on the results and presented graphs showing how a finite data set of size N should be partitioned between training and test sets for various values of N. However, Kanal and Chandrasekaran [112] showed that Highleyman's analysis and the resulting graphs are valid only when N is sufficiently large, whereas the problem of estimation of misclassification is of most concern when N is small. Additional work on obtaining confidence intervals and partitioning the data set can be found in [16], [17], [50], [51], [118], [127], and [143]. Researchers using the R and H methods soon reported large discrepancies between $\hat{P}_e[R]$ and $\hat{P}_e[H]$. Some of the important works that discuss these discrepancies are [11], [18], [31], [45], [46], [88], and [142]. It was observed that $\Delta\hat{P}_e(H - R) \triangleq \hat{P}_e[H] - \hat{P}_e[R]$ was usually positive, and it was conjectured [45], [88], that the value of $\Delta\hat{P}_e(H - R)$ was inversely proportional to sample size and that

$$\lim_{N\to\infty} \{\Delta\hat{P}_e(H - R)\} = 0.$$

As it turns out, although the R method uses the data efficiently, it is an overly optimistic estimate of performance. Furthermore, unless N is large, the H method tends to give an overly pessimistic estimate of performance, as well as an unreliable one because the value of $\hat{P}_e[H]$ for a given data set depends on the partitioning of $\{X,\theta\}$. The H method also uses the data in an inefficient manner. It can, however, be made more reliable by averaging $\hat{P}_e[H]$ over all possible partitions of fixed size.

1) Partition $\{X,\theta\}$ into K randomly chosen pairs of sets of equal size

$$\{X,\theta\}_\alpha^1 : \{X,\theta\}_\beta^1, \cdots, \{X,\theta\}_\alpha^K : \{X,\theta\}_\beta^K$$

such that for $i = 1,2,\cdots,K$, $\{X,\theta\}_\alpha^i$ and $\{X,\theta\}_\beta^i$ are mutually exclusive.

2) For $i = 1,2,\cdots,K$ train the classifier on $\{X,\theta\}_\alpha^i$ and test it on $\{X,\theta\}_\beta^i$, letting the resulting proportion of errors be denoted by $\hat{P}_e[H]_i$.

3) An estimate of the expected value of $\hat{P}_e[H]$ over the partitions is then given by

$$\frac{1}{K}\sum_{i=1}^{K} \hat{P}_e[H]_i. \tag{1}$$

This method of improving the reliability of the estimate was mentioned by Duda and Hart [46], and is known in some circles as "data shuffling" [68]. Although the estimate in (1) uses the data more efficiently than the H method, it still uses only half of the available data for training each time. Furthermore, the final result is still overly pessimistic.

A method which has come to be known in North American circles as the U method or "leave-one-out" method goes a long way towards making efficient use of the data and yielding an estimate of performance with a small amount of bias compared to the previous methods.

Method 3—(U Method)

1) Take one pattern sample (X_i,θ_i) out of $\{X,\theta\}$. Then define

$$\{X,\theta\}_i \triangleq \{X_1, \theta_1; \cdots; X_{i-1}, \theta_{i-1}; X_{i+1}, \theta_{i+1}; \cdots; X_N, \theta_N\}.$$

2) Train the classifier on $\{X,\theta\}_i$.

3) Test the classifier on (X_i,θ_i). If X_i is classified into the category associated with θ_i, set $e_i = 0$; otherwise set $e_i = 1$, where e_i acts as an error indicator.

4) Do steps 1)–3) for $i = 1,2,\cdots,N$ to obtain values for e_i, $i = 1,2,\cdots,N$.

5) The estimate of $\hat{P}_e$, denoted by $\hat{P}_e[U]$, is then computed as follows:

$$\hat{P}_e[U] = \frac{1}{N}\sum_{i=1}^{N} e_i. \tag{2}$$

In the statistics literature the U method is attributed to Lachenbruch, [90], [165], who published results on it as early as 1967 [119]. However, the U method has been under investigation in the pattern recognition literature since the early 1960's. Lunts and Brailovskiy [128] attribute the U method, which they refer to as a "sliding" estimate, to Weinzweig, and they themselves published experimental and theoretical work on it as early as 1964 [21], [22], and [128]. An experimental comparison of the U method with the R method and the actual error probability for different ratios of sample size to feature size (dimensionality) for different nonnormal distributions is given in [124].

In spite of its advantages with regard to bias, the U method suffers from at least two disadvantages. Denote by $E\{\hat{P}_e[U]\}$ the expected value of $\hat{P}_e[U]$ over the distribution of training sets. Although it is desirable to have $E\{\hat{P}_e[U]\}$ "close" to the actual error probability, it is probably more important to use an estimator with a small variance. Hence, an estimator which is more biased than the U method but has a much smaller variance may be preferred by a researcher who may then have more confidence about his particular result on his particular data set. This problem has been considered by Lunts and Brailovskiy [128], who also derive an expression for the variance of $\hat{P}_e[U]$ under certain restrictions. Glick has shown that the U method has much greater variance than the R method for discrete distributions and, in fact, the U method in some sense achieves bias reduction in exactly the "worst" way for the discrete case.[1] Recently Lissack and Fu [126] have proposed a method which they call the F method, and have reported experimental results on Gaussian data. They found that the F method was less biased and had smaller variance than the U method. A second practical disadvantage of the U method is that it requires excessive computation in the distribution-free-case, in the form of N training sessions, unless N is very small. For the case of Gaussian distributions a certain amount of computation can be saved [63], [64], [119]. To combat this disadvantage of the U method the following method, also referred to as the rotation or Π method, was proposed in [171] and [173].

Method 4—(Π *Method*)

1) Take a small subset of pattern samples

$$\{X,\theta\}_i^{TS} \triangleq \{X_1, \theta_1; X_2, \theta_2; \cdots; X_P, \theta_P\}$$

such that $1 \leq P \ll N$ and N/P is an integer, $P/N \leq \frac{1}{2}$. Then

$$\{X,\theta\}_i^{TR} \triangleq \{X_{p+1}, \theta_{p+1}; \cdots; X_N, \theta_N\}.$$

2) Train the classifier on $\{X,\theta\}^{TR}$.

3) Test the classifier on $\{X,\theta\}_i^{TS}$ to obtain a proportion of errors denoted by $\hat{P}_e[\Pi]_i$.

4) Do steps 1)–3) for $i = 1,2,\cdots,N/P$ such that $\{X,\theta\}_i^{TS}$ and $\{X,\theta\}_j^{TS}$ are disjoint for $i = 1,2,\cdots,N/P$, $J = 1,2,\cdots,N/P$, and $i \neq j$.

5) The resulting estimate of $\hat{P}_e$ is computed as

$$\frac{P}{N}\sum_{i=1}^{N/P} \hat{P}_e[\Pi]_i. \quad (3)$$

[1] Ned Glick, personal communication.

Note that when $P = 1$ the Π method reduces to the U method. On the other hand, when $P = N/2$ the Π method reduces essentially to the H method, where the roles of training and testing are interchanged. This is the well-known "cross-validation in both directions" method [139].[2] The Π method is also considered in [128]. Obviously, the Π method is a compromise between the U and H methods. One would expect the Π method to be less biased than the H method (depending on the values of P, N, and λ, where λ denotes feature size, dimensionality, or the number of parameters to be estimated) and to require less computation than the U method. Therefore, it is a method well suited to "medium-sized" data sets. Some experimental results on this method of estimating $\hat{P}_e$ are given in [99], [100], [172], and [174]. This method of cross-validation has the flavor of the estimation methods used in statistics to reduce bias that are referred to as "jackknifing" procedures [138].

Two problems closely related to the estimation of the probability of misclassification from a given data set are: 1) reducing the bias of the estimates of the parameters that results when designing the classifier, especially when the training set is small, and 2) estimating the stability of the classifier or estimated parameters based on the given data set. The jackknife [138] serves the dual purpose of eliminating bias in the estimates of the parameters and giving an honest measure of variability, based on the training data itself. For example, consider a linear discriminant function $g(X)$. Let the data be divided into k subgroups and let $g_{\text{all}}(X)$ and $g_j(X)$ denote the discriminant functions computed using the entire data set and using all the data left after omitting the jth subgroup, respectively. The jackknifed discriminant function is then given by

$$g^*(X) = kg_{\text{all}}(X) - \frac{k-1}{k}\sum_{j=1}^{k} g_j(X). \quad (4)$$

In [139] Mosteller and Tukey propose a "leave-two-out" method[3] in which jackknifing and cross-validation are carried out simultaneously. At each step one pattern sample is put aside for cross-validation while another is successively removed from the remaining group of size $N - 1$ in order to obtain a jackknifed classifier design. These methods have been applied to an authorship classification problem in [138]–[141].

Several studies [56], [57] show that these estimates of $\hat{P}_e$ converge to $\hat{P}_e$ as $N \to \infty$. In particular, a quantity such

[2] This method is referred to as "double cross-validation" in the psychology literature [137], [145]. A further extension of these methods is possible, as indicated by Norman [145]. For example, one can use "triple cross-validation" [145] to estimate the probability of misclassification of the best subset of n out of N features for a specified feature-selection criterion. The data set is first partitioned into three subsets. With knowledge of each subset of data, a subset of n features is chosen with the specified feature-selection criterion. For each of the three subsets of n features the classifier is trained with a data subset not used in the feature subset selection procedure. Finally, the classifier incorporating a particular feature subset is tested on the third data subset. The average of the three results is a measure of the performance of the best n features according to a given feature-selection criterion.

[3] It should be kept in mind that this "leave-two-out" method is not the same as the "second-order-jackknife." The latter involves leaving two out for the purpose of bias reduction and has nothing to do with cross-validation. Work on the "second-order-jackknife" can be found in Adams *et al.*, *Ann. Math. Statist.*, vol. 42, pp. 1606–1612, 1971.

as $E\{\hat{P}_e[R]\}$ approaches $\hat{P}_e$ from below whereas another quantity such as $E\{\hat{P}_e[\Pi]\}$ approaches $\hat{P}_e$ from above. Therefore, another estimate for $\hat{P}_e$ can be defined as

$$\hat{P}_e^* = W(N,P,\lambda)\frac{P}{N}\sum_{i=1}^{N/P}\hat{P}_e[\Pi]_i + [1 - W(N,P,\lambda)]\hat{P}_e[R] \qquad (5)$$

where $0 \leq W(N,P,\lambda) \leq 1$. In fact, since (3) and $\hat{P}_e[R]$ are estimates of $\hat{P}_e$ biased in opposite directions, it should be possible to determine the function $W(N,P,\lambda)$, at least empirically, such that $\hat{P}_e^*$ is an essentially unbiased estimate of $\hat{P}_e$. For example, in the work of Foley [56], the average of the results on the test set and training set provides quite a good estimate of the actual error probability, even for small N. In [174], $\hat{P}_e^*$ was applied to a problem in medical diagnosis and it was found empirically that for $W(N,P,\lambda) =$ constant $= 1/2$ and $P/N = 1/10$, where $N = 300$, $\hat{P}_e^*$ was essentially equal to $\hat{P}_e[U]$. Furthermore, a tremendous saving was realized, because 300 training sessions were needed to obtain $\hat{P}_e[U]$, whereas for $\hat{P}_e^*$ only 11 training sessions were needed—one to obtain $\hat{P}_e[R]$ and ten to obtain (3).

Studying the error probability on the training and testing sets as a function of N, the number of pattern samples, is not the whole story. The estimation of $\hat{P}_e$ is also intimately related to the number of features or measurements used by the classifier.[4] Early experimental observations of this dependence in pattern recognition, discriminant analysis, and disease diagnosis can be found in [4], [5], [33], [38], [49], [67], [73], and [175]. Some theoretical work along the same lines is given in [1], [28], [29], [46], [56], [57], [96], [98], [111], and [154]. The problem of estimating $\hat{P}_e$ is further complicated by the fact that it depends on whether there exist dependencies among the features and ultimately on the actual distributions for the problem at hand. One measure of error probability not yet defined here is the "problem-average" error rate or, as defined by Hughes [96], the "mean-recognition-accuracy" denoted by $\bar{P}_e(L,N)$, where N is the number of samples and L is the number of "cells" or values X can take in the discrete case. $\bar{P}_e(L,N)$ represents the error probability averaged over all possible pattern recognition problems or distributions on X. Further results on $\bar{P}_e(L,N)$ are given in [1], [28], [29], [98], and [111].

The literature contains a wide variety of other methods (the parametric methods) for estimating various measures of probability of misclassification when certain *a priori* information concerning the distributions is available. These methods usually invoke the normality assumption. An example is the D method in [123], where it is assumed that there are two classes ($M = 2$) with means μ_1 and μ_2, and equal covariance matrix Σ. Obviously, if the parameters were known there would be no problem and the class-conditional Bayes probabilities of misclassification would be given by

$$P_{e|C_1}^B = P_{e|C_2}^B = \Phi(-\delta/2)$$

where $\delta^2 = (\mu_1 - \mu_2)^T\Sigma^{-1}(\mu_1 - \mu_2)$ is the Mahalanobis distance, Φ is the cumulative normal distribution, and T denotes the transpose. When the parameters are not known the D method yields an estimate of $P_{e|C_i}^B$, $i = 1,2$, which is given by

$$P_i = \Phi(-D/2)$$

where D^2 is the Mahalanobis sample distance when the sample means $\bar{X}_1$ and $\bar{X}_2$ and the sample covariance matrix S are substituted for μ_1, μ_2, and Σ, respectively. Various modifications of this D method exist, in which different types of estimates of the Mahalanobis distance are used. Discussions and comparisons of all these methods can be found in [23], [119], [120], [122], [123], [151], [162]–[165], and [167]. It should be noted that the D method yields the "apparent" error rate discussed earlier for the case of normal distributions.

The parametric approach to estimation of misclassification involves two other theoretical aspects of the problem: the distributions of classification statistics on one hand [19], [20], [84], [102]–[110], [133]–[135], [146], [158], [159], and the convergence properties of the estimators on the other [54], [55], [74]–[76], [176]. For example, in a typical approach, for the two-category problem with Gaussian distributions and known equal covariance matrices, John [102] proposes a classification procedure based on the calculation of a classification statistic and derives an analytic expression, in the form of an infinite series, for the probability of misclassification as a function of N_1 and N_2, where $N_1 + N_2 = N$ and N_i is the number of training pattern samples in the ith category. Furthermore, for the case of M categories, $M > 2$, he derives an upper bound on the probability of misclassification. In order to set up the classification procedure and to study performance characteristics, such as the probability of misclassification, it is necessary to know the distribution of the statistic used in the classification procedure. In [104] John gives the exact distribution of several classification statistics. Glick [75], [76] extensively covers what he calls "plug-in" estimates (for Gaussian distributions, actually the D method of Lachenbruch and Mickey [123]) and "deletion-counting" estimates (actually the "sliding" estimates in [128] or the U method in [123]). He also considers these estimates for various decision rules such as the nearest-neighbor rule.

The "deleted nearest-neighbor" estimate of $\hat{P}_e$ was first proposed by Cover [39]. Since then further theoretical work has been done on the estimate and on an interesting modification of it in [178], [179], and [187]. The modification is essentially a recursively updated nearest-neighbor estimate as new pattern samples are added. Experimental work with the deleted nearest-neighbor estimate can be found in [174] and [184]. Additional work on the convergence of nearest-neighbor estimates is given in [41], [42], [78], [82], [85], [147]–[150]. Estimating error probabilities using nearest-neighbor rules requires a great

[4] Anderson and Isenhour [6] have recently done extensive Monte Carlo studies on dimensionality λ versus sample size N as related to linear separability. They found that even for constant N/λ the probability of error on the testing set tends to decrease as λ increases for values of $N/\lambda < 3$.

deal of storage when data sets are large. Hence some attempts have been made at decreasing the size of the training data; in some cases better estimates of $\hat{P}_e^B$ are obtained than those obtained by using the entire training set [53], [83], [87], [147], [170], and [186].[5]

Some further miscellaneous work concerning the estimation of $\hat{P}_e$ and related problems can be found in [3], [12], [13], [15], [34], [36], [37], [58], [81], [116], [125], [152], [156], and [166]. Friedman defines $\Delta = \hat{P}_e^B - P_e^B$ as the "error determined by a classifier," the parameters of which are estimated from a particular training set. For the two-class problem with equal *a priori* probabilities, he derives expected values of Δ and examines their asymptotic behavior for a few simple univariate Gaussian cases. Wilkins and Ford [185] discuss the effects of unrepresentative samples present in the training sets.

The reader should be reminded that estimating the error on a given data set by making proper use of the best procedures available is only half the problem. One may have a large enough data set relative to the number of parameters to be estimated, but does it adequately represent the variability in the data for the problem one is trying to solve? Hence a problem of perhaps even greater importance than the previous one is the adequacy of the data set itself. For example, in speech recognition and alphanumeric handprinted character recognition, thousands of samples are required to represent the true variability in the data from the population at large. This is the price which must be paid when the underlying class-conditional distributions are not known.

Acknowledgment

The author is grateful to the referees for their helpful comments and to T. Cover for reading the manuscript and suggesting stylistic changes, as well as removing ambiguities. The references on cross-validation in the psychology literature were compiled by L. Goldberg and brought to my attention by E. Mark Gold, who also contributed to stimulating discussions on the jackknife and cross-validation methods. Thanks are due to all those who kindly sent in reprints of their work. The author would be grateful to be informed of any additional references on these topics that readers may be aware of and that have been left out of this bibliography.

References

[1] K. Abend, T. J. Harley, Jr., B. Chandrasekaran, and C. F. Hughes, "Comments 'On the mean accuracy of statistical pattern recognizers'," *IEEE Trans. Inform. Theory* (Corresp.), vol. IT-15, pp. 420–423, May 1969.

[2] A. A. Afifi and S. P. Azen, *Statistical Analysis: A Computer Oriented Approach.* New York: Academic Press, 1972, pp. 244–245.

[3] R. Albreht and W. Werner, "Error analysis of a statistical decision method," *IEEE Trans. Inform. Theory*, vol. IT-10, pp. 34–38, Jan. 1964.

[4] D. C. Allais, "Selection of measurements for prediction," Stanford Electron. Res. Lab., Stanford, Calif., Rep. SEL-64-115, TR 6103-9, Nov. 1964.

[5] ——, "The problem of too many measurements in pattern recognition and prediction," in *IEEE Int. Conv. Rec.*, vol. 14, pt. 2, 1966, pp. 124–130.

[6] D. N. Anderson and T. L. Isenhour, "Empirical studies of separability and prediction using threshold logic units," *Pattern Recognition*, vol. 5, pp. 249–258, Sept. 1973.

[7] T. W. Anderson, "Classification by multivariate analysis," *Psychometrika*, vol. 16, pp. 31–50, 1951.

[8] ——, "Asymptotic evaluation of the probabilities of misclassification by linear discriminant functions," in *Discriminant Analysis and Applications*, T. Cacoullos, Ed. New York: Academic Press, 1973, pp. 17–35.

[9] ——, "An asymptotic expansion of the distribution of the studentized classification statistic," *Ann. Statist.*, vol. 1, pp. 964–972, Sept. 1973.

[10] T. W. Anderson, S. D. Gupta, and G. P. Styan, *A Bibliography of Multivariate Statistical Analysis.* New York: Wiley, 1972.

[11] P. Armitage, "Recent developments in medical statistics," *Rev. Int. Stat. Inst.*, vol. 34, pp. 27–42, 1966.

[12] S. P. Azen and A. A. Afifi, "Asymptotic and small-sample behaviour of estimated Bayes rules for classifying time dependent observations," *Biometrics*, vol. 28, pp. 898–998, Dec. 1972.

[13] ——, "Two models for assessing prognosis on the basis of successive observations," *Mathematical Biosciences*, vol. 14, pp. 169–176, 1972.

[14] M. S. Bartlett, "An inverse matrix adjustment arising in discriminant analysis," *Ann. Math. Statist.*, vol. 22, pp. 107–111, 1951.

[15] M. S. Bartlett and N. W. Please, "Discrimination in the case of zero mean differences," *Biometrika*, vol. 50, pp. 17–21, 1963.

[16] L. S. Belobragina and V. K. Eliseev, "Statistical investigation of a recognition algorithm for type-written symbols," *Kibernetika*, vol. 3, no. 6, pp. 65–72, 1967; see also English translation in *Cybernetics*, vol. 3, no. 6, pp. 51–57, 1967.

[17] ——, "Statistical estimation of recognition error probability from experimental data," *Kibernetika*, vol. 3, no. 4, pp. 81–89, 1967; see also English translation in *Cybernetics*, vol. 3, no. 4, pp. 67–73, 1967.

[18] W. W. Bledsoe, "Further results on the N-tuple pattern recognition method," *IRE Trans. Electron. Comput.* (Corresp.), vol. EC-10, p. 96, Mar. 1961.

[19] A. H. Bowker, "A representation of Hotelling's T^2 and Anderson's statistic W in terms of simple statistics," *Contributions to Probability and Statistics.* Stanford, Calif.: Stanford Univ. Press, 1960, pp. 142–150.

[20] A. H. Bowker and R. Sitgreaves, "Asymptotic expansion for the distribution function of the W-classification statistic," in *Studies in Item Analysis and Prediction*, H. Solomon, Ed. Stanford, Calif.: Stanford Univ. Press, 1961.

[21] V. L. Brailovskiy, "An object recognition algorithm with many parameters and its applications," *Eng. Cybern.* (USSR), no. 2, pp. 22–30, 1964.

[22] V. L. Brailovskiy and A. L. Lunts, "The multiparameter recognition problem and its solution," *Eng. Cybern. (USSR)*, no. 1, pp. 13–22, 1964.

[23] J. D. Broffitt, "Estimating the probability of misclassification based on discriminant function techniques," Ph.D. dissertation, Colorado State Univ., Fort Collins, 1969.

[24] ——, "Minimum variance estimators for misclassification probabilities in discriminant analysis," *J. Multivariate Analysis*, vol. 3, pp. 311–327, Sept. 1973.

[25] J. D. Broffitt and J. S. Williams, "Distributions of functions of $A = (ZZ')^{-1/2}Z$ where the density of Z satisfies certain symmetry conditions," Dep. Statistics, Univ. Iowa, Iowa City, Tech. Rep. 7, 1971.

[26] L. S. Chan, "The treatment of missing values in discriminant analysis," M.S. thesis, Univ. California, Los Angeles, 1970.

[27] L. S. Chan and O. J. Dunn, "The treatment of missing values in discriminant analysis—1. The sampling experiment," *J.A.S.A.*, vol. 67, no. 338, 473–477, June 1972.

[28] B. Chandrasekaran, "Independence of measurements and the mean recognition accuracy," *IEEE Trans. Inform. Theory*, vol. IT-17, pp. 452–456, July 1971.

[29] B. Chandrasekaran and A. K. Jain, "Quantization of independent measurements and recognition performance," presented at the 1972 IEEE Int. Symp. Information Theory.

[30] Z. Chen and K. S. Fu, "Nonparametric Bayes risk estimation for pattern classification," in *Proc. IEEE Conf. on Systems, Man, and Cybernetics*, Boston, Mass., Nov. 5–7, 1973.

[31] C. K. Chow, "A recognition method using neighbour dependence," *IRE Trans. Electron. Comput.*, vol. EC-11, pp. 683–690, Oct. 1962.

[32] ——, "On optimum recognition error and reject tradeoff," *IEEE Trans. Inform. Theory*, vol. IT-16, pp. 41–46, Jan. 1970.

[33] J. T. Chu and J. C. Chueh, "Error probabilities in decision functions for character recognition," *J. Ass. Comput. Mach.*, vol. 14, pp. 273–280, Apr. 1967.

[34] W. G. Cochran, "On the performance of linear discriminant functions," *Bull. Int. Statist. Inst.*, vol. 34, pp. 435–447, 1961;

[5] Applications of these methods to judicial decisions can be found in [129].

also in *Technometrics*, vol. 6, pp. 179–190, 1964.
[35] ——, "Commentary on estimation of error rates in discriminant analysis," *Technometrics*, vol. 10, pp. 204–205, Feb. 1968.
[36] W. G. Cochran and C. E. Hopkins, "Some classification problems with multivariate qualitative data," *Biometrics*, vol. 17, pp. 10–32, 1961.
[37] J. Cornfield, "Joint dependence of risk on coronary heart disease on serum cholesterol and systolic blood pressure: a discriminant function analysis," *Fed. Proc.* (Abstr.), vol. 21, no. II, pp. 58–61, 1962.
[38] ——, "Discriminant functions," *Rev. Int. Statist. Inst.*, vol. 35, pp. 142–153, 1967.
[39] T. M. Cover, "Learning in pattern recognition," *Methodologies of Pattern Recognition*, S. Watanabe, Ed. New York: Academic Press, 1969, pp. 111–132.
[40] ——, "Geometrical and statistical properties of linear inequalities with applications in pattern recognition," *IEEE Trans. Electron. Comput.*, vol. EC-14, pp. 326–334, June 1965.
[41] ——, "Rates of convergence of nearest neighbor decision procedures," presented at 1st Annu. Hawaii Conf. Systems Theory, Jan. 1968, pp. 413–415.
[42] T. M. Cover and P. E. Hart, "Nearest neighbor pattern classification," *IEEE Trans. Inform. Theory*, vol. IT-13, pp. 21–27, Jan. 1967.
[43] E. E. Cureton, "Approximate linear restraints and best predictor weights," *Educational and Psychological Measurement*, vol. 11, pp. 12–15, 1951.
[44] ——, "Validity, reliability, and boloney," *Educational and Psychological Measurement*, vol. 10, pp. 94–96, 1950.
[45] R. O. Duda and H. Fossum, "Pattern classification by iteratively determined linear and piecewise linear discriminant functions," *IEEE Trans. Electron. Comput.*, vol. EC-15, pp. 220–232, Apr. 1966.
[46] R. O. Duda and P. E. Hart, *Pattern Classification and Scène Analysis*. New York: Wiley, 1973.
[47] O. J. Dunn, "Some expected values for probabilities of correct classification in discriminant analysis," *Technometrics*, vol. 13, pp. 345–353, May 1971.
[48] O. J. Dunn and P. D. Varady, "Probabilities of correct classification in discriminant analysis," *Biometrics*, vol. 22, pp. 908–924, 1966.
[49] S. E. Estes, "Measurement selection for linear discriminants used in pattern classification," Ph.D. dissertation, Stanford University, Stanford, Calif., 1965.
[50] V. K. Eliseev, "Statistical methods of the experimental investigation of reliability (quality) of recognition systems," in *Proc. Seminar Pattern Recognition and Construction of Reading Automata* (in Russian), no. 1, Kiev, 1966.
[51] ——, "Statistical investigation of the reliability of a reading automaton with optical correlation," collection in *Reading Automata* (in Russian), izd-vo Naukova dumka, Kiev, 1965.
[52] T. B. Farver, "Stepwise selection of variables in discriminant analysis," Ph.D. dissertation, Univ. California, Los Angeles, 1972.
[53] F. P. Fischer, "A preprocessing algorithm for nearest neighbour decision rules," in *Proc. Nat. Electron. Conf.*, Chicago, Ill., Dec. 7–9, 1970, pp. 481–485.
[54] E. Fix and J. L. Hodges, "Discriminatory analysis: nonparametric discrimination: small sample performance," U.S. School of Aviation Medicine, Randolph Field, Tex., Project 21-49-004, Rep. 11, AF 4(128)-31, 1952.
[55] ——, "Nonparametric discrimination: consistency properties," U.S. School of Aviation Medicine, Randolph Field, Tex., Project 21-49-004, Rep. 4, AF 41(128)-31, 1951.
[56] D. H. Foley, "Considerations of sample and feature size," *IEEE Trans. Inform. Theory*, vol. IT-18, pp. 618–626, Sept. 1972.
[57] ——, "The probability of error on the design set as a function of the sample size and feature size," Ph.D. dissertation, Syracuse Univ., Syracuse, N.Y., June 1971; also Tech. Rep. RADC-TR-71-171.
[58] I. Francis, "Inference in the classification problem," Ph.D. dissertation, Harvard Univ., Cambridge, Mass., 1966.
[59] H. D. Friedman, "On the expected error in the probability of misclassification," *Proc. IEEE*, vol. 53, pp. 658–659, June 1965.
[60] K. Fukunaga, *Introduction to Statistical Pattern Recognition*. Academic Press, 1972, ch. 5.
[61] K. Fukunaga and D. Kessell, "Nonparametric Bayes error estimation using unclassified samples," *IEEE Trans. Inform. Theory*, vol. IT-19, pp. 434–439, July 1973.
[62] ——, "Application of optimum error-reject functions," *IEEE Trans. Inform. Theory* (Corresp.), vol. IT-18, pp. 814–817, Nov. 1972.
[63] ——, "Error evaluation and model validation in statistical pattern recognition," Sch. Elec. Eng., Purdue Univ., Tech. Rep. TR-EE 72-23, Aug. 1972.
[64] ——, "Estimation of classification error," *IEEE Trans. Comput.*, vol. C-20, pp. 1521–1527, Dec. 1971.
[65] ——, "A model for error estimation," in *Proc. 1971 IEEE Conf. Decision and Control* (including *10th Symp. Adaptive Processes*), Miami Beach, Fla., Dec. 15–17, pp. 351–352.
[66] K. Fukunaga and T. F. Krile, "Calculation of Bayes recognition error for two multivariate Gaussian distributions," *IEEE Trans. Comput.*, vol. C-18, pp. 220–229, Mar. 1969.
[67] W. R. Gaffey, "Discriminatory analysis: perfect discrimination as the number of variables increases," U.S. School of Aviation Medicine, Randolph Field, Tex., Project 21-49-004, Feb. 1951.
[68] M. F. Gardiner *et al.*, "The interpretation of statistical measures from discriminant analysis in evoked response experiments," in *Proc. 5th Hawaii Int. Conf. Systems Sciences, Computers in Biomedicine*, 1972, pp. 235–237.
[69] S. Geisser, "Predictive discrimination," in *Proc. Int. Symp. Multivariate Analysis*, P. R. Krishnaiah, Ed. New York: Academic Press, 1966, pp. 149–163.
[70] ——, "Posterior odds for multivariate normal classification," *J. Roy. Stat. Soc.*, series B, vol. 26, pp. 69–76, 1964.
[71] ——, "Estimation associated with linear discriminants," *Ann. Math. Statist.*, vol. 38, pp. 807–817, 1967.
[72] S. G. Ghurye and I. Olkin, "Unbiased estimation of some multivariate probability densities and related functions," *Ann. Math. Statist.*, vol. 40, no. 4, pp. 1261–1271, 1969.
[73] E. S. Gilbert, "On discrimination using qualitative variables," *J. Amer. Statist. Ass.*, vol. 63, pp. 1399–1412, Dec. 1968.
[74] N. Glick, "Sample-based classification procedures derived from density estimators," *J.A.S.A.*, vol. 67, pp. 116–122, Mar. 1972.
[75] ——, "Sample-based multinomial classification," *Biometrics*, vol. 29, pp. 241–256, June 1973.
[76] ——, "Classification procedures based on random samples from a mixture," Univ. Chicago, Chicago, Ill., Tech. Rep., 69 pp. (obtainable from author, Dep. Mathematics, Univ. British Columbia, Vancouver, B.C., Canada).
[77] E. Mark Gold, "Simple formulae for jackknife crossvalidation," July 1972, informal report available from the author, Department d'Informatique, Univ., Montreal, Montreal, P.Q., Canada.
[78] M. Goldstein, "k_n-Nearest neighbour classification," *IEEE Trans. Inform. Theory*, vol. IT-18, pp. 627–630, Sept. 1972.
[79] H. L. Gray and W. R. Schucany, *The Generalized Jackknife Statistic*. New York: Marcel Dekker, Inc., 1973.
[80] S. D. Gupta, "Theories and methods in classification: a review," in *Discriminant Analysis and Applications*, T. Cacoullos, Ed. New York: Academic Press, 1973, pp. 77–137.
[81] T. J. Harley, L. N. Kanal, and N. C. Randall, "System considerations for automatic imagery screening," in *Pictorial Pattern Recognition*, G. C. Cheng *et al.*, Eds. Washington, D.C.: Thompson, 1968, pp. 15–31.
[82] P. E. Hart, "An asymptotic analysis of the nearest neighbour decision rule," Stanford Electronics Labs., Stanford, Calif., Tech. Rep. 1828-2, May 1966.
[83] ——, "The condensed nearest neighbour rule," *IEEE Trans. Inform. Theory* (Corresp.), vol. IT-14, pp. 515–516, May 1968.
[84] H. L. Harter, "On the distribution of Wald's classification statistic," *Ann. Math. Statist.*, vol. 22, pp. 58–67, 1951.
[85] M. E. Hellman, "The nearest neighbour classification rule with a reject option," *IEEE Trans. Syst. Sci. Cybern.*, vol. SSC-6, pp. 179–185, July 1970.
[86] P. Herzberg, "The parameters of cross-validation," *Psychometrika* (Suppl.), vol. 34, no. 16, 1969.
[87] R. P. Heydorn, "Nonparametric classification," Ph.D. dissertation, Ohio State Univ., Columbus, Ohio, 1971.
[88] W. H. Highleyman, "Linear decision function, with application to pattern recognition," *Proc. IRE*, vol. 50, pp. 1501–1514, June 1962.
[89] ——, "The design and analysis of pattern recognition experiments," *Bell Syst. Tech. J.*, vol. 41, pp. 723–744, Mar. 1962.
[90] M. Hills, "Allocation rules and their error rates," *J. Roy. Statist. Soc.*, series B, no. 28, pp. 1–31, 1966.
[91] ——, "Discrimination and allocation with discrete data," *J. Roy. Statist. Soc.*, series C, vol. 16, no. 2, pp. 237–250, 1967.
[92] P. G. Hoel and R. P. Peterson, "A solution to the problem of optimum allocation," *Ann. Math. Statist.*, vol. 20, pp. 433–438, 1949.
[93] H. Hudimoto, "On the distribution-free classification of an individual into one of two groups," *Ann. Inst. Stat. Math.*, vol. 8, pp. 105–112, 1956.
[94] ——, "A note on the probability of the correct classification when the distributions are not specified," *Ann. Inst. Stat. Math.*, vol. 9, pp. 31–36, 1958.
[95] ——, "On a distribution-free two-way classification," *Ann. Inst. Stat. Math.*, vol. 16, pp. 247–253, 1964.
[96] G. F. Hughes, "On the mean accuracy of statistical pattern recognizers," *IEEE Trans. Inform. Theory*, vol. IT-14, pp. 55–63, Jan. 1968.
[97] G. F. Hughes and J. A. Lebo, "Data reduction using information theoretic techniques," Rome Air Development Center, Griffiss Air Force Base, Rome, N.Y., RADC Rep. TR-67-67, Mar. 1967, pp. 45–46.
[98] G. F. Hughes, "Number of pattern classifier design samples per

class," *IEEE Trans. Inform. Theory* (Corresp.), pp. 615–618, Sept. 1969.
[99] A. B. S. Hussain, G. T. Toussaint, and R. W. Donaldson, "Results obtained using a simple character recognition procedure on Munson's handprinted data," *IEEE Trans. Comput.* (Short Notes), vol. C-20, pp. 201–205, Feb. 1972.
[100] A. B. S. Hussain, "Sequential decision schemes for statistical pattern recognition problems with dependent and independent hypotheses," Ph.D. dissertation, Univ. British Columbia, Vancouver, B.C., Canada, June 1972.
[101] S. John, "Errors in discrimination," *Ann. Math. Statist.*, vol. 32, pp. 1125–1144, 1961.
[102] ——, "On some classification problems—I," *Sankhya: Ind. J. Stat.*, vol. 22, pp. 301–308, 1960.
[103] ——, "On classification by the statistics R and Z," *Ann. Inst. Stat. Math.*, vol. 14, pp. 237–246, 1962.
[104] ——, "On some classification statistics," *Sankhya: Ind. J. Stat.*, vol. 22, pp. 309–316, 1960.
[105] ——, "The distribution of Wald's classification statistic when the dispersion matrix is known," *Sankhya: Ind. J. Stat.*, vol. 21, pp. 371–376, 1959.
[106] ——, "Corrigenda to a paper 'On some classification problems—I'," *Sankhya: Ind. J. Stat.*, vol. 23, ser. A, p. 308, 1961.
[107] ——, "Corrigenda to a paper 'On some classification statistics'," *Sankhya: Ind. J. Stat.*, vol. 23, ser. A, p. 308, 1961.
[108] ——, "Further results on classification by W," *Sankhya: Ind. J. Stat.*, vol. 26, ser. A, pp. 39–46, 1964.
[109] ——, "Corrections to 'On classification by the statistics R and Z'," *Ann. Inst. Stat. Math.*, vol. 17, p. 113, 1965.
[110] D. G. Kabe, "Some results on the distribution of two random matrices used in classification procedures," *Ann. Math. Statist.*, vol. 34, p. 181, 1964 (a correction to this article appeared in *Ann. Math. Statist.*, vol. 34, p. 924, 1964).
[111] R. Y. Kain, "The mean accuracy of pattern recognizers with many pattern classes," *IEEE Trans. Inform. Theory* (Corresp.), vol. IT-15, pp. 424–425, May 1969.
[112] L. Kanal and B. Chandrasekaran, "On dimensionality and sample size in statistical pattern classification," in *Proc. Nat. Electron. Conf.*, vol. 24, pp. 2–7, 1968; also in *Pattern Recognition*, vol. 3, pp. 225–234, Oct. 1971.
[113] L. Kanal and N. C. Randall, "Recognition system design by statistical analysis," in *Proc. 19th Nat. Conf. Ass. Computing Machinery*, pp. D2-5-1–D2-5-10, 1964.
[114] R. A. Katzell, "Cross-validation of item analyses," *Educational and Psychological Measurement*, vol. 11, pp. 16–22, 1951.
[115] M. G. Kendall and A. Stuart, *The Advanced Theory of Statistics*, vol. 3. London: Griffin, 1966, pp. 328–329.
[116] C. F. Kossack, "A handbook of statistical classification techniques," Purdue Univ., Lafayette, Ind., Res. Rep. 601-866, 1964.
[117] A. Kudo, "The classificatory problem viewed as a two-decision problem," *Memoirs Faculty of Science*, Kyushu University, series A, vol. 13, pp. 96–125, 1959.
[118] E. F. Kushner, "Experiments on the application of the correlation method for the recognition of figures and letters written by hand," in *Proc. Seminar Pattern Recognition and Construction of Reading Automata* (in Russian), Kiev, 1966.
[119] P. A. Lachenbruch, "An almost unbiased method of obtaining confidence intervals for the probability of misclassification in discriminant analysis," *Biometrics*, vol. 23, pp. 639–645, Dec. 1967.
[120] ——, "On expected probabilities of misclassification in discriminant analysis, necessary sample size, and a relation with the multiple correlation coefficient," *Biometrics*, vol. 24, pp. 823–834, Dec. 1968.
[121] ——, "Some results on the multiple group discriminant problem," in *Discriminant Analysis and Applications*, T. Cacoullos. Ed. New York: Academic Press, 1973, pp. 193–211.
[122] ——, "Estimation of error rates in discriminant analysis," Ph.D dissertation, Univ. California, Los Angeles, 1965.
[123] P. A. Lachenbruch and R. M. Mickey, "Estimation of error rates in discriminant analysis," *Technometrics*, vol. 10, no. 1, pp. 1–11, 1968.
[124] P. A. Lachenbruch, C. Sneeringer, and L. T. Revo, "Robustness of the linear and quadratic discriminant functions to certain types of non-normality," *Communications in Statistics*, vol. 1, no. 1, pp. 39–56, 1972.
[125] L. E. Larsen, *et al.*, "On the problem of bias in error rate estimation for discriminant analysis," *Pattern Recognition*, vol. 3, pp. 217–224, Oct. 1971.
[126] T. Lissack and K. S. Fu, "A separability measure for feature selection and error estimation in pattern recognition," Sch. Elec. Eng., Purdue Univ., Lafayette, Ind., Tech. Rep. TR-EE-72-15, May 1972.
[127] V. I. Loginov, "Probability estimates of the quality of a pattern recognition decision rule," *Eng. Cybern.* (USSR), no. 6, pp. 112–117, 1968.
[128] A. L. Lunts and V. L. Brailovskiy, "Evaluation of attributes obtained in statistical decision rules," *Eng. Cybern.* (USSR), no. 3, pp. 98–109, 1967.
[129] E. Mackaay and P. Robillard, "Predicting judicial decisions: the nearest neighbour rule and visual representation of case patterns," Publication no. 131, Department d'Informatique, Univ. Montreal, Montreal, P.Q., Canada.
[130] S. Marks, "Discriminant functions when covariance matrices are unequal," Ph.D. dissertation, Univ. California, Los Angeles, 1970.
[131] D. C. Martin and R. R. Bradley, "Probability models, estimation, and classification for multivariate dichotomous populations," *Biometrics*, vol. 28, pp. 203–222, 1972.
[132] G. J. McLachlan, "An asymptotic expansion for the variance of the errors of misclassification of the linear discriminant function," *Aust. J. Statist.*, vol. 14, pp. 68–72, 1972.
[133] A. Z. Memon, "Z statistic in discriminant analysis," Ph.D. dissertation, Iowa State Univ., Ames, Iowa, 1968.
[134] A. Z. Memon and M. Okamoto, "The classification statistic W^* in covariate discriminant analysis," *Ann. Math. Statist.*, vol. 41, pp. 1491–1499, 1970.
[135] ——, "Assymptotic expansion of the distribution of the Z statistic in discriminant analysis," *J. Multivariate Analysis*, vol. 1, pp. 294–307, Sept. 1971.
[136] J. Michaelis, "Simulation experiments with multiple group linear and quadratic discriminant analysis," in *Discriminant Analysis and Applications*, T. Cacoullos, Ed. New York: Academic Press, 1973, pp. 225–238.
[137] C. I. Mosier, "Problems and designs of cross-validation," *Educational and Psychological Measurement*, vol. 11, pp. 5–11, 1951.
[138] F. Mosteller, "The jackknife," *Rev. Int. Statist. Inst.*, vol. 39, no. 3, pp. 363–368, 1971.
[139] F. Mosteller and J. W. Tukey, "Data analysis, including statistics," in *Revised Handbook of Social Psychology*, vol. 2, G. Lindzey and E. Aronson, Eds. Reading, Mass.: Addison-Wesley, 1968, ch. 10, pp. 80–203.
[140] F. Mosteller and D. L. Wallace, "Inference in an authorship problem," *J.A.S.A.*, vol. 58, pp. 275–309, 1963.
[141] ——, *Inference in an Authorship Problem: The Federalist.* Reading, Mass.: Addison-Wesley, 1964.
[142] J. H. Munson, R. O. Duda, and P. E. Hart, "Experiments with Highleyman's data," *IEEE Trans. Comput.* (Short Notes), pp. 399–401, Apr. 1968.
[143] R. A. Nashlyunas and A. V. Lashas, "The problem of estimating the reliability of recognition algorithms," collection in *Automatics and Computational Technology* (in Russian), izd-vo Mintis, Vil'nyus, 1965.
[144] G. E. Nicholson, Jr., "Prediction in future samples," in *Contributions to Probability and Statistics*, I. Olkin *et al.*, Eds. Stanford, Calif.: Stanford Univ. Press, 1960, pp. 322–330.
[145] W. T. Norman, "Double-split cross-validation: an extension of Mosier's design, two undesirable alternatives, and some enigmatic results," *J. Appl. Psychol.*, vol. 49, pp. 348–357, 1965.
[146] M. Okamoto, "An asymptotic expansion for the distribution of the linear discriminant function," *Ann. Math. Statist.*, vol. 34, pp. 1286–1301, 1963. Correction in *Ann. Math. Statist.*, vol. 39, p. 1358, 1968.
[147] E. A. Patrick, *Fundamentals of Pattern Recognition.* Englewood Cliffs, N.J.: Prentice-Hall, 1972, ch. 4.
[148] E. A. Patrick and F. P. Fisher, "Generalized k nearest neighbour decision rule," *Inform. Contr.*, vol. 16, pp. 128–152, Apr. 1970.
[149] C. R. Pelto, "Adaptive nonparametric classification," *Technometrics*, vol. 11, pp. 775–792, Nov. 1969.
[150] D. W. Peterson, "Some convergence properties of a nearest neighbour decision rule," *IEEE Trans. Inform. Theory*, vol. IT-16, pp. 26–31, Jan. 1970.
[151] R. E. Pogue, "Some investigations of multivariate discrimination procedures, with applications to diagnosis clinical electrocardiography," Ph.D. dissertation, Univ. Minnesota, Minneapolis, 1966.
[152] C. R. Rao, "On a general theory of discrimination when the information on alternate hypotheses is based on samples," *Ann. Math. Statist.*, vol. 25, pp. 651–670, 1954.
[153] P. R. Rayment, "The identification problem for a mixture of observations from two normal populations," *Technometrics*, vol. 14, pp. 911–918, Nov. 1972.
[154] J. Sammon, D. H. Foley, and A. Proctor, "Considerations of dimensionality versus sample size," in *Proc. 1970 IEEE Symp. Adaptive Processes*, Dec. 7–9, Austin, Tex.
[155] W. Schaafsma, "Classifying when populations are estimated," in *Discriminant Analysis and Applications*, T. Cacoullos, Ed. New York: Academic Press, 1973, pp. 339–364.
[156] N. Sedransk, "Contributions to discriminant analysis," Ph.D. dissertation, Iowa State University, Ames, 1969.
[157] N. Sedransk and M. Okamoto, "Estimation of the probabilities of misclassification for a linear discriminant function in the univariate normal case," *Ann. Inst. Stat. Math.*, vol. 23, no. 3, pp. 419–435, 1971.
[158] R. Sitgreaves, "On the distribution of two random matrices

used in classification procedures," *Ann. Math. Statist.*, vol. 23, pp. 263–270, 1952.
[159] ——, "Some results on the distribution of the *W*-classification statistic," in *Studies in Item Analysis and Prediction.* Stanford, Calif.: Stanford Univ. Press, 1961, pp. 241–261.
[160] ——, "Some operating characteristics of linear discriminant functions," in *Discriminant Analysis and Applications*, T. Cacoullos, Ed. New York: Academic Press, 1973, pp. 365–374.
[161] C. A. B. Smith, "Some examples of discrimination," *Ann. Eugen.*, vol. 18, p. 272, 1947.
[162] M. Sorum, "Estimating the expected and the optimal probabilities of misclassification," *Technometrics*, vol. 14, pp. 935–943, Nov. 1972.
[163] ——, "Estimating the probability of misclassification," Ph.D. dissertation, Univ. Minnesota, Minneapolis, 1968.
[164] ——, "Three probabilties of misclassification," *Technometrics*, vol. 14, pp. 309–316, May 1972.
[165] ——, "Estimating the conditional probability of misclassification," *Technometrics*, vol. 13, pp. 333–343, May 1971.
[166] ——, "Estimating the expected probability of misclassification for a rule based on the linear discriminant function: univariate normal case," *Technometrics*, vol. 15, pp. 329–340, May 1973.
[167] M. Sorum and R. J. Buehler, "Some conditional estimation problems with applications to estimating the probability of misclassification," Statist. Dep., Univ. Minnesota, Minneapolis, Tech. Rep. 112, 1968.
[168] M. S. Srivastava, "Evaluation of misclassification errors," *Can. J. Statist.*, vol. 1, no. 1, pp. 35–50, 1973.
[169] D. Stoller, "Univariate two-population distribution-free discrimination," *J.A.S.A.*, vol. 49, pp. 770–777, 1954.
[170] C. W. Swonger, "Sample set condensation for a condensed nearest neighbour decision rule for pattern recognition," in *Frontiers of Pattern Recognition*, Satosi Watanabe, Ed. New York: Academic Press, 1972, pp. 511–526.
[171] G. T. Toussaint, "Machine recognition of independent and contextually constrained contour-traced handprinted characters," M.A.Sc. thesis, Univ. British Columbia, Vancouver, Canada, Dec. 1969.
[172] ——, "Feature evaluation criteria and contextual decoding algorithms in statistical pattern recognition," Ph.D. dissertation, Univ. British Columbia, Vancouver, Canada, Oct. 1972.
[173] G. T. Toussaint and R. W. Donaldson, "Algorithms for recognizing contour-traced handprinted characters," *IEEE Trans. Comput.*, vol. C-19, pp. 541–546, June 1970.
[174] G. T. Toussaint and P. M. Sharpe, "An efficient method for estimating the probability of misclassification applied to a problem in medical diagnosis," *Computers in Biology and Medicine*, to be published.
[175] J. R. Ullman, "Experiments with the *n*-tuple method of pattern recognition," *IEEE Trans. Comput.*, vol. C-18, pp. 1135–1137, Dec. 1969.
[176] J. Van Ryzin, "Bayes risk consistency of classification procedures using density estimation," *Sankhya: Ind. J. Stat.*, vol. A28, pts. 2 and 3, pp. 261–270, 1966.
[177] ——, "Nonparametric Bayesian decision procedures for (pattern) classification with stochastic learning," in *Trans. 4th Prague Conf. Information Theory, Statistical Decision Functions, Random Processes.* Prague: Czechoslovak Academy of Sciences, 1967.
[178] T. J. Wagner, "Convergence of the nearest neighbour rule," *IEEE Trans. Inform. Theory*, vol. IT-17, pp. 566–571, Sept. 1971.
[179] ——, "Deleted estimates of the Bayes risk," *Ann. Statist.*, vol. 1, pp. 359–362, Mar. 1973.
[180] A. Wald, "On a statistical problem in the classification of an individual into one of two groups," *Ann. Math. Statist.*, vol. 15, pp. 145–162, 1944.
[181] W. G. Wee, "On computational aspects and properties of a pattern classifier," presented at 5th Hawaii Int. Conf. System Sciences, Jan. 1972, pp. 598–600.
[182] R. J. Wherry, "Comparison of cross-validation with statistical inference of betas and multiple *R* from a single sample," *Educational and Psychological Measurement*, vol. 11, pp. 23–28, 1951.
[183] J. Wiggin, *Personality and Prediction.* Reading, Mass.: Addison-Wesley, 1973, pp. 46–49.
[184] A. W. Whitney, "A direct method of nonparametric measurement selection," *IEEE Trans. Comput.*, vol. C-20, pp. 1100–1103, Sept. 1971.
[185] B. R. Wilkins and N. L. Ford, "The analysis of training sets for adaptive pattern classifiers," in *Proc. Conf. Machine Perception of Patterns and Pictures*, Teddington, England, London, England, Apr. 12–14, 1972, pp. 267–275.
[186] D. L. Wilson, "Asymptotic properties of nearest neighbour rules using edited data," *IEEE Trans. Syst., Man, Cybern.*, vol. SMC-2, pp. 408–420, July 1972.
[187] C. T. Wolverton, "Strong consistency of an estimate of the asymptotic error probability of the nearest neighbour rule," *IEEE Trans. Inform. Theory*, vol. IT-19, pp. 119–120, Jan. 1973.
[188] M. Zielezny, "A two-stage classification rule based on expected cost," Ph.D. dissertation, Univ. California, Los Angeles, 1971.

ON DIMENSIONALITY AND SAMPLE SIZE IN STATISTICAL PATTERN CLASSIFICATION[1]

Laveen Kanal[2] and B. Chandrasekaran[3]

Philco-Ford Corp.
Blue Bell, Penna.

I. INTRODUCTION

Some questions on dimensionality and sample size which arise in the statistical approach to the design of pattern classification systems are: what is the best way to use a fixed size sample to design a classification system and evaluate its performance? When a certain finite number of samples is available what should be the dimensionality of the pattern vector, i.e., how many variables should be used, and if one can get as many samples as one wants, can the probability of error be made arbitrarily small by increasing the number of samples?

Surprising as it may seem now, in much of the earlier work in pattern classification, especially that based on adaptive algorithms, the entire set of available samples was first used for design and future performance was then predicted to be that achieved on this design set. By now it is well known that this procedure is biased, resulting in too optimistic an estimate of performance.

The choice between competing design procedures can only be based on predicted performance. We would like the ranking of procedures based on performance estimated from a fixed size sample to correspond to the ranking that would occur given actual performance. Moreover we want the estimated performance of the system finally selected to be a "good" predictor of its actual performance. Both the sizes of the design and test sample sets influence the accuracy of these estimates. We are then faced with the problem of the optimum use of a fixed size sample for maximizing the accuracy of these estimates. This can be considered without reference to the specific competing design procedures.

Pattern vector dimensionality enters into the effectiveness of the design based on finite samples. In statistical classification, estimation, and prediction, it has often been noted that, with finite samples, performance does not always improve as the number of variables is arbitrarily increased. Sometimes it may even deteriorate. This added to the increase in system complexity for more variables, makes the relationship of pattern vector dimensionality to design sample size, worth investigation.

Some answers to these questions have been previously proposed. In this paper we (1) examine the specific formulation and applicability of the proposed solutions and consider modifications which make the results more useful; (2) formulate a tradeoff between the number of variables and the number of samples, and (3) consider the role of structural assumptions in questions concerning dimensionality and sample size.

II. DESIGN AND TESTING

Suppose we have alternate design procedures applicable to a problem and have a finite sample set. Eventually we want to choose the best design procedure and then use it to design a system with all available samples. But first we do the alternate designs using only part of the total sample set and then test their performance on the remainder. This method is hereafter referred to as the holdout or H method.

For the selection of the best design procedure based on performance data we need to maximize our confidence in the test results obtained. On the other hand we would like the systems designed with a subset of the available samples to reflect faithfully the design based on the entire set. This leads to the problem of optimum use of a sample set to maximize overall confidence in the design and testing of the system.

To our knowledge, Ref. 1 is the only publication presenting analytical results for this problem. The paper suggests partitioning the total sample set into disjoint design and test sets and obtains the optimum partitioning to minimize the variance of the estimated error rate. The assumptions underlying the analysis are: the error rate, e, can be expressed as a function of a finite number of estimated parameters; it can be expanded into a Taylor series about the error rate, e_o, of the optimum system based on infinite design samples; and the deviations $(e - e_o)$ are small enough for terms, in the expansion, higher than second order to be neglected. The result of the analysis is a set of curves showing the fractions of the available sample set, which should be used for design and testing, versus a function of the ideal error, e_o, the total number of samples, t, and a quantity which measures the effectiveness of the design.

The H method analysed in Ref. 1 and the recommendations given there are interesting. However, it has not been recognized that they are valid only when the total sample size is large. When a prescription is most needed, i.e., in the small sample case, the analysis breaks down because the deviations $(e - e_o)$ can no longer be considered small enough to be approximated by just two terms of the Taylor expansion. In this case the resulting recommendations are not applicable. Fortunately, approaches other than the H method are possible and do apply to the small sample case. They also give a better estimate of the error rate for the system designed with all the available samples, something for which there is no provision in the

---

[1] Invited talk, Pattern Recognition Session, Natl. Electr. Conf., Chicago, 1968.

[2] Work contributed in support of Contract F33615-67-C-1836 at Philco-Ford Corp., and Research Grant AFOSR-68-1390 at Lehigh Univ.

[3] Work supported by Contract F33615-67-C-1836, Aerospace Medical Research Laboratories, Aerospace Medical Division, Air Force Systems Command, Wright-Patterson AFB, Ohio.

Reprinted with permission from *Proc. Nat. Electron. Conf.*, vol. XXIV, Dec. 9-11, 1968, pp. 2-7.

H method.

We suggest the use of the following method, which is the most promising general procedure among the various procedures that have been experimentally evaluated in Ref. 2. The problem considered in this paper is more general than the one posed in Ref. 1, but this only enhances the usefulness of the results. If m is the total number of samples, take all possible partitions of size 1 for the test set and m-1 for the design set. This results in successively omitting one sample in the design procedure. The estimates of error obtained are unbiased estimates of the error rate for a design based on m-1 samples. Following Ref. 2, we term this the U method.

The H method is quite uneconomical with samples; the U method is definitely superior in this respect. However, it requires the computation of m designs for each candidate procedure. If the design calls for the inversion of a covariance matrix, the prospect of computing m inverses might appear formidable. Fortunately an identity by Bartlett leads to a method which requires only one explicit inversion for each class covariance matrix (only one for the whole problem if covariance matrices are assumed equal). The details are given in Refs. 2 and 3.

Having considered the first question mentioned in the introduction we turn to the relationship between dimensionality and sample size. We consider first the ideal situation.

III. INFINITE SAMPLE SIZE

Optical Character Recognition is an example of situations in which the designer has, potentially, a large, essentially infinite sample. Models leading to very optimistic and rather pessimistic results have been presented for classification based on an infinite sample set. Representative of optimistic results are those presented in Refs. 4, 5, and 6. Ref. 4, which appears to have gone unnoticed during the last decade, assumes multivariate Gaussian distributions. Its results are sharper than those presented in Ref. 6 which are more general since they do not invoke the Gaussian assumption. However, Ref. 6 assumes independent variables. Ref. 5 evaluates bounds for the error rate for independent, Gaussian variables. These references derive conditions whereby the probability of error can be made arbitrarily close to zero as the number of variables increases.

In the multivariate normal case, with $\mu_k^{(i)}$ and σ_k denoting respectively the mean and variance of the kth variate in class i, with variances assumed equal for both classes, this result is obtained, when the variables are independent, if

$$\Delta_k = \left|\frac{\mu_k^{(1)} - \mu_k^{(2)}}{\sigma_k}\right| > \delta > 0 \text{ for all k,}$$

and $\sum_{k=1}^{\infty} \Delta_k^2$ diverges. If the variables are not independent, but the lower bound δ for the Δ_k's exists, then the sufficient condition becomes, roughly speaking, that all the elements r^{kj} of the reciprocal of the correlation matrix be non-zero. Or we have the equivalent necessary condition that the series

$$\sum_{k=1}^{s} \sum_{j=1}^{s} r^{kj} \Delta_k \Delta_j \quad \text{diverge.}$$

If we do not assume normal distributions and let $f_1(x_k)$ and $f_2(x_k)$ be the probability density functions of the variable X_k for classes 1 and 2 respectively, then defining a distance by

$$d_k = \int_{X_k} |f_1(x_k) - f_2(x_k)| \, dx_k,$$

the condition, $\sum_{k=1}^{\infty} d_k$ diverges, is sufficient for the probability of error to be arbitrarily close to zero when the number of variables is increased indefinitely.

The implication of these conditions is that if each variable, being considered for inclusion in the decision function, contributes ever so little to the discrimination, by using sufficient numbers of them, we can eventually get perfect discrimination. A corrolary is that, by adding another variable, even if we don's do any better, we can never do any worse.

How much do these optimistic results help us in practice? First the assumption of independence for arbitrarily large numbers of observables is unrealistic. In most practical problems the observables represent bandlimited functions such as two dimensional visual patterns and time functions. Even if we are prepared to process all the observables there are just so many independent ones available. Secondly, in practice it is even more difficult to determine if they are truly independent than if

$$\sum_{k=1}^{\infty} d_k \quad \text{or} \quad \sum_{k=1}^{\infty} \Delta_k^2 \quad \text{diverges.}$$

Thirdly, these results do not give any idea of the danger involved in the statement "the more, the better" applied to the number of variables, when the number of samples available for estimating the decision function is not large. This last point is quite important in a number of contexts (e.g. Ref.7).

The extreme among pessimistic results is that presented in Ref. 8. This reference considers the problem of finding the average probability of error over all problems with a fixed number of measurement states. The number of measurement states can be computed as follows. If we have N variables and the kth variable can take on one of r_k values, then the total number of measurement states is

$$\prod_{k=1}^{N} r_k.$$

No assumption of statistical independence or dependence between the variables is made, nor is there a metric in the measurement space. The latter point, broadly speaking, means that no parametric families of distributions can be reasonably fitted on the probability functions in the measurement space. This statistical model is general enough and even, as we shall see, too general. In this model, in making the decision about class membership, we need the probabilities $P[S_i/\alpha]$ where S_i are the measurement states and α the class index. When S_i occurs, the class for which $P(\alpha)\ P(S_i/\alpha)$ is highest is decided upon as the class from which the pattern came. If we know these probabilities, or equivalently if we have an infinite number of samples from which to estimate them, then for two class problems with equal prior probabilities, Ref. 8 establishes that, on the average, even if we increase the number of measurement states (or the number of variables) indefinitely the probability of correct recognition only approaches 0.75.

This result takes into account that in some problems the variables may be independent, in some others correlated; in some the probability densities may be continuous while in others they may be essentially discontinuous. The figure 0.75 for the probability of correct recognition over all such problems is admittedly a consequence of the particular probability distribution over the problem-space. This particular distribution is summarized by the statement that the quantities $p(S_i/\alpha)$ are for all α's, uniformly distributed in the n-1 dimensional simplex

$$\left\{[p(S_1/\alpha), \ldots p(S_{n-1}/\alpha)]: p(S_i/\alpha) \geq 0, i=1,\ldots n-1; \sum_{i=1}^{n-1} p(S_i/\alpha) \leq 1\right\} \quad \text{and } p(S_n/\alpha)$$

$$\text{is } 1 - \sum_{i=1}^{n-1} p(S_i/\alpha).$$

Here n is the total number of discrete measurement values that are assumed possible. The results based on this model are further examined in the section on probability structure and sample size.

IV. FINITE SAMPLE SIZE

In many problems such as target recognition and fault diagnosis, the available sample size is finite and usually small. The relationship of measurement-space dimensionality to sample size is considered in Ref. 8, within the framework of a statistical model which is very general, assuming practically no structure. The model is the same as that described for Ref. 8 previously except that $P(S_i/\alpha)$ are now not known but need to be estimated from samples; a suitable decision rule is based on these estimates.

Defining measurement complexity as the total number of measurement states allowed, the mean correct recognition probability is calculated as an average of performance over all classification problems falling within the purview of the model and having a specified measurement complexity and prior class probabilities. The reason for considering prior probabilities as a separate parameter is that some interesting phenomena occur for the case of unequal prior probabilities. Some paradoxes present in Ref. 8, have been clarified in Refs. 9, and 10. We now consider the consequences of the general model of Ref. 8, taking into account the contributions of Refs. 9, and 10.

Let m_1 and m_2 be the number of samples available for estimating the parameters for both the classes and let n be the measurement complexity. Let r_i and s_i be the numbers of times out of m_1 and m_2 respectively, that the measurement value S_i occurred for classes 1 and 2. Let the prior probabilities of the classes be given by p_{c_1} and p_{c_2}. The Bayes decision rule (Ref. 9) is then to compare the quantities

$$\left(p_{c_1} \frac{r_i + 1}{m_1 + n}\right) \text{ and } \left(p_{c_2} \frac{s_i + 1}{m_2 + n}\right)$$

and assign S_i to class 1 if the first is greater than the second, and assign it to class 2 otherwise.

When the a priori probabilities of the classes are equal, this decision rule leads to an average performance curve in which, for a fixed number of samples, when the measurement complexity is increased, the mean classification accuracy increases until an optimum value is reached after which performance falls off. At infinite measurement complexity the performance is no better than that based on prior probabilities. As would be expected, the value of the optimum measurement complexity increases with the number of samples. The values obtained are astonishingly pessimistic. For instance, when 500 samples are available from each class, the optimum measurement complexity is 23. For a vector of binary variables, this allows less than 5 variables. As shown in Ref. 10 some interesting variations on this behaviour occur for the case of unequal prior probabilities. The existence of an optimum measurement complexity is a likely characteristic of all statistical classification systems designed with a finite sample.

Performance as a function of the dimensionality of the variables and the sample has been considered in Ref. 11. Although it deals with the prediction problem assuming Gaussian statistics, the important similarities between prediction and pattern classification make the results worth discussing.

The decision function considered in Ref. 11 is the maximum likelihood estimator of the ideal prediction function, based on known parameters, and derived from a minimum mean square error criterion. Assuming an N-dimensional multivariate normal vector with a non-singular, in general, non-diagonal correlation matrix and assuming that the predictand and the variable vector are jointly normal, the expected value of the error, ϵ, is given by

$$E(\epsilon) = \begin{cases} \rho^2\left(\frac{m+1}{m}\right)\left(1 + \frac{N}{m-N-2}\right) & \text{for } N < m-2 \\ \infty & \text{for } N = m-2 \\ \text{undefined} & \text{for } N \geq m-1, \end{cases}$$

where m is the number of samples available to estimate the predictor function, and ρ^2 is the minimum mean square error achievable when all the parameters are known. The ideal error ρ^2 is in general a monotonically non-increasing function of the dimensionality, N, such that, if the variables satisfy the conditions of Ref. 4, mentioned in the previous section,

$$\lim_{N \to \infty} \rho^2 = 0.$$

For $N < m-2$, there is an optimum value of N at which $E(\epsilon)$ is a minimum. The value of this optimum dimensionality depends on the particular form taken by $\rho^2(N)$. For instance (Ref. 11) if $\rho^2(N) = \frac{1}{1+0.03N}$ and m = 200, 82 variables provide the minimum expected error. Increasing the number of variables above this value only decreases the performance of the predictor.

V. A TRADE-OFF PROBLEM

We now formulate a trade-off between the number of samples and the number of variables. In many situations a cost is associated with acquiring one more sample or one more block of r samples. A cost is also associated with mechanizing sensor systems to measure one more variable. The motivation for considering the trade-off is that even when it is certain that increasing the number of variables is going to result in improved performance, it may be more cost-effective to achieve the same improvement by increasing the number of samples.

For illustration, consider the prediction problem of Ref. 11. For simplicity let us ignore the term $(m+1)/m$, which enters into the expression for the expected error, so that

$$\bar{\epsilon}(N,m) = \rho^2\left(\frac{m-2}{m-N-2}\right) \text{ for } N < m-2,$$

where m is the number of samples and N the number of variables. Let C_m be the cost associated with obtaining one more sample and C_N the cost to mechanize the system to measure one more variable. Assume that ρ^2, the ideal error, decreases as a function of N in the manner $\rho^2 = 1/1 + aN$, so that the N for which the minimum error is attained is

$$N_{opt} = \frac{(m-2)}{2} - \frac{1}{2a}.$$

The question then is: what are the optimum numbers of samples and variables which achieve a given error rate and minimize the cost ? Since the cost is $C = C_m \cdot m + C_N \cdot N$, letting the error rate $\bar{\epsilon} = E$, we can minimize the cost under this constraint. Substituting for m and ρ^2 from the expressions given above C can be written as

$$C = C_m\left[\frac{E(N+2)(1+aN) -2}{E(1+aN) -1}\right] + C_N \cdot N.$$

Setting dC/dN equal to zero gives the optimum number of variables corresponding to the error rate E:

$$N_{opt} = \frac{1}{aE}\left[(1-E) + \sqrt{(1-E)^2 + \frac{E(2C_N + C_m) - C_N}{(C_m + C_N)} - E^2}\right]$$

For $E \ll 1$, this expression can be reduced to

$$aEN_{opt} \approx (1-E) + \sqrt{(1-2E) + \frac{(2E-1)\frac{C_N}{C_m} + E}{1 + C_N/C_m}} = Q.$$

For $\frac{C_N}{C_m} \to 0$, $Q \to (1-E) + \sqrt{1-E} = (\sqrt{1-E})(\sqrt{1-E} + 1) \approx 2$;

for $\frac{C_N}{C_m} \to \infty$, $Q \to (1-E) \approx 1$.

Substituting $N_{opt} = Q/aE$ into the expression for $\bar{\epsilon}$ gives

$$m_{opt} - 2 \approx \frac{1}{aE}\left[\frac{Q(Q+E)}{Q-(1-E)}\right].$$

Thus, for $C_N/C_m \to 0$, $m_{opt} \to 4/aE = 2N_{opt}$; for $C_N/C_m \to \infty$, $m_{opt} \to \infty$.

These results prescribe, simply, that when variables are cheap relative to samples, having specified the optimum number of variables corresponding to the error rate E, we need only use twice that many samples; when variables are very expensive compared to samples we pick only half as many variables, viz, $1/aE$, and use a very large number of samples.

VI. PROBABILITY STRUCTURE AND SAMPLE SIZE

The optimum dimensionality corresponding to a given sample size depends on the probability structure assumed for the problem and the correspondence between the assumed structure and reality. Further, optimal decision procedures differ for different underlying probability structures. For instance decision procedures involving estimated covariance matrices when nothing is known, about the dependence or independence of the variables, are non-optimal when in fact the variables are independent.

The optimum dimensionality for a given sample size increases, in general, with the increased structure in the problem formulation, with a corresponding increase in the maximum probability of correct recognition. For example with a finite sample size and N binary variables, assuming no structure at all the problem is equivalent to the model in Ref. 8 where the measurement complexity is 2^N; with 500 samples from each class, the optimum number of variables is 5 and the optimal probability of correct recognition is 0.74. In contrast consider the problem generated by increasing the structure considerably by imposing the following constraints (Ref. 12, p. 25). Let $X = (X_1, \ldots X_N)$ and $Y = (Y_1, \ldots Y_N)$ denote respectively, the pattern vectors from class 1 and class 2, where the X_i's and Y_i's are independent, binary random variables with $P[x_i = 1] = \gamma$ and $P[Y_i = 1] = \beta = (1-\gamma)$ for all i. Let γ be estimated using m samples from each class. If sample $Z = (Z_1, \ldots Z_N)$ of unknown origin, to be classified into one of the two classes, contains r ones and N-r zeros, the Bayes decision rule is: decide class 1 if $r < N/2$ and $\hat{\gamma} < \frac{1}{2}$ or if $r > N/2$ and $\hat{\gamma} > 1/2$; and decide class 2 if $r < N/2$ and $\hat{\gamma} > 1/2$ or if $r > N/2$ and $\hat{\gamma} < \frac{1}{2}$. The probability of error is derived in Ref. 12. Going one step beyond Ref. 12 we arrive at the result of interest here. It can be verified that $\lim_{N\to\infty} P_e = 0$ for finite m and $\lim_{m\to\infty} P_e \neq 0$ for finite N. In this example, for any finite sample size, arbitrarily increasing the number of variables always improves performance. Thus the optimal measurement complexity for this highly structured problem is infinite. The case of non-identically distributed independent variables lies inbetween those of Ref. 8 and 12, and numerical results remain to be worked out.

Another aspect of the relationship between probability structure, sample size and measurement-space dimensionality is brought out rather clearly in any decision procedure involving the estimation of covariance matrices. Let a sample of size m be available from an N-variate population. Regardless of the actual population covariance matrix, if $N > m-1$, the estimated ocvariance matrix is singular. If samples from both classes are pooled to estimate a single covariance matrix, then with m now representing the total of samples from classes 1 and 2, the estimated covariance matrix is singular for $N > m - 2$. Traditionally this point was avoided by restricting consideration to those cases where the number of variables is less than m-2, although Hottelling (Ref. 13) explicitly mentions an example with four samples and five observables. In Ref. 13 Hottelling says "some of the information must be allowed to go to waste" and discards three of the five random variables. He admits his dissatisfaction with this procedure and with the alternate approach of removing the singularity problem by assuming independent variables. A rationale against reducing the number of variables to get around the singularity problem in the small sample case, is presented in Ref. 14. When the estimated covariance matrix is of rank $r < N$, then all the sample points lie on an r dimensional hyperplane. The suggestion by many authors of using the Generalized Inverse, which exists even for singular matrices, is undesirable as it constrains the estimated population to the r dimensional hyperplane of sample points. Ref. 15 presents a class of ''psuedo estimates'' for the covariance matrix, obtained by adding a term proportional to the average variance to each diagonal element of the sample estimate of the covariance matrix. It also contains examples showing the superiority of the suggested estimates over the Generalized Inverse solution. The Bayesian version and justification for the ad-hoc approach of Ref. 15 appears in Ref. 16. We note that from a Bayesian point of view the Generalized Inverse procedure is untenable since it implies a prior distribution which assigns zero probability to some part of the space of variates.

Consideration of the structural assumptions of the model of Ref. 8 leads to an explanation of the rather pessimistic results for measurement complexity. First, there is no provision in the model for the case of independent variables and consequently for the use of more variables than allowed by the general model. The mean performance is calculated as an average over all problems with various degrees of correlations between variables. This tends to lower the average performance from the value corresponding to the case of independent variables. However, in the abscence of any knowledge of independence it is not unreasonable to obtain average performance over all correlations that are possible.

Another important assumption responsible for the conservative results on measurement complexity is that of lack of continuity in probability values of neighboring measurement cells. To illustrate this consider just two variables Y_1 and Y_2 each taking values from 1 to 10, with increments of 1. Let us index the 100 measurement states as follows. States S_1 to S_{10} represent states for which $(Y_1, Y_2) = (i, 1)$ where i goes from 1 to 10; states S_{11} to S_{20} represent $(i, 2)$, $1 \leq i \leq 10$ and so on. If we construct three dimensional probability diagrams where one horizontal axis represents the ten values of Y_1, a second horizontal axis ten values of Y_2, and the vertical axis the probabilities associated with these values, we would normally not expect highly discontinuous changes in these probabilities. Ref. 8 gives an example where the estimated probabilities in a real problem are indeed discontinuous. However there are very many other problems where this does not apply, and in these cases the usefulness of the conservative results for maximum measurement complexity is questionable.

A further examination of this assumption provides meaning to these numbers and also an insight for tightening the design procedure. Continuity provides redundancy and redundancy is generally helpful in reducing error. However if estimates of the nature of this redundancy are unreliable performance can worsen rather than improve. When we do not have enough information for estimating redundancy, it can be removed by quantizing the variables no finer than is absolutely necessary. That is we provide just enough levels so that knowledge of $P[S_i/\alpha]$ does not increase our knowledge of $P[S_j/\alpha]$ where $j \neq i$. Another way to reduce the measurement complexity, when it is necessary to improve average performance, is to eliminate relatively insignificant variables. Various suggestions for the selection and evaluation of features have been made. A useful but not well known reference on this subject is Ref. 17.

VII. CONCLUSIONS

On the question of the optimum use of a fixed size sample to maximize overall confidence in the design and testing of pattern classification systems, the only published theoretical analysis of the simple partitioning of samples between design and test sets, and the recommendations based on it, are invalid in the small sample case. In this case a definitely superior alternate method is available.

On the question of how many variables to use in designing a classification system, the probability structure assumed and its correspondence to the real problem at hand determine the relationship between the design sample size, the number of variables and the probability of error. Earlier investigations led to very optimistic results while recent results have been very pessimistic. As we have shown, these are only extremes of a range of possibilities.

VIII. ACKNOWLEDGEMENTS

We are indebted to our collegues Kenneth Abend and Thomas J. Harley, Jr. for many helpful discussions.

IX. REFERENCES

1. Highleyman, W. H., ''The Design and Analysis of Pattern Recognition Experiments'', Bell Syst. Tech. Jour., March 1962, p. 723-744.
2. Lachenbruch, P. A., and M. R Mickey, ''Estimation of Error Rates in Discriminant Analysis'', Technometrics, Vol. 10, No. 1., Feb. 1968, p. 715-725.
3. Lachenbruch, P. A., Estimation of Error Rates in Discriminant Analysis, Ph.D. Dissertation, Univ. of Calif., Los Angeles, 1965.
4. Gaffey, W. R., '' Discriminatory Analysis: Perfect Discrimination as the Number of Variables Increases'', Report No. 5, Project No. 21-49-004, USAF School of Aviation Medicine, Randolf Field, Texas, Feb. 1951.
5. Albrecht, R., and W. Werner, '' Error Analysis of a Statistical Decision Method'', IEEE Trans. on Info. Theory, Vol. IT-10, No. 1, Jan. 1964, p. 34-38.
6. Chu, J. T., and J. C. Chueh, '' Error Probability in Decision Functions for Character Recognition'', Assn. Computing Machy. Jour., Vol. 14, No. 2, April 1967, p. 273-280.
7. Harley, T. J., L. N. Kanal, and N. C. Randall, '' System Considerations for Automatic Imagery Screening'', p. 15-31 in G. C. Cheng et al. (Editors), Pictorial Pattern Recognition, Thompson Book Co., Wash. D. C., 1968.
8. Hughes, G. F., '' On the Mean Accuracy of Statistical Pattern Recognizers'', IEEE Trans. on Info. Theory, Vol. IT-14, No. 1, Jan 1968, p. 55-63.
9. Abend, K., and T. J. Harley, '' On the Maximum Mean Accuracy of Statistical Pattern Recognizers'', correspondence submitted Apr. 1968 to IEEE. Trans. on Info. Theory.
10. Chandrasekaran, B., and T. J. Harley, ''Comments on the Mean Accuracy of Statistical Pattern Recognizers'', correspondence submitted July 1968 to IEEE Trans. on Info Theory.
11. Allais, D. C., '' The Selection of Measurements for Prediction'', Tech. Report. No. 6103-9, Stanford Electr. Lab. Nov. 1964; AD456770.

12. Abend, K., Compound Decision Procedures for Pattern Classification, Ph.D. Dissertation, Univ. of Pennsylvania, Philadelphia, Dec. 1966; also Report. No. AMRL-TR-67-10, Aerospace Medical Research Labs, Aerospace Medical Division, Air Force Systems Command, Wright-Patterson AFB, Ohio, Dec. 1967.
13. Hottelling, H., "Multivariate Analysis", Chap. 4 in O. Kempthorne(Editor), Statistics and Mathematics in Biology, 1954; reprint, New York: Hafner, 1964.
14. Kanal, L., and N. C Randall, "Recognition System Design by Statistical Analysis", Proc. 19th Natl. Conf. A.C.M., New York, Assoc. for Computing Machy. 1964, p. D2.5-1 to D2.5-10.
15. Harley, T. J., "Psuedoestimates versus Psuedo-Inverses for Singular Sample Covariance Matrices", Sect. 2 in Report No. 5, Contract DA-36-039-SC-90742, Sept. 1963 (AD427172); also M.S. thesis, More School of E.E. Univ. of Penn. 1965.
16. Ando, A., and G. M. Kaufman, 'Bayesian Analysis of the Independent Multinormal Process - Neither Mean nor Precision Known", Journ. Am. Stat. Assoc. Vol 60, No. 309, March 1965, p. 347-358.
17. Bargmann, R. E., Representative Ordering and Selection of Variables, Final Report, Project No. 1132, Virginia Polytechnic Institute, Blacksburg, June 1962.

Considerations of Sample and Feature Size

DONALD H. FOLEY, MEMBER, IEEE

Abstract—In many practical pattern-classification problems the underlying probability distributions are not completely known. Consequently, the classification logic must be determined on the basis of vector samples gathered for each class. Although it is common knowledge that the error rate on the design set is a biased estimate of the true error rate of the classifier, the amount of bias as a function of sample size per class and feature size has been an open question. In this paper, the design-set error rate for a two-class problem with multivariate normal distributions is derived as a function of the sample size per class (N) and dimensionality (L). The design-set error rate is compared to both the corresponding Bayes error rate and the test-set error rate. It is demonstrated that the design-set error rate is an extremely biased estimate of either the Bayes or test-set error rate if the ratio of samples per class to dimensions (N/L) is less than three. Also the variance of the design-set error rate is approximated by a function that is bounded by $1/8N$.

Introduction

IN MANY practical pattern-recognition problems, the underlying class conditional probability densities are either partially or completely unknown. Consequently, the classification logic must be designed from information based on representative samples from each class. The difficult question of how many samples are needed for an adequate classifier design naturally arises and has received some attention.

The deleterious effects of inadequate sample size have been discussed in the past. For multivariate normal distributions with common covariance, John [1] and Sitgreaves [2] discuss the distribution of the Fisher linear discriminant.[1] Estes [3] shows that the error rate using the Fisher linear discriminant deviates severely from the theoretical optimum when the ratio of sample size (N) to feature[2] size (L) is small. For the related problem of linear prediction, assuming normal statistics, Allais [4] derives a comparable result. Hughes [5] and Abend *et al.* [6] show that the average probability of correct classification over all possible discrete class distributions deteriorates as the ratio of samples to measurement states decreases. Ullman [7] has reported a similar phenomenon occurring in his experiments in the numeric handprint character-recognition problem. All of these results pertain to the expected performance of a classifier on future test samples when the classifier has been designed using a design set of finite size.

A number of people have noticed that the error rate on the design set gives an optimistically biased estimate of the true performance or error rate of the classifier. Hills [8] showed for multivariate normal distributions that the expected value of the estimated error rate of a classifier that was designed and tested on the same data (i.e., the design set) is always less than the true error rate. Lachenbruch and Mickey [9], Lachenbruch [10], and Fukunaga [11] have experimentally verified this result. Cover [12] has derived some results, which may be interpreted as follows: regardless of the true performance of a two-class classifier, if the total number of samples is less than twice the number of features, there exists a linear hyperplane such that the probability of error on the design set is always zero.[3]

Kanal and Chandrasekaran [13] have considered two questions. 1) What is the best way to design a classification system and evaluate its performance given a fixed sample size? 2) When a finite number of samples is available, how many features should be used? In answering the first question, Kanal recommends the "hold-one-out" method originally proposed by Lachenbruch [10]. In this method, a classifier is designed on $N - 1$ samples and tested on the one remaining sample. This procedure is then repeated for all N samples. In answering the second question, Kanal [13] points out that the number of features that can be used for a fixed sample size depends upon the probability structure assumed for the problem.

Generally speaking, the greater the knowledge of the underlying probability structure, the greater the number of features that can be used without degrading the performance of the classifier.

In this paper, the error rate on the design set as a function of the number of samples per class (N) and the number of features (L) is derived and related to both the true error rate of the classifier and the Bayes error rate for the corresponding minimum-probability-of-error classifier. The underlying probability structure consists of a) a two-class problem with equal *a priori* probabilities; b) a cost of 1 for any error and zero for any correct decision; c) N independent and identically distributed samples for each class from two multivariate normal distributions with common covariance.

The emphasis on the design set is for two reasons. First, although a number of authors have noted that the error rate on the design set is a biased estimate of the true error rate of the classifier, the amount of the bias as a function of sample size per class (N) and feature size (L) has been an open question until now. Secondly, in some problems the

Manuscript received January 27, 1971; revised January 12, 1972. This paper is part of a dissertation submitted to Syracuse University, Syracuse, N.Y., in partial fulfillment of the requirements for the Ph.D. degree.

The author was with the Rome Air Development Center, Griffiss Air-Force Base, Rome, N.Y. He is now with Pattern Analysis and Recognition, Inc., Rome, N.Y., and with the Department of Systems and Information Sciences, Syracuse University, Syracuse, N.Y.

[1] The Fisher linear discriminant $\boldsymbol{d}$ is $\Sigma^{-1}(\tilde{\mu}_1 - \tilde{\mu}_2)$ where Σ, $\hat{\mu}_1$, and $\hat{\mu}_2$ are the estimated common covariance and the estimated means of class 1 and 2.

[2] In the literature, the terms feature, measurement, variable, and dimensionality are used interchangeably.

[3] Actually, Cover [12] shows that the design-set error rate ε_d is zero when $(2N/L) < 1$ and that ε_d rapidly approaches zero when $(2N/L) < 2$ and L increases without bound. Also note that Cover refers to the total number of samples in a two-class problem. This is equivalent to $2N$ in this paper since N is the sample size per class.

Reprinted from *IEEE Trans. Inform. Theory*, vol. IT-18, pp. 618–626, Sept. 1972.

hold-one-out method of estimating the error rate of a classifier is too time consuming. Consequently, the data must be divided into a design set and a test set. Unfortunately, this makes poor use of the data since a classifier designed on the entire data set will on the average perform better than a classifier designed on only a portion of the data. Therefore, if a designer is satisfied with the test-set results, he would normally recombine the two data sets and redesign the classifier based on all the samples. Although this makes better use of the data for design purposes, the evaluation of the performance must be based only on design-set results. Consequently, knowledge of both the amount of the bias and the relationship between the design estimate and true performance is required.

Experimental Illustration

In this section, some new experimental results point out a statistical trap involved in using the error rate on the design set $\mathscr{E}_d$ as a measure of the true performance of the classifier when the ratio of the sample size per class (N) to feature size (L) is small. In addition, the average error rate on the design set is computed for a number of experimental runs. The results indicate that the ratio of the sample size to feature size (N/L) can be related to the amount of bias between the error rates on the design and test sets.

Suppose that a researcher has selected L features that hopefully contain enough information to allow two classes to be reasonably distinguished. N representative samples are gathered from each class. One possible classification procedure would be to orthogonally project the samples from the two classes onto the optimal discriminant plane[4] [14]. Next, the researcher could attempt to construct a piecewise linear boundary in the discriminant plane that would separate the samples from the two classes.

In one particular experiment, ten samples for each of two classes were randomly generated from their twenty eight-dimensional class-conditional distributions. The OLPARS[5] system [15] was used to project the samples onto the discriminant plane, shown in Fig. 1. It is obvious that a linear boundary will separate the two classes perfectly. Consequently, on the basis of these results, a researcher might conclude that he had selected a useful set of features and an excellent decision rule for this particular problem. However, in this experiment the samples for these two classes were generated from identical uniform distributions! In effect, a class has been perfectly distinguished from itself. This contradiction glaringly illustrates the deceiving results on the design set when the ratio N/L is small. The results are deceiving in this case since the true error rate (assuming equal *a priori* probabilities) for any classifier without reject regions is 0.5. This "statistical trap" may have been the source of some exaggerated claims in the past. These results are compatible with Cover's results [12] since the ratio of the total number of samples to features ($2N/L$) is less than two.

Fig. 2 shows the resulting discriminant plane when a larger ratio of sample size to feature size is used. No matter what linear boundary is drawn in this plane, the resulting error rate on the design set will give a more realistic indication of the true error rate.

Since it is only hypothesized by the designer that he has selected a useful set of features, the example is not unreasonable. For instance, in a signal-recognition problem, the first L discrete power spectrum coefficients may be selected as features. If the difference between the two classes lies in higher frequencies than represented by the Lth coefficient, then the two class-conditional densities are identical. If the ratio of the sample to feature size is small enough, the designer will have no indication of the poor quality of his feature extractor.

Instead of just investigating whether the error rate on the design set ($\mathscr{E}_d$) is a biased estimate of the true performance, we ran experiments to determine the effect of the ratio of the sample size per class (N) to the feature size (L) on $\mathscr{E}_d$.

Consider the following two-class problem. Each class has equal *a priori* probability. Each class has identical L-dimensional class-conditional probability densities. The density along each of the L features is statistically independent and uniform over the interval $[0,1]$. Two sets of N L-dimensional samples were randomly generated on a computer. One set was arbitrarily labeled class 1; the other was labeled class 2. The Fisher linear discriminant $\boldsymbol{d}$ was computed using the OLPARS system. The threshold ϕ was placed halfway between the estimated means along $\boldsymbol{d}$. Any sample that was arbitrarily labeled as class i and assigned by the above classifier to class j ($i \neq j$) was considered in error.

Selected values of L and N were chosen. A number of runs were made for every pair of values of L and N. The error rate on the design set was computed for each run. Fig. 3 shows the average error rate on the design set as a function of sample to feature size (N/L) with L as a parameter. The curves for L equal to 21, 28, and 45 are nearly identical.

It appears that the error rate on the design set is very misleading for cases where the ratio of N/L is small. The curves appear to level off for ratios greater than three. For instance, when N/L is three, the difference between the average estimate and the true error rate (0.5 in this case) is approximately 0.15. When N/L is ten, the difference has only been reduced to approximately 0.08. This leveling off of the curve for values of N/L greater than three is even more apparent in the theoretical curves obtained in the following section.

Expected Design-Set Error Rate

Consider a two-class pattern-recognition problem. Let each class have equal *a priori* probability. Let the design set consist of N independent and identically distributed L dimensional samples from each class. Let the class-conditional densities be L-dimensional normal distributions

[4] The x axis of the discriminant plane is the Fisher direction, while the y axis is the direction that maximizes the same criterion as the Fisher direction subject to the constraint that the two directions are orthogonal.

[5] The on-line pattern analysis and recognition system was developed by Sammon and is presently implemented at RADC.

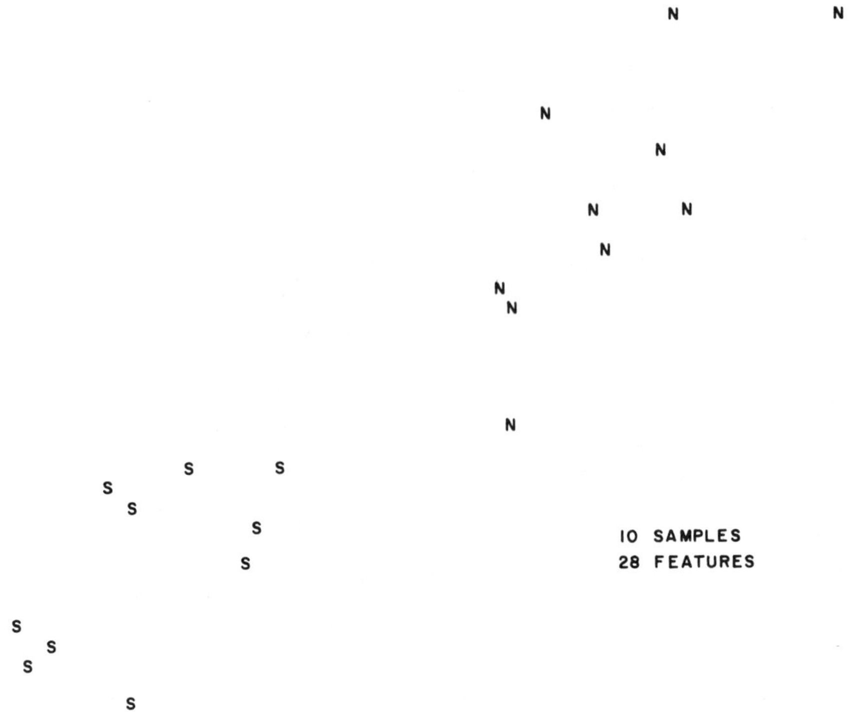

Fig. 1. Discriminant plane ($N/L = 0.36$).

with means $\boldsymbol{\mu}_1$ and $\boldsymbol{\mu}_2$, respectively, and with common covariance Σ, i.e.,

$$\boldsymbol{x}/c_1 \sim \Phi_L(\boldsymbol{\mu}_1,\Sigma)$$

$$\boldsymbol{x}/c_2 \sim \Phi_L(\boldsymbol{\mu}_2,\Sigma).$$

For the minimum-probability-of-error classifier, it is well known that the error rate ε is given by

$$\varepsilon = \tfrac{1}{2} - \operatorname{erf}(\delta/2),$$

where

$$\operatorname{erf}(y) = \int_0^y (2\pi)^{-1/2} e^{-t^2/2}\, dt$$

is the standard error function and

$$\delta^2 = (\boldsymbol{\mu}_1 - \boldsymbol{\mu}_2)'\Sigma^{-1}(\boldsymbol{\mu}_1 - \boldsymbol{\mu}_2)$$

is a measure of the separability of the two distributions.

Suppose a researcher, ignorant of the underlying distributions except for knowledge of the common covariance Σ, attempts to design and evaluate a classifier on the basis of N samples per class. A classification procedure that is reasonable, simple, and commonly used is the linear discriminant $\boldsymbol{d}$ given by

$$\boldsymbol{d} = \Sigma^{-1}(\hat{\boldsymbol{\mu}}_1 - \hat{\boldsymbol{\mu}}_2),$$

where

$$\hat{\boldsymbol{\mu}}_i = (1/N) \sum_{j=1}^{N} \boldsymbol{x}_{ij}$$

is the sample (or estimated) mean of class i and $\boldsymbol{x}_{ij}$ is the jth sample of class i. The threshold θ is given by

$$\theta = [(\hat{\boldsymbol{\mu}}_1 - \hat{\boldsymbol{\mu}}_2)/2]'\boldsymbol{d}.$$

Therefore, a sample $\boldsymbol{x}$ is assigned to class 1 if $\boldsymbol{x}'\boldsymbol{d} \geq \theta$ and to class 2 otherwise.

The error rate on the design set is a random variable since it is a function of the particular $2N$ samples that are collected. In Appendix A, the expected value of the error rate on the design set $\overline{\mathscr{E}}_d$ is shown to be the probability that an arbitrary sample $\boldsymbol{x}_{ij}$ in the design set is misclassified. In Appendix B, this expected value is derived as a function of the feature size (L), sample size per class (N), and the separation, δ, and is given by

$$E\{\mathscr{E}_d(L,N,\delta^2)\} = \sum_{r=0}^{\infty} e^{-(N\delta^2/4)} \frac{1}{r!} (N\delta^2/4)^r \cdot \frac{\Gamma(r + L/2 + \frac{1}{2})}{\Gamma(\frac{1}{2})\Gamma(L/2 + r)} I_2(L + 2r, N),$$

where

$$I_2(L + 2r, N) = \int_0^A \sin^{L+2r-1} \theta \, d\theta$$

and

$$A = \tan^{-1} (2N - 1)^{1/2},$$

which may be written recursively as

$$I_2(L + 2r, N) = \frac{L + 2r - 2}{L + 2r - 1} I_2(L + 2r - 2) - \frac{1}{L + 2r - 1} \frac{1}{\sqrt{2N - 1}} \left[\frac{2(N - 1)}{2N - 1}\right]^{(L+2r-2)/2}$$

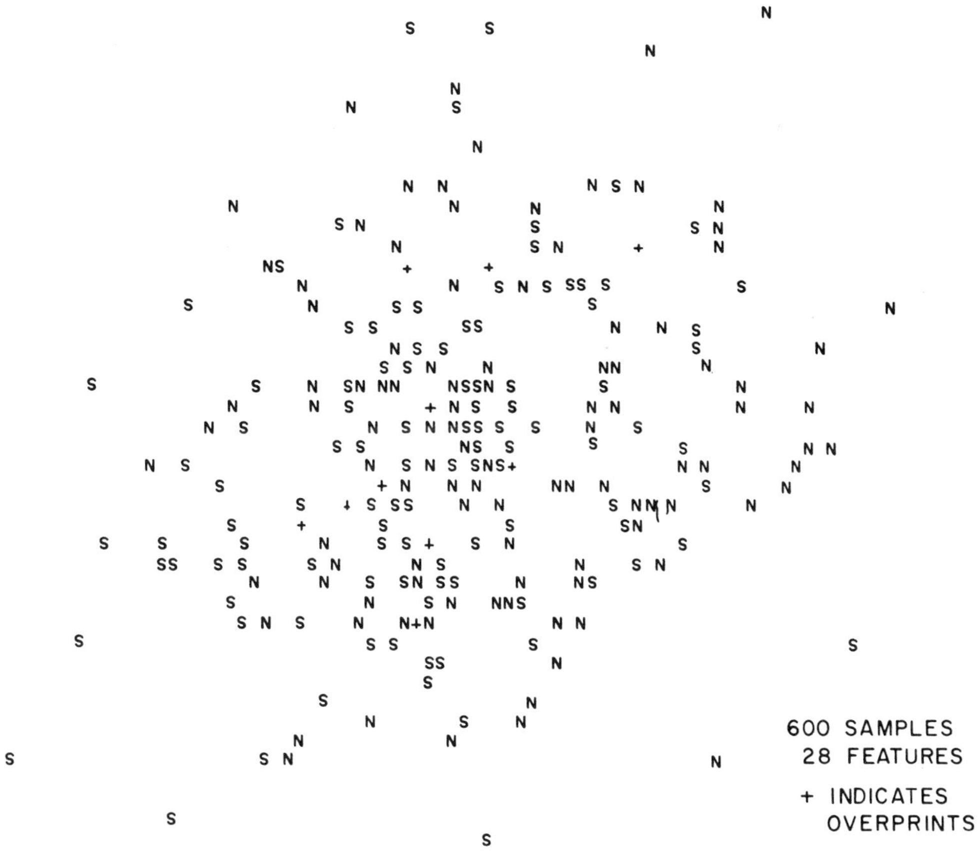

Fig. 2. Discriminant plane ($N/L = 21.7$).

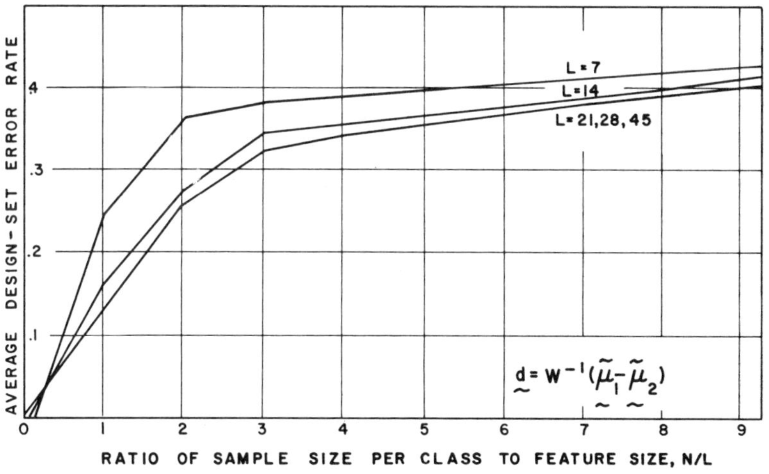

Fig. 3. Experiment results: Identical uniform distributions.

Note that as a corollary the same result holds if the common covariance is diagonal ($\Sigma = \sigma^2 I$) and nearest estimated mean vector logic is used.

A computer program was written to calculate

$$E\{\mathscr{E}_d(L,N,\delta^2)\}$$

for various values of L, N, and δ^2. Curves of $E\{\mathscr{E}_d(L,N,\delta^2)\}$ for $\delta^2 = 0.0$, 1.0, and 2.0 as a function of N/L with L as a parameter are shown in Figs. 4–6, respectively. The corresponding error rates ($\varepsilon = 0.5$, 0.309, and 0.240) for the minimum probability of error classifier are also shown.

A number of limiting cases are of interest. For one sample per class ($N = 1$), $E\{\mathscr{E}_d(L,1,\delta^2)\} = 0$; and consequently the curves all begin with $E\{\mathscr{E}_d\} = 0$ at $1/L$. This is expected since the probability that the single sample from class 1 is exactly the same as the single sample from class 2, is zero.

At the other extreme, Hoel and Peterson [16] show that as the sample size increases without bound the design-set error approaches the optimum $\mathscr{E}$. This is reasonable since as N increases without bound, the sample means approach the true means and consequently the classification rule

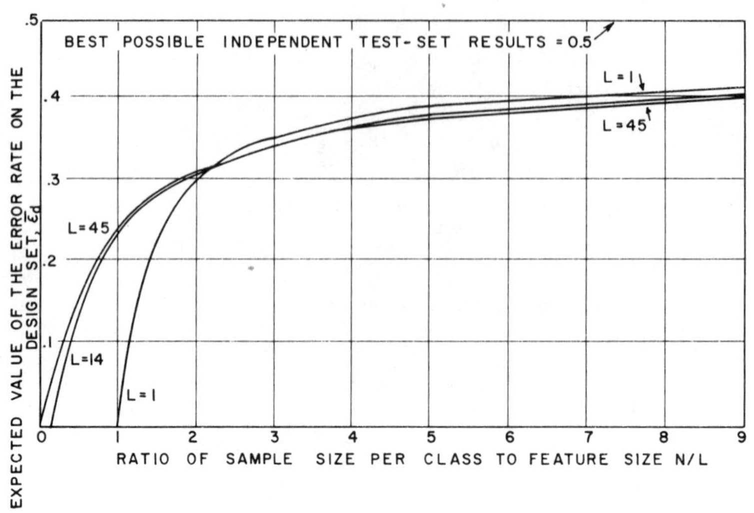

Fig. 4. Expected error rates ($\delta^2 = 0.0$).

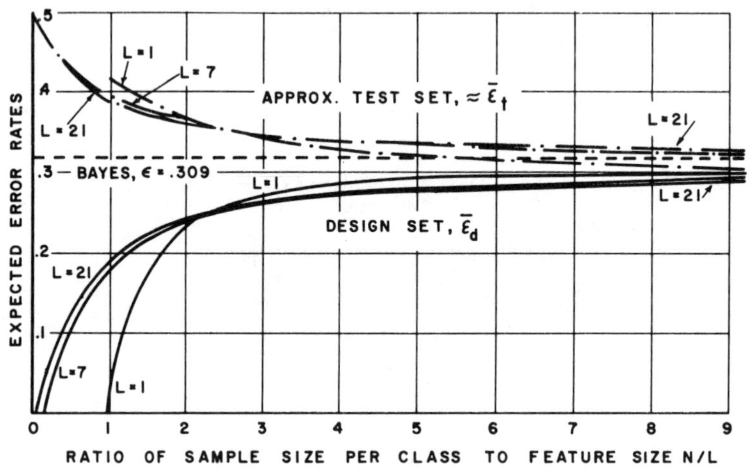

Fig. 5. Expected error rates ($\delta^2 = 1.0$).

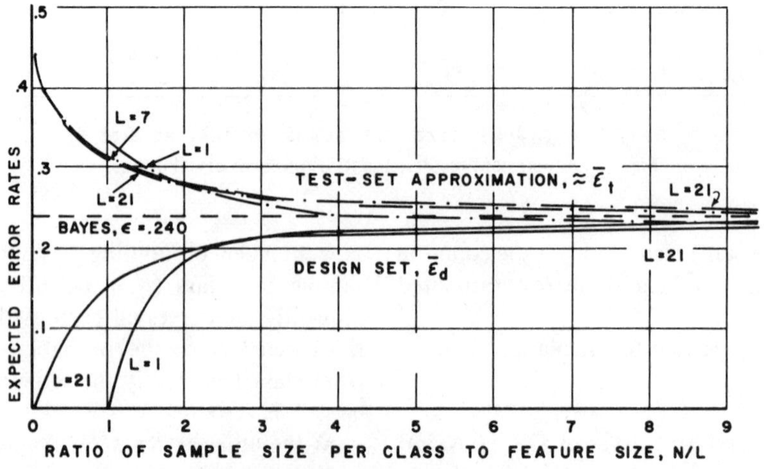

Fig. 6. Expected error rates ($\delta^2 = 2.0$).

based on the sample means approaches the optimum discriminant.

For the case where $\delta^2 = 0$, the two class-conditional distributions are identical. In essence, Fig. 4 indicates that when the ratio of samples to features is small, it is possible to discriminate between samples of the same class on the design set. In fact, Foley [17] shows that as the number of features increase without bound,

$$\lim_{L\to\infty} E\{\mathscr{E}_d(L, N, \delta^2 = 0)\} = 0.$$

Recalling that L represents the number of features for which there is no difference in the class-conditional distributions, this implies that the error rate on the design-set can, on the average, be reduced by selecting more and more useless features. However, since this has no effect in improving the true performance of the system, the researcher should be cognizant of this phenomenon of "beating his problem to death."

Another extreme case is letting both L and N increase without bound, while constraining the ratio of N/L to be a fixed constant. The computer runs shown in Fig. 4 indicate that under these conditions $E\{\mathscr{E}_d\}$ converges to an asymptotic solution very rapidly. However, no limiting form has been obtained.

Comparison of Design- and Test-Set Error Rates

For the same underlying probability structure considered in the previous section, John [1] derives the expected value of the error rate on an independent test set given that the classifier was derived from a design set of N samples per class. Unfortunately, the expression (except for $L = 1$) is so complicated that a computer run would be too time consuming. However, John [1] also derives a useful approximation. For completeness, these expressions are written in Appendix C.

Computer programs were written to obtain graphic results. Figs. 7 and 8 show a comparison of the approximate and true test-set error rates for $L = 1$ and $\delta^2 = 1.0$ and 2.0, respectively. The approximation appears to be slightly low. John [1] comments that the approximation involved is of the same order as that involved in assuming that the cube root of a noncentral chi-square variable has a normal distribution. For purposes of comparison, Figs. 5–8 show the relationship between the expected design and the test-set error rates. The curves indicate that when the ratio of the sample size per class to the feature size is large enough such that the design-set error rate gives a reasonable indication of the true error rate of the classifier, the true error rate of the classifier is close to the optimum probability of error ε achievable by the minimum-probability-of-error classifier.

Variance of the Design-Set Error Rate

Although the expected value of the design-set error rate $\bar{\mathscr{E}}_d$ has been derived, little is known about the distribution of $\mathscr{E}_d$ until its variance is determined. In Appendix A, it is shown that an approximation for the variance σ^2 is

$$\sigma^2 \cong [\bar{\mathscr{E}}_d(1 - \bar{\mathscr{E}}_d)]/2N.$$

Foley [17] gives some results indicating the closeness of the true and approximate values for σ^2. Since the maximum of $y(1 - y)$ for $y \in [0,1]$ is $\frac{1}{4}$ at $y = \frac{1}{2}$, an upper bound for the approximation is

$$\sigma^2 \cong [\bar{\mathscr{E}}_d(1 - \bar{\mathscr{E}}_d)]/2N \leq 1/8N.$$

For instance, if N is 50, then no matter what value $\bar{\mathscr{E}}_d$ assumes, the variance and standard derivation are approximated by functions that are bounded by 0.0025 and 0.05, respectively.

Note that as N increases without bound the variance approaches zero and consequently the design-set error rate is a consistent estimate of the test-set error rate, since the expected value of both the design- and test-set error rates approach the minimum probability of error ε.

Summary

New experimental results indicate the statistical trap involved in using the design-set error rate as an estimate of the true error rate of the classifier when the ratio of sample size to feature size is small.

The expected value for the design-set error rate has been derived and related to the test-set error rate for a two-class pattern-recognition problem with underlying multivariate normal class-conditional distributions. Although it is well known that the design-set error rate is a biased estimate of the test-set error rate, the amount of bias is shown to be dependent upon the ratio of the sample size per class to the feature size (N/L). Although it is recognized that the greater the ratio of N/L the better the results, a reasonable engineering rule of thumb for this particular probability structure appears to be that if the ratio of sample to feature size is greater than three, then on the average the design-set error rate is reasonably close to the test-set error rate, and also the test-set error rate is close to the optimum error rate attained by the minimum probability of error classifier. As Kanal and Chandrasekaran [13] point out, if less is known about the underlying probability structure, an even greater ratio of sample size to feature size is needed.

In addition, the variance of $\mathscr{E}_d$ is shown to be approximated by a function that is bounded by $1/8N$. This indicates that even if the number of features is small, enough samples must still be used in order to minimize the variance of $\mathscr{E}_d$.

As expected, it was shown that the design-set error rate can be decreased by adding more and more useless features. Of course, since these features add no discriminatory information no improvement in the test-set results can be expected.

Although these results were proved only for underlying multivariate normal distributions, the results may be more general. In the proof (Appendix B), two key variables (z_k, Δ_k) are each linear sums of identically and independently distributed samples from their underlying distributions. For reasonable distributions, these variables will approach normal distributions.

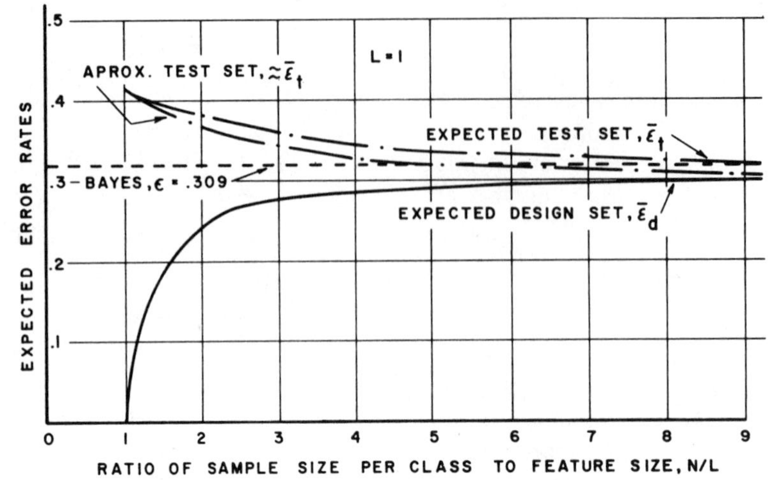

Fig. 7. Comparison of true and approximate test set results ($\delta^2 = 1.0$).

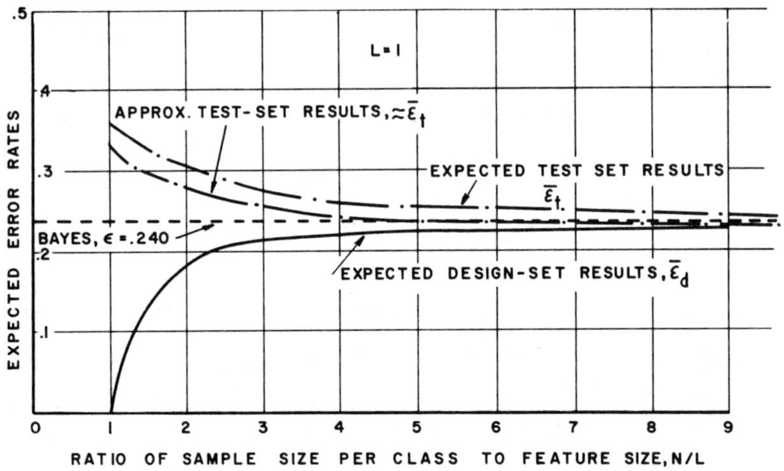

Fig. 8. Comparison of true and approximate test set results ($\delta^2 = 2.0$).

Acknowledgment

The author would like to express his gratitude to J. W. Sammon, Jr., A. H. Proctor, K. Mehrotra, H. Webb, R. Szkody, and F. Borasz for their advice and help.

Appendix A

In order to determine the expected value and the variance of the design-set error rate $\mathscr{E}_d$, consider the new random variables,

$$T_{i_j} = \begin{cases} 1, & \text{if the } j\text{th sample from the } i\text{th class is misclassified} \\ 0, & \text{otherwise} \end{cases}$$

$i = 1,2$ and $j = 1,2,\cdots,N$. By definition, the design-set error rate is the total number of misclassified samples from the design set divided by $2N$, i.e.,

$$\mathscr{E}_d = \sum_i^2 \sum_j^N T_{ij}/2N.$$

Since the samples from each class are identically distributed, and since the probability of misclassifying a sample from class 1 is the same as misclassifying a sample from class 2,

$$\bar{\mathscr{E}}_d = \sum_i^2 \sum_j^N E\{T_{ij}\}/2N = E\{T_{kl}\},$$

where T_{kl} represents an arbitrary sample. However,

$$E\{T_{kl}\} = 0 \cdot \Pr\{T_{kl} = 0\} + 1 \cdot \Pr\{T_{kl} = 1\}$$
$$= \Pr\{\text{arbitrary sample is misclassified}\}.$$

To determine the variance of $\mathscr{E}_d$, first consider $\bar{\mathscr{E}}_d^{\,2}$. By definition

$$\bar{\mathscr{E}}_d^{\,2} = \frac{1}{4N^2} \sum_i^2 \sum_j^N \sum_k^2 \sum_l^N E\{T_{ij}T_{kl}\}$$

$$= \frac{1}{2N}[E\{T_{ij}\} + (N-1)E\{T_{ip}T_{iq}\} + NE\{T_{1r}T_{2s}\}$$

$$= \frac{1}{2N}[\Pr(A_{ij}) + (N-1)\Pr(A_{ip}A_{iq})$$

$$+ N \Pr\{A_{1r}A_{2s}\}],$$

where A_{ij} is the event that the jth sample from the ith class is misclassified; $\Pr(A_{ip}A_{ip})$ is the probability that two arbitrary samples from the same class are misclassified; $\Pr(A_{1r}A_{2s})$ is the probability that two arbitrary samples from different classes are misclassified. However, if the number of samples is large, let us make the approximations that

$$\Pr(A_{ip}A_{iq}) \cong \Pr(A_{ip})\Pr(A_{iq})$$

$$\Pr(A_{1r}A_{2s}) \cong \Pr(A_{1r})\Pr(A_{2s}).$$

Therefore

$$\overline{\mathscr{E}_d^2} \cong [\overline{\mathscr{E}}_d + (2N-1)\overline{\mathscr{E}}_d^2]/2N$$

and

$$\sigma^2 = \overline{\mathscr{E}_d^2} - \overline{\mathscr{E}}_d^2 \cong \overline{\mathscr{E}}_d(1-\overline{\mathscr{E}}_d)/2N.$$

Appendix B

The complete derivation of the expected value of the design set error rate $E\{\mathscr{E}_d\}$, as a function of the feature size (L), sample size per class (N), and the separation (δ^2) is given in Foley [17]. The main steps are presented here. Using the previous notation, let y_{ij} be the jth sample of the ith class. Each sample from class i is independent and identically distributed with a L-dimensional normal distribution, denoted by

$$y_{ij} \sim \Phi_L(\mu_i,\Sigma).$$

The classification rule $R(y)$ uses the linear discriminant, $\Sigma^{-1}(\hat{\mu}_1 - \hat{\mu}_2)$ and is given by comparing

$$[y - (\hat{\mu}_1 + \hat{\mu}_2)/2]'\Sigma^{-1}(\hat{\mu}_1 - \hat{\mu}_2)$$

to zero, where $\hat{\mu}_i$ is the estimated or sample mean of class i. Since Σ is positive definite, there exists an orthogonal transformation T such that

$$T'\Sigma T = \Lambda,$$

where Λ is a diagonal matrix with diagonal elements $\lambda_1,\cdots,\lambda_L$. Actually the ith column of T is the ith eigenvector of the covariance matrix Σ, with λ_i equal to the variance along the ith eigenvector. Let $x = \Lambda^{-1/2}T'y$ and $\eta_i = \Lambda^{-1/2}T'\mu_i$, then $x_{ij} \sim \Phi_L(\eta_i, I)$. Also the classification rule $R(x)$ may be rewritten in terms of

$$[x - (\hat{\eta}_1 + \hat{\eta}_2)/2]'(\hat{\eta}_1 - \hat{\eta}_2).$$

It was shown that $E\{\mathscr{E}_d\}$ is the probability that an arbitrary sample is misclassified. For concreteness, consider x_{11}. Then

$$\begin{aligned}\overline{\mathscr{E}}_d &= \Pr\{x_{11} \text{ is misclassified}\}\\ &= \Pr\{w = [x_{11} - (\hat{\eta}_1 + \hat{\eta}_2)/2]'(\hat{\eta}_1 - \hat{\eta}_2) < 0\}\\ &= \int_{-\infty}^{0} p(w)\,dw.\end{aligned}$$

Consequently, the key to determining $E\{\mathscr{E}_d\}$ is the determination of the probability density $p(w)$. However, it is not necessary to obtain $p(w)$ explicitly. It is only necessary to obtain the conditional density of w given another random variable α. One can then express the density of w and the probability of error as

$$p(w) = \int p(w/\alpha)p(\alpha)\,d\alpha$$

$$\overline{\mathscr{E}}_d = \int_{-\infty}^{0}\int p(w/\alpha)p(\alpha)\,d\alpha\,dw.$$

Although $p(w)$ is left in integral form, $\overline{\mathscr{E}}_d(L,N)$ can be obtained explicitly by defining the appropriate transformation into polar coordinates.

Following the procedure just outlined, let

$$\begin{aligned}z_k &= 2Nx_{11k} - N\hat{\mu}_{1k} - N\hat{\mu}_{2k}\\ &= (2N-1)x_{11k} - \sum_{j=2}^{N} x_{1jk} - \sum_{j=1}^{N} x_{2jk}\\ \Delta_k &= N\hat{\mu}_{1k} - N\hat{\mu}_{2k} = \sum_{j=1}^{N}(x_{1jk} - x_{2jk}).\end{aligned}$$

Since each x_{ijk} is statistically independent and since linear sums of statistically independent normal random variables are still normal, (z_k,Δ_k) are jointly normal random variables with means and covariance

$$\begin{pmatrix}\bar{z}_k\\ \bar{\Delta}_k\end{pmatrix} = \begin{pmatrix}N(\eta_{1k} - \eta_{2k})\\ N(\eta_{1k} - \eta_{2k})\end{pmatrix} \qquad K = \begin{pmatrix}2N(2N-1) & 2N\\ 2N & 2N\end{pmatrix}.$$

Also the conditional distributions can be obtained.

$$\begin{aligned}z_k \mid \Delta_k &\sim \Phi_1[\Delta_k, 4N(N-1)]\\ \Delta_k z_k \mid \Delta_k &\sim \Phi_1[\Delta_k^2, 4N(N-1)\Delta_k^2]\\ \Delta_k &\sim \Phi_1[N(\eta_{1k} - \eta_{2k}), 2N].\end{aligned}$$

Using the definitions of z_k and Δ_k, w may be expressed as

$$w = \sum_{k=1}^{L} \Delta_k z_k.$$

Since $w \mid \Delta_1,\cdots,\Delta_L$ is a linear sum of statistically independent normal random variables, $w \mid \Delta$ is normal with additive means and variances, i.e.,

$$w|\Delta \sim \Phi_1\left[\sum_{k=1}^{L}\Delta_k^2, 4N(N-1)\sum_{k=1}^{L}\Delta_k^2\right].$$

Let

$$\alpha = \sum_{k=1}^{L}\Delta_k^2.$$

Then

$$\overline{\mathscr{E}}_d = \int_{-\infty}^{0}\int_{0}^{\infty} p(w/\alpha)p(\alpha)\,d\alpha\,dw, \tag{B1}$$

where α has a noncentral chi-square density with L degrees of freedom and parameter of noncentrality

$$\begin{aligned}\lambda^2 &= \sum_{k=1}^{L}[N(\eta_{1k} - \eta_{2k})]^2/2N = (N/2)\sum_{k=1}^{L}(\eta_{1k} - \eta_{2k})^2\\ &= (N/2)(\eta_1 - \eta_2)'(\eta_1 - \eta_2)\\ &= (N/2)(\hat{\mu}_1 - \hat{\mu}_2)'\Sigma^{-1}(\mu_1 - \mu_2) = N\delta^2/2\end{aligned}$$

and

$$\begin{aligned}p(\alpha) &= x_L^2(N\delta^2/2)\\ &= (1/2N)[\exp(-N\delta^2/4)]\\ &\quad\cdot\sum_{r=0}^{\infty}(N\delta^2/4)^r[\exp(-\alpha/2N)](\alpha/2N)^{r+L/2-1}\\ &\quad\cdot(r!\,\Gamma(r + L/2)2^{r+L/2})^{-1}.\end{aligned}$$

Substituting for $p(\alpha)$ and $p(w/\alpha)$ in (B1), exchanging the order of integration and summation (Foley [17] shows that $p(w/\alpha)p(\alpha)$ is a uniformly convergent series), and applying the transformations

$$t = -(w - \alpha)/(4N(N-1)\alpha)^{1/2}$$
$$\gamma = (\alpha/2N)^{1/2}$$

and

$$p^2 = \gamma^2 + t^2$$
$$\theta = \tan^{-1}(\gamma/t)$$

it can be shown that

$$\bar{\mathscr{E}}_d(L,N,\delta^2) = \sum_{r=0}^{\infty} [\exp(-N\delta^2/4)](N\delta^2/4)^r \cdot \Gamma(r + L/2 + \tfrac{1}{2})[\Gamma(\tfrac{1}{2})\Gamma(L/2 + r)]^{-1} \cdot I(L + 2r, N),$$

where

$$I(M,N) = \int_0^A \sin^{M-1}\theta \, d\theta$$
$$A = \tan^{-1}\sqrt{2(N-1)}.$$

In addition $I(M,N)$ may be recursively written as

$$I(M,N) = [(M-2)/(M-1)]I(M-2, N) - [2(N-1)/(2N-1)]^{L/2}[(L-1)\sqrt{2N-1}]^{-1},$$

where

$$I(1,N) = \tan^{-1}\sqrt{2(N-1)}$$

and

$$I(2,N) = \frac{1}{2}\left[1 - \frac{1}{\sqrt{2N-1}}\right].$$

Appendix C

For completeness, and to give the reader some appreciation of their complex nature, expressions given by John [1] are presented here.

For the linear discriminant $d = \Sigma^{-1}(\hat{\mu}_1 - \hat{\mu}_2)$, and the case of N samples per class, the expected value of the test set error rate $\bar{\mathscr{E}}_t$ given by John reduces to

$$\bar{\mathscr{E}}_t = e^{-(\lambda_1+\lambda_2)} \sum_{r=0}^{\infty}\sum_{s=0}^{\infty} \frac{\lambda_1^2}{r!}\frac{\lambda_2^2}{s!} I_{1/2}(s + L/2, r + L/2), \tag{C1}$$

where

$$\lambda_1 = (N/8)[1 - (2N+1)^{-1/2}]^2\delta^2$$
$$\lambda_2 = (N/8)[1 + (2N+1)^{-1/2}]^2\delta^2$$

$I_\chi(p,q)$ is the incomplete beta function and

$$I_\chi(p,q) = [\Gamma(p+q)/\Gamma(p)\Gamma(q)] \int_0^\chi \mu^{p-1}(1-\mu)^{q-1}\, du.$$

The approximation given by John is

$$\bar{\mathscr{E}}_t \approx \int_{-\infty}^{a} (2\pi)^{-1/2} \exp(-y^2/2)\, dy, \tag{C2}$$

where

$$a = (18)^{-1/2}[r_1^{-1/3}(1 + b_1) + r_2^{-1/3}(1 + b_2)]^{-1/2} \cdot \{2[r_2^{-2/3}(1 + b_2) - r_1^{-2/3}(1 + b_1)] + 9(r_1^{1/3} - r_2^{1/3})\}$$

and

$$r_i = L + 2\lambda_i$$
$$b_i = 2(L + 2\lambda_i)^{-1}\lambda_i.$$

For one dimension, John gives the exact value for $\bar{\mathscr{E}}_t$ as

$$\bar{\mathscr{E}}_t = G(a_{11})G(a_{21}) + G(a_{12})G(a_{22}), \tag{C3}$$

where

$$a_{11} = -a_{12} = \sqrt{N/2}\,\delta$$
$$a_{21} = -a_{22} = -\sqrt{2N/(2N) + 1}\,(\delta/2)$$

and

$$G(x) = \int_{-\infty}^{\chi} (2\pi)^{-1/2} \exp(-y^2/2)\, dy.$$

References

[1] S. John, "Errors in discrimination," *Ann. Math. Statist.*, vol. 32, 1961.
[2] Sitgreaves, "On the distribution of two random matrices used in classification procedures," *Ann. Math. Statist.*, vol. 23, 1952.
[3] S. E. Estes, "Measurement selection for linear discriminants used in pattern classification," San Jose Res. Lab., IBM Res. Rep. RJ-331, Apr. 1965.
[4] D. C. Allais, "Selection of measurements for prediction," Stanford Electron. Lab., Stanford, Calif., Rep. SEL-64-115, Nov. 1964.
[5] G. F. Hughes, "On the mean accuracy of statistical pattern recognizers," *IEEE Trans. Inform. Theory*, vol. IT-14, pp. 55–63, Jan. 1968.
[6] K. Abend, T. J. Harley, and B. Chandrasekaran, "Comments on the mean accuracy of statistical pattern recognizers," *IEEE Trans. Inform. Theory*, vol. IT-15, pp. 420–423, May 1969.
[7] J. R. Ullmann, "Experiments with the *n*-tuple method of pattern recognition," *IEEE Trans. Comput.* (Short Notes), vol. C-18, pp. 1135–1137, Dec. 1969.
[8] M. Hills, "Allocation rules and their error rates," *J. Roy. Statist. Soc.*, ser. B, no. 28, 1966.
[9] P. A. Lachenbruch and M. R. Mickey, "Estimation of error rates in discriminant analysis," *Technometrics*, vol. 10, no. 1, Feb. 1968.
[10] P. A. Lachenbruch, "Estimation of error rates in discriminant analysis," Ph.D. dissertation, Univ. Southern California, Los Angeles, 1965.
[11] K. Fukunaga and D. L. Kessell, "Estimation of classification errors," in *Proc. 1970 IEEE Symp. Adaptive Processes*, Dec. 1970.
[12] T. M. Cover, "Geometrical and statistical properties of linear inequalities with applications in pattern recognition," *IEEE Trans. Electron. Comput.*, vol. EC-14, pp. 326–334, June 1965.
[13] L. Kanal and B. Chandrasekaran, "On dimensionality and sample size in statistical pattern classification," in *Proc. 1968 National Electronics Conf.*, pp. 2–7.
[14] J. W. Sammon, Jr., "An optimal discriminant plane," *IEEE Trans. Comput.* (Short Notes), vol. C-19, pp. 826–829, Sept. 1970.
[15] ——, "Interactive pattern analysis and classification," *IEEE Trans. Comput.*, vol. C-19, pp. 594–616, July 1970.
[16] P. G. Hoel and R. P. Peterson, "A solution to the problem of optimum allocation," *Ann. Math. Statist.*, pp. 20, 433–438, 1949.
[17] D. H. Foley, "The probability of error on the design set as a function of the sample size and feature size," Ph.D. dissertation, Syracuse Univ., Syracuse, N.Y., June 1971; also RADC-TR-71-171.

Estimation of Error Rates in Discriminant Analysis

Peter A. Lachenbruch and M. Ray Mickey

University of North Carolina and University of California, Los Angeles

Several methods of estimating error rates in Discriminant Analysis are evaluated by sampling methods. Multivariate normal samples are generated on a computer which have various true probabilities of misclassification for different combinations of sample sizes and different numbers of parameters. The two methods in most common use are found to be significantly poorer than some new methods that are proposed.

1. Introduction

The general two-group discrimination problem may be characterized as follows: on the basis of measurements alone, an individual must be assigned to one of two groups. It is assumed that the two groups are the only possible choices and that an assignment must be made. After the assignment procedure has been established, it may also be desired to estimate the proportion of individuals in each group that will be wrongly classified. One approach to the classification problem has been to form a linear combination of the observations to form a single number. Then an individual is classified into one or the other group depending on this number. We shall consider several means of estimating error rates for a given discriminant function.

Suppose there is an initial sample of n_1 multivariate observations from group 1 and n_2 multivariate observations from group 2. The discriminant function will be constructed from this sample. Let $x_k = (x_{1k}, \cdots, x_{pk})'$ denote the kth sample value of a p-dimensional multivariate column vector $k = 1, \cdots, n_1 + n_2 = m$. The within groups sample covariance between the ith and jth variables will be denoted by s_{ij}. The mean values from the group samples are denoted by $\bar{x}_1 = (\bar{x}_{11}, \cdots, \bar{x}_{p1})'$ and $\bar{x}_2 = (\bar{x}_{12}, \cdots, \bar{x}_{p2})'$.

Fisher (3) suggested finding a linear combination of observations that would maximize the difference between groups relative to the standard deviation within groups. This leads to the choice of discriminant function: $S^{-1}(\bar{x}_1 - \bar{x}_2)$ where S is the sample covariance matrix. Then classify as group 1 if $x'S^{-1}(\bar{x}_1 - \bar{x}_2)$ is greater than some constant C and as group 2 otherwise.

An alternate way to determine the discriminant function is due to Welch (11). If the density functions are denoted by f_1 and f_2, the likelihood ratio criterion leads to the rule: assign an individual to group 1 if $f_1/f_2 > k$ and otherwise to group 2. The choice of k depends on the relative costs of misclassification, and the proportion of each group in the general population.

Received May 1966; revised November 1966.

Reprinted with permission from *Technometrics*, vol. 10, pp. 1-11, Feb. 1968.

In this study we assume $k = 1$. If f_1 and f_2 are multivariate normal distributions with the same covariance matrix Σ, but different means μ_1 and μ_2, some algebra shows that the likelihood ratio criterion is equivalent to classifying as group 1 if $D_t(x) = x'\Sigma^{-1}(\mu_1 - \mu_2) - \frac{1}{2}(\mu_1 + \mu_2)'\Sigma^{-1}(\mu_1 - \mu_2)$. The first part of this expression is the theoretical analogue of the function suggested by Fisher. If we knew the population parameters of the distributions, this expression would be optimal. However, we do not, in general, know them so it is necessary to estimate them. Thus, the discriminant function we shall be concerned with is $D_s(x) = x'S^{-1}(\bar{x}_1 - \bar{x}_2) - \frac{1}{2}(\bar{x}_1 + \bar{x}_2)S^{-1}(\bar{x}_1 - \bar{x}_2)$. This was denoted by Anderson (1) as W. We shall let $y = \bar{x}_1 + \bar{x}_2$ and $z = \bar{x}_1 - \bar{x}_2$, so $D_s(x) = x'S^{-1}z - \frac{1}{2}y'S^{-1}z$.

We wish to estimate the probabilities of misclassification based on the sample discriminant function, namely $P_1 = P(D_s(x) < 0 \mid G_1, \bar{x}_1, \bar{x}_2, S)$ and $P_2 = P(D_s(x) > 0 \mid G_2, \bar{x}_1, \bar{x}_2, S)$. The exact distribution of $D_s(x)$ is quite complicated. It has been studied by Wald (10), Anderson (1), Sitgreaves (8), Kabe (4) and Okamoto (7) among others. If we knew the parameters of the distribution, the problem would be trivial and reduce to $P_1 = P_2 = \Phi(-\delta/2)$ where $\delta^2 = (\mu_1 - \mu_2)'\Sigma^{-1}(\mu_1 - \mu_2)$ is Mahalanobis' distance (6), and Φ is the cumulative normal distribution. This represents a limiting value which we cannot improve upon, and unfortunately do not know. In this study, we shall evaluate several estimates of the probability of misclassification for discriminant functions. Three of these estimates (the D, R, and H methods) have been used regularly; the other methods were considered in (5).

2. Estimates of Error Rates

Several techniques are currently used to estimate error rates of sample discriminant functions. None are satisfactory for sample sizes that are small relative to the number of parameters, although for large samples they are not too bad. Several new techniques will be suggested and evaluated along with the older ones.

The techniques may be divided into two classes: those using a sample to evaluate a given discriminant function, and those using properties of the normal distribution. The former may be considered empirical methods while the latter are dependent on the normality of the distribution for their validity.

If the initial samples are sufficiently large, we may choose a subset of observations from each group, compute a discriminant function from them, and use the remaining observations to estimate the error probabilities. The number of errors in each group will be binomially distributed with probabilities P_1 and P_2. After these estimates have been obtained we may recompute the discriminant function using the entire sample. There are several drawbacks to this method. First, in many applications large samples are not available. This is particularly true in biomedical uses when the data is usually expensive and difficult to obtain. Second, the discriminant function that is evaluated is not the one that is used. There may be a considerable difference in the performance of the two. Third, there are problems connected with the size of the holdout sample. If it is large, a good estimate of the performance of the discriminant function will be obtained, but that function is likely to be poor. If the holdout sample is small, the discriminant function will be better, but the estimate of its performance will be highly variable. Finally, this method is quite uneconomical with data. A larger sample than is necessary to obtain a good discriminant function must be selected to obtain estimates of performance. For these reasons, we did not evaluate this method empirically. We shall refer to this method as the H method or the holdout method. It is an empirical method.

The second commonly used technique will be referred to as the resubstitution method. C. A. B. Smith suggested that the sample used to compute the discriminant function would be reused to estimate the error.

> We may get approximate values of such an error in two ways. First, taking the distribution of x to be $f_A x dx$ in population A, we may get from it the distribution of Lx (the discriminant function), and from that the probability that $Lx < L_0$. Unhappily the integrals needed are frequently not very simple, and, in addition, if we have taken the wrong form for the distribution f_A, the value of E_A (the error) may be quite wrong. The other way is to take a sample from population A, and see how frequently $Lx < L_0$ in this sample. We have, in fact, such a sample, namely, the one which was used in working out the form of the distribution of $f_A x$. However, it is necessary to keep in mind that if this sample is used to get E_A, the standard error of E_A will not have its binomial value $\sqrt{E_A(1 - E_A)/n_A}$, although it will probably not be greatly different. (9)

We have found this technique to be quite misleading; if the sample used to compute the discriminant function is not large, this method gives too optimistic an estimate of the probabilities of misclassification. The main point, it seems, is not that the estimate does not have the binomial standard error, but that it can be a badly biased estimate. In further discussion, we shall refer to this empirical technique as the R method.

The probability of misclassification, P_1, may be written as

$$P_1 = P\left\{t < \frac{(-\mu_1 + \frac{1}{2}y)'S^{-1}z}{\sqrt{z'S^{-1}\Sigma S^{-1}z}}\right\},$$

where t is a standard normal deviate.

If we replace μ_1 and Σ by $\bar{x}_1$ and S (or μ_2 by $\bar{x}_2$ and Σ by S in the case of P_2), we see that for normally distributed variables, the estimate of P_1 (or P_2) is $\Phi(-D/2)$ where $D^2 = z'S^{-1}z$ is Mahalanobis sample distance. If the degrees of freedom are large, this is a fairly accurate estimate of P_1 since D^2 is consistent for δ^2. If the degrees of freedom are not large, this may be badly biased and give much too favorable an impression of the probability of error. Another way to derive this estimate is that since $P_1 = \Phi(-\delta/2)$ when the parameters are known, by estimating the parameters, μ_1, μ_2, and Σ by $\bar{x}_1$, $\bar{x}_2$, and S we should arrive at a reasonable result. This method will be denoted as the D method.

If n_1 and n_2 are not large relative to p, it may be desired to use an unbiased estimate of δ^2 based on D^2. This may be written as

$$D^{*2} = \{D^2 - (m-2)mp/n_1n_2(m-p-3)\}\cdot(m-p-3)/(m-2).$$

Unfortunately, when this is most useful (when n_1, n_2 are small relative to p and D^2 is also small) D^{*2} is frequently negative. Instead of using D^{*2} one may construct estimates of δ^2 using the quantity $DS = (m - p - 3)D^2/(m - 2)$ This merely ignores the constant which is subtracted from D to obtain an unbiased estimate for δ^2. This partially corrects for the bias in D^2, is consistent for δ^2, and is not negative for the range of values we are interested in. We shall denote the estimate $P_1 = \Phi(-\sqrt{DS}/2)$ as the DS method. It appears to have some advantages over the D method.

The next method for estimating P_1 is based on a result of Okamoto (7). He gave an asymptotic approximation for P_1 in terms of n_1, n_2, p, and δ^2. The approximation of P_2 is obtained by interchanging n_1 and n_2 in the expansion for P_1. Thus, this enables us to get different estimates for P_1 and P_2 which we could not do with the D or DS methods. We may estimate δ^2 by D^2 or DS. In computational work, we have found this approximation to be poor when δ^2 is small and the sample sizes are not large. For large values of D^2, this method and the D method give similar results because the correction terms are proportional to $1/D^2$. For moderately sized values of D^2 (say between 1 and 10) there is evidence that this method is better than the D method. We shall refer to this as the O method if D^2 is used and the OS method if DS is used as an estimate of δ^2.

A desirable empirical method would make use of all the observations, as in the R method, yet not have the disadvantages of serious bias. A procedure which has the advantages of both the R and the H method is as follows: take all possible splits of size 1 in one group and the remainder in the other. This has the effect of successively omitting one observation from the computation of the discriminant function. The estimates of error obtained are unbiased estimates of the error rates for a discriminant function based on $n_1 - 1$ and n_2 observations. Three questions remain: first, is it feasible? second, how large is the standard error? and third, how good is the method? This method requires the computation of m discriminant functions. Since the computation of each discriminant function requires a matrix inversion, a method had to be devised which would reduce the number of inversions required. Otherwise, for large dimensional problems, this method would be too time-consuming. The method that was developed requires only one explicit inversion, namely, the inversion of the sample covariance matrix based on the entire sample. An identity first given by Bartlett (2) was used. If $B = A + uv'$, then $B^{-1} = A^{-1} - (A^{-1}uv'A^{-1}/1 + v'A^{-1}u)$ where B and A are square nonsingular matrices, and u and v are column vectors. Let $U_i = x_i - \bar{x}_k$ when x_i belongs to the kth group, n_k denote the number of cases in the kth group, α_i be $U_i'S^{-1}U_i$, and let $c_k = n_k/((n_k - 1)(m - 2))$. Then the discriminant function for x_i as computed without the sample point x_i is given by

$$D_i(x_i) = \frac{m-3}{m-2}\{x_i - \tfrac{1}{2}y + U_i/(2(n_k - 1))\}S_{(i)}^{-1}(z + (-1)^k U_i/(n_k - 1))$$

where $\bar{x}_1$, $\bar{x}_2$, and S are computed from the whole sample, and $S_{(i)}^{-1} = S^{-1} + (c_k S^{-1}U_iU_i'S^{-1}/1 - c_k\alpha_i)$. (In the derivation it is necessary to note that the mean of the kth group and S must both be adjusted.) The estimates of the probabilities of misclassification are then computed by summing the number of cases that were misclassified from each group and dividing by the number in each group. Thus, the method is feasible. The second question is difficult to answer exactly. Because there is correlation between $D_i(x_i)$ and $D_j(x_j)$, $i \neq j$, the standard error is not the simple binomial value. A 50 replicate experiment was performed with various values of n_1, n_2, $p = 10$ and δ such that the true value $P_1 = P_2$ was .10 or .30. In all cases, the correlation was quite small (<.01). This method will be denoted as the U method.

Finally, we may consider a method which combines features of an empirical method and the use of the normal distribution. To use the U method we must find the value of the discriminant function based on $m - 1$ observations for each observation. We propose to take the mean and variance within each group to estimate P_1 by $\Phi(-\bar{D}_1/s_{D1})$ and P_2 by $\Phi(\bar{D}_2/s_{D2})$. This method will be denoted as the $\bar{U}$ method. The R method has not been mentioned in this context because the estimates one would obtain reduce to the D method.

3. The Sampling Experiments

We have described eight techniques to estimate error. We attempted to evaluate seven of them (the H method was not considered for reasons given above) by sampling experiments. A computer program was written to calculate the estimates of the error rates by each method. The cutoff point was assumed to be zero. The probability of error for a discriminant function is invariant under linear transformations of the variates. Thus, for any multivariate normal distribution, we can find a transformation so that the covariance matrix of the new variates is the identity matrix, and the means are the same except for the first variate. Because the distribution of the discriminant function is independent of the covariance matrix and depends only on δ^2, n_1, n_2, and p, we used $\Sigma = I$ and $\mu_1 = 0$, $\mu_2 = (\delta, 0, \cdots, 0)$. Since the mean vector for each group was known, it was possible to determine the exact probability of misclassification for each sample discriminent function. This enabled us to compare the performance of the various methods of estimation by using generated data.

A total of 288 samples was taken from normal populations. Their true distances were distributed as in Table 1. The values were combined so that for each combination of n_1, n_2, and p, twelve cases were generated, two for each of the six levels of $\Phi(-\delta/2) = .05(.05).30$. Table 2 gives the distribution of sample size with respect to p. The ratio of sample sizes was 1 : 1, 1 : 2, or 1 : 3. We wished to determine whether the ratio of sample sizes was of importance in the performance of the empirical methods.

4. Results of Experiments.

For a given discriminant function we denoted the true probability of misclassification in the first group as P_1, and the estimates given by the various

Table 1

Number of Samples (n) at Given Distance δ^2

δ^2	1.098	1.817	2.836	4.293	6.574	11.482
$\Phi(-\delta/2)$	.30	.25	.20	.15	.10	.05
n	48	48	48	48	48	48

TABLE 2

Samples Sizes and Number of Parameters

	p = 2	4	8	20
n_1, n_2	4,4	8,8	8,8	15,15
	4,8	8,16	8,16	15,30
	4,12	8,24	8,24	15,45
	16,16	20,20	20,20	25,25
	16,32	20,40	20,40	25,50
	16,48	20,60	20,60	25,75

methods by P_{1x}, where x is O, OS, D, DS, $\bar{U}$, U, or R. Table 3 and Figure 1 give the numbers and the cumulative number of samples whose estimates of error rate were within the specified distance of the true error rate. The quantity e is defined as $|P_1 - P_{1x}|$ for the various values of x. The last eight sections of Table 3, have been stratified on p and $m - p - 1$ to represent each value of the parameters and small versus large numbers of degrees of freedom in testing T^2.

TABLE 3

Number of Samples Within Given Error

	$e<.05$	$.05<e<.10$	$.10<e<.15$	$.15<e<.20$	$e>.20$		Sample Size
O	97	68	42	28	53	Overall	288
OS	118	81	45	23	21		
D	87	52	37	40	72		
DS	94	73	50	36	35		
Ū	107	70	48	25	38		
U	73	82	62	29	42		
R	64	60	46	30	88		
O	14	4	4	5	9	$p = 2$	36
OS	8	10	6	6	6		
D	14	3	5	5	9	$m-p-1\leq 20$	
DS	11	8	6	4	7		
Ū	11	8	6	0	11		
U	7	6	6	3	14		
R	6	8	5	3	14		
O	10	7	3	2	2	$p = 4$	24
OS	7	11	2	2	2		
D	11	5	4	2	2	$m-p-1\leq 20$	
DS	11	6	4	1	2		
Ū	10	3	5	3	3		
U	5	8	6	1	4		
R	6	4	8	1	5		

TABLE 3 (continued)

Number of Samples Within Given Error

	$e<.05$	$.05<e<.10$	$.10<e<.15$	$.15<e<.20$	$e>.20$		Sample Size
O	3	7	3	5	6	$p = 8$	24
OS	9	5	4	1	5		
D	1	4	7	5	7	$m-p-1\leq 20$	
DS	6	6	2	3	7		
U	7	3	3	2	9		
U	5	4	3	6	6		
R	2	2	5	6	9		
O	4	4	2	4	10	$p = 20$	24
OS	12	4	5	1	2		
D	1	0	3	7	13	$m-p-1\leq 25$	
DS	1	4	8	3	8		
Ū	9	6	6	0	3		
U	6	6	5	4	3		
R	1	1	3	3	16		
O	15	11	8	1	1	$p = 2$	36
OS	16	11	6	2	1		
D	17	8	8	2	1	$m-p-1>20$	
DS	17	8	8	2	1		
Ū	19	8	5	3	1		
U	14	9	10	2	1		
R	16	8	7	4	1		
O	21	15	9	1	2	$p = 4$	48
OS	26	9	9	2	2		
D	22	15	3	6	2	$m-p-1>20$	
DS	23	14	7	3	1		
Ū	24	12	5	5	2		
U	15	15	10	5	3		
R	17	16	8	2	5		
O	22	9	9	4	4	$p = 8$	48
OS	23	15	5	5	0		
D	17	12	5	4	10	$m-p-1>20$	
DS	18	19	3	7	1		
Ū	16	19	6	4	3		
U	9	18	15	3	3		
R	13	12	4	7	12		
O	8	11	4	6	19	$p = 20$	48
OS	17	16	8	4	3		
D	4	5	2	9	28	$m-p-1>25$	
DS	7	8	12	13	8		
Ū	11	11	12	8	6		
U	12	16	7	5	8		
R	3	9	6	4	26		

Note that this table is not stratified on δ.

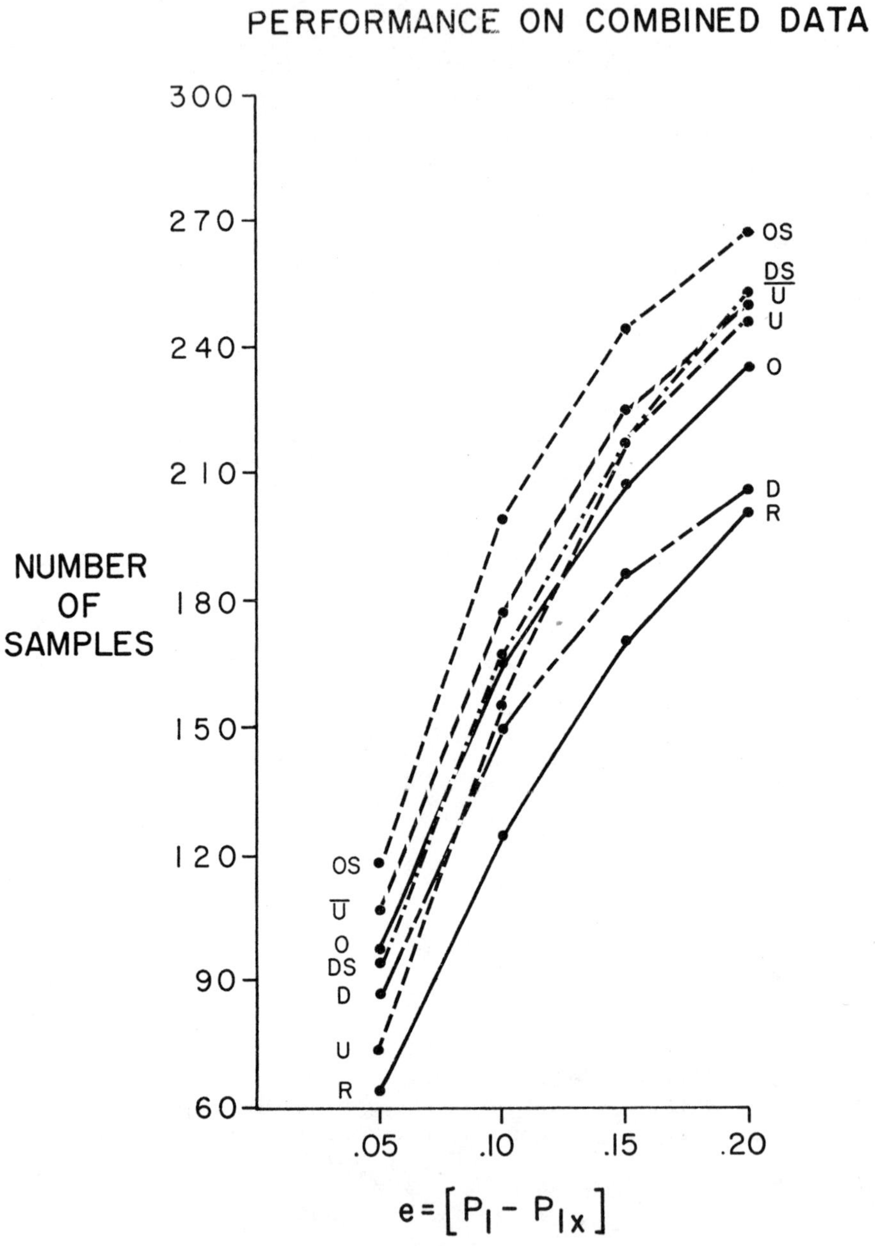

Figure 1

Several interesting points were noted in constructing this table. First, P_{1R} was less than or equal to P_{1U} in almost all cases. This evidently resulted from re-using the observations to estimate the error. Second, for $p = 20$, the OS, $\bar{U}$, and U methods were far superior to the others. For small dimensional problems, the methods were approximately equivalent. The $\bar{U}$ and U methods also appeared to be better than the other methods when δ was small (i.e., P_1

was relatively large) than when δ was large. The superiority of the OS, $\bar{U}$ and U methods lay in the fact that they performed at least as well as the other methods when the true probability of misclassification was small, and did better when it was large. The D and O methods yield similar results for $p = 2, 4$, or 8. For $p = 20$, the O method was somewhat better. A separate comparison of these two methods was made for equal n_1 and n_2. The result was that the O method was closer to the true value in thirty-six cases, the D method was closer in eight cases, and in forty-four cases, there was no difference. The "no difference" category is present because if D^2 or n_1 and n_2 are large, the O method does not add a correction term large enough to affect the value of P_1. The likelihood ratio test that the 36 to 8 split can be accounted for by sampling variation yielded $\chi^2 = 21.02$, $p < .001$ with 1 df.

Of the methods based on the normal distribution, the OS and $\bar{U}$ methods are the best. Figure 1 shows the cumulative curve of the methods (truncated at $e = .20$) over all values of p and $m - p - 1$. Kolmogorov–Smirnov tests were applied to all possible pairs of these cumulative distributions and ordered them as follows: $\underline{OS\ \bar{U}}\ \ \underline{O\ DS\ U}\ \ \underline{D\ R}$. The underlining indicates no significant differences (at the .05 level) between methods under a single line. Quality decreases from left to right. Thus, the two methods in common use at the present time, the D and R methods, are significantly poorer than any of the methods we have proposed. If the sample sizes are not large, the D and R methods are quite poor. If D^2 or n_1 and n_2 are small the OS method is not recommended because of the difficulties with the Okamoto approximation. In this case, the $\bar{U}$ method should be used if approximate normality may be assumed. If not, then the U method should be satisfactory. Note that whenever the OS method is ruled out, the O and DS methods are also ruled out. For large values of p, the OS, $\bar{U}$ or U methods should be used. None of the other methods appears to give accurate estimates. Instances where p is large and $m - p - 1$ is small arise frequently in biomedical applications in which the cost of obtaining data is high. Not many observations will be available in these cases, but p is frequently large.

The holdout, or H, method has not been included in the foregoing comparisons since the number of hold-out cases in each group that are incorrect by classified is binomially distributed. The ease with which the error rates can be estimated, by both point and interval estimates, together with the lack of dependence of the distribution of the estimates upon the form of the population sampled, form the main attractions of the method. The distributional results apply only to the discriminant function obtained from the part of the data designated for analysis, and do not hold for the discriminant function computed from all of the data. Thus we do not consider the H method to have any inherent superiority to the U method; the H method has the disadvantage of requiring larger samples than the other methods. However, in some large sample problems using real data, estimates of error rates obtained using the H method did not differ appreciably from those obtained by application of the other methods.

An additional check was made with different data generated in a similar manner to determine if the ratio of sample sizes made a difference in the performance of the two empirical methods. Table 4 summarizes their behavior

TABLE 4

Performance of U and R Methods for Various Ratios of Sample Sizes

Ratio	$e < .05$	$.05 < e < .10$	$.10 < e < .15$	$.15 < e < .20$	$e > .20$
U					
1:1	8	3	3	4	3
1:2	8	6	3	1	4
1:3	7	8	1	2	2
R					
1:1	2	1	3	2	11
1:2	0	0	1	2	19
1:3	0	1	1	3	15

for $p = 8, 20, m - p - 1 < 15$. For the U method the χ^2 was 3.01 with 4 df. For the R method the χ^2 was 1.02 with 3 df. Neither value was significantly large. Thus, the ratio of sample size did not appear to affect the performance of the empirical methods.

5. Summary and Recommendations

We have described several methods of estimation of error rates of discriminant analysis, and have made a comparative evaluation on the basis of a series of Monte Carlo experiments. No one method is uniformly best for all situations, although some methods, the D and R, appear to be relatively poor. It is of some interest to note that the O method does fairly well overall. This is somewhat surprising since the O method estimates

$$P_1^* = P\{D_s(x) < 0 \mid G_1\} = E(P(D_s(x) < 0 \mid G_1, \bar{x}_1, \bar{x}_2, S)) = E(P_1)$$

and we are trying to estimate P_1. However, if we examine Table 3 we find that the O method does well in those cases in which p is small and thus D^2 may be expected to be close to δ^2. For larger values of p we note that the O method is substantially poorer than the S, $\bar{U}$ or U methods. The OS appears generally preferable to the O, and the DS to the D method. One of the more commonly used methods, the R method appeared to be fairly consistently poorer than the others. For large values of P, the OS, $\bar{U}$ or U methods are far superior to the other methods. If approximate normality can be assumed, the OS and $\bar{U}$ methods are good. The U method does not take advantage of the assumption of approximate normality. If D^2 is small, or the sample size is small relative to the number of parameters, the OS method should not be used. In particular, if D^2 is small (say $D^2 < 1.0$), the OS method may lead one astray. For this reason, the $\bar{U}$ method or the U method should be used. Finally, the U method should be used if normality is questionable (e.g., when a large number of dichotomies are used as variables) and the sample size is small relative to the number of variables.

Acknowledgements

The authors wish to acknowledge assistance from the Health Sciences Computing Facility, University of California, Los Angeles supported by grant

FR-3 of the Division of Facilities and Resources, National Institutes of Health. One of us (P. A. L.) held a traineeship in Biostatistics sponsored by grant TG-49, National Institutes of Health during graduate study, when this work was performed.

REFERENCES

1. ANDERSON, T. W., 1951. Classification by multivariate analysis. *Psychometrika, 16*, p. 31.
2. BARTLETT, M. S., 1952. An inverse matrix adjustment arising in discriminant analysis. *Ann. Math. Stat. 22*, p. 107.
3. FISHER, R. A., 1936. The use of multiple measurements in taxonomic problems. *Ann. Eugen., 7*, p. 179.
4. KABE, D. G., 1963. Some results on the distribution of two random matrices used in classification procedures. *Ann. Math. Stat., 34*, p. 181 (a correction to this article appeared appeared in *Ann. Math. Stat.*, 1964, *34*, p. 924).
5. LACHENBRUCH, P. A., 1965. Estimation of error rates in discriminant analysis. Ph.D. Dissertation (unpublished) University of California, Los Angeles.
6. MAHALANOBIS, P. C., 1936. On the generalized distance in statistics. *Proc. Nat. Inst. Sci. India, 2*, p. 49.
7. OKAMOTO, M., 1963. An asymptotic expansion for the distribution of the linear discriminant function. *Ann. Math. Stat., 34*, p. 1286.
8. SITGREAVES, ROSEDITH., 1952. On the distribution of two random matrices used in classification procedures. *Ann. Math. Stat., 23*, p. 263.
9. SMITH, C. A. B., 1947. Some examples of discrimination. *Ann. Eugen., 18*, p. 272.
10. WALD, A., 1944. On a statistical problem in the classification of an individual into one of two groups. *Ann. Math. Stat., 15*, p. 145.
11. WELCH, B. L., 1939. Note on discriminant functions. *Biometrika, 31*, p. 218.

On Optimum Recognition Error and Reject Tradeoff

C. K. CHOW, SENIOR MEMBER, IEEE

Abstract—The performance of a pattern recognition system is characterized by its error and reject tradeoff. This paper describes an optimum rejection rule and presents a general relation between the error and reject probabilities and some simple properties of the tradeoff in the optimum recognition system. The error rate can be directly evaluated from the reject function. Some practical implications of the results are discussed. Examples in normal distributions and uniform distributions are given.

I. Introduction

THE ERROR rate and the reject rate are commonly used to describe the performance level of pattern recognition systems. A complete description of the recognition performance is given by the error–reject tradeoff, i.e., the functional relation of the error rate and reject rate at all levels. An error or misrecognition occurs when a pattern from one class is identified as that of a different class. The error is sometimes referred to as a substitution error or undetected error. A reject occurs when the recognition system withholds its recognition decision, and the pattern is rejected for exceptional handling, such as rescan or manual inspection.

Because of uncertainties and noise inherent in any pattern recognition task, errors are generally unavoidable. The option to reject is introduced to safeguard against excessive misrecognition; it converts potential misrecognition into rejection. However, the tradeoff between the errors and rejects is seldom one for one. Whenever the reject option is exercised, some would-be correct recognitions are also converted into rejects. We are interested in the best error–reject tradeoff in the optimum rejection scheme.

An optimum rejection scheme was derived in [1]. The error–reject tradeoff curves have been used to describe and compare the empirical performances of recognition methods [2] and [3], and they have also been found useful in the actual system design of an optical page reader [4]. However, few theoretical results on the error–reject tradeoff are available.

This paper first describes an optimum rejection rule and then derives a general relation between the error and reject probabilities. The error rate can be directly evaluated from the reject function. This result provides a basis for calculating the error rates from the empirical rejection curve without actually identifying the errors. Some simple properties of the optimum tradeoff are presented. Examples in normal distributions and uniform distributions are given.

II. Optimum Recognition Rule

A recognition rule is optimum if for a given error rate (error probability) it minimizes the reject rate (reject probability). It is known [1] that the optimum rule is to reject the pattern if the maximum of the a posteriori probabilities is less than some threshold. More explicitly, the optimum recognition rule δ is given as

$$\text{(a)} \qquad \delta(d_k \mid v) = 1 \qquad (k \neq 0) \tag{1}$$

i.e., to accept the pattern v for recognition and to identify it as of the kth pattern class whenever

$$p_k F(v \mid k) \geq p_j F(v \mid j) \qquad \text{for all} \quad j = 1, 2, \cdots n,$$

Manuscript received March 24, 1969; revised June 2, 1969. Some results of the paper were described at the IEEE 1968 International Workshop on Pattern Recognition, Delft, the Netherlands; a summary of the paper was presented at the 1969 International Symposium on Information Theory, Ellenville, N. Y.

The author is with the Thomas J. Watson Research Center, IBM Corporation, Yorktown Heights, N. Y. 10598, and is currently visiting the Department of Electrical Engineering, Massachusetts Institute of Technology, Cambridge, Mass. 02139.

Reprinted from *IEEE Trans. Inform. Theory*, vol. IT-16, pp. 41–46, Jan. 1970.

and

$$p_k F(v \mid k) \geq (1 - t) \sum_{i=1}^{n} p_i F(v \mid i) \tag{2}$$

(b)

$$\delta(d_0 \mid v) = 1 \tag{3}$$

i.e., to reject the pattern whenever

$$\max_i [p_i F(v \mid i)] < (1 - t) \sum_{i=1}^{n} p_i F(v \mid i) \tag{4}$$

where v is the pattern vector, n is the number of classes, $(p_1, p_2, \cdots, p_n)$ is the a priori probability distribution of the classes, $F(v \mid i)$ is the conditional probability density for v given the ith class, d_i $(i \neq 0)$ is the decision that v is identified as of the ith class while d_0 is the decision to reject, and t is a constant between 0 and 1 $(0 \leq t \leq 1)$. The probability of error, or error rate, is

$$E(t) = \int_V \sum_{i=1}^{n} \sum_{\substack{j=1 \\ j \neq i}}^{n} \delta(d_j \mid v) p_i F(v \mid i) \, dv \tag{5}$$

and the probability of reject or reject rate is

$$R(t) = \int_V \delta(d_0 \mid v) \sum_{i=1}^{n} p_i F(v \mid i) \, dv \tag{6}$$

where V is the pattern space. Both the error and reject rates are implicit functions of the parameter t.

The probability of correct recognition is

$$C(t) = \int_V \sum_{i=1}^{n} \delta(d_i \mid v) p_i F(v \mid a_i) \, dv = 1 - E(t) - R(t) \tag{7}$$

and the probability of acceptance (or acceptance rate) is defined as

$$A(t) = C(t) + E(t). \tag{8}$$

Now let $m(v)$ denote the random variable

$$m(v) = \frac{\max_i p_i F(v \mid i)}{F(v)} \tag{9}$$

where $F(v)$ is the absolute probability density

$$F(v) = \sum_{i=1}^{n} p_i F(v \mid i). \tag{10}$$

The variable $m(v)$ is the maximum of the a posteriori probabilities of the classes given the pattern v.

The optimum rule δ can then be restated as:

1) accept the pattern v whenever

$$m(v) \geq 1 - t, \tag{2'}$$

2) reject the pattern v whenever

$$m(v) < 1 - t. \tag{4'}$$

The optimum rule is to reject the pattern v whenever its maximum of the a posteriori probabilities $m(v)$ is small (less than $1 - t$). The optimality can be seen by observing that $m(v)$ is the conditional probability of correctly recognizing a given pattern v. A detailed proof is given in [1].

III. Rejection Threshold

The parameter t in the decision rule will be called the "rejection threshold." For any fixed value of t $(0 \leq t \leq 1)$, the decision rule δ partitions the pattern space V into two disjoint sets (or regions) ($V_A(t)$ and $V_R(t)$) where (2) and (4), respectively, hold, namely:

$$V_A(t) = \{v \mid m(v) \geq (1 - t)\} \tag{11}$$

$$V_R(t) = \{v \mid m(v) < (1 - t)\}. \tag{12}$$

Without loss of generality, it will be assumed that $F(v)$ is nonzero over the entire space V, otherwise the set over which $F(v)$ is zero is first deleted. V_A and V_R are called, respectively, the "acceptance region" and the "reject region" of the decision rule. An example is depicted in Fig. 1(a) where the shaded region is V_R and the unshaded region is V_A.

In terms of these regions, the various probabilities can be written as

$$R(t) = \int_{V_R(t)} F(v) \, dv \tag{6'}$$

$$A(t) = \int_{V_A(t)} F(v) \, dv \tag{8'}$$

and

$$C(t) = \int_{V_A(t)} \max_i [p_i F(v \mid i)] \, dv = \int_{V_A(t)} m(v) F(v) \, dv \tag{7'}$$

$$E(t) = \int_{V_A(t)} \left\{ \sum_{i=1}^{n} p_i F(v \mid i) - \max_i [p_i F(v \mid i)] \right\} dv = \int_{V_A(t)} [1 - m(v)] F(v) \, dv. \tag{5'}$$

We shall now present some simple properties of the rejection threshold t.

1) Both the error and reject rates are monotonic in t.
2) t is an upper bound of the error rate.
3) t is a differential error-reject tradeoff ratio [see (20)].

A. Monotonicity

It follows immediately from the definitions of (11) and (12) that for any t_1 and t_2 in [0, 1] if $t_1 < t_2$, then

$$V_A(t_1) \subset V_A(t_2)$$

and

$$V_R(t_1) \supset V_R(t_2).$$

All the integrands in the integrals of (5′) to (8′) are

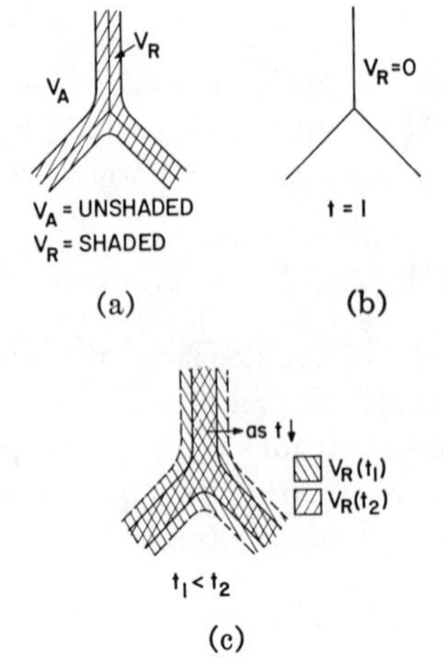

Fig. 1. Reject regions in the pattern space.

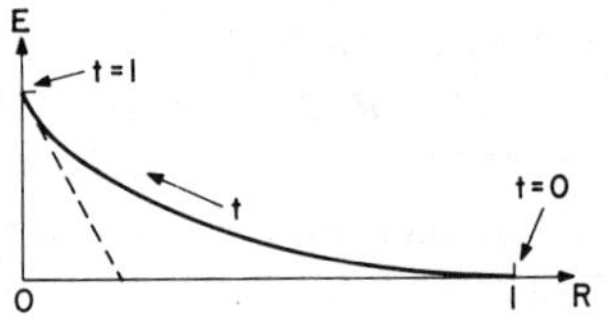

Fig. 2. Error–reject tradeoff curve.

nonnegative, hence if the domain of integration expands, the value of the integral increases. More specifically, if $t_1 < t_2$, then $V_A(t_1) \subset V_A(t_2)$ and $V_R(t_1) \supset V_R(t_2)$; therefore, $E(t_1) \leq E(t_2)$ and $R(t_1) \geq R(t_2)$. In other words, E increases and R decreases with increasing t. In particular, when $t = 0$, $E = 0$, and when $t = 1$, $A = 1$ and $R = 0$. Whenever $t \geq 1 - 1/n$, $R = 0$.

B. An Upper Bound of Error Rate

We shall now show that

$$E(t) \leq t.$$

For any v in $V_A(t)$, we have

$$m(v) \geq (1 - t).$$

Therefore (5′) gives

$$E(t) \leq \int_{V_A(t)} F(v)\, dv.$$

Hence

$$E(t) \leq tA(t) \leq t.$$

IV. Error-Reject Tradeoff

A complete description of the performance of recognition systems is given by the error–reject tradeoff, i.e., the functional relation of E and R at all levels. A typical tradeoff curve is given in Fig. 2. Since both E and R of the optimum recognition systems are monotonic functions of the rejection threshold t, one can compute the tradeoff E versus R from $E(t)$ and $R(t)$.

We shall now show that the rejection function $R(t)$ alone suffices to completely characterize the optimum recognition performance. In other words, E can be derived from $R(t)$. The central result is a simple functional relation between E and R; $E(t)$ is a Stieltjes integral of t with respect to $R(t)$, namely,

$$E(t) = -\int_{t=0}^{t} t\, dR(t). \tag{13}$$

This relation is valid for all optimum decision rules as defined in (1)–(4). No explicit forms for the density functions $F(v/i)$ are required in deriving the integral. If $R(t)$ is differentiable with respect to t, then the above Stieltjes integral reduces to the ordinary Riemann integral

$$E = \int_R^1 t(R)\, dR. \tag{14}$$

It is noted that the integral of (14) is not always meaningful; for example, when $R(t)$ is discontinuous (as in the case of Section VI-B). On the other hand, the Stieltjes integral of (13) always exists, as $R(t)$ is always bounded, monotonic, and thus of bounded variation.

Consider a decremental change in the rejection threshold from t to $t - \Delta t$; the reject region expands from $V_R(t)$ to $V_R(t - \Delta t)$. Let $\Delta V_R(t)$ denote the incremental region $V_R(t - \Delta t) - V_R(t)$. For any v in $\Delta V_R(t)$, it was accepted at the threshold t and is now rejected at the lower threshold $t - \Delta t$. Equations (2) and (4) now give

$$(1 - t)F(v) \leq \max_i p_i F(v \mid i) < (1 - t + \Delta t)F(v) \qquad \text{for } v \in \Delta V_R(t). \tag{15}$$

By integrating the last expression over the incremental region ΔV_R, one obtains

$$(1 - t)\, \Delta R \leq -\Delta C < (1 - t + \Delta t)\, \Delta R \tag{16}$$

where ΔR and ΔC are, respectively, the increments in the rejection rate and correct recognition rate, namely,

$$\Delta R = \int_{\Delta V_R} F(v)\, dv$$

$$\Delta C = \int_{\Delta V_R} \max_i \left[p_i F(v \mid i)\right] dv.$$

Of course, the increment in the error rate is simply

$$\Delta E = -\Delta R - \Delta C. \tag{17}$$

By substituting (17) into (16), one has

$$-t\Delta R \leq \Delta E < -(t - \Delta t)\, \Delta R. \tag{18}$$

One then sums (18) with t steadily decreasing throughout the range of interest from t to 0 to obtain

$$-\sum t\Delta R \leq E(t) \leq -\sum t\Delta R - \sum \Delta t \Delta R$$

and then lets Δt tend to zero. As Δt tends to zero, the last sum of the above expression vanishes and (13) is thus obtained.

When $R(t)$ is differentiable, (13) becomes

$$E(t) = -\int_0^t t\frac{dR}{dt}\,dt = -\int_{R(0)}^{R(t)} t(R)\,dR = \int_R^1 t\,dR$$

since $R(0) = 1$. This relation is depicted in Fig. 3. The area under the entire rejection curve is the (forced decision) error rate when no rejection is allowed. Through an integration by parts and as indicated in Fig. 3, (13) can also be written as

$$E = \int_0^t R(t)\,dt - tR(t). \tag{19}$$

Equation (14) gives

$$\frac{dE}{dR} = -t \leq 0. \tag{20}$$

The rejection threshold is the differential error–reject tradeoff. In particular, the initial slope of the error–reject curve is $-1 + 1/n$ or greater, while the final slope is 0. Equation 20 also gives

$$\frac{d^2E}{dR^2} = -\frac{dt}{dR} \geq 0. \tag{21}$$

The optimum error–reject curve is always concave upward and the slope increases from -1 to 0 as R increases from 0 to 1 (Fig. 2).

V. Rejection Threshold of a Minimum-Risk Rule

It is known [1] that the optimum decision rule given in (1) to (4) is also a minimum-risk rule if the cost function is uniform within each class of decisions, i.e., if no distinction is made among the errors, among the rejects, and among the correct recognition. The rejection threshold is then related to the costs as follows:

$$t = \frac{W_r - W_c}{W_e - W_c} \tag{22}$$

where W_e, W_r, and W_c are the costs for making an error, reject, and correct recognition, respectively. Usually $W_e > W_r > W_c$. The rejection threshold is simply the normalized cost for the rejection. We can take $W_c = 0$ and $W_e = 1$, and the minimum risk is

$$\text{risk}\ (t) = E(t) + tR(t) = \int_0^t R(t)\,dt \tag{23}$$

which is also depicted in Fig. 3.

VI. Examples

For numerical illustration, two examples are given here. In these examples, the pattern vector v is 1-dimensional and there are two pattern classes with equal a priori probability of occurrence, i.e., $p_1 = p_2 = \frac{1}{2}$. The examples are concerned with the normal distributions and uniform distributions, respectively.

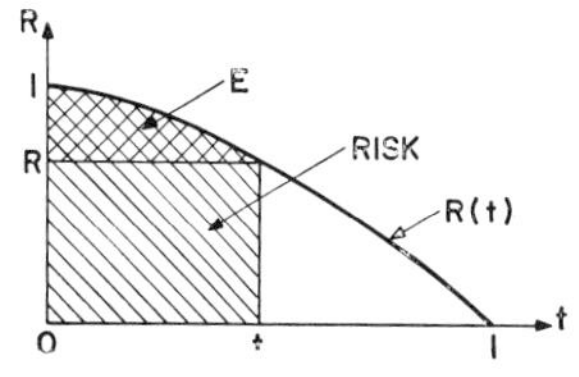

Fig. 3. Reject curve.

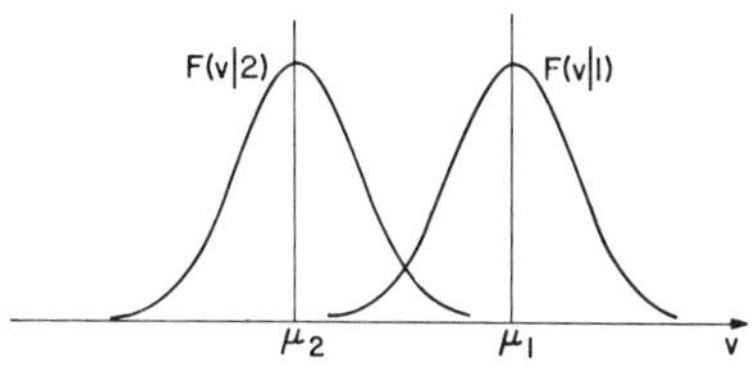

Fig. 4. Example in normal distribution.

For two classes, the condition for rejection, namely, (4), can never be satisfied when $t > \frac{1}{2}$; hence the reject rate is always zero if the reject threshold t exceeds $\frac{1}{2}$. The effective range of t for problems of two classes is, therefore, from 0 to $\frac{1}{2}$. With $n = 2$ and $0 \leq t \leq \frac{1}{2}$ it can be readily verified that the condition for rejection (4) is equivalent to

$$\frac{t}{1-t} \leq \frac{p_1F(v \mid 1)}{p_2F(v \mid 2)} \leq \frac{1-t}{t} \tag{24}$$

A. *Normal Distributions of Equal Variance*

Consider two normal distributions with means μ_1 and μ_2 and equal covariance σ^2, as shown in Fig. 4. Take $\mu_1 > \mu_2$. The density function is, $i = 1$ or 2,

$$F(v \mid i) = \frac{1}{\sigma\sqrt{2\pi}} \exp\left[-\frac{(v-\mu_i)^2}{2\sigma^2}\right]. \tag{25}$$

With (25) and some algebraic manipulations, (24) can be transformed to

$$|v - \tfrac{1}{2}(\mu_1 + \mu_2)| \leq \frac{\sigma^2}{\mu_1 - \mu_2} \ln\left(\frac{1}{t} - 1\right), \tag{26}$$

i.e., the optimum rule is to reject whenever the pattern lies within a certain distance of the midpoint between the two means. The corresponding error and reject rates are

$$E(t) = \Phi(a) \tag{27}$$

$$R(t) = \Phi(b) - \Phi(a) \tag{28}$$

where Φ is the normal cumulative distribution function, namely,

$$\Phi(z) = \frac{1}{\sqrt{2\pi}} \int_{-\infty}^{z} e^{-(x^2/2)}\,dx \tag{29}$$

and the parameters are

$$a = -\tfrac{1}{2}s - \frac{1}{s}\ln\left(\frac{1}{t} - 1\right) \tag{30a}$$

$$b = -\tfrac{1}{2}s + \frac{1}{s}\ln\left(\frac{1}{t} - 1\right) \tag{30b}$$

$$s = \frac{\mu_1 - \mu_2}{\sigma}. \tag{30c}$$

The parameter s is the (normalized) separation between the means of the distributions and is the only (composite) parameter of the distributions that $R(t)$ and $E(t)$ depend upon. It is straightforward to verify (14) for this example. A set of the error, reject, and tradeoff curves, for $s = 1, 2, 3$, and 4, is depicted in Fig. 5.

B. Uniform Distributions

Consider two uniform distributions:

$$F(v \mid 1) = \begin{cases} 1 & \text{when } 0 \le v \le 1 \\ 0 & \text{elsewhere} \end{cases} \tag{31a}$$

$$F(v \mid 2) = \begin{cases} \frac{1}{2} & \text{when } \frac{1}{2} \le v \le \frac{5}{2} \\ 0 & \text{elsewhere} \end{cases} \tag{31b}$$

as shown in Fig. 6.

The reject function $R(t)$ is simply

$$R(t) = \begin{cases} \frac{3}{8} & \text{when } 0 \le t \le \frac{1}{3} \\ 0 & \text{when } \frac{1}{3} < t \le 1, \end{cases} \tag{32}$$

which is discontinuous [Fig. 7(a)], and the integral of (13) is evaluated to

$$E(t) = \begin{cases} 0 & \text{when } 0 \le t \le \frac{1}{3} \\ \frac{1}{8} & \text{when } \frac{1}{3} < t \le 1, \end{cases} \tag{33}$$

which is shown in Fig. 7(b) and the tradeoff can assume only two values, namely $(E, R) = (\frac{1}{8}, 0)$ or $(0, \frac{3}{8})$ [Fig. 7(c)]. However, if a randomized scheme is used in the range $\frac{1}{2} \le v \le 1$, R may vary continuously from $\frac{1}{8}$ to 0 as shown by the dotted line in Fig. 7(c).

VII. Some Practical Implications

Most of our results on the error–reject tradeoff seem consistent with our intuition, although the simple integral relation between the error and reject rates is somewhat unexpected.

Since the slope of the error–reject tradeoff curve (Fig. 2) is the value of the rejection threshold, the tradeoff is most effective initially (i.e., at the low level of rejection) and it gets more difficult as the error rate is lower. This is certainly common in our practical experience; excessive rejection is generally required to reduce residual errors.

Practical applications of the present results are in the areas of system design and performance evaluation of the recognition systems. The general characteristics of the error–reject tradeoff curve provide the system de-

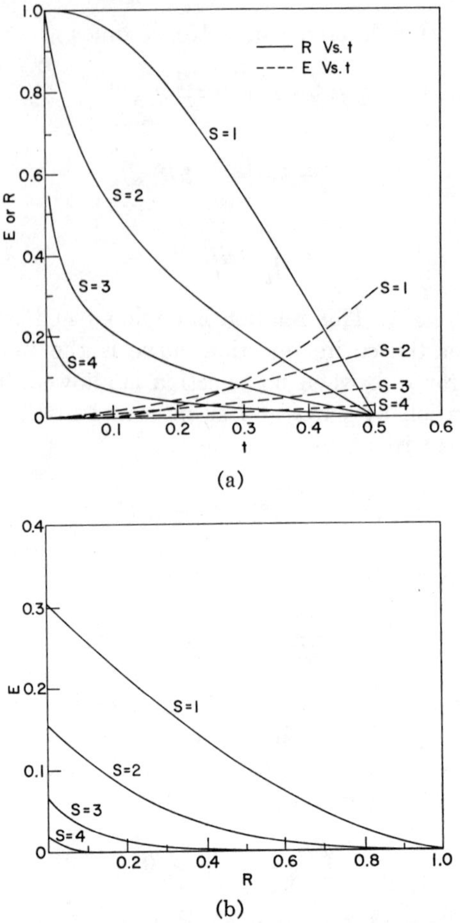

Fig. 5. Normal distributions. (a) Reject and error curves. (b) Tradeoff curve.

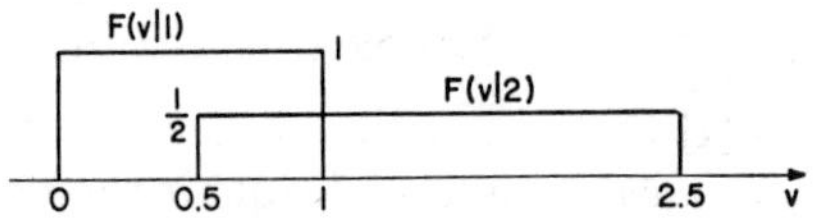

Fig. 6. Example in uniform distributions.

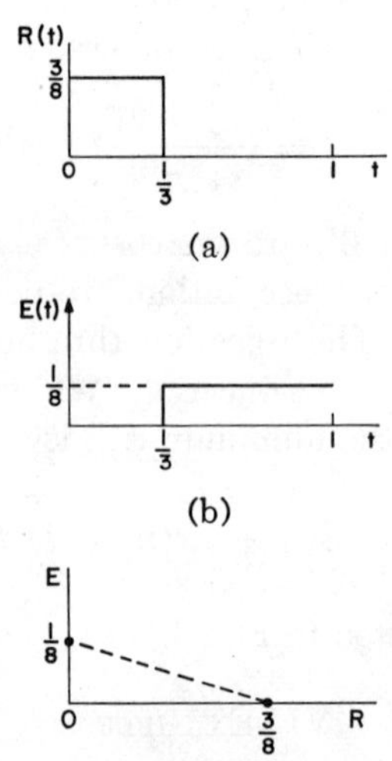

Fig. 7. Uniform distributions. (a) Reject curve. (b) Error curve. (c) Tradeoff curve.

signer with a convenient means of verifying the basic assumption on the underlying probability distributions. The integral of (13) makes it possible to calculate error rates and consequently, the tradeoff curve from the empirically observed reject rates. No class identification of the sample patterns are required in obtaining the empirical rejection curve. Or equivalently, one can just obtain an empirical density function of the maximum of the a posteriori probabilities, and then calculate the error and reject rates.

In most recognition tasks, the underlying probability distributions of the patterns are not completely known and the design of the recognition systems is generally based on empirical data. A common design procedure is to assume, on the basis of available (usually limited) a priori information and the designer's intuition, some functional forms of the distributions, to derive the system structure based on these assumptions, and to adjust the system parameters by using the empirical data. It is not always a simple matter to verify the validity of the assumptions on which the system structure is based. However, one can always, though laboriously, obtain the empirical error–reject tradeoff curve and compute the theoretical one from the basic assumptions. A comparison of the empirical and theoretical tradeoff curves can quickly reveal how well the theoretical model agrees with the empirical data, and it can serve as a checkpoint for initiating the process of revising and improving the theoretical model.

The data used in any meaningful evaluation of a recognition system are usually large, and it is extremely costly and time consuming to detect the recognition errors. To identify a recognition error additional information, usually human inspection, at some stage is required. On the other hand, the rejection is the explicit result of a definite decision, and the rejects can be readily recorded and tallied. Equation (13) provides a simple means of calculating the error rate from the reject curve without actually identifying the errors.

VIII. Conclusion

A general error and reject tradeoff relation is derived for the (Bayes) optimum recognition system with an option to reject. The error probability is a Stieltjes integral of the rejection threshold with respect to the reject probability. The error function can be directly evaluated from the reject function. Hence, the reject function determines the recognition error and reject tradeoff and completely characterizes the performance of the optimum recognition system. The error–reject integral provides a simple means of calculating the error rate from the empirical reject curve without actually identifying the recognition errors.

References

[1] C. K. Chow, "An optimum character recognition system using decision functions," *IRE Trans. Electronic Computers*, vol. EC-6, pp. 247–254, December 1957.

[2] C. K. Chow and C. N. Liu, "An approach to structure adaptation in pattern recognition," *IEEE Trans. Systems Science and Cybernetics*, vol. SSC-2, pp. 73–80, December 1966.

[3] R. Bakis, N. Herbst, and G. Nagy, "An experimental study of machine recognition of hand-printed numerals," *IEEE Trans. Systems Science and Cybernetics*, vol. SSC-4, pp. 119–132, July 1968.

[4] R. B. Hennis, "The IBM 1975 optical page reader, Part I: System design," *IBM J. Res. and Develop.*, vol. 12, pp. 346–353, September 1968.

Estimation of Classification Error

KEINOSUKE FUKUNAGA, MEMBER, IEEE, AND DAVID L. KESSELL,
STUDENT MEMBER, IEEE

Abstract—This paper discusses methods of estimating the probability of error for the Bayes' classifier which must be designed and tested with a finite number of classified samples. The expected difference between estimates is discussed. A simplified algorithm to compute the leaving-one-out method is proposed for multivariate normal distributions wtih unequal covariance matrices. The discussion is extended to nonparametric classifiers by using the Parzen approximation for the density functions. Experimental results are shown for both parametric and nonparametric cases.

Index Terms—Bayes' classifier, estimation, finite number of samples, pattern recognition, probability of error.

I. Introduction

IN MANY classification problems the designer is faced with the problem of designing and evaluating the performance of a pattern classifier on the basis of a limited number of classified samples. In this paper we assume the classifier is of the form of the Bayes' classifier (minimum probability of error classifier), with incomplete information available about the distributions to be classified. Since with a finite number of samples the distributions cannot be estimated exactly, the resulting classifier design is nonoptimum. The evaluation of the performance of this classifier, as measured by the probability of error to be expected when it is applied to further samples, is the subject of this paper.

Many of the early evaluations of classifier performance were obtained by using all available samples to design the classifier and then using the same samples to test it. It has been known for some time that this procedure, which we denote as the C method, produces unreliable results. This has led several investigators to search for better methods of evaluating classifier error rates.

Hills [1] presented the general relationships between various error estimates and the minimum attainable error, and pointed out, along with other facts, that the C method gives an expected error which is less than the true error.

Highleyman [2] published optimum partitions of the total sample set into design and test sets to obtain minimum variance estimates of the minimum attainable error rate. He concluded that the test sample size should never be smaller than the design sample size. As was later pointed out by Kanal and Chandrasekaran [3], Highleyman's results are valid only for a large sample size. Also since not all available samples are used to build the classifier, one would expect a poorer classifier design, and since not all samples are used in the evaluation of the classifier, one also expects a larger variance in the estimate of probability of error.

Another important method is called the leaving-one-out method (the L method) [4]. This gives a nearly unbiased estimate of the error rate and uses all available samples effectively. In Section II we discuss this method and general relations between error rates. The disadvantage of the L method is that it required the same number of classifier designs as there are samples. In order to eliminate this difficulty, we provide, in Section III, a simpler computational procedure for implementing the L method for unequal covariance multivariate normal densities. If N is the available number of samples, we find that the difference in the likelihood ratios produced by the C and L methods decreases as $1/N$ while the standard deviation of the estimated likelihood ratio decreases as $1/\sqrt{N}$.

All of the previous discussion assumes a parametric approach to the classification problem. In order to extend the L and C methods to a nonparametric case, in Section IV we examine classification using Parzen multidimensional approximations of the respective density functions.

In Section V, the experimental results are shown for both parametric and nonparametric cases with cight dimensional samples.

II. Estimation of Errors

In this section, general relations between various error estimates are discussed.

Let us consider two distributions in an n-dimensional vector space. If we classify these two distributions according to the Bayes' optimum classifier so as to minimize the probability of error, the decision rule is given by

$$L(X, \Theta) = \frac{p(\omega_1)p(X \mid \omega_1)}{p(\omega_2)p(X \mid \omega_2)} \begin{matrix} > 1 \rightarrow X \in \omega_1 \\ < 1 \rightarrow X \in \omega_2 \end{matrix} \tag{1}$$

where $p(\omega_i)$ is the *a priori* probability of class i, $p(X|\omega_i)$ is the conditional density function of $\boldsymbol{X}$, assuming class i, and X is a column vector with n components. $L(X, \Theta)$ is a function of a set of parameters Θ, which characterize the $p(\omega_i)$'s and $p(X/\omega_i)$'s.

In practice Θ is unknown and an estimate $\hat{\Theta}$, is made of Θ from a finite number of classified samples. The actual probability of error that will be realized by (1) will be a function of the actual parameters of the distributions being classified. Thus the probability of error $\mathcal{E}$, is a function of two arguments as follows:

$$\mathcal{E}(\Theta_1, \Theta_2) \tag{2}$$

Manuscript received October 16, 1970; revised March 19, 1971. This work was supported in part by the National Science Foundation under Grant GJ-1099.

K. Fukunaga is with the School of Electrical Engineering, Purdue University, Lafayette, Ind. 47907.

D. L. Kessell is with Bell Telephone Laboratories, Inc., Murray Hill, N. J., on educational assignment at the School of Electrical Engineering, Purdue University, Lafayette, Ind. 47907.

Reprinted from *IEEE Trans. Comput.*, vol. C-20, pp. 1521–1527, Dec. 1971.

where

Θ_1 Set of parameters used in the design.
Θ_2 Set of parameters of the data being classified.

Since the formulation (1) minimizes the probability of error,

$$\mathcal{E}(\Theta, \Theta) \leq \mathcal{E}(\Theta', \Theta) \quad (3)$$

where Θ and Θ' are not equal.

For a particular problem, assume that the set of true parameters is Θ and that $\hat{\mathbf{\Theta}}_N$ is the estimate of Θ made from a random selection of N samples from the true distributions. Thus $\hat{\mathbf{\Theta}}_N$ is a random vector. For any particular value of $\hat{\mathbf{\Theta}}_N$, Θ_N, the following inequalities follow from (3):

$$\mathcal{E}(\Theta, \Theta) \leq \mathcal{E}(\hat{\Theta}_N, \Theta) \quad (4)$$

$$\mathcal{E}(\hat{\Theta}_N, \hat{\Theta}_N) \leq \mathcal{E}(\Theta, \hat{\Theta}_N). \quad (5)$$

Since (4) and (5) are true for every realization $\hat{\Theta}_N$, it follows that

$$\mathcal{E}(\Theta, \Theta) \leq E\{\mathcal{E}(\hat{\mathbf{\Theta}}_N, \Theta)\} \quad (6)$$

and

$$E\{\mathcal{E}(\hat{\mathbf{\Theta}}_N, \hat{\mathbf{\Theta}}_N)\} \leq E\{\mathcal{E}(\Theta, \hat{\mathbf{\Theta}}_N)\}. \quad (7)$$

If

$$E\{\mathcal{E}(\Theta, \hat{\mathbf{\Theta}}_N)\} = \mathcal{E}(\Theta, \Theta) \quad (8)$$

then (6), (7), and (8) give [1]

$$E\{\mathcal{E}(\hat{\mathbf{\Theta}}_N, \hat{\mathbf{\Theta}}_N)\} \leq \mathcal{E}(\Theta, \Theta) \leq E\{\mathcal{E}(\hat{\mathbf{\Theta}}_N, \Theta)\}. \quad (9)$$

Equation (8) is not true in general. However, it is true when the estimated densities, obtained by substituting $\hat{\mathbf{\Theta}}$ for the true parameter Θ, are unbiased estimates of the true densities. The left-hand side of (9) has not been verified in general, but this behavior is frequently experimentally observed [2], [3].

An estimate of $E\{\mathcal{E}(\hat{\mathbf{\Theta}}_N, \hat{\mathbf{\Theta}}_N)\}$, $\hat{\mathcal{E}}(\hat{\Theta}_N, \hat{\Theta}_N)$, is called the C-method estimate in this paper. This estimate of the probability of error is calculated as follows.

The C Method

1) $X_1, \cdots, X_N$ are randomly selected from the true distributions to calculate $\hat{\Theta}_N$.

2) Calculate $L(X_k, \hat{\Theta}_N)$ for $k=1, 2, \cdots, N$.

3) Count the number of X_k for which

$$L(X_k, \hat{\Theta}_N) > 1 \quad \text{and} \quad X_k \notin \omega_1$$
$$L(X_k, \hat{\Theta}_N) < 1 \quad \text{and} \quad X_k \notin \omega_2. \quad (10)$$

To the degree that the C-method estimate is a good estimate of $\mathcal{E}(\hat{\mathbf{\Theta}}_N, \hat{\mathbf{\Theta}}_N)$ and for those situations in which (8) holds we see that (9) indicates this method may be expected to give an optimistically biased estimate.

On the other hand, $\hat{\mathcal{E}}(\hat{\mathbf{\Theta}}_N, \Theta)$ is the estimate in which independent sets of samples are used for determining the Bayes' classifier and testing. The leaving-one-out method gives an approximately unbiased estimate of $E\{\hat{\mathcal{E}}(\hat{\mathbf{\Theta}}_N, \Theta)\}$, $\hat{\mathcal{E}}(\hat{\Theta}_{N-1}, \Theta)$, utilizing all available samples as effectively as possible [4].

The L Method

1) Assuming that N samples $X_1, X_2, \cdots, X_N$ are available, $N-1$ samples, omitting X_K, are used to calculate $\hat{\Theta}_{N-1}^{(k)}$.

2) Calculate $L(X_k, \hat{\Theta}_{N-1}^{(k)})$ for $k=1, 2, \cdots, N$.

3) Count the number of X_k for which

$$L(X_k, \hat{\Theta}_{N-1}^{(k)}) > 1 \quad \text{and} \quad X_k \notin \omega_1$$
$$L(X_k, \hat{\Theta}_{N-1}^{(k)}) < 1 \quad \text{and} \quad X_k \notin \omega_2. \quad (11)$$

The L method makes efficient use of the available samples. However, the disadvantage of this method is that designing N Bayes' classifiers may be too laborious.

In this paper, we propose a method to overcome this disadvantage both for parametric and nonparametric cases.

III. The L Method for Normal Distribution

In this section, a simple way of implementing the L method for normal distributions will be proposed, eliminating the calculation of N Bayes' classifiers.

For normal distributions, the likelihood ratio (1) is conveniently written as the log-likelihood ratio

$$\begin{aligned} l(X, \Theta) &= -2 \ln L(X, \Theta) \\ &= (X - M_1)^T \Sigma_1^{-1} (X - M_1) \\ &\quad - (X - M_2) \Sigma_2^{-1} (X - M_2) \\ &\quad + \ln \frac{|\Sigma_1|}{|\Sigma_2|} - 2 \ln \frac{p(\omega_1)}{p(\omega_2)} \end{aligned} \quad (12)$$

where M_i and Σ_i are the mean vectors and covariance matrices of $\omega_i (i=1, 2)$. The Bayes' classifier then is, instead of (1),

$$\text{if } l(X, \Theta) < 0 \quad \text{then } X \in \omega_1$$
$$\text{if } l(X, \Theta) > 0 \quad \text{then } X \in \omega_2. \quad (13)$$

Let $\Theta_N = \{\hat{M}_i, \hat{\Sigma}_i, \hat{p}(\omega_i): (i=1, 2)\}$ be the set of parameters estimated from the available N classified samples and let $\hat{\Theta}_{N-1}^{(k)} = \{\hat{M}_{ik}, \hat{\Sigma}_{ik}, \hat{p}_k(\omega_i): (i=1, 2)\}$ be the set of parameters estimated from the $N-1$ samples left when sample X_k is excluded. Assuming that the N independent samples consist of N_1 samples from ω_1 and N_2 samples from ω_2, these parameters are given and related as follows for $X_j \in \omega_i$:

$$\hat{M}_i = \frac{1}{N_i} \sum_{j=1}^{N_i} X_j \quad (14)$$

$$\begin{aligned} \hat{M}_{ik} &= \frac{1}{N_i - 1} \left\{ \left(\sum_{j=1}^{N_i} X_j \right) - X_k \right\} \\ &= \hat{M}_i - \frac{1}{N_i - 1} (X_k - \hat{M}_i) \end{aligned} \quad (15)$$

$$\hat{\Sigma}_i = \frac{1}{N_i - 1} \sum_{j=1}^{N_i} (X_j - \hat{M}_i)(X_j - \hat{M}_i)^T \tag{16}$$

$$\hat{\Sigma}_{ik} = \frac{1}{N_i - 2}\left[\left\{\sum_{j=1}^{N_i} (X_j - \hat{M}_{ik})(X_j - \hat{M}_{ik})^T\right\} - (X_k - \hat{M}_{ik})(X_k - \hat{M}_{ik})^T\right]$$

$$= \hat{\Sigma}_i + \frac{1}{N_i - 2} \cdot \left[\hat{\Sigma}_i - \frac{N_i}{N_i - 1}(X_k - \hat{M}_i)(X_k - \hat{M}_i)^T\right] \tag{17}$$

$$\hat{p}(\omega_i) = \frac{N_i}{N} \quad \text{and} \quad \hat{p}(\omega_j) = \frac{N_j}{N} \tag{18}$$

$$\hat{p}_k(\omega_i) = \frac{N_i - 1}{N - 1} \quad \text{and} \quad \hat{p}_k(\omega_j) = \frac{N_j}{N - 1}, \quad (i \neq j), \quad \text{for} \quad X_k \in \omega_i. \tag{19}$$

According to (11), in the L method we have to calculate

$$l(X_k, \hat{\Theta}_{N-1}^{(k)}) = (X_k - \hat{M}_{1k})^T \hat{\Sigma}_{1k}^{-1}(X_k - \hat{M}_{1k}) - (X_k - \hat{M}_2)^T \hat{\Sigma}_2^{-1}(X_k - \hat{M}_2) + \ln \frac{|\hat{\Sigma}_{1k}|}{|\hat{\Sigma}_2|} - 2 \ln \frac{\hat{p}_k(\omega_1)}{\hat{p}_k(\omega_2)}, \quad X_k \in \omega_1. \tag{20}$$

A similar expression can be obtained for $X_k \in \omega_2$.

As is shown in the Appendix, using (14) through (19), $l(X_k, \hat{\Theta}_{N-1}^{(k)})$ of (20) can be expressed as the deviation from $l(X_k, \hat{\Theta}_N)$, which is the estimate of the likelihood ratio by the C method, as follows:

$$l(X_k, \hat{\Theta}_{N-1}^{(k)}) = l(X_k, \hat{\Theta}_N) \pm g(N_i, \hat{d}_i^2(X_k)), \quad + \text{ for } X_k \in \omega_1, \quad - \text{ for } X_k \in \omega_2 \tag{21}$$

where

$$g(N_i, \hat{d}_i^2(X_k)) = \frac{(N_i^2 - 3N_i + 1)\hat{d}_i^2(X_k)/(N_i - 1) + N_i \hat{d}_i^4(X_k)}{(N_i - 1)^2 - N_i \hat{d}_i^2(X_k)} + \ln\left(1 - \frac{N_i}{(N_i - 1)^2}\hat{d}_i^2(X_k)\right) + 2 \ln \frac{N_i}{N_i - 1} + n \ln \frac{N_i - 1}{N_i - 2} > 0 \tag{22}$$

and

$$\hat{d}_i^2(X_k) = (X_k - \hat{M}_i)^T \hat{\Sigma}_i^{-1}(X_k - \hat{M}_i). \tag{23}$$

From (21), (22), and (23) the following three observations can be made.

1) When the C method is used to calculate the probability of error, $l(X_k, \hat{\Theta}_N)$ and $\hat{d}_i^2(X_k)(i=1, 2)$ must be computed for $k=1, 2, \cdots, N$. Therefore, the computation of the scalar function of (22) for each k is a negligible load to a computer in comparison with the computation of $l(X_k, \hat{\Theta}_N)$ for each k. Thus, the computation time of both the L and C methods becomes almost equivalent to the computation time of the C method alone.

2) As is proved in the Appendix, $g(\cdot)$ of (22) is always positive no matter what N_i, $\hat{d}_i^2(X_k)$ and n are. Therefore, from (21),

$$l(X_k, \hat{\Theta}_{N-1}^{(k)}) > l(X_k, \hat{\Theta}_N), \qquad X_k \in \omega_1 \tag{24}$$

and

$$l(X_k, \hat{\Theta}_{N-1}^{(k)}) < l(X_k, \hat{\Theta}_N), \qquad X_k \in \omega_2. \tag{25}$$

According to the decision rule of (13), we can conclude that: if X_k is misclassified by the C method, X_k is also misclassified by the L method; and there may be some X_k's that are correctly classified by the C method but misclassified by the L method. This conclusion for normal distributions is a stronger statement than the inequality of (9), because the inequality of (9) holds only for the expectations of errors while our conclusion is for individual samples of individual tests.

3) For $N_i \gg 1$ and $\hat{d}_i^2(X_k)/N_i \ll 1$, a simpler approximation of (22) can be obtained as follows:

$$g(N_i, \hat{d}_i^2(X_k)) \cong \frac{\hat{d}_i^2(X_k) + \hat{d}_i^4(X_k)}{N_i - \hat{d}_i^2(X_k)} - \frac{\hat{d}_i^2(X_k)}{N_i} + \frac{n+2}{N_i} \cong \frac{\hat{d}_i^4(X_k) + n + 2}{N_i}. \tag{26}$$

Thus we see that the difference in the likelihood-ratio rule at a particular point decreases as $1/N_i$. In an effort to compare this difference with the statistical variation of the likelihood ratio, an approximation to the variance of the likelihood ratio at a particular point was obtained. Omitting the lengthy derivation we show only the result for fixed X_k,

$$E\{[l(X_k, \hat{\Theta}_N) - l(X_k, \Theta)]^2\} \cong \frac{2}{N_1}\{\hat{d}_1^4(X_k) + n\} + \frac{2}{N_2}\{\hat{d}_2^4(X_k) + n\}. \tag{27}$$

Thus the standard deviation decreases as $1/\sqrt{N_i}$. This indicates that for large N_i the statistical variation is of more importance than the difference between the C and L estimates.

IV. A Nonparametric Approach

In this section, we extend the previous discussions for normal distributions to a nonparameteric setting, and compare the C and L methods. The nonparametric approach used here is to use the Parzen approximation to density functions.

The Parzen approximation of a density function is given by

$$p_{N_i}(X \mid \omega_i) = \frac{1}{N_i} \sum_{j=1}^{N_i} \frac{1}{r(N_i)^n} K\left(\frac{X - X_j}{r(N_i)}\right) \quad (28)$$

where $p_{N_i}(X|\omega_i)$ is a random function due to the selection of N_i samples. Under certain assumptions about the kernel $K(\cdot)$, it has been shown [6], [8] that

$$\lim_{N_i \to \infty} E^{1/2}\left[\sup_X \mid p_{N_i}(X \mid \omega_i) - p(X \mid \omega_i) \mid\right] = 0 \quad (29)$$

if

$$p_{N_i}(X \mid \omega_i) \quad (30)$$

is uniformly continuous,

$$\lim_{N_i \to \infty} r(N_i) = 0 \quad (31)$$

and

$$\lim_{N_i \to \infty} N_i r(N_i)^{2n} = \infty. \quad (32)$$

In this paper, we use a normal function as the kernel [8] as

$$\frac{1}{r(N_i)^n} K\left(\frac{X - X_j}{r(N_i)}\right) = \frac{N_i^{\alpha}}{2\pi^{n/2}\sqrt{|\Sigma_i|}} \cdot \exp\left[-\tfrac{1}{2}N_i^{2\alpha/n}(X - X_j)^T\Sigma_i^{-1}(X - X_j)\right] \quad (33)$$

where

$$r(N_i) = N_i^{-\alpha/n}. \quad (34)$$

In order to satisfy (31) and (32), α must be in the range

$$\tfrac{1}{2} > \alpha > 0. \quad (35)$$

In the C method, we use the following decision rule for a specified sample X_k

$$\frac{N_1}{N} p_{N_1}(X_k \mid \omega_1) \gtrless \frac{N_2}{N} p_{N_2}(X_k \mid \omega_2) \rightarrow X_k \in \begin{cases}\omega_1 \\ \omega_2.\end{cases} \quad (36)$$

Or, using (28) and (33)

$$\frac{N_1^{\alpha}}{\sqrt{|\Sigma_1|}} \sum_{j=1}^{N_1} \exp\left[-\tfrac{1}{2}N_1^{2\alpha/n}d_1^2(X_k, X_j)\right] \gtrless \frac{N_2^{\alpha}}{\sqrt{|\Sigma_2|}} \sum_{l=1}^{N_2} \exp\left[-\tfrac{1}{2}N_2^{2\alpha/n}d_2^2(X_k, X_l)\right] \rightarrow X_k \in \begin{cases}\omega_1 \\ \omega_2\end{cases} \quad (37)$$

where $d_i^2(X_k, X_j)$ is a distance between X_k and X_j and is given by

$$d_i^2(X_k, X_j) = (X_k - X_j)^T\Sigma_i^{-1}(X_k - X_j). \quad (38)$$

In the L method, for $X_k \in \omega_1$, X_k is removed from the approximation to $p_{N_1}(X|\omega_1)$, and N_1 and N are replaced by $N_1 - 1$ and $N - 1$, respectively. Therefore, the left-hand side of (37) is modified as

$$\frac{(N_1 - 1)^{\alpha}}{\sqrt{|\Sigma_1|}}\left[\left[\sum_{j=1}^{N_1} \cdot \exp\left\{-\tfrac{1}{2}(N_1 - 1)^{2\alpha/n}d_1^2(X_k, X_j)\right\}\right] - 1\right]. \quad (39)$$

For $X_k \in \omega_2$, the right-hand side of (44) should be modified as (39).

The calculation of error for nonparametric cases is laborious mainly because we have to calculate all pairs of distances of (38), that is, $N(N-1)/2$ combinations. However, there is no difference between the computation times of the C and L methods, because in the L method $d_1^2(X_k, X_j)$ is multiplied by $(N_1 - 1)^{2\alpha/n}$ instead of by $N_1^{2\alpha/n}$ in the C method before the exponential function is computed.

V. Experimental Results

A. Parametric Approach

An experiment was conducted by using the mean vectors and covariance matrices for measurements on the letter A and B, as published by Marill and Green [5]. Eight dimensional samples were generated so as to be normal according to the above parameters. This was done for sample sizes $N_1 = N_2 = 100$, 200, and 400 for each class. Each time a set of data was generated, the sample means and covariances, $\hat{M}_i$ and $\hat{\Sigma}_i$, were calculated and the C and L methods were applied to calculate the estimates of the probability of error, $\hat{\varepsilon}(\hat{\Theta}_N, \hat{\Theta}_N)$ and $\hat{\varepsilon}(\hat{\Theta}_{N-1}, \Theta)$. Forty sets of samples were generated for $N_1 = N_2 = 100$, 200, and 400 to calculate the experimental means and variances of $\hat{\varepsilon}(\hat{\Theta}_N, \hat{\Theta}_N)$ and $\hat{\varepsilon}(\hat{\Theta}_N, \Theta)$ which are random variables due to the selection of N samples. The results are shown in Table I.

We have shown that the difference in the estimated likelihood ratios decreases approximately as $1/N_i$. We see from Table I that the same behavior is present for the difference in the C and L estimates of error. We also note that the standard deviation of the error estimates decreases approximately as $1/\sqrt{N_i}$ for the sample sizes indicated.

B. Nonparametric Approach

The nonparametric approach of this paper was applied to the same data sets as in the parametric example.

First, since no information on the appropriate value for α could be found except the condition $0.5 > \alpha > 0$ of (35), an experiment was conducted with 100 samples per class with $\alpha = 1/3$, 1/5, and 1/7. The results are shown in Table II. Although there is some variation in the performance, it does not appear that the choice of α is of critical importance.

Based on the above information, α was selected as 1/3.

TABLE I

ESTIMATION OF ERRORS FOR A PARAMETRIC EXAMPLE

Number of Samples per Class $N_1 = N_2$	C Method, $\hat{\mathcal{E}}(\hat{\Theta}_N, \hat{\Theta}_N)$		L Method, $\hat{\mathcal{E}}(\hat{\Theta}_{N-1}, \Theta)$		Mean Difference Between the C and L Methods
	Mean (percent)	Standard Deviation (percent)	Mean (percent)	Standard Deviation (percent)	
100	1.44	0.8	2.15	1.0	0.71
200	1.56	0.7	2.00	0.7	0.44
400	1.83	0.5	1.97	0.5	0.14

TABLE II

EFFECT OF α FOR A NONPARAMETRIC APPROACH ($N_1 = N_2 = 100$)

α	C Method $\hat{\mathcal{E}}(\hat{\Theta}_N, \hat{\Theta}_N)$ (percent)	L Method, $\hat{\mathcal{E}}(\hat{\Theta}_{N-1}, \hat{\Theta})$ (percent)
1/3	0.1	2.9
1/5	0.2	2.6
1/7	0.4	2.5

TABLE III

ESTIMATION OF ERRORS FOR A NONPARAMETRIC EXAMPLE

Number of Samples per Class $N_1 = N_2$	C Method, $\hat{\mathcal{E}}(\hat{\Theta}_N, \hat{\Theta}_N)$ Mean (percent)	L Method, $\hat{\mathcal{E}}(\hat{\Theta}_{N-1}, \hat{\Theta})$ Mean (percent)
100	0.1	2.9
200	0.45	2.35
400	0.65	2.2

Five sets of samples were generated for each of $N_1 = N_2 = 100$, 200 and, 400. The results are shown in Table III.

C. Discussion of the Experiments

For the original data Marill and Green reported a 2.75 percent error rate for the Bayes' classifier using the C method to evaluate its performance on 200 samples per class. This compares to the 1.56 percent average error and 0.7 percent standard deviation for 200 samples per class reported in Table I. Thus the 2.75 percent error rate is less than two standard deviations away from the mean and is not unreasonable. In addition it is improbable that the original data exactly fit the normal model.

Tables II and III indicate that the bias introduced by using the C method to evaluate the nonparametric classifier is so large as to make the estimate of little value. The errors by the nonparametric method appear to be greater than those by the parametric classifier. This is to be expected since we use the additional information that the densities are normal in the parametric case. For nonnormal data the nonparametric classifier may be superior at the cost of greater computation.

For two classes normally distributed with the known pa-

rameters used in these two experiments, a 1.9 percent error rate has been reported for the optimum Bayes' classifier [9]. We note that for the two examples presented and for the sample sizes indicated we have the average of the C and L estimates bounding the optimum error rate as indicated by (9). It should be emphasized, however, that the present work does not in general guarantee (9) since (8) has not been verified.

VI. SUMMARY

This paper discusses the estimation of the probability of error to be expected if one uses a classifier constructed by using estimates calculated from a finite sample set for the parameters in a Bayes' optimum classifier. The major results follow.

1) A simple procedure is given for implementing the L method for the likelihood-ratio rule resulting from the multivariate normal assumption.

2) The difference in the likelihood-ratio rule for the C and L methods is proportional to $1/N_i$ while the standard deviation is proportional to $1/\sqrt{N_i}$. Experimental results indicate the $1/N_i$ dependence for the difference in the error rates and $1/\sqrt{N_i}$ dependence for the standard deviation of the error rate estimates.

3) A nonparametric version of both C and L methods is discussed by using the Parzen approximation to density functions. The experimental results by this approach are shown and are found to be similar to the results obtained by the parametric approach.

APPENDIX

The proof of (21) consists of three parts: the quadratic term, the determinant term, and the *a priori* probability term in (20).

Quadratic Terms

We rewrite (17) as

$$\hat{\Sigma}_{ik} = \frac{N_i - 1}{N_i - 2} \hat{\Sigma}_i - \frac{N_i}{(N_i - 1)(N_i - 2)} \cdot (X_k - \hat{M}_i)(X_k - \hat{M}_i)^T. \quad (40)$$

The inverse matrix of $\hat{\Sigma}_{ik}$ is

$$\hat{\Sigma}_{ik}^{-1} = \left(\frac{N_i - 2}{N_i - 1}\right) \cdot \left[\hat{\Sigma}_i^{-1} + \frac{N_i\hat{\Sigma}_i^{-1}(X_k - \hat{M}_i)(X_k - \hat{M}_i)^T\hat{\Sigma}_i^{-1}}{(N_i - 1)^2 - N_i\hat{d}_i^2(X_k)}\right] \quad (41)$$

where $\hat{d}_i^2(X_k)$ is given in (23). Then, using (15), the quadratic term is given by

$$\begin{aligned}(X_k - \hat{M}_{ik})^T\hat{\Sigma}_{ik}^{-1}(X_k - \hat{M}_{ik}) &= \left(\frac{N_i}{N_i-1}\right)^2 (X_k - \hat{M}_i)^T\hat{\Sigma}_{ik}^{-1}(X_k - \hat{M}_i)\\ &= \left(\frac{N_i}{N_i-1}\right)^2\left(\frac{N_i-2}{N_i-1}\right) \cdot \left[\hat{d}_i^2(X_k) + \frac{N_i\hat{d}_i^4(X_k)}{(N_i-1)^2 - N_i\hat{d}_i^2(X_k)}\right]\\ &= \hat{d}_i^2(X_k) + \frac{(N_i^2 - 3N_i + 1)\hat{d}_i^2(X_k)/(N_i-1) + N_i\hat{d}_i^4(X_k)}{(N_i-1)^2 - N_i\hat{d}_i^2(X_k)}. \end{aligned} \quad (42)$$

Determinant Terms

Using (40), the determinant of $\hat{\Sigma}_{ik}$ can be calculated as follows:

$$|\hat{\Sigma}_{ik}| = \left(\frac{N_i - 1}{N_i - 2}\right)^n |\hat{\Sigma}_i| \cdot \left| I - \frac{N_i}{(N_i - 1)^2}\hat{\Sigma}_i^{-1}(X_k - \hat{M}_i)(X_k - \hat{M}_i)^T \right|. \quad (43)$$

Let $\lambda_1, \lambda_2, \cdots, \lambda_n$ be the eigenvalues of the matrix $\hat{\Sigma}_i^{-1}(X_k - \hat{M}_i)(X_k - \hat{M}_i)^T$. Then the last determinant of (43) is

$$\left| I - \frac{N_i}{(N_i - 1)^2}\hat{\Sigma}_i^{-1}(X_k - \hat{M}_i)(X_k - \hat{M}_i)^T \right| = \prod_{i=1}^{n}\left(1 - \frac{N_i}{(N_i - 1)^2}\lambda_i\right). \quad (44)$$

The rank of the matrix $(X_k - \hat{M}_i)(X_k - \hat{M}_i)^T$ is one. Consequently, the rank of the matrix $\hat{\Sigma}_i^{-1}(X_k - \hat{M}_i)(X_k - \hat{M}_i)^T$ is also one. Therefore, the λ's should satisfy the following conditions:

$$\lambda_1 \neq 0, \qquad \lambda_2 = \lambda_3 = \cdots = \lambda_n = 0, \quad (45)$$

and

$$\begin{aligned}\sum_{i=1}^{n} \lambda_i = \lambda_1 &= \operatorname{tr}\,[\hat{\Sigma}_i^{-1}(X_k - \hat{M}_i)(X_k - \hat{M}_i)^T]\\ &= (X_k - \hat{M}_i)^T\hat{\Sigma}_i^{-1}(X_k - \hat{M}_i)\\ &= \hat{d}_i^2(X_k). \end{aligned} \quad (46)$$

Using these results, (44) becomes

$$\left| I - \frac{N_i}{(N_i - 1)^2}\hat{\Sigma}_i^{-1}(X_k - \hat{M}_i)(X_k - \hat{M}_i)^T \right| = 1 - \frac{N_i}{(N_i - 1)^2}\hat{d}_i^2(X_k). \quad (47)$$

From (43),

$$\ln |\hat{\Sigma}_{ik}| = \ln |\hat{\Sigma}_i| + n \ln\frac{N_i - 1}{N_i - 2} + \ln\left(1 - \frac{N_i}{(N_i - 1)^2}\hat{d}_i^2(X_k)\right). \quad (48)$$

A Priori Probabilities

If we assume $X_k \in \omega_i$, from (18) and (19)

$$\hat{p}_k(\omega_i) = \frac{N_i - 1}{N - 1} = \frac{N_i}{N}\frac{N}{N - 1}\cdot\frac{N_i - 1}{N_i} = \hat{p}(\omega_i)\cdot\frac{N}{N - 1}\cdot\frac{N_i - 1}{N_i}. \quad (49)$$

Also

$$\hat{p}_k(\omega_j) = \frac{N_j}{N - 1} = \frac{N_j}{N}\cdot\frac{N}{N - 1} = \hat{p}(\omega_j)\cdot\frac{N}{N - 1}\cdot(j \neq i). \quad (50)$$

Therefore,

$$\frac{\hat{p}_k(\omega_i)}{\hat{p}_k(\omega_j)} = \frac{\hat{p}(\omega_i)}{\hat{p}(\omega_j)}\cdot\frac{N_i - 1}{N_i}. \quad (51)$$

Equations (42), (48), and (51) give all terms of (21) and (22). Thus the proof is completed.

Proof of $g(\cdot) > 0$ *of* (22)

Assuming $N_i > 2$, $|\hat{\Sigma}_{ik}|$ of (43) should be positive because $\hat{\Sigma}_{ik}$ is a sample covariance matrix and should be a positive definite matrix. Therefore, the determinant of (47) should also be positive. That is,

$$1 - \frac{N_i}{(N_i - 1)^2}\hat{d}_i^2(X_k) > 0. \quad (52)$$

Thus

$$0 < \hat{d}_i^2(X_k) < (N_i - 1)^2/N_i. \quad (53)$$

To find the minimum of g we examine

$$\frac{d\{g(N_i, \hat{d}_i^2(X_k))\}}{d\{\hat{d}_i^2(X_k)\}} = \frac{-N_i^2\hat{d}_i^4(X_k) + (2N_i^3 - 3N_i^2 + 2N_i)\hat{d}_i^2(X_k) + (-2N_i^2 + 3N_i - 1)}{[(N_i - 1)^2 - N_i\hat{d}_i^2(X_k)]^2} = 0 \quad (54)$$

which has solution $\hat{d}_i^2(X_k)=1/N_i$ satisfying (53). By substituting $1/N_i$ and 0 for $\hat{d}_i^2(X_k)$ in (22) it can easily be shown that

$$g(N_i, 0) > g(N_i, 1/N_i) > 0. \tag{55}$$

This proves that $\hat{d}_i^2(X_k)=1/N_i$ is a minimum and that $g(\cdot)>0$ for $\hat{d}_i^2(X_k)$ satisfying (53).

References

[1] M. Hills, "Allocation rules and their error rates," *J. Stat. Royal Soc.*, series B, vol. 28, pp. 1–31, 1966.

[2] W. H. Highleyman, "The design and analysis of pattern recognition experiments," *Bell Syst. Tech. J.*, vol. 41, pp. 723–744, Mar. 1962.

[3] L. Kanal and B. Chandrasekaran, "On dimensionality and sample size in statistical pattern classification," in *Proc. Nat. Electronics Conf.*, vol. 24, 1968, pp. 2–7.

[4] P. A. Lachenbruch and R. M. Mickey, "Estimation of error rates in discriminant analysis," *Technometrics*, vol. 10, no. 1, pp. 1–11, 1968.

[5] T. Marill and D. M. Green, "On the effectiveness of receptors in recognition systems," *IEEE Trans. Inform. Theory*, vol. IT-19, pp. 11–17, Jan. 1963.

[6] E. Parzen, "An estimation of a probability density function and mode," *Ann. Inst. Statist. Math.*, vol. 33, pp. 1065–1076, 1962.

[7] R. P. Heydorn, "An upper bound estimate on classification error," *IEEE Trans. Inform. Theory* (Corresp.), vol. IT-14, pp. 783–784, Sept. 1968.

[8] T. Cacoullos, "Estimation of a multivariate density," *Ann. Inst. Statist. Math.*, vol. 18, pp. 179–189, 1966.

[9] K. Fukunaga and T. F. Krile, "Calculation of Bayes' recognition error for two multivariate Gaussian distributions," *IEEE Trans. Comput.*, vol. C-18, pp. 220–229, Mar. 1969.

Application of Optimum Error-Reject Functions

KEINOSUKE FUKUNAGA AND DAVID L. KESSELL

Abstract—**In an optimum pattern-recognition system the error rate is determined by the reject function. This correspondence describes how this property may be exploited to provide quantitative tests of model validity using unclassified test samples. These tests are basically goodness-of-fit tests for a function of the observations. One of these tests is shown to provide an improved estimate of error in Monte Carlo studies of complex systems. Results are given for normal distributions when parameters are estimated. In this case error estimates obtained from the empirical reject rate underestimate the actual error and performance depends on the ratio of design samples to dimension.**

I. INTRODUCTION

Let X be a random n-dimensional pattern vector that must be classified as belonging to one of m classes, $\omega_1, \omega_2, \cdots, \omega_m$. Allow the possibility of rejection or withheld classification. Let P_i be the prior probability of class ω_i and $p_i(X)$ the conditional probability density function of X given that it belongs to class ω_i. For the mixture density

$$p(X) = \sum_{i=1}^{m} P_i p_i(X), \tag{1}$$

we have that

$$r(X) = 1 - \frac{\max_i \{P_1 p_1(X), \cdots, P_m p_m(X)\}}{p(X)} \tag{2}$$

is the conditional probability of error given X when an observation is classified using a Bayes' procedure. Chow [1] has shown that the optimum classification-rejection strategy is to reject whenever

$$r(X) \geq t \tag{3}$$

and choose the class with maximum *a posteriori* probability otherwise. The probability of rejection, or reject function, is given by

$$\begin{aligned} R(t) &= \Pr\{r(X) > t\} \\ &= 1 - F(t), \end{aligned} \tag{4}$$

where $F(t)$ is the cumulative distribution function of the random variable $r(X)$. The error function may be evaluated directly from the reject function as

$$\begin{aligned} E(t) &= \int_0^t y\, dF(y) \\ &= -\int_0^t y\, dR(y). \end{aligned} \tag{5}$$

Equation (5) emphasizes that $R(t)$ specifies the error function, because $1 - R(t)$ is the distribution of the conditional probability of error $r(X)$.

If we assume specific P_i and $p_i(X)$, an empirical estimate of the reject function (4) may be determined from unclassified data. Using (5), this provides an empirical error estimate. Chow has suggested that the empirical error-reject functions can be compared with the theoretical functions in order to test the validity of a system model. As is clear from (4), this is simply a goodness-of-fit test for the assumed distribution. This correspondence discusses three methods of making this comparison to ascertain the correctness of the assumptions. These methods give quantitative measures of the effect of a finite amount of data. (This is an extension of the authors' previous work [2], [3].) Using (5) as an estimate of error probability provides improved Monte Carlo estimates as compared to the usual error-estimation techniques. Simulation results are given for the case in which parameters of distributions in the model are estimated.

II. COMPARISON OF EMPIRICAL ESTIMATES WITH THE MODEL

In this section we discuss three specific comparisons of observed and predicted error and reject rates. Each will allow the rejection of the model at a given significance level.

A. A Test Based on the Mean of $r(X)$

As indicated in (5), the expected value of $r(X)$ is just the probability of error with no rejections, which we denote by E. E is equal to $E(t)$ for $t = 1 - 1/m$. Given N_t independent identically distributed test samples $X_1, X_2, \cdots, X_{N_t}$, distributed according to $p(X)$, an unbiased estimate of E is

$$\hat{E} = \frac{1}{N_t} \sum_{i=1}^{N_t} r(X_i). \tag{6}$$

The variance of the estimate is simply $\sigma^2(r(X))N_t^{-1}$. By the central limit theorem $N_t^{1/2}(\hat{E} - E)$ has approximately the $n(0, \sigma^2(r(X)))$ distribution. For $\sigma^2(r(X))$ unknown, the sample variance

$$s^2 = \frac{1}{N_t} \sum_{i=1}^{Nt} (r(X_i) - \hat{E})^2 \tag{7}$$

converges in probability to $\sigma^2(r(X))$, so that the test is to reject the model whenever

$$|N_t^{1/2}(\hat{E} - E)/s| > c_\alpha. \tag{8}$$

The significance level (probability of rejecting the model when it is valid) is given by

$$\alpha = 1 - \frac{2}{\sqrt{2\pi}} \int_{-\infty}^{c_\alpha} e^{-z^2/2}\, dz. \tag{9}$$

The fact that the above test uses unclassified test samples is an advantage over the usual error-counting technique. This is usually of great economic importance. Another advantage is that $\sigma^2(r(X))$ is significantly less than the variance $E(1 - E)$ associated with the usual error count. To see this consider the distribution of $r(X)$ that gives the largest variance $\sigma^2(r(X))$ for a given value of E. This distribution is

$$F(t) = \begin{cases} 0, & t < 0 \\ 1 - \dfrac{m}{m-1} E, & 0 \leq t < 1 - (1/m). \\ 1, & 1 - (1/m) \leq t. \end{cases} \tag{10}$$

Now

$$\begin{aligned} \sigma^2(r(X)) &\leq E^2 \left(1 - \frac{m}{m-1} E\right) + \left(1 - \frac{1}{m} - E\right)^2 \frac{m}{m-1} E \\ &= E(1 - E) - E/m. \end{aligned} \tag{11}$$

Manuscript received October 29, 1971; revised May 1, 1972. This work was supported in part by the National Science Foundation under Grant GJ-1099.

K. Fukunaga is with the School of Electrical Engineering, Purdue University, Lafayette, Ind.
D. Kessell was with the School of Electrical Engineering, Purdue University, Lafayette, Ind. He is now with the Bell Telephone Laboratories, Inc., Greensboro, N.C.

Reprinted from *IEEE Trans. Inform. Theory*, vol. IT-18, pp. 814–817, Nov. 1972.

Thus the estimate $\hat{E}$ of (6) gives a reduction in variance of at least E/m.

This result may seem paradoxical, since given N_t labeled samples a better estimate may be obtained by ignoring the labels. One reason is that the frequency-of-error estimate quantizes the error on a test sample to two values while $r(X_i)$ allows the assignment of a real-valued estimate. There may be an even better estimate that uses the label information.

The reduction in variance is important in Monte Carlo studies. In many applications the assumed models become too complicated to solve analytically for the unknown Bayes' error. In this case it is common practice to generate pseudorandom vectors and count the errors. Equation (11) shows that an error estimate can be obtained more efficiently by using the estimate of (6).

B. χ^2 Goodness-of-Fit Test

Suppose that $X_1, X_2, \cdots, X_{N_t}$ is a random test sample from the distribution with density $p(X)$ defined in (1). Suppose furthermore that the P_i and $p_i(X)$ are known for each class ω_i. Define the empirical reject function

$$R_{N_t}(t) = \frac{1}{N_t} (\text{number of } r(X_1), r(X_2), \cdots, r(X_{N_t}) > t). \quad (12)$$

Comparison of $R_{N_t}(t)$ with the predicted $R(t)$ is actually, by (4) and (12), the comparison of the empirical cumulative distribution function $1 - R_{N_t}(t)$ with the predicted distribution function $F(t)$. Thus the standard χ^2 test is appropriate.

Let $\{t_i, i = 0, \cdots, k\}$ be a partition into cells independent of the data satisfying

$$0 = t_0 < t_1 \cdots < t_k = 1 - 1/m. \quad (13)$$

Define the probabilities

$$\pi_i = R(t_{i-1}) - R(t_i) \quad (14)$$

and the random numbers N_i such that

$$N_i = N_t[R_{N_t}(t_{i-1}) - R_{N_t}(t_i)], \qquad i = 1, \cdots, k. \quad (15)$$

Then the statistic

$$Q = \sum_{i=1}^{k} \left[\frac{(N_i - N_t\pi_i)^2}{N_t\pi_i} \right] \quad (16)$$

has an approximate chi-square distribution with $k - 1$ degrees of freedom. Q "large" implies a large difference between the empirical function $R_{N_t}(t)$ and the assumed $R(t)$ and calls for the rejection of the model. Tables of the χ^2 distribution that give the significance level and critical values are readily available. A commonly quoted rule of thumb is to choose the t_i such that each $N_t \cdot \pi_i$ is greater than five [4].

C. Kolmogorov–Smirnov Test for $R(t)$

For completeness the application of the well-known Kolmogorov–Smirnov one- and two-sample goodness-of-fit tests to the present problem should be discussed. Implementation requires the ordering of all observations so that the empirical cumulative distribution function (cdf) (12) is specified at each observation. The one-sample test will test whether the sample giving the empirical cdf $(1 - R_{N_t}(t))$ is drawn from a population with cdf $(1 - R(t))$, where $R(t)$ is specified at each point the comparison is made. As mentioned previously there are many assumptions of $P = \{P_1p_1(X), \cdots, P_mp_m(X)\}$ that imply reject functions $R(t)$ that may not be easily computed. However, it is usually possible to generate pseudorandom vectors $Z_1, Z_2, \cdots, Z_M$ according to the resulting density $p(X)$. This will yield an empirical cdf $(1 - R_M(t))$. The two-sample Kolmogorov–Smirnov test is a test of whether the empirical samples giving the respective cdf's $(1 - R_{N_t}(t))$ and $(1 - R_M(t))$ were drawn from populations with the same, but unknown cdf. Thus, without computing $R(t)$, the two-sample Kolmogorov–Smirnov test gives a test of the assumed statistical model. For details regarding the use, definition, and critical values of these tests, the reader is referred to [5].

D. Comparison and Discussion

Each of the preceding tests provides tests of the validity of the system model. Each allows the rejection of the model at a specified significance level. They differ obviously in the complexity of implementation and almost certainly in power (probability of rejecting assumptions when in fact they are false).

The ordering in terms of increasing computational complexity is Section II-A < Section II-B < Section II-C. Section II-A requires only the accumulation of a sum and a single comparison, Section II-B the accumulation of k sums and k comparisons, and Section II-C the ordering of N_t observations and N_t comparisons. With each comparison an evaluation of $E(t)$ or $R(t)$ is required.

The ordering in terms of power is Section II-A < Section II-B < Section II-C. Section II-A tests only one moment of the distribution, the mean. Section II-B tests the probability that the distribution being tested assigns the same probability to each of the k intervals as does the assumed distribution. Section II-C takes a finer look at the distributions, testing the maximum difference in the empirical and assumed distribution. Of course, as pointed out above, Section II-A is quite useful in Monte Carlo studies because of its variance-reducing property.

III. Reject Rule With Parameters Estimated; Effect of N_d

A much more difficult problem in the application of optimum error-reject rules is that the distributions are not usually completely known. In some settings, however, the parametric forms are known but the parameters are unknown. These unknown parameters are estimated from a set of N_d design samples, i.e., a set of N_d random vectors of known classification from the respective classes. Even with this simplifying assumption, we are not aware of a general solution. Attention here is restricted to multivariate normal populations. Theoretical results are attainable for the two-class multivariate-normal problem where the covariance matrices are equal. The key parameters are found to be the Mahalonobis distance squared and the ratio ν of the number of design samples N_d to the dimension n. Simulation for the two-class multivariate-normal problem with unequal covariance matrices shows the effect of N_d to be approximately the same as in the equal-covariance case.

A. Equal Covariance Matrices

In this section the mean performance for the two-class equal-covariance multivariate-normal problem is investigated. When all parameters are known the condition (3) for rejection of a random observation X is equivalent to

$$\frac{t}{1-t} \leq \frac{P_1p_1(X)}{P_2p_2(X)} \leq \frac{1-t}{t}. \quad (17)$$

If the sample means and the sample covariances are unknown, they may be estimated from N_1 random vectors from class 1 and N_2 random vectors from class 2. Substituting the parameter estimates for the unknown parameters in (17) gives the estimated rejection condition

$$-\ln\left(\frac{1-t}{t}\right) \le W + \ln(P_1/P_2) \le \ln\left(\frac{1-t}{t}\right), \qquad (18)$$

where

$$W = [X - \tfrac{1}{2}(\hat{M}_1 + \hat{M}_2)]^T\hat{\Sigma}^{-1}(\hat{M}_1 - \hat{M}_2) \qquad (19)$$

and $\hat{M}_1$, $\hat{M}_2$, and $\hat{\Sigma}$ are the sample mean vectors and covariance matrix and X is the random observation presented for classification.

Then the mean probability of rejection $\tilde{R}(t)$ and the mean probability of error $\tilde{E}(t)$ are functions of the probability distribution of W. Thus the specification of $\tilde{R}(t)$ and $\tilde{E}(t)$ reduces to specifying the distribution of W. Unfortunately, no exact solution that lends itself to computation exists. Okamoto [6], [7] does provide, however, an asymptotic expansion of the distribution of W that lends itself to machine computation. He gives the expansion through all terms of order N_i^{-2}. The coefficients are functions of the dimension and the Mahalonobis distance. This expansion was used to obtain $\tilde{E}(t)$ versus $\tilde{R}(t)$ for two values of the actual Mahalonobis squared distance D^2 defined by

$$D^2 = (M_1 - M_2)^T\Sigma^{-1}(M_1 - M_2) \qquad (20)$$

with $P_1 = P_2$ and $N_1 = N_2$.

Fig. 1 shows curves of $\tilde{E}$ versus $\tilde{R}$ for $D = 3$ and 4, $\nu = N_i/n = 2$, 10, and 50, and dimension $n = 5$, 20, and 100, where $N_i = N_1 = N_2$. From these curves it can be seen that for a given D and any dimension n, the mean performance depends almost entirely on the ratio ν. Thus the number of design samples required for a given level of approximation to the optimum performance depends upon the dimension n. This conclusion for the whole of the error-reject curves is an extension of the same conclusion for the error rate with no rejections [8]. As a rule of thumb it appears that ν must be 10 or greater for mean performance reasonably to approximate the optimum.

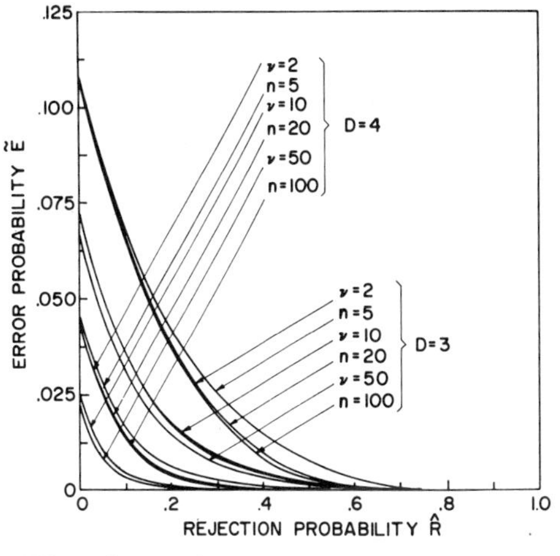

Fig. 1. Effect of $\nu = Nd/n$ for $D = 3$ and 4 and $n = 5$, 20, and 100.

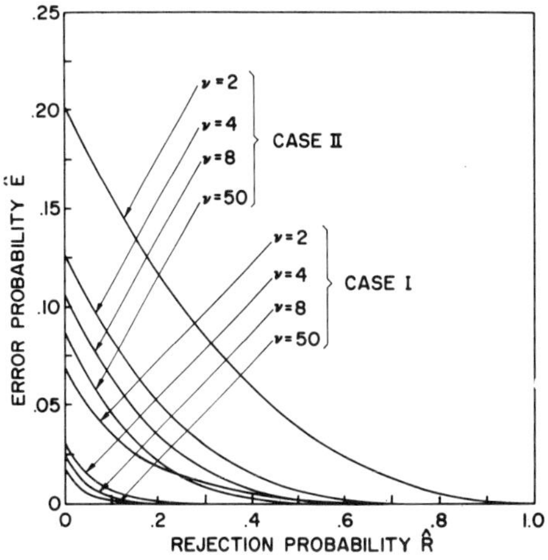

Fig. 2. Unequal covariance: average error versus rejection probability.

B. Unequal Covariance Matrices

If the covariance matrices for the two populations are not equal, the resulting approximate rejection condition is

$$-\ln\left(\frac{1-t}{t}\right) \le \ln(P_1/P_2) + U \le \ln\left(\frac{1-t}{t}\right), \qquad (21)$$

where

$$U = \tfrac{1}{2}[(X - \hat{M}_2)^T\hat{\Sigma}_2^{-1}(X - \hat{M}_2) - (X - \hat{M}_1)^T\hat{\Sigma}_1^{-1}(X - \hat{M}_1) + \ln(|\hat{\Sigma}_2|/|\hat{\Sigma}_1|)]. \qquad (22)$$

Since the distribution of U is not known, simulation experiments were run to compare with the equal-covariance case. For case I, pseudorandom vectors were generated according to two eight-dimensional normal distributions with unequal mean vectors and covariance matrices reported for measurements on the letters A and B [9], [10]. Ratios $\nu = 2$, 4, 8, and 50 were used to determine the sample size for parameter estimation. For each ratio 25 repetitions were made. To determine the empirical reject and error count for each repetition, 2000 vectors were drawn with probability 0.5 from each class. An estimated error rate $\hat{E}$ was calculated from the empirical reject rate $R_{N_t}(t)$. For case II the vectors were generated with the same covariance matrices as used in case I, but with the same mean vector for both classes. Fig. 2 shows the $\tilde{E}$ versus $\hat{R}$ curve for both cases. The general dependency on the ratio $N_i/n = \nu$ is present, but now a somewhat larger number of design samples is needed for good results. Fig. 3 illustrates, for case II, the behavior observed for the normal problem in general. With estimated parameters the error estimate, $\hat{E}$ drastically underestimates the errors actually incurred $\tilde{E}$. This indicates that using the empirical reject rate to predict error rates can produce very inaccurate results if the model used in the classifier design is inaccurate.

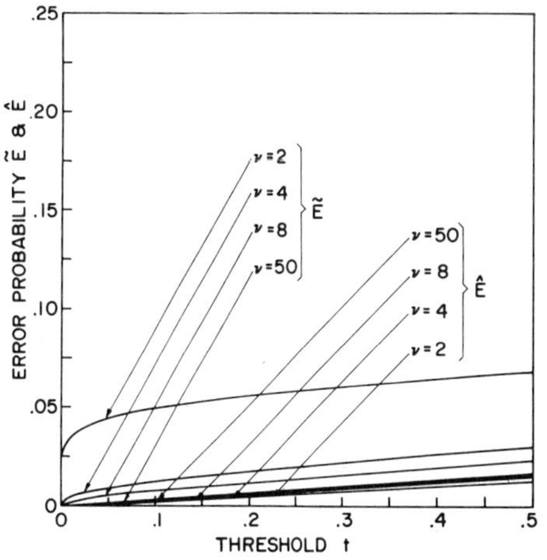

Fig. 3. Unequal covariance: case II, $\bar{E}$ and $\hat{E}$ versus t.

References

[1] C. K. Chow, "On optimum recognition error and reject tradeoff," *IEEE Trans. Inform. Theory*, vol. IT-16, pp. 41–46, Jan. 1970.
[2] K. Fukunaga and D. L. Kessell, "Estimation of classification error," *IEEE Trans. Computers*, vol. C-20, pp. 1521–1527, Dec. 1971.
[3] K. Fukunaga, *Introduction to Statistical Pattern Recognition.* New York: Academic Press, 1972, ch. 5.
[4] R. V. Hogg and A. T. Craig, *Introduction to Mathematical Statistics.* New York: MacMillan, 1969, p. 301.
[5] G. E. Noether, *Elements of Non-Parametric Statistics.* New York: Wiley, 1967, ch. 4.
[6] M. Okamoto, "An asymptotic expansion for the distribution of the linear discriminant function," *Ann. Math. Statist.*, vol. 34, pp. 1286–1301, 1963.
[7] ——, "Correction to 'An asymptotic expansion for the distribution of the linear discriminant function'," *ibid.*, vol. 39, p. 135, 1968.
[8] S. E. Estes, "Measurement selection for linear discriminants used in pattern classification," IBM Res. Rep. RJ-331, Apr. 1965.
[9] T. Marill and D. M. Green, "On the effectiveness of receptors in recognition systems," *IEEE Trans. Inform. Theory*, vol. IT-9, pp. 11–17, Jan. 1963.
[10] K. Fukunaga and T. F. Krile, "Calculation of Bayes recognition error for two multivariate Gaussian distributions," *IEEE Trans. Comput.*, vol. C-18, pp. 220–229, Mar. 1969.

Nonparametric Bayes Error Estimation Using Unclassified Samples

KEINOSUKE FUKUNAGA AND DAVID L. KESSELL

Abstract—**A new nonparametric method of estimating the Bayes risk using an unclassified test sample set as well as a classified design sample set is introduced. The classified design set is used to obtain nonparametric estimates of the conditional Bayes risk of classification at each point of the unclassified test set. The average of these risk estimates is the error estimate. For large numbers of design samples the new error estimate has less variance than does an error-count estimate for classified test samples using the optimum Bayes classifier.**

The first application of the nonparametric method uses k-nearest neighbor (k-NN) estimates of the posterior probabilities to form the risk estimate. A large-sample analysis is made of this estimate. The expected value of this estimate is shown to be a lower bound on the Bayes error. A simple modification provides unbiased estimates of the k-NN classification error, thus providing an upper bound on the Bayes error. The second application of the method uses Parzen approximation of the density functions to obtain estimates of the risk and subsequently the Bayes error. Results of experiments on simulated data illustrate the small-sample behavior.

I. Introduction

A PATTERN recognition system may be viewed as a decision rule which transforms measurements into class assignments. The Bayes error (Bayes risk for a 0–1 loss function) is the minimum achievable error, where the minimization is with respect to all decision rules. The Bayes error is a function of the prior probabilities and the probability density functions of the respective classes. Unfortunately, in many applications, the probability density functions are unknown and therefore the Bayes error is unknown.

Since it is such an important measure of optimum system performance, several suggestions have been put forth to provide nonparametric estimates of, or bounds for, the Bayes error. The best known in the engineering literature are the k-nearest neighbor (k-NN) estimated bounds. It has been suggested [1] that since the asymptotic k-NN error bounds the Bayes error, the empirical error rate found by simply counting the errors when the k-NN rule is used provides good estimated bounds of the Bayes error. Properties of the k-NN rules may be found in [2]–[6]. A second method is to use Parzen nonparametric estimates [7]–[9] of the unknown density functions to form an estimated Bayes decision rule. The estimate is then obtained directly from an empirical count of the errors made by this estimated rule [10], [11].

Manuscript received May 18, 1972; revised January 12, 1973. This work was supported in part by the National Science Foundation under Grants GJ-1099 and GJ-35722, and by the Bell Laboratories, Greensboro, N.C.

K. Fukunaga is with the School of Electrical Engineering, Purdue University, Lafayette, Ind. 47907.

D. L. Kessell is with the Bell Laboratories, Greensboro, N.C. 27420.

In this paper an alternate approach is introduced. Nonparametric estimates of the unknown conditional Bayes risk in classifying a fixed sample are given. These nonparametric estimates are averaged over each test sample to provide the error estimate. The test samples may be of unknown classification. It is shown that asymptotically the variance of the resulting estimate is considerably less than the variance of the error-counting procedures outlined in the previous paragraph. The use of unclassified test samples may be of great economic importance when it is difficult to obtain independent verification of class identity. Chow [12] first proposed the use of unclassified test samples. Unfortunately he gave no results for the case in which the density functions are unknown. Fukunaga and Kessell [13] extend Chow's work, using unclassified samples to test assumptions about the class distribution.

The first estimate discussed uses the representation of the respective classes in the k-NN to the test sample to estimate the class densities. These are used to form an estimate of the Bayes conditional risk in classifying the test sample. The risk estimates for all test samples are averaged to obtain the error estimate. Properties of this estimate are given for large N_d, the number of design samples. The expected value of this error estimate is a lower bound on the Bayes error. Simple modification yields an unbiased estimate of the k-NN classification error. As k increases, the bounds approach the Bayes error. The variance of the estimate is given for all k.

The second estimate introduced uses Parzen estimates of the class densities at each test sample to estimate the Bayes conditional risk at the test sample. These estimates are averaged over the unclassified test samples to provide the error estimate. Large-sample properties are equivalent to those of the k-NN procedure. However, for small numbers of design samples this procedure appears to be superior.

Simulation results are given for a two-dimensional example illustrating the theoretical results obtained. These also provide an indication of the small-sample behavior of the proposed Bayes error estimates.

II. $r(X)$ as an Error Estimate

Since the estimation procedure introduced in this paper is a nonparametric approximation to the Bayes procedure, we give the Bayes procedure for reference and to introduce notation. Let X be a random n-dimensional measurement vector belonging to one of two classes ω_1 or ω_2. Let P_i be the prior probabilities of the two classes and $p_i(X)$ be the probability density function of the random vector X evaluated at X, given that it belongs to class ω_i. Let the

Reprinted from *IEEE Trans. Inform. Theory*, vol. IT-19, pp. 434–440, July 1973.

mixture density be given by

$$p(X) = P_1 p_1(X) + P_2 p_2(X) \tag{1}$$

and let

$$\eta_i(X) = \frac{P_i p_i(X)}{p(X)} \tag{2}$$

denote the posterior probability, i.e., the conditional probability of a measurement X belonging to class ω_i. Then the Bayes decision is to choose the class with maximum $\eta_i(X)$. Thus the conditional probability of error when $\boldsymbol{X}$ is classified according to the Bayes decision rule is

$$r(\boldsymbol{X}) = \min \{\eta_1(\boldsymbol{X}), \eta_2(\boldsymbol{X})\}. \tag{3}$$

Taking the expectation with respect to the random vector $\boldsymbol{X}$ gives the Bayes error

$$R = E\{r(\boldsymbol{X})\}. \tag{4}$$

Thus, if we know $r(X)$ as a function of X, $r(X)$ has two significant properties as follows.

1) The Bayes error can be estimated by the sample mean of $r(\boldsymbol{X}_i)$ for N_t test samples as

$$\hat{\boldsymbol{R}} = \frac{1}{N_t} \sum_{i=1}^{N_t} r(\boldsymbol{X}_i) \tag{5}$$

where the $\boldsymbol{X}_i$'s are drawn from the mixture density $p(X)$ and the class assignments of the X_i are not needed. Since the $\boldsymbol{X}_i$'s are independent and identically distributed random vectors, the $r(\boldsymbol{X}_i)$'s are independent and identically distributed random variables. Therefore, from (4), the estimate of (5) is unbiased as

$$E\{\hat{\boldsymbol{R}}\} = \frac{1}{N_t} \sum_{i=1}^{N_t} E\{r(\boldsymbol{X}_i)\} = R. \tag{6}$$

2) Since

$$0 \le r(\boldsymbol{X}) \le \tfrac{1}{2} \tag{7}$$

gives

$$r^2(\boldsymbol{X}) \le \tfrac{1}{2} r(\boldsymbol{X}) \tag{8}$$

and

$$E\{r^2(\boldsymbol{X})\} \le \tfrac{1}{2} R \tag{9}$$

a bound on the variance of $r(\boldsymbol{X})$, $\sigma^2(r(\boldsymbol{X}))$ is

$$\begin{aligned}\sigma^2(r(\boldsymbol{X})) &= E\{r^2(\boldsymbol{X})\} - R^2 \\ &\le \tfrac{1}{2}R - R^2 \\ &= R(1-R) - \tfrac{1}{2}R.\end{aligned} \tag{10}$$

Thus the variance of $\hat{\boldsymbol{R}}$ is given by

$$\operatorname{var}[\hat{\boldsymbol{R}}] = \frac{\sigma^2(r(\boldsymbol{X}))}{N_t}. \tag{11}$$

On the other hand, if class identification were available for the N_t test vectors and an empirical error count were made, the error count would also give an unbiased estimate $\hat{R}'$ of the Bayes error. The variance of this estimate is known to be

$$\operatorname{var}[\hat{\boldsymbol{R}}'] = \frac{R(1-R)}{N_t}. \tag{12}$$

Thus we can achieve a reduction in variance of at least $0.5RN_t^{-1}$ by using $\hat{\boldsymbol{R}}$. Both estimates are asymptotically normal when properly normalized.

Unfortunately, in many instances the probability densities $p_i(X)$ needed to specify the function $r(X)$ are not known. However, because of the reduction in variance and effective use of unclassified samples, it is reasonable to search for nonparametric approximations to $r(X)$, thus providing improved nonparametric estimates of the Bayes error. Two such approximations will be discussed in the remainder of this paper.

III. k-NN Estimate of $r(X)$

Suppose a random design set of N_d samples $\{\boldsymbol{X}_i, \boldsymbol{\theta}_i\}_{i=1}^{N_d}$ is given, where $\boldsymbol{\theta}_i$ is the true class of $\boldsymbol{X}_i$ and the design set is drawn according to the unknown underlying distributions. It is then possible to estimate the conditional error at a new unclassified observation X by investigating the representation of the respective classes in the k-NN to X. In this section we define such estimates, study their asymptotic properties, and relate them to the errors incurred by the k-NN classification rule.

A. 2-NN Estimates

Consider first the 2-NN estimate at a fixed point X. Let $\boldsymbol{X}^1$ and $\boldsymbol{X}^2$ be the first and second NN to X and $\boldsymbol{\theta}^1$ and $\boldsymbol{\theta}^2$ their respective classes. Then it is reasonable to assume that the unknown conditional risk $r(X)$ is more likely to be large if $\boldsymbol{\theta}^1 \ne \boldsymbol{\theta}^2$ and small if $\boldsymbol{\theta}^1 = \boldsymbol{\theta}^2$. To be specific, we have 2 samples and we make the crude estimate of the posterior probabilities $\eta_i(X)$ as

$$\hat{\boldsymbol{\eta}}_i(X) = \begin{cases} \frac{0}{2}, & \text{for } \boldsymbol{\theta}^1 = \boldsymbol{\theta}^2 \ne \omega_i \\ \frac{1}{2}, & \text{for } \boldsymbol{\theta}^1 \ne \boldsymbol{\theta}^2 \\ \frac{2}{2}, & \text{for } \boldsymbol{\theta}^1 = \boldsymbol{\theta}^2 = \omega_i. \end{cases} \tag{13}$$

Then the 2-NN estimate of $r(X)$, $\boldsymbol{r}_2(X)$, may be taken as

$$\begin{aligned}\boldsymbol{r}_2(X) &= \min\{\hat{\boldsymbol{\eta}}_1(X), \hat{\boldsymbol{\eta}}_2(X)\} \\ &= \begin{cases} \frac{0}{2}, & \text{for } \boldsymbol{\theta}^1 = \boldsymbol{\theta}^2 \\ \frac{1}{2}, & \text{for } \boldsymbol{\theta}^1 \ne \boldsymbol{\theta}^2. \end{cases}\end{aligned} \tag{14}$$

Since for fixed X,

$$\begin{aligned}P_r\{\boldsymbol{r}_2(X) = \tfrac{1}{2}\} &= P_r\{\boldsymbol{\theta}^1 \ne \boldsymbol{\theta}^2 \mid \boldsymbol{X} = X, \boldsymbol{X}^1 = X^1, \boldsymbol{X}^2 = X^2\} \\ &= \eta_1(X^1)\eta_2(X^2) + \eta_2(X^1)\eta_1(X^2)\end{aligned} \tag{15}$$

and $\eta_i(X^1) \to \eta_i(X)$ and $\eta_i(X^2) \to \eta_i(X)$ as $N_d \to \infty$ [2], the conditional expectation of $\boldsymbol{r}_2(X)$ is given by

$$\begin{aligned}r_2(X) &= E\{\boldsymbol{r}_2(\boldsymbol{X}) \mid \boldsymbol{X} = X\} \\ &= \eta_1(X)\eta_2(X) \\ &= r(X)[1 - r(X)].\end{aligned} \tag{16}$$

Now, $0 \le r(X) \le 0.5$, so (16) gives

$$r_2(X) \le r(X) \le 2r_2(X). \tag{17}$$

Thus the conditional expectation of the estimate, using only two nearest neighbors, bounds the true conditional error $r(X)$. Equation (17) is somewhat weaker than the result in [1] in which nearest-neighbor risks are used to estimate the Bayes risk. Defining $c_k(X)$ to be the conditional error using the k-NN classification rule, we observe from (16) and [2] that

$$c_1(X) = 2r_2(X). \tag{18}$$

Taking the expectation over $\boldsymbol{X}$ gives

$$R_2 \leq R \leq 2R_2 \equiv C_1. \tag{19}$$

At no point in the previous discussion was the unknown classification of $\boldsymbol{X}$ used. Thus unclassified samples may be used in estimating the bounds of (19) just as they were used in Section II with all statistics known. Specifically, if $\boldsymbol{X}_1,\boldsymbol{X}_2,\cdots,\boldsymbol{X}_{N_t}$ is a random unclassified set of test vectors drawn according to $p(X)$, then

$$\hat{\boldsymbol{R}}_2 = \frac{1}{N_t} \sum_{i=1}^{N_t} r_2(\boldsymbol{X}_i) \tag{20}$$

is an unbiased estimate of R_2. Furthermore, $2\hat{\boldsymbol{R}}_2$ is an unbiased estimate of C_1.

B. General k-NN Estimates

We now extend the preceding estimate to the general k-NN case. All results are asymptotic as $N_d \to \infty$ and $kN_D^{-1} \to 0$. Of the k-NN of a fixed X, $\boldsymbol{k}_1$ are from class ω_1 and $\boldsymbol{k}_2$ are from class ω_2. Then we use the estimate

$$\boldsymbol{r}_k(X) = \min \{\hat{\boldsymbol{\eta}}_1(X),\hat{\boldsymbol{\eta}}_2(X)\}$$
$$= \min \left\{\frac{\boldsymbol{k}_1}{k}, \frac{\boldsymbol{k}_2}{k}\right\} \tag{21}$$

where $\boldsymbol{k}_1 + \boldsymbol{k}_2 = k$. The possible values of $\boldsymbol{r}_k(X)$ are

$$\boldsymbol{r}_k(X) = \begin{cases} 0, \quad \frac{1}{k}, \frac{2}{k}, \cdots, \frac{k/2}{k}, & k \text{ even} \\ 0, \quad \frac{1}{k}, \frac{2}{k}, \cdots, \frac{(k-1)/2}{k}, & k \text{ odd.} \end{cases} \tag{22}$$

The probability that $\boldsymbol{r}_k(X)$ equals the preceding values for $i \neq k/2$ is

$$P_r\left\{\boldsymbol{r}_k(X) = \frac{i}{k} \mid \boldsymbol{X} = X\right\}$$
$$= \binom{k}{i} \eta_i(X)^i \eta_2(X)^{k-i} + \binom{k}{k-i} \eta_1(X)^{k-i}\eta_2(X)^i \tag{23}$$

and for $i = k/2$

$$P_r\left\{\boldsymbol{r}_k(X) = \frac{k/2}{k} \mid \boldsymbol{X} = X\right\} = \binom{k}{k/2} \eta_1(X)^{k/2}\eta_2(X)^{k/2}. \tag{24}$$

For k odd the conditional expectation of $\boldsymbol{r}_k(X)$ is

$$r_k(X) = E\{\boldsymbol{r}_k(X) \mid \boldsymbol{X} = X\}$$
$$= \sum_{i=0}^{(k-1)/2} \frac{i}{k} \binom{k}{i} [\eta_i(X)^i\eta_2(X)^{k-i} + \eta_1(X)^{k-i}\eta_2(X)^i] \tag{25}$$

and for k even

$$r_k(X) = E\{\boldsymbol{r}_k(X) \mid \boldsymbol{X} = X\}$$
$$= \frac{1}{2}\binom{k}{k/2} \eta_1(X)^{k/2}\eta_2(X)^{k/2} + \sum_{i=0}^{k/2-1} \frac{i}{k}\binom{k}{i}$$
$$\cdot\ [\eta_1(X)^i\eta_2(X)^{k-i} + \eta_1(X)^{k-i}\eta_2(X)^i]. \tag{26}$$

Equations (25) and (26) are summarized in a single form as

$$r_k(X) = \sum_{i=1}^{[k/2]} \frac{1}{i}\binom{2i-2}{i-1} (\eta_1(X)\eta_2(X))^i$$
$$= \sum_{i=1}^{[k/2]} \frac{1}{i}\binom{2i-1}{i-1} r_2{}^i(X) \tag{27}$$

where $[a]$ is the greatest integer less than or equal the real number a.

On the other hand, from (16), $r(X)$ can be expressed by

$$r(X) = \tfrac{1}{2} - \tfrac{1}{2}\sqrt{1 - 4r_2(X)}. \tag{28}$$

Therefore, the MacLaurin series of (28) gives

$$r(X) = \sum_{i=1}^{\infty} \frac{1}{i}\binom{2i-2}{i-1} r_2{}^i(X). \tag{29}$$

Comparison of (29) with (27) indicates the following.

1) Since all terms of (27) are positive, $r_k(X)$ is a lower bound on $r(X)$ and

$$r_2(X) = r_3(X) < r_4(X) = r_5(X) < \cdots$$
$$< r_{2k}(X) = r_{2k+1}(X) < \cdots < r(X). \tag{30}$$

2) Each term of (27) or its expectation can be evaluated by

$$\frac{1}{k}\binom{2k-2}{k-1} r_2{}^k(X) = r_{2k}(X) - r_{2k-2}(X)$$

or

$$\frac{1}{k}\binom{2k-2}{k-1} E\{r_2{}^k(X)\} = E\{r_{2k}(X)\} - E\{r_{2k-2}(X)\}. \tag{31}$$

The use of $r(\boldsymbol{X})$, utilizing unclassified samples, was shown in Section II to provide a reduction in variance in comparison to the usual error-counting techniques. By using the k-NN estimate of $r(\boldsymbol{X})$ this advantage is retained. The variance of $\boldsymbol{r}_k(\boldsymbol{X})$,

$$\operatorname{var}\{\boldsymbol{r}_k(\boldsymbol{X})\}$$
$$= E\{E\{\boldsymbol{r}_k{}^2(\boldsymbol{X}) \mid \boldsymbol{X}\}\} - R_k{}^2$$
$$= E\left\{\sum_{i=0}^{(k-1)/2} \left(\frac{i}{k}\right)^2 \binom{k}{i} [\eta_1{}^i\eta_2^{k-i} + \eta_1^{k-i}\eta_2{}^i]\right\} - R_k{}^2 (k \text{ odd})$$
$$= E\left\{\sum_{i=0}^{k} \left(\frac{i}{k}\right)^2 \left[\frac{k}{2} - \left|i - \frac{k}{2}\right|\right]^2 \binom{k}{i} \eta_1{}^i\eta_2^{k-i}\right\} - R_k{}^2 \text{ (all } k)$$
$$= R_k(1 - R_k) - \left(\frac{k-1}{k}\right) R_2$$
$$\leq R_k(1 - R_k) - \left(\frac{k-1}{k}\right)\left(\frac{R}{2}\right) \tag{32}$$

where we have used the well-known properties of binomial distributions and the fact that (25) and (26) can both be written as

$$E\{r_k(X) \mid X = X\} = \frac{1}{2} - \frac{1}{k}\sum_{i=0}^{k}\binom{k}{i}|i - (k/2)|\eta_1{}^i\eta_2^{k-i}. \tag{33}$$

Equation (32) shows the variance-reducing property for the k-NN estimates of (21) that was seen in (10) for $r(X)$ known exactly.

In summary, given test samples $X_1,X_2,\cdots,X_{N_t}$ drawn according to $p(X)$, we use the k nearest design samples to X_i to calculate $r_k(X_i)$ of (21). Then the sample mean

$$\hat{R}_k = \frac{1}{N_t}\sum_{i=1}^{N_t} r_k(X_i) \tag{34}$$

has expectation

$$E\{\hat{R}_k\} = \sum_{i=1}^{[k/2]} \frac{1}{i}\binom{2i-2}{i-1} E\{r_2{}^i(X)\} \tag{35}$$

and variance given by (32). From (29), this expected value is a lower bound on the Bayes error, R.

C. Estimates of k-NN Error and Approximation of Bayes Error

It is known that the k-NN classification procedure gives the upper bound of the Bayes error. The conditional k-NN error $c_k(X)$ is given for k odd [2] by

$$c_k(X) = \eta_1(X)\sum_{j=0}^{(k-1)/2}\binom{k}{j}\eta_1{}^j(X)\eta_2(X)^{k-j} + \eta_2(X)\sum_{j=(k+1)/2}^{k}\binom{k}{j}\eta_1{}^j(X)\eta_2^{k-j}(X). \tag{36}$$

This can be rewritten in terms of $r_k(X)$ as

$$c_{2k-1}(X) = r_{2k}(X) + \frac{1}{2}\binom{2k}{k}[\eta_1(X)\eta_2(X)]^k = r_{2k}(X) + \frac{1}{2}\binom{2k}{k} r_2{}^k(X). \tag{37}$$

Thus both $r_k(X)$ and $c_k(X)$ may be written as polynomials in $r_2(X) = \eta_1(X)\eta_2(X)$. With increasing k, $c_k(X)$, and $r_k(X)$ are high-order polynomial approximations to $r(X)$ as written in (28). Furthermore, $c_k(X)$ is a decreasing upper bound on $r(X)$ and $r_k(X)$ is an increasing lower bound. Representative curves are shown in Fig. 1.

The relationship given by (37) suggests a modification of the definition of the risk estimate, $r_k(X)$, to provide an unbiased estimate of the conditional k-NN classification risk. In order to accomplish this, replace (21) by the modified version

$$r_k'(X) = \alpha_i, \qquad \text{for } \min\{k_1,k_2\} = i. \tag{38}$$

From (37) it is clear that the α_i should be chosen to add

$$\frac{1}{2}\binom{2k}{k}\eta_1{}^k(X)\eta_2{}^k(X)$$

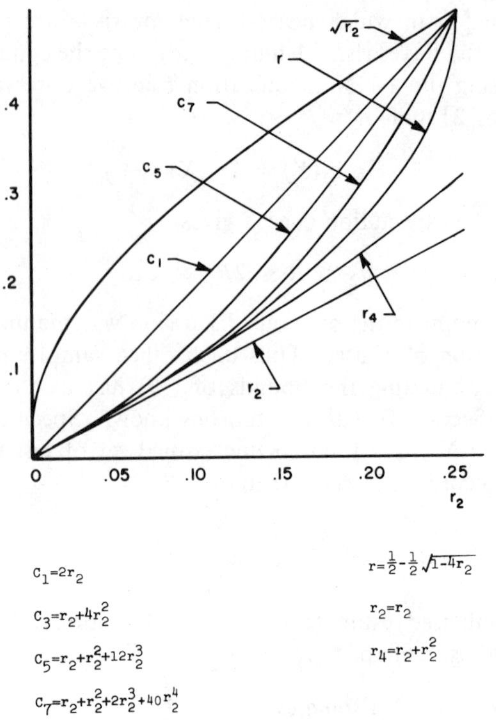

Fig. 1. $r(X)$, $r_k(X)$, and $c_k(X)$ versus $r_2(X)$.

to $r_{2k}(X)$. Examining (25) and (26), it is easily shown that this is accomplished by defining the α_i as follows:

$$r_{2k}'(X) = \begin{cases} \dfrac{i}{2k}, & i < k \\ 1, & i = k \end{cases}, \qquad i = \min\{k_1,k_2\} \tag{39}$$

$$r_{2k+1}'(X) = \begin{cases} \dfrac{i}{2k+1}, & i < k \\ \dfrac{3k+1}{4k+2}, & i = k \end{cases}, \qquad i = \min\{k_1,k_2\}. \tag{40}$$

Then we have the relationship

$$c_{2k-1}(X) = r_{2k}'(X) = r_{2k+1}'(X) \tag{41}$$

where

$$r_{2k}'(X) = E\{r_{2k}'(X) \mid X = X\}. \tag{42}$$

Thus for unclassified test samples $X_1,X_2,\cdots,X_{N_T}$,

$$C_{2k-1} = \frac{1}{N_t}\sum_{i=1}^{N_t} r_{2k}'(X_i) \tag{43}$$

is an unbiased estimate of the $(2k-1)$-NN classification error. Equations (34) and (43) give estimated lower and upper bounds on the Bayes error using information from both classified design and unclassified test samples.

In addition to the previous, the curves of Fig. 1 show the following interesting facts.

1) Equations (28) and (37), or the curves of Fig. 1, provide a quick comparison of the Bayes risk $r(X)$ and the nearest neighbor risk $c_k(X)$. If the largest ratio between the

TABLE I
β_k SUCH THAT $C_k \le \beta_k R$.

k	1	3	5	7	9	11	13
β_k	2.0	1.316	1.218	1.173	1.147	1.130	1.117

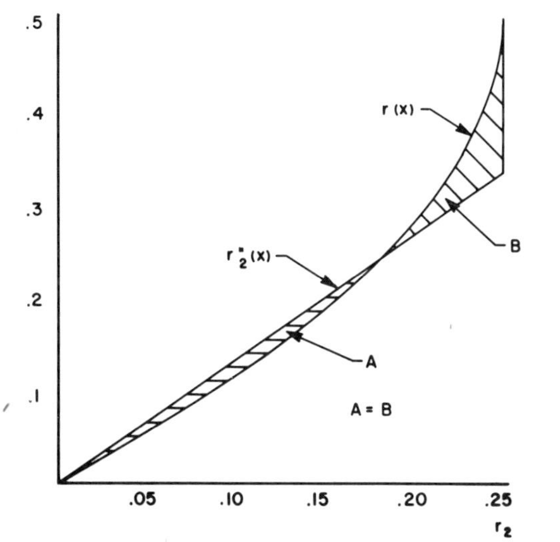

Fig. 2. Equal area criteria; $r(X)$, $r_2''(X)$ versus $r_2(X)$.

c_k-curve and r-curve in Fig. 1 is β_k, then

$$c_k(X) < \beta_k r(X) \tag{44}$$

so that

$$C_k < \beta_k R. \tag{45}$$

Thus we can obtain a rough bound on the relation of C_k to R. These β_k's are given in Table I.

2) It has been shown that $r_k(X) < r(X)$ and $r_k'(X) > r(X)$. An alternative viewpoint is to introduce an estimate which has conditional expectation approximating $r(X)$ rather than bounding it. It may be shown that modifying the last coefficient as

$$r_{2k}''(X) = \begin{cases} \dfrac{i}{2k}, & i < k \\ \frac{2}{3}, & i = k \end{cases}, \quad i = \min\{k_1, k_2\} \tag{46}$$

$$r_{2k+1}''(X) = \begin{cases} \dfrac{i}{2k+1}, & i < k \\ \dfrac{k+1}{12k+6}, & i = k \end{cases}, \quad i = \min\{k_1, k_2\} \tag{47}$$

gives the reasonable property that

$$\int [r_k''(X) - r(X)]\, dX = 0. \tag{48}$$

Fig. 2 illustrates the approximation for $k = 2$. Obviously, the degree of this approximation depends upon the distribution of r_2. However, the examples we have run show that the approximation is good for reasonable distributions.

3) The Bhattacharyya bound on R is given by

$$B = \int P(X)\sqrt{r_2(X)}\, dx > R. \tag{49}$$

Also, $\sqrt{r_2(X)}$ versus $r_2(X)$ is plotted in Fig. 1. Clearly $B \ge C_1$, so that the 1-NN expected error is a better bound on R than is the parametric Bhattacharyya bound.

In summary, for "large" N_d, experimental bounds on the Bayes error R may be obtained by taking the arithmetic average of the estimated conditional risk $r_k(X)$ and the modification $r_k'(X)$ over unclassified points, X, drawn from the unknown mixture density. The upper bound has expectation equal to the k-NN error. With increasing k, the bound becomes arbitrarily tight so that estimates of R may be obtained. Furthermore, the variance of these estimates is shown to be considerably smaller than that obtained by counting the errors made by the optimum classification rule on classified samples. Applications of this technique for finite N_d will be shown in Section V.

IV. Parzen Estimate of $r(X)$

In the previous section the posterior probabilities were estimated by the fraction of representation in the k-NN to X. An alternative procedure is to use the available design samples to provide nonparametric estimates of the probability density functions and the prior probabilities if they are also unknown. We use the multivariate extension of the Parzen density function estimate.

Given a sequence of independent, identically distributed random n-dimensional vectors, $X_1, X_2, \cdots, X_N$, from a distribution with probability density function $p(X)$, the Parzen estimate of $p(X)$ is [8]

$$p_N(X) = \frac{1}{Nh(N)^n} \sum_{i=1}^{N} K\left(\frac{X - X_i}{h(N)}\right). \tag{50}$$

With proper choice of the weighting function $h(N)$ and kernel $K(\cdot)$, $p_N(X)$ tends uniformly in probability to $p(X)$. We arbitrarily use the normal kernel as

$$h(N)^{-n} K\left(\frac{X - X_j}{h(N)}\right) = \frac{(2\pi)^{-n/2} N^{1/2}}{\sqrt{|\Sigma|}} \exp\left[-\frac{N^{1/n}}{2}(X - X_j)^T \Sigma^{-1} (X - X_j)\right] \tag{51}$$

where Σ is the sample covariance matrix of the data.

As in the previous section, the estimate of $r(X)$ is made from the N_d random labeled design vectors $\{X_i, \theta_i\}$. Of the N_d vectors, N_i are observed from class ω_i, so the prior probabilities are estimated by

$$\hat{P}_i = \frac{N_i}{N_d}. \tag{52}$$

The Parzen estimate of the conditional error for any X is taken as

$$r_p(X) = \frac{\min\{\hat{P}_1 p_{N_1}(X), \hat{P}_2 p_{N_2}(X)\}}{\hat{P}_1 P_{N_1}(X) + \hat{P}_2 p_{N_2}(X)}. \tag{53}$$

$r_p(X)$ is calculated for each unclassified test observation and the average is calculated to form the error estimate.

For N_t test samples, $X_1, \cdots, X_{N_t}$, this estimate is given by

$$\hat{R}_p = \frac{1}{N_t} \sum_{i=1}^{N_t} r_p(X_i). \tag{54}$$

V. Simulation Experiments

In order to demonstrate the application of the methods proposed in this paper, the results of simulation experiments are now given. The data simulated was two-class, two-dimensional, equal-covariance normal with a Mahalanobis distance of 2.56. Each class was chosen, both in the design and test sets, with probability 0.5. Thus the Bayes probability of error, R, for this example is 10 percent.

The primary objective was to demonstrate the convergence of the estimates $\hat{R}_k$ to R with increasing k and to verify the small-variance properties. For each trial, $N_D =$ 400 design samples and 500 test samples were drawn from the preceding pooled distribution. The $\hat{R}_k$ of (34), $\hat{C}_k$ of (43), and $\hat{C}_k'$, the error count estimate using the k-NN classification rule, were calculated. This was repeated for 10 trials, and the results are shown in Fig. 3. The convergence of $\hat{R}_k$ to R is clearly evident. There is fair agreement between $\hat{C}_k$ and $\hat{C}_k'$, with both converging to the Bayes error R. Thus in this "large sample" case the proposed method provides reasonable bounds for R. The Parzen approximation $\hat{R}_p$ for this data gives 0.0976 as an average estimate using (51)–(53).

In order to investigate the variance we examine the sample statistics for a typical trial. For $N_d = 400$ and $N_t = 500$ the sample standard deviation was found to be as given in Fig. 4. Comparing this with $\sqrt{R(1-R)} = 0.3$ shows a 50 percent reduction in standard deviation. The sample standard deviation for the Parzen estimate of $r(X)$ was 0.18, also showing a large reduction.

Finally, in order to demonstrate the small-sample characteristics of the proposed estimation method, the experiment outlined previously was repeated with varying values of N_d. The average results for ten trials for each number of design samples is shown in Fig. 5. From this we see that the Parzen estimate is good even for small samples for this data and our choice of $h(N)$ and $K(\cdot)$. No general rule for choosing $h(N)$ is available and the effect of its choice on the result is not known. $\hat{R}_2$ and $\hat{C}_1$ also appear to be quite stable, but for larger k and small N_d the expected deterioration in performance is observed. For fixed design data the variance remains small as given in Fig. 4 even for small N_d. However, for small N_d the variation from trial to trial becomes appreciable, the standard deviation of $\hat{R}_2$, $\hat{R}_6$, and $\hat{R}_p$ for the 10 trials being, respectively, 0.0205, 0.0287, and 0.0281 for 25 design samples per class. This, of course, may be expected with any estimation procedure.

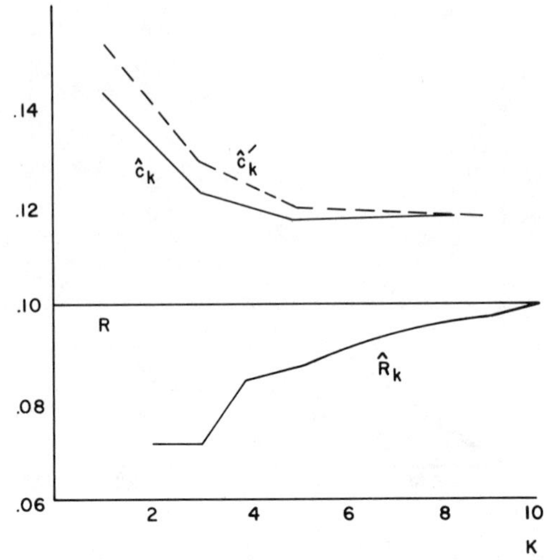

Fig. 3. Average $\hat{R}_k$, $\hat{C}_k$, $\hat{C}_k'$ versus k.

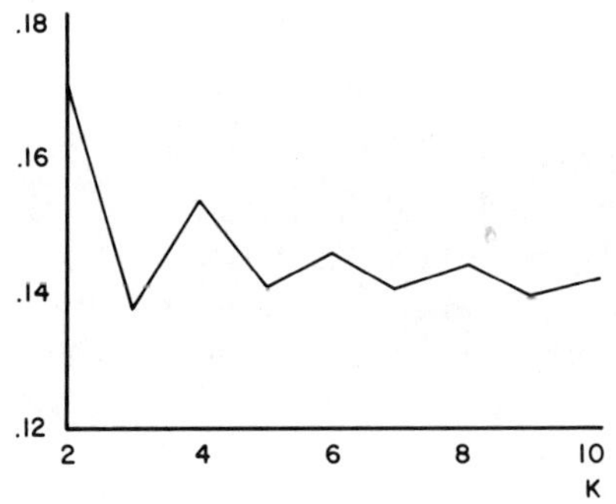

Fig. 4. Standard deviation of $\mathbf{r}_k(\mathbf{X})$ versus k (typical).

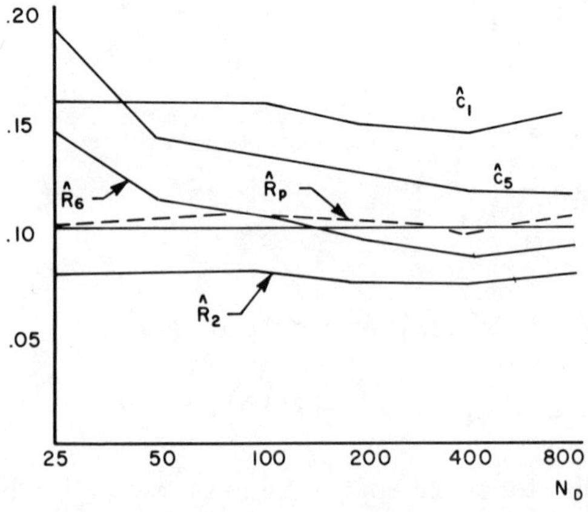

Fig. 5. Average $\hat{C}_k$, $\hat{R}_n$, $\hat{R}_p$ versus number of design samples.

VI. Summary

A new nonparametric method for Bayes error estimation has been developed. Classified design samples are required, as in existing methods, but test samples may be unclassified samples. This may be of great economic advantage in those situations in which independent verification of the class identity of test samples is impractical or very expensive. Furthermore, at least asymptotically, the error estimate has less variance than an error estimate made from an error count for the (unknown) Bayes classifier classifying classified samples. In addition, simulation indicates there may be a wide class of situations in which this method, using unclassified samples, performs well even for small numbers of design samples.

REFERENCES

[1] T. M. Cover, "Learning in pattern recognition," in *Methodologies in Pattern Recognition*, M. Watanabe, Ed. New York: Academic Press, 1969.

[2] T. M. Cover and P. E. Hart, "Nearest neighbor pattern classification," *IEEE Trans. Inform. Theory*, vol. IT-13, pp. 21–27, Jan. 1967.

[3] A. W. Whitney and S. J. Dwyer, "Performance and implementation of the k-nearest neighbor decision rule with incorrectly identified training samples," in *Proc. 4th Annu. Allerton Conf. Circuit and System Theory*, pp. 96–106, Oct. 1966.

[4] D. W. Peterson, "Some convergence properties of a nearest neighbor decision rule," *IEEE Trans. Inform. Theory*, vol. IT-16, pp. 26–31, Jan. 1970.

[5] T. J. Wagner, "Convergence of the nearest neighbor rule," *IEEE Trans. Inform. Theory*, vol. IT-17, pp. 566–571, Sept. 1971.

[6] M. E. Hellman, "The nearest neighbor classification rule with a reject option," *IEEE Trans. Syst. Sci. Cybern.*, vol. SSC-6, pp. 179–185, July 1970.

[7] E. Parzen, "On estimation of a probability density function and mode," *Ann. Math. Statist.*, vol. 33, pp. 1065–1076, 1962.

[8] T. Cacoullos, "Estimation of a multivariate density," *Ann. Inst. Statist. Math.*, vol. 18, pp. 179–189, 1966.

[9] D. F. Specht, "Series estimation of a probability density function," *Technometrics*, vol. 13, pp. 409–424, May 1971.

[10] K. Fukunaga and D. L. Kessell, "Estimation of classification error," *IEEE Trans. Comput.*, vol. C-20, pp. 1521–1527, Dec. 1971.

[11] S. C. Fralich and R. W. Scott, "Nonparametric Bayes-Risk estimation," *IEEE Trans. Inform. Theory*, vol. IT-17, pp. 440–444, July 1971.

[12] C. K. Chow, "On optimum recognition error and reject tradeoff," *IEEE Trans. Inform. Theory*, vol. IT-16, pp. 41–46, Jan. 1970.

[13] K. Fukunaga and D. L. Kessell, "Application of optimum error-reject functions," *IEEE Trans. Inform. Theory*, vol. IT-18, pp. 814–817, Nov. 1972.

Independence, Measurement Complexity, and Classification Performance

B. CHANDRASEKARAN, MEMBER, IEEE, AND ANIL K. JAIN, MEMBER, IEEE

Abstract—**If $f(x)$ and $g(x)$ are the densities for the N-dimensional measurement vector x, conditioned on the classes c_1 and c_2, and if finite sets of samples from the two classes are available, then a decision function based on estimates $\hat{f}(x)$ and $\hat{g}(x)$ can be used to classify future observations. In general, however, when the measurement complexity (the dimensionality N) is increased arbitrarily and the sets of training samples remain finite, a "peaking phenomenon" of the following kind is observed: classification accuracy improves at first, peaks at a finite value of N, called the *optimum measurement complexity*, and starts deteriorating thereafter. We derive, for the case of statistically independent measurements, general conditions under which it can be guaranteed that the peaking phenomenon will not occur, and the correct classification probability will keep increasing to value unity as $N \to \infty$. Several applications are considered which together indicate, contrary to general belief, that independence of measurements alone does not guarantee the absence of the peaking phenomenon.**

I. INTRODUCTION

THE DESIGNER of a statistical pattern classification system is often faced with the following situation: finite sets of samples, or paradigms, from the various classes are available along with a set of measurements, or features, to be computed from the patterns. The designer usually proceeds by estimating the class-conditional densities of the measurement vector on the basis of the available samples and uses these estimates to arrive at a classification function. Naive intuition suggests that if the dimensionality of the measurement vector is increased, then the classification error rate should generally decrease. In the case where the added measurements do not contribute in any way to classification, then the error rate should at least stay the same. For, after all, is not more information being utilized in the design? However, in practice quite often the performance of the classifier based on estimated densities improved up to a point, then started deteriorating as further measurements were added, thus indicating the existence of an *optimal measurement complexity* when the number of training samples is finite. Many recent investigations [1]–[6] have concerned themselves with explicating this counter-intuitive experimental observation. Hughes [2] mathematically demonstrated the existence of this phenomenon in the context of a Bayesian model in which no specific assumptions are made about the dependence or lack of it between the measurements. An intuitive notion of the role played by measurement dependence can be obtained by recalling that, in the case of normal distributions, the estimated covariance matrix becomes singular if the dimensionality is greater than the number of samples. Since the decision function involves inverting the covariance matrix, clearly the dimensionality ought to be kept smaller than the sample size. Nevertheless, if the measurements are known to be independent, this problem does not arise, since only the diagonal elements of the covariance matrix need to be estimated. Thus, in the general problem, the increased structure in the model resulting from the assumption of independence might be expected to lead to qualitatively different results. Indeed, in [5] the following result is obtained. Let the measurements be independent and of binary quantization ($x_i = 0$ or 1). The parameters $\Pr(x_i = 1 \mid c_1) = p_i$ and $\Pr(x_i = 1 \mid c_2) = q_i$ are unknown and are to be estimated from samples of the two classes. If one assumes an *a priori* distribution on these parameters and thus sets up the optimal Bayesian decision function, then it can be shown that $\bar{P}_{cr}$, the mean probability of correct classification, monotonically increases with N, the number of measurements, until as $N \to \infty$ perfect classification is obtained. For practical purposes, this result implies that for this model at any rate the number of independent measurements can be increased without fear that at some point the performance will start deteriorating.

Manuscript received August 27, 1973; revised September 3, 1974. This work was supported by Grant AFOSR 72-2351.

B. Chandrasekaran is with the Department of Computer and Information Science, Ohio State University, Columbus, Ohio 43210.

A. K. Jain was with the Communications and Control Systems Laboratory, Department of Electrical Engineering, Ohio State University, Columbus, Ohio. He is now with the Computer Science Department, Michigan State University, East Lansing, Mich., on leave from the Computer Science Section, Department of Mathematics, Wayne State University, Detroit, Mich.

Reprinted from *IEEE Trans. Syst., Man, Cybern.*, vol. SMC-5, pp. 240–244, Mar. 1975.

It is not clear, however, how far this qualitative conclusion can be extended if the underlying model is not Bayesian.

In this paper we consider the following general question: If the measurements are independent, what are the most general conditions under which, as the dimensionality is increased, the classification accuracy will keep improving steadily? For reasons mentioned earlier, we do not wish to confine ourselves to Bayesian estimates of unknown parameters, as was done in [2] and [5]. This assumption, by requiring knowledge of *a priori* distributions, restricts the scope of possible applications. As a comparison bench mark, it is useful to consider first the case corresponding to infinite sample sets, i.e., known class-conditional density functions.

II. Infinite Sample Sets

Let $f_N(x)$ and $g_N(x)$ be the class-conditional densities of the classes c_1 and c_2, respectively, where N is the dimensionality of the measurement vector x. Assuming equal prior probabilities for the classes, the probability of correct recognition based on optimal Bayes decision rule is given by

$$P_{cr} = \frac{1}{2}\left[\Pr\left\{\log \frac{g_N(x)}{f_N(x)} \leq 0 \mid x \in c_1\right\} + \Pr\left\{\log \frac{f_N(x)}{g_N(x)} > 0 \mid x \in c_2\right\}\right]. \quad (1)$$

It is known [7] that if f_N and g_N are density functions defining different probability distributions with the same range, then for every N

$$E_f(\log f_N(x)) > E_f(\log g_N(x)),$$

where E_f denotes the expectation with respect to the f-distribution. Paralleling the proof in [7] in connection with the consistency of the likelihood estimates, let

$$f_N(x_1,\cdots,x_N) = \prod_{i=1}^{N} f_i(x_i)$$

$$g_N(x_1,\cdots,x_N) = \prod_{i=1}^{N} g_i(x_i)$$

and further assume that for all i and almost all ξ

$$f_i(\xi) \neq g_i(\xi). \quad (2)$$

Then it can be shown that

$$E_f\left\{\log \frac{f_N(x)}{g_N(x)}\right\} = 0(N)$$

and

$$\sigma_f^2\left\{\log \frac{f_N(x)}{g_N(x)}\right\} = 0(N).$$

Therefore, for large N, $\log (f_N(x)/g_N(x))$ is a random variable of which the expected value E_f is large relative to its standard deviation. This implies that as $N \to \infty$, $f_N > g_N$ with an f-probability that approaches unity and $g_N > f_N$ with a g-probability that approaches unity, and thus perfect discrimination is achieved under condition (2). This result can be summarized informally as follows. When the densities are known, as long as each measurement contributes something towards classification, then as more and more of them are included, the probability of correct classification keeps increasing steadily towards an asymptotic value of unity.

III. Finite Sample Sets

With a slight change in notation from the previous section, let

$$f(x) = \prod_{i=1}^{N} f_i(x_i) \qquad g(x) = \prod_{i=1}^{N} g_i(x_i) \quad (3)$$

be the two class-conditional densities. Let $\hat{f}_i$ and $\hat{g}_i$, $i = 1,\cdots,N$, be some estimates of f_i and g_i, the class prior probabilities be equal, and the decision function be

$$\text{if } \hat{f}(x) \equiv \prod_{i=1}^{N} \hat{f}_i(x_i) \geq \hat{g}(x) \equiv \prod_{i=1}^{N} \hat{g}_i(x_i), \text{ then } c_1; \text{ otherwise } c_2 \quad (4)$$

Consider $x \in c_1$. Then

$$\Pr\{\hat{f}(x) \geq \hat{g}(x) \mid x \in c_1\} = \Pr\left\{\sum_{i=1}^{N} (\log \hat{f}_i(x_i) - \log \hat{g}_i(x_i)) \geq 0 \mid x \in c_1\right\}.$$

Let $\boldsymbol{x}_i$ be the set of samples from c_i, $\boldsymbol{x} = \boldsymbol{x}_1 \cup \boldsymbol{x}_2$, and V the quantity

$$\left(\sum_{i=1}^{N} \text{var}_{\boldsymbol{x}_1} \log \hat{f}_i + \text{var}_{\boldsymbol{x}_2} \log \hat{g}_i\right)^{1/2}.$$

The preceding probability becomes

$$\Pr\left\{\frac{\sum (\log \hat{f}_i - \log \hat{g}_i) - E_{\boldsymbol{x}}(\sum (\log \hat{f}_i - \log \hat{g}_i))}{V} \geq \frac{-E_{\boldsymbol{x}}(\sum (\log \hat{f}_i - \log \hat{g}_i))}{V} \,\middle|\, x \in c_1\right\} \quad (5)$$

where the summations are from one to N. Observe that $\hat{f}$ and $\hat{g}$ are random quantities, and the expected values and the variances are with respect to the sample sets. Denote the random quantity on the left side of the inequality by Z. Then, by the central limit theorem, Z is normally distributed with zero mean and unit variance, for sufficiently large N.[1] Thus

$$\lim_{N\to\infty} \Pr(\hat{f}(x) \geq \hat{g}(x) \mid x \in c_1) = \lim_{N\to\infty} \left(\Pr\left(Z \geq \frac{E_{\boldsymbol{x}}(\sum (\log \hat{g}_i - \log \hat{f}_i))}{V} \,\middle|\, x \in c_1\right)\right).$$

[1] To be rigorous, we have to verify that the conditions of the central limit theorem hold, which cannot be done until the f_i and the g_i are specified more fully. However, it can be verified that the conditions are satisfied for the applications considered in the next section. Most textbooks on probability theory give sufficient conditions of varying degrees of complexity. The following conditions of Lindberg are given in [11]. Let X_k, $k = 1,\ldots$, be mutually independent variables, and let $\mu_k = E(X_k)$, $\sigma_k^2 = \text{var}(X_k)$, and $s_n^2 = \sigma_1^2 + \cdots + \sigma_n^2$. Then the central limit theorem holds whenever, for every $\varepsilon = 0$, the truncated variables U_k defined by $U_k = X_k - \mu_k$ if $|X_k - \mu_k| \leq \varepsilon s_n$, $U_k = 0$ otherwise, satisfy the conditions $s_n \to \infty$ and

$$1/s_n^2 \sum_{1}^{n} E(U_k^2) \to 1.$$

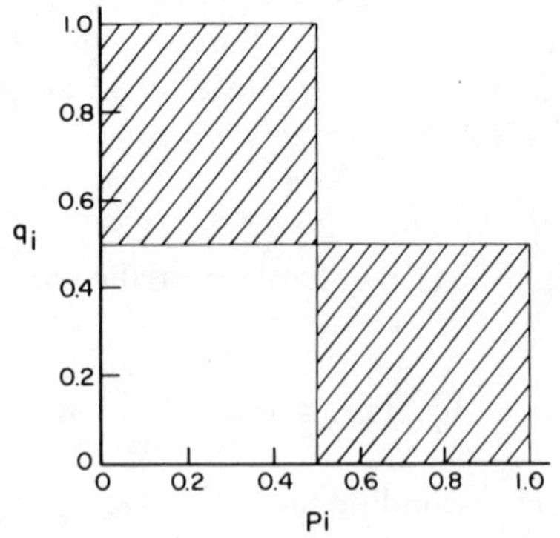

Fig. 1. Permissible region for p_i and q_i, Section IV-A: $m = 1$.

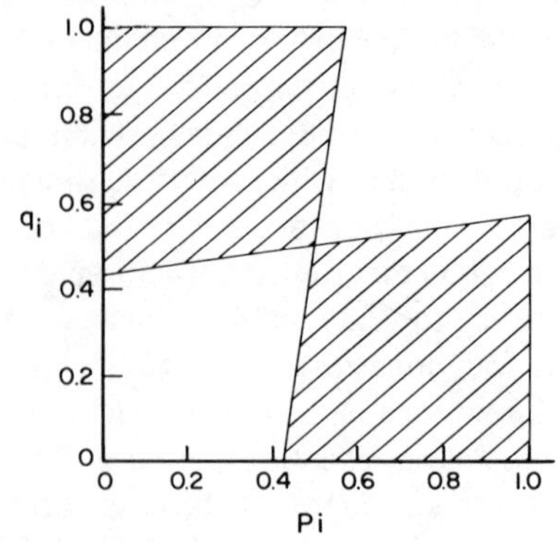

Fig. 2. Permissible region for p_i and q_i, Section IV-B: $m = 2$.

Then for the probability of correct classification for class c_1 to approach unity as $N \to \infty$, we show in the Appendix that it is necessary and sufficient that

$$\lim_{N\to\infty} E_{x\in c_1} E_{\mathbf{x}} \sum_{i=1}^{N} (\log \hat{f}_i - \log \hat{g}_i) = \infty. \tag{6a}$$

Similarly, for class c_2, the probability of correct classification approaches unity as $N \to \infty$, if and only if

$$\lim_{N\to\infty} E_{x\in c_2} E_{\mathbf{x}} \sum_{i=1}^{N} (\log \hat{g}_i - \log \hat{f}_i) = \infty. \tag{6b}$$

We thus have two compact conditions to test whether the dimensionality can be arbitrarily increased. As a result it is, now possible to consider a wide class of problems without starting from first principles every time. A few remarks on the interpretation of (6a) and (6b) are in order. Notice that the form of the conditions is similar to those in the infinite sample case, except for the addition of the expectation operator over the samples. The left side of the equations can be viewed as distance measures. This viewpoint has been explored in a recent paper by the authors [10]. In the next section we present several examples in which the preceding conditions are used to derive results some of which are rather surprising.

IV. Applications

Example A.

The first example will generalize the result in [5] by direct application of the conditions derived in the previous section. A perusal of [5] will reveal how much complex analysis has been saved, while at the same time obtaining generalizations that were previously intractable.

Let the measurements be independent, of binary quantization ($x_i = 0$ or 1), and let p_i and q_i, $i = 1,\cdots,N$, be $\Pr(x_i = 1 \mid c_1)$ and $\Pr(x_i = 1 \mid c_2)$, respectively. Let m be the number of training samples available from each class, and let s_i and r_i be the numbers of times x_i takes the value one for the two classes in the set of training samples. Following [5] we adopt a Bayesian model. Let the *a priori* densities on p_i and q_i, for all i, be uniform in the interval [0,1]. The Bayesian estimates for the parameters are

$$\hat{p}_i = \frac{s_i + 1}{m + 2} \qquad \hat{q}_i = \frac{r_i + 1}{m + 2}. \tag{7}$$

Since we are interested here in the mean recognition accuracy, we need another expectation operator $\tilde{E}$ to stand for averaging over the priors on p_i and q_i. Equation (6a) now becomes

$$\lim_{N\to\infty} \tilde{E} E_{x\in c_1} E_{\mathbf{x}} \sum \log [\hat{p}_i^{x_i}(1 - \hat{p}_i)^{1-x_i}] - \log [\hat{q}_i^{x_i}(1 - \hat{q}_i)^{1-x_i}] = \infty.$$

Now

$$\begin{aligned}
&\tilde{E} E_{x\in c_1} E_{\mathbf{x}} \log [\hat{p}_i^{x_i}(1 - \hat{p}_i)^{1-x_i}] \\
&= E_{\mathbf{x}} \tilde{E}[p_i \log \hat{p}_i + (1 - p_i) \log (1 - \hat{p}_i)] \\
&= \sum_{s_i=0}^{m} \left\{ \int_0^1 \binom{m}{s_i} p_i^{s_i+1}(1 - p_i)^{m-s_i} \log \frac{s_i + 1}{m + 2}\, dp_i \right. \\
&\qquad \left. + \int_0^1 \binom{m}{s_i} p_i^{s_i}(1 - p_i)^{m-s_i+1} \log \left(1 - \frac{s_i + 1}{m + 2}\right) dp_i \right\} \\
&= 2 \sum_{s_i=0}^{m} \frac{s_i + 1}{(m + 1)(m + 2)} \log \frac{s_i + 1}{m + 2}.
\end{aligned}$$

In a similar manner it can be shown that

$$\tilde{E} E_{x\in c_1} E_{\mathbf{x}} \log [\hat{q}_i^{x_i}(1 - \hat{q}_i)^{1-x_i}] = \sum_{r_i=0}^{m} \frac{1}{m + 1} \log \frac{r_i + 1}{m + 2}.$$

Thus (6a) is equivalent to

$$\sum_{s_i=0}^{m} \left(\frac{2(s_i + 1)}{m + 2} - 1\right) \log \frac{s_i + 1}{m + 2} > 0$$

which can be checked by straightforward manipulation to be true. Equation (6b) can also be shown to be satisfied in a similar manner. This is a generalization of the result in [5] to arbitrary m.

The application of the conditions can handle further generalizations. We will consider two that yield somewhat surprising results. The result in the previous paragraph concerns only the average performance over a variety of problems and furthermore, is a consequence of the fact that $\tilde{E}[|p_i - q_i|] > 0$. However, what about the performance in an individual problem, even though the estimates are Bayesian for the assumed uniform *a priori*'s? In order to highlight some new phenomena that occur, we consider two cases, $m = 1$ and $m = 2$. We will use the conditions without the $\tilde{E}$ operator, since we will be concerned with performance over individual problems and not average performance.

For $m = 1$, (6a) and (6b) are equivalent to demanding that

$$\lim_{N\to\infty} \sum_{i=1}^{N} (p_i - q_i)(2p_i - 1) = \infty$$

$$\lim_{N\to\infty} \sum_{i=1}^{N} (q_i - p_i)(2q_i - 1) = \infty$$

when the estimates are as in (7). The interesting point to note here is that it is not sufficient that $|p_i - q_i| > 0$, for all i. As $N \to \infty$, it is necessary that infinitely often we have either $p_i > \frac{1}{2}$ and $q_i < \frac{1}{2}$ or $p_i < \frac{1}{2}$ and $q_i > \frac{1}{2}$. The permissible regions for p_i and q_i are shaded in Fig. 1. For $m = 2$, the necessary and sufficient conditions for perfect classification with estimates as in (7) are

$$\lim_{N\to\infty} \sum (p_i - q_i)[(3p_i + q_i) \log 3 - (p_i + q_i) \log 4 - \log \tfrac{9}{4}] = \infty$$

and a similar equation with p_i and q_i reversed. This leads to an equivalent condition that infinitely often, for each i, $p_i \neq q_i$ and the values of p_i and q_i must lie in the shaded region in Fig. 2. As m becomes larger the regions not permitted become smaller and smaller. However, as long as m remains finite, if p_i and q_i do not infinitely often take values in the corresponding permissible region, $P_{cr}, \to \frac{1}{2}$, as $N \to \infty$. It is worth noting that qualitatively similar phenomena will occur if other *a priori* densities are assumed and corresponding Bayesian estimates of the parameters are used in the decision function.

The foregoing application involved Bayesian estimates. In many practical applications maximum likelihood estimates are quite often preferred both for simplicity and because *a priori* densities on unknown parameters are difficult to obtain. Thus we next consider the use of maximum likelihood estimates of the parameters p_i and q_i. The conditions (6a) and (6b) can be used, but we take a slightly different approach. Consider x such that all the x_i are one for simplicity. Then the decision rule based on maximum likelihood estimate is

$$s_1 \cdots s_N > r_1 \cdots r_N \Rightarrow c_1; \text{ otherwise } c_2.$$

We have arbitrarily assigned c_2 for the case $s_1 \cdots s_N = r_1 \cdots r_N$. The result that follows is valid for the other assignment also. It is easy to see that $\Pr(s_i = 0) \neq 0$ and $\Pr(r_i = 0) \neq 0$, for any finite m, as long as $p_i \neq 1$ and $q_i \neq 1$. Now

$$\begin{aligned}\Pr(s_1 \cdots s_N = r_1 \cdots r_N) &\\ \geq \Pr(s_1 \cdots s_N = 0) \Pr(r_1 \cdots r_N = 0)&\\ = \prod_{i=1}^{N} (1 - \Pr(s_i \neq 0))(1 - \Pr(r_i \neq 0)).&\end{aligned}$$

It follows that

$$\lim_{N\to\infty} \Pr(s_1 \cdots s_N = r_1 \cdots r_N) = 1$$

since $\Pr(s_i \neq 0)$ and $\Pr(r_i \neq 0)$ are both strictly less than one, except when p_i and q_i are unity. Thus the probability of correct classification for this x and similarly for all the other x goes to $\frac{1}{2}$ as $N \to \infty$. It is true, however, as N increases, performance improves at first, and when it peaks before falling off, both the measurement complexity (i.e., the dimensionality of the pattern vector) at which the peak occurs and the correct classification probability at that point increase as m increases.

Note that in the Bayesian estimate case, as m increases, the region in which p_i and q_i can lie becomes less restrictive. On the other hand, in the maximum likelihood estimate case, as m increases, the optimum measurement complexity N_{opt} is increased, but for all finite m, N_{opt} remains finite.

Example B.

In this example we consider independent measurements that are continuous and normally distributed. Specifically, $f_i(x_i) = \mathcal{N}(\theta_i,1)$ and $g_i(x_i) = \mathcal{N}(\phi_i,1)$, where $\mathcal{N}(u,\sigma^2)$ is the normal density with mean u and variance σ^2. Let $\hat{\theta}_i$ and $\hat{\phi}_i$ be the maximum likelihood estimates based on m_1 and m_2 samples, respectively. It is well known that $\hat{\theta}_i \sim (\theta_i,1/m_1)$ and $\hat{\phi}_i \sim (\phi_i,1/m_2)$. Equations (6a) and (6b) become

$$\lim_{N\to\infty} E_{x\in c_1} E_x \left(\sum_{i=1}^{N} (x_i - \hat{\phi}_i)^2 - (x_i - \theta_i)^2\right)$$

and a similar equation with c_2 in place of c_1 and θ_i and ϕ_i reversed. Equivalently, the conditions are

$$\lim_{N\to\infty} \sum \left\{(\phi_i - \theta_i)^2 + \frac{1}{m_2} - \frac{1}{m_1}\right\} = \infty$$

$$\lim_{N\to\infty} \sum \left\{(\theta_i - \phi_i)^2 + \frac{1}{m_1} - \frac{1}{m_2}\right\} = \infty. \quad (8)$$

If $m_1 = m_2$, it is clear that, even with finite number of samples, as long as θ_i and ϕ_i differ infinitely often, perfect classification is achieved as $N \to \infty$. That is, independence assures that optimum measurement complexity for finite m is infinite. However, if $m_1 \neq m_2$, then even if $\theta_i \neq \phi_i$, for every i, it can happen that $\lim_{N\to\infty} P_{cr} = \frac{1}{2}$, if it is not true that $(\theta_i - \phi_i)^2 > |1/m_2 - 1/m_1|$ infinitely often.

It is possible to interpret the preceding result in a surprising manner. Consider the case where $(\theta_i - \phi_i)^2 > 0$ but $\not> |1/m_2 - 1/m_1|$ sufficiently often. It appears that by discarding excess samples from the class more often represented in the samples, (8) can be satisfied, and perfect classification as $N \to \infty$ can be restored. This is certainly counter-intuitive. However, a Montecarlo simulation [8] confirms the correctness of the result by exhibiting a curve in which expected performance increases and then drops off for an unequal number of samples.

It is instructive to examine what is happening somewhat more closely. It can be readily shown that if suitable *a priori* densities are assumed on θ_i and ϕ_i and the corresponding Bayesian decision function is used, then performance averaged over the problem space generated by the *a priori* densities keeps improving monotonically with N, similar to the case of binary measurements discussed in the earlier example. The problem is that maximum likelihood estimate-based decision functions do not have this property of optimality in the sense of minimum probability of error. Furthermore, while Bayesian estimate-based decision functions use estimates of density functions that automatically incorporate a weighting factor taking into account different sample sizes, the decision function that results from substituting maximum likelihood estimates for parameters in the Bayes decision function does not have this weighting. It appears that it is indeed possible to weight the density function estimates such that the paradoxical behavior under discussion does not arise. This is a subject of current investigation.

V. Concluding Remarks

In the problem of the relationship between classification accuracy and the dimensionality of the measurement vector in the context of a finite set of learning samples, previous results raised the hope that independence of measurements might guarantee that the optimal dimensionality would be infinite, i.e., extra measurements could be added without fear that performance would peak at a finite dimensionality and deteriorate thereafter and that this phenomenon of peaking could be relegated to the case of dependent measurements. We have derived a set of conditions which, by making it possible to investigate a variety of cases in a relatively efficient manner, show that this hope (e.g., [9, p. 77]) is overoptimistic. That is, there exist numerous circumstances in which independence of measurements is not sufficient to make the optimum measurement complexity infinite.

Appendix

In this appendix, we give some of the details of the derivation of (6a). Equation (6b) can be derived in a similar manner. For ease of handling as well as to emphasize its dependence on x, denote the quantity

$$\frac{E_x(\sum \log \hat{f}_i - \log \hat{g}_i)}{V}$$

by $T(x)$. Then the correct recognition probability for a particular $x \in c_1$ can be represented by $\nu(-T(x))$, where $\nu(u)$ stands for

$$\frac{1}{\sqrt{2\pi}} \int_u^\infty \exp\left[-\tfrac{1}{2}(u' - u)^2\right] du'.$$

Note that $\nu(u)$ has the property $\lim_{T\to\infty} \nu(-T) = 1$. Since x is a vector of independent random variables, T is a sum of random variables. The ith term of the sum has the expected value

$$E_{x\in c_1} E_x(\log \hat{f}_i - \log \hat{g}_i) \triangleq \overline{T}_i$$

and a variance, which it is sufficient for our purposes to represent by V_1'. Again, by the application of the central limit theorem, $T(x)$ is normally distributed with mean $\sum \overline{T}_i$ and variance $\sum V_i'$. The probability of correct recognition $\to 1$, if and only if $T(x) \to \infty$. It can be seen that $\Pr(T(x) \to \infty) = 1$, if and only if $\sum \overline{T}_i \to \infty$, and the V_i' are sufficiently well behaved. Hence the condition (6a).

References

[1] D. C. Allais, "The selection of measurements for prediction," Stanford Electron. Labs, Stanford, Calif., Tech. Rep. 6103-9, Nov. 1964; also available as AD 456770.

[2] G. F. Hughes, "On the mean accuracy of statistical pattern recognizers," *IEEE Trans. Inform. Theory*, vol. IT-14, pp. 55–63, Jan. 1968.

[3] K. Abend, T. J. Harley, Jr., B. Chandrasekaran, and G. F. Hughes, Comments "On the mean accuracy of statistical pattern recognizers," *IEEE Trans. Inform. Theory* (Corresp.), vol. IT-15, pp. 420–423, May 1969.

[4] L. Kanal and B. Chandrasekaran, "On dimensionality and sample size in statistical pattern classification," *Pattern Recognition*, vol. 3, pp. 225–234, 1971.

[5] B. Chandrasekaran, "Independence of measurements and the mean recognition accuracy," *IEEE Trans. Inform. Theory*, vol. 17, pp. 452–456, July 1971.

[6] B. Chandrasekaran and A. K. Jain, "Quantization complexity and independent measurements," *IEEE Trans. Comput.*, (Corresp.), vol. C-23, pp. 102–106, Jan. 1974.

[7] S. D. Silvey, "A note on maximum likelihood in the case of dependent random variables," *J. Roy. Statist. Soc.*, Ser. B, vol. 23, pp. 444–452, 1961.

[8] A. K. Jain and B. Chandrasekaran, "Some aspects of dimensionality and sample size problems in statistical pattern recognition," Commun. and Control Systems Lab., Ohio State Univ., Columbus, Tech. Rep., 1973.

[9] R. O. Duda and P. E. Hart, *Pattern Classification and Scene Analysis*. New York: Wiley, 1973.

[10] B. Chandrasekaran and A. K. Jain, "Distance functions for independent measurements and finite sample size," in *Proc. 2nd Int. Joint Conf. Pattern Recognition*, 1974.

[11] W. Feller, *An Introduction to Probability Theory and Its Applications*, vol. 1, 3rd Ed. New York: Wiley, pp. 254–256.

[Note added by the authors November 17, 1976]
Some corrections and clarifications of this paper can be found in the following notes to appear in IEEE Trans. Systems, Man & Cybernetics in early 1977:

1) R.P.W. Duin, "Comments on 'Independence, measurement complexity and classification performance'."
2) B. Chandrasekaran and A.K. Jain, Reply to 1) above.
3) J. W. Van Ness, "Dimensionality and classification performance with independent coordinates."

On Pattern Classification Algorithms Introduction and Survey

YU-CHI HO, SENIOR MEMBER, IEEE, AND ASHOK K. AGRAWALA

Invited Paper

Abstract—**This paper attempts to lay bare the underlying ideas used in various pattern classification algorithms reported in the literature. It is shown that these algorithms can be classified according to the type of input information required and that the techniques of estimation, decision, and optimization theory can be used to effectively derive known as well as new results.**

I. Introduction

PATTERN classification or recognition covers an extremely broad spectrum of problems. Most of us are only concerned with one or two of these at any given time. For example, there is the engineering aspect of the pattern classification problem, which is mainly concerned with the implementation and design of actual recognition devices. At the other extreme, there is the artificial intelligence aspect of the problem, which is concerned with the philosophical question of learning and intelligence. It is both stimulating and controversial [19], [38]. Similarly, the study of recognition mechanisms in biological systems is another accepted field of study [20].

In this paper, we shall not touch on any of the above-mentioned areas.[1] Our survey will be concentrated on what might be called the analytical aspects of the pattern classification problem. By this we mean that the problem is viewed as one of making decisions under uncertainty and the mathematical techniques of decision, estimation, and optimization theory are brought to bear on the problem. These techniques are familiar tools to modern control engineers. One purpose of this paper is to point out pattern classification as a potential area of research and development for workers in automatic control. Conversely, the results in pattern classification are useful or potentially useful in control system design where a great deal of uncertainty is involved. Various papers in adaptive and learning control represent attempts in this direction. However, we shall not engage in a detailed survey of this aspect of the problem.[2]

As it is usually understood, there are two fundamental problems associated with this aspect of pattern classification.

1) Characterization Problem: Given a pattern, signal, or waveform, before any decision can be made concerning the pattern, it is often convenient as well as necessary to convert the pattern, signal, or waveform into a set of *features* or *attributes* that characterize the pattern under consideration. These features are usually denoted by the real variables $x_1, \cdots, x_m$ and the vector x is called the *pattern vector*. If we represent the original scanned pattern or sampled waveform as a vector z, then the characterization or feature selection problem can be simply but vaguely stated as finding a map from z to x, i.e.,

$$x = \phi(z) \tag{1}$$

such that x adequately characterizes the original z for purposes of classification but the dimension of x is much smaller than that of z.

2) Abstraction and Generalization Problem: Once a set of features has been selected, and certain data concerning the patterns and their features are given, the next problem is the determination of a decision function of these features based on the data given such that

$$f(x) = \begin{cases} \geq 0 & x \in \text{class } H^1 \\ < 0 & x \in \text{class } H^0. \end{cases} \qquad (2)^3$$

The problem of abstracting the necessary information from the given data to produce the decision function $f(x)$[4] is called *abstraction.* It is often convenient but not absolutely necessary to process the given data sequentially or iteratively in order to determine $f(x)$. This iterative procedure for calculating $f(x)$ is known as *training procedure*, *adaptation*, or *learning*.[5] Once a decision function $f(x)$ has been found,

Manuscript received July 12, 1968. This work represents an expanded version of a talk given by Y. C. Ho at the 10th Anniversary Seminar of the Statistics Dept., Harvard University, April, 1967. It was made possible through support extended to the Div. of Engrg. and Appl. Phys., Harvard University, by the U. S. Army Research Office, the USAFOSR, and the USONR under Joint Services Electronics Program Contracts N00014-67-A-0298-0006, -0005, and -0008 and by NASA Grant NGR 22-007-068.

This paper was invited for publication in the IEEE Transactions on Automatic Control, where it appears this month. It is also printed here because of its wide interest to readers of the Proceedings.—*The Editor.*

The authors are with the Division of Engineering and Applied Physics, Harvard University, Cambridge, Mass.

[1] A survey of *all* different aspects of pattern recognition was recently done by Nagy [41].

[2] We refer readers to Sklansky's survey article for this aspect of the problem [53].

[3] In the main, we shall restrict ourselves to two-class problems. In Section IX, we shall discuss the extension to multiclass problems.

[4] Sometimes $f(x)$ is also referred to as a decision surface in m-dimensional x space.

[5] In the context of this paper, these words simply represent entrenched terminology. No philosophical or metamathematical meaning should be attached to them.

Reprinted from *Proc. IEEE*, vol. 56, pp. 2101–2114, Dec. 1968.

the *generalization problem* attempts to assess the goodness of the $f(x)$ through the determination of various error probabilities. Fundamental to this assessment is the knowledge (given or calculated) of the quantity $P(H^1/x)=1-P(H^0/x)$. In fact, the generalization problem can be viewed simply as that of the determination of $P(H^1/x)$.

The distinction between problems 1) and 2), of course, is not always clear cut, nor can their solutions always be separately considered. For example, how well the characterization problem is solved clearly affects the success of an abstraction algorithm and the ability of the resultant decision function to generalize. In fact, it is generally recognized that problem 1) is really the principal problem in pattern recognition.

The present paper is devoted to a survey of the various algorithms for the solution of the abstraction problem of pattern classification only. Without minimizing their importance, the characterization and generalization problems will be discussed only to the extent that they are related to the abstraction problem.

II. Types of Available or Assumed Data

The various abstraction algorithms to be discussed require or assume different types of available data. In this section, we shall list these and establish a common notation to be used in the rest of the paper.

There are two pattern classes, H^1 and H^0. The probability of occurrence of patterns from the ith class is denoted by $P(H^i)$. If this probability is not explicitly given, then we shall assume it to be equal to $\frac{1}{2}$, i.e., both classes occur equally often. The pattern vectors will be denoted by x with the understanding that the components x_i are features determined as a result of the solution of the characterization problem. Four types of data concerning x will be considered.

1) Functional Form of the Conditional Density $p(x/H^i, \theta)$*:* By this we mean that the form of the conditional density functions of x for both classes is given to within the specification of a set of parameters θ. For example, it may be given that the pattern vectors from both classes are Gaussianly distributed with unknown mean and covariances.

2) Parameters of $p(x/H^i, \theta)$*:* By this it is meant that the values of the parameters θ are also known.

3) Sample Patterns with Known Classification: As part of the given data for the abstraction problem, one is often supplied with a set of training sample patterns of known classification. We denote the two sets

$$\{x^1(1), x^1(2), \cdots, x^1(n_1)\} \triangleq \chi^1(n_1)$$

$$\{x^0(1), x^0(2), \cdots, x^0(n_0)\} \triangleq \chi^0(n_0).$$

In this case we have two sets of n_1 and n_0 samples for classes H^1 and H^0, respectively. For notational compactness, the two sets are often joined to make a matrix, each row of which is a sample pattern from one of the two classes as shown below:

$$A = \begin{bmatrix} 1 & x^1(1)^T \\ \hline 1 & x^1(2)^T \\ \hline & \vdots \\ \hline 1 & x^1(n_1)^T \\ \hline -1 & -x^0(1)^T \\ \hline & \vdots \\ \hline -1 & -x^0(n_0)^T \end{bmatrix} (n_1 + n_0) \times (1 + m) \text{ matrix.}$$

The first column of ones and minus ones is used to indicate the known classification of the patterns.

4) Samples of Unknown Classification: In so-called problems of "training without a teacher," sample patterns of unknown classification are given. In this case they are simply indicated as

$$\chi(n) \triangleq \{x(1), x(2), \cdots, x(n)\}.$$

In connection with data types 3) and 4), it is always assumed that the samples are independently chosen. The order of appearance of these patterns is of no significance.

Depending on the combinations of data types 1)–4) that are supplied, different abstraction algorithms result. The following sections will classify and discuss the various algorithms on the basis of these available data and the natural mathematical techniques used in each case.

III. Case A—Data Types 1) and 2) Are Given

When the conditional density functions $p(x/H^i, \theta)$, including the values of θ are given, the problem reduces to that of simple hypothesis testing in statistics. The basic quantity of interest here is the *likelihood ratio* defined as

$$L(x) = \frac{p(x/H^i)}{p(x/H^0)}. \tag{3}$$

A decision function formed by comparing $L(x)$ against a threshold value η, i.e.,

$$f(x) = L(x) - \eta, \tag{4}$$

is known to be optimal for the following variety of criteria depending on the specific value of η (see, for example, Selin [52], ch. 2).

1) Neyman–Pearson Criterion: Let $X^1 \triangleq \{x|f(x) \geq 0\}$, $X^0 \triangleq \{x|f(x) < 0\}$, and let

$$\alpha \triangleq \int_{X^1} p(x/H^0)dx = \text{error probability of type 1} \tag{5}$$

$$\beta \triangleq \int_{X^0} p(x/H^1)dx = \text{error probability of type 2.} \tag{6}$$

If we select the value of η in (4) to yield a fixed value of α, then the decision function $f(x)$ has the property that it minimizes the value of β as compared to any other $f(x)$ yielding the same or smaller α.

2) Bayes Criterion: If the prior probabilities of occurrence of the two classes $P(H^i)$ as well as the cost of wrong decisions C_1 and C_2 for the two error types are given, then selecting

$$\eta = \frac{P(H^0)C_1}{P(H^1)C_2} \tag{7}$$

will minimize the average risk of making wrong decisions.

3) Minimax Criterion: If the prior probabilities $P(H^i)$ are unknown, then we may wish to choose the value of η so as to minimize the average risk against the worst value of $P(H^i)$. This is given implicitly by

$$C_1\alpha = C_2\beta. \tag{8}$$

Special Case of the Gaussian $p(x/H^i, \theta)$

In the case when $p(x/H^i, \theta)$ are Gaussian, the likelihood ratio can be explicitly written in terms of the means μ_i and covariances Σ_i, $i=0, 1$. Since the logarithm function is monotone, it is also customary to write $f(x)=\ln L(x)-\ln \eta$, and we have

$$f(x) = \frac{1}{2}[(x - \mu_0)^T\Sigma_0^{-1}(x - \mu_0) - (x - \mu_1)^T\Sigma_1^{-1}(x - \mu_1)] + \frac{1}{2}\ln\frac{|\Sigma_0|}{|\Sigma_1|} - \ln \eta, \tag{9}$$

i.e., the optimal decision functions are quadratic. If we furthermore assume that $\Sigma_1=\Sigma_0=\Sigma$, then (9) simplifies to a linear decision function:[6]

$$\begin{aligned} f(x) &= x^T\Sigma^{-1}(\mu_1 - \mu_0) + \text{constant term} \\ &\triangleq \alpha^T x + \alpha_0. \end{aligned} \tag{10}$$

In communication terminology, we let components of x represent the successive samples of an input waveform that may be a known signal plus noise or noise only. The components of α are then the impulse response of a linear discrete "matched filter" whose output at a given time is the value of the decision function $f(x)$. This is the solution to the problem of detecting the presence of a known signal in Gaussian noise.

A linear decision function of the type of (10) also arises naturally in other pattern classification approaches to be described later. Their ease of implementation is a major factor of their popularity. In fact, one is often led to consider only the determination of the best linear decision function based on the given input data. For the Gaussian case discussed here, this question has been resolved by Anderson and Bahadur [6].

[6] The α here is not to be confused with the α of (5).

Other Optimal Quadratic $f(x)$

A quadratic $f(x)$ of the type of (9) is actually optimal[7] for the more general type of distributions than Gaussian. Some of these generalizations have been studied by Cooper [12], [13]. Consider the case where $p(x/H^i)$ is given by

$$p(x/H^i) = A_i|\Sigma_i|^{-\frac{1}{2}}h[(x - \mu_i)^T\Sigma_i^{-1}(x - \mu_i)] \tag{11}$$

where h is a function integrable in m-space and monotone, i.e., $h(\alpha)$ decreases monotonically for increasing α, $0\leq\alpha<\infty$, and A_i is a constant adjusted to insure $\int p(x/H^i)dx=1$. It can be shown that μ_i and Σ_i are the mean and covariance matrices, respectively, of $p(x/H^i)$ and that the class encompasses a wide range of distributions including the normal, Laplace, and rectangular distributions. In the special case, when the determinants $|\Sigma_1|=|\Sigma_0|$, then the $f(x)$ is the optimal separating surface for spherical normal, Pearson II, and Pearson VII types of distributions [12].

Sequential Decision Procedures

In many classification problems, the features or attributes of a sample pattern, x_i, are received sequentially in a natural way, e.g., the x_i's are the sampled value of a waveform in time. In other cases, it may be advantageous to arrange to examine the features in decreasing order of significance with the hope that a classification can be reliably made without having to go through all the features of a pattern most of the time. In either case, one is led to the consideration of sequential decision functions.

The main tool used here is the sequential probability ratio test (SPRT) developed by Wald [59]. This is a natural extension of (3). Let

$$L_j(x) \triangleq L(x_1, \cdots, x_j) = \frac{p(x_1, \cdots, x_j/H^1)}{p(x_1, \cdots, x_j/H^0)}. \tag{12}$$

Instead of a binary choice of decisions after j features, we use the following analog of (4):

$$\begin{aligned} &L_j(x) - \eta_A \geq 0 && x \in H^1 \\ &L_j(x) - \eta_B \leq 0 && x \in H^0 \\ &\eta_B < L_j(x) < \eta_A && \text{Observe the next feature } x_{j+1}. \end{aligned} \tag{13}$$

It is well known that if we set

$$\eta_A = \frac{1 - \beta}{\alpha} \qquad \eta_B = \frac{\beta}{1 - \alpha} \tag{14}$$

where α and β are the misclassification probabilities defined in (5) and (6), then the decision function of (13) has the property that among all sequential tests with the same specified α and β this SPRT will require the smallest number of features to reach a classification decision, on the average.[8]

Computationally, the main problem in the use of SPRT is the recursive evaluation of the likelihood function. In

[7] In the sense of the Bayes criterion with equal cost of misclassification.

[8] This statement is true to within the accuracy of the so-called "excess over boundary" represented by $L_j(x)-\eta_A$ or $L_j(x)-\eta_B$ [59].

general, for real-time application one would like a formula of the type

$$L_{j+1}(x) = L_j(x) \times (\text{term involving } x_{j+1} \text{ only}) \tag{15}$$

or

$$\ln\left[L_{j+1}(x)\right] = \ln\left[L_j(x)\right] + \ln\left[x_{j+1} \text{ term}\right]. \tag{15a}$$

This turns out to be possible if the x_i belong to a fairly general class of Gaussian sequences. In particular, let

$$\begin{aligned} x_j &= Hy_j + v_j \\ y_j &= \Phi\, y_{j-1} + w_{j-1} \end{aligned} \tag{16}$$

where H is the measurement matrix and v_j and w_j are independent white Gaussian sequences with

$$\begin{aligned} E(v_j) &= 0 \qquad E(v_j v_i^T) = R_j \delta_{ij} \\ E(w_j) &= \bar{w}_j \qquad E\left[(w_j - \bar{w}_j)(w_i - \bar{w}_i)^T\right] = Q_j \delta_{ij}, \end{aligned} \tag{17}$$

i.e., the features are noise-corrupted linear combinations of the state of a vector Gauss-Markov sequence. Then a set of finite-dimensional sufficient statistics of the features exists in the form of conditional mean and covariances of the state y, $(\hat{y}, P_y)$, that is,

$$p(x_j/x_1, \cdots, x_{j-1}, H^i) \Leftrightarrow p(x_j/\hat{y}, P_y, H^i). \tag{18}$$

These statistics can be recursively updated in terms of the Kalman filter, well known in control theory [30].

The relationship (18) and the observation

$$\begin{aligned} &p(x_j, x_{j-1}, \cdots, x_1/H^i) \\ &\quad = p(x_j/x_1, \cdots, x_{j-1}, H^i)p(x_1, \cdots, x_{j-1}/H^i) \end{aligned} \tag{19}$$

immediately leads to (15). This powerful technique apparently has not been greatly exploited in detection theory and to an even lesser extent in the pattern classification literature.

Fu and his associates have studied various aspects of sequential methods as applied to pattern recognition. Fu and Chen [24] considered the reordering of the unobserved features so as to next observe the feature containing most significant information about the pattern. A straightforward SPRT is then applied to the features selected. For a SPRT with two parallel stopping boundaries as in (13) one can easily compute the average number of features required for a decision. This, however, does not guarantee that the decision process will terminate in every case. In practice it may not be possible to observe more than a finite number of features. Fu and Chien [11], [25] have suggested using a time-varying stopping boundary to assure a termination in a finite time.

Consider the features $x_1, x_2, \cdots, x_n$ approximated by a continuous time function $x(t)$. Our two hypotheses now involve determining $x(t)$ as samples from one of the two stochastic processes H^0 or H^1. Again the likelihood ratio can be formed and a continuous analog of a SPRT used for decision purposes:

$$L[x(t)] = \frac{p[x(t)/H^1]}{p[x(t)/H^0]}. \tag{20}$$

The modified SPRT is stated by the following inequalities:

$$\eta_B(t) < L[x(t)] < \eta_A(t) \tag{21}$$

where $\eta_B(t)$ and $\eta_A(t)$ are nondecreasing and nonincreasing functions of time, respectively. The decision is made as to class H^0 or H^1 when left or right inequality is violated. By making $\eta_A(t)$ and $\eta_B(t)$ functions of observation time, it is possible to insure that a decision is reached in a finite time.

The expected time of reaching a decision and the probabilities of error, of course, will be different from the usual SPRT. But they may be calculated and controlled in advance.

By arbitrarily assuming the form for the stopping boundary with undetermined parameters, an optimal modified SPRT with respect to the assumed structure can be designed. If we know the costs of continuing the observations and the cost of making a wrong decision using available information at every instant, the idea of dynamic programming can be used to arrive at the best stopping boundary, using the standard idea of backward sweep and the principle of optimality. In a practical situation, this may result in excessively large amounts of data that cannot be handled.

Summarizing, we may say that Case A is characterized by direct application of decision-theoretic ideas to pattern recognition. Because of the assumed availability of prior data, usually no iteration is involved in the determination of the decision function or separating surface.

IV. Case B—Data Types 1) and 3) Are Given

When the functional form of conditional density function $p(x/H^i, \theta)$ is given but θ are unknown parameters, the obvious modification involves the use of the given sample patterns with known classification to estimate these parameters before performing hypothesis testing. The basic quantity of interest still is the *likelihood ratio*, which is now defined as

$$L(x) = \frac{p(x/x^1(1)\cdots x^1(n), H^1)}{p(x/x^0(1)\cdots x^0(n), H^0)} \triangleq \frac{p(x/\chi^1(n), H^1)}{p(x/\chi^0(n), H^0)}. \tag{22}$$

We may write

$$p(x/\chi^i(n), H^i) = \int p(x/\theta, H^i)p(\theta/\chi^i(n), H^i)d\theta. \tag{23}$$

Assuming that the computation of (23) is straightforward, though it may be laborious, the determination of the conditional density $p(\theta/\chi^i(n)\, H^i)$ becomes the principal problem. We have, by Bayes' rule,

$$p[\theta/\chi^i(n)] = \frac{p[x^i(n)/\theta, \chi^i(n-1)]}{\int p[x^i(n)/\theta, \chi^i(n-1)]p[\theta/\chi^i(n-1)]d\theta} \cdot p[\theta/\chi^i(n-1)]$$

$$= \frac{p(x^i(n)/\theta)}{\int p(x^i(n)/\theta)p[\theta/\chi^i(n-1)]d\theta} p[\theta/\chi^i(n-1)] \tag{24}$$

where the simplification in the second step comes about due to the assumed conditional independence of the sample patterns.[9] We have also dropped the explicit dependence of $p[\theta/\chi^i(n)]$ in H^i for notational simplicity. It is understood that (24) has to be carried out for each class.

Equation (24) is a recursive computational procedure that is often referred to as "learning with a teacher." The computational feasibility of (24) depends critically on the existence of a fixed-dimensional sufficient statistic for the relevant prior and posterior density functions. In other words, one would like to be able to compute recursively a vector $\hat{\theta}_n^i$ with the property that

$$p(\theta/\hat{\theta}_n^i) \Leftrightarrow p[\theta/\chi^i(n)]. \tag{25}$$

Then instead of doing recursion on functions, which is the case for (24), one is only concerned with updating a set of numbers $\hat{\theta}_n^i$. Prior and posterior density functions that satisfy this requirement are called conjugate or reproducing pairs. They have been extensively studied by Raiffa and Schlaifer [49] and Spragins [55], [57]. It can be shown that in the limit of an infinite number of learning samples, the reproducing densities have the property that

$$\lim_{n\to\infty} \hat{\theta}_n \to \theta \tag{26}$$

in some appropriate sense. Thus, this learning scheme used with any of the decision functions of Case A is at least asymptotically optimal and in the limit produces results as good as if θ were known. In fact, if one interprets the α and β as average error probabilities with

$$\alpha \triangleq \int_{X^1} p(x/\theta, H^0)p(\theta/\chi^0(n), H^0)d\theta$$
$$\beta \triangleq \int_{X^0} p(x/\theta, H^1)p(\theta/\chi^1(n), H^1)d\theta \tag{27}$$

then optimality for a finite number of learning samples can also be claimed. In general, however, the relationship between system performance and this learning scheme for finite samples is only qualitative and has not been investigated thoroughly. Putting it less precisely, we have the question: Given the optimal decision function as a function of θ and the best estimate of θ, does the overall optimal decision function simply involve the replacement of θ by its estimate?

Special Case of Gaussian $p(x/H^i, \theta)$

Consider the case where $p(x/H^i, \theta)$ is $N(\theta^i, \Sigma)$, Σ given, and let $p(\theta^i)$ be $N(\bar{\theta}^i, P)$. An easy way to treat this problem is to consider

$$x^i = \theta^i + v \tag{28}$$

where v is $N(0, \Sigma)$. Then $p(\theta^i/\chi^i(n))$ is Gaussian with mean $\hat{\theta}_n^i$ and covariance P_n where

$$\hat{\theta}_n^i = \hat{\theta}_{n-1}^i + P\Sigma_n^{-1}(x^i(n) - \hat{\theta}_{n-1}^i), \qquad \hat{\theta}_0^i = \bar{\theta}^i \tag{29}$$
$$P_n = P_{n-1} - P_{n-1}(P_{n-1} + \Sigma)^{-1}P_{n-1}, \qquad P_0 = P. \tag{30}$$

This reduces $p(x/\chi_n^i, H^i)$ to a Gaussian distribution with mean $\hat{\theta}_n^i$ and covariance $P_n + \Sigma$. The numbers $\hat{\theta}_n^i$ and P_n constitute a set of finite-dimensional sufficient statistics for $\chi^i(n)$. If Σ is the same for the two categories, we have the linear decision function as

$$f(x) = \alpha^T x + \alpha_0$$
$$\alpha^T = (P_n + \Sigma)^{-1}(\hat{\theta}_n^1 - \hat{\theta}_n^0).$$

Note that (29) and (30) are a special case of the Kalman filter mentioned in (16) and (17) (with $\Phi = 0$ and $w_i = 0$). This was first worked out independently by Abramson and Braverman [1].

If Σ is also unknown, then the conjugate density is Gauss-Wishart (Keehn [33]). If Σ_i are known but different or if θ^i are time varying and can be represented by a Gauss-Markov process, then the theory of the Kalman filter can again be directly used to develop decision functions (or, equivalently, estimates for θ^i) that *tracks* the variations.

It should be pointed out that convergence of the estimates of θ using reproducing densities as suggested by (24) and (29) ignores the problem of round-off errors in the computations associated with these equations. In practical calculations using computers with finite word length there will be a steady-state estimation error depending on the size of the round-off error. This fact is well known to control engineers using the Kalman-Bucy filter of (29) and (30). In the context of pattern classification Cover [14] has discussed this problem and suggested some alternate approaches.

Special Case of Discrete Distribution

In the discussion so far, the learning of $L(x)$ [from (22)–(24)] and the determination of $f(x)$ [from (4)] are two separate problems. In certain simplified cases it is possible to devise a learning procedure for $f(x)$ directly. Sklansky [54] has considered the classification of a sequence of independent binary signals transmitted over a noisy channel. Let $x(j)$ be the channel outputs; we consider a decision function

$$f(x) = x - \eta. \tag{31}$$

If the distribution of x as well as the choice of η values is discrete, then for a given procedure of changing η values after each wrong decision, the probabilities of η at the various permissible values form a Markov chain. The property and convergence of this Markov chain can be straightforwardly calculated once the transition probabilities (i.e., the learning procedures) are given. From this, the error probabilities of $f(x)$ follow.

[9] By conditional independence we mean $p(x^i(n)/\theta) = p[x^i(n)/\theta, x^i(n-1), \cdots, x^i(1)]$.

The performance of a scheme of this type depends to a large extent on the type of updating for η. Kaplan and Sklansky [31] have analyzed the properties of Markov chains resulting from some typical learning procedures specified on an intuitive basis.

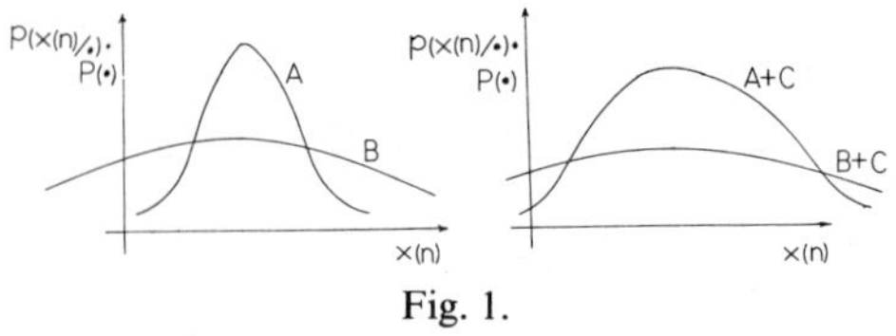

Fig. 1.

V. Case C—Data Types 1) and 4) Are Given

In this case, the given set of sample patterns will be used again to learn the parameters θ. But now the given learning samples are unclassified, bringing in additional uncertainty Appropriately, this type of learning is often called "learning without a teacher." In 1962 Daly [16] suggested a scheme that works in this case, but the computation grows exponentially. Later Fralick suggested a bounded scheme [21], [22], that was further extended by Patrick and Hancock [46].

The basic ideas in Section IV still apply here. We may rewrite (24) as

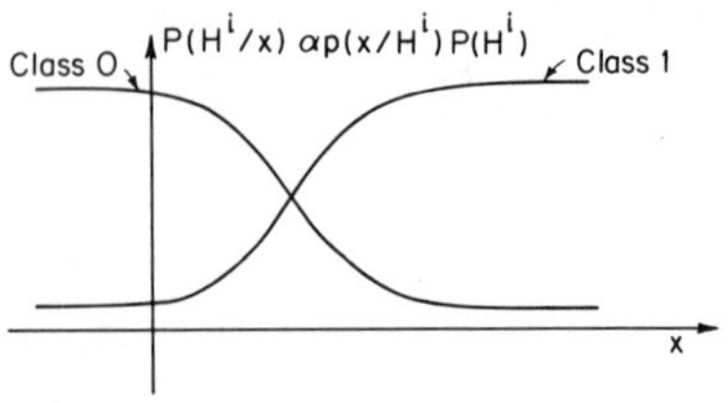

Fig. 2.

As $n \to \infty$ all three schemes will show similar learning behavior, and the learning behavior of 1) and 2) will be the same even for finite n.

$$\begin{aligned} p(\theta/\chi(n)) &= \frac{p(x(n)/\theta, \chi(n-1))}{p(x(n)/\chi(n-1))} p(\theta/\chi(n-1)) \\ &= \frac{p\{x(n)/\theta, \chi(n-1), H^0\}P(H^0) + p\{x(n)/\theta, \chi(n-1), H^1\}P(H^1)}{p(x(n)/\chi(n-1), H^0)P(H^0) + p(x(n)/\chi(n-1), H^1)P(H^1)} p(\theta/\chi(n-1)). \end{aligned} \tag{32}$$

The only difference occurs in the way we compute the ratio between prior and posterior density. The added term essentially represents a form of hedging.

Heuristically, we can see the effect as follows. Consider the case where only class 1 contains the unknown parameter θ. Now the multiplying factor on the right-hand side of (32) is in the form $(C+A)/(C+B)$ where $C=p[x(n)/\chi(n-1), H^0]P(H^0)$, $A=p[x(n)/\chi(n-1),\ \theta,\ H^1]P(H^1)$, and $B=p[x(n)/\chi(n-1), H^1]P(H^1)$. For the case where $x(n)$ actually came from class 1, we generally will have the density function of A and B and $A+C$ and $B+C$ appear as in Fig. 1. Since the convergence of (32) depends on the "peakness" of the multiplying factor, this tends to indicate that the process of learning will be slower in the case of "learning without a teacher." Essentially, we are paying for the uncertainty about the classification of learning samples in terms of slower learning. Viewed in this light, the difference between learning with or without a teacher is conceptually minimal. Another example illustrates this point. Consider the classification problem shown in Fig. 2.

Suppose

1) A set of samples $\chi(n)$ was taken, correct classification was attached to these, and a scheme of Section IV was used.
2) A set of samples $\chi(n)$ was taken, classifications were assigned according to the probability $P(H^i/x)$, and a scheme of Section IV was used.
3) A set of samples $\chi(n)$ was taken and a scheme of Sectior V was used.

Computationally, (32) is much more difficult than its counterpart, (24). With the presence of the additional terms the reproducing property is lost.

Interpretation of (32) also requires some care. Since learning samples are unclassified, (32) cannot be carried out separately for each class in general. Let θ represent the unknown parameters in both classes, θ^1 and θ^0. If, in addition, we assume $p(\theta^1, \theta^0/\chi(n))=p(\theta^1/\chi(n))p(\theta^0/\chi(n))$, then we can separate (32) as:

$$p(\theta^i/\chi(n)) = \frac{\sum_{j=0}^{1} p(x(n)/\theta^i, \chi(n-1), H^j)p(H^j)}{\sum_{j=0}^{1} p(x(n)/\chi(n-1), H^j)p(H^j)} p(\theta^i/\chi(n-1) \qquad i = 0, 1. \tag{33}$$

Furthermore, we can usually write $p(x(n)/\theta^i, \chi(n-1), H^j) = p(x(n)/\chi(n-1), H^j)$, $j \neq i$. Equation (33) is essentially Fralick's scheme. Note that if $p(\theta^i/\chi(n))$ is identical for $i=0, 1$ and $P(H^0)=P(H^1)$, then no learning can take place. In the work of Patrick and Hancock [46] the independence assumption of θ^0 and θ^1 is not made and computation must take place via the single equation (32) with the resultant added complexity. The only simplification is to note that $p(x(n)/\theta, \chi(n-1, H^j) = p(x(n)/\theta^j, \chi(n-1), H^j)$ for $j=0, 1$.

The main advantage of learning without a teacher results from the fact that when actual processing of data is in progress (after initial learning from the sample patterns with classification) learning can still continue and eventually a machine learning this way may do much better than a machine that is trained only by initial learning with classified samples.

Very little computational result has been reported in the literature [56] although our society seems to abound with real-life examples of "learning without a teacher" or even "learning in spite of the teacher."

VI. Case D—Data Type 3) Given Only (Deterministic Methods)

The previous three sections dealt with algorithms that require knowledge of the structural forms of the underlying distributions of the pattern classes. Criticism has often been raised that in practice information concerning data type 1) is seldom available. This has prompted development of algorithms for the construction of decision functions that do not require 1). Basically, the idea is to find an $f(x)$ that works well at least on the given samples of known classification.

Two implicit assumptions of this approach are as follows.

1) A sufficient number of samples from both classes is available to constitute two representative groups.
2) The characteristic problem (i.e., $x=\phi(z)$) has been solved using a sufficiently rich class of $\phi(z)$'s so that it is only necessary to examine the class of linear $f(x)$ to solve the abstraction problem.

Assumption 2) is often justified on the basis of the Weierstrass approximation theorem. However, this merely transfers the difficulty to the characterization problem since one is still faced with the problem of finding a class of complete $\phi(z)$'s that can efficiently represent the pattern. Furthermore, relatively little work has been done on defining the adjectives "sufficient," "representative," and "efficient." The works of Cover [14], Nilsson [44], Allais [4], and Watanabe [60] bear on this aspect of the problem. We shall discuss them separately later.

Accepting assumptions 1) and 2), one can now restate the problem of abstraction more succinctly. Let there be a total of N patterns given (n_1 in class H^1, n_0 in H^0, $n_0+n_1=N$) and consider the linear decision function

$$f(x) = \mathfrak{a}^T x + \mathfrak{a}_0. \tag{34}$$

The problem of determining an $f(x)$ that classifies all the given patterns correctly is equivalent to the problem of finding a solution to the vector inequality

$$Aw > 0 \tag{35}$$

where

$$A = \begin{bmatrix} 1 & x^{1^T}(i) \\ -1 & -x^{0^T}(i) \end{bmatrix} \begin{matrix} \} \, i = 1, \cdots, n_1; \text{class 1 samples} \\ \} \, i = 1, \cdots, n_0; \text{class 0 samples} \end{matrix} \tag{36}$$

$$w = \begin{bmatrix} \mathfrak{a}_0 \\ \mathfrak{a} \end{bmatrix} \tag{37}$$

A common procedure for solving linear inequalities is to transform the problem into an optimization problem, the solution of which also guarantees a solution for (35). For example, consider

$$\min_w J(w) \triangleq \min_w \| \, |Aw| - Aw \, \|^2. \tag{38}$$

The solution for (35), if it exists, must correspond to the minimum of (38), which is zero. If we try a gradient descent procedure for minimizing (38), then we are led immediately to

$$\begin{aligned} w(j+1) &= w(j) + \rho \left.\frac{\partial J}{\partial w}\right|_{w=w(j)} \\ &= w(j) + \rho A^T[|Aw(j)| - Aw(j)]; \qquad \rho > 0 \end{aligned} \tag{39}$$

or[10]

$$w(j+1) = w(j) + \rho \sum_{i=1}^{N} x(i)[|x(i)^T w(j)| - x^T(i) w(j)]. \tag{39a}$$

Algorithms of the type of (39) are often referred to as *many pattern adaptation* in the sense that all given pattern samples are used in one iteration of the weighting vector w. The corresponding *single pattern adaptation* of (39) is

$$w(j+1) = w(j) + \rho x(j)(|x(j)^T w(j)| - x(j)^T w(j)). \tag{40}$$

For $\rho=2$, (40) is simply the well-known perceptron algorithm (Novikoff [45]) which was originally developed on the simple idea of reward and punishment and which is known to converge in a finite number of steps.

The idea of viewing a learning algorithm as an iterative and deterministic optimization procedure for some criterion function can be used to interpret other algorithms and to discover new ones. In fact, our ability to create new algorithms is only limited by our ability to find meaningful new criteria. Table I identifies a set of algorithms as gradient procedures for a corresponding set of criterion functions.

The Generalization Question

One of the basic problems of the algorithms of this type is the question of generalization. In the absence of any probabilisitic information, the only result along this line seems to be the important result of Cover [14]. Cover shows that in general the number of samples N must be at least equal to or larger than twice the number of attributes m for the algorithm of this case to yield meaningful results. If we allow ourselves the luxury of Gaussian x_i, then Allais demonstrates a more explicit relationship between N, m, and the LMS algorithm of Table I [4]. Another interesting property of the LMS algorithm is pointed out by Groner [27]. It turns out that the $w \triangleq \{\mathfrak{a}_0, \mathfrak{a}\}$ which minimizes $\|Aw - \beta_0\|^2$ can also be expressed as

[10] In (39a), we have abused our notation to let $x(i)$ represent the vector $\begin{bmatrix} \pm 1 \\ x(i) \end{bmatrix}$

TABLE I*

Authors	Algorithms	Criterion $J(w)$
Widrow-Hoff [61]†	$w(j+1) = \rho A^T(Aw(j) - \beta_0)$	$J(w) = \lVert Aw - \beta_0 \rVert^2,\ \beta_0^T = [1, 1, \cdots, 1]$
Agmon-Mays [2], [36]	$w(j+1) = w(j) + \rho A^T[\lvert Aw(j) - \beta_0 \rvert - (Aw(j) - \beta_0)]$	$J(w) = \lVert (Aw - \beta_0) - \lvert Aw - \beta_0 \rvert \rVert^2,\ \beta_0^T = [1, 1, \cdots, 1]$
Wong-Eisenberg [62]‡	$Aw(j+1) = Aw(j) + \rho A(A^TA)^{-1}A^T[\beta_0 - \operatorname{sgn}(Aw(j))]$	
Ho-Kashyap [29]	$w(j+1) = w(j) + \rho SA^T[Aw(j) - \beta(j)]$ $\beta(j+1) = \beta(j) + [(Aw(j) - \beta(j) + \lvert Aw(j) - \beta(j) \rvert]$ where ρ and S are chosen to insure $[\rho^2 SA^TAS - 2\rho S] < 0$	$J(w, \beta) = \lVert Aw - \beta \rVert^2,\ \beta > 0$

* For a more detailed table see [17].
† Solution of this algorithm is not equivalent to the solution of $Aw > 0$.
‡ This algorithm is different from the Ho-Kashyap algorithm with $S = (A^TA)^{-1}$ only in the sense that β_0 is constant here.

$$\alpha = (\Sigma_s^1 + \Sigma_s^0)^{-1}(\mu_s^1 - \mu_s^0)$$
$$\alpha_0 = (\mu_s^1 + \mu_s^0)(\Sigma_s^1 + \Sigma_s^0)(\mu_s^1 + \mu_s^0) \tag{41}$$

where

μ_s^i = sample mean of class H^i
Σ_s^i = sample covariance of class H^i.

Furthermore, the α in (41) also maximizes the Mahalanobis distance criterion [5]

$$J = \frac{[\alpha^T(\mu_s^1 - \mu_s^0)]^2}{\alpha^T(\Sigma_s^1 + \Sigma_s^0)\alpha} \tag{42}$$

which has the simple interpretation of maximizing interclass distance and minimizing total dispersion of the projections of the patterns onto the decision surface $f(x)$.

Equation (41) can be further generalized. Peterson and Mattson [48] have shown that for a linear decision function of the type of (32) and a criterion function J which depends only on sample means and covariances of the two classes, the optimal α is given via

$$\alpha = (k_1\Sigma_s^1 + k_0\Sigma_s^0)^{-1}(\mu_s^1 - \mu_s^0) \tag{43}$$

where k_0 and k_1 are constants that can be determined.[11]

While these connections of the linear decision function and the statistical parameters of the sample patterns are interesting, they do not completely answer the generalization question in terms of the error probabilities α and β of (5) and (6).

A recent important result of Cover and Hart [15] is an exception to this point. They show that if we classify a sample by the classification of its nearest (according to some distance measure) neighboring sample of known classification (an extremely simple-minded approach), the probability of such a decision for large number of samples is *bounded from above* by twice the optimal Bayes error probabilities of Section III [criterion 2)] where all the underlying probabilities are known. This tends to suggest that the schemes described in this section, which are more sophisticated than the nearest neighbor algorithm, should also have similar bounds on error. Communications with experimental workers in the field tend to confirm this. This nearest neighbor decision function is originally due to Fix and Hodges [23].

Two other statistical techniques commonly used in data analysis called "jacknife" and "leaving-one-out" [39] may be useful in shedding further light on this question. The latter technique consists of successively solving a series of optimization problems, each time leaving out a different sample pattern. Variation in the solutions of these problems will then indirectly provide a quantitative answer to the adequateness of assumption 1). This approach apparently has not been exploited in the usual pattern classification literature.

The Characterization Problem

Although we conveniently avoided the question of how to choose a mapping $\phi: z \rightarrow x$, the question is nevertheless an important one. There do not seem to be many generally applicable schemes which possess noteworthy properties that are independent of the particular type of recognition problems in question. An important result due to Watanabe [60] does, however, fill the requirement. Consider the (sample) covariance matrices of each class Σ_{z^1} and Σ_{z^0} and the linear combination

$$\Sigma = P(H^1)\Sigma_{z^1} + P(H^0)\Sigma_{z^0}. \tag{44}$$

Let the dimension $(z) = p$, which is usually very large compared to the desired dimension for x, m. Let the vectors $t_1, t_2, \cdots, t_p$ be the normalized eigenvectors of Σ ordered according to $\lambda_1(\Sigma) \geq \lambda_2(\Sigma) \geq \cdots \geq \lambda_p(\Sigma)$. The t_i form a basis in p-space.[12] We may write

$$z = \sum_{i=1}^{p} x_i t_i \quad \text{with} \quad x_i = z^T t_i. \tag{45}$$

The magnitude of x_i or, more accurately, $P(H^1)(x_i^1)^2 + P(H^0)(x_i^0)^2 \triangleq e_i$ can be considered as a good measure of the extent to which the coordinate vector t_i is useful in representing the members of the two classes. It turns out in this setup that the following properties are true.

1) The t_i coordinate system has the least square approximation property:

[11] The validity of (43) is, of course, still good if we replace sample means and covariances by true means and covariances.

[12] They constitute the Karhunen-Loeve coordinate system.

$$E\left\{P(H^1)(z^1 - \sum_{i=1}^{m} x_i t_i)^2 + P(H^0)(z^0 - \sum_{i=1}^{m} x_i t_i)^2\right\}$$
$$= \min_{s_i} E\left\{P(H^1)(z^1 - \sum_{i=1}^{m} x_i s_i)^2 + P(H^0)(z^0 - \sum_{i=1}^{m} x_i s_i)^2\right\} \quad \text{for all } m. \tag{46}$$

2) The t_i coordinate system minimizes the entropy function

$$S(t_i) \triangleq -\sum_{i=1}^{p} e_i \ln e_i \tag{47}$$

among all possible coordinate systems, where e_i are as defined above. Properties 1) and 2) imply that there exists a natural [according to (46) and (47)] characterization of the attributes in terms of the large eigenvectors of the composite covariance matrix of the problem. This phenomenon is related to the method of factor analysis and we shall encounter it again in Section VIII.

Extension to Nonlinear $f(x)$

Once the approach for the linear case is clear, the extension to the nonlinear case is conceptually straightforward. Instead of linear inequalities, we deal with nonlinear inequalities or piecewise linear [44] inequalities. Various established or *ad hoc* techniques in nonlinear programming can be brought to bear on the abstraction problem [34], [35], [51].

Arkadev and Braverman [7] have suggested an algorithm that tries to arrive at a piecewise linear $f(x)$ from the given set of classified x. The algorithm proceeds to find the best hyperplane to separate the given samples. As more samples come and this plane fails to classify them, more hyperplanes are connected to it until all given samples are correctly classified. Finally, all redundant portions of the planes are deleted, giving a piecewise linear $f(x)$.

VII. Case E—Data Type 3) Only Given (Stochastic Methods)

The algorithms described in Section VI, with the exception of the nearest neighbor algorithm, despite their simplicity and practical usefulness, suffer one general drawback in terms of relating the decision functions obtained to a quantitative evaluation of its generalization capabilities. Since the latter question is best answered in terms of error probabilities, or equivalently the knowledge of $P(H^i/x)$, some probabilistic structure will have to be put back into the formulation of the problem, implicitly or explicitly.

One approach to this problem is to consider that $P(H^i/x)$ as a function of x can be expanded in a series. Let us consider

$$f(x) \triangleq P(H^1/x) - P(H^0/x) \triangleq 2P(H^1/x) - 1 \triangleq \sum_{j=0}^{\infty} \alpha_j \phi_j(x) \tag{48}$$

where $\phi_i(x)$ is some class of complete (possibly orthonormal) functions which one conveniently assumes to be given as a result of solving the characterization problem. For every given sample pattern, there corresponds a $\phi[x(i)]$ or $\phi(i)$. The problem is then simply reduced to the determination of the parameters α_j of a function $f(x)$ when the values of the function are measured at randomly selected points. This is essentially the approach taken by Aizerman, Braverman, and Rozonoer [3], Tsypkin [58], Blaydon and Ho [9], Kashyap and Blaydon [32], Patterson, Wagner, and Womack [47], and Nicolic and Fu [43].[13] Define a classification variable $\zeta[x(i)]$ by

$$\zeta[x(i)] = \begin{cases} 1 & x(i) \in H^1 \\ -1 & x(i) \in H^0. \end{cases} \tag{49}$$

One may visualize $\zeta(i)$ as a *noisy* measurement of the value of the function $f(x)$ at the sample point (pattern) $\zeta(i)$:

$$\zeta(i) \triangleq f[\phi(i)] + v(i) \tag{50}$$

where $v(i)$ are independent random variables with

$$\begin{aligned} E[v(i)] &= [1 - f(i)]P[H^1/x(i)] \\ &\quad + [-1 - f(i)][1 - P(H^1/x(i))] \\ &= 2[1 - P(H^1/x(i))]P(H^i/x(i)) \\ &\quad - 2P(H^1/x(i))(1 - P(H^1/x(i))] = 0. \end{aligned} \tag{51}$$

Now consider the minimization of the regression function

$$J = \min_{\alpha} E\{\|\zeta - \alpha^T\phi\|^2\} \tag{52}$$

which in view of (50) and (51) can be shown to be equivalent to

$$J^1 = \min_{\alpha} E\{\|f(x) - \alpha^T\phi\|^2\}. \tag{53}$$

Thus, if one finds a finite-dimensional α that minimizes J in (52), then one has also found the optimal mean square approximation to $f(x)$. A well-known method for minimization of regression functions is via stochastic approximation using the given noisy sample values of the function. We have

$$\alpha(i+1) = \alpha(i) + \rho(i)\phi(i)[\zeta(i) - \alpha^T(i)\phi(i)] \tag{54}$$

with

$$\sum_{i=1}^{\infty} \rho(i) = \infty; \qquad \sum_{i=1}^{\infty} \rho^2(i) < \infty. \tag{55}$$

With mild assumptions on ϕ, the algorithm of (54) is known to converge with probability 1 to α^* where

$$\alpha^* = \arg\min E\{\|\zeta - \alpha^T\phi\|^2\}. \tag{56}$$

Hence,

$$\alpha^* = \arg\min E\{\|f(x) - \alpha^T\phi\|^2\}.$$

[13] These methods are also called "potential function" methods [7] in the Russian literature.

This constitutes a learning scheme with a teacher which is asymptotically optimal in a mean square sense with respect to the classification probabilities. Another way of visualizing (54) is to note that

$$\phi(i)[\zeta(i) - \alpha^T(i)\phi(i)] = \left.\frac{\partial\|\zeta - \alpha^T\phi\|^2}{\partial\alpha}\right|_{\phi(i)}$$

and (54) is simply the stochastic analog of the gradient method for minimization. In fact, if one considers instead

$$\alpha(i+1) = \alpha(i) + \rho(i)S\phi(i)[\zeta(i) - \alpha^T(i)\phi(i)] \qquad (54a)$$

where

$$S \triangleq [E(\phi\phi^T)]^{-1} \qquad (57)$$

one has the analog of the second-order descent method, which generally converges faster. Since S in (57) is not given in general, one may substitute instead

$$S(i) = \left[\frac{1}{i}\sum_{j=1}^{i}\phi(j)\phi(j)^T\right]^{-1} \triangleq iP(i). \qquad (58)$$

Not surprisingly, the recursive computation of $P(i)$ is governed by

$$P(i+1) = P(i) - P(i)\phi(i)\{\phi(i)^T P(i)\phi(i) + 1\}^{-1}\phi(i)^T P(i);$$
$$P(1) = I \qquad (59)$$

which is a special case of (56). Furthermore, $\alpha(i+1)$ from (54) has the property that

$$\alpha(i+1) = \arg\min \sum_{j=1}^{i+1} [\zeta(j) - \alpha^T\phi(j)]^2.$$

In other words, it is also the solution of the LMS algorithm of Section VI. Using the method of stochastic approximation, one can show [9] that (54a) also converges with probability 1 to α^*, thus furnishing additional rationalization for the LMS algorithm.

Of course, the criterion of (52) is not the only one that can be used in this approach. A table similar to Table I of Section VI can be constructed. For details see [17].

In practice, the convergence of most stochastic approximation methods is notoriously slow. Sometimes they appear not to converge at all. Largely, this is due to the problem of round-off error mentioned in Section IV. Thus, until real (not academic) success stories have been reported, the practicality of the above scheme is not overwhelmingly strong.

The choice of the base function set ϕ has also been so far left open. A particular approach to the problem has been suggested by Brick [10]. Instead of expanding $f(x)$ in a series, $p(x/H^i)$ may be expanded in a series of orthonormal functions, the normalized hermite functions. Brick has shown that these coefficients appear as some ensemble average that, given certain *a priori* information, can be precomputed. In the case of ergodic processes, however, these ensemble averages can be replaced by time averages and can be easily determined experimentally, given a set of classified samples for initial learning. Furthermore, if the system parameters are known to change gradually, a bootstrap updating of these coefficients is possible during the run, improving continuously on the "learned" coefficients.

The main advantage of this scheme is the possibility of implementation in circuit form for ergodic processes, where the coefficients appear only as amplifier gains that can be easily preadjusted or changed automatically. The number of terms to be used in the expansion depends, however, on the complexity of the form of $p(x/H^i)$. In practical situations the implementation may not be feasible for any moderately complex system.

VIII. Case F—Data Type 4) Given Only

This is the extreme case in pattern classification where minimal information is available for the design of $f(x)$. Not much has been reported in the literature about the approaches for this case, which are often heuristic or experimental, justified only by the fact that they work in some sense according to the author. Conceptually the problem can be resolved in either one of two ways.

Method 1

The first method consists of reintroducing, explicitly or implicitly, some criterion of separation onto the set of unclassified sample patterns. This is used in conjunction with the same algorithms of Case D (Section VI) in a bootstrap fashion, i.e., one uses the result of classification at one iteration to produce the classified learning sample for the learning cycle. For example, a bootstrap algorithm results if we try to rewrite (52) as

$$J = \min_{\alpha} E\{\|\alpha^T\phi - \operatorname{sgn}(\alpha^T\phi)\|^2\}. \qquad (60)$$

Miller [37] has examined this criterion function for a linear $f(x)$, i.e., where ϕ is only x. For this case J becomes

$$J' = \min_{\alpha} E\{\|\alpha^T x - \operatorname{sgn}(\alpha^T x)\|^2\} \qquad (60a)$$

and an algorithm parallel to (54) may be given as

$$\alpha(k+1) = \alpha(k) - 2\rho(k)[\alpha^T(k)x(k) - \operatorname{sgn}\{\alpha^T(k)x(k)\}]x(k) \qquad (61)$$

with

$$\sum_{k=1}^{\infty}\rho(k) = \infty; \qquad \sum_{k=1}^{\infty}\rho^2(k) < \infty.$$

Miller found that the J' surface, in general, has saddle points and local minima. In the case of Gaussian distributions with the same covariance matrix and $\mu_1 = -\mu_0$, the J' surface has two local minima with the same minimum value and the algorithm of (61) converges to one of the two minima with probability 1. However, in this case the value of α at one minimum is the negative of the value at the other. As the decision takes place according to $\alpha^T x \gtrless 0$, the decision surface using either value merely results in the relabeling of the classes.

It should be pointed out that if this externally imposed

criterion of separation happens to resemble the natural criterion of separation, then all is well. For instance, consider the two-dimensional example shown in Fig. 3 where the actual identity of the sample points is unknown to the classifier. One can nevertheless require that a separating plane (linear decision function) be constructed with the normal α coinciding with the direction of the maximal eigenvector of the covariance matrix of the sample points, that is:

$$\alpha \text{ parallel to the maximal eigenvector of } (A^T A) \quad (62)$$

where

$$A = \begin{bmatrix} x^T(1) \\ ---- \\ \vdots \\ ---- \\ x^T(N) \end{bmatrix}. \quad (63)$$

If this eigenvector direction is determined via the usual iterative power method, then one has derived a learning scheme that works. However, it is equally obvious that had the two classes been distributed as in Fig. 4 the learning scheme would have failed. This approach actually forms the essence of a very successful bootstrap self-correction scheme by Nagy and Shelton [42] for character recognition and is closely related to the method of principal components in factor analysis.

A slightly different approach to introducing a criterion has been taken by Rogers and Tanimoto [50]. A distance measure d_{ij} for x_i and x_j may be defined as

$$d_{ij} = g(x_i, x_j). \quad (64)$$

Assuming there are only two classes, we define a homogeneity function for each class. The function has d_{ij}, the interpair distances of the various sample patterns, as its arguments. The assignment of a given sample pattern to a particular class changes the value of the homogeneity function of that class. The criterion of classification is that the two homogeneity functions have minimal difference in their value. Analytically we may visualize this as follows.

Let

$$u_1(d_{12}, d_{13}, \cdots, d_{n-1,n}; \eta)$$
$$u_0(d_{12}, d_{13}, \cdots, d_{n-1,n}; \eta)$$

be the homogeneity functions involved. η is a parameter that assigns the usage of a particular d_{ij} to the evaluation of u_0 or u_1.[14] Classification then involves the choice of η such that the difference $u_1 - u_0$ is minimized.

This scheme can very easily be generalized to a multiclass case where the number of classes is not known *a priori*. We shall encounter it again in this light in Section IX.

[14] For example, Rogers and Tanimoto successively include more and more d_{ij} in the evaluation of u_0 or u_1 until they exceed a certain value. The assumption here is that each class should be homogeneously similar. If for a given η, $u_1 \gg u_0$, then some member of class 1 should be class 0 and vice versa.

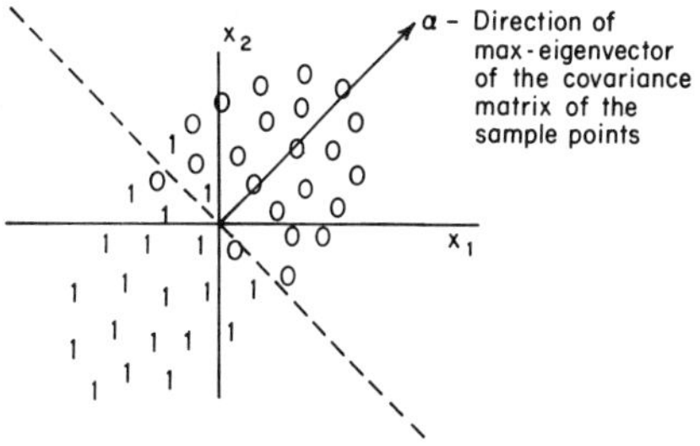

Fig. 3.

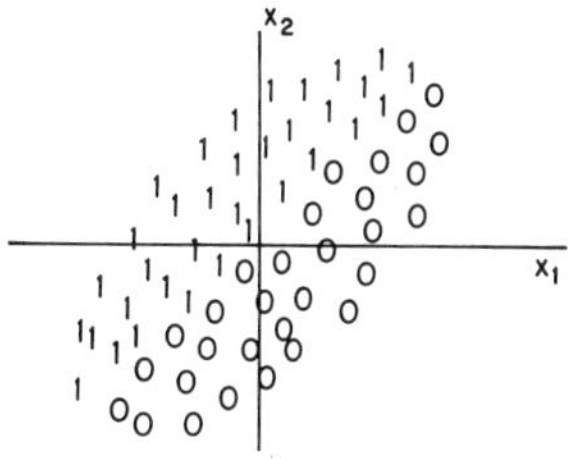

Fig. 4.

The above examples can all be viewed as special cases in which the algorithm attempts to separate the given unknown samples into distinct clusters in feature space. The most recent survey of clustering techniques was done by Ball [8].

Method 2

Attempt a more or less brute force computation of the learning equation (32) in Section V. The pertinent probability density functions are approximated by histograms using the given data. Patrick and Hancock claim convergence of this computational procedure [46]. However, little or no actual experiences have been reported. Due to the lack of sufficient statistics and the large amount of data usually required for histograms to yield good approximations, the feasibility of such a scheme remains to be demonstrated.

IX. Multiclass Problem

So far we have concerned ourselves only with two-class problems. A few words about multiclass problems are in order.

In a multiclass problem we have to decide to which of m classes $H^1, H^2, H^3, \cdots, H^m$ the given pattern vector x belongs. For problems having a probabilistic structure, i.e., from Cases A, B, C, and E, the extension to a multiclass case is straightforward. Instead of considering the likelihood ratio formed by the two conditional probabilities and testing it against a threshold for a two-class case, we may directly consider $p(x/H^i)$ or $P(H^i/x)$ and pick the largest of these.[15] This procedure is optimal in the sense that it minimizes the error probability.

More generally, we may define a set of decision functions $f^i(x)$ and take decisions as x belonging to H^i if

$$f^i(x) > f^j(x) \qquad \text{for all } j \neq i; \quad (65)$$

[15] $p(x/H^i)$ minimizes error probability only if $p(H^i)$ are equal.

for the problems of Cases A, B, C, and E

$$f^i(x) = p(x/H^i) \quad \text{or} \quad P(H^i/x). \tag{66}$$

In the case of deterministic algorithms (nonprobabilistic structure) the extension to multiclass problems is not as natural. A multiclass problem is usually reduced to a collection of two-class problems. This reduction depends on the separability that exists in the multiclass problem and may be of three types, as follows.

1) Each class may be separable from all the rest by a single decision surface. Then we may take the decision according to

$$f^i(x) \begin{matrix} > 0 & \text{if } x \in H^i \\ < 0 & \text{otherwise.} \end{matrix}$$

This reduces the multiclass problem to $m-1$ two-class problems.

2) Each class may be separable from each other class. Now we have $m(m-1)/2$ two-class problems and as many decision functions such that

$$f^{ij}(x) \begin{matrix} > 0 & \text{if } x \in H^i \\ < 0 & \text{if } x \in H^j \end{matrix} \quad \text{given that } x \text{ belongs to } H^i \text{ or } H^j. \tag{67}$$

The unknown x is classified as H^i *only if* [16]

$$f^{ij}(x) > 0 \qquad \text{for all } j \neq i.$$

3) There exist m $f^i(x)$ such that x belongs to H^i only if

$$f^i(x) > f^j(x) \qquad \text{for all } j \neq i. \tag{68}$$

Note that this is a special case of 2) as we may define

$$f^{ij}(x) = f^i(x) - f^j(x) \qquad \text{for all } j \neq i. \tag{69}$$

In Cases A, B, C, and E, as we noted earlier, $f^i(x)$ of (68) are the conditional probabilities. For deterministic Case D, a criterion of separation is introduced. For example, one may consider the inverse of distance criterion, which is the extension of the "nearest neighbor" approach to this case.

The way we may try to reduce a multiclass problem to a set of two-class problems depends on the individual problem. It should be pointed out that if we are not restricting $f^i(x)$ to be of a particular form (linear or quadratic, etc.) then the distinction of these three types is artificial, as we can always find suitable $f^i(x)$ to use with any of the desired three types.

Though we have presented all the algorithms as they are applicable to two-class problems, they have often been extended to the multiclass case. The number of classes is assumed known in all these schemes. One exception is the paper by Rogers and Tanimoto [50] mentioned under Case F. The procedure they use is independent of the knowledge of the number of classes. By computing an auxiliary index of "typicality," they permit the procedure to adjust itself to produce automatically the number of classes that will satisfy a homogeneity criterion.

[16] Some irrelevant results will be obtained in the process from the cases where x coming from H^k, $k \neq i, j$ is being tried.

X. Conclusion

Based on the above survey and analysis, a few remarks (perhaps controversial) seem in order.

1) Roughly speaking, classification algorithms can be broadly divided into two groups: probabilistically based and nonprobabilistically based. The former group, comprising Cases A–C, enjoys the obvious advantage of being easily able to assess the generalization ability of the results. On the other hand, it is often difficult to justify the availability of the assumed data. The latter group, representing Cases D–F, is just the reverse. By being more realistic on input data requirements, it makes precise quantitative evaluation of performance much more involved and difficult, although it seems reasonable to assume that as our analytical ability advances this difficulty will gradually ease. The main learning tool for the first group is the recursive application of the Bayes rule, while that of the latter is the iterative solution of an optimization criterion. Both techniques are fundamental to stochastic and deterministic control theory. It is expected that further cross-fertilization will take place between these two fields.

2) Characterization remains as a major open problem.

3) Relatively little experimentation with these algorithms has been carried out with real-life classification problems compared to the number of proposed approaches. This is not so much a general criticism of the papers but a comment on the difficulties of obtaining real data. An often overlooked and unappreciated problem is that of collecting, converting, and generating *enough* samples of $x(i)$ from original data in real problems.[17] Enormous data processing time or specially designed data processing machines are needed. In fact, it is the authors' belief that this often represents the major cost of a pattern classification project. Once this is done, the solution of the abstraction problem tends to be straightforward.

In this paper we have attempted a classification of the various pattern classification techniques that have been reported in the literature. The purpose has been to try to lay bare the underlying statistical and mathematical principles used in the development of these algorithms. Only when such a classification is complete can meaningful comparisons among the numerous approaches be made. Furthermore, deficiencies as well as advantages of the various schemes hopefully can be made obvious, and progress of the field as a whole can be speeded up.

A complete coverage of the literature in this field is neither possible nor desirable. It is nevertheless believed that our classification is reasonably complete and workable and future approaches can be fitted into this framework, i.e., our scheme possesses the generalization property. There are many other papers that have appeared in the

[17] We quote from the next-to-last paragraph of [40]: "We feel that larger and higher-quality data sets are needed for work aimed at achieving useful results. Such data sets may contain hundreds, or even thousands, of samples in each class. We know, for example, that investigators at SRI and IBM have used data sets containing over ten thousand samples, and we expect that even larger data sets will be collected."

literature. We leave it as an exercise for the reader to find their case classifications. The authors welcome additions to their bibliography for the various cases and apologize in advance for any unintended omissions.

REFERENCES

[1] N. Abramson and D. Braverman, "Learning to recognize patterns in a random environment," *IRE Trans. Information Theory*, vol. IT-8, pp. 58–63, September 1962.
[2] S. Agmon, "The relaxation method for linear inequalities," *Canad. J. Math.*, vol. 6, pp. 382–392, 1956.
[3] M. A. Aizerman, E. M. Braverman, and L. I. Rozonoer, "Method of potential functions in the problem of restoration of functional converter characteristic by means of points observed randomly," *Automation and Remote Control*, vol. 25, December 1964.
[4] D. C. Allais, "Selection of measurement for prediction," Stanford University, Stanford, Calif., Tech. Rept. 6103-9, November 1964.
[5] T. W. Anderson, *An Introduction to Multivariate Statistical Analysis*. New York: Wiley, 1958.
[6] T. W. Anderson and R. Bahadur, "Classification into two multivariate normal distributions with different covariance matrices," *Ann. Math. Stat.*, vol. 33, pp. 422–431, 1962.
[7] A. G. Arkadev and E. M. Braverman, *Computers and Pattern Recognition*. Washington, D. C.: Thompson, 1967.
[8] G. H. Ball, "Data analysis on the social sciences: What about the details?" *Proc. Fall Joint Computer Conf.*, pp. 533–559, 1965.
[9] C. C. Blaydon and Y. C. Ho, "Recursive algorithms for pattern classification," *Proc. Nat'l Electronics Conf.*, 1966.
[10] D. B. Brick, "Wiener's nonlinear expansion procedure applied to cybernetics problems," *IEEE Trans. Systems Science and Cybernetics*, vol. SSC-1, pp. 67–74, November 1965.
[11] Y. T. Chien and K. S. Fu, "Sequential recognition using a nonparameter ranking procedure," *IEEE Trans. Information Theory*, vol. IT-13, pp. 484–492, July 1967.
[12] P. W. Cooper, "Quadratic discriminant functions in pattern recognition," *IEEE Trans. Information Theory (Correspondence)*, vol. IT-11, pp. 313–315, April 1965.
[13] ——, "Hyperplanes, hyperspheres and hyperspadrices as decision boundaries," in *Computer and Information Science*. Washington, D. C.: Spartan Books, 1964, pp. 111–139.
[14] T. M. Cover, "Geometrical and statistical properties of systems of linear inequalities with applications in pattern recognition," *IEEE Trans. Electronic Computers*, vol. EC-14, pp. 326–334, June 1965; also Stanford University, Stanford, Calif., Tech. Rept. 6107-1, May 1964.
[15] T. M. Cover and P. E. Hart, "Nearest neighbor pattern classification," *IEEE Trans. Information Theory*, vol. IT-13, pp. 21–27, January 1967.
[16] R. F. Daly, "The adaptive binary—Detection problem on the real line," Stanford University, Stanford, Calif., Tech. Rept. 2003-3, February 1962.
[17] I. P. Devyaterikov, A. I. Pripoi, and Ya. Z. Tsypkin, "Iterative learning algorithms for pattern recognition," *Automation and Remote Control*, pp. 108–117, January 1967.
[18] R. O. Duda and H. Fossum, "Pattern classification by iteratively determined linear and piecewise linear discriminant functions," *IEEE Trans. Electronic Computers*, vol. EC-15, pp. 220–232, April 1966.
[19] H. L. Dreyfus, "Alchemy and artificial intelligence," RAND Corp., Rept. P-3244, December 1965.
[20] J. L. Flanagan, *Speech Analysis, Synthesis and Perception*. New York: Academic Press, 1965.
[21] S. C. Fralick, "The synthesis of machines which learn without a teacher," Stanford University, Stanford, Calif., Tech. Rept. 6103-8, April 1964.
[22] ——, "Learning to recognize patterns without a teacher," *IEEE Trans. Information Theory*, vol. IT-13, pp. 57–65, January 1967; also System Theory Lab., Stanford University, Stanford, Calif., Tech. Rept. 6103-10, March 1965.
[23] E. Fix and J. L. Hodges, "Discriminatory analysis, nonparametric discrimination," USAF School of Aviation Medicine, Randolph Field, Tex., Project 21-49-004, Rept. 4, Contract AF 41-(128) 31, February 1951.
[24] K. S. Fu and C. H. Chen, "Sequential decisions, pattern recognition and machine learning," Purdue University, Lafayette, Ind., Tech. Rept. TR-EE65-6, April 1965.
[25] K. S. Fu and Y. T. Chien, "On the finite stopping rules and nonparameter techniques in a feature ordered sequential recognition system," Purdue University, Lafayette, Ind., Tech. Rept. TR-3366-16, October 1966.
[26] K. S. Fu, Y. T. Chien, and G. P. Cardillo, "A dynamic programming approach to sequential pattern recognition," *IEEE Trans. Electronic Computers*, vol. EC-16, pp. 790–803, December 1967.
[27] G. F. Groner, "Statistical analysis of adaptive linear classifiers," Electronics Labs., Stanford University, Stanford, Calif., Tech. Rept. 6761, April 1964.
[28] Y. C. Ho and A. K. Agrawala, "On the self-learning scheme of Nagy and Shelton," *Proc. IEEE (Letters)*, vol. 55, pp. 1764–1765, October 1967.
[29] Y. C. Ho and R. L. Kashyap, "A class of iterative procedures for linear inequalities," *J. SIAM Control*, vol. 4, no. 1, pp. 112–115, 1966.
[30] R. E. Kalman, "A new approach to linear filtering and prediction problems," *Trans. ASME, J. Basic Engrg.*, ser. D, vol. 82, pp. 35–45, 1960.
[31] K. R. Kaplan and J. Sklansky, "Analysis of Markov chain models of adaptive processes," Aerospace Medical Research Labs., Rept. AMRL-TR-65-3, January 1965.
[32] R. L. Kashyap and C. C. Blaydon, "Recovery of functions from noisy measurements taken at randomly selected points and its application to pattern classification," *Proc. IEEE (Letters)*, vol. 54, pp. 1127–1128, August 1966.
[33] D. G. Keehn, "A note on learning for Gaussian properties," *IEEE Trans. Information Theory*, vol. IT-11, pp. 126–132, January 1965.
[34] A. G. Konheim, "Linear and nonlinear methods in pattern classification," *IBM J. Research and Develop.*, July 1964.
[35] O. L. Mangasarian, "Linear and nonlinear separation of patterns by linear programming," *Operations Research*, vol. 13, pp. 444–452, 1965.
[36] C. H. Mays, "Effect of adaptation parameters on convergence time and tolerance for adaptive threshold elements," *IEEE Trans. Electronic Computers (Short Notes)*, vol. EC-13, pp. 465–468, August 1964.
[37] W. C. Miller, "A modified mean square criterion for use in unsupervised learning," Center for Systems Research, Stanford University, Stanford, Calif., Tech. Rept. 6778-2, August 1967.
[38] M. Minsky, "Steps toward artificial intelligence," *Proc. IRE*, vol. 49, pp. 8–30, January 1961.
[39] F. Mosteller and J. W. Tukey, "Data analysis, including statistics," in *Handbook of Social Psychology*. G. Lindzey and E. Aronsen, Eds. Reading, Mass.: Addison-Wesley, 1968.
[40] J. H. Munson, R. O. Duda, and P. E. Hart, "Experiments with Highleyman's data," *IEEE Trans. Computers (Short Notes)*, vol. C-17, pp. 399–401, April 1968.
[41] G. Nagy, "State of the art in pattern recognition," *Proc. IEEE*, vol. 56, pp. 836–862, May 1968.
[42] G. Nagy and G. L. Shelton, "Self-corrective character recognition system," *IEEE Trans. Information Theory*, vol. IT-12, pp. 215–222, April 1966.
[43] Z. J. Nikolic and K. S. Fu, "A mathematical model of learning in an unknown random environment," *Proc. Nat'l Electronics Conf.*, vol. 22, pp. 607–612, October 1966.
[44] N. J. Nilsson, *Learning Machines*. New York: McGraw-Hill, 1965.
[45] A. Novikoff, "On convergence proofs for perceptrons," *Proc. Symp. on Mathematical Theory of Automata*. Brooklyn, N. Y.: Polytechnic Inst. of Brooklyn, 1962, pp. 615–622.
[46] E. A. Patrick and J. C. Hancock, "Nonsupervised sequential classification and recognition of patterns," *IEEE Trans. Information Theory*, vol. IT-12, pp. 362–372, July 1966.
[47] J. D. Patterson, T. J. Wagner, and B. F. Womack, "A mean-square performance criterion for adaptive pattern classification systems," *IEEE Trans. Automatic Control (Short Papers)*, vol. AC-12, pp. 195–197, April 1967.
[48] D. W. Peterson and R. L. Mattson, "A method of finding linear discriminant functions for a class of performance criteria," *IEEE Trans. Information Theory*, vol. IT-12, pp. 380–387, July 1966.
[49] H. Raiffa and R. Schlaifer, *Applied Statistical Decision Theory*. Boston, Mass.: Harvard Business School, 1961.
[50] D. J. Rogers and T. T. Tanimoto, "A computer program for classifying plants," *Science*, vol. 132, pp. 1115–1118, October 1960.
[51] J. B. Rosen, "Pattern separation by convex programming," *J. Math.*

Analysis and Applications, vol. 10, pp. 123–134, 1965.
[52] I. Selin, *Detection Theory*. Princeton, N. J.: Princeton University Press, 1965.
[53] J. Sklansky, "Learning systems for automatic control," *IEEE Trans. Automatic Control*, vol. AC-11, pp. 6–19, January 1966.
[54] ——, "Threshold training of two-mode signal detection," *IEEE Trans. Information Theory*, vol. IT-11, pp. 353–362, July 1965.
[55] J. Spragins, "A note on the iterative application of Bayes' rule," *IEEE Trans. Information Theory*, vol. IT-11, pp. 544–549, October 1965.
[56] ——, "Learning without a teacher," *IEEE Trans. Information Theory*, vol. IT-12, pp. 223–229, April 1966.
[57] ——, "Reproducing distributions for machine learning," Stanford University, Stanford, Calif., Tech. Rept. 6103-7, November 1963.
[58] Y. Z. Tsypkin, "Adaptation, training and self-organization in automatic systems," *Automation and Remote Control*, vol. 27, pp. 16–52, January 1966.
[59] A. Wald, *Sequential Analysis*. New York: Wiley, 1947.
[60] S. Watanabe, "Karhunen-Loeve expansion and factor analysis, theoretical remarks and applications," *Information Theory, Statistical Decision Functions, Random Processes, Trans. 4th Prague Conf.*, pp. 635–660, 1965.
[61] B. Widrow and M. E. Hoff, "Adaptive switching circuits," Electronic Labs., Stanford University, Stanford, Calif., Tech. Rept. 1553-1, June 1960.
[62] E. Wong and E. Eisenberg, "Iterative synthesis of threshold functions," *J. Math. Analysis and Applications*, vol. 11, pp. 226–235, 1965.

DISCRIMINATORY ANALYSIS

NONPARAMETRIC DISCRIMINATION: CONSISTENCY PROPERTIES

EVELYN FIX, Ph. D.
J. L. HODGES, JR., Ph. D.

University of California
Berkeley, California

1. Introduction

The discrimination problem (two population case) may be defined as follows: a random variable Z, of observed value z, is distributed over some space (say, p-dimensional) either according to distribution F, or according to distribution G. The problem is to decide, on the basis of z, which of the two distributions Z has.

The problem may be classified in various ways into subproblems. One pertinent method of classification is according to the amount of information assumed to be available about F and G. We may distinguish three stages:

(i) F and G are completely known

(ii) F and G are known except for the values of one or more parameters

(iii) F and G are completely unknown, except possibly for assumptions about existence of densities, etc.

Subproblem (i) has been, in a sense, completely solved. The solution is implicit in the Neyman-Pearson lemma [1], and was made explicit by Welch [2]. We may without loss of generality assume the existence of density functions, say f and g, corresponding to F and G, since F and G are absolutely continuous with respect to F + G. If f and g are known, the discrimination should depend only on $\frac{f(z)}{g(z)}$. An appropriate (positive) constant c is chosen, and the following rule is observed:

Reprinted with permission from USAF School of Aviation Medicine, Randolph AFB, TX, Project 21-49-004, Rep. 4, Feb. 1959; first published Feb. 1951.

If $\frac{f(z)}{g(z)} > c$, we decide in favor of F

If $\frac{f(z)}{g(z)} < c$, we decide in favor of G

If $\frac{f(z)}{g(z)} = c$, the decision may be made in an arbitrary manner.

These procedures are known to have optimum properties with regard to control of probability of misclassification (probability of wrong decision). We shall refer to this as the "likelihood ratio procedure," and denote it by L(c).

For simplicity, we shall assume throughout the paper that the borderline case $f(z) = cg(z)$ can be neglected. Formally, we postulate that

$$P\{ f(Z) = cg(Z)\} = 0$$

regardless of whether Z comes from F or G. Since the classification is arbitrary when $f(z) = cg(z)$, it hardly seems worth while to introduce complications into the methods to allow for it. However, it is not difficult to extend our methods to take care of the situation which arises when

$$P\{ f(Z) = cg(Z) \} > 0.$$

The choice of c depends on considerations relating to the relative importance of the two possible errors: saying Z is distributed according to G when in fact it is distributed according to F, and conversely. Two choices of c have been widely advocated:

(a) Take $c = 1$

(b) Choose c so that the two probabilities of error are equal.

Choice (a) has been called "logical"; choice (b) yields the minimax procedure. In this paper we shall not concern ourselves with the choice of c, but shall assume that a given positive c is a datum of the problem.

The usual approach to subproblem (ii) is as follows. We assume there are available samples from the two distributions, say

$$X_1, X_2, \ldots, X_m : \text{sample from } F$$

$$Y_1, Y_2, \ldots, Y_n : \text{sample from } G.$$

We assume further that F and G are known in form: that is, that we know them except for the values of some real parameters, which may be denoted collectively by θ. We may denote the distributions corresponding to a given θ by F_θ, G_θ. The procedure currently employed is to use the X's and Y's to estimate θ, by, say, $\hat{\theta}$, and then to proceed as under (i), using the distributions $F_{\hat{\theta}}$, $G_{\hat{\theta}}$ as though they were known to be correct.

The most familiar example of this process is the linear discriminant function [3]. There, it is (tacitly) assumed that F and G are p-variate normal distributions having the same (unknown) covariance matrix, and unknown expectation vectors. The two expectation vectors and the covariance matrix are estimated from the samples, and the likelihood ratio procedure is then employed, using the estimated values as though they were known to be correct.

Not much is known about the desirability of the usual method of attack on (ii). We give in Section 3 a theorem concerning asymptotic properties of the method. Undoubtedly, this procedure is reasonable <u>provided</u> the assumed parametric form is correct. But the validity of the use of the linear discriminant function with data obviously not normal or, if normal, with obviously unequal covariance matrices has been of general concern. Presumably, very bad results may ensue if a procedure is used, based on certain assumptions about parametric form, when those assumptions are not even approximately correct.

There seems to be a need for discrimination procedures whose validity does not require the amount of knowledge implied by the normality assumption, the homoscedastic assumption, or any assumption of parametric form. The present paper is, as far as the authors are aware, the first one to attack subproblem (iii): can reasonable discrimination procedures be found which will work even if no parametric form can be assumed?

It is not to be expected that any procedure can be guaranteed to give good results without any restriction whatsoever on the distributions F and G. To clarify this point, we need to state a precise meaning for "good results." This is done in Section 2, with the introduction of the concept of "consistency." We then proceed in Section 4 to prove, under weak restrictions on the densities f and g, the consistency of a class of nonparametric procedures there proposed. A modification of these procedures is then considered in Section 5.

It may be noted that all of the methods and results of this paper can be extended without difficulty to the situation in which there are more than two populations to be discriminated.

The authors are engaged in further work along the lines here laid down. Specifically, some sampling experiments are being conducted, intended to throw some light on the performance of the procedures for moderate sample sizes; and asymptotic properties of a class of sequential nonparametric discriminatory procedures is being investigated. It is intended to prepare further reports setting forth the results.

2. The notion of consistency.

In setting out to define an optimum property in statistical inference, it is useful to have in mind the limit of excellence beyond which it is not possible to go. The procedures L(c) described in Section 1 provide such a limit in the case of nonparametric discrimination: we cannot, with any nonparametric classification procedure, expect to do better than the best which is possible when the densities themselves are assumed to be known. This fact is intuitively obvious, but if desired an exact proof is easily given. When f and g are known, Z is sufficient for the classification, with respect to $(Z; X_1, X_2, \ldots, X_m; Y_1 Y_2, \ldots, Y_n)$, and we may (by using randomization) exactly duplicate (with a procedure based on Z) the performance characteristic of any procedure based on $(Z; X_1 X_2, \ldots, X_m; Y_1, Y_2, \ldots, Y_n)$.

Thus, no nonparametric procedure can have probabilities of error less than those of a likelihood ratio procedure. On the other hand, we shall propose in Sections 4 and 5 classes of (sequences of) nonparametric procedures which, in the limit as m and n tend to infinity, have the same probabilities of error as the procedures L(c). We may therefore reasonably say that our procedures are consistent with the likelihood ratio procedures.

There are two different notions of consistency for sequences of statistical decision functions, and it may be worth while to distinguish them. Suppose that the decision space is finite (as is the case in discriminatory analysis when there are finitely many populations). Let the possible decisions be denoted by $\delta_1, \delta_2, \ldots, \delta_r$. Now suppose we are considering two sequences of decision functions, say $\{\Delta'_n\}$ and $\{\Delta''_n\}$. How should we define the notion that these two sequences tend to agree with each other, or be consistent with each other, as $n \longrightarrow \infty$? On the one hand, we might require that in the limit there should be close agreement between the probabilities of decision; on the other hand we might require that in the limit there be high probability of agreement of decision. The former requirement relates to the performance characteristics of the decision functions; the latter requirement relates to the decision functions themselves. We have then two definitions:

Definition 1. We shall say that the sequences $\{\Delta'_n\}$ and $\{\Delta''_n\}$ are consistent in the sense of performance characteristics if, whatever be the true distributions, and whatever be $\varepsilon > 0$, there exists a number N such that whenever $m > N$ and $n > N$,

$$\left| P\{\Delta'_m = \delta_i\} - P\{\Delta''_n = \delta_i\} \right| < \varepsilon$$

for every decision δ_i.

Definition 2. We shall say that the sequences $\{\Delta'_n\}$ and $\{\Delta''_n\}$ are consistent in the sense of decision functions if, whatever be the true distributions, and whatever be $\varepsilon > 0$, there exists a number N such that whenever $m > N$ and $n > N$,

$$P\{\Delta'_m = \Delta''_n\} > 1 - \varepsilon.$$

We observe that consistency in the second sense implies that in the first, since $P(\Delta'_m \neq \Delta''_n)$ is not less than each of the quantities

$$P(\Delta'_m = \delta_i \text{ and } \Delta''_n \neq \delta_i) \geq P(\Delta'_m = \delta_i) - P(\Delta''_n = \delta_i).$$

The definitions are not equivalent however, as the following trivial example shows. If Δ' and Δ'' each denotes (for any m,n) the process of choosing between two alternatives δ_1 and δ_2 by tossing a coin, then $P(\Delta' = \Delta'') = \frac{1}{2}$, while

$$P(\Delta' = \delta_i) = P(\Delta'' = \delta_i) = \frac{1}{2} \text{ for } i = 1, 2.$$

Inasmuch as it is customary to evaluate decision functions solely in terms of their performance characteristics, Definition 1 is the more natural. However all proofs of consistency given in this paper provide consistency in the stronger sense of the second definition, and consequently we shall adopt it.

Since our procedures are based on two samples, we must consider a double limit process as both m and n tend to infinity. To avoid difficulties which would otherwise arise in Section 5, we shall assume throughout that m and n approach infinity at the same speed. Precisely, we assume $\frac{m}{n}$ and $\frac{n}{m}$ are both bounded away from 0 as $n,m \longrightarrow \infty$. Whenever we write "$m,n \longrightarrow \infty$" this restriction should be understood. Our restriction has the effect of reducing the limiting process from a double to a single one.

In the sequel we shall be comparing certain discriminatory procedures with procedures of the type L(c). It is convenient to introduce:

<u>Definition</u> 3. A sequence $\{\Delta_{m,n}\}$ of discriminatory procedures, based on Z and on samples $X_1,X_2,\ldots,X_m$ from F and $Y_1,Y_2,\ldots,Y_n$

from G, is said to be <u>consistent with</u> $L(c)$ if, whatever be the distributions F and G, regardless of whether Z is distributed according to F or according to G, and whatever be $\varepsilon > 0$, we can assure

$$P\left\{\Delta_{m,n} \text{ and } L(c) \text{ yield the same classification of } Z\right\} > 1 - \varepsilon$$

provided only that m and n are sufficiently large.

We may also define a corresponding notion of uniform consistency. If, in Definition 3, the bound on probability of agreement can be assured for all F and G with a single size specification on m and n, we say that $\{\Delta_{m,n}\}$ is uniformly consistent with $L(c)$.

3. Consistency for the parametric case.

We shall now demonstrate that the analogy of the notion of consistency just introduced with the like-named notion in point estimation, is more than formal. Consider the problem of parametric discrimination (subproblem (ii)) of Section 1.

We shall from time to time have occasion to consider probabilities computed under the assumption that Z is distributed according to F, or according to G. It is convenient to let P_1 and P_2 denote probabilities computed under these respective assumptions.

Let $\mathfrak{F}$ and $\mathfrak{G}$ be classes of densities parametrized by parameters denoted collectively by θ. Let there be a notion of convergence introduced in the space Θ of parameter values. Suppose there is given a sequence $\{\hat{\theta}_{m,n}\}$ of estimates for θ, $\hat{\theta}_{m,n}$ being a function of $X_1, X_2, \ldots, X_m$ and $Y_1, Y_2, \ldots, Y_n$.

Theorem 1. If

(a) the estimates $\{\hat{\theta}_{m,n}\}$ are consistent,

(b) for every θ, $f_\theta(z)$ and $g_\theta(z)$ are continuous functions of θ for every z except perhaps for $z \in Z_\theta$, where $P_i(Z_\theta) = 0$, $i = 1, 2$, then the sequence of discrimination procedures $\{\hat{L}_{m,n}(c)\}$ obtained by applying the likelihood ratio principle with critical value $c > 0$ to $f_{\hat{\theta}_{m,n}}(z)$ and $g_{\hat{\theta}_{m,n}}(z)$ is consistent with $L(c)$.

Proof. The idea of the proof is very simple: Since $\hat{\theta}_{m,n}$ is consistent, $\hat{\theta}_{m,n}$ will probably be near θ if m and n are large. But since f_θ and g_θ are continuous, this means that $f_{\hat{\theta}_{m,n}}$ will probably be near f_θ, and $cg_{\hat{\theta}_{m,n}}$ will probably be near cg_θ. Therefore, it is not likely to make much difference whether we compare f_θ and cg_θ or $f_{\hat{\theta}_{m,n}}$ and $cg_{\hat{\theta}_{m,n}}$.

Fix $c > 0$, $\varepsilon > 0$, and $\theta \in \Theta$. Find $\delta > 0$ so small that $P_i\{\,|f_\theta(Z) - cg_\theta(Z)| \leq \delta\} < \frac{1}{2}\varepsilon$, $i = 1, 2$. (This is possible since $P_i\{|f_\theta(Z) - cg(Z)| \leq u\}$ is the cumulative function of the random variable $|f_\theta(Z) - cg_\theta(Z)|$ and hence is continuous on the right, and by assumption takes on the value 0 when $u = 0$). We now assume that z does not lie in Z_θ, thus excluding an event of zero probability. Since $f_\theta(z)$ is a continuous function of θ for all z, we can associate with every z a quantity $\eta_1(z) > 0$ such that

$$|f_{\hat{\theta}}(z) - f_\theta(z)| < \frac{\delta}{2} \quad \text{whenever} \quad |\hat{\theta} - \theta| < \eta_1(z).$$

A like function $\eta_2(z)$ arises if f is replaced by cg. Let $\eta(z) = \min\{\eta_1(z), \eta_2(z)\}$ and find $\eta > 0$ such that $P_i(\eta(Z) < \eta) < \frac{1}{4}\varepsilon$, $i = 1, 2$.

Using finally the consistency of the estimates, choose M and N large enough so that whenever $m > M$ and $n > N$, $P\{|\hat{\theta}_{m,n} - \theta| > \eta\} < \frac{1}{4}\varepsilon$. Combining the above, a disagreement between $L(c)$ and $\hat{L}_{m,n}(c)$ will arise with probability less than ε.

Remarks. (1) The dependence of the discontinuity sets Z_θ on θ is important. Were we to demand the stronger property that $f_\theta(z)$ and $g_\theta(z)$ be continuous in θ for all $z \notin Z$, Z a fixed set, $P_i(Z) = 0$, $i = 1, 2$, we should exclude many cases which are included under the theorem as given.

(2) Two notions of convergence in Θ are involved: that with respect to which the estimates are consistent, and that with respect to which the densities are continuous. These need not be the same, provided the former implies the latter.

(3) If uniformity is added to the hypotheses of theorem 1, it may also be added to the conclusions. Specifically, if the estimates $\hat{\theta}_{m,n}$ are uniformly consistent, if the densities f and g are uniformly continuous functions of θ, uniformly in z, and if the δ of the proof of theorem 1 may be fixed independently of θ, then that proof goes through for all θ using the same value of ε. We can then conclude the uniform consistency of $\{\hat{L}_{m,n}(c)\}$.

4. Nonparametric discrimination and its consistency.

Let us next consider the discrimination problem of the third kind delineated in Section 1. We admit the possibility that the densities f for X and g for Y may be any in certain classes $\mathfrak{F}$ and $\mathfrak{G}$ of densities which are too large to be characterized by a finite number of parameters. Thus, $\mathfrak{F}$ and $\mathfrak{G}$ may consist of all uniformly continuous densities, or of all continuous densities, or of all densities continuous save at most at countably many points. Can we have any discrimination procedures which are reasonable to use when so little is assumed about the populations being discriminated?

Recall that, once c has been selected and Z has been observed to have the value z, the only information needed to carry out the procedure L(c) are the two real numbers f(z) and g(z). In the procedure $\hat{L}_{m,n}(c)$, we employed the estimate for θ as a means of obtaining estimates for $f_\theta(z)$ and $g_\theta(z)$. In the nonparametric case there is no θ to be estimated, but we may instead proceed to estimate the numbers f(z) and g(z) directly. Once estimates have been obtained, we may apply the procedure L(c), using these estimates instead of f(z) and g(z). We shall designate such procedures by $L^*(c, \hat{f}, \hat{g})$, where $\hat{f}$ and $\hat{g}$ are the estimates for f and g.

Before considering the problem of estimating the densities, let us note the properties which such estimates should have if we are to be able to prove the consistency of $L^*(c, \hat{f}, \hat{g})$ with L(c).

<u>Theorem 2</u>. <u>If</u> $\hat{f}_{m,n}(z)$ <u>and</u> $\hat{g}_{m,n}(z)$ <u>are consistent estimates for</u> f(z) <u>and</u> g(z) <u>for all</u> z <u>except possibly</u> $z \in Z_{f,g}$ <u>where</u> $P_i(Z_{f,g}) = 0$, $i = 1, 2$, <u>then</u> $\{L^*_{m,n}(c, \hat{f}, \hat{g})\}$ <u>is consistent with</u> L(c).

The proof follows lines similar to that of theorem 1, and will be omitted.

Our problem is now to find consistent estimates for $f(z)$ and $g(z)$. We shall for brevity consider $f(z)$ only, as analogous remarks apply to $g(z)$. We fix z, since the argument is the same for each value. Our basic idea is this: the proportion of the m X's which fall in a stated (small) neighborhood of z may be used to estimate the X-probability in that neighborhood. The ratio of this estimated probability to the measure of the neighborhood is then an estimate of the average value of $f(x)$ near z. This is in turn an estimate of $f(z)$ itself if we make some assumption about the smoothness of f. To obtain consistency, we may let the neighborhood shrink down to z as $m \to \infty$, so that the average of $f(x)$ over the neighborhood will approach $f(z)$; but we will take care to have the neighborhood shrink slowly enough so that the proportion of the X's therein will have a positive expectation. This will assure that the proportion of X's in the neighborhood is a consistent estimate of the probability.

It is obvious that we cannot hope to estimate $f(z)$ from $X_1, X_2, \ldots, X_m$ unless some continuity assumption is made. For, otherwise we could alter $f(z)$ arbitrarily without in any way changing the distribution of $X_1, X_2, \ldots$, and thus without changing the distribution of any sequence of estimates based on $X_1, X_2, \ldots$.

Now let μ denote Lebeague measure in our (p-dimensional) sample space, and let $|x - y|$ denote the (Euclidean) distance between points x and y of this space.

Lemma 3. *If* $f(x)$ *is continuous at* $x = z$, *and if* $\{\Delta_m\}$ *is a sequence of sets such that*

$$\lim_{m \to \infty} \sup_{d \in \Delta_m} |z-d| = 0.$$

<u>and</u> $\lim m \cdot \mu(\Delta_m) = \infty$, <u>and if</u> M <u>is the number of</u> $X_1, X_2, \ldots, X_m$ <u>which lie in</u> Δ_m, <u>then</u> $\left\{\frac{M}{m\,\mu(\Delta_m)}\right\}$ <u>is a consistent estimate for</u> f(z).

<u>Proof</u>. Observe that $\frac{P(\Delta_m)}{\mu(\Delta_m)} \longrightarrow f(z)$ as $m \longrightarrow \infty$. If $f(z) > 0$, $m\,P(\Delta_m) \longrightarrow \infty$. Since $\mu(\Delta_m) \longrightarrow 0$, $P(\Delta_m) \rightarrow 0$ and we conclude $\frac{M}{mP(\Delta_m)} \xrightarrow[p]{} 1$. Combining $\frac{M}{m\,\mu(\Delta_m)} \xrightarrow[p]{} f(z)$ as was to be shown. If $f(z) = 0$, $E\left(\frac{M}{m\,\mu(\Delta_m)}\right) = \frac{P(\Delta_m)}{\mu(\Delta_m)} \rightarrow 0$ and the Markoff lemma completes the proof.

We have in lemma 3 a class of estimates, any of which, by virtue of theorem 2, will provide consistent discrimination of any (nonparametric) classes $\mathfrak{F}$ and $\mathfrak{G}$ whose members are continuous (except possibly for a set of values of zero measure).

5. Alternative procedures.

While the procedures $L^*\left(c, \frac{M}{m\,\mu(\Delta_m)}, \frac{N}{n\,\mu(\Delta_m)}\right)$ of the last section provide consistent discrimination, the question of their applicability when m and n are not large remains open. (Like criticism may of course be applied to any asymptotic theorem.) We shall in the present section suggest some alternative estimates for f(z) and g(z), which seem on intuitive grounds more likely to give good results than the estimates proposed before. The former estimates are the natural ones when thinking of the simplicity of consistency proofs, but need not be desirable in practice.

The main practical difficulty in using the former estimates lies in the choice of the regions $\{\Delta_m\}$, (and the corresponding regions for g, say $\{\Lambda_n\}$). If these regions are made too small, the numbers M and N of sample points falling into them will be too small, so that the proportions $\frac{M}{m}$ and $\frac{N}{n}$ will not be accurate estimates for the corresponding probabilities $P_1(\Delta_m)$, $P_2(\Lambda_n)$. On the other hand, if the regions are made too large, these probabilities will not be good approximations for $f(z)\mu(\Delta_m)$ and $g(z)\mu(\Lambda_n)$. We are between twin perils and must steer a middle course. We might, for example, decide the smallest values of M and N we could tolerate, and choose Δ_m and Λ_n just big enough to include the chosen number of points. But to do so alters the probabilistic properties; now M and N are fixed and Δ and Λ are random. Are the results of lemma 3 still valid?

Even if they are we may still be in difficulties. It may happen that near z there are numerous X's, but few Y's; but by going a little further we find the situation reversed. The indication is clearly for π_1, but if we take separate Δ and Λ the estimated f and g may be close. To avoid this difficulty the following idea is suggested: Choose a number k, and take in the neighborhood of z a single region, $\Delta_{m,n}$, containing a total of k points of either sample. Intuitively this procedure seems sound, but since $M + N = k$ we have introduced dependence of our estimates and further altered the probabilistic properties. The question which now arises is whether or not estimates for $f(z)$ and $g(z)$ based on M and N, when so determined, are still consistent.

As a first step in answering these questions, observe that we may by means of a preliminary transformation reduce our space from p dimensions to one. Let $\rho(x,y)$ denote a non-negative real valued function of pairs (x,y) of points in the sample space. Suppose ρ is so constructed that when $x_n \longrightarrow x$, $\rho(x_n, x) \longrightarrow 0$, and suppose further that for each z, except perhaps for $z \in Z_{f,g}$ where $P_i(Z_{f,g}) = 0$, $i = 1, 2$, $\rho(X,z)$ and $\rho(Y,z)$ are random variables possessing densities, say $f_z(x)$ and $g_z(x)$, continuous and not both 0 at 0. (These properties are satisfied, for example, by $\rho(x,y) = \sqrt[p]{|x-y|}$). We now replace the problem of deciding whether $f(z)$ or $cg(z)$ is the larger, by the problem of deciding whether $f_z(0)$ or $cg_z(0)$ is larger; and further replace the samples $X_1,X_2,\ldots,X_m$ and $Y_1,Y_2,\ldots,Y_n$ by $\rho(X_1,z)$, $\rho(X_2,z),\ldots,$ $\rho(X_m,z)$ and $\rho(Y_1,z)$, $\rho(Y_2,z),\ldots,\rho(Y_n,z)$, respectively. We may now, without real loss of generality, assume that f and g are densities of non-negative univariate random variables, and that $z = 0$.

Theorem 4. *Let X and Y be non-negative. Let f and g be positive and continuous at 0. Let $k(m,n)$ be a positive-integer-valued function such that $k(m,n) \longrightarrow \infty$, $\frac{1}{m} k(m,n) \longrightarrow 0$, and $\frac{1}{n} k(m,n) \longrightarrow 0$, as m and $n \longrightarrow \infty$. (This tendency being restricted so that $\frac{m}{n}$ is bounded away from 0 and ∞). Define*

$U = k^{th}$ *smallest value of combined samples of* X's *and* Y's,

M = number of X's $\leq U$,

N = number of Y's $\leq U$.

Then $\frac{M}{mU}$ <u>is a consistent estimate for</u> $f(0)$ <u>and</u> $\frac{N}{nU}$ <u>is a consistent estimate for</u> $g(0)$.

<u>Proof</u>. Fix $\varepsilon > 0$ and $\delta > 0$. Define $k_1(m,n)$ and $k_2(m,n)$ by $k_1(m,n) + k_2(m,n) = k(m,n)$ and $\frac{k_1(m,n)}{k_2(m,n)} = \frac{mf(0)}{ng(0)}$.

Define $v(m,n) = \frac{k_1(m,n)}{mf(0)(1+\delta)^2}$ and $w(m,n) = \frac{k_1(m,n)}{mf(0)(1-\delta)^2}$.

Observe $v(m,n) = \frac{k_2(m,n)}{ng(0)(1+\delta)^2}$ and $w(m,n) = \frac{k_2(m,n)}{ng(0)(1-\delta)^2}$.

Define

$$M^v_{m,n} = \text{number of } X\text{'s} < v(m,n),$$

$$M^w_{m,n} = \text{number of } X\text{'s} < w(m,n),$$

$$N^v_{m,n} = \text{number of } Y\text{'s} < v(m,n),$$

$$N^w_{m,n} = \text{number of } Y\text{'s} < w(m,n).$$

Using the continuity and positiveness of f and g at 0, find $q > 0$ so small that when $0 \leq x \leq q$, $\left| \frac{f(x)}{f(0)} - 1 \right| < \delta$ and $\left| \frac{g(x)}{g(0)} - 1 \right| < \delta$. Find m_1, n_1 such that when $m > m_1$ and $n > n_1$, $w(m,n) < q$, and make these restrictions. Observe

$$E(M^v_{m,n}) = m \int_0^{v(m,n)} f(x)dx \text{ and hence}$$

$$mf(0)\ v(m,n)(1-\delta) < E(M^v_{m,n}) < mf(0) \cdot v(m,n)(1+\delta).$$

Similarly observe

$$mf(0)\, w(m,n)(1-\delta) < E(M^w_{m,n}) < mf(0)\, w(m,n)(1+\delta)$$

$$ng(0)\, v(m,n)(1-\delta) < E(N^v_{m,n}) < ng(0)\, v(m,n)(1+\delta)$$

$$ng(0)\, w(m,n)(1-\delta) < E(N^w_{m,n}) < ng(0)\, w(m,n)(1+\delta)$$

Thus, $E(M^v_{m,n}) < \dfrac{k_1(m,n)}{1+\delta}$, $\quad E(M^w_{m,n}) > \dfrac{k_1(m,n)}{1-\delta}$,

$$E(N^v_{m,n}) < \frac{k_2(m,n)}{1+\delta}, \qquad E(N^w_{m,n}) > \frac{k_2(m,n)}{1-\delta}.$$

The random variables involved are binomials, whose expectations tend to ∞, but more slowly than the numbers of trials, as $m,n \to \infty$. Therefore, if we take m_2, n_2 large enough, we can assure

$$P\left(M^v_{m,n} < k_1(m,n)\right) > 1 - \varepsilon$$

$$P\left(N^v_{m,n} < k_2(m,n)\right) > 1 - \varepsilon$$

$$P\left(M^w_{m,n} > k_1(m,n)\right) > 1 - \varepsilon \cdot$$

$$P\left(N^w_{m,n} > k_2(m,n)\right) > 1 - \varepsilon$$

as soon as $m > m_2$ and $n > n_2$, which restriction we now make. Combining, using the fact that U will exceed $v(m,n)$ if $M^v_{m,n} + N^v_{m,n} < k(m,n)$, we have

$$P\left(U > v(m,n)\right) > 1 - 2\varepsilon,$$

$$P\left(U < w(m,n)\right) > 1 - 2\varepsilon.$$

The event $U > v(m,n)$ implies the event that all X's $< v(m,n)$ are among the first k X's and Y's and hence the event $M^V_{m,n} \leq M$. Therefore, $P(M^V_{m,n} \leq M) \geq P\left(U > v(m,n)\right) > 1 - 2\varepsilon$.

Similarly, $P(M^W_{m,n} \geq M) > 1 - 2\varepsilon$. Restricting $m > m_3$, $n > n_3$, we can further assure

$$P\left(M^V_{m,n} > mf(0)\ v(m,n)(1-\delta)^2\right) > 1 - \varepsilon,$$

$$P\left(M^W_{m,n} < mf(0)\ w(m,n)(1+\delta)^2\right) > 1 - \varepsilon.$$

Combining,

$$P\left(\frac{M}{m} < f(0)\ w(m,n)(1+\delta)^2\right) > 1 - 3\varepsilon,$$

$$P\left(\frac{M}{m} > f(0)\ v(m,n)(1-\delta)^2\right) > 1 - 3\varepsilon.$$

Hence $P\left\{f(0).\ \frac{v(m,n)}{w(m,n)}(1-\delta)^2 < \frac{M}{mU} < f(0).\ \frac{w(m,n)}{v(m,n)}(1+\delta)^2\right\} > 1 - 10\varepsilon.$

Since $\frac{v(m,n)}{w(m,n)} = \frac{(1-\delta)^2}{(1+\delta)^2}$, the conclusion $\frac{M}{mU} \xrightarrow[p]{} f(0)$ is at hand.

A similar argument shows $\frac{N}{nU} \xrightarrow[p]{} g(0)$.

A situation in which one of the densities is 0 at 0 can be dealt with by a corresponding but simpler argument which we omit. The effect of theorem 4 is to assure us of satisfactory large sample results if we employ procedures of the following kind:

Choose k, a positive integer which is large but small compared to the sample sizes. Specify a metric in the sample space, for example ordinary Euclidean distance. Pool the two samples and find, of the k values in the pooled samples which are nearest to z, the number M

which are X's. Let $N = k-M$ be the number which are Y's. Proceed with the likelihood ratio discrimination, using however $\frac{M}{m}$ in place of $f(z)$ and $\frac{N}{n}$ in place of $g(z)$. That is, assign Z to F if and only if

$$\frac{M}{m} < c\,\frac{N}{n}\,.$$

REFERENCES

1. J. NEYMAN and E. S. PEARSON, "Contributions to the theory of testing statistical hypotheses," Stat. Res. Memoirs, Vol. 1 (1936), pp. 1-37.
2. B. L. WELCH, "Note on discriminant functions," Biometrika, Vol. 31 (1939), pp. 218-220.
3. R. A. FISHER, "The use of multiple measurements in taxonomic problems," Annals of Eugenics, Vol. 7 (1936), pp. 179-188.

DISCRIMINATORY ANALYSIS

Nonparametric Discrimination: Small Sample Performance

EVELYN FIX, Ph.D.
J.L. HODGES, Jr., Ph.D.
University of California, Berkeley

1. Introduction

In an earlier paper [1] concerned with the problem of nonparametric discrimination, the present authors proposed several classes of nonparametric discrimination procedures and proved that these procedures have asymptotic optimum properties for large samples. The ideas and results of [1] are briefly summarized in section 2 for the convenience of the reader.

The present paper is concerned with the performance of some of these procedures where the samples are small. While the large sample optimum properties given in [1] are general, the investigation of small sample properties is necessarily special since small sample performance depends greatly upon a number of variables connected with the underlying distributions assumed. We have examined in detail certain special cases which seemed of interest and have tried to give some indication of the performance in others. The scope of the present study is given in section 3. The results obtained are presented in the remaining sections.

A related paper, "Nonparametric Discrimination: Consistency Properties," was published as Report No. 4 of this project, February 1951.

Reprinted from USAF School of Aviation Medicine, Randolph AFB, TX, Project 21-49-004, Rep. 11, Aug. 1952.

2. A class of nonparametric discriminators and their large sample properties

In the present section we summarize some of the ideas and results of [1]. Let $X_1, X_2, \cdots, X_m$ be a sample from the p-variate distribution F and let $Y_1, Y_2, \cdots, Y_n$ be a sample from the p-variate distribution G. We do not suppose that F and G are known, nor even that their parametric form is known. Let Z be an observation known to be either from F or from G; our problem is to decide which. To this end, define in the p-dimensional space a notion of "distance," in terms of which the $m + n$ observations in the combined samples can be ranked according to their "nearness" to Z. The general idea of the discrimination procedures of [1] is that Z should be assigned to F if most of the nearby observations are X's; otherwise Z should be assigned to G. To simplify matters, suppose the sample sizes are equal $(m = n)$, and select an odd integer k. A specific procedure of the general class is obtained by assigning Z to that distribution from which came the majority of the k nearest observation.

In [1], it was shown that several classes of these nonparametric discriminators have asymptotically optimum performance as m and n tend to infinity, in the sense that the probabilities of misclassification,

$$P_1 = P\{Z \text{ is assigned to } G | Z \text{ came from } F\},$$

$$P_2 = P\{Z \text{ is assigned to } F | Z \text{ came from } G\},$$

and, as m and n tend to infinity, to the theoretical minimum values which they could have even if F and G were completely known. The results do not require any restrictive assumptions on the form of F and G, or on the definition of nearness which is used.

3. Scope of the present study

The optimum large sample property mentioned above, together with the applicational simplicity of the procedures, suggests that nonparametric discriminators may be useful alternatives to the commonly employed linear discriminant function. The latter is a reasonable procedure if (i) F and G are p-variate normal distributions and (ii) F and G have the same covariance matrix. Many users and also potential users of the linear discriminant function have been disturbed by the apparent and often considerable failure to satisfy conditions (i) and/or (ii) in cases where the procedure has been applied. In the absence of knowledge of the performance of the linear discriminant function under other conditions than (i) and/or (ii), such uneasiness leads to an interest in methods whose theoretical justification is free of these restrictions.

It would not be reasonable, however, to propose an alternative to the linear discriminant function solely on the basis of asymptotic properties. In particular, it is necessary to ask how much discriminating power is lost through the use of a nonparametric procedure when samples are small and when assumptions (i) and (ii) are valid so that the linear discriminant function is appropriate. The answer to this question requires a comparison of the probabilities of error, P_1 and P_2, which result when the linear discriminant function is used with the corresponding probabilities P_1 and P_2 obtained when some alternative discriminating procedure is used.

The number of parameters on which these probabilities of error seem to depend is considerable: (i) the dimensionality p of the observation space (that is, the number of measurements made on each individual), (ii) the $\frac{p(p+1)}{2}$ parameters of the common covariance matrix, (iii) the $2p$ coordinates of the two vector expectations and, finally, (iv) the specification of the distance function used in the nonparametric procedures to order the sample observations according to their nearness to Z.

We may note that the distance function does not need to be a metric although any metric will serve. All that is required is that, of two points u and v, the distance function specify which is closer to a point z. Geometrically, this amounts to establishing for each point z a system of loci, each locus consisting of those points at the same distance from z. For example, if we use Euclidean distance, the loci are just the surfaces of p-dimensional hyperspheres centered at z. As a second example, consider the distance defined by

$$\Delta(x, z) = \max_{i=1}^{p} |x_i - z_i|.$$

Here the locus of points at a given distance from z consists of the surface of a hypercube, centered at z, with faces parallel to the coordinate hyperplanes. The distance $\Delta(x, z)$ has the advantage of being easily computed. It is, incidentally, a metric.

We now observe that the problem can be substantially reduced by considering linear transformations on the observation space. First, it is always possible by such a transformation to insure that F and G will have the identity covariance matrix; that is, that the p transformed measurements are independent in each population, and that each measurement has unit variance. Second, we can put the expectation vector of F at the origin and the expectation vector of G on the positive first axis. Thus, only two parameters are required to specify the transformed populations, namely, p and λ where

$$\lambda = E(\text{first coordinate of } Y)$$
$$= \text{distance between the means of the transformed populations.}$$

It is well known that P_1 and P_2 for the linear discriminant function are unchanged by this transformation. Thus, in so far as the linear discriminant function is concerned, there is no loss of generality.

What about the nonparametric procedures? Associated with each z and each distance from z, there was a locus of points in the original space. We may consider the transformed loci, in the new space, as providing a transformed distance function. Since the totality of possible distance functions in the original space is mapped one-one into the totality in the new space, our transformation loses no generality for the nonparametric procedure either. Therefore, it is sufficient to consider the transformed populations with the two parameters, p and λ.

It is clear that the totality of possible distance functions forms a very large class; in fact, it is not even a parametric class. It is also easy to see that the values of P_1 and P_2 will depend very heavily upon the distance function used. For example, if we use

$$\delta(x, z) = |x_2 - z_2|$$

as distance (remembering that in the transformed populations the expectation vector of F is at the origin and the expectation vector of G is on the positive first axis), we would have no discriminating power at all and $P_1 = P_2 = 1/2$. At the other extreme,

$$\delta'(x, z) = |x_1 - z_1|$$

would give quite good discrimination, even with small samples (see section 4). In using the nonparametric discriminators proposed here, the judgment of the statistician as to the relative importance of the various measurements is of great consequence. In a sense, the linear discriminant function makes great demands on the populations being discriminated but asks of the statistician only a routine (though lengthy) computation--while the nonparametric discriminators which ask little or nothing of the populations demand considerable judgment on the part of the statistician. Of course, this is not a clear cut distinction since, for instance, with the linear discrimination function, judgment is needed to decide whether or not assumptions (i) and (ii) are sufficiently true in the case under consideration to permit its use.

We are now able to define the scope of the present study. Throughout the entire paper we assume that the sizes of the samples taken from each population are equal, $m = n$. Most of the computations have been made using Δ (defined in section 3) as distance function. Also a great part of the work has dealt with the case where Z is assigned to that population from which came the individual of the pooled samples who most closely resembles Z, that is, $k = 1$. The values of $P_1 = P_2$, when Δ is used as distance function, are given in sections 4 and 5 for $p = 1$ and 2; $\lambda = 1, 2, 3$; $n = 1, 2, 3, 4, 5, 10, 20, 50$ and ∞; $k = 1$. In section 6, values of $k > 1$ have been considered. Section 7 has a discussion of the effect of distance function alternative to Δ. A brief investigation for $p > 3$ is reported in section 8.

Unfortunately, we are unable to say how the values of $P_1 = P_2$ obtained here compare with those of the linear discriminant function, since the latter is not yet tabled. A preliminary survey indicated that an adequate treatment of the performance characteristic of the linear discriminant function would require a large computational program. The result would be of great value and interest but was beyond our means at this time. We have given the results in the univariate case (section 4) where it is easily obtained.

4. Univariate case

When $p = 1$, the obvious and natural distance function is ordinary Euclidean distance which in this case coincides with Δ. The linear discriminant function is also greatly simplified, since no matrix computation enters. One simply computes the arithmetic mean of the sample means,

$$\frac{\bar{X} + \bar{Y}}{2},$$

and assigns Z to that population whose sample mean lies on the side of $(\bar{X} + \bar{Y})/2$ as does Z itself. In this case the probabilities of error of the linear discriminant function are easily computed and this we now proceed to do.

From the symmetry of the problem it is clear that $P_1 = P_2$, so it suffices to compute P_1, that is, we assume that Z is distributed according to F. As shown in section 3, we lose no generality by putting $E(X) = 0$, $E(Y) = \lambda > 0$, $\sigma_X^2 = \sigma_Y^2 = 1$. Introduce the new variables

$$U = \bar{Y} - \bar{X}, \qquad V = \bar{X} + \bar{Y} - 2Z$$

where $n\bar{X} = \sum_{i=1}^{n} X_i$, $n\bar{Y} = \sum_{i=1}^{n} Y_i$. Since, as is well known, $\bar{Y} - \bar{X}$ and $\bar{X} + \bar{Y}$ are independent, we see that U and V are independent normal random variables, with

$$E(U) = \lambda, \quad \sigma_U^2 = 2/n, \quad E(V) = \lambda, \quad \sigma_V^2 = 4 + 2/n.$$

Furthermore, an error is committed by the linear discriminant function if and only if

$$\text{(i)} \quad Z > \frac{\bar{X} + \bar{Y}}{2} \quad \text{and} \quad \bar{Y} > \bar{X}$$

or

$$\text{(ii)} \quad Z < \frac{\bar{X} + \bar{Y}}{2} \quad \text{and} \quad \bar{Y} < \bar{X}.$$

Thus, an error occurs if and only if $UV < 0$. Therefore, it follows that for the linear discriminant function, when $p = 1$,

$$(4.1) \quad P_1 = P_2 = \left[1 - \phi\left(-\frac{\sqrt{n}\lambda}{\sqrt{2}}\right)\right] \phi\left(-\frac{\sqrt{n}\,\lambda}{\sqrt{2+4n}}\right) + \phi\left(-\frac{\sqrt{n}\lambda}{\sqrt{2}}\right)\left[1 - \phi\left(-\frac{\sqrt{n}\lambda}{\sqrt{2+4n}}\right)\right]$$

where

$$\phi(x) = \int_{-\infty}^{x} \frac{1}{\sqrt{2\pi}} e^{-\frac{1}{2}u^2} du.$$

The limiting value for $n = \infty$ is $\phi(-\lambda/2)$ since with infinite samples the population means become surely known and P_1 just the probability that Z exceeds $\lambda/2$. Table I gives the values of $P_1 = P_2$ for various values of n and λ. The results are pictured graphically in figures 1 and 2.

Let us now consider nonparametric discriminators. The simplest of these procedures is the one corresponding to $k = 1$ which consists in assigning Z to that population from which came the sample individual nearest to Z. This "rule of nearest neighbor" has considerable elementary intuitive appeal and

Table I

Probability of error, linear discriminant function, univariate normal distributions

n	$\lambda = 1$	$\lambda = 2$	$\lambda = 3$
1	.4175	.2532	.1235
2	.3821	.1999	.0910
3	.3611	.1819	.0826
4	.3472	.1744	.0787
5	.3376	.1707	.0763
10	.3175	.1646	.0716
20	.3110	.1616	.0692
50	.3094	.1599	.0678
∞	.3085	.1587	.0668

n = size of sample taken from each population

λ = distance between the means of the two populations

Probability of error = $P\{Z \text{ is assigned to } G | Z \text{ came from } F\}$

$= P\{Z \text{ is assigned to } F | Z \text{ came from } G\}$

(see formula 4.1)

probably corresponds to practice in many situations. For example, it is possible that much medical diagnosis is influenced by the doctor's recollection of the subsequent history of an earlier patient whose symptoms resemble in some way

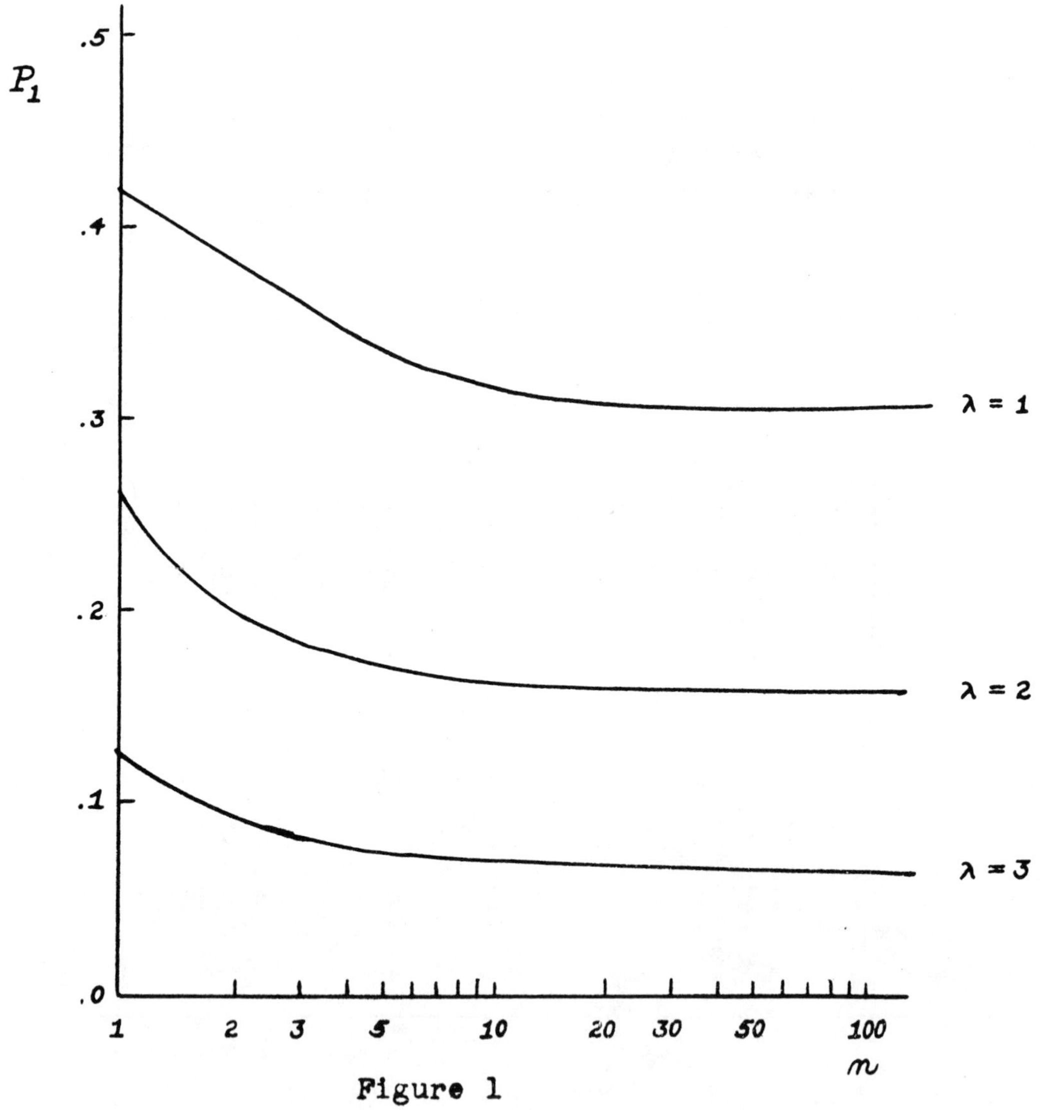

Figure 1

Probability of error P_1 of the linear discriminant function for two univariate normal distributions with distance between means = λ. n = size of sample from each population.

those of the current patient. At any rate it seemed advisable to begin computations with the simplest procedure, that is, to begin with the computation of the probability P_1 that the nearest neighbor to Z is one of the Y's, given that Z has the distribution of an X.

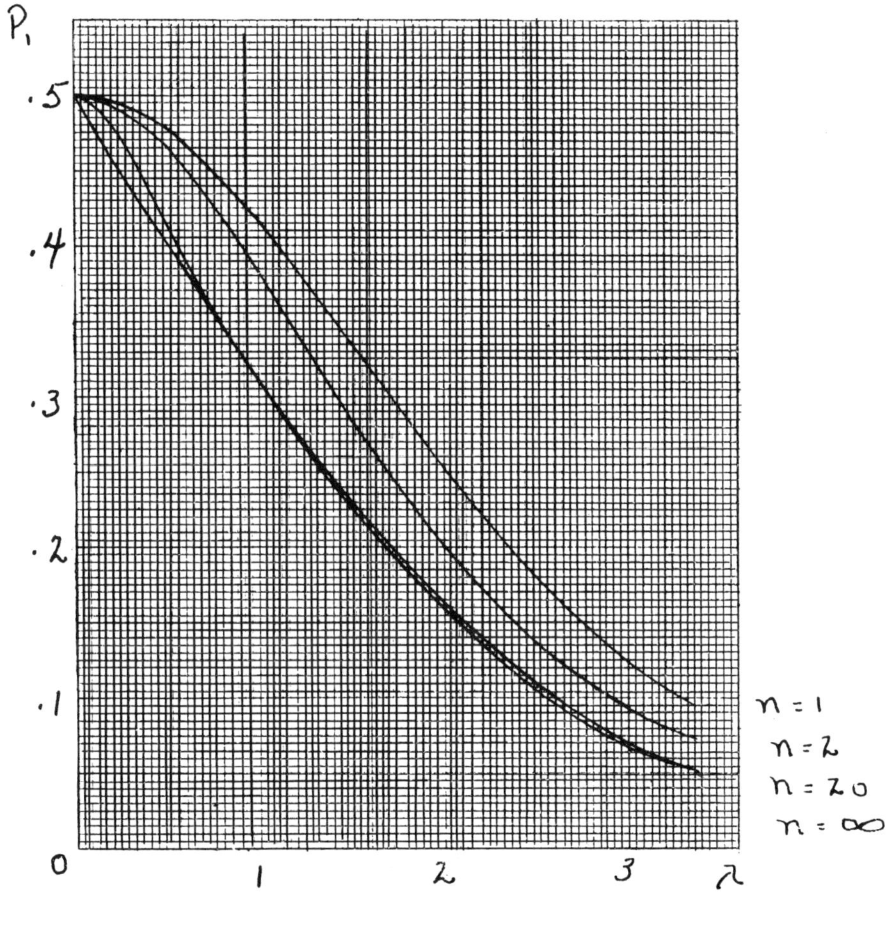

Figure 2

Probability of error P_1 of the linear discriminant function for two univariate normal distributions with distance between the means = λ, plotted as a function of λ. n = size of sample from each population.

Our technique for performing this computation is as follows. Suppose it is given that $Z = z$, and let $P_1(z)$ denote the conditional probability that the nearest of the $2n$ sample observations to Z is a Y, given that $Z = z$. Then

$$(4.2) \qquad P_1 = E[P_1(Z)] = \int_{-\infty}^{\infty} \frac{1}{\sqrt{2\pi}} e^{-\frac{1}{2}z^2} P_1(z)\, dz.$$

The calculation of $P_1(z)$ is quite straight forward. Let

$$(4.3) \qquad \begin{aligned} H_z(\delta) &= P\{|X - z| < \delta\} \\ &= P\{z - \delta < X < z + \delta\} \\ &= \Phi(z + \delta) - \Phi(z - \delta), \end{aligned}$$

while

$$(4.4) \qquad \begin{aligned} K_z(\delta) &= P\{|Y - z| < \delta\} \\ &= P\{z - \lambda - \delta < Y - \lambda < z - \lambda + \delta\} \\ &= \Phi(z - \lambda + \delta) - \Phi(z - \lambda - \delta). \end{aligned}$$

The event, "the nearest sample value to z is a Y" may be classified into the n exclusive events, "the nearest sample value to z is Y_i", $i = 1, 2, \cdots, n$. By symmetry these n events are equiprobable. The event, "the nearest sample value to z is Y_1" may be broken down according to the distance from z to Y_1. Thus,

$$(4.5) \qquad P_1(z) = n \int_0^\infty [1 - H_z(\delta)]^n [1 - K_z(\delta)]^{n-1} \, dK_z(\delta).$$

Formulae (4.2) and (4.5) are the basis of all our computations for the "nearest neighbor rule," no matter what the value of p. If $p > 1$, $H_z(\delta)$ and $K_z(\delta)$ are not, of course, given by the explicit formulae (4.3) and (4.4). Their definition is analogous if one replaces $P\{|X - z| < \delta\}$ by $P\{\text{the distance of } X \text{ from } z < \delta\}$ in (4.3) and similarly $P\{|Y - z| < \delta\}$ by $P\{\text{the distance of } Y \text{ from } z < \delta\}$ in (4.4). The specific evaluation depends then upon the distance function used.

Aside from the case $p = 1$, $n = 1$, which is given explicitly by formula (4.1) with $n = 1$, the bulk of the computation was carried out by straightforward numerical integration. For $p = 1$,

$$dK_z(\delta) = \frac{1}{\sqrt{2\pi}} \left[e^{-\frac{(z-\lambda+\delta)^2}{2}} + e^{-\frac{(z-\lambda-\delta)^2}{2}} \right] d\delta .$$

The values of $H_z(\delta)$, $K_z(\delta)$ and $dK_z(\delta)$ were taken from tables [2] and [3]. In the calculation of $P_1(z)$ the fineness of the mesh and the quadrature rule used depended to some extent on the location of z. After the values of $P_1(z)$ had been obtained, a final quadrature (4.2) was effected to obtain the value of P_1. The results given in table II were computed in this way.

The computations that led to the values recorded in table II are quite heavy. This is especially true in the bivariate case, $p = 2$, with which we began computations. Therefore a search for a simple and sufficiently accurate approximate method was instituted. Of the numerous approximate formulae tried, the following was the most successful. Let δ denote the distance from z at which the nearest sample value lies. The conditional value of $P_1(z)$, given δ, may be seen to be

$$(4.6) \qquad \frac{\dfrac{dK_z(\delta)}{1 - K_z(\delta)}}{\dfrac{dK_z(\delta)}{1-K_z(\delta)} + \dfrac{dH_z(\delta)}{1-H_z(\delta)}} = q(z, \delta).$$

It is notable that $q(z, \delta)$ is independent of n. The idea of the approximation is that $P_1(z)$ may be replaced by its conditional value, $q(z, \delta^*)$ where δ^* is in some reasonable sense an average value of δ. In order that $q(z, \delta)$ be an adequate replacement for $P_1(z)$, it is clear that δ^* will be a monotonic decreasing function of n. The function of δ^* which served best was arrived at by treating the n observations from each population as a pooled sample of size $2n$. An average value of δ was thought to be one which would make the probability that at least one of the combined sample values would fall within the prescribed δ distance of z equal to the probability that a sample value would fall outside this prescribed distance. The value of

δ^* for a given n was then chosen to satisfy the following equation:

$$(4.7) \quad \left[\frac{\{1-H_z(\delta^*)\} + \{1-K_z(\delta^*)\}}{2}\right]^{2n} = e^{-\frac{\{1-H_z(\delta^*)\} + \{1-K_z(\delta^*)\}}{2}}$$

It was found easier to solve the above equation for the value of n, say n^*, corresponding to a given value of δ. Then, if $q(z, \delta)$ is regarded as a function of n^*, the value of $q(z, \delta)$ corresponding to a given n can be found by interpolation, using Aitken's method. Table II was extended to larger values of n in this way and the results are shown in table II-A. Figure 3 is based on the combined data of tables II and II-A.

The approximation by means of (4.6) and (4.7) was developed specifically for the bivariate case and it appears to be a better approximation for small n under these conditions than in the univariate case. Time permitted us to make only a limited search for an approximation which would be more satisfactory for the univariate normal distributions. It may be of some interest to give the first terms of the expansion of (4.5). We are indebted to Mr. T. A. Jeeves of this Laboratory for bringing this expansion to our attention. In this connection, see [4] and [5].

Table II
Probability of error, nonparametric discriminator with k = 1, univariate normal distribution

n	$\lambda = 1$	$\lambda = 2$	$\lambda = 3$
1	.4175	.2532	.1235
2	.4086	.2364	.1084
3	.4052	.2307	.1036
4	.4032	.2280	.1014

Table II-A
Approximate probability of error, nonparametric discriminator with k = 1, univariate normal distribution

n	$\lambda = 1$	$\lambda = 2$	$\lambda = 3$
4	.403	.226	.102
5	.401	.225	.100
10	.399	.223	.098
20	.398	.224	.098
50	.398	.225	.098
∞	.398	.225	.098

n = size of sample from each population

λ = distance between the means of the two populations

k = odd integer such that Z is assigned to that population from which came the majority of the k nearest observations--k = 1 is the "rule of nearest neighbor."

Probability of error = $P\{Z \text{ is assigned to } G | Z \text{ came from } F\}$
$= P\{Z \text{ is assigned to } G | Z \text{ came from } G\}$

(see formulae 4.2 - 4.5)

Distance function = $\Delta(x,z) = |x - z|$

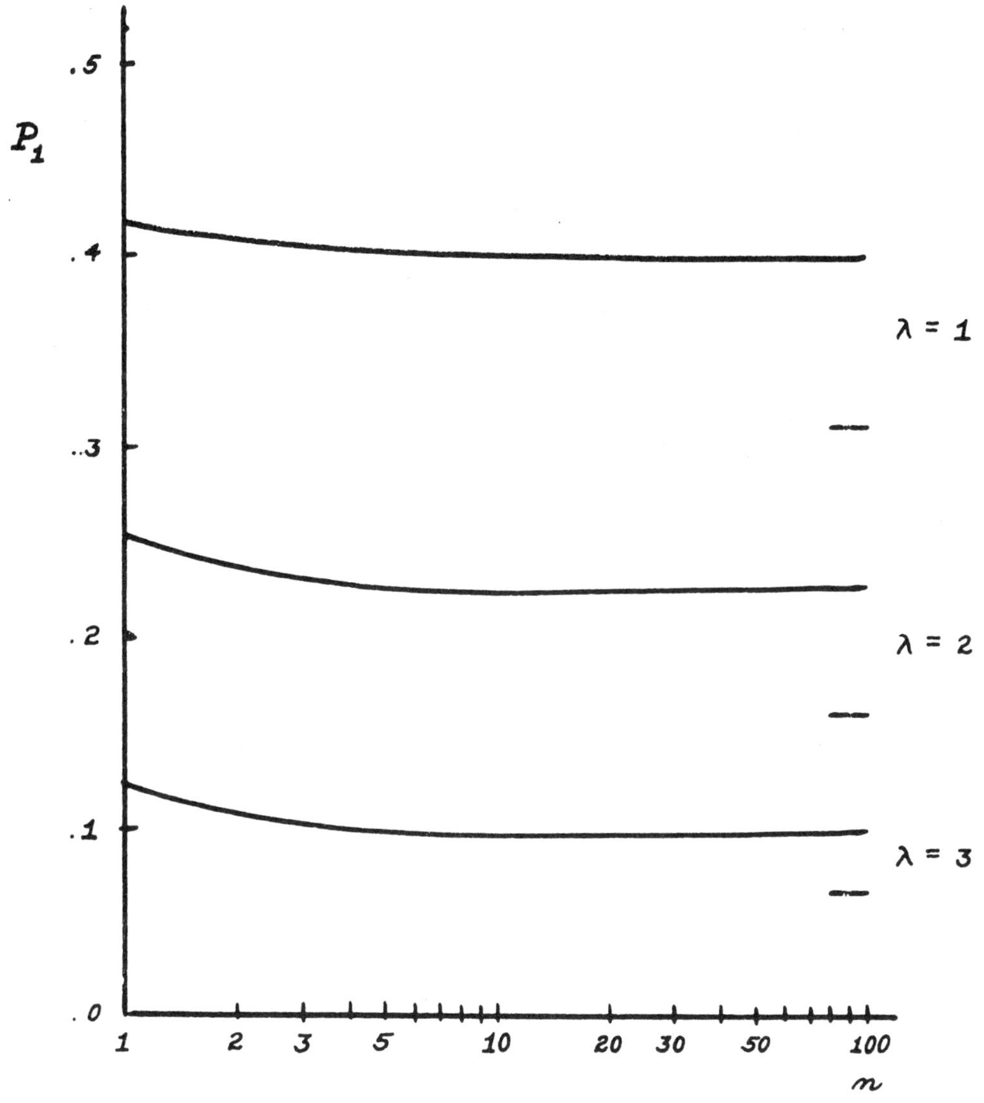

Figure 3

Probability of error P_1 of the nonparametric discriminator, with Δ as distance function, for two univariate normal distributions with distance between means = λ. n = size of sample from each population. k = 1, the rule of nearest neighbor. --- indicates the optimum likelihood ratio procedure.

$$P_1(z) = \frac{dK_z(0)}{dH_z(0)+dK_z(0)}$$

$$- \frac{1}{n} \frac{dH_z(0)dK_z(0)[dH_z(0)-dK_z(0)]}{[dH_z(0)+dK_z(0)]^2}$$

$$+ \frac{1}{n^2[dH_z(0)+dK_z(0)]^3} \left\{ \frac{d^3K_z(0)dH_z(0)-dK_z(0)d^3H_z(0)}{dH_z(0)+dK_z(0)} \right.$$

$$\left. + \frac{dH_z(0)dK_z(0)[dH_z(0)-dK_z(0)][(dH_z(0))^2-4dH_z(0)dK_z(0)+(dK_z(0))^2]}{[dH_z(0)+dK_z(0)]^2} \right\}$$

$$+ O(n^{-3}).$$

The limiting value for $n \to \infty$ may be approached in another way. When n is large, δ will be small, so that in the limit, $P_1(z)$ will simply be $q(z,0) = \dfrac{dK_z(0)}{dK_z(0)+dH_z(0)} = \dfrac{g(z)}{f(z)+g(z)}$, where f and g are the density functions corresponding to F and G, respectively. This argument is quite general: for large n,

$$P_1 \cong E\left[\frac{g(Z)}{g(Z)+f(Z)}\right] = \int_{-\infty}^{\infty} \frac{f(z)g(z)}{f(z)+g(z)}\, dz.$$

simple application of Schwartz's inequality shows the latter integral to be at most 1/2. We can thus assert that, whatever be the populations being discriminated, the "rule of nearest neighbor" will have in the limit, as $m = n \longrightarrow \infty$, equal probabilities of error at most 1/2. While this remark is of no practical interest, it is theoretically interesting because the "optimum" maximum likelihood rule, "assign Z to that population with the larger density at z," possesses no such nontrivial general bound on the individual probabilities of error.

The easiest and most vivid method of comparing the figures of tables I, II and II-A is graphically. Therefore, in figure 4, the probabilities of misclassification for paired values of λ are plotted against n while figure 5 shows the same values plotted this time against λ for selected values of n. It seems needless to discuss the graphs at length since in any practical case the experimenter must make up his mind whether or not the simplicity of operation given by the nonparametric discriminator makes up for the loss of efficiency. In the univariate case the question seems somewhat pointless since the linear discriminant function is easy to compute and also it is little work to derive its performance characteristic. The univariate investigation was undertaken for the sake of completeness of presentation and because it provides a simple case on which to illustrate the use on nonparametric discriminators.

Next to the "rule of nearest neighbor," the simplest nonparametric discriminator is obtained by setting $k = 3$ and using the "rule of two out of three," that is, assign to that population from which came the majority of the nearest three observations in the pooled samples. For finite n, the problem of misclassification reduces to the following.

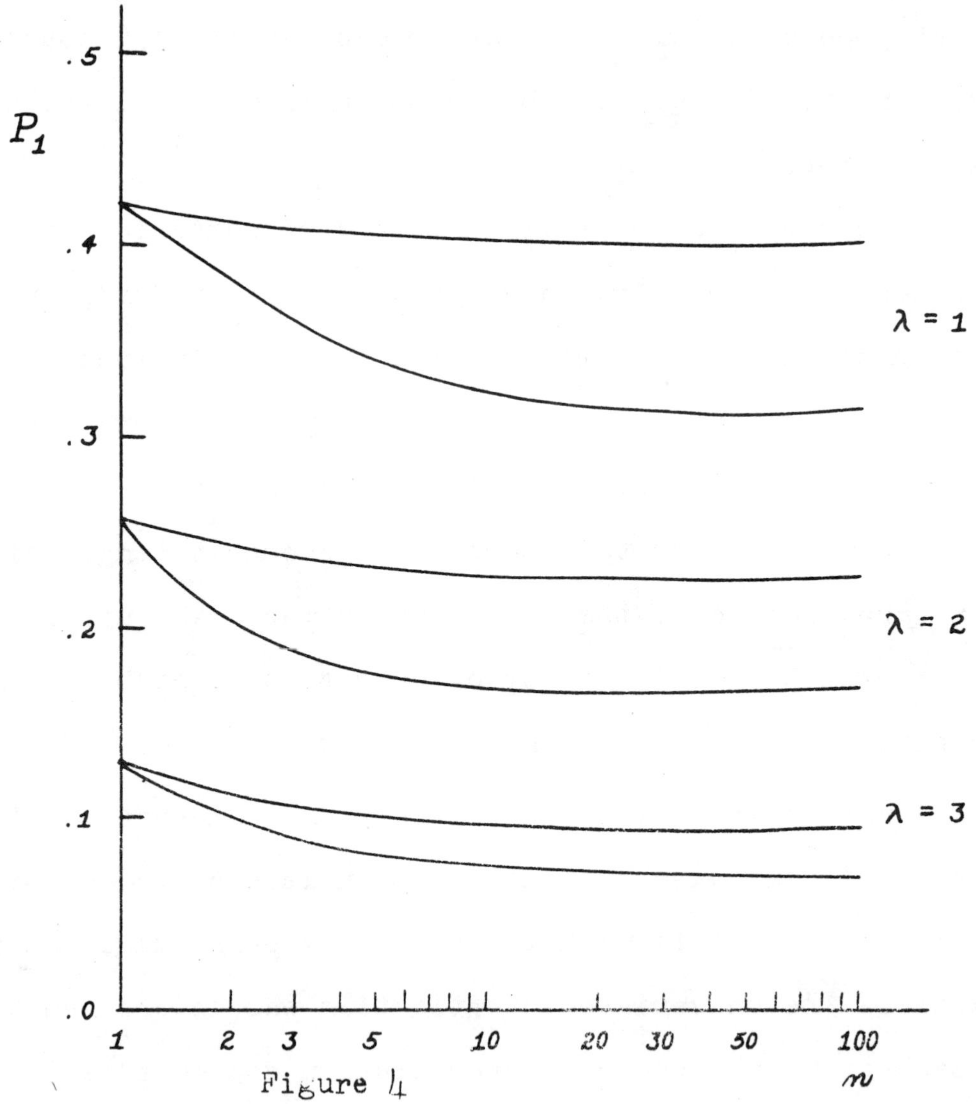

Figure 4

Comparison of the probability of error P_1 as a function of n for the linear discriminant function and the non-parametric discriminator, distance function $= \Delta$, $k = 1$, for two normal univariate populations with distance between means $= \lambda$. n = size of sample from each population.

Let X_1, X_2, X_3 denote the values obtained from F and Y_1, Y_2, Y_3 the values from G. Then the conditional probability that two of the three values nearest to Z will be Y's given that Z belongs to F and Z = z is

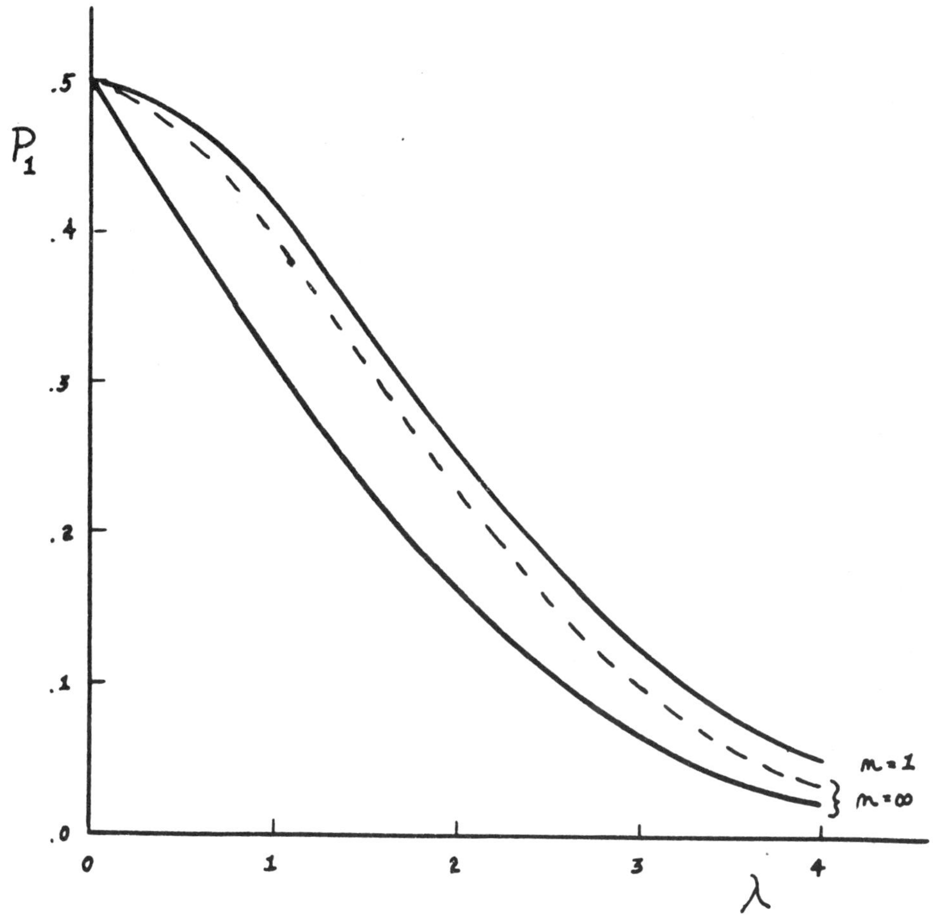

Figure 5

Comparison of the probability of error P_1 as a function of λ, the distance between the means, for the linear discriminant function and the nonparametric discrimnator, distance function = Δ, k = 1, for two normal univariate populations n = size of sample from each population. n = 1 is identical for both. --- indicates the nonparametric procedure.

$$P_1^{(3)}(z) = 6P\{\text{all } Y\text{'s and } X_1 \text{ are nearer to } z \text{ than } X_2 \text{ while } X_3 \text{ is farther from } z \text{ than } X_2\}$$

$$+ 18P\{Y_1, Y_2, X_1 \text{ are nearer } z \text{ than } X_2 \text{ while } X_3 \text{ and } Y_3 \text{ are farther from } z \text{ than } X_2\}$$

$$= 6 \int_0^\infty K_z^3(\delta)\, H_z(\delta)\, [1 - H_z(\delta)]\, dH_z(\delta)$$

$$+ 18 \int_0^\infty K_z^2(\delta)\, H_z(\delta)\, [1 - H_z(\delta)][1 - K_z(\delta)]\, dH_z(\delta).$$

Then, as before,

$$P_1^{(3)} = E\left[P_1^{(3)}(z)\right].$$

As $n \longrightarrow \infty$, $P_1^{(3)}$ may be shown (the argument is similar to the one used when $n \longrightarrow \infty$, $k = 1$) to approach

$$P_1^{(3)} = \int_{-\infty}^{\infty} \frac{[g(z)]^3 + 3[g(z)]^2 f(z)}{[f(z) + g(z)]^3}\, f(z)\, dz.$$

It is noteworthy that as $n \longrightarrow \infty$, the value of $P_1^{(3)}$ for fixed values of k, however small, are independent of the dimensionality p of the sample space.

From this formula, the middle column of table III was computed. Corresponding results from tables I and II-A are repeated for comparison. As shown in [1], as $n \longrightarrow \infty$ and

$k \longrightarrow \infty$ (more slowly, however, than n), the linear discriminant function and the nonparametric discriminators have a common limiting behavior, shown in line three of table III. Thus, for $\lambda = 2$, $p = 1$, and large n, the "rule of two out of three" has a 19.2 per cent chance of misclassification as against 15.9 per cent for the optimum. Figure 6 illustrates these results graphically.

Table III

Limiting probabilities of error as $n \to \infty$, for the p-variate normal distribution

λ	$k = 1$	$k = 3$	$k = \infty$
0	.500	.500	.500
1	.398	.368	.309
2	.225	.192	.159
3	.098	.080	.067
4	.034	.027	.023
5	.009	.007	.006

n = size of sample from each population

= distance between the means of the transformed populations

k = odd integer such that Z is assigned to that population from which λ came the majority of the k nearest observations.

Probability of error = $P\{Z \text{ is assigned to } G \mid Z \text{ came from } F\}$

= $P\{Z \text{ is assigned to } F \mid Z \text{ came from } G\}$.

The probability of error for n large is independent of p.

5. Bivariate normal distribution

For $p = 2$, we have employed methods analogous to those described in section 4, to obtain the probabilities of error for the nonparametric discriminators with $k = 1$; $\lambda = 1, 2, 3$;

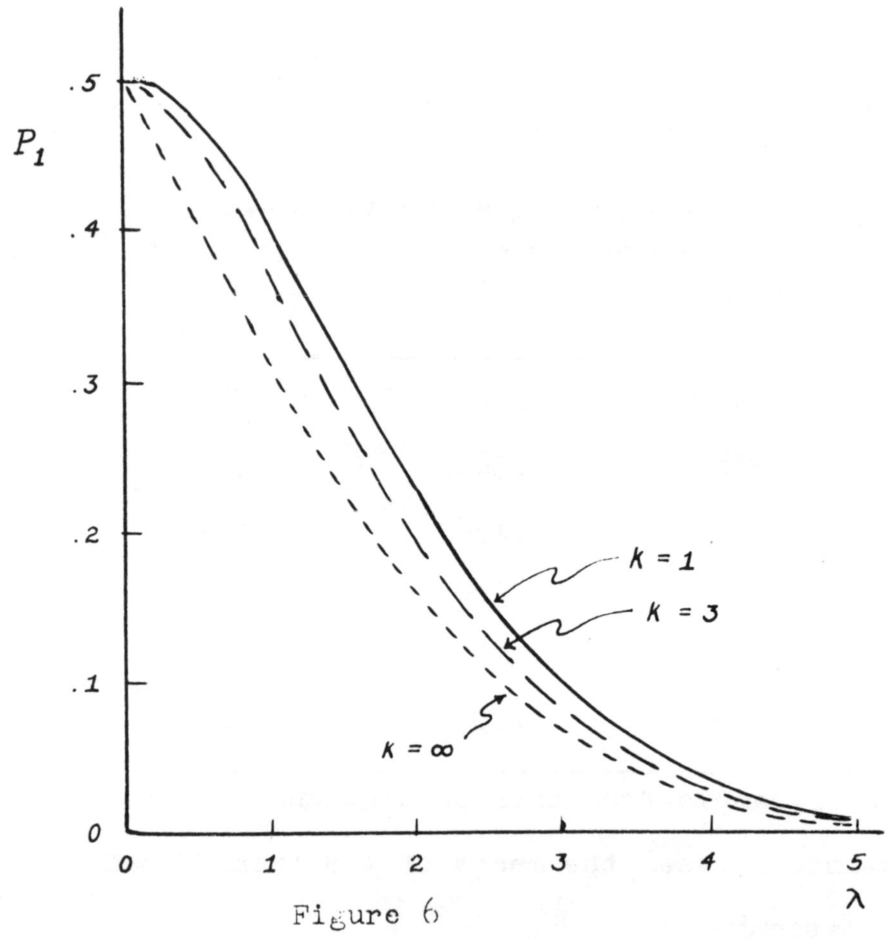

Figure 6

Limiting probabilities of error P_1 as n, the size of sample from each population, $\rightarrow \infty$, for two p-variate normal distributions. Distance function = Δ, k = number of nearest individuals on which the nonparametric procedure is based.

and $n = 1, 2, 3, 4, 5, 10, 20, 50, \infty$. The results are summarized in table IV. All finite values of $n > 4$ were obtained by the approximate method discussed in the last section. A comparison of the values obtained by numerical integration with those given by the approximation are shown in table IV-A.

To enable the reader to get a clearer picture of the change in probabilities of misclassification with a change in λ, figure 7 shows the values of table IV plotted against λ.

Unfortunately we do not have available the comparable figures for the linear discriminant function. However, as a measure of the efficiency of the nonparametric discriminators we have included the optimum limiting behavior to which both the nonparametric discriminator and the linear discriminant function tend.

6. $k \geqq 3$ for the univariate and bivariate normal distributions

As k is increased the computations become much more laborious, so much so that the actual numerical integrations were carried out in only a very few instances for the "two out of three rule." The following method may, however, be used to estimate the effect of $k \geqq 3$. Let us consider an alternative discriminator which we shall denote as (r, n', k'). Suppose $k = rk'$ and $n = rn'$. Partition the $2n$ sample values at random into r sets of $2n'$ each and for each set observe the population-or-origin of the majority of the k' observations nearest to Z. Assign Z to that population whose elements are in the majority for a majority of the r sets. It is easy to show that this discriminator will determine the

Table IV

Probabilities of error, nonparametric discriminators, k = 1, bivariate normal distribution

n	$\lambda = 1$	$\lambda = 2$	$\lambda = 3$
1	.435	.292	.157
2	.429	.269	.135
3	.423	.259	.125
4	.420	.252	.120
5	.417	.250	.117
10	.411	.240	.109
20	.406	.234	.104
50	.402	.230	.100
∞	.398	.225	.098

Table IV-A

Comparison of the values obtained by numerical integration with those obtained by the approximate method

n	λ	numerical integration	approximation
1	1	.4354	.4370
1	2	.2920	.2951
2	2	.2693	.2721
3	2	.2586	.2612
4	2	.2525	.2548
1	3	.1572	.1560

n = size of sample from each population

λ = distance between the means of the transformed populations

Probability of error = P{Z is assigned to F|Z came from G}

= P{Z is assigned to G|Z came from F}

k = odd integer such that Z is assigned to that population from which came the majority of the k nearest observations. k = 1 is "nearest neighbor rule."

Distance function = Δ = $\max\{|x_1 - z_1|, |x_2 - z_2|\}$

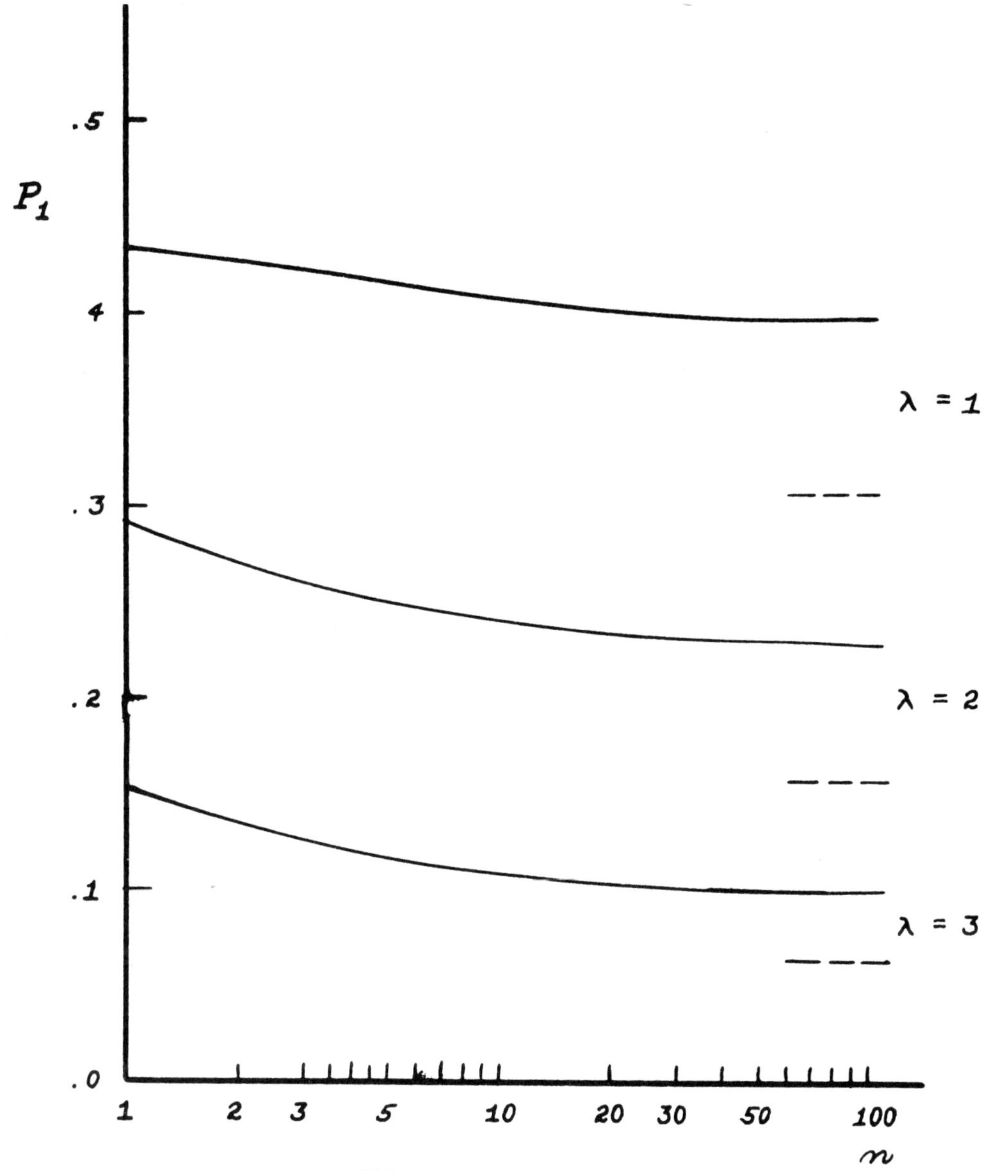

Figure 7

Probability of error P_1 of the nonparametric discriminator with Δ as distance function, for two bivariate normal distributions with distance between means = λ. n = size of sample from each population. k = 1, the rule of nearest neighbor. --- indicates the optimum likelihood ratio procedure.

Assignment of Z on the basis of observations less close to Z than would be the case if we employed the ordinary discriminator using the k closest of the entire sample of 2n. Hence it is intuitive that the probabilities of error of (r, n', k') will exceed those of the usual rule (n,k). We do not know a proof of this, however.

The computation of P_1 for (r, n', k') once P_1 has been obtained for (n', k') is relatively easy. For fixed z, the r sets can be regarded as r independent trials each with constant probability $P_1(z)$ for (n', k') of success (success is here defined as the event that Z will be misclassified). The values of $P_1(z)$ for (r, n', k') can then be found from the tables of the binomial distribution [6].

Tables V and VI give the results for the univariate and bivariate normal distributions, respectively. The first line in table VI has the values calculated for the two out of three rule. The second line gives the probability of error when a sample of three observations from each population is considered as a set of three independent trials and the individual Z is assigned to that population in which the majority of the trials placed him. One notices that while the corresponding probabilities in the two lines are extremely close the figures bear out one's intuition mentioned above. The tables have been arranged so that comparison between different uses of the same total number of individuals in the sample will be convenient and an idea of the most effective discriminator (r, n', k') can be obtained. The same results are illustrated graphically in figures 8 and 9.

Table V

Probabilities of error, nonparametric discriminator, univariate normal distribution

n	r	n'	k'	$\lambda = 1$	$\lambda = 2$
3	1	3	1	.405	.231
3	3	1	1	.385	.203
9	9	1	1	.345	.173
10	1	10	1	.399	.223
29	29	1	1	.324	.164
50	1	50	1	.398	.225

n = total size of sample from each population

r = number of sets in the partition of the total sample

n' = size of each of the r sets; n = n'r

k' = 1 = rule of nearest neighbor

λ = distance between the means of the transformed populations

Probability of error = $P\{Z \text{ is assigned to } G | Z \text{ came from } F\}$

$= P\{Z \text{ is assigned to } F | Z \text{ came from } G\}$

Distance function = Δ .

Table VI

Probabilities of error, nonparametric discriminator, bivariate normal distribution

n	r	n'	k'	$\lambda = 1$	$\lambda = 2$	$\lambda = 3$
3	1	3	3	.408	.238	.110
3	3	1	1	.408	.239	.112
15	1	15	1	.408*	.236*	
15	3	5	1	.386	.207	
15	5	3	1	.375	.198	
15	15	1	1	.353*	.188*	
5	5	1	1	.391	.218	.096
12	3	4	1	.389	.209	.090
29	29	1	1	.332	.184	
30	3	10	1	.379	.201	.083
150	3	50	1	.371	.195	.077

n = total size of sample from each population

r = number of sets in the partition of the total sample

n' = size of each of the r sets; n = n'r

k' = 1 = rule of nearest neighbor

k' = 3 = rule of two out of three

λ = distance between the means of the transformed populations

Probability of error = $P\{Z \text{ is assigned to } G | Z \text{ came from } F\}$

$= P\{Z \text{ is assigned to } F | Z \text{ came from } G\}$

Distance function = Δ .

*The starred values were read from graphs

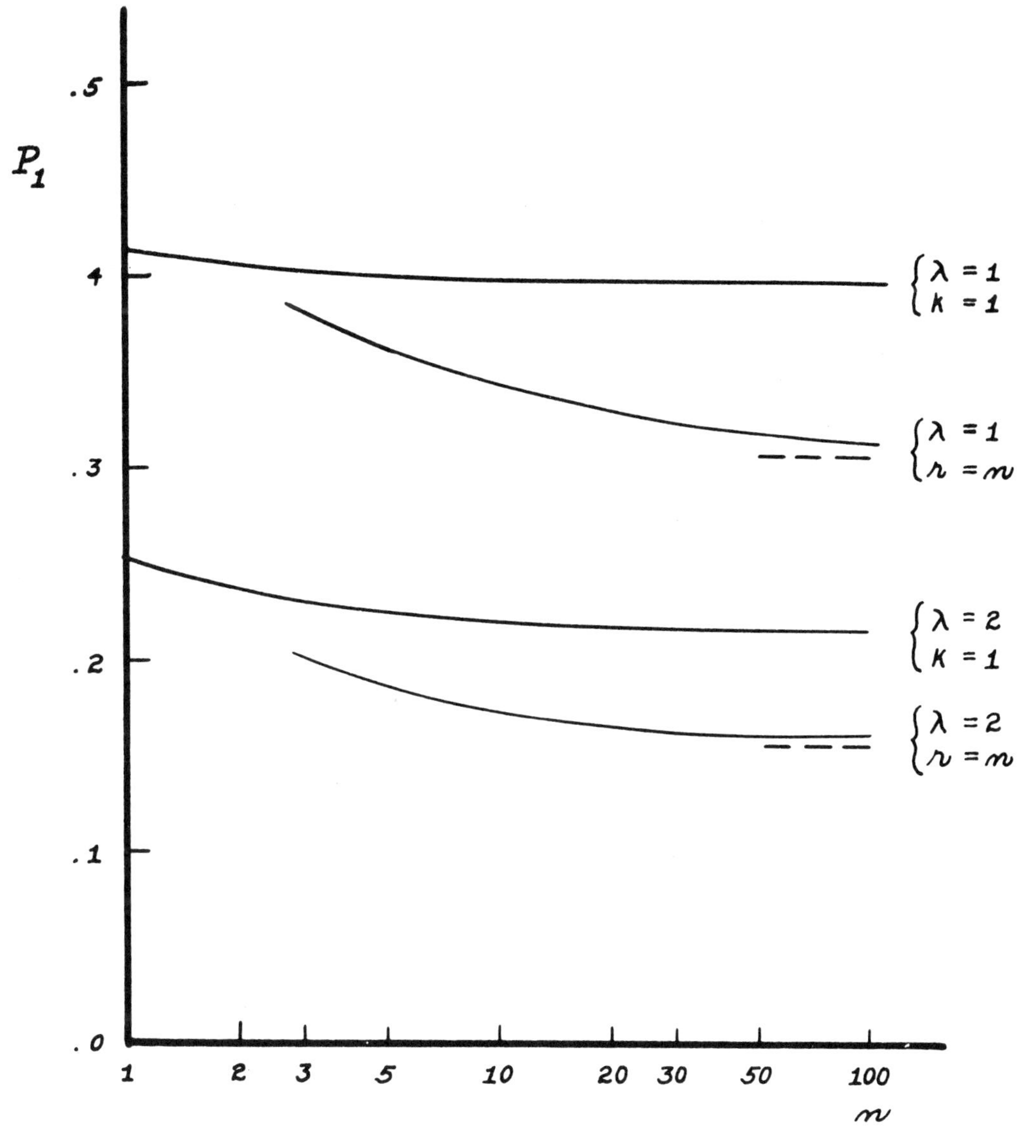

Figure 8

Probability of error P_1 of the nonparametric discriminator, distance function = Δ, for two bivariate normal populations with distance between means = λ. n = size of sample from each population. k = k' = 1 and r = 1 for k = 1; r = n for k' = 1. --- indicates the optimum procedure.

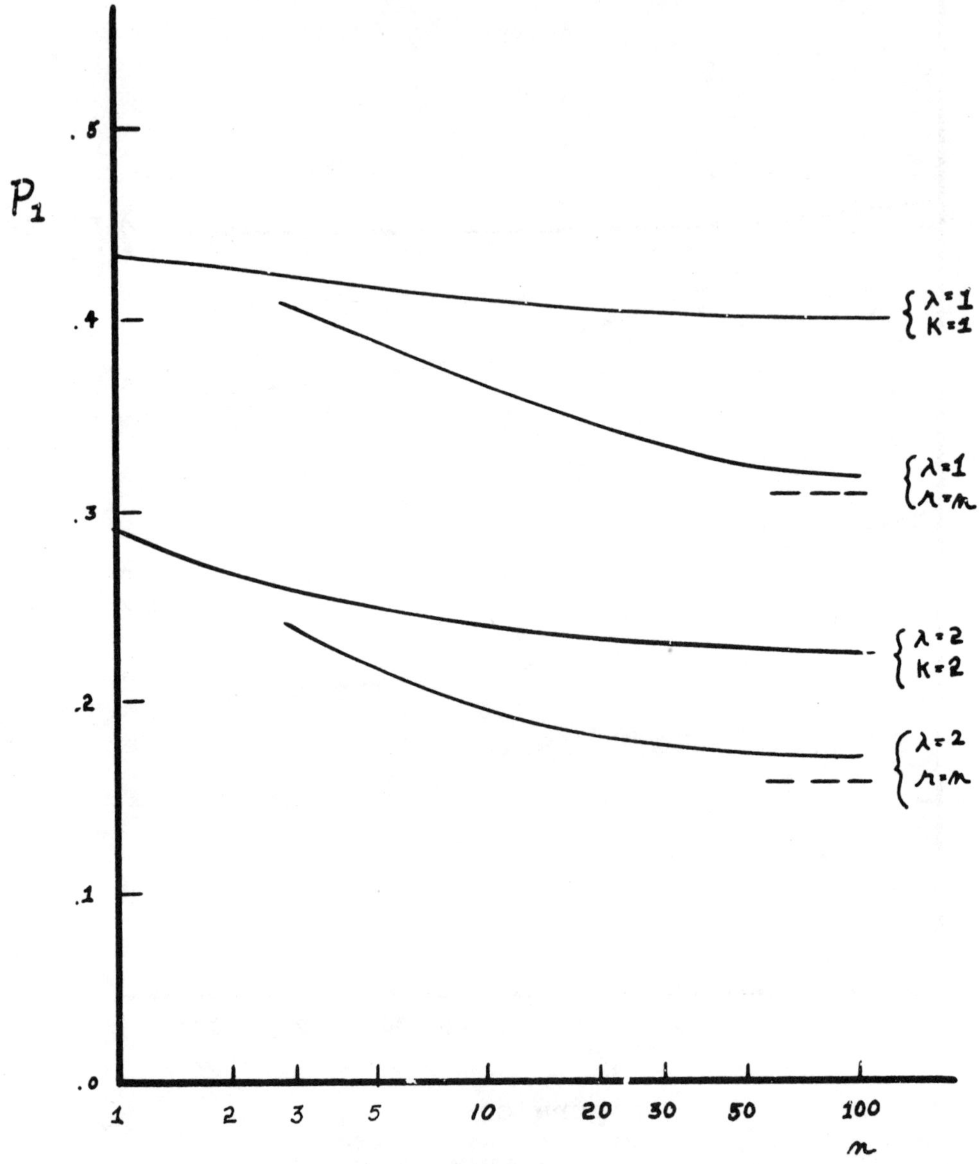

Figure 9

Probability of error P_1 of the nonparametric discriminator, distance function = Δ, for two bivariate normal distributions, $r = 1$ with $k' = 1$ and $r = n$ with $k' = 1$.

7. Alternative distance functions for the normal bivariate distribution

The dependence of P_1 on the distance function was emphasized in section 3. The numerical results which are given in this section are intended to show the magnitude of the effect on P_1 of certain moderate changes in the distance function.

During the computations which are reported in section 5, we noticed that the value of $P_1(0,0)$, the conditional probability of error given that Z is at the origin (the expected position of Z), was remarkably consistent with the value of P_1. Since we felt that it would be more worthwhile to survey a larger area of problems than to concentrate on the complete answer to one, we decided to make use of the fact noted above and to recalculate the values of $P_1(0,0)$ for various distance functions. In table VII, the values of $P_1(0,0)$ and P_1 are given, together with the difference $P_1 - P_1(0,0)$. The fourth column gives and approximation for P_1 obtained by adding a crude correction term to $P_1(0,0)$, namely,

$$\frac{1}{3}\,\frac{.5 - P_1(0,0)}{\lambda/2},$$

.5 being the value of $P_1(\lambda/2, x_2)$. It is our belief that the order of the magnitude of the change in P_1 with the change of distance function will be shown by the effect of the distance function on $P_1(0,0)$.

Table VII

Comparison of the probabilities of error P_1 with the conditional probability of error $P_1(0,0)$ given that Z is at the origin. Nonparametric discriminator, normal p-variate distribution, p = 1, 2, k = 1, 3.

n	P_1	$P_1(0,0)$	D	$\tilde{P}_1$	P_1	$P_1(0,0)$	D	$\tilde{P}_1$
	$\lambda = 1$, p = 2, k = 1				$\lambda = 2$, p = 2, k = 1			
1	.435	.391	.044	.464	.292	.184	.108	.289
2	.429	.385	.044	.462	.269	.159	.110	.273
3	.423	.383	.040	.461	.259	.149	.110	.266
4	.420	.382	.038	.461	.252	.142	.110	.261
5	.417	.381	.036	.460	.250	.139	.111	.259
10	.411	.379	.032	.460	.240	.130	.110	.253
20	.406	.379	.027	.460	.234	.125	.109	.250
50	.402	.378	.024	.459	.230	.121	.109	.247
∞	.398	.378	.020	.459	.225	.119	.106	.246
	$\lambda = 1$, p = 2, k = 3				$\lambda = 2$, p = 2, k = 3			
3	.408	.339	.069	.446	.238	.088	.150	.225
	$\lambda = 3$, p = 2, k = 1				$\lambda = 1$, p = 1, k = 1			
1	.157	.051	.106	.151	.418	.365	.053	.455
2	.135	.027	.108	.132	.409	.365	.043	.455
3	.125	.024	.101	.130	.405	.367	.038	.456
4	.120	.021	.099	.127	.403	.368	.035	.456
5	.117	.019	.098	.126	.401	.369	.032	.456
10	.109	.015	.094	.123	.399	.373	.026	.458
20	.104	.013	.091	.121	.398	.375	.023	.458
50	.100	.012	.088	.120	.398	.376	.021	.459
∞	.098	.011	.087	.120	.398	.378	.020	.459
	$\lambda = 3$, p = 2, k = 3							
3	.110	.007	.103	.117				
	$\lambda = 2$, p = 1, k = 1				$\lambda = 3$, p = 1, k = 1			
1	.253	.145	.108	.263	.124	.033	.090	.137
2	.236	.125	.112	.250	.108	.019	.090	.126
3	.231	.119	.112	.246	.104	.015	.089	.123
4	.228	.116	.111	.244	.101	.013	.088	.121
5	.225	.115	.109	.243	.099	.012	.087	.120
10	.223	.115	.108	.243	.098	.011	.087	.120
20	.224	.116	.108	.244	.098	.011	.087	.120
50	.225	.119	.105	.246	.098	.011	.088	.120
∞	.225	.119	.106	.246	.098	.011	.087	.120

$D = P_1 - P_1(0,0)$

$$\tilde{P}_1 = P_1(0,0) + \frac{2[.5 - P_1(0,0)]}{3}$$

In selecting the alternative distances, we had in mind that, in general, we were dealing with a transformed space and were interested in the effect on the probability of error if Δ itself were used as a distance function in the original space. The distance functions chosen are as follows. The definition of Δ is repeated for the sake of completeness.

$$\text{(i)} \quad \Delta[(x_1,x_2),(z_1,z_2)] = \max\{|x_1 - z_1|, |x_2 - z_2|\}.$$

The locus of points at a given distance from z is a square, centered at z, with sides parallel to the axes.

$$\text{(ii)} \quad \Delta_1[(x_1,x_2),(z_1,z_2)] = \sqrt{(x_1 - z_1)^2 + (x_2 - z_2)^2}.$$

Thus Δ_1 is ordinary Euclidean distance (perhaps a more natural distance function than Δ). The locus of points at a given distance from z is a circle centered at z.

$$\text{(iii)} \quad \Delta_2[(x_1,x_2),(z_1,z_2)] = \max\{|x_1 - z_1|, 3|x_2 - z_2|\}.$$

The locus of points at a given distance from z is a rectangle centered at z whose sides are parallel to the axes and in the ratio of one to three.

$$\text{(iv)} \quad \Delta_3[(x_1,x_2),(z_1,z_2)] = \max\{3|x_1 - z_1|, |x_2 - z_2|\}.$$

The locus of points at a given distance from z is a rectangle centered at z with sides parallel to the axes and in the ratio of three to one.

Distance functions Δ_2 and Δ_3 are the transforms if the original distributions is independent normal bivariate but the variances of the two measurements are unequal.

(v) Distance functions denoted by Δ (ρ = a). The locus of points is a square centered at z but whose sides are not parallel to the axes. The values of ρ are a = .25, .50, .75. This is the transform of Δ if the original distribution is joint normal bivariate with the two variates having unit variances and covariance = ρ.

The comparison of values of $P_1(0,0)$ for the various distance functions is given in table VIII and in figure 10. It will be seen that for all practical purposes it makes no difference whether Δ or Δ_1 (Euclidean distance) is used. However, the effect of the other distance functions is marked. This bears out the statement made previously that a burden is placed upon the statistician for selecting the appropriate distance function.

8. $p \geqq 2$ for the p-variate normal distribution

This section is an attempt to give an indication of the influence that an increase in p, the number of dimensions of the sample space, will produce on the probability of misclassification. We have again computed only the conditional probability $P_1(0)$ for z at the origin. Two alternative distance functions were used, namely,

Table VIII

Probabilities of error, nonparametric discriminator, normal bivariate distribution, $k = 1$.

		Δ		Δ_1		Δ_2		Δ_3	
λ	n	$P_1(0,0)$	P_1	$P_1(0,0)$	$\tilde{P}_1$	$P_1(0,0)$	$\tilde{P}_1$	$P_1(0,0)$	$\tilde{P}_1$
1	1	.391	.435	.389	.463				
2	1	.184	.292	.184	.289	.383	.422	.146	.225
2	2	.300	.269			.300	.367	.128	.211
2	3	.254	.259			.254	.336	.123	.207
2	4	.226	.252			.226	.317	.122	.206
3	1	.051	.157	.053	.152				
		$\Delta = \Delta(\rho=0)$		$\Delta(\rho=.25)$		$\Delta(\rho=.50)$		$\Delta(\rho=.75)$	
2	1	184	.292	.179	.286	.165	.277	.137	.258
	2	.159	.269	.152	.268	.129	.253	.084	.223
	3	.149	.259	.140	.260	.112	.241	.062	.208
	4	.142	.252	.133	.255	.102	.235	.049	.199

λ = distance between the means of the transformed populations

n = size of sample from each population

k = 1 = **nearest** neighbor rule

$P_1(0,0)$ = conditional probability that for z at the origin, Z will be misclassified

P_1 = probability of misclassification

$\tilde{P}_1$ = rough estimate of P_1. The figures to be compared are the $P_1(0,0)$

Distance functions Δ's are as defined in the preceding paragraphs

$$\Delta[(x_1,\cdots,x_p),(z_1,\cdots,z_p)] = \max_{i=1}^{p} |x_i - z_i|$$

and

$$\Delta_1[(x_1,\cdots,x_p),(z_1,\cdots,z_p)] = \sqrt{\sum_{i=1}^{p} (x_i - z_i)^2},$$

and the computations were carried out for $n = 1$, $k = 1$.

The results are shown in table IX and figure 11. As one would expect the results depend rather heavily on the dimen-

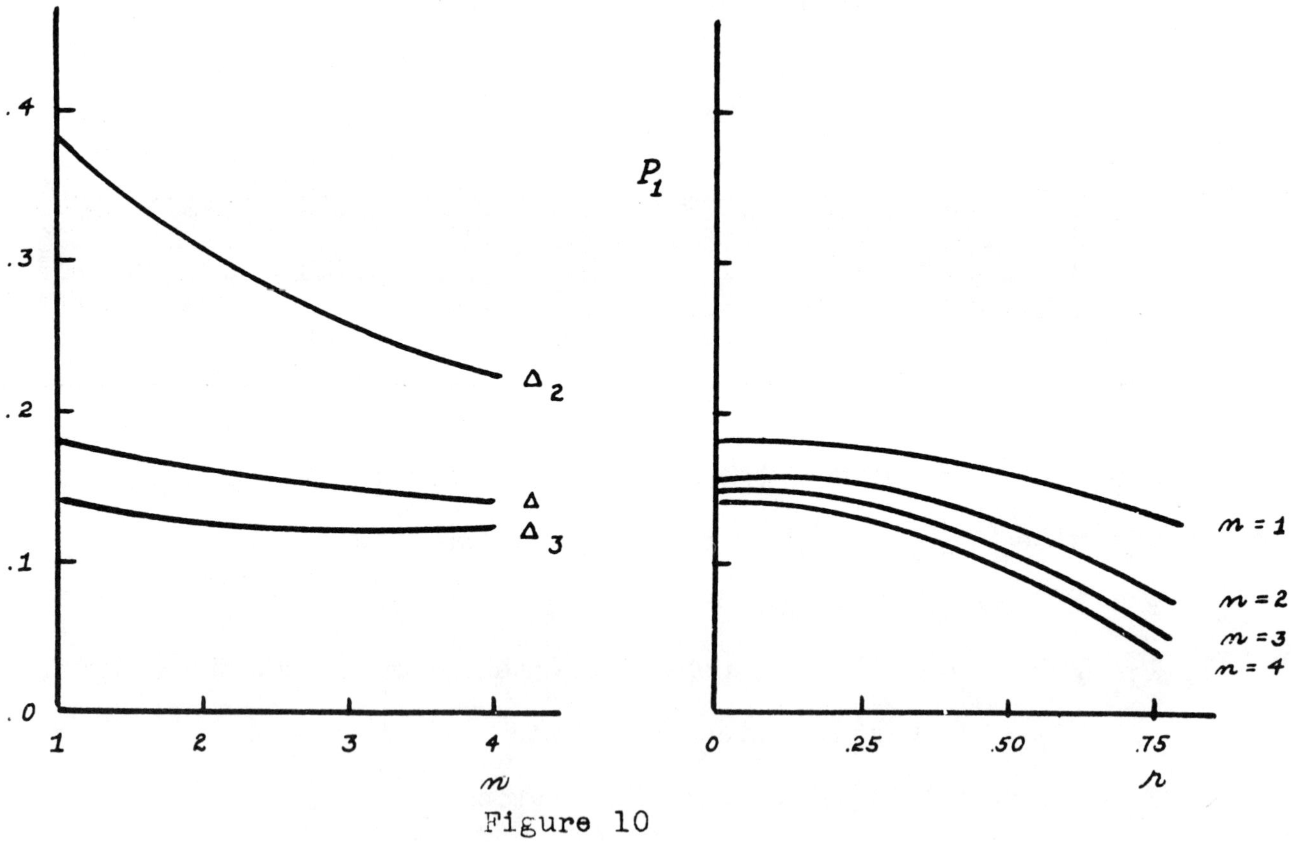

Figure 10

Probability of error P_1 of nonparametric discriminator for two bivariate normal distributions with distance between the means equal to 2 for various distance function. $n = k = 1$.

Table IX

Conditional probabilities $P_1(0,0)$ of error given that Z is at the origin, nonparametric discriminator, normal p-variate distribution, n = 1, k = 1

p	$\lambda = 1$ Δ_1	$\lambda = 2$ Δ	$\lambda = 2$ Δ_1	$\lambda = 3$ Δ_1
2	.389	.184	.184	.053
4	.414	.228	.230	.082
6	.427	.255	.259	.105
10		.288	.295	

sionality of the space when n is fixed. Admittedly, this is a most cursory glance at the situation for p dimensions. The fact that the figures refer to n = 1, k = 1, means of course that the figures have no practical value. Nevertheless, we decided to include them since it seemed that the behavior in this simplest case might provide some indication of what might be expected as the dimensionality p is increased.

9. Conclusion

The choice between parametric and nonparametric rules will in any given situation depend upon (i) the strength of the statistician's belief in his parametric model, (ii) the loss he would suffer by using the nonparametric rule if in fact the parametric form is correct and (iii) the loss he would suffer by using the parametric rule if the actual densities depart from the parametric form assumed. In [1], it was ascertained that if the sample size increases and at the same time the number of nearest neighbors on which the nonparametric procedures base its decision is increased but more slowly than the sample size, then in the limit the probabilities of error will be those of the optimum likelihood ratio rule whatever the population densities. However,

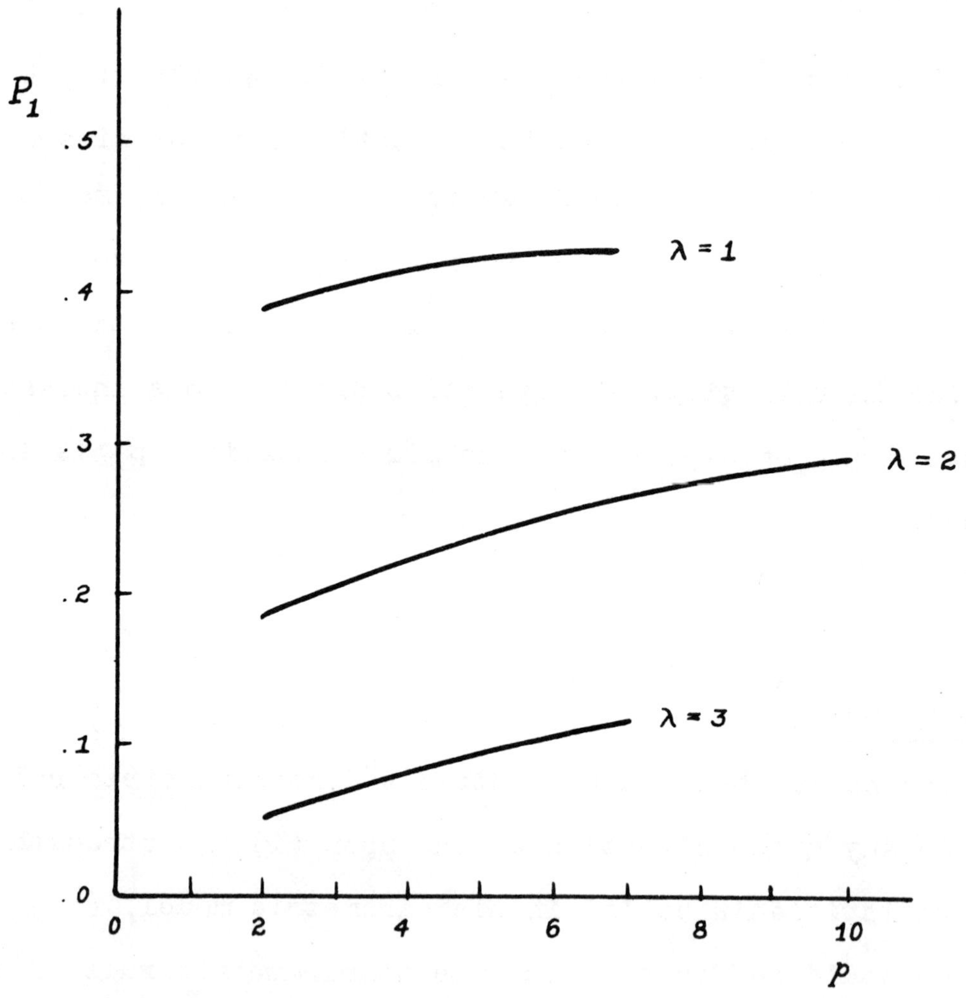

Figure 11

Probability of error P_1 of nonparametric discriminator, distance function $= \Delta$, for two p-variate distributions with distance between the means $= \lambda$. $n = 1$, $k = 1$.

the matter of greatest practical interest is the performance of the rules when the samples are small.

In this paper, we have been concerned with (ii) for the special case of greatest interest, the linear discriminant function. We succeeded in finding the probabilities of misclassification for some nonparametric procedures. However, the computation of the performance characteristic of the linear discriminant function proved to be too lengthy. It would be of extreme value, especially when one thinks of the wide use to which the linear discriminant function is put if its probabilities of misclassification in representative situations would be tabulated.

In summary, let us indicate the nature of the situations in which a nonparametric discriminator may be preferable to the linear discriminant function, and conversely. If the populations to be discriminated are well known, and have been investigated to establish that the normal distribution gives a good fit and that the variances and correlations do not change much when the means are changed, and if the classification to be made warrants the labor of matrix inversion, then the linear discriminant function should certainly be used. If on the other hand, the populations are either not well known, or are known not to be approximately normal, or to have very different covariance matrices; or if the discrimination is one in which small decreases in probability of error are not worth extensive computations, then the simple nonparametric rule, perhaps with $k \geq 3$, seems to have the edge.

In conclusion, we would like to express our appreciation to the many people to whom we are indebted for help in the preparation of this paper. Especially we would like to thank Mrs. Jeanne Lovasich and Mrs. Eloise Putz, who computed the tables for us.

REFERENCES

[1] EVELYN FIX and J. L. HODGES, Jr., "Nonparametric discrimination. I. Consistency properties," Technical report prepared under contract between University of California and School of Aviation Medicine, Randolph Field, Texas, 22 pp.

[2] Tables of probability functions. Vol. 2, Federal Works Agency, Mathematical Tables Project, National Bureau of Standards, 1942.

[3] KARL PEARSON, Tables for statisticians and biometricians parts 1 and 2. Cambridge University Press, 1930.

[4] T. A. JEEVES, "Functions of large numbers. Asymptotic expansions," from Probability methods in physics--seminar by Michel Loeve and appendix by participants, pp. 187-201. Mimeographed, University of California, 1948-1949.

[5] O. PERRON, K. Akad. der Wis., Munick, Sitz. Math. Phy. Kl., 1917, pp. 191-219.

$\frac{D^2}{S} = \max$

$D = \lambda \cdot (d^1 - d^2)$ if multiplied out

$= \lambda S_B \lambda^T$

THE USE OF MULTIPLE MEASUREMENTS IN TAXONOMIC PROBLEMS

By R. A. FISHER, Sc.D., F.R.S.

I. Discriminant functions

When two or more populations have been measured in several characters, $x_1, \ldots, x_s$, special interest attaches to certain linear functions of the measurements by which the populations are best discriminated. At the author's suggestion use has already been made of this fact in craniometry (*a*) by Mr E. S. Martin, who has applied the principle to the sex differences in measurements of the mandible, and (*b*) by Miss Mildred Barnard, who showed how to obtain from a series of dated series the particular compound of cranial measurements showing most distinctly a progressive or secular trend. In the present paper the application of the same principle will be illustrated on a taxonomic problem; some questions connected with the precision of the processes employed will also be discussed.

II. Arithmetical procedure

Table I shows measurements of the flowers of fifty plants each of the two species *Iris setosa* and *I. versicolor*, found growing together in the same colony and measured by Dr E. Anderson, to whom I am indebted for the use of the data. Four flower measurements are given. We shall first consider the question: What linear function of the four measurements

$$X = \lambda_1 x_1 + \lambda_2 x_2 + \lambda_3 x_3 + \lambda_4 x_4$$

will maximize the ratio of the difference between the specific means to the standard deviations within species? The observed means and their differences are shown in Table II. We may represent the differences by d_p, where $p = 1, 2, 3$ or 4 for the four measurements.

The sums of squares and products of deviations from the specific means are shown in Table III. Since fifty plants of each species were used these sums contain 98 degrees of freedom. We may represent these sums of squares or products by S_{pq}, where p and q take independently the values 1, 2, 3 and 4.

Then for any linear function, X, of the measurements, as defined above, the difference between the means of X in the two species is

$$D = \lambda_1 d_1 + \lambda_2 d_2 + \lambda_3 d_3 + \lambda_4 d_4,$$

while the variance of X within species is proportional to

$$S = \sum_{p=1}^{4} \sum_{q=1}^{4} \lambda_p \lambda_q S_{pq}.$$

The particular linear function which best discriminates the two species will be one for

Reprinted with permission from *Ann. Eugenics*, vol. 7, pp. 179–188, 1936.

Table I

Iris setosa				*Iris versicolor*				*Iris virginica*			
Sepal length	Sepal width	Petal length	Petal width	Sepal length	Sepal width	Petal length	Petal width	Sepal length	Sepal width	Petal length	Petal width
5·1	3·5	1·4	0·2	7·0	3·2	4·7	1·4	6·3	3·3	6·0	2·5
4·9	3·0	1·4	0·2	6·4	3·2	4·5	1·5	5·8	2·7	5·1	1·9
4·7	3·2	1·3	0·2	6·9	3·1	4·9	1·5	7·1	3·0	5·9	2·1
4·6	3·1	1·5	0·2	5·5	2·3	4·0	1·3	6·3	2·9	5·6	1·8
5·0	3·6	1·4	0·2	6·5	2·8	4·6	1·5	6·5	3·0	5·8	2·2
5·4	3·9	1·7	0·4	5·7	2·8	4·5	1·3	7·6	3·0	6·6	2·1
4·6	3·4	1·4	0·3	6·3	3·3	4·7	1·6	4·9	2·5	4·5	1·7
5·0	3·4	1·5	0·2	4·9	2·4	3·3	1·0	7·3	2·9	6·3	1·8
4·4	2·9	1·4	0·2	6·6	2·9	4·6	1·3	6·7	2·5	5·8	1·8
4·9	3·1	1·5	0·1	5·2	2·7	3·9	1·4	7·2	3·6	6·1	2·5
5·4	3·7	1·5	0·2	5·0	2·0	3·5	1·0	6·5	3·2	5·1	2·0
4·8	3·4	1·6	0·2	5·9	3·0	4·2	1·5	6·4	2·7	5·3	1·9
4·8	3·0	1·4	0·1	6·0	2·2	4·0	1·0	6·8	3·0	5·5	2·1
4·3	3·0	1·1	0·1	6·1	2·9	4·7	1·4	5·7	2·5	5·0	2·0
5·8	4·0	1·2	0·2	5·6	2·9	3·6	1·3	5·8	2·8	5·1	2·4
5·7	4·4	1·5	0·4	6·7	3·1	4·4	1·4	6·4	3·2	5·3	2·3
5·4	3·9	1·3	0·4	5·6	3·0	4·5	1·5	6·5	3·0	5·5	1·8
5·1	3·5	1·4	0·3	5·8	2·7	4·1	1·0	7·7	3·8	6·7	2·2
5·7	3·8	1·7	0·3	6·2	2·2	4·5	1·5	7·7	2·6	6·9	2·3
5·1	3·8	1·5	0·3	5·6	2·5	3·9	1·1	6·0	2·2	5·0	1·5
5·4	3·4	1·7	0·2	5·9	3·2	4·8	1·8	6·9	3·2	5·7	2·3
5·1	3·7	1·5	0·4	6·1	2·8	4·0	1·3	5·6	2·8	4·9	2·0
4·6	3·6	1·0	0·2	6·3	2·5	4·9	1·5	7·7	2·8	6·7	2·0
5·1	3·3	1·7	0·5	6·1	2·8	4·7	1·2	6·3	2·7	4·9	1·8
4·8	3·4	1·9	0·2	6·4	2·9	4·3	1·3	6·7	3·3	5·7	2·1
5·0	3·0	1·6	0·2	6·6	3·0	4·4	1·4	7·2	3·2	6·0	1·8
5·0	3·4	1·6	0·4	6·8	2·8	4·8	1·4	6·2	2·8	4·8	1·8
5·2	3·5	1·5	0·2	6·7	3·0	5·0	1·7	6·1	3·0	4·9	1·8
5·2	3·4	1·4	0·2	6·0	2·9	4·5	1·5	6·4	2·8	5·6	2·1
4·7	3·2	1·6	0·2	5·7	2·6	3·5	1·0	7·2	3·0	5·8	1·6
4·8	3·1	1·6	0·2	5·5	2·4	3·8	1·1	7·4	2·8	6·1	1·9
5·4	3·4	1·5	0·4	5·5	2·4	3·7	1·0	7·9	3·8	6·4	2·0
5·2	4·1	1·5	0·1	5·8	2·7	3·9	1·2	6·4	2·8	5·6	2·2
5·5	4·2	1·4	0·2	6·0	2·7	5·1	1·6	6·3	2·8	5·1	1·5
4·9	3·1	1·5	0·2	5·4	3·0	4·5	1·5	6·1	2·6	5·6	1·4
5·0	3·2	1·2	0·2	6·0	3·4	4·5	1·6	7·7	3·0	6·1	2·3
5·5	3·5	1·3	0·2	6·7	3·1	4·7	1·5	6·3	3·4	5·6	2·4
4·9	3·6	1·4	0·1	6·3	2·3	4·4	1·3	6·4	3·1	5·5	1·8
4·4	3·0	1·3	0·2	5·6	3·0	4·1	1·3	6·0	3·0	4·8	1·8
5·1	3·4	1·5	0·2	5·5	2·5	4·0	1·3	6·9	3·1	5·4	2·1
5·0	3·5	1·3	0·3	5·5	2·6	4·4	1·2	6·7	3·1	5·6	2·4
4·5	2·3	1·3	0·3	6·1	3·0	4·6	1·4	6·9	3·1	5·1	2·3
4·4	3·2	1·3	0·2	5·8	2·6	4·0	1·2	5·8	2·7	5·1	1·9
5·0	3·5	1·6	0·6	5·0	2·3	3·3	1·0	6·8	3·2	5·9	2·3
5·1	3·8	1·9	0·4	5·6	2·7	4·2	1·3	6·7	3·3	5·7	2·5
4·8	3·0	1·4	0·3	5·7	3·0	4·2	1·2	6·7	3·0	5·2	2·3
5·1	3·8	1·6	0·2	5·7	2·9	4·2	1·3	6·3	2·5	5·0	1·9
4·6	3·2	1·4	0·2	6·2	2·9	4·3	1·3	6·5	3·0	5·2	2·0
5·3	3·7	1·5	0·2	5·1	2·5	3·0	1·1	6·2	3·4	5·4	2·3
5·0	3·3	1·4	0·2	5·7	2·8	4·1	1·3	5·9	3·0	5·1	1·8

Table II. *Observed means for two species and their difference (cm.)*

	Versicolor	*Setosa*	Difference ($V-S$)
Sepal length (x_1)	5·936	5·006	0·930
Sepal width (x_2)	2·770	3·428	−0·658
Petal length (x_3)	4·260	1·462	2·798
Petal width (x_4)	1·326	0·246	1·080

Table III. *Sums of squares and products of four measurements, within species* ($cm.^2$)

	Sepal length	Sepal width	Petal length	Petal width
Sepal length	19·1434	9·0356	9·7634	3·2394
Sepal width	9·0356	11·8658	4·6232	2·4746
Petal length	9·7634	4·6232	12·2978	3·8794
Petal width	3·2394	2·4746	3·8794	2·4604

which the ratio D^2/S is greatest, by variation of the four coefficients λ_1, λ_2, λ_3 and λ_4 independently. This gives for each λ

$$\frac{D}{S^2}\left\{2S\frac{\partial D}{\partial \lambda}-D\frac{\partial S}{\partial \lambda}\right\}=0,$$

or

$$\frac{1}{2}\cdot\frac{\partial S}{\partial \lambda}=\frac{S}{D}\frac{\partial D}{\partial \lambda},$$

where it may be noticed that S/D is a factor constant for the four unknown coefficients Consequently, the coefficients required are proportional to the solutions of the equations

$$\left.\begin{aligned}S_{11}\lambda_1+S_{12}\lambda_2+S_{13}\lambda_3+S_{14}\lambda_4&=d_1,\\ S_{12}\lambda_1+S_{22}\lambda_2+S_{23}\lambda_3+S_{24}\lambda_4&=d_2,\\ S_{13}\lambda_1+S_{23}\lambda_2+S_{33}\lambda_3+S_{34}\lambda_4&=d_3,\\ S_{14}\lambda_1+S_{24}\lambda_2+S_{34}\lambda_3+S_{44}\lambda_4&=d_4.\end{aligned}\right\} \quad \text{......(1)}$$

If, in turn, unity is substituted for each of the differences and zero for the others, the solutions obtained constitute the matrix of multipliers reciprocal to the matrix of S; numerically we find:

Table IV. *Matrix of multipliers reciprocal to the sums of squares and products within species* ($cm.^{-2}$)

	Sepal length	Sepal width	Petal length	Petal width
Sepal length	0·1187161	−0·0668666	−0·0816158	0·0396350
Sepal width	−0·0668666	0·1452736	0·0334101	−0·1107529
Petal length	−0·0816158	0·0334101	0·2193614	−0·2720206
Petal width	0·0396350	−0·1107529	−0·2720206	0·8945506

These values may be denoted by s_{pq} for values of p and q from 1 to 4.

Multiplying the columns of the matrix in Table IV by the observed differences, we have the solutions of the equation (1) in the form

$$\lambda = -0\cdot0311511,\quad \lambda_2 = -0\cdot1839075,\quad \lambda_3 = +0\cdot2221044,\quad \lambda_4 = +0\cdot3147370,$$

so that, if we choose to take the coefficient of sepal length to be unity, the compound measurement required is

$$X = x_1 + 5\cdot9037x_2 - 7\cdot1299x_3 - 10\cdot1036x_4.$$

If in this expression we substitute the values observed in *setosa* plants, the mean, as found from the values in Table I, is

$$5\cdot006 + (3\cdot428)\,(5\cdot9037) - (1\cdot462)\,(7\cdot1299) - (0\cdot246)\,(10\cdot1036) = 12\cdot3345 \text{ cm.};$$

for *versicolor*, on the contrary, we have

$$5\cdot936 + (2\cdot770)\,(5\cdot9037) - (4\cdot260)\,(7\cdot1299) - (1\cdot326)\,(10\cdot1036) = -21\cdot4815 \text{ cm.}$$

The difference between the average values of the compound measurements being thus 33·816 cm.

The distinctness of the metrical characters of the two species may now be gauged by comparing this difference between the average values with its standard error. Using the values of Table III, with the coefficients of our compound, we have

$$19\cdot1434 + (9\cdot0356)\,(5\cdot9037) - (9\cdot7634)\,(7\cdot1299) - (3\cdot2394)\,(10\cdot1036) = -29\cdot8508,$$

$$9\cdot0356 + (11\cdot8658)\,(5\cdot9037) - (4\cdot6232)\,(7\cdot1299) - (2\cdot4746)\,(10\cdot1036) = 21\cdot1224,$$

$$9\cdot7634 + (4\cdot6232)\,(5\cdot9037) - (12\cdot2978)\,(7\cdot1299) - (3\cdot8794)\,(10\cdot1036) = -89\cdot8206,$$

$$3\cdot2394 + (2\cdot4746)\,(5\cdot9037) - (3\cdot8794)\,(7\cdot1299) - (2\cdot4604)\,(10\cdot1036) = -34\cdot6699,$$

and finally,

$$-29\cdot8508 + (21\cdot1224)\,(5\cdot9037) + (89\cdot8206)\,(7\cdot1299) + (34\cdot6699)\,(10\cdot1036) = 1085\cdot5522.$$

The average variance of the two species in respect of the compound measurements may be estimated by dividing this value (1085·5522) by 95; the variance of the difference between two means of fifty plants each, by dividing again by 25. For single plants the variance is 11·4269, so that the mean difference, 33·816 cm., between a pair of plants of different species has a standard deviation of 4·781 cm. For means of fifty the same average difference has the standard error 0·6761 cm., or only about one-fiftieth of its value.

III. Interpretation

The ratio of the difference between the means of the chosen compound measurement to its standard error in individual plants is of interest also in relation to the probability of misclassification, if the specific nature were judged wholly from the measurements. For reasons to be discussed later we shall estimate the variance of a single plant by dividing 1085·5522 by 95, giving 11·4269 cm.^{2} for the variance, and 3·3804 cm. for the standard deviation. Supposing that a plant is misclassified, if its deviation in the right direction exceeds half the difference, 33·816 cm., between the species, the ratio to the standard as estimated is 5·0018. (33·816/2)/3·3804

The table of the normal distribution (*Statistical Methods*, Table II) shows that a ratio 4·89164 is exceeded five times in a million, and 5·32672 only once in two million trials. By logarithmic interpolation the frequency appropriate to a ratio 5·0018 is about 2·79 per million. If the variances of the two species are unequal, this frequency is somewhat overestimated by this method, since we ought to divide the specific difference in proportion to the two standard deviations, and for constant sum of variances the sum of the standard deviations is greatest when they are equal. We may, therefore, at once conclude that if the measurements are nearly normally distributed the probability of misclassification, using the compound movement only is less than three per million.

The same ratio is of interest from another aspect. If the chosen compound X is analysed in respect to its variation within and between species, the sum of squares between species must be $25D^2$. Numerically we have, therefore,

Table V. *Analysis of variance of the chosen compound X, between and within species*

	Degrees of freedom	Sum of squares
Between species	4	28588·05
Within species	95	1085·55
Total	99	29673·60

Of the total only 3·6583 per cent. is within species, and 96·3417 per cent. between species. The compound has been chosen to maximize the latter percentage. Since, in addition to the specific means, we have used three adjustable ratios, the variation within species must contain only 95 degrees of freedom.

In making up the variate X, we have multiplied the original values of λ by $-32·1018$ in order to give to the measurement sepal length the coefficient unity. Had we used the original values, the analysis of Table V would have appeared as:

Table VI. *Analysis of variance of the crude compound X, between and within species*

	Degrees of freedom	Sum of squares	
Between species	4	27·74160	$=25D^2$
Within species	95	1·05341	$= \quad D = S$
Total	99	28·79501	$D(1+25D)$

On multiplying equations (1) by λ_1, λ_2, λ_3 and λ_4 and adding, it appears that $S = \Sigma\lambda d = D$, the specific difference in the crude compound X. The proportion (3·6 per cent.) of the sum of squares within species could therefore have been found simply as $1/(1+25D)$.

IV. The analogy of partial regression

The analysis of Table VI suggests an analogy of some interest. If to each plant were assigned a value of a variate y, the same for all members of each species, the analysis of variance of y, between the portions accountable by linear regression on the measurements $x_1, \ldots, x_4$, and the residual variation after fitting such a regression, would be identical with Table VI, if y were given appropriate equal and opposite values for the two species.

In general, with different numbers of representatives of the two species, n_1 and n_2, if the values of y assigned were

$$\frac{n_2}{n_1+n_2} \quad \text{and} \quad \frac{-n_1}{n_1+n_2},$$

differing by unity, the right-hand sides of the equations for the regression coefficients, corresponding to equation (1), would have been

$$\frac{n_1 n_2}{n_1+n_2} d_p,$$

where d_p is the difference between the means of the two species in any one of the measurements. The typical coefficient of the left-hand side would be

$$S_{pq} + \frac{n_1 n_2}{n_1+n_2} d_p d_q.$$

Transferring the additional fractions to the right-hand side, we should have equations identical with (1), save that the right-hand sides are now

$$\frac{n_1 n_2}{n_1+n_2} d_p (1 - \Sigma\lambda' d),$$

where λ' stands for a solution of the new equations; hence

$$\lambda' = \frac{n_1 n_2}{n_1+n_2} (1 - \Sigma\lambda' d)\, \lambda,$$

multiply these equations by d and add, so that

$$\Sigma\lambda' d = \frac{n_1 n_2}{n_1+n_2} \Sigma\lambda d\, (1 - \Sigma\lambda' d),$$

or

$$(1 - \Sigma\lambda' d)\left(1 + \frac{n_1 n_2}{n_1+n_2} \Sigma\lambda d\right) = 1,$$

and so in our example

$$1 - \Sigma\lambda' d = \frac{1}{1+25D}.$$

The analysis of variance of y is, therefore,

Table VII. *Analysis of variance of a variate y determined exclusively by the species*

	Degrees of freedom	Sum of squares	
Regression	4	24·0854	$25^2D/1+25D$
Remainder	95	0·9146	$25/1+25D$
Total	99	25·0000	

The total $S(y^2)$ is clearly in general $\frac{n_1 n_2}{n_1+n_2}$; the portion ascribable to regression is

$$\frac{n_1 n_2}{n_1+n_2}\Sigma\lambda' d = \frac{25^2 D}{1+25D}.$$

In this method of presentation the appropriate allocation of the degrees of freedom is evident.

The multiple correlation of y with the measurements $x_1, \ldots, x_4$ is given by

$$R^2 = 25D/1+25D.$$

V. Test of significance

It is now clear in what manner the specific difference may be tested for significance, so as to allow for the fact that a variate has been chosen so as to maximise the distinctness of the species. The regression of y on the four measurements is given 4 degrees of freedom, and the residual variation 95; the value of z calculated from the sums of squares in any one of Tables V, VI or VII is 3·2183 or

$$\tfrac{1}{2}(\log 95 - \log 4 + \log 25 + \log D),$$

a very significant value for the number of degrees of freedom used.

VI. Applications to the theory of allopolyploidy

We may now consider one of the extensions of this procedure which are available when samples have been taken from more than two populations. The sample of the third species given in Table I, *Iris virginica*, differs from the two other samples in not being taken from the same natural colony as they were—a circumstance which might considerably disturb both the mean values and their variabilities. It is of interest in association with *I. setosa* and *I. versicolor* in that Randoph (1934) has ascertained and Anderson has confirmed that, whereas *I. setosa* is a "diploid" species with 38 chromosomes, *I. virginica* is "tetraploid", with 70, and *I. versicolor*, which is intermediate in three measurements, though not in sepal breadth, is hexaploid. He has suggested the interesting possibility that *I. versicolor* is a polyploid hybrid of the two other species. We shall, therefore, consider whether, when we use the linear compound of the four measurements most appropriate for discriminating three such species, the mean value for *I. versicolor* takes an intermediate value, and, if so, whether it differs twice as much from *I. setosa* as from *I. virginica*, as might be expected, if the effects of genes are simply additive, in a hybrid between a diploid and a tetraploid species.

If a third value lies two-thirds of the way from one value to another, the three deviations from their common mean must be in the ratio 4 : 1 : −5. To obtain values corresponding with the differences between the two species we may, therefore, form linear compounds of their mean measurements, using these numerical coefficients. The results are shown in Table VIII where, for example, the value 7·258 cm. for sepal length is four times the mean

13-2

sepal length for *I. virginica* plus once the mean sepal length for *I. versicolor* minus five times the value for *I. setosa*.

Table VIII

Means	S_{pq}			
	Iris virginica. Fifty plants			
6·588	19·8128	4·5944	14·8612	2·4056
2·974	4·5944	5·0962	3·4976	2·3338
5·552	14·8612	3·4976	14·9248	2·3924
2·026	2·4056	2·3338	2·3924	3·6962
	Iris versicolor. Fifty plants			
5·936	13·0552	4·1740	8·9620	2·7332
2·770	4·1740	4·8250	4·0500	2·0190
4·260	8·9620	4·0500	10·8200	3·5820
1·326	2·7332	2·0190	3·5820	1·9162
	Iris setosa. Fifty plants			
5·006	6·0882	4·8616	0·8014	0·5062
3·428	4·8616	7·0408	0·5732	0·4556
1·462	0·8014	0·5732	1·4778	0·2974
0·246	0·5062	0·4556	0·2974	0·5442
	$4ri + ve - 5se$			
7·258	482·2650	199·2244	266·7762	53·8778
−2·474	199·2244	262·3842	74·3416	50·7498
19·158	266·7762	74·3416	286·5618	49·2954
8·200	53·8778	50·7498	49·2954	74·6604

Since the values for the sums of squares and products of deviations from the means within each of the three species are somewhat different, we may make an appropriate matrix corresponding with our chosen linear compound by multiplying the values for *I. virginica* by 16, those for *I. versicolor* by one and those for *I. setosa* by 25, and adding the values for the three species, as shown in Table VIII. The values so obtained will correspond with the matrix of sums of squares and products within species when only two populations have been sampled.

Using the rows of the matrix as the coefficients of four unknowns in an equation with our chosen compound of the mean measurements, e.g.

$$482{\cdot}2650\lambda_1 + 199{\cdot}2244\lambda_2 + 266{\cdot}7762\lambda_3 + 53{\cdot}8778\lambda_4 = 7{\cdot}258,$$

we find solutions which, when multiplied by 100, are

Coefficient of sepal length	−3·308998
sepal breadth	−2·759132
petal length	8·866048
petal breadth	9·392551

defining the compound measurement required.

It is now easy to find the means and variances of this compound measurement in the three species. These are shown in the table below (Table IX):

Table IX

	Mean	Sum of squares	Mean square	Standard deviation
I. virginica	38·24827	923·7958	18·8530	4·342
I. versicolor	22·93888	873·5119	17·8268	4·222
I. setosa	− 10·75042	292·8958	5·9775	2·444

From this table it can be seen that, whereas the difference between *I. setosa* and *I. versicolor*, 33·69 of our units, is so great compared with the standard deviations that no appreciable overlapping of values can occur, the difference between *I. virginica* and *I. versicolor*, 15·31 units, is less than four times the standard deviation of each species.

The differences do seem, however, to be remarkably closely in the ratio 2 : 1. Compared with this standard, *I. virginica* would appear to have exerted a slightly preponderant influence. The departure from expectation is, however, small, and we have the material for making at least an approximate test of significance.

If the differences between the means were exactly in the ratio 2 : 1, then the linear function formed by adding the means with coefficients in the ratio 2 :−3 : 1 would be zero. Actually it has the value 3·07052. The sampling variance of this compound is found by multiplying the variances of the three species by 4, 9 and 1, adding them together and dividing by 50, since each mean is based on fifty plants. This gives 4·8365 for the variance and 2·199 for the standard error. Thus on this test the discrepancy, 3·071, is certainly not significant, though it somewhat exceeds its standard error.

In theory the test of significance is not wholly exact, since in estimating the sampling variance of each species we have divided the sum of squares of deviations from the mean by 49, as though these deviations had in all 147 degrees of freedom. Actually three degrees of freedom have been absorbed in adjusting the coefficients of the linear compound so as to discriminate the species as distinctly as possible. Had we divided by 48 instead of by 49 the standard error would have been raised by a trifle to the value 2·231, which would not have affected the interpretation of the data. This change, however, would certainly have been an over-correction, since it is the variances of the extreme species *I. virginica* and *I. setosa* which are most reduced in the choice of the compound measurement, while that of *I. versicolor* contributes the greater part of the sampling error in the test of significance.

The diagram, Fig. 1, shows the actual distributions of the compound measurement adopted in the individuals of the three species measured. It will be noticed, as was anticipated above, that there is some overlap of the distributions of *I. virginica* and *I. versicolor*, so that a certain diagnosis of these two species could not be based solely on these four measurements of a single flower taken on a plant growing wild. It is not, however, impossible that in culture the measurements alone should afford a more complete discrimination.

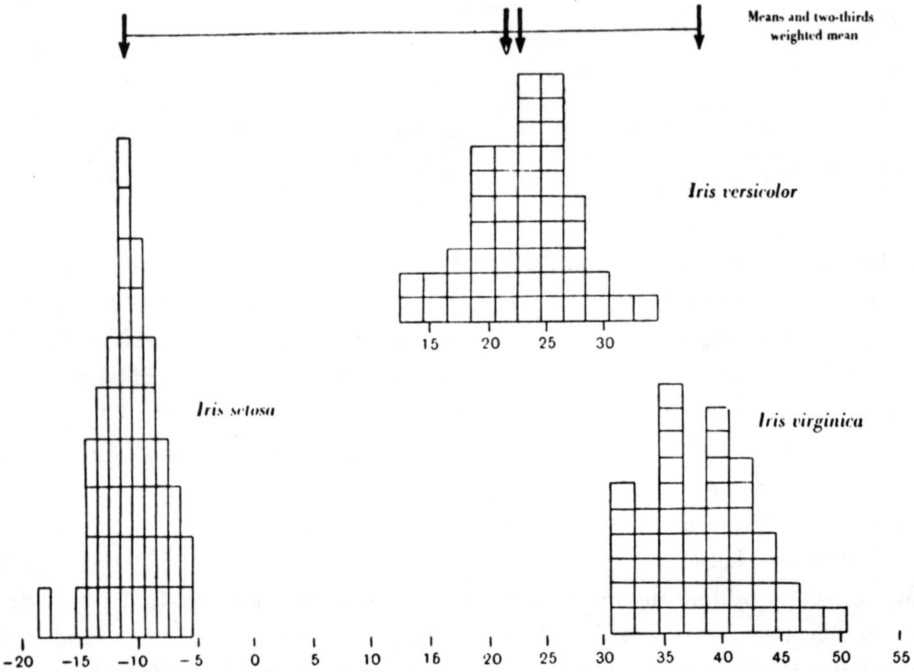

Fig. 1. Frequency histograms of the discriminating linear function, for three species of *Iris*.

REFERENCES

RANDOLPH, L. F. (1934). "Chromosome numbers in native American and introduced species and cultivated varieties of Iris." *Bull. Amer. Iris Soc.* **52**, 61–66.

ANDERSON, EDGAR (1935). "The irises of the Gaspe Peninsula." *Bull. Amer. Iris Soc.* **59**, 2–5.

—— (1936). "The species problem in *Iris*." *Ann. Mo. bot. Gdn.* (in the Press).

Nearest Neighbor Pattern Classification

T. M. COVER, MEMBER, IEEE, AND P. E. HART, MEMBER, IEEE

Abstract—**The nearest neighbor decision rule assigns to an unclassified sample point the classification of the nearest of a set of previously classified points. This rule is independent of the underlying joint distribution on the sample points and their classifications, and hence the probability of error R of such a rule must be at least as great as the Bayes probability of error R^*—the minimum probability of error over all decision rules taking underlying probability structure into account. However, in a large sample analysis, we will show in the M-category case that $R^* \leq R \leq R^*(2 - MR^*/(M-1))$, where these bounds are the tightest possible, for all suitably smooth underlying distributions. Thus for any number of categories, the probability of error of the nearest neighbor rule is bounded above by twice the Bayes probability of error. In this sense, it may be said that half the classification information in an infinite sample set is contained in the nearest neighbor.**

I. Introduction

IN THE CLASSIFICATION problem there are two extremes of knowledge which the statistician may possess. Either he may have complete statistical knowledge of the underlying joint distribution of the observation x and the true category θ, or he may have no knowledge of the underlying distribution except that which can be inferred from samples. In the first extreme, a standard Bayes analysis will yield an optimal decision procedure and the corresponding minimum (Bayes) probability of error of classification R^*. In the other extreme, a decision to classify x into category θ is allowed to depend only on a collection of n correctly classified samples (x_1, θ_1), (x_2, θ_2), $\cdots$, (x_n, θ_n), and the decision procedure is by no means clear. This problem is in the domain of nonparametric statistics and no optimal classification procedure exists with respect to all underlying statistics.

If it is assumed that the classified samples (x_i, θ_i) are independently identically distributed according to the distribution of (x, θ), certain heuristic arguments may be made about good decision procedures. For example, it is reasonable to assume that observations which are close together (in some appropriate metric) will have the same classification, or at least will have almost the same posterior probability distributions on their respective classifications. Thus to classify the unknown sample x we may wish to weight the evidence of the nearby x_i's most heavily. Perhaps the simplest nonparametric decision procedure of this form is the *nearest neighbor* (NN) rule, which classifies x in the category of its nearest neighbor. Surprisingly, it will be shown that, in the large sample case, this simple rule has a probability of error which

Manuscript received February 23, 1966; revised April 29, 1966. This work has been supported at Stanford University by U. S. Army Electronics Command under Contract DA28-043-AMC-01764(E) and by USAF under Contract AF49(638)1517; and at the Stanford Research Institute, Menlo Park, Calif., by RADC under Contract AF30(602)-3945.

T. M. Cover is with the Department of Electrical Engineering, Stanford University, Stanford, Calif.

P. E. Hart is with the Stanford Research Institute, Menlo Park, Calif.

Reprinted from *IEEE Trans. Inform. Theory*, vol. IT-13, pp. 21–27, Jan. 1967.

is less than twice the Bayes probability of error, and hence is less than twice the probability of error of any other decision rule, nonparametric or otherwise, based on the infinite sample set.

The first formulation of a rule of the nearest neighbor type and primary previous contribution to the analysis of its properties, appears to have been made by Fix and Hodges [1] and [2]. They investigated a rule which might be called the k_n-nearest neighbor rule. It assigns to an unclassified point the class most heavily represented among its k_n nearest neighbors. Fix and Hodges established the consistency of this rule for sequences $k_n \to \infty$ such that $k_n/n \to 0$. In reference [2], they investigate numerically the small sample performance of the k_n-NN rule under the assumption of normal statistics.

The NN rule has been used by Johns [3] as an example of an empirical Bayes rule. Kanal [4], Sebestyen [5] (who calls it the proximity algorithm), and Nilsson [6] have mentioned the intuitive appeal of the NN rule and suggested its use in the pattern recognition problem. Loftsgaarden and Quesenberry [7] have shown that a simple modification of the k_n-NN rule gives a consistent estimate of a probability density function. In the above mentioned papers, no analytical results in the nonparametric case were obtained either for the finite sample size problem or for the finite number of nearest neighbors problem.

In this paper we shall show that, for any number n of samples, the single-NN rule has strictly lower probability of error than any other k_n-NN rule against certain classes of distributions, and hence is admissible among the k_n-NN rules. We will then establish the extent to which "samples which are close together have categories which are close together" and use this to compare in Section VI the probability of error of the NN-rule with the minimum possible probability of error.

II. The Nearest Neighbor Rule

A set of n pairs $(x_1, \theta_2), \cdots, (x_n, \theta_n)$ is given, where the x_i's take values in a metric space X upon which is defined a metric d, and the θ_i's take values in the set $\{1, 2, \cdots, M\}$. Each θ_i is considered to be the index of the category to which the ith individual belongs, and each x_i is the outcome of the set of measurements made upon that individual. For brevity, we shall frequently say "x_i belongs to θ_i" when we mean precisely that the ith individual, upon which measurements x_i have been observed, belongs to category θ_i.

A new pair (x, θ) is given, where only the measurement x is observable by the statistician, and it is desired to estimate θ by utilizing the information contained in the set of correctly classified points. We shall call

$$x_n' \in \{x_1, x_2, \cdots, x_n\}$$

a nearest neighbor to x if

$$\min d(x_i, x) = d(x_n', x) \quad i = 1, 2, \cdots, n. \tag{1}$$

The nearest neighbor rule decides x belongs to the category θ_n' of its nearest[1] neighbor x_n'. A mistake is made if $\theta_n' \neq \theta$. Notice that the NN rule utilizes only the classification of the nearest neighbor. The $n - 1$ remaining classifications θ_i are ignored.

III. Admissibility of Nearest Neighbor Rule

If the number of samples is large it makes good sense to use, instead of the single nearest neighbor, the majority vote of the nearest k neighbors. We wish k to be large in order to minimize the probability of a non-Bayes decision for the unclassified point x, but we wish k to be small (in proportion to the number of samples) in order that the points be close enough to x to give an accurate estimate of the posterior probabilities of the true class of x.

The purpose of this section is to show that, among the class of k-NN rules, the single nearest neighbor rule (1-NN) is admissible. That is, for the n-sample problem, there exists no k-NN rule, $k \neq 1$, which has lower probability of error against all distributions. We shall show that the single NN rule is undominated by exhibiting a simple distribution for which it has strictly lower probability of error P_e. The example to be given comes from the family of distributions for which simple decision boundaries provide complete separation of the samples into their respective categories. Fortunately, one example will serve for all n.

Consider the two category problem in which the prior probabilities $\eta_1 = \eta_2 = \frac{1}{2}$, and the conditional density f_1 is uniform on the unit disk D_1 centered at $(-3, 0)$, and the conditional density f_2 is uniform on the unit disk D_2 centered at $(3, 0)$ as shown in Fig. 1. In the n-sample problem, the probability that j individuals come from category 1, and hence have measurements lying in D_1, is $(\frac{1}{2})^n\binom{n}{j}$. Without loss of generality, assume that the unclassified x lies in category 1. Then the NN rule will make a classification error only if the nearest neighbor x_n' belongs to category 2, and thus, necessarily, lies in D_2. But, from inspection of the distance relationships, if the nearest neighbor to x is in D_2, then each of the x_i must lie in D_2. Thus the probability $P_e(1; n)$ of error of the NN rule in this case is precisely $(\frac{1}{2})^n$—the probability that $x_1, x_2, \cdots, x_n$ all lie in D_2. Let $k = 2k_0 + 1$. Then the k-NN rule makes an error if k_0 or fewer points lie in D_1. This occurs with probability

$$P_e(k; n) = (\tfrac{1}{2})^n \sum_{j=0}^{k_0} \binom{n}{j}. \tag{2}$$

Thus in this example, the 1-NN rule has strictly lower P_e than does any k-NN rule, $k \neq 1$, and hence is admissible in that class. Indeed

[1] In case of ties for the nearest neighbor, the rule may be modified to decide the most popular category among the ties. However, in those cases in which ties occur with nonzero probability, our results are trivially true.

$$P_e(k;n) \uparrow \tfrac{1}{2} \quad \text{in} \quad k, \quad \text{for any} \quad n,$$
$$P_e(k;n) \downarrow 0 \quad \text{in} \quad n, \quad \text{for any} \quad k > 0, \tag{3}$$

and

$$P_e(k_n;n) \to 0, \quad \text{if} \quad 0 < \frac{k_n}{n} \le \alpha < 1, \quad \text{for all} \quad n.$$

In general, then, the 1-NN rule is strictly better than the $k \neq$ 1-NN rule in those cases where the supports of the densities $f_1, f_2, \cdots, f_M$ are such that each in-class distance is greater than any between-class distance.

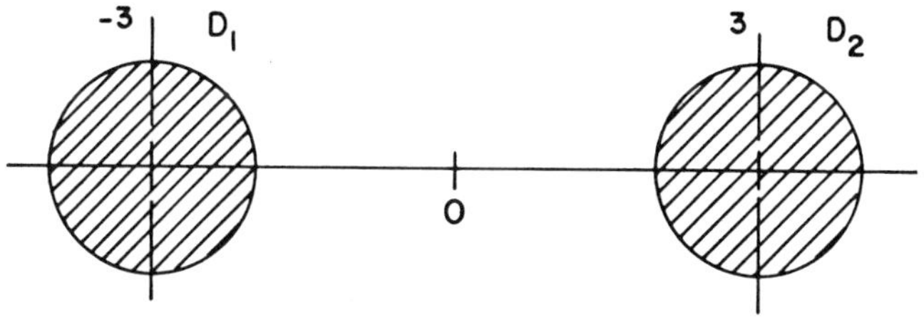

Fig. 1. Admissibility of nearest neighbor rule.

IV. Bayes Procedure

In this section we shall present the simplest version of the Bayes decision procedure for minimizing the probability of error in classifying a given observation x into one of M categories. All the statistics will be assumed known. Bear in mind, however, that the NN rule is nonparametric, or distribution free, in the sense that it does not depend on any assumptions about the underlying statistics for its application. The Bayes risk serves merely as a reference—the limit of excellence beyond which it is not possible to go.

Let x denote the measurements on an individual and X the sample space of possible values of x. We shall refer to x as the observation. On the basis of x a decision must be made about the membership of the individual in one of M specified categories.

For the purposes of defining the Bayes risk, we assume $f_1(x), f_2(x), \cdots, f_M(x)$, probability densities at x with respect to a σ-finite measure ν, such that an individual in category i gives rise to an observation x according to density f_i. Let $L(i, j)$ be the loss incurred by assigning an individual from category i to category j.

Let $\eta_1, \eta_2, \cdots, \eta_M, \eta_i \ge 0, \sum \eta_i = 1$, be the *prior* probabilities of the M categories. The conditional probability $\hat{\eta}_i(x)$ of an individual with measurements x belonging to category i is, by the Bayes theorem,

$$\hat{\eta}_i = \frac{\eta_i f_i}{\sum \eta_j f_j}, \qquad i = 1, 2, \cdots, M. \tag{4}$$

Thus the random variable x transforms the prior probability vector η into the *posterior* probability vector $\hat{\eta}(x)$. If the statistician decides to place an individual with measurements x into category j, the conditional loss is

$$r_j(x) = \sum_{i=1}^{M} \hat{\eta}_i(x) L(i, j). \tag{5}$$

For a given x the conditional loss is minimum when the individual is assigned to the category j for which $r_j(x)$ is lowest. Minimizing the conditional expected loss obviously minimizes the unconditional expected loss. Thus the minimizing decision rule δ^*, called the Bayes decision rule with respect to η, is given by deciding the category j for which r_j is lowest. Using δ^*, the conditional Bayes risk $r^*(x)$ is

$$r^*(x) = \min_j \left\{ \sum_{i=1}^{M} \hat{\eta}_i(x) L(i, j) \right\}, \tag{6}$$

and the resulting overall minimum expected risk R^*, called the Bayes risk, is given by

$$R^* = E r^*(x), \tag{7}$$

where the expectation is with respect to the compound density

$$f(x) = \sum_{i=1}^{M} \eta_i f_i(x). \tag{8}$$

V. Convergence of Nearest Neighbors

Most of the properties of the NN rules hinge on the assumption that the conditional distributions of θ_n' and θ approach one another when $x_n' \to x$. In order to put bounds on the NN risk for as wide a class of underlying statistics as possible, it will be necessary to determine the weakest possible conditions on the statistics which guarantee the above convergence.

Lemma (Convergence of the Nearest Neighbor)

Let x and $x_1, x_2, \cdots$ be independent identically distributed random variables taking values in a separable metric space X. Let x_n' denote the nearest neighbor to x from the set $\{x_1, x_2, \cdots, x_n\}$. Then $x_n' \to x$ with probability one.

Remark: In particular, $x_n' \to x$ with probability one for any probability measure in Euclidean n-space. We prove the lemma in this generality in order to include in its coverage such standard pathological candidates for counterexamples as the Cantor ternary distribution function defined on X the real line.

Since the convergence of the nearest neighbor to x is independent of the metric, the bounds on the risks of the NN rule will be independent of the metric on X.

Proof: Let $S_x(r)$ be the sphere $\{\bar{x} \in X: d(x, \bar{x}) \le r\}$ of radius r centered at x, where d is the metric defined on X.

Consider first a point $x \in X$ having the property that every sphere $S_x(r)$, $r > 0$, has nonzero probability measure. Then, for any $\delta > 0$,

$$P\{\min_{k=1,2,\cdots,n} d(x_k, x) \ge \delta\} = (1 - P(S_x(\delta)))^n \to 0 \tag{9}$$

and therefore, since $d(x_k, x)$ is monotonically decreasing in k, the nearest neighbor to x converges to x with probability one.

It remains to argue that the random variable x has this property with probability one. We shall do so by proving that the set N of points failing to have this property has probability measure zero. Accordingly, let N be the set of all x for which there exists some r_x sufficiently small that $P(S_x(r_x)) = 0$.

By the definition of the separability of X, there exists a countable dense subset A of X. For each $x \in N$ there exists, by the denseness of A, a_x in A for which $a_x \in S_x(r_x/3)$. Thus, there exists a small sphere $S_{a_x}(r_x/2)$ which is strictly contained in the original sphere $S_x(r_x)$ and which contains x. Thus $P(S_{a_x}(r_x/2)) = 0$. Then the possibly uncountable set N is contained in the countable union (by the countability of A) of spheres $\bigcup_{x \in N} S_{a_x}(r_x)$. Since N is contained in the countable union of sets of measure zero, $P(N) = 0$, as was to be shown.

VI. Nearest Neighbor Probability of Error

Let $x_n' \in \{x_1, x_2, \cdots, x_n\}$ be the nearest neighbor to x and let θ_n' be the category to which the individual having measurement x_n' belongs. If θ is indeed the category of x, the NN rule incurs loss $L(\theta, \theta_n')$. If $(x, \theta), (x_1, \theta_1), \cdots, (x_n, \theta_n)$ are random variables, we define the n-sample NN risk $R(n)$ by the expectation

$$R(n) = E[L(\theta, \theta_n')] \tag{10}$$

and the (large sample) *NN risk* R by

$$R = \lim_{n \to \infty} R(n). \tag{11}$$

Throughout this discussion we shall assume that the pairs $(x, \theta), (x_1, \theta_1), \cdots, (x_n, \theta_n)$ are independent identically distributed random variables in $X \times \Theta$. Of course, except in trivial cases, there will be some dependence between the elements x_i, θ_i of each pair.

We shall first consider the $M = 2$ category problem with probability of error criterion given by the $0 - 1$ loss matrix

$$L = \begin{bmatrix} 0 & 1 \\ 1 & 0 \end{bmatrix}, \tag{12}$$

where L counts an error whenever a mistake in classification is made. The following theorem is the principal result of this discussion.

Theorem

Let X be a separable metric space. Let f_1 and f_2 be such that, with probability one, x is either 1) a continuity point of f_1 and f_2, or 2) a point of nonzero probability measure. Then the NN risk R (probability of error) has the bounds

$$R^* \le R \le 2R^*(1 - R^*). \tag{13}$$

These bounds are as tight as possible.

Remarks: In particular, the hypotheses of the theorem are satisfied for probability densities which consist of any mixture of δ-functions and piecewise continuous density functions on Euclidean d-space. Observe that $0 \le R^* \le R \le 2R^*(1 - R^*) \le \frac{1}{2}$; so $R^* = 0$ if and only if $R = 0$, and $R^* = \frac{1}{2}$ if and only if $R = \frac{1}{2}$. Thus in the extreme cases of complete certainty and complete uncertainty the NN probability of error equals the Bayes probability of error. Conditions for equality of R and R^* for other values of R^* will be developed in the proof.

Proof: Let us condition on the random variables x and x_n' in the n-sample NN problem. The conditional NN risk $r(x, x_n')$ is then given, upon using the conditional independence of θ and θ_n', by

$$\begin{aligned} r(x, x_n') &= E[L(\theta, \theta_n') \mid x, x_n'] = P_r\{\theta \ne \theta_n' \mid x, x_n'\} \\ &= P_r\{\theta = 1 \mid x\}P_r\{\theta_n' = 2 \mid x_n'\} \\ &\quad + P_r\{\theta = 2 \mid x\}P_r\{\theta_n' = 1 \mid x_n'\} \end{aligned} \tag{14}$$

where the expectation is taken over θ and θ_n'. By the development of (4) the above may be written as

$$r(x, x_n') = \hat{\eta}_1(x)\hat{\eta}_2(x_n') + \hat{\eta}_2(x)\hat{\eta}_1(x_n'). \tag{15}$$

We wish first to show that $r(x, x_n')$ converges to the random variable $2\hat{\eta}_1(x)\hat{\eta}_2(x)$ with probability one.

We have not required that f_1, f_2 be continuous at the points x of nonzero probability measure $\nu(x)$, because these points may be trivially taken into account as follows. Let $\nu(x_0) > 0$; then

$$P_r\{x_0 \ne x_n'\} = (1 - \nu(x_0))^n \to 0. \tag{16}$$

Since x_n', once equalling x_0, equals x_0 thereafter,

$$r(x, x_n') \to 2\hat{\eta}_1(x_0)\hat{\eta}_2(x_0) \tag{17}$$

with probability one.

For the remaining points, the hypothesized continuity of f_1 and f_2 is needed. Here x is a continuity point of f_1 and f_2 with conditional probability one (conditioned on x such that $\nu(x) = 0$). Then, since $\hat{\eta}$ is continuous in f_1 and f_2, x is a continuity point of $\hat{\eta}$ with probability one. By the lemma, x_n' converges to the random variable x with probability one. Hence, with probability one,

$$\hat{\eta}(x_n') \to \hat{\eta}(x) \tag{18}$$

and, from (15), with probability one,

$$r(x, x_n') \to r(x) = 2\hat{\eta}_1(x)\hat{\eta}_2(x), \tag{19}$$

where $r(x)$ is the limit of the n-sample conditional NN risk.

As shown in (6) the conditional Bayes risk is

$$\begin{aligned} r^*(x) &= \min\{\hat{\eta}_1(x), \hat{\eta}_2(x)\} \\ &= \min\{\hat{\eta}_1(x), 1 - \hat{\eta}_1(x)\}. \end{aligned} \tag{20}$$

Now, by the symmetry of r^* in $\hat{\eta}_1$, we may write

$$\begin{aligned} r(x) &= 2\hat{\eta}_1(x)\hat{\eta}_2(x) = 2\hat{\eta}_1(x)(1 - \hat{\eta}_1(x)) \\ &= 2r^*(x)(1 - r^*(x)). \end{aligned} \tag{21}$$

Thus as a by-product of the proof, we have shown in the large sample case, that with probability one a randomly chosen x will be correctly classified with probability $2r^*(x)(1 - r^*(x))$. For the overall NN risk R, we have, by definition,

$$R = \lim_n E[r(x, x_n')] \tag{22}$$

where the expectation is taken over x and x_n'. Now L, and hence r, is bounded by one; so applying the dominated convergence theorem,

$$R = E[\lim_n r(x, x_n')]. \tag{23}$$

The limit, from (19) and (21), yields

$$\begin{aligned} R &= E[r(x)] \\ &= E[2\hat{\eta}_1(x)\hat{\eta}_2(x)] \\ &= E[2r^*(x)(1 - r^*(x))]. \end{aligned} \tag{24}$$

Since the Bayes risk R^* is the expectation of r^*, we have

$$R = 2R^*(1 - R^*) - 2 \operatorname{Var} r^*(x). \tag{25}$$

Hence

$$R \leq 2R^*(1 - R^*), \tag{26}$$

with equality iff $\operatorname{Var} r^* = 0$, which holds iff $r^* = R^*$ with probability one. Investigating this condition we find that for $R = 2R^*(1 - R^*)$ it is necessary and sufficient that

$$\frac{\eta_1 f_1(x)}{\eta_2 f_2(x)} = R^*/(1 - R^*) \quad \text{or} \quad (1 - R^*)/R^* \tag{27}$$

for almost every x (with respect to the probability measure ν).

Rewriting (24), we have

$$\begin{aligned} R &= E[r^*(x) + r^*(x)(1 - 2r^*(x))] \\ &= R^* + E[r^*(x)(1 - 2r^*(x))] \\ &\geq R^* \end{aligned} \tag{28}$$

with equality if and only if $r^*(x)(1 - 2r^*(x)) = 0$ almost everywhere (with respect to ν). Thus the lower bound $R = R^*$ is achieved if and only if r^* equals 0 or $\frac{1}{2}$ almost everywhere and $Er^* = R^*$. Examples of probability distributions achieving the upper and lower bounds will be given at the end of this section following the extension to M categories.

Consider now the M-category problem with the probability of error criterion given by the loss function $L(i, j) = 0$, for $i = j$, and $L(i, j) = 1$, for $i \neq j$. The substitution trick of (21) can no longer be used when $M \neq 2$.

Theorem (Extension of Theorem 1 to $M \neq 2$)

Let X be a separable metric space. Let $f_1, f_2, \cdots, f_M$ be probability densities with respect to some probability measure ν such that, with probability one, x is either 1) a continuity point of $f_1, f_2, \cdots, f_M$, or 2) a point of nonzero probability measure. Then the NN probability of error R has the bounds

$$R^* \leq R \leq R^*\left(2 - \frac{M}{M - 1} R^*\right). \tag{29}$$

These bounds are as tight as possible.

Proof: Since $x_n' \to x$ with probability one, the posterior probability vector $\hat{\eta}(x_n') \to \hat{\eta}(x)$ with probability one. The conditional n-sample NN risk $r(x, x_n')$ is

$$r(x, x_n') = E[L(\theta, \theta_n') \mid x, x_n'] = \sum_{i \neq j}^{M} \hat{\eta}_i(x)\hat{\eta}_j(x_n') \tag{30}$$

which converges with probability one to the large sample conditional risk $r(x)$ defined by

$$r(x) = \sum_{i \neq j} \hat{\eta}_i(x)\hat{\eta}_j(x) = 1 - \sum_{j=1}^{M} \hat{\eta}_j^2(x). \tag{31}$$

The conditional Bayes risk $r^*(x)$, obtained by selecting, for a given x, the maximum $\hat{\eta}_j(x)$, say $\hat{\eta}_k(x)$, is given by

$$r^*(x) = 1 - \max_j \{\hat{\eta}_j(x)\} = 1 - \hat{\eta}_k(x). \tag{32}$$

By the Cauchy-Schwarz inequality

$$\begin{aligned} (M - 1) \sum_{j \neq k}^{M} \hat{\eta}_j^2(x) &\geq \left[\sum_{j \neq k}^{M} \hat{\eta}_j(x)\right]^2 \\ &= [1 - \hat{\eta}_k(x)]^2 = (r^*(x))^2. \end{aligned} \tag{33}$$

Adding $(M - 1)\hat{\eta}_k^2(x)$ to each side,

$$\begin{aligned} (M - 1) \sum_{j=1}^{M} \hat{\eta}_j^2(x) &\geq (r^*(x))^2 + (M - 1)\hat{\eta}_k^2(x) \\ &= (r^*(x))^2 + (M - 1)(1 - r^*(x))^2 \end{aligned} \tag{34}$$

or

$$\sum_{j=1}^{M} \hat{\eta}_j^2(x) \geq \frac{(r^*(x))^2}{M - 1} + (1 - r^*(x))^2 \tag{35}$$

Substituting (35) into (31),

$$r(x) \leq 2r^*(x) - \frac{M}{M - 1} (r^*(x))^2. \tag{36}$$

Taking expectations, and using the dominated convergence theorem as before,

$$R = 2R^* - \frac{M}{M - 1} (R^*)^2 - \frac{M}{M - 1} \operatorname{Var} r^*(x). \tag{37}$$

Hence

$$R \leq R^*\left(2 - \frac{M}{M - 1} R^*\right) \tag{38}$$

with equality if and only if $\operatorname{Var} r^*(x) = 0$. Of course, $\operatorname{Var} r^* = 0$ implies $r^*(x) = R^*$ with probability one.

The upper bound is attained for the no-information experiment $f_1 = f_2 = \cdots = f_M$, with $\eta_1 = 1 - R^*$, and $\eta_i = R^*/(M-1); i = 2, \cdots, M$. The lower bound $R = R^*$ is attained, for example, when $\eta_i = 1/M$, $i = 1, 2, \cdots, M$, and

$$f_i(x) = \begin{cases} 1, & 0 \le x \le \dfrac{MR^*}{M-1} \text{ or } i \le x \le i + 1 - \dfrac{MR^*}{M-1} \\ 0, & \text{elsewhere.} \end{cases} \tag{39}$$

VII. Example

Let the real valued random variable x have triangular densities f_1 and f_2 with prior probabilities $\eta_1 = \eta_2 = \frac{1}{2}$, as shown in Fig. 2. The density $f = \eta_1 f_1 + \eta_2 f_2$ on x is uniform on [0, 1], thus facilitating calculation of the distribution of the nearest neighbor x_n'.

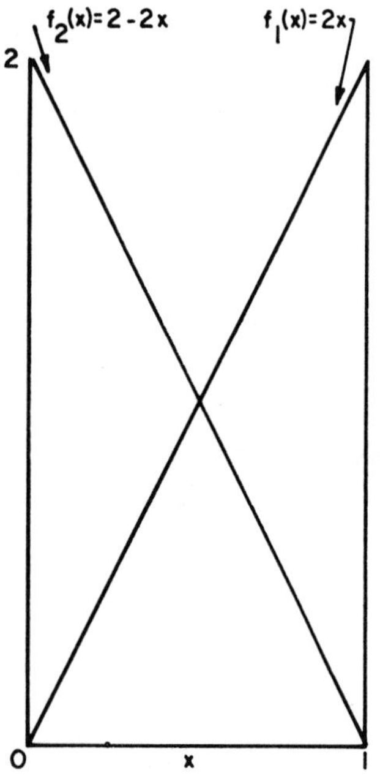

Fig. 2. Triangle densities for example.

The probability of error for this example in the n-sample single NN case is

$$\begin{aligned} R(n) &= E[\eta_1\eta_2 f_1(x) f_2(x_n') + \eta_1\eta_2 f_2(x) f_1(x_n')] \\ &= E[x(1 - x_n') + (1 - x)x_n']. \end{aligned} \tag{40}$$

Upon performing a lengthy but straightforward calculation, we obtain

$$R(n) = \frac{1}{3} + \frac{1}{(n+1)(n+2)}. \tag{41}$$

Thus

$$R = \lim_{n\to\infty} R(n) = \tfrac{1}{3}. \tag{42}$$

The NN risk R is to be compared to the Bayes risk

$$\begin{aligned} R^* &= \int \min\{\eta_1 f_1, \eta_2 f_2\}\, d\nu \\ &= \int_0^1 \min\{x, 1 - x\}\, dx = \tfrac{1}{4}. \end{aligned} \tag{43}$$

Exhibiting corresponding terms we have

$$R^* \le R \le 2R^*(1 - R^*)$$

or

$$\tfrac{1}{4} \le \tfrac{1}{3} \le \tfrac{3}{8}. \tag{44}$$

In this example we have found an exact expression for the NN risk $R(n)$ for any finite sample size. Observe that $R(1) = \frac{1}{2}$, in agreement with simpler considerations, and that $R(n)$ converges to its limit approximately as $1/n^2$.

VIII. The k-NN Rule

From Section V it is also possible to conclude that the kth nearest neighbor to x converges to x with probability one as the sample size n increases with k fixed. Since each of the nearest neighbors casts conditionally independent votes as to the category of x, we may conclude, in the 2-category case for odd k, that the conditional k-NN risk $r_k(x)$ is given in the limit (with probability one) as n increases, by

$$\begin{aligned} r_k(x) &= \hat{\eta}_1(x) \sum_{j=0}^{(k-1)/2} \binom{k}{j} \hat{\eta}_1^j(x)(1 - \hat{\eta}_1(x))^{k-j} \\ &\quad + (1 - \hat{\eta}_1(x)) \sum_{j=(k+1)/2}^{k} \binom{k}{j} \hat{\eta}_1^j(x)(1 - \hat{\eta}_1(x))^{k-j}. \end{aligned} \tag{45}$$

Note that the conditional NN risks $r_k(x)$ are monotonically decreasing in k (to $\min\{\hat{\eta}_1(x), 1 - \hat{\eta}_1(x)\}$), as we might suspect. Thus the least upper bounds on the unconditional NN risks R_k will also be monotonically decreasing in k (to R^*).

Observe that in (45) r_k is symmetric in $\hat{\eta}_1$ and $1 - \hat{\eta}_1$. Thus r_k may be expressed solely in terms of $r^* = \min\{\hat{\eta}_1, 1 - \hat{\eta}_1\}$ in the form

$$\begin{aligned} r_k &= \rho_k(r^*) \\ &= r^* \sum_{j=0}^{(k-1)/2} \binom{k}{j} (r^*)^j (1 - r^*)^{k-j} \\ &\quad + (1 - r^*) \sum_{j=(k+1)/2}^{k} \binom{k}{j} (r^*)^j (1 - r^*)^{k-j}. \end{aligned} \tag{46}$$

Now let $\tilde{\rho}_k(r^*)$ be defined to be the least concave function greater than $\rho_k(r^*)$. Then

$$r_k = \rho_k(r^*) \le \tilde{\rho}_k(r^*), \tag{47}$$

and, by Jensen's inequality,

$$R_k = Er_k = E\rho_k(r^*) \le E\tilde{\rho}_k(r^*) \le \tilde{\rho}_k(Er^*) = \tilde{\rho}_k(R^*). \tag{48}$$

So $\tilde{\rho}_k(R^*)$ is an upper bound on the large sample k-NN risk R_k. It may further be shown, for any R^*, that $\tilde{\rho}_k(R^*)$ is the least upper bound on R_k by demonstrating simple statistics which achieve it. Hence we have the bounds

$$R^* \leq R_k \leq \tilde{\rho}_k(R^*) \leq \tilde{\rho}_{k-1}(R^*) \leq \cdots \leq \tilde{\rho}_1(R^*) = 2R^*(1 - R^*) \qquad (49)$$

where the upper and lower bounds on R_k are as tight as possible.

IX. Conclusions

The single NN rule has been shown to be admissible among the class of k_n-NN rules for the n-sample case for any n. It has been shown that the NN probability of error R, in the M-category classification problem, is bounded below by the Bayes probability of error R^* and above by $R^*(2 - MR^*/(M - 1))$. Thus *any* other decision rule based on the infinite data set can cut the probability of error by at most one half. In this sense, half of the available information in an infinite collection of classified samples is contained in the nearest neighbor.

References

[1] E. Fix and J. L. Hodges, Jr., "Discriminatory analysis, nonparametric discrimination," USAF School of Aviation Medicine, Randolph Field, Tex., Project 21-49-004, Rept. 4, Contract AF41(128)-31, February 1951.

[2] ——, "Discriminatory analysis: small sample performance," USAF School of Aviation Medicine, Randolph Field, Tex., Project 21-49-004, Rept. 11, August 1952.

[3] M. V. Johns, "An empirical Bayes approach to non-parametric two-way classification," in *Studies in Item Analysis and Prediction*, H. Solomon, Ed. Stanford, Calif.: Stanford University Press, 1961.

[4] L. N. Kanal, "Statistical methods for pattern classification," Philco Rept., 1963; originally appeared in T. Harley et al., "Semi-automatic imagery screening research study and experimental investigation," *Philco Reports*, V043-2 and V043-3, Vol. I, sec. 6, and Appendix H, prepared for U. S. Army Electronics Research and Development Lab. under Contract DA-36-039-SC-90742, March 29, 1963.

[5] G. Sebestyen, *Decision Making Processes in Pattern Recognition*. New York: Macmillan, 1962, pp. 90–92.

[6] Nils Nilsson, *Learning Machines*. New York: McGraw-Hill, 1965, pp. 120–121.

[7] D. O. Loftsgaarden and C. P. Quesenberry, "A nonparametric estimate of a multivariate density function," *Annals Math Stat.*, vol. 36, pp. 1049–1051, June 1965.

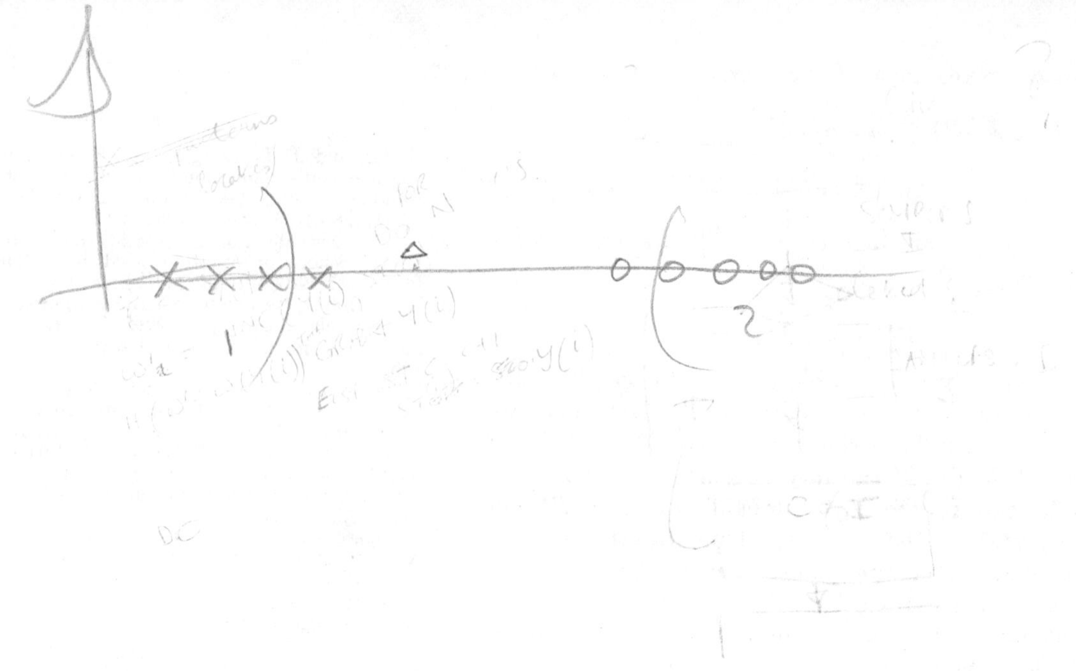

The Condensed Nearest Neighbor Rule

The purpose of this note is to introduce the condensed nearest neighbor decision rule (CNN rule) and to pose some unsolved theoretical questions which it raises. The CNN rule, one of a class of *ad hoc* decision rules which have appeared in the literature in the past few years, was motivated by statistical considerations pertaining to the nearest neighbor decision rule (NN rule). We briefly review the NN rule and then describe the CNN rule.

The NN rule[1]–[4] assigns an unclassified sample to the same class as the nearest of n stored, correctly classified samples. In other words, given a collection of n reference points, each classified by some external source, a new point is assigned to the same class as its nearest neighbor. The most interesting theoretical property of the NN rule is that under very mild regularity assumptions on the underlying statistics, for any metric, and for a variety of loss functions, the large-sample risk incurred is less than twice the Bayes risk. (The Bayes decision rule achieves minimum risk but requires complete knowledge of the underlying statistics.) From a practical point of view, however, the NN rule is not a prime candidate for many applications because of the storage requirements it imposes. The CNN rule is suggested as a rule which retains the basic approach of the NN rule without imposing such stringent storage requirements.

Before describing the CNN rule we first define the notion of a consistent subset of a sample set. This is a subset which, when used as a stored reference set for the NN rule, correctly classifies all of the remaining points in the sample set. A minimal consistent subset is a consistent subset with a minimum number of elements. Every set has a consistent subset, since every set is trivially a consistent subset of itself. Obviously, every finite set has a minimal consistent subset, although the minimum size is not, in general, achieved uniquely. The CNN rule uses the following algorithm to determine a consistent subset of the original sample set. In general, however, the algorithm will not find a minimal consistent subset. We assume that the original sample set is arranged in some order; then we set up bins called STORE and GRABBAG and proceed as follows.

Manuscript received November 24, 1966; revised October 5, 1967.

1) The first sample is placed in STORE.

2) The second sample is classified by the NN rule, using as a reference set the current contents of STORE. (Since STORE has only one point, the classification is trivial at this stage.) If the second sample is classified correctly it is placed in GRABBAG; otherwise it is placed in STORE.

3) Proceeding inductively, the ith sample is classified by the current contents of STORE. If classified correctly it is placed in GRABBAG; otherwise it is placed in STORE.

4) After one pass through the original sample set, the procedure continues to loop through GRABBAG until termination, which can occur in one of two ways:

   a) The GRABBAG is exhausted, with all its members now transferred to STORE (in which case, the consistent subset found is the entire original set), or

   b) One complete pass is made through GRABBAG with no transfers to STORE. (If this happens, all subsequent passes through GRABBAG will result in no transfers, since the underlying decision surface has not been changed.)

5) The final contents of STORE are used as reference points for the NN rule; the contents of GRABBAG are discarded.

Qualitatively, the rule behaves as follows: If the Bayes risk is small, i.e., if the underlying densities of the various classes have small overlap, then the algorithm will tend to pick out points near the (perhaps fuzzy) boundary between the classes. Typically, points deeply imbedded within a class will not be transferred to STORE, since they will be correctly classified. If the Bayes risk is high, then STORE will contain essentially all the points in the original sample set, and no important reduction in sample size will have been achieved. No theoretical properties of the CNN rule have been established.

The CNN rule has been tried on a number of problems, both real and artificial. In order to investigate the behavior of the rule when the classes are (essentially) disjoint—the case in which the CNN rule is of greatest interest—several experiments similar to the following were run. The underlying probability structure for a two-class problem was assumed to consist of two probability densities, each a uniform distribution on the supports shown in Fig. 1. The set of all vectors with integer components lying within each

Reprinted from *IEEE Trans. Inform. Theory*, vol. IT-14, pp. 515–516, May 1968.

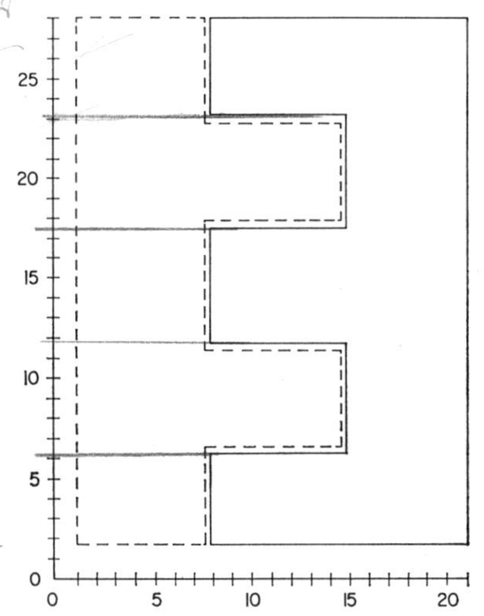

Fig. 1. Class boundaries.

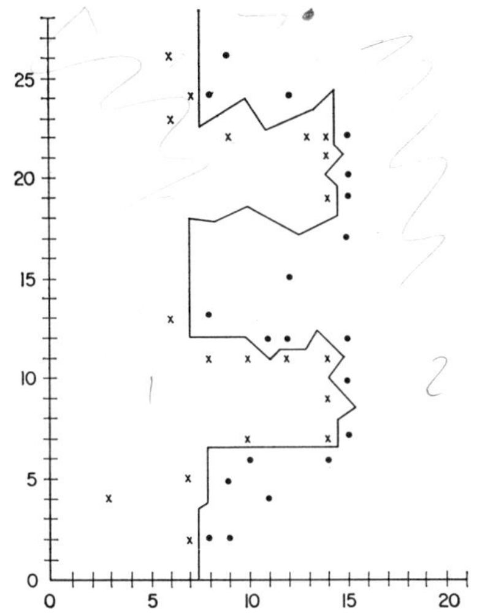

Fig. 2. Samples selected and induced decision surface.

support was taken to simulate a random sampling from each population. The 482 points thus obtained were ordered by a random mechanism and processed using the algorithm described above.

The algorithm terminated after four interations through GRABBAG, at which time STORE contained 40 samples. Fig. 2 shows the final 40 samples and the decision surface induced by the NN rule using these 40 samples as a stored reference set.

Since all samples had integer-valued components, ties occurred with nonzero probability, and these were broken arbitrarily. This accounts for the fact that occasionally the decision surface lies properly within one or the other of the supports rather than between them. The points most deeply imbedded within each class were the first two points in the random ordering.

A more realistic experiment was performed using data supplied by Nagy of IBM.[5] This data consisted of approximately 12 000 96-dimensional binary vectors drawn from 25 different statistical populations. (The data represent upper-case typewritten characters, excluding "I," typed with nine different styles of fonts.) The 12 000 samples were divided into a training set and a testing set of approximately equal size, and the CNN algorithm was used on the training set. The algorithm terminated after four iterations through GRABBAG, at which time STORE contained 197 of the original 6295 samples. An error rate of 1.28 percent was obtained on the independent test set. This was somewhat disappointing in view of the fact that a number of simpler classifiers (the ternary reference classifier,[5] linear machine,[6] and piecewise-linear machine[6]), using considerably less computer time, achieved error rates on the order of 0.3-0.5 percent.[7],[8] It was also a little surprising, since (necessarily) the 197 stored points correctly classified all the 6295 samples in the training set.

These and similar experiments have persuaded us that the CNN rule offers interesting possibilities, but that a great deal more work of both a theoretical and experimental nature will be needed before the rule is thoroughly understood. For example, under suitably restrictive assumptions on the underlying statistics:

1) What is the expected number of iterations before termination?
2) What is the expected reduction in the size of the stored sample set?
3) What is the expected increase in CNN risk over NN risk for a sample set of given size?

In view of the desirable theoretical properties of the k-NN rule,[1],[2]—the rule that makes a decision on the basis of votes cast by each of the k nearest neighbors—we pose a final obvious question which should, perhaps, be answered experimentally. How would the CNN rule perform if the vote of, say, the three nearest neighbors was substituted for the decision of the single nearest neighbor everywhere in the algorithm?

PETER E. HART
Applied Physics Lab.
Stanford Research Institute
Menlo Park, Calif. 94025

REFERENCES

[1] P. E. Hart, "An asymptotic analysis of the nearest-neighbor decision rule," Stanford Electronics Labs., Stanford, Calif., Tech. Rept. 1828-2 (SEL-66-016), May 1966.
[2] T. M. Cover and P. E. Hart, "Nearest-neighbor pattern classification," *IEEE Trans. Information Theory*, vol. IT-13, pp. 21–27, January 1967.
[3] T. M. Cover, "Estimation by the nearest-neighbor rule," *IEEE Trans. Information Theory*, vol. IT-14, pp. 50–55, January 1968.
[4] A. W. Whitney and S. J. Dwyer, III, "Performance and implementation of the k-nearest neighbor decision rule with incorrectly identified training samples," *1966 Proc. 4th Allerton Conf. Circuit and System Theory.*
[5] C. N. Liu and G. L. Shelton, Jr., "An experimental investigation of a mixed-font print recognition system," *IEEE Trans. Electronic Computers*, vol. EC-15, pp. 916-925, December 1966.
[6] N. J. Nilsson, *Learning Machines-Foundations of Trainable Pattern Classifying Systems.* New York: McGraw-Hill, 1965.
[7] R. G. Casey *et al.*, "An experimental comparison of several design algorithms used in pattern recognition," IBM Corp., Research Rept. RC 1500, November 1965.
[8] D. S. Nee, "Multifont character-recognition experiments using trainable classifiers," Stanford Research Institute, Menlo Park, Calif., Tech. Note 1, Contract AF 30(602)-3945, August 1966.

An Algorithm for Finding Nearest Neighbors

JEROME H. FRIEDMAN, FOREST BASKETT, AND LEONARD J. SHUSTEK

Abstract—**An algorithm that finds the k nearest neighbors of a point, from a sample of size N in a d-dimensional space, with an expected number of distance calculations**

$$E[n_d] \lesssim \pi^{-1/2}[kd\Gamma(d/2)]^{1/d}(2N)^{1-(1/d)}$$

is described, its properties examined, and the validity of the estimate verified with simulated data.

Index Terms—**Best match, nearest neighbors, nonparametric discrimination, searching, sorting.**

INTRODUCTION

Nearest-neighbor techniques have been shown to be important nonparametric procedures for multivariate density estimation and pattern classification [1]–[6]. For classification, a sample of prototype feature vectors is drawn from each category, correctly labeled by an external source. For each test point to be classified, the set of k closest prototype points (feature vectors) is found and the test point is assigned to that category having the largest representation in this set. For density estimation, the volume, $V(k)$, containing the closest k points to each of the N sample points, is used to estimate the local sparsity $\hat{s}$ (inverse density) by $\hat{s} = NV(k)/k - 1$.

The application of these techniques has been severely limited by the computational resources required for finding the nearest neighbors. The feature vectors for the complete set of samples must be stored, and the distances to them calculated for each classification or density estimation. Several modifications to the k-nearest-neighbor rule have been suggested that are computationally more tractable but whose statistical properties are unknown [7], [8]. The condensed nearest-neighbor rule [9] mitigates both the storage and processing requirements by choosing a subset of the prototype vectors such that the nearest-neighbor rule correctly classifies all of the original prototypes.

Fisher and Patrick [10] suggest a preprocessing scheme for reducing the computational requirements of nearest-neighbor classifications when the test sample is much larger than the prototype set. For this case, it is worthwhile to use considerable computation preprocessing the prototypes so that processing can be reduced for each test sample. Their technique orders the prototypes so that each point tends to be far away from its predecessors in the ordered list. By examining these prototype points in this order and having precalculated distances between prototypes, the triangle inequality can be applied to eliminate distance calculations from the test vector to many of the prototypes. (All of the prototypes must be examined, however.) The algorithm is examined only for $k = 1$ in two dimensions where for bivariate normal data a median number of approximately 58 distance calculations is required for 1000 prototypes, after preprocessing.

This correspondence describes a straightforward preprocessing technique for reducing the computation required for finding the k nearest neighbors to a point from a sample of size N in a d-dimensional space. This procedure can be profitably applied to both density estimation and classification, even when the number of test points is considerably smaller than the number of prototypes. This preprocessing requires no distance calculations. (It can, however, require up to $dN \log_2 N$ comparisons.) The distance function (dissimilarity measure) is not required to satisfy the triangle inequality. With a Euclidean distance measure[1] the average number of prototypes that need be examined is bounded by

$$E[n_d] \lesssim \pi^{-1/2}[kd\Gamma(d/2)]^{1/d}(2N)^{1-(1/d)}, \tag{1}$$

after preprocessing.

For the case of bivariate normal data with $d = 2$, $k = 1$, and $N = 1000$, (1) predicts an average of 36 distance calculations, whereas simulations have shown that 24 are actually required. The performance of the algorithm is compared to (1), with simulated data for several values of k, d, N, and underlying density distributions of the prototype sample points.

BASIC PROCEDURE

The preprocessing for this algorithm consists basically of ordering the prototype points on the values of one of the coordinates. For

Manuscript received June 24, 1974; revised February 7, 1975. This work was supported in part by the U. S. Atomic Energy Commission under Contract AT(043)515.

J. H. Friedman is with Stanford Linear Accelerator Center, Stanford, Calif. 94305.

F. Baskett and L. J. Shustek are with the Computer Science Department, Stanford University, Stanford, Calif.

[1] Similar formulas for other distance measures are discussed below.

Reprinted from *IEEE Trans. Comput.*, vol. C-24, pp. 1000–1006, Oct. 1975.

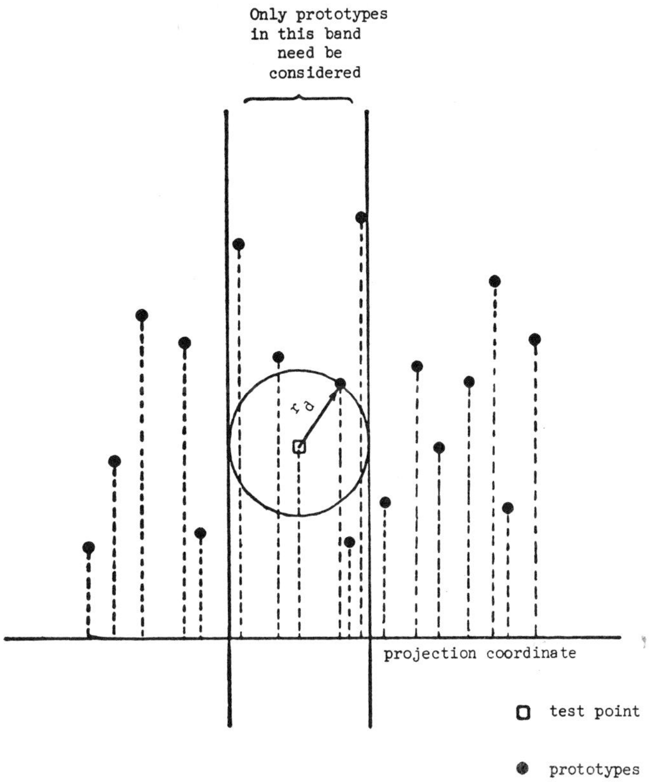

Fig. 1. Illustration of the basic procedure for the nearest neighbor ($k = 1$) in two dimensions.

each test point, the prototypes are examined in the order of their projected distance from the test point on the sorted coordinate. When this projected distance becomes larger than the distance (in the full dimensionality) to the k closest point of those prototypes already examined, no more prototypes need be considered; the k closest prototypes of the examined points are those for the complete set. Fig. 1 illustrates this procedure for the nearest neighbor ($k = 1$) in two dimensions.

A simple calculation gives an approximation to the expected number of prototypes that need be examined before the above stopping criterion is met. For simplicity, consider N prototypes uniformly distributed in a d-dimensional unit hypercube and a Euclidean distance measure. Assume also that N is large enough so that effects due to the boundaries are not important. For this case, the volume v of a d-dimensional sphere, centered at the test point and containing exactly k-prototypes, is a random variable distributed according to a beta distribution

$$p(v)\,dv = \frac{N!}{(k-1)!(N-k)!} v^{k-1}(1-v)^{N-k}\,dv, \qquad 0 \le v \le 1. \tag{2}$$

The radius of this sphere, given by

$$r_d = \left[\frac{d\Gamma(d/2)}{2\pi^{d/2}} v\right]^{1/d}, \tag{3}$$

is also a random variable. Let

$$\zeta_d = [2\pi^{d/2}/d\Gamma(d/2)]^{1/d}.$$

Then $v = (\zeta_d r_d)^d$ and the distribution for r_d becomes

$$p(r_d)\,dr_d = \frac{N!\,d\zeta_d}{(k-1)!(N-k)!} (\zeta_d r_d)^{dk-1}[1-(\zeta_d r_d)^d]^{N-k}\,dr_d. \tag{4}$$

The stopping criterion is met when the projected distance from the test point to a prototype along the sorted coordinate is greater than r_d. This projected distance is uniformly distributed. The expected fraction of prototypes, then, that must be examined is just twice the expected value of r_d given by (4).[2] Various other statistics, such as the variance, median, and percentiles, can also be calculated from (4). These calculations must be done numerically since the integrals cannot be evaluated analytically.

A close upper bound[3] on $E[r_d]$ can be derived from (2) and (3) by

$$E[r_d] \lesssim \hat{r}_d = \left[\frac{d\Gamma(d/2)}{2\pi^{d/2}} E[v]\right]^{1/d}, \tag{5}$$

where from (2),

$$E[v] = \frac{k}{N+1}. \tag{6}$$

The upper bound on the expected fraction of prototypes that must be examined is then $2\hat{r}_d$, and the upper bound on the expected *number* of prototypes $E[n_d]$ is $2\hat{r}_d N$. Combining these results,

$$E[n_d] \le \hat{n}_d = 2\left[\frac{d\Gamma(d/2)}{2\pi^{d/2}} \frac{k}{N+1}\right]^{1/d} N. \tag{7}$$

Simplifying this expression and approximating $N + 1$ by N, one has the result shown in (1). The variance of n_d is similarly approximated by

$$E[n_d - E(n_d)]^2 \lesssim 4\left[\left(\frac{d\Gamma(d/2)}{2\pi^{d/2}}\right)^2 \frac{k(N-k+1)}{(N+1)^2(N+2)}\right]^{1/d} N \tag{8}$$

[2] Prototypes must be examined for a projected distance r_d both above and below the test point position.

[3] Taking the dth root of the average rather than the average of the dth root will cause a slight overestimation that decreases with increasing d. For $d = 2$, this overestimation is around 10 percent, while for $d = 8$ it is 6 percent.

so that the coefficient of variation

$$C(n_d) = \left[\frac{E[n_d - E(n_d)]^2}{E^2[n_d]}\right]^{1/2}$$

becomes (to the same approximation)

$$C(n_d) \lesssim \left[\frac{N - k + 1}{k(N + 2)}\right]^{1/(2d)} \qquad (9)$$

Other statistics of the distribution can be similarly calculated.

These calculations all presuppose a uniform distribution of the prototype sample. This is seldom the case in application. However, as discussed below under the full procedure, a uniform distribution of prototypes represents a worst case for the performance of the algorithm, so that the preceding calculations can serve as upper bounds for the performance in the more general cases.

FULL PROCEDURE

The nonuniformity of the axis projections can be used to advantage to increase the efficiency of the algorithm. For a given expected radius $E[r_d]$, the points that need to be considered on the average are those that lie in the interval $\Delta x \simeq 2E[r_d]$, centered at the projected test point. That projection axis, for which the number of such prototypes is least, should be chosen for maximum efficiency. If the points are ordered only along one coordinate in the preprocessing (basic procedure), then the one with the smallest average projected density (largest spread) should be chosen. In the full procedure, the points are ordered on several or all of the coordinates and the one with the smallest local projected density in the neighborhood of the test point is chosen.

For each test point, the local projected sparsity on each axis is estimated as

$$s_i = | X_{i,p_i+n/2} - X_{i,p_i-n/2} | \qquad (10)$$

where X_{ij} is the ith coordinate of the jth ordered prototype and p_i is the position of the test point in the ith projection (n is discussed below). The prototype ordering on that particular coordinate for which s_i is maximum is chosen.

The number of prototypes n over which the sparsity is averaged on each projection should correspond to a distance of about $2E[r_d]$. For a uniform distribution, this is given approximately by (5). The number of prototypes within this interval (again for a uniform distribution) is $E[n_d]$, given by (1). For nonuniform distributions, both $E[r_d]$ and the various projected $E[n_d]$'s will be different. Since the density distribution of the prototypes is usually unknown, a reasonable approximation is to use the uniform distribution results,[4] that is $n = E[n_d]$, as given by (1).

Prototypes are examined in order of their increasing projected distance from the test point until the stopping condition

$$d_k^2 \leq (X_{i,p_i} - X_{i,l})^2 \qquad (11)$$

is met for some point l. Here d_k^2 is the distance squared to the kth nearest prototype of those examined up to that point. The current list of k closest prototypes is then correct for the entire sample.

The expected number of prototype points $E_{\text{full}}[n_d]$ that need to be considered when applying this full procedure of choosing the optimum ordering coordinate individually for each test point can be calculated using arguments and assumptions similar to those that led to (1). The result is

$$E_{\text{full}}[n_d] \simeq E[(\prod_{i=1}^{d} s_i)^{1/d} / \max_{1\leq i\leq d} \{s_i\}] E[n_d] \qquad (12)$$

[4] Simulation results indicate that the performance of the algorithm is very insensitive to the choice of n.

where the s_i's are the local projected sparsities on each of the coordinates near each test point, and $E[n_d]$ is the expected number if all projected sparsities were the same. For uniformly distributed prototypes, $E[n_d]$ is given by (1) and the s_i's are distributed normally about their average values.

Actual values for $E_{\text{full}}[n_d]$ are difficult to calculate, but (12) can be used to gain insight into the effect of employing the full procedure. For example, if the spread of one of the coordinates is a factor of R larger, on the average, than the others which all have approximately equal spread, then (12) gives

$$E_{\text{full}}[n_d] \simeq \frac{1}{R^{1-(1/d)}} E[n_d]. \qquad (13)$$

Equation (12) clearly shows that the full procedure will always increase the efficiency of the algorithm and be most effective when the variation of the prototype density is greatest.

GENERAL DISSIMILARITY MEASURES

Although the above discussion has centered on the Euclidean distance

$$d(X_m, X_n) = [\sum_{i=1}^{d} (X_{im} - X_{in})^2]^{1/2} \qquad (14)$$

as a measure of dissimilarity between feature vectors, nowhere in the general procedure is it required. In fact, the triangle inequality is not required. This technique can be applied with any dissimilarity measure

$$d(X_m, X_n) = g[\sum_{i=1}^{d} f_i(X_{im}, X_{in})] \qquad (15)$$

as long as the functions f and g satisfy the basic properties of symmetry

$$f(x,y) = f(y,x) \qquad (16a)$$

and monotonicity

$$g(x) \geq g(y), \qquad \text{if } x > y$$

$$f(x,z) \geq f(x,y), \qquad \begin{cases} \text{if } z \geq y \geq x \\ \text{or if } z \leq y \leq x. \end{cases} \qquad (16b)$$

The performance of the algorithm does depend upon the dissimilarity measure and, in particular, the result contained in (1) applies only to the Euclidean metric. The dependence on k and N contained in (1) is the same for any Minkowski p metric

$$d(X_m, X_n) = [\sum_{i=1}^{d} | X_{im} - X_{in} |^p]^{1/p}, \qquad (p \geq 1) \qquad (17)$$

since for these distance measures the volume of a d-dimensional "sphere" grows with radius r as $v \propto r^d$. Because of their computational advantage, the two most often used Minkowski metrics, besides the Euclidean metric ($p = 2$), are the city-block or taxicab distance ($p = 1$) and the maximum coordinate distance, $d(X_m, X_n) = \max_{1\leq i\leq d} \{| X_{im} - X_{in} |\}$ ($p = \infty$). Upper bounds on the average number of distance calculations $E[n_d]$, analogous to (1), can be derived in a similar manner for these distance measures. The results are

$$E_1[n_d] \lesssim (k\, d!)^{1/d} N^{1-(1/d)}, \qquad (p = 1) \qquad (1a)$$

$$E_\infty[n_d] \lesssim k^{1/d} N^{1-(1/d)}, \qquad (p = \infty). \qquad (1b)$$

SIMULATION EXPERIMENTS

In order to gain insight into the performance of the algorithm and compare it to the upper bound predicted by (1), several simulation experiments were performed. For each simulation, $N + 1$ random d-dimensional points were drawn from the appropriate

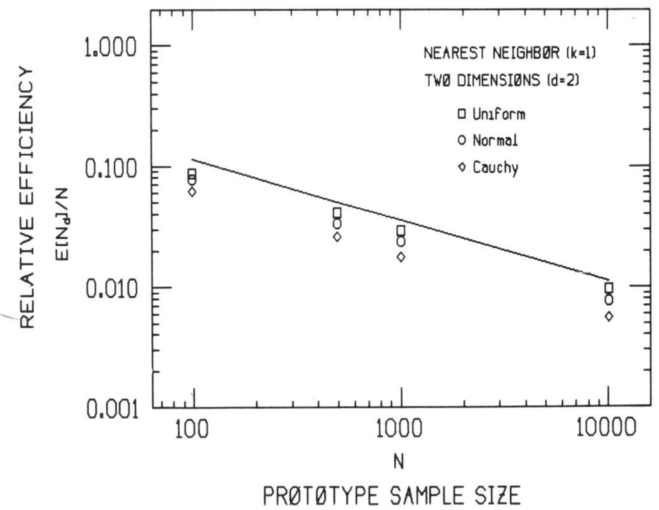

Fig. 2. Relative efficiency of this algorithm to the brute force method, for finding the nearest neighbor ($k = 1$) for bivariate uniform (□), normal (○), and Cauchy (◇) density distributions as a function of prototype sample size N. The solid line represents the predictions of (1).

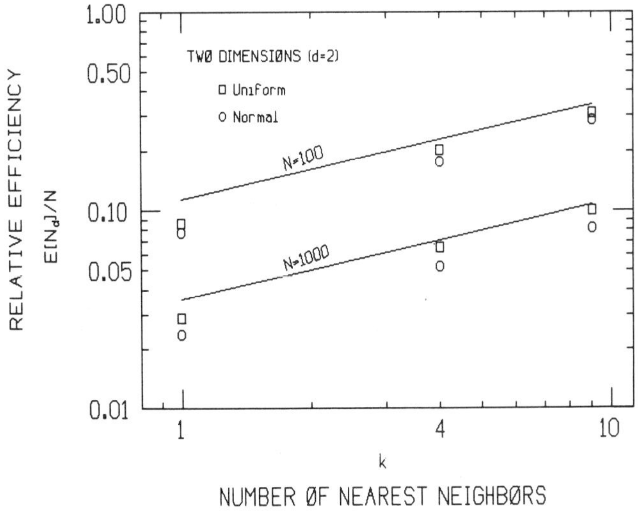

Fig. 3. Relative efficiency of this algorithm to the brute force method, for finding the k nearest neighbors, with bivariate uniform (□) and normal (○) density for 100 and 1000 prototypes. The solid lines represent the predictions of (1).

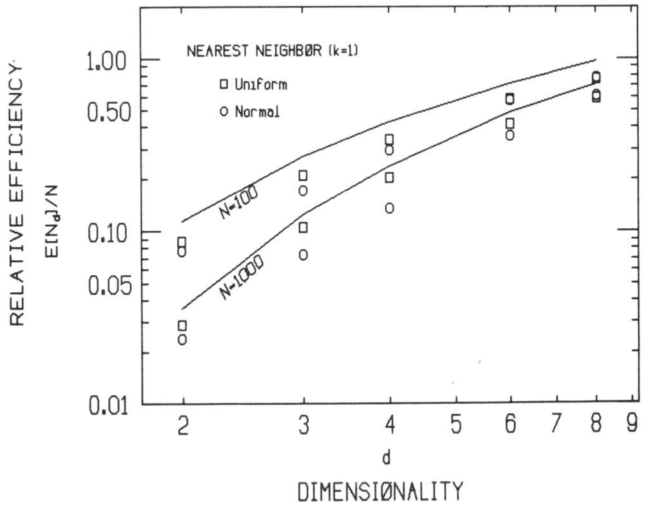

Fig. 4. Relative efficiency of this algorithm to the brute force method, for finding the nearest neighbor with uniform (□) and normal (○) density distributions for 100 and 1000 prototypes as a function of dimensionality d. The solid lines represent the predictions of (1).

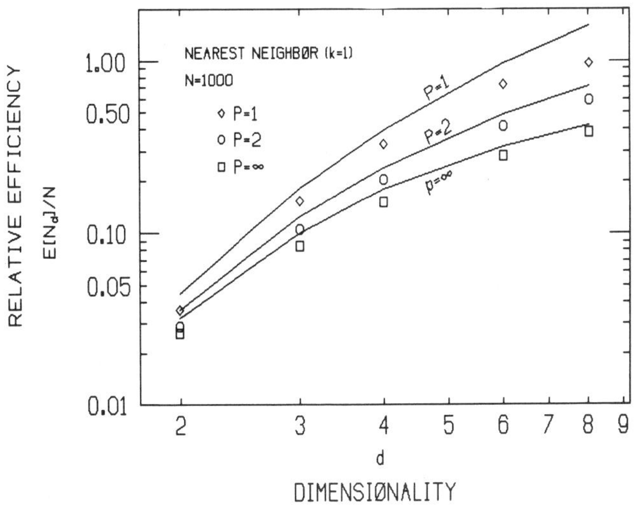

Fig. 5. Variation with dimensionality d of the relative efficiency of this method to the brute force method, for finding the nearest neighbor ($k = 1$, $N = 1000$, uniform distribution) for several Minkowski p metrics, $p = 1$ (◇), $p = 2$ (○), $p = \infty$ (□). The solid lines represent the predictions of (1), (1a), and (1b).

probability density function. The number of distance calculations required to find the k nearest neighbors to each point, using the full procedure (sorting on all coordinates), was determined and then averaged over all of the points. This procedure was then repeated ten times with different random points from the same probability density function. The average of these ten trials was then taken as the result of the experiment, and the statistical uncertainty was taken to be $1/(10)^{1/2}$ times the standard deviation about the mean for the ten trials. These uncertainties were all less than 1 percent and for the larger samples were around 0.1 percent.

These simulation results are presented in Figs. 2–5. The variation with N,k,d, underlying distribution, and distance measure of the relative efficiency of this algorithm to the brute force method (calculating distances to all of the prototypes) is compared to the upper bound predicted by (1) (solid lines). Fig. 2 shows the dependence on N ($d = 2$, $k = 1$) for several underlying distributions. These distributions are uniform on the unit square, bivariate normal with unit dispersion matrix, and bivariate Cauchy

$$p(x_1,x_2) = \frac{\pi^2}{(1 + x_1^2)(1 + x_2^2)}. \tag{18}$$

Fig. 3 shows the dependence on k ($d = 2$, $n = 100$ and 1000) for uniform and normal data. Fig. 4 shows the dependence on d ($k = 1$, $N = 100$ and 1000) again, for both uniformly and normally distributed data. Fig. 5 shows the dependence on d ($k = 1$, $N = 1000$, uniform distribution) for several different Minkowski p metrics, namely $p = 1$ (city block distance), $p = 2$ (Euclidean distance), and $p = \infty$ (maximum coordinate distance).

DISCUSSION

These simulation experiments show that (1), (1a), and (1b) do, indeed, provide a close upper bound on the average number of distance calculations required by the algorithm to find nearest neighbors. Although these formulas always slightly overestimate the actual number, they quite accurately reflect the variation with N, k, d, and p. As predicted by (12), the number of distance calculations tends to diminish for increasing density variation of the sample points. It is interesting to note that for $d = 2$ and $k = 1$, this algorithm requires a smaller average number of distance calculations for 10 000 prototypes than does the brute force method for 100 prototypes.

The relative efficiency of this algorithm (as compared with the brute force method) decreases slightly with increasing k and more rapidly with increasing dimensionality d. In eight dimensions for 1000 prototypes ($k = 1$) the average number of distance evaluations is reduced by approximately 40 percent. Although not dramatic, this is still quite profitable in terms of the preprocessing requirements.

As indicated by (1), (1a), and (1b) and verified in Fig. 5, the growth of $E[n_d]$ with dimensionality depends strongly on the choice of the distance measure. For Minkowski p metrics, it is easy to show that $E_p[n_d]$ grows more slowly with d for increasing p. The results of (1b) and Fig. 5 indicate that if a distance measure is chosen on the basis of rapid calculation, the maximum coordinate distance ($p = \infty$) is the natural choice since it also minimizes the number of distance calculations, especially for high dimensionality.

A crude calculation gives a rough idea of how many test points N_t are required (in terms of the number of prototypes N_p, k, and d) for the preprocessing procedure to be profitable. The preprocessing requires approximately $dN_p \log_2 N_p$ compares, memory fetches, and stores. Each distance calculation requires around d multiplies, subtractions, additions, and memory fetches. Assuming all of these operations require equal computation, then the preprocessing requires about $3dN_p \log N_p$ operations, while it saves approximately $4\, dN_t(N_p - E[n_d])$ operations. Thus, for the procedure to be profitable

$$4dN_t(N_p - E[n_d]) > 3dN_p \log N_p$$

or crudely[5]

$$N_t > N_0 \approx \frac{N_p \log_2 N_p}{N_p - E[n_d]}. \tag{19}$$

$E[n_d]$ is given approximately by (1) (Euclidean metric). For $d = 2$, $k = 1$, and 1000 prototypes, N_0 is around 10, whereas for $d = 8$, $k = 1$, and 1000 prototypes, one has $N_0 \approx 25$.

Although these results are quite crude, it is clear that the number of test points need not be large, compared to the number of prototypes, before the algorithm can be profitably applied. For density estimation, where $N_t = N_p = N$, the procedure is profitable so long as N_0/N is small compared to one.

The only adjustable parameter in this algorithm is the number of projection coordinates m on which the data are sorted. This parameter can range in value from one (basic procedure) to d (full procedure). The value chosen for this parameter is governed principally by the amount of memory available. This algorithm requires mN additional memory locations, and for $m = d$, doubles the memory over that required by the brute force method. If less than the full procedure is employed, then those axes with the largest spread should be chosen. Arguments similar to those that lead to (13) can be used to estimate the efficiency for this case. For the case where all coordinates have approximately equal spread, (12) can be used to show that the increase in efficiency, as additional sorted coordinates are added, is proportional to $1/m$. Results of simulations (not shown) verify this dependence.

The tendency toward decreasing relative efficiency with increasing dimensionality cannot be mitigated by requiring the distance measure to satisfy the triangle inequality

$$d(x_m,x_n) \geq | d(x_m,x_l) - d(x_l,x_n) |. \tag{20}$$

In this case distance calculations can be avoided for those prototypes x_n for which

$$d(x_t,x_k) < | d(x_t,x_l) - d(x_l,x_n) | \tag{21}$$

[5] This calculation is extremely dependent on the specific computer upon which the algorithm is implemented, and the results of (19) should be regarded as only a crude estimate.

where x_t is the test point, x_k is the kth nearest prototype of those already examined and x_l is a prototype for which $d(x_t,x_l)$ and $d(x_l,x_n)$ have already been evaluated (and saved). The use of (21) will be most effective when the dispersion of interpoint distances in the prototype sample is greatest. In this case, $d(x_t,x_k)$ will tend to be small whereas $d(x_t,x_l)$ and $d(x_l,x_n)$ will quite often be dissimilar, making the right-hand side on (21) large. Since distance varies as the dth root of the volume, the distance variation will decrease with increasing dimensionality for a given density variation.

For a uniform density distribution in a d-dimensional space, the coefficient of variation of the interpoint distance is

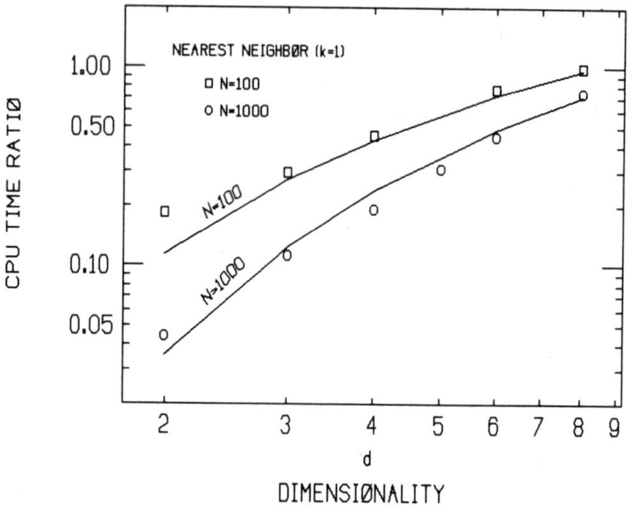

Fig. 6. Ratio of actual running times of this algorithm to the brute force method for finding the nearest neighbor for 100 and 1000 normally distributed prototypes, as a function of the dimensionality d. The solid lines represent the predictions of (1).

$$\left[\frac{\langle r_d^2\rangle - \langle r_d\rangle^2}{\langle r_d\rangle^2}\right]^{1/2} = [d(d+2)]^{-1/2} \tag{22}$$

which decreases as $1/d$ for increasing d. Thus, the usefulness of the triangle inequality is affected by the "curse of dimensionality" in the same manner as the algorithm discussed above.

The performance of this algorithm has been discussed in terms of the number of prototypes that need to be examined and distances calculated. This measure has the advantage of being independent of the specific implementation of the algorithm and the computer upon which it is executed. It has the disadvantage that it does not measure the additional "overhead" computation that may be present in the algorithm. The brute force method spends nearly all of its time performing distance calculations and has very little such overhead. The method discussed here introduces additional computation exclusive of the distance calculations. Fig. 6 indicates that this overhead computation is not excessive. Shown in Fig. 6 is the ratio of actual running times of this algorithm to the brute force method[6] for the same situations presented in Fig. 4. Comparisons of corresponding results in these two figures show that the performance of this algorithm, as reflected in number of distance calculations, closely corresponds to its actual performance when implemented on a computer.[7]

[6] These ratios were obtained by executing both algorithms on an IBM 370/168 computer. Both algorithms were coded in Fortran IV and compiled with the IBM Fortran H compiler at optimization level two.

[7] The largest discrepancies occur for low dimensionality where distance calculations are relatively inexpensive. For higher dimensionalities, the correspondence becomes closer.

CONCLUSION

A simple algorithm has been presented for finding nearest neighbors with computation proportional to $k^{1/d}N^{1-(1/d)}$ and preprocessing proportional to $dN \log N$. The algorithm can be used with a general class of dissimilarity measures, not just those that satisfy the triangle inequality. The algorithm takes advantage of local variations in the structure of the data to increase efficiency. Formulas that enable one to calculate a close upper bound on the expected performance for common metrics have been derived. Simulation experiments have been presented that illustrate the degree to which these formulas bound the actual performance.

ACKNOWLEDGMENT

The authors would like to thank W. H. Rogers, S. Steppel, and J. E. Zolnowsky for helpful discussions.

REFERENCES

[1] E. Fix and J. L. Hodges, Jr., "Discriminatory analysis; small sample performance," USAF School of Aviation Medicine, Randolf Field, Tex., Project 21-49-004, Rep. 11, Aug. 1952.
[2] D. O. Loftsgaarden and C. P. Quesenberry, "A nonparametric density function," *Ann. Math Statist.*, vol. 36, pp. 1049–1051, 1965.
[3] T. M. Cover and P. E. Hart, "Nearest neighbor pattern classification," *IEEE Trans. Inform. Theory*, vol. IT-13, pp. 21–27, Jan. 1967.
[4] T. M. Cover, "Rates of convergence of nearest neighbor decision procedures," in *Proc. 1st Annu. Hawaii Conf. Systems Theory*, Jan. 1968, pp. 413–415.
[5] T. J. Wagner, "Convergence of the nearest neighbor rule," *IEEE Trans. Inform. Theory*, vol. IT-17, pp. 566–571, Sept. 1971.
[6] K. Fukunaga and L. D. Hostetler, "Optimization of k-nearest-neighbor density estimates," *IEEE Trans. Inform. Theory*, vol. IT-19, pp. 320–326, May 1973.
[7] C. Barns, "An easily mechanized scheme for an adaptive pattern recognizer," *IEEE Trans. Electron. Comput.* (Corresp.), vol. EC-15, pp. 385–387, June 1966.
[8] E. A. Patrick and F. P. Fisher, "Generalized k-nearest neighbor decision rule," *J. Inform. Contr.*, vol. 16, pp. 128–152, Apr. 1970.
[9] P. E. Hart, "The condensed nearest neighbor rule," *IEEE Trans. Inform. Theory* (Corresp.), vol. IT-14, pp. 515–516, May 1968.
[10] F. P. Fisher and E. A. Patrick, "A preprocessing algorithm for nearest neighbor decision rules," in *Proc. Nat. Electronics Conf.*, vol. 26, Dec. 1970, pp. 481–485.

A Classifier Design Technique for Discrete Variable Pattern Recognition Problems

JAMES C. STOFFEL, MEMBER, IEEE

Abstract—This paper presents a new computerized technique to aid the designers of pattern classifiers when the measurement variables are discrete and the values form a simple nominal scale (no inherent metric). A theory of "prime events" which applies to patterns with measurements of this type is presented. A procedure for applying the theory of "prime events" and an analysis of the "prime event estimates" is given. To manifest additional characteristics of this technique, an example optical character recognition (OCR) application is discussed.

Index Terms—Classification, discrete variables, interactive pattern recognition, nonparametric pattern recognition, n-tuple selection, optical character recognition (OCR), pattern recognition, prime events.

I. INTRODUCTION

THE DESIGN of automatic classification devices often relies on one or a number of mathematical procedures which manifest the statistical structure of samples from the classes to be discriminated. Such mathematical procedures have been effectively incorporated in interactive computer environments (see Kanal [1]). There exist few mathematical techniques, however, to deal with patterns whose measurement variables have discrete, type-II values. The following will describe the unique characteristics of discrete type-II variables, the difficulties in dealing with these variables in pattern-recognition problems, and a new theoretical and practical procedure to handle such variables.

II. TYPES OF VARIABLES

In a classical manner, a pattern will be represented hereafter as a vector, $v = [v_1 v_2 \cdots v_d]$. The elements v_i in the vector represent the values of specific measurements, and the dimension of the vector d corresponds to the number of measurements used to represent the pattern. The measurement variables will be divided into three categories. Following the definitions of Sammon [2], the categories will be labeled continuous, discrete, type-I, and discrete, type-II.

The continuous category is composed of variables which may take on any value in a prescribed range of the real line.

The second type of variable is defined as discrete, type-I. This group will include those variables which take on only discrete values, but which represent samples from some underlying continuum. An example of these discrete, type-I variables is age. Although it is typically given as integer years, the measurement value is a sample from a quantized continuum, time since birth.

A variable in the third category, called discrete, type-II, may take on discrete values, but there is no apparently significant ranking of these values. An example of such a variable is the blood type of a sample. The possible values are: A, AB, O, etc. These values are discrete and represent a nominal, rather than an ordinal scale.

For cases when the measurement variables are discrete, type-II, significant practical difficulties may arise in the design of accurate classifiers. It is characteristic of the discrete, type-II variables that a change of a single variable value, from one level to another, may represent a significant change in the measured item. For example, two specimens which have identical measurement values, with the exception of blood type, may have significantly different responses to certain pathogens.

Unlike the continuous category there is no incremental variation in the discrete, type-II variable values which will leave the pattern effectively unaltered. Due to this factor and the lack of an inherent ordering principle for the variable values, it is difficult to describe the probability distribution of the measurement vectors by a simple parametric model. If a generally applicable model existed with relatively few parameters, the designer might confidently estimate the parameters of the distribution and then approximate an optimal discriminate rule such as Bayes' (Kanal [3]).

As an example, consider the case when the measurement vector has a finite dimension and each variable takes on a finite number of values. From a statistical point of view, it would appear useful to estimate the probabilities of *each* of the possible measurement vectors. For this "multinomial model" (Foley [4]), assume that all measurements are binary valued and that the measurement vector has dimension ten. These conditions imply that there are 1024 parameters, probabilities for the measurement vectors, to estimate. Since a number of these parameters will be less than one one-thousandth, a large number of samples of each class must be obtained to guarantee confidence in these estimates. Foley [4] implies that 3072 to 4096 samples per class should be utilized to yield confidence in the classifier design. Such large sample sets are often unobtainable, however.

Manuscript received March 6, 1973; revised September 24, 1973. This work was supported in part by a research grant to Syracuse University from the Rome Air Development Center, Rome, N. Y.
The author is with the Research Laboratories Department, Xerox Corporation, Rochester, N. Y. 14644.

Reprinted from *IEEE Trans. Comput.*, vol. C-23, pp. 428–441, Apr. 1974.

Augmenting the statistical tools which aid the practical classifier designer are procedures which are based on "geometric principles." Rather than estimate statistical parameters, a designer may begin to treat the set of possible measurement vectors as members of a vector space, wherein he seeks a relatively simple discriminate rule to be specified in terms of a metric for that space. Exemplars of this approach are "nearest neighbors" classification rules (Fix, Hodges [5]), and Fisher's Linear Discriminant (Fisher [6], Sammon [7]).

For measurement vectors with discrete, type-II variables, however, the Euclidean metric is not generally applicable as a similarity measure (Hills [8]). Furthermore, the arbitrary nature of the nominal scale makes alternate metrics difficult to derive (Lance, Williams [9]). The geometric principles which lead to useful design tools for classification tasks with continuous variable measurement vectors are not generally applicable to the cases with discrete, type-II variables.

III. APPROACHES TO HANDLING DISCRETE VARIABLES

This paper attempts to present a general "tool" to assist the classifier designer in extracting classificatory information from data with discrete, type-II variables. This technique, like all other in pattern recognition, will not solve every classification problem; however, it will add to the designer's ability to handle discrete variable data. The initiative for the work reported here was the work done in the development of a "discrete variable subsystem" for OLPARS, by Sammon [10]. It is the author's belief that the analytical techniques developed in this paper are best suited to an interactive environment such as described by Kanal [1].

Various approaches have been taken to deal with the difficulties of discrete, type-II variables as cited above. Linhart [11] and Cochran and Hopkins [12] were among the first to publish the inherent difficulties in handling classification problems with discrete, type-II variables. A number of others have utilized a variety of techniques in an attempt to overcome the difficulties with variables of this category.

Viewing the problem statistically, a number of restrictions have been imposed on the general multinomial model of the probability distribution of the measurement vectors. If one assumes that the variables are mutually independent, then there are only d parameters to estimate for measurement vectors of dimension d with binary-valued variables. Regarding this as too restrictive, one might assume the "latent class" model of Lazarsfeld [13] to represent a class of measurement vectors. This model would represent the class as a summation of subclasses, each of which has variables which are mutually independent. If there were s subclasses, then one would have to estimate $s \times (d + 1)$ parameters for measurement vectors of dimension d whose measurements were binary valued. Investigations of the parameter estimation of this model have been carried out, by Anderson [14] and McHugh [15]; however, this is not a generally applicable model.

Another restricted model which has been proposed is the "logit" model. For this model, the logarithm of the probability distribution of the measurement vectors is represented as follows:

$$\log \{P(v_1,v_2,\cdots,v_d)\} = a_0 + \sum_{i=1}^{d} (-1)^{v_i} a_i \tag{1}$$

where $v_i \in \{0,1\}$ and a_i are constants. Schaefer [16] utilized this model for binary-valued measurement variables, which are by definition discrete, type-II. (A generalization of this model and additional details may be found in Good [17], Gilbert [18], and Cox [19].) This model, as well as the restricted models given above, represents assumptions about the classes being dealt with. For practical applications these various assumptions must be justified before the models become of value.

An alternate technique which has been employed is to develop a finite series expansion for the general multinomial probability distribution. By a judicious choice of the basis set, a concise description of the total probability distribution may be possible if problem information constrains some coefficients to zero. Examples of this approach are Bahadur [20], Abend *et al.* [21], and Chow [22], [23]. This approach has yielded limited results.

A variety of "geometric" techniques have also been applied to the discrete, type-II variable classifier design task. The "near neighbor" concept of Fix and Hodges [5] was applied unsuccessfully by Hills [8] to discriminate discrete, type-II data. Gilbert [18] examined the applicability of Fisher's *linear discriminant* to the classification of a restricted class of measurement vectors with binary variables. Furthermore, numerous *similarity metrics* have been proposed and applied to classification tasks. Among these are the "matching metric" of Sokal and Sneath [24], the "hierarchical" clustering metrics of Lance and Williams [9], and a "probabilistic" metric defined by Goodall [25].

Still another alternative for dealing with discrete, type-II variables is to transform them into continuous variables. Examples of such transformations may be found in Sammon [2].

The above techniques have not been valueless, but there remains a need for a general approach to extracting classificatory information from the sample data. An approach which makes few *a priori* decisions about the data is "measurement selection." This technique attempts to eliminate from the measurement vector variables which contribute little or nothing to the classification accuracy. Hills [8], for example, selects the "best" subset of measurement variable by estimating the information divergence, Fortier and Solomon [26] incorporate the product moment correlations of the variables in a figure-of-merit selection algorithm, and McQuitty [27] applies a clustering algorithm. These procedures tend to be ineffective or to require exhaustive, impractical computation for discrete, type-II variable data. Some theoretical justification for the lack of positive results in this area may be found in Elashoff *et al.* [28] and Toussaint [29].

IV. PRIME EVENTS

A new theoretical point of view is presented in this section which deals with discrete, type-II variable measurement vectors. The theory is generally applicable to this type of data; i.e., no *a priori* decisions about the form of the underlying probability distributions are required.

A pattern is available to a classifier designer in the form of a d-dimensional vector, $\boldsymbol{v} = (v_1, v_2, \cdots, v_d)$, the measurement vector. The set of possible measurement vectors is thus comprised of vectors whose elements lie in the range of the measurement functions associated with each element in the vector. The set of possible measurement vectors forms a set of *events* in a sample space.

An event in the sample space described above is completely specified by a d-dimensional vector. The term, event, will be utilized hereafter to denote a measurement vector in which a subset of the d elements have specified values. The remaining elements are unspecified and will be represented by a "—" in the vector. Hence, event $e_1 = (1,2,5)$ represents the state that measurements one, two, and three take on values 1, 2, and 5, respectively. Furthermore, event $e_2 = (1,2,—)$ is defined to represent the state that measurements one and two take on values 1 and 2, respectively. Measurement three is *not specified.*

One of the significant characteristics of an event is its ability to "**cover**" other events. An event e_1 will be said to cover an event e_2 if and only if every element of e_1 which has a specified value equals the value of the corresponding item in e_2. Furthermore, if an element in e_1 is not specified, then any value or a "not specified" value may exist for the corresponding element of e_2.

To exemplify the covering principle, examine the following events:

$$e_1 = (2,—,—)$$

$$e_2 = (2,1,0)$$

$$e_3 = (2,2,—).$$

Using the above definition, one may see that event e_1 covers e_2 and e_3. However, e_2 does not cover e_1 or e_3, and e_3 does not cover e_1 or e_2.

Due to the covering capacity of an event, one may note that an event partitions the set of possible measurement vectors into two subsets. One subset comprises the measurement vectors which are covered by the event, and the other subset contains all measurement vectors not covered by the event. The above principle is easily incorporated in the design of a classifier. For each class, a collection of events which will henceforth be termed the *definition set* is assigned. The classification rule is, then, to assign a measurement vector to the class whose definition set contained an event which covered the measurement vector. If the measurement vector is not covered by a member of any definition set, then it is rejected.

To implement the simple classification procedure described above, a number of major questions must be answered. First of all, what events should theoretically be contained within the definition sets of each class? The number of possible events is typically quite large. For example, a ten-dimensional measurement vector with binary-valued elements will have 3^{10} events which must be considered in making up a definition set. Further, the sets of events may overlap one another in varying degrees, and various percentages of the one or more classes may be covered by one event. Hence, there are potentially complex tradeoffs in the error rates for various sets of events used as a definition set.

Second, for a specific classification problem, how does one generate the theoretically ideal events as defined by the answer to question one?

Finally, how does sample information from a practical design problem become incorporated in the design of definition sets for each class?

The remainder of this section will be devoted to answering the first question; the next section will deal with questions two and three. Therefore, the immediate goal is to ascertain just what events should be contained within the definition set of a particular class.

Two types of errors are of concern when using events to discriminate between classes. Type-I errors will be defined as the occurrence of a measurement vector from class C_j which is covered by an event in the definition set of class C_i, for $i \neq j$. Type-II errors will be defined as the occurrence of a measurement vector from class C_j which is not covered by an event in the definition set for class C_j. It is not always possible to reduce the occurrence of errors to zero, since classes may overlap. The optimality criterion which is utilized, therefore, is the minimization of the *average probability of error.*

Another criterion is placed on the theoretically optimal solution. This second criterion states that the set of events which comprise the definition set for each class must be minimal in number. Among other things, this criterion introduces the practical consideration of storage for a classification algorithm.

The first criterion for the optimal definition set may be met by Bayes' rule, Kanal [3]. For the case under consideration, the rule states that the minimum average probability of error is obtained when the classifier assigns a measurement vector to the class which yields the largest *a posteriori* probability. Using the notation $p(\boldsymbol{v} \mid C_j)$ for the conditional probability of measurement vector $\boldsymbol{v}$, given class C_j as a source and $p(C_j)$ as the probability of occurrence of a vector from class C_j, then the optimal rule assigns to class C_j a sample $\boldsymbol{v}$ whenever $p(\boldsymbol{v} \mid C_j)p(C_j) \geq p(\boldsymbol{v} \mid C_i)p(C_i)$ for all i.

From the above, one may deduce that a definition set comprised of a measurement vectors which the above rule has assigned to a specific class would satisfy criterion one. However, criterion two may not be satisfied by the collection of measurement vectors. Hence, the optimal set of events is not immediately obtained.

A particular set of events will be shown to be a sufficient collection from which an optimal definition set may be selected. The members of this set are labeled "**prime events.**" A prime event is defined as an event which *covers* only those measurement vectors which a Bayes' Rule would assign to *one class*; furthermore, a prime event may not be covered by another prime event.

The fact that the optimal definition sets may be composed of events from the set of prime events may be easily proved by contradiction. Under the assumption that the optimal design set includes a nonprime event e_j, it follows that e_j must either be covered by a prime event e_p, and thus e_p may replace e_j in the design set, or e_j covers measurement vectors assigned by Bayes' Rule to more than one class. The second alternative is not possible, since the optimal definition set will not contradict Bayes' Rule; therefore, the prime events form a sufficient set.

In order to clarify the ideas expressed above, an example will be given utilizing the set of three-dimensional binary-valued measurement vectors. The example is that of a two-class problem plus reject class, and the class conditional probabilities for the measurement vectors are given below. The example shows the assignment of the measurement vectors and the prime events associated with the problem. The optimal design sets for each class are then listed.

Example 1

Measurement vectors	$p(v_i \mid C_1)$	$p(v_i \mid C_2)$	$p(v_i \mid R)$
000	0	0	0.25
001	0	0	0.25
010	0.4	0.2	0
011	0.4	0.2	0
100	0.1	0.3	0
101	0.1	0.2	0
110	0	0.1	0
111	0	0	0.50

Assume that the probability of each class is 0.45; namely, $p(C_1) = p(C_2) = 0.45$ and $p(R) = 0.10$. The decision rule described above may be rewritten as follows.

Assign v_i to class C_j whenever

$$p(v_i \mid C_j)p(C_j) \geq p(v_i \mid C_k)p(C_k)$$

for $C_j,C_k \in \{C_i,C_2,R\}$.

Utilizing this rule, the measurement vectors will be assigned in the following fashion:

$$\text{Class } C_1 = \{(0,1,0),\ (0,1,1)\}$$

$$\text{Class } C_2 = \{(1,0,0),\ (1,0,1),\ (1,1,0)\}$$

$$\text{Reject} = \{(0,0,0),\ (0,0,1),\ (1,1,1)\};$$

the prime events for class C_1: $\{(0,1-)\}$, for class C_2: $\{(1,0,—),\ (1,—,0)\}$; the chosen optimal design sets are:

$$E_1 = \{(0,1,—)\}$$

$$E_2 = \{(1,0,—),\ (1,—,0)\}.$$

Example 1 is intentionally simple and does not reflect some of the more complex characteristics of prime events and definition sets. There is a potentially large number of prime events which may be associated with a particular classification problem. The number of these prime events may be as large as the number of measurement vectors which they cover. The magnitude of their number and their characteristics are, furthermore, problem-dependent facts.

The potential variability in the number of prime events and their complex covering properties results in definition sets of various sizes and (problem-dependent) characteristics. In addition, the definition sets for a particular classification problem are not unique, even though they may be composed of only prime events.

The suggested procedure for designing a classifier requires that one first generate the prime events for the specific problem at hand. The next step is to select a minimal size set of prime events to make up the definition sets. These procedures are discussed in the next section.

V. GENERATION OF EVENTS

The next question to be dealt with is the method of creating the optimal design set for a specific class. In what follows, a procedure will be given which is capable of creating all of the prime events associated with a specified set of measurement vectors. A procedure for selecting the final design set will then be described.

It is intended that the generation procedure be performed for each class to yield the optimal set of events for that class. Thus, for a six-class problem six sets of events will be generated. The reject class then becomes the remainder of the set of measurement vectors which are not covered by any of the six sets of events.

As throughout the discussion of prime events, the procedure described below will make use of the knowledge of the class conditional probabilities of the measurement vectors, along with the probabilities of occurrence of the classes. These quantities must be estimated in most practical cases.

The first step in the generation procedure is to form two lists of measurement vectors, L and NL. List L is comprised of all the measurement vectors which the Bayes' decision rule would assign to the chosen class. List NL is comprised of all the measurement vectors which are not assigned to the chosen class.

The procedure of generating prime events uses the list L to create new events and forms a new list, LP, of potential prime events. The creation of new lists continues until no new events are generated.

New events are created from list L by combining a pair of events in the list. The combining process for two events in L is performed using the lattice binary operation "join" for each variable. To make clear this procedure, the operation of combining variables will first be dealt with.

The result of combining variables may be expressed as a binary operation with a simple rule. If the two variable values differ, then the result is a "don't care" value. If the variables are the same, the resultant variable has that same value. When combining a "don't care" value with anything, the result is a "don't care" value. For ternary-valued variables, the table below will demonstrate the combination rules described above:

v'	v''	$(v' + v'')$
0	0	0
0	1	—
0	2	—
0	—	—
1	0	—
1	1	1
1	2	—
1	—	—
2	0	—
2	1	—
2	2	2
2	—	—
—	0	—
—	1	—
—	2	—
—	—	—

where "—" signifies a "don't care."

Now, to combine two events in L which have ternary-valued variables, the above operation will be applied "pointwise" to each variable. The combination of the following two events will help clarify this concept:

$$(2,—,1) + (2,1,0) = (2,—,—).$$

In this way, any two events derived from the same measurement space may be combined to form a new event. The process of combining events will henceforth be termed "merging."

The procedure for generating the set of prime events begins by merging all pairs of events in the list L. Each new event, the result of merging two events in L, is checked to see if it covers any members of NL. If it does cover a member of NL, then the event will not be a prime event nor will any event which covers this new event. This follows from the restriction that a prime event may not cover measurement vectors which a Bayes' decision strategy would assign to two different classes. The new event is then disregarded.

On the other hand, if the result of merging two events in L does not cover any member of NL, then this event will be a potential prime event, and it is stored in list LP. All new events generated from L are checked and only those new events which are truly *potential prime events* are stored in LP. Also added to LP is any event in L which did not yield a *potential prime* event when it was merged with any of the other events in L.

The procedure forms all pairwise mergers in list L and adds to list LP those new events which only cover measurement vectors assigned to a specific class. The list LP will also include those events from L which did not yield a potential prime event upon merging with any of the events in L.

The list LP is next treated as list L and the merging process is repeated as before. Each pair of events in LP is merged and a check is performed to see if the new event is a potential prime event.

This formation of new lists continues until list L equals list LP. This occurs when no merger of a pair of events in L yields an event which is a potential prime event and is different from each member of L.

An example of the generation procedure will be given below to help clarify the specific details of the algorithm. The example problem is a two-class problem with three-dimensional ternary-valued variables. The procedure will be applied to derive the set of prime events associated with one of the classes, C_1.

Let the set of measurement vectors which a Bayes' decision rule would assign to class C_1 be as follows: $\{(2,0,0), (2,1,0), (2,2,0), (2,0,1)\}$. The remaining measurement vectors will be either in class C_2 or a reject class. The algorithm begins by forming list L.

List L

1: (2,0,0)
2: (2,1,0)
3: (2,2,0)
4: (2,0,1)

Indices have been assigned to each measurement vector so that they may be referenced more easily, i.e., $e_1 \triangleq (2,0,0)$.

Next, one merges events e_1 and e_2:

$$(2,0,0) + (2,1,0) = (2,—,0) \triangleq e_{12}.$$

This event is checked against the list NL with the result that no member of that list is covered by event e_{12}. Thus, e_{12} is placed in list LP.

The events e_1 and e_3 are then merged:

$$(2,0,0) + (2,2,0) = (2,—,0) = e_{13}.$$

Since the event e_{13} is already in LP, no further processing is required.

The remaining combinations yield:

$$e_{14} \triangleq (2,0,—)$$

$$e_{23} \triangleq (2,—,0)$$

$$e_{24} \triangleq (2,—,—)$$

$$e_{34} \triangleq (2,—,—).$$

The events e_{14}, e_{24}, e_{34} are not retained, since they cover members of NL. Event e_{23} is already stored on LP and hence is disregarded.

Event e_4 is next added to list LP since it merged with no member of L to yield a potential prime event.

$$LP = \{(2,—,0), (2,0,1)\}.$$

Checking LP and L, one will find them different. Therefore, LP becomes list L and a new empty list is introduced as LP:

List L	List LP
$e_{12}(2,—,0)$	(Null).
$e_4(2,0,1)$	

Repeating the merging process:

$$(2,—,0) + (2,0,1) = (2,—,—) \triangleq e_{124}.$$

Event e_{124} covers elements of list NL and therefore is disregarded.

No further mergers are possible in list L, and thus e_{12} and e_4 are added to LP:

$$LP = \{2,—,0), (2,0,1)\}.$$

Checking LP and L, it will be seen that they are identical, and thus the procedure *stops*. The set of prime events for class C_1 is in both lists, L and LP.

It can be shown that the above procedure will generate all, and only, the prime events for a specific classification problem. To manifest that the procedure will generate *all* of the prime events, this fact will be negated and a contradiction will be shown to follow. Pursuing this method, let there exist some prime event e_p which is not generated by the procedure described above. Event e_p covers a set of measurement vectors which by Bayes' rule will be classified as belonging to one class. Thus a pair or any subset of these vectors, when merged, will yield an event which is covered by e_p and hence covers no member of another class. The generative procedure described above discards only those mergers which cover measurement vectors of two or more classes. Hence, the mergers of measurement vectors which are covered by e_p will be retained. Successive, exhaustive, pairwise merging of the retained events which are covered by e_p will eventually generate event e_p, as it represents the merger of all measurement vectors which it covers. But this contradicts the assumption that there exists a prime event which is not generated by the above procedure.

To show that *only* prime events are generated via the above procedure, a proof by contradiction will also suffice. Assume that an event e_n is generated but that e_n is not a prime event. There are two restrictions of prime events which e_n may have violated. First of all, e_n may cover measurement vectors from two or more classes. This may be ruled out since the above generative procedure does not retain events as potential prime events for a specific class if that event also covers measurement vectors of another class, members of NL. The second prime event restriction is that a prime event may not be covered by another prime event. Event e_n may not be covered by some prime event e_p, however, since the generative procedure would attempt to merge e_n and e_p and yield event e_p, which would be retained. Event e_n would not remain with the final list of prime events which was shown above to be complete. Therefore, the assumption that event e_n exists is false, and the generative procedure has been shown to yield only prime events.

The final theoretical step in the creation of the optimal definition sets for the classes of a specific problem is the selection of the *minimum* size set of the generated prime events. The measurement vectors which a definition set must cover are the same vectors which were placed in list L to generate the prime events. The goal is, therefore, to select a minimal-size cover for these measurement vectors.

One method of selecting the minimal-size covering is to exhaustively examine the power set of the set of prime events. One could then select from this set the smallest set of prime events which covered the required measurement vectors. Alternate procedures for selecting this minimal-size cover may be found in the procedures developed to "minimize Boolean functions," Prather [30]. For a theoretical analysis, the existence of some procedure is sufficient. Thus, the problem of selecting a minimal cover will be considered answered until the practical application of this theory is discussed in the next section.

The Prime-Event-Generation (PEG) algorithm will operate to minimize a function of the discrete variables. Algorithms which minimize the "cost" of a Boolean function, e.g., Prather [30], yield similar results. Both procedures generate covers for a set of discrete points. However, the PEG algorithm will operate on other than binary-valued variables, with various mixes of multivalued variables, and with more than the three classes of points, "trues," "falses," and "don't cares," which define Boolean functions.

This section has provided theoretical answers to the questions of what events should be utilized in a classifier and how these events may be generated and selected. The next section will deal with the practical classifier design task and the application of the theory of prime events to it.

VI. APPLICATION OF PRIME EVENT THEORY

The following is the proposed method for dealing with design problems wherein the probabilities of the measurement vectors are not known. When one is not aware of the class conditional probabilities of the measurement vectors, optimal design procedures may only be estimated. The set of prime events will serve as a goal for the design methods described below. However, only sample information will be utilized in the procedure.

The proposed method of dealing with sample information is to form estimates of the true prime events for the particular classes. The mechanism for creating these estimates is to incorporate samples of the classes as the assigned measurement vectors were incorporated in the prime-event-generation algorithm described in the previous section. To obtain the prime events associated with a class C, one places the samples from class C in list L and the samples from all other classes in list NL. The prime-event-generation algorithm then proceeds, as described above, to merge the samples in list L and to add potential prime events (truly estimates) to list LP. Proceeding as previously described, the generation algorithm will halt when list L equals list LP.

The task of extracting the minimal size cover as a definition set is also encumbered by the practicality of dealing only with estimates of prime events. For practical classifiers, it is economically advantageous to store as few prime event estimates as possible. However, the selection of the smallest set which simultaneously covers the set of samples of that specific class is not guaranteed to yield the best classifier accuracy; it may, in fact, degrade the performance over that of a larger set. Thus, the selection of the definition set may incorporate a tradeoff in the number of prime event estimates and their ability to cover all, and only, the measurement vectors which Bayes' rule would assign to that class. When the number of prime event estimates is large, a cover-selection algorithm such as given by Prather [30] may be incorporated. If but a few estimates are generated, it may be practical to include all of them in the definition set. This decision is often dependent on problem constraints which are specific to the design tasks; hence, no rule is given here. An example-selection procedure is described in the design application presented in Section VII.

Two new facilities are added to the fundamental prime-event-generation procedure to increase its flexibility when dealing with sample information. The first facility is a threshold, θ_A, which is utilized when checking if an event covers a member of list NL. An event will be treated as though it did not cover a member of NL if the event truly covered less than or equal to θ_A percent of list NL.

The normal setting of θ_A is 0. It may be raised to other percentage values, however. This flexibility may prove helpful when a measurement vector occurs as a sample in two different classes. If sufficient numbers of samples are available to confidently estimate the Bayes' rule for classifying such measurement vectors, they may simply be removed from classes other than the properly assigned class. The generation procedure may then proceed as before. However, if insufficient confidence is established with the available samples, then threshold θ_A may be raised above 0.

The second facility which is added to the fundamental generation algorithm is a threshold, θ_B. An event will be considered to cover a measurement vector in list NL if the number of specified variables in the event which differ from those of the measurement vector is less than θ_B.

To exemplify the use of θ_B, assume that vector (2,1,0,1,0) is in list NL. If θ_B is set at the normal value 1, then the event (2,—,1,—,0) will be considered, as described in the previous section, not to cover the measurement vector. However, if θ_B is raised to 2, then the event will be treated as though it covers the measurement vector, since only one specified variable in the event differs in value from that of the measurement vector.

Both θ_A and θ_B are utilized to compensate for the finite sample sizes in practical problems. By raising θ_A above 0, one is not forced to make decisions based on a small number of samples in a very large measurement space. The variable θ_B is utilized to provide greater confidence that a generated event will not cover samples of a class represented in list NL. An increase in θ_B from 1 to 2 will compensate for the absence of a sample in NL which is different in only one variable value from a sample presently in NL. In this way one may compensate for some deficiencies in the samples on list NL.

The method of incorporating samples in the basic prime-event-generation algorithm provides a mechanism for extracting the classificatory information from the discrete, type-II variable data. This algorithm with the added flexibilities provided by θ_A and θ_B is defined as the Prime-Event-Generation algorithm (PEG) and it represents the fundamental analytic mechanism which is presented as a classifier design tool.

The important qualities of the prime-event-estimation procedures are noted below. An example application of these procedures is discussed in the section which follows.

The first notable characteristic of the prime-event-estimation procedure is its generality. The technique makes no *a priori* decisions about the form of the underlying probability distributions for the measurement vectors. The PEG algorithm is a tool for extracting from the samples of the classes that "structural" information which will make possible the discrimination of these classes, regardless of the underlying probability distributions associated with each class.

A second characteristic of the PEG procedure which should be noted concerns the statistical confidence of estimated parameters. As noted earlier, for discrete, type-II variable classifier design tasks, the number of possible measurement vectors is often too large in number to obtain confident estimates of their probabilities of occurrence using practical sample sizes. The merging process of the PEG algorithm yields events which may have a number of variables not specified in value. These events may truly be considered as members of the subspace defined by the variables which are specified. Hence, there will be less possible variation in that subspace and greater confidence may be placed in an estimate of the probability of the event occurring than in the estimate of measurement vectors.

To exemplify the above concept, assume there exists a two-class recognition problem with ten-dimensional, binary-valued measurement vectors. If one treats the vectors as a positional binary number, then the measurement vectors may be denoted by a decimal number in the range from 0 to 1024. Using this notation, let the samples of class C_1 be the set $\{0,1,2,\cdots,255\}$, and let the samples of class C_2 be the set $\{256,257,\cdots,767\}$ (see Fig. 1).

For the example described above, one may estimate the probabilities for each of the possible measurement vectors. However, there is at most one sample of any of the possible measurement vectors. Also, the greatest difference in the number of samples of a specific measurement vector for the two classes is one. Furthermore, there are only 768 samples with which to estimate the 2048 class-conditional probabilities of the measurement vectors. Little statistical confidence may be placed in these estimates.

On the other hand, one may note that all samples in class C have the first two measurements equal to 0. Furthermore, class C_2 samples have measurements one and two equal to the two-tuple (0,1) or (1,0). A discriminatory event for class C_1 could thus be (0,0,—,—,—,—,—,—,—,—) and a pair for class C_2 could be (0,1,—,—,—,—,—,—,—,—) and (1,0,—,—,—,—,—,—,—,—). All of these events cover 256 samples each, and greater confidence may be placed in estimating an accurate classification rule for these events than for the measurement vectors considered above.

A third point to note about the PEG procedure is that it extracts from the samples the within-class similarities which simultaneously discriminate the specific classes from one another. The prime-event estimates simultaneously fit a specific class and discriminate this class from the other classes. Classifier design tools which simultaneously perform these two functions are rare. Often a procedure relies strictly on its facility to discriminate the samples, e.g., Ho-Kashyap [31]. The application of such a procedure requires care (see Foley [4] and Cover [32]). Furthermore, the possibility of a reject class is annulled.

On the other hand, there are procedures which concentrate on fitting each class with some description; then, classification becomes a matter of determining the best description for a sample from the set of class descriptions. However, a useful description for classification will emphasize the features which are different in separate classes, and not merely describe a class in some least mean-square error sense (see Fukanga [33]). The prime-event-generation procedure provides fitting information, but by definition the events have the ability to discriminate the classes.

Another major point which should be emphasized is the ability of the PEG algorithm to detect high-order statistical structure without requiring exhaustive searches. For many practical classification problems, the dimension of the measurement vector is such that only first- and second-order statistics are examined. Higher order statistical analysis would be too time consuming. The example below will help manifest the ability of the PEG procedure to enable higher order statistical analysis.

Assume that a two-class discrimination problem had fifty-dimensional, binary-valued measurement vectors. Let the probabilities for measurements ten, twenty, and thirty, when treated as a three-tuple, be:

$v' = (v_{10}$	v_{20}	$v_{30})$	$P(v' \mid C_1)$	$P(v' \mid C_2)$
0	0	0	$\frac{1}{4}$	0
0	0	1	0	$\frac{1}{4}$
0	1	0	0	$\frac{1}{4}$
0	1	1	$\frac{1}{4}$	0
1	0	0	0	$\frac{1}{4}$
1	0	1	$\frac{1}{4}$	0
1	1	0	$\frac{1}{4}$	0
1	1	1	0	$\frac{1}{4}$

Finally, assume that all other measurements have a fifty percent probability of being a 1 for both classes.

Class C_1 Samples		Class C_2 Samples	
v_0 :	(0,0,0,0,0,0,0,0,0,0)	v_{256}:	(0,1,0,0,0,0,0,0,0,0)
v_1 :	(0,0,0,0,0,0,0,0,0,1)	v_{257}:	(0,1,0,0,0,0,0,0,0,1)
v_2 :	(0,0,0,0,0,0,0,0,1,0)	v_{258}:	(0,1,0,0,0,0,0,0,1,0)
.		.	
.		.	
.		.	
v_{255}:	(0,0,1,1,1,1,1,1,1,1)	.	
		v_{767}:	(1,0,1,1,1,1,1,1,1,1)

Fig. 1. Sample measurement vectors for class C_1 and class C_2.

The two classes above have identical first- and second-order statistics. Hence, discrimination techniques which rely on such statistics will be useless. Furthermore, there are 1225 second-order statistics for this problem. Examination of this many parameters and incorporation of these in a classifier may be expensive in terms of time and storage.

On the other hand, the PEG procedure will be able to extract from samples of the classes, the significant third-order events. (The *order* of an event is defined as the *number of specified variables.*) Specifically, as the number of samples grows in size, the PEG procedure will generate the following events with a probability approaching one.

Events for Class C_1

Measurement Number	1,2,⋯,9	10	11,⋯,19	20	21,⋯,29	30	31,⋯,50
e_1:	(— — ⋯ —	0	— ⋯ —	0	— ⋯ —	0	— ⋯ —)
e_2:	(— — ⋯ —	0	— ⋯ —	1	— ⋯ —	0	— ⋯ —)
e_3:	(— — ⋯ —	1	— ⋯ —	0	— ⋯ —	1	— ⋯ —)
e_4:	(— — ⋯ —	1	— ⋯ —	1	— ⋯ —	0	— ⋯ —)

Events for Class C_2

Measurement Number	1,2,3,⋯,9	10	11,⋯,19	20	21,⋯,29	30	31,⋯,50
e_5	(— — ⋯ —	0	— ⋯ —	0	— ⋯ —	1	— ⋯ —)
e_6	(— — ⋯ —	0	— ⋯ —	1	— ⋯ —	1	— ⋯ —)
e_7	(— — ⋯ —	1	— ⋯ —	0	— ⋯ —	0	— ⋯ —)
e_8	(— — ⋯ —	1	— ⋯ —	1	— ⋯ —	1	— ⋯ —)

Not only will the events shown above provide accurate classification information for classes C_1 and C_2, the events represent components of a classifier which are economical with respect to the storage which they require.

Another point should be made about statistics which are greater than second order. High-order events may exist which accurately characterize different classes. It may be scientifically helpful not only to discriminate such classes, but also to specify what the different class characteristics are. Such information with regard to disease classes, for example, may point toward better knowledge of causes or cures. Prime events may manifest such characteristics.

The theory of prime events and the PEG procedure for generating estimates of prime events are offered as the basis for a classifier design tool. The effectiveness of this approach depends upon the problem being dealt with and the particular samples which are obtained. Operational characteristics, such as computation time, storage, and accuracy, need to be stated in terms of the characteristics of a particular problem. Hence, an example of the application of the prime event theory will be described briefly in the next section to show additional practical details.

VII. EXAMPLE APPLICATION

The example application of the theory of prime events discussed here is the design of a classifier for optical character recognition (OCR). The characters are the numerals, 0 through 9, which are printed by a computer-output line printer. The numerals are represented by a 12×8 binary array; Fig. 2 shows samples of these numerals. There are relatively large variations in the characters, as may be seen in Fig. 2, and these characters are not members of a font specifically designed for OCR.

The example OCR task was to discriminate the ten classes of numerals discussed above. Furthermore, practical constraints of time and storage were imposed on this design task. Using a specific processor architecture, the classifier was restricted to be a stored-program algorithm which would require no more than 8K bytes of memory. The speed of classification was constrained to classify 500 characters per second.

The above classifier design task, one of a large variety of practical recognition problems which have discrete, type-II variables, was selected as an example because a large group of readers could understand and interpret the results, statistically and visually, without a great deal of interpretation by the author. This design task was a nontrivial multiclass recognition problem which had extremely large dimensional-measurement vectors. The unique features of the prime-event approach, as discussed in the last section, might therefore be manifest.

The sample characters were represented as 96-dimensional binary-valued vectors. An event, therefore, may be viewed as a 96-dimensional ternary-valued vector, and a set of events, the, *definition set* was selected for each class. The method of classification was to assign a sample character to the class whose *definition set* contained the event which covered the sample character.

The practical time and storage constraints described above inhibited straightforward application of prime-event theory. Time is required to compute whether an event covers a sample character and, naturally, the events in the definition sets must be stored in the classifier. To meet the practical constraints in this problem, it was judged that, at most, three events could be stored for each definition set.

Another practical complication of the example problem was that only a finite set of sample numerals was available, thus inhibiting exhaustive statistical analysis. One hundred samples of each numeral were made available for design purposes.

An initial application of the PEG algorithm for the class of 8's, with parameters θ_A and θ_B set to 0 and 1, respectively, yielded one prime-event estimate. Testing this event on samples outside of the design set revealed that over 1 percent of the new 8's were not covered by the

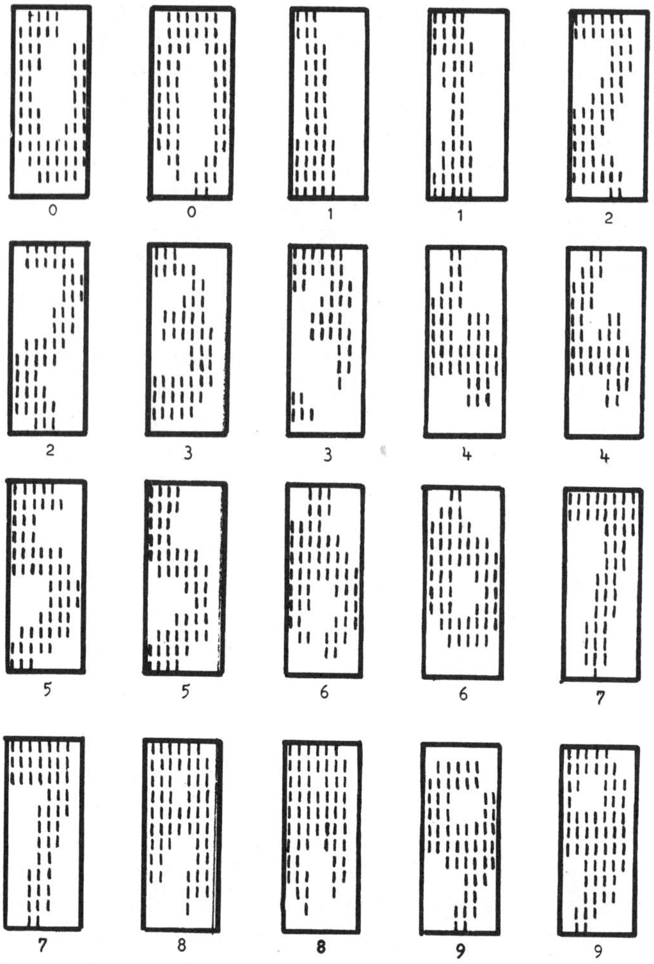

Fig. 2. Sample OCR characters represented as 12×8 binary arrays.

generated prime event. The uncovered samples of 8's, however, had a small number of variables (less than five) which differed from the specified variables in the prime-event estimate.

Based on the above results, the concept of covering was expanded to include a measure termed the covering distance. The covering distance from an event to a sample is defined as the number of variable values in the measurement vector which differ from the corresponding specified variables in the event. The rule for classifying a sample was altered to incorporate this principle. The covering distance to each prime-event estimate was computed, and the sample was assigned to the class whose *definition set* contained the event with the smallest covering distance. If the smallest covering distance was greater than five, the sample was rejected.

For the classification procedure stated above, it was determined that 22 events could be stored and incorporated in the software classification algorithm. The goal thus became one of selecting the best 22 events which had covering-distance properties enabling classification accuracy on the order of one substitution error or one rejection of a completed, humanly recognizable character in 10 000 samples. The method for meeting this goal was to increase θ_B when generating prime-event estimates.

(Parameter θ_A was maintained at zero throughout the design.) This resulted in prime events which had covering distances of larger magnitudes to the samples of other classes. This also resulted in larger numbers of prime events being generated.

The large numbers of prime events generated by the PEG algorithm had to be further examined to select a *definition set.* To overcome this design difficulty, a single-list mode of the PEG algorithm, PEG1, which is described in Appendix A, was employed. This procedure generates a subset of the prime-event estimates generated by the PEG algorithm and this subset is guaranteed to cover all samples initially placed in list L. In this way, the definition sets for the ten classes were selected. In Fig. 3, the definition sets which were automatically generated are shown. Table I shows the values of θ_B which were utilized when the definition sets were generated. The results of testing this classifier on, roughly, 9000 samples, which were independent of the design samples, are as follows.

The number of "valid" samples which were correctly classified was 8855. The number of misclassified samples was 0. A number of samples which represented electronic malfunctions, noise, etc. appeared in the test data; these were defined by the designer as reject characters. All eleven of these were correctly rejected by the classifier. No valid characters were rejected.

VIII. ANALYSIS

The procedure of incorporating "masks" or "n-tuples" in an OCR classifier is not a novel technique (see Nagy [34], Bowman [35]). However, the method of determining the specific n-tuples to be incorporated is new. Historically, the n-tuples which were generated were random selections of variables from a select set of variables. Membership in this select set was based upon the fact that maximum-likelihood first-order statistical estimates for a variable value of 0 or 1 exceeded some threshold. The frequency of occurrence of the selected n-tuple within the set of design samples was not known. The estimates of the number n of variables to be specified in the mask was typically based on first-order statistics (Bowman [35]). Furthermore, if two or more n-tuples could be utilized in a classifier, the random selection procedure, alluded to above, provides little assistance in selecting two or more complementary representations of a class.

The method of generating prime-event estimates yields n-tuple masks which have guaranteed characteristics, different from those generated by the random-selection procedure. The prime-event estimates reflect the interdependence of the variables and do not rely solely on first-order statistics. Furthermore, the prime-event estimates represent distinct "modes" of the samples of a class. The frequency of occurrence of the events may be estimated by the percentage of the class samples which the event covers; this value is available in the PEG1 algorithm and was printed out with each generated event. Furthermore, through the use of a selection procedure such as the PEG1 method, multiple masks may be selected which have complementary covering capabilities. These represent superior "fitting properties" of the prime events over the random n-tuple masks. It should also be noted that the prime-event estimates have specific discriminatory properties as defined by parameter θ_B in the generation algorithm. Such properties are neither known nor examined by the random n-tuple selection methods.

Another property of prime events which may be demonstrated visually is their ability to denote the subclasses or the modes of the statistical structure. Evidence of this property was obtained during the classifier design task; but to provide clearer proof of this property, the classes were combined so that only two classes remained. Class C_1

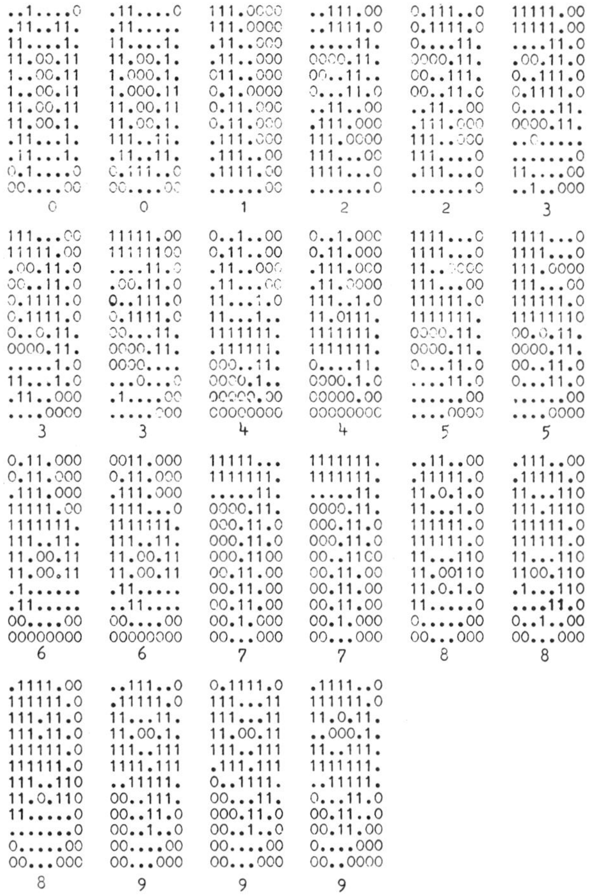

Fig. 3. Automatically generated prime-event estimates arranged as 12 × 8 arrays and depicting the ten definition sets. A "." indicates an unspecified value.

TABLE I
VALUES OF θ_B USED FOR GENERATING EACH DEFINITION SET

Character	θ_B
zero	10
one	11
two	9
three	10
four	10
five	8
six	9
seven	10
eight	9
nine	9

was defined to contain numerals 0 through 4 and class C_2, numerals 5 through 9. Samples of classes C_2 and C_1 were placed in list L and NL, respectively, of the PEG1 algorithm. The algorithm then generated the prime-event estimates, which are shown in Fig. 4, while parameters θ_A and θ_B were set to 0 and 14, respectively. The structure of the numerals 5 through 9 may be seen in the different prime events. Furthermore, some of the prime events in Fig. 4 represent subclasses which are composed of pairs of numerals which have similar graphical representations in areas of the 12 × 8 array. These pairs of numerals have thus created new subclasses with specific *graphical* structure.

The above example is intended to manifest the method of applying the theory of prime events and the unique properties of the prime-event estimates. The details of the example, the 12 × 8 array representation of a character, the accuracy of classification, the number of samples utilized, and the potential of this method of OCR, are not at issue here. The OCR classifier design task gives evidence of how the theory of prime events may be applied and of what the results might be.

No special section on caveats for potential users of prime-event theory was included above. It should be understood that all computerized procedures which operate on samples to provide classificatory information require processor time and storage, and that these are functions of the types of samples which are utilized. It is appropriate to note here, however, that the PEG algorithm demanded magnitudes of storage and time which were exponentially related to the number of OCR samples incorporated in the above example. This was in contrast to the PEG1 algorithm, which had an approximately linear demand for time and storage as the number of incorporated samples was varied. The PEG1 algorithm was selected for the OCR classifier design task, and it required less than 60 seconds and 110 000 bytes of storage for any generation of a class *definition set.* (The algorithm was written in Fortran and run on an IBM 370/155.)

IX. CONCLUSION

The problems of designing a classifier for discrete, type-II, variable-measurement vectors have been examined above. The theory of prime events was introduced, and a procedure of generating prime-event estimates was proposed as a tool to aid the classifier designer. An example classifier design task, using a prime-event-generation procedure, was reviewed and the results were examined visually and statistically. This paper introduces a new method of dealing with sample data and provides a new theoretical viewpoint from which to view the classificatory information which has been defined in terms of prime events.

APPENDIX

The following is a description of an additional mode of operation which has been provided for the basic prime event generation algorithm. For some design tasks, a generation procedure which is less exhaustive and faster than the basic prime event generation algorithm may be useful. The PEG algorithm will yield all events which will satisfy the properties of a prime event with respect to the initial lists, L and NL, of samples. The resultant set of estimates of prime events may be "overly complete," "too large," or "too time consuming" to create for some problems. The next design task is to select a practical size set of the resultant events which one estimates will cover all of the chosen class. This also may prove too time consuming for some classification problems.

To cope with these difficulties, it is possible to run the PEG algorithm in a *single list mode.* In this mode, the successive generation of lists is eliminated. Only lists L and NL will be incorporated. Furthermore, this mode of operation will perform the selection of a sufficient set of events to cover the initial list L. This will eliminate the task of comparing covers made up of events generated by PEG.

The following discussion will include a description of the PEG1 algorithm, an example of its operation, and a flow chart of the specific operations in the algorithm. It will be instructive to include the example with the description of the procedure.

The algorithm begins by placing samples of one class in list L and the remaining samples in list NL. As an example, let class C_1 be made up of the following set of four-dimensional, binary-valued vectors. Class C_2, and hence list NL, will be all remaining vectors from the set of four-dimensional binary-valued vectors.

	L	PF	TF	NL
1:	(1 0 1 0)	0	0	(remaining measurement vectors)
2:	(1 0 1 1)	0	0	
3:	(1 1 0 0)	0	0	
4:	(0 1 1 0)	0	0	
5:	(1 0 0 1)	0	0	
6:	(1 0 0 0)	0	0	

PF and TF are vectors of dimension the size of list L and they are initialized to zero.

The basic operations of merging events and checking their ability to cover list NL are retained. The algorithm begins by merging the first pair of samples in list L. Let this be labeled event e_{12}:

$$e_{12} \triangleq (1,0,1,0) + (1,0,1,1) = (1,0,1,—).$$

This event is then checked to see if it covers any member of NL. As shown above, there are two flag vectors, the "temporary flag," TF, and the "permanent flag," PF, which are initialized to zero. These are utilized to keep track of those members of list L which are, or have been, covered by an event previously generated. Event e_{12} covers no member of NL and thus "temporary flags" $TF(1)$ and $TF(2)$ are set to 1. If the event e_{12} did cover some members of NL, then the flags would remain 0.

The next step in the algorithm would be to merge e_{12}

```
1111...0   00110000   .11111.0   ..111.00   .1111.00
1111...0   01110000   11111110   .11111.0   111111.0
111.0000   1111.000   ...01110   11...1.0   11.0.110
111.0000   11111..0   ..00.11.   111011.0   ..00011.
111111.0   1111111.   ...0111.   111111.0   111.111.
11111110   111..111   ....11..   111111.0   1111111.
0000.11.   11100.11   0..111.0   11...110   ..111110
0000011.   11100111   00.111.0   11.0.110   00.111.0
000.1110   .111111.   00.11..0   11.0.110   00.11..0
0..11110   ..11111.   00.11.00   11.....0   00.11.00
..111.00   00...000   00.11000   0.....00   0....000
..1.0000   00000000   00.1.000   00...000   00..0000

111111.0   00111000   ..1111..   0.11..00   .11111.0
111111.0   0.111000   .111111.   ..11...0   111111.0
111.0000   11110000   .....11.   11.....0   11.00...
111...00   11111.00   ...0..11   11111..0   11.00...
111111.0   11111110   ...0.11.   11111110   111111..
11111110   11111111   ....111.   111111..   1111111.
0000.11.   11100.11   0..111..   11.0..1.   00...11.
0000.11.   11.00011   00.111..   11.00.1.   000..110
000.1110   11..011.   000.11.0   111..11.   00..11.0
00.111.0   .11.111.   00011..0   .111111.   00.11..0
0.1...00   00..11..   00011.00   00.11.00   00.1.000
0...0000   00000000   000.0000   00000000   00..0000

1111..00   ..111000   111111..   .111..00
1111..00   ..111.00   1111111.   .11111.0
11.00000   .1....00   .....11.   11.0.110
111.0000   111.1.00   .000.11.   11...110
11111100   111111.0   ....11.0   111.11.0
11111110   111111.0   ....11.0   11111110
0000.11.   11.00.1.   00.111.0   .11.1110
0000.11.   11.00.1.   00.11.00   ..0..110
000111.0   1110...0   00.11.00   ..1.11.0
011111.0   .111..00   00.11000   ..111..0
11111000   00...000   00...000   0011.000
111.0000   00000000   00..0000   00000000
```

Fig. 4. Automatically generated definition set for the class made up of numerals 5 through 9. A "." indicates an unspecified value.

and measurement vector 3:

$$e_{123} \triangleq (1,0,1,—) + (1,1,0,0) = (1,—,—,—).$$

Checking list NL shows that vector (1,1,0,1) is in NL, and thus e_{123} will not be a retained event since it covers a vector in NL.

Next, form the event e_{124} as above. This too covers some event in NL and is thus not retained. Event e_{125} is then formed: $e_{125} = (1,0,—,—)$. This event covers nothing in NL and hence flag $TF(5)$ is set to 1.

Continuing down list L, the algorithm notes that measurement vector 6 is covered by e_{125}. Thus flag $TF(6)$ is set to 1.

The algorithm now proceeds to the top of list L in an attempt to merge additional vectors. Vector 1 was the "*start vector*" and therefore this "pass" terminates. The permanent flag vector is then updated by forming the pointwide logical "or" of the entries in TF and PF. The event e_{125} is stored, as one of the selected events, in list E, and TF is reset to all 0's. Henceforth, PEG1 will make two "passes" through the samples.

The above procedure is now restarted with one of the measurement vectors not covered thus far. The flag $PF(3)$ is 0 and thus vector 3 becomes the "restart vector." The first step is to merge vector 3 with another vector which is not covered thus far. The flag vectors at this point are as follows:

	1	2	3	4	5	6
PF:	(1	1	0	0	1	1)
TF:	(0	0	0	0	0	0).

From PF one can see that vector 4 is uncovered. Forming, during the first "pass," $e_{34} \triangleq (1,1,0,0) + (0,1,1,0) = (—,1,—,0)$, and checking NL, one notes that (1,1,1,0) is in NL and thus covered by e_{34}. The event e_{34} is disregarded and the algorithm then searches PF for another uncovered vector. If it found one, the result of its merger with vector 3 would be checked to determine if it covered some vector in NL. If no vectors in NL were covered, the search for another 0 in PF would begin again. If the new event covered something in NL, then the event would be disregarded. However, no other 0 was found in PF. The algorithm now attempts to merge vector 3 with any vector in L, not just the uncovered ones. This is referred to as the second "pass."

The event e_{35} is formed and checked against NL. Successfully covering an element in NL, this event is ignored. Event e_{36} is formed and covers no event in NL. However, merging any additional events with e_{36} will yield an event which covers something in NL. Thus, event e_{36} is added to the list E, $PF(3)$ is set to 1, and the next uncovered vector is selected as a restart vector. Two passes are always performed on the list L when generating a potential prime event.

The restart vector is vector 4. Finding no other uncovered measurement vectors, the algorithm proceeds to attempt merging vector 4 with all other elements of list L. Each merger covers something in NL. The result is that vector 4 must be retained in E as the only "potential prime event" covering vector 4. $PF(4)$ is then set to 1.

The algorithm now searches for another uncovered sample in L. All entries in PF are 1, however. When this occurs, the algorithm halts. The set E then contains a subset of the estimated prime events which may be generated by PEG. The resultant set is a sufficient set to cover all the design samples in list L.

The details of the PEG1 algorithm may be obtained from the flow graph of Fig. 5. List L initially contains

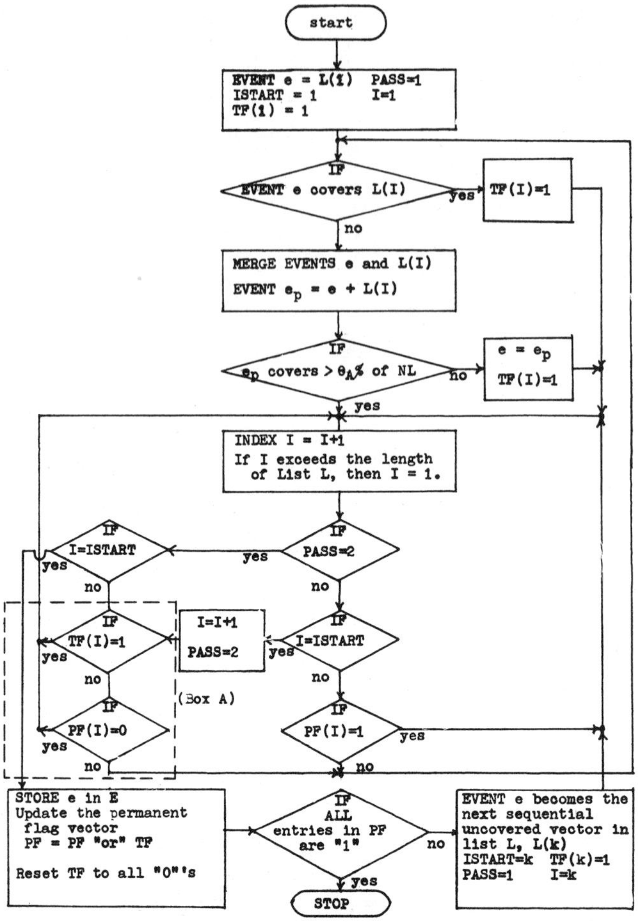

Fig. 5. Flow graph of the PEG1 algorithm.

the samples from the chosen class, and list NL will contain the samples from the other classes. The variable PASS serves to indicate whether the algorithm is attempting a merger with the as yet uncovered samples, PASS = 1, or the covered samples, PASS = 2. Variable ISTART is the index of the member of list L where PEG1 begins its search for mergers. Also, in the PEG1 procedure, as with the PEG algorithm, the definition of "cover" is potentially expandable through the incorporation of parameters θ_A and θ_B, as described previously in Section VI. The purpose of the checking which is performed in Box A is to reduce the amount of redundant merging and checking in the two-pass algorithm.

It should be noted that PEG1 will generate a subset of those events generated by PEG. A sufficient set to cover List L is generated, and this subset may be the same as that generated by PEG.

ACKNOWLEDGMENT

The author would like to thank Dr. J. Sammon for supplying the OCR data which were utilized for the example described in Section VII. Furthermore, credit is due Dr. Sammon for stimulating the author's interest in the discrete variable problem discussed in this paper.

REFERENCES

[1] L. N. Kanal, "Interactive pattern analysis and classification systems: A survey and commentary," *Proc. IEEE*, vol. 60, pp. 1200–1215, Oct. 1972.
[2] J. Sammon, "Techniques for discrete, type-II data processing on-line (AMOLPARS)," Rome Air Development Center, Rome, N. Y., Tech. Rep. RADC-TR-71-232, 1971.
[3] L. Kanal, "Adaptive modeling of likelihood classification," Rome Air Development Center, Rome, N. Y., Tech. Rep. TR-66-190, 1966.
[4] D. Foley, "The probability of error on the design set," Ph.D. dissertation, Dep. of Electrical Engineering, Syracuse Univ., Syracuse, N. Y., 1971.
[5] E. Fix and J. Hodges, "Discriminatory analysis," USAF School of Aviation Med., Randolph Field, San Antonio, Tex., Project Rep. 21-49-004, no. 11, 1961.
[6] R. Fisher, "The use of multiple measurements in taxonomic problems," *Ann. Eugen.*, vol. 7, pp. 179–188, Sept. 1936.
[7] J. W. Sammon, Jr., "An optimal discriminant plane," *IEEE Trans. Comput.* (Short Notes), vol. C-19, pp. 826–829, Sept. 1970.
[8] M. Hills, "Discrimination and allocation with discrete data," *Appl. Statist.*, vol. 16, 1967.
[9] G. Lance and W. Williams, "Computer programs for hierarchical polythetic classification (similarity analysis)," *Nature*, vol. 207, p. 159, 1965.
[10] J. W. Sammon, Jr., "Interactive pattern analysis and classification," *IEEE Trans. Comput.*, vol. C-19, pp. 594–616, July 1970.
[11] H. Linhart, "Techniques for discriminant analysis with discrete variables," *Metrika*, vol. 2, pp. 138–140, 1959.
[12] W. G. Cochran and C. Hopkins, "Some classification problems with multivariate qualitative data," *Biometrics*, vol. 17, pp. 11–31, 1961.
[13] P. F. Lazarsfeld, "The algebra of dichotomous systems," in *Studies in Item Analysis and Prediction*, H. Solomon, Ed. Stanford, Calif.: Stanford Univ. Press, 1961.

[14] T. W. Anderson, "On estimation of parameters in latent structure analysis," *Psychometrika*, vol. 12, no. 1, pp. 1–10, 1964.
[15] R. McHugh, "Efficient estimation and local identification in latent class analysis," *Psychometrika*, vol. 21, no. 4, pp. 331–347, 1966.
[16] E. L. Schaefer, "On discrimination using qualitative variables," unpublished Ph.D. dissertation, Univ. of Michigan, Ann Arbor, 1967.
[17] I. J. Good, "Maximum entropy for hypothesis formulation, especially for multidimensional contingency tables," *Ann. Math. Statist.*, vol. 34, pp. 911–934, 1963.
[18] E. S. Gilbert, "On discrimination using qualitative variables," *Amer. Statist. Assoc. J.*, vol. 40, pp. 1399–1413, 1968.
[19] D. R. Cox, *Analysis of Binary Data.* London: Methuen, 1970.
[20] R. R. Bahadur, "A representation of the joint distribution of responses to *n* dichotomous items," in *Studies in Item Analysis*, H. Solomon, Ed. Stanford, Calif.: Stanford Univ. Press, 1961.
[21] K. Abend, T. J. Hartley, and L. N. Kanal, "Classification of binary random patterns," *IEEE Trans. Inform. Theory*, vol. IT-11, pp. 538–544, Oct. 1965.
[22] C. K. Chow, "A recognition method using neighbor dependence," *IRE Trans. Electron. Comput.*, vol. EC-11, pp. 683–690, Oct. 1962.
[23] C. K. Chow, "A class of nonlinear recognition procedures," *IEEE Trans. Syst. Sci. and Cybern.*, vol. SSC-2, pp. 101–109, Dec. 1966.
[24] R. Sokal and P. Sneath, *Principles of Numerical Taxonomy.* San Francisco: W. H. Freeman, 1963.
[25] D. W. Goodall, "On a new similarity index based on probability," *Biometrics*, vol. 22, pp. 668–670, Dec. 1966.
[26] J. J. Fortier and H. Solomon, "Clustering procedures," in *Item Analysis, Test Design, Classification*, H. Solomon, Ed. Co-op. Res. Project 1327. Stanford, Calif.: Stanford Univ. Press, 1965.
[27] L. McQuitty and J. Clark, "Clusters from iterative intercolumnar correlational analysis," *Educ. Psychol. Meas.*, vol. 28, pp. 2–20, 1968.
[28] J. Elashoff, R. Elashoff, and G. Goldman, "On the choice of variables in classification problems with dichotomous variables," *Biometrics*, vol. 23, pp. 668–670, 1967.
[29] G. T. Toussaint, "Note on optimal selection of independent binary-valued features for pattern recognition," *IEEE Trans. Inform. Theory* (Corresp.), vol. IT-17, p. 618, Sept. 1971.
[30] R. Prather, *Introduction to Switching Theory.* Boston: Allyn and Bacon, 1967.
[31] Y. C. Ho and R. L. Kashyap, "An algorithm for linear inequalities and its application," *IEEE Trans. Electron. Comput.*, vol. EC-14, pp. 683–688, 1965.
[32] T. M. Cover, "Geometrical and statistical properties of systems of linear inequalities with applications in pattern recognition," *IEEE Trans. Electron. Comput.*, vol. EC-14, pp. 326–334, June 1965.
[33] K. Fukanaga and W. L. G. Koontz, "Application of the Karhunen–Loève expansion to feature selection and ordering," *IEEE Trans. Comput.*, vol. C-19, pp. 311–318, Apr. 1970.
[34] R. Casey and G. Nagy, "Recognition of printed Chinese characters," *IEEE Trans. Electron. Comput.*, vol. EC-15, pp. 91–101, Feb. 1966.
[35] R. M. Bowman, "On *n*-tuple optimization and *a priori* error specification for minimum distance pattern classifiers," Ph.D. dissertation, Dep. Elec. Eng., Univ. of Virginia, Charlottesville, 1970.

THE ANALYSIS OF CELL IMAGES*

Judith M. S. Prewitt and Mortimer L. Mendelsohn
Department of Radiology, University of Pennsylvania, Philadelphia, Pennsylvania

Introduction

Automation of the acquisition and interpretation of data in microscopy has been a focus of biomedical research for almost a decade. In spite of many serious attempts,[1-5] mechanical perception of microscopic fields with a reliability that would inspire routine application still eludes us.

Many facets of the problem appear to be well within the grasp of present-day technology. Thus, available histochemical techniques make it possible to prepare biological materials so that morphological integrity is preserved, key constituents are stained stoichiometrically, and the specimens are favorably dispersed for effective imaging one by one. Scanning microscopes now have the requisite sensitivity, resolution, and stability to sample such objects and make photometric measurements over a wide range of magnifications and wavelengths within the visible and near-visible spectrum. Furthermore, modern large capacity, high speed data facilities at last provide the ability to manipulate the hitherto unmanageable quantities of optical information contained within all but the simplest images.

With the basic materials for achieving automation via mensuration finally at hand, attention has been turned toward generating and evaluating methods for extracting meaning from quantitative optical information. Definitive concepts for image structuring and image characterization have yet to be realized, to be given satisfactory operational definitions, and to be assembled within a machine-oriented perceptual framework.[6] Criteria for effective and efficient discrimination and interpretation of images must be evolved. It would be a serious mistake to presuppose that mechanical perception must mimic the human's perceptual apparatus in organizing images as complexes of picture elements. Likewise it would be serious to ignore traditional descriptive morphology and established taxonomies. In steering a middle course, the exploration of many complementary approaches and the introduction of numeric methods which fully utilize measurements of light intensity of optical density seemed to us to hold the most promise for augmenting and explicating the existing, largely verbal tradition of microscopic morphology.

To realize these objectives, we have designed a system with three basic components: 1) a sensor which rigorously and effectively scans microscopic fields and converts the optical information into digital form; 2) human analysts who contribute heuristics, devise image processing methods and en-

*This work was supported by Contract PH 43-62-432 from the Diagnostic Research Branch, National Cancer Institute, Bethesda, Maryland, and by Research Career Award 5-K6-CA-18, 540 from the National Cancer Institute.

Reprinted with permission from *Ann. N.Y. Acad. Sci.*, vol. 128, pp. 1035–1053, Jan. 31, 1966.

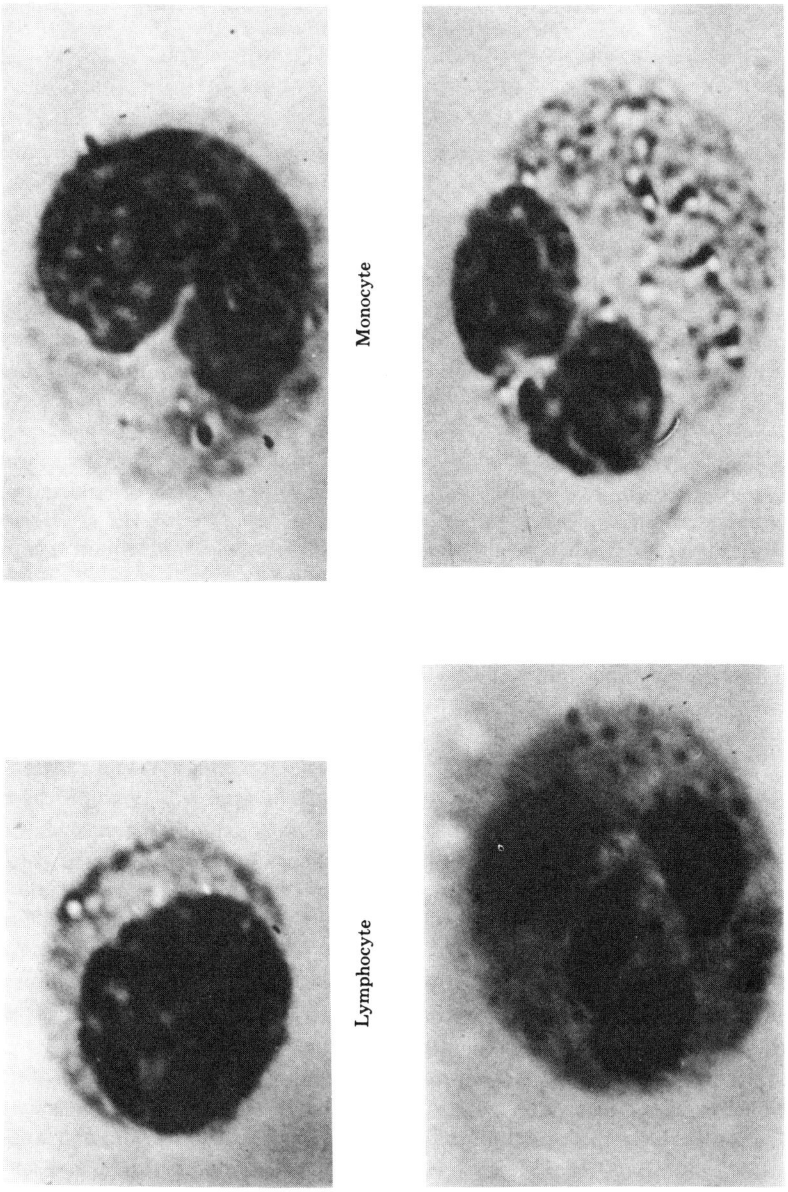

FIGURE 1. Representative cells of the four types used in this study. The photomicrographs have been deliberately distorted to conform to the 5:4 horizontal to vertical distortion of the printouts in FIGURES 3 and 4.

sembles of discrimination criteria, program and supervise the other components, systematically set standards, and select and prepare the material to be studied; and 3) a large general purpose digital computer which assimilates the enormous volumes of quantitative optical information and renders the machine interpretation of images. Preprocessing of the optical information by the sensor is kept to a minimum, and the quantity and quality of the optical information transmitted to the computer approaches the theoretical limit imposed by the microscope itself. Thus, the heuristic and algorithmic aspects of image processing can interact without restraints forced by the hardware, and a facile and free interplay is encouraged between the analyst and the computer.[7-9]

Methods and General Principles

As a pilot study in image characterization and discrimination, we have selected the normal human peripheral blood smear and have concentrated our attention on a small sample of typical members of four easily distinguished classes of leukocytes. An example of each of the four leukocyte types is shown in FIGURE 1. The cells were prepared by a flotation technique which eliminated the red cells.[10] They were then air-dried rapidly and stained with gallocyanin chrome alum and naphthol yellow S. Discrimination of these four leukocytes is an easily-enough learned task for even a layman, although monocyte-lymphocyte ambiguities are sometimes hard to resolve. To a machine, however, they represent a complex unsolved discrimination problem.

The CYDAC scanning and recording cytophotometer used as the sensor in this study consists of a flying spot microscope, a digital converter, and a magnetic tape recorder.[11] The scanner uses a cathode ray tube to sweep a blue-green spot of light through a rectilinear raster. Entering the microscope through the eyepiece, the focused spot of light is reduced to 0.3 micron diameter in the plane of a mounted specimen. The optical density of the specimen is measured along lines spaced 0.25 microns apart, with the interval between successive samples on one line also fixed at 0.25 microns.[12] These measurements of optical density can span a 256-level gray scale. A 50×50 micron field is sensed and represented on magnetic tape as 40,000 eight-bit optical density measurements.

On reading a CYDAC tape, the digital computer receives a primary representation of the scanned field as a matrix of optical density values in which spatial and gray-scale relationships are preserved. A set of graded alphanumeric symbols simulating a 32-level gray scale can be used to reconstitute CYDAC scans on the high-speed printer.[13] Such computer reconstitutions of the images of human blood cells, originally scanned by CYDAC at 256 gray levels, retain sufficient information for ready morphological discrimination by eye. As we shall show below, the primary representations

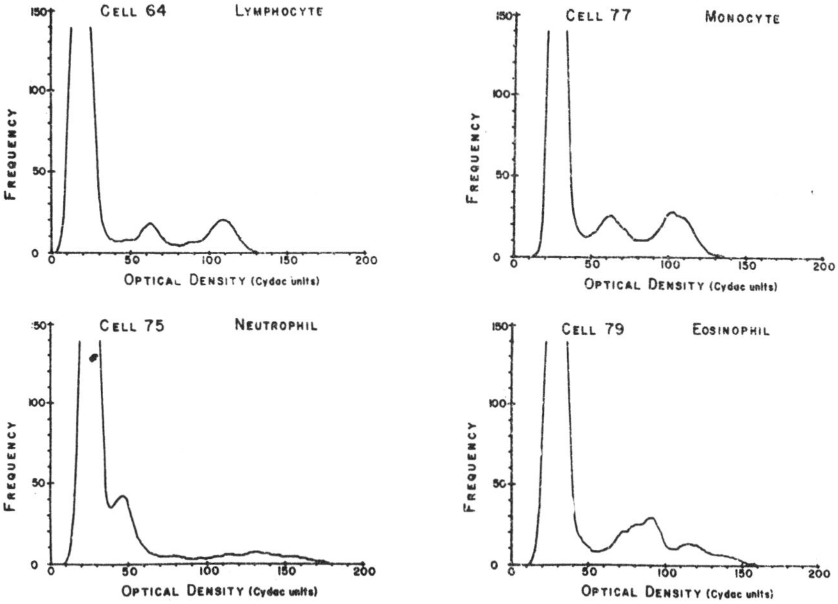

FIGURE 2. Optical density frequency distributions of the four cell types. The principal peaks, corresponding to background, have been abbreviated for purposes of display, and the curves have been smoothed by an analytic procedure that conserves the number of observations and the integrated optical density locally. Note the minima representing low frequency optical density values from boundary regions, and note also the difference in shape of the four curves.

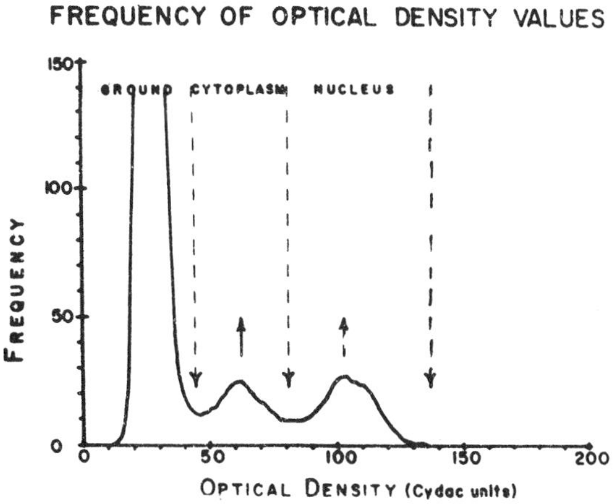

FIGURE 3. Boundary determination for a monocyte. The graph reproduces the frequency distribution in FIGURE 2 with the local minima identified. The upper illustration shows a computer printout with a standard 32-level gray scale, and the lower illustration shows a 3-level gray scale as defined by thresholds taken from the location of the local minima. A comparison of the two printouts and the photomicrograph of the same cell in FIGURE 1 indicates the effectiveness of this method of boundary identification.

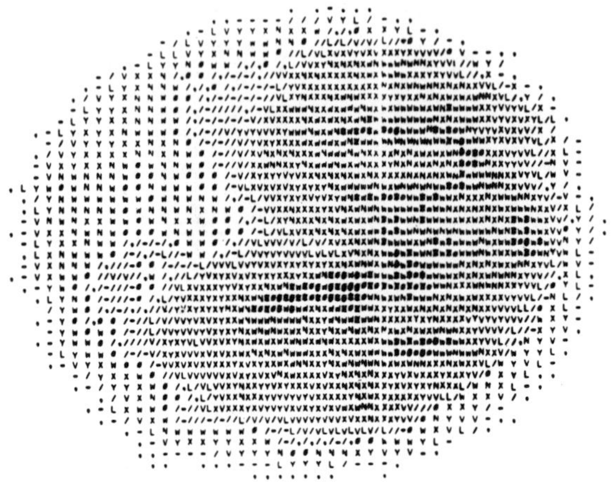

FIGURE 3. (cont.)

themselves contain sufficient information for morphological discriminations by machine.

The analysis of digitized images involves five principal phases:

1. delineation of figure and ground;
2. description of images by numeric and non-numeric parameters, and by relational descriptors;
3. determination of the range of variation and the discriminatory power of these parameters and descriptors;

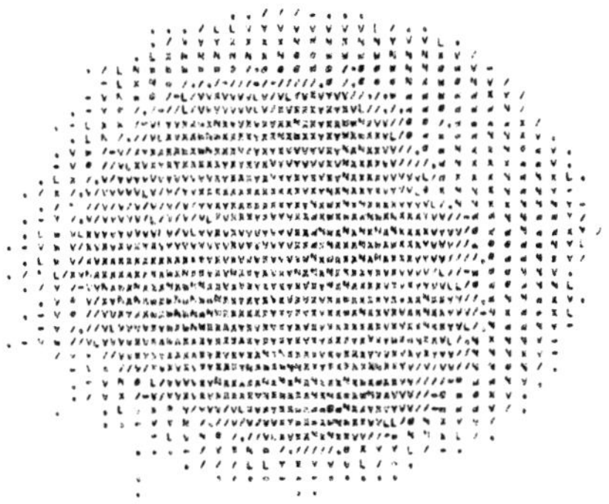

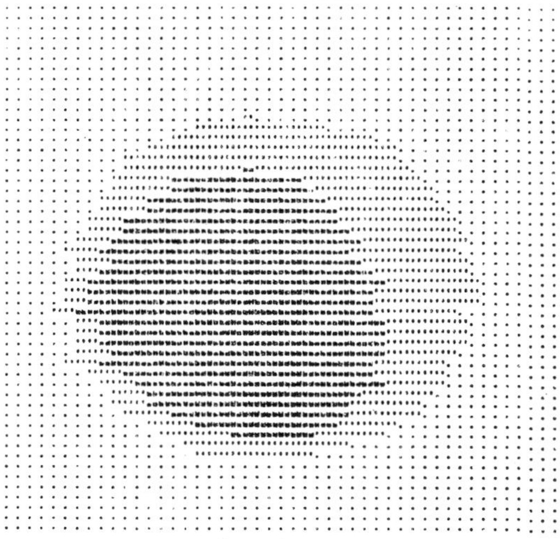

Lymphocyte

FIGURE 4. Boundary determinations. The same procedure has been followed as in FIGURE 3, and again the images should be compared to the photomicrographs in FIGURE 1. Note that four gray levels were used for the eosinophil in an attempt to delineate the denser regions of cytoplasmic granules in addition to the cell and nuclear-cytoplasmic boundaries.

4. development of appropriate decision functions and taxonomies for classification; and
5. identification of unknown specimens.

Delineation of figure and ground in its simplest form involves the dissection of entities from surroundings, and as such, constitutes an operational definition of "objects of interest." Depending on the material being studied and the aims of the investigation, the delineation or depth of dissection can also extend to detail within the object of interest. The need to formally identify substructure varies considerably with the method of analysis being used. For example, discrimination of leukocytes in the present study can be accomplished by some sets of parameters only after specific identification of the nucleus and cytoplasm of the cell; other parameters in the present study accomplished the same end, yet required no more than the distinction between cell and background.

Choosing a specific set of parameters for describing an image is equivalent to entertaining a composite hypothesis about the relevance of (i) a corresponding set of features of the image, (ii) constructs which purport to abstract these features, and (iii) implementations which purport to give reproducible and reliable measures of these features. Parameter collections which include

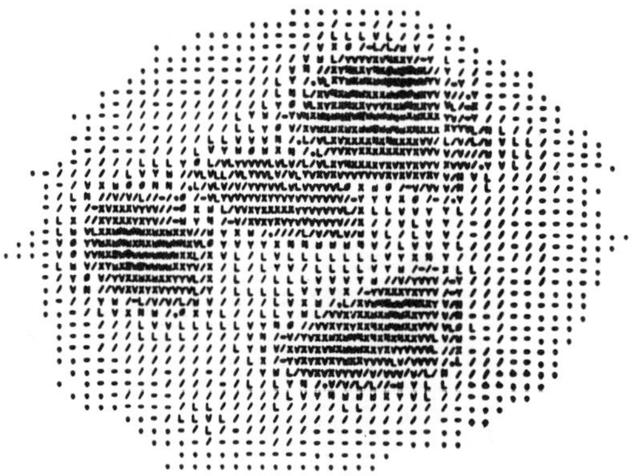

Neutrophil

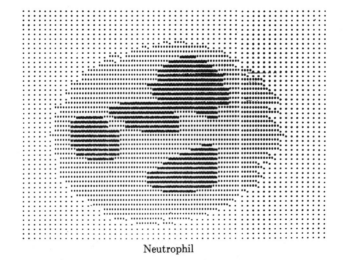

FIGURE 4. (cont.)

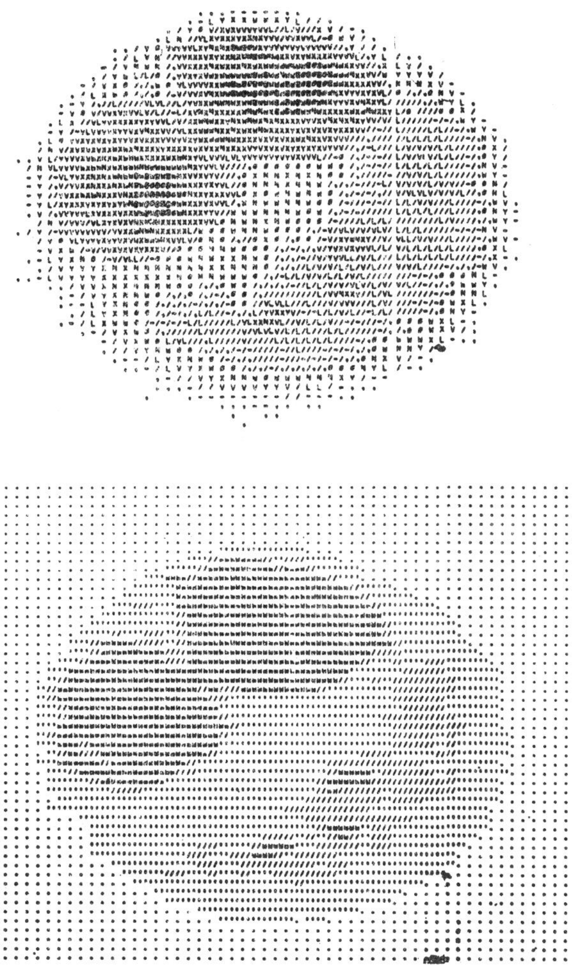

Eosinphil

partially redundant as well as independent elements will be needed for reliable discrimination. The chosen parameters must have certain invariance qualities, including relative insensitivity to orientation and position of specimens in the field of view, to distortions of scanning and sampling, to noise, and to inconsequential variations inherent in biological materials or secondary to artifacts of preparation.

It is our basic premise that pattern classes and subclasses of images can be ascertained and explicated from the behavior of relevant parameters. Assigning each numeric parameter of an image to a coordinate axis in a multidimensional property or parameter space, the image can be represented as a single vector, the components of which are the actual values of the

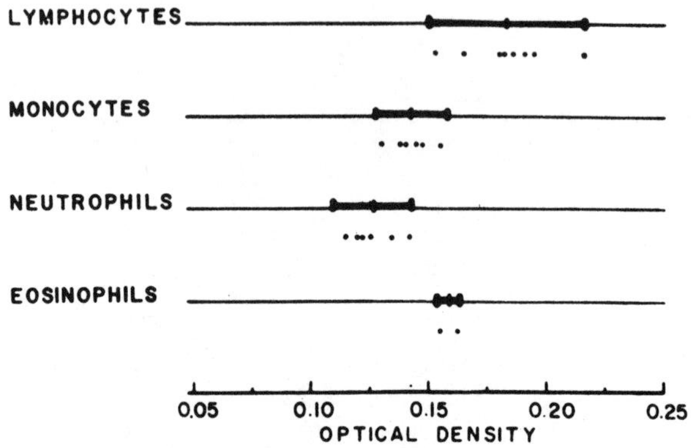

FIGURE 5. A one-dimensional representation of mean optical density. The dots indicate the individual cell measurements and the bars represent the means ± two standard deviations for each cell type. Mean optical density has a replicate coefficient of variation of 1.27 per cent, but in spite of this dimensional stability it does not discriminate effectively among the cell types.

parameters. In principle, the more alike two images are, the closer together their vectors will lie in the property space. The vectors of images within the same pattern classes should therefore cluster into neighborhoods within the parameter space. These neighborhoods are initially identified by studying exemplars of a population, and their margins remain fluid in response to cumulative experience with the population. Neighborhoods can be defined and analyzed by means of metrics, statistical computations, or clustering procedures.[14] Once one has some insight into the nature of the property space, the analysis of an individual image consists of a pattern detection phase in which the parameters are extracted and represented vectorially, and a pattern

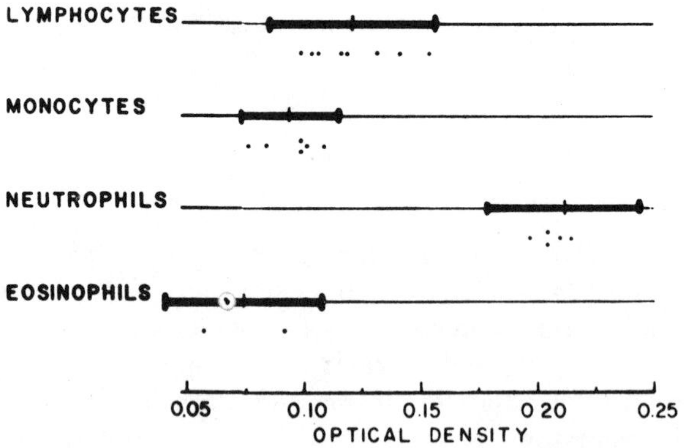

FIGURE 6. A one-dimensional representation of nuclear-cytoplasmic contrast. This parameter expresses the distance between the right-hand peaks of the optical density frequency distribution. The neutrophils generate a neighborhood that does not overlap with those of the other cell types. With the parameters we have studied so far, the neutrophil is by far the easiest cell type to distinguish. None of the parameters by itself distinguishes all four cell types.

TABLE 1
THIRTY-FIVE PARAMETERS OF THE OPTICAL DENSITY FREQUENCY DISTRIBUTION WHICH RELATE TO LEUKOCYTE DISCRIMINATION

Kind of range of variation for four cell types	Type[1]	Parameter	Key to cell types[2] 1 2 3 4	Discrimination[3] Results
1 2 3 4	I	skewness of nuclear o.d. distribution		L,M,N,E
		kurtosis of nuclear o.d. distribution		L,M,N,E
		nuclear o.d. range: cell o.d. range		L,M,N,E
		cytoplasmic o.d. range: cell o.d. range		L,M,N,E
1 2 3 4	II	nuclear-cytoplasmic contrast, measure 1	N L M E	N/L,M,E
		nuclear-cytoplasmic contrast, measure 2	N L M E	N/L,M,E
		skewness of cytoplasmic o.d. distribution	N L M E	N/L,M,E
		cytoplasmic integrated o.d.	E L M N	E/L,M,N
		mean o.d. ratio, nucleus: cytoplasm	N L M E	N/L,M,E
		nuclear area	M L N E	M/L,N,E
		kurtosis of cytoplasmic o.d. distribution	N L M E	N/L,M,E
		o.d. mode for cell	N L M E	N/L,M,E
		std. deviation of cell o.d.	N L M E	N/L,M,E
		std. deviation of nuclear o.d.	N L M E	N/L,M,E
		coef. of variation of cell o.d.	N L M E	N/L,M,E
		coef. of variation of cytoplasm o.d.	N L M E	N/L,M,E
1 2 3 4	II	nuclear integrated o.d.	M N L E	M/N,L,E;L/E
		o.d. mode for cytoplasm	N L M E	N/L,M,E;M/E
1 3 2 4	III	skewness of cell o.d. distribution	L M N E	L,M/N,E
		cell integrated o.d.	L N M E	L,N/M,E

1 2 4 3	IV	cell mean o.d. nuclear mean o.d. area ratio, nucleus: cytoplasm integrated o.d. ratio, nucleus:cytoplasm cell area o.d. mode for cell o.d. mode for cytoplasm kurtosis of cell o.d. distribution std. deviation of cytoplasmic o.d.	M L E N L N E M L N E M L M N E N M E L M N E L M N E L N L M E L N E M	L,E/N N,E/M N,E/M M,N/E M,E/L N,E/L N,E/L L,M/E N,E/M
1 2 3 4	IV	frequencies ratio for o.d. modes, nucleus:cytoplasm nuclear o.d. mode frequency at nuclear o.d. mode	L M N E L M N E E M L N	M/N/E M/N/E M/N/L
1 2 3 4	IV	coef. of variation of nuclear o.d.	L M N E	N/E
1 2 3 4	IV	cytoplasmic mean o.d. cytoplasmic area	L N E M M E L N	E/N,M; L/N L/E,N; M/E

Legend (1) Type of discrimination achieved:
- I. No discrimination of the four leukocyte types.
- II. Discrimination of one cell type from the other three types.
- III. Discrimination of two cell types from the other two types.
- IV. Partial discrimination.

(2) Cell types:
L lymphocyte M monocyte N neutrophil E eosinophil

(3) Discrimination results:
X,Y/Z indicates that types X and Y were not distinguished from each other, but both were distinguished from type Z.

identification phase in which the image is assigned to the established neighborhood in or nearest to which its associated property vector falls.

To implement these ideas, a flexible collection of mixed language programs is being evolved. Preference is given to using problem-oriented languages and pure procedures which facilitate fluent computer-scientist communication. Initial programs were written in Automath and Argus for the Honeywell 800, but with the addition of a one-half inch tape facility to CYDAC, current work is being done in Fortran II/IV and MAP for the IBM 7040 data processor. The programs for picture analysis will be serviced by auxiliary programs which prepare CYDAC data for processing, maintain a library of cell images, monitor picture generation by CYDAC, and follow picture manipulation and transformation in the course of computer analysis. An artificial image generator, which produces simple combinations and superpositions of "gray-tone" convex picture elements is available for testing algorithms and debugging. Finally, rules for adjusting the level of resolution in stored images and the level of detail in the analysis will be incorporated.

Applications to Blood Cells

The salient anatomic features of blood cells suggest that delineation should involve the dissection of the image into background, cytoplasm, and nucleus as a minimum, with the possibility that demarcation of granules, chromatin, and nucleoli will also be required. The boundaries between these compartments of the image appear to be regions of abrupt change in average optical density. However, it is not clear to the eye how consistent the optical

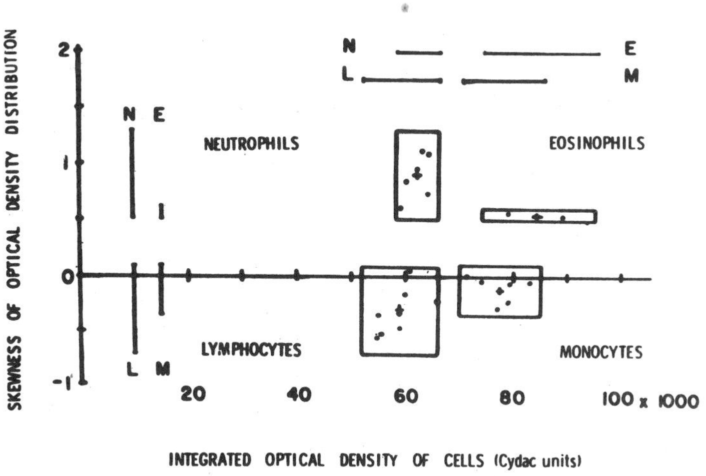

FIGURE 7. A two-dimensional representation of a pair of parameters. The labeled lines depict the results for each parameter in one-space, and the dots and 95 per cent confidence rectangles represent the interaction of the parameters in two-space. This is one of four combinations giving quadriparitite discrimination with only two parameters.

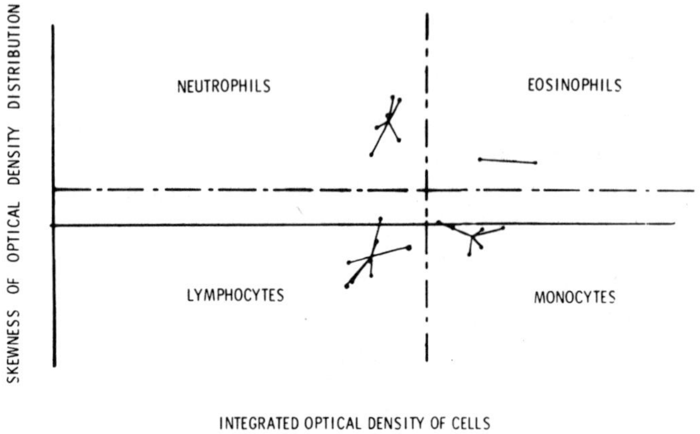

FIGURE 8. A decision space in two-dimensions. The data points are the same as in FIGURE 7, and the dotted lines now indicate a possible orthogonal division of the parameter space into four diagnostic quadrants.

density differences for specific structures are, not only in different cell images, but from one part of the same cell image to another.

Delineation of figure and ground can be accomplished satisfactorily by several independent approaches which use either thresholding or spatial differentiation. Thresholding presupposes the relative constancy of optical density over an object of interest, and a discernible difference in optical density between figure and ground. Differentiation methods presume that optical density changes most rapidly in the vicinity of the margins of principal cell structures; thus they seek maximal brightness gradients in the image. Our earliest results with blood cell images indicated that preset thresholds (i.e., fixed thresholds defined by experience and supplied to the analysis programs) would not effect an adequate separation of nucleus and cytoplasm. A maximal gradient-seeking routine, although successful, required a substantial amount of processing time for each cell image. For the present study, a novel method of implicit spatial differentiation which uses data-generated relative thresholds was devised, and proved to be both satisfactory and efficient for defining boundaries. This method, the frequency distribution method, is described in detail elsewhere.[15]

The frequency distribution method combines gradient-maximizing and thresholding by identifying those gray levels which are embedded in steep gradients. Scan elements on a steep gradient of optical density will contribute sparsely to the frequency of occurrence of optical density values spanning the gradient. At least in the case of blood cells, these transitional points can be identified as local minima in a frequency histogram of the optical density values of the entire image. In a field containing an intact leukocyte, the local minimum with the lowest optical density corresponds to the cytoplasmic boundary and provides a threshold optical density value which is

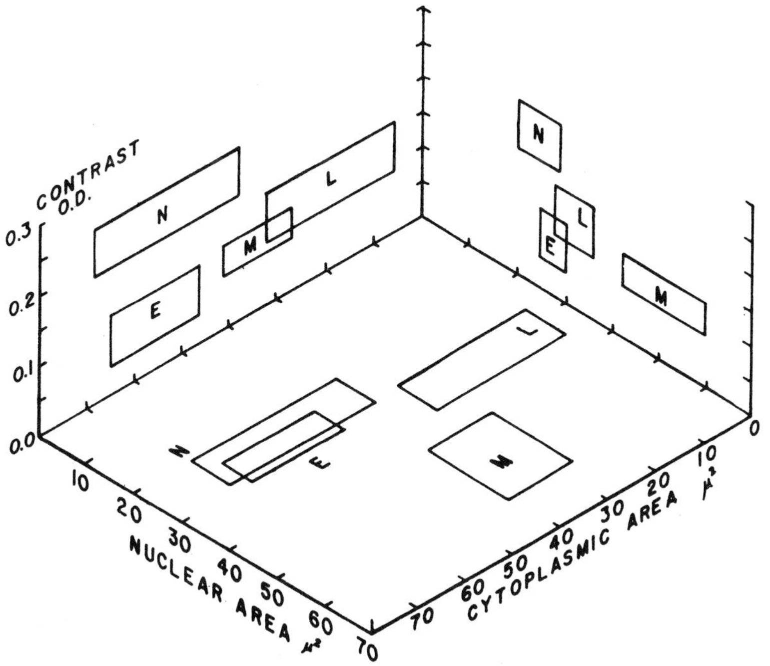

FIGURE 9. Three independent pairs of parameters. In each case the overlapping rectangles indicate incomplete discrimination with just two parameters.

effectively an upper bound for background elements and a lower bound for cell elements. The local minimum with the highest optical density defines the nuclear boundary and divides the cell into cytoplasmic and nuclear elements. FIGURE 2 gives an optical density frequency distribution for each type of leukocyte in this study. FIGURE 3 depicts the application of the method to a monocyte, and FIGURE 4 illustrates pictorially the effectiveness of the method in the three other types of cells. Over 50 cells have been processed by this method, and as in the examples shown, the computer-selected boundaries have always agreed closely with the boundaries selected by a morphologist.

The optical density frequency distributions from cells of the same type are strikingly superimposable, but as indicated in FIGURE 2, the distributions are qualitatively different for the four different cell types. These differences in shape reflect differences in the quantity, variability, and contrast of absorbing material in the cells. To give two examples, the skewness of the optical density distribution of the neutrophil is indicative of a large low-density cytoplasm and a small dark nucleus. And the separation of secondary peaks in all of the distributions is a measure of nuclear-cytoplasmic contrast. This separation is greater for neutrophils than for eosinophils, confirming the readily visible difference in internal contrast between these cell types.

The absence of explicit topological information in the optical density frequency distribution is compensated for by the relation between local minima and principal geographic boundaries, and these distributions represent an extremely efficient condensation of the data, preserving many important morphological features of the image, yet reducing the amount of data by roughly fifteenfold. Taking advantage of the internal organization of information in a blood cell image, a wide variety of parameters can be calculated from the optical density frequency distributions without retaining the scanned image in computer memory. Thus both the hardware and software requirements for the analysis are materially simplified. At present, approximately 90 parameters can be extracted from an optical density frequency distribution by the programs available in the CYDAC system, and this processing requires no more than six seconds per image or roughly the same time required to perform and record the original scan.

A selection of 35 available parameters of the optical density frequency distribution which are pertinent to distinguishing the four types of leukocytes appear in TABLE 1, along with notations of their relevance as judged from the results obtained with the 22 leukocytes included in this study. The stability of the measures has been assessed by a replication experiment using one monocyte and one neutrophil. This experiment included three identical

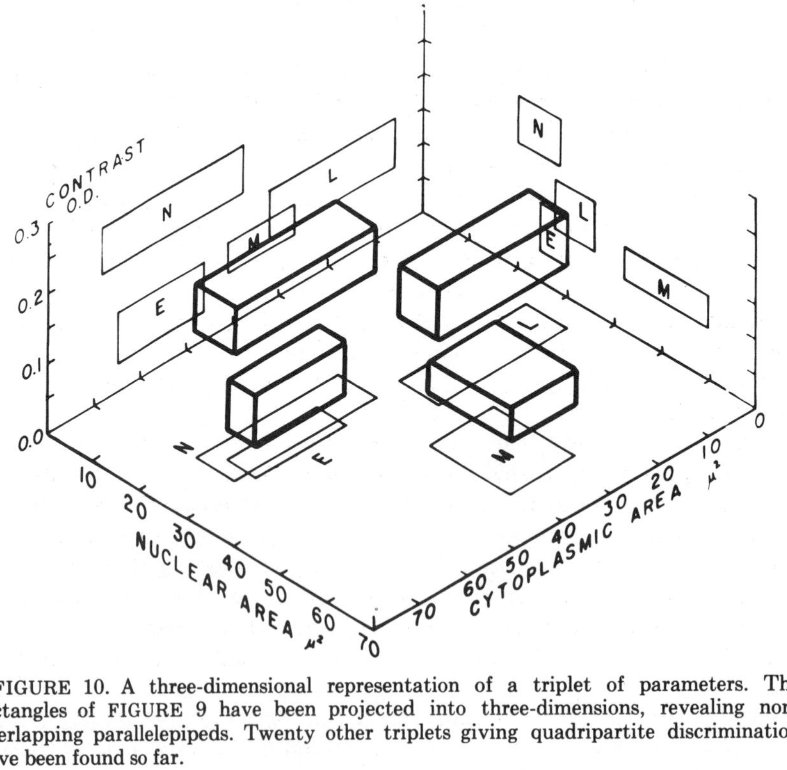

FIGURE 10. A three-dimensional representation of a triplet of parameters. The rectangles of FIGURE 9 have been projected into three-dimensions, revealing non-overlapping parallelepipeds. Twenty other triplets giving quadripartite discrimination have been found so far.

scans with the cell in the center of the field of view, and four other scans with the cell rotated or displaced away from the center. Using these scans, coefficients of variation ranging from 0.1 to 9 per cent were obtained for various members of the parameter set, the higher values being associated with measures having mean values approaching zero.

For each of the four cell types, means and standard deviations of the available measurements were calculated for every parameter. Neighborhoods for particular cell types were established along the coordinate axis for each parameter by setting the neighborhood boundaries at two standard deviations on both sides of the mean. Discrimination was defined as a non-overlapping of neighborhoods, and within the limits imposed by the small statistical samples, the results should therefore apply to at least 95 per cent of the population of each cell group. This procedure is depicted in one-space for two representative parameters in FIGURES 5 and 6. In FIGURE 5, the mean optical density of the cell gives overlapping neighborhoods and no discriminations (as defined above) among the four cell types. Nuclear-cytoplasmic contrast, depicted in FIGURE 6, is an example of one of the 14 parameters that permitted the discrimination of a single cell type. No single parameter gave quadripartite discrimination.

Taking the parameters in pairs and analyzing the data in two-space, complete discrimination of all four cell types was accomplished by four independent combinations. An example of one of these combinations, skewness of the optical density distribution and integrated optical density of the whole cell, is shown in FIGURE 7. Along each of the parameter axes, the cell images fall into two rather than four categories; in two-space however, there are four discrete pattern neighborhoods. With two decision lines parallel to the parameter axes as in FIGURE 8, this two-dimensional parameter space can be divided into quadrants representing the four cell types. In this particular case it is of interest that the two parameters, skewness and integrated optical density, are properties of the total cell and do not require delineation of the nuclear-cytoplasmic boundary.

FIGURE 9 shows 95 per cent confidence rectangles for three independent pairings of the parameters, nuclear area, cytoplasmic area, and nuclear-cytoplasmic contrast. In each of the two-dimensional property-spaces, there is overlapping of some rectangles, indicating that no two of these parameters gives total discrimination. When the parameters are considered collectively in a three-dimensional property space, the four cell types have associated non-overlapping 95 per cent confidence parallelepipeds (FIGURE 10). The three-dimensional analogy to the use of orthogonal separating lines in two-dimensional space is shown in FIGURE 11. Orthogonal planes have now divided the three-space into compartments which effect a quadripartite discrimination of the parallelepipeds representing the neighborhoods for each cell type. Twenty-one independent triplets of the available parameters have been found to give total discrimination as in FIGURES 10 and 11.

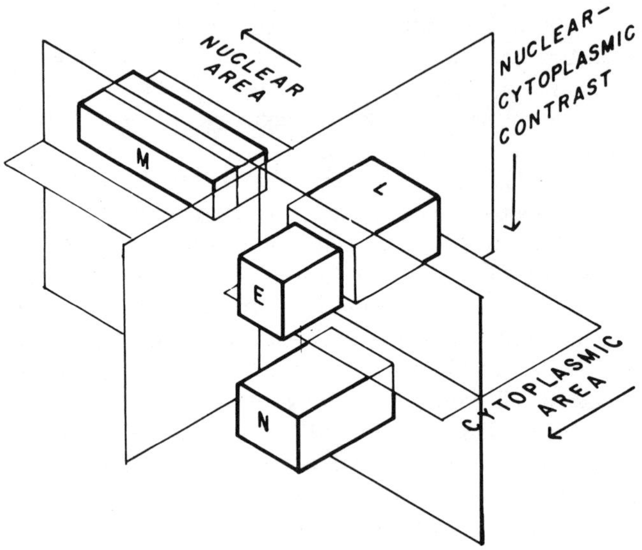

FIGURE 11. A decision space in three-dimensions. This represents the same data as FIGURE 10, but the direction of the axes has been reversed and three decision planes now separate the four parallelepipeds. It is impossible to depict the effect of additional dimensions, but the increasing discriminatory power as the argument goes from one to two to three dimensions can be carried into multi-dimensional space by appropriate analytic methods.

Discussion

With enlargement of the blood cell sample and the inclusion of hard-to-identify specimens, and with the examination of more complex biological systems, the need to make the method of analysis more sophisticated would hardly be surprising. Elaboration of the method is probable along two different lines: (1) extending the kinds of image-characterizing parameters used in analysis, and (2) employing a more complex parameter space and decision-making procedure.

The parameters described in this report were derived exclusively from the optical density frequency distribution, and as such they do not exploit obvious topological features such as nuclear shape and number of nuclear lobes. Additional procedures involving shape descriptors, analytical moments, and measures of fine texture are in various stages of development. These require the availability of the primary scan data during the course of an analysis, but they are well within the capacity and performance characteristics of current computers.

As more and more cells are subjected to analysis, the ranges of variation of numeric parameters may turn out to overlap to such a degree that no two or three parameters would give effective discrimination. In addition, discrimination procedures using linear and orthogonal partitions of the property space may be inappropriate. Higher dimensional property spaces, partially redundant parameters, and nonorthogonal as well as nonlinear discrimination might then be required to realize adequate classification and identification.

Summary

The CYDAC System has been designed to explore the extent to which mechanical perception can complement human perception in the domain of microscopic diagnosis, not merely in performing lesser tasks, but in stimulating fundamental new insights in cytomorphology. Emphasis has been put on: (1) finely discriminated gray-scale information taken at high optical resolution, (2) the use of optical density frequency distributions of images to perform the preliminary organization of quantitative optical information, and (3) the extraction and evaluation of large collections of potential image-characterizing parameters within a decision-theoretic framework. Using these methods, four major types of blood cells have been distinguished by applying simple combinations of criteria to a limited and carefully selected population. This preliminary success encourages us to try the method on larger and more inclusive populations, but future research alone will tell whether this approach will yield the discriminatory power to master the normal blood smear and to go beyond it.

Acknowledgments

The authors are appreciative of the assistance given by several members of the Department of Radiology, University of Pennsylvania: Drs. W. A. Kolman and B. H. Mayall prepared and scanned the specimens; Messrs. B. H. Perry and T. J. Conway programmed input/output; Miss J. M. Gogel prepared the manuscript; and Mr. W. H. Jenkins photographed the illustrations. The authors are also grateful for the administrative support of the Diagnostic Research Branch of the National Cancer Institute, in particular, Drs. E. M. Nadel and J. H. Carleton.

References

1. MONTGOMERY, P. O'B., ed. 1962. Scanning Techniques in Biology and Medicine. Ann. N. Y. Acad. Sci. **97:** 329–526.
2. TOLLES, W. E., ed. 1962. Applications and Methods of Counting and Sizing in Medicine and Biology. Ann. N. Y. Acad. Sci. **99:** 231–334.
3. BOSTROM, R. C., H. S. SAWYER & W. E. TOLLES. 1959. Instrumentation for automatically pre-screening cytological smears. Proceedings of the IRE **47:** 1893–1900.
4. SPENCER, C. C. & R. C. BOSTROM. 1962. Performance of the cytoanalyzer in recent clinical trials. J. Natl. Cancer Inst. **29:** 267–276.
5. NADEL, E. M. 1965. Computer analysis of cytophotometric fields by CYDAC and its historical evolution from the Cytoanalyzer. Acta Cytologica **9:** 203–206.
6. HEMPEL, C. G. 1952. Fundamentals of Concept Formation in Empirical Science. University of Chicago Press, Chicago, Ill.

7. MENDELSOHN, M. L., W. A. KOLMAN & R. C. BOSTROM. 1964. Initial approaches to the computer analysis of cytophotometric fields. Ann. N. Y. Acad. Sci. **115:** 998–1009.
8. MENDELSOHN, M. L., W. A. KOLMAN, B. PERRY & J. M. S. PREWITT. 1964. Morphological analysis of cells and chromosomes by digital computer. 6th IBM Medical Symposium.
9. MENDELSOHN, M. L., W. A. KOLMAN, B. PERRY & J. M. S. PREWITT. 1965. Computer analysis of cell images. Postgraduate Medicine (in press).
10. BØYUM, ARNE. 1964. Separation of white blood cells. Nature **204:** 793–794.
11. BOSTROM, R. C. & W. G. HOLCOMB. 1963. A digital scanning cytophotometer. IEEE International Convention Record Part **9:** 110–119.
12. PREWITT, J. M. S. 1965. The selection of sampling rate for digital scanning. IEEE Transactions on Bio-Medical Engineering **12:** 16–24.
13. PERRY, B. & M. L. MENDELSOHN. 1964. Picture generation with a standard line printer. Communications of the ACM **7:** 311–313.
14. SEBESTYEN, G. S. 1962. Decision-making processes in pattern recognition. The Macmillan Co., New York, N. Y.
15. PREWITT, J. M. S. & M. L. MENDELSOHN. 1965. The use of optical density distribution functions in effecting cytomorphological discriminations (in preparation).

Digital Image-Processing Activities in Remote Sensing for Earth Resources

GEORGE NAGY, SENIOR MEMBER, IEEE

Abstract—The United States space program is in the throes of a major shift in emphasis from exploration of the moon and nearby planets to the application of remote sensing technology toward increased scientific understanding and economic exploitation of the earth itself. Over one hundred potential applications have already been identified. Since data from the unmanned Earth Resources Technology Satellites and the manned Earth Resources Observation Satellites are not yet available, the experimentation required to realize the ambitious goals of these projects is carried out through approximation of the expected characteristics of the data by means of images derived from weather satellite vidicon and spin-scan cameras, Gemini and Apollo photographs, and the comprehensive sensor complement of the NASA earth resources observation aircraft.

The extensive and varied work currently underway is reviewed in terms of the special purpose scan and display equipment and efficient data manipulation routines required for high-resolution images; the essential role of interactive processing; the application of supervised classification methods to crop and timber forecasts, geological exploration, and hydrological surveys; the need for nonsupervised classification techniques for video compaction and for more efficient utilization of ground-control samples; and the outstanding problem of mapping accurately the collected data on a standard coordinate system.

An attempt is made to identify among the welter of "promising" results areas of tangible achievement as well as likely bottlenecks, and to assess the contribution to be expected of digital image-processing methods in both operational and experimental utilization of the forthcoming torrent of data.

I. Introduction

THE OBJECT of this survey is to give an account of experimental developments in digital image processing prompted by the major environmental remote sensing endeavors currently underway, such as the already operational weather satellite program of the National Oceanographic and Atmospheric Agency (NOAA), the projected Earth Resources Technology Satellite (ERTS) and Skylab experiments, the NASA Earth Resources Aircraft Program (ERAP), and the Department of the Interior's Earth Resources Observation System (EROS).

Sources of Information: The most comprehensive and readily accessible source of material in this area is the seven volumes published so far of the *Proceedings of the International Symposium on Remote Sensing of Environment*, held annually under the auspices of the Center for Remote Sensing Information and Analysis of the University of Michigan.

Other useful sources of information are the *NASA-MSC Annual Earth Resources Program Reviews*, the *Proceedings of the Princeton University Conference on Aerospace Methods for Revealing and Evaluating Earth's Resources*, the publications of the American Society of Photogrammetry and of the Society of Photo-Optical Instrumentation Engineers, the *Journal of Applied Meteorology*, the *Proceedings of the IEEE* (pertinent special issues in April 1969 and in July 1972), the *IEEE Transactions on Computers* and the *IEEE Transactions on Man, Machines, and Cybernetics*, the Journals of *Remote Sensing of Environment* and of *Pattern Recognition*, and the proceedings of several symposia and workshops on picture processing and on pattern and target recognition. Previous introductory and survey articles include Shay [185], Colwell and Lent [37], Leese *et al.* [120], Park [167], Dornbach [48], and George [67].

As is the case with most emerging fields of research, the assiduous reader is likely to encounter considerable redundancy, with many experiments republished without change in the electrical engineering and computer literature, in the publications dealing with aerial photography and photogrammetry, in the various "subject matter" journals (agronomy, meteorology, geophysics), in the pattern recognition press, and in the increasing number of collections devoted exclusively to remote sensing.

A depository of relevant published material, government agency reports, and accounts of contractual investigations is maintained by NASA at the Earth Resources Research Data Facility at the Manned Spaceflight Center in Houston, Texas (Zeitler and Bratton [223]). The Facility also maintains a file of most of the photographs obtained by the NASA satellites and earth observation aircraft, and by other cooperating agencies, institutions, and organizations. Provisions are made for convenient browsing through both the printed material and the vast amounts of photography. The Center publishes *Mission Summary Reports* and detailed *Screening and Indexing Reports* of each data-collection operation and acts in principle as a clearinghouse for the exchange of such material. All of its holdings are cataloged by subject, location, and author, but in its periodically published computer compiled *Index* [155]; documents cannot, unfortunately, be located by either author or title. An annotated list of references to the literature is, however, also available [154].

For background information, the book *Remote Sensing*, embodying the report of the Committee on Remote Sensing for Agricultural Purposes appointed by the National Academy of Sciences, is recommended as much for its comprehensive coverage (the chapters on "Imaging with Photographic Sensors," "Imaging with Nonphotographic Sensors," "Applications," and "Research Needs," are particularly interesting) as for the quality of its photographic illustrations [161]. The reports of the other Committees are also available [185].

The International Geographic Union is compiling a survey of current work, including a list of participating scientists, in geographic data sensing and processing. The long-range plans of the United States, as presented to the Committee on Science and Astronautics of the U. S. House of Representatives, are set forth in [197], [38], and [60].

Contents of the Paper: Although much of the current ac-

Manuscript received January 31, 1972; revised June 30, 1972.

The author was with IBM Thomas J. Watson Research Center, Yorktown Heights, N.Y. 10598. He is now with the Department of Computer Science, University of Nebraska, Lincoln, Neb. 68508.

Reprinted from *Proc. IEEE*, vol. 60, pp. 1177–1200, Oct. 1972.

tivity is sponsored by NASA, most of the early work in remote sensing was initiated by military intelligence requirements; in particular, the development of imaging sensors was greatly accelerated by the deployment of high-altitude photoreconnaissance aircraft and surveillance satellites. Very little information is, however, available in the open literature about the actual utilization of the collected imagery. The few published experiments for instance, in the *Proceedings of the Symposium on Automatic Photo Interpretation* (Cheng *et al.* [31]), deal almost exclusively with idealized target recognition or terrain classification situations far removed from presumed operational requirements. In view of the scarcity of up-to-date information, this aspect of remote sensing will be discussed here only in passing despite its evident bearing and influence even on strictly scientific and economic applications.

We shall also largely avoid peripheral application of digital computers to the collection or preparation of pictorial material intended only for conventional visual utilization, as in the calculation of projective coefficients in photogrammetry or the simulation of accelerated transmission methods independent of the two-dimensional nature of the imagery. Nor shall we be concerned with statistical computations arising from manually derived measurements, as in models of forest growth and riparian formations based on aerial photographs, or in keys and taxonomies using essentially one-dimensional densitometric cross sections or manual planimetry.

Omitted too is a description of the important and interesting Sideways Looking Airborne Radar all-weather sensors. Such equipment will not be included in the forthcoming satellite experiments. Its potential role in remote sensing is discussed by Simonett [187], Hovis [94], and Zelenka [224].

The diffuse and unstructured nature of terrestrial scenes does not lend itself readily to elegant mathematical modeling techniques and tidy approximations; an empirical approach is well-nigh unavoidable. The first ERTS vehicle is not, however, expected to be launched until the second half of 1972, and the Skylab project is scheduled for 1973, hence, preparatory experimentation must be based on other material. Although none of the currently available sources of imagery approximates closely the expected characteristics of ERTS and Skylab, some reflect analogous problems, and several are of interest on their own merits as large scale data-collection systems. These sensor systems, including both spaceborne and airborne platforms, are described in Section II.

A large portion of the overall experimental effort has been devoted to developing means for entering the imagery into a computer, for storing and retrieving it, and for visual monitoring—both of the hardware available for scanning and displaying high-resolution imagery, and of the software packages necessary for efficient manipulation of large amounts of two-dimensional (and often multiband) imagery in widely disparate formats. These matters are discussed in Section III.

Section IV is devoted to image registration, the difficult problem of superimposing two different pictures of the same area in such a way that matching elements are brought into one-to-one correspondence. This problem arises in preparing color composites from images obtained simultaneously through separate detectors mounted on the same platform, in constructing mosaics from consecutive overlapping pictures from a single sensor, in obtaining a chronological record of the variations taking place in the course of a day or a year, and in comparing aspects of the scenery observed through diverse sensor systems. The most general objective here consists of mapping the images onto a set of standard map coordinates.

Section V is concerned with the application of automatic classification techniques to the imagery. The major problem is the boundless variability of the observed appearance of every class of interest, due to variations inherent in the features under observation as well as in atmospheric properties and in illumination. The difficulty of defining representative training classes under these circumstances has led to renewed experimentation with adaptive systems and unsupervised learning algorithms. From another point of view, the classification of observations into previously undefined classes is an efficient form of data compression, an objective of importance in its own right in view of the quantity of data to be collected.

By way of conclusion, we attempt to gauge the progress accomplished thus far in terms of what still remains to be done if automatic digital image processing is to play a significant part in the worthwhile utilization of the remote sensing products about to become widely available.

The remainder of this Introduction lists some of the proposed applications for ERTS and Skylab, outlines the functional specifications for the image collection systems designed for these platforms, and describes the central data processing facility intended to accelerate widespread utilization of the ERTS image products.

A. Objects of the United States Remote Sensing Program

It is too early to tell whether expectations in dozens of specific application areas are unduly optimistic [185], [38], [60]. Certainly, few applications have emerged to date where satellite surveillance has been conclusively demonstrated to have an economic edge over alternative methods; it is only through the combined benefits accruing from many projects that this undertaking may be eventually justified.

Typical examples of proposed applications are crop inventory and forecasting, including blight detection, in agriculture [61], [169]; pasture management in animal husbandry [97], [32]; watershed management and snow coverage measurement in hydrology [135], [22]; ice floe detection and tracking in oceanography [93], [196]; demarcation of lineaments and other geographic and geomorphological features in geology and in cartography [219], [59]; and demographic modeling [209].

Much of the digital image processing development work to date has been directed at removing the multifarious distortions expected in the imagery and in mapping the results on a standard reference frame with respect to the earth. This process is a prerequisite not only to most automatic classification tasks but also to much of the conventional visual photointerpretation studies of the sort already successfully undertaken with the Apollo and Gemini photographs [37].

The pattern recognition aspects of the environmental satellite applications are largely confined to terrain classification based on either spectral characteristics or on textural distinctions. Object or target recognition as such is of minor importance since few unknown objects of interest are discernible even at the originally postulated 300 ft per line-pair resolution of the ERTS-A imaging sensors.

B. Plans for ERTS and Skylab

The ERTS satellites will be launched in a 496-nmi 90-min near-polar (99°) sun-synchronous orbit. The total payload is about 400 lb.

The two separate imaging sensor systems on ERTS-A (the first of the two Earth Resources Technology Satellites) consist 1) of three high-resolution boresighted return-beam vidicons sensitive to blue–green, yellow–red, and deep-red solar infrared regions of the spectrum, and 2) of an oscillating-mirror transverse-sweep electromechanical multispectral scanner with four channels assigned to blue–green, orange, red, and reflective infrared (IR) bands. ERTS-B will carry a fifth MSS channel in the thermal infrared.

The target of the vidicon tubes is exposed for a period of 12 ms/frame; the readout takes 5 s. This design represents a compromise between the requirements of minimal motion smear, sufficient illumination for acceptable signal-to-noise ratio, and low bandwidth for transmission or recording. In the oscillating-mirror scanner high signal-to-noise ratio is preserved through the use of multiple detectors for each band.

The field of view of both types of sensors will sweep out a 100-nmi swath of the surface of the earth, repeating the full coverage every 18 days—with 10-percent overlap between adjacent frames. Every 100-nmi square will thus correspond to seven overlapping frames consisting of approximately 3500 by 3500 picture elements for each vidicon and 3000 by 3000 elements for each channel of the mirror scanner, digitized at 64 levels of intensity.

The resolution on the ground will be at best 160 m/line-pair for low-contrast targets in the vidicon system and 200 m/line-pair in the mirror scanner [126], [159], [160], [12]. A comparison of the various resolution figures quoted for the Gemini/Apollo photography and for the ERTS/Skylab sensors, and more pessimistic estimates of the resolving power of the ERTS sensors, can be found in [34].

The pictures will be either transmitted directly to receiving stations at Fairbanks, Alaska, Mojave, Calif., and Rosman, N. C., if within range, or temporarily stored on video tape. The vidicon data will then be transmitted in frequency-modulated form in an analog mode while the scanner information is first digitized and then transmitted by pulse-code modultation (PCM) [67]. Canadian plans to capture and utilize the data are described in [198].

The center location of each picture will be determined within one half mile from the ephemeris and attitude information provided in the master tracking tapes which will also be made available to the public.

The sources of geometric and photometric distortion and the calibration systems provided for both sensors are described in some detail in Section IV, where digital implementation of corrective measures is considered. We note here only that estimates for digital processing on an IBM 360/67 computer of a single set of seven ERTS images ranges from 2 min for geometric distortion correction only to 136 min for complete precision processing including photometric correction [217].

The Skylab program will utilize a combined version of the Apollo command-and-service module and a Saturn third stage with a total vehicle weight of 130 000 lb in a low (250-nmi) orbit permitting observation of the earth between latitudes 50° N and 50° S.

The major imaging systems of the Skylab EREP (Earth Resources Experimental Package) consist of a 13-band multispectral scanner covering the ranges 0.4–2.3 μ and 10–12 μ, and of six 70-mm cartographic cameras having suitable film–filter combinations for four bands between 0.4 and 0.9 μ. The instantaneous field of view of the multispectral scanner will be 80 m^2 with a 78-km swath. The low-contrast resolution of the camera system will be 30 m/line-pair with a 163-km^2 surface coverage. A number of nonimaging sensors, such as a lower resolution infrared spectrometer, microwave radiometer/scatterometer altimeter, will also be on board, as well as an optical telescope [215], [168].

The multispectral data will be recorded on board in PCM on 20 000 BPI 28-track tape and returned with the undeveloped film at the end of each manned period of Skylab.

C. *Throughput Requirements*

Only the relatively well-defined processing load of the centralized NASA facility for the ERTS imagery will be considered here, since it is clear that the quantity of data required for each application ranges from the occasional frame for urban planning [165], to the vast quantities needed for global food supply forecasts [71]. The expected requirements of the user community are discussed in some detail in [72] and [146]. The coverage extended for the North American continent is of the order of

$$\frac{3000 \text{ nmi} \times 3000 \text{ nmi (area)}}{100 \text{ nmi} \times 100 \text{ nmi (frame size)} \times 18 \text{ days (period)}} = 50 \text{ sets}$$

of seven pictures per day. Each set of pictures contains approximately 10^8 bits of data, thus each day's output is the equivalent of 125 reels of 1600 bit/in magnetic tape. This estimate neglects the effects of cloud cover, which is discussed in [190] and [68].

At the NASA Data Processing Facility all of the imagery will be geometrically corrected to within at most 0.5 nmi in linearity and at most 1 nmi in location, and distributed in the form of 70-mm annotated black-and-white transparencies prepared by means of a computer-controlled electronic-beam recorder. In addition, about 5 percent of the images will undergo precision processing designed to reduce registration and location errors with both sensors to within 200 ft (to allow the preparation of color composites), and to reduce photometric degradation to under 1 percent of the overall range. All of the precision-processed data, 5 percent of the raw MSS data, and 1 percent of the raw RBV data will be made available on standard digital tape [220], [217], [138]. The current plan is to use the ephemeris and tracking data for the bulk processing and analog cross correlation against film chips of easily observable landmarks for the precision processing [138].

This is, of course, only the beginning; the subcontinent represents but 15 percent of the total area of the globe. While nations other than the U. S. and Canada may eventually obtain the data by direct transmission from the satellite [62], much of the original demand will be funneled through the NASA facility. The initial capacity of the photographic laboratories is to be 300 000 black-and-white and 10 000 color prints or transparencies per week; it is clear that the major emphasis is *not* on the digital products.

II. Characteristics of the Data Currently Available for Experimentation

At the initial stages of an image-processing experiment, the actual content of the pictorial data under investigation is sometimes less important than its format, resolution, distortion, and grey-tone characteristics, and its relation to other pictorial coverage of the same area. Fortunately, a large variety of data, much of it already digitized, is available to the tenacious investigator, and the supply is being replenished perhaps faster than it can be turned to profitable use.

The sources covered in this section include the vast collection of the National Environmental Satellite Center, the photography from the Gemini and Apollo missions, and both

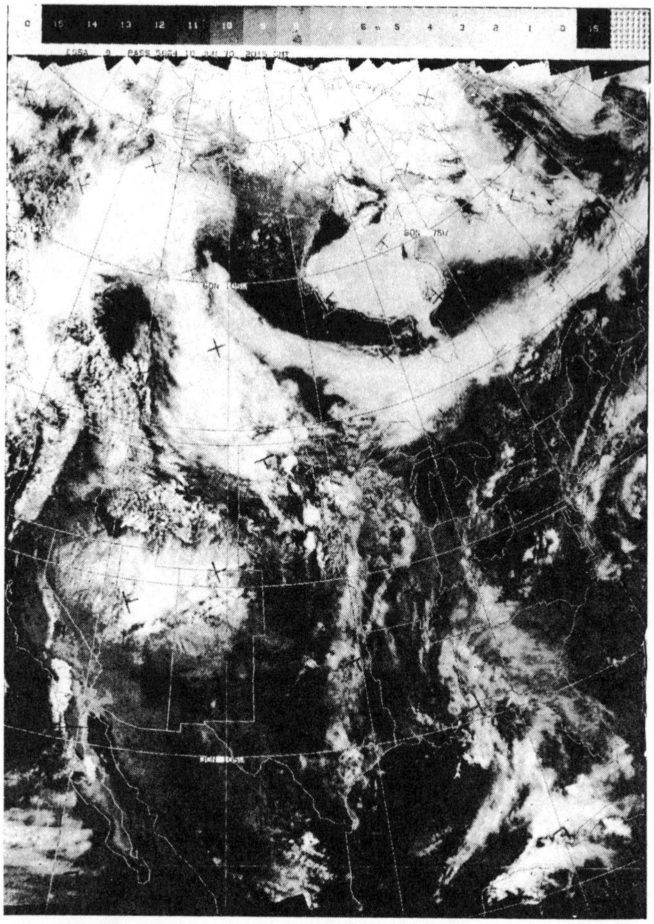

Fig. 1. ESSA-9 mosaic of North America. Traces of the reconstruction from the separate video frames are evident from the fiducial marks. The deviation of the overlay from the true coast lines shows a registration error carried into the mapping program. A programming error, since corrected, may be seen in the checkerboard in NW corner. Note gray wedge and annotation.

photographic and multispectral coverage of over two hundred specially selected test sites obtained by the NASA earth observation fleet.

A. Weather Satellites

Data have been obtained so far from 25 individual satellites beginning in 1959 with Vanguard and Explorer and continuing in the early 1960's with the ten satellites of the TIROS series and later with the Environmental Survey Satellites (ESSA) of the Tiros Operational Satellite System. The current operational series (ITOS) has been delayed because of the premature failure of ITOS-A. Data have also been collected by the Applications Technology Satellites in high geosynchronous orbits and by the experimental Nimbus series.

At present the major meteorological function of these systems is to provide worldwide cloud and wind-vector information for both manual and automated forecasting services, but extensions to other atmospheric characteristics are also underway [222], [41]. The newer satellites provide, for instance, accurate sea-level temperatures in cloud-free regions [123], [174], cloud-height distributions (through the combination of infrared sensor information with ground-based National Meteorological Center pressure and temperature observations [47]), and somewhat less accurate altitude-temperature and humidity profiles (based on the differential spectral absorption characteristics of the atmosphere). Other applications are mapping snow and ice boundaries and observation of sea state [135]. In addition, over 4000 storm advisories have been issued as a result of satellite observed disturbances [120].

The individual frames of Advanced Vidicon Camera System video, obtained from the latest operational polar-orbiting satellites, contain approximately 800 by 800 points at a resolution varying from 1.5 mi at the subsatellite point to 3.0 mi at the edges. The video is quantized to 64 levels of grey, with nine fiducial marks (intended to allow removal of geometric camera distortion), appearing in black on white. The overlap between successive frames is about 50 percent in the direction of the orbit and about 30 percent laterally at the equator; each frame covers about 1700 by 1700 nmi [23]. The two-channel Scanning Radiometer operates at about half the resolution of the AVCS [29].

Digital mosaics are available on a daily basis in either Universal Transverse Mercator or Polar Stereographic projections (Fig. 1). Each "chip" contains 1920 by 2238 points digitized at 16 levels, covering an area of about 3000 by 3000 mi^2. Multiday composites including average, minimum, and maximum brightness charts for snow, ice, and precipitation studies, are also issued periodically. The positional accuracy of any individual point is usually good to within 10 mi. On the high-quality facsimile output provided by the National Environmental Satellite Service geodesic gridlines and coastlines are superimposed on the video to facilitate orientation, but the only extraneous signals in the actual digital data are the fiducial marks from the vidicon camera [26], [24].

The geosynchronous ATS's are equipped with telescopic spin-scan cloud cameras which take advantage of the spin of the satellite itself to provide one direction of motion. The signal from these sensors can be monitored with relatively simple equipment; currently over 600 receiving stations throughout the world take advantage of the wide-angle coverage provided of the Atlantic and Pacific Oceans (Fig. 2). The average altitude is of the order of 20 000 mi, but the high angular resolution of the spin-scan camera allows ground definition comparable to that of the ITOS vidicons. Each frame consists of approximately 2000 by 2000 points. The maximum repetition rate is one frame every 24 min [28].

The Nimbus satellites are used mainly for experimentation with instrumentation to be eventually included in operational systems. Nimbus III, for instance, launched in 1969, carries a triad of vidicon cameras, a high-resolution infrared radiometer, an infrared spectrometer, an ultraviolet monitor, an image dissector camera system, and an interrogation, recording, and location system for data-collection from terrestrial experimental platforms.

At present, the imagery from the various satellites is archived at the original resolution only in graphic form, but the last few days' coverage is usually available from the National Environmental Satellite Service Center at Suitland, Md., on digital magnetic tape. Medium-scale archival data tapes going back to January 1962 are maintained by the National Weather Record Center in Asheville, N. C. [23].

An excellent summary of the history, status, and prospects of meteorological satellites data processing, including an extensive bibliography, is contained in [120] and updated in [41].

B. Gemini and Apollo Photography

Most of the 2000 photographs collected on the six Gemini missions between 1964 and 1968 were obtained with hand-held cameras. The astronauts appear to have favored high-oblique

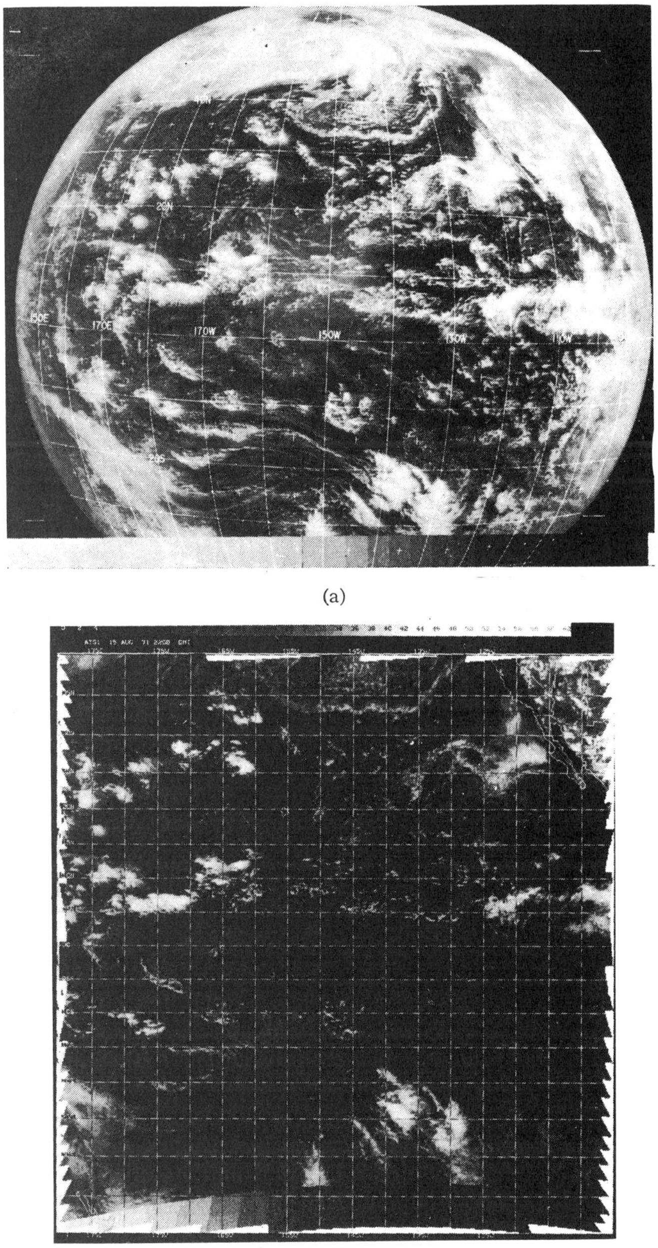

(a)

(b)

Fig. 2. ATS image. Raw video and Mercator projection of the Pacific Ocean from the first ATS. These illustrations were obtained through the courtesy of the National Environmental Satellite Center.

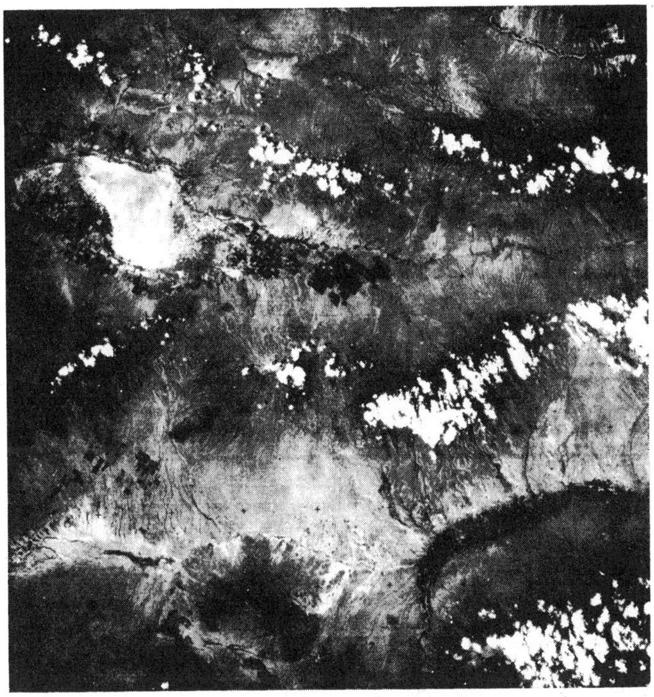

Fig. 3. Digitized Apollo photograph. This photograph of central Arizona was digitized at a resolution corresponding to 4200 lines on a drum scanner and was then recorded on film using the same device. The fiducial marks were introduced in the digital data for testing certain reseau detection algorithms [10], [11].

shots, with considerable variation in the scale and orientation of photographs of the same area [151].

For registration experiments, three Gemini photographs of Cape Kennedy obtained within a three-year interval are quite suitable. Two of these photographs are almost at the same scale and show little foreshortening, while the third is an oblique view extending clear across Florida [10].

In addition to hand-held cameras, some of the Apollo missions were equipped with a bank of four boresighted 70-mm Hasselblad cameras. The SO-65 project on the Apollo-9, in particular, was designed to assess the capabilities and limitations of multiband photography in a variety of applications. The satellite photography was carefully coordinated with aerial photography from almost a dozen aircraft flying at altitudes ranging from 3000 to 60 0000 ft, with airborne multispectral scanner coverage, and with the simultaneous collection of terrain information ("ground truth") from several test sites [152].

For agricultural purposes, the most popular test site appears to be the Imperial Valley of California. Extensive coverage is available for this area, with overlapping frames both in the same orbit of the Apollo-9 and in successive orbits several days apart. Each photo-quadruplet consists of three black-and-white negatives in the green, red, and infrared, and of a false-color composite including all three of these bands. The scale of the vertical photography is about 1:1 500 000 [153].

The photographs are obtainable in the form of third-generation prints, negatives, or 35-mm slides from the Technology Application Center of the University of New Mexico. Several dozen photographs, including some of the Imperial Valley and Cape Kennedy pictures mentioned above, have been digitized by Fairchild Camera and Instrument Corporation, Optronics International, Inc., and IBM (among others), at a resolution corresponding to 4000 lines/frame (Fig. 3). The quality of the pictures gives little justification for higher resolution [5].

C. High-Altitude Photography

The MSC Earth Resources Aircraft Program operates half-a-dozen specially equipped airplanes gathering data over some 250 NASA designated test sites [48]. The particular missions flown are decided largely on the advice of 200 or so principal investigators of diverse affiliations appointed for specific research tasks involving remote sensing. About 500 000 frames are collected annually, and are available from NASA "by special request."

Detailed descriptive material is available for each mission, including flight log summaries, charts showing flight lines, lists of camera characteristics (some missions fly as many as a dozen different cameras (see Fig. 4), film and filter combinations, roll and frame numbers, and plots of the earth loca-

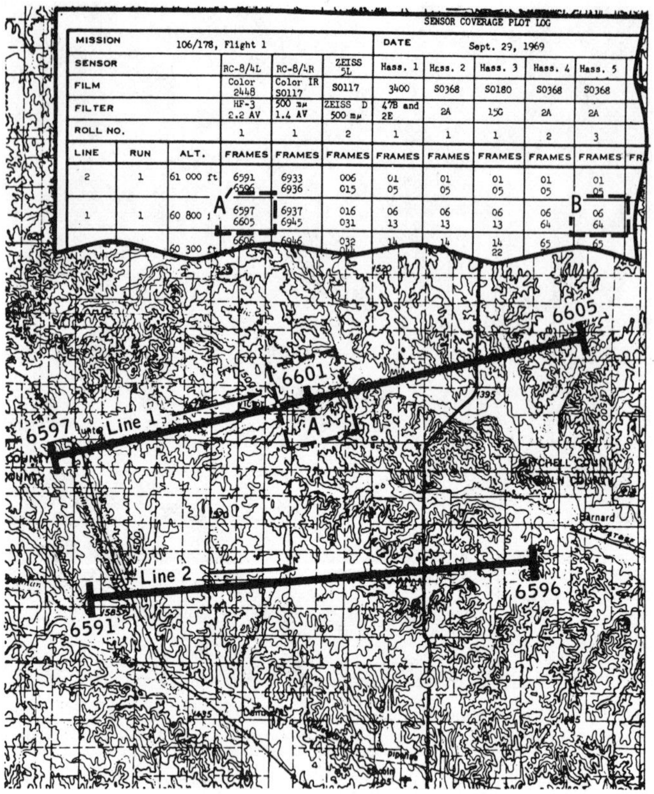

Fig. 4. NASA-ERAP documentation. Example of photographic coverage plot and corresponding plot for a high-altitude flight of the Earth Resources Observation Program (excerpted from NASA-MSC Screening and Indexing Report, Mission 123, Houston, Tex., July 1970).

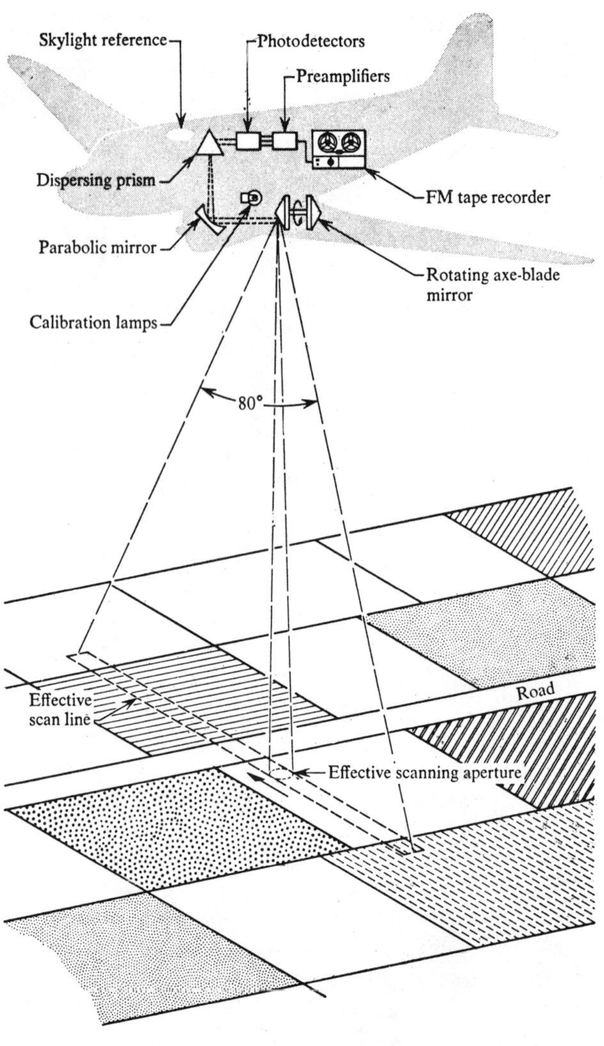

Fig. 5. Multispectral data collection. Schematic diagram showing how the light reflected or radiated from the ground is decomposed into its spectral components, converted into an electric signal, and recorded on board in analog form for subsequent digitization.

tion of selected frames. For simulation of future satellite data, the most suitable imagery is probably that obtained by the 60 000-ft ceiling RB-57 twin jet reconnaissance aircraft and by the recently acquired "ERTS-simulator" U-2's equipped with four multiband cameras (red, green, pan-IR, color-IR) with 40-mm lenses imaging the earth at only twice the resolution of the expected ERTS coverage.

Several of the aircraft are equipped with line scanners of various types. Such instruments will be described in the next section.

D. Airborne Multispectral Scanners

In instruments of this type, one scan direction is provided by the forward motion of the aircraft and the other by the rotation or oscillation of a prism or mirror (Fig. 5). Emitted or reflected radiation from the ground is imaged onto an array of detectors sensitive to various bands in the spectrum; the recorded output is an array of multidimensional vectors where each vector represents a specific position on the ground and each component corresponds to a spectral channel [92].

Scanners in operation today have anywhere from one to twenty-four spectral channels of varying bandwidths; cover all or part of the spectrum from the ultraviolet to the thermal infrared; offer a spatial resolution of 2 mrad down to about 0.1 rad; and differ widely with respect to calibration sources, attitude control and tracking accuracy, and method of recording the information. In general, most of the instruments can be flown in various configurtions in conjunction with other sensors including photographic cameras, nonimaging probes, and radar [126].

Most of the published work is based on data obtained by means of the scanners mounted on an unpressurized (10 000-ft ceiling) C-47 aircraft operated for NASA by the University of Michigan. Since 1966, over 150 missions have been completed, with such varied purposes as the study of soil distribution, arctic ice, bark attack on ponderosa pine, water depth, sinkhole-prone conditions, water-fowl habitats, urban features, and most recently and extensively, corn blight. Only a small fraction of the collected information has been automatically analyzed; the remainder is printed out in analog form for visual examination [148].

Digitized data from one of the Michigan flights are typically in the form of an array of 12-dimensional vectors (there are additional channels available but due to separate mounts they are not all in spatial register), with 220 samples perpendicular to the flight direction and up to several thousand samples along the flight line. Ground resolution at 5000-ft flight altitude is of the order of 60 ft.

Several calibration sources are viewed and recorded during the period that neither surface of the rotating axe-blade mirror is looking at the ground. These sources include lamps filtered to match the solar spectrum as closely as possible, black-body thermal references, and background illumination collected through a diffuser [112], [124].

After the flight, the analog signal recorded on FM tape is

digitized, corrected for roll angle, unskewed, and normalized with respect to the calibration signals. Noise bursts, out-of-sync conditions, and other anomalies are detected by elaborate preprocessing programs which also provide appropriate coordinate labels for subsequent identification with respect to photographs or other sources of independent terrain information.

Michigan is currently testing the new M7 scanner which is designed for recording wavelengths from 0.34 to 12 μ [39]. In addition, NASA is testing a 24-channel scanner on a C-130 Hercules (30 000-ft) aircraft equipped with an elaborate automatic data annotation system for facilitating earth location of the imagery [111], [221], [218], [69]. Other scanners with a smaller number of channels and less flexible arrangements are flown on smaller aircraft (such as Bendix's Beechcraft, and Colorado State's Aerocommander) for special missions.

The design of a 625-line color television system intended for airborne service is described in [142].

III. Image-Processing Systems

Although the availability of a large general-purpose digital computer is a valuable asset for experimentation with processing techniques, special hardware is required for converting the raw data into computer-readable form, for monitoring the results of the processing operation and for entering ground truth or other ancillary data pertaining to observed features of the image.

Many experimenters feel that parallel processors must also be available for performing the calculations at the speed necessary to evaluate the results on a significant enough variety of imagery. With conventional processors a large amount of programming work of a rather stultifying nature is required to decompose two-dimensional arrays containing up to 10^7 bytes into fragments of a size suitable for manipulation within the constraints imposed by core size, sequential tape access, blocked disk formats, and, possibly, multiprogrammed operating systems, and to reconstitute these arrays after transformations which may involve changes in the relations between, as well as within, the segments. Some alternatives to sequential digital processing are discussed by Preston elsewhere in this issue.

The large initial investment necessary to begin coming to grips with the more interesting problems offered by *real* data (as opposed to mathematical abstractions or shreds of hand-picked and selected imagery) accounts for the domination of this area of research by a few relatively large institutions, as reflected in the bibliography accompanying this paper.

It is not, as mentioned before, indispensable for each institution to provide means for digitizing the raw data. In principle, this is a one-time operation. In practice, however, it is a very ticklish procedure, and shortcomings may be discovered only after considerable experience with the digitized imagery. For this reason, many experimenters believe it necessary to develop their own scanners and other analog-to-digital conversion equipment, a challenge usually outlasting their purse and patience.

The equipment required for precision conversion of multispectral FM recordings and directly captured weather satellite pictures is so specialized that it will not be described here. Some of the calibration and synchronization problems encountered are described in [148] and [28]. Optical scanners suitable for diverse applications are, however, commercially available and will be briefly discussed.

There is no question that adequate grey-tone output must be conveniently available for experimentation, but opinion seems divided as to whether a television-type screen display with some interactive capability or a high-quality hardcopy output is preferable. A common compromise is a low-resolution CRT display with higher resolution (because flicker-free operation is not required) Polaroid recording capability.

Other less easily defined aspects of processing *large* pictures discussed in this section are the operating systems and utility programs necessary for any sort of coherent experimentation, special processors for anticipated quantity production, and the role of man–machine interaction in both experimental and operational systems.

Some examples of digital-computer-oriented remote sensing facilities, and of the equipment they contain are as follows:[1]

NOAA's National Environmental Satellite Center at Suitland, Md.: three CDC 6600's, CDC 160A, two ERM 6130's and 6050's, CDC 924, three 5000 by 5000 element Muirhead recorders, Link 35-mm archival microfilm unit [28], [29];

NASA–MSC's complex for the analysis of multispectral recordings and photography: 160 by 111 digital color display, closed-circuit television display, Xerox hardcopy output, Grafacon tablet, keypack, analog tape drives, IBM 360/44 processor [56], [58];

Caltech's JPL operation: film-scanner, CRT display, FM tape conversion, facsimile hardcopy, IBM 360/75 [18], [162];

University of Michigan multispectral facility: SPARC analog computer, drum scanner, analog film recorder, CRT display, FM tape conversion, CDC 3600 [131];

Purdue University's Laboratory for Applications of Remote Sensing: 577 by 768 element flicker-free 16-level digital TV display, light pen, continuous image motion, selective Polaroid or negative hardcopy without obstruction of display, FM tape conversion, IBM 360/67 [116], [117], [203];

University of Kansas KANDIDATS (Kansas Digital Image Data System) and IDECS (Image Discrimination, Enhancement, and Combination System): three flying-spot scanners for transparencies (25 mm to 3 by 4 in) and a vidicon camera controlled by a PDP 15/20, electronic congruencing unit (rotation, translation, and change of scale), 20 by 20 element linear processor and level selector, 24-channel digital disk storage, monochrome and color displays with built-in crosshatch generator, film output, GE-635 computer [77];

Computing Science Center of the University of Maryland: flying-spot film scanner, drum scanner/recorder, CRT display, vidicon, Univac 1108 [171];

University of Southern California Image Processing Laboratory: IER 1000 by 1000 element flying-spot color scanner and display, Muirhead rotating-drum color scanner and recorder, digital color television and display, Adage vector display with joystick and light pen, IBM 360/44, IBM 370/155, and HP 2100 computers connected to ARPA net [173];

Perkin-Elmer's Sampled Image Laboratories: drum scanner/recorder, flying-spot scanner, high-resolution traveling-stage microscope image-plane scanner, CRT and storage tube displays, precision plotting table, linked IBM 360/67, XDS 930, H-516, and Varian 620-i computers [212];

[1] Some of this information, obtained through personal communication, is more recent than the references would indicate.

IBM Research Division's facility at Yorktown Heights: film scanner, CRT output, image dissector, digital color TV display, graphic tablets, 360/91, 360/67, and 1800 computer net [85].

Another group of facilities is dedicated primarily to automatic photointerpretation, with only fragmentary information available about the work. Examples of this group are as follows:

McDonnell Douglas Astronautics: a compact vidicon scanner with 70-mm film scanner and a minicomputer, and a larger interactive system with a 1024-line (nominal) image dissector, scan converter, rear-projection viewer, 16-level digital TV display, alphanumeric display, joystick, XDS 930 computer [104], [105];

SOCRATES (Scope's Own Conditioned-Reflex Automatic Trainable Electronic System), a 20 by 20 photodiode and threshold logic array, the successor to Conflex I [164], [211];

SARF, General Motors' phoenix-like interactive Signature Analysis Research Facility [192];

MULTIVAC, Hughes Research Laboratories' 10 by 10 element binary array processor [8];

Litton Industries' Automatic Target Recognition Device, a hybrid system with a programmable CRT scanner, Recomp II process control computer, and interactive operation [205];

Cornell Aeronautical Laboratories' adaptive image processing operation using 35/70-mm CRT scanner, storage scope output, PDP-9, IBM 360/65 and 370/165 [134], [143];

ASTRID, Ohio State's Automatic Recognition and Terrain Identification Device, a hybrid computer system oriented toward processing line segments [163].

A good review of image enhancement facilities for remote sensing throughout the country is available in [37]. Among the systems discussed are the following: the NASA–USDA Forestry Remote Sensing Laboratory Optical Color Combiner at Berkeley, Calif.; the University of Kansas IDECS system; the two-band 1000-line Philco-Ford Image-Tone Enhancement System; and the Long Island University Multispectral Camera-Viewer. Abroad, we know of sustained activity only at the Institute for Information Processing and Transmission of Karlsruhe University [106], [89], [107], though some earlier European work is described in [21].

A. Optical Scanners

Since the data most closely resembling the expected ERTS and Skylab imagery in terms of resolution are available in the form of photography, optical scanners are necessary to translate the grey-tone (or color) information into computer-readable code.

CRT flying-spot scanners and television cameras (image dissectors or vidicons) are the most inexpensive and fastest devices available, but beyond a degree of resolution corresponding to about 500 by 500 picture elements quantized at 16 levels of intensity, the nonlinearities introduced by such scanners tend to exceed the degradation and distortion present in the photography itself. Owing to the nonuniform sensitivity, scanning the pictures section by section introduces even graver problems in juxtaposing adjacent sections.

Mechanical-drum and flatbed microdensitometers (50 000 dollars and up) are easily capable of the accuracy required for almost any type of photography, with even the less expensive digitizers (15 000 dollars) producing 2000 by 2000 arrays with up to eight bits of grey-scale quantization. Owing to the narrow spectral range of the source of illumination and matching detector configuration, most of these machines cannot be readily converted to color work. For this purpose, one must turn to scanners specially designed for the simultaneous production of color-separation plates in the printing industry, suitably modified by the addition of an analog-to-digital interface. The low speed of operation of such scanners (of the order of $\frac{1}{4}$ s/scan-line) generally requires off-line operation or an elaborate interrupt structure [141], [210], [171], [212].

Due to the lower contrast of opaque prints, positive or negative transparencies constitute the preferred medium for scanning. Because of multiple surface reflections, transparencies cannot be scanned with a reflection scanner by simply providing a uniform reflective background. Drum scanners designed for film have either a glass drum or some self-supporting arrangement with edge guides.

B. Grey-Tone Output Devices

Many flying-spot scanners and drum microdensitometers can be modified to operate in a write mode. This is a particularly convenient arrangement since the format conversion problems are altogether eliminated, and compatible resolution and sensitivity characteristics are guaranteed. The only drawback is that closely controlled wet processing with attendant time delay is usually required for consistent grey-tone reproduction. Film recorders may also be used with Ozalid foil overlays to produce high-quality color transparencies [130].

Facsimile recorders are less expensive and can provide 16 levels of grey on a 4000 by 4000 array (Fig. 2). Programmable flying-spot recorders with special character masks, such as the widely used Datagraphics 4020, provide about 500 by 500 distinct elements, but elaborate programming is necessary, with frequent recalibration, to secure even eight reasonably uniformly distributed intensity levels on either paper or film. Spatial resolution may, however, be traded off for grey-scale resolution by resorting to halftone techniques [79], [183].

Although all of these devices are generally used in a fixed-raster mode of operation, control of the beam deflection in an electron-beam recorder being developed by CBS Laboratories is the intended mechanism for the correction of "bulk-processed" video tapes at the NASA–ERTS Data Processing Facility [138]. This is an essentially analog system under control of an XDS Sigma 3 digital computer. A laser-beam recorder with a 10-μ spot over a 20 by 20-cm area has been developed at ITEK Corporation [125].

Line-printer overstrike programs are still useful for quick turn around, particularly with elongated formats such as that of the Michigan MSS. The visual qualities of this form of output are greatly improved by judicious use of watercolors and transparent overlays; modifications intended for on-line terminal use are, however, agonizingly slow. Isometric, perspective, and isodensity Calcomp plots offer another alternative for the impecunious investigator.

Television-type grey-scale displays are generally refreshed either from a high-speed core buffer or from a digital video disk. A single-line buffer is sufficient to fill the video disk, but a full-frame buffer (typically 520 by 600 bytes or picture elements) renders it much easier to change only parts of a picture without regenerating the entire frame.

Color displays need three times as much buffer storage as black-and-white pictures, but offer no particular difficulty if registered color separations are available in digital form. The calibration procedures necessary to produce color composites from *multiband* photography (filtered black-and-white exposures) are discussed in [19].

It is possible to circumvent the need for an image buffer by resorting to the now available grey-scale storage scope. Such a device requires a much simpler interface than a refreshed system, but the saving is to some extent illusory since most of the cost resides in the programming system necessary to select, retrieve, edit, and otherwise manipulate the displayed pictures.

Without a sophisticated programming system, the display can be used only to show the coarsest changes in the picture or as a conversation piece with lay visitors. For meaningful experimentation, it is desirable to be able to show two or more versions of the same picture simultaneously, to form overlays, to label specified features, to display intensity histograms and other computed functions, to vary the density modulation to bring into prominence regions of different intensity or to compensate for the amplitude nonlinearities of both the data collection system and the display itself, and to to perform many other more specific functions quickly and effortlessly.

Just how good a display must be to prove useful is a moot point and depends largely on the ingenuity of the user in casting the relevant information in a form compatible with the available display capabilities. So far, there is insufficient evidence to evaluate, in realistic terms, the contribution of display systems to the development of specific image-processing algorithms.

C. Operating Subsystems and Utility Programs

As already mentioned in several different connections, the major part of the programming effort required to cope effectively with large image arrays (four orders of magnitude larger than binary character arrays and about two orders of magnitude larger than most biomedical pictures) must be devoted to conceptually trivial matters such as: the decomposition and reconstitution of pictures; edge effects; efficient packing and unpacking routines for the various modes of point representation; variations in the basic byte and word sizes between different machines; aspect-ratio and other format changes among scanner, analog-to-digital converter, internal processor, and output devices; tape and disk compatibility; storage-protect and filing devices to ensure the preservation of valuable "originals" without undue accumulation of intermediate results; diagnostic routines permitting inspection of the actual values of relatively small segments at given image coordinate locations; left–right, up–down, black–white confusions; and myriad other frustrating details.

To avoid having to reprogram all these ancillary routines for each new function to be performed on the pictures, it is desirable to set up a procedure-oriented language or system within the framework of which new programs can be readily incorporated. Such a system may provide the necessary interface with the special-purpose hardware, allow access to a library of subroutines, supervise extensive runs in the batch mode on large computers, and offer special image-oriented debugging and diagnostic facilities in a time-shared mode of operation [125], [85].

Since most functions to be performed on a picture are local operations in the sense that the values of only a small subset of all the picture elements need be known in order to compute the value of an element in the output picture, the provision of a generalized storage policy is essential for the efficient performance of arbitrary window operations. For instance a window of size $n \times m$ may take n disk accesses if the image is stored line by line. A worst case example is a horizontal edge-finding operation on an image stored by vertical scans. With large images in such cases it is usually worth rewriting the array in an appropriate format before proceeding with the calculation; flexible means for accomplishing the reshuffling must be a part of any image-processing system worthy of the name unless an entire image can be accommodated in the fast random-access memory. A valuable discussion of the computational aspects of two-dimensional linear operations on very large arrays (up to 4000 by 4000 elements) is presented in [99].

Among the best known image-processing systems are the various versions of PAX developed in conjunction with the Illiac III, and later rewritten for the CDC 3600, IBM 7094 and System/360, and also for the Univac 1108. In PAX, images are treated as stacks of two-dimensional binary arrays. Arithmetic operations on integer-valued image elements are replaced by logical operations performed in parallel on the corresponding components (such as the 2^3 level) of several picture elements. Planes are defined in multiples of the word size of the machine, but aside from a few such restrictions, PAX II is conveniently imbedded in Fortran IV, with the debugging facilities of the latter available in defining new subroutines. Both a conversational mode and batch demand processing have been implemented at the Computing Center of the University of Maryland. The major subroutines are designed for the definition of planes, masks, and windows, logical functions of one or more planes or windows, neighborhood operations, area and edge determination, preparation of mosaics, tracing of connectivity, creation of specific geometric figures such as circles and disks, distance measurements, grey-scale overprint, grey-scale histograms and normalization, superimposition of grids, noise generation, moment-of-inertia operations, translation, rotation and reflections, and include as well a number of basic "macro" operations intended to facilitate expansion of the program library [149], [170], [30], [101], [102].

Other examples of comprehensive programming systems described in the literature are Purdue's LARSYSAA [116], [202], [203], General Motors' SARF [192], and the University of Kansas KANDIDATS [76]. Such systems are generally difficult to evaluate because the publication of interesting research results developed with the system (as opposed to contrived examples) tends to lag indefinitely behind the system description. Furthermore, very seldom is there any indication of the breakdown between the amount of effort expended in the development of the system and the time required to conduct given experiments.

D. Special-Purpose Digital and Hybrid Systems

At a time of continually waning interest in special-purpose processors for pattern recognition, there are two main arguments for their use in remote sensing. The first is the inability of even the largest digital computers to cope with element-by-element classification at a speed approaching the rate of collection of the data; an airborne MSS typically spews out 10^8 samples/h while the 360/44 can ingest only about 10^5 bytes/h on a ten-class problem [133]. The second argument is based on the need for on-board processing owing to the excessive bandwidth requirements for transmitting data from a spaceborne platform.

An example of a hybrid classification system is the SPARC machine at the Infrared and Optics Laboratory of the University of Michigan [130]. SPARC has 48 analog multipliers operating in parallel, and performs quadratic maximum-likelihood decisions on 12-component vectors at the rate of one every 10 μs.

Because of the difficulty of calibrating the machine, requiring manual setting of the potentiometers corresponding to the entries in up to four previously computed 12×12 class-covariance matrices, exact duplication of results is almost impossible and the machine is therefore of marginal utility in strictly experimental investigations. A successor featuring direct digital control and an interactive display capability is on the drawing boards [132], [133].

The proposed NASA–ERTS data processing facility makes use of optical correlation techniques against chips containing easily identifiable landmarks for registering the data, and special digital hardware for point-by-point correction of vignetting in the vidicons and other systematic errors [71], [138].

So far, no on-board satellite image processor has been installed, but a feasibility study based on several hundred photographs of clouds and diverse lunar terrain features concludes that an acceptable classification rate can be attained [45].

Another study, using photographs of six "typical" terrain features, proposes a simple adaptive processor based on coarsely quantized average intensity levels, spatial derivatives, and bandpass spatial filter output [100]. Electrooptical preprocessing techniques using image intensifier tubes are described in [83].

The highly circumscribed test material used in these experiments leaves some doubt as to their relevance to the output of currently available spaceborne sensors.

In spite of the commercial availability of relatively inexpensive FFT hardware and long shift-register correlators, there appears to have been no attempt so far to apply these devices to digital image processing for remote sensing.

E. *Interactive Processing*

Interactive processing in remote sensing does not necessarily imply the kind of lively dialogue between man and machine envisioned by early proponents of conversational systems and already realized to some extent in computer-aided design and information retrieval, and in certain areas of pattern recognition (see paper by Kanal elsewhere in this issue).

The prime objective of on-line access to the imagery is to provide an alternative to laborious and error-prone off-line identification, by row and column counts on printouts or interpolation from measurements on hardcopy output, of features which are easily identifiable by eye yet difficult to describe algorithmically without ambiguity. Examples of such features are landmarks—such as mountains, promontories, and confluences of rivers—for use in accurate registration of photographs, and the demarcation of field boundaries for crop-identification studies based on multispectral recordings.

Even a system without immediate visual feedback, such as a graphic tablet on which a facsimile rendition of the digitized image can be overlaid, is considerably superior to keying in the measured coordinate values. One step better is the displacement of a cursor on the display under control of a tablet, joystick, or mouse. The ideal is direct light-pen interaction, but this is not easy to implement on a high-resolution digital display. For really accurate work, a zoom option on the display is necessary for accurate location of the features of interest, but the amount of computation required is prohibitive in terms of response time [84].

A thoroughly tested system for locating nonimaging sensor data in relation to a closed-circuit television display of simultaneously obtained photography is described in [55] and [58]. The accuracy of the computer-generated overlays is shown to be better than 0.5° by reference to salient landmarks [54].

There has also been discussion of on-line design of spatial filters, decision boundaries, and compression algorithms. Here again, however, the waiting time between results is lengthy, and the operator must transmit so little information to the machine—typically just a few parameter values—that batch processing with high-quality hardcopy output is preferable in many instances. With multiprogrammed systems, the difference between on-line and off-line operation tends to blur in any case, with the distinction sometimes reduced to whether one enters the necessary commands at a terminal in the office or at a nearby remote job entry station.

Another possible desideratum is a display browsing mode, allowing inspection of large quantities of images. Here also, however, reams of hardcopy output, with on-line operation, if any, confined to pictures of interest, may be preferable.

It would thus appear that the most appropriate applications of interactive concepts, in the context of remote sensing, are 1) the debugging of program logic, where small image arrays may be used to keep the response time within acceptable limits, and 2) the entry of large quantities of positional information, where practically no computation is required and no viable off-line alternatives exist.

IV. Image Restoration and Registration

The need for exact (element-by-element) superimposition of two images of the same scene upon one another arises in the preparation of color composites, chronological observations, and sensor-to-sensor comparisons. The spatial, temporal, and spectral aspects of image congruence are discussed in [3]. Here we shall attempt to categorize the types of differences which may be encountered between two pictures of the same scene on the basis of the processing requirements necessary to produce a useful combined version. Only digital techniques are presented; the advantages and disadvantages of optical techniques are discussed elsewhere in this issue by Preston, and in [165], [166].

Geometric distortions in electronically scanned imagery are due to changes in the attitude and altitude of the sensor, to nonlinearities and noise in the scan-deflection system, and to aberrations of the optical system.

Photometric degradation (occasionally also referred to as "distortion," with questionable propriety) arises due to modulation transfer-function defects including motion blur, nonlinear amplitude response, shading and vignetting, and channel noise.

The atmospheric effects of scattering and diffraction, and variations in the illumination, also degrade the picture, but these effects are in a sense part of the scene and cannot be entirely eliminated without ancillary observations.

Once the pictures to be matched have been corrected for these sources of error, resulting in the digital equivalent of perfect orthophotos, the *relative* location of the pictures must still be determined before objective point-by-point comparisons can be performed. In reality, this is a chicken-or-egg problem, since the pictures cannot be fully corrected without locating a reference image, but the location cannot be determined accurately without the corrections.

Tracking and ephemeris data usually provide a first approximation to the position of the sensor at the time of exposure, but for exact registration more accurate localization is required. In operator-aided systems, such as the operational NESC mapping program, the landmarks are located by eye, while in fully automatic systems some correlation process is usually employed. A compromise is preliminary location of the landmarks by the operator, with the final "tuning" carried out by computer [191] in a manner analogous to the widely used track measurement programs for bubble-chamber photographs, described by Strand elsewhere in this issue.

A major difficulty in multispectral correlation or matched filtering of perfectly corrected images is the existence of *tone reversals*, or negative correlations, between spectral bands. This phenomenon, however, constitutes the very essence of most of the spectral discrimination techniques described in Section V.

Many of the current image restoration and enhancement techniques are intended to facilitate the task of visual interpretation. These matters are discussed in detail in the July 1972 special issue of the *Proceedings of the IEEE*, and in [96]. Difficulties arise because the transformations required to reveal or emphasize one set of features may, in fact, degrade features desirable for another purpose, yet such techniques have consistently produced visually startling results in Mars images [176]. An excellent discussion of the necessary compromises is offered by Billingsley [20].

A. Mathematical Formulation

The registration problem is cumbersome to state mathematically in its entire generality, but the following formulation may help in understanding the work currently in progress.

The scene under observation is considered to be a two-dimensional intensity distribution $f(x, y)$. The recorded image is another (digitized) two-dimensional distribution $g(u, v)$. The image is related to the "true" scene $f(x, y)$ through an unknown transformation T:

$$g(u, v) = T(f(x, y)).$$

Thus in order to recover the original information from the recorded observations, we must first determine the nature of the transformation T, and then execute the inverse operation T^{-1} on the image.

When independent information is available about T, such as calibration data on distortion and degradation, or a model of atmospheric effects, or attitude data concerning the angle of view, then the two operations may be separated.

Often, however, only indirect information about T is available, usually in the form of another image or a map of the scene in question. In this case, our goal must be to transform one of the pictures in such a manner that the result looks as much as possible like the other picture. The measure of similarity is seldom stated explicitly, since even if the two pictures are obtained simultaneously, the details perceptible to the two sensors may be markedly different. Thus for instance, in registering photographs of the same scene obtained simultaneously through different color filters we would want shorelines and rivers, but not the intensity levels, to correspond. On the other hand, if the photographs are obtained years apart with the purpose of observing the erosion of the shoreline or the shift in drainage patterns, then we must expect changes in the location of such features. Seasonal variations also give rise to problems of this type.

In some studies it is assumed that except for the effect of some well-defined transformation of interest, the image of a given scene is produced either by the addition of independently distributed Gaussian white noise, or by multiplication by exponentially distributed noise. While these assumptions lead to the expected two-dimensional generalization of the familiar formulas of detection, estimation and identification theory, they bear little relation to the observed deviations in many situations of practical interest.

The case of known (or derivable) T is sometimes known as image restoration, as opposed to the classical registration problem where T must be obtained by repeated comparison of the processed image with some standard or prototype. This dichotomy fails, however, when the parameters of T are obtained by visual location of outstanding landmarks followed by automatic computation of the corrected image.

B. Single-Point Photometric Corrections

To make any headway on either problem, at least the form of the unknown transformation must be known. We can then parametrize the transformations and write $g(x, y) = T_{\mathbf{c}}(f(x, y))$ to indicate that the true value (grey level) of a point with coordinates (x, y) depends only on the observed value at (x, y). The components of $\mathbf{c}$ specify the regions where a given correction factor is applicable.

Examples of such degradation are the vignetting due to the reduced amount of light reaching the periphery of the image plane in the sensor, and the shading due to sun-angle in the TIROS and ESSA vidicon data. Since the combined degradation is quite nonlinear with respect to both intensity and position, the appropriate correction factors are prestored for selected intensity levels on a 54 by 54 reference lattice, and the individual values in the 850 by 850 element picture are interpolated by cubic fit. Camera warmup time through each orbit, as well as the sawtooth effect owing to the non-uniformly reciprocating focal-plane shutter, are taken into account, but contamination by the residual images on the photocathode is neglected. The final output is claimed to be photometrically accurate (or at least consistent) within 5 percent, which is sufficient for the production of acceptable montages for visual inspection [26], [24].

If the preflight calibration does not yield a sufficiently accurate description of the response of the post-launch system, as was the case with the early Mariner pictures, then the correction may be based on the average grey-scale distribution of many pictures on the assumption that the true distribution is essentially uniform [156].

Spectral calibration of digitized aerial color photography can be performed on the basis of the measured reflectance characteristics of large ground calibration panels [52].

Single-point photometric corrections have also been extensively applied to airborne multispectral imagery. A comprehensive discussion of the various factors contributing to variations in the output of the multispectral scanner, including the crucial non-Lambertian reflectance characteristics of vegetative ground cover, is contained in [112]. This study also offers an experimental evaluation of various normalization methods based on *relative* spectral intensities, and a formula for eliminating channel errors resulting in "unlikely" observations. A followup study [113] describes interactive techniques based on visual examination of certain amplitude averages. Good examples of the importance of amplitude preprocessing in extending the range of multispectral recognition are shown in [88], [188].

A more theoretical approach to automatic derivation of the complicated relation between sun-angle and look-angle is presented in [43] and an analysis of scattering phenomena in different layers of the atmosphere in [172].

C. Multipoint Photometric Correction

This class of operations may be symbolized as

$$g(x, y) = T_c(f(n(x, y)))$$

where $n(x, y)$ denotes a *neighborhood* of the point (x, y). In the simplest case, the corrected value at (x, y) depends on the observations at two adjacent points:

$$g(x, y) = T_c(f(x-1, y), f(x, y)).$$

Such linear filtering operations (the properties of the filter are characterized by $\mathbf{c}$) are common in correcting for motion blur (the convolution of the true video with a rectangular pulse corresponding to the length of the exposure), for loss of resolution due to modulation transfer function (MTF) rolloff, for periodic system noise, and for scan-line noise [18], [156], [179], [157], [50], [10], [217], [184], [177].

The desired filtering operation may be performed directly in the space domain as a local operation [179], [10], [11], [156], with typical operators ranging from 3 by 3 neighborhoods for motion blur to 21 by 41 elements for more complex sources of low-frequency noise, by convolution with the fast Fourier transform [80], [50], [2], [186], or through optical techniques [96]. In processing speed the local operators show an advantage as long as only very-high-frequency effects are considered and they are also less prone to grid effects in the final results [184], [7]. Optical processing has not yet been used on an operational basis on nonphotographic imagery, principally because of the difficulty of interfacing the digital and optical operations [95].

D. Geometric Distortion

Geometric distortion affects only the position rather than the magnitude of the grey-scale values. Thus

$$f(u, v) = f(T_c(x, y))$$

where T_c is a transformation of the coordinates.

If the transformation is linear, the parameter vector contains only the six components necessary to specify the transformation, i.e., $\mathbf{c} = (A, B, C, D, E, F)$ where

$$u = Ax + By + C$$
$$v = Dx + Ey + F$$
$$f(u, v) = f(Ax + By + C, Dx + Ey + F).$$

Important subcases are pure translation ($A = E = 1$, $B = D = 0$), pure rotation ($C = F = 0$, $A^2 + B^2 = D^2 + E^2 = 1$), and change of scale ($A/B = D/E$, $C = F = 0$). From an operational point of view, the transformation is specified by the original and final location of three noncollinear points. In executing a linear transformation on the computer, it is sufficient to perform the computations for a small segment of the image in high-speed storage, and transform the remainder, segment by segment, by successive table lookup operations. Aside from the saving in high-speed storage requirements, this technique results in approximately a tenfold decrease in computation over direct implementation of the transformation.

Along the same lines, a projective transformation is specified by eight parameters, which may be derived from the location of four pairs of picture elements. The execution of this transformation is, however, more complicated, since the relative displacement of the picture elements is not uniform throughout the frame.

It is important to note that owing to the quantization of the coordinate axes, the actual computation of the corrected image is usually performed in reverse in the sense that the program proceeds by determining the *antecedent* of each element or set of elements in the new image. Were the transformation performed directly, one would be faced with the possibility of the occurrence of gaps in the case of dilations and the superposition of several elements in the case of contractions. Since the computed coordinates of the antecedents do not in general fall on actual grid points, it is customary to adopt a nearest neighbor rule for selecting the appropriate element, though local averages are sometimes used instead.

Translation, rotation, and perspective transformations occur in practice owing to changes in the position and attitude of the sensor platform, while scale changes are frequently required by format considerations in input–output. The most bothersome distortions cannot, however, be described in such a simple form. Properties of the transducer itself, such as pincushion distortion, barreling, optical aberrations, and noise in the deflection electronics are best characterized by their effect on a calibration grid scanned either prior to launching or during the course of operation. In addition, fiducial marks are usually etched on the faceplate of the camera in order to provide *in situ* registration marks.

The expected sources of distortion in ERTS-A RBV imagery are discussed in quantitative terms in [136] with particular reference to correction by means of analog techniques such as optical projection and rectification, line-scan modulation, orthophoto correlation, and analytically (digital computer) controlled transformation of incremental areas. Because of the nonuniformity of the distortions over the entire format, and the possibility of tone reversals from object to object in the spectral bands, only the last system is accorded much chance of success.

The precise measurement of the location of the 81 (9×9 array) fiducial marks (also called reseau marks) on the faceplate as well as on the output image of a number of return-beam vidicons destined for the ERTS-A satellite is described in detail in [137]. It is shown that to provide a frame of reference for eventual correction of the imagery to within one-half resolution element, the vidicon parameters must be established to the accuracy shown in Table I.

The detection of the fiducial marks in the ERTS vidicon images, with experiments on simulated pictures derived from digitized Apollo photographs, is described in [11], [16], [129]. The basic technique is "shadow casting" of the intensity distributions on the x and y axes of the picture. This is shown to correspond, for the selected fiducial-mark geometry, to matched-filter detection.

The actual correction, by interpolation between the grid coordinates of the distortion on extraterrestrial images, is reported in [156], on TIROS vidicon data in [26], and on ATS spin-scan cloud-camera pictures in [28]. The correction of geometrical distortions may be efficiently combined with the production of rectified orthophotos (equivalent to a 90° angle of view) [156] and with the generation of standard cartographic products such as Mercator and Polar Stereographic projections [27], [23], [29].

TABLE I

CALIBRATION REQUIREMENTS FOR PARAMETERS OF THE RETURN-BEAM VIDICON FOR ERTS-A
(from [137])

Parameter	System Accuracy	Calibration Accuracy
Reseau coordinates	$\pm$ 10 μm	$\pm$ 3 μm
Lens:		
Focal length	+270 μm −980 μm	$\pm$20 μm
Principal point	$\pm$ 65 μm	$\pm$ 5 μm
Radial distortion	$\pm$ 30 μm	$\pm$ 5 μm
Electronic distortion	$\pm$750 μm[a] (about 125 TVL of 6 μm each)	$\pm$ 5 μm
Orientation between cameras	$\pm 7.0\times10^{-4}$ rad (about 2.4 ft)	$\pm 1.5\times10^{-5}$ rad (about 3 in)

[a] Recent data indicate that the 750-μm value may be too high. However, the complete RBV–transmission–EBR system has not been tested yet.

A fast algorithm suitable for digital computers equipped with MOVE BYTE-STRING instructions has been reported in [217], [10], [11]. This algorithm is intended for the correction of small distortions, such as those due to the camera characteristics, and is based on the fact that relatively large groups of adjacent picture elements retain their spatial relationship in the corrected picture. The program computes the maximum number of adjacent elements that may be moved together without exceeding a preset error (typically one coordinate increment). Experimental results [17], [129] show that the boundaries between such groups are not visually detectable.

When the imagery is intended mainly for visual use rather than for further computer processing, the technique of "gridding" offers an expedient alternative to mapping [27]. With this method the picture elements are left in their original location and the positional information is inserted by the superposition of latitude and longitude coordinates over the image. Since only the locations of selected image points need be computed for this purpose, the method is quite rapid and is extensively used with the specially modified output devices of the National Environmental Satellite Center.

E. *Automatic Determination of Anchor Points*

Finding corresponding points in two pictures of the same scene can be accomplished by correlating a "window function" from one picture with selected portions of the other picture. If the two images differ only by a shift or translation, then only a two-dimensional search is involved. If, however, a rotation and a change of scale are also necessary, then the time required for exhaustive search exceeds all practicable bounds.

Once one window function has been adequately matched, the location of the maximum value of the correlation function usually gives a good idea of where the search for the next window function should be centered, even if the transformation is not quite linear.

In terms of our earlier formulation, we are trying to evaluate the parameter vector $\boldsymbol{c}$ under the assumption that both $f(x, y)$ and $g(x, y)$ are available and that parameters representative of the entire image can be derived by establishing the correspondence of selected subimages. This usually involves maximization of a similarity function subject to the constraints imposed by the postulated transformation.

The similarity function to be maximized may take on several forms. If, for instance, we take two $m\times m$ images Y_1 and Y_2 considered as vectors in an m^2-dimensional space, then an $n\times n$ window function V_1 and the trial segment V_2 may be considered as projections of Y_1 and Y_2 onto the n^2-dimensional subspaces spanned by the coordinates corresponding to the elements in the two subimages. Reasonable choices for the similarity function are as follows

1) $$V_1 \cdot V_2$$

2) $$\frac{V_1 \cdot V_2}{Y_1 \cdot Y_2}$$

3) $$\frac{V_1 \cdot V_2}{|V_1| \cdot |V_2|}.$$

The first of these functions suffers from the defect that false maxima may be obtained by positioning the window function over some high-intensity region of the target picture. Normalizing the entire image 2) does not circumvent this difficulty completely. Alternative 3) is thus usually chosen, representing the angle between the window function and the trial segment considered as vectors, in spite of the fact that this procedure requires renormalization of the trial segment for each displacement.

A good account of the problems encountered in an experimental investigation of this problem, viewed as "one of determining the location of matching context points in multiple images and alteration of the geometric relationship of the images such that the registration of context points is enhanced," is given in [3], [4]. Both 14-channel multispectral images obtained one month apart and digitized Apollo-9 photographs were tested. Window functions ranging in size from 4 by 4 to 24 by 24 picture elements and located at the vertices of a grid were used to obtain least squares estimates of a "generalized spatial distance" incorporating the translational, rotational, and scale parameters of the required transformation. The information derived at each vertex was used to center the search space at the next vertex at the most likely values of the parameters. The actual correlation function was the correlation coefficient[2]

$$\phi(k, l) = \frac{\sum_{i=1}^{n}\sum_{j=1}^{n} f(i + k + s, j + l + s) g(i, j)}{\sum_{i=1}^{n}\sum_{j=1}^{n} f^2(i + k, j + l) \sum_{i=1}^{n}\sum_{j=1}^{n} g^2(i, j)}$$

where the image f is of size $m\times m$; the window is of size $n\times n$; $s=(m-n)/2$; and k and l range from $-s$ to s.

The average values were previously subtracted from f and g to yield zero-mean functions; $\phi(k, l)$ is then bounded by -1 and $+1$. In order to circumvent the problem of tone reversals, experiments were also conducted on gradient enhancement techniques designed to extract significant edge information from the images, but this is of less value than might be expected, owing to the noisy nature of the data. The computation was carried out by means of FFT routines, which are shown to yield an average improvement of an order of magnitude in speed over the direct method. The displacements determined by the program are of the order of 2–3 elements in the multispectral data and 10 elements in the photographs; safeguards are included to reject maxima obtained under certain suspect circumstances (for instance on patches of uniform intensity).

[2] The formula is given in this form in [4]; the more customary formulation has a square root in the denominator.

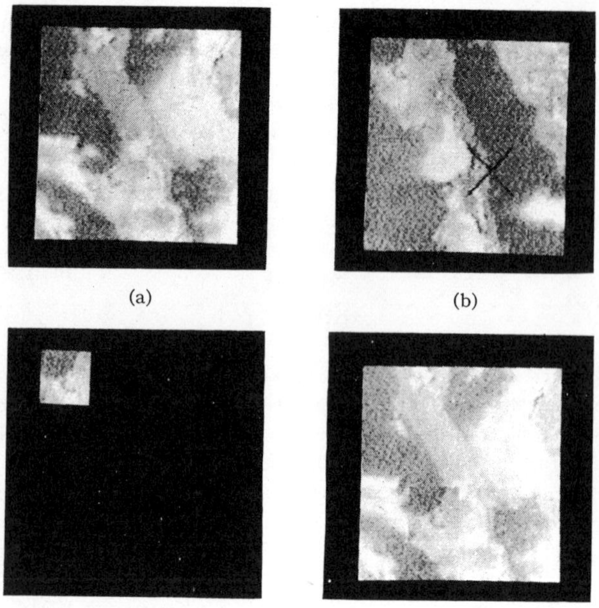

Fig. 6. ITOS-1 registration experiment. A 32 by 32 window function (c) extracted from the top left corner of picture #1 (b) is tried in every possible position of the search area (a) by means of the sequential similarity detection algorithm. The position of the best match determined by the algorithm is shown in (d), where the window function is inserted into the search area. Note the discontinuities due to the change in cloud coverage between the times of exposure of the two pictures.

Similar work has been reported on a pair of black-and-white Gemini photographs of Cape Kennedy, obtained thirty months apart, and on a SO 65 color-separation triplet [10]. On the black-and-white pictures, windows of size 16 by 16 and 32 by 32 elements gave fairly consistent results, but on the SO-65 IR–red, and IR–green pairs, 128 by 128 elements were necessary even with preprocessing by means of an edge-enhancement technique using the coefficient of dispersion or mean-to-variance ratio over 3×3 subregions. These experiments were carried out on a terminal-based system in a time-shared environment.

Impressive savings in processing time can be demonstrated on the basis of the observation that when two windows do not match, the cumulative distance function rises on the average much more rapidly with each pair of picture elements examined than when the windows do match [13]. The class of *sequential similarity detection algorithms*, as the method is called, was analyzed on the assumption that the deviation between two pictures in register is exponentially and independently distributed, and optimal stopping rules were derived under various conditions. The number of operations required was tabulated according to the size of the search space and the size of the window. It is shown, for example, that for a search area of dimensions 2048 by 2048 and a window size of 256 by 256 elements (much larger than in the experiments actually carried out), the direct method would require about 10^{12} operations, the FFT, 10^{10} operations, and the best of the sequential algorithms, 2×10^7 operations. The test vehicle in this instance consisted of pairs of ITOS AVCS frames obtained two days apart over the Baja California and Gulf Coast regions (Fig. 6).

Another shortcut for multiple template matching, based on prior selection of "rare" configurations, is compared to the conventional systematic search in [147].

F. Cloud Motion

An interesting twist on the registration problem occurs when the camera remains stationary and the scene shifts. This is precisely the case in attempting to determine wind-velocity vectors from changes in the location of cloud masses in the 30-min intervals between successive readouts from the geostationary ATS spin-scan cloud cameras.

An excellent account of the importance of this problem in the context of the Global Atmospheric Research Program, which requires wind-velocity measurements accurate to within 3 knots, is presented in [191]. An interactive computer facility (WINDCO) for tracing cloud motion by means of 32 by 32 element FFT correlation on a Univac 1108 computer is also described. A highlight of this paper is the thorough treatment of the computations necessary to determine the satellite orbit and attitude from least squares approximations of the measured location of landmarks appearing in the pictures. It is shown that the parameters necessary for mapping operations can be determined to an accuracy superior to the resolution of the individual picture elements.

Correlation techniques using the FFT were also applied to 64 by 64 element windows extracted from preprocessed (i.e., projected on standard map coordinates) versions of the large ATS pictures by Leese and his colleagues. They report an approximately twentyfold improvement over direct calculation of the lagged product. The metric selected was the correlation coefficient; the observed peak value was usually about 0.7. The results are claimed to be comparable to or better than visually obtained values when only a single layer of clouds is present or when the wind velocity is constant with altitude. The major source of inaccuracy, in addition to the gradual deformation of the cloud masses, is the occurrence of relative mapping errors between the two pictures [121], [122].

Essentially similar results were obtained with a binary matching technique operating on edge configurations extracted from ATS cloud pictures quantized to only two levels. This method is a factor of two or more faster than the FFT method, but is also unable to cope with multilayer cloud patterns drifting in different directions. The human observer, however, has little difficulty in separating such motion components on the basis of accelerated "loop movies" showing twenty or more successive exposures [121].

Yet another sustained attempt at generating wind-velocity maps from ATS pictures is taking place at the Stanford Research Institute. In this work the bright points (clouds) are aggregated by means of a clustering algorithm, and the ground location is determined through successively finer-grained cross correlation against preselected 20 by 20 element templates. At the last stage a directed-search technique is used, as if the cross-correlation function were monotonic, but the results are checked by means of several independently chosen starting points. The major remaining difficulties are said to be connected with changes in sun angle [73], [53].

G. Parallax Measurements

The determination of parallax from stereo photographs differs from the problems just discussed in that the displacement function may vary quite rapidly from point to point; therefore, the use of window functions based on uniform displacements is inappropriate.

Good results in estimating parallax on a single digitized low-altitude stereo pair were obtained with the assumptions that the difference in the grey levels of corresponding trial pairs of points in the two pictures is a zero-mean Gaussian process and that the departure of the displacement function from its average value over a small neighborhood is also of the same form. Since in this formulation the grey-level difference distribution is conditional upon the parallax, for which the Gaussian continuity condition gives an *a priori* distribution, Bayes' rule may be invoked to estimate the *a posteriori* dependence of the parallax on the observed video distribution.

The computation of the altitude contour lines from the parallax information is a straightforward problem in analytic geometry. Some results of applying the complete procedure to the estimation of forest-tree heights are shown in [9].

It should be noted that there exist automatic and semiautomatic photogrammetric image-correlating devices (*stereoplotters*) which recognize corresponding subsections on a stereopair of photographs and simultaneously transform and print one of the images in an orthographic projection or generate altitude contour lines. Several types of equipment are available, with electronic (scanned) or direct optical image transfer, digital or mechanical implementation of the projective parameters, manual or automatic correlation, and on-line or off-line printout [207], [98]. These sophisticated and expensive precision instruments are not, however, considered to be sufficiently adaptable to cope with the types of distortion expected from the various satellite sensors [136].

V. Classification Techniques

Experimental work in automatic classification through remote sensing may be neatly dichotomized according to whether the primary features consist of spectral or spatial characteristics. Examples of the former are largely based on the output of the Michigan multispectral scanner, while examples of the latter include aerial photographs, high-resolution photographs of the moon, and satellite cloud pictures.

The reason why the expected development of methods based on both spatial *and* spectral characteristics has not yet taken place to any significant degree is that the spatial resolution of the airborne multispectral scanner is too low to allow discrimination of most objects of interest. With multiband aerial photography, on the other hand, automatic registration techniques have not yet come far enough along to permit the preparation of digital color composites in sufficient numbers for significant experimentation.

The typical classification experiment in either domain is open to criticism on several counts. The data, collected in a single region under favorable conditions by airborne or spaceborne sensors, are *examined in their entirety by the experimenter*, who decides which areas are most representative of the region as a whole. The samples from these areas are assembled to form the training set, which is characterized by ground-truth information delineating certain categories of interest. A statistical categorizer or decision box is constructed on the basis of the statistical parameters extracted from the training set.

The classification performance is evaluated on another portion of the data (the test set), also carefully *selected to enhance the probability of correct classification*, where the location and extent of the different types of cover is known to the experimenter. If the error rate is unacceptably high, then offending portions of the test set may be included in the training set for another iteration through the whole cycle!

The details of the various experiments differ with respect to the source of data, the method of labeling the training and test sets, the number and nature of the classes to be identified, the degree of statistical sophistication of the categorizer, and the method of evaluating the results, but the general scheme of classifying samples of the test set according to their similarity to the training set remains the same.

Since it is impossible to review in detail the many dozen pattern-recognition experiments reported in the literature, we shall confine our attention to a few tasks which have been the object of sustained efforts and will examine other contributions in terms of their deviation from the specimen tasks. Rather than offer a description of each classification problem, method of collecting the data, and decision algorithm, we shall concentrate on the experimental procedure, the manner of evaluating the results, and the validity of the derived inferences. For background, the reader cannot do better than turn to the excellent discussion of these matters in relation to conventional photointerpretation in [36], which includes many fine examples drawn from Gemini pictures and coordinated low-altitude oblique aerial photography.

A. Crop Recognition

In the United States, the recognition of crop species by means of multispectral *signatures*, or distinctive spectral characteristics, has been extensively studied since 1966 with a view to providing timely information for fertilization practices, blight control, harvesting schedules, and yield forecasts [61], [90], [124]. There has been much discussion of the importance of systematic coverage throughout the growing season [167], [195], but most of the experiments reported use only data collected in a single day.

Almost all of the earlier work in automatic classification is based on data collected by the Michigan scanner at altitudes ranging from 3000 to 10 000 ft in intensively farmed areas of the Midwest, though a number of missions were also flown in the Imperial Valley agricultural test site of southern California in conjunction with the Apollo-9 experiments. As a rule only the twelve bands spanning the visible and near-IR range of the spectrum are used, because the other channels of the Michigan scanner do not produce data in register with the first twelve channels and cannot be readily transformed into the same spatial coordinate system [25].

Ground truth is generally obtained either through ground surveys or by means of color, IR, and black-and-white photography obtained during the overflights. The performance of skilled photointerpreters using the various types of imagery has been most recently evaluated in [14], with still valid ideas on the most appropriate roles for manual and automatic techniques discussed in [35] and [118].

Most of the classification experiments were performed by investigators associated with the Infrared and Optics Laboratory of the University of Michigan and with the Laboratory for Applications of Remote Sensing of Purdue University. The primary instruments for experimentation were a CDC 3600 at Michigan and IBM 360/44 and 360/67 computers at Purdue. A number of results were also obtained with the Michigan SPARC analog processor.

Extensive programming systems were developed at both installations to allow data editing, data normalization, inspection of statistical attributes of spectral distributions, selection of spectral bands, derivation of categorizer parameters, execution of classification procedures, and evaluation of results [115], [202], [112], [148], [87]. Both organizations take pride in the accessibility and ease of assimilation of their software packages as attested, for instance, in [206] and [208].

The ground swath covered in each flight by the Michigan scanner is normally twice as wide as the flight altitude. i.e.,

$\frac{1}{2}$ to 2 mi, with the flight lines varying in length from 2 to 20 mi. With a few notable exceptions [88], however, not all of the data collected are run through the training and classification algorithms, and even when all of the data are actually classified, the determination of the accuracy of classification over the entire region is usually hampered by the difficulty of entering into the computer the complete ground-truth description.

The specific fields chosen for training and for classification are usually selected for uniform appearance and for nearness to the centerline of the swath since recognition tends to be worse at oblique look-angles [113]. Sometimes the central portions of certain fields are chosen for the training set, with the remainder of the field used for checking the "generalization" capability of the categorizer [63].

The training areas are frequently augmented by including areas where "preliminary" classification runs show poor recognition rates [202], [131]. In view of the variability of widely spaced samples, this procedure usually requires the specification of several subclasses for each category of interest [131], [113]. Automatic mode determination by means of clustering algorithms has also been attempted with fair success [201], [63], [6], [65], [66].

The ratio of the size of the training set to the size of the test set has been steadily decreasing as it is discovered that in multispectral recognition the quantity of samples collected in any given field is much less important than the judicious inclusion of small "representative" regions along, and particularly across, the flight line. Though excellent results have been obtained under favorable conditions over large areas up to 90 mi away from the training fields, even these experiments show that the experimenter must ever be on the alert to change the configuration of training and test fields should an inopportune fluff of cloud intrude on the original experimental design [88].

Much effort has been devoted to the selection of suitable subsets of the spectral channels in order to increase throughput. Among the feature selection methods tested are principal component analysis, divergence, and minimax pairwise linear discriminants. All reports agree that four to six channels perform as well as the full set of ten or twelve (and sometimes better, owing to the use of suboptimal classifiers), but, as expected, the best subset varies from application to application. Linear combinations of channels have also been used, with similar results, but the necessary computation can be justified only for problems involving a large number of categories [116], [117], [140], [64]–[66].

Theoretical attempts to relate the laboratory-observed spectral characteristics of plants to remote observations through the atmosphere are discussed in [51] and [91].

Michigan and Purdue seem to agree that quadratic decision boundaries derived from the maximum likelihood ratio based on Gaussian assumptions constitute the preferred method of classification. Almost all of the experiments discussed in this section made use of this technique, though linear decisions, sequential tree logic, potential functions, and nearest neighbor classification have been shown to yield very similar results, at least on small samples [193], [63], [158], [65], [66]. The quadratic decision rule is to choose the class (or subclass) i which exhibits the largest value

$$g(x) = (\boldsymbol{x} - \boldsymbol{M}_i)^T \tilde{K}_i (\boldsymbol{x} - \boldsymbol{M}_i) + C_i$$

where $\boldsymbol{x}$ is a multispectral measurement vector; $\boldsymbol{M}_i$ is the class mean vector estimated from the training samples; $\tilde{K}_i$ is the class covariance matrix; and C_i is a constant related to the *a priori* probability of class i.

This decision function can be computed rather rapidly (0.3 ms per six-dimensional sample, eight classes, on an IBM 360/44) by making use of table lookup and sequential search procedures [57].

One means of improving the recognition results achieved by such methods is "per-field" classification, where the individual sample vectors are replaced by the average values of the spectral components in each field. Not only does this ease the computational requirements, but it also reduces the contribution to the error rate of weedy patches, irrigation ditches, and other irregularities [6], [14], [65]. Efforts are underway to develop automatic methods for deriving the field boundaries in order to give real meaning to these per-field figures, but while the majority of the boundary segments may be readily obtained by "local operators," linking them up in the desired topological configuration is a difficult matter [4], [213], [214].

Recognition results range from 90 to 98 percent on a single crop (wheat) versus "background" [131], [88], through 91 percent on eight classes in the same flight line, dropping to 65 percent with only four classes across flight lines [63], to 30 percent on really difficult-to-distinguish crops with training and test samples selected from different fields [70].

In comparing the classification performance of a given system to how well one might be expected to do by chance alone, the *a priori* probabilities which are obtained from the ground truth associated with the training set should be taken into account. On the above four-class problem, for instance, almost half the samples were drawn from soybeans, hence one would reach approximately 50-percent correct recognition without any reference at all to the multispectral information.

Crop-recognition experiments have also been conducted on digitized samples of color and color-IR photography. These experiments are based on sample sizes ranging from minuscule to small: 59 samples used for a comparison of several different recognition algorithms [193]; a few hundred samples from carefully chosen densitometric *transects* (single scans) with six classes (including "low-reflectance," "medium-reflectance," and "high-reflectance" water!), and no differentiation between training and test data [175]; 6000 pixels of training data from 60 000-ft RB-57 multiband and multiemulsion photography, divided into four classes (corn, soybeans, pasture, and trees) with 95-percent accuracy [87]; seven fields from a dissector-digitized photograph (81-percent accuracy on dry cotton, 33-percent accuracy on wet cotton) [70]; and 50 000 samples (about 1 percent of one frame) of automatically digitized Apollo SO-65 photography [127], [5], [6]. Recognition rates on the latter material range from 30 to 70 percent, with about 3 percent of the carefully selected specimen areas used for training, and the rest for test. In comparing the results on satellite data to the performance obtained by airborne sensors on similar tasks, it must be observed that the photographs were scanned at a resolution corresponding to about 200 ft on the ground, and no photometric calibration was attempted.

The largest series of experiments to date are the Summer 1971 corn-blight surveys flown by the Michigan (and other) aircraft and divided up for processing between Michigan and Purdue. Strong United States Department of Agriculture (USDA) logistic support for these experiments was presumably based on the promising results obtained in August and September of 1970 [128], [14]. At the time of writing no published information was available on the 1971 experiments, but the results will be eventually released by the Corn Blight Information Center in Washington, D. C.

B. Terrain Classification Based on Spectral Characteristics

The entry of ground-truth information for crop classification, difficult as it is, is a relatively straightforward matter compared to the problems encountered in other types of terrain classification, because the geometry of cultivated fields tends to be quite simple, and it can be safely assumed that each field corresponds to one crop type or to a standard mixture.

In the absence of similar simplifying features in other problem areas there has been no attempt so far to enter ground-truth information into the computer with a view to objective quantitative evaluation of the results. Instead, classification maps are generated which are visually compared to maps or aerial photographs of the area. The results of such comparisons are invariably "promising."

Among applications which have been tackled so far with the help of the Michigan scanner are: the location of areas of potential sink-hole activity in Florida [130], [33]; a beautifully illustrated and ecologically captivating study of hydrobiological features within the Everglades [110]; and soils mapping in Indiana (where difficulties were encountered in attempting to extend the classification to samples located 4 km from the training set) [114], [206]. In addition, there have been innumerable other projects where prints of the unprocessed MSS output, or simple thresholded versions thereof, have so far proved sufficient for the purpose at hand, but where automatic processing may be eventually required as research findings are translated into operational requirements.

Terrain classification has also been attempted by means of digitized aerial photographs. Here also the difficulty of preparing detailed ground-truth maps for the entire area under investigation presents an insurmountable obstacle to quantitative evaluation of the results. In one study, for example, the investigators had to resort to marking isolated patches containing "marked vegetative zonation or relatively homogeneous stands of a dominant species" with 18-in plastic strips which were discernible in the photographs. This particular experiment is also distinguished by conscientious spectral calibration by means of large colored panels displayed on the ground at flight time and subsequently scanned with the remainder of the imagery [52].

For some other applications of interest, and some novel insights, the reader may consult [40], [109].

C. Shape Detection

The major methodological difference between research aimed at automating the production of land usage maps and research concerned with the classification and recognition of objects on the basis of their geometrical properties (including texture) is an inevitable consequence of the relative scarcity of objects of interest. In multispectral crop classification, for instance, every decision results in a positive contribution, but if we are looking for houses, roads, tornadoes, or eagle's nests, then many more pictures will have to be examined to obtain statistically significant results [78].

To gain some idea of the preliminary (and often unreported) manipulation necessary to obtain acceptable results in this area, we shall examine in some detail a rather extensive feasibility study intended to explore alternative designs for a satellite-based recognition system. Various aspects of this study have been reported in outside publications [44], [45], [103], [46], but most of the information presented here is obtained from an internal contract report [49].

The pictures originally selected by the contracting agency, as representative of the material the satellite-borne classifier would encounter, consisted of 311 black-and-white prints containing 198 lunar features, such as craters, rimas, and rilles, and 323 Nimbus cloud samples of various types.

One hundred and 47 of the better prints were selected for digitization on the basis of *visual examination.* In the cloud pictures, fiducial marks and certain "long black lines" were eliminated by means of a water-color retouching kit. The prints were then rotated *by the experimenters* to align the shadow directions to reduce variation due to changes in the solar illumination. The resolution of the slow-scan television camera used to convert the pictures to an intermediate analog tape was set *by the operator* on each pattern in such a way that the maximum size variation was kept below 1.5:1. The resolution was then further reduced by averaging to 50 by 50 picture elements for the lunar patterns, and 75 by 75 elements for the clouds. The dynamic range was also individually adjusted *by the operator* to let each pattern "fill" the 3-bit digital grey scale.

A file of 1000 training samples and 200 test samples was produced for both moonscapes and clouds by a digital editing process consisting of replicating individual patterns by means of translations of up to 15 percent of the effective frame size and rotations of up to 15°. To avoid letting "difficult" patterns predominate, not all patterns were replicated the same number of times. Due care was taken, however, to avoid including replicas of the same pattern in both the training and test set.

Each pattern was characterized by the output of *property filters* consisting either of intuitively designed measurements or of features derived by statistical means. Eight different classification schemes, gleaned from a literature search resulting in 167 titles, were tried on a subset of the data, but none of the eight methods (forced adaptive learning, "error correction," Madaline, another piecewise-linear method, mean-square error criterion, "iterative design," Bayes weights, and direct estimation of the distributions) proved notably superior to the others. Of greatest benefit to accurate classification, it turned out, was the "reduced aperture" technique, whereby insignificant portions of the picture are eliminated prior to the feature-extraction stage! The best combination of features, decision methods, and reduced aperture consistently achieved better than 90-percent correct classification on a half-dozen different ways of grouping the patterns into classes.

Experiments were also conducted on pattern segmentation. The data for these tests consisted of side-by-side montages of cloud patterns which had been correctly classified in isolated form. In this way it was possible to demonstrate that the *input* to the decision units on successive segments generally gives a reliable indication of the location of the boundary between the different cloud types (at least as long as the progression of segments is limited to the direction perpendicular to the boundary)!

Hardware configurations were evaluated for parallel/analog, sequential/hybrid, and sequential/digital methods of implementation. While all three configurations were capable of meeting the desired real-time operation criterion under the particular choice of assumptions, the last design showed a definite advantage in terms of *weight.*

Studies in a similar vein, but with more emphasis on parallel methods of implementation, have been conducted for several years by Hawkins and his colleagues [81]–[83]. The objects of interest here, extracted from aerial photographs, are orchards, oiltank farms, woods, railroad yards, roads, and lakes. The photographs were scanned with a flying-spot scanner under program control (PDP-7), with examples of various local feature-extraction operations, such as matched filters, gradient detection, contrast enhancement, and thresholding demonstrated by means of electrooptical techniques.

Another point of view altogether, but surprisingly similar conclusions regarding the feature-extraction stage, are represented by the M.I.T. pilot study of a semiautonomous Mars Rover. The input to this low-resolution system is provided by a stereo television system under control of a PDP-9, but the output, following a hierarchical multilayer model of the vertebrate visual subsystem, remains in the realm of conjecture [200].

A good description of the application of Golay rotation-invariant hexagonal-neighborhood logic to both local and global feature extraction, including measurements of object diameter, area, perimeter, curvature, and particle counts, is given in [108]. Experimental results are presented on two 500 by 500 arrays extracted from aerial photographs.

Diverse analog and digital methods for implementing texture measurements are considered in [204]. Haralick in a very thorough series of experiments, has classified 54 scenes (each $\frac{1}{8}$ by $\frac{1}{8}$ inch in area) from 1:20000 scale photographs into 9 classes on the basis of the statistical dependence of the grey levels in adjoining picture elements. He compared the results obtained (average 70 percent correct) to those of five trained photointerpreters using the entire 9 by 9 in photograph (81 percent correct) [76].

An early experiment to detect broken and continuous cloud cover in Tiros imagery on the basis of texture is reported in [178]. Local operators containing 5 by 5 picture elements were used for purely textural characteristics, with 15 by 15 element operators for distinction based on size and elongation. A follow-up study introduces additional criteria such as amount of edge per unit area and number of grey-level extrema per unit area [181], [182].

A good review of cloud-cover work, emphasizing the difference between classifying a given segment and producing a cloud map, can be found in [199]. This paper also presents new heuristic algorithms for delineating cloudy regions.

D. Nonsupervised Classification

Nonsupervised learning or *cluster seeking* are names applied to methods of data analysis where *only* the observed values are used explicitly to group samples according to some intrinsic measure of similarity. It is true that closer examination inevitably reveals that some additional information, such as the expected number of groups and some suitable metric, was used by the experimenter to achieve the desired results, but the nature of the ground-truth information associated with the samples enters the algorithm only in a circuitous manner.

In remote-sensing experiments this approach has been used 1) to alleviate the problem of multimodal probability distributions in supervised classification methods, 2) to circumvent the need for *a priori* selection of training samples, 3) to extract the boundaries between homogeneous regions in multispectral arrays, and 4) to condense the amount of information stored or transmitted.

Experiments showing the application of nonparametric clustering techniques to discover the "natural constituents" of the distributions characterizing the various terrain classes are described in [63] and [65] on multispectral scanner observations and in [5], [6], [87] on digitized multiband photographs. We learn, for example, that *mode estimation* yields a good approximation to the mean values of the spectral components in individual fields, or that seven different subclasses of "bare soil" were found in a certain batch of data, but there is not sufficient information presented to determine how much clustering reduces the error rate in comparison to using a single quadratic boundary per class, or alternatively, whether clustering permits the substitution of simpler boundary equations. In each of the papers mentioned the clustering procedure is conducted on an even smaller number of samples than the main supervised classification experiments, because the algorithms used so far tend to be very complicated and time-consuming, frequently involving repeated merging and partitioning of the tentative cluster assignments.

When the clustering technique is used on all of the available observations without any regard to the class descriptions, then it may be considered equivalent to a stratified or two-stage sampling design insuring the efficient collection of the ground-truth information [119], [1]. In other words, the classifier is allowed to designate the appropriate areas for the collection of class-identifying information on the basis of the data itself, rather than on *a priori* considerations. The necessary ground truth may then be collected after the analysis rather than before, reducing the risk that the areas sampled may not be typical of significant portions of the data. One of the few complete experiments testing this idea is described in [193], but the test data unfortunately contained only a few dozen digitized samples. A somewhat larger experiment on nine classes extracted from aerial color photographs by means of a trichromatic microdensitometer is reported in [189]; here the clustering was performed by inspection on two-dimensional projections of the three-dimensional measurement space pending the completion of suitable programmed algorithms. Finally, 2500 samples of high-altitude photography were classified by clustering in [87], but since the study was oriented toward other objectives, these results were not evaluated in detail.

The extraction of boundary information for registration or other purposes is even more difficult on noisy multispectral data than on black-and-white images. A comparison of gradient techniques with clustering is reported in [214], with both methods applied to congruencing data obtained at different times in [4]. A related problem is the conversion of gray-scale imagery to binary arrays by thresholding; here a clustering technique oriented towards the joint occurrence of certain gray-level values in adjacent picture elements has been shown to yield better results than thresholds based on the intensity histogram alone [180].

Both iterative and single-pass clustering algorithms have been thoroughly investigated by Haralick and his colleagues for the purpose of discovering data structures in remote-sensing observations that may reduce storage and transmission requirements for such data. The single-pass algorithms, tried on 80×80 microdensitometric samples of three-band aerial photography, are based on a chaining technique operating in either the image space or in the measurement space [74]. The iterative technique depends on preliminary mapping of the data in a high-dimensional binary space and adjusting the coefficients of prototype vectors to minimize the least square deviation; it proved relatively unsuccessful in reaching an acceptable error rate in compacting 27 000 twelve-dimensional multispectral observations of Yellowstone National Park [75]. An exhaustive experimental investigation of various aspects of the performance of the iterative clustering algorithm on five distributions (three arbitrary, and two tenuously connected with remote observations) is described at length in [46], and a theoretical analysis of the same family of algorithms is presented in [42].

VI. Conclusions

It would appear that few of the results demonstrated to date warrant our sanguine expectations regarding *automatic* processing of the output of the first generation of earth resources survey satellites. Even making allowances for the ever-accelerating march of science, some of the current preparations are uncomfortably reminiscent of the early attempts at automatic translation and "universal" pattern recognition.

The first grounds for scepticism concern the question of instrumentation. Is it really possible to measure consistently the reflectance of 4000 by 4000 distinct picture elements with satellite-borne vidicon cameras and multispectral sensors when meticulously tuned electronic scanning equipment (as opposed to mechanical microdensitometers) in image processing laboratories throughout the country yield only about one quarter as many usable points? The Michigan scanner has an effective transverse resolution of 220 lines (though the optical system is nearly five times as good), the ITOS camera system has barely 800 lines; improvements in this area have not, historically, taken order-of-magnitude jumps. Even if specifications are met, how much can we learn from 200 by 200-ft picture elements?

In regard to the crucial question of automatic registration, very little can be said until the accuracy of the satellite attitude and ephemeris information and the magnitude of the geometric and photometric degradation are firmly established. It should be noted, however, that so far no completely automatic techniques have been developed even for the registration of weather satellite imagery, where far greater errors could be tolerated. Although it is frequently implied that the major obstacle to the implementation of digital registration methods based on correlation is the inordinate amount of computation required, none of the work performed to date indicates that the required accuracy could be attained at *any* cost.

Many of our troubles can, of course, be attributed to the lack of representative raw data. Whatever will be the significant characteristics of the ERTS and Skylab coverage, it is safe to predict that it will bear little resemblance to the digitized photographs and low-altitude multispectral observations which are currently available for experimentation. The weather satellite pictures, which are in many ways most representative, are not nearly detailed enough for most of the suggested earth resources applications. Although there have been attempts at simulating the scale and resolution of the expected data [15], these simulations did not include some of the essential features of the electronic data-collection systems, and were, in any case, largely ignored by the image-processing community.

A related source of frustration is due to our failure to take advantage of the economies of scale resulting from large well-coordinated efforts. The tendency seems to be for each research group to attempt to build its own "complete" image-processing system independently of what may be available elsewhere. Since such an undertaking exceeds the resources of most laboratories, a small part of the overall problem is selected for special attention, with the remainder treated in cursory fashion without regard for previous work on the subject. If, for instance, the selected topic is feature extraction, then the feature extraction algorithms are exercised with minimal preprocessing and normalization of the data, and without any attempt at relating the performance achieved to the manner in which the results are to be utilized. Yet chances are that, as in any large programming effort, the "interface" problems will in the end dwarf the contributions necessary to develop the individual modules.

Leaving aside for the moment the essential but so far tremulous infrastructure in image registration and restoration, we come to the more glamorous aspects of automatic data classification. Without further insistence on the many sins in experimental design (i.e., lack of separate training and test sets, and failure to select the test data *independently* of the training data), and on the widespread and arrant disregard for the statistical rules of inference governing small-sample behavior, we shall take at face value the 60-, 75-, and 90-percent recognition rates achieved on favorable test sites on a half-dozen carefully selected terrain categories or crop species. Studies of the error rates tolerable in various applications would leave little doubt that such performance levels, though perhaps not totally useless, can be reached far more economically by means of other than satellitic surveillance, but seldom in the pattern-recognition literature is there any reference to the minimum acceptable classification rates.

Perhaps an absolute standard is too much to ask. Yet, with only a handful of major test sites under study for automatic classification, are there any published comparisons of relative recognition rates obtained by *different* investigators under similar circumstances? The same photographs and printouts appear in publication after publication, but a sufficient number of conditions are changed in each study to render all comparison meaningless.

Significant progress in this area cannot be expected until sophisticated interactive systems are developed for entering ground-truth information directly in the reference frame of the digitized images. This, in turn, requires high-resolution gray-scale display devices, with attendant software facilities for pinpointing landmarks and outlining boundaries, implementing projective and other transformations, preparing mosaics, comparing the images with digitized maps, serial photographs and other prestored information, and in general, easing the burden of programming the sundry necessary details.

These observations are not meant to imply that digital methods will not play an important role in processing the torrent of data that will soon be released by the survey satellites. It is likely, however, that the computer will for a time continue to be relegated to such relatively unexciting tasks as format conversion, "cosmetic" transformations, merging the image stream and the ephemeris and attitude information, correction of systematic distortions, keeping track of the distribution list and other bookkeeping chores, while interpretation of the images is left to the ultimate user. The prototype operation is likely to be modeled on that of the successful and efficient National Environmental Satellite Center, where over one hundred frames are smoothly processed and assembled daily, with dozens of computer products distributed on a routine basis to the four corners of the globe.

The situation is more encouraging with regard to data collected by relatively low-flying aircraft. Here the scattering effects of the atmosphere are not quite so debilitating, the sensor configuration can be optimized for specific objectives, the flights can, in principle, be timed for the best combination of illumination and terrain conditions, and bore-sighted cameras and navigational subsystems can be used to ensure adequate ground location of the electronic images. The yield of usable pictures should then be sufficiently high to allow fairly sophisticated automatic analysis of the data in selected applications. An example of a plausible if modest candidate for digital processing is the bispectral airborne forest-fire detection system described in [86].

In spite of the many difficulties, the long-range objective must of course remain the eventual combination of spaceborne and airborne sensor systems with conventional ground observations in a grand design for a worldwide hierarchical data-collection system enabling more rational utilization of our planet's plentiful but by no means unlimited natural resources.

We conclude with a plea for more cohesive exploitation of the talent and funds already committed, increased exchange of data sets in a readily usable form, more collaboration and standardization in image-processing software, formulation of realistic goals, and persistence.

References

[1] R. C. Aldrich, "Space photos for land use and forestry," *Photogrammetric. Eng.* (*Special Issue on Remote Sensing*), vol. 37, pp. 389–401, 1971.

[2] H. C. Andrews, *Computer Techniques and Image Processing.* New York: Academic Press, 1970.

[3] P. E. Anuta, "Digital registration of multispectral video imagery," *SPIE J.*, vol. 7, pp. 168–175, 1969.

[4] ——, "Spatial recognition of multispectral and multitemporal digital imagery using fast Fourier transform techniques," *IEEE Trans. Geosci. Electron.*, vol. GE-8, pp. 353–368, Oct. 1970.

[5] P. E. Anuta, S. J. Kristof, D. W. Levandowski, R. B. MacDonald, and T. L. Phillips, "Crop, soil and geological mapping from digitized multispectral satellite photography," in *Proc. 7th Int. Symp. Remote Sens. Environ.* (Ann Arbor, Mich.), pp. 1983–2016, 1971.

[6] P. E. Anuta and R. B. MacDonald, "Crop surveys from multiband satellite photography using digital techniques," *J. Remote Sens. Environ.*, vol. 2, pp. 53–67, 1971.

[7] R. J. Arguello, H. R. Sellner, and J. A. Stuller, "Transfer function compensation of sampled imagery," in *Proc. Symp. Two-Dimensional Image Processing* (Columbia, Mo.), pp. 11-2-1–11-2-12, 1971.

[8] R. H. Asendorf, "The remote reconnaissance of extraterrestrial environments," in *Pictorial Pattern Recognition*, Cheng *et al.*, Eds. Washington, D. C.: Thompson, 1968, pp. 223–238.

[9] R. Bakis and P. G. Langley, "A method for determining the height of forest trees automatically from digitized 70 mm color aerial photographs," in *Proc. 7th Int. Symp. Remote Sens. Environ.* (Ann Arbor, Mich.), pp. 705–714, 1971.

[10] R. Bakis, M. A. Wesley, and P. M. Will, "Digital image processing for the Earth Resources Technology Satellite data," in *Proc. IFIP Congress 71* (Ljubljana, Yugoslavia), 1971.

[11] ——, "Digital correction of geometric and radiometric errors in ERTS data," in *Proc. 7th Int. Symp. Remote Sens. Environ.* (Ann Arbor, Mich.), pp. 1427–1436, 1971.

[12] G. Barna, "Frame type imaging sensors," in *Proc. Princeton Univ. Conf. Aerospace Methods for Revealing Earth's Resources* (Princeton, N. J.), p. 1.1, June 1970.

[13] D. Barnea and H. F. Silverman, "A class of algorithms for fast digital image registration," *IEEE Trans. Comput.*, vol. C-21, pp. 179–186, Feb. 1972; also IBM Res. Rep. RC-3358, 1971.

[14] M. E. Bauer, R. M. Swain, R. I. Mroczynski, P. E. Anuta, and R. B. MacDonald, "Detection of southern corn leaf blight by remote sensing techniques," in *Proc. 7th Int. Symp. Remote Sens. Environ.* (Ann Arbor, Mich.), pp. 693–704, 1971.

[15] D. J. Belcher, E.E. Hardy, and E.S. Phillips, "Land use classification with simulated satellite photography," *USDA Econ. Res. Serv.*, Agriculture Information Bull. 352, 1971.

[16] R. Bernstein, H. Branning, and D. G. Ferneyhough, "Geometric and radiometric correction of high resolution images by digital image processing techniques," presented at the IEEE Annu. Int. Geoscience Electronics Symp., Washington, D. C., 1971.

[17] R. Bernstein and H. F. Silverman, "Digital techniques for Earth resource image data processing," presented at the AIAA 8th Annu. Meeting, Sept. 1971; also IBM–FSD Tech. Rep. FSC 71-6017, Gaithersburg, Md.

[18] F. C. Billingsley, "Digital image processing at JPL," in *SPIE Computerized Imaging Techniques Seminar* (Washington, D. C.), pp. II 1–10, 1967.

[19] F. C. Billingsley, A. F. H. Goetz, and J. N. Lindsley, "Color differentiation by computer image processing," *Photogr. Sci. Eng.*, vol. 14, pp. 28–35, Jan.–Feb. 1970.

[20] F. C. Billingsley, "Photo reconnaissance applications of computer processing of images," in *Proc. Symp. Two-Dimensional Image Processing* (Columbia, Mo.), pp. 7-2-1–7-2-12, 1971.

[21] W. T. Blackband, Ed., "Advanced techniques for aerospace surveillance," Advisory Group for Aerospace Research and Development (AGARD), U. S. Dep. Commerce, NADO ASTIA Doc. AD 73887.

[22] P. Bock, "Space acquired data: Hydrological requirements," in *Proc. Princeton Univ. Conf. Aerospace Methods for Revealing Earth's Resources* (Princeton, N. J.), p. 14.1, June 1970.

[23] A. L. Booth and V. R. Taylor, "Meso-scale archive and products of digitized video data from ESSA satellite," *Bull. Amer. Meteorol. Soc.*, vol. 50, pp. 431–438, 1969; also U. S. Dep. Commerce Tech. Memo. NESCTM-9.

[24] R. E. Bradford and J. F. Gross, "Conditioning of digitized TIROS and ESSA satellite vidicon data," in *SPIE Computerized Imaging Techniques Seminar* (Washington, D. C.), pp. VII 1–8, 1967.

[25] J. Braithwaite, "Airborne multispectral sensing and applications," *SPIE J.*, vol. 8, pp. 139–144, 1970.

[26] C. L. Bristor, W. M. Callicott, and R. E. Bradford, "Operational processing of satellite cloud pictures by computer," *Mon. Weather Rev.*, vol. 94, pp. 515–527, 1966.

[27] C. L. Bristor, "Computer processing of satellite cloud pictures," U. S. Dep. Commerce, Washington, D. C., Tech. Memo. NESCTM-3, 1968.

[28] ——, "The earth location of geostationary satellite imagery," *Pattern Recogn.*, vol. 2, pp. 269–277, 1970.

[29] C. L. Bristor and J. A. Leese, "Operational processing of ITOS scanning radiometer data," presented at IEEE Int. Conf. Telemetry, 1971, NESC Preprint.

[30] E. B. Butt and J. W. Snively, "The Pax II picture processing system," Univ. of Md. Comput. Sci. Cen., Rep. 68-67, 1969.

[31] G. C. Cheng, R. S. Ledley, D. K. Pollock, and A. Rosenfeld, Eds., *Pictorial Pattern Recognition.* Washington, D. C.: Thompson, 1968.

[32] L. J. Cihacek and J. V. Drew, "Infrared photos can map soils," *Farm, Ranch and Home Quart.*, Univ. of Nebr., pp. 4–8, Spring 1970.

[33] A. E. Coker, R. E. Marshall, and N. S. Thomson, "Application of multispectral data processing techniques to the discrimination of sinkhole activity in Florida," in *Proc. 6th Int. Symp. Remote Sens. Environ.* (Ann Arbor, Mich.), pp. 65–78, 1969.

[34] A. P. Colvocoresses, "Image resolution for ERTS, SKYLAB, and GEMINI/APOLLO," *Photogrammetr. Eng.*, vol. 37, 1972.

[35] R. N. Colwell, "The extraction of data from aerial photographs by human and mechanical means," *Photogrammetria*, vol. 20, pp. 211–228, 1965.

[36] ——, "Determining the usefulness of space photography for natural resource inventory," in *Proc. 5th Int. Symp. Remote Sens. Environ.* (Ann Arbor, Mich.), pp. 249–289, 1968.

[37] R. N. Colwell and J. D. Lent, "The inventory of Earth resources on enhanced multiband space photography," in *Proc. 6th Int. Symp. Remote Sens. Environ.* (Ann Arbor, Mich.), pp. 133–143, 1969.

[38] R. N. Colwell, "The future for remote sensing of agricultural, forest, and range resources," presented before the Comm. Science and Astronautics, U. S. House of Representatives, Jan. 26, 1972.

[39] J. J. Cook and J. E. Colwell, "Michigan M7 scanner," Cent. for Remote Sensing Informat. and Analysis, Willow Run Labs., Univ. of Mich., Ann Arbor, Mich., Newsletter, 1971.

[40] M. Cook, "Remote sensing in the Isles of Langerhans," in *Proc. 7th Int. Symp. Remote Sens. Environ.* (Ann Arbor, Mich.), pp. 905–918, 1971.

[41] D. S. Cooley, "Applications of remote sensing and operational weather forecasting," in *Proc. 7th Int. Symp. Remote Sens. Environ.* (Ann Arbor, Mich.), pp. 941–950, 1971.

[42] P. W. Cooper, "Theoretical investigation of unsupervised learning techniques," NASA Contract NAS 12-697, Final Rep., 1970.

[43] R. B. Crane and M. M. Spencer, "Preprocessing techniques to reduce atmospheric and sensor variability in multispectral scanner data," in *Proc. 7th Int. Symp. Remote Sens. Environ.* (Ann Arbor, Mich.), pp. 1345–1356, 1971.

[44] E. M. Darling and R. D. Joseph, "An experimental investigation of video pattern recognition," in *Pictorial Pattern Recognition*, Cheng *et al.*, Eds. Washington, D. C.: Thompson, 1968, pp. 457–469.

[45] ——, "Pattern recognition from satellite altitudes," *IEEE Trans. Syst. Sci. Cybern.*, vol. SSC-4, pp. 38–47, Mar. 1968.

[46] E. M. Darling and J. G. Raudseps, "Non-parametric unsupervised learning with application to image classification," *Pattern Recog.*, vol. 2, pp. 313–336, 1970.

[47] A. G. DeCotiis and E. Conlan, "Cloud information in three spatial dimensions using thermal imagery and vertical temperature profile data," in *Proc. 7th Int. Symp. Remote Sens. Environ.* (Ann Arbor, Mich.), pp. 595–606, 1971.

[48] J. E. Dornbach, "Manned systems for sensing Earth's resources," in *Proc. Princeton Univ. Conf. Aerospace Methods for Revealing Earth's Resources* (Princeton, N. J.), p. 6.1, June 1970.

[49] Douglas Aircraft Co., "Research on the utilization of pattern recognition techniques to identify and classify objects in video data," NASA Contract Rep. CR-999, 1968.

[50] J. A. Dunne, "Mariner 1969 television image processing," *Pattern Recogn.*, vol. 2, pp. 261–268, 1970.
[51] D. L. Earing and I. W. Ginsberg, "A spectral discrimination technique for agricultural applications," in *Proc. 6th Int. Symp. Remote Sens. Environ.* (Ann Arbor, Mich.), pp. 21–32, 1969.
[52] W. G. Egan and M. E. Hair, "Automated delineation of wetlands in photographic remote sensing," in *Proc. 7th Int. Symp. Remote Sens. Environ.* (Ann Arbor, Mich.), pp. 2231–2252, 1971.
[53] R. M. Endlich, D. E. Wolf, D. J. Hall, and A. E. Brain, "Use of pattern recognition techniques for determining cloud motion from sequences of satellite photographs," *J. Appl. Meteorol.*, vol. 10, pp. 105–117, 1971.
[54] W. G. Eppler, "Accuracy of determining sensor boresight position during aircraft flight test," in *Proc. 6th Int. Symp. Remote Sens. Environ.* (Ann Arbor, Mich.), pp. 205–226, 1969.
[55] W. G. Eppler and R. D. Merrill, "Relating remote sensor signals to ground-truth information," *Proc. IEEE*, vol. 57, pp. 665–675, Apr. 1969.
[56] W. G. Eppler, D. L. Loe, E. L. Wilson, S. L. Whitley, and R. J. Sachen, "Interactive display/graphics systems for remote sensor data analysis," in *3rd Annu. Earth Resources Program Review* (NASA-MSC, Houston, Tex.), p. 44-1, Dec. 1970.
[57] W. G. Eppler, C. A. Helmke, and R. H. Evans, "Table look-up approach to pattern recognition," in *Proc. 7th Int. Symp. Remote Sens. Environ.* (Ann Arbor, Mich.), pp. 1415–1426, 1971.
[58] W. G. Eppler, D. L. Loe, E. L. Wilson, S. L. Whitley, and R. J. Sachen, "Interactive system for remote sensor data analysis," in *Proc. 7th Int. Symp. Remote Sens. Environ.* (Ann Arbor, Mich.), pp. 1293–1306, 1971.
[59] W. A. Fischer, "User needs in geology and cartology," in *Proc. Princeton Univ. Conf. Aerospace Methods for Revealing Earth's Resources* (Princeton, N. J.), p. 11.1, June 1970.
[60] J. C. Fletcher, "NASA's long-range earth resources survey program," presented before the Comm. Science and Astronautics, U. S. House of Representatives, Jan. 26, 1972.
[61] H. T. Frey, "Agricultural application of remote sensing—The potential from space platforms," USDA Agricultural Information Bull. N-328, Washington, D. C.
[62] A. W. Frutkin, "Status and prospects of international Earth Resources Satellite programs," in *Proc. Princeton Univ. Conf. Aerospace Methods for Revealing Earth's Resources* (Princeton, N. J.), p. 17.1, June 1970.
[63] K. S. Fu, D. A. Landgrebe, and T. L. Phillips, "Information processing of remotely sensed agricultural data," *Proc. IEEE*, vol. 57, pp. 639–653, Apr. 1969.
[64] K. S. Fu, P. J. Min, and T. J. Li, "Feature selection in pattern recognition," *IEEE Trans. Syst. Sci. Cybern.*, vol. SSC-6, pp. 33–39, Jan. 1970.
[65] K. S. Fu, "On the application of pattern recognition techniques to remote sensing problems," Purdue Univ. School of Elect. Eng. Rep. TR-EE 71-73, 1971.
[66] ——, "Pattern recognition in remote sensing," in *Proc. 9th Allerton Conf. Circuits and Systems Theory* (Univ. of Illinois), Oct. 1971.
[67] T. A. George, "Unmanned spacecraft for surveying Earth's resources," in *Proc. Princeton Univ. Conf. Aerospace Methods for Revealing Earth's Resources* (Princeton, N. J.), p. 7.1, June 1970.
[68] F. A. Godshall, "The analysis of cloud amount for satellite data," in *Trans. N. Y. Acad. Sci.*, Ser. 2, vol. 33, pp. 436–453, 1971.
[69] I. L. Goldberg, "Design considerations for a multispectral scanner for ERTS," in *Proc. Purdue Centennial Year Symp. Information Theory* (Lafayette, Ind.), pp. 672–680, 1969.
[70] V. W. Goldsworthy, E. E. Nelson, and S. S. Viglione, "Automatic classification of agricultural crops from multispectral and multicamera imagery," presented at Symp. Automatic Photointerpretation and Recognition, Washington, D. C., 1971; also McDonnell Douglas Astronautics Co., Rep. WD.
[71] H. M. Gurk, C. R. Smith, and P. Wood, "Data handling for Earth Resources Satellite data," in *Proc. 6th Int. Symp. Remote Sens. Environ.* (Ann Arbor, Mich.), pp. 247–259, 1969.
[72] H. M. Gurk, "User data processing requirements," in *Proc. Princeton Univ. Conf. Aerospace Methods for Revealing Earth's Resources* (Princeton, N. J.), p. 9.1, June 1970.
[73] D. J. Hall, R. M. Endlich, D. E. Wolf, and A. E. Brain, "Objective methods for registering landmarks and determining cloud motions from satellite data," in *Proc. Symp. Two-Dimensional Image Processing* (Columbia, Mo.), pp. 10-1-1–10-1-7, 1971.
[74] R. M. Haralick and G. L. Kelly, "Pattern recognition with measurement space and spatial clustering for multiple images," *Proc. IEEE*, vol. 57, pp. 654–665, Apr. 1969.
[75] R. M. Haralick and I. Dinstein, "An iterative clustering procedure," presented at EIA Symp. Automatic Photointerpretation and Recognition, Baltimore, Md., Dec. 1970; also in *Proc. 9th IEEE Symp. Adaptive Processes* (Austin, Tex.), Dec. 1970.
[76] R. M. Haralick and D. E. Anderson, "Texture-tone study with application to digitized imagery," presented at Symp. Automatic Photointerpretation and Recognition, Washington, D. C.; also Univ. of Kansas, CRES Tech. Rep. 182 2, 1971.
[77] R. M. Haralick, "Data processing at the University of Kansas," presented at the *4th Ann. Earth Resources Program Review* (NASA-MSC, Houston, Tex.) 1972.
[78] T. J. Harley, L. N. Kanal, and N. C. Randall, "System considerations for automatic imagery screening," in *Pictorial Pattern Recognition*, Cheng *et al.*, Eds. Washington, D. C.: Thompson, 1968, pp. 15–32.
[79] L. D. Harmon and K. C. Knowlton, "Picture processing by computer," *Science*, vol. 164, pp. 19–29, 1969.
[80] J. C. Harris, "Computer processing of atmospherically degraded images," in *SPIE Computerized Imaging Techniques Seminar* (Washington, D. C.), pp. xv 1–5, 1967.
[81] J. K. Hawkins, G. T. Elerding, K. W. Bixby, and P. A. Haworth, "Automatic shape detection for programmed terrain classification," in *Proc. Soc. Photo-Optical Instrument. Eng., Filmed Data and Computers Seminar*, Boston, (Mass.), 1966.
[82] J. K. Hawkins and G. T. Elerding, "Image feature extraction for automatic terrain classification," in *SPIE Computerized Imaging Techniques Seminar* (Washington, D. C.), pp. vi 1–8, 1967.
[83] J. K. Hawkins, "Parallel electro-optical picture processing," in *Pictorial Pattern Recognition*, Cheng *et al.*, Eds. Washington, D. C.: Thompson, 1968, pp. 373–386.
[84] N. M. Herbst and P. M. Will, "Design of an experimental laboratory for signal and image processing," in *Advanced Computer Graphics*, Parslow and Green, Eds. New York: Plenum, 1971.
[85] ——, "An experimental laboratory for pattern recognition and signal processing," *Commun. Ass. Comput. Mach.*, vol. 15, pp. 231–244, 1972.
[86] S. M. Hirsch, F. A. Madden, and R. F. Kruckeberg, "The bispectral forest fire detection system," in *Proc. 7th Int. Symp. Remote Sens. Environ.* (Ann Arbor, Mich.), pp. 2253–2272, 1971.
[87] R. M. Hoffer, P. E. Anuta, and T. L. Phillips, "Application of ADP techniques to multiband and multiemulsion digitized photography," in *Proc. Amer. Soc. Photogrammetry 37th Ann. Meeting* (Washington, D. C.), 1972.
[88] R. M. Hoffer and F. E. Goodrick, "Variables and automatic classification over extended remote sensing test sites," in *Proc. 7th Int. Symp. Remote Sens. Environ.* (Ann Arbor, Mich.), pp. 1967–1982, 1971.
[89] F. Holderman and H. Kazmierczak, "Generation of line drawings from grey-scale pictures," Tech. Rep. Res. Group for Information Processing and Transmission of the Univ. of Karlsruhe, under German Ministry of Defense Contract T 0230/92340/91354.
[90] R. A. Holmes, "An agricultural remote sensing information system," in *EASCON '68 Rec.*, pp. 142–149, 1968.
[91] R. A. Holmes and R. B. MacDonald, "The physical basis of system design for remote sensing in agriculture," *Proc. IEEE*, vol. 57, pp. 629–639, Apr. 1969.
[92] M. R. Holter and W. L. Wolfe, "Optical-mechanical scanning techniques," *Proc. IRE*, vol. 47, pp. 1546–1550, Sept. 1959.
[93] R. Horvath and D. S. Lowe, "Multispectral survey in the Alaskan Arctic," in *Proc. 5th Int. Symp. Remote Sens. Environ.* (Ann Arbor, Mich.), pp. 483–496, 1968.
[94] W. Hovis, "Passive microwave sensors," in *Proc. Princeton Univ. Conf. Aerospace Methods for Revealing Earth's Resources* (Princeton, N. J.), p. 3.1, June 1970.
[95] T. S. Huang and H. L. Kasnitz, "The combined use of digital computer and coherent optics in image processing," in *Computerized Imaging Techniques Seminar* (Washington, D. C.), pp. xvii 1–6, 1967.
[96] T. S. Huang, W. F. Schreiber, and O. J. Tretiak, "Image processing," *Proc. IEEE*, vol. 59, pp. 1586–1609, Nov. 1971.
[97] H. F. Huddlestone and E. H. Roberts, "Use of remote sensing for livestock inventories," in *Proc. 5th Int. Symp. Remota Sens. Environ.* (Ann Arbor, Mich.), pp. 307–323, 1968.
[98] T. A. Hughes, A. R. Shope, and F. S. Baxter, "The USGS automatic orthophoto system," in *Proc. Amer. Soc. Photogrammetry 37th Ann. Meeting* (Washington, D. C.), pp. 792–817, 1971.
[99] B. R. Hunt, "Computational considerations in digital image enhancement," in *Proc. Symp. Two-Dimensional Image Processing* (Columbia, Mo.), pp. 1-4-1–1-4-7, 1971.
[100] J. M. Idelsohn, "A learning system for terrain recognition," *Pattern Recogn.*, vol. 2, pp. 293–302, 1970.
[101] E. G. Johnston, "The PAX II picture processing system," in *Picture Processing and Psychopictorics*, B. S. Lipkin and A. Rosenfeld, Ed. New York: Academic Press, 1970, pp. 427–512.
[102] E. G. Johnston, M. N. Fritz, and A. Rosenfeld, "A study of new image processing techniques," Univ. of Maryland Comput. Sci. Cent. Rep. AFCRL-71-0434, 1971.
[103] R. D. Joseph, R. G. Burge, and S. S. Viglione, "Design of a satellite-borne pattern classifier," in *Proc. Purdue Centennial Year Symp. on Information Theory* (Lafayette, Ind.), 1969, pp. 681–700.
[104] ——, "A compact programmable pattern recognition system," presented at the Symp. Application of Reconnaissance Technology to Monitoring and Planning Environmental Change, Rome, N. Y., 1970; also McDonnell Douglas Astronautics Co. Rep. WD 1409.
[105] R. D. Joseph and S. S. Viglione, "Interactive imagery analysis," in *Proc. Symp. on Two-Dimensional Image Processing* (Columbia, Mo.), pp. 7-1-1–7-1-6, 1971; also McDonnell Douglas Astro-

nautics Co. Paper WD 1754, Aug. 1971.
[106] H. Kazmierczak and F. Holderman, "The Karlsruhe system for automatic photointerpretation," in *Pictorial Pattern Recognition*, Cheng *et al.*, Eds. Washington, D. C.: Thompson, 1968, pp. 45–62.
[107] H. Kazmierczak, "Informationsreduktion und Invarianz-Leistung bei der Bildverarbeitung mit einen Computer," in *Pattern Recognition in Biological and Technical Systems*. New York: Springer, 1971.
[108] S. J. Kishner, "Feature extraction using Golay logic," in *Proc. Perkin-Elmer Symp. on Sampled Images* (Norwalk, Conn.), pp. 7-1–7-8, 1971.
[109] M. C. Kolipinski and A. L. Higer, "On the detection of pesticidal fallout by remote sensing techniques," in *Proc. 6th Int. Symp. Remote Sens. Environ.* (Ann Arbor, Mich.), p. 989, 1969.
[110] M. C. Kolipinski, A. L. Higer, N. S. Thomson, and F. J. Thomson, "Automatic processing of multiband data for inventorying hydrobiological features," in *Proc. 6th Int. Symp. Remote Sens. Environ.* (Ann Arbor, Mich.), pp. 79–96, 1969.
[111] C. L. Korb, "Physical considerations in the channel selection and design specification of an airborne multispectral scanner," in *Proc. Purdue Centennial Year Symp. Information Theory* (Lafayette, Ind.), pp. 646–657, 1969.
[112] F. J. Kriegler, W. Malika, R. F. Nalepka, and W. Richardson, "Preprocessing transformations and their effects on multispectral recognition," in *Proc. 6th Int. Symp. Remote Sens. Environ.* (Ann Arbor, Mich.), pp. 97–132, 1969.
[113] F. J. Kriegler, "Implicit determination of multispectral scanner variation over extended areas," in *Proc. 7th Int. Symp. Remote Sens. Environ.* (Ann Arbor, Mich.), pp. 759–778, 1971.
[114] S. J. Kristof, A. L. Zachary, and J. E. Cipra, "Mapping soil types from multispectral scanner data," in *Proc. 7th Int. Symp. Remote Sens. Environ.* (Ann Arbor, Mich.), pp. 2095–2108, 1971.
[115] D. A. Landgrebe and T. L. Phillips, "A multichannel image data handling system for agricultural remote sensing," in *SPIE Computerized Imaging Techniques Seminar* (Washington, D. C.), pp. xii 1–10, 1967.
[116] D. A. Landgrebe, P. J. Min, P. H. Swain, and K. S. Fu, "The application of pattern recognition techniques to a remote sensing problem," Purdue Univ., Lafayette, Ind., 1968, LARS Information Note 080568.
[117] D. A. Landgrebe, "The development of machine technology processing for Earth resource survey," in *3rd Ann. Earth Resources Program Review* (NASA-MSC, Houston, Tex.), p. 40-1, Dec. 1970.
[118] P. G. Langley, "Automating aerial photointerpretation in forestry —How it works and what it will do for you," in *Proc. Ann. Meet. Soc. Amer. Forestry* (Detroit, Mich.), 1965.
[119] ——, "New multistage sampling techniques using space and aircraft imagery for forest inventory," in *Proc. 6th Int. Symp. Remote Sens. Environ.* (Ann Arbor, Mich.), pp. 1179–1192, 1969.
[120] J. A. Leese, A. L. Booth, and F. A. Godshall, "Archiving and climatological application of meteorological satellite data," U. S. Dep. Commerce, Environ. Sci. Serv. Admin., Rockville, Md., Rep. to the World Meteorol. Org. Comm. for Climatol.; also ESSA Tech. Rep. NESC 53, July 1970.
[121] J. A. Leese, C. S. Novak, and V. R. Taylor, "The determination of cloud pattern motion from geosynchronous satellite image data," *Pattern Recogn.*, vol. 2, pp. 279–292, 1970.
[122] J. A. Leese, C. S. Novak, and B. B. Clark, "An automated technique for obtaining cloud motion for geosynchronous satellite data using cross-correlation," *J. Appl. Meteorol.*, vol. 10, pp. 110–132, 1971.
[123] J. A. Leese, W. Pickel, B. Goddard, and R. Bower, "An experimental model for automated detection, measurement and quality control of sea-surface temperature from ITOS-IR data," in *Proc. 7th Int. Symp. Remote Sens. Environ.* (Ann Arbor, Mich.), pp. 625–646, 1971.
[124] R. R. Legault, "Summary of Michigan Multispectral Investigations program," in *3rd Ann. Earth Resources Program Review* (NASA-MSC, Houston, Tex.) p. 37-1, Dec. 1970.
[125] S. H. Lerman, "Digital image processing at ITEK," in *Proc. Symp. on Two-Dimensional Image Processing* (Columbia, Mo.), pp. 5-5-1–5-5-4, 1971.
[126] D. S. Lowe, "Line scan devices and why use them," in *Proc. 5th Int. Symp. Remote Sens. Environ.* (Ann Arbor, Mich.), pp. 77–100, 1968.
[127] R. B. MacDonald, "The application of remote sensing to corn blight detection and crop yield forecasting," in *3rd Ann. Earth Resources Program Review* (NASA-MSC, Houston, Tex.), p. 28-1, Dec. 1970.
[128] ——, "The application of automatic recognition techniques in the Apollo IX SO-65 experiment," in *3rd Ann. Earth Resources Program Review* (NASA-MSC, Houston, Tex.), p. 39-1, Dec. 1970.
[129] H. Markarian, R. Bernstein, D. G. Ferneyhough, C. E. Gregg, and F. S. Sharp, "Implementation of digital techniques for correcting high resolution images," presented at the ASP-ACSM Fall Convention, Sept. 1971; also IBM-FSD, Gaithersburg, Md., Tech. Rep. FSC 71-6012.
[130] R. E. Marshall, "Application of multispectral recognition techniques for water resources investigations in Florida," in *Proc' Purdue Centennial Year Symp. Information Theory* (Lafayette Ind.), pp. 719–731, 1969.
[131] R. E. Marshall, N. S. Thomson, and F. J. Kriegler, "Use of multispectral recognition techniques for conducting wide area wheat surveys," in *Proc. 6th Int. Symp. Remote Sens. Environ.* (Ann Arbor, Mich.), pp. 3–20, 1969.
[132] R. E. Marshall and F. J. Kriegler, "Multispectral recognition system," in *Proc. 9th IEEE Symp. Adaptive Processes, Decision, and Control* (Austin, Tex.), p. xi-2, 1970.
[133] ——, "An operational multispectral survey system," in *Proc. 7th Int. Symp. Remote Sens. Environ.* (Ann Arbor, Mich.), pp. 2169–2192, 1971.
[134] H. M. Maynard, L. F. Pemberton, and C. W. Swonger, "Application of image processing research to the retrieval of filmed data," in *Proc. Soc. Photo-Optical Instrument. Eng., Filmed Data and Computers Seminar* (Boston, Mass.), pp. xvii 1–10, 1966.
[135] E. P. McClain, "Potential use of Earth satellites for solving problems in oceanography and hydrology," presented at the Nat. Meeting of the Amer. Astronaut. Soc., Las Cruces, N. Mex., 1970.
——, "Application of environmental satellite data to oceanography and hydrology," U. S. Dep. Commerce, Washington, D. C., Tech. Memo. NES CTM 19.
[136] R. B. McEwen, "An evaluation of analog techniques for image registration," U. S. Geol. Survey Prof. Paper 700-D, pp. D305–D311, 1970.
[137] ——, "Geometric calibration of the RBV system for ERTS," in *Proc. 7th Int. Symp. Remote Sens. Environ.* (Ann Arbor, Mich.), pp. 791–808, 1971.
[138] E. P. McMahon, "Earth Resources Technology Satellite system data processing," in *Proc. EASCON 70*, pp. 24–27, 1970.
[139] T. M. Mendel and K. S. Fu, Eds., *Adaptive, Learning and Pattern Recognition Systems*. New York: Academic Press, 1971.
[140] P. J. Min, D. A. Landgrebe, and K. S. Fu, "On feature selection in multiclass pattern recognition," in *Proc. 2nd Ann. Princeton Conf. Information Sciences and Systems*, pp. 453–457, 1968.
[141] R. T. Moore, M. C. Stark, and L. Cahn, "Digitizing pictorial information with a precision optical scanner," *Photogrammetr. Eng.*, vol. 30, pp. 923–931, 1964.
[142] M. Mozer and P. Serge, "High resolution multispectral TV camera systems," in *Proc. 7th Int. Symp. Remote Sens. Environ.* (Ann Arbor, Mich.), pp. 1475–1482, 1971.
[143] J. L. Muerle and D. C. Allen, "Experimental evaluation of techniques of automatic segmentation of objects in a complex scene," in *Pictorial Pattern Recognition*, Cheng *et al.*, Eds. Washington, D. C.: Thompson, 1968, pp. 3–14.
[144] J. L. Muerle, "Some thoughts on texture discrimination by computer," in *Picture Processing and Psychopictorics*. New York: Academic Press, 1970, pp. 371–379.
[145] A. H. Muir, "Some shifting relationships between the user community and the Earth Resources Program," in *Proc. 7th Space Cong.* (Cocoa Beach, Fla.), pp. 2-11–2-14, 1970.
[146] L. E. Mumbower, "Ground data processing considerations for Earth resources information," in *Proc. Princeton Univ. Conf. Aerospace Methods for Revealing Earth's Resources* (Princeton, N. J.), p. 8.1, June 1970.
[147] R. Nagel and A. Rosenfeld, "Ordered search techniques in template matching," *Proc. IEEE* (Lett.), vol. 60, p. 242, Feb. 1972; also Univ. of Maryland Comput. Sci. Cent. Rep. TR-166.
[148] R. F. Nalepka, "Investigation of multispectral discrimination techniques," Infrared and Optics Lab., Inst. Sci. and Technol. of the Univ. of Michigan, Ann Arbor, Mich., Rep. 2264-12-F, 1970.
[149] R. Narasimhan, "Labeling schemata and syntactic description of pictures," *Inform. Contr.*, vol. 7, pp. 151–179, 1964.
[150] NASA-MSFC, "Skylab in-flight experiments," Skylab Program Summary Description, June 1971.
[151] NASA, "Earth photographs from Gemini VI through XII," Washington, D. C., NASA SP-171, 1969.
[152] NASA, "Apollo-9 photographic plotting and indexing report," NASA-MSC, Mapping Sci. Lab. for Earth Resour. Div., Sci. and Appl. Directorate, Houston, Tex., 1969.
[153] NASA, NASA-MSC Earth Resour. Aircraft Program, Houston, Tex., Mission 89 Summary Rep., 1969.
[154] NASA, "Remote sensing of Earth resources: A literature survey with indexes," NASA Publ. SP-7036, 1970.
[155] NASA, "Earth resources research facility index, vol. I—Documentary data, vol. II—Sensor data," Houston, Tex., NASA-MSC-02576, 1971.
[156] R. Nathan, "Picture enhancement for the Moon, Mars and Man," in *Pictorial Pattern Recognition*, Cheng *et al.*, Eds. Washington, D. C.: Thompson, 1968, pp. 239–266.
[157] ——, "Spatial frequency filtering," in *Picture Processing and Psychopictorics*, B. S. Lipkin and A. Rosenfeld, Eds. New York: Academic Press, 1970, pp. 151–163.
[158] R. Newman and B. Reisine, "Practical applications of sequential pattern recognition techniques," in *Proc. 7th Space Cong.* (Cocoa Beach, Fla.), pp. 2.1–2.9, 1970.

[159] V. T. Norwood, "Optimization of a multispectral scanner for ERTS," in *Proc. 6th Int. Symp. Remote Sens. Environ.* (Ann Arbor, Mich.), pp. 227–236, 1969.
[160] ——, "Scanning type imaging sensors," in *Proc. Princeton Univ. Conf. Aerospace Methods for Revealing Earth's Resources* (Princeton, N. J.), p. 2.1, June 1970.
[161] National Research Council (Comm. on Remote Sensing for Agricultural Purposes), *Remote Sensing with Special Reference to Agriculture and Forestry.* Washington, D. C.: Natl. Acad. Sci., 1970.
[162] D. O'Handley and W. B. Green, "Recent developments in digital image processing at the Image Processing Laboratory at the Jet Propulsion Laboratory," *Proc. IEEE*, vol. 60, pp. 821–828, July 1972.
[163] K. W. Olson, "An operational pattern recognition system," in *Pictorial Pattern Recognition*, Cheng *et al.*, Eds. Washington, D. C.: Thompson, 1968, pp. 63–73.
[164] R. F. Owens, R. W. VanDuinen, and L. D. Sinnamon, "The Socrates adaptive image processor," in *SPIE Computerized Imaging Techniques Seminar* (Washington, D. C.), pp. v 1–5, 1967.
[165] J. J. O. Palgen, "Applicability of pattern recognition techniques to the analysis of urban quality from satellites," *Pattern Recogn.*, vol. 2, pp. 255–260, 1970.
[166] ——, "Application of optical processing for improving ERTS data," Allied Research Associates Tech. Rep. 16, NASA Contract NAS-10343, 1970.
[167] A. B. Park, "Remote sensing of time dependent phenomena," in *Proc. 6th Int. Symp. Remote Sens. Environ.* (Ann Arbor, Mich.), pp. 1227–1236, 1969.
[168] ——, "The role of man in an observatory/laboratory spacecraft," in *Proc. EASCON 70*, pp. 21–23, 1970.
[169] ——, "User needs in agriculture and forestry," *Proc. Princeton Univ. Conf. Aerospace Methods for Revealing Earth's Resources* (Princeton, N. J.), p. 13.1, June 1970.
[170] J. L. Pfaltz, J. W. Snively, and A. Rosenfeld, "Local and global picture processing by computer," in *Pictorial Pattern Recognition*, Cheng *et al.*, Eds. Washington, D. C.: Thompson, 1968, pp. 353–372.
[171] A. Pilipchuk, "Mechanical scanner for off-line picture digitization," Comput. Sci. Cent., Univ. of Maryland Rep. 69-92, 1969.
[172] J. F. Potter, "Scattering and absorption in the Earth's atmosphere," in *Proc. 6th Int. Symp. Remote Sens. Environ.* (Ann Arbor, Mich.), pp. 415–430, 1969.
[173] W. K. Pratt, "Semi-annual technical report of the USC Image Processing Laboratory," Univ. of South. California Rep. 411, Mar. 1972.
[174] P. K. Rao and A. E. Strong, "Sea surface temperature mapping off the eastern United States using NOAA's ITOS satellite," in *Proc. 7th Int. Symp. Remote Sens. Environ.* (Ann Arbor, Mich.), pp. 683–692, 1971.
[175] A. J. Richardson, R. J. Torline, and W. A. Allen, "Computer identification of ground patterns from aerial photographs," in *Proc. 7th Int. Symp. Remote Sens. Environ.* (Ann Arbor, Mich.), pp. 1357–1376, 1971.
[176] T. C. Rindfleisch, "Getting more out of Ranger pictures by computer," *Astronaut. Aeronaut.*, vol. 7, 1969.
[177] T. C. Rindfleisch, J. A. Dunne, H. F. Frieden, and W. D. Stromberg, "Digital processing of the Mariner 6 and 7 pictures," *J. Geophys. Res.*, vol. 76, pp. 394–417, 1971.
[178] A. Rosenfeld, C. Fried, and J. Ortan, "Automatic cloud interpretation," *Photogrammet. Eng.*, vol. 31, p. 991, 1965.
[179] A. Rosenfeld, *Picture Processing by Computer.* New York: Academic Press, 1969.
[180] A. Rosenfeld, H. Huang, and V. B. Schneider, "An application of cluster detection to text and picture processing," *IEEE Trans. Inform. Theory*, vol. IT-15, pp. 672–681, Nov. 1969; also Univ. of Maryland Comput. Sci. Cent. Rep. TR-68-68.
[181] A. Rosenfeld and E. B. Troy, "Visual texture analysis," Comput. Sci. Cent., Univ. of Maryland, Tech. Rep. TR70-116.
[182] A. Rosenfeld and M. Thurston, "Edge and curve enhancement for visual scene analysis," *IEEE Trans. Comput.*, vol. C-20, pp. 562–569, May 1971.
[183] L. Rossol, "Generation of halftones by computer-controlled microfilm recorder," *IEEE Trans. Comput.* (Short Note), vol. C-20, pp. 662–664, June 1971.
[184] H. R. Sellner, "Transfer function compensation of sampled imagery," in *Proc. Perkin-Elmer Symp. on Sampled Images* (Norwalk, Conn.), pp. 4-1–4-14, 1971.
[185] J. R. Shay, "Systems for Earth resources information," in *Proc. Purdue Centennial Year Symp. Information Theory* (Lafayette, Ind.), pp. 635–643, 1969.
[186] H. F. Silverman, "On the use of transforms for satellite image processing," in *Proc. 7th Int. Symp. Remote Sens. Environ.* (Ann Arbor, Mich.), 1971, pp. 1377–1386.
[187] D. S. Simonett, "Potential of radar remote sensors as tools in reconnaissance geomorphic, vegetation and soil mapping," in *9th Int. Cong. Soil Sci. Trans.*, vol. IV, Paper 20, pp. 271–280, 1968; also Univ. of Kansas CRES Rep. 117-2.
[188] H. W. Smedes, M. M. Spencer, and F. J. Thomson, "Processing of multispectral data and simulation of ERTS data channels to make computer terrain maps of a Yellowstone National Park test site," in *3rd Annu. Earth Resources Program Review* (NASA-MSC Houston, Tex.), p. 10-1, Dec. 1970.
[189] H. W. Smedes, H. J. Linnerud, S. G. Hawks, and L. B. Woolamer, "Digital computer mapping of terrain by clustering techniques using color film on a three-band sensor," in *Proc. 7th Int. Symp. Remote Sens. Environ.* (Ann Arbor, Mich.), pp. 2057–2072, 1971.
[190] C. R. Smith and T. F. Shafman, "Cloud cover limitations on satellite photography of the United States," in *Trans. 49th Annu. Meeting of the Amer. Geophys. Union* (Washington, D. C.), p. 188, 1968.
[191] E. A. Smith and D. R. Phillips, "Automated cloud tracking using precisely aligned digital ATS pictures," in *Proc. Symp. Two-Dimensional Image Processing* (Columbia, Mo.), pp. 10-2-1–10-2-26, 1971.
[192] G. L. Stanely, W. C. Nienow, and G. G. Lendaris, "SARF—An interactive signature analysis research facility," in *Proc. Purdue Centennial Year Symp. Information Theory* (Lafayette, Ind.), pp. 436–445, 1969.
[193] D. Steiner, "A methodology for the automated photo-identification of rural land use types," in *Automatic Interpretation and Classification of Images*, A. E. Grasselli, Ed. New York: Academic Press, 1969, p. 235.
[194] D. Steiner, K. Baumberger, and H. Maurer, "Computer processing and classification of multi-variate information from remote sensing imagery," in *Proc. 6th Int. Symp. Remote Sens. Environ.* (Ann Arbor, Mich.), pp. 895–908, 1969.
[195] D. Steiner, "Time dimension for crop surveys from space," *Photogrammetr. Eng.*, vol. 36, pp. 187–194, 1970.
[196] R. E. Stevenson, "Oceanographic data requirements for the development of an operational satellite system," in *Proc. Princeton Univ. Conf. Aerospace Methods for Revealing Earth's Resources* (Princeton, N. J.), p. 12.1, June 1970.
[197] H. G. Stever, Keynote Address to the 13th Meeting of the Panel on Sci. and Technol., Comm. Sci. and Astronaut., U. S. House of Representatives, Jan. 25, 1972.
[198] W. M. Strome, "Canadian data-handling facility for ERTS," in *Proc. Canadian Computer Conf.*, pp. 423101–423118, 1972.
[199] J. P. Strong, "Automatic cloud cover mapping," Univ. of Maryland Comput. Sci. Cent. Rep. TR-163.
[200] L. L. Sutro and W. S. McCulloch, "Steps toward the automatic recognition of unknown object," in *Proc. Inst. Elec. Eng. NPL Conf. Pattern Recognition* (Teddington, U. K.), pp. 117–133, 1968.
[201] P. H. Swain and K. S. Fu, "On the application of a nonparametric technique to crop classification problems," in *Proc. Nat. Electronics Conf.*, 1968.
[202] P. H. Swain and D. A. Germann, "On the application of man-machine computing systems to problems in remote sensing," in *Proc. 11th Midwest Symp. Circuit Theory* (Notre Dame, Ind.), May, 1968; also *Software Age*, vol. 2, pp. 13–20, 1968.
[203] P. H. Swain, "Data processing I: Advancements in machine analysis of multispectral data," Purdue Univ. LARS Informat. Note 012472, to be included in the *4th Annu. Earth Resources Program Review* (NASA-MSC, Houston, Tex.), 1972.
[204] G. D. Swanlund, "Design requirements for texture measurements," in *Proc. Symp. Two-Dimensional Image Processing* (Columbia, Mo.), pp. 8-3-12–8-3-19, 1971.
[205] W. Swoboda and J. W. Gerdes, "A system for demonstrating the effects of changing background on automatic target recognition," in *Pictorial Pattern Recognition*, Cheng *et al.*, Eds. Washington, D. C.: Thompson, 1968, pp. 33–42.
[206] M. G. Tanguay, R. M. Hoffer, and R. D. Miles, "Multispectral imagery and automatic classificaton of spectral response for detailed engineering soils mapping," in *Proc. 6th Int. Symp. Remote Sens. Environ.* (Ann Arbor, Mich.), pp. 33–64, 1969.
[207] M. M. Thompson, Ed., *Manual of Photogrammetry.* Falls Church, Va.: Amer. Soc. of Photogrammetry, 1966.
[208] F. J. Thomson, "User oriented data processing at the University of Michigan," in *3rd Annu. Earth Resources Program Review* (NASA-MSC, Houston, Tex.), p. 38-1, Dec. 1970.
[209] W. R. Tobler, "Problems and prospects in geographical photointerpretation," in *Pictorial Pattern Recognition*, Cheng *et al.*, Eds. Washington, D. C.: Thompson, 1968, pp. 267–274.
[210] D. R. Tompson, "An IBM special cartographic scanner," in *Proc. ASP-ACSM Conv.* (Washington, D. C.), 1967.
[211] M. R. Uffelman, "Target detection, prenormalization, and learning machines," in *Pictorial Pattern Recognition*, Cheng *et al.*, Eds. Washington, D. C.: Thompson, 1968, pp. 503–521.
[212] R. M. Vesper and D. N. Rosenzweig, "Sampled image laboratories and facilities," in *Proc. Perkin-Elmer Symp. Sampled Images* (Norwalk, Conn.), pp. 10-1–10-8, 1971.
[213] A. G. Wacker, "A cluster approach to finding spatial boundaries in multispectral imagery," LARS Informat. Note 122969, 1969.
[214] A. G. Wacker and D. A. Landgrebe, "Boundaries in multispectral images by clustering," in *Proc. 1970 9th IEEE Symp. Adaptive Processes* (Austin, Tex.), pp. 322–330, 1970.

[215] R. N. Watts, "Skylab scheduled for 1972," *Sky Telesc.*, pp. 146–148, 1970.

[216] G. R. Welti and S. H. Durrain, "Communication system configuration for the Earth Resources Satellite," in *Communication Satellites for the 70's Systems*, N. E. Feldman and C. M. Kelly, Eds. (vol. 26 of *Progress in Astronautics and Aeronautonics*). Cambridge, Mass.: M.I.T. Press, 1971, pp. 289–314.

[217] P. M. Will, R. Bakis, and M. A. Wesley, "On an all-digital approach to Earth Resources Satellite image processing," Yorktown Heights, N. Y., IBM Tech. Rep. RC-3027, 1970.

[218] C. L. Wilson, M. M. Beilock, and E. M. Zaitzeff, "Design considerations for aerospace multispectral scanning systems," in *Proc. Purdue Centennial Year Symp. on Information Theory* (Lafayette, Ind.), pp. 658–671, 1969.

[219] F. J. Wobber, "Space age prospecting," *World Mining*, p. 25, June 1968.

[220] P. Wood, "User requirements for Earth Resources Satellite data," in *Proc. EASCON 70*, pp. 14–20, 1970.

[221] E. M. Zaitzeff, C. L. Wilson, and D. H. Ebert, "MSDS: An experimental 24-channel multispectral scanner system," *Bendix Tech. J.*, pp. 20–32, 1970.

[222] B. Zavos, "Application of remote sensing to the World Weather Watch and the Global Atmospheric Research Program," in *Proc. 7th Int. Symp. Remote Sens. Environ.* (Ann Arbor, Mich.), pp. 207–220, 1971.

[223] E. O. Zeitler and R. O. Bratton, "Uses of Earth Resources data in the NASA/MSC Earth Resources research data facility," in *Proc. 7th Int. Symp. Remote Sens. Environ.* (Ann Arbor, Mich.), pp. 925–936, 1971.

[224] J. S. Zelenka, "Imaging radar techniques in remote sensing applications," in *Proc. 9th Annu. Allerton Conf. Circuit and System Theory*, pp. 975–986, 1971.

Digital Analysis of the Electroencephalogram, the Blood Pressure Wave, and the Electrocardiogram

JEROME R. COX, JR., MEMBER, IEEE, FLOYD M. NOLLE, MEMBER, IEEE, AND R. MARTIN ARTHUR, MEMBER, IEEE

Abstract—The electroencephalogram (EEG), the blood pressure wave, and the electrocardiogram (ECG), produce patterns that the eye of the physician has empirically correlated with important aspects of health. Digital computer techniques for the recognition of these patterns are made particularly difficult by the realities of pattern context sensitivity, frequent signal artifact, real-time operation, finite storage limitations, and reasonable cost. Evaluations of these techniques are handicapped by the absence of absolute standards, the wide signal variability associated with pathologic states, and the sheer mechanics of comparison with human analysis.

Computer analysis of the EEG has been directed toward monitoring sleep and certain pathologic states, leaving the more difficult problem of diagnosis to the trained neurologist. Automatic pattern recognition of the blood pressure wave has been implemented with straightforward techniques for diagnostic use in the cardiac catheterization laboratory and for monitoring in the intensive care unit. Computer analysis of the ECG has been directed toward morphological and rhythm diagnosis, having great potential utility in clinical heart stations, and toward rhythm monitoring, a most practical application arising in coronary intensive care units.

Promising systems are emerging, but years of evaluation and adjustment will be necessary to meet the need for both accuracy and economy.

Manuscript received May 19, 1972; revised June 22, 1972. This work was supported in part by the National Institutes of Health under Grants RR 00396 and RR 06115 from the Division of Research Resources and under Contract NIH-71-2481 from the National Heart and Lung Institute.

J. R. Cox, Jr., is with the Biomedical Computer Laboratory and the Department of Electrical Engineering, Washington University, St. Louis, Mo.

F. M. Nolle is with the Biomedical Computer Laboratory and the Department of Medicine, Washington University, St. Louis, Mo.

R. M. Arthur is with the Department of Electrical Engineering, Washington University, St. Louis, Mo.

I. Introduction

PHYSICIANS have used patterns to aid in patient care for centuries—patterns of symptoms, patterns of cells, tissues or organs and, more recently, patterns of physiological signals. Many of the techniques we have come to expect to find in digital pattern recognition are useful in each of these three classes of problems. The first class forms patterns only in the mind of the diagnostician and computer aids to this process have been reviewed by Ledley [1]. The second class may be described as patterns of biomedical images [2].

In this review we concentrate on the final class, physiological signals, displayed against time and yielding familiar patterns to the skilled eye of the physician or nurse. Simpler in many respects than two-dimensional biomedical images, the classic form of these patterns consists of a single-valued function of time plotted with stylus or pen on chart paper

Reprinted from *Proc. IEEE*, vol. 60, pp. 1137–1164, Oct. 1972.

moving at a constant speed. We will concentrate here on signals that have been available to and scrutinized by the clinician for many decades with the result that a rich body of empirical correlations have been developed between the health of the patient and the patterns formed by the signals.

We will examine in some detail work that has been done in automatic pattern recognition for the electroencephalogram (EEG), the blood pressure wave, and the electrocardiogram (ECG), the three most frequently used physiological signals for patient monitoring and diagnosis. Although our major emphasis will be on digital techniques, occasional consideration of analog and hybrid techniques will be included. Patterns formed by the recording of these three signals have been well studied by physicians, and the correlations with disease states are often surprisingly sophisticated and definitive. For all three signals, however, other clinical signs and symptoms must be integrated by the physician along with the pattern-recognition results before a final judgment or diagnosis is justified. The signals are at best indirect indicators of the answers sought by the physician. Signal artifact, bizarre clinical circumstances, multiple pathologies, and the lack of a unique relation between signal and pathology can each serve to foil even the most sophisticated attempts at programmed decision making based on pattern recognition. These same factors frequently confuse the clinician when he must use the physiological signals alone for his decision. Usually he has the advantage of a substantially larger base of information, parts of which are difficult to obtain in coded form.

The analysis of a clinically useful physiological signal often needs to be accomplished within minutes and rarely can be delayed by more than a day. A 1-min record should not take hours to process. Hundreds of samples per second are common for these signals so that computing-time requirements must be carefully examined. This torrent of data can quickly fill any reasonably sized buffer memory, forcing a serious study of storage requirements. These difficult requirements often come into conflict with the need for economy. To be clinically useful, a digital pattern-recognition system must have an expectation that it will soon be less expensive than will be available alternatives. Surprisingly, several systems are on the threshold of meeting this trio of requirements involving time, storage, and economy.

II. The Electroencephalogram

A. The Mechanism of Generation

The electrical activity of the brain manifests itself on the surface of the scalp in minute electrical potential differences (typically 50 μV). Since the pioneering work of Berger [3] in 1924, neurologists have used tracings of these EEG potentials to aid in the evaluation of brain function and more recently to provide means for the assessment of psychotropic drugs. Intracellular recordings of neural activity from exposed cortex reveal a multitude of local electrical generators within nerve cells and nerve fibers. In contrast to the waveforms observed in the nerve fibers, the signals recorded from the scalp reflect graded rather than all-or-none signals, are two or three orders of magnitude lower in amplitude and exhibit a power spectrum with negligible rather than substantial energy above 25 Hz. The cortical sources can be viewed as an assembly of dipoles embedded in a conducting medium surrounded by the less conductive skull. Simulations of their aggregate neural activity [4] explain many but not all aspects of the surface recordings. Although the nerve fibers themselves and supporting glial cells have been implicated, recent reports [5]–[7] indicate that spontaneous neural activity producing graded waveforms at synapses can account for most of the normal EEG as seen on the scalp. The all-or-none responses of the nerve fibers probably produce only local effects generally not seen in the EEG.

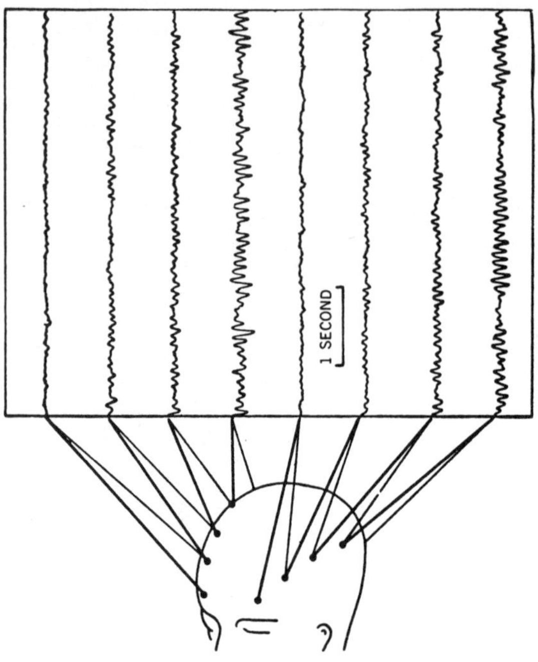

Fig. 1. Typical multitrace EEG of a normal waking adult. Note the predominance of alpha rhythm in the posterior part of the head. From Brazier [9].

B. Analysis of EEG Patterns

Clinical practice for diagnostic EEG's utilizes pairs of electrodes fixed to the scalp at standard locations [8] to produce eight or more simultaneous tracings (Fig. 1). The identification of EEG patterns that correlate with clinical problems is carried out on a routine basis by neurologists through examination of tracings like those of Fig. 1. During the past 40 years of clinical study a surprising variety of correlations have been described [9], [10]—brain infections, cerebrovascular lesions, trauma, epilepsy, certain congenital brain defects, and barbiturate poisoning. Most of these clinical states require evidence in addition to the EEG, but its diagnostic usefulness is well established because it is atraumatic and noninvasive. The EEG is also useful as a monitoring technique [11] although use is by no means as widespread as in diagnosis. With careful interpretation of the tracings, detection is possible of brain ischemia, coma, death, and the return of brain function after cardiac arrest or barbiturate poisoning. The stages of sleep as reflected in the EEG were first classified by Loomis [12] and subsequently applied to a wide variety of research including psychotropic drug evaluation, mental disease, dreaming, and the effects of space flight. Response patterns in the EEG evoked by sensory stimuli have been observed [13] and subsequently used in research in perception [14].

All four classes of EEG analysis—diagnosis, monitoring, sleep staging, and evoked responses—have, in recent years, been approached with automatic pattern-recognition techniques. Most work has been done with sleep staging and

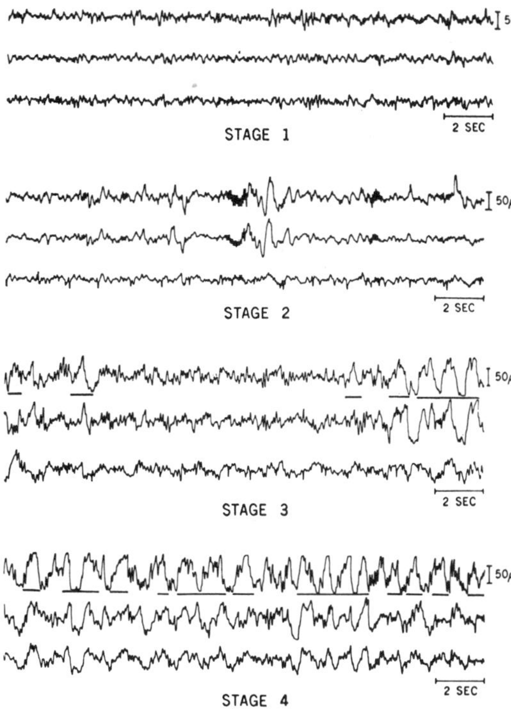

Fig. 2. Three-trace EEG records, each about 20 s long for sleep stages 1, 2, 3, and 4 (see Table I) for a single normal subject. The stage 1 tracings show some vertex sharp waves, but otherwise relatively low voltage, 2–7-Hz activity. The stage 2 tracings show mixed-frequency activity with amplitude generally greater than stage 1. The K complex in the center of the record is preceded by a sleep spindle. Other more brief sleep spindles may be seen elsewhere in the record. The underline in the stage 3 tracings shows the occurrence of delta waves exceeding 75 μV for about a quarter of the time. In the stage 4 tracings the delta waves occupy about three quarters of the time. Adapted from Rechtschaffen *et al.* [17].

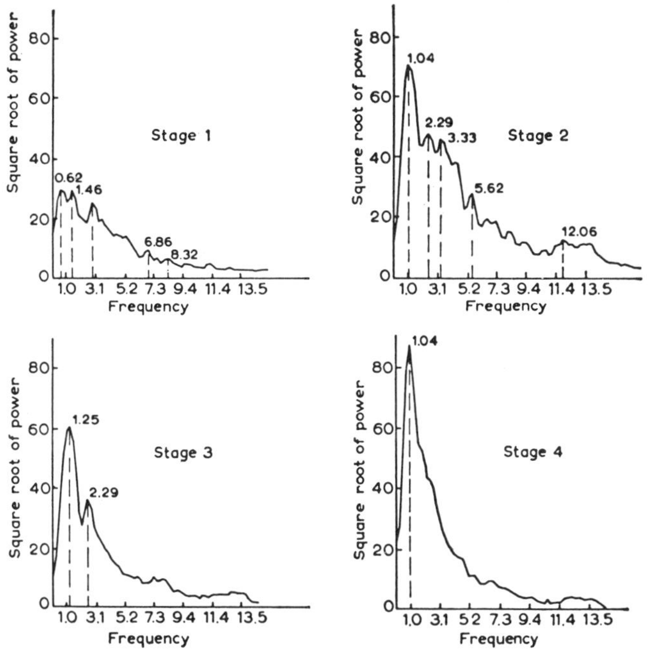

Fig. 3. Autospectra of sleep stages 1, 2, 3, and 4 for a single normal subject at a resolution of 0.208 Hz. From Hord *et al.* [23].

evoked responses, fields in which the applications have been primarily to research rather than to clinical use.

1) Automatic Recognition of Sleep Stages: Most investigators use a scheme similar to that proposed by Dement and Kleitman [15] who identified six distinct EEG states—waking (W), four sleep stages (1, 2, 3, 4) indicating increasing depth of sleep, and a special sleep stage whose EEG pattern is similar to sleep stage 1, but characterized by rapid eye movement (REM), and often associated with dreaming. Unambiguous detection of REM sleep requires recording of the electrooculogram (EOG) in addition to the EEG. Some investigators also record muscle activity (EMG), typically at the chin. These EEG states show differences in both the time domain (Fig. 2) and the frequency domain (Fig. 3).

The first step in human scoring of sleep stages is carried out by examination of 20-s or 30-s epochs and estimating the location of peaks in the spectrum through the measurement of the average period of prominent rhythmic waves. These periodic components of the EEG may be assigned to several frequency bands whose boundaries are traditional rather than standardized: delta (1–4 Hz), theta (4–8 Hz), alpha (8–12 Hz), sigma (12–14 Hz), and beta (14–35 Hz). Variability of 1 Hz in the specification of these boundaries is common, and some investigators may ignore or coalesce one or two of the bands. One particular band, sigma (12–14 Hz), is particularly characteristic of sleep and the human scorer looks for "sleep spindles," rhythmic bursts in this band consisting of multiple cycles, 5 to 20 or more in number, which appear superimposed on a low-voltage mixed-frequency EEG background.

TABLE I

CHARACTERISTICS OF EEG IN VARIOUS SLEEP STAGES

Stage	Description of EEG
W[a]	Alpha and/or low-voltage[c] mixed-frequency activity for more than 50 percent of the time.
REM[b]	Relatively low-voltage,[d] mixed-frequency activity and rapid eye movements.
1	Relatively low-voltage 2–7-Hz activity with an occasional vertex sharp wave not exceeding 200 μV.
2	Sleep spindles and K complexes superimposed on relatively low-voltage mixed-frequency activity.
3	Delta waves exceeding 75 μV for 20 to 50 percent of the time; low-voltage intervening activity with occasional spindles.
4	Delta waves exceeding 75 μV for greater than 50 percent of the time.

[a] Wakefulness.
[b] Rapid eye movement.
[c] Low voltage is characterized by no rhythmic activity above 10 μV and no activity above 20 μV.
[d] Relatively low voltage is greater than low voltage, but does not exceed 75 μV.

The human scorer also recognizes certain aperiodic patterns called vertex sharp waves and K complexes [16]. A K complex is a well-delineated negative sharp wave immediately followed by a positive component. This biphasic wave should have a total duration 0.5 to 1.0 s and be seen simultaneously in several leads. The human scorer combines this information with an estimate of the frequency of the rhythmic bursts and the presence or absence of REM to arrive at a classification into one of six stages (W, REM, 1, 2, 3, 4) [17]. Table I abbreviates and summarizes one statement of these criteria. Minor variations exist from laboratory to laboratory, particularly with regard to sleep stage 3.

The task of manually scoring sleep records is time-consuming (a record of a single subject's sleep during a single 8-h session covers about 300 m of chart paper). Analysis of enough records to produce statistically significant results may well involve kilometers of EEG recordings. As a result many attempts have been made to develop automatic methods for the classification of EEG sleep records.

Amplitude analysis, introduced by Drohocki [18], has been applied to sleep by Agnew *et al.* [19]. The method provides a continuous cumulative measurement of the area under the rectified EEG for the interval analyzed. The result correlates well with sleep stages 1, 3, and 4. Stage 2 and REM sleep require additional information to be separated from the former three. A similar technique using only components of the EEG within a 2–6-Hz band has been described [20].

Frequency analysis, introduced by Grass and Gibbs [21] and applied by Knott *et al.* [22] to sleep, required human interpretation of the resulting spectrogram. Hord *et al.* [23] and Walter *et al.* [24] confirmed the shift to lower frequencies with increasing depth of sleep. The use of these spectral changes to classify automatically the stages of sleep has been pursued by Lubin *et al.* [25], Larsen and Walter [26], [27], and Ruspini [28]. Evaluation of these automatic techniques revealed the delta frequency band as the most useful discriminant, with alpha and sigma bands next in importance.

Using linear discriminant analysis and by considering only certain pairs of transitions between stages, Lubin *et al.* [25] were able to achieve performance on a test set that ranged from no better than chance for transitions between stages 3 and 4 and between stages 1 and REM, to performance comparable to human scoring (96-percent agreement) for transitions between stages 1 and 2 and between stages 2 and REM. They conclude that other aperiodic events (spindles, K complexes, REM bursts) will have to be added to frequency analysis to bring the performance of any automatic system close to that of human scorers.

Larsen and Walter [26], [27] show by use of a two-stage multivariate discriminant analysis with quadratic boundaries some improvement in performance for stages 2, 3, and 4, but the basic problem with an analysis based solely on frequency-domain techniques remains unchanged. Fig. 4 shows the overlapping clusters resulting from their single stage processing.

Period analysis, introduced by Burch and his co-workers [29], [30], utilizes only zero-crossing information in the EEG and its first and second derivatives. Motivated by the intelligibility of infinitely clipped speech as demonstrated by Licklider [31], Burch shows that period analysis contains much of the same information as does frequency analysis, but has the advantage of computational simplicity. Although more like the process carried out by the human scorer than is frequency analysis, period analysis can be at variance with the human within episodes of substantial baseline excursions during which baseline crossings may be completely absent.

Fink *et al.* [32] and Itil *et al.* [33], [34] have used period analysis as the basis of several digital computer programs which classify all-night sleep records of the EEG. They have ignored the zero crossing of the second derivative of the EEG and classified the observed periods into several categories for both the EEG and its derivative. Percentage agreement with human scorers [33] ranges from 55 to 74 percent, somewhat less than the best results from frequency analysis. Roessler *et al.* [35] describe a similar scheme which agrees with human scoring for 69 percent of the epochs studied.

Lessard and his co-workers [36], [37] use period analysis along with amplitude analysis to extract some 50 features in each 1-min interval of a night's EEG record. A multivariate linear discriminant analysis was performed reducing the number of useful features to 23. On a single subject, 85-percent agreement with human scoring was obtained, but it was observed that other aperiodic events must be included to achieve scores across subjects that are comparable to human scoring. Noting that delta activity contained the most reliable information about the sleep stage, this group has also described a system that plots the amount of this slow-wave activity in 1-min intervals [38]. Legewie and Probst [39] have also combined period and amplitude analysis.

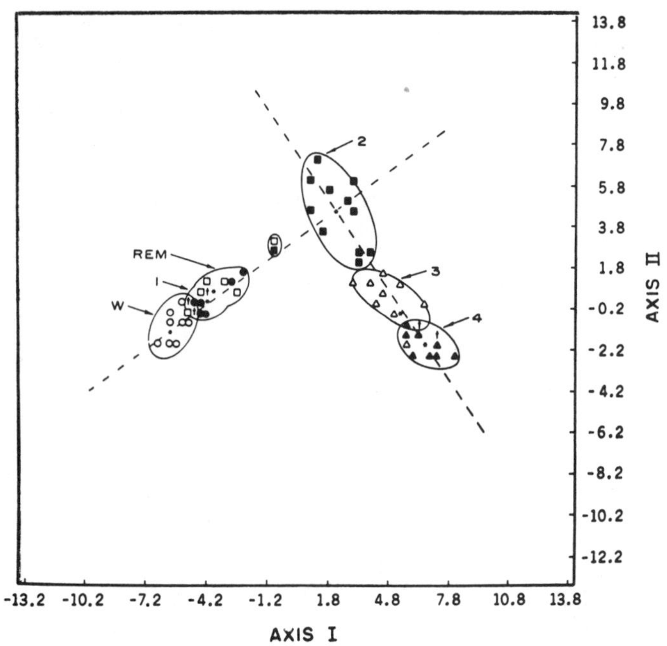

Fig. 4. A plot of EEG sleep data after frequency analysis, quadratic preprocessing, and transformation into a discriminant space of 2 dimensions. Asterisks indicate group means, and daggers indicate overlap of points. Waking points are indicated by open circles, stage 1 by open squares, REM by closed circles, stage 2 by closed squares, stage 3 by open triangles, and stage 4 by closed triangles. Broken lines represent translated and rotated axes in the discriminant space. From Larsen and Walter [27].

Other time-domain analyses having computational advantages like period analysis have been reported. Hjorth [40] computes the variance of the EEG and its first and second derivatives. These three variances along with certain ratios of the variances are used for automatic sleep staging. Haar functions [41] as a method to recognize sleep stages have been proposed by Bishop *et al.* [42]. These functions are orthonormal, and the calculation of the coefficients for a Haar-function expansion of the EEG on the interval analyzed (0.8 s) required very few multiplications. Preliminary results on a training set using a moving-window approach appear promising, but it is hard to see advantages over frequency analysis beyond computational simplicity.

Heuristic methods using features extracted by frequency or period analysis and by the recognition of certain events in the time domain are a promising approach to automatic classification of sleep records [43]–[47]. Techniques to detect specific significant events in the sleep EEG have been reported: REM bursts [48], [49]; sleep spindles [50]; alpha bursts [51], and K complexes [52]. A variety of analog and digital techniques have been used for these devices, but no careful evaluations have yet been reported.

Frost [45] describes a system that makes use of the decrease in average frequency of the EEG with the progression from W through stages 1, 2, 3, and 4. Hysteresis is incorpo-

TABLE II

COMPARISON OF HUMAN AND ANALYZER SLEEP-SCORING RESULTS (After Smith [47])

Human	Automatic W	1	2	3	4
W	449[a]	64	43	11	1
	79.05%	11.27%	7.57%	1.94%	0.18%
1	39	1519	226	28	2
	2.15%	83.74%	12.46%	1.54%	0.11%
2	23	74	2688	268	35
	0.74%	2.40%	87.05%	8.68%	1.13%
3	2	0	68	216	160
	0.45%	0.00%	15.25%	48.43%	35.87%
4	0	1	4	84	874
	0.00%	0.10%	0.42%	8.72%	90.76%

[a] Number of minutes scored in each category.

ated to prevent rapid fluctuations between stages. Separate sections of the system detect motion artifact from an accelerometer signal and REM from a combination of the EEG and the EOG signals. The outputs from these latter two sections are used to override the classifications based on average frequency.

Another system with a heuristic approach is reported by Smith [47]. It uses analog bandpass filters to detect alpha, sigma, delta, and artifact in the EEG record. Digital logic combines the outputs of these filters to automatically classify the sleep stage. Results of a performance evaluation of the system are shown in Table II, but a K-complex detector [52] and a REM detector [48] developed by Smith and his coworkers were not yet incorporated into the system at the time of the study.

2) Automatic Diagnosis and Monitoring: Even though 40 years of study of the EEG have produced many clinical correlations, systematic development of automatic techniques for diagnosis and monitoring of EEG records has not yet begun. A few exploratory studies have been reported, but no evaluations, even of a preliminary nature, have appeared. Expectations for the application of computers to EEG have been high [53]–[55], but most work has focused on EEG signal processing that seeks to produce a transformation of the input data revealing information not seen in the original tracing.

Diagnosis of the EEG as carried out by the electroencephalographer correlates information in each of the eight or more tracings, uses pattern recognition of both periodic and aperiodic waves, and applies contextual cues that can be distributed over several minutes of the record. In addition to bursts of alpha activity, the human EEG reader looks for a variety of patterns such as the "spike-dome discharge," an alternating occurrence of a sharp wave with a duration of about 1/15 s, and a slower wave with duration of about 1/3 s. This pair of waves can be repeated from 2–15 times.

Farley *et al.* [51] developed a program for the recognition of alpha bursts. After filtering they identified successive peaks and valleys in the record. If the amplitude of the wave between peak and valley exceeded a threshold, and if the interval between successive waves fell in the alpha range, a string of candidate waves was identified. Strings exceeding a fixed length (typically five waves) were recognized as alpha bursts (Fig. 5). Features extracted from a record were the total alpha activity and the total number of bursts, allowing classification of the EEG's of several subjects and identification of the state of consciousness of a single subject.

Leader *et al.* [56] began work on the much more ambitious task of pattern recognition in the clinical EEG. Using feature extraction techniques similar to Farley [51], they counted waves in an array of 128 categories (8 amplitude ranges by 16 frequency bands) during successive 4-s epochs. By testing against a set of 13 clinical pattern descriptions, each such epoch was classified. No evaluation data were presented.

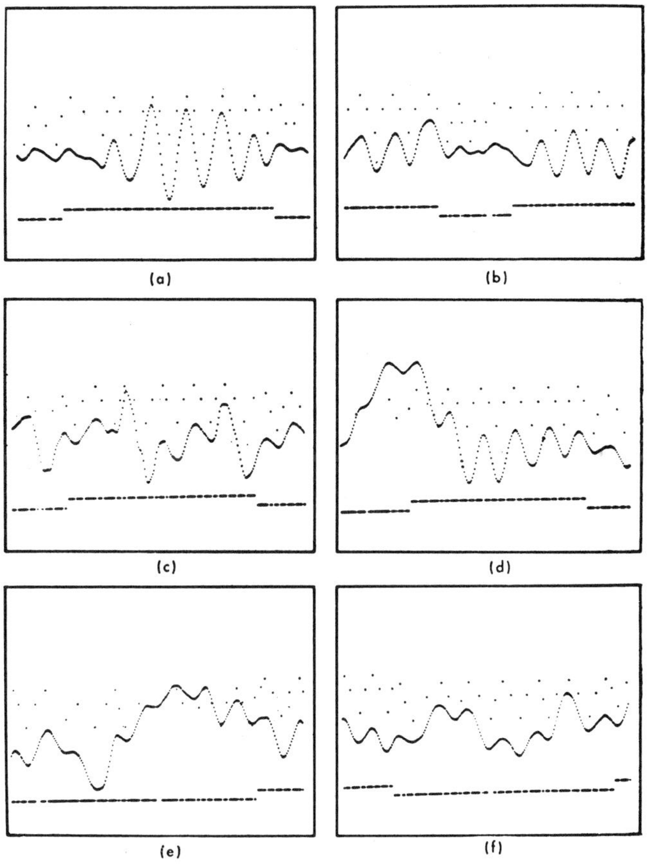

Fig. 5. Automatic recognition of alpha bursts indicated by the raised portions of the dashed line at the bottom of the panels. (a) A rhythmic burst is marked. (b) The interval between bursts is unmarked. (c), (d) Irregular bursts are marked. (e), (f) Two irregular regions not qualifying as alpha bursts are shown. The dots above the tracing show computer identified peaks and valleys along with midpoints between the peaks and valleys. From Farley *et al.* [51].

Monitoring of the EEG by automatic techniques during anesthesia is described in a preliminary report [57] which includes a few interesting results using an autoregressive analysis for the classification of various states of consciousness.

Bickford *et al.* [58] describe a computer system which eliminates electrocardiographic artifact from the EEG. This technique is particularly relevant in the determination of brain death when the amplitude of the EEG becomes vanishingly small. The signal recorded from the scalp is averaged, triggered by the *QRS* complex of the ECG recorded from chest leads. The resultant average reveals the ECG as seen on the scalp. This waveform can then be subtracted from successive epochs of the scalp record to yield the uncontaminated EEG. Recognition of the states of coma or brain death are made by comparison of the rectified average EEG voltage with three threshold voltages.

Other studies [59], [60] indicate that distinguishing states of consciousness within patients is possible, but that separation of states across patients is more difficult.

3) Evoked Responses: Davis [13] showed that sensory stimuli could evoke a response at the scalp of man. Although the evoked response component of the EEG is almost always obscured by spontaneous activity, a number of instruments have been described [61]–[64] that reveal the evoked response by averaging together the portions of the EEG record that follow each of a sequence of stimuli. Extraction of the median rather than the average response has also been suggested [65]. These new instruments and techniques have spawned an enormous number of investigations [14], [66], [67], but we confine ourselves here to the specific problem of pattern recognition.

Most investigators interested in automatic pattern recognition for evoked responses tested the EEG record against two hypotheses H_0 or H_1. For example the test might seek to determine which of two stimuli was presented or in which of two states of consciousness was the subject. Each response or group of responses containing n sampled data points can be viewed as a point in n-dimensional feature space. Classification of a response into H_0 or H_1 has been achieved by linear discriminant analysis [68], the multivariate analog of Student's t test [69], [70], principal component analysis [71], [72], step-wise discriminant analysis [73], [74], correlograms [75], [76], the sequential probability ratio test of Wald [68], and sequential decision theory [77].

In general, some training mechanism has been used to discriminate EEG patterns not readily classified by eye. Recourse to clinically familiar evoked response patterns has not been made, partly because of the individual and temporal variability in evoked responses and partly because evoked response techniques have had a relatively short period of clinical use. Derbyshire [76], however, uses a pattern or "template" which corresponds to the classic negative-positive-negative late auditory evoked response. Correlograms of this template with the EEG (Fig. 6) show an evoked response to a single presentation of the word "raisin." Variability is great between listeners, however, with some listeners' correlograms yielding results only slightly better than chance.

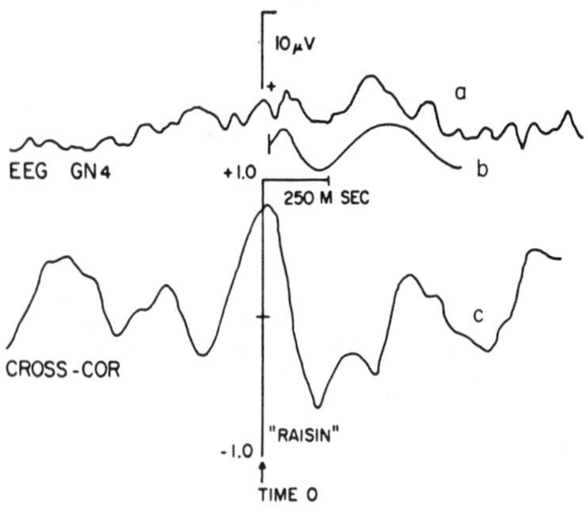

Fig. 6. Cross-correlogram method for the detection of an evoked response. a, the raw EEG trace from one listener in an evoked response study is shown (surface negative upward). A template b is set so it starts at the time of maximum cross correlation, 15 ms after time zero. The cross correlogram is shown, c, where the vertical line gives the possible range of cross correlation from -1.0 to $+1.0$. From Derbyshire *et al.* [76].

C. Discussion

The applications of automatic pattern recognition of the EEG can be divided into two categories: 1) attempts to extract information not seen by the clinician in the EEG principally through multivariate statistical techniques and 2) attempts to emulate the clinician's pattern recognition through heuristic techniques.

Frequently the statistical techniques assume the EEG is stationary, ergodic, and derived from a Gaussian process. In evoked response studies it is also assumed that the EEG is formed from a linear combination of response and ongoing activity. Careful confirmation of these assumptions is lacking. An important problem for these techniques is their validation [78]. Randomly selected, but distinct, training and test sets have been used, but difficulties may arise even when such a validation is carefully done. For example, hidden bias in the selection of both the training and test sets may invalidate the results for apparently similar sets drawn from the population at large.

Statistical techniques have to date involved much computation and relatively little data (only kilometers of EEG tracings rather than hundreds of kilometers). Thus it has been possible to handle artifact by human editing of records. Any scheme which eventually must operate in an unattended fashion needs a means to detect and react appropriately to artifact in the record. None of the statistical techniques reported have yet attended to this problem.

The heuristic techniques do not require assumptions about stochastic models of the EEG, but they do lean heavily on accumulated clinical experience. Unfortunately, the reading of EEG's is a highly developed skill without clear and uniform standards and algorithms. Electroencephalographers trained in one department of neurology use pattern-recognition algorithms sometimes different from algorithms used by those trained elsewhere. The clinical diagnosis of patients will likely turn out the same because crucial differences between schools or preceptors are generally recognized and eliminated and because the diagnosis depends only partially on EEG findings. However, these different algorithms if translated directly into an automatic system may result in a quite different EEG analysis on certain patients. Only with integration of other modifying clinical data can the two algorithms be rationalized.

Even without the consideration of the different pattern-recognition algorithms used, the heuristic techniques suffer from the imperfect correlation of clinical observation with disease. Rarely are there but two hypotheses, H_0 and H_1, and rarely can they be tested incontrovertibly. Rather there exist a variety of disease entities, graded in extent and confounded by individual variability. Surgery or autopsy is not, in general, available to resolve uncertainties. Modeling the diagnostician's behavior in reading EEG's, for all the difficulties of his situation, has at least the virtue of familiarity and immediate utility.

Only in sleep research have automatic techniques developed sufficiently for performance evaluations to have been accomplished. Here the heuristic techniques appear to be on the threshold of effective operation. In diagnosis only a few of the first steps have been taken; conversely, some monitoring applications, profiting by experience in sleep research, may move to clinical usefulness relatively quickly. Progress toward pattern recognition in evoked response work is hampered by response variability and the lack of sufficient experience to provide a rich catalog of patterns along with their clinical correlates.

III. The Blood Pressure Wave

A. The Mechanism of Generation

For routine use and in common office practice the indirect method of arterial blood pressure measurement via sphygmomanometer is preferred. For the critically ill, direct observation of the arterial blood pressure wave by means of a pressure transducer connected to a flexible tube (catheter) inserted into an artery is frequently essential, but bears some added hazard.

Of most interest from a pattern-recognition viewpoint is the central arterial pressure (Fig. 7). The waveform correlates closely with dynamic events taking place in the heart and arterial system during a cardiac cycle. In Fig. 7(a) a normal waveform is shown where the pressure minima correspond to the end of one cardiac cycle and the beginning of the next. The rapid upstroke indicates the contraction of the muscular walls of the left ventricle of the heart, forcing blood into the aorta and the distensible trunk of the arterial tree. During systole, the ejection phase of the cardiac cycle, the blood pressure rises to a peak and then falls as the ventricle relaxes until the pressure applied by the compliant aorta and the central arterial system exceeds that applied by the ventricle. The aortic valve of the heart closes, marking the end of the systolic phase of the cardiac cycle. The dicrotic notch identifies this event in the pressure wave. The central arterial pressure sometimes rises slightly for a moment then falls as the trunk of the arterial tree contracts elastically continuing to perfuse the peripheral circulation during the diastolic phase of the cardiac cycle. The important events for an automatic system to identify in the blood pressure wave are 1) the end-diastolic pressure marking the transition from one cardiac cycle to the next, 2) the peak-systolic pressure, and 3) the dicrotic notch, a characteristic inflection in the pressure wave following peak systole and at a substantially lower pressure.

Fig. 7(b), (c), and (d) shows some abnormal shapes of the arterial pressure wave as reported in a popular text [79], but the three important points in each are still easily identifiable. Contrast the waveforms obtained under monitoring conditions shown in Fig. 8. Peak systole is still unambiguous, but end diastole and the dicrotic notch require a more sophisticated interpretation.

The blood pressure wave measured more peripherally in the arterial system has much in common with the central arterial pressure. Some smoothing and delay of the waveform occurs, but the basic characteristics remain substantially unchanged for normal circulation even in blood vessels a fraction of a millimeter in diameter. Pulsations also appear in the venous system, but they are much smaller in amplitude and result from pressure changes transmitted upstream from the atria or transmurally from nearby arteries.

B. Monitoring of the Arterial Pressure Wave

For the critically ill patient, the importance of the direct measurement of the arterial pressure wave has been accepted for decades. Analog techniques have been used to display the arterial pressure wave and to record the diastolic, mean, and systolic pressures. Even so, the sphygmomanometer has also been used regularly as a check, an independent calibration, and a secondary device in the event of failure of the direct measurement system. Computer techniques in monitoring the arterial pressure of critically ill patients were introduced by Warner *et al.* [80], [81]. They also estimated cardiac output (liters per minute) from measurements on the central arterial pressure wave [82], [83]. This method, which has been critically reviewed and modified by others [84]–[87] requires the location of the dicrotic notch as well as end diastole and peak systole.

In monitoring applications, artifact detection is essential.

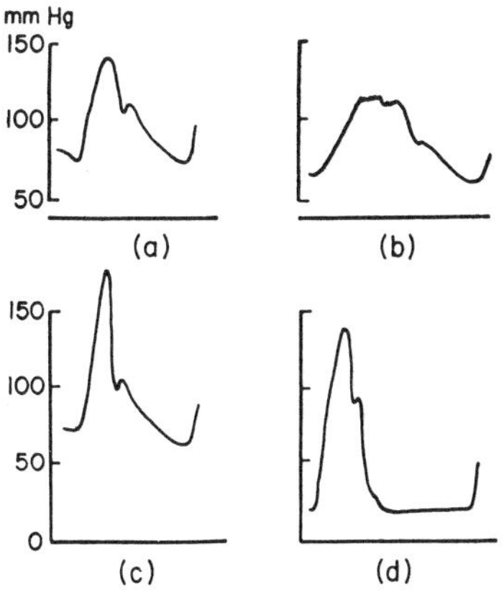

Fig. 7. Some shapes of the central arterial pressure wave. (a) Normal. (b) Aortic stenosis. (c) Arteriosclerosis. (d) Aortic insufficiency. From Burton [79].

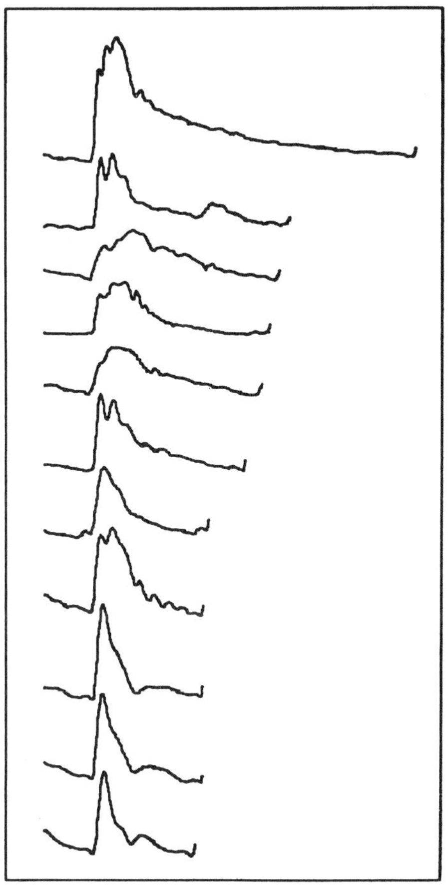

Fig. 8. Central arterial pressure waves observed from a variety of patients in a surgical intensive-care unit.

With blood pressure signals the most prevalent artifact is caused by manipulation of the patient or his catheter by the nurse. Because of their unpredictable nature, no automatic sensing of such artifacts appears to be completely reliable.

A procedure suggested by Strand [88] may be an alternative to artifact sensing when each beat need not be analyzed. In monitoring pulmonary artery pressure he synchronized the record of a cardiac cycle by means of the ECG, stored a dozen or so cardiac cycles, and selected the median of all recorded pressures at each instant of the cardiac cycle. This technique reduces variation in measured results caused

TABLE III

ALGORITHM FOR LOCATION OF DICROTIC NOTCH
(After Stauffer [95])

Arterial Pressure Sampled Every 10 ms
1) Establish beginning of search range 8 samples after peak systole. Set trial notch to this sample.
2) Establish end of search range 25 samples after peak systole or 8 samples before next end diastole, whichever comes first.
3) Consider the samples from the sixth before to the sixth after the trial notch. Weight them as follows: 1, 0, 1, 0, 1, −1, −4, −1, 1, 0, 1, 0, 1.
4) Sum the weighted samples and modify by adding 1 mmHg for each sample from peak systole to the trial notch.
5) Save modified weighted sum, advance trial notch 1 sample, test for end of search range, and if not done go back to 3).
6) Reset trial notch to 4 samples before first sample with maximum modified weighted sum.
7) Consider 3 samples centered on trial notch. Weight them 1, −2, 1 and calculate second difference.
8) Save second difference, advance trial notch 1 sample, test for limit at 4 samples beyond sample with maximum modified weighted sum, and if limit is not yet reached go back to 7).
9) Set final notch to first sample with maximum second difference.

by respiration, occasional arrhythmias, occasional mislocation of temporal reference points, or brief artifact. A somewhat similar approach is used by Harrison and Miller [89] in their catheterization laboratory system.

The formation of clots at the catheter tip can cause severe loss of high-frequency response of the system and consequent mismeasurement of waveforms. A constant very slow infusion of heparinized saline through the catheter to reduce the formation of such clots is used by several groups as an alternative to schemes which sense the loss of high-frequency components in the signal and thereupon automatically advise the nurse to flush the catheter.

C. Cardiac Catheterization Laboratory

The measurement of pressure waveforms in the chambers of the heart and its surrounding vessels has become an important and increasingly popular diagnostic procedure during the past decade. The associated computations often require as much time as the procedure itself and, consequently, several groups [89]–[96] have developed computer systems for the real-time analysis of hemodynamic data from the cardiac catheterization laboratory. Most of these systems make use of pattern-recognition techniques like those required for monitoring.

Only Harrison *et al.* [97] have reported an evaluation of their system's performance. While overall results appear quite useful—correlations with human measurements are above 0.9—the measurement of the end-diastolic pressure in the left ventricle was reported to be occasionally seriously in error (for example, 38 mmHg by computer against 20 mmHg by cardiologist). Efforts to eliminate this deficiency are underway.

D. Automatic Recognition of the Dicrotic Notch

Illustrative of the kind of pattern-recognition task encountered with the blood pressure wave is the identification of the dicrotic notch. Usually straightforward, but occasionally quite difficult, this recognition task can mislead the unwary. Several groups have developed algorithms for the location of the notch. Two basic approaches have been used: 1) linear digital filters [95], [98], [99] and 2) an interpolating preprocessor [100]. An example of the former approach from Stauffer [95] is described in Table III. Note that two searches

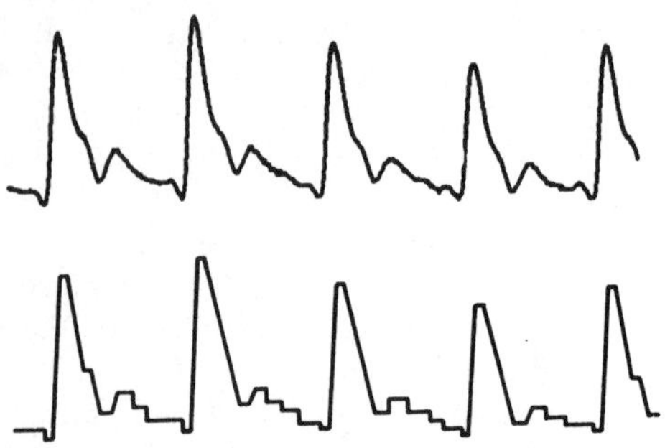

Fig. 9. Central arterial pressure waves (upper trace) and as preprocessed by Aztec (lower trace). In this example the dicrotic notch is identified by searching for the first extremum following the peak-systolic pressure. After DeBakey and Glaeser [100].

are conducted, the first a gross search for the notch and the second a more local search. In the first search a term linearly related to the time after peak systole is added to bias the search somewhat toward late smaller inflections. The search range is limited to avoid spurious inflections near peak systole often encountered in aortic stenosis (Fig. 7(b)) and to avoid fluctuations late in diastole caused by inertial components in the response of the circulatory system [101].

Pryor [98] uses a single weighted sum for location of both the notch and the onset of systole. Starmer [99] calculates a five-sample weighted sum (−2, −1, 0, 1, 2) that turns out to be the slope of least squares parabolic fit to that region of the signal. He looks for a maximum second derivative by subtracting adjacent slope estimates and identifies that maximum with the dicrotic notch. Using the occurrence of the *QRS* as observed on an ECG channel Starmer is able to calculate the preejection period as well as the onset of systole, the onset of diastole, and the ejection time. The use of the *QRS* to identify the region most likely to contain the onset of ejection in the pressure wave decreases the algorithm's exposure to noise during the major portion of diastole.

DeBakey and Glaeser [100] use the Aztec preprocessor described by Cox *et al.* [102] to initiate their search for the important points in the central arterial pressure wave. This scheme codes the waveform as a series of flat sections and slopes (Fig. 9). The dicrotic notch is located by proceeding forward in the search range until two consecutive flat sections, or a single flat section that is an extremum, or a flat section followed by a slope whose amplitude is less than 8 mmHg is found.

E. Discussion

The blood pressure wave is more highly structured than the EEG and even possibly the ECG. However, there are fewer clinically significant patterns, and the work on automatic analysis has centered on the recognition of certain important events and the measurement of a few features related to these events. Digital pattern-recognition techniques have been used in both monitoring and catheterization laboratory applications.

Acceptance by physicians of these digital techniques in the monitoring setting will probably come with the advent of an economical system. Analog monitors usually measure the absolute maximum pressure, as well as the absolute minimum pressure over several beats. Alternating strong and weak contractions (pulsus alternans) yield an indicated pulse pressure that may be substantially larger than it should be. The measurement error by sphygmomanometer may also be serious for pulsus alternans or very low diastolic pressures. With good transducer and catheter responses and effective artifact sensing the performance of an automatic pressure-monitoring system should easily exceed that from an analog monitor or a sphygmomanometer.

On the other hand, performance of an automatic analysis system in the cardiac catheterization laboratory may be inferior to the trained eye of the cardiologist for some time to come. Here in contrast to the monitoring application, the automatic system has a much more demanding objective. Many abnormal pressure waves are encountered and even infrequent measurement errors could cause serious diagnostic mistakes. Transducers and catheter systems may differ somewhat from laboratory to laboratory altering waveforms enough to cause marginal performance of certain pattern-recognition algorithms. Perhaps a semiautomated procedure will be developed to query the cardiologist whenever questionable patterns are encountered. In any case, general acceptance in the catheterization laboratory may be slow unless the cardiologist can verify the accuracy of all-automatic pattern recognition.

IV. The Electrocardiogram

A. The Mechanism of Generation

Mechanical events of the cardiac cycle are initiated and synchronized by electrical events. This relationship is exploited in empirically determining the anatomical and physiological condition of the heart. Although all myocardial cells possess a dual electrical and mechanical nature, specialized tissue groups have great influence on the sequence of activation. A discussion of anatomical studies of the conduction system [103], [104] and the electrophysiology of cardiac tissue [105], [106] is beyond the scope of this review.

Cells of the sinoatrial node in the right atrium are astable and normally possess the shortest natural period of all potentially astable groups of cells, thus pacing the heart's rhythmic electrical activity. By virtue of its strategic location, the atrioventricular node controls impulse passage between the atria and ventricles. Finally, the rapidly conducting Purkinje system spreads excitation to the ventricular masses much faster than conduction through working muscle tissue. The normal spread of ventricular depolarization has been extensively studied [107], [108]. Less is known of the normal repolarization process, although indications are that repolarization is not propagated [109], [110].

Each cell's contribution to the electrical field at a distance can be represented by a current dipole [111]. Body tissues are linear, isotropic in the bulk medium, and resistive, but with conductivities that vary with the tissue type [112]. The distribution of current dipoles in a volume conductor, the torso, gives rise to the surface ECG, fluctuating potential differences (typically 1 mV) measured between points on the torso. Reconstruction of the actual sources cannot be determined from these surface measurements [113]. Biophysical models of ventricular sources and principal component analysis indicate only about ten independent equivalent cardiac generators with surface contributions greater than the noise level [114]–[117].

Abnormalities of activation may be localized or widespread. Thus impulse propagation around a necrotic muscle segment may only perturb the overall sequence. In another instance, abnormality of a specialized conduction system structure may totally change the activation pattern. The exact consequences of most abnormal conditions on the electrical sources are not known. Instead, a wide variety of empirical data relates patterns in the surface ECG directly to the condition of the heart. To aid visualization of these relationships, a simple heart model consisting of a single spatial dipole (3 independent orthogonal generators) is usually employed. Two recent reviews [118], [119] on electrocardiography may be referred to for additional information.

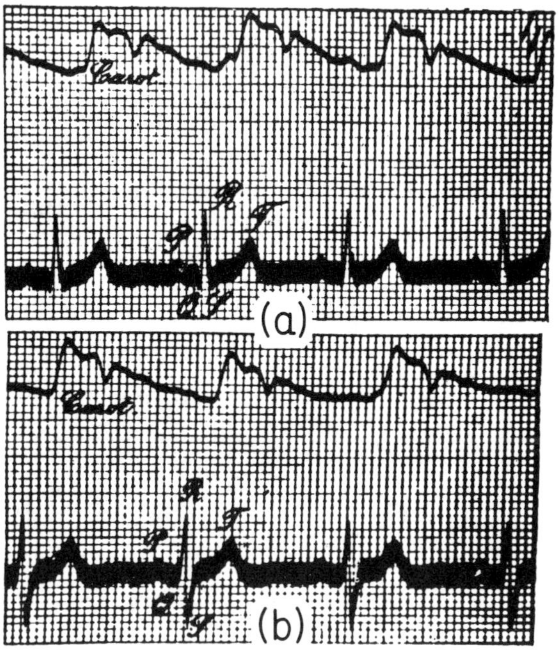

Fig. 10. (a) "Lead I, patient lying on the left side." (b) "The same person with the same lead, lying on the right side." This figure was one of many illustrating Einthoven's systematic investigation into the effects of respiration, body position, and heart rate on the ECG's of 10 healthy subjects. From Einthoven *et al.* [121].

B. Analysis of ECG Patterns

The gross patterns or waves readily observable in the surface ECG were given an arbitrary designation by Einthoven [120]. Fig. 10 shows the P wave and the QRS complex, now associated with the spread of depolarization in the atria and ventricles, respectively, and the T wave associated with ventricular recovery. The electrocardiographer studies the timing and shape of these patterns, inferring activity in pacemaker and conduction-system structures. Conventional ECG waves may overlap each other in time, making unambiguous measurements impossible, even in the multiple-lead ECG. The human handles this problem by scanning the raw waveform repeatedly, performing feature extraction and classification in parallel.

Diagnostic statements concerning operation of the heart as evidenced by the ECG are divided into two classes: 1) Morphological statements are primarily based on ECG wave shapes and attempt to describe the state of working muscle masses. 2) Rhythm statements are primarily concerned with the site and rate of cardiac pacemakers and the propagation of impulses through the specialized conduction system. The actual ECG diagnostic process is quite complicated, having an iterative trial-and-error nature with uncertain convergence properties.

ECG pattern-recognition efforts usually follow the conventional two-step approach of feature extraction and subsequent classification. Feature extraction involves detection of ECG waves, delimitation of wave boundaries, description of wave morphology, and measurement of interwave intervals.

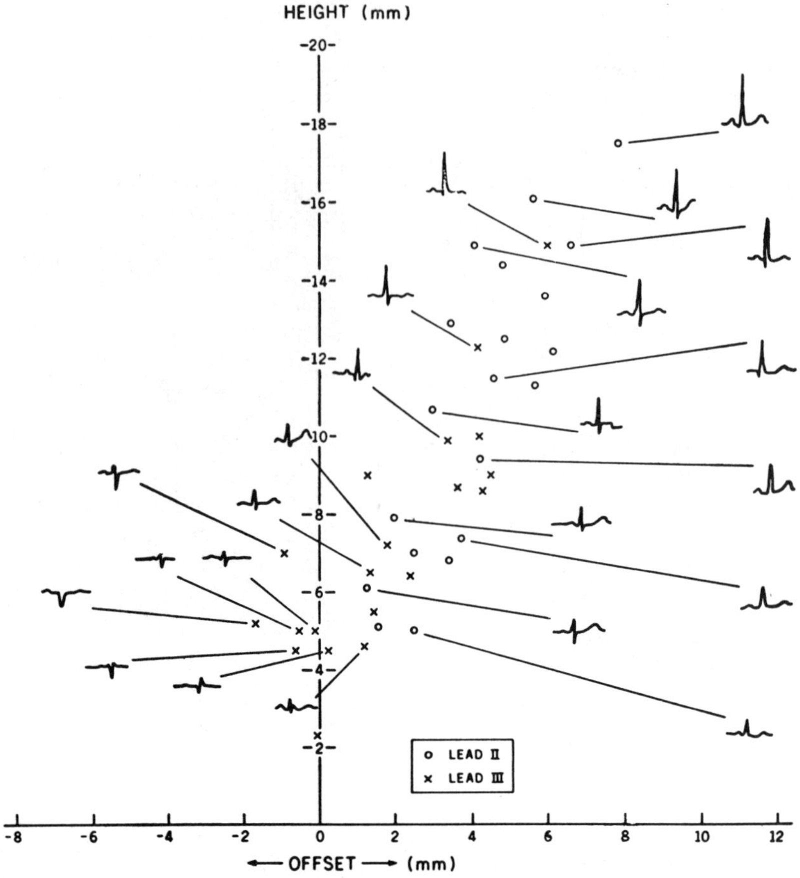

Fig. 11. *QRS* height (maximum amplitude minus minimum amplitude) and offset (the mean of the maximum and minimum amplitudes) are just two features that may be selected for classification purposes. Twenty randomly selected heart station ECG's having normal measurements show lead II *QRS* complexes (circles, illustrative waveforms to the right) intermingling with those of lead III (crosses, waveforms to the left) in the height-offset plane.

Classification techniques have been quite diverse, individual methods favoring either heuristic logic or more formal statistical methods. The basic extraction and classification procedures are often similar in morphological and rhythm analysis. Practical differences in the application of these two modes of analysis, however, make separate discussions appropriate.

The first step in feature extraction for most digital systems for automatic ECG analysis is to detect a *QRS* complex, usually via some suitably defined derivative function. Search procedures of varying complexity, generally initiated by *QRS* detection, are used for *P* and *T* detection. Specific detection algorithms for other waves such as flutter, fibrillation, and artificial pacemaker spikes are rare.

Delimitation of wave boundaries constitutes a difficult feature-extraction problem. Even so, most systems determine *QRS* boundaries and algorithm complexities range from a one-pass forward scan to multiple-pass scans both backward and forward. Generalized algorithms to recognize the complexities of an abnormal wave have difficulty in excluding small amounts of artifact or portions of a different proximal wave.

Descriptions of wave morphology fall into two classes: 1) time-ordered (sampled data, first difference, extrema, segment sequences, etc.) and 2) time-independent (envelope measures such as duration, amplitude, and polarity, also area, maximum derivative, etc.). A time-ordered morphology description may result in a feature space with a variable number of dimensions. The location of a complex in this space can be quite sensitive to the location of its fiducial mark. Time-independent measures generally have fixed dimensions and are less sensitive to fiducial-mark location, but usually do not allow unique reconstruction. Measurement of interwave intervals is dependent on wave detection and delimitation capabilities. The relative time of successive *QRS* complexes is variously measured as the interval between *QRS* detection points or *R*-wave peaks (*RR*) or as the interval between initial *QRS* boundaries (*QQ*).

Although patterns clearly associated with cardiac events appear in the ECG, classification of the ECG is difficult for two reasons: 1) measurement at a distance obscures cardiac processes (see Section IV-A above) and 2) complex variabilities are inherent in the phenomena. This variability has long been known but is often overlooked. Fig. 10 shows the striking change Einthoven [121] observed in the *QRS* of a subject who merely changed position. Fig. 11 shows the wide intraclass variability of two features of the normal ECG. The manifestation of a cardiac event may vary with the location of the recording site, as well. A wave morphology, bizarre at one location, can simultaneously appear quite normal at another as in Fig. 12.

Inconsistency of the human observer adds another form of variability to the problem of ECG analysis. In a study in which 125 ECG's were analyzed twice by nine experienced interpreters, the results were consistent on the average in just 73 percent of the cases [122]. Machine processing using ob-

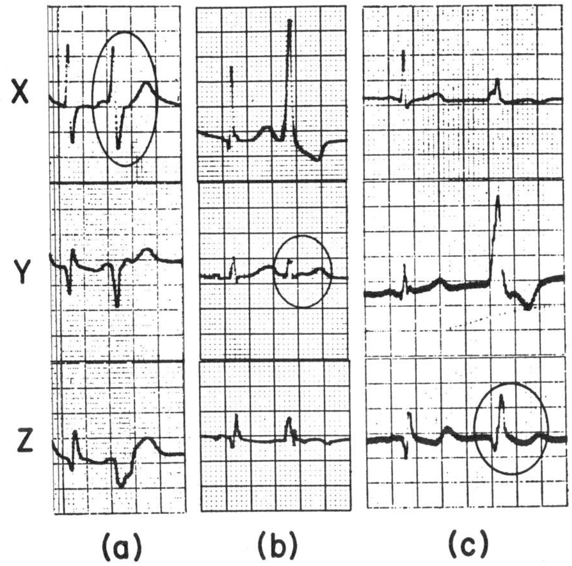

Fig. 12. PVC morphologies may bear a striking resemblance to the normally conducted *QRS* complex in any single lead, even to indistinguishability [174]. From 10 randomly selected-heart station ECG's showing PVC's in the Frank leads, these 3 records were chosen as showing PVC's (encircled) bearing the strongest similarity to the immediately preceding normal *QRS* complexes. (a) *X* lead. (b) *Y* lead. (c) *Z* lead. Their manifestations in simultaneously recorded leads immediately above and below demonstrate their true bizarre nature and lengthened conduction time.

jective measurement and classification criteria may provide more nearly reproducible analysis [123]. For example, computer measurement can reduce variation in the *P* and *QRS* durations, in the *QT* interval, and in the values of wave amplitudes in the *QRS* compared to visual determinations [124]. Beat-to-beat changes in the ECG itself cannot be eliminated, of course. The minimum variation from beat to beat in a given feature, however, establishes a practical lower bound on measurement accuracy [125].

ECG features are obtained clinically by recording from electrodes placed at specified anatomical locations. A combination of two or more potential sensing electrodes, which may be interconnected with an appropriate weighting network is known as a lead. Lead systems, as practical entities, have evolved empirically and as the result of biophysical analysis. They usually represent a compromise which attempts to maximize the information content without being redundant and to minimize the number of electrodes, thus reducing application time or interference with the patient. The minimum number of electrodes required to reconstruct all the potentials on the torso surface has been investigated by Barr and co-workers [126]. They selected 10 ECG isopotential maps in 45 pediatric patients. Using principal component analysis and a minimum mean-square estimation method, 24 properly placed electrodes were found to be necessary to accurately reconstruct maps determined from recordings at 150 sites.

A single lead, just two electrodes, has been the common choice for rhythm monitoring, originally designed to warn of extreme arrhythmias in coronary care units. Observation of the single-lead ECG is certainly sufficient for diagnosis of ventricular fibrillation or standstill. For this reason, single-lead ECG rhythm analysis became a common practice, often being performed by nurses and other trained personnel in the temporary absence of a skilled electrocardiographer. In the course of this intensive observation it soon became apparent that even a single lead revealed a wide variety of other rhythm disturbances. As indicated in Fig. 12, however, a multiple-lead ECG may be preferred and is sometimes required for consistent diagnosis.

The most commonly utilized multiple-lead system is the conventional 12-lead set. Either it or one of the 3-lead corrected orthogonal systems which give the components of an equivalent cardiac dipole is the usual choice for morphological analysis. The choice is limited, at present, because the accumulation of sufficient criteria to reliably characterize a lead system is a very difficult, lengthy, and exacting process.

The 12-lead set uses 9 electrodes and consists of 3 limb leads [120], [127], 3 augmented limb leads [128], and 6 precordial leads [129]. Among the vectorcardiographic (VCG) configurations are the 7-electrode Frank system [130], the 14-electrode SVEC III system [131], the 7-electrode Helm system [132], and the 11-electrode axial system [133].

Unfortunately, criteria for one VCG system may not apply to another because lead systems derived using different model assumptions are not generally interchangeable [134], [135]. Even though specific criteria may differ, the information content of VCG and conventional ECG leads appears to be substantially the same [136], [137]. Thus the four-to-one data reduction possible with orthogonal systems gives them an important advantage for automatic analysis. Because both conventional ECG and VCG leads are incomplete, the more familiar ECG leads may still be preferable [138]. In a direct comparison of diagnostic accuracy by ten cardiographers, analysis of scalar ECG's gave 54-percent correct disease classification while VCG analysis was only 49-percent correct [139].

The best extraction and classification procedures may fail if the necessary features are not adequately emphasized or are not present at all in the input stream. Information that is present in a lead system but which is not manifest can be brought out by an appropriate transformation. Batchlor and co-workers [140] have successfully determined lead directions derived from VCG's which optimally separate normals from patients with left or right ventricular hypertrophy (LVH, RVH). One measurement in a single lead for LVH and one in another for RVH equaled the diagnostic performance of eight features from twelve leads. Kelly and co-workers [141] have proposed a linear lead transformation that minimized the mean-square error between a patient's VCG and a standard VCG. This technique assumes the primary differences between diagnostic classes will be nonlinear.

Multiple-dipole and multipole-source descriptions have been investigated as refinements of the simple dipole model in order to extract more information from the torso ECG's. Holt, Barnard, and Lynn [142], recorded ECG's from a 126-electrode grid to determine a 12-dipole cardiac model. The ventricles and septum were segmented into 12 regions, each represented by a dipole fixed in location and orientation and constrained to be nonnegative. These dipoles performed better than either the 12 scalar or 3 vector leads in diagnosing left ventricular hypertrophy. The strength of local cardiac activity can also be examined with aimed leads [143] constructed from multipole coefficients. A multipole expansion containing dipole and quadrupole terms has proved successful in extracting the significant features of torso maps from a single subject [144]. Trost [145] developed a reliable, 17-electrode, dipole plus quadrupole lead system and used it to investigate aimed leads and other transforms in 50 normal and 9 abnormal subjects. Although the VCG transforms and nondipolar lead systems are not yet clinically important, they represent valid logical ways to expand the ECG information available for morphological classification.

C. *Automatic Morphological Analysis*

This section reflects the usual two-step pattern-recognition procedure. Under *Feature Extraction*, we describe data acquisition, digital preprocessing, and wave-measurement methods. *Classification Techniques* are divided into heuristic and statistical methods.

1) Feature Extraction: Clearly, the characteristics of the ECG acquisition system affect the values determined by any subsequent measurement routine. Although almost all machine processing is now done digitally, special analog preprocessing steps such as identification of critical slope changes or generation of fiducial marks for averaging have been used [146], [147]. The recommendations of the Committee on Electrocardiography of the American Heart Association [148] suggest a conversion rate of 500 samples/s with a 9-bit precision. In practice, rates from 200 to 1000 samples/s have been utilized with 8-bit to 12-bit precision [149]. Digital smoothing is often employed to reduce noise which could confuse the feature-extraction routines. As a result, the upper frequency limit for most systems is well below 100 Hz.

Digital preprocessing: One or more new functions may be derived from weighted sums of the sampled values to aid in feature extraction. Smoothing is often done digitally because it can be better controlled and more easily implemented than with an equivalent analog filter [150]. Averaging of the signals from successive cardiac cycles to improve the signal-to-noise ratio is usually employed only if the artifact problem is severe, for example, as is the case with exercise ECG's. Differentiating the ECG yields the basic information used for *QRS* detection. The derivative is also important in delimiting wave boundaries.

Although the three basic mathematical formulations of the digital filter problem (convolution, recursion, and z transforms) lead to specific implementation forms, the simplest, a weighted sum, has usually been chosen for smoothing in ECG analysis. The weighting function must be symmetrical to avoid the introduction of a phase shift relative to the original sampled data. Uniform weighting yields a running average [151], [152]. Steinberg *et al.* [153] and Stark *et al.* [154] smoothed the ECG by using a least squares error criterion to fit the sampled data with a parabola whose value at the center sample replaces that sample. Stallmann and Pipberger [155] and Macfarlane [156] employed cosine weights for smoothing, with values chosen to yield a null at the power line frequency. An approximation to an ideal filter using weights derived from a truncated $(\sin x)/x$ function is described by Pryor [157]. Fig. 13 compares the frequency response of these four filter types.

The digitized ECG signal can be differentiated one scalar lead at a time. Alternatively, the spatial velocity, the derivative of the equivalent cardiac dipole or of a pseudovector composed of arbitrary leads, may be obtained. The first-difference method is commonly utilized, but because of its asymmetric nature, it introduces a phase shift with respect to the sampled data, possibly contributing to errors in wave-boundary delimitation. The coefficient of the linear term in the least squares parabola also estimates the derivative. Both first-difference and parabola techniques provide additional smoothing to reduce the sensitivity of the derivative to high-frequency noise. A factor of $\sin(2\pi f/r)/(2\pi f/r)$, where f is the frequency of interest and r the sampling rate, relates the derivative to the first difference. Smoothing is even greater for the parabolic method, involving a factor that includes higher multiples of (f/r).

Wave measurement: After the *QRS* complex is located, wave boundaries are determined, and a baseline is found. Whereas scalar leads sampled sequentially must be processed independently, simultaneous sampling permits direct temporal comparison of critical points. This comparison, possible for most systems using VCG leads, may provide an important aid in wave delimitation. The measured quantities include: peak and instantaneous amplitudes, durations, interwave intervals, areas, and spatial angles of the cardiac dipole. Values from several beats may be compared and selected measurements averaged. The procedure is straightforward for a quiet stylized waveform such as the one depicted in Fig. 14(a). Programs quickly become very complex as they are adapted to handle real signals (Fig. 14(b)).

A scalar-lead program with more than 10 000 instructions was developed by Caceres and co-workers [153], [158], [159] at the Medical Systems Development Laboratory (MSDL). Using a parabolic filter and derivative method, the most negative derivatives in a 5-s record locate the downslope of the *R* waves. Tests are included to eliminate *P* or *T* waves, ectopic beats, and other arrhythmias from the set of acceptable *R* waves. Fixed intervals after the downslope of the *R* and before its peak are searched for minima to define *S* and *Q*, respectively. The derivative is used to determine the *QRS* onset and end while the *P* onset fixes the baseline. Processing of the *P* and *T* waves is similar. The end-of-*P* routine, for example, has 47 steps, each of which either specifies a test or makes a comparison followed by a branch to the appropriate subsequent step in the routine. An evaluation of measurements in 200 single-lead records using a version of this program showed computed and visually determined wave durations agreed within 20 ms in about 90 percent of the cases except for *ST* and *T* (30 ms) and *QT* (50 ms) [160]. Wave amplitude agreement within 100 μV occurred in about 90 percent of the cases. Milliken and Wartak [161]–[163] have modified the MSDL routines, characterizing wave detection and delimitation rules in decision tables and using a histogram to determine the baseline. A similarly structured digital measurement system, which relies on analog preprocessing for *QRS* detection and *P*, *QRS*, and *T* delimitation has been reported by Kimura [152]. Wortzman *et al.* [146] describe a 12-lead program in which measurements are made on a template initially constructed from the first beat analyzed, then refined by subsequent beats. Compared to visual determination the differences for both *PR* intervals and *QRS* durations were within 15 ms and for *QT* intervals, within 35 ms in about 90 percent of 143 cases.

Pipberger pioneered the analysis of VCG leads, simultaneously sampling 6 s of the Frank leads [155], [164]–[167] and using the first-difference spatial velocity to detect the *QRS* and establish a fiducial mark. The *QRS* boundaries are then found by moving backward and forward from the fiducial

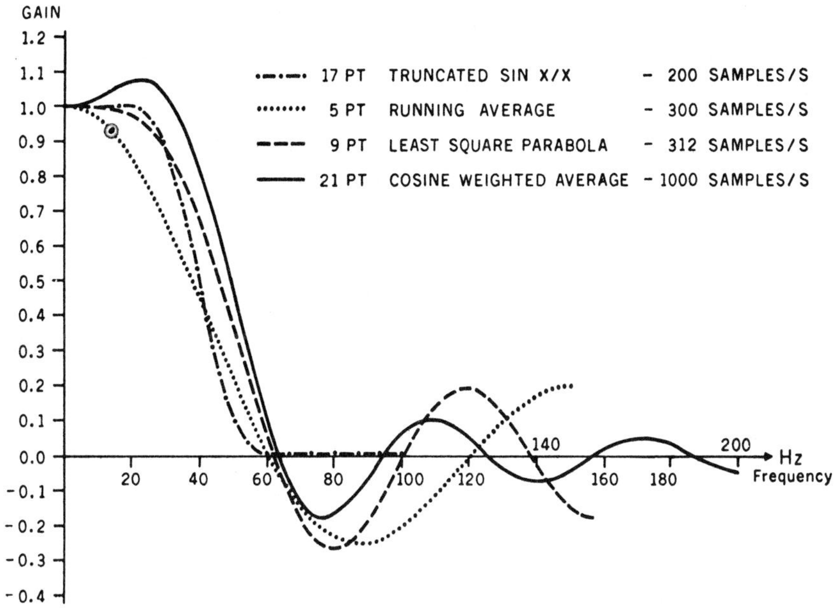

Fig. 13. Frequency response of 4 types of digital smoothing used with ECG data. The five-point running average for data converted at 300 samples/s was chosen to go to zero at 60 Hz. The least-squares parabola response is calculated using the weights given in [153], but at one-half the sampling rate. The response of the cosine weighted average is described in [155], and the truncated sin x/x weights are tabulated in [157]. Those curves that do not extend to 200 Hz are terminated at the folding frequency.

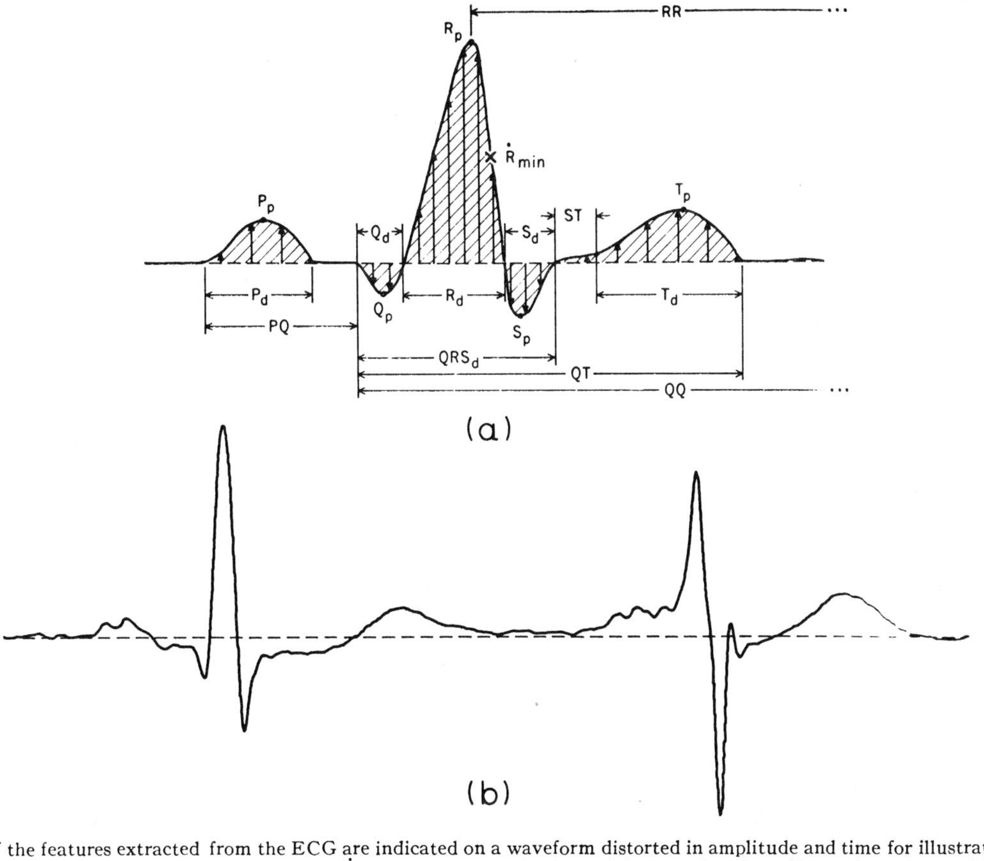

Fig. 14. (a) Some of the features extracted from the ECG are indicated on a waveform distorted in amplitude and time for illustrative purposes. Features designated are the point of minimum derivative ($\dot{R}_{min}$), peak amplitudes (R_p, etc.), wave durations (R_d, etc.), and several interwave intervals (*RR*, etc.). The vertical arrows correspond to instantaneous values, usually time-normalized over a wave or complex. The number of instantaneous values selected as features is usually greater over the *QRS* than for the *P* or *T* waves. Wave areas, the crosshatched regions, are also commonly calculated wave features. (b) The difficulties of obtaining these features in practice are suggested by the deviations from the stylized waveform in (a), which occur for real ECG's (b), shown here sampled at 500 samples/s and with a different time scale than in (a).

mark until the spatial velocity falls below a variable threshold. After P and T delimitation, the various waves are described with more than 300 features including wave amplitudes and durations, time-normalized vectors, polar vectors, eigenvectors, wave integrals, and amplitude ratios. In a test of the system on 106 records, the agreement between computed and visually determined values was within 25 ms for about 90 percent of the PR intervals and QRS durations and also for about 80 percent of the P-wave durations and QT intervals [155].

Wave amplitudes and durations are determined for X, Y, and Z leads by Arvedson [168] with a system that plots the sampled data for any interval in which the waves are not recognized by the computer. The results of cross correlation with a template are used by van Bemmel and co-workers [169] to delimit waves in a 30-s record of X, Y, and Z leads—one of the longest records analyzed. Stark and co-workers [170], [154] describe P, QRS, and T complexes of SVEC III and Frank leads by amplitude-normalized voltages at time-normalized instants, after delimiting procedures based on the spatial magnitude and velocity.

A number of other investigators have also analyzed the Frank leads. Nomura and co-workers [151] use a derivative of the X lead to detect the QRS. Tests of magnitudes and the spatial velocity in fixed intervals specified the onset of P and Q and the end of P, S, and T to within 10 ms of visual values in about 90 out of 100 cases. The waves are represented by critical point amplitudes and baseline intercepts. About 30 features related to the intervals, amplitudes, and durations of waves are determined by Yasui *et al.* [171], [172]. The procedure sets a fiducial mark in the QRS corresponding to the maximum sum of the absolute value of the X, Y, and Z derivatives. Weaver and co-workers [150] use the spatial velocity to detect the R wave and the PR and ST segments. Beginning with rough estimates, the wave onsets and ends are then fixed at points at which normalized moveable window integrals on the spatial magnitude exceed a threshold. In a study by Pryor [173], after R detection, a threshold is determined for each lead equal to 1/6 the maximum difference in that lead. The QRS limits are set where five successive 3-point differences are below threshold in all three leads. The output of this program provides durations, amplitudes, intervals, integrals, and ratios of the various waves.

Several systems have been designed to handle both 3-lead and 12-lead sets. Parts of programs developed at Mt. Sinai Hospital and the Mayo Clinic have been incorporated into two expanded versions, so that each can analyze both conventional and vector leads [174]. Bonner and Pordy [175]–[177] produced a system at Mt. Sinai to record standard and Frank leads in five sets of three simultaneous leads to yield both 12-lead and VCG diagnostics. See Section IV-D1) for some details of the feature extraction portion of this program. Smith and Hyde [178]–[180] at the Mayo Clinic record 10 s of both Frank lead and 12-lead data using up to six simultaneous input channels. A time difference function which uniformly weights points 10 and 15 ms on either side of the sample of interest is the key criterion in the delimiting process. A comparison of visual and computer determination of P duration and PR interval in 248 cases showed a mean difference of 14.8 and 11.9 ms, respectively. A program for analyzing vector leads and 12-lead sets processed in four pseudo-orthogonal groups has been described by Macfarlane [156]. The spatial velocity and its equivalent is used to specify approximate wave onset and end with a 3-mV/s and 1.5-mV/s threshold for QRS and T, respectively. P delimitation is related to the maximum spatial velocity in the interval before the QRS. A panel of cardiologists found the maximum incidence of clinically significant wave duration errors to be 3.4 percent.

Some of the difficulties in the wave-extraction process can be avoided by transforming the ECG to another feature space. Of course, the QRS first must be detected to provide the original fiducial mark. The measurement routine becomes just the calculation of a set of features describing the new representation. Cady and co-workers [181] expressed the ECG as a Fourier series. The dimensionality of the feature space, however, is reduced most efficiently by eigenvector analysis. The resulting orthogonal vectors are known variously as intrinsic components [182], principal factors [117], and elements in a Karhunen–Loève expansion [183]. Representation in terms of these orthogonal vectors requires diagonalizing a correlation matrix derived from the ECG waveform. Young and Huggins [116], who investigated intrinsic components, elected to use six pairs of matched orthonormal exponentials as basis functions because they are easier to compute.

2) Classification Techniques: The diagnostic category into which a particular ECG morphology falls can be determined in a variety of ways. The simplest approach is to match the waveform to a set of templates using an appropriate similarity criterion [150]. Where large variations occur within the patterns of a given category, such as is the case in electrocardiography, the choice of template and matching criterion are extremely difficult [184]. Consequently, features which are presumably invariant within a given disease category are selected for classification. There are two basic approaches that deal with extracted features. The most obvious approach is to automate the clinical procedure used by a cardiologist. In this approach binary decisions which test the wave measurements against established criteria lead to appropriate categories [185]. Most heart-station programs are constructed in this way. The object is to approximate the performance of a cardiologist, so that he only has to verify the computer findings. In an alternate approach, statistical decision methods are applied with the aim of improving diagnostic accuracy beyond that possible for an unassisted cardiologist.

Binary decision trees: A heuristic linear discriminant function implements the comparison of measurements and criteria at the node of a decision tree in most heart-station programs. These discriminant functions are not unique as can be seen in Table IV. Criteria are shown for just one condition, left ventricular hypertrophy. Programs also differ in the number of possible diagnostic categories, in the number of paths to a given category, and in the interaction between paths.

Table V shows partial results of evaluations of several heart-station programs. Percent agreement gives the percentage of correct classifications in all categories and naturally depends on the number of possible categories. The false-positive percentage is the rate at which normal ECG's are classified as abnormal. The false-negative rate gives the percentage of abnormals classified as normal. In all but one case the programs use a heuristic approach with the "correct" classification determined by one or more cardiologists, often after reviewing the computer findings. The Veteran's Administration (VA) program [167] utilizes a statistical approach with selection of records for a given category made independently of the ECG, i.e., based entirely on medical history, physical exami-

TABLE IV
EXAMPLES OF CRITERIA COMPATIBLE WITH LEFT-VENTRICULAR HYPERTROPHY

	After Weihrer *et al.* [159]	After Pordy *et al.* [176]
12 Lead	eliminate left bundle branch block and { (R_p in II) >1.5 mV or (R_p in a VL) >1.0 mV or (S_p in V_1) + (R_p in V_5 or V_6) >3.5 mV } or (S_p in V_1 or V_2) + (R_p in V_5 or V_6) >4.6 mV (consistent with LVH)	eliminate left bundle branch block and { (R_p in V_5 or V_6) >2.7 mV or (Q_p or S_p in V_1) + (R_p in V_5 or V_6) >3.5 mV or (R_p in a VL) ≥ 1.3 mV or (R_p in I) + (S_p in III) ≥ 2.6 mV } and age >30 years
	After Nomura *et al.* [197]	After Pryor *et al.* [173]
VCG	$QRS_d < 126$ ms and (S_p/R_p in X) <0.4 and { (R_p in X) ≥ 1.7 mV or { (R_p in X) ≤ 1.7 mV and (R_p in X) + (S_p in Z) ≥ 2.5 mV } }	$QRS_d < 120$ ms and (S_p/R_p in Z) <7 and (integral over first 40 ms of QRS in Y) ≥ -500 and (integral over first 40 ms of QRS in X) ≥ -500 and (R_p in X) + (S_p in Z) ≥ 3.5 mV

Note: Assumptions have been made to make the notation consistent with Fig. 14.

TABLE V
SCREENING RESULTS OF SELECTED HEART-STATION EVALUATIONS

Source of Program	Source of Records	Date of Test	Reference	Leads	Agreement (%)	Normals (Negative) Number of Records	True Negative (%)	False Positive (%)	Abnormals (Positive) Number of Records	True Positive (%)	False Negative (%)
Medical Systems Development Laboratory	George Washington University Hospital	1966	[186]	ECG	73	148	72	28	598	99.2	0.8
Medical Systems Development Laboratory	Hartford Hospital	1967	[190]	ECG	87	113	100	0	253	81	19
Medical Systems Development Laboratory	Hartford Hospital	1967	[191]	ECG	78	276	80	20	52	67	33
Medical Systems Development Laboratory	George Washington University Hospital	1968	[187]	ECG	81	178	97.3	2.2	469	96.6	3.4
MSDL and Queen's University	Queen's University Teaching Hospital	1969	[194]	ECG	82	112	86	14	88		
MSDL and Queen's University	Hotel Diev Hospital and Kingston General Hospital	1970	[193]	ECG	85	762	90	10	1257	96	4
Mt. Sinai Hospital	Mt. Sinai Hospital	1967	[176]	ECG	91	996	91	9	1064	94	6
Mayo Clinic	University of Washington and Group Health Hospitals	1970	[198]	VCG	74	289	75	25	84	76	24
Latter-day Saints Hospital	Latter-day Saints Hospital	1969	[173]	VCG	95	195	99	1	92	91	9
Osaka Center for Adult Diseases	Osaka Center for Adult Diseases	1966	[197]	VCG	82	100	80	20	105	84	16
Iowa Methodist Hospital	Iowa Methodist Hospital	1967	[196]	I, II, $V2$		1708	99.7	0.3	3090	91	9
Mt. Sinai Hospital and Mayo Clinic	l'Hospital Brugmann	1970	[199]	VCG ECG	81 85	105 432	83 91.5	17 8.5	 1303		
Mt. Sinai Hospital and Mayo Clinic	l'Hospital Brugmann	1971	[200]	VCG ECG	67 89	2589 1487	78 95	22 5	603 5334	95.6	4.4
Mt. Sinai Hospital and Mayo Clinic	CHU Bretonneau à Tours	1971	[201]	ECG ECG+VCG	85 87	73 73	93	7	427 427	83	17
Royal Infirmary Glasgow	Royal Infirmary Glasgow	1971	[202]	VCG ECG	81 82	205 205	73 73	27 27	419 419	85 86	15 14
VA Research Center	VA Hospitals	1971	[167]	VCG	74	597	90	10	2005	89	11

nations, and laboratory and autopsy data.

The first comprehensive work implementing a binary decision tree was begun at MSDL [186]. This program has been tested at heart stations [186], [187], used for mass screening [188], [189], evaluated remotely from a community hospital [190], and applied to records taken in routine physicals [191]. Milliken and Wartak [192]–[194] adapted the MSDL program, systematizing the classification process in decision tables similar to the ones they used for wave measurement rules. Conventional lead interpretation has been investigated by Staples and co-workers using manually extracted features [195]. They have also compared a 3-lead screening system to 12-lead findings [196]. In a 3-lead program developed by Nomura and co-workers [197] tentative diagnoses are made based on measurements of the $P-PQ$, QRS, and $ST-T$ complexes considered separately, and are then combined for a final diagnosis. Pryor and co-workers [173] considered several other interpretation schemes, including the use of predictive filters, before deciding on a method similar to a cardiologist's heuristic procedure. The Mayo Clinic [178] and Mt. Sinai Hospital [176] systems are the only ones in addition to the MSDL program which have been evaluated by investigators other than the developers [198]–[201]. Although the tests of the Mt. Sinai program revealed greater errors for VCG than for 12-lead analysis, Macfarlane [202] found no substantial difference. Variations in the evaluation results of Table V reflect, for a given system, its evolution, differing interpretation standards, transition from training set to test set, and varied populations.

Statistical methods possess the capability of simultaneously handling more factors than can be managed by humans. Since they can also be constructed to maximize the likelinood of correct classification, they may have greater diagnostic power than present heuristic techniques. An important consideration in optimizing the decision making process is the selection of features which best separate measurements from patients belonging to different disease categories. Von der Groeben [203] addressed the problem of adequately determining decision regions for 12-lead and VCG measurements. Mucciardi and Gose [204] examined statistical, information theoretic, and sequential techniques for selecting significant features from a set of measured quantities. They found a weighted sum of 1) the probability of error when used alone and 2) the average of correlation coefficients with the other features the best of seven heuristically chosen methods.

A set of measurements, presumably of significant features, can be optimally classified using a Bayes decision rule. The decision rule in its simplest form permits, with the use of Bayes's theorem, calculation of the probability that a given measurement belongs to each of the disease categories. Kimura *et al.* [205] and Wartak [206] applied Bayes's theorem to electrocardiographic data. Kimura used a 47-dimensional 2-level space so that the *a priori* probabilities for all possible measurements could be tabulated. Wartak calculated probabilities at new measurement points by assuming normal distributions for the clusters. Distributions with finely quantized features are not used because the sample population would have to be enormous for statistical convergence. Yasui and associates [172] describe a decision tree in which branching is done on the basis of joint probabilities calculated as the product of individual wave-amplitude and wave-duration probabilities, each assumed to be normally distributed independent random variables.

Multivariate normal distributions were assumed to characterize 12 wave features in a study by Rikli and co-workers [207]. The statistical significance of differences between feature means, variances, and correlation coefficients was determined for normals and two disease states—hypertension and aortic insufficiency. Pipberger and co-workers applied a Bayes rule to multivariate normal distributions [164], [166], [208] to generate linear discriminant functions for a data base that now contains more than 20 000 patient records. With the use of this technique, optimal features were sought in the diagnosis of ventricular hypertrophy [209], ventricular conduction defects [210], pulmonary emphysema [211], and myocardial infarction [212]. In each case over 300 features were considered. The best individual features were selected using various simple statistical procedures. For a set of about 30 features the best discriminators were then chosen by multivariate analysis. These discriminators included both clinically familiar features and instantaneous vectors. The investigators suggest that to obtain reproducible results the number of features should be less than the square root of the number of members in each cluster. Multivariate analysis did as well as, or improved significantly upon, previous reports with empirical criteria. For example, in a study on 1002 myocardial infarction cases, discriminant-function classification was 84-percent correct with a 6-percent false-positive rate [212]. The 12-lead classification scheme known as the Minnesota Code [213] was only 49-percent correct for the same false-positive rate.

Linear discriminant functions have been constructed in a variety of other ways. Young and Huggins [214] determined a diagnostic matrix to relate exponential basis functions representing ECG's to a feature vector useful in establishing the subject's membership in a disease category. Cady [181] employed a stepwise search to construct a linear discriminant function in which the Fourier coefficient of the ECG that minimized the error in estimating patient status was added at each step. Later, Cady [215] calculated discriminant multipliers for R-wave and T-wave amplitudes to separate patients with left ventricular strain, myocardial infarction, and coronary insufficiency using a technique based on characterizing cluster envelopes with ellipsoidal boundaries. Another form of linear discriminant is the correlation or matched filter technique which extracts a single feature of the ECG, its cross-correlation coefficient with a reference waveform. The dimensionality of the measurement space has usually been fixed by time-normalizing the waveforms. Balm [216] applied a correlation technique to the QR portion of lead I (left to right arm) records to screen normals from four disease categories.

Correlation techniques are usually easy to implement, and in addition the reference waveform or matched filter can be made adaptive. Stark and co-workers [170], [217], [218], [154] have shown that this approach compares favorably to the classification done by humans. A waveform in the training set is added to a particular filter if the cross-correlation coefficient exceeds a threshold. The threshold level determines the number of different filters required to classify all the ECG's in a given population. A similar learning procedure was described by Sano *et al.* [219] who utilized adaptive linear discriminant functions at the nodes of a decision tree.

Multivariate transformations can be used to appropriately weight discriminants to emphasize both the separation of different categories and the clustering of measurements from a given category [220]. In some cases, however, it may be necessary to describe the surface-separating clusters in more detail than that provided by the hyperplane representing a linear discriminant function. McFee and Baule [221] compute the squared distance from measurement point to cluster center, a quadratic discriminant function, assuming independent normal distributions. Specht [222] has demonstrated a general polynomial discriminant technique which makes no assumption about the cluster distributions. Rather, they are estimated by a sum of exponentials. Coefficients of the polynomials representing the separating boundaries can be deter-

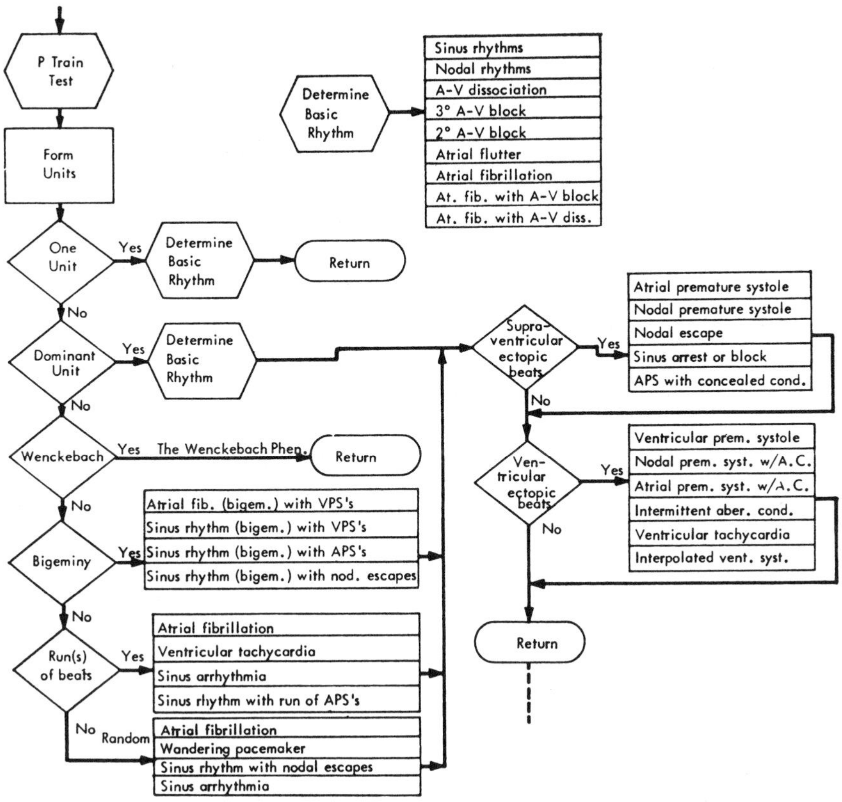

Fig. 15. A flowchart of the gross rhythm-analysis logic for individual leads in an ECG diagnostic system orders tests by reliability for basic rhythms and complicating irregularities. Diagnoses for individual leads are then logically combined to select 1 of 27 basic rhythm statements and 1 or more of 21 suffix statements concerning ectopic beats and other basic rhythm disturbances. From Bonner and Schwetman [226].

mined adaptively. Using a Bayes decision rule, any decision strategy from hyperplane separation to nearest neighbor selection can be implemented depending on the smoothness with which the actual distributions are estimated. For smoothing which is chosen to give highest correct diagnosis in separating normals and abnormals for a 246-case training set, the polynomial contained 27 linear terms, 2 squared terms, and a constant [223].

D. *Automatic Rhythm Analysis*

Cardiac rhythm terms, confined primarily to the domain of the electrocardiographer slightly over a decade ago, now enjoy widespread familiarity in the medical and biomedical community. In particular, the premature ventricular contraction (PVC), bizarre and elephantine in its appearance in the ECG and variously known as a ventricular premature beat or extrasystole, has achieved notoriety as a harbinger of ventricular fibrillation [224].

Interest in the manifestations of extrasystoles and other cardiac arrhythmias is not recent with published references dating to the 6th century B. C. [225]. The first ECG tracings of arrhythmias were shown by Einthoven in his initial publication [120]. He also described the first instance of ECG rhythm monitoring in this paper, detecting and reporting PVC's by remote telephone line.

1) Heart-Station Rhythm Diagnosis: Arrhythmia classification logic is found in varying degrees in digital computer ECG diagnostic systems [146], [154], [159], [174], [226]–[230]. Rhythm analysis advantages enjoyed by these systems are 1) access to multiple and sometimes simultaneous ECG leads, 2) signal quality control by human for each record, and 3) absence of real-time processing constraints. A significant disadvantage is the limited record length analyzed, typically a few seconds per lead.

The available literature indicates that progress in automatic rhythm analysis has lagged morphological analysis. In those efforts going beyond simple rhythm screening, logic-tree rhythm classification has been used, following textbook criteria, but often neglecting the many exceptions to the rules. Although evaluations have been rare, present rhythm classification potential appears strongly limited by the scope and quality of the extracted features.

Advanced work on rhythm diagnosis for the 12-lead ECG plus two additional 20-s rhythm leads has been described by Bonner and Schwetman [226]. In the flowchart of Fig. 15, the *P*-train test clusters together *PP* intervals and then tests the representative interval for each cluster to determine whether a significant "*P*-train interval" exists. In the absence of an obvious *P*-train interval, extensive logic is included to account for *P* waves which are possibly buried in *QRS* complexes or *T* waves. *QRS* complexes are clustered by comparing amplitudes and durations of their subcomplexes. The relative morphology of each *QRS* having been typed, clusters of adjacent pairs of *QRS* complexes are formed, based on morphology and *QQ* interval. A variety of other feature clusterings are made during traversal of the classification logic tree, many taking into account potential errors in the extracted feature data.

A detailed description of the feature extraction logic for this system has also been given [175]. A hardware preprocessor [231] was used to flag points in the 400 samples/s data stream for which the signal derivative passes from one zone to another. A digital "fine tuning" adjustment of the locations of these points was then performed. Several adjacent straight-line sections of the waveform described by these points were then grouped together into simple upright, inverted, or tilted V or U shapes. These overlapping shapes were scanned repeatedly to detect and measure conventional ECG waves, including atrial flutter wave activity, but not including artificial pacemaker spikes.

An explanation by the authors of the reasoning behind much of this logic points out some of the wave-feature extraction problems which are universally encountered. In a given lead, the sloping segments of bizarre *QRS* complexes may be much more gradual than the steepest slope of the "dominant" *QRS*, causing problems in differentiating all steep *T* waves from all *QRS* complexes. In determining the onset of a *QRS*, a portion of a nearby *P* may resemble a slurred beginning of the *QRS*. In comparing wave shapes for similarity, the results may be in error because the wave boundaries or other fiducial marks were measured inconsistently. Context-sensitive algorithms and measurements previously made on other leads were used by Bonner to help resolve these and other ambiguous situations [175].

In an evaluation [176] of the performance of the system containing this logic, basic rhythm statements and extra statements regarding ectopic beats were considered separately. For basic rhythm, in approximately 2000 cases of sinus rhythm, only 1 percent were falsely labeled abnormal. Of 70 cases of atrial fibrillation or of atrial flutter, only 6 percent were missed completely, but over 50 percent of 22 other abnormal rhythms were missed completely. The false-positive rate for ectopic-beat statements was higher than for basic rhythm, occurring in 7 percent of 1777 records not requiring them. Of 283 records requiring ectopic-beat statements, only 6 percent had none, but some ectopic beats were mislabeled as to type. More specifically, PVC statements were correctly given in 81 percent of the 133 cases requiring them and falsely given in approximately 2.5 percent of 1927 cases not requiring them.

2) *Automatic ECG Rhythm Monitoring:* Of all signals used for continuous monitoring of patient status, the ECG is most commonly employed. Hardware instruments providing computation of average ventricular heart rate with extremes leading to activation of high-rate or low-rate alarms have enjoyed widespread usage in hospitals for several decades. In the early 1960's, the first coronary care units (CCU's) were established using these instruments to aid immediate detection of ventricular fibrillation and other catastrophic arrhythmias in patients recovering from myocardial infarction. As CCU's proliferated, evidence accumulated that catastrophic arrhythmias were often preceded by lesser premonitory arrhythmias, and the emphasis of CCU treatment shifted from resuscitation to aggressive prophylactic therapy [224]. For most of today's CCU patients, monitoring of their ECG rhythm is performed by intensive visual observation of oscilloscope tracings augmented by automatic heart-rate alarms, a situation virtually unchanged from a decade ago.

Automatic rhythm analysis of long segments of ECG records poses special problems in addition to the inherent complexities of ECG rhythm patterns. Economic considerations cannot be neglected. While a cost of one dollar for a 20-s heart-station rhythm diagnosis may not be unreasonable, a cost of only one cent for monitoring each of the 4320 20-s rhythm strips of a single CCU patient in a single day is impractical. A complicating factor is that one may expect at best only infrequent human quality control of the input waveforms. In addition, continuous real-time analysis requires special techniques to stay abreast of the data.

Interwave interval clustering may be used to extract more information than is utilized by monitors of average or instantaneous ventricular heart rate. For example, the *RR*-interval histogram demonstrates patterns which may be visually correlated with different arrhythmias, and serial observation allows detection of rhythm changes [232], [233]. Gersch *et al.* [234] transformed *RR*-interval sequences into a three-symbol (short, regular, long) Markov chain sequence and successfully applied an automatic classification procedure for six arrhythmia classes in the training set of 35 cases of 100 beats each. Working with 189 records of 30 s each, Haisty *et al.* [235] recently investigated linear discriminant-function analysis of *RR* intervals. Utilizing the temporal locations of *P*-wave and *R*-wave peaks as measured by a human observer on 112 records of 60 beats each, Whipple and co-workers [236], [237] investigated digital computer logic for arrhythmia classification based on a "smoothed" *RR*-interval histogram. They concluded from an evaluation of the results that further development using wave-morphology information was necessary.

Most absolute measures of ECG wave morphology have little intrinsic value in single-lead rhythm monitoring. Duration of the *QRS* is probably the most important absolute measure since the spread of depolarization from an ectopic ventricular focus is usually slower than for a normally conducted beat. The apparent *QRS* duration, however, may be erroneously lengthened by noise which mimics small *Q* or *S* waves. The presence of AV bundle branch block or other intraventricular conduction defects also results in wide "normal" beats. Moreover, the *QRS* of a PVC may appear narrow because its initial or terminal portions are isoelectric. Nevertheless, relative comparisons of duration and other *QRS* morphology measures are used by the human.

A commercially available hybrid device utilizing *QRS* duration for rhythm monitoring has been described in some detail by Horth [238]. Three parallel processors provide *QRS* occurrence detection, *QRS* width measurement, and artifact detection. Manual initiation of a "stored normal" sequence tailors the feature-extraction characteristics to the patient's ECG at that time. In this case, thresholds for *QRS* detection and delimitation are set automatically, and a reference *QRS* width is measured. Moreover, manual switches allow the user to tailor device operation as an "ectopic beat" detector, selecting combinations of widened beats (*QRS* width at least 12 ms greater than the reference) and premature beats (*RR* interval at least 20 percent less than a running average) for data logging, alarm generation, and strip-chart presentation.

Manual tailoring of monitoring device operation to the patient is traditional and seen in varying degrees in most arrhythmia monitoring efforts. The degree to which device performance is dependent on operator performance thus becomes an important consideration in system evaluation, especially if frequent manual intervention is required. This may be a major reason for the lack of published performance data on simple heart-rate monitors. Whether the situation will recur for more sophisticated rhythm monitoring apparatus is an open question.

A variety of other hybrid devices measuring more than *RR* interval have been described as suitable for ECG rhythm monitoring. One compares the duration of each subwave of the *QRS* to a manually selected threshold for purposes of PVC detection [239]. The width of the *R* and the area inscribed by the *QRST* were also utilized [240]. Another device utilized a measure of *QRS* duration and polarity [241]. Detection of PVC's via measurement of *T* amplitude [242] and circuitry to sense ventricular fibrillation waves [243] have also been reported. Kezdi and co-workers [244], [245] have illustrated operation of a device for counting premature atrial contractions and premature ventricular contractions based on measures of *QRS* width, polarity (direction of the initial *QRS* deflection), and height (maximum amplitude of the rectified differentiated signal). Another ectopic-beat detector has been described [246], [247] in which the morphology of the patient's normal *QRS* complex is continually updated, but no details have been given. In a commercial ectopic-beat detector described by Harris *et al.* [248]–[253], utilizing waveforms consisting of products of the ECG signal and its derivative, each *QRS* complex is automatically classified into one of eight morphology states corresponding to eight prototypic *QRS* types (*R, Rs, rS, Q, Qr, qR*, broad *R*, broad *Q*). All morphology states corresponding to the patient's normal *QRS* are established during a 15-s learning period.

A different approach to wave morphology comparison was taken by Feezor *et al.* [254], [255] who constructed and tested a matched filter for a prototype PVC waveform (*QRS* and *T*). Its usage as a preprocessor in a digital computer system has also been described [256], [257]. A real-time filter matched to a prototype normal *QRS* complex for lead II has also been implemented [258]. Finally, a hybrid device for more complex rhythm diagnosis [259], [260] and other digital computer efforts utilizing hardware feature extraction [261], [262], have also been attempted.

Most computer scientists investigating ECG rhythm monitoring have been unwilling to rely on analog or hybrid preprocessors for anything more than simple filtering, preferring to retain algorithmic control over *QRS* detection and all other logic associated with feature extraction and classification. While simple rhythm-monitoring techniques have used a reference interval and wave morphology for comparison purposes, recent trends are toward automatic multiple clusterings of intervals and morphologies.

An early effort of this sort directed toward continuous ECG rhythm analysis of tape-recorded data sampled at 125 samples/s and utilizing the "stored normal" concept for classification of *QRS* morphology was performed by Lynch and Barnett [263]. A measure of the distance between the sample vectors for the reference and subsequent test waves was compared to a threshold to differentiate normal *QRS* complexes from those having a "significantly different shape." A logic-tree diagnosis was performed to identify some supraventricular and ventricular arrhythmias, and a summary was printed at regular intervals. An on-line display allowed a knowledgeable operator to monitor the computer's operation and to rapidly alter crucial controls.

With respect to more automatic operation, an attempt was made to monitor the single-lead ECG with elements of a diagnostic system operating intermittently at 500 samples/s [264], [265]. Approximately 4-s segments of ECG were acquired and then analyzed by computer in 2 s. Summary diagnoses were produced at 90-s intervals describing technical problems, rhythms, and wave morphology changes. Examples of computer output show relatively nonspecific rhythm diagnosis: "Atypical *QRS* or artifact, . . . rule out premature contractions." Dissatisfaction with arrhythmia classification accuracy was evident [264]. Future plans were strongly oriented toward statistical analysis of the extracted feature data, hoping to quantify clinically significant changes.

Monitoring extracted features of the cardiac cycle has also been done by Haywood and co-workers [266]–[269]. For their system, operating continuously on 240 samples/s data, the *RR* interval and four features of each wave (wave height, wave onset, peak, and termination times) in a *P–QRS–T* cycle are measured, and 10-percent variations from the reference values are reported. Reference values are obtained on startup by averaging eight cycles whose lengths pass a test for outliers. Recent reports on this work indicate additional comparisons for *QRS* width and adjacent *RR* intervals [270], [271].

A more circumscribed problem, detection of ectopic beats, has been pursued by Feldman and co-workers [272]–[275]. In this work, extensive development of feature extraction logic is bypassed in favor of a computationally demanding morphology-classification technique. A 300-ms segment of 200 samples/s data centered on the *QRS* detection point is compared with a stored normal *QRS* by computing the cross-correlation coefficient. A threshold value for differentiating normals and abnormals is set to the smaller of 0.875 or $2\rho_s - 1$, where ρ_s is a running average of the coefficient. Beats classed abnormal are also correlated with the first beat which was premature and followed by a compensatory pause. The computer operator is allowed selection of ventricular premature beat classification criteria, as well as *R*-detection thresholds and several other program parameters.

For monitoring post-surgical intensive care patients, Lewis and associates [276], [277] worked with ECG data at 60 samples/s, measuring *QRS* duration and *RR* interval for consecutive sets of 50 *QRS* complexes to produce some 23 different rhythm statements. Their plans, however, were to increase the sampling rate to obtain better resolution on the extracted features. In recent work by Cady [278] on 100 samples/s data, *QRS* morphology comparison is also based on the distance between sample vectors. The *QRS* detection logic is more selective, looking for a V-shaped signal in which the derivative exceeds both a positive and a negative threshold within 150 ms. Program output is oriented toward reporting on excessive change in *RR* or *PR* intervals or in the *QRS* shape. Other investigators have pursued PVC detection with methods for comparing *QRS* morphology. In a recent report by Geddes and Warner [279], the shape of a reference normal *QRS* complex is coded as a 160-ms sequence of derivatives quantized to three levels. For subsequent *QRS* complexes, segments of 120-ms duration are compared to the reference by computing a distance function. To allow for jitter in the *QRS* detection point, the test signal is shifted 20 ms to the left and right of the *QRS* detection point in 5-ms increments, and the minimum distance is chosen. In another recent paper by Gerlings *et al.* [280], *QRS* morphology is described by the minimum value of the first derivative and the total time duration during which the derivative is below a threshold level. A sampling rate of 500 samples/s was chosen to provide good resolution.

The cross-correlation coefficient has become a popular technique for stored normal *QRS* morphology comparison [281]–[283]; it currently forms the basis for development of a number of commercial monitoring systems. Young and Kohn [281] utilize a 300-ms segment of 200 samples/s data,

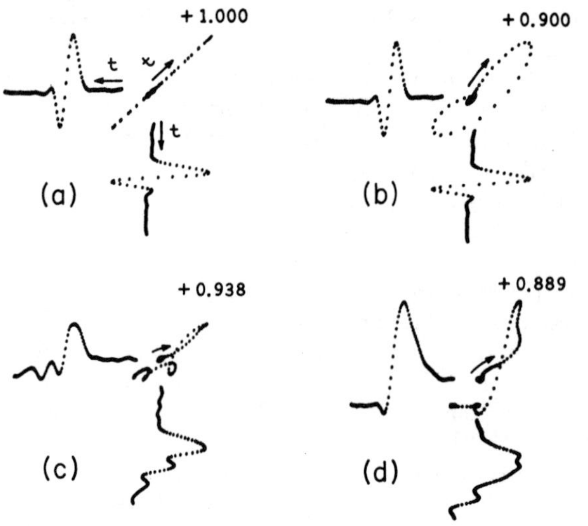

Fig. 16. The cross-correlation coefficient is shown for pairs of *QRS* complexes in approximately 200 ms of context at 500 samples/s. Waveforms selected for comparison are plotted along vertical and horizontal axes. The direction of increasing time is indicated in (a). The corresponding *X–Y* scatter plots show loop-like patterns familiar to the vector-cardiographer. (a) The straight-line scatter plot for a waveform time-aligned on itself has unity coefficient. (b) A 4-ms time shift causes a drop to 0.9. (c) Two adjacent normal beats. (d) Multifocal PVC beats were time-aligned at the point of maximum coefficient.

as did Feldman and co-workers [275], for comparison with a stored normal *QRS*, but do not state the threshold value used although they indicate a broad-band separating normals and abnormals. Abnormal waves are further correlated with up to seven stored PVC references. Kempner *et al.* [282] have used the cross-correlation coefficient with other measures of *QRS* morphology (*QRS* width, *R* and *S* amplitudes, absolute *QRS* area) in a Fortran analysis program. This effort also used a sampling rate of 200 samples/s, but no further details concerning usage of the coefficient were given. Another group [283] has recently illustrated beat-to-beat variations in the cross-correlation coefficient, using analog *QRS* detection for waveform synchronization.

Some insight to the workings of this classic statistical measure in comparing waveforms digitized with a time resolution of 2 ms is provided by Fig. 16. A slight time skew between identical waveforms reduces the cross-correlation coefficient below unity and is accompanied by a change in the straight-line scatter plot of Fig. 16(a) to the kidney-shaped loop of Fig. 16(b). For the similar, but not identical beats of Fig. 16(c), any algorithmic misalignment would cause a further decrease in their coefficient from the peak value of 0.938 shown here. In Fig. 16(d), two different PVC's from a single record form a more complex loop than that of Fig. 16(b), although a difference of only 0.011 is seen in their cross-correlation coefficients.

Several current efforts have devoted much work to feature extraction. Rey *et al.* [284], [285] have used Fortran to work with an approximation to the spatial velocity waveform for the *X*, *Y*, and *Z* leads of the Frank system. This group has concentrated on *P*-wave detection algorithms, although *QRS* and *T* detection and delimitation are also performed on the data sampled at 100 samples/s. Continuous ECG rhythm monitoring using 500 samples/s data for *QRS* measurements has been the goal of an effort by Whiteman and co-workers [286]. Complex algorithms for detection and delimitation of *P* and *T* waves on digitally preprocessed data at 125 samples/s are also under development, the effort devoted to *P*-wave searches probably exceeding any previous work on single rhythm leads.

To gain additional appreciation for the potential complexity of automatic rhythm monitoring, one may turn to work performed by Bonner [287]–[289]. During a two-year developmental effort, some 20K of machine-language instructions were packaged into a multiple-patient rhythm monitoring system. The overall approach is similar to his previously described work in ECG rhythm diagnosis. A preprocessing algorithm, operating on a smoothed derivative, is used to select specific samples from the original 240 samples/s data. Feature extraction, while somewhat simpler than for the diagnostic program, includes detection, delimitation, and description of all ECG waves including artificial pacemaker spikes and ventricular fibrillation waves. *QRS* waves are clustered into permanent "reference complex" or temporary "candidate complex" groups. Reference complex groups are labeled normal or PVC. Candidate complex groups having five members are either admitted as a new reference group or discarded as being artifactual or of unknown etiology. In order to handle a larger number of patients, preprocessed data are collected for 6 min and analysis is then performed, causing a gap in the monitoring, although continuous monitoring for "catastrophic events" was later added. At the present stage of development, an elaborate setup procedure is required. Work on this system has been dormant in recent times and equipment is expensive, but many of the concepts involved are possibly indicative of the future in ECG rhythm monitoring.

A highly structured approach to continuous ECG rhythm monitoring was initiated some seven years ago at the Washington University School of Medicine. In initial work on 500 samples/s data, computing time and data storage requirements were found to increase rapidly with algorithm complexity, especially as longer contextual segments of sampled data were included. Moreover, the hundreds of sampled data points contained in even short contextual segments prevented convenient visualization of the detailed operation of a particular algorithm on a particular waveform. The severity of these problems could have been reduced somewhat by decreasing the sampling rate but it seemed advisable to consider a different approach which might have some general applicability to later work.

Accordingly, a method of transforming the sampled ECG data to some other more compact waveform representation was sought. The result was a data compression scheme termed Aztec [102], producing a sequence of flat lines and sloping segments caricaturing the original ECG at a rate of approximately 25 elements/s. Algorithms for scanning the Aztec data for *QRS* feature extraction appeared practical and, most importantly, the operation of these procedures could be readily visualized. The Aztec algorithm became the first of a series of processing stages, each stage transforming data from the preceding stage by reducing redundancy to produce a reduced-data-rate output stream [290]. The second processing stage, termed Primitive, provided detection, delimitation, and description of ECG waves. The third-stage processor, Cycle, grouped together waves of similar shape as shown in Fig. 17 and provided efficient coding of interwave intervals. Finally, the task of the fourth-stage processor, Sequence, was production of rhythm analysis terms familiar to the clinician.

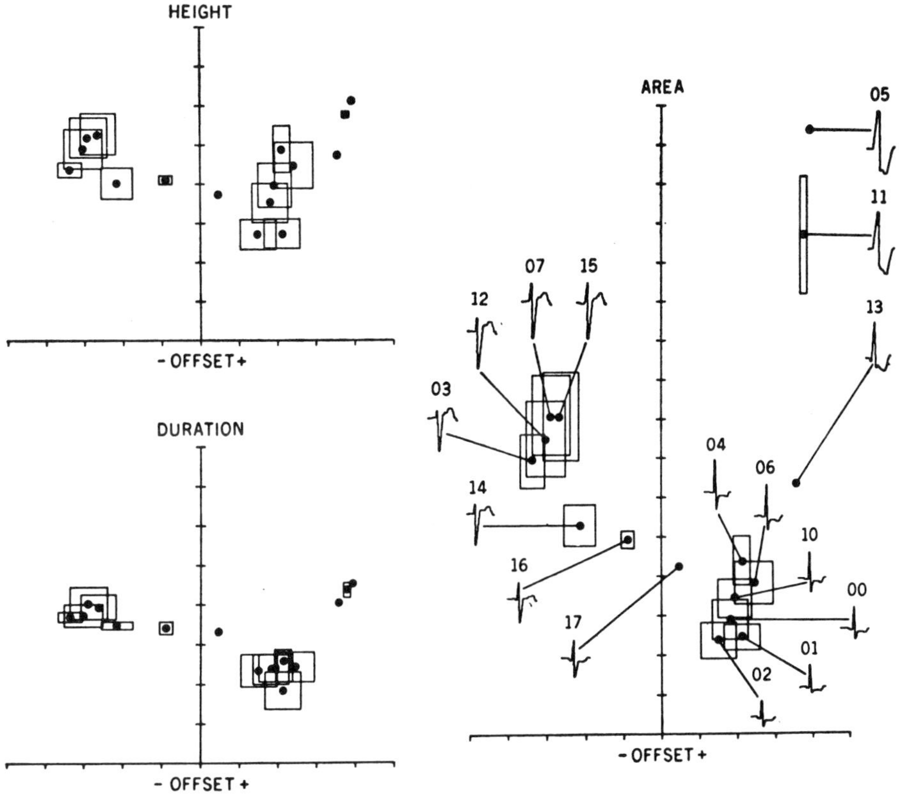

Fig. 17. The Argus cycle processor catalogs every *QRS* described by 4 morphology measures (duration, height, area, offset) in 1 of 16 dynamic families of similar complexes enclosed by 4-dimensional boxes. This snapshot of a patient's ECG families also shows typical members by waveform and number (base eight) in the area-offset plane. A normal morphology label had propagated to each family in the cluster 0, 1, 2, 4, 6, and 10, having a total of 463 members. Of these, 42 early members had been classed borderline during the families' evolutions. PVC's from 2 or more foci form the heads of 2 additional clusters tailing into the normals. Of 52 beats in these clusters, 51 were classed abnormal, the single member of family 17 having been classed borderline. After Nolle and Clark [295].

These processing stages utilized the resources of a single general purpose digital computer on a regularly scheduled priority basis [291].

The outgrowth of this project has been a system termed Argus (*A*rrhythmia *Gu*ard *S*ystem) which has been in round-the-clock clinical operation at the Barnes Hospital Coronary Care Unit since November of 1969. Argus's external appearance to the nurse and clinician is quite simple at present; automatic identification of PVC's in the presence of other rhythm complications for any two selected patients in the CCU, with trend-data displays and ECG paper writeout verification on PVC bursts which may be premonitory indicators [292], [293]. The present Argus system utilizes two small prototype patient computers but is amenable to a variety of modern hardware arrangements to monitor multiple patients [294]. The hierarchy of cascaded data transformation stages allowed orderly evolution and documentation of relatively compact algorithms [102], [290], [295], [296], but progress in producing clinically familiar rhythm terms has been slow, reflecting a quite conservative but apparently realistic view of the need for extracted data of high quality.

A beat-by-beat evaluation of Argus's performance in detection of PVC's has been performed by Oliver *et al.* [297]. Following a rigidly defined protocol, records of 34 patients having an average PVC rate of almost one out of every twelve beats were studied, and approximately 50 000 beats were analyzed independently by one of two cardiologists and correlated with the computer analysis. The overall results of this study are shown in Table VI. Referring to the intersection of the cardiologists' PVC column and Argus's PVC row 78 percent of the 4010 total PVC's were so labeled by Argus. Other rows intersecting this column show the fate of the remaining 22 percent. Only 38 normals (less than 0.1 percent) were falsely called PVC's, but 122 falsely detected *QRS* complexes were also called PVC's.

E. Discussion

The ECG constitutes a data base of extraordinary accessibility and size. Correspondingly, efforts in ECG pattern recognition are now so widespread that no single review can hope to provide a comprehensive picture. A detailed review of research aspects has been recently provided by McFee and Baule [118].

In this review, work on development of practical ECG analysis systems has been separated into morphological and rhythm analysis. Work has been further subdivided into feature extraction and subsequent classification. Finally, techniques have often been characterized as heuristic or statistical in nature, especially for classification. Such distinctions are somewhat artificial.

A good deal of underlying structure is imposed by detailed knowledge of excitation and conduction processes within the heart, causing a natural separation of ECG waves having a relatively large signal-to-noise ratio into *P*, *QRS*, and *T* waves. Identification and measurement of these waves has been viewed as feature extraction, a gross simplification for the complex records sometimes encountered. A wealth of material has related the form of these waves to the condition

TABLE VI
DETAILED SUMMARY OF ARGUS'S PERFORMANCE
(After Oliver *et al.* [297])

Argus's Classifications	Cardiologists' Classifications: Normal *QRS*	Aberrantly Conducted Beat Questionable Beat Ventricular Escape Beat	Premature Ventricular Contraction	*QRS* Falsely Detected	Argus's Totals
Significant artifact detected	2985— 6.6%	35— 7.7%	168— 4.2%	NA[a]	3188
QRS not detected	17— 0.04%	20— 4.4%	213— 5.3%	NA[a]	250
Normal *QRS* morphology	38 595— 85.1%	24— 5.3%	50— 1.2%	0— 0%	38 669
Borderline *QRS* morphology—non-PVC	3646— 8.0%	114— 25.2%	298— 7.4%	18— 13%	4076
Abnormal *QRS* morphology—non-PVC	83— 0.18%	158— 34.9%	152— 3.8%	3— 2%	396
Abnormal or borderline morphology—PVC	38— 0.08%	102— 22.5%	3129— 78.0%	122— 85%	3391
Cardiologists' totals	45 364—100%	453—100%	4010—100%	143—100%	

[a] Not applicable.

of the working muscle masses. Association of these forms with epidemiological groups is termed morphological analysis, a useful but not usually conclusive tool in medical diagnosis. Finally, a large number of temporal aberrancies in surface waves have become associated with events in smaller tissue groups producing no measurable surface waves. Matching these known aberrancies with the observed wave sequences of an individual's ECG has become a discipline termed rhythm analysis, seemingly a prerequisite to morphological analysis.

All automatic ECG analysis systems are at least partially heuristic in nature, especially with regard to sensing *P*, *QRS*, and *T*. Subsequent feature extraction steps, while primarily heuristic, may also use more formal mathematical techniques. Rhythms can only be inferred from the extracted features, usually with empirical criteria adjusted to their information content. Subsequent morphological classifications, whether empirical or statistical, seem quite at the mercy of the earlier stages.

Work on ECG pattern recognition has not suffered from a lack of ideas. Periodic evaluation, crucial to productive development, is frequently more difficult than development. Perturbations in program logic are easily made. Their consequences are measured with difficulty. Documented data bases in a form suitable for further work are scarce, despite the wealth of raw ECG's. Investigations of classification techniques are thus frequently started from scratch.

Despite profuse publications, algorithms have not circulated well. Sterile flow-chartings and logical listings give little insight to the problems being solved. Examples are helpful, evaluations are crucial. Feature-extraction algorithms have been described in some detail here, giving occasional glimpses of the underlying motivations. Extensive repetition of the textbook type of classification logic was avoided. Statistical classification methods, lending themselves to concise description, were enumerated more thoroughly.

Extensive evaluations of morphological analysis systems are now appearing with increasing frequency. Evaluations of rhythm analysis have been rare. In addition to the two cited in detail [176], [297], other special-purpose tests have been made for heart station rhythm diagnosis [190], [194], [198], [199], [201], [227], [230], and for rhythm monitoring [239], [275], [285], [286], [298]–[300]. Because of the differing data bases and methods, direct comparisons of results are not usually possible. Indications are that much more effort is now being given to the problem of evaluation.

At present, the number of man years devoted to morphological analysis is probably an order of magnitude greater than for rhythm analysis and monitoring. In both areas, however, some efforts have recently formed the basis of commercial systems. This suggests that automated ECG analysis is on the verge of becoming an accepted medical tool. The next several years may thus be crucial for answering questions with facts.

V. CONCLUSION

This review has examined the pattern-recognition techniques used for the analysis of the EEG, the blood pressure wave, and the ECG. All three signals present difficulties in the clinical setting in spite of the apparent simplicity of the task when assessed on the basis of textbook waveforms. Limitations on computing time and memory space are obvious difficulties for these high data-rate signals, but less obvious are the serious problems associated with artifact, context sensitivity, and performance evaluation.

Artifacts may arise from power line interference, muscle potentials, and movement (both voluntary and as a result of manipulation of the patient by a nurse or physician). Careful attention to electrodes, transducers, and signal conditioners can generally eliminate most of the effects of the power lines. The other sources of artifact are less predictable and consequently more difficult to manage. On occasion the recognition of artifact requires the best efforts of highly trained human observers. How many episodes of artifact have masqueraded as real phenomena can never be known. At present the expedients of human editing of records, automatic elimination of suspicious portions of a record, or automatic multitrace comparisons may have to suffice.

A difficulty faced with all signals of physiological origin, but encountered acutely with the ECG, is context sensitivity. A pattern often can be classified in more than one way according to the context in which it is embedded. A million bits of input data may be required to establish the context of a pattern described by only a few hundred bits. Serious practical problems arise if the epoch under study is lengthened in an attempt to establish patterns of sufficiently long duration to contain most contextual clues. One such practical problem concerns the lack of a method to partition a continuous record into independent epochs. Another concerns the computing time and storage requirements associated with patterns analyzed most conveniently only in a space of many dimensions.

Performance evaluation of an automatic pattern-recognition system for physiological signals is essential for its improvement and acceptance by clinicians. Early in its development a system's performance can be evaluated by quite informal techniques. Enough gross errors are distressingly obvious to keep the developers happily occupied. As the system approaches clinical usefulness, an improvement in one attribute of performance may only be obtained at the expense of the safety margins for other attributes. Only a carefully controlled performance evaluation on a sufficiently large test set can determine whether the most recent "improvement" should be retained.

Few of the systems reported in the literature have undergone performance evaluations. Many are still in an early stage. Others should be evaluated, but the difficulties surrounding the task have been a deterrent. Even so, a few evaluations have been accomplished and they were reported in some detail here because of the importance of any evaluative information to a critical review.

The performance evaluation of automated pattern-recognition systems for physiological signals shares with all medical trials a host of problems. Frequently, there are no convenient absolute standards for the classification of patterns according to the pathological state of the patient. In some special cases autopsy or surgery can give definitive answers, but even then classification can be blurred by the concurrence of more than one disease. Selection of a test set with completely unambiguous classifications may not give a representative evaluation since the strict criteria imposed on the test set may force selection of a biased subset of the population on which the system is to be used.

The test set must be of adequate size. The variability of patterns in normal patients is often surprising and the increase in variability can be manyfold when a wide spectrum of pathological states are included in the set. The test set should include typical artifact—not so severe and ubiquitous as to reward unduly systems biased toward artifact, but sufficient to penalize systems overly sensitive to artifact. The combinations of many normal and abnormal patterns with a wide variety of forms of artifact increases the size of the test set dramatically.

The results of performance evaluations can often be misleading. For a valid comparison between two studies, both clinical and technical circumstances must be the same, a goal difficult to achieve. The amount of human interaction with a system needs to be quantified and controlled. Clearly, an evaluation of a system that takes advantage of continuous human adjustment cannot be compared directly with the evaluation of one that operates unattended. Finally, an improved method for reporting results is required to emphasize the difference between errors that occur randomly throughout all patients and those that occur consistently within a single patient's record or within a single disease category.

Such considerations lead to concern about the convergence of performance evaluations that are too broadly conceived. Will each new member of the test set reveal new phenomena in the system's performance? How many members are needed before one can have confidence that few surprises await the user? Perhaps only when performance evaluations are limited to a specific clinical environment can they be expected to converge to useful results. In any case, the time has passed for the presentation of new unevaluated approaches. Difficult as it may be, performance evaluation is the next major task for the developers of pattern-recognition systems that are to be applied to the EEG, the blood pressure wave, and the ECG.

With the above list of problems and concerns the reader can be justifiably wary of unqualified claims of success. Judging by early signs of clinical acceptance, however, several systems appear to be on the threshold of success in specific applications. They seem to share the common attribute that they have evolved within a clinical setting where theory has given way to pragmatism and where the system emulates human pattern recognition based on many decades of medical experience. Perhaps, in the future, the more systematic approaches suggested by theory will bear fruit as we learn the strengths and weaknesses of the present pragmatic approaches through careful objective performance evaluations.

Acknowledgment

The authors wish to acknowledge the early guidance and support of Dr. H. Fozzard, now at the University of Chicago. Our special thanks also go to Dr. C. Oliver for his continuing collaboration over the years and during the preparation of this review. To many colleagues throughout the country who were helpful in person and by telephone and letter we are also indebted, particularly to Dr. D. Glaeser of Baylor College of Medicine for valuable discussions and some of the data we used. Thanks also go to members of our staff who helped with the preparation of several of the figures.

References

[1] R. S. Ledley, "Practical problems in the use of computers in medical diagnosis," *Proc. IEEE*, vol. 57, pp. 1900–1918, Nov. 1969.

[2] J. M. S. Prewitt, "Digital images in biology and medicine: Processing and recognition," to be published.

[3] H. Berger, "Über das Elektrenkephalogramm des Menschen," *Arch. Psychiat. Nervenkrankheiten*, vol. 87, pp. 527–570, 1929.

[4] B. G. Farley, "A neural network model and the 'slow potentials' of electrophysiology," in *Computers in Biomedical Research*, vol. 1, R. W. Stacy and B. D. Waxman, Eds. New York: Academic Press, 1965, pp. 265–294.

[5] D. R. Humphrey, "Re-analysis of the antidromic cortical response —II: On the contribution of cell discharge and PSPs to the evoked potentials," *Electroenceph. Clin. Neurophysiol.*, vol. 25, pp. 421–442, 1968.

[6] C. D. Creutzfeldt, "Neuronal mechanisms underlying the EEG," in *Basic Mechanisms of the Epilepsies*, H. H. Jasper, A. A. Ward, Jr., and A. Pope, Eds. Boston, Mass.: Little, Brown, 1969, pp. 397–410.

[7] D. A. Pollen, "On the generation of neocortical potentials," in *Basic Mechanisms of the Epilepsies*, H. H. Jasper, A. A. Ward, Jr., and A. Pope, Eds. Boston, Mass.: Little, Brown, 1969, pp. 411–420.

[8] Committee on Clinical Examination in EEG, "The ten twenty electrode system of the international federation," *Electroenceph. Clin. Neurophysiol.*, vol. 10, pp. 371–375, 1958.

[9] M. A. B. Brazier, *The Electrical Activity of the Nervous System*, 3rd ed. London, England: Pitman Medical Publishing Co.; Baltimore, Md.: Williams and Wilkins, 1968.

[10] J. S. Garvin, Moderator, "The practical value of EEG for solving difficult clinical problems," round-table discussion at 5th Annual Meeting of Amer. Med. Electroenceph. Ass.; also *Clin. Electroenceph.*, vol. 2, pp. 118–129, 1971.

[11] M. S. Sadove, S. Hatano, and T. Redlin, "Electroencephalographic monitoring and the anesthesiologist," *Clin. Electroenceph.*, vol. 2, pp. 130–135, 1971.

[12] A. L. Loomis, E. N. Harvey, and G. A. Hobart, III, "Cerebral states during sleep, as studied by human brain potentials," *J. Exp. Psychol.*, vol. 21, pp. 127–144, Aug. 1937.

[13] P. A. Davis, "Effects of acoustic stimuli on the waking human brain," *J. Neurophysiol.*, vol. 2, pp. 494–499, 1939.

[14] R. Katzman, Ed., *Sensory Evoked Response in Man (Ann. N. Y. Acad. Sci.)*, vol. 112. New York: New York Academy of Sciences, 1964.

[15] W. Dement and N. Kleitman, "Cyclic variations in EEG during sleep and their relation to eye movements, body motility, and dreaming," *Electroenceph. Clin. Neurophysiol.*, vol. 9, pp. 673–690, 1957.

[16] M. Roth, J. Shaw, and J. Green, "The form, voltage distribution and physiological significance of the K-complex," *Electroenceph. Clin. Neurophysiol.*, vol. 8, pp. 385–402, 1956.

[17] A. Rechtschaffen and A. Kales, Eds., *A Manual of Standardized Terminology, Techniques and Scoring System for Sleep Stages of Human Subjects.* Washington, D. C.: GPO, Public Health Service, 1968.

[18] Z. Drohocki, "An electronic integrator for the automatic measurement of average tension in the EEG" (Abstract), *Electroenceph.*

Clin. Neurophysiol., vol. 8, pp. 706–707, 1956.
[19] H. W. Agnew, Jr., J. C. Parker, W. B. Webb, and R. L. Williams, "Amplitude measurement of the sleep electroencephalogram," *Electroenceph. Clin. Neurophysiol.*, vol. 22, pp. 84–86, 1967.
[20] R. L. Maulsby, J. D. Frost, Jr., and M. H. Graham, "A simple electronic method for graphing EEG sleep patterns," *Electroenceph. Clin. Neurophysiol.*, vol. 21, pp. 501–503, 1966.
[21] A. M. Grass and F. A. Gibbs, "A Fourier transform of the electroencephalogram," *J. Neurophysiol.*, vol. 1, pp. 521–526, 1938.
[22] J. R. Knott, F. A. Gibbs, and C. E. Henry, "Fourier transforms of the electroencephalogram during sleep," *J. Exp. Psychol.*, vol. 31, pp. 465–477, 1942.
[23] D. J. Hord, L. C. Johnson, A. Lubin, and M. T. Austin, "Resolution and stability in the autospectra of EEG," *Electroenceph. Clin. Neurophysiol.*, vol. 19, pp. 305–308, 1965.
[24] D. O. Walter, R. T. Kado, J. M. Rhodes, and W. R. Adey, "Electroencephalographic baselines in astronaut candidates estimated by computation and pattern recognition techniques," *Aerosp. Med.*, vol. 38, pp. 371–379, Apr. 1967.
[25] A. Lubin, L. C. Johnson, and M. T. Austin, "Discrimination among states of consciousness using EEG spectra," *Agressologie*, vol. 10, pp. 593–600, 1969.
[26] L. E. Larsen and D. O. Walter, "On automatic methods of sleep staging by spectra of electroencephalograms," *Agressologie*, vol. 10, pp. 1–13, 1969.
[27] ——, "On automatic methods of sleep staging by EEG spectra," *Electroenceph. Clin. Neurophysiol.*, vol. 28, pp. 459–467, 1970.
[28] E. H. Ruspini, "New cluster analysis techniques: Fuzzy and probabilistic clustering and some of their applications," in *Proc. 5th Hawaii Int. Conf. System Sciences—Computers in Biomedicine* (Honolulu, Hawaii), pp. 186–188, 1972.
[29] N. R. Burch, "Automatic analysis of the electroencephalogram: A review and classification of systems," *Electroenceph. Clin. Neurophysiol.*, vol. 11, pp. 827–834, 1959.
[30] ——, "Period analysis of the electroencephalogram on a general-purpose digital computer," *Ann. N. Y. Acad. Sci.*, vol. 115, pp. 827–843, 1964.
[31] J. C. R. Licklider, "Effects of various types of nonlinear distortion upon the intelligibility of speech" (Abstract), *J. Acoust. Soc. Amer.*, vol. 24, p. 114, 1952.
[32] M. Fink, T. M. Itil, and D. M. Shapiro, "Digital computer analysis of the human EEG in psychiatric research," *Compr. Psychiatry*, vol. 8, pp. 521–538, Dec. 1967.
[33] T. M. Itil, D. M. Shapiro, M. Fink, and D. Kassebaum, "Digital computer classifications of EEG sleep stages," *Electroenceph. Clin. Neurophysiol.*, vol. 27, pp. 76–83, 1969.
[34] T. M. Itil *et al.*, "The effects of smoking withdrawal on quantitatively analyzed EEG," *Clin. Electroenceph.*, vol. 2, pp. 44–51, 1971
[35] R. Roessler, F. Collins, and R. Ostman, "A period analysis classification of sleep stages," *Electroenceph. Clin. Neurophysiol.*, vol. 29, pp. 358–362, 1970.
[36] C. S. Lessard, G. E. Ford, and H. M. Hughes, "Decomposition and variability of EEG information during sleep," in *Conf. Rec.* (Part V: 7), *12th Midwest Symp. Circuit Theory* (Austin, Tex., 1969). New York: IEEE, 1969.
[37] C. S. Lessard and H. M. Hughes, "Digital simulation aid in designing an automatic EEG analyzer," USAF Rep., SAM-TR-70-33, June 1970.
[38] C. S. Lessard and R. C. Paschall, Jr., "A system for quantifying EEG slow wave activity," *Electroenceph. Clin. Neurophysiol.*, vol. 29, pp. 516–520, 1970.
[39] H. Legewie and W. Probst, "On-line analysis of EEG with a small computer (period-amplitude analysis)," *Electroenceph. Clin. Neurophysiol.*, vol. 27, pp. 533–535, 1969.
[40] B. Hjorth, "EEG analysis based on time domain properties," *Electroenceph. Clin. Neurophysiol.*, vol. 29, pp. 306–310, 1970.
[41] J. L. Hammond, Jr., and R. S. Johnson, "A review of orthogonal square-wave functions and their application to linear networks," *J. Franklin Inst.*, vol. 273, pp. 211–225, 1962.
[42] A. O. Bishop, Jr., R. W. Snelsire, L. C. Wilcox, and W. P. Wilson, "The moving window approach to on-line real-time waveform recognition," in *Proc. San Diego Biomedical Symp.* (San Diego, Calif.), pp. 77–83, 1970.
[43] J. Gaillard, A. E. Simmen, and R. Tissot, "Analyse automatique des enregistrements polygraphiques de sommeil," *Electroenceph. Clin. Neurophysiol.*, vol. 30, pp. 557–561, 1971.
[44] J. D. Frost, Jr., "An automatic sleep analyzer," *Electroenceph. Clin. Neurophysiol.*, vol. 29, pp. 88–92, 1970.
[45] ——, "Development and testing of a prototype operational system for automatic monitoring of sleep during manned space flight," Contract NAS9-10747, Final Rep., 1971.
[46] J. R. Smith, M. Negin, and A. H. Nevis, "Automatic analysis of sleep electroencephalograms by hybrid computation," *IEEE Trans. Syst. Sci. Cybern.*, vol. SSC-5, pp. 278–284, Oct. 1969.
[47] J. R. Smith and I. Karacan, "EEG sleep stage scoring by an automatic hybrid system," *Electroenceph. Clin. Neurophysiol.*, vol. 31, pp. 231–237, 1971.
[48] J. R. Smith, M. J. Cronin, and I. Karacan, "A multichannel hybrid system for rapid eye movement detection (REM detection)," *Comput. Biomed. Res.*, vol. 4, pp. 275–290, 1970.
[49] J. G. Minard and D. Krausman, "Rapid eye movement definition and count: An on-line detector," *Electroenceph. Clin. Neurophysiol.*, vol. 31, pp. 99–102, 1971.
[50] G. Sciarretta and A. Bricolo, "Automatic detection of sleep spindles by analysis of harmonic components," *Med. Biol. Eng.*, vol. 8, pp. 517–519, 1970.
[51] B. G. Farley, L. S. Frishkopf, W. A. Clark, Jr., and J. T. Gilmore, Jr., "Computer techniques for the study of patterns in the electroencephalogram," *IRE Trans. Bio-Med. Electron.*, vol BME-9, pp. 4–12, Jan. 1962.
[52] G. Bremer, J. R. Smith, and I. Karacan, "Automatic detection of the *K*-complex in sleep electroencephalograms," *IEEE Trans. Bio-Med. Eng.*, vol. BME-17, pp. 314–323, Oct. 1970.
[53] M. A. B. Brazier, Ed., "Computer techniques in EEG analysis," in *Proc. Conf. Sponsored by Brain Research Institute, University of California* (Los Angeles, Oct. 1960), Suppl. 20 to *Electroenceph. Clin. Neurophysiol.*, 1961.
[54] W. A. Rosenblith, Ed. *Processing Neuroelectric Data.* Cambridge, Mass.: M.I.T. Press, 1959.
[55] M. A. B. Brazier, "The application of computers to electroencephalography," in *Computers in Biomedical Research*, vol. 1, R. W. Stacy and B. D. Waxman, Eds. New York: Academic Press, 1965, pp. 295–315.
[56] H. S. Leader, R. Cohn, A. L. Weihrer, and C. A. Caceres, "Pattern reading of the clinical electroencephalogram with a digital computer," *Electroenceph. Clin. Neurophysiol.*, vol. 23, pp. 566–570, 1967.
[57] G. F. Franklin and D. H. Utter, "Parameter identification from EEG data taken during anesthesia," in *Proc. 5th Hawaii Int. Conf. on System Sciences–Computers in Biomedicine* (Honolulu, Hawaii), pp. 15–17, 1972.
[58] R. G. Bickford *et al.*, "A computer and enunciator system for estimation of brain death," in *Proc. San Diego Biomedical Symp.* (San Diego, Calif.), vol. 10, pp. 117–123, 1971.
[59] J. M. Rhodes, D. O. Walter, and W. R. Adey, "Discriminant analysis of 'activated' EEG," *Psychon. Sci.*, vol. 6, pp. 439–440, 1966.
[60] D. O. Walter, J. M. Rhodes, and W. R. Adey, "Discriminating among states of consciousness by EEG measurements. A study of four subjects," *Electroenceph. Clin. Neurophysiol.*, vol. 22, pp. 22–29, 1967.
[61] G. D. Dawson, "A summation technique for the detection of small evoked potentials," *Electroenceph. Clin. Neurophysiol.*, vol. 6, pp. 65–84, 1954.
[62] W. A. Clark *et al.*, "The average response computer (ARC): a digital device for computing averages and amplitude and time histograms of electrophysiological response," *IRE Trans. Bio-Med. Electron.*, vol. BME-8, pp. 46–51, Jan. 1961.
[63] J. R. Cox, Jr., "Special purpose digital computers in biology," in *Computers in Biomedical Research*, vol. 2, R. W. Stacy and B. D. Waxman, Eds. New York: Academic Press, 1965, pp. 67–99.
[64] H. Davis and A. F. Niemoeller, "A system for clinical evoked response audiometry," *J. Speech Hear. Disorders*, vol. 33, pp. 33–37, Feb. 1968.
[65] R. P. Borda and J. D. Frost, Jr., "Error reduction in small sample averaging through the use of the median rather than the mean," *Electroenceph. Clin. Neurophysiol.*, vol. 25, pp. 391–392, 1968.
[66] N. W. Perry, Jr., and D. G. Childers, *The Human Visual Evoked Response: Method and Theory.* Springfield, Ill.: Charles C Thomas, 1969.
[67] E. Donchin and D. B. Lindsley, Eds., *Average Evoked Potentials: Methods, Results and Evaluations.* Washington, D. C.: National Aeronautics and Space Admin., 1969.
[68] J. L. Poage and K. P. S. Prabhu, "Pattern classification applied to electro-encephalographs," Harvard Univ., Cambridge, Mass., Tech. Rep. 1, Grant NGR 22-007-143, for National Aeronautics and Space Admin., Sept. 1969.
[69] D. Arnal and P. Gerin, "Comparaison des potentiels évoqués moyens à l'aide d'un test T^2 généralisé. Application au problème de l'interférence des résponses évoquées visuelles successives," *Electroenceph. Clin. Neurophysiol.*, vol. 26, pp. 325–331, 1969.
[70] P. Naitoh, "The use of Hotelling's zero-mu T^2 for analysis of evoked responses," in *Proc. 5th Hawaii Int. Conf. System Sciences–Computers in Biomedicine* (Honolulu, Hawaii), pp. 232–234, 1972.
[71] E. Donchin, "A multivariate approach to the analysis of average evoked potentials," *IEEE Trans. Bio-Med. Eng.*, vol. BME-13, pp. 131–139, July 1966.
[72] D. Arnal, "Contribution a l'etude des potentiels evoques moyens visuels et a leur application en ophthalmologie," Ph.D. dissertation, Univ. Claude-Bernard de Lyon, Lyon, France, July 1971.
[73] E. Donchin, "Disciminant analysis in average evoked response studies: The study of single trial data," *Electroenceph. Clin. Neurophysiol.*, vol. 27, pp. 311–314, 1969.
[74] E. Donchin, E. Callaway, III, and R. T. Jones, "Auditory evoked potential variability in schizóphrenia—II: The application of discriminant analysis," *Electroenceph. Clin. Neurophysiol.*, vol. 29, pp. 429–440, 1970.
[75] A. J. Derbyshire, G. J. Driessen, and C. W. Palmer, "Technical

advances in the analysis of single, acoustically evoked potentials," *Electroenceph. Clin. Neurophysiol*, vol. 22, pp. 476–481, 1967.
[76] A. J. Derbyshire, S. B. Osenar, L. R. Hamilton, and M. E. Joseph, "Problems in identifying an acoustically evoked potential to a single stimulus," *J. Speech Hear. Res.*, vol. 14, pp. 160–171, 1971.
[77] K. P. S. Prabhu, "On feature reduction with application to electroencephalograms," Harvard Univ., Cambridge, Mass., Tech. Rep. 615, Contract N00014-67-A-0298-0006 NR-372-012, and Grant NGL 22-007-143, for Office of Naval Research and National Aeronautics and Space Admin., Sept. 1970.
[78] M. F. Gardiner, R. J. Sclabassi, N. F. Enns, and N. S. Namerow, "The interpretation of statistical measures from discriminant analysis in evoked response experiments," in *Proc. 5th Hawaii Int. Conf. System Sciences–Computers in Biomedicine* (Honolulu, Hawaii), pp. 235–237, 1972.
[79] A. C. Burton, *Physiology and Biophysics of the Circulation.* Chicago, Ill.: Yearbook Medical Publishers, 1965.
[80] H. R. Warner, R. M. Gardner, and A. F. Toronto, "Computer-based monitoring of cardiovascular functions in postoperative patients," Suppl. II to *Circulation*, vols. XXXVII and XXXVIII, pp. II-68–74, Apr. 1968.
[81] H. R. Warner, "Computer-based patient monitoring," in *Computers in Biomedical Research*, vol. III, R. W. Stacy and B. D. Waxman, Eds. New York: Academic Press, 1969, pp. 239–251.
[82] H. R. Warner *et al.*, "Quantitation of beat-to-beat changes in stroke volume from the aortic pulse contour in man," *J. Appl. Physiol.*, vol. 5, pp. 495–507, 1953.
[83] H. R. Warner, "Some computer techniques of value for study of circulation," in *Computers in Biomedical Research*, vol. II, R. W. Stacy and B. D. Waxman, Eds. New York: Academic Press, 1965, pp. 239–268.
[84] N. T. Kouchoukos, L. C. Sheppard, D. A. McDonald, and J. W. Kirklin, "Estimation of stroke volume from the central arterial pressure contour in postoperative patients," *Surg. Forum*, vol. XX, pp. 180–181, 1969.
[85] N. T. Kouchoukos, L. C. Sheppard, and D. A. McDonald, "Estimation of stroke volume in the dog by a pulse contour method," *Circ. Res.*, vol. XXVI, pp. 611–623, May 1970.
[86] W. M. Stauffer, "Comparison of dye dilution curve and pressure pulse methods of determining cardiac output in patients undergoing anesthesia," in *Dig. 1969 IEEE Computer Group Conf.*
[87] J. C. Greenfield, Jr., C. F. Starmer, and A. Walston, II, "Measurement of aortic blood flow in man by the computed pressure derivative method," *J. Appl. Physiol.*, vol. 31, pp. 792–795, Nov. 1971.
[88] E. M. Strand, "Extraction of pulmonary artery end diastolic pressure," in *Proc. 24th Ann. Conf. Engineering in Medicine and Biology* (Las Vegas, Nev.), p. 151, 1971.
[89] D. Harrison and H. Miller, *Calculating Cardiac Catheterization Data With an On-line Computer System.* Waltham, Mass.: Hewlett-Packard Co., Medical Electronics Div., May 1971.
[90] R. E. Stenson, L. Crouse, W. L. Henry, and D. C. Harrison, "A time-shared digital computer system for on-line analysis of cardiac catheterization data," *Comput. Biomed. Res.*, vol. 1, pp. 605–614, 1968.
[91] W. L. Henry, L. Crouse, R. Stenson, and D. C. Harrison, "Computer analysis of cardiac catheterization data," *Amer. J. Cardiol.*, vol. 22, pp. 696–705, Nov. 1968.
[92] R. A. Carleton, M. Passovoy, and J. S. Graettinger, "A computer program for processing, storage, and reporting of cardiac catheterization data," *Med. Res. Eng.*, vol. 8, pp. 18–21, 26, Mar.–Apr. 1969.
[93] H. R. Warner *et al.*, "A system for on-line computer analysis of data during heart catheterization," in *Pathophysiology of Congenital Heart Disease*, F. H. Adams, H. J. C. Swan, and V. E. Hall, Eds. Berkeley and Los Angeles, Calif.: Univ. of California Press, 1970, pp. 409–418.
[94] G. C. Oliver and W. V. Glenn, Jr., "Computer in the cardiac catheterization laboratory," Biomedical Computer Lab., Washington Univ. School of Medicine, St. Louis, Mo., Monograph 133, May 1970.
[95] W. M. Stauffer (Automated Medical Systems, Minneapolis, Minn.). private communication.
[96] P. G. Hugenholtz, A. C. Miller, G. T. Meester (Thoraxcentrum, Rotterdam, The Netherlands) and J. A. Courtier, F. M. Harris (Digital Equipment Corp., Maynard, Mass.), private communication.
[97] D. C. Harrison *et al.*, "Real-time analysis of cardiac catheterization data using a computer system," *Circulation*, vol. XLIV, pp. 709–718, Oct. 1971.
[98] T. A. Pryor, "Some techniques for extraction of useful features from biological signals," in *Proc. 5th Hawaii Int. Conf. System Sciences—Computers in Biomedicine* (Honolulu, Hawaii), pp. 1–3, 1972.
[99] F. Starmer (Duke Univ., Durham, N. C.), private communication.
[100] M. E. DeBakey and D. H. Glaeser, "Waveform analysis of the central arterial pressure using a technique of data compression," *J. Ass. Advan. Med. Instrum.*, vol. 6, pp. 60–64, Jan.–Feb. 1972.
[101] R. M. Goldwyn and T. B. Watt, Jr., "Arterial pressure pulse contour analysis via a mathematical model for the clinical quantification of human vascular properties," *IEEE Trans. Bio-Med. Eng.*, vol. BME-14, pp. 11–17, Jan. 1967.
[102] J. R. Cox, F. M. Nolle, H. A. Fozzard, and G. C. Oliver, Jr., "AZTEC, a preprocessing program for real-time ECG rhythm analysis," *IEEE Trans. Bio-Med. Eng.* (Short Commun.), vol. BME-15, pp. 128–129, Apr. 1968.
[103] T. N. James, "Anatomy of the conduction system of the heart," in *The Heart*, J. W. Hurst and R. B. Logue, Eds. New York: McGraw-Hill, 1970, pp. 47–58.
[104] T. N. James and L. Sherf, "Ultrastructure of the myocardium," in *The Heart*, J. W. Hurst and R. B. Logue, Eds. New York: McGraw-Hill, 1970, pp. 58–73.
[105] B. F. Hoffman and P. F. Cranefield, *Electrophysiology of the Heart.* New York: McGraw-Hill, 1960.
[106] H. A. Fozzard and W. R. Gibbons, "The action potential and contraction of heart muscle," to be published in *Amer. J. Cardiol.*
[107] A. M. Scher and A. C. Young, "Ventricular depolarization and the genesis of QRS," *Ann. N. Y. Acad. Sci.*, vol. 65, pp. 768–778, Aug. 1957.
[108] D. Durrer *et al.*, "Total excitation of the isolated human heart," *Circulation*, vol. XLI, pp. 899–912, June 1970.
[109] A. M. Scher, "Electrical correlates of the cardiac cycle," in *Physiology and Biophysics*, T. C. Ruch and H. D. Patton, Eds. Philadelphia, Pa.: Saunders, 1965, pp. 565–599.
[110] K. Harumi, M. J. Burgess, and J. A. Abildskov, "A theoretic model of the T wave," *Circulation*, vol. 34, pp. 657–688, Oct. 1966.
[111] D. B. Geselowitz and O. H. Schmitt, "Electrocardiography," in *Biological Engineering*, H. P. Schwan, Ed. New York: McGraw-Hill, 1969, pp. 333–390.
[112] R. Plonsey and D. B. Heppner, "Considerations of quasi-stationarity in electrophysiological systems," *Bull. Math. Biophys.*, vol. 29, pp. 657–664, 1967.
[113] R. Plonsey, "Limitations on the equivalent cardiac generator," *Biophys. J.*, vol. 6, pp. 163–173, 1966.
[114] M. S. Lynn, A. C. L. Barnard, J. H. Holt, and L. T. Sheffield, "A proposed method for the inverse problem in electrocardiology," *Biophys. J.*, vol. 7, pp. 925–945, 1967.
[115] R. M. Arthur, D. B. Geselowitz, S. A. Briller, and R. F. Trost, "Quadrupole components of the human surface electrocardiogram," *Amer. Heart J.*, vol. 83, pp. 663–677, May 1972.
[116] T. Y. Young and W. H. Huggins, "On the representation of electrocardiograms," *IEEE Trans. Bio-Med. Electron.*, vol. BME-10, pp. 86–95, July 1963.
[117] L. G. Horan, N. C. Flowers, and D. A. Brody, "Principal factor waveforms of the thoracic QRS complex," *Circ. Res.*, vol. XV, pp. 131–145, Aug. 1964.
[118] R. McFee and G. M. Baule, "Research in electrocardiography and magnetocardiography," *Proc. IEEE*, vol. 60, pp. 290–321, Mar. 1972.
[119] R. Plonsey, "The biophysical basis for electrocardiography," *Crit. Rev. Bioeng.*, vol. 1, pp. 1–48, Oct. 1971.
[120] W. Einthoven, "The telecardiogram," *Arch. Int. Physiol.*, vol. 4, pp. 132–161, 1906. (Transl.: F. A. L. Mathewson and H. Jackh, *Amer. Heart J.*, vol. 49, pp. 77–82, 1955, and H. W. Blackburn, Jr., *Amer. Heart J.*, vol. 53, pp. 602–615, 1957.)
[121] W. Einthoven, G. Fahr, and A. de Waart, "On the direction and manifest size of the variations of potential in the human heart and on the influence of the position of the heart on the form of the electrocardiogram," *Pflüger's Arch. Gesamte Physiol.*, vol. 150, pp. 275–315, 1913. (Transl.: H. E. Hoff and P. Sekelj, *Amer. Heart J.*, vol. 40, pp. 163–193, 1950.)
[122] K. Yamada *et al.*, "Observer variation in electrocardiographic interpretation," *Ann. Rep. Res. Inst. Environ. Med.* (Nagoya Univ., Nagoya, Japan), vol. 16, pp. 27–41, 1968.
[123] C. A. Caceres, "A basis for observer variation in electrocardiographic interpretation," *Progr. Cardiov. Dis.*, vol. 5, pp. 521–532, Mar. 1963.
[124] K. Ishikawa, C. Batchlor, and H. V. Pipberger, "Reduction of electrocardiographic beat-to-beat variation through computer wave recognition," *Amer. Heart J.*, vol. 81, pp. 236–241, Feb. 1971.
[125] E. Fischmann, J. Cosma, and H. V. Pipberger, "Beat to beat and observer variation of the electrocardiogram," *Amer. Heart J.*, vol. 75, pp. 465–473, Apr. 1968.
[126] R. C. Barr, M. S. Spach, and G. S. Herman-Giddens, "Selection of the number and positions of measuring locations for electrocardiography," *IEEE Trans. Bio-Med. Eng.*, vol. BME-18, pp. 125–138, Mar. 1971.
[127] W. Einthoven, "Weiteres über das Elektrokardiogramm," *Pflüger's Arch. Gesamte Physiol.*, vol. 122, pp. 517–584, 1908.
[128] E. Goldberger, "A simple, indifferent, electrocardiographic electrode of zero potential and a technique of obtaining augmented, unipolar, extremity leads," *Amer. Heart J.*, vol. 23, pp. 483–492, 1942.
[129] F. N. Wilson *et al.*, "Recommendations for standardization of electrocardiographic and vectorcardiographic leads," *Circulation*, vol. X, pp. 564–573, 1954.
[130] E. Frank, "An accurate, clinically practical system for spatial vectorcardiography," *Circulation*, vol. XIII, pp. 737–749, May 1956.
[131] O. H. Schmitt and E. Simonson, "The present status of vectorcardiography," *AMA Arch. Intern. Med.*, pp. 574–590, 1955.

[132] R. A. Helm, "An accurate lead system for spatial vectorcardiography," *Amer. Heart J.*, vol. 53, pp. 415–424, Mar. 1957.
[133] R. McFee and A. Parungao, "An orthogonal lead system for clinical electrocardiography," *Amer. Heart J.*, vol. 62, pp. 93–100, July 1961.
[134] D. A. Brody and R. C. Arzbaecher, "A comparative analysis of several corrected vectorcardiographic leads," *Circulation*, vol. XXIX, pp. 533–545, Apr. 1964.
[135] L. G. Horan, N. C. Flowers, and D. A. Brody, "The interchangeability of vectorcardiographic systems," *Amer. Heart J.*, vol. 70, pp. 365–376, Sept. 1965.
[136] H. V. Pipberger, S. M. Bialek, J. K. Perloff, and H. W. Schnaper, "Correlation of clinical information in the standard 12-lead ECG and in a corrected orthogonal 3-lead ECG," *Amer. Heart J.*, vol. 61, pp. 34–43, Jan. 1961.
[137] J. A. Abildskov and R. S. Wilkinson, Jr., "The relation of precordial and orthogonal leads," *Circulation*, vol. XXVII, pp. 58–63, Jan. 1963.
[138] R. H. Okada, "A critical review of vector electrocardiography," *IEEE Trans. Bio-Med. Electron.*, vol. BME-10, pp. 95–98, July 1963.
[139] E. Simonson, N. Tuna, N. Okamoto, and H. Toshima, "Diagnostic accuracy of the vectorcardiogram and electrocardiogram," *Amer. J. Cardiol.*, vol. 17, pp. 829–878, June 1966.
[140] C. D. Batchlor, A. S. Berson, I. A. Naval, and H. V. Pipberger, "Computer search for electrocardiographic directions to optimize diagnostic differentiation," *Circulation*, vol. XXXVI, pp. 320–330, Aug. 1967.
[141] K. K. Kelly, T. W. Calvert, R. L. Longini, and J. P. Brown, "Feature enhancement of vectorcardiograms by linear normalization," *IEEE Trans. Comput.* (Corresp.), vol. C-20, pp. 1109–1111, Sept. 1971.
[142] J. H. Holt, Jr., A. C. L. Barnard, and M. S. Lynn, "A study of the human heart as a multiple dipole electrical source. II. Diagnosis and quantitation of left ventricular hypertrophy," *Circulation*, vol. XL, pp. 697–710, Nov. 1969.
[143] D. B. Geselowitz and R. M. Arthur, "Derivation of aimed electrocardiographic leads from the multipole expansion," *J. Electrocardiol.*, vol. 4, pp. 291–298, 1971.
[144] D. B. Geselowitz, "Use of the multipole expansion to extract significant features of the surface electrocardiogram," *IEEE Trans. Comput.* (Short Notes), vol. C-20, pp. 1086–1089, Sept. 1971.
[145] R. F. Trost, "Experimental studies of a human dipole plus quadrupole lead system for electrocardiography," Ph.D. dissertation, Univ. of Pennsylvania, Philadelphia, 1970.
[146] D. Wortzman, B. Gilmore, H. D. Schwetman, and J. I. Hirsch, "A hybrid computer system for the measurement and interpretation of electrocardiograms," *Ann. N. Y. Acad. Sci.*, vol. 128, pp. 876–899, 1966.
[147] L. D. Cady and B. Mitchell, "Computer components for electrocardiographic processing," *Amer. J. Med. Electron.*, vol. 5, pp. 40–43, 1966.
[148] Report of Committee on Electrocardiography, American Heart Association, "Recommendations for standardization of leads and of specifications for instruments in electrocardiography and vectorcardiography," *Circulation*, vol. XXXV, pp. 583–602, Mar. 1967.
[149] J. Wartak, J. A. Milliken, and D. W. Lywood, "Theoretical and practical aspects of analog-to-digital conversion of the electrocardiogram," *Med. Res. Eng.*, vol. 9, pp. 21–23, Sept. 1970.
[150] C. S. Weaver *et al.*, "Digital filtering with applications to electrocardiogram processing," *IEEE Trans. Audio Electroacoust.*, vol. AU-16, pp. 350–391, Sept. 1968.
[151] Y. Nomura, Y. Takaki, and S. Toyama, "Automatic measurement of the electrocardiogram by digital computer," *Jap. Circ. J.*, vol. 30, pp. 21–28, Jan. 1966.
[152] E. Kimura, "Automatic interpretation of electrocardiogram by electronic computer," *Jap. J. Med.*, vol. 8, pp. 182–184, 1969.
[153] C. A. Steinberg, S. Abraham, and C. A. Caceres, "Pattern recognition in the clinical electrocardiogram," *IRE Trans. Bio-Med. Electron.*, vol. BME-9, pp. 23–30, Jan. 1962.
[154] L. Stark, J. F. Dickson, G. H. Whipple, and H. Horibe, "Remote real-time diagnosis of clinical electrocardiograms by a digital computer system," *Ann. N. Y. Acad. Sci.*, vol. 126, pp. 851–872, Aug. 1967.
[155] F. W. Stallmann and H. V. Pipberger, "Automatic recognition of electrocardiographic waves by digital computer," *Circ. Res.*, vol. IX, pp. 1138–1143, Nov. 1961.
[156] P. W. Macfarlane, "ECG waveform identification by digital computer," *Cardiovasc. Res.*, vol. 5, pp. 141–146, 1971.
[157] T. A. Pryor, "A note on filtering electrocardiograms," *Comput. Biomed. Res.*, vol. 4, pp. 542–547, 1971.
[158] C. A. Caceres *et al.*, "Computer extraction of electrocardiographic parameters," *Circulation*, vol. XXV, pp. 356–362, Feb. 1962.
[159] A. L. Weihrer, J. R. Whiteman, A. Zimmerman, and C. A. Caceres, "Computer programs for an automated electrocardiographic system," in *Clinical Electrocardiography and Computers*, C. A. Caceres and L. S. Dreifus, Eds. New York: Academic Press, 1970, pp. 81–108.
[160] R. J. Dobrow *et al.*, "Accuracy of electrocardiographic measurements by computer," *Amer. J. Med. Electron.*, vol. 4, pp. 121–126, 1965.
[161] J. A. Milliken *et al.*, "Use of computers in the interpretation of electrocardiograms," *Can. Med. Ass. J.*, vol. 101, pp. 39–43, Oct. 4, 1969.
[162] J. A. Milliken *et al.*, "Computer recognition of electrocardiographic waveforms," *Can. Med. Ass. J.*, vol. 103, pp. 365–370, Aug. 1970.
[163] J. Wartak, J. A. Milliken, and J. Karchmar, "Computer program for pattern recognition of electrocardiograms," *Comput. Biomed. Res.*, vol. 4, pp. 344–374, 1970.
[164] H. V. Pipberger, F. W. Stallmann, K. Yano, and H. W. Draper, "Digital computer analysis of the normal and abnormal electrocardiogram," *Prog. Cardiov. Dis.*, vol. 5, pp. 378–392, Jan. 1963.
[165] F. W. Stallmann, "A computer program for automatic analysis of electrocardiograms," *Amer. Heart J.*, vol. 67, pp. 136–137, Jan. 1964.
[166] H. V. Pipberger, "Computer analysis of the electrocardiogram," in *Computers in Biomedical Research*, vol. I, R. W. Stacy and B. D. Waxman, Eds. New York: Academic Press, 1965, pp. 377–407.
[167] H. V. Pipberger, J. Cornfield, and R. A. Dunn, "Diagnosis of the electrocardiogram," in *Proc. Conf. Diagnostic Process*, J. Jaques, Ed. Fort Lauderdale, Fla.: Charles C Thomas, 1972, in press.
[168] O. Arvedson, "Evaluation of ECG's with the IBM 1620 computer" (Abstract), *Scand. J. Clin. Lab. Invest.*, vol. 17, Suppl. 86, p. 123, 1965.
[169] J. H. van Bemmel *et al.*, "Statistical processing methods for recognition and classification of vectorcardiograms," in *Proc. XI Int. Symp. Vectorcardiography* (New York, 1970). Amsterdam, The Netherlands: North-Holland, in press.
[170] L. Stark, M. Okajima, and G. H. Whipple, "Computer pattern recognition techniques: electrocardiographic diagnosis," *Commun. Ass. Comput. Mach.*, pp. 527–531, Oct. 1962.
[171] S. Yasui *et al.*, "On-line diagnostic system of electrocardiogram by small scale digital computer," *Jap. Circ. J.*, vol. 32, pp. 1597–1601, Nov. 1968.
[172] S. Yasui *et al.*, "Computer diagnosis of electrocardiograms by means of joint probability," *Israel J. Med. Sci.*, vol. 5, pp. 913–916, July–Aug. 1969.
[173] T. A. Pryor, R. Russell, A. Budkin, and W. G. Price, "Electrocardiographic interpretation by computer," *Comput. Biomed. Res.*, vol. 2, pp. 537–548, 1969.
[174] D. C. Alexander, "Multichannel simultaneous analysis of the electrocardiogram using simultaneously recorded 3-lead sets," in *Clinical Electrocardiography and Computers*, C. A. Caceres and L. S. Dreifus, Eds. New York: Academic Press, 1970, pp. 149–156.
[175] R. E. Bonner and H. D. Schwetman, "Computer diagnosis of electrocardiograms. II. A computer program for EKG measurements," *Comput. Biomed. Res.*, vol. 1, pp. 366–386, 1968.
[176] L. Pordy *et al.*, "Computer diagnosis of electrocardiograms. IV. A computer program for contour analysis with clinical results of rhythm and contour interpretation," *Comput. Biomed. Res.*, vol. 1, pp. 408–433, 1968.
[177] L. Pordy *et al.*, "Computer analysis of the electrocardiogram: A joint project," in *Clinical Electrocardiography and Computers*, C. A. Caceres and L. S. Dreifus, Eds. New York: Academic Press, 1970, pp. 133–147.
[178] R. E. Smith and C. M. Hyde, "A computer system for electrocardiographic analysis," in *Proc. 3rd Ann. Rocky Mountain Bio-Engineering Symp.* (Univ. of Colorado, Boulder, May 1966).
[179] E. M. Strand, C. M. Hyde, and R. E. Smith, "A computerized technique for the recognition and characterization of ECG atrial activity," in *Dig. 7th Int. Conf. Medical and Biological Engineering* (Stockholm, Sweden), pp. 99–100, 1967.
[180] R. E. Smith, "How 'automated heart stations' have begun. V: The Mayo Group program," in *Clinical Electrocardiography and Computers*, C. A. Caceres and L. S. Dreifus, Eds. New York: Academic Press, 1970, pp. 225–227.
[181] L. D. Cady, Jr., M. A. Woodbury, L. J. Tick, and M. M. Gertler, "A method for electrocardiogram wave-pattern estimation," *Circ. Res.*, vol. IX, pp. 1078–1082, Sept. 1961.
[182] T. Y. Young and W. H. Huggins, "The intrinsic component theory of electrocardiography," *IRE Trans. Bio-Med. Electron.*, vol. BME-9, pp. 214–221, Oct. 1962.
[183] S. Karlsson, "Representation of ECG records by Karhunen-Loève expansions," in *Dig. 7th Int. Conf. Medical and Biological Engineering* (Stockholm, Sweden), p. 105, 1967.
[184] K. S. Fu, *Sequential Methods in Pattern Recognition and Machine Learning*. New York: Academic Press, 1968.
[185] J. Wartak and J. A. Milliken, "Logical approach to diagnosing electrocardiograms," *J. Electrocardiol.*, vol. 2, pp. 253–260, 1969.
[186] J. R. Whiteman *et al.*, "Automation of electrocardiographic diagnostic criteria," *J. Am. Med. Ass.*, vol. 200, pp. 932–938, June 12, 1967.

[187] P. A. Gorman and J. M. Evans, "Computer analysis of the electrocardiogram: Evaluation of experience in a hospital heart station," *Amer. Heart J.*, vol. 80, pp. 515–521, Oct. 1970.
[188] H. M. Hochberg, *et al.*, "Automatic electrocardiogram analysis in rapid mass screening," *Arch. Environ. Health*, vol. 15, pp. 390–398. Sept. 1967.
[189] P. J. Schneider, J. K. Cooper, A. A. Birch, and E. M. Dwyer, "Computer analysis of electrocardiograms with six and twelve leads," *Public Health Rep.*, vol. 85, pp. 853–858, Oct. 1970.
[190] R. J. Dobrow *et al.*, "Transmission of electrocardiograms from a community hospital for remote computer analysis," *Amer. J. Cardiol.*, vol. 21, pp. 687–698, May 1968.
[191] J. K. T. Ormrod, D. T. Book, and J. G. Irving, "Computer interpretation by telephone of electrocardiograms in the home office of a life insurance company," *Trans. Ass. Life Insur. Med. Dir. Amer.*, vol. 53, pp. 48–60, 1969.
[192] J. A. Milliken *et al.*, "Diagnostic evaluation of ECG data by a computer," *Can. Med. Ass. J.*, vol. 104, pp. 801–805, May 8, 1971.
[193] J. A. Milliken *et al.*, "Validity of computer interpretation of the electrocardiogram," *Can. Med. Ass. J.*, vol. 105, pp. 1147–1150, Dec. 4, 1971.
[194] J. Wartak, J. A. Milliken, and J. Karchmar, "Computer program for diagnostic evaluation of electrocardiograms," *Comput. Biomed. Res.*, vol. 4, pp. 225–238, 1971.
[195] L. F. Staples, J. E. Gustafson, G. J. Balm, and W. A. Tate, "Computer interpretation of electrocardiograms," *Amer. Heart J.*, vol. 72, pp. 351–358, Sept. 1966.
[196] L. F. Staples, J. E. Gustafson, and G. J. Balm, "A three-lead electrocardiographic screening system," *J. Iowa Med. Soc.*, vol. LVII, pp. 820–823, Aug. 1967.
[197] Y. Nomura, Y. Takaki, and S. Toyama, "A method for computer diagnosis of the electrocardiogram," *Jap. Circ. J.*, vol. 30, pp. 499–508, May 1966.
[198] R. A. Bruce *et al.*, "Reliability and normal variations of computer analysis of Frank electrocardiogram by Smith–Hyde program (1968 version)," *Amer. J. Cardiol.*, vol. 29, pp. 389–396, Mar. 1972.
[199] J. Enderle, "Application de l'ordinateur au diagnostic electrocardiographique en pratique hospitaliere," *Acta Cardiol.*, vol. 35, pp. 357–377, 1970.
[200] ——, "Analyse de l'electrocardiogramme par ordinateur," Clinique Médicale de l'Hôpital Universitaire Brugmann, Brussels, Belgium, private communication.
[201] P. Raynaud *et al.*, "Analyse automatique par ordinateur de l'électocardiogramme couplé au vecto-cardiogramme," *Antenne Médicale*, vol. 6, pp. 315–338, 1971.
[202] P. W. Macfarlane, A. R. Lorimer, and T. D. V. Lawrie, "3 and 12 lead electrocardiogram interpretation by computer—A comparison on 1093 patients," *Brit. Heart J.*, vol. 33, pp. 266–274, 1971.
[203] J. von der Groeben, "Decision rules in electrocardiography and vectorcardiography," *Circulation*, vol. XXXVI, pp. 136–147, July 1967.
[204] A. N. Mucciardi and E. E. Gose, "A comparison of seven techniques for choosing subsets of pattern recognition properties," *IEEE Trans. Comput.*, vol. C-20, pp. 1023–1031, Sept. 1971.
[205] E. Kimura, Y. Mibukura, and S. Miura, "Statistical diagnosis of electrocardiogram by theorem of Bayes," *Jap. Heart J.*, vol. 4, pp. 469–488, Sept. 1963.
[206] J. Wartak, "Computer-aided recognition of electrocardiograms," *Acta Cardiol.*, vol. 22, pp. 350–361, 1967.
[207] A. E. Rikli *et al.*, "Computer analysis of electrocardiographic measurements," *Circulation*, vol. XXIV, pp. 643–649, Sept. 1961.
[208] H. V. Pipberger, R. A. Dunn, and J. Cornfield, "First and second generation computer programs for diagnostic ECG and VCG classification," in *Proc. XII Int. Colloq. Vectorcardiographicum* (Brussels, Belgium). Amsterdam, The Netherlands: North-Holland, 1972, in press.
[209] R. Gamboa, J. D. Klingeman, and H. V. Pipberger, "Computer diagnosis of biventricular hypertrophy from the orthogonal electrocardiogram," *Circulation*, vol. XXXIX, pp. 72–82, Jan. 1969.
[210] M. J. Goldman and H. V. Pipberger, "Analysis of the orthogonal electrocardiogram and vectorcardiogram in ventricular conduction defect with and without myocardial infarction," *Circulation*, vol. XXXIX, pp. 243–250, Feb. 1969.
[211] A. Kerr, Jr., A. Adicoff, J. D. Klingeman, and H. V. Pipberger, "Computer analysis of the orthogonal electrocardiogram in pulmonary emphysema," *Amer. J. Cardiol.*, vol. 25, pp. 34–45, Jan. 1970.
[212] E. E. Eddleman, Jr., and H. V. Pipberger, "Computer analysis of the orthogonal electrocardiogram and vectorcardiogram in 1,002 patients with myocardial infarction," *Amer. Heart J.*, vol. 81, pp. 608–621, May 1971.
[213] H. Blackburn *et al.*, "The electrocardiogram in population studies—A classification system," *Circulation*, vol. XXI, pp. 1160–1175, June 1960.
[214] T. Y. Young and W. H. Huggins, "Computer analysis of electrocardiograms using a linear regression technique," *IEEE Trans. Bio-Med. Eng.*, vol. BME-11, pp. 60–67, July 1964.
[215] L. D. Cady, Jr., E. Simonson, H. Blackburn, and H. L. Taylor, "Computed cardiographic pattern diagnosis," *Method. Inform. Med.*, vol. 4, pp. 92–96, 1965.
[216] G. J. Balm, "Crosscorrelation techniques applied to the electrocardiogram interpretation problem," *IEEE Trans. Bio-Med. Eng.*, vol. BME-14, pp. 258–262, Oct. 1967.
[217] M. Okajima, L. Stark, G. Whipple, and S. Yasui, "Computer pattern recognition techniques: Some results with real electrocardiographic data," *IEEE Trans. Bio-Med. Electron.*, vol. BME-10, pp. 106–114, July 1963.
[218] S. Yasui, G. H. Whipple, and L. Stark, "Comparison of human and computer electrocardiographic wave-form classification and identification," *Amer. Heart J.*, vol. 68, pp. 236–242, Aug. 1964.
[219] T. Sano, S. Tsuchiya, and F. Suzuki, "A use of Adaline as an automatic method for interpretation of the electrocardiogram and the vectorcardiogram," *Jap. Circ. J.*, vol. 33, pp. 537–544, May 1969.
[220] J. Klingeman and H. V. Pipberger, "Computer classification of electrocardiograms," *Comput. Biomed. Res.*, vol. 1, pp. 1–17, 1967.
[221] R. McFee and G. M. Baule, "Numerical diagnosis using 'stat-rules'," *IEEE Trans. Bio-Med. Eng.*, vol. BME-16, pp. 27–39, Jan. 1969.
[222] D. F. Specht, "Generation of polynomial discriminant functions for pattern recognition," *IEEE Trans. Electron. Comput.*, vol. EC-16, pp. 308–319, June 1967.
[223] ——, "Vectorcardiographic diagnosis using the polynomial discriminant method of pattern recognition," *IEEE Trans. Bio-Med. Eng.*, vol. BME-14, pp. 90–95, Apr. 1967.
[224] B. Lown, M. D. Klein, and P. I. Hershberg, "Coronary and precoronary care," *Amer. J. Med.*, vol. 46, pp. 705–724, May 1969.
[225] D. Scherf and A. Schott, *Extrasystoles and Allied Arrhythmias.* Melbourne, Australia: William Heinemann Medical Books, 1953.
[226] R. E. Bonner and H. D. Schwetman, "Computer diagnosis of electrocardiograms. III. A computer program for arrhythmia diagnosis," *Comput. Biomed. Res.*, vol. 1, pp. 387–407, 1968.
[227] M. Yokoi *et al.*, "On-line computer diagnosis of arrhythmias on ECG using by small scale digital computer system," *Jap. Circ. J.*, vol. 33, pp. 129–138, Feb. 1969.
[228] P. W. Macfarlane, A. R. Lorimer, and T. D. V. Lawrie, "ECG reporting by computer," *Scot. Med. J.*, vol. 15, pp. 363–369, 1970.
[229] J. Wartak, *Computers in Electrocardiography.* Springfield, Ill.: Charles C Thomas, 1970.
[230] J. L. Willems and H. V. Pipberger, "Arrhythmia detection by digital computer," *Comput. Biomed. Res.*, vol. 5, pp. 263–278, 1972.
[231] D. C. Alexander and D. Wortzman, "Computer diagnosis of electrocardiograms. I. Equipment," *Comput. Biomed. Res.*, vol. 1, pp. 348–365, 1968.
[232] D. W. Simborg, R. S. Ross, K. B. Lewis, and R. H. Shepard, "The R-R interval histogram—A technique for the study of cardiac rhythms," *J. Amer. Med. Ass.*, vol. 197, pp. 145–148, Sept. 12, 1966.
[233] R. E. Goldstein and G. O. Barnett, "A statistical study of the ventricular irregularity of atrial fibrillation," *Comput. Biomed. Res.*, vol. 1, pp. 146–161, 1967.
[234] W. Gersch, D. M. Eddy, and E. Dong, Jr., "Cardiac arrhythmia classification: A heart-beat interval—Markov chain approach," *Comput. Biomed. Res.*, vol. 4, pp. 385–392, 1970.
[235] W. K. Haisty, Jr., C. Batchlor, J. Cornfield, and H. V. Pipberger, "Discriminant function analysis of RR intervals: An algorithm for on-line arrhythmia diagnosis," *Comput. Biomed. Res.*, vol. 5, pp. 247–255, 1972.
[236] H. Miyahara *et al.*, "Cardiac arrhythmia diagnosis by digital computer. Considerations related to the temporal distribution of P and R waves," *Comput. Biomed. Res.*, vol. 1, pp. 277–300, 1968.
[237] G. H. Whipple, "Identification of complex cardiac arrhythmias by digital computation," in *Clinical Electrocardiography and Computers*, C. A. Caceres and L. S. Dreifus, Eds. New York: Academic Press, 1970, pp. 373–385.
[238] T. Horth, "Arrhythmia monitor," *Bio-Med. Eng.*, vol. 4, pp. 308–312, July 1969.
[239] D. L. Sulman, "Regulation of digitalis administration by testing for repetitive ventricular response," M.S. thesis, Mass. Inst. Technol., Cambridge, Sept. 1969.
[240] A. Pedersen, "Automatic detection of cardiac arrhythmias in long-term patient monitoring," in *Patient Monitoring*, J. F. Crul and J. P. Payne, Eds. Baltimore, Md.: Williams and Wilkins, 1970, pp. 96–105.
[241] W. P. Holsinger, K. M. Kempner, and M. H. Miller, "A bedside arrhythmia preprocessor," in *Proc. 8th Int. Conf. Medical and Biological Engineering* (Chicago, Ill., July 1969).
[242] H. N. Uhley *et al.*, "Automatic surveillance of heart rate and rhythm and T wave contour," *Amer. J. Cardiol.*, vol. 26, pp. 375–379, Oct. 1970.
[243] C. W. Ragsdale, "The army heart monitor—An automatic diagnostic cardiac waveform," in *Proc. 8th Int. Conf. Medical and Biological Engineering* (Chicago, Ill., July 1969).

[244] P. Kezdi, W. S. Naylor, R. Rambousek, and E. Stanley, "A practical heart rate and ectopic beat detector," *J. Electrocardiol.*, vol. 1, pp. 213–219, 1968.
[245] W. S. Naylor, E. L. Stanley, K. E. Robins, and P. Kezdi, "A reliable electrocardiogram R-wave detection applicable to normal and abnormal rhythms," in *Dig. 7th Int. Conf. Medical and Biological Engineering* (Stockholm, Sweden), p. 306, 1967.
[246] J. M. Neilson, "A special purpose computer for 'on-line' detection of ventricular ectopic complexes in a monitoring ECG signal," presented at the Conf. the Place of the Digital Computer in the Intensive Care Unit, Rotterdam, The Netherlands, Sept. 1970.
[247] C. W. Vellani and J. M. M. Neilson, "Computer analysis of ventricular ectopic rhythms in myocardial infarction" (Abstract), *Brit. Heart J.*,vol. 33, p. 145, 1971.
[248] G. J. Harris, "Ectopic beat detection based on temporal and morphological patterns," *NEREM Rec.*, vol. 11, pp. 22–23, 1969.
[249] G. J. Harris, M. D. Klein, P. R. Brooks, Jr., and B. Lown, "Ectopic beat detection in coronary patients," in *Proc. 8th Int. Conf. Medical and Biological Engineering* (Chicago, Ill., July 1969).
[250] G. J. Harris, "Multiform ventricular premature beat detector," U. S. Patent 3 616 790, Nov. 2, 1971.
[251] ——, "Electrocardiographic morphology recognition system," U. S. Patent 3 616 791, Nov. 2, 1971.
[252] ——, "Electrocardiographic R-wave detector," U. S. Patent 3 590 811, July 6, 1971.
[253] G. J. Harris and C. C. Day, "Automatic gain presetting circuit," U. S. Patent 3 579 138, May 18, 1971.
[254] M. D. Feezor, "A real-time electrocardiogram waveform analyzer for detection of premature ventricular contractions," Ph.D. dissertation, Univ. of North Carolina, Chapel Hill, 1969.
[255] M. D. Feezor, A. G. Wallace, and R. W. Stacy, "A real-time waveform analyzer for detection of ventricular premature beats," *J. Appl. Physiol.*, vol. 29, pp. 541–545, 1970.
[256] P. Kezdi, W. S. Naylor, J. W. Spickler, and R. W. Stacy, "Preprocessing of the electrocardiogram and blood pressure for on-line monitoring," in *Proc. 1970 San Diego Biomedical Symp.* (San Diego, Calif.), pp. 69–76, 1970.
[257] M. D. Feezor, "Analog preprocessing of electrocardiograms in a computer monitoring system," in *Proc. 1970 San Diego Biomedical Symp.* (San Diego, Calif.), pp. 129–131, 1970.
[258] C. A. Braun and F. B. Vogt, "Detection of the normal QRS complex by a hybrid matched filter technique," in *Proc. 24th Ann. Conf. Engineering in Medicine and Biology* (Las Vegas, Nev.), p. 148, 1971.
[259] T. Akazome, K. Ohbayashi, G. Kasai, and E. Kimura, "ECG wave measurement by a hybrid computer for automatic diagnosis of arrhythmias," in *Dig. 7th Int. Conf. Medical and Biological Engineering* (Stockholm, Sweden), p. 102, 1967.
[260] T. Suzuki *et al.*, "Automatic ECG analyzer: An almost analog device," in *Proc. 8th Int. Conf. Medical and Biological Engineering* (Chicago, Ill., July 1969).
[261] L. Sasmor and G. King, "On line computer arrhythmia analysis using an analog preprocessor," in *Proc. 24th Ann. Conf. Engineering in Medicine and Biology* (Las Vegas, Nev.), p. 152, 1971.
[262] Y. Abe *et al.*, "Computer analysis of ECG for patients monitoring," in *Proc. 8th Int. Conf. Medical and Biological Engineering* (Chicago, Ill., July 1969).
[263] J. T. Lynch, "Arrhythmia detection and classification using a digital computer on electrocardiographic data," M.S. thesis, Mass. Inst. Technol., Cambridge, June 1965.
[264] H. M. Hochberg *et al.*, "Monitoring of electrocardiograms in a coronary care unit by digital computer," *J. Amer. Med. Ass.*, vol. 207, pp. 2421–2424, Mar. 31, 1969.
[265] H. M. Hochberg, B. Wolk, N. Koss, and C. A. Caceres, "Methods for trend analysis in electrocardiogram monitoring," in *Clinical Electrocardiography and Computers*, C. A. Caceres and L. S. Dreifus, Eds. New York: Academic Press, 1970, pp. 439–454.
[266] L. J. Haywood, G. Harvey, S. Saltzberg, and V. K. Murthy, "An algorithm for real time continuous ECG waveform analysis and the statistical problems associated with on-line monitoring," in *Proc. 8th Int. Conf. Medical and Biological Engineering* (Chicago, Ill., July 1969).
[267] L. J. Haywood, G. A. Harvey and W. L. Kirk, Jr., "On-line digital computer for electrocardiogram monitoring in a coronary care unit," *J. Ass. Advan. Med. Instrum.*, vol. 3, pp. 165–169, Sept. 1969.
[268] L. J. Haywood, V. K. Murthy, G. A. Harvey and S. Saltzberg, "On-line real time computer algorithm for monitoring the ECG waveform," *Comput. Biomed. Res.*, vol. 3, pp. 15–25, 1970.
[269] S. Saltzberg, L. J. Haywood, G. Harvey, and D. Vereeke, "Electrocardiographic monitoring and wave form analysis utilizing interactive computer graphics," *J. Ass. Advan. Med. Instrum.*, vol. 5, pp. 91–96, Mar.–Apr., 1971.
[270] L. J. Haywood, G. A. Harvey, and S. A. Saltzberg, "Significance of interectopic intervals in automated arrhythmia monitoring" (Abstract), *J. Ass. Advan. Med. Instrum.*, vol. 6, p. 169, 1972.
[271] L. J. Haywood *et al.*, "Clinical use of R-R interval prediction for ECG monitoring: Time series analysis by autoregressive models," *J. Ass. Advan. Med. Instrum.*, vol. 6, pp. 111–116, 1972.
[272] C. L. Feldman, M. Hubelbank, and P. G. Amazeen, "A real-time ectopic heart beat detection system," in *Proc. 21st Ann. Conf. Engineering in Medicine and Biology* (Houston, Tex., Nov. 1968).
[273] ——, "Real-time cardiac arrhythmia monitoring with the PDP-7," *DECUS Proc.*, pp. 345–353, Spring 1969.
[274] P. G. Amazeen, "Detection of premature ventricular beats in the electrocardiogram," Ph.D. dissertation, Worcester Polytech. Inst., Worcester, Mass., May 1970.
[275] C. L. Feldman, P. G. Amazeen, M. D. Klein, and B. Lown, "Computer detection of ventricular ectopic beats," *Comput. Biomed. Res.*, vol. 3, pp. 666–674, 1971.
[276] F. J. Lewis *et al.*, "On-line monitoring with a dedicated computer," in *Proc. 1970 San Diego Biomedical Symp.* (San Diego, Calif.), pp. 1–3, 1970.
[277] S. T. Rabin *et al.*, "A real-time computer system for the diagnosis of cardiac arrhythmias," in *Proc. 1970 San Diego Biomedical Symp.* (San Diego, Calif.), pp. 125–128, 1970.
[278] L. D. Cady, and J. Albus, "Arrhythmia monitor for cardiac patients," in *Proc. 24th Ann. Conf. Engineering in Medicine and Biology* (Las Vegas, Nev.), p. 150, 1971.
[279] J. S. Geddes and H. R. Warner, "A PVC detection program," *Comput. Biomed. Res.*, vol. 4, pp. 493–508, 1971.
[280] E. D. Gerlings, D. L. Bowers, and G. A. Rol, "Detection of abnormal ventricular activation in a coronary care unit," *Comput. Biomed. Res.*, vol. 5, pp. 14–24, 1972.
[281] I. T. Young and M. S. Kohn, "Recognition of cardiac arrhythmias," in *Proc. UMR—Mervin J. Kelly Communications Conf.* (Univ. of Missouri, Rolla, 1970).
[282] K. M. Kempner, M. H. Miller, and W. P. Holsinger, "A computer approach to arrhythmia monitoring," in *Proc. 8th Int. Conf. Medical and Biological Engineering* (Chicago, Ill., July 1969).
[283] A. J. Berni and D. E. Dick, "Cross correlation to detect extrasystoles," in *Proc. 24th Ann. Conf. Engineering in Medicine and Biology* (Las Vegas, Nev.), p. 346, 1971.
[284] W. Rey, "The heart electrical activity and the cardiac monitoring," M.B.L.E.-Lab. de Recherches, Brussels, Belgium, Rep. R151, Jan. 1971.
[285] W. Rey, J. D. Laird, and P. G. Hugenholtz, "P-wave detection by digital computer," *Comput Biomed. Res.*, vol. 4, pp. 509–522, 1971.
[286] J. R. Whiteman and F. A. Siegel, "Progress report on the development of a computerized cardiac arrhythmia monitor," Health Care Technology Div., National Center for Health Services Research and Development, Feb.–Aug. 1970.
[287] R. E. Bonner, "A computer system for ECG monitoring," IBM Corp., Yorktown Heights, N. Y., Tech. Rep. 17–241, 1969.
[288] ——, "Electrocardiogram monitoring by computer," in *Clinical Electrocardiography and Computers*, C. A. Caceres and L. S. Dreifus, Eds. New York: Academic Press, 1970, pp. 455–463.
[289] ——, "On-line electronic data processing of cardiac arrhythmias," presented at the Symp. Cardiac Arrhythmias, Elsinore, Denmark, Apr. 23–25, 1970.
[290] J. R. Cox, Jr., H. A. Fozzard, F. M. Nolle, and G. C. Oliver, "Some data transformations useful in electrocardiography," in *Computers in Biomedical Research*, vol. 3, R. W. Stacy and B. D. Waxman, Eds. New York: Academic Press, 1969, pp. 181–206.
[291] F. M. Nolle and J. R. Cox, Jr., "How to keep up with the ECG," in *Dig. 1969 IEEE Computer Group Conf.*, pp. 182–185.
[292] F. M. Nolle, "Argus, a clinical computer system for monitoring electrocardiographic rhythms," D.Sc. dissertation, Washington Univ., St. Louis, Mo., 1972.
[293] F. M. Nolle *et al.*, "A clinical computer system for monitoring electrocardiographic rhythms," in *Proc. 24th Ann. Conf. Engineering in Medicine and Biology* (Las Vegas, Nev.), p. 154, 1971.
[294] J. R. Cox, Jr., and R. D. Logue, "Some observations on the economics of computer systems for monitoring electrocardiographic rhythms," *Comput. Biomed. Res.*, vol. 4, pp. 447–459, 1971.
[295] F. M. Nolle and K. W. Clark, "Detection of premature ventricular contractions using an algorithm for cataloging QRS complexes," in *Proc. 1971 San Diego Biomedical Symp.* (San Diego, Calif.), pp. 85–97, 1971.
[296] J. R. Cox, Jr., and F. M. Nolle, "Arrhythmia monitoring algorithms for real time applications," in *Proc. 5th Hawaii Int. Conf. System Sciences–Computers in Biomedicine* (Honolulu, Hawaii), pp. 120–122, 1972.
[297] G. C. Oliver *et al.*, "Detection of premature ventricular contractions with a clinical system for monitoring electrocardiographic rhythms," *Comput. Biomed. Res.*, vol. 4, pp. 523–541, 1971.
[298] M. S. Kohn, "Characterization of ectopic heartbeats," M.S. thesis, Mass. Inst. Technol., Cambridge, 1968.
[299] H. N. Hultgren and D. F. Specht, "Clinical evaluation—Smith Kline instruments computerized arrhythmia monitoring system" (Abstract), *J. Ass. Advan. Med. Instrum.*, vol. 6, p. 170, 1972.
[300] G. M. Vincent, G. N. Webb, R. S. Ross, and W. H. Guier, "QRS-wave detector evaluation," *Amer. Heart J.*, vol. 83, pp. 475–480, Apr. 1972.

comparative religion in character recognition machines

by
A. W. Holt
Rabinow Laboratory
Control Data Corporation

I. Introduction

The man in the street, when discussing Character Recognition, used to be able to get by with friendly phrases like "Best Match" and "Feature." [1,2] Due to the influence of Pattern Recognition Theory, however, it is now the rule to be able to spell "Hyperplane Dichotomies" and "Piecewise Linear Discriminant Function."[2,3,4] Techniques using complex optical transformations are also becoming practical.[2] It is the intent of this paper to describe a few of these different philosophies in terms which are hopefully common to most of the ideas. This is done by introducing the concept of "stage analysis." Peripheral problems such as character separation, paper handling, control, applications, etc., will be given only scant attention.

Stage analysis is a way of classifying character recognition machinery with a minimum of reference to the specific components used. Viewed as a black box, the job of all such machines is to convert a set of data having a high information content into a character name having a much lower information content. If this is accomplished by a single level of decision, the machine is called a "one stage" reader. In many readers, however, intermediate decisions are made before the final decision; each one of these decision levels terminates a "stage." Although the stage concept is related to the idea of a "layer," as used in Pattern Recognition theory, it is believed that a classification of Character Recognition machinery has not previously been attempted in these terms.

What is character recognition? Character recognition is the conversion into digital codes of any well known group of patterns commonly used for human communication. These include:

a. Those stylized fonts which are humanly readable.
b. Non-stylized machine imprinted fonts such as ordinary typewriter fonts, high speed printer, bookkeeping fonts.
c. Hand printed numeric and alpha-numeric sets which have good spacing between characters.
d. Cursive script.
e. Ideographs (Chinese).

Note that this collection of conversions which we call character recognition does not include mark sensing, at one end of the scale, nor does it include the recognition of all types of generalized patterns and pictures at the other end of the scale.

The usefulness of character recognition machines in our society can be summed up in one phrase: it lets computers snuggle up a little closer to human beings. In the early stages of computer development the only way for humans to enter programs or data into a computer was to have a human read the information in whatever form it was and strike keys on a machine which immediately translated the key stroke into a digital code. The best known of these machines is the key punch. Another well known method is to punch holes in a paper tape.

In contrast, the major attractiveness of character recognition is that it is entirely compatible with the way humans communicate among themselves. Why is compatibility good? Because humans produce better accuracy, better verification, and better flexibility using a single language than using a double language. Also, a document may have to be read both by humans and machines; humans do not easily read machine language.

A brief note on the organization of this paper. Section II presents the concept of stage analysis in some detail; imaginary machines are designed and discussed in order to illustrate the types of decisions. This is in preparation for Section III, in which a list is presented of the more outstanding and interesting character recognition machines, organized by the number of stages. In Section IV we speculate on the possible significance of the number of stages as a function of the difficulty of the task to be performed.

Reprinted from *IEEE Comput. Group News*, vol. 2, pp. 3–11, Nov. 1968.

II. Central Recognition Philosophy as Classified By Stage Analysis

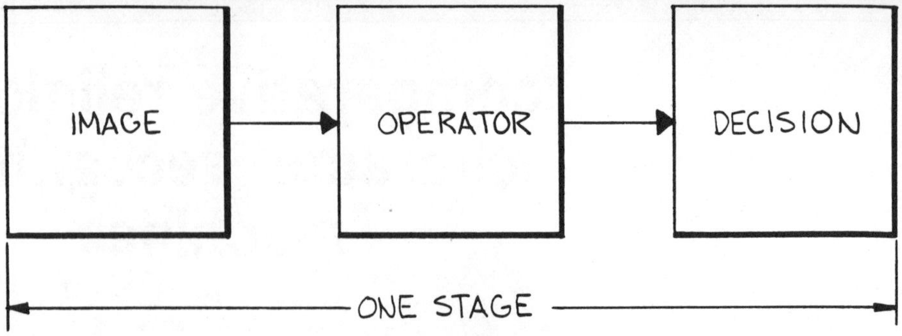

FIGURE 1. The "Stage" Concept in Character Recognition Machines.

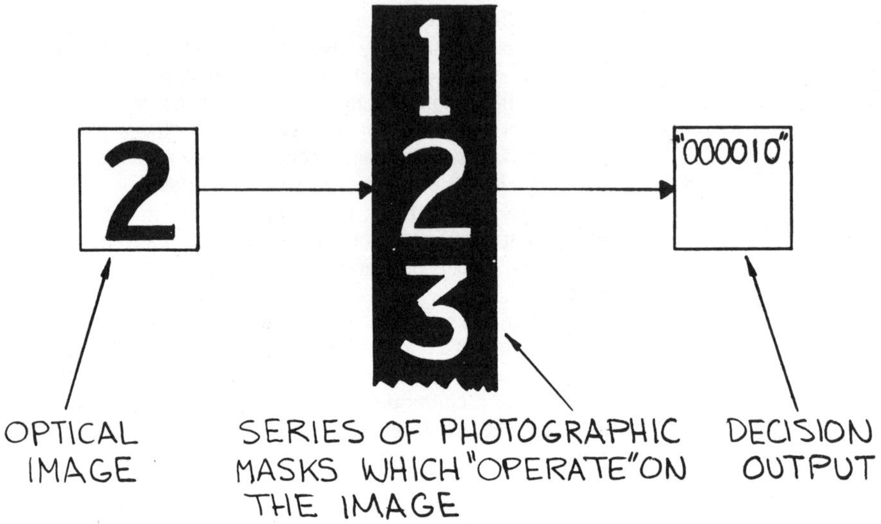

FIGURE 2. A Simplified Example of a Single Stage Reading Machine.

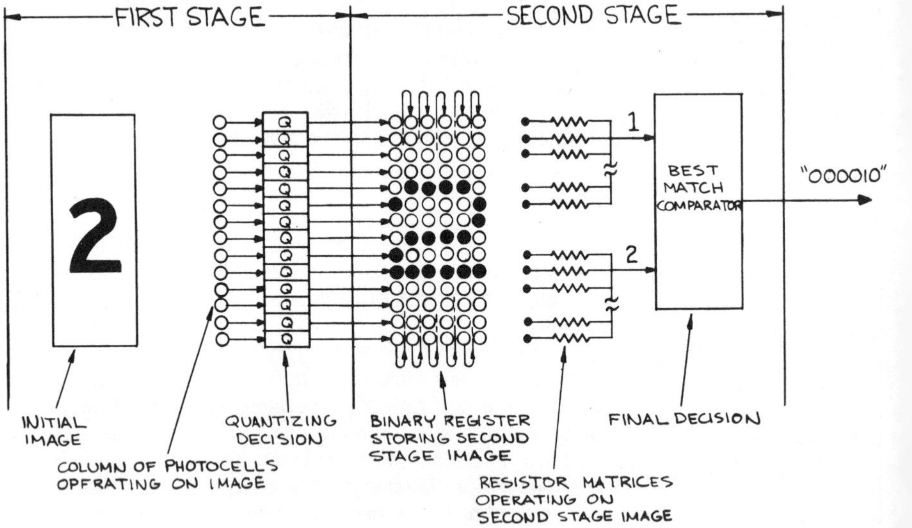

FIGURE 3. A Simplified Example of a Two Stage Reading Machine.

In the following paragraphs we will discuss the manner in which stages are defined, and then go on to give illustrative examples of one, two, and three stage machines.

A stage consists in general of an "image" (may be in optical, magnetic, or electronic form), one or more operations upon that image, and a decision. This is illustrated in Figure 1. A single stage machine, for example, may have an optical image operated upon by being passed through transparent templates which are more or less complete pictures of the characters to be recognized. The decision is made on the basis of which template is matched best by the unknown image. A two stage machine is one in which intermediate decisions are made at the first stage, a new image is formed, a new operation is performed, and a final decision is made on the basis of this last operation. Similarly, a three stage machine is one in which there are three decision levels.

The discovery of the decision point is the critical task in stage analysis. We define a decision as a logical point at which a group of data is given a new name. If many decisions are made independently of each other, and have approximately the same degree of complexity, this is defined as a single decision level. The information content is always reduced by making a decision. To find whether the information content has been reduced, test for reversibility.

By way of illustrating the stage concept, let us generate three machines which may or may not exist today. Figure 2 is a diagrammatic representation of a single stage machine. In this machine the initial image is to be an optical image of the whole character. This optical image is projected through photographs of the various character shapes which are to be recognized. These optical masks, or templates, form the operator. The operation is simply area correlation. The result of this correlation is detected by a photocell which is sensitive to the total light of the image modified by the photographic masks. The final decision is made by choosing the character template which best fits the unknown image. The essential feature to be noted here is that no decisions are made intermediate to the final decision.

A typical two stage machine is illustrated in Figure 3. Here, we again start off with an optical image, but in this case we will have an intermediate decision level as well as the final decision level. For this illustration we have chosen the first operator to be a column of discrete photocells across which the optical image has been transported horizontally. Decisions are made at appropriate time intervals as to whether the small unitary area seen by each photocell should be called black or white. (More complex decisions based on various normalizing processes are possible here). The second stage image of this imaginary machine is a point set of binary values representing the black and white components of the original image. Image storage is provided by a shift register, which has particular utility for handling vertical mis-registration, as we shall discuss in later paragraphs. Shifting can be considered to be a second stage operator. The other sec-

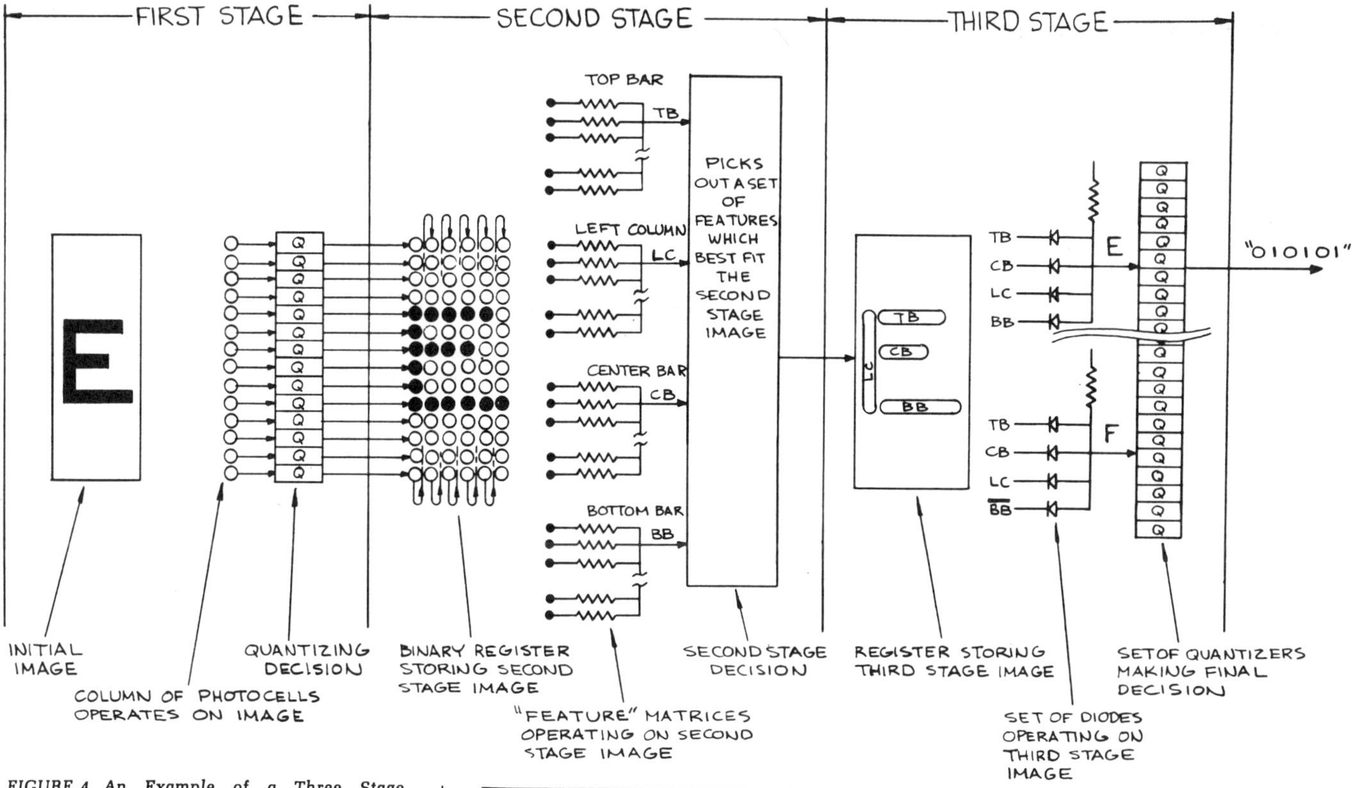

FIGURE 4. An Example of a Three Stage Reading Machine.

ond stage operator is a set of resistor matrices. The final decision is made by choosing which resistor matrix best matches the unknown character. Such a decision method is known as a "best match" and also as a "minimum distance categorizer."

Figure 4 illustrates a three stage machine. Let us assume that the image is again optical and is scanned by a column of photocells, the decision being simply whether each unitary point is black or white. The result of the first stage is to produce a second stage image which is again a point set representing the whole character. The operators of the second stage do not perform transformations on the character as a whole as it would in the two stage machine; instead the operator will be so designed as to separate certain types of features which are parts of the characters. Typical second stage operators would be resistor matrices designed to separate a left vertical bar, a high horizontal bar, a middle horizontal bar, and a low horizontal bar. Second stage decisions choose one of these preprogrammed features to represent groups of unitary points in each of many appropriate areas. The result of the second stage is a third stage image which consists of a set of features. This may again be stored in a shift register, but more commonly it will be stored in flip flops. The third stage operator in our imaginary machine is shown as a logic tree. Note that "AND" gates are separated into a logical operator and a quantizer. The quantizer represents the decision level. Such a decision method is often called "absolute" as opposed to the best match.

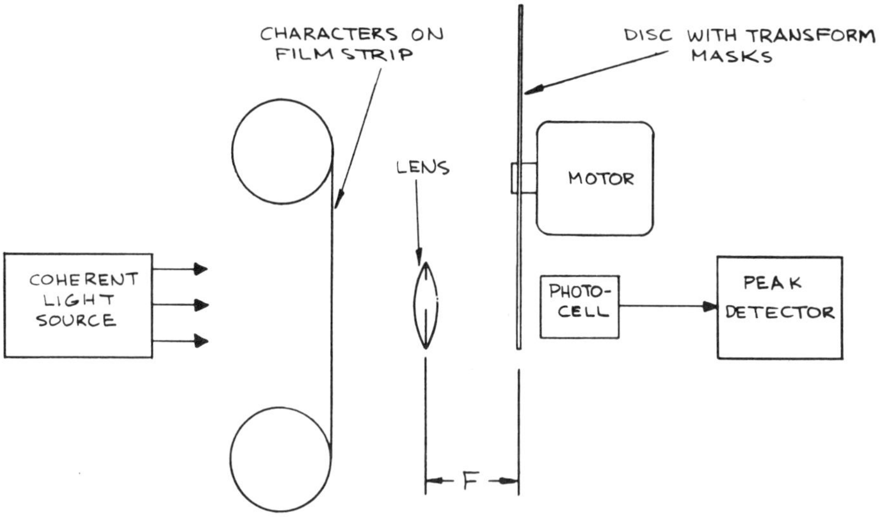

FIGURE 5. Fourier Transform Character Recognition Machine.

These three examples of hypothetical machines should be taken as merely tutorial. In general, there are no theorems which describe how many stages are desirable. In practice it turns out that extra stages are added to take care of vertical registration, to increase speed, or to reduce the number of character templates required.

Before advancing to our description of present day machines it is advisable to briefly discuss the problem of "vertical registration." Rough positioning of characters within the field of the sensors is usually accomplished by paper motion or mechanical motion of mirrors (except when a flying spot CRT is used). Fine positioning is not needed with the holographic or the Fourier methods, as described in Section III. Most template matching machines, however, provide specific equipment to ensure that the image will pass through nearly perfect registration at some time. For a single stage machine such as illustrated in Figure 2, vertical registration can be accomplished by moving the templates mechanically with respect to unknown characters. In Figure 3 (the two stage machine) registration is accomplished by using the shift register to rapidly move the second stage image through all possible vertical positions.

III. Machine Descriptions

In this section we will attempt to turn the tables on reading machines by categorizing the categorizers. The most important material is contained in Tables 1, 2, and 3, while the text is mainly commentary.

A. One Stage Machines

Table No. 1 illustrates only a few machines chosen from the very large number of possible machines which use a single stage of recognition. The first entry in this table is called a photographic mask machine. In this case the initial image is an entire image of the character in an optical form. This image is focused on a plane of a series of photographic masks, which is the first (and only) operator. The final decision is accomplished by measuring the area correlation between the unknown image and the photographic masks and choosing the best correlation. Such machines were among the very earliest built by the pioneers in this field. Vertical registration is accomplished by having the image move mechanically with respect to the templates or vice-versa. The templates can either be presented for correlation serially (for example, they may be mounted inside a rotating drum) or they may be presented in parallel, a beam splitter being used to make multiple images. There are

TABLE 1. SINGLE STAGE CHARACTER RECOGNITION MACHINES

NAME	TYPE OF INITIAL IMAGE	OPERATORS	FIRST (AND FINAL) DECISION	REMARKS
Photographic Mask Reader	Optical	Photographic Masks Perform Area Correlation.	Best Match chooses least transmitted light.	Slow, cheap, registration by mechanical motion. Not used commercially. Font: Any single numeric set.
Bar Code Reader for COC5 Font (GE #DRD200)	Optical	1. Narrow slit, long axis vertical. 2. Photocell. 3. Timing Gates.	Decides either narrow white space or wide white space between bars.	Font: COC5 only. The wide-narrow decisions come serially and become the BCD output code. Numerics + 1 symbol. See Figure 7. May shortly become a high volume commercial machine. High Speed. Vert. Reg.: inherent.
MICR (Single Head) (GE, NCR, Lundy)	Magnetic	1. Single narrow magnetic head, long axis vertical. 2. Image stored in delay line. 3. Resistor summing network from delay line taps.	Best Match.	High volume commercial. Highly stylized font, E13b, hard to print. Numerics + 4 symbols. See Figure 7. High Speed. Vert. Reg.: inherent.
Fourier Transform Reader	Optical (Must be derived from transparency)	Fourier transform mask at focal point of lens performs area correlation on transform of unknown.	Best Match chooses least transmitted light.	Not used commercially. Coherent light required. Registration independent.
Hologram Reader	Optical (Must be derived from transparency)	Holograms (Autocorrelation)	Look for bright spots.	Not used commercially. Coherent light required. Registration independent.

TABLE 2. TWO STAGE CHARACTER RECOGNITION MACHINES

NAME	TYPE OF INITIAL IMAGE	FIRST STAGE OPERATORS	FIRST STAGE DECISIONS	SECOND STAGE IMAGE	SECOND STAGE OPERATORS	FINAL DECISION	REMARKS
Control Data 915 Page Reader	Optical	1. High speed mirror. 2. Row of photocells. 3. Timing Gates.	Black or white decision on each point.	5 wide by 18 high, set of binary points stored in shift register. Stored image represents whole character.	1. Shift Register 2. Resistor Matrices (one per character).	Best Match.	Font: USASI-A (64 char.) Medium Speed. Commercial product. Vert. Reg.: High Speed Mirror + Shift Register.
Farrington Credit Card Reader	Optical	1. Rotating Mechanical Scanner. 2. Photocell. 3. Timing Gates. 4. Integrators for selected areas.	Outputs of integrators are quantized.	Set of flip-flops, each representing a feature such as Left Vertical Bar, Top Horiz. Bar, etc.	Logic Tree.	Absolute.	Font: 7B (Numeric only). Vertical Registration accomplished by Mechanical Scanner, which scans in Vertical Direction, in cooperation with triggered timing circuits. Medium speed. Commercial product.
Multiple Head MICR IBM #1419	Magnetic	1. Column of 30 magnetic heads in contact with paper. 2. Timing Gates.	Black or white decision on each point.	Set of binary points stored in shift register.	1. Shift Register. 2. Logic Tree. Some alternate paths allowed.	Absolute.	Font: E13b (Numeric + 4) High Speed. Vert. Reg.: Extra heads above and below char. + shift register. Commercial product.
Control Data Ft. Monmouth Multi-font Reader, AN/FST-6	Optical	1. Column of photocells. 2. Timing Gates.	Black or white decision on each point.	25 wide by 60 high. Set of binary points stored in shift register.	1. Shift Register. 2. Resistor matrices (One character per matrix.) 3. Similar categories from various fonts are "OR" gated at input to comparator.	Best Match.	Resembles "piece-wise linear" machine. Fonts: 12 pitch Elite, U.C. + L.C., 10 pitch Pica, U.C. + L.C., USASI-A. Total of 200 characters. Medium speed. Vert. Reg.: Extra photocells above and below char. + Shift Register. Only one machine built.
Adaptive Machine Using Hyperplane Dichotomies	Either Optical or Magnetic	Any General Scanner	Break up analog image into discrete points. Output may be either analog or digital.	Set of "d" measurements representing a point in "d" dimensional space.	Resistor Matrices. Each matrix defines a hyperplane in d dimensional space. two modes are possible — see text.	1. Minimum Distance Categorizer. (Best Match). 2. Threshold Logic Units (TLU).	If TLU method is used there are only P matrices, where 2^P = R categories. Not used commercially
Adaptive Machine Using "Piece-wise Linear" Dichotomies	Either Optical or Magnetic	Any General Scanner	Break up analog image into discrete points. Output may be either analog or digital.	Set of d measurements representing a point in d dimensional space.	Piecewise Linear Discriminant Functions (Multiple resistor matrices per category). Each matrix may represent a "dirty" prototype point or it may represent a clean prototype from a different font, same category.	Minimum Distance Categorizer. Multiple matrices representing boundaries of one category are "OR" gated at input to comparator.	Resembles Rabinow Ft. Monmouth Multi-font Reader. Not used commercially

TABLE 3. THREE STAGE CHARACTER RECOGNITION MACHINES

NAME	TYPE OF INITIAL IMAGE	FIRST STAGE OPERATORS	FIRST STAGE DECISIONS	SECOND STAGE IMAGE	SECOND STAGE OPERATORS	SECOND STAGE DECISIONS	THIRD STAGE IMAGE	THIRD STAGE OPERATORS	FINAL DECISION	REMARKS
IBM 1287 Hand print Number Reader	Optical	Flying Spot CRT performs small spiral motions to follow outline of character.	Set of decisions about whether or not a line was touched.	Set of sequential measurements on the X and Y deflections which resulted from following the character outline.	1. Smoothing. 2. Circuits to measure trace angle.	Quantizing of the trace angle in 45° increments.	Closed Loop Word (Base 8) describing angular changes around periphery of character.	Shift Register probably drives resistor templates.	Probably Best Match.	Commercial Product. Hand printed numerals + a few selected alpha characters. Vert. Reg. drops out. Medium Speed.
Control Data Optical Watchbird Hand Print Number Reader	Optical	Any raster scan.	Black or white decision on each unitary point.	30 x 30 set of binary points.	Line Trackers.	Line beginnings, endings, splits, and joints.	Image of Features.	Logic Tree.	Absolute.	Laboratory Model. Hand printed numerals. Vert. Reg. drops out.
IBM 1975 Omni-Font Reader	Optical	CRT + normalization in height, gray level, stroke width.	Black or white decision on each unitary point.	650 bit complete image stored in shift register.	Logic Operators describe many features.	Recognizes features.	100 bit feature vector.	Reference vectors are in ternary form.	Best Match.	Reads more than 200 alpha numeric fonts. Only one machine built. Vert. reg.: Shift Register
"N" Tuple Adaptive Machine	Optical	Any general scanner.	Breakup analog image into discrete points. Output may be either analog or digital.	Set of "d" measurements representing a point in "d" dimensional space.	"Y" dichotomies each with "N" weights (can be random, fixed, or trainable).	Y Threshold Logic Units. Each TLU is independent.	Set of "Y" binary measurements representing a point in Y dimensional space.	"R" dichotomies, (trainable weights).	Minimum Distance categorizer chooses one out of R categories.	With N=6, Y=6, R=50, this machine works quite well.

usually both "assertion masks" and "negation masks," the assertion mask being transparent in the area where the black character is expected to be, and the negation mask being transparent in the area where white is expected to be. The correlation is obtained by summing the output of the assertion photocell together with the inverted output of the negation photocell – for a perfect match no light is transmitted to the assertion photocell and a maximum amount of light is transmitted to the negation photocell.

The next entry in Table 1 discusses a machine which we shall call a vertical bar code reader. This type of machine depends absolutely on having a very stylized font for its operation and cannot read ordinary typewritten characters at all. There are two major fonts for which this machine is philosophically suited – the European CMC7 (alphanumeric) and the U.S. COC5 (numeric only). The character is made up of vertical bars. The space between these bars are either wide or narrow and form a code. An example of the COC5 is shown in Figure 7. The initial image for these machines is optical and there are three operators: 1) a narrow slit with its long axis vertical, 2) a photocell, and 3) a set of timing gates. The job of the decision maker is to decide whether each space is wide or narrow. These wide-narrow decisions are made serially (but independently) and become the output code directly. Note that the machine is a single stage machine, since no further reduction of information needs to be made on this code. The major advantage of this type of machine is that the reading logic is inexpensive, but the font appearance is esthetically

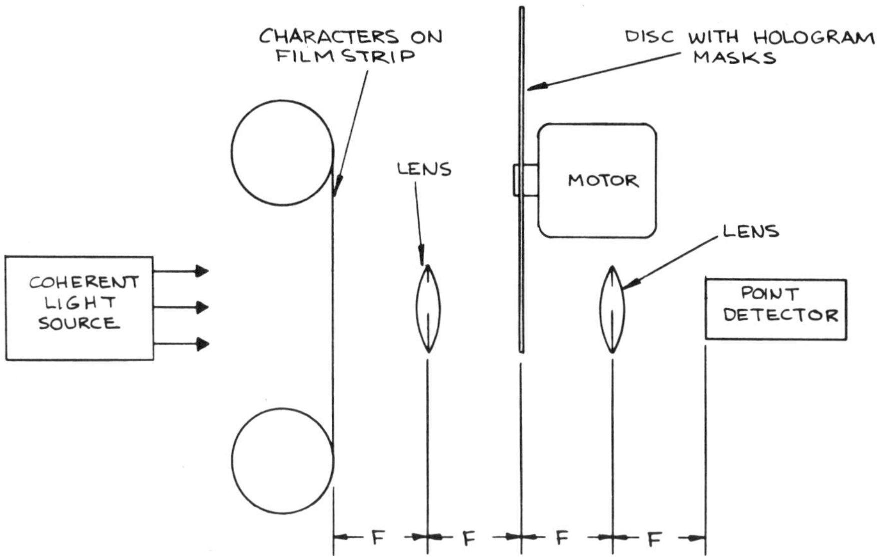

FIGURE 6. Holographic Character Recognition Machine.

poor. Such fonts are also difficult to print.

The next single stage reader to be considered is the magnetic ink character reader (MICR) which uses a single head. Used for banking applications, machines of this type are currently in commercial production by GE, NCR, and Lundy; the number produced probably exceeds 700. The font is "E13b," which is composed of 10 highly stylized numerals and 4 symbols. This font is illustrated in Figure 7. This machine is a single stage reader, since it only has a single level of decision. The initial image is, of course, magnetic, and it must therefore be scanned by a magnetic head in contact with the paper. This magnetic head can be considered to be the first operator. It is a single narrow magnetic head, with its long axis vertical. Its output is proportional to the rate of change of the magnetic flux passing the gap; the signal is zero volts while traversing a horizontal line and rises suddenly to a maximum when crossing a vertical column of magnetic ink. Since the head is taller than the character the output will be independent of the vertical position of the character. Note that this is a valuable way of reducing the information content without making any decisions – after the scanning no knowledge remains about the position of any black marks relative to each other in any vertical slice. Signals are temporarily stored in an electro-magnetic delay line, and this may be considered to be a form of temporary image register. A set of summing matrices are attached to various taps on this delay line, and these summing matrices can be considered to be another operator. The final (and only) decision is made by comparing the outputs of the summing matrices and choosing that matrix which produces the best match.

Another example of a single stage reader is the Fourier transform machine[2] shown schematically in Figure 5. Although this is by no means commercially developed it represents an interesting concept. The intial image is optical and the operators are photographic masks. Coherent, or nearly coherent, light must be used. Unlike the photographic mask machine explained above, the pattern on the mask is not the normal picture of a character. Rather, it is more like the picture of a diffraction pattern caused by the character shape. In the reading machine these photographs of the Fourier transforms are placed at the principal focus of the optical system rather than being placed in the plane of the real image, as is done in the simple photographic mask machine. Viewing the correlation between the Fourier transform of the initial image and the Fourier transform templates is a photocell or set of photocells. The simple magnitude of light is a measure of the correlation, and the minimum represents best correlation. The decision as to which template fits best is again done on a best match basis. The most novel characteristic of this type of machine is that the output is, to the first order, independent of the registration of the character with respect to the fixed position of the mask. There are, however, difficulties arising from the fact that the transforms are invariant under 180° rotation of the character. Since the phase relationships of the light must be preserved, the unknown character must be presented to the reader in the form of a transparency.

The hologram reading machine[2] uses optical transforms of an even more sophisticated nature. It is illustrated in Figure 6. Again, this type of machine is not in commercial use, but the principles involved are of extreme interest. A hologram is a photograph which captures on film not only the amplitude but also the phase of the light which passes through a given plane. In making the hologram, this phase information is captured by "beating" a reference light source against the modulated image, and a kind of interference pattern is thus formed. In the reading machine, a cross correlation is performed between a modulated image of the unknown character and the hologram. A good correlation between the unknown transparency and the hologram is evidenced by a single point of light in the image plane which the photomultiplier looks at, and this plane must therefore be scanned. The decision involves choosing which one of the points of light is most cleanly defined. As in the Fourier machine, the unknown character must be in the form of a transparency.

B. Two Stage Character Recognition Machines

The first example shown of a two stage character recognition machine is the Control Data® 915 Page Reader. Figure 8 shows an overall view of the 915, and Figure 9 shows a diagram of the optical scanning system. The initial image here is a complete optical image of the character. The line scanning mirror merely provides rough positioning. There are three operations carried out on the image before the first decision. The first operation is performed by a high speed mirror, oscillating at 3750 Hertz. This mirror transports the optical image up and down past a horizontal row of six photocells which constitute the second operator. Only five of these photocells are used for character scanning. A third operation is performed by timing gates. The first level decision is made as to whether each one of these photocells is seeing a black or white point. The output of each one of these photocells is quantized 54 times in one vertical half-sweep. These decisions are timed to be 6 mils apart vertically (referenced to the actual character size) and the photocells are spaced about 14 mils apart horizontally. This ends the first stage. The second stage starts with an image of the character formed by the binary decisions developed from the first stage. This image is stored in a shift register which shifts vertically downwards when the mirror is traveling upwards, and upwards when the mirror is traveling down. This shift register has 5 columns, each 18 stages high. Each shift register column is driven by only one photocell. Note that the number of elements scanned vertically by the photocells is more than three times as many as the shift register has room for. The result is that (while the mirror is going down) the image of a character is shifted up through the shift register and disappears off the top of the register. During the next half-cycle the image is again presented to the row of photocells and is shifted downwards through the shift register. The second level operator is a set of resistor matrices, of which there is one matrix per character. These matrices are driven by elements of the shift register, with points which are supposed to be black being implemented with a pure resistor. Especially important points which are supposed to be white are implemented by a diode in series with a resistor. The reason a diode is used here is that we don't want the presence of white to help the correlation voltage, but black should hurt the correlation. Within the resistor matrix for one character many shift register elements are not connected to the matrix at all; these represent "don't care" points. The final decision is made by choosing the best match. The great advantage of two stage machines over one stage machines is that the templates which are used for final recognition can be driven in parallel without having to build complex optical devices for image splitting. The combination of high speed mirror and shift register provide the ability to handle characters which are mis-registered in the vertical direction as much as plus or minus a full character height.

Next, in Table 2, is the Farrington Credit Card Reader, which was probably the first commercially successful character reader. It is a rare example of a two stage "feature" machine. It reads Farrington 7B, a numeric font used on Esso, Shell, Sunoco and many other credit cards. Operating on the optical image are four distinct mechanisms: 1) a rotating mechanical disk scanner, 2) a photocell, 3) timing gates, and 4) integrators for selected areas. The paper moves horizontally in the direction of the line of characters, while the disk scans vertically. A timing sequence, started by the recognition of a character being present, generates gating signals which distribute the video into the appropriate integrator circuits. These integrators store "black" over many scans for areas such as the Left Vertical Bar, Top Bar, etc. The first stage decisions are performed by quantizers looking at the integrators. The second stage image merely stores these decisions for later use by the logic tree. Decision is the "Absolute" mode.

The third entry in Table 2 is the IBM 1419 multiple head magnetic ink character reader. Operating on the magnetic image is a column of about 33 magnetic heads in contact with the paper. The paper (normally a bank check) is traveling in the horizontal direction – i.e., in the direction parallel to the line of characters. The first decision level is a series of black-white decisions for each magnetic head. This completes the first stage. The second stage begins with a shift register which catches the image of the character presented by the first stage. This register is approximately 15 elements wide by 33 elements high, the character being nominally 11 elements high. The image is shifted horizontally at a rate equal to the paper motion, and super-imposed upon this is the vertical shifting necessary to move the character image through all possible positions of vertical registration. The second stage operator is a pure logic tree which does not use resistor matrices. Enough alternate logic paths are provided, however, so that many somewhat "noisy" versions of the characters are allowed to be recognized. The final decision is therefore of the so-called absolute type, and is not a best match. The font read by this machine is E13b, which has been standardized for use in the American banking industry. It is to be expected that the IBM 1419 machine should be able to read characters which are "noiser" than single stage readers can, since much more information has been picked up from the magnetic image.

The fourth entry in Table 2 is the Control Data Multifont Reader built for Fort Monmouth. This machine was built specifically for a message entry system to be used in various military communications centers. It reads the following sets of characters: Upper and lower case 12 pitch elite, upper and lower case 10 pitch pica, and the USASI-A font. The optical image is scanned by a column of 100 photocells disposed in the vertical direction. These are placed at 3.5 mil intervals. The decision at the first stage is simply to determine whether each unitary point is to be called black or white. The second image is a set of binary elements contained in a shift register 25 wide x 64 high. The output of the photocells is switched so that the average vertical position of the characters falls in the center of the 64 high shift register. Three operations are performed on this image, the first of which is the vertical positioning accomplished by running the shift register in the vertical direction. The second is the operation of a set of resistor matrices, of which there is one matrix per character style. There are over 200 resistor matrices in the Fort Monmouth machine. In this multifont categorizer, a third operation is performed – the outputs of resistor matrices representing similar characters are OR-gated together before being presented to the minimum distance categorizer. That is to say, the matrix which represents the capital elite "A" is OR-gated with the matrix which represents the capital pica "A" and with the matrix which represents the USASI "A." Similarly, all the capital "B's" will be OR gated together, etc. Therefore, only the best correlation for each character named is presented to the comparator for categorization. This is sometimes called a

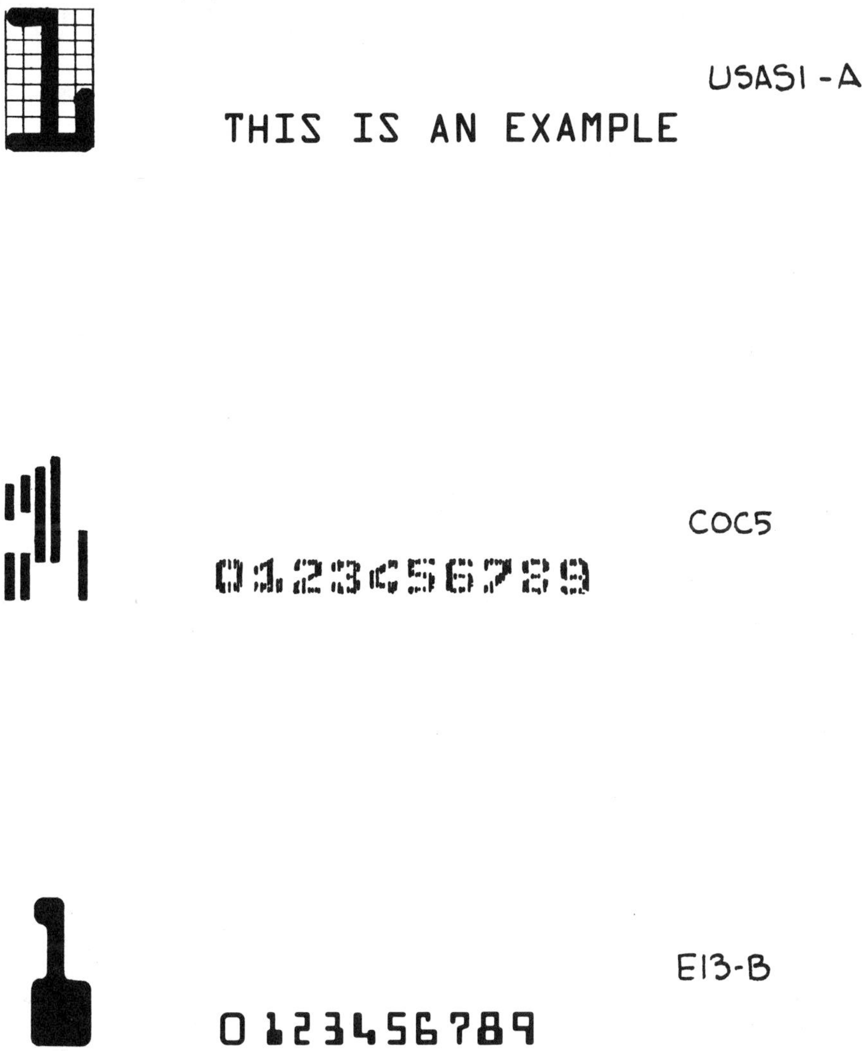

FIGURE 7. Several Varieties of Stylized Font

"best of best match." The OR-gate used here is merely several diodes with their cathodes tied together; its function is to put the highest voltage from any of several sources on to a single wire. Note that it does not represent another stage in our systematic description of reading machines, since no decision was made by employing the OR-gate. Information content is reduced, however, since the operation is not reversible. Where the font type is known ahead of time, the unused resistor matrices for the other fonts can be gated off, and somewhat more reliable decisions accrue to this mode of operation. The technique of OR gating several operators into a single category resembles somewhat the "piece-wise linear" machine which is described in Entry 6 of Table 2.

Turning now to more exotic ideas, we will next consider machines which are capable of categorizing much more general patterns than the preceding entries in the list. They are also capable of "learning" or "adaptation." This more general field is called "Pattern Recognition," and is, at present, characterized by a very large amount of mathematical theory but not a whole lot of practice. To be sure, a number of the proposals have been evaluated on computers but unless there is a good deal of work behind closed doors, it is a good guess that generalized pattern recognition machines are still very much in the realm of theory. It seems certainly fair to say that no generalized pattern recognition machines have been applied to commercial endeavors.

The Fifth Entry in Table 2 is the "Adaptive Machine Using Hyperplane Dichotomies." A hyperplane dichotomy may be implemented by a resistor matrix, for the purposes of this discussion. An adaptive machine will normally be able to change the weights of the resistors during the training program or during normal operation. The initial image can be either optical or magnetic and any suitable scanner can be used. A typical first decision would be simply to quantize the image into a set of discrete points. The values of light recorded for each of these points may be either a binary number or they may be recorded as continuous shades of grey. This decision level terminates the first stage. The second stage image is then stored in some form of register. In mathematical terms this image is described as a set of "d" measurements representing a point in "d" dimensional space. In other words, instead of viewing this second stage image as a representation of a character in two dimensions, the attack here is to consider that each of the discrete measurements made by the first operator in the first stage is an independent degree of freedom. The second stage operator can be a set of resistor matrices, each matrix defining a hyperplane in "d" dimensional space. Either one of two modes can be used at this point. A close analogy to commercial character readers (See, for example, the Control Data 915) is obtained if "R" resistor matrices are used, where R is the number of categories to be separated. A minimum distance categorizer (best match) selects the appropriate output code. The other mode is to use only "P" resistor matrices, where $2^{P} = R$. In this case, decisions are made by "Threshold Logic Units" (TLU), each decision being binary and independent of the others.

The next entry in Table 2 is an "Adaptive Machine Using Piece-wise Linear Dichotomies." This is a machine quite similar in philosophy to the previous adaptive machine described except that it is more powerful. This extra "power" may be obtained by describing more than one prototype point for each decision category. Philosophically, this also resembles the Control Data Fort Monmouth Multifont Reader. Using the more precise language of pattern recognition theory, the Piecewise Linear Machine uses a set of discriminant functions each of which is the maximum of a group of subsidiary discriminant functions. The initial image will be an optical image; any general scanner may be used, and the first decision will be simply to break up the analog image into a set of discrete points. The values of these discrete points, which are measurements of the amount of light falling on a particular part of the image, may be either two-valued or continuous. This decision level terminates the first stage. The image which starts the second stage is exactly as in the preceding machine: a set of "d" measurements representing a point in "d" dimensional space. The Piecewise Linear Machine diverges at this point, however, from the simple hyperplane machine. In the hyperplane machine there was just one "d" dimensional dichotomy used to perform each separation. In this machine several descriptions of prototypes from each category can be used, and the minimum distance within each category is OR-gated to the final comparator. In other words, we may have a machine which is trying to read three different shapes of A and three different shapes of B, etc. A prototype matrix can be used for each of these different shapes. This is particularly valuable when an average description might fall within the boundaries of some other category entirely. If there are "R" categories, only "R" wires will go into the comparator and this will select the winner from among these "R" wires. The training of these adaptive machines is a subject beyond the scope of this paper, but it is well treated in the references.

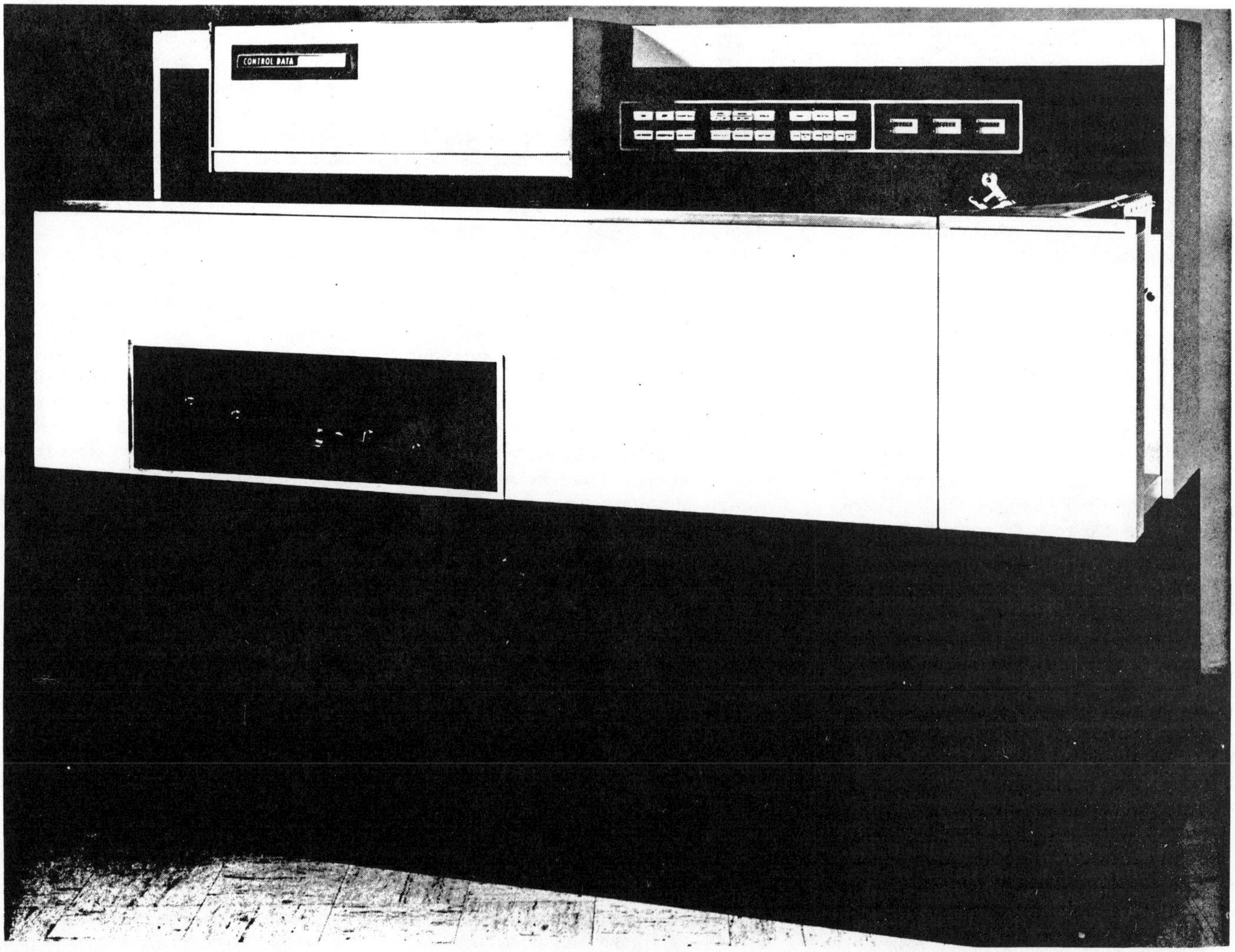

FIGURE 8. Control Data 915 Page Reader

C. Three Stage Character Recognition Machines

Table 3 lists a few examples of machines using three levels of decision. The first is the IBM 1287, which can read carefully hand printed numerals with only the constraint that the characters shall be printed inside a box. It is a highly successful commercial machine. The scanner is a cathode ray tube which tracks the outline of a character until the beam returns to its starting point. Smoothing and quantizing circuits operate on the deflection voltages to produce the third stage image. This image is compared with stored templates to produce a final decision.

Item 2 in Table 3 is a laboratory machine for reading handprinted numbers which differs considerably from the IBM 1287. A column of photocells operates on the optical image and produces a second stage image of unitary points. This is operated upon by line trackers and decisions are made about features such as line beginnings, endings, splits, and joints. These form a third image, which is operated upon by a Logic Tree. The final decision is absolute.

The IBM 1975 Omni-Font Reader is an extremely powerful machine which was constructed for the purpose of reading the quarterly reports made by corporations to the Social Security Administration. This equipment recognizes an enormous variety of fonts – exactly how many is not known – and seems to do an excellent job, so long as the quality of characters is reasonably good. The organization of this machine in terms of decision levels follows fairly well the philosophy shown in Figure 4, with the major exception that normalization is used extensively. A pre-scan is used with this machine to locate the characters and to develop some of the normalization factors, but we will not consider this pre-scan as part of the character recognition. The first operator is a flying spot cathode ray tube. The CRT, having once located the character, applies a raster scan to the character, but decisions as to whether a point should be called black or white are influenced by the black density of its neighbors, a complex decision operator being used for this. The second image stage is a 650 bit binary image stored in a shift register. This image still has the same general shape as the original character. A series of measurements which relate to features are performed by logic operators, and decisions transform the 650 bit image into a third stage image of 100 bits. This binary word is called a feature vector. The feature vector no longer has the same dimensions as a real character. This third stage image is operated upon by a complex library of decision rules which produces a final decision.

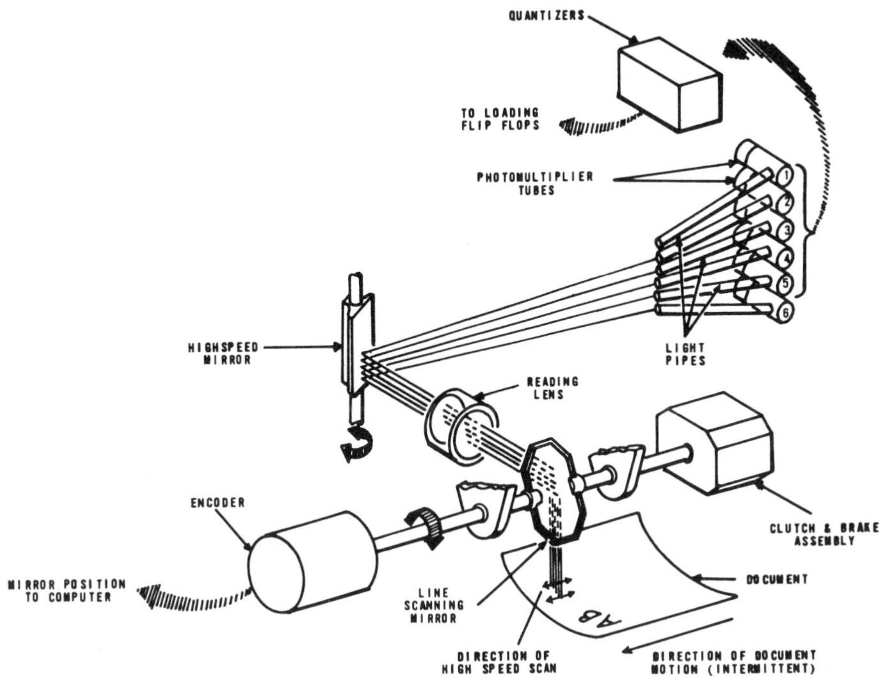

FIGURE 9. Optical Scanning System For Control Data 915 Page Reader

The last reader to be discussed is the "N" Tuple Adaptive Machine. The organization, in the broad outline of Table 3, shows many similiarities to the IBM 1975. Critical points of difference exist in the second and third stage operators, however, In the Omni-Font reader the second stage feature detectors are very carefully chosen to pick up particular types of line segments. On the other hand, a random choice of non-parametric points is often used in the "N" Tuple philosophy. At the third stage, the operators are chosen in both machines after much study of training data, but it is strongly significant that the study is done by people for the IBM 1975 and by computer program for the "N" Tuple. The "N" Tuple Machine, operating as a program within a computer and using the parameters listed in Table III, has demonstrated ability to read the imprints from Addressograph plates quite well.

IV. Conclusion

This brief discussion has concentrated on pointing out some of the significant similarities and differences between central recognition philosophies. One point, in particular, stands out: the number of stages used seems to be proportional to the complexity of the character recognition problem. This is not suggested by any present theory, and its treatment would be a valuable advance.

Machines with more than three stages have been proposed, and it seems likely that the reading of cursive script will be first accomplished by using a large number of decision levels.

Many important machines were omitted from discussion. The major reason for these omissions is that detailed knowledge of commercial machines is often not available. In addition, this situation has probably caused errors in the descriptions which were attempted.

Thanks are due to Mr. James D. Hill, of the Rabinow Laboratory of Control Data Corporation for his many valuable suggestions.

REFERENCES:

1. Holt, A. W. "What Was Promised – What We Have – and What is Being Promised in Character Recognition," *Proceedings of the Fall Joint Computer Conference*, December, 1968.
2. "Pattern Recognition," *Proceedings of the IEEE Workshop on Pattern Recognition*, held at Dorado, Puerto Rico, ed. Laveen N. Kanal. Thompson Book Co., 1968. This contains a good deal of material on Character Recognition.
3. Nilsson, Nils J., *Learning Machines*, McGraw-Hill, 1965.
4. Nagy, George, "State of the Art in Pattern Recognition," *Proceedings of the IEEE*, vol. 56, no. 5, May, 1968.

Excellent bibliographies are included in references 2, 3, and 4.

Design of a Linguistic Statistical Decoder for the Recognition of Continuous Speech

FREDERICK JELINEK, FELLOW, IEEE, LALIT R. BAHL, MEMBER, IEEE, AND ROBERT L. MERCER

Abstract—**Most current attempts at automatic speech recognition are formulated in an artificial intelligence framework. In this paper we approach the problem from an information-theoretic point of view. We describe the overall structure of a linguistic statistical decoder (LSD) for the recognition of continuous speech. The input to the decoder is a string of phonetic symbols estimated by an acoustic processor (AP). For each phonetic string, the decoder finds the most likely input sentence. The decoder consists of four major subparts: 1) a statistical model of the language being recognized; 2) a phonemic dictionary and statistical phonological rules characterizing the speaker; 3) a phonetic matching algorithm that computes the similarity between phonetic strings, using the performance characteristics of the AP; 4) a word level search control. The details of each of the subparts and their interaction during the decoding process are discussed.**

I. Introduction

MOST CURRENT attempts at automatic speech recognition are formulated in an artificial intelligence framework. A mini-universe of discourse is selected (e.g., repair of faucets [1], geophysical inquiry [2], or chess playing [3]) and described syntactically and semantically. This description deterministically limits the permissible set of utterances. A complex interaction of acoustic, syntactic, and semantic processors then directs the search for the spoken sentence. The search is often based on confidence, fit, and frequency metrics derived in an ad hoc intuitive manner.

In this paper we describe the structure of a linguistic statistical decoder (LSD) that will be implemented by the Speech Processing Group of the IBM Thomas J. Watson Research Center. It constitutes an attempt to model statistically various aspects of speech production and recognition and to use decision procedures familiar in the field of information transmission in order to recognize and transcribe speech. A statistics-based system was previously implemented by Dixon and Tappert [4], [5] at IBM, Raleigh, N.C.; this serves as the starting point for the efforts here.

Four problems of particular interest to information theorists will be introduced. None of these problems has received adequate analytic treatment in the literature. First, we must decode in a system in which the codewords are not under the control of the system designer. The information sequence is a sentence, and the corresponding transmitted codeword is the phonetic representation of the sentence, which is completely determined by the phonology of the language and the speaker. Second, there is a probabilistic relationship between the information sequence and the codeword that is transmitted. This is due to the fact that even a single speaker can pronounce the same sentence in many different ways. Third, the number of symbols in a codeword is a random variable, since word lengths and sentence lengths are variable. Finally, the recognition channel commits insertion and deletion errors in addition to the usual substitution errors. The insertion and deletion errors are due to imperfect segmentation, and the substitution errors are due to imperfect classification.

Fig. 1 is a block diagram of the speech recognition system. The acoustic processor (AP) uses signal processing and pattern recognition techniques to extract phonetic information from the acoustic signal. In the AP that we will consider here, this phonetic information is in the form of a phonetic string. In general, the AP may provide more detailed information and may even provide probabilistic information. The linguistic decoder then uses the structure of the language—its vocabulary, phonological rules, syntax, and semantics—to produce an orthographic transcription of the phonetic string.

The aim of this work is to recognize carefully spoken utterances that are produced in a relatively noiseless environment. The utterances are drawn from a corpus, which at present consists of two million words of patent applications in the field of laser technology. The vocabulary is roughly 10 000 words. We use this corpus to construct a statistical model of the language, and this is used by the LSD during the decoding process. The details of this model are discussed in Section IV. Sections II and III describe the speaker and AP models and the estimation of probabilities for them. In Sections V and VI we explain the principles and the implementation of the LSD. Section VII deals with some refinements of the model and decoder.

II. Front End Model

Fig. 2 is a diagram of the speaker-AP model, which will be referred to as the front end. It consists of three parts—an essentially phonemic dictionary, a set of phonological rules that models the speaker, and a noisy channel that models the AP. The front end accepts orthographic text as input and produces as output a string of symbols from a phonetic alphabet $A = (a_1,a_2,\cdots,a_K)$.

The phonemic dictionary and phonological rules are described in detail by Cohen and Mercer [6]. The phonemic dictionary contains a set of phonemic base forms for each word of the vocabulary. Each of these represents a basic pronunciation of the word from which a number of other

Manuscript received March 29, 1974.
F. Jelinek and R. L. Mercer are with the Computer Sciences Department, IBM Thomas J. Watson Research Center, Yorktown Heights, N.Y.
L. R. Bahl is with the Computer Sciences Department, IBM Thomas J. Watson Research Center, Yorktown Heights, N.Y., and also the Department of Electrical Engineering and Computer Science, Columbia University, New York, N.Y.

Reprinted from *IEEE Trans. Inform. Theory*, vol. IT-21, pp. 250–256, May 1975.

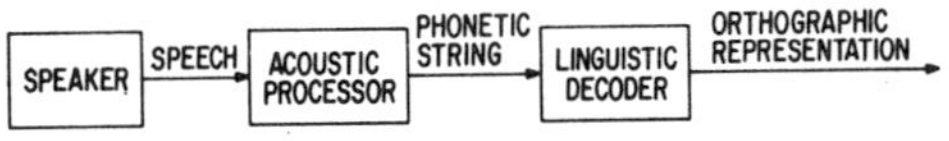

Fig. 1. Block diagram of speech recognition system.

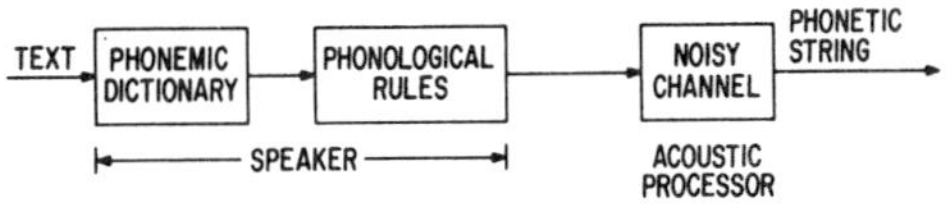

Fig. 2. Block diagram of front end model.

pronunciations are to be derived by the application of the phonological rules. For example, the word *library* has at least three phonemic base forms: /laˈbrɛri/, /laˈbrəri/, /laˈbɛri/.

The phonological rules account for variations in pronunciation due to surrounding words, differences in dialect and idiolect, rate of speech, etc. A typical phonological rule has the form $\alpha \rightarrow \beta/\gamma \_\_ \delta$, where α and β are strings over the phonetic alphabet A, and γ and δ are sets of such strings that define the context in which the rule can be applied. All rules are optional and apply on a single left-to-right pass through the base-form string.

The phonemic dictionary and the phonological rules comprise the speaker model in the following way. Given the string of words corresponding to a complete utterance, base forms for each of the words are selected with speaker-dependent probabilities. The phonological rules then apply to the base-form string with further speaker-dependent probabilities. Conceptually, this process generates all the possible pronunciations with associated probabilities. These are conveniently represented by a directed graph with a single starting node and a single ending node [7], such that any path through this graph traces out a possible pronunciation, with its associated probability obtained by forming the product of the probabilities on the branches. The actual application of the phonological rules to a base-form string is a very time-consuming process. Except for rules that operate across word boundaries, the rules are preapplied to the base forms to obtain a directed-graph representation of each word. To account for the rules that do involve word boundaries, the graphs have multiple starting and ending nodes that are labeled with the conditions that must be met by the preceding and following words, respectively. As an example, Fig. 3 shows the directed-graph lexical entries for *apprentice* and *sorcerer* and the resulting directed graph for *apprentice sorcerer* when preceded and followed by silence. Nodes that arise from application of the same set of phonological rules have the same probability distribution on their outgoing transitions. Those nodes in the graph through which all paths must pass are called confluent nodes. The phonology is such that, except for a few very short words, each directed-graph lexical entry has at least one confluent node.

The AP model is intended to account for the segmentation and classification errors that occur during the signal processing and pattern recognition process. The output alphabet of the AP is denoted by $B = (b_1,\cdots,b_J)$. Because

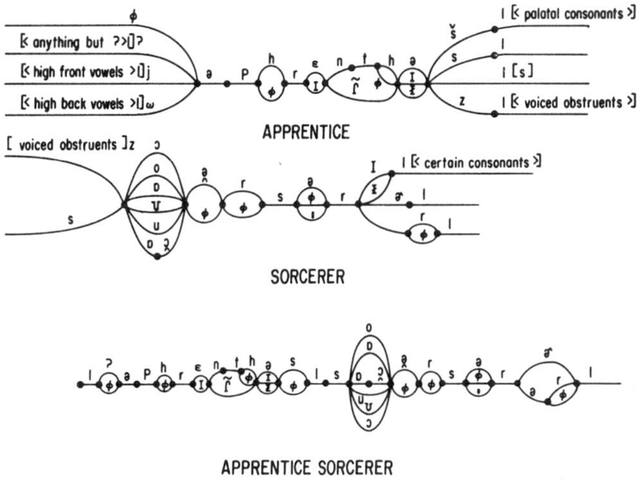

Fig. 3. Directed-graph lexical entries for *apprentice* and *sorcerer* and resultant graph for *apprentice sorcerer*.

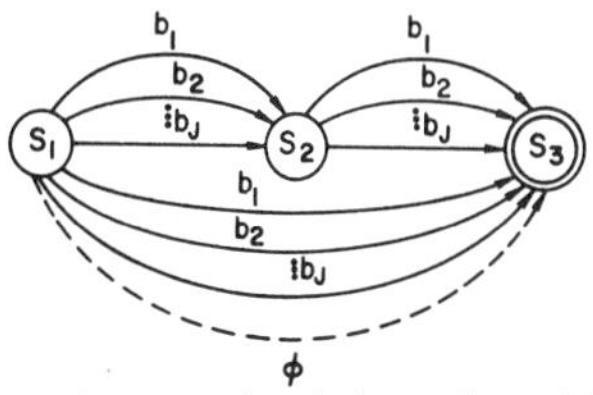

Fig. 4. Simple example of channel model for AP.

of segmentation errors, the channel model must handle insertion and deletion errors as well as substitution errors. Models for such channels are discussed in detail by Bahl and Jelinek [8]. A simple example of such a model is one in which we associate with each input symbol $a_k \in A$ a probabilistic finite-state machine $F(a_k)$ that generates the possible outputs for the input a_k. Fig. 4 shows the state transition diagram of such a machine, which has initial state S_1 and final state S_3. Associated with states S_1 and S_2 are probability distributions on their outgoing transitions, and associated with each transition is an output produced by that transition. Some transitions, called null transitions, have no associated output. These are drawn in dotted lines and labeled with a ϕ in the state transition diagram. In the example of Fig. 4, the null transition from state S_1 to state S_3 represents a deletion, the remaining transitions from S_1 to S_3 represent substitutions, the paths from S_1 to S_3 via S_2 produce two outputs and, therefore, represent insertions. To accurately reflect the types of errors made by the AP, it may be necessary that the machines $F(\cdot)$ be associated not with single symbols from A but with strings of symbols from A. It may, of course, also be necessary to consider machines with more than three states.

Both the directed-graph lexical entries and the probabilistic finite-state machines $F(\cdot)$ are Markov chains. Given a word sequence $W_{1,m} = w_1,w_2,\cdots,w_m$, we can construct a composite Markov chain that generates all of the possible front end sequences for $W_{1,m}$ by first concatenating the directed-graph lexical entries for the words $w_1,w_2,\cdots,w_m$ and then embedding in each transition the finite-state machine $F(\cdot)$ associated with the label of that transition.

III. Estimation of Probabilities for Front End Model

To carry out the decoding process, we must know 1) the probabilities of the transitions in each directed-graph lexical entry, and 2) the probabilities of the transitions in each of the probabilistic finite-state machines $F(\cdot)$. One way of determining these probabilities is to transcribe by hand a large amount of speech data for each speaker. Regarding this transcription as the true input of the AP, one can in principle estimate the probabilities associated with the machines $F(\cdot)$ by comparison with the actual AP output for the same utterance. One could also estimate the probabilities associated with the directed-graph lexical entries by determining which path in the directed graph of the utterance is identical to the transcription. The amount of speech that must be transcribed to make reliable determinations in this manner is very large. Since hand transcription of speech is a very slow and expensive process, this makes the approach an unattractive one. Furthermore, different transcribers often produce different transcriptions for the same utterance, which leads us to question the consistency of this approach.

We now propose a method for estimating probabilities that does not involve hand transcription. Baum, Petrie, Soules, and Weiss [9] have described an iterative method for obtaining the maximum-likelihood estimate of the parameters of a Markov chain, given a sample of the output generated by the chain. Each iteration can be carried out by using the algorithm of Bahl, Cocke, Jelinek, and Raviv [10]. This method can be applied to the problem. We proceed as follows. Text is read by the speaker and processed by the AP, which produces a phonetic string. The composite Markov chain for this text is constructed by the method described in the previous section. The manner in which this chain is constructed places constraints on the probabilities associated with its transitions. For example, each subchain corresponding to a particular machine $F(a_k)$ must have the same probabilities. The method of Baum *et al.* may be applied to obtain maximum-likelihood estimates of the probabilities on the composite Markov chain. The probabilities associated with each subchain $F(a_k)$ can then be obtained by combining the probabilities associated with each occurrence of this subchain in the composite chain. This method requires some initial crude estimates of the probabilities, which can be obtained by examining a small amount of data.

Although the probabilities for the phonemic dictionary and phonological rule models will certainly be speaker dependent, those for the AP model will be much less so because the AP itself is trained to the individual speaker. Once probabilities have been estimated for many different speakers, it will be relatively easy to estimate probabilities for a new speaker by choosing as an initial estimate those of the known speaker who is dialectally most similar.

IV. Language Model

The aim of any speech recognition system is to determine for an acoustic signal A and a language L that sequence of words $W \in L$ which maximizes the *a posteriori* probability $\Pr\{W \mid A;L\}$. Now $\Pr\{W \mid A;L\} = \Pr\{W \mid L\} \cdot \Pr\{A \mid W;L\}/\Pr\{A \mid L\}$. The front end model provides us with $\Pr\{A \mid W;L\}$, and it is the function of the language model (LM) to provide us with $\Pr\{W \mid L\}$. The term $\Pr\{A \mid L\}$ in the denominator is independent of W and, therefore, need not be known.

We employ a probabilistic finite-state model to define the language L and provide us with the probabilities $\Pr\{W \mid L\}$. The probabilities associated with the model will be derived from the laser patent corpus. It should be noted that the decoding procedure is in no way dependent on the finite-state nature of the LM; it asks only for the probabilities $\Pr\{W \mid L\}$, caring nothing about how they are obtained.

We are well aware of the opinion held by linguists that finite-state models cannot account for the performance or competence of speakers of a natural language. The following arguments can be advanced in favor of finite-state models.

Current linguistic research and even many speech recognition efforts are primarily concerned with semantic interpretation, while the aim here is simply transcription. We know of no syntactic-semantic theory that is sufficiently developed to support a real corpus as large as ours. Furthermore, most of the arguments against finite-state models have been directed at word n-gram models in which the possible state transitions are determined by observing the $(n + 1)$-grams that occur. For finite-state models in which the states are not word n-grams and in which the state transitions are determined by more sophisticated techniques, these criticisms are unfounded. No research into the adequacy of more general finite-state models has been done. With the availability of large computers, this appears to be an opportune moment to make such an investigation. Finally, one more advantage is that while there are many efficient computational techniques known for finite-state models, few techniques are available for models of any other type.

The states of the model are vectors of the form $S = (w_{-1},\cdots,w_{-k},s_{-1},\cdots,s_{-l},c_{-1},\cdots,c_{-m})$, where, $w_{-1},\cdots,w_{-k}$ are the k most recent words, $s_{-1},\cdots,s_{-l}$ are the parts of speech of the $l(\geq k)$ most recent words, and $c_{-1},\cdots,c_{-m}$ are the representatives of the m content classes (defined later) immediately preceding word w_{-k}. The purpose of including the most recent parts of speech in the states of the model is to make use of local grammaticality, while the purpose of the content classes is to use some information about long-range semantic content. As an example, consider the sentence: *The future of America depends on the availability of cheap energy.* Using D for determiner, N for noun, P for preposition, V for verb, and A for adjective, the corresponding part-of-speech sequence is *DNPNVPDNPAN*. If we assume that the only words that belong to content classes are *future* and *depend*, then for $k = 1$, $l = 2$, $m = 1$, the resulting state sequence would be (ϕ,ϕ,ϕ,ϕ), (The,D,ϕ,ϕ), (future,N,D,ϕ), (of,P,N,future(N)), (America,N,P,future(N)), (depends,V,N,future(N)), (on,P,V,depend(V)), $\cdots$, $(\cdot,\cdot,N$,depend(V)), where $S_0 = (\phi,\phi,\phi,\phi)$ is the initial state and $(\cdot,\cdot,N$,depend(V)) is a terminal state. Associated with a transition from state S_i to S_j is a word and its part of speech and the probability of that transition, which is denoted by $P(S_j \mid S_i)$.

We propose to obtain the transition probabilities by statistical analysis of the corpus. Thus it is necessary to label the corpus with parts of speech and to determine for it an appropriate set of content classes. Currently we are using a classification system of 29 parts of speech that have been obtained by conglomeration of the 133 parts of speech used by the Harvard Multiple-Path Syntactic Analyzer for English [12]. The part-of-speech labeling of the corpus is carried out by a probabilistic algorithm described elsewhere [13]. The algorithm agrees with human labeling roughly 98 percent of the time.

In the state description we have included the k most recent words explicitly. However, some words have significant statistical influence over a range of text; such words are called content words. Only adjectives, adverbs, nouns, and verbs are considered as possible content words. Since content words are of interest for their long-range effect, grammatical inflection due to number, tense, etc., is considered unimportant. Content words are, therefore, divided into equivalence classes called content classes, and one member of a class acts as a representative of that class.

For example, light (verb) represents the class {light (verb), lighted (verb), lighting (verb), lights (verb), lit (verb)}, while light (noun) represents the class {light (noun), lights (noun)}. Not all adjectives, adverbs, verbs, and nouns have long-range statistical influence. We have adopted the following procedure to determine those which do. After the text has been labeled with parts of speech, each of the potential content words is replaced by its representative. For each pair of representatives we determine the number of times they occur together within a specified span. If for any representative the co-occurrence statistics are significantly different from the average, then the class it represents is taken as a content class.

Once the text is labeled and the content classes determined, one may estimate the probabilities of transitions by determining the state sequence for the text and counting the transitions that actually occur. In estimating the probabilities, transitions that have never occurred should not necessarily be assigned zero probabilities. We are investigating several ways of estimating the probabilities of such transitions.

V. Decoding Principles

We now consider the decoding of the AP output on a sentence-by-sentence basis. Given the AP output $Y_{1,N} = y_1,y_2,\cdots,y_N$, we wish to find that sequence of LM state transitions $S_{0,M} = S_0,S_1,\cdots,S_M$ such that $\Pr\{S_{0,M}\} \cdot \Pr\{Y_{1,N} \mid S_{0,M}\}$ is maximized. State S_0 must be a sentence initial state and state S_M a sentence final state in the LM.

Corresponding to any state sequence $S_{0,m} = S_0,S_1,\cdots,S_m$, there is a unique word sequence $W_{1,m} = w_1,w_2,\cdots,w_m$ determined by the state transitions. The probability that the LM assigns to $S_{0,m}$ is denoted by $P(S_{0,m}) = P(S_1 \mid S_0) \cdot P(S_2 \mid S_1) \cdot \cdots \cdot P(S_m \mid S_{m-1})$.

Let $G(S_{0,m})$ be the graph embodying all possible phonetic realizations of the word sequence $W_{1,m-1}$ when followed by w_m, which provides the necessary phonological right context. Let g be a particular path through the graph (denoted by $g \in G(S_{0,m})$), and let $u(g)$ be the probability associated with g as determined by the speaker model. Now for a given front end output $Y_{1,n} = y_1,y_2,\cdots,y_n$ and a state sequence $S_{0,m}$, we define the conditional probability $Q(Y_{1,n} \mid S_{0,m})$ to be the probability that input $W_{1,m-1}$ (when followed by w_m) produces the output $Y_{1,n}$. Clearly,

$$Q(Y_{1,n} \mid S_{0,m}) = \sum_{g \in G(S_{0,m})} \Pr\{Y_{1,n} \mid g\} u(g). \tag{1}$$

Let $Q(Y_{1,N} \mid S_{0,m})$ denote the $(N+1)$-vector

$$\{Q(\phi \mid S_{0,m}), Q(Y_{1,1} \mid S_{0,m}), Q(Y_{1,2} \mid S_{0,m}), \cdots, Q(Y_{1,N} \mid S_{0,m})\}.$$

An efficient method for computing $Q(\cdot \mid \cdot)$ is given in Bahl and Jelinek [8].

We assign to $S_{0,m}$ the likelihood $L(S_{0,m})$ given by

$$L(S_{0,m}) = P(S_{0,m}) \sum_{n=0}^{N} Q(Y_{1,n} \mid S_{0,m}) \cdot \Pr\{Y_{n+1,N} \mid Y_{1,n}, w_{m-1}, w_m, S_m\}. \tag{2}$$

The term $P(S_{0,m})$ is, of course, the *a priori* probability of the state sequence $S_{0,m}$. $\Pr\{Y_{n+1,N} \mid Y_{1,n}, w_{m-1}, w_m, S_m\}$ is the probability that the remainder of the output sequence $Y_{n+1,N}$ is produced by w_m (w_{m-1} merely provides the necessary left context) followed by some sequence of words ending in a period that can be produced from state S_m. Since we cannot know exactly how much of the output sequence $Y_{1,N}$ is accounted for by input $W_{1,m-1}$, it is necessary to sum over all possible values of n in (2). It should be noted that whereas $P(S_{0,m})$ involves the first m words, $Q(Y_{1,n} \mid S_{0,m})$ uses only the first $m-1$ words, with w_m providing the right context for the directed-graph lexicon (DGL). Assuming that the pronunciation of the final word (which must be sentence terminal punctuation) is complete silence, the likelihood of (2) for a complete sentence $S_{0,M}$ becomes $P(S_{0,M}) \cdot \Pr\{Y_{1,N} \mid S_{0,M}\}$, which is exactly what we are trying to maximize. In fact,

$$\Pr\{Y_{n+1,N} \mid Y_{1,n}, w_{m-1}, w_m, S_m\} = \sum_i \Pr\{Y_{n+1,N}, I = i \mid Y_{1,n}, w_{m-1}, w_m, S_m\}$$

where I is a random variable whose value is the sentence length. When S_m is a terminal state, the only contribution to the sum is that for $I = m$, and thus $\Pr\{Y_{n+1,N} \mid Y_{1,n}, w_{m-1}, w_m, s_m\}$ reduces to δ_{nN} (Kronecker delta).

In practice, the probabilities $\Pr\{Y_{n+1,N} \mid Y_{1,n}, w_{m-1}, w_m, S_m\}$ cannot be obtained exactly, but we can make a reasonable approximation by neglecting the dependence of $Y_{n+1,N}$ on w_{m-1}, w_m, S_m. It is possible to make a simple Markov model for the AP output and estimate its parameters by direct observation. Such a model will provide us with probabilities $\Pr\{Y_{n+1,N} \mid Y_{1,n}\}$, which we use instead of $\Pr\{Y_{n+1,N} \mid Y_{1,n}, w_{m-1}, w_m, S_m\}$ in (2). With this approximation, the likelihood function is, of course, no longer exact for incomplete sentences.

The LSD uses the stack algorithm of sequential decoding [14], [15] to find the most likely state sequence corresponding to a given front end output $Y_{1,N}$. Each partially decoded sequence $S_{0,m}$ is represented in the stack by an entry of the form $(S_{0,m};L(S_{0,m}))$. Entries in the stack are arranged in descending order of their likelihoods. We define the successors of an entry $(S_{0,m};L(S_{0,m}))$ to be the entries $(S_{0,m+1} = S_{0,m},S_{m+1};L(S_{0,m+1}))$ and $(S_{0,m}' = S_{0,m-1},S_m'; L(S_{0,m}'))$, where S_{m+1} is chosen such that $P(S_{m+1} \mid S_m) = \max_S \{P(S \mid S_m)\}$, and S_m' is chosen such that $P(S_m' \mid S_{m-1}) = \max_S \{P(S \mid S_{m-1}) \mid P(S \mid S_{m-1}) < P(S_m \mid S_{m-1})\}$. We assume that no two transitions out of S_{m-1} have identical probabilities. If they do, then the usual minor adjustment must be made in the definition of S_m'. Occasionally no S_m' exists, in which case there is only one successor.

Decoding proceeds as follows.

0) Initialize the stack to contain the single entry $(S_{0,1};P(S_{0,1}) \cdot \Pr\{Y_{1,N}\})$, where $S_{0,1} = S_0,S_1$ is chosen such that $P(S_1 \mid S_0) = \max_S P(S \mid S_0)$.
1) Let $(S_{0,m};L(S_{0,m}))$ denote the entry at the top of the stack, i.e., the one having maximum likelihood. If S_m is a final state, then we stop and accept $W_{1,m}$ corresponding to $S_{0,m}$ as the most likely input. Otherwise, we replace $(S_{0,m};L(S_{0,m}))$ by its successors, reorder the stack, and repeat step 1.

VI. Decoder Implementation

The decoding algorithm of the previous section is feasible only if an efficient technique can be devised for evaluating the likelihoods $L(S_{0,m})$. The probabilities $P(S_{0,m})$ are easily obtained from the LM using the recursion $P(S_{0,m}) = P(S_{0,m-1}) \cdot P(S_m \mid S_{m-1})$. The probabilities $\Pr\{Y_{n+1,N} \mid Y_{1,n}, w_{m-1},w_m,S_m\}$ have been approximated by $\Pr\{Y_{n+1,N} \mid Y_{1,n}\}$, which need to be computed only once for the output sequence $Y_{1,N}$. This leaves the evaluation of the probabilities $Q(Y_{1,N} \mid S_{0,m})$. An algorithm for computing these probabilities is discussed in [8]. The complexity of the calculation is roughly proportional to the product of the number of nodes in $G(S_{0,m})$ and N, the number of symbols in the output sequence. When computing $Q(Y_{1,N} \mid S_{0,m+1})$ and $Q(Y_{1,N} \mid S_{0,m}')$, it is not necessary to deal with the complete graphs for $G(S_{0,m+1})$ and $G(S_{0,m}')$ but only with the parts that differ from $G(S_{0,m})$. Let us denote by $G^*(S_{0,m})$ the subgraph of $G(S_{0,m})$ up to the rightmost confluent node and by $Q^*(Y_{1,n} \mid S_{0,m})$ the probabilities

$$Q^*(Y_{1,n} \mid S_{0,m}) = \sum_{g \in G^*(S_{0,m})} \Pr\{Y_{1,n} \mid g\} u(g), \qquad n = 0,1,\cdots,N.$$

The probabilities $Q^*(Y_{1,N} \mid S_{0,m})$ are obtained as a by-product of the computation of $Q(Y_{1,N} \mid S_{0,m})$. To compute the probabilities $Q(Y_{1,N} \mid S_{0,m+1})$ and $Q(Y_{1,N} \mid S_{0,m}')$, one need only know $Q^*(Y_{1,N} \mid S_{0,m})$ and those portions of the graphs $G(S_{0,m+1})$ and $G(S_{0,m}')$ that differ from $G^*(S_{0,m})$. Therefore, we store the vector $Q^*(Y_{1,N} \mid S_{0,m})$ with the stack entry for $S_{0,m}$.

Fig. 5 is a block diagram of the LSD. The decoding process is controlled by the word level search controller (WLSC), which maintains the likelihood stack. Each entry in the stack contains the path $S_{0,m}$, the likelihood $L(S_{0,m})$, the probability $P(S_{0,m})$, and the vector $Q^*(Y_{1,N} \mid S_{0,m})$.

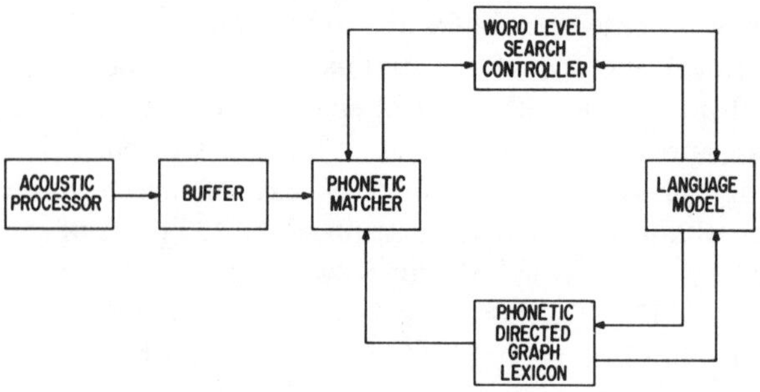

Fig. 5. Block diagram of LSD.

One iteration in the decoding process is as follows. The WLSC locates the path $S_{0,m}$ having the highest likelihood. The successors of $S_{0,m}$ must now be determined. To do so the WLSC sends the last three states of path $S_{0,m}$ to the LM. The LM determines S_{m+1} and the probability $P(S_{m+1} \mid S_m)$ and returns this information to the WLSC. Simultaneously the LM sends the word triplet w_{m-1},w_m,w_{m+1} corresponding to the state sequence $S_{0,m+1}$ to the DGL. The DGL uses these to determine the rightmost confluent node R of $G(S_{0,m})$ and $G^+(S_{0,m+1})$, which is that part of $G(S_{0,m+1})$ that lies to the right of R. The phonology is such that in virtually all cases R can be determined from w_{m-1} and w_m. At most, the DGL will need to know w_{m-2}, which could be provided by the WLSC through the LM if desired. The DGL sends $G^+(S_{0,m+1})$ to the matching algorithm. The matcher also receives $Q^*(Y_{1,N} \mid S_{0,m})$ from the WLSC and computes $Q(Y_{1,N} \mid S_{0,m+1})$ and $Q^*(Y_{1,N} \mid S_{0,m+1})$, both of which it returns to the WLSC. The WLSC can now complete the entry for $S_{0,m+1}$ and insert it in the stack. The procedure for computing the entry for the other successor $S_{0,m}'$ is similar. The WLSC terminates the decoding process when the top of the stack corresponds to a complete sentence.

The LM that we have described generates word and part of speech pairs, and consequently the decoder finds the most likely sequence of words and parts of speech for a given utterance. The likelihood of a word sequence can be obtained by summing up the likelihoods of all the state sequences that give rise to that word sequence. The decoder could then operate on these likelihoods to find the most likely word sequence. We believe, however, that the loss of performance caused by using state sequence likelihoods rather than word sequence likelihoods will be negligible.

VII. Refinements

One possible shortcoming of the LM is that it does not take advantage of any phonetic similarity between different words. The LM can be modified in the manner shown in Fig. 6. Fig. 6(a) shows a portion of the state transition diagram of the LM. All the transitions indicated have words whose phonetic representation starts with the phonetic sequence corresponding to *non*. The phonetic representations of *nonsense* and *nonsensical* agree even further as do those of *nonagenarian* (N) and *nonagenarian* (A). Fig. 6(b) shows a portion of a modified transition diagram that produces the same words with the same

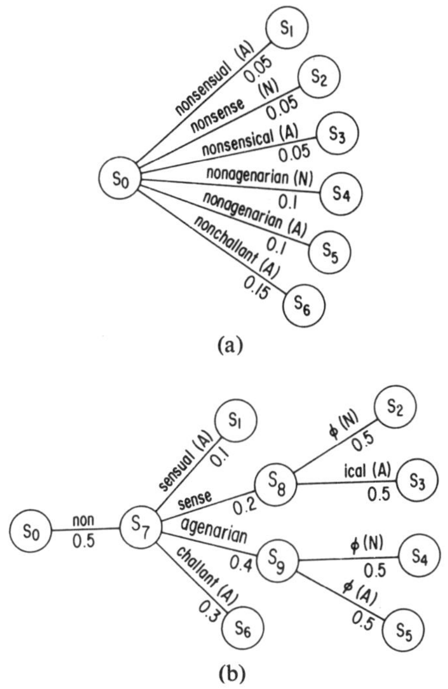

Fig. 6. Modification of LM state transition diagram to take advantage of phonetic similarity.

probabilities as Fig. 6(a), but takes advantage of the phonetic similarity of the words. The advantages of such a modification are twofold. First, the time used in computing $Q(Y_{1,N} \mid S_{0,m})$ is reduced because we need to compute these for *non* only once and use them for any word that starts with *non*. Second, the actual order of search may be altered beneficially, e.g., in Fig. 6(a), the transition S_0,S_6 will be investigated before either of the transitions S_0,S_4 or S_0,S_5, while in Fig. 6(b) S_7,S_9 (which is a combination of S_0,S_4 and S_0,S_5 in Fig. 6(a)) is investigated before S_7,S_6 (which corresponds to S_0,S_6 in Fig. 6(a)).

Although we have described the decoding algorithm as replacing the top stack entry with its successors, it may be better to consider replacing the top several entries with their successors simultaneously. Furthermore, it may be worthwhile to construct more than two successors for each stack entry.

Another possible modification to the decoding algorithm would be to allow a two-way search, i.e., a search in which we decode the received utterance simultaneously in the forward and the reverse directions. To construct a reverse decoder we must of course build a reverse LM which produces the sentences for the language in reverse order. This reverse model can be easily obtained for any finite-state machine by reversing the arrows in the state transition diagram and replacing the probability $P(S_j \mid S_i)$ by ${}^rP(S_i \mid S_j) = P(S_j \mid S_i) \cdot P(S_i)/P(S_j)$, where $P(S_i)$ is the probability that a path through the state transition diagram will include S_i. The initial states of the reverse machine are the final states of the original machine and *vice versa*. The forward machine defined by $P(S_j \mid S_i)$ and the reverse machine defined by ${}^rP(S_i \mid S_j)$ are then isomorphic under sequence reversal. We will use a left superscript r to indicate quantities related to the reverse model. A state sequence ${}^r\boldsymbol{S}_{m_1,M}$ in the reverse machine corresponds to the transitions $S_{m_1} \leftarrow S_{m_1+1} \leftarrow \cdots \leftarrow S_M$, where S_M is a final state. The speaker and channel models are similarly reversible, since they too are finite state. Once the reverse models have been obtained, a reverse decoder that decodes from the end of the received sequence $Y_{1,N}$ can be implemented in exactly the same manner as the forward decoder of Sections V and VI. We can combine the forward and reverse decoders to give us a two-way decoder. This decoder would have two stacks, one for the forward paths and one for the reverse, and we would extend the top stack entry that has the greater likelihood. When extending a forward path, we would not only construct the two successors discussed in Section V, but also those successors that connect this forward path to a reverse path. Let $\boldsymbol{S}_{0,m_1}$ be a forward path and ${}^r\boldsymbol{S}_{m_2,M}$ be a reverse path and let us assume that the transition $S_{m_1} \to S_{m_2}$ is possible in the LM. Then we would construct the successor $\boldsymbol{S}_{0,m_2} = \boldsymbol{S}_{0,m_1}S_{m_2}$ and determine the likelihood for the complete path $\boldsymbol{S}_{0,M} = \boldsymbol{S}_{0,m_1}S_{m_2}{}^r\boldsymbol{S}_{m_2,M}$ from the entries for $\boldsymbol{S}_{0,m_2}$ and ${}^r\boldsymbol{S}_{m_2,M}$. The *a priori* probability of the complete path is given by

$$P(\boldsymbol{S}_{0,M}) = \frac{P(\boldsymbol{S}_{0,m_2}) \cdot P({}^r\boldsymbol{S}_{m_2,M})}{P(S_{m_2})}. \tag{3}$$

The probability $\Pr\{\boldsymbol{Y}_{1,N} \mid \boldsymbol{S}_{0,M}\}$ is obtained as

$$\Pr\{\boldsymbol{Y}_{1,N} \mid \boldsymbol{S}_{0,M}\} = \sum_{n=0,N} \Pr\{\boldsymbol{Y}_{1,n} \mid \boldsymbol{W}_{1,m_2}\} \cdot \Pr\{\boldsymbol{Y}_{n+1,N} \mid {}^r\boldsymbol{W}_{m_2+1,M}\} \tag{4}$$

where $\boldsymbol{W}_{1,m_2}$ and ${}^r\boldsymbol{W}_{m_2+1,M}$ are the word sequences corresponding to $\boldsymbol{S}_{0,m_2}$ and ${}^r\boldsymbol{S}_{m_2,M}$. The probabilities on the right side of (4) are, of course, easily obtained by extending $Q^*(\boldsymbol{Y}_{1,N} \mid \boldsymbol{S}_{0,m_2})$ and ${}^rQ^*(\boldsymbol{Y}_{1,N} \mid {}^r\boldsymbol{S}_{m_2,M})$, respectively. The likelihood of the complete path $\boldsymbol{S}_{0,M}$ is obtained by multiplying $P(\boldsymbol{S}_{0,M})$ and $\Pr\{\boldsymbol{Y}_{1,N} \mid \boldsymbol{S}_{0,M}\}$, which have been obtained from (3) and (4). Similarly when extending a reverse path, we would try to connect to partial forward paths.

It would, of course, require considerable computation to check which partial reverse paths are connectable to a forward path being extended. A simple heuristic technique for limiting the search is as follows. For any $\boldsymbol{S}_{0,m}$, let $n_{\max}(\boldsymbol{S}_{0,m})$ be that value of n (presumed unique) which maximizes $\Pr\{\boldsymbol{Y}_{1,n} \mid \boldsymbol{S}_{0,m}\}$. Then $n_{\max}(\boldsymbol{S}_{0,m})$ is the most likely right boundary for $\boldsymbol{S}_{0,m}$. Similarly, we can define $n_{\max}({}^r\boldsymbol{S}_{m,M})$ to be the most likely left boundary for ${}^r\boldsymbol{S}_{m,M}$. When trying to connect $\boldsymbol{S}_{0,m_1}$ to ${}^r\boldsymbol{S}_{m_2,M}$, we check if $n_{\max}({}^r\boldsymbol{S}_{m_2,M}) - n_{\max}(\boldsymbol{S}_{0,m_1}) \leq e$, where e is a small integer. If this condition is not met, we do not try to connect the two paths. To facilitate in checking this condition, we can keep for each $n = 0,1,\cdots,N$, a list of all forward paths $\boldsymbol{S}_{0,m}$ such that $n_{\max}(\boldsymbol{S}_{0,m}) = n$. Similar lists can be kept for reverse paths. To decide if $\boldsymbol{S}_{0,m}$ should be connected to any reverse path, we consider only those reverse entries that are in the reverse path lists for $n_{\max}(\boldsymbol{S}_{0,m}) + n'$, $n' \leq e$. The basic idea here is that $n_{\max}(\boldsymbol{S}_{0,m})$ gives us the most likely right boundary for $\boldsymbol{S}_{0,m}$, and we should try to connect $\boldsymbol{S}_{0,m}$ only to those reverse paths that have a likely left boundary close to

$n_{\max}(S_{0,m})$. At any time we need only save one complete path—i.e., the one with the highest likelihood—and if its likelihood is higher than the partial paths in both stacks, decoding is terminated.

Acknowledgment

The authors are grateful for the many suggestions they have received from the members of the Speech Processing Group, especially P. Cohen. They also wish to express their thanks to Dr. John Cocke for many stimulating discussions.

References

[1] D. E. Walker, "Speech understanding through syntactic and semantic analysis," in *Proc. 3rd Int. Joint Conf. Artificial Intelligence*, 1973, pp. 208–215.
[2] W. A. Woods, J. Makhoul, J. Wolf, and P. Rovner, "Organizing a system for continuous speech understanding," presented at the 85th Meeting of the Acoustical Society of America, Boston, Mass., Apr. 1973.
[3] D. R. Reddy, L. D. Erman, R. D. Fennell, and R. B. Neely, "The hearsay speech understanding system," in *Proc. 3rd Int. Joint Conf. Artificial Intelligence*, 1973, pp. 185–193.
[4] N. R. Dixon and C. C. Tappert, "Intermediate performance evaluation of a multi-stage system for automatic recognition of continuous speech," Tech. Rep. RADC-TR-73-16, 1973.
[5] C. C. Tappert, N. R. Dixon, and A. S. Rabinowitz, "Application of sequential decoding for converting phonetic to graphemic representation in automatic recognition of continuous speech (ARCS)," *IEEE Trans. Audio Electroacoust.*, vol. AU-21, pp. 225–228, June 1973.
[6] P. S. Cohen and R. L. Mercer, "The phonological component of an automatic speech-recognition system," in *Proc. IEEE Symp. Speech Recognition*, 1974, pp. 177–188.
[7] R. Alter, "Utilization of contextual constraints in automatic speech recognition," *IEEE Trans. Audio Electroacoust.*, vol. AU-16, pp. 6–11, Jan. 1968.
[8] L. R. Bahl and F. Jelinek, "Decoding for channels with insertions, deletions, and substitutions, with applications to speech recognition," to appear in *IEEE Trans. Inform. Theory*.
[9] L. E. Baum, T. Petrie, G. Soules, and N. Weiss, "A maximization technique occurring in the statistical analysis of probabilistic functions of Markov chains," *Ann. Math. Statist.*, vol. 41, no. 1, pp. 164–171.
[10] L. R. Bahl, J. Cocke, F. Jelinek, and J. Raviv, "Optimal decoding of linear codes for minimizing symbol error rate," *IEEE Trans. Inform. Theory*, vol. IT-20, pp. 284–287, Mar. 1974.
[11] N. Chomsky, *Syntactic Structures*. New York: Humanities, 1957.
[12] S. Kuno, "The multiple-path syntactic analyzer for English," Mathematical Linguistics and Automatic Translation, Computation Lab. Harvard Univ., Rep. NSF-8, 1963.
[13] L. R. Bahl and R. L. Mercer, "Part-of-speech assignment by a statistical decision algorithm," IBM Res. Rep., to appear.
[14] F. Jelinek, "A stack algorithm for faster sequential decoding of transmitted information," IBM Res. Rep., RC-2441, Apr. 1969.
[15] ——, "A fast sequential decoding algorithm using a stack," *IBM J. Res. Develop.*, vol. 13, pp. 675–685, Nov. 1969.

Application of Pattern Recognition to Steady-State Security Evaluation in a Power System

CHOK K. PANG, ANTTI J. KOIVO, AND AHMED H. EL-ABIAD

Abstract—Power system operation is outlined and system security is defined. The need for security evaluation in power system operation is discussed, and the evaluation is presented as a pattern recognition problem. A suitable straightforward and quick procedure is used to select a small number of variables as features from a large set of variables which are normally available in power systems. Comparison is made on the security classification performances of a number of different types of classifiers. The training of classifiers is carried out by a search algorithm which seeks to minimize the number of classification errors. The procedure to determine the security functions (classifiers) is illustrated by an example, and simulation results on the steady-state security of the CIGRE 225-kV system show that the pattern recognition approach to security evaluation is encouraging. Some uses of security functions in the control and operation of power systems are outlined. The effect of many of these uses cannot be achieved as easily by other existing methods. Finally, some of the problems associated with the application of pattern recognition to power system security evaluation are discussed.

I. Introduction

PRESENT-DAY power systems are large and complex. With the current rise in the demand of electrical energy, power systems will continue to grow both in size and complexity. Also, our dependence on electricity is so great that it is essential to have uninterrupted supply of electrical power within set limits of frequency and voltage levels. Due to economic reasons and uncertainties in the forecast of loads and the completion date of new facilities, power supply reliability does not attain the 100-percent level. The building of extra high voltage (EHV) tie lines has resulted in further propagation of the effects of disturbances. Consequently, the burden on system operators to ensure that all customers are satisfied has increased tremendously. Therefore it becomes a necessity to develop methods for effective control and operation of power systems [1], [2].

A quick security evaluation of power system performance using real time data will aid the operation of the system. In fact, the operators will be able to detect conditions which may lead to possible failures or deteriorations of the quality of the power supply before they actually occur. The evaluation will forewarn the operators that the system is insecure under certain conditions and that appropriate precautions and/or actions should be taken quickly.

Manuscript received January 22, 1973; revised June 15, 1973. This work was supported by the NSF under grant GK-16245. This paper is part of a dissertation by C. K. Pang submitted to Purdue University, Lafayette, Ind., in partial fulfillment of the requirements for the Ph.D. degree.

C. K. Pang is with Power Technologies, Inc., Schenectady, N.Y.
. J. Koivo and A. H. El-Abiad are with the School of Electrical neering, Purdue University, Lafayette, Ind. 47907.

Security evaluation using computer simulation on current system status has been recently proposed [3], [4]. Essentially, load flow and transient stability studies are performed from time to time. This usually involves rather long computer time, and the results generated are voluminous.

Pattern recognition technique can be used to overcome the shortcomings of computer simulation in security evaluation. In pattern recognition the main bulk of the simulation is done off-line. Using the off-line results, security evaluation could be carried out in a very short time [4], [5].

This paper gives an outline of power system operation and presents the evaluation of system security as a pattern recognition problem. The latter involves the determination of security functions which describe the security of a power system, and these functions depend on certain current measurement or data. A pattern recognition approach to steady-state security evaluation for the CIGRE 225-kV system (Appendix) is described. Though fast repetitive load flows [4] and distribution factors [6] programs are capable of evaluating steady-state security quickly, they do not possess the same potentiality of pattern recognition in many of the uses which are discussed in the later part of the paper. At present transient stability programs demand far too much computing time to be of use in on-line evaluation of transient security [4], and hybrid simulation [7] might be an alternate solution to this problem. In view of the negligible computing requirement once security functions have been determined, the superiority of pattern recognition approach may be exploited in this area. Encouraging results have been reported on the application of pattern recognition to transient security evaluation [4], [8]. However, the approach described herein has been shown to give much better classification performance, and to be more suitable for use in power systems [19] than those in [4] and [8]. Though only results on steady-state security are presented, it may be stressed that the same procedure can be used for transient or dynamic security when proper training sets are available. But problems such as excess computing effort required to generate the necessary training sets and the choice of variables as features could present additional difficulties for the application of pattern recognition to transient or dynamic security.

II. Power System Operation

The primary aim of a power system is to provide adequate uninterrupted supply of power of certain quality to meet all the demands of the customers. To achieve this aim, the operation of power system involves many interrelated

Reprinted from *IEEE Trans. Syst., Man, Cybern.*, vol. SMC-3, pp. 622–631, Nov. 1973.

studies [9], [10]. These include the following:

load flow studies
stability studies
fault analysis
economic dispatch
unit commitment
maintenance planning
spinning and reserve requirement
load-frequency control
load forecasting.

A power system network comprises a number of nodes or buses which are linked by branches or lines. Connected to some buses are generating units, while to some other buses are the loads. Components such as transformers and condensers may also be found at some of the buses. Power is transferred from bus to bus through the connecting lines.

The power flow is strictly governed by the electric network equations. The flow pattern depends mainly on the load and the generation distributions and the network configuration. The amount of power generated by each unit is constrained by its capacity. The power flowing in each line is limited by its rating, and so is that handled by each transformer. For system security purposes, constraints may be imposed on the bus voltage angle across the lines. Voltage levels are to be within acceptable range. All the preceding conditions may be expressed in the following mathematical equalities and inequalities [9]:

$$PG_i - PL_i = V_i \sum_{j=1}^{N} V_j Y_{ij} \cos(\delta_i - \delta_j - \theta_{ij}) \quad (1)$$

$$QG_i - QL_i = V_i \sum_{j=1}^{N} V_j Y_{ij} \sin(\delta_i - \delta_j - \theta_{ij}) \quad (2)$$

$$PG_{\max i} \geq PG_i \geq PG_{\min i} \quad (3)$$

$$QG_{\max i} \geq QG_i \geq QG_{\min i} \quad (4)$$

$$V_{\max i} \geq V_i \geq V_{\min i} \quad (5)$$

$$\alpha_{ij} \geq |\delta_{ij}| = |\delta_i - \delta_j|, \qquad i = 1,2,\cdots,N, \quad j = i+1,\cdots,N \quad (6)$$

where

PG_i real power generation at bus i
PL_i real power demand at bus i
QG_i reactive power generation at bus i
QL_i reactive power demand at bus i
V_i voltage magnitude of bus i
δ_i voltage angle of bus i
Y_{ij} magnitude of (i,j) element in bus admittance matrix
θ_{ij} angle of (i,j) element in bus admittance matrix
$V_{\max i}$ maximum voltage magnitude at bus i
$V_{\min i}$ minimum voltage magnitude at bus i
$PG_{\max i}$ maximum real power generation at bus i
$PG_{\min i}$ minimum real power generation at bus i
$QG_{\max i}$ maximum reactive power generation at bus i
$QG_{\min i}$ minimum reactive power generation at bus i
α_{ij} maximum voltage angle between bus i and bus j.

The equalities and inequalities (1)–(6) may be expressed in a more compact form [11]:

$$g(x,u) = 0 \quad (7)$$

$$h(x,u) \leq 0 \quad (8)$$

where u is a set of independent variables and x is a set of dependent variables.

A. Normal Operating State

When all the equality and inequality constraints, $g(x,u) = 0$ and $h(x,u) \leq 0$, are satisfied, the power system is said to be in the normal operating state. Under this condition all the demands are met at the specified frequency and voltages, and all the system components are loaded within acceptable limits. For economic reasons the operating cost at this state is minimized. Much fuel cost savings are obtained through economic dispatch and unit commitment of the available generators.

It is the aim of the operators to maintain the system in the normal operating state under foreseeable circumstances. Controls chosen by the operator to achieve this aim are thus preventive in nature. Such controls are termed preventive controls.

B. Emergency Operating State

When all equality constraints $g(x,u) = 0$ are satisfied and a subset of the inequality constraints $h(x,u) \leq 0$ is violated, the power system is said to be in the emergency operating state. This could come about when some components are overloaded or when the specified quality of the supply cannot be maintained. It is also possible that the system is in the process of losing synchronism.

Under the preceding circumstances, the system will continue to deteriorate if no control actions are taken. The supply to some customers may have to be curtailed as a measure to save the system from falling apart. Control is needed to bring the system to a state such that the whole set of inequality constraints is satisfied. At the same time, maximum demand should be met so as to cause minimum inconvenience to the customers. Actions taken constitute the emergency control.

C. Restorative Operating State

When a subset of the equality constraints $g(x,u) = 0$ is violated and all the inequality constraints $h(x,u) \leq 0$ are satisfied, the power system is said to be in the restorative operating state. This normally occurs after an emergency during which the supply to some customers has been curtailed.

Now, the control objective is to restore all the supply and return the system to the normal operating state in minimum time. All controls designed to achieve this end come under the name restorative control.

III. System Security

In practice it is not sufficient just to maintain a system in the normal operating state. Under certain conditions, the occurrence of some disturbances may cause the system to go into an emergency such as the overloading of lines and violation of voltage limits. In this framework, the security of a system will next be defined. A set of most probable disturbances (contingencies) is first specified. This set of disturbances may consist of the following:

a single line out
a loss of a generator
sudden loss of a load
sudden change of flow in an inter-tie
a three-phase fault in the system
loss of lines on the same right-of-way.

Suppose that a power system in the normal operating state is subjected to the set of disturbances, one at a time. If for every single disturbance in the specified set, the system remains in the normal operating state, then the system is said to be secure. Otherwise, it is insecure.

It is apparent that the larger the set of disturbances the more stringent is the security standard. The members of the set of disturbances will depend on the system involved and the standard of security required. We may call the secure normal operating state the preferred state and the insecure normal operating state the alert state. A power system should therefore be maintained at the preferred state as long as possible. Should the system go into the alert state, actions like shifting of generation and changing of transformer tappings may have to be taken to bring the system to the preferred state. Such control actions constitute the security controls.

Power system security may be divided into three modes, namely: 1) steady-state security which deals with the steady-state condition of a system; 2) transient security which concerns the transient stability of a system when it is subjected to a disturbance [12]; and 3) dynamic security which pertains to the system responses of the order of a few minutes [13]. Only studies on the first one will be presented herein. However, they can be applied to transient and dynamic securities in the same fashion.

IV. Security Evaluation as a Pattern Recognition Problem

In order to provide satisfactory service to all customers at all times, it is essential for the power system to be secure under all circumstances. The conditions of the environment, like the weather and the load demand by customers, are always changing, hence the state of the power system is never static. Therefore some kind of security evaluation or analysis must be carried out from time to time to check if the system is secure or not. An on-line evaluation will reveal to the operators whether control is needed to ensure system security. For off-line purposes, security evaluation could aid in many planning and operating routines which may be very vital to the security of the system. These include unit commitment, maintenance of components, economic dispatch, and addition of new components or any general system expansion.

Any incorrect information could lead to wrong actions which may result in breakdown of components and interruption of supply to customers. Many power system phenomena happen so fast that both the decisions and actions have to be made quickly. Economic factors are always present in any venture. Until such time when a power system can be fully automated, human operators will be involved in the maintenance of system security. Owing to forced and scheduled outages of components plus the continual rise in the demand of power, the system is subjected to frequent changes. In view of the preceding facts, any security evaluation scheme should possess certain characteristics. The scheme should be

accurate
consistent
quick
easy to implement
adaptable to system changes
of reasonable cost
able to provide results which can be easily interpreted.

In order to be able to have accurate and consistent evaluation of the security of power systems, the measurements of the various variables obtained must be accurate. In general, these measurements are not very accurate and have varying degree of accuracy. The inaccuracy could be due to the presence of noise in the measuring devices and communication channels. Sometimes malfunctioning of equipment components could give rise to grave errors in the measurements. However, the effects of noise can be reduced and the accuracy of the measurements improved with the use of state estimation. Such applications of state estimation to power systems have been proposed recently [14]–[16]. In fact, commercial state estimation programs are presently available to the utility companies. Hence it is reasonable to assume that accurate measurements of variables are available for security evaluation purposes and other aspects of power system operation. Such an assumption is made in this paper.

Some of the questions that will be encountered in security evaluation are as follows.

Is a normal operation state of a power system an alert or a preferred state?

If the system is in an alert state, what mode of insecurity is it?

Does a disturbance result in insecurity?

Will a certain type of insecurity occur when a system is subjected to specified disturbances?

It is clear that each question will have two or more answers. In cases where there are more than two answers, the questions can be broken up and rephrased so that each question will have two answers.

From the preceding, it may be desirable to have an indicator for each mode of security discussed in the previous section. The indicator could be represented by one or more decision criteria which can be specified by mathematical functions. These shall be termed security functions herein. Security functions for each of the disturbances may be found also. These will point out if a particular disturbance would result in insecurity. Security functions showing the type of insecurity, such as violation of voltage limits and overload of components, may be useful in helping to decide the controls to be initiated. This series of security functions will invariably assist the operators to maintain a power system in the preferred state.

In the pattern recognition terminology, the preceding security functions are classifiers or discriminating functions. Classifiers can be designed to provide the answers to the many questions that will be encountered in security evaluation. Some of these questions have been listed already. It can be seen that two-class classifiers will be suitable for use in security evaluation purposes. Each set of measurements describing a state of the power system is termed a pattern. There are many measurements available and some of them are bus voltage magnitudes and angles, power generation and load at individual buses, power losses, and the flow of power in each transmission line.

Pattern recognition has a number of attractive features for use in security evaluation. The major bulk of the studies involves the determination of the weights associated with each security function or classifier, and this can be done off-line. Once the weights have been obtained, information of the current state of the power system is used to compute the value of the function which is a measure of the security. Normally, this computational requirement is very little and hence such approach is suitable for on-line security evaluation. If security functions with the capability of giving acceptable percentage of correct classification can be found, it can be seen that the pattern recognition approach to security evaluation could meet most of the requirements listed earlier in this section. In addition, by having the security functions as added constraints to economic dispatch and scheduling programs, the power system is then restricted to operate in the secure state most of the time. From the preceding one can conclude that pattern recognition approach to security evaluation is promising. The following section describes such an approach for the CIGRE 225-kV system. The description of the system is given in the Appendix.

V. Numerical Example

The application of pattern recognition to security evaluation of a power system is illustrated below. The description of the power system used in this work is provided in the Appendix. Only studies on the steady state security for the system will be presented (herein, "the system" will mean the CIGRE 225-kV system). As mentioned before, the studies can be applied to transient and dynamic securities in the same fashion.

A. Steady-State Security

Ten single-line outages (one at a time) form the set of disturbances to be tested for the steady-state security in the system. Outages on two of the thirteen lines are not included in the disturbance set as they will cause the system to break up into two separate systems, and hence complicate the problem. Studies show that in most of the load flows for the outage of line 3–9, feasible solutions cannot be found, so line 3–9 outage is not included as a member in the set of disturbances. This could be due to the low limits imposed on certain lines; in practice such a condition will not be encountered in a well-designed system. Hence only ten single-line outages are considered instead of the possible thirteen.

For a given normal operating state (a pattern), ten outage load flows are made. The total generation cost to meet the load is minimized and the penalty method [17] is used in the optimal load flow solution. If the system remains in the normal operating state for all the ten single-line outages (i.e., a feasible solution is obtained for each of the ten outage load flows), then the pattern is a secure pattern (preferred state), otherwise it is an insecure pattern (alert state).

B. Training Set

Having defined the steady-state security in the previous section, the next step is to generate a training set. The system loads are examined. Out of the given 168 hourly loads (for a week), 35 are chosen such that the rest can be regarded as small deviations from these loads. This is done by assigning levels to the load at individual buses and studying the combinations of these load levels for each of the 168 h. The total active load of the system varies from 675 to 2030 MW. The total system load is broken into five ranges, namely: 1) 600 to 900 MW; 2) 900 to 1200 MW; 3) 1200 to 1500 MW; 4) 1500 to 1800 MW; and 5) 1800 to 2100 MW. For each range, six sets of unit commitment are selected with spinning reserve varying from 5 to 20 percent of the maximum load. This is to reflect on the different schedule of units that may be encountered in practice. The preceding choice of loads and unit commitments should be able to ensure a good representation of the actual range of operating conditions.

To simplify the optimal load flow problem, an equivalent quadratic cost function for each generating bus is computed using the given quadratic cost functions of the committed units at that bus. Optimal load flows which minimize the total generation cost are performed for the 210 cases (35 loads $\times$ 6 unit commitments). It is found that 179 cases give feasible solutions (i.e., the system operation is in the normal state). The other 31 cases do not have feasible solutions and are of no interest in this study. The preceding 179 cases or patterns make up the training set for the study of steady-state security.

Ten outage load flows (one for each of the single-line outages in the disturbance set) are made on each of the patterns in the training set to determine if it belongs to the secure or the insecure class. Load flow results show that 75 patterns are secure and the other 104 patterns insecure. (This large proportion of insecure patterns may be explained by the low limits imposed on some line flows and the arbitrary choice of unit commitments.) Table I gives the outcome of the outage load flows.

Some patterns in the training set can be obtained from planning studies. In certain utility companies where contingency evaluations are performed during system operation, additional patterns are available for inclusion in the training set. These will help to reduce the amount of effort required in off-line studies to generate the training set.

It must be stressed that the training set obtained should be representative of the whole range of the system operating conditions. This is an important requirement. Otherwise, the classifiers determined may not be able to classify future patterns correctly. In most pattern recognition problems the preceding requirement is verified. This is normally done by generating many training sets randomly and testing their corresponding resulting classifiers for consistent classification results. When generating the training set, care has been taken to ensure that such requirement is satisfied, hence its verification is not very essential. Furthermore, the cost in generating the training set for the determination of security functions may be substantial, and thus should be kept to a minimum whenever possible.

C. Features Selection

For each of the patterns in the training set, the following variables are considered:

V	voltage magnitude at a bus
δ	voltage angle at a bus
PG	active power generation at a bus
QG	reactive power generation at a bus
PL	active load at a bus
QL	reactive load at a bus
P_{loss}	total active power loss in the system
Q_{loss}	total reactive power loss in the system
$PGRA$	$PG_{max} - PG$
$PGRB$	$PG - PG_{min}$
$QGRA$	$QG_{max} - QG$
$QGRB$	$QG - QG_{min}$

where

PG_{max}	maximum active power generation at a bus
PG_{min}	minimum active power generation at a bus
QG_{max}	maximum reactive power generation at a bus
QG_{min}	minimum reactive power generation at a bus.

Also included are the sums of some of the aforementioned variables; they are: $\sum PG$, $\sum QG$, $\sum PL$, $\sum QL$, $\sum PGRA$, $\sum PGRB$, $\sum QGRA$, and $\sum QGRB$. Neglecting those trivial variables at certain buses (such as zero load and zero generation), there are altogether 85 variables. Thus each pattern will have 85 components. Variables such as individual line flows and bus injection powers may be included if required. It is felt that 85 variables should be sufficient for the study at this stage. Power systems with a few hundred buses are common in practice. Therefore the number of variables that are available is very large for these systems.

TABLE I
OUTAGE LOAD FLOW RESULTS FOR TRAINING SET

Line Outage	Number of Cases: Feasible	Infeasible
Line 1-3	156	23
Line 1-4	104	75
Line 2-3	144	35
Line 2-10	155	24
Line 3-4	147	32
Line 4-6	166	13
Line 4-9	175	4
Line 4-10	135	44
Line 6-8	138	41
Line 8-9	173	6

It can be seen that the number of variables obtainable for a pattern can be very large in power system security evaluation. For transient and dynamic securities this number would be even larger as additional variables may have to be included. Therefore it is desirable to determine a small number of features from the large set of variables for classification purposes. Normally feature extraction involves the use of all the components of the pattern vector and mathematical formulation, such as the Karhunen–Loève expansion. Thus each of the features obtained is a function of the components of the pattern vector; as a special case the features form a subset of the components of such a vector. This is more relevant and suitable to power system purposes as it will restrict the number of variables that need to be obtained accurately.

The following F function is used as a criterion in the selection of a variable as feature:

$$F = \frac{|m_s - m_i|}{\sigma_s + \sigma_i} \tag{9}$$

where

m_s	mean of the variable in the secure class
m_i	mean of the variable in the insecure class
σ_s^2	variance of the variable in the secure class
σ_i^2	variance of the variable in the insecure class.

This function provides a measure of the classification errors that could arise when the variable is used as the only feature. The larger the value of F, the lesser would be the classification errors. Hence variables to be used as features should have high values of F. The preceding function is invariant as far as any scaling is concerned. This is particularly an advantage as the values of certain variables could differ by a few orders.

Feature extraction begins with the computation of the F values for all the components (variables) of the pattern vectors in the training set. The variable with the largest F is selected as the first feature; without loss of generality, let this variable be x_1. When selecting other features, redundant information has to be noted as it is unnecessary. Hence the correlation coefficients between x_1 and each of the rest of the variables are determined. A simple procedure is to discard all variables which are highly correlated to x_1 (say, with correlation coefficient greater than 0.9) thereby removing most of the redundant information. Now, from the remaining variables, the one with the largest F value is selected as the second feature, say x_2. The preceding procedure is repeated until the required number of features has been reached, or the F values of the remaining variables are small. It can be seen that this process is straightforward, quick, and suitable for power system problems in view of the very large number of variables available. The features selected and their respective F values are given in Table II.

D. Training Procedure

Having selected the features $(z_1,z_2,\cdots,z_m)$, the next step is to determine the decision function, or classifier; in this case it is the security function. This is achieved using the training set. A simple security function is a linear (first order) function of the features as follows:

$$S(z) = \omega_0 + \sum_{i=1}^{m} \omega_i z_i = z\omega^T \tag{10}$$

where $z = (z_1,z_2,\cdots,z_m,1)$ and $\omega = (\omega_1,\omega_2,\cdots,\omega_m,\omega_0)$, and the superscript T denotes the transpose of a vector or matrix. The weighting coefficients or weights $(\omega_1,\omega_2,\cdots,\omega_m,\omega_0)$ are determined such that $S(z) \geq 0$ if z is a secure pattern and $S(z) < 0$ if z is an insecure pattern.

In addition to the aforementioned linear function, more sophisticated functions can be used. One is of multiple function which may be composed of a number of linear functions. Its classification procedure is one of the following.

1) The pattern z is secure if $S_i(z) \geq 0$, for all $i = 1,2,\cdots,p$, where each $S_i(z)$ is a linear function of z, and p is some integer. Otherwise, z is insecure.

2) The pattern z is insecure if $S_i(z) \leq 0$, for all $i = 1,2,\cdots,p$, where each $S_i(z)$ is a linear function of z, and p is some integer. Otherwise, z is secure.

The weights are determined by a training algorithm used in the solution of linear inequalities [18]. This training procedure, termed the optimal search herein, seeks to minimize the number of classification errors iteratively. In the studies it has been found to be desirable to have higher percentage of correct classification than those obtained by the first-order functions. Hence second-order functions (11) have also been studied:

$$S(z) = \omega_0 + \sum_{i=1}^{m} \omega_i z_i + \sum_{i=1}^{m} \sum_{j=i}^{m} \omega_{ij} z_i z_j. \tag{11}$$

By considering the product terms $z_i z_j$ as individual features the function becomes a first-order one, and the training can be done in the same manner.

In some cases it may be desirable to introduce a bias on the classifiers. Biasing affects the frequency of occurrence of the following two types of errors:

1) false alarm: secure pattern is classed as insecure
2) false dismissal: insecure pattern is classed as secure.

TABLE II
FEATURES FOR STEADY-STATE SECURITY

Features	F-Values
δ_4	0.74
PLOSS	0.62
$QGRB_3$	0.61
V_3	0.57
V_{10}	0.57
QG_3	0.57

A bias in favor of insecure patterns will tend to reduce the number of false dismissals while a bias favoring the secure patterns will decrease the false alarm errors. It can be seen that false dismissals should be kept to a minimum in power system security evaluation. Either one of the preceding types of biasing can be included in the optimal search method. Also, the degree of biasing can be adjusted without much difficulty. Classifiers or security functions with a bias are determined using the optimal search method. The performance of the classifiers obtained are presented and discussed in the following section.

E. Simulation Results and Discussions for Steady-State Security

The classifiers (security functions) obtained from training are first checked by using them to classify the 179 patterns in the training set. Next, a test set of patterns is generated in the manner to be described later. This test set is used to determine the performance of the classifiers. Herein, the kind of classifier used in each case is denoted by a numeral preceding an alphabet. The numeral denotes the number of functions. The alphabet f indicates first-order functions and s second order. For example, a $2f$ classifier is made up of two first-order functions while a $1s$ one is made up of one second-order function.

Classification of Patterns in the Training Set: Table III contains the results of classification of patterns in the training set by various classifiers and using the features in Table II. It can be seen that second-order classifiers always have less classification errors than first-order ones. Also, the use of two-function classifiers gives higher percentage of correct classification than those with one function only. The effects of biasing in favor of a class of patterns during training are clearly shown in Table III. It can be seen that the number of false alarms (secure pattern classified incorrectly) or false dismissals (insecure patterns classed as secure) can be greatly reduced (if necessary, to zero for the patterns in the training set) by biasing the classifier properly. The results with over 90-percent correct classification are definitely encouraging.

One way to aid the operator in the choice of control actions when a system goes into the alert state is to identify the disturbances which would cause the system to go into an emergency. Thus single-disturbance classifiers are obtained for each member of the disturbance set. Such

TABLE III
STEADY-STATE SECURITY CLASSIFICATION RESULTS ON TRAINING SET

Classifier		1f	1s	2f	2s	4f*	4s*	4f+	4s+
Number of	Secure	3	4	4	6	0	1	31	11
Misclassed	Insecure	24	8	12	1	14	2	2	0
Patterns	Total	27	12	16	7	14	3	33	11
Percent Correct		78.2	93.3	91.1	96.1	92.2	98.3	81.6	93.9

*Bias on classifier - secure:insecure = 10:1

+Bias on classifier - secure:insecure = 1:10

TABLE V
OUTAGE LOAD FLOW RESULTS FOR TEST SET

Line Outage	Number of Cases: Feasible	Number of Cases: Infeasible
Line 1-3	79	11
Line 1-4	55	35
Line 2-3	78	12
Line 2-10	78	12
Line 3-4	74	16
Line 4-6	83	7
Line 4-10	68	22
Line 6-8	70	20

TABLE IV
STEADY-STATE SECURITY CLASSIFICATION RESULTS ON TRAINING SET FOR SINGLE-DISTURBANCE CLASSIFIERS

Disturbance	Percent Correct Classification: 1st Order Fn.	Percent Correct Classification: 2nd Order Fn.
Line 1-3 out	97.2	98.9
Line 1-4 out	87.1	93.3
Line 2-3 out	95.0	96.6
Line 2-10 out	94.4	98.9
Line 3-4 out	96.6	98.2
Line 4-6 out	94.4	96.6
Line 4-10 out	97.2	98.2
Line 6-8 out	97.2	97.9

TABLE VI
STEADY-STATE SECURITY CLASSIFICATION RESULTS ON TEST SET FOR DIFFERENT CLASSIFIERS

Purpose of Classifier	Percent Correct Classification: 1st Order Fn.	Percent Correct Classification: 2nd Order Fn.
Security	84.4	87.8
Line 1-3 out	96.7	92.2
Line 1-4 out	77.8	84.4
Line 2-3 out	95.6	92.2
Line 2-10 out	91.1	87.8
Line 3-4 out	94.4	88.9
Line 4-6 out	86.7	34.4
Line 4-10 out	87.8	91.1
Line 6-8 out	96.7	95.6

classifiers will indicate if a pattern will remain in the normal operating state should a particular disturbance occur. Table I shows that line 4–9 and line 8–9 result in very few cases of insecurity, so there is no great need to have classifiers for these two disturbances. In cases where they do, one or more other line outages also result in insecurity. For each of the other eight disturbances, feature extraction and training are carried out in the manner described earlier. A set of six features are obtained for each disturbance. The results of classifying the patterns in the training set using the weighting vectors determined are given in Table IV.

It can be seen that for each of the eight disturbances, the classification results are good and encouraging, over 90 percent being correct in most cases. In fact, single second-order classifiers have correct classification close to 100 percent in all cases except one with 93.3 percent. The results of first- and second-order single-function classifiers are also compared. On the average, a second-order function produces only about half as many misclassified patterns as a first-order function.

Classification of Patterns in the Test Set:

A test set of patterns is generated in the following manner. Thirteen loads are chosen from the 168 hourly loads (for a week) with none of them the same as the 35 loads selected to generate the training set. These 13 loads cover about the same range as the weekly system load. Additional unit commitments are selected in the same manner described earlier. Using the 13 loads and all the unit commitments (including those obtained for the training set), the test set of 90 patterns is generated following the procedure used in generating the training set. Forty of these patterns are secure while the other 50 are insecure. The results of the individual outage load flows are given in Table V.

The classifiers obtained in the training process (by means of the optimal search) are used to classify the patterns in the test set. Using single-function classifiers and the features determined, the classification results are shown in Table VI. All cases except one have over 80-percent correct classification; in fact, half of them exceed 90 percent. A final study is made by including the test set in the training set to form a larger training set with 269 (90 + 179) patterns. One hundred fifteen of these are secure while 154 are insecure. It can be seen that this new training set is a better representation of the range of the system operating condition than the previous one. Hence the new classifiers obtained by the use of new training set should give better classification results than those before. The weights for the new classifiers can be determined by the optimal search method using the old weights as the initial values. Table VII shows the classification results using classifiers newly determined by optimal search to classify patterns in the new training set. All but two cases have over 90-percent correct classification. In fact, most of them are greater than 95 percent with many nearing 100 percent. For all but two cases, second-order

TABLE VII
STEADY-STATE SECURITY CLASSIFICATION RESULTS ON NEW TRAINING SET FOR DIFFERENT CLASSIFIERS

Purpose of Classifier	Percent Correct Classification 1f	2f	1s	2s
Security	87.7	90.7	91.8	95.5
Line 1-3 out	98.1	98.5	97.4	98.5
Line 1-4 out	87.0	90.7	92.6	93.3
Line 2-3 out	94.8	94.8	96.3	97.4
Line 2-10 out	94.4	96.3	97.8	98.9
Line 3-4 out	97.0	97.0	97.8	98.9
Line 4-6 out	95.2	96.3	97.0	97.4
Line 4-10 out	96.7	97.0	97.8	98.5
Line 6-8 out	97.8	97.8	97.8	98.5

function classifiers have less errors than their corresponding first-order function classifiers. Also two-piece-function classifiers always improve the correct classification of the single-function counterparts.

The preceding simulation results indicate that the procedure of determining the classifiers for steady-state security evaluation on actual systems is promising. In the following section some uses of the classifiers or security functions in power system operations are discussed.

VI. Additional Uses of Security Functions

The simulation results on the CIGRE 225-kV system in the preceding section show that high accuracy (small errors in classification) security functions are realizable using pattern recognition. What is of interest at this point is how applicable these security functions are in the operation of power systems. Possible uses of security functions include:

1) monitoring of system security
2) secure economic dispatch
3) identification of potential causes of insecurity
4) determination of precontingency corrective actions
5) scheduling of units for secure operation.

As pointed out in [19], distribution factors and computer simulation can be used in areas (1) and (3). The distribution factors method is restricted to steady-state security only. Furthermore, these two methods cannot be used explicitly for areas (2), (4), and (5). In this section the applications of security functions to the preceding five areas will be outlined and discussed [19].

A. Monitoring of System Security

The measurements or values of the features at any time instant are obtained and the values of the security functions are computed. This will indicate if the system is secure or not. Since the computation involves only a number of multiplications and additions, computing time required is very short. Also the storage requirement for the weighting coefficients is very small. Hence security functions are suitable for on-line evaluation of system security.

Monitoring the values of the security functions provides a warning to the operators whenever the system goes into an alert state [1]. This will help the operators to ensure continual supply of electrical power to all customers at specified standards without overloading system components.

B. Identification of Potential Causes of Insecurity

Identifying the would-be causes of insecurity is a step towards finding the proper corrective actions to maintain the system in the preferred normal state. When the values of the security functions indicate that the system is insecure (alert state), the values of the individual disturbance security functions are computed. These values will point out which disturbances, if they occur, would result in the system going into an emergency.

Once the would-be causes of insecurity are known, relevant simulation studies could be performed to determine the best strategy to divert possible emergencies.

C. Determination of Precontingency Corrective Actions

When a system is in an alert state, corrective actions are needed to bring the system to the preferred normal state. The actions can be found by performing an optimal load flow with the necessary security functions as added constraints. If a feasible solution is found, then the necessary actions are obtained. If no feasible solution is found, two alternatives may be taken. One is to increase the generating capacity and/or import power until a feasible solution is obtained in the optimal load flow. The other is to run an optimal load flow with minimum load shedding as objective function instead of minimum operating cost.

D. Secure Economic Dispatch

Most economic dispatch studies do not include the security of a system. In cases where they do, security is only implied by more stringent constraints on certain variables [20].

Secure economic dispatch has been proposed recently [21], and the formulation of this approach is also given in [19]. This involves a regular optimal load flow with added constraints which reflect on the effects of outages or contingencies. Linear programming formulation for this method has been reported elsewhere [22]. It must be pointed out that the added constraints cannot take into account transient or dynamic security. It is felt that such a method is a brute force one and may not be applicable for large systems.

Reference [23] describes an ac optimal load flow constrained by dc flows. This method has no assurance that the voltages will be acceptable should a disturbance occur. As in the case of [21], the proposed method is applicable to only steady-state security.

By adding the security functions to the constraints in an on-line optimal load flow, preferred normal operating (secure) states are dispatched. This does not cause appreciable increase in the computational requirement for an optimal load flow. The use of security functions is superior to the methods of [21] and [23] in that less computer memory and computing time are required [19]. This is due to the fact that the number of security functions to be used as added constraints is very much smaller than the number of additional constraints required by the other methods for secure economic dispatch.

E. Scheduling of Units for Secure Operation

Unit schedules or commitments which are capable of providing secure operation of a power system will result in less corrective actions to maintain a system in the preferred operating state. Such schedules can be obtained by using security functions as added constraints in the optimal load flow studies when selecting the units to be put on line. This approach can be implemented and is discussed in the following section. Another possible approach is to have security functions with features which reflect on the distribution of generation reserves in the system. Such an approach could be formulated into a linear programming problem. It provides a quick check which ensures that units to be scheduled would be able to provide secure system operation. This approach is discussed in [19, appendix], where the scheduling is formulated as a mixed-integer linear programming problem.

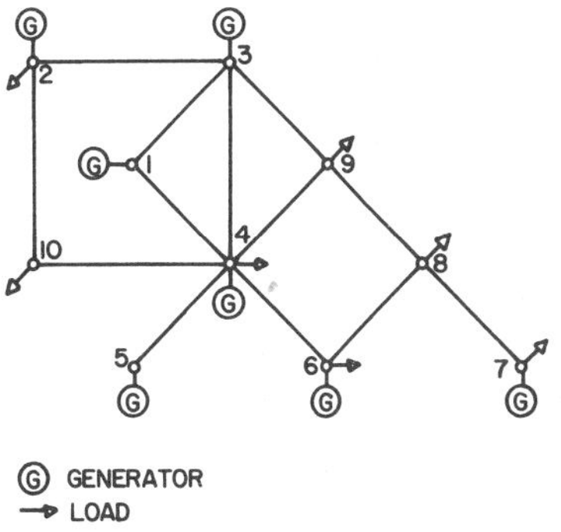

Fig. 1. CIGRE 225-kV system.

TABLE VIII
LINE PARAMETERS

Bus i	Bus j	R(ohm)	X(ohm)	ωC/2(mho)	Max$\|\delta_{ij}\|$*
1	3	5.0	24.5	.0002	6.0
1	4	5.0	24.5	.0001	6.0
2	3	22.8	62.6	.0002	14.0
2	10	8.25	32.3	.0003	8.5
3	4	6.0	39.5	.0003	7.0
3	9	5.75	28.0	.0002	10.5
4	5	2.0	10.0	.0002	5.0
4	6	3.75	24.75	.0001	6.0
4	9	24.7	97.0	.0002	15.0
4	10	8.25	33.0	.0003	8.5
6	8	9.5	31.8	.0002	8.5
7	8	6.0	39.5	.0003	7.0
8	9	24.7	97.0	.0002	15.0

*Maximum voltage angle across line i-j in degrees.

VII. CONCLUSIONS AND DISCUSSIONS

The presentation of power system security evaluation as a pattern recognition problem has been given. Despite the relatively simple approach being used, the preceding numerical example shows that security functions (classifiers) with the capability of giving high percentage of correct classification are realizable. Some uses of security functions in power system operation have been outlined and the effect of many of these uses cannot be achieved as easily by other existing methods.

It may be pointed out at this juncture that the sample study assumed that the system is operated under the base configuration (i.e., all the lines and generators are in-service). This is not always true in practice as scheduled maintenance and forced outages of components (lines and generators) will result in configurations which are different from the base case. One possible solution is to have a set of security functions for each likely configuration. Another way is to include patterns with different configurations in the training set. However, both would require the generation of large numbers of training patterns and the computing effort could be too demanding even though this is done off-line. Hence in the case of transient security such requirement may prohibit the use of pattern recognition. Power systems with several hundreds of buses are not uncommon and, therefore, the dimensionality of the problem could increase many folds in actual systems.

For certain planning routines such as unit commitment and maintenance of system components, it is desirable to consider the stochastic nature in the forecasting of loads. Hence statistical pattern recognition approach will be preferred to the deterministic one presented herein. However, there are many problems associated with a statistical approach. Generally, the forecast loads can be assumed to be normally distributed. But other variables such as voltage magnitude and angles are coupled to the loads through highly nonlinear equations (power equations). Furthermore, the allocation of power generation amongst the individual generating buses is an independent process. Another problem is that the frequency of occurrence of alert state in a well-designed system is very small compared to that of preferred state. It is the alert state which is of most concern to the system operators.

The electric power industry forms an integral and important part of the nation's life and progress, and has been largely neglected by those working in the pattern recognition area. It is hoped that this paper will generate greater interest in the investigation of various pattern recognition techniques for possible uses in power systems and certain problems that would be encountered, some of these problems having been discussed previously and elsewhere [19].

APPENDIX
CIGRE 225-KV SYSTEM

The CIGRE 225-kV system is shown in Fig. 1. It has 10 buses and 13 lines. There are 7 generating buses, and the loads are located at 7 of the buses. Each generating bus has two to five generating units. For a generating unit, its quadratic cost coefficients and power generation limits are given. One hundred sixty-eight hourly loads (for a week) are available. The total active load ranges from 675 to 2030 MW. The line parameters and the upper limit of the voltage angle across each line are shown in Table VIII. The upper and lower limits on the voltage magnitude of any bus are 240 and 205 kV, respectively.

References

[1] A. H. El-Abiad, "New directions in power systems reliability and security," presented at the Third Southeastern Symp. System Theory, Georgia Institute of Technology, Atlanta, Apr. 1971.
[2] T. E. Dy Liacco, "The emerging concept of security control," in *Proc. Purdue 1970 Symp. Power Systems*, Purdue Univ., Lafayette, Ind., May 1970.
[3] S. Hayashi *et al.*, "Power system security assessing by digital computer simulation-basis control," presented at the PICA Conf., Denver, Colo., May 18–21, 1969.
[4] "Bulk power security assessment," IBM Research Div., San Jose, Calif., Final Tech. Rep. for Edison Electric Institute, Nov. 1970.
[5] C. K. Pang, "Security assessment in power systems," in *Proc. Midwest Power Symp.*, Univ. Michigan, Ann Arbor, Oct. 21–22, 1971.
[6] H. D. Limmer, "Techniques and applications of security calculations applied to dispatching computers," in *Third Power Systems Computation Conf. Proc.*, Paper STY4, Rome, June 1969.
[7] L. H. Michaels, "The AC/hybrid power system simulator and its role in system security," *IEEE Trans. Power App. Syst.*, vol. PAS-91, pp. 128–136, Jan./Feb. 1972.
[8] "On-line stability analysis study," North American Rockwell Information Systems Co., Anaheim, Calif., Tech. Rep. for Edison Electric Institute, Oct. 1970.
[9] G. W. Stagg and A. H. El-Abiad, *Computer Methods in Power System Analysis*. New York: McGraw-Hill, 1968.
[10] J. R. Neuenswander, *Modern Power Systems*. Scranton: International Text., 1971.
[11] F. J. Jaimes, "Optimal power flows," Ph.D. dissertation, Purdue Univ., Lafayette, Ind., June 1971.
[12] E. W. Kimbark, *Power System Stability*, vol. 1. New York: Wiley, 1948.
[13] K. N. Stanton, "Dynamic energy balance studies for simulation of power-frequency transients," *IEEE Trans. Power App. Syst.*, vol. PAS-91, pp. 110–117, Jan./Feb. 1972.
[14] R. E. Larson *et al.*, "State estimation in power systems: parts I and II," *IEEE Trans. Power App. Syst.*, vol. PAS-89, pp. 345–363, Mar. 1970.
[15] F. C. Schweppe *et al.*, "Power system static state estimation: parts I, II, and III," *IEEE Trans. Power App. Syst.*, vol. PAS-89, pp. 120–135, Jan. 1970.
[16] F. D. Galiana and E. Handschin, "Combined network and power station dynamic state estimation," in *4th Power Systems Computation Conf. Proc.*, Paper 3.3/4, Grenoble, Sept. 1972.
[17] A. E. Bryson and Y. C. Ho, *Applied Optimal Control*. Waltham, Mass.: Blaisdell, 1969.
[18] P. H. Mengert, "Solution of linear inequalities," *IEEE Trans. Comput.*, vol. C-19, pp. 124–131, Feb. 1970.
[19] C. K. Pang, "Studies on security evaluation by pattern recognition and unit commitment by dynamic programming in power systems," School Elec. Eng., Purdue Univ., Lafayette, Ind., Tech. Rep. TR-EE-73-3, Jan. 1973.
[20] A. Thanikachalam and J. R. Tudor, "Optimal rescheduling of power for system reliability," *IEEE Trans. Power App. Syst.*, vol. PAS-90, pp. 2186–2192, Sept./Oct. 1971.
[21] J. Peschon *et al.*, "A generalized approach for determining optimal solutions to problems involving system security and savings," Systems Control, Inc., Palo Alto, Calif., Final Rep. for Edison Electric Institute, July 1970.
[22] J. C. Kaltenbach and L. P. Hajdu, "Optimal corrective rescheduling for power system security," *IEEE Trans. Power App. Syst.*, vol. PAS-90, pp. 843–851, Mar./Apr. 1971.
[23] B. Cory and P. Henser, "Economic dispatch with security using nonlinear programming," in *4th Power Systems Computation Conf. Proc.*, Paper 2.1/5, Grenoble, Sept. 1972.

Author Index

A

Abend, K., 151
Agrawala, A. K., 247
Arthur, R. M., 405

B

Bahl, L. R., 442
Baskett, F., 342
Bellman, R., 49

C

Chandrasekaran, B., 151, 155, 192, 242
Chow, C. K., 27, 218
Cover, T. M., 333
Cox, J. R., Jr., 405

E

El-Abiad, A. H., 449
Elashoff, J. D., 139
Elashoff, R. M., 139

F

Fisher, R. A., 323
Fix, E., 261, 280
Foley, D. H., 130, 198
Friedman, J. H., 175, 342
Fukunaga, K., 108, 224, 231, 235

G

Goldman, G. E., 139
Gose, E. E., 115

H

Halle, M., 44
Harley, T. J., Jr., 75, 151
Hart, P. E., 333, 340
Ho, Y. C., 247
Hodges, J. L., Jr., 261, 280
Holt, A. W., 433
Hughes, G. F., 142, 151

J

Jain, A. K., 242
Jelinek, F., 442

K

Kac, M., 56
Kain, R. Y., 160
Kalaba, R., 49
Kanal, L. N., 1, 59, 75, 192
Kessell, D. L., 224, 231, 235
Koivo, A. J., 449
Koontz, W. L. G., 108

L

Lachenbruch, P. A., 207

M

Mendelsohn, M. L., 362
Mercer, R. L., 442
Mickey, M. R., 207
Mucciardi, A. N., 115

N

Nagy, G., 124, 381
Nolle, F. M., 405

P

Pang, C. K., 449
Preston, K., Jr., 92
Prewitt, J. M. S., 362

R

Randall, N. C., 75
Rosenblatt, F., 35

S

Sammon, J. W., Jr., 130, 162, 166
Shustek, L. J., 342
Stevens, K, 44
Stoffel, J. C., 348

T

Toussaint, G. T., 184
Tukey, J. W., 175

Z

Zadeh, L., 49

Subject Index

A

Abstraction and generalization
  associated with pattern classification, 49
Aerial reconnaissance
  imagery, 75
Air Force
  application of pattern classification, 280
Algorithms
  for finding nearest neighbor, 342
  for grouping data, 108
  for multivariate data, 166
  pattern classification, 247
  projection pursuit for data analysis, 175
Allopolyploidy, 323
Analog computers
  use for pattern recognition, 92
Automatic control
  use of pattern classification, 247
Automatic imagery screening, 75
Automatic pattern recognition, 1, 348, 405
Automatic speech recognition, 442

B

Bayes classifiers, 224
Bayes error estimation
  using unclassified samples, 235
Bayes probability of error, 333
Bibliographies
  estimation of misclassification, 184
  remote sensing for earth resources, 381
  use of pattern recognition for biomedical applications, 405
Binary patterns
  feature extraction, 124
Binary pulses, 56
Biomedical images, 405
Blood cells
  images, 362
  recognition, viii
Blood pressure waves
  digital analysis, 405

C

Cell images
  analysis, 362
Character recognition machines, 433
Character separation, 433
Chromosome spread detection, 92
CIGRE 225-kV power system, 449
Classification errors, 224
Classification procedures, 280
Clustering, 124, 166, 175
Computer-aided design
  of pattern classifiers, 348
Condensed nearest neighbor decision rule, 340
Continuous speech
  recognition, 442
Craniometry, 323
Cytophotometers, 362

D

Data analysis
  projection pursuit algorithm, 175
Data grouping, 108
Data structure analysis, 166
Decision functions, 27, 242
Decision making, 115
Decision rules, 333, 340
Decision theory
  application, 27
Decoders
  for speech recognition, 442
Diagnostics, 405
Dichotomous variables, 139
Digital computers
  use for pattern recognition, 92
Digital image processing, 381
Digital pattern recognition, 92
Dimensionality reductions, 162, 166, 175, 192
Discriminant analysis, 207, 261, 280
Discriminant vectors, 130
Discrimination, viii, 139, 162, 207, 323, 342
  of images, 362

E

Earth resources
  analysis, 92
  remote sensing, 381
Electrocardiograms, 115
  digital analysis, 405
Electroencephalograms
  digital analysis, 405
Error correction
  applied to signal detection, 56
Error probability, 333
Error rates, 198, 218, 231
  estimation, 207
  minimum, 27
Error-reject functions, 231
Error estimation, 1, 207, 224, 231, 235
Estimation
  of classification error, 224
  of error rates, 207
  of misclassification, 184
Events generation, 348

F

Feature extraction, viii, 1, 115, 130
  automatic, 124
Feature selection, 130
Feature size, 198
Fingerprint identification, 92
Flowers
  measurements, 323
Fuzzy sets, 49

G

Gaussian data
  grouping, 108
Geometric features, 124
Grouping
  of data, 108

I

Image characterization and discrimination, 362

Image processing
  digital, 381
Interactive pattern analysis and classification, 59
Interactive pattern recognition, 348

K

Karhunen–Loeve transforms, 130

L

Land use
  analysis, 92
Language models, 442
Learning and learning machines, 56, 59
Linguistic statistical decoders
  for speech recognition, 442

M

Machine pattern recognition, viii
Mapping, 166, 175
Mean accuracy, 155, 160
  of statistical pattern recognizers, 142, 151
Mean recognition accuracy, 155
Measurement complexity
  of pattern classification, 242
Microscopy, 362
Misclassification
  bibliography, 184
Models
  of language, 442
  of speech recognition, 44
Morphology, 362, 405
Multidimensional scaling, 166, 175
Multiple measurements
  use in taxonomic problems, 323
Multivariable data
  algorithms, 166
  analysis, 115, 130, 162, 166, 175
  grouping, 108
Multivariate normal distribution and samples, 207, 224, 280

N

NASA projects, 381
Nearest neighbors, 333, 340, 342
Nonlinear mapping
  for data structure analysis, 166
Nonparametric classifiers, 224
Nonparametric discrimination, 342
  consistency properties, 261
  small sample performance, 280
Nonparametric estimates, 235

O

On-line pattern analysis and recognition, 162
Optical character recognition, viii, 348
Optimal discriminant plane, 162
Optimum pattern recognition
  using decision functions, 27
Optimum recognition error, 218

P

Pattern analysis, 59, 162
Pattern classes, 160
Pattern discrimination, 35
Pattern classification and classifiers, 49, 75, 142, 160, 247
  accuracy, 242, 280
  algorithms, 247
  application for Air Force, 280
  choice of variables, 139
  computer-aided design, 348
  decision making, 247
  design, 192, 198, 348
  discrimination and discriminants, 162, 261, 280
  error probability, 333
  error rates, 198
  errors, 224
  graphic systems, 162
  interactive, 59
  measurement complexity, 242
  nearest neighbors, 333, 340
  statistical, 192, 242
  use in automatic control, 247
Pattern recognition and recognizers, 142, 160
  analog versus digital techniques, 92
  applications, 1, 27, 405, 449
  automatic, 1, 348, 405, 442
  bibliographic references, viii, 1
  books, 1
  design methodology, 1
  digital versus analog techniques, 92
  dimensionality, 1, 130
  discrete variables, 348
  error-free, 27
  errors, 218, 231
  expected risk, 27
  interactive, 348
  journals, 1
  machine, viii
  mapping, 166, 175
  mean accuracy, 142, 151, 155, 160
  mean recognition probability, 160
  measurements, 155
  nonparametric, 175, 224, 235, 348
  on-line systems, 162
  optimum, 27, 218, 231
  properties, 115
  reject tradeoff, 218
  sample size, 155
  statistical methods, 1, 142, 151
  subsets choice, 115
  survey of period 1968–1974, 1
  two-class type, 130
Perception simulation, 35
Perceptrons, 35
Perceptual learning, 35
Phoneme identification, 44
Power systems
  security evaluation, 449
Prime events theory, 348
Probability
  of misclassification, 184
Projection pursuit algorithm
  for exploratory data analysis, 175

R

Radar signal processing, 92
Reading machines, 433
Recognition
  of speech, 44, 442
Recognition machines
  characters, 433
Recognition models
  of speech, 44
Reconnaissance imagery, 75
Reject rate, 218, 231
Remote sensing
  for earth resources, 381

Risk estimates, 235

S

Sample size, 1, 155, 192, 198
Satellites
  NASA projects, 381
Security evaluation
  in power systems, 449
Segmentation problem, 44
Signal detection, 56
Signal processing
  radar, 92
  speech, 44
Space programs, 381
Speech production, 44
Speech recognition, viii, 44, 442
Statistical pattern recognizers, 142, 160
  comments, 151
Subsets choosing
  of pattern recognition, 115
System security
  definition, 449

T

Tactical reconnaissance, 75
Target detection, 75
Taxonomic problems
  use of multiple measurements, 323
Ternary features, 124
Threshold detectors
  operating on noisy binary pulses, 56

V

Vectorcardiograms, 115

W

Word recognition, 92

Editor's Biography

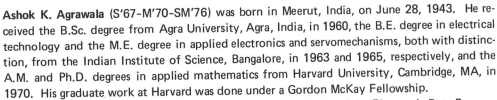

Ashok K. Agrawala (S'67-M'70-SM'76) was born in Meerut, India, on June 28, 1943. He received the B.Sc. degree from Agra University, Agra, India, in 1960, the B.E. degree in electrical technology and the M.E. degree in applied electronics and servomechanisms, both with distinction, from the Indian Institute of Science, Bangalore, in 1963 and 1965, respectively, and the A.M. and Ph.D. degrees in applied mathematics from Harvard University, Cambridge, MA, in 1970. His graduate work at Harvard was done under a Gordon McKay Fellowship.

From 1968 to 1970 he was with the Applied Research Group of the Electronic Data Processing Division, Honeywell, Inc., Waltham, MA. During this period he was involved in various aspects of the design of computer systems. From 1970 to 1971 he was with the Optical Character Recognition Product Development Group of Honeywell Information Systems, Minneapolis, MN. In 1971 he joined the Computer Science Faculty of the University of Maryland, College Park. He has been actively involved in teaching and research in computer systems, simulation and modeling, performance evaluation, pattern recognition, and interactive systems. He is the author of many papers in these fields.

Dr. Agrawala is a member of Sigma Xi, the Association for Computing Machinery, and the Pattern Recognition Society.

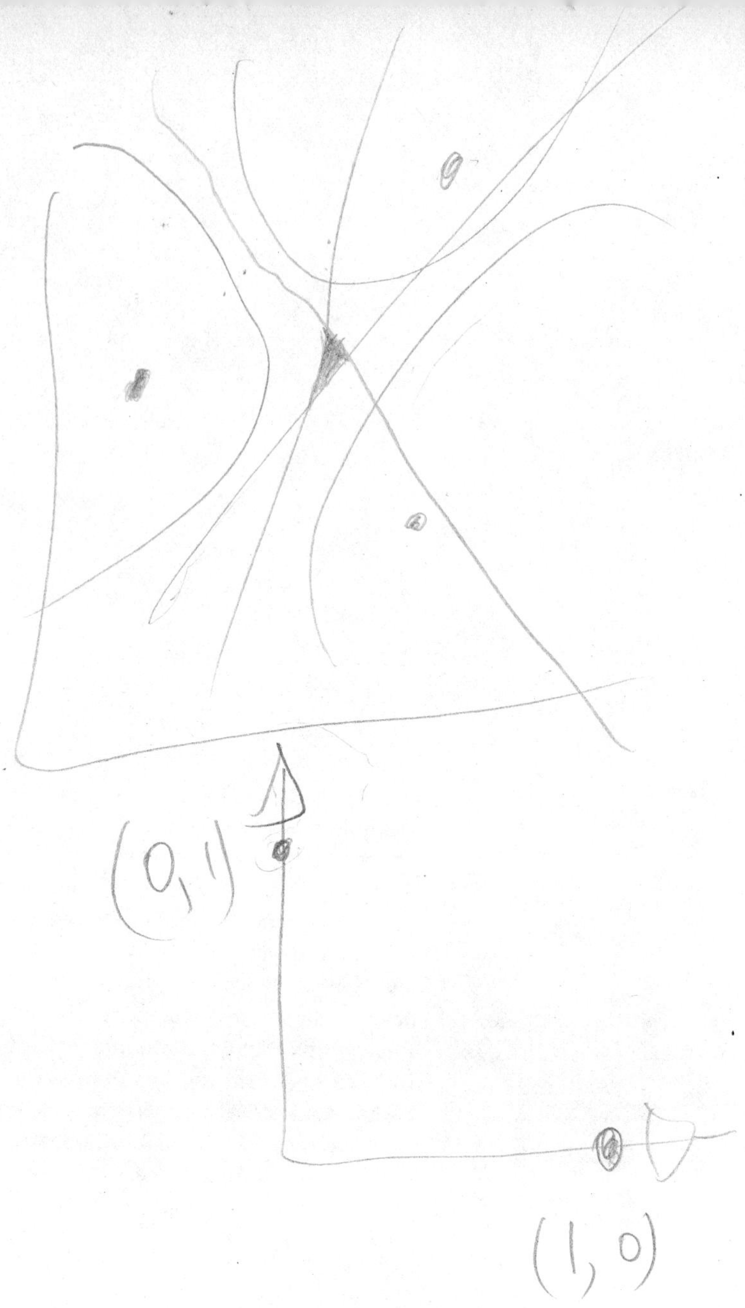

C
Coooo c,ooo